Function and Macro Definitions

(**Bold** page numbers indicate source code implementation)

UNIX Network Programming Volume 1

Second Edition

Networking APIs: Sockets and XTI

by W. Richard Stevens

To join a Prentice Hall PTR Internet mailing list, point to
http://www.prenhall.com/mail_lists/

ISBN 0-13-490012-X

Prentice Hall PTR
Upper Saddle River, NJ 07458

Library of Congress Cataloging-in-Publication Data
Stevens, W. Richard
    UNIX network programming / by W. Richard Stevens. -- 2nd ed.
        p.   cm.
    Includes index.
    ISBN 0-13-490012-X
    1. UNIX (Computer file) 2. Computer networks. 3. Internet
programming.   I. Title.
QA76.76.O63S755 1997
005.7'127768--dc21   97-31761
                                                CIP

Editorial/Production Supervision: *Eileen Clark*
Acquisitions Editor: *Mary Franz*
Marketing Manager: *Miles Williams*
Buyer: *Alexis R. Heydt*
Cover Design: *Scott Weiss*
Cover Design Direction: *Jerry Votta*
Editorial Assistant: *Noreen Regina*

© 1998 Prentice Hall PTR
Prentice-Hall, Inc.
A Simon & Schuster Company
Upper Saddle River, NJ 07458

Prentice Hall books are widely used by corporations and government agencies for training, marketing, and resale. The publisher offers discounts on this book when ordered in bulk quantities.
For more information, contact

        Corporate Sales Department,
        Phone: 800-382-3419; FAX: 201-236-7141
        E-mail (Internet): corpsales@prenhall.com
Or write: Prentice Hall PTR
        Corp. Sales Department
        One Lake Street
        Upper Saddle River, NJ 07458

Printed in the United States of America

10 9 8 7 6 5 4 3 2

ISBN 0-13-490012-X

Prentice-Hall International (UK) Limited, *London*
Prentice-Hall of Australia Pty. Limited, *Sydney*
Prentice-Hall Canada Inc., *Toronto*
Prentice-Hall Hispanoamericana, S.A., *Mexico*
Prentice-Hall of India Private Limited, *New Delhi*
Prentice-Hall of Japan, Inc., *Tokyo*
Simon & Schuster Asia Pte. Ltd., *Singapore*
Editora Prentice-Hall do Brasil, Ltda., *Rio de Janeiro*

To Sally, Bill, Ellen, and David.
Aloha nui loa.

Contents

Part 2. Elementary Sockets   55

Chapter 3.   Sockets Introduction   57

Chapter 4.   Elementary TCP Sockets   85

Chapter 5.   TCP Client–Server Example   111

Preface

Introduction

Network programming involves writing programs that communicate with other programs across a computer network. One program is normally called the *client* and the other the *server*. Most operating systems provide precompiled programs that communicate across a network—common examples in the TCP/IP world are Web clients (browsers) and Web servers, and the FTP and Telnet clients and servers—but this book describes how to write our own network programs.

We write network programs using an *application program interface* or *API*. We describe two APIs for network programming:

1. sockets, sometimes called "Berkeley sockets" acknowledging their heritage from Berkeley Unix, and

2. XTI (X/Open Transport Interface), a slight modification of the Transport Layer Interface (TLI) developed by AT&T.

All the examples in the text are from the Unix operating system, although the foundation and concepts required for network programming are, to a large degree, operating system independent. The examples are also based on the TCP/IP protocol suite, both IP versions 4 and 6.

To write network programs one must understand the underlying operating system and the underlying networking protocols. This book builds on the foundation of my other four books in these two areas, and these books are abbreviated throughout this text as follows:

- APUE: *Advanced Programming in the UNIX Environment* [Stevens 1992],
- TCPv1: *TCP/IP Illustrated, Volume 1* [Stevens 1994],
- TCPv2: *TCP/IP Illustrated, Volume 2* [Wright and Stevens 1995], and
- TCPv3: *TCP/IP Illustrated, Volume 3* [Stevens 1996].

This second edition of *UNIX Network Programming* still contains information on both Unix and the TCP/IP protocols, but many references are made to these other four texts to allow interested readers to obtain more detailed information on various topics. This is especially the case for TCPv2, which describes and presents the actual 4.4BSD implementation of the network programming functions for the sockets API (socket, bind, connect, and so on). If one understands the implementation of a feature, the use of that feature in an application makes more sense.

Changes from the First Edition

This second edition is a complete rewrite of the first edition. These changes have been driven by the feedback I have received teaching this material about once a month during 1990–1996, and by following certain Usenet newsgroups during this same time, which lets one see the topics that are continually misunderstood. The following are the major changes with this new edition:

- This new edition uses ANSI C for all examples.
- The old Chapters 6 ("Berkeley Sockets") and 8 ("Library Routines") have been expanded into 25 chapters. Indeed this sevenfold expansion (based on a word count) of this material is probably the most significant change from the first to the second edition. Most of the individual sections in the old Chapter 6 have been expanded into an entire chapter with more examples added.
- The TCP and UDP portions from the old Chapter 6 have been separated and we now cover the TCP functions and a complete TCP client–server, followed by the UDP functions and a complete UDP client–server. This is easier for newcomers to understand than describing all the details of the connect function, for example, with its different semantics for TCP versus UDP.
- The old Chapter 7 ("System V Transport Layer Interface") has been expanded into seven chapters. We also cover the newer XTI instead of the TLI that it replaces.
- The old Chapter 2 ("The Unix Model") is gone. This chapter provided an overview of the Unix system in about 75 pages. In 1990 this chapter was needed because few books existed that adequately described the basic Unix programming interface, especially the differences between the Berkeley and System V implementations that existed in 1990. Today, however, more readers have a fundamental understanding of Unix, so concepts such as a process ID, password files, directories, and group IDs, need not be repeated. (My APUE book is a 700-page expansion of this material for readers desiring additional Unix programming details.)

Some of the advanced topics from the old Chapter 2 are covered in this new edition, but their coverage is moved to where the feature is used. For example, when showing our first concurrent server (Section 4.8) we cover the `fork` function. When we describe how to handle the `SIGCHLD` signal with our concurrent server (Section 5.9), we describe many additional features of Posix signal handling (zombies, interrupted system calls, etc.).

- Whenever possible this text describes the Posix interface. (We say more about the Posix family of standards in Section 1.10.) This includes not only the Posix.1 standard for the basic Unix functions (process control, signals, etc.), but also the forthcoming Posix.1g standard for the sockets and XTI networking APIs, and the 1996 Posix.1 standard for threads.

  The term "system call" has been changed to "function" when describing functions such as `socket` and `connect`. This follows the Posix convention that the distinction between a system call and a library function is an implementation detail that is often irrelevant for a programmer.

- The old Chapters 4 ("A Network Primer") and 5 ("Communication Protocols") have been replaced with Appendix A covering IP versions 4 (IPv4) and 6 (IPv6), and Chapter 2 covering TCP and UDP. This new material focuses on the protocol issues that network programmers are certain to encounter. The coverage of IPv6 was included, even though IPv6 implementations are just starting to appear, since during the lifetime of this text IPv6 will probably become the predominant networking protocol.

  I have found when teaching network programming that about 80% of all network programming problems have nothing to do with network programming, per se. That is, the problems are not with the API functions such as `accept` and `select`, but the problems arise from a lack of understanding of the underlying network protocols. For example, I have found that once a student understands TCP's three-way handshake and four-packet connection termination, many network programming problems are immediately understood.

  The old sections on XNS, SNA, NetBIOS, the OSI protocols, and UUCP have been removed, since it has become obvious during the early 1990s that these proprietary protocols have been eclipsed by the TCP/IP protocols. (UUCP is still popular and is not proprietary, but there is little we can show from a network programming perspective using UUCP.)

- The following new topics are covered in this second edition:
  - IPv4/IPv6 interoperability (Chapter 10),
  - protocol-independent name translation (Chapter 11),
  - routing sockets (Chapter 17),
  - multicasting (Chapter 19),
  - threads (Chapter 23),
  - IP options (Chapter 24),
  - datalink access (Chapter 26),

- client–server design alternatives (Chapter 27),
- virtual networks and tunneling (Appendix B), and
- network program debugging techniques (Appendix C).

Unfortunately, the coverage of the material from the first edition has been expanded so much that it no longer fits into a single book. Therefore at least two additional volumes are planned in the *UNIX Network Programming* series.

- Volume 2 will probably be subtitled *IPC: Interprocess Communication* and will be an expansion of the old Chapter 3, along with coverage of the 1996 Posix.1 real-time IPC mechanisms.

- Volume 3 will probably be subtitled *Applications* and will be an expansion of Chapters 9–18 of the first edition.

Even though most of the networking applications will be covered in Volume 3, a few special applications are covered in this volume: Ping, Traceroute, and `inetd`.

Readers

This text can be used as either a tutorial on network programming, or as a reference for experienced programmers. When used as a tutorial or for an introductory class on network programming, the emphasis should be on Part 2 ("Elementary Sockets," Chapters 3 through 9) followed by whatever additional topics are of interest. Part 2 covers the basic socket functions, for both TCP and UDP, along with I/O multiplexing, socket options, and basic name and address conversions. Chapter 1 should be read by all readers, especially Section 1.4, which describes some wrapper functions used throughout the text. Chapter 2 and perhaps Appendix A should be referred to as necessary, depending on the reader's background. Most of the chapters in Part 3 ("Advanced Sockets") can be read independently of the others in that part.

To aid in the use as a reference, a thorough index is provided, along with summaries on the end papers of where to find detailed descriptions of all the functions and structures. To help those reading topics in a random order, numerous references to related topics are provided throughout the text.

Although the sockets API has become the de facto standard for network programming, XTI is still used, sometimes with protocol suites other than TCP/IP. While the coverage of XTI in Part 4 is smaller than the coverage of sockets in Parts 2 and 3, much of the sockets coverage describes *concepts* that apply to XTI as well as sockets. For example, all of the concepts regarding the use of nonblocking I/O, broadcasting, multicasting, signal-driven I/O, out-of-band data, and threads, are the same, regardless of which API (sockets or XTI) is used. Indeed, many network programming problems are fundamentally similar, independent of whether the program is written using sockets or XTI, and there is hardly anything that can be done with one API that cannot be done with the other. The concepts are the same—just the function names and arguments change.

Source Code and Errata Availability

The source code for all the examples that appear in the book is available from `ftp://ftp.kohala.com/pub/rstevens/unpv12e.tar.gz`. The best way to learn network programming is to take these programs, modify them, and enhance them. Actually writing code of this form is the *only* way to reinforce the concepts and techniques. Numerous exercises are also provided at the end of each chapter, and most answers are provided in Appendix E.

A current errata for the book is also available from my home page, listed at the end of the Preface.

Acknowledgments

Supporting every author is an understanding family, or nothing would ever get written! I am grateful to my family, Sally, Bill, Ellen, and David, first for their support and understanding when I wrote my first book (the first edition of this book), and for enduring this "small" revision. Their love, support, and encouragement helped make this book possible.

Numerous reviewers provided invaluable feedback (totaling 190 printed pages or 70,000 words), catching lots of errors, pointing out areas that needed more explanation, and suggesting alternative presentations, wording, and coding: Ragnvald Blindheim, Jim Bound, Gavin Bowe, Allen Briggs, Joe Doupnik, Wu-chang Feng, Bill Fenner, Bob Friesenhahn, Andrew Gierth, Wayne Hathaway, Kent Hofer, Sugih Jamin, Scott Johnson, Rick Jones, Mukesh Kacker, Marc Lampo, Marty Leisner, Jack McCann, Craig Metz, Bob Nelson, Evi Nemeth, John C. Noble, Steve Rago, Jim Reid, Chung-Shang Shao, Ian Lance Taylor, Ron Taylor, Andreas Terzis, and Dave Thaler. A special thanks to Sugih Jamin and his students in EECS 489 ("Computer Networks") at the University of Michigan who beta tested an early draft of the manuscript during the spring of 1997.

The following people answered email questions of mine, sometimes lots of questions, which improved the accuracy and presentation of the text: Dave Butenhof, Dave Hanson, Jim Hogue, Mukesh Kacker, Brian Kernighan, Vern Paxson, Steve Rago, Dennis Ritchie, Steve Summit, Paul Vixie, John Wait, Steve Wise, and Gary Wright.

A special thanks to Larry Rafsky and the wonderful team at Gari Software for handling lots of details and for many interesting technical discussions. Thank you, Larry, for everything.

Numerous individuals and their organizations went beyond the normal call of duty to provide either a loaner system, software, or access to a system, all of which were used to test some of the examples in the text.

- Meg McRoberts of SCO provided the latest releases of UnixWare, and Dion Johnson, Yasmin Kureshi, Michael Townsend, and Brian Ziel, provided support and answered questions.

- Mukesh Kacker of SunSoft provided access to a beta version of Solaris 2.6 and answered many questions about the Solaris TCP/IP implementation.

- Jim Bound, Matt Thomas, Mary Clouter, and Barb Glover of Digital Equipment Corp. provided an Alpha system and access to the latest IPv6 kits for Digital Unix.

- Michael Johnson of Red Hat Software provided the latest releases of Red Hat Linux.

- Steve Wise and Jessie Haug of IBM Austin provided an RS/6000 system and access to the latest IPv6 for AIX.

- Rick Jones of Hewlett-Packard provided access to a beta version of HP-UX 10.30 and he and William Gilliam answered many questions about it.

Many people helped with the Internet connectivity used throughout the text. My thanks once again to the National Optical Astronomy Observatories (NOAO), Sidney Wolff, Richard Wolff, and Steve Grandi, for providing access to their networks and hosts. Dave Siegel, Justis Addis, and Paul Lucchina answered many questions, Phil Kaslo and Jim Davis provided an MBone connection, Ran Atkinson and Pedro Marques provided a 6bone connection, and Craig Metz provided lots of DNS help.

The staff at Prentice Hall, especially my editor Mary Franz, along with Noreen Regina, Sophie Papanikolaou, and Eileen Clark, have been a wonderful asset to a writer. Many thanks for letting me do so many things "my way."

As usual, but contrary to popular fads, I produced camera-ready copy of the book using the wonderful Groff package written by James Clark. I typed in all 291,972 words using the vi editor, created the 201 illustrations using the gpic program (using many of Gary Wright's macros), produced the 81 tables using the gtbl program, performed all the indexing, and did the final page layout. Dave Hanson's loom program and some scripts by Gary Wright were used to include the source code in the book. A set of awk scripts written by Jon Bentley and Brian Kernighan helped in producing the final index.

I welcome electronic mail from any readers with comments, suggestions, or bug fixes.

Tucson, Arizona
September 1997

W. Richard Stevens
rstevens@kohala.com
http://www.kohala.com/~rstevens

Part 1

Introduction and TCP/IP

1

Introduction

1.1   Introduction

Most network applications can be divided into two pieces: a *client* and a *server*. We can draw the communication link between the two as shown in Figure 1.1.

Figure 1.1   Network application: client and server.

There are numerous examples of clients and servers that most readers are probably familiar with: a Web browser (a client) communicating with a Web server; an FTP client fetching a file from an FTP server; a Telnet client that we use to log in to a remote host through a Telnet server on that remote host.

Clients normally communicate with one server at a time, although using the Web browser as an example, we might communicate with many different Web servers over, say, a 10-minute time period. But from the server's perspective at any given point in time it is not unusual for a server to be communicating with multiple clients. We show this in Figure 1.2. Later in this text we will cover several different ways for a server to handle multiple clients at the same time.

Although we think of the client application communicating with the server application, networking protocols are involved. In this text we focus on the TCP/IP protocol suite, also called the Internet protocol suite. For example, Web clients and servers communicate using the TCP protocol. TCP, in turn, uses the IP protocol, and IP communicates with a datalink layer of some form. For example, if the client and server are on the same Ethernet, we would have the arrangement shown in Figure 1.3.

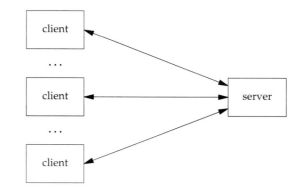

Figure 1.2 Server handling multiple clients at the same time.

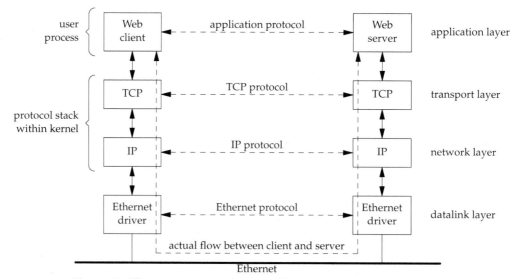

Figure 1.3 Client and server on the same Ethernet communicating using TCP.

Even though the client and server communicate using an application protocol, the transport layers communicate using TCP, and so on, we note that the actual flow of information between the client and server goes down the protocol stack on one side, across the network, and up the protocol stack on the other side.

We also note that the client and server are typically user processes, while the TCP and IP protocols are normally part of the protocol stack within the kernel. We have labeled the four layers on the right side of Figure 1.3.

TCP and IP are not the only protocols that we discuss. Some clients and servers use the UDP protocol instead of TCP and we discuss both protocols in more detail in Chapter 2. Furthermore, we have used the term "IP" but the protocol, which has been in use since the early 1980s, is officially called *IP version 4* (IPv4). A new version, *IP version 6* (IPv6) was developed during the mid-1990s and will probably replace IPv4 in the years to come. Initial implementations of IPv6 were available at the time of this writing, and this text covers the development of network applications using both IPv4 and IPv6. Appendix A provides a comparison of IPv4 and IPv6, along with other protocols that we will encounter.

The client and server need not be attached to the same *local area network* (LAN) as we show in Figure 1.3. Instead, in Figure 1.4 we show the client and server on different LANs, with the both LANs connected to a *wide area network* (WAN) using *routers*.

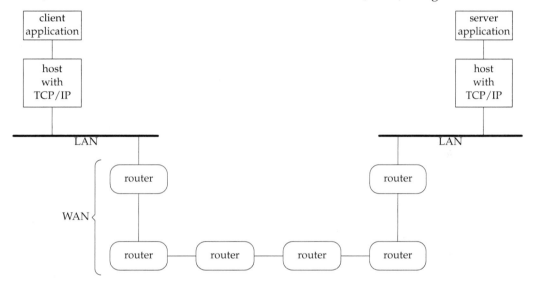

Figure 1.4 Client and server on different LANs connected through a WAN.

Routers are the building blocks of WANs. The largest WAN today is the *Internet*, although many companies build their own WANs and these private WANs may or may not be connected to the Internet.

The remainder of this chapter provides an introduction and overview to the various topics that are covered in detail later in the text. We start with a complete example of a TCP client, albeit a simple one, that demonstrates many of the function calls and concepts that we encounter throughout the text. This client works with IP version 4 only, and we show the changes required to work with IP version 6. A better solution is to write protocol-independent clients and servers, and we discuss this in Chapter 11. This chapter also shows a complete TCP server that works with our client.

To simplify all the code that we write, we define our own wrapper functions for most of the system functions that we call throughout the text. We can use these most of the time to check for an error, print an appropriate message, and terminate when an error occurs. We also show the test network, hosts, and routers used for most examples in the text, along with their hostnames, IP addresses, and operating systems.

Most discussions of Unix these days include the term *Posix*, which is the standard that most vendors have adopted. We describe the history of Posix and how it affects the APIs that we describe in this text, along with the other players in the standards area.

1.2   A Simple Daytime Client

Let us consider a specific example to introduce many of the concepts and terms that we will encounter throughout the book. Figure 1.5 is an implementation of a TCP time-of-day client. This client establishes a TCP connection with a server and the server simply sends back the current time and date in a human-readable format.

———————————————————————————————— *intro/daytimetcpcli.c*

```
 1 #include     "unp.h"

 2 int
 3 main(int argc, char **argv)
 4 {
 5     int     sockfd, n;
 6     char    recvline[MAXLINE + 1];
 7     struct sockaddr_in servaddr;

 8     if (argc != 2)
 9         err_quit("usage: a.out <IPaddress>");

10     if ( (sockfd = socket(AF_INET, SOCK_STREAM, 0)) < 0)
11         err_sys("socket error");

12     bzero(&servaddr, sizeof(servaddr));
13     servaddr.sin_family = AF_INET;
14     servaddr.sin_port = htons(13);   /* daytime server */
15     if (inet_pton(AF_INET, argv[1], &servaddr.sin_addr) <= 0)
16         err_quit("inet_pton error for %s", argv[1]);

17     if (connect(sockfd, (SA *) &servaddr, sizeof(servaddr)) < 0)
18         err_sys("connect error");

19     while ( (n = read(sockfd, recvline, MAXLINE)) > 0) {
20         recvline[n] = 0;          /* null terminate */
21         if (fputs(recvline, stdout) == EOF)
22             err_sys("fputs error");
23     }
24     if (n < 0)
25         err_sys("read error");

26     exit(0);
27 }
```

———————————————————————————————— *intro/daytimetcpcli.c*

Figure 1.5 TCP daytime client.

This is the format that we use for all the source code in the text. Each nonblank line is numbered. The text describing portions of the code begins with the starting and ending line numbers in the left margin, as shown shortly. Sometimes the paragraph is preceded by a short descriptive bold heading, providing a summary statement of the code being described.

The horizontal rules at the beginning and end of the code fragment specify the source code filename: the file daytimetcpcli.c in the directory intro for this example. Since the source code for all the examples in the text is freely available (see the Preface), this lets you locate the appropriate source file. Compiling, running, and especially modifying these programs while reading this text is an excellent way to learn the concepts of network programming.

Throughout the text we will use indented, parenthetical notes such as this to describe implementation details and historical points.

If we compile the program into the default a.out file and execute it, we have the following output.

```
solaris % a.out 206.62.226.35          our input
Fri Jan 12 14:27:52 1996               the program's output
```

Whenever we display interactive input and output we show our typed input in a **bold font**, and the computer output like this. *Comments are added on the right side in italics.* We always include the name of the system as part of the shell prompt (solaris in this example) to show on which host the command was run. Figure 1.16 shows the systems used to run most of the examples in this book. The hostnames usually describe the operating system.

There are many details to now consider in this 27-line program. We mention them briefly here, in case this is your first encounter with a network program, and provide more information on these topics later in the text.

Include our own header

1   We include our own header, unp.h, which we show in Section D.1. This header includes numerous system headers that are needed by most network programs and defines various constants that we use (e.g., MAXLINE).

Command-line arguments

2-3   This is the definition of the main function along with the command-line arguments. We have written the code in this text assuming an ANSI (American National Standards Institute) C compiler.

Create a TCP socket

10-11   The socket function creates an Internet (AF_INET) stream (SOCK_STREAM) socket, which is a fancy name for a TCP socket. The function returns a small integer descriptor that we use to identify the socket in all future function calls (e.g., the calls to connect and read that follow).

The if statement contains a call to the socket function , an assignment of the return value to the variable named sockfd, and then a test of whether this assigned value is less than 0. While we could break this into two C statements,

```
sockfd = socket(AF_INET, SOCK_STREAM, 0);
if (sockfd < 0)
```

it is a common C idiom to combine the two lines. The set of parentheses around the function call and assignment are required, given the precedence rules of C (the less-than operator has a higher precedence than assignment). As a personal style issue, the author always places a space between the two opening parentheses, as a visual indicator that the left-hand side of the comparison is also an assignment. (The author first saw this style in the Minix source code [Tanenbaum 1987] and has copied it ever since.) We use this same style in the while statement later in the program.

We will encounter many different uses of the term *socket*. First, the *application programming interface*, or API, that we are using is called the *sockets API.* In the preceding paragraph we refer to a function named `socket` that is part of the sockets API. In the preceding paragraph we also refer to a "TCP socket," which is synonymous with a "TCP endpoint."

If the call to `socket` fails, we abort the program by calling our own `err_sys` function. It prints our error message along with a description of the system error that occurred (e.g., "Protocol not supported" is one possible error from `socket`) and terminates the process. This function, and a few others of our own that begin with `err_`, are called throughout the text. We describe them in Section D.4.

Specify server's IP address and port

12–16   We fill in an Internet socket address structure (a `sockaddr_in` structure named `servaddr`) with the server's IP address and port number. We set the entire structure to 0 using `bzero`, set the address family to `AF_INET`, set the port number to 13 (which is the well-known port of the daytime server on any TCP/IP host that supports this service, as shown in Figure 2.13), and set the IP address to the value specified as the first command-line argument (`argv[1]`). The IP address and port number fields in this structure must be in specific formats: we call the library function `htons` ("host to network short") to convert the binary port number, and we call the library function `inet_pton` ("presentation to numeric") to convert the ASCII command-line argument (such as `206.62.226.35` when we ran this example) into the proper format.

> `bzero` is not an ANSI C function. It is derived from early Berkeley networking code. Nevertheless, we use it throughout the text, instead of the ANSI C `memset` function, because `bzero` is easier to remember (with only two arguments) than `memset` (with three arguments). Almost every vendor that supports the sockets API also provides `bzero`, and if not, we provide a macro definition of it in our `unp.h` header.

> Indeed, the author made the mistake of swapping the second and third arguments to `memset` in 10 occurrences in the first printing of TCPv3. A C compiler cannot catch this error because both arguments are of the same type. (Actually, the second argument is an `int` and the third argument is `size_t`, which is typically an `unsigned int`, but the values specified, 0 and 16, respectively, are still OK for the other type of argument.) The call to `memset` still worked but did nothing: the number of bytes to initialize was specified as 0. The programs still worked, because only a few of the socket functions actually require that the final 8 bytes of an Internet socket address structure be set to 0. Nevertheless, it was an error, and one that can be avoided by using `bzero`, because swapping the two arguments to `bzero` will always be caught by the C compiler if function prototypes are used.

> This may be your first encounter with the `inet_pton` function. It is new with IP version 6 (which we talk more about in Appendix A). Older code uses the `inet_addr` function to convert an ASCII dotted-decimal string into the correct format, but this function has numerous limitations that `inet_pton` corrects. Do not worry if your system does not (yet) support this function; we provide an implementation of it in Section 3.7.

Establish connection with server

17–18   The `connect` function, when applied to a TCP socket, establishes a TCP connection with the server specified by the socket address structure pointed to by the second argument. We must also specify the length of the socket address structure as the third argument to `connect`, and for Internet socket address structures we always let the compiler calculate the length using C's `sizeof` operator.

In the unp.h header we #define SA to be struct sockaddr, that is, a generic socket address structure. Every time one of the socket functions requires a pointer to a socket address structure, that pointer must be cast to a pointer to a generic socket address structure. This is because the socket functions predate the ANSI C standard, so the void * pointer type was not available in the early 1980s when these functions were developed. The problem is that "struct sockaddr" is 15 characters and often causes the source code line to extend past the right edge of the screen (or page in the case of a book), so we shorten it to SA. We talk more about generic socket address structures with Figure 3.3.

Read and display server's reply

19-25   We read the server's reply and display the result using the standard I/O fputs function. We must be careful when using TCP because it is a *byte-stream* protocol with no record boundaries. The server's reply is normally a 26-byte string of the form

        Fri Jan 12 14:27:52 1996\r\n

where \r is the ASCII carriage return and \n is the ASCII linefeed. With a byte-stream protocol these 26 bytes can be returned in numerous ways: a single TCP segment containing all 26 bytes of data, in 26 TCP segments each containing 1 byte of data, or any other combination that totals to 26 bytes. Normally a single segment containing all 26 bytes of data is returned, but with larger data sizes we cannot assume that the server's reply is returned by a single read. Therefore, when reading from a TCP socket we *always* need to code the read in a loop and terminate the loop when either read returns 0 (i.e., the other end closed the connection) or less than 0 (an error).

In this example the end of record is being denoted by the server closing the connection. This technique is also used by HTTP, the Hypertext Transfer Protocol. Other techniques are available. For example, FTP (File Transfer Protocol) and SMTP (Simple Mail Transfer Protocol) both mark the end of a record with the 2-byte sequence of an ASCII carriage return followed by an ASCII linefeed. Sun RPC (Remote Procedure Call) and the DNS (Domain Name System) place a binary count containing the record length in front of each record that is sent when using TCP. The important concept here is that TCP itself provides no record markers: if the application wants to delineate the end of records, it must do so itself and there are a few common ways to accomplish this.

Terminate program

26   exit terminates the program. Unix always closes all open descriptors when a process terminates, so our TCP socket is now closed.

As we mentioned, the text goes into much more detail on all the points that we just described.

1.3   Protocol Independence

Our program in Figure 1.5 is *protocol dependent* on IP version 4 (IPv4). We allocate and initialize a sockaddr_in structure, we set the family of this structure to AF_INET, and we specify the first argument to socket as AF_INET.

If we want to modify the program to work under IP version 6 (IPv6) we must change the code. Figure 1.6 shows a version that works under IPv6, with the changes highlighted in a bolder font.

intro/daytimetcpcliv6.c

```
 1 #include    "unp.h"

 2 int
 3 main(int argc, char **argv)
 4 {
 5     int     sockfd, n;
 6     char    recvline[MAXLINE + 1];
 7     struct sockaddr_in6 servaddr;

 8     if (argc != 2)
 9         err_quit("usage: a.out <IPaddress>");

10     if ( (sockfd = socket(AF_INET6, SOCK_STREAM, 0)) < 0)
11         err_sys("socket error");

12     bzero(&servaddr, sizeof(servaddr));
13     servaddr.sin6_family = AF_INET6;
14     servaddr.sin6_port = htons(13);    /* daytime server */
15     if (inet_pton(AF_INET6, argv[1], &servaddr.sin6_addr) <= 0)
16         err_quit("inet_pton error for %s", argv[1]);

17     if (connect(sockfd, (SA *) &servaddr, sizeof(servaddr)) < 0)
18         err_sys("connect error");

19     while ( (n = read(sockfd, recvline, MAXLINE)) > 0) {
20         recvline[n] = 0;    /* null terminate */
21         if (fputs(recvline, stdout) == EOF)
22             err_sys("fputs error");
23     }
24     if (n < 0)
25         err_sys("read error");

26     exit(0);
27 }
```

intro/daytimetcpcliv6.c

Figure 1.6 Version of Figure 1.5 for IP version 6.

Only five lines are changed, but what we now have is another protocol-dependent program, this time dependent on IP version 6. It is better to make the program *protocol independent*. Figure 11.7 shows a version of this client that is protocol independent by using the getaddrinfo function.

Another deficiency in our programs is that the user must enter the server's IP address as a dotted-decimal number (e.g., 206.62.226.35 for the IPv4 version). Humans work better with names instead of numbers (e.g., laptop.kohala.com or just laptop). In Chapters 9 and 11 we discuss the functions that convert between host-names and IP addresses, and between service names and ports. We purposely put off the discussion of these functions and continue using IP addresses and port numbers so we know exactly what goes into the socket address structures that we must fill in and examine. This also avoids complicating our discussion of network programming with the details of yet another set of functions.

1.4   Error Handling: Wrapper Functions

In any real-world program it is essential to check *every* function call for an error return. In Figure 1.5 we check for errors from `socket`, `inet_pton`, `connect`, `read`, and `fputs`, and when one occurs we call our own functions `err_quit` and `err_sys` to print an error message and terminate the program. We find that most of the time this is what we want to do. Occasionally we want to do something other than terminate when one of these functions returns an error, as in Figure 5.12, when we must check for an interrupted system call.

Since terminating on an error is the common case, we can shorten our programs by defining a *wrapper function* that performs the actual function call, tests the return value, and terminates on an error. The convention we use is to capitalize the name of the function, as in

```
sockfd = Socket(AF_INET, SOCK_STREAM, 0);
```

Our wrapper function is shown in Figure 1.7.

—— *lib/wrapsock.c*
```
172 int
173 Socket(int family, int type, int protocol)
174 {
175     int    n;

176     if ( (n = socket(family, type, protocol)) < 0)
177         err_sys("socket error");
178     return (n);
179 }
```
—— *lib/wrapsock.c*

Figure 1.7   Our wrapper function for the `socket` function.

Whenever you encounter a function name in the text that begins with an uppercase letter, that is a wrapper function of our own. It calls a function whose name is the same but beginning with the lowercase letter.

When describing the source code that is presented in the text, we always refer to the lowest level function being called (e.g., `socket`*) and not the wrapper function (e.g.,* `Socket`*).*

While these wrapper functions might not seem like a big savings, when we discuss threads in Chapter 23 we will find that the thread functions do not set the standard Unix `errno` variable when an error occurs; instead the `errno` value is the return value of the function. This means that every time we call one of the pthread functions we must allocate a variable, save the return value in that variable, and then set `errno` to this value before calling `err_sys`. To avoid cluttering the code with braces, we can use C's comma operator to combine the assignment into `errno` and the call of `err_sys` into a single statement, as in the following:

```
int     n;

if ( (n = pthread_mutex_lock(&ndone_mutex)) != 0)
    errno = n, err_sys("pthread_mutex_lock error");
```

Alternately we could define a new error function that takes the system's error number as an argument. But we can make this piece of code much easier to read as just

```
Pthread_mutex_lock(&ndone_mutex);
```

by defining our own wrapper function, shown in Figure 1.8.

── *lib/wrappthread.c*
```
72 void
73 Pthread_mutex_lock(pthread_mutex_t *mptr)
74 {
75     int     n;

76     if ( (n = pthread_mutex_lock(mptr)) == 0)
77         return;
78     errno = n;
79     err_sys("pthread_mutex_lock error");
80 }
```
── *lib/wrappthread.c*

Figure 1.8 Our wrapper function for `pthread_mutex_lock`.

> With careful C coding we could use macros instead of functions, providing a little run-time efficiency, but these wrapper functions are rarely, if ever, the performance bottleneck of a program.
>
> Our choice of capitalizing the first character of the function name is a compromise. Many other styles were considered: prefixing the function name with an e (as done on p. 184 of [Kernighan and Pike 1984]), appending _e to the function name, and so on. Our style seems the least distracting while still providing a visual indication that some other function is really being called.
>
> This technique has the side benefit of checking for errors from functions whose error returns are often ignored: `close` and `listen`, for example.

Throughout the rest of this book we will use these wrapper functions unless we need to check for an explicit error and handle it in some form other than terminating the process. We do not show the source code for all our wrapper functions, but the code is freely available (see the Preface).

Unix `errno` Value

When an error occurs in a Unix function (such as one of the socket functions), the global variable `errno` is set to a positive value indicating the type of error and the function normally returns −1. Our `err_sys` function looks at the value of `errno` and prints the corresponding error message string (e.g., "Connection timed out" if `errno` equals `ETIMEDOUT`).

The value of `errno` is set by a function only if an error occurs. Its value is undefined if the function does not return an error. All of the positive error values are constants with an all uppercase name beginning with E and are normally defined in the
`<sys/errno.h>` header. No error has the value of 0.

Storing `errno` in a global variable does not work with multiple threads that share
all global variables. We talk about solutions to this problem in Chapter 23.

Throughout the text we use phrases of the form "the `connect` function returns
ECONNREFUSED" as shorthand to mean that the function returns an error (typically a
return value of −1) with `errno` set to the specified constant.

1.5   A Simple Daytime Server

We can also write a simple version of a TCP daytime server, which will work with the
client from Section 1.2. We use the wrapper functions that we described in the previous
section and show this server in Figure 1.9.

intro/daytimetcpsrv.c

```
 1 #include      "unp.h"
 2 #include      <time.h>

 3 int
 4 main(int argc, char **argv)
 5 {
 6      int       listenfd, connfd;
 7      struct sockaddr_in servaddr;
 8      char      buff[MAXLINE];
 9      time_t  ticks;

10      listenfd = Socket(AF_INET, SOCK_STREAM, 0);

11      bzero(&servaddr, sizeof(servaddr));
12      servaddr.sin_family = AF_INET;
13      servaddr.sin_addr.s_addr = htonl(INADDR_ANY);
14      servaddr.sin_port = htons(13);  /* daytime server */

15      Bind(listenfd, (SA *) &servaddr, sizeof(servaddr));

16      Listen(listenfd, LISTENQ);

17      for ( ; ; ) {
18          connfd = Accept(listenfd, (SA *) NULL, NULL);

19          ticks = time(NULL);
20          snprintf(buff, sizeof(buff), "%.24s\r\n", ctime(&ticks));
21          Write(connfd, buff, strlen(buff));

22          Close(connfd);
23      }
24 }
```

intro/daytimetcpsrv.c

Figure 1.9 TCP daytime server.

Create a TCP socket

10   The creation of the TCP socket is identical to the client code.

Bind server's well-known port to socket

11–15   The server's well-known port (13 for the daytime service) is bound to the socket by filling in an Internet socket address structure and calling `bind`. We specify the IP address as `INADDR_ANY`, which allows the server to accept a client connection on any interface, in case the server host has multiple interfaces. Later we will see how we can restrict the server to accepting a client connection on just a single interface, if we so desire.

Convert socket to listening socket

16   By calling `listen` the socket is converted into a listening socket, on which incoming connections from clients will be accepted by the kernel. These three steps, `socket`, `bind`, and `listen`, are the normal steps for any TCP server to prepare what we call the *listening descriptor* (`listenfd` in this example).

The constant `LISTENQ` is from our `unp.h` header. It specifies the maximum number of client connections that the kernel will queue for this listening descriptor. We say much more about this queueing in Section 4.5.

Accept client connection, send reply

17–21   Normally the server process is put to sleep in the call to `accept`, waiting for a client connection to arrive and be accepted. A TCP connection uses what is called a *three-way handshake* to establish a connection and when this handshake completes, `accept` returns, and the return value from the function is a new descriptor (`connfd`) that is called the *connected descriptor*. This new descriptor is used for communication with the new client. A new descriptor is returned by `accept` for each client that connects to our server.

> The style used throughout the book for an infinite loop is
>
> ```
> for ( ; ; ) {
>     . . .
> }
> ```

The current time and date is returned by the library function `time`, which returns the number of seconds since the Unix Epoch: 00:00:00 January 1, 1970, UTC (Coordinated Universal Time). The next library function, `ctime`, converts this integer value into a human-readable string such as

```
Fri Jan 12 14:27:52 1996
```

A carriage return and linefeed are appended to the string by `snprintf` and the result is written to the client by `write`.

> This may be your first encounter with `snprintf`. Lots of existing code calls `sprintf` instead, but `sprintf` cannot check for overflow of the destination buffer. `snprintf`, on the other hand, requires that the second argument be the size of the destination buffer, and this buffer will not be overflowed.

snprintf is not yet part of the ANSI C standard but is being considered for a revision of the standard, currently called *C9X*. Nevertheless, many vendors are providing it as part of the standard C library. We use snprintf throughout the text, providing our own version that just calls sprintf when it is not provided.

It is remarkable how many network break-ins have occurred by a hacker sending data to cause a server's call to sprintf to overflow its buffer. Other functions that we should be careful with are gets, strcat, and strcpy, normally calling fgets, strncat, and strncpy instead. Additional tips on writing secure network programs are in Chapter 23 of [Garfinkel and Spafford 1996].

Terminate connection

22   The server closes its connection with the client by calling close. This initiates the normal TCP connection termination sequence: a FIN is sent in each direction and each FIN is acknowledged by the other end. We say much more about TCP's three-way handshake and the four TCP packets used to terminate a TCP connection in Section 2.5.

As with the client in the previous section, we have only examined this server briefly, saving all the details for later in the book. Note the following points:

- As with the client, the server is protocol dependent on IPv4. We will show a protocol-independent version in Figure 11.9 that uses the getaddrinfo function.

- Our server handles only one client at a time. If multiple client connections arrive at about the same time, the kernel queues them, up to some limit, and returns them to accept one at a time. This daytime server, which requires calling two library functions, time and ctime, is quite fast. But if the server took more time to service each client (say a few seconds or a minute), we would need some way to overlap the service of one client with another client. The server that we show in Figure 1.9 is called an *iterative server*, because it iterates through each client, one at a time. There are numerous techniques for writing a *concurrent server*, one that handles multiple clients at the same time. The simplest technique for a concurrent server is to call the Unix fork function (Section 4.7), creating one child process for each client. Other techniques are to use threads instead of fork (Section 23.4) or to pre-fork a fixed number of children when the server starts (Section 27.6).

- If we start a server like this from a shell command line, we might want the server to run for a long time, since servers often run for as long as the system is up. This requires that we add code to the server to run correctly as a Unix *daemon*: a process that can run in the background, unattached to a terminal. We cover this in Section 12.5.

1.6   Road Map to Client–Server Examples in the Text

Two client–server examples are used predominantly throughout the text to illustrate the various techniques used in network programming:

- a daytime client–server (which we started in Figures 1.5, 1.6, and 1.9), and
- an echo client–server (which starts in Chapter 5).

To provide a road map for the different topics that are covered in this text, we summarize the programs that we develop, and the starting figure number and page number in which the source code appears. Figure 1.10 lists the versions of the daytime client, two versions of which we have already seen. Figure 1.11 lists the versions of the daytime server. Figure 1.12 lists the versions of the echo client and Figure 1.13 lists the versions of the echo server.

Figure	Page	Description
1.5	6	TCP/IPv4, protocol dependent
1.6	10	TCP/IPv6, protocol dependent
9.8	253	TCP/IPv4, protocol dependent, calls `gethostbyname` and `getservbyname`
11.7	287	TCP, protocol independent, calls `getaddrinfo` and `tcp_connect`
11.12	295	UDP, protocol independent, calls `getaddrinfo` and `udp_client`
15.11	411	TCP, uses nonblocking `connect`
28.13	779	TCP/IPv4, XTI, protocol dependent
29.7	795	TCP, XTI, protocol independent, calls `netdir_getbyname` and `tcp_connect`
31.3	823	UDP, XTI, protocol independent, calls `netdir_getbyname` and `udp_client`
31.4	826	UDP, XTI, protocol independent, receives asynchronous errors
31.7	830	UDP, XTI, protocol independent, reads datagrams in pieces
33.8	857	TCP, protocol dependent, uses TPI instead of sockets or XTI
E.1	929	TCP, protocol dependent, generates `SIGPIPE`
E.5	932	TCP, protocol dependent, prints socket receive buffer sizes and MSS
E.13	942	TCP, protocol dependent, allows hostname (`gethostbyname`) or IP address
E.14	943	TCP, protocol independent, allows hostname (`gethostbyname`)

Figure 1.10 Different versions of the daytime client developed in the text.

Figure	Page	Description
1.9	13	TCP/IPv4, protocol dependent
11.9	290	TCP, protocol independent, calls `getaddrinfo` and `tcp_listen`
11.10	292	TCP, protocol independent, calls `getaddrinfo` and `tcp_listen`
11.15	298	UDP, protocol independent, calls `getaddrinfo` and `udp_server`
12.5	338	TCP, protocol independent, runs as stand-alone daemon
12.12	345	TCP, protocol independent, spawned from `inetd` daemon
30.5	805	TCP, XTI, protocol independent, calls `netdir_getbyname` and `tcp_listen`
31.6	828	UDP, XTI, protocol independent, calls `netdir_getbyname` and `udp_server`

Figure 1.11 Different versions of the daytime server developed in the text.

Figure	Page	Description
5.4	114	TCP/IPv4, protocol dependent
6.9	157	TCP, uses `select`
6.13	162	TCP, uses `select` and works in a batch mode
8.7	216	UDP/IPv4, protocol dependent
8.9	219	UDP, verifies server's address
8.17	227	UDP, calls `connect` to obtain asynchronous errors
13.2	352	UDP, timeout when reading server's reply using `SIGALRM`
13.4	354	UDP, timeout when reading server's reply using `select`
13.5	355	UDP, timeout when reading server's reply using `SO_RCVTIMEO`
14.4	380	Unix domain stream, protocol dependent
14.6	381	Unix domain datagram, protocol dependent
15.3	400	TCP, uses nonblocking I/O
15.9	408	TCP, uses two processes (`fork`)
15.21	423	TCP, establishes connection then sends RST
18.5	476	UDP, broadcasts with race condition
18.6	479	UDP, broadcasts with race condition
18.7	481	UDP, broadcasts, race condition fixed by using `pselect`
18.9	483	UDP, broadcasts, race condition fixed by using `sigsetjmp` and `siglongjmp`
18.10	485	UDP, broadcasts, race condition fixed by using IPC from signal handler
20.6	545	UDP, reliable using timeout, retransmit, and sequence number
21.14	583	TCP, heartbeat test to server using out-of-band data
23.2	606	TCP, uses two threads
24.6	642	TCP/IPv4, specifies a source route

Figure 1.12 Different versions of the echo client developed in the text.

Figure	Page	Description
5.2	113	TCP/IPv4, protocol dependent
5.12	128	TCP/IPv4, protocol dependent, reaps terminated children
6.21	165	TCP/IPv4, protocol dependent, uses `select`, one process handles all clients
6.25	172	TCP/IPv4, protocol dependent, uses `poll`, one process handles all clients
8.3	214	UDP/IPv4, protocol dependent
8.24	234	TCP and UDP/IPv4, protocol dependent, uses `select`
13.14	367	TCP, uses standard I/O library
14.3	379	Unix domain stream, protocol dependent
14.5	380	Unix domain datagram, protocol dependent
14.15	393	Unix domain stream, with credential passing from client
20.4	537	UDP, receive destination address and received interface; truncated datagrams
20.15	554	UDP, bind all interface addresses
21.15	585	TCP, heartbeat test to client using out-of-band data
22.4	594	UDP, uses signal-driven I/O
23.3	607	TCP, one thread per client
23.4	610	TCP, one thread per client, portable argument passing
24.6	642	TCP/IPv4, prints received source route
25.30	689	UDP, uses `icmpd` to receive asynchronous errors
E.17	955	UDP, bind all interface addresses

Figure 1.13 Different versions of the echo server developed in the text.

1.7   OSI Model

A common way to describe the layers in a network is the International Organization for Standardization (ISO) *open systems interconnection* model (OSI) for computer communications. This is a seven-layer model, which we show in Figure 1.14, along with the approximate mapping to the Internet protocol suite.

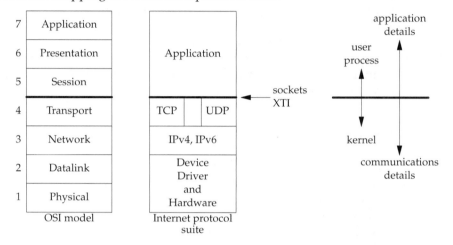

Figure 1.14   Layers in OSI model and Internet protocol suite.

We consider the bottom two layers of the OSI model as the device driver and networking hardware that are supplied with the system. Normally we need not concern ourselves with these layers other than being aware of some properties of the datalink, such as the 1500-byte Ethernet MTU (which we describe in Section 2.9).

The network layer is handled by the IPv4 and IPv6 protocols, both of which we describe in Appendix A. The transport layers that we can choose from are TCP and UDP, and we describe these in Chapter 2. We show a gap between TCP and UDP in Figure 1.14 to indicate that it is possible for an application to bypass the transport layer and use IPv4 or IPv6 directly. This is called a *raw socket* and we talk about this in Chapter 25.

The upper three layers of the OSI model are combined into a single layer called the application. This is the Web client (browser), Telnet client, the Web server, the FTP server, or whatever application we are using. With the Internet protocols there is rarely any distinction between the upper three layers of the OSI model.

The two programming interfaces that we describe in this book, sockets and XTI, are interfaces from the upper three layers (the "application") into the transport layer. This is the focus of this book: how to write applications using either sockets or XTI that use either TCP or UDP. We already mentioned raw sockets and in Chapter 26 we will see that we can even bypass the IP layer completely to read and write our own datalink layer frames.

Why do both sockets and XTI provide the interface from the upper three layers of the OSI model into the transport layer? There are two reasons for this design, which we note on the right side of Figure 1.14. First, the upper three layers handle all the details of the application (FTP, Telnet, or HTTP, for example) and know little about the communication details. The lower four layers know little about the application but handle all the communication details: sending data, waiting for an acknowledgment, sequencing data that arrives out of order, calculating and verifying checksums, and so on. The second reason is that the upper three layers often form what is called a *user process* while the lower four layers are normally provided as part of the operating system kernel. Unix provides this separation between the user process and the kernel, as do many other contemporary operating systems. Therefore the interface between layers 4 and 5 is the natural place to build the application programming interface (API).

1.8   BSD Networking History

The sockets API originated with the 4.2BSD system, released in 1983. Figure 1.15 shows the development of the various BSD releases, noting the major TCP/IP developments. A few changes to the sockets API also took place in 1990 with the 4.3BSD Reno release, when the OSI protocols went into the BSD kernel.

The path down the page from 4.2BSD through 4.4BSD are the releases from the Computer Systems Research Group (CSRG) at Berkeley that required the recipient to already have a source code license for Unix. But all of the networking code, both the kernel support (such as the TCP/IP and Unix domain protocol stacks and the socket interface), along with the applications (such as the Telnet and FTP clients and servers), were developed independently from the AT&T-derived Unix code. Therefore starting in 1989 Berkeley provided the first of the BSD networking releases, which contained all of the networking code and various other pieces of the BSD system that were not constrained by the Unix source code license. These releases were "publicly available" and eventually available by anonymous FTP to anyone on the Internet.

The final releases from Berkeley were 4.4BSD-Lite in 1994 and 4.4BSD-Lite2 in 1995. We note that these two releases were then used as the base for other systems: BSD/OS, FreeBSD, NetBSD, and OpenBSD, all four of which are still being actively developed and enhanced. More information on the various BSD releases, and on the history of the various Unix systems in general, can be found in Chapter 1 of [McKusick et al. 1996].

Many Unix systems started with some version of the BSD networking code, including the sockets API, and we refer to these implementations as *Berkeley-derived implementations*. Many commercial versions of Unix are based on System V Release 4 (SVR4) and some of these have Berkeley-derived networking code (e.g., UnixWare 2.x), while the networking code in other SVR4 systems has been independently derived (e.g., Solaris 2.x). We also note that the Linux system, a popular, freely available implementation of Unix, does *not* fit into the Berkeley-derived classification: its networking code and sockets API were developed from scratch.

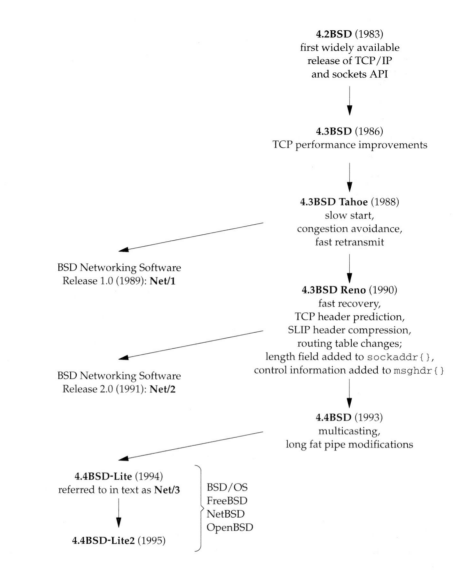

Figure 1.15   History of various BSD releases.

1.9   Test Networks and Hosts

Figure 1.16 shows the various networks and hosts used in the examples throughout the text. For each host we show the operating system and the type of hardware (since some of the operating systems run on more than one type of hardware). The name within each box is the hostname that appears in the text.

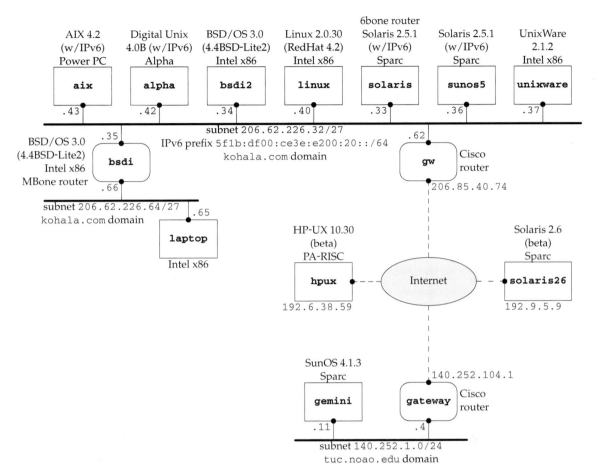

Figure 1.16 Networks and hosts used for most examples in the text.

The hosts on the top two Ethernets with the subnet addresses 206.62.226.32/27 and 206.62.226.64/27 are all in the kohala.com domain. The hosts on the bottom Ethernet with the subnet address 140.252.1.0/24 are all in the tuc.noao.edu domain, which is run by the National Optical Astronomy Observatories. The notation /27 and /24 indicates the number of consecutive bits starting from the leftmost bit of the address used to identify the network and subnet. Figures A.6 and A.5 show these two IPv4 addresses in more detail and Section A.4 talks about the /n notation used today to designate subnet boundaries.

Also in Figure 1.16 we draw nodes that function as routers with rounded corners, and nodes that are only hosts with square corners. We follow this convention throughout the book, as sometimes the distinction between a host and a router is important.

> We note that the real name of the Sun operating system is SunOS 5.x and not Solaris 2.x, but everyone calls it Solaris.

Discovering Network Topology

We show the network topology in Figure 1.16 for the hosts used for the examples throughout this text, but you need to know your own network topology to run the examples and exercises on your own network. Although there are no current Unix standards with regard to network configuration and administration, two basic commands are provided by most Unix systems and can be used to discover details of a network: `netstat` and `ifconfig`. We show examples on some different systems from Figure 1.16. Check the manual pages for these commands on your system to see the details on the information that is output. Also be aware that some vendors place these commands in an administrative directory, such as `/sbin` or `/usr/sbin`, instead of the normal `/usr/bin`, and these directories might not be in your normal shell search path (`PATH`).

1. `netstat -i` provides information on the interfaces. We also specify the `-n` flag to print numeric addresses, instead of trying to find names for the networks. This shows us the interfaces and their names.

```
linux % netstat -ni
Kernel Interface table
Iface   MTU Met   RX-OK RX-ERR RX-DRP RX-OVR   TX-OK TX-ERR TX-DRP TX-OVR Flags
lo     3584   0      32      0      0      0      32      0      0      0 BLRU
eth0   1500   0  483929      0      0      0  449881      0      0      0 BRU
```

The loopback interface is called `lo` and the Ethernet is called `eth0`. The next example shows a host with IPv6 support.

```
alpha % netstat -ni
Name  Mtu    Network        Address                         Ipkts Ierrs    Opkts Oerrs Coll
ln0   1500   <Link>         08:00:2b:37:64:26               11220     0     4893     0    4
ln0   1500   DLI            none                            11220     0     4893     0    4
ln0   1500   206.62.226.    206.62.226.42                   11220     0     4893     0    4
ln0   1500   IPv6 FE80::800:2B37:6426                       11220     0     4893     0    4
ln0   1500   IPv6 5F1B:DF00:CE3E:E200:20:800:2B37:6426 11220 0 4893     0    4
lo0   1536   <Link>         Link#3                          12432     0    12432     0    0
lo0   1536   127            127.0.0.1                       12432     0    12432     0    0
lo0   1536   IPv6           ::1                             12432     0    12432     0    0
tun0   576   <Link>         Link#4                              0     0        0     0    0
tun0   576   IPv6           ::206.62.226.42                     0     0        0     0    0
```

2. `netstat -r` shows the routing table, which is another way to determine the interfaces. We normally specify the `-n` flag to print numeric addresses. This also shows the IP address of the default router.

```
aix % netstat -rn
Routing tables
Destination        Gateway           Flags  Refs   Use   MTU   Netif Expire

Route tree for Protocol Family 2 (Internet):
default            206.62.226.62     UG       0     0     -     en0
127/8              127.0.0.1         U        0     0     -     lo0
206.62.226.32/27   206.62.226.43     U        4    475    -     en0
```

```
Route tree for Protocol Family 24 (Internet v6):
::/96                 0.0.0.0            UC      0      0  1480   sit0   - =>
default        fe80::2:0:800:2078:e3e3  UG      0      0    -     en0
::1                   ::1               UH      0      0 16896   lo0
5f1b:df00:ce3e:e200:20::/80
                      link#2            UC      0      0  1500   en0    -
fe80::/16             link#2            UC      0      0  1500   en0    -
fe80::2:0:800:2078:e3e3
                      link#2            UHDL    1      0  1500   en0    -
ff01::/16             ::1               U       0      0    -     lo0
ff02::/16      fe80::800:5afc:2b36      U       0      3  1500   en0
ff11::/16             ::1               U       0      0    -     lo0
ff12::/16      fe80::800:5afc:2b36      U       0      0  1500   en0
```

(We have wrapped some of the longer lines to align the output fields.)

3. Given the interface names, we execute `ifconfig` to obtain the details for each interface.

```
linux % ifconfig eth0
eth0 Link encap:10Mbps Ethernet  HWaddr 00:A0:24:9C:43:34
     inet addr:206.62.226.40  Bcast:206.62.226.63  Mask:255.255.255.224
     UP BROADCAST RUNNING MULTICAST  MTU:1500  Metric:1
     RX packets:484461 errors:0 dropped:0 overruns:0
     TX packets:450113 errors:0 dropped:0 overruns:0
     Interrupt:10 Base address:0x300
```

This shows the IP address, subnet mask, and broadcast address. The MULTICAST flag is often an indication that the host supports multicasting.

```
alpha % ifconfig ln0
ln0: flags=c63<UP,BROADCAST,NOTRAILERS,RUNNING,MULTICAST,SIMPLEX>
     inet 206.62.226.42 netmask fffffe0 broadcast 206.62.226.63 ipmtu 1500
```

Some implementations provide a -a flag that prints the information on all configured interfaces.

4 One way to find the IP address of many hosts on the local network is to `ping` the broadcast address (which we found in the previous step).

```
bsdi % ping 206.62.226.63
PING 206.62.226.63 (206.62.226.63): 56 data bytes
64 bytes from 206.62.226.35: icmp_seq=0 ttl=255 time=0.316 ms
64 bytes from 206.62.226.40: icmp_seq=0 ttl=64 time=1.369 ms (DUP!)
64 bytes from 206.62.226.34: icmp_seq=0 ttl=255 time=1.822 ms (DUP!)
64 bytes from 206.62.226.42: icmp_seq=0 ttl=64 time=2.27 ms (DUP!)
64 bytes from 206.62.226.37: icmp_seq=0 ttl=64 time=2.717 ms (DUP!)
64 bytes from 206.62.226.33: icmp_seq=0 ttl=255 time=3.281 ms (DUP!)
64 bytes from 206.62.226.62: icmp_seq=0 ttl=255 time=3.731 ms (DUP!)
^?                                      type our interrupt key (DEL)
--- 206.62.226.63 ping statistics ---
1 packets transmitted, 1 packets received, +6 duplicates, 0% packet loss
round-trip min/avg/max = 0.316/2.215/3.731 ms
```

1.10 Unix Standards

Most activity these days with regard to Unix standardization is being done by Posix and
The Open Group.

POSIX

Posix is an acronym for "Portable Operating System Interface." Posix is not a single
standard, but a family of standards being developed by the Institute for Electrical and
Electronics Engineers, Inc., normally called the *IEEE*. The Posix standards are also
being adopted as international standards by ISO (the International Organization for
Standardization) and IEC (the International Electrotechnical Commission), called
ISO/IEC.

The first of the Posix standards was IEEE Std 1003.1–1988 (317 pages) and it specified the C language interface into a Unix-like kernel covering the following areas: process primitives (`fork`, `exec`, signals, timers), the environment of a process (user IDs,
process groups), files and directories (all the I/O functions), terminal I/O, the system
databases (password file and group file), and the `tar` and `cpio` archive formats.

> The first Posix standard was a trial use version in 1986 known as "IEEEIX." The name Posix
> was suggested by Richard Stallman.

This standard was updated in 1990 by IEEE Std 1003.1–1990 (356 pages), which was
also International Standard ISO/IEC 9945–1: 1990. Minimal changes were made from
the 1988 to the 1990 version. Appended to the title was "Part 1: System Application
Program Interface (API) [C Language]" indicating that this standard was the C language API.

The next of the Posix standards was IEEE Std 1003.2–1992, and its title contained
"Part 2: Shell and Utilities." It was published in two volumes, totaling about 1300
pages. This part defines the shell (based on the System V Bourne shell) and about 100
utilities (programs normally executed from a shell, from `awk` and `basename` to `vi` and
`yacc`). Throughout this text we refer to this standard as *Posix.2*.

Next came IEEE Std 1003.1b–1993, formerly known as IEEE P1003.4. This was an
update to the 1003.1–1990 standard to include the realtime extensions developed by the
P1003.4 working group. The 1003.1b–1993 standard added the following items to the
1990 standard: file synchronization, asynchronous I/O, semaphores, memory management (`mmap` and shared memory), execution scheduling, clocks and timers, and message queues. The 1003.1b–1993 standard totaled 590 pages.

The next Posix standard was IEEE Std 1003.1, 1996 Edition [IEEE 1996], which
includes 1003.1–1990 (the base API), 1003.1b–1993 (realtime extensions), 1003.1c–1995
(pthreads), and 1003.1i–1995 (technical corrections to 1003.1b). This standard is also
called ISO/IEC 9945–1: 1996. Three chapters on threads were added for a total size of
743 pages. Throughout this text we refer to this standard as *Posix.1*.

> Over one-quarter of the 743 pages are an appendix titled "Rationale and Notes." This ratio-
> nale contains historical information and reasons why certain features were included or omit-
> ted. Often the rationale is as informative as the official standard.

This standard also contains a Foreword stating that ISO/IEC 9945 consists of the following parts:

- Part 1: System application program interface (API) [C language],
- Part 2: Shell and utilities, and
- Part 3: System administration (under development).

The Posix work that affects most of this book is IEEE Std 1003.1g: Protocol Independent Interfaces (PII), a product of the P1003.1g working group. This is the networking API standard and it defines two APIs, which it calls DNIs (Detailed Network Interfaces):

1. DNI/Socket, based on the 4.4BSD sockets API.

2. DNI/XTI, based on the X/Open XPG4 specification.

Work on this standard started in the late 1980s as the P1003.12 working group (later renamed P1003.1g), but as of this writing, the standard is not complete (but getting close!). Draft 6.4 (May 1996) was the first draft to obtain more than 75% approval from the balloting group. Draft 6.6 (March 1997) appears to be the final draft [IEEE 1997a]. Sometime in 1998 or 1999 a new version of IEEE Std 1003.1 should be printed to include the P1003.1g standard.

Even though the P1003.1g standard is not officially complete, this book uses the features from Draft 6.6 of this standard whenever possible. Throughout this text we refer to this draft as *Posix.1g*. For example, the third argument to the `connect` function (Section 4.3) is shown as a `socklen_t` datatype, even though this is new with Posix.1g. Similarly we describe the new Posix.1g `sockatmark` function (Section 21.3) and provide an implementation of it using the `ioctl` function. We also use the Posix.1g protocol value of `AF_LOCAL` instead of `AF_UNIX` for Unix domain sockets. Differences between current practice and Posix.1g are noted throughout the book. Although no vendors today support Posix.1g (since it is not final), once the standard is complete vendor support should be forthcoming.

Work on all of the Posix standards continues and it is a moving target for any book that attempts to cover it. The current status of the various Posix standards is available from `http://www.pasc.org/standing/sd11.html`.

The Open Group

The Open Group was formed in 1996 by the consolidation of the X/Open Company (founded in 1984) and the Open Software Foundation (OSF, founded in 1988). It is an international consortium of vendors and end-user customers from industry, government, and academia.

X/Open published the *X/Open Portability Guide*, Issue 3 (XPG3) in 1989. Issue 4 was published in 1992 followed by Issue 4, Version 2 in 1994. This latest version was also known as "Spec 1170," with the magic number 1170 being the sum of the number of system interfaces (926), the number of headers (70), and the number of commands (174). The latest name for this set of specifications is the "X/Open Single Unix Specification" although it is also called "Unix 95."

In March 1997 Version 2 of the Single Unix Specification was announced. Products conforming to this specification can be called "Unix 98." We refer to this specification as just "Unix 98" throughout this text. The number of interfaces required by Unix 98 increases from 1170 to 1434, although for a workstation this jumps to 3030, because it includes the CDE (Common Desktop Environment), which in turn requires the X Window System and the Motif user interface. Details are available in [Josey 1997] and `http://www.opengroup.org/public/tech/unix/version2`.

We are interested in the networking services that are part of Unix 98. These are defined in [Open Group 1997] for both the sockets and XTI APIs. This specification is nearly identical to Draft 6.6 of Posix.1g.

> Unfortunately X/Open refers to their networking standards as *XNS*: X/Open Networking Services. The version of this document that defines sockets and XTI for Unix 98 ([Open Group 1997]) is called "XNS Issue 5." In the networking world XNS has always been the acronym for the Xerox Network Systems architecture. We avoid this use of XNS and refer to this X/Open document as just the Unix 98 network API standard.

Internet Engineering Task Force

The *IETF*, the Internet Engineering Task Force, is a large open international community of network designers, operators, vendors, and researchers concerned with the evolution of the Internet architecture and the smooth operation of the Internet. It is open to any interested individual.

The Internet standards process is documented in RFC 2026 [Bradner 1996]. Internet standards normally deal with protocol issues and not with programming APIs. Nevertheless, two RFCs ([Gilligan et al. 1997] and [Stevens and Thomas 1997]) specify the sockets API for IP version 6. These are informational RFCs, not standards, and were produced to speed the deployment of portable applications by the numerous vendors working on early releases of IPv6. Standards bodies tend to take a long time. Nevertheless, at some time the IPv6 APIs will probably be standardized more formally.

Unix Versions and Portability

Most Unix systems today conform to some version of Posix.1 and Posix.2. We must use the qualifier "some" because as updates to Posix occur (e.g., the realtime extensions in 1993 and the pthreads addition in 1996) it takes vendors a year or two (sometimes more) to incorporate these latest changes.

Historically most Unix systems show either a Berkeley heritage or a System V heritage, but these differences are slowly disappearing as most vendors adopt the Posix standards. The main differences still existing deal with system administration, one area that no Posix standard currently addresses.

The focus of this book is on the forthcoming Posix.1g standard, with our main focus on the sockets API. Whenever possible we use the Posix functions.

1.11 64-bit Architectures

During the mid to late 1990s the trend is toward 64-bit architectures and 64-bit software. One reason is for larger addressing within a process (i.e., 64-bit pointers) that can address large amounts of memory (more than 2^{32} bytes). The common programming model for existing 32-bit Unix systems is called the *ILP32* model, denoting that integers (I), long integers (L), and pointers (P) occupy 32 bits. The model that is becoming most prevalent for 64-bit Unix systems is called the *LP64* model, meaning only long integers (L) and pointers (P) require 64 bits. Figure 1.17 compares these two models.

Datatype	ILP32 model	LP64 model
char	8	8
short	16	16
int	32	32
long	32	64
pointer	32	64

Figure 1.17 Comparison of number of bits to hold various datatypes for ILP32 and LP64 models.

From a programming perspective the LP64 model means we cannot assume that a pointer can be stored in an integer. We must also consider the effect of the LP64 model on the existing APIs.

ANSI C invented the size_t datatype, and this is used, for example, as the argument to malloc (the number of bytes to allocate), and the third argument to read and write (the number of bytes to read or write). On a 32-bit system size_t is a 32-bit value, but on a 64-bit system it must be a 64-bit value, to take advantage of the larger addressing model. This means a 64-bit system will probably contain a typedef of size_t to be an unsigned long. The networking API problem is that some drafts of Posix.1g specified that function arguments containing the size of a socket address structures have the size_t datatype (e.g., the third argument to bind and connect). Some XTI structures also had members with a datatype of long (e.g., the t_info and t_opthdr structures). If these had been left as is, both would change from 32-bit values to 64-bit values when a Unix system changes from the ILP32 to the LP64 model. In both instances there is no need for a 64-bit datatype: the length of a socket address structure is a few hundred bytes at the most, and the use of long for the XTI structure members was a mistake.

What we will see are new datatypes invented to handle these scenarios. The sockets API uses the socklen_t datatype for lengths of socket address structures and XTI uses the t_scalar_t and t_uscalar_t datatypes. The reason for not changing these values from 32 bits to 64 bits is to make it easier to provide binary compatibility on the new 64-bit systems for application compiled under the 32-bit systems.

1.12 Summary

Figure 1.5 shows a complete, albeit simple, TCP client that fetches the current time and date from a specified server and Figure 1.9 shows a complete version of the server. These two examples introduce many of the terms and concepts that are expanded on throughout the rest of the book.

Our client was protocol dependent on IPv4 and we modified it to use IPv6 instead. But this just gave us another protocol-dependent program. In Chapter 11 we develop some functions that let us write protocol-independent code, which will be important as the Internet starts using IPv6.

Throughout the text we will use the wrapper functions developed in Section 1.4 to reduce the size of our code, yet still check every function call for an error return. Our wrapper functions all begin with a capital letter.

The IEEE Posix standards—Posix.1 defining the basic C interface to Unix, Posix.2 defining the standard commands, and Posix.1g defining the networking APIs—have been the standards that most vendors are moving toward. The Posix standards, however, are rapidly being absorbed and expanded by the commercial standards, notably The Open Group's Unix standards, such as Unix 98.

Readers interested in the history of Unix networking should consult [Salus 1994] for a description of the Unix history, and [Salus 1995] for the history of TCP/IP and the Internet.

Exercises

1.1 Go through the steps at the end of Section 1.9 to discover information about your network topology.

1.2 Obtain the source code for the examples in this text (see the Preface). Compile and test the TCP daytime client in Figure 1.5. Run the program a few times, specifying a different IP address as the command-line argument each time.

1.3 Modify the first argument to socket in Figure 1.5 to be 9999. Compile and run the program. What happens? Find the errno value corresponding to the error that is printed. How can you find more information on this error?

1.4 Modify Figure 1.5 by placing a counter in the while loop, counting the number of times read returns a value greater than 0. Print the value of the counter before terminating. Compile and run your new client.

1.5 Modify Figure 1.9 as follows. First change the port number assigned to the sin_port member from 13 to 9999. Next, change the single call to write into a loop that calls write for each byte of the result string. Compile this modified server and start it running in the background. Next modify the client from the previous exercise (which prints the counter before terminating), changing the port number assigned to the sin_port member from 13 to 9999. Start this client, specifying the IP address of the host on which the modified server is running as the command-line argument. What value is printed as the client's counter? If possible, also try to run the client and server on different hosts.

2

The Transport Layer:
TCP and UDP

2.1 Introduction

This chapter provides an overview of the TCP/IP protocols that are used in the examples throughout the book. Our goal is to provide enough detail to understand how to use the protocols from a network programming perspective and provide references to more detailed descriptions of the actual design, implementation, and history of the protocols.

This chapter focuses on the transport layer, the TCP and UDP protocols, because most client–server applications use either TCP or UDP. These two protocols in turn use the network-layer protocol IP, either IP version 4 (IPv4) or IP version 6 (IPv6). While it is possible to use IPv4 or IPv6 directly, bypassing the transport layer, this technique (called *raw sockets*) is used less frequently. Therefore, we place a more detailed description of IPv4 and IPv6, along with ICMPv4 and ICMPv6, in Appendix A.

UDP is a simple, unreliable, datagram protocol, while TCP is a sophisticated, reliable, byte-stream protocol. We need to understand the services provided by these two transport layers to the application, so that we know what is handled by the protocol and what we must handle in the application.

There are features of TCP that, when understood, make it easier for us to write robust clients and servers. Also, when we understand these features it becomes easier to debug our clients and servers using commonly provided tools such as `netstat`. We cover various topics in this chapter that fall into this category: TCP's three-way handshake, TCP's connection termination sequence, TCP's TIME_WAIT state, TCP and UDP buffering by the socket layer, and so on.

2.2   The Big Picture

Although the protocol suite is called "TCP/IP," there are more members of this family than just TCP and IP. Figure 2.1 shows an overview of these protocols.

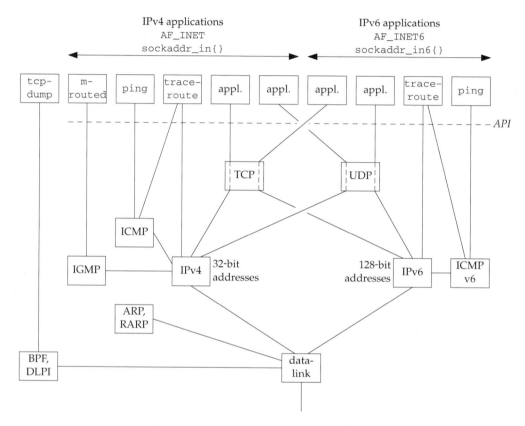

Figure 2.1   Overview of TCP/IP protocols.

We show both IPv4 and IPv6 in this figure. Moving from right to left in this figure, the rightmost four applications are using IPv6 and we talk about the AF_INET6 constant in Chapter 3 along with the sockaddr_in6 structure. The next five applications use IPv4.

The leftmost application, tcpdump, communicates directly with the datalink using either BPF (BSD Packet Filter) or DLPI (Data Link Provider Interface). We mark the dashed line beneath the nine applications on the right as the *API*, which is normally sockets or XTI. The interface to either BPF or DLPI does not use sockets or XTI.

> There is an exception to this, which we describe in more detail in Chapter 25: Linux provides access to the datalink using a special type of socket called SOCK_PACKET.

We also note in Figure 2.1 that the `traceroute` program uses two sockets: one for IP and another for ICMP. In Chapter 25 we develop IPv4 and IPv6 versions of both `ping` and `traceroute`.

We now describe each of the protocol boxes in this figure.

IPv4   *Internet Protocol, version 4.* IPv4, which we often denote as just IP, has been the workhorse protocol of the Internet protocol suite since the early 1980s. It uses 32-bit addresses (Section A.4). IPv4 provides the packet delivery service for TCP, UDP, ICMP, and IGMP.

IPv6   *Internet Protocol, version 6.* IPv6 was designed in the mid-1990s as a replacement for IPv4. The major change is a larger address comprising 128 bits (Section A.5), to deal with the explosive growth of the Internet in the 1990s. IPv6 provides the packet delivery service for TCP, UDP, and ICMPv6.

We often use the adjective *IP*, as in *IP layer* and *IP address*, when the distinction between IPv4 and IPv6 is not needed.

TCP   *Transmission Control Protocol.* TCP is a connection-oriented protocol that provides a reliable, full-duplex, byte stream for a user process. TCP sockets are an example of *stream sockets*. TCP takes care of details such as acknowledgments, timeouts, retransmissions, and the like. Most Internet application programs use TCP. Notice that TCP can use either IPv4 or IPv6.

UDP   *User Datagram Protocol.* UDP is a connectionless protocol and UDP sockets are an example of *datagram sockets*. Unlike TCP, which is a reliable protocol, there is no guarantee that UDP datagrams ever reach their intended destination. As with TCP, UDP can use either IPv4 or IPv6.

ICMP   *Internet Control Message Protocol.* ICMP handles error and control information between routers and hosts. These messages are normally generated by and processed by the TCP/IP networking software itself, not user processes, although we show the Ping program, which uses ICMP. We sometimes refer to this protocol as ICMPv4 to distinguish it from ICMPv6.

IGMP   *Internet Group Management Protocol.* IGMP is used with multicasting (Chapter 19), which is optional with IPv4.

ARP   *Address Resolution Protocol.* ARP maps an IPv4 address into a hardware address (such as an Ethernet address). ARP is normally used on broadcast networks such as Ethernet, token ring, and FDDI but is not needed on point-to-point networks.

RARP   *Reverse Address Resolution Protocol.* RARP maps a hardware address into an IPv4 address. It is sometimes used when a diskless node such as an X terminal is booting.

ICMPv6   *Internet Control Message Protocol, version 6.* ICMPv6 combines the functionality of ICMPv4, IGMP, and ARP.

BPF   *BSD Packet Filter.* This interface provides access to the datalink for a process. It is normally found on Berkeley-derived kernels.

DLPI   *Data Link Provider Interface.* This interface provides access to the datalink and is normally provided with SVR4.

All the Internet protocols are defined by *Request for Comments (RFCs)*, which are their formal specifications. The solution to Exercise 2.1 shows how to obtain RFCs.

We use the terms *IPv4/IPv6 host* and *dual-stack host* to denote a host that supports both IPv4 and IPv6.

Additional details on the TCP/IP protocols themselves are in TCPv1. The 4.4BSD implementation of TCP/IP is described in TCPv2.

2.3   UDP: User Datagram Protocol

UDP is a simple transport-layer protocol. It is described in RFC 768 [Postel 1980]. The application writes a *datagram* to a UDP socket, which is *encapsulated* as either an IPv4 datagram or an IPv6 datagram, which is then sent to its destination. But there is no guarantee that a UDP datagram ever reaches its final destination.

The problem that we encounter with network programming using UDP is its lack of reliability. If we want to be certain that a datagram reaches its destination, we must build lots of features into our application: acknowledgments from the other end, time-outs, retransmissions, and the like.

Each UDP datagram has a length and we can consider a datagram as a *record*. If the datagram reaches its final destination correctly (that is, the packet arrives without a checksum error), then the length of the datagram is passed to the receiving application. We have already mentioned that TCP is a *byte-stream* protocol, without any record boundaries at all (Section 1.2), which differs from UDP.

We also say that UDP provides a *connectionless* service as there need not be any long-term relationship between a UDP client and server. For example, a UDP client can create a socket and send a datagram to a given server and then immediately send another datagram on the same socket to a different server. Similarly a UDP server can receive five datagrams in a row on a single UDP socket, each from five different clients.

2.4   TCP: Transmission Control Protocol

The service provided by TCP to an application is different from the service provided by UDP. (TCP is described in RFC 793 [Postel 1981c]). First, TCP provides *connections* between clients and servers. A TCP client establishes a connection with a given server, exchanges data with that server across the connection, and then terminates the connection.

TCP also provides *reliability*. When TCP sends data to the other end, it requires an acknowledgment in return. If an acknowledgment is not received, TCP automatically retransmits the data and waits a longer amount of time. After some number of retransmissions, TCP will give up, with the total amount of time spent trying to send data typically between 4 and 10 minutes (depending on the implementation). TCP contains algorithms to estimate the *round-trip time* (RTT) between a client and server dynamically so that it knows how long to wait for an acknowledgment. For example, the RTT on a LAN can be milliseconds while across a WAN it can be seconds. Furthermore, TCP can measure an RTT of 1 second between a client and server and then 30 seconds later measure an RTT of 2 seconds on the same connection, caused by variations in the network traffic.

TCP also *sequences* the data by associating a sequence number with every byte that it sends. For example, assume an application writes 2048 bytes to a TCP socket, causing TCP to send two segments, the first containing the data with sequence numbers 1–1024 and the second containing the data with sequence numbers 1025–2048. (A *segment* is the unit of data that TCP passes to IP.) If the segments arrive out of order, the receiving TCP will reorder the two segments based on their sequence numbers before passing the data to the receiving application. If TCP receives duplicate data from its peer (say the peer thought a segment was lost and retransmitted it, when it wasn't really lost, the network was just overloaded), it can detect that the data has been duplicated (from the sequence numbers), and the duplicate data is discarded.

> There is no reliability provided by UDP. UDP itself does not provide anything like acknowledgments, sequence numbers, RTT estimation, timeouts, or retransmissions. If a UDP datagram is duplicated in the network, two copies can be delivered to the receiving host. Also, if a UDP client sends two datagrams to the same destination, they can be reordered by the network and arrive out of order. UDP applications must handle all these cases, as we show in Section 20.5.

TCP provides *flow control*. TCP always tells its peer exactly how many bytes of data it is willing to accept from the peer. This is called the advertised *window*. At any time, the window is the amount of room currently available in the receive buffer, guaranteeing that the sender cannot overflow the receiver's buffer. The window changes dynamically over time: as data is received from the sender, the window size decreases, but as the receiving application reads data from the buffer, the window increases. It is possible for the window to reach 0: TCP's receive buffer for this socket is full and it must wait for the application to read data from the buffer before it can take any more data from the peer.

> UDP provides no flow control. It is easy for a fast UDP sender to transmit datagrams at a rate that the UDP receiver cannot keep up with, as we show in Section 8.13.

Finally, a TCP connection is also *full-duplex*. This means that an application can send and receive data in both directions on a given connection at any time. This means that TCP must keep track of state information such as sequence numbers and window sizes for each direction of data flow: sending and receiving.

> UDP can be full-duplex.

2.5   TCP Connection Establishment and Termination

To aid our understanding of the `connect`, `accept`, and `close` functions and to help us debug TCP applications using the `netstat` program, we must understand how TCP connections are established and terminated, and TCP's state transition diagram. This is an example of increased knowledge of the underlying protocols helping us with network programming.

Three-Way Handshake

The following scenario occurs when a TCP connection is established:

1. The server must be prepared to accept an incoming connection. This is normally done by calling `socket`, `bind`, and `listen` and is called a *passive open*.

2. The client issues an *active open* by calling `connect`. This causes the client TCP to send a SYN segment (which stands for "synchronize") to tell the server the client's initial sequence number for the data that the client will send on the connection. Normally there is no data sent with the SYN: it just contains an IP header, a TCP header, and possible TCP options (which we talk about shortly).

3. The server must acknowledge the client's SYN and the server must also send its own SYN containing the initial sequence number for the data that the server will send on the connection. The server sends its SYN and the ACK of the client's SYN in a single segment.

4. The client must acknowledge the server's SYN.

The minimum number of packets required for this exchange is three; hence this is called TCP's *three-way handshake*. We show a picture of the three segments in Figure 2.2.

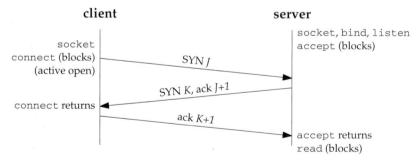

Figure 2.2 TCP three-way handshake.

We show the client's initial sequence number as *J* and the server's initial sequence number as *K*. The acknowledgment number in an ACK is the next expected sequence number for the end sending the ACK. Since a SYN occupies 1 byte of the sequence number space, the acknowledgment number in the ACK of each SYN is the initial sequence number plus one. Similarly the ACK of each FIN is the sequence number of the FIN plus one.

> An everyday analogy for establishing a TCP connection is the telephone system [Nemeth 1997]. The socket function is the equivalent of having a telephone to use. bind is telling other people your telephone number so that they can call you. listen is turning on the ringer so that you will hear when an incoming call arrives. connect requires that we know the other person's phone number and dial it. accept is when the person being called answers the phone. Having the client's identity returned by accept (where the identify is the client's IP address and port number) is similar to having the caller ID feature show the caller's phone number. One difference, however, is that accept returns the client's identity only after the connection has been established, whereas the caller ID feature shows the caller's phone number before we choose whether to answer the phone or not. If the Domain Name System is used (Chapter 9), it provides a service analogous to a telephone book. gethostbyname is similar to looking up a person's phone number in the phone book. gethostbyaddr would be the equivalent of having a phone book sorted by telephone numbers that we could search, instead of sorted by name.

TCP Options

Each SYN can contain TCP options. Commonly used options are the following:

- MSS option. With this option the TCP sending the SYN announces its *maximum segment size*, the maximum amount of data that it is willing to accept in each TCP segment, on this connection We will see how to fetch and set this TCP option with the TCP_MAXSEG socket option (Section 7.9).

- Window scale option. The maximum window that either TCP can advertise to the other TCP is 65535, because the corresponding field in the TCP header occupies 16 bits. But high-speed connections (45 Mbits/sec and faster, as described in RFC 1323 [Jacobson, Braden, and Borman 1992]) or long-delay paths (satellite links) require a larger window to obtain the maximum throughput possible. This newer option specifies that the advertised window in the TCP header must be scaled (left-shifted) by 0–14 bits, providing a maximum window of almost one gigabyte (65535×2^{14}). Both end systems must support this option for the window scale to be used on a connection. We will see how to effect this option with the SO_RCVBUF socket option (Section 7.5).

  > To provide interoperability with older implementations that do not support this option, the following rules apply. TCP can send the option with its SYN as part of an active open. But it can scale its windows only if the other end also sends the option with its SYN. Similarly the server's TCP can send this option only if it receives the option with the client's SYN. This logic assumes that implementations ignore options that they do not understand, which is required and common, but unfortunately, not guaranteed with all implementations.

- Timestamp option. This option is needed for high-speed connections to prevent possible data corruption caused by lost packets that then reappear. Since it is a newer option, it is negotiated similarly to the window scale option. As a network programmer there is nothing we need worry about with this option.

The MSS option is supported by most implementations, while the window scale and timestamp options are newer. These latter two are sometimes called the "RFC 1323 options" as that RFC [Jacobson, Braden, and Borman 1992] specifies the options. They are also called the "long fat pipe" options, since a network with either a high bandwidth or a long delay is called a *long fat pipe*. Chapter 24 of TCPv1 contains more details on these newer options.

TCP Connection Termination

While it takes three segments to establish a connection, it takes four to terminate a connection.

1. One application calls `close` first, and we say that this end performs the *active close*. This end's TCP sends a FIN segment, which means it is finished sending data.

2. The other end that receives the FIN performs the *passive close*. The received FIN is acknowledged by TCP. The receipt of the FIN is also passed to the application as an end-of-file (after any data that may already be queued for the application to receive), since the receipt of the FIN means the application will never receive any additional data on the connection.

3. Sometime later the application that received the end-of-file will `close` its socket. This causes its TCP to send a FIN.

4. The TCP on the system that receives this final FIN (the end that did the active close) acknowledges the FIN.

Since a FIN and an ACK are required in each direction, four segments are normally required. We use the qualifier "normally" because in some scenarios the FIN in step 1 is sent with data. Also, the segments in steps 2 and 3 are both from the end performing the passive close and could be combined into one segment. We show these packets in Figure 2.3.

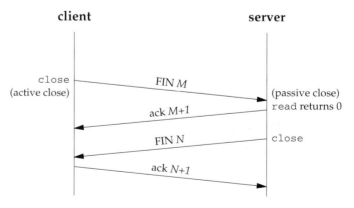

Figure 2.3 Packets exchanged when a TCP connection is closed.

A FIN occupies 1 byte of sequence number space just like a SYN. Therefore the ACK of each FIN is the sequence number of the FIN plus one.

Between steps 2 and 3 it is possible for data to flow from the end doing the passive close to the end doing the active close. This is called a *half-close* and we talk about this in detail with the shutdown function in Section 6.6.

The sending of each FIN occurs when the socket is closed. We indicated that the application calls close for this to happen but realize that when a Unix process terminates, either voluntarily (calling exit or having the main function return) or involuntarily (receiving a signal that terminates the process), all open descriptors are closed, which will also cause a FIN to be sent on any TCP connection that is still open.

Although we show the client in Figure 2.3 performing the active close, either end—the client or the server—can perform the active close. Often the client performs the active close, but with some protocols (notably HTTP), the server performs the active close.

TCP State Transition Diagram

The operation of TCP with regard to connection establishment and connection termination can be specified with a *state transition diagram*. We show this in Figure 2.4.

There are 11 different states defined for a connection and the rules of TCP dictate the transitions from one state to another, based on the current state and the segment received in that state. For example, if the application performs an active open in the CLOSED state, TCP sends a SYN and the new state is SYN_SENT. If TCP next receives a SYN with an ACK, it sends an ACK and the new state is ESTABLISHED. This final state is where most data transfer occurs.

The two arrows leading from the ESTABLISHED state deal with the termination of a connection. If the application calls close before receiving an end-of-file (an active close), the transition is to the FIN_WAIT_1 state. But if the application receives a FIN while in the ESTABLISHED state (a passive close), the transition is to the CLOSE_WAIT state.

We denote the normal client transitions with a darker solid line and the normal server transitions with a darker dashed line. We also note that there are two transitions that we have not talked about: a simultaneous open (when both ends send SYNs at about the same time and the SYNs cross in the network) and a simultaneous close (when both ends send FINs at the same time). Chapter 18 of TCPv1 contains examples and discussion of both scenarios, which are possible but rare.

One reason for showing the state transition diagram is to show the 11 TCP states with their names. These states are displayed by netstat, which is a useful tool when debugging client–server applications. We will use netstat to monitor the state changes in Chapter 5.

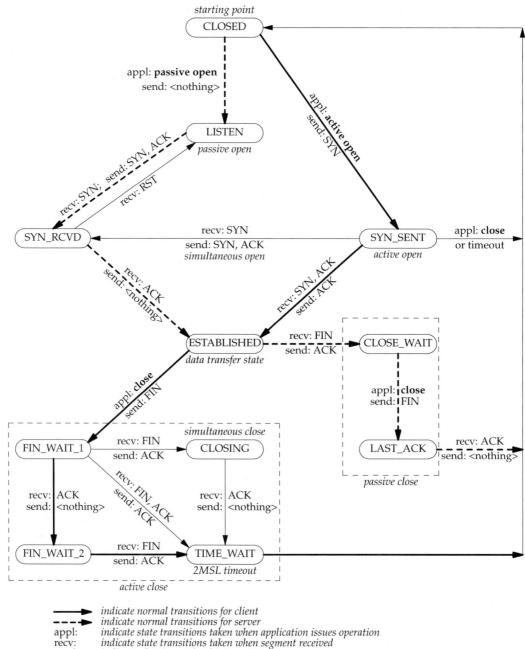

starting point

Figure 2.4 TCP state transition diagram.

Watching the Packets

Figure 2.5 shows the actual packet exchange that takes place for a complete TCP connection: the connection establishment, data transfer, and connection termination. We also show the TCP states through which each endpoint passes.

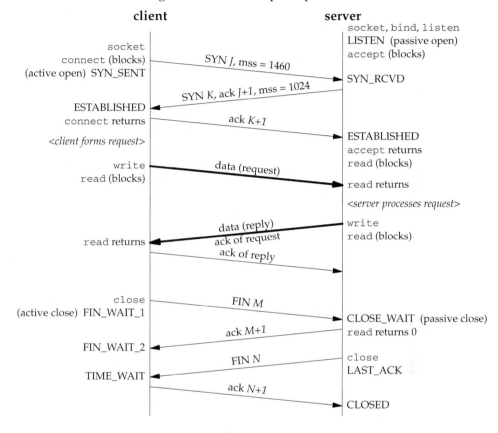

Figure 2.5 Packet exchange for TCP connection.

The client in this example announces an MSS of 1460 (typical for IPv4 on an Ethernet) and the server announces an MSS of 1024 (typical for older Berkeley-derived implementations on an Ethernet). It is OK for the MSS to be different in each direction. (See also Exercise 2.5.)

Once the connection is established, the client forms a request and sends it to the server. We assume this request fits into a single TCP segment (i.e., less than 1024 bytes given the server's announced MSS). The server processes the request and sends a reply, and we assume that the reply fits in a single segment (less than 1460 in this example).

We show both data segments as bolder arrows. Notice that the acknowledgment of the client's request is sent with the server's reply. This is called *piggybacking* and will normally happen when the time it takes the server to process the request and generate the reply is less than around 200 ms. If the server takes longer, say 1 second, we would see the acknowledgment followed later by the reply. (The dynamics of TCP data flow are covered in detail in Chapters 19 and 20 of TCPv1.)

We then show the four segments that terminate the connection. Notice that the end that performs the active close (the client in this scenario) enters the TIME_WAIT state. We discuss this in the next section.

It is important to notice in Figure 2.5 that if the entire purpose of this connection was to send a one-segment request and receive a one-segment reply, there are eight segments of overhead involved when using TCP. If UDP were used instead, only two packets would be exchanged: the request and the reply. But switching from TCP to UDP removes all the reliability that TCP provides to the application, pushing lots of these details from the transport layer (TCP) into the UDP application. Another important feature provided by TCP is congestion control, which must then be handled by the UDP application. Nevertheless, it is important to understand that many applications that are built using UDP do so because the application exchanges small amounts of data and UDP avoids the overhead of the TCP connection establishment and connection termination.

> An alternative to UDP in this scenario is T/TCP: TCP for Transactions. We describe this in Section 13.9.

2.6   TIME_WAIT State

Undoubtedly, the most misunderstood aspect of TCP with regard to network programming is its TIME_WAIT state. We can see in Figure 2.4 that the end that performs the active close goes through this state. The duration that this endpoint remains in this state is twice the MSL (*maximum segment lifetime*), sometimes called 2MSL.

Every implementation of TCP must choose a value for the MSL. The recommended value in RFC 1122 [Braden 1989] is 2 minutes, although Berkeley-derived implementations have traditionally used a value of 30 seconds instead. This means the duration of the TIME_WAIT state is between 1 and 4 minutes. The MSL is the maximum amount of time that any given IP datagram can live in an internet. We know this time is bounded because every datagram contains an 8-bit hop limit (the IPv4 TTL field in Figure A.1 and the IPv6 hop limit field in Figure A.2) with a maximum value of 255. Although this is a hop limit and not a true time limit, the assumption is made that a packet with the maximum hop limit of 255 cannot exist in an internet for more than MSL seconds.

The way in which a packet gets "lost" in an internet is usually the result of routing anomalies. A router crashes or a link between two routers goes down and it takes the routing protocols seconds or minutes to stabilize and find an alternate path. During that time period routing loops can occur (router A sends packets to router B, and B sends them back to A) and packets can get caught in these loops. In the meantime, assuming the lost packet is a TCP segment, the sending TCP times out and retransmits the packet, and the retransmitted packet gets to the final destination by some alternate path. But sometime later (up to MSL seconds after the lost packet started on its journey) the routing loop is corrected and the packet that was lost in the loop is sent to the final destination. This original packet is called a *lost duplicate* or a *wandering duplicate*. TCP must handle these duplicates.

There are two reasons for the TIME_WAIT state:

1. to implement TCP's full-duplex connection termination reliably, and

2. to allow old duplicate segments to expire in the network.

The first reason can be explained by looking at Figure 2.5 and assuming that the final ACK is lost. The server will resend its final FIN so the client must maintain state information allowing it to resend the final ACK. If it did not maintain this information, it would respond with an RST (a different type of TCP segment), which would be interpreted by the server as an error. If TCP is performing all the work necessary to terminate both directions of data flow cleanly for a connection (its full-duplex close), then it must correctly handle the loss of any of these four segments. This example also shows why the end that performs the active close is the end that remains in the TIME_WAIT state: because that end is the one that might have to retransmit the final ACK.

To understand the second reason for the TIME_WAIT state, assume we have a TCP connection between 206.62.226.33 port 1500 and 198.69.10.2 port 21. This connection is closed and then sometime later we establish another connection between the same IP addresses and ports: 206.62.226.33 port 1500 and 198.69.10.2 port 21. This latter connection is called an *incarnation* of the previous connection since the IP addresses and ports are the same. TCP must prevent old duplicates from a connection from reappearing at some time later and being misinterpreted as belonging to a new incarnation of the same connection. To do this TCP will not initiate a new incarnation of a connection that is currently in the TIME_WAIT state. Since the duration of the TIME_WAIT state is twice the MSL, this allows MSL seconds for a packet in one direction to be lost, and another MSL seconds for the reply to be lost. By enforcing this rule we are guaranteed that when we successfully establish a TCP connection, all old duplicates from previous incarnations of this connection have expired in the network.

> There is an exception to this rule. Berkeley-derived implementations will initiate a new incarnation of a connection that is currently in the TIME_WAIT state if the arriving SYN has a sequence number that is "greater than" the ending sequence number from the previous incarnation. Pages 958–959 of TCPv2 talk about this in more detail. This requires the server to perform the active close, since the TIME_WAIT state must exist on the end that receives the next SYN. This capability is used by the `rsh` command. RFC 1185 [Jacobson, Braden, and Zhang 1990] talks about some pitfalls in doing this.

2.7 Port Numbers

At any given time, multiple processes can use either UDP or TCP. Both TCP and UDP use 16-bit integer *port numbers* to differentiate between these processes.

When a client wants to contact a server, the client must identify the server with which it wants to communicate. Both TCP and UDP define a group of *well-known ports* to identify well-known services. For example, every TCP/IP implementation that supports FTP assigns the well-known port of 21 (decimal) to the FTP server. TFTP servers, for the Trivial File Transfer Protocol, are assigned the UDP port of 69.

Clients, on the other hand, use *ephemeral ports*, that is, short-lived ports. These port numbers are normally assigned automatically by TCP or UDP to the client. Clients normally do not care about the value of the ephemeral port; the client just needs to be certain that the ephemeral port is unique on the client host. The TCP and UDP codes guarantee this uniqueness.

RFC 1700 [Reynolds and Postel 1994] contains the list of port number assignments from the *Internet Assigned Numbers Authority* (IANA). But usually the file `ftp://ftp.isi.edu/in-notes/iana/assignments/port-numbers` is more up to date than the RFC. The port numbers are divided into three ranges:

1. The *well-known ports*: 0 through 1023. These port numbers are controlled and assigned by the IANA. When possible, the same port is assigned to a given service for both TCP and UDP. For example, port 80 is assigned for a Web server, for both protocols, even though all implementations currently use only TCP.

2. The *registered ports*: 1024 through 49151 . These are not controlled by the IANA, but the IANA registers and lists the uses of these ports as a convenience to the community. When possible, the same port is assigned to a given service for both TCP and UDP. For example, ports 6000 through 6063 are assigned for an X Window server, for both protocols, even though all implementations currently use only TCP. The upper limit of 49151 for these ports is new, as RFC 1700 [Reynolds and Postel 1994] lists the upper range as 65535.

3. The *dynamic* or *private* ports, 49152 through 65535. The IANA says nothing about these ports. These are what we call *ephemeral* ports.

(The magic number 49152 is three-fourths of 65536.) Figure 2.6 shows this division along with the common allocation of the port numbers.

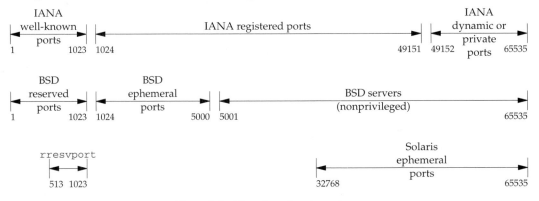

Figure 2.6 Allocation of port numbers.

We note the following points from this figure.

- Unix systems have the concept of a *reserved port*, which is any port less than 1024. These ports can only be assigned to a socket by a superuser process. All the IANA well-known ports are reserved ports; hence the server allocating this port (such as the FTP server) must have superuser privileges when it starts.

- Historically, Berkeley-derived implementations (starting with 4.3BSD) have allocated ephemeral ports in the range 1024–5000. This was fine in the early 1980s, when server hosts were not capable of handling too many clients at once, but it is easy today to find a host that can support more than 3977 clients at any given time. Therefore some systems allocate ephemeral ports differently (e.g., Solaris as we show in Figure 2.6) to provide more ephemeral ports.

  > As it turns out, the upper limit of 5000 for the ephemeral ports, which many systems currently implement, was a typo [Borman 1997a]. The limit should have been 50,000.

- There are a few clients (not servers) that require a reserved port as part of the client–server authentication: the `rlogin` and `rsh` clients are the common examples. These clients call the library function `rresvport` to create a TCP socket and assign an unused port in the range 513–1023 to the socket. This function normally tries to bind port 1023 and if that fails, tries to bind 1022, and so on, until it either succeeds, or fails on port 513.

  > Notice that the BSD reserved ports and the `rresvport` function both overlap with the upper half of the IANA well-known ports. This is because the IANA well-known ports used to stop at 255. RFC 1340 (a previous "Assigned Numbers" RFC) in 1992 started assigning well-known ports between 256 and 1023. The previous "Assigned Numbers" document, RFC 1060 in 1990, called ports 256–1023 the *Unix Standard Services*. There are numerous Berkeley-derived servers that picked their well-known ports in the 1980s starting at 512 (leaving 256–511 untouched). The `rresvport` function chose to start at the top of the 512–1023 range and work down.

Socket Pair

The *socket pair* for a TCP connection is the 4-tuple that defines the two endpoints of the connection: the local IP address, local TCP port, foreign IP address, and foreign TCP port. A socket pair uniquely identifies every TCP connection on an internet.

The two values that identify each endpoint, an IP address and a port number, are often called a *socket*.

We can extend the concept of a socket pair to UDP, even though UDP is connectionless. When we describe the socket functions (`bind`, `connect`, `getpeername`, etc.), we will note which functions specify which values in the socket pair. For example, `bind` lets the application specify the local IP address and local port, for both TCP and UDP sockets.

2.8   TCP Port Numbers and Concurrent Servers

With a concurrent server, where the main server loop spawns a child to handle each new connection, what happens if the child continues to use the well-known port number while servicing a long request? Let's examine a typical sequence. First, the server is started on the host bsdi (Figure 1.16), which is multihomed with IP addresses 206.62.226.35 and 206.62.226.66 and the server does a passive open using its well-known port number (21, for this example). It is now waiting for a client request which we show in Figure 2.7.

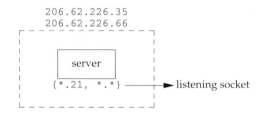

Figure 2.7   TCP server with a passive open on port 21.

We use the notation {*.21, *.*} to indicate the server's socket pair. The server is waiting for a connection request on any local interface (the first asterisk), on port 21. The foreign IP address and foreign port are not specified and we denote them as *.*. We also call this a *listening socket*.

> We use a period to separate the IP address from the port number because that is what netstat uses. This is sometimes confusing because decimal points are used in both domain names (solaris.kohala.com.21) and in IPv4 dotted-decimal notation (206.62.226.33.21).

When we specify the local IP address as an asterisk, it is called the *wildcard* character. If the host on which the server is running is multihomed (as in this example), the server can specify that it wants only to accept incoming connections that arrive destined to one specific local interface. This is a one-or-any choice for the server. The server cannot specify a list of multiple addresses. The wildcard local address is the "any" choice. In Figure 1.9 the wildcard address was specified by setting the IP address in the socket address structure to INADDR_ANY before calling bind.

At some later time a client starts on the host with IP address 198.69.10.2 and executes an active open to the server's IP address of 206.62.226.35. We assume the ephemeral port chosen by the client TCP is 1500 for this example. This is shown in Figure 2.8. Beneath the client we show its socket pair.

When the server receives and accepts the client's connection, it forks a copy of itself, letting the child handle the client, as we show in Figure 2.9. (We describe the fork function in Section 4.7.)

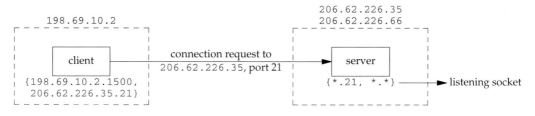

Figure 2.8 Connection request from client to server.

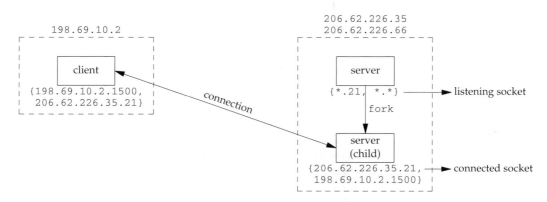

Figure 2.9 Concurrent server has child handle client.

At this point we must distinguish on the server host between the listening socket and the connected socket. Notice that the connected socket uses the same local port (21) as used for the listening socket. Also notice that on the multihomed server the local address is filled in for the connected socket (206.62.226.35) once the connection is established.

The next step assumes that another client process on the client host requests a connection with the same server. The TCP code on the client host assigns the new client socket an unused ephemeral port number, say 1501. This gives us the scenario shown in Figure 2.10. On the server the two connections are distinct: the socket pair for the first connection differs from the socket pair for the second connection because the client's TCP chooses an unused port for the second connection (1501).

Notice from this example that TCP cannot demultiplex incoming segments by looking at just the destination port number. TCP must look at all four elements in the socket pair to determine which endpoint receives an arriving segment. In Figure 2.10 we have three sockets with the same local port (21). If a segment arrives from 198.69.10.2 port 1500 destined for 206.62.226.35 port 21, it is delivered to the first child. If a segment arrives from 198.69.10.2 port 1501 destined for 206.62.226.35 port 21, it is delivered to the second child. All other TCP segments destined for port 21 are delivered to the original server with the listening socket.

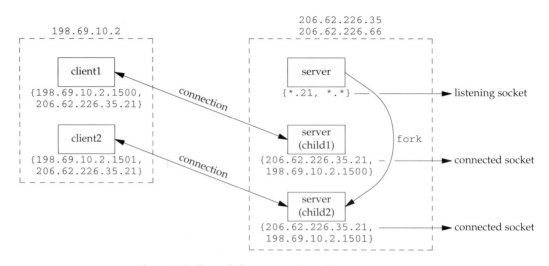

Figure 2.10 Second client connection with same server.

2.9   Buffer Sizes and Limitations

There are certain limits that affect the size of IP datagrams. We first describe these limits and then tie them all together with regard to how they affect the data an application can transmit.

- The maximum size of an IPv4 datagram is 65535 bytes, including the IPv4 header. This is because of the 16-bit total length field in Figure A.1.

- The maximum size of an IPv6 datagram is 65575 bytes, including the 40-byte IPv6 header. This is because of the 16-bit payload length field in Figure A.2. Notice that the IPv6 payload length field does not include the size of the IPv6 header, while the IPv4 total length field does include the header size.

    IPv6 has a jumbo payload option, which extends the payload length field to 32 bits, but this option is supported only on those datalinks with an MTU that exceeds 65535. (This is intended for host-to-host interconnects, such as HIPPI, which often have no inherent MTU.)

- Many networks have an *MTU, maximum transmission unit*, which can be dictated by the hardware. For example, the Ethernet MTU is 1500 bytes. Other datalinks, such as point-to-point links using the PPP protocol, have a configurable MTU. Older SLIP links often used an MTU of 296 bytes.

    The minimum link MTU for IPv4 is 68 bytes. The minimum link MTU for IPv6 is 576 bytes.

- The smallest MTU in the path between two hosts is called the *path MTU*. Today, the Ethernet MTU of 1500 bytes is often the path MTU. The path MTU need not be the same in both directions between any two hosts, because routing in the Internet is often asymmetric [Paxson 1996]. That is, the route from A to B can differ from the route from B to A.

- When an IP datagram is to be sent out an interface, if the size of the datagram exceeds the link MTU, *fragmentation* is performed by both IPv4 and IPv6. The fragments are never *reassembled* until they reach the final destination. IPv4 hosts perform fragmentation on datagrams that they generate and IPv4 routers perform fragmentation on datagrams that they forward. But with IPv6 only hosts perform fragmentation on datagrams that they generate; IPv6 routers do not fragment datagrams that they are forwarding.

> We must be careful with our terminology. A box labeled an IPv6 router may indeed perform fragmentation, but only on datagrams that the router itself generates, never on datagrams that it is forwarding. When this box generates IPv6 datagrams, it is really acting as a host. For example, most routers support the Telnet protocol and this is used for configuration of the router by administrators. The IP datagrams generated by the router's Telnet server are generated by the router, not forwarded by the router.
>
> You may notice that fields exist in the IPv4 header (Figure A.1) to handle IPv4 fragmentation, but there are no fields in the IPv6 header (Figure A.2) for fragmentation. Since fragmentation is the exception, rather than the rule, IPv6 contains an option header with the fragmentation information.

- If the DF bit ("don't fragment") is set in the IPv4 header (Figure A.1) it specifies that this datagram must not be fragmented, either by the sending host or by any router. A router that receives an IPv4 datagram with the DF bit set whose size exceeds the outgoing link's MTU generates an ICMPv4 "destination unreachable, fragmentation needed but DF bit set" error message (Figure A.15).

  Since IPv6 routers do not perform fragmentation, there is an implied DF bit with every IPv6 datagram. When an IPv6 router receives a datagram whose size exceeds the outgoing link's MTU, it generates an ICMPv6 "packet too big" error message (Figure A.16).

  The IPv4 DF bit and its implied IPv6 counterpart can be used for *path MTU discovery* (RFC 1191 [Mogul and Deering 1990] for IPv4 and RFC 1981 [McCann, Deering, and Mogul 1996] for IPv6). For example, if TCP uses this technique with IPv4, then it sends all of its datagrams with the DF bit set. If some intermediate router returns an ICMP "destination unreachable, fragmentation needed but DF bit set" error, TCP decreases the amount of data it sends per datagram and retransmits. Path MTU discovery is optional with IPv4 but should be supported by all IPv6 implementations.

- IPv4 and IPv6 define a *minimum reassembly buffer size*: the minimum datagram size that we are guaranteed any implementation must support. For IPv4 this is 576 bytes. IPv6 raises this to 1500 bytes. With IPv4, for example, we have no idea whether a given destination can accept a 577-byte datagram or not. Therefore many IPv4 applications that use UDP (DNS, RIP, TFTP, BOOTP, SNMP) prevent the application from generating IP datagrams that exceed this size.

- TCP has an *MSS, maximum segment size*, that announces to the peer TCP the maximum amount of TCP data that the peer can send per segment. We saw the MSS option on the SYN segments in Figure 2.5. The goal of the MSS is to tell the peer the actual value of the reassembly buffer size and to try to avoid fragmentation. The MSS is often set to the interface MTU minus the fixed sizes of the IP and TCP headers. On an Ethernet using IPv4 this would be 1460, and on an Ethernet using IPv6 this would be 1440. (The TCP header is 20 bytes for both, but the IPv4 header is 20 bytes and the IPv6 header is 40 bytes.)

The MSS value in the TCP MSS option is a 16-bit field, limiting the value to 65535. This is fine for IPv4, since the maximum amount of TCP data in an IPv4 datagram is 65495 (65535 minus the 20-byte IPv4 header and minus the 20-byte TCP header). But with the IPv6 jumbo payload option, a different technique is used (RFC 2147 [Borman 1997b]). First, the maximum amount of TCP data in an IPv6 datagram without the jumbo payload option is 65515 (65535 minus the 20-byte TCP header). Therefore the MSS value of 65535 is considered a special case that designates "infinity." This value is used only if the jumbo payload option is being used, which requires an MTU that exceeds 65535. If TCP is using the jumbo payload option and receives an MSS announcement of 65535 from the peer, the limit on the datagram sizes that it sends is just the interface MTU. If this turns out to be too large (i.e., there is a link in the path with a smaller MTU) then path MTU discovery will determine the smaller value.

TCP Output

Given all these terms and definitions, Figure 2.11 shows what happens when an application writes data to a TCP socket.

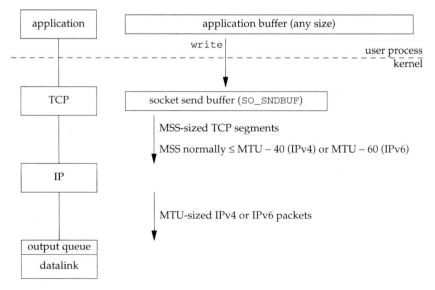

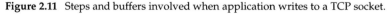

Figure 2.11 Steps and buffers involved when application writes to a TCP socket.

Every TCP socket has a send buffer and we can change the size of this buffer with the SO_SNDBUF socket option (Section 7.5). When the application calls `write`, the kernel copies all the data from the application buffer into the socket send buffer. If there is insufficient room in the socket buffer for all of the application's data (either the application buffer is larger than the socket send buffer, or there is already data in the socket send buffer), the process is put to sleep. This assumes the normal default of a blocking socket. (We talk about nonblocking sockets in Chapter 15.) The kernel will not return from the `write` until the final byte in the application buffer has been copied into the socket send buffer. Therefore the successful return from a `write` to a TCP socket only tells us that we can reuse our application buffer. It does *not* tell us that either the peer TCP has received the data, or that the peer application has received the data. (We talk about this more with the SO_LINGER socket option in Section 7.5.)

TCP takes the data in the socket send buffer and sends it to the peer TCP, based on all the rules of TCP data transmission (Chapters 19 and 20 of TCPv1). The peer TCP must acknowledge the data, and as the ACKs arrive from the peer, only then can our TCP discard the acknowledged data from the socket send buffer. TCP must keep a copy of our data until it is acknowledged by the peer.

TCP sends the data to IP in MSS-sized chunks or smaller, prepending its TCP header to each segment, where the MSS is the value announced by the peer, or 536 if the peer did not send an MSS option. IP prepends its header, searches the routing table for the destination IP address (the matching routing table entry specifies the outgoing interface), and passes the datagram to the appropriate datalink. IP might perform fragmentation before passing the datagram to the datalink, but as we said earlier, one goal of the MSS option is to try to avoid fragmentation and newer implementations also use path MTU discovery. Each datalink has an output queue and if this queue is full, the packet is discarded and an error is returned up the protocol stack: from the datalink to IP and then from IP to TCP. TCP will note this error and try sending the segment later. The application is not told of this transient condition.

UDP Output

Figure 2.12 shows what happens when an application writes data to a UDP socket. This time we show the socket send buffer as a dashed box because it doesn't really exist. A UDP socket has a send buffer size (which we can change with the SO_SNDBUF socket option, Section 7.5), but this is simply an upper limit on the maximum sized UDP datagram that can be written to the socket. If an application writes a datagram larger than the socket send buffer size, EMSGSIZE is returned. Since UDP is unreliable, it does not need to keep a copy of the application's data and does not need an actual send buffer. (The application data is normally copied into a kernel buffer of some form as it passes down the protocol stack, but this copy is discarded by the datalink layer after the data is transmitted.)

UDP simply prepends its 8-byte header and passes the datagram to IP. IPv4 or IPv6 prepends its header, determines the outgoing interface by performing the routing function, and then either adds the datagram to the datalink output queue (if it fits within the MTU) or fragments the datagram and adds each fragment to the datalink output queue.

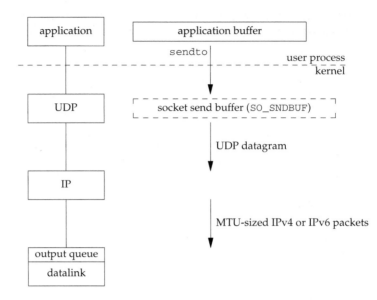

Figure 2.12 Steps and buffers involved when application writes to a UDP socket.

If a UDP application sends large datagrams (say 2000-byte datagrams), there is a much higher probability of fragmentation than with TCP, because TCP breaks the application data into MSS-sized chunks, something that has no counterpart in UDP.

The successful return from a write to a UDP socket tells us that either the datagram or all fragments of the datagram have been added to the datalink output queue. If there is no room on the queue for the datagram or one of its fragments, ENOBUFS is often returned to the application.

> Unfortunately some implementations do not return this error, giving the application no indication that the datagram was discarded without even being transmitted.

2.10 Standard Internet Services

Figure 2.13 lists several standard services that are provided by most implementations of TCP/IP. Notice that all are provided using both TCP and UDP and the port number is the same for both protocols.

Name	TCP port	UDP port	RFC	Description
echo	7	7	862	Server returns whatever the client sends.
discard	9	9	863	Server discards whatever the client sends.
daytime	13	13	867	Server returns the time and date in a human-readable format.
chargen	19	19	864	TCP server sends a continual stream of characters, until the connection is terminated by the client. UDP server sends a datagram containing a random number of characters each time the client sends a datagram.
time	37	37	868	Server returns the time as a 32-bit binary number. This number represents the number of seconds since midnight January 1, 1900, UTC.

Figure 2.13 Standard TCP/IP services provided by most implementations.

Often these services are provided by the `inetd` daemon on Unix hosts (Section 12.5). These standard services provide an easy testing facility, using the standard Telnet client. For example, the following tests both the daytime and echo servers.

```
solaris % telnet bsdi daytime
Trying 206.62.226.35...                        output by Telnet client
Connected to bsdi.kohala.com.                  output by Telnet client
Escape character is '^]'.                       output by Telnet client
Tue Mar 19 11:06:49 1996                        output by daytime server
Connection closed by foreign host.              output by Telnet client (server closes connection)

solaris % telnet bsdi echo
Trying 206.62.226.35...                        output by Telnet client
Connected to bsdi.kohala.com.                  output by Telnet client
Escape character is '^]'.                       output by Telnet client
hello, world                                    we type this
hello, world                                    and it is echoed back by the server
^]                                              we type control and right bracket to talk to Telnet client
telnet> quit                                    and tell client we are done
Connection closed.                              client closes the connection this time
```

In these two examples we type the name of the host and the name of the service (`daytime` and `echo`). These service names are mapped into the port numbers shown in Figure 2.13 by the `/etc/services` file, as we describe in Section 9.9.

Notice that when we connect to the `daytime` server, the server performs the active close, while with the `echo` server, the client performs the active close. Recall from Figure 2.4 that the end performing the active close is the end that goes through the TIME_WAIT state.

2.11 Protocol Usage by Common Internet Applications

Figure 2.14 summarizes the protocol usage of various common Internet applications.

Application	IP	ICMP	UDP	TCP
Ping		•		
Traceroute		•	•	
OSPF (routing protocol)	•			
RIP (routing protocol)			•	
BGP (routing protocol)				•
BOOTP (bootstrap protocol)			•	
DHCP (bootstrap protocol)			•	
NTP (time protocol)			•	
TFTP (trivial FTP)			•	
SNMP (network management)			•	
SMTP (electronic mail)				•
Telnet (remote login)				•
FTP (file transfer)				•
HTTP (the Web)				•
NNTP (network news)				•
DNS (domain name system)			•	•
NFS (network file system)			•	•
Sun RPC (remote procedure call)			•	•
DCE RPC (remote procedure call)			•	•

Figure 2.14 Protocol usage of various common Internet applications.

The first two applications, Ping and Traceroute, are diagnostic applications that use ICMP. Traceroute builds its own UDP packets to send and reads ICMP replies. The three popular routing protocols demonstrate the variety of transport protocols used by routing protocols. OSPF uses IP directly, using a raw socket, while RIP uses UDP and BGP uses TCP.

The next five are UDP-based applications, followed by five TCP applications. The final four are applications that use both UDP and TCP.

2.12 Summary

UDP is a simple, unreliable, connectionless protocol, while TCP is a complex, reliable, connection-oriented protocol. While most applications on the Internet use TCP (the Web, Telnet, FTP, and email), there is a need for both transport layers. In Section 20.4 we discuss the reasons to choose UDP instead of TCP.

TCP establishes connections using a three-way handshake and terminates connections using a four-packet exchange. When a TCP connection is established, it goes from the CLOSED state to the ESTABLISHED state, and when it is terminated, it goes back to the CLOSED state. There are 11 states in which a TCP connection can be, and a state transition diagram gives the rules on how to go between the states. Understanding this diagram is essential to diagnosing problems using the `netstat` command and understanding what happens when we call functions such as `connect`, `accept`, and `close`.

TCP's TIME_WAIT state is a continual source of confusion with network programmers. This state exists to implement TCP's full-duplex connection termination (i.e., to handle the case of the final ACK being lost), and to allow old duplicate segments to expire in the network.

Exercises

2.1   We have mentioned IP versions 4 and 6. What happened to version 5 and what were versions 0, 1, 2, and 3? (*Hint*: Find the latest "Assigned Numbers" RFC. Feel free to skip ahead to the solution if you do not know how to obtain RFCs electronically.)

2.2   Where would you look to find more information about the protocol that is assigned IP version 5?

2.3   With Figure 2.11 we said that TCP assumes an MSS of 536 if it does not receive an MSS option from the peer. Why is this value used?

2.4   Draw a figure like Figure 2.5 for the daytime client–server in Chapter 1, assuming the server returns the 26 bytes of data in a single TCP segment.

2.5   A connection is established between a host on an Ethernet, whose TCP advertises an MSS of 1460, and a host on a token ring, whose TCP advertises an MSS of 4096. Neither host implements path MTU discovery. Watching the packets we never see more than 1460 bytes of data in either direction. Why?

2.6   In Figure 2.14 we said that OSPF uses IP directly. What is the value of the protocol field in the IPv4 header (Figure A.1) for these OSPF datagrams?

Part 2

Elementary Sockets

3

Sockets Introduction

3.1 Introduction

This chapter begins the description of the sockets API (application program interface). We begin with socket address structures, which will be found in almost every example in the text. These structures can be passed in two directions: from the process to the kernel, and from the kernel to the process. The latter case is an example of a value–result argument, and we will encounter other examples of these arguments throughout the text.

The address conversion functions convert between a text representation of an address and the binary value that goes into a socket address structure. Most existing IPv4 code uses `inet_addr` and `inet_ntoa`, but two new functions, `inet_pton` and `inet_ntop`, handle both IPv4 and IPv6.

One problem with these address conversion functions is that they are protocol dependent on the type of address being converted: IPv4 or IPv6. We develop a set of functions whose names begin with `sock_` that work with socket address structures in a protocol-independent fashion. We will use these throughout the text to make our code protocol independent.

3.2 Socket Address Structures

Most of the socket functions require a pointer to a socket address structure as an argument. Each supported protocol suite defines its own socket address structure. The names of these structure begins with `sockaddr_` with a unique suffix for each protocol suite.

IPv4 Socket Address Structure

An IPv4 socket address structure, commonly called an "Internet socket address structure," is named `sockaddr_in` and defined by including the `<netinet/in.h>` header. Figure 3.1 shows the Posix.1g definition.

```
struct in_addr {
  in_addr_t    s_addr;           /* 32-bit IPv4 address */
                                 /* network byte ordered */
};

struct sockaddr_in {
  uint8_t         sin_len;       /* length of structure (16) */
  sa_family_t     sin_family;    /* AF_INET */
  in_port_t       sin_port;      /* 16-bit TCP or UDP port number */
                                 /* network byte ordered */
  struct in_addr  sin_addr;      /* 32-bit IPv4 address */
                                 /* network byte ordered */
  char            sin_zero[8];   /* unused */
};
```

Figure 3.1 The Internet (IPv4) socket address structure: `sockaddr_in`.

There are several points we need to make about socket address structures in general, using this example.

- The length member, `sin_len`, was added with 4.3BSD-Reno, when support for the OSI protocols was added (Figure 1.15). Before this release, the first member was `sin_family`, which was historically an `unsigned short`. Not all vendors support a length field for socket address structures and Posix.1g does not require this member. The datatype that we show, `uint8_t`, is typical, and datatypes of this form are new with Posix.1g (Figure 3.2).

  Having a length field simplifies the handling of variable-length socket address structures.

- Even if the length field is present, we need never set it and need never examine it, unless we are dealing with routing sockets (Chapter 17). It is used within the kernel by the routines that deal with socket address structures from various protocol families (e.g., the routing table code).

  > The four socket functions that pass a socket address structure from the process to the kernel, `bind`, `connect`, `sendto`, and `sendmsg`, all go through the `sockargs` function in a Berkeley-derived implementation (p. 452 of TCPv2). This function copies the socket address structure from the process and explicitly sets its `sin_len` member to the size of the structure that was passed as an argument to these four functions. The five socket functions that pass a socket address structure from the kernel to the process, `accept`, `recvfrom`, `recvmsg`, `getpeername`, and `getsockname`, all set the `sin_len` member before returning to the process.

  > Unfortunately there is normally no simple compile-time test to determine whether an implementation defines a length field for its socket address structures. In our code we test our own

`HAVE_SOCKADDR_SA_LEN` constant (Figure D.2), but whether to define this constant or not requires trying to compile a simple test program that uses this optional structure member and seeing if the compilation succeeds or not. We will see in Figure 3.4 that IPv6 implementations are required to define `SIN6_LEN` if socket address structures have a length field. Some IPv4 implementations (e.g., Digital Unix) provide the length field of the socket address structure to the application based on a compile-time option (e.g., `_SOCKADDR_LEN`). This feature provides compatibility for older programs.

- Posix.1g requires only three members in the structure: `sin_family`, `sin_addr`, and `sin_port`. It is acceptable for a Posix-compliant implementation to define additional structure members, and this is normal for an Internet socket address structure. Almost all implementations add the `sin_zero` member so that all socket address structures are at least 16 bytes in size.

- We show the Posix.1g datatypes for the `s_addr`, `sin_family`, and `sin_port` members. The `in_addr_t` datatype must be an unsigned integer type of at least 32 bits, `in_port_t` must be an unsigned integer type of at least 16 bits, and `sa_family_t` can be any unsigned integer type. The latter is normally an 8-bit unsigned integer if the implementation supports the length field, or an unsigned 16-bit integer if the length field is not supported. Figure 3.2 lists these three Posix-defined datatypes, along with some other Posix.1g datatypes that we will encounter.

Datatype	Description	Header
`int8_t`	signed 8-bit integer	`<sys/types.h>`
`uint8_t`	unsigned 8-bit integer	`<sys/types.h>`
`int16_t`	signed 16-bit integer	`<sys/types.h>`
`uint16_t`	unsigned 16-bit integer	`<sys/types.h>`
`int32_t`	signed 32-bit integer	`<sys/types.h>`
`uint32_t`	unsigned 32-bit integer	`<sys/types.h>`
`sa_family_t`	address family of socket address structure	`<sys/socket.h>`
`socklen_t`	length of socket address structure, normally `uint32_t`	`<sys/socket.h>`
`in_addr_t`	IPv4 address, normally `uint32_t`	`<netinet/in.h>`
`in_port_t`	TCP or UDP port, normally `uint16_t`	`<netinet/in.h>`

Figure 3.2 Datatypes required by Posix.1g.

- You will also encounter the datatypes `u_char`, `u_short`, `u_int`, and `u_long`, which are all unsigned. Posix.1g defines these with the note that they are obsolescent. They are provided for backward compatibility.

- Both the IPv4 address and the TCP or UDP port number are always stored in the structure in network byte order. We must be cognizant of this when using these members. (We say more about the difference between host byte order and network byte order in Section 3.4.)

- The 32-bit IPv4 address can be accessed in two different ways. For example, if `serv` is defined as an Internet socket address structure, then `serv.sin_addr` references the 32-bit IPv4 address as an `in_addr` structure, while `serv.sin_addr.s_addr` references the same 32-bit IPv4 address as an `in_addr_t` (typically an unsigned 32-bit integer). We must be certain that we are referencing the IPv4 address correctly, especially when it is used as an argument to a function, because compilers often pass structures differently from integers.

> The reason the `sin_addr` member is a structure, and not just an `unsigned long`, is historical. Earlier releases (4.2BSD) defined the `in_addr` structure as a `union` of various structures, to allow access to each of the 4 bytes and to both of the 16-bit values contained within the 32-bit IPv4 address. This was used with class A, B, and C addresses to fetch the appropriate bytes of the address. But with the advent of subnetting and then the disappearance of the various address classes with classless addressing (Section A.4), the need for the `union` disappeared. Most systems today have done away with the `union` and just define `in_addr` as a structure with a single `unsigned long` member.

- The `sin_zero` member is unused, but we *always* set it to 0 when filling in one of these structures. By convention, we always set the entire structure to 0 before filling it in, not just the `sin_zero` member.

> Although most uses of the structure do not require that this member be 0, when binding a non-wildcard IPv4 address, this member must be 0 (pp. 731–732 of TCPv2).

- Socket address structures are used only on a given host: the structure itself is not communicated between different hosts although certain fields (e.g., the IP address and port) are used for communication.

Generic Socket Address Structure

Socket address structures are *always* passed by reference when passed as an argument to any of the socket functions. But the socket functions that take one of these pointers as an argument must deal with socket address structures from *any* of the supported protocol families.

A problem is how to declare the type of pointer that is passed. With ANSI C the solution is simple: `void *` is the generic pointer type. But the socket functions predate ANSI C and the solution chosen in 1982 was to define a *generic* socket address structure in the `<sys/socket.h>` header, which we show in Figure 3.3.

```
struct sockaddr {
  uint8_t       sa_len;
  sa_family_t   sa_family;    /* address family: AF_xxx value */
  char          sa_data[14];  /* protocol-specific address */
};
```

Figure 3.3 The generic socket address structure: `sockaddr`.

The socket functions are then defined as taking a pointer to the generic socket address structure, as shown here in the ANSI C function prototype for the `bind` function:

```
int bind(int, struct sockaddr *, socklen_t);
```

This requires that any calls to these functions must cast the pointer to the protocol-specific socket address structure to be a pointer to a generic socket address structure. For example,

```
struct sockaddr_in   serv;       /* IPv4 socket address structure */

/* fill in serv{} */

bind(sockfd, (struct sockaddr *) &serv, sizeof(serv));
```

If we omit the cast "(struct sockaddr *)" the C compiler generates a warning of the form "warning: passing arg 2 of 'bind' from incompatible pointer type" assuming the system's headers have an ANSI C prototype for the bind function.

From an application programmer's point of view, the *only* use of these generic socket address structures is to cast pointers to protocol-specific structures.

> Recall in Section 1.2 that in our unp.h header we define SA to be the string "struct sockaddr" just to shorten the code that we must write to cast these pointers.

> From the kernel's perspective another reason for using pointers to generic socket address structures as arguments is that the kernel must take the caller's pointer, cast it to a struct sockaddr * and then look at the value of sa_family to determine the type of structure. But from an application programmer's perspective, it would be simpler if the pointer type were void *, omitting the need for the explicit cast.

IPv6 Socket Address Structure

The IPv6 socket address is defined by including the <netinet/in.h> header, and we show it in Figure 3.4.

```
struct in6_addr {
  uint8_t   s6_addr[16];          /* 128-bit IPv6 address */
                                  /* network byte ordered */
};

#define SIN6_LEN        /* required for compile-time tests */

struct sockaddr_in6 {
  uint8_t         sin6_len;       /* length of this struct (24) */
  sa_family_t     sin6_family;    /* AF_INET6 */
  in_port_t       sin6_port;      /* transport layer port# */
                                  /* network byte ordered */
  uint32_t        sin6_flowinfo;  /* priority & flow label */
                                  /* network byte ordered */
  struct in6_addr sin6_addr;      /* IPv6 address */
                                  /* network byte ordered */
};
```

Figure 3.4 IPv6 socket address structure: sockaddr_in6.

The extensions to the sockets API for IPv6 are defined in RFC 2133 [Gilligan et al. 1997]. Posix.1g says nothing about IPv6. But some of the datatypes in Figure 3.4 differ from RFC 2133 because we use what would be the Posix.1g datatypes in the figure, but these were finalized in a Posix.1g draft that came after RFC 2133.

Note the following points about Figure 3.4:

- The `SIN6_LEN` constant must be defined if the system supports the length member for socket address structures.

- The IPv6 family is `AF_INET6`, whereas the IPv4 family is `AF_INET`.

- The members in this structure are ordered so that if the `sockaddr_in6` structure is 64-bit aligned, so is the 128-bit `sin6_addr` member. On some 64-bit processors, data accesses of 64-bit values are optimized if stored on a 64-bit boundary.

- The `sin6_flowinfo` member is divided into three fields:

  ▫ the low-order 24 bits are the flow label,
  ▫ the next 4 bits are the priority,
  ▫ the next 4 bits are reserved.

The flow label and priority fields are described with Figure A.2. We note that the use of the priority field is still a research topic.

Comparison of Socket Address Structures

Figure 3.5 shows a comparison of the four socket address structures that we encounter in this text: IPv4, IPv6, Unix domain (Figure 14.1), and datalink (Figure 17.1). In this figure we assume that the socket address structures all contain a 1-byte length field, that the family field also occupies 1 byte, and that any field that must be at least some number of bits is exactly that number of bits. Two of the socket address structures are fixed length, while the Unix domain structure and the datalink structure are variable length. To handle variable-length structures whenever we pass a pointer to a socket address structure as an argument to one of the socket functions, we pass its length as another argument. We show the size in bytes (for the 4.4BSD implementation) of the fixed-length structures beneath each structure.

The `sockaddr_un` structure itself is not variable length (Figure 14.1), but the amount of information—the pathname within the structure—is variable length. When passing pointers to these structures, we must be careful how we handle the length field, both the length field in the socket address structure itself (if supported by the implementation), and the length to and from the kernel.

This figure shows a style that we follow throughout the text: structure names are always shown in a bolder font followed by braces, as in **sockaddr_in{}**.

We noted earlier that the length field was added to all the socket address structures with the 4.3BSD Reno release. Had the length field been present with the original release of sockets,

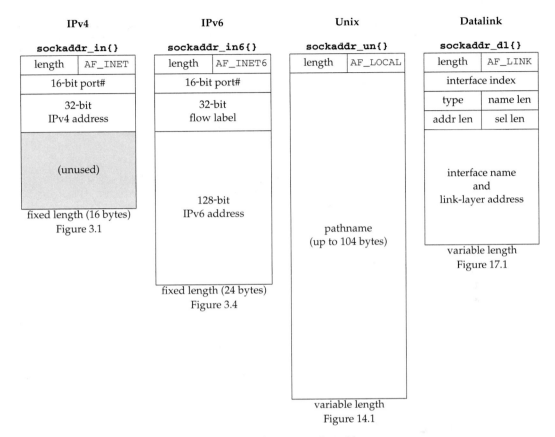

Figure 3.5 Comparison of various socket address structures.

there would be no need for the length argument to all the socket functions: the third argument to `bind` and `connect`, for example. Instead, the size of the structure could be contained in the length field of the structure.

3.3 Value–Result Arguments

We mentioned that when a socket address structure is passed to any of the socket functions, it is always passed by reference. That is, a pointer to the structure is passed. The length of the structure is also passed as an argument. But the way in which the length is passed depends on which direction the structure is being passed: from the process to the kernel, or vice versa.

1. The three functions `bind`, `connect`, and `sendto` pass a socket address structure from the process to the kernel. One argument to these three functions is the pointer to the socket address structure and another argument is the integer size of the structure, as in

```
struct sockaddr_in  serv;

/* fill in serv{} */
connect(sockfd, (SA *) &serv, sizeof(serv));
```

Since the kernel is passed both the pointer and the size of what the pointer points to, it knows exactly how much data to copy from the process into the kernel. Figure 3.6 shows this scenario.

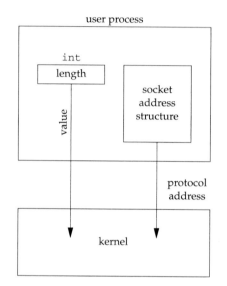

Figure 3.6   Socket address structure passed from process to kernel.

We will see in the next chapter that the datatype for the size of a socket address structure is actually `socklen_t` and not `int`, but Posix.1g recommends that `socklen_t` be defined as `uint32_t`.

2. The four functions `accept`, `recvfrom`, `getsockname`, and `getpeername` pass a socket address structure from the kernel to the process, the reverse direction from the previous scenario. Two of the arguments to these four functions are the pointer to the socket address structure along with a pointer to an integer containing the size of the structure, as in

```
struct sockaddr_un  cli;   /* Unix domain */
socklen_t  len;

len = sizeof(cli);          /* len is a value */
getpeername(unixfd, (SA *) &cli, &len);
/* len may have changed */
```

The reason that the size changes from an integer to be a pointer to an integer is because the size is both a *value* when the function is called (it tells the kernel the size of the structure, so that the kernel does not write past the end of the structure when filling it in) and a *result* when the function returns (it tells the process how much information the kernel actually stored in the structure). This type of argument is called a *value–result* argument. Figure 3.7 shows this scenario.

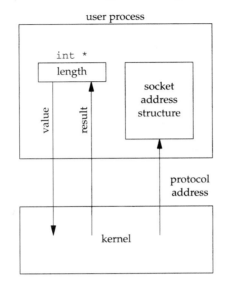

Figure 3.7 Socket address structure passed from kernel to process.

We will see an example of value–result arguments in Figure 4.11.

> We have been talking about socket address structures being passed between the process and the kernel. For an implementation such as 4.4BSD, where all the socket functions are system calls within the kernel, this is correct. But in some implementations, notably System V, the socket functions are just library functions that execute as part of a normal user process. How these functions interface with the protocol stack in the kernel is an implementation detail that normally does not affect us. Nevertheless, for simplicity we continue to talk about these structures as being passed between the process and the kernel by functions such as bind and connect. (We will see in Section C.1 that System V implementations do indeed pass user's socket address structures between the process and the kernel, but as part of streams messages.)

> Two other functions pass socket address structures: recvmsg and sendmsg (Section 13.5). But we will see that the length field is not a function argument but a structure member.

When using value–result arguments for the length of socket address structures, if the socket address structure is fixed length (Figure 3.5), the value returned by the kernel will always be that fixed size: 16 for an IPv4 sockaddr_in and 24 for an IPv6 sockaddr_in6, for example. But with a variable-length socket address structure (e.g., a Unix domain sockaddr_un) the value returned can be less than the maximum size of the structure (as we will see with Figure 14.2).

With network programming the most common example of a value–result argument is the length of a returned socket address structure. But we will encounter other value–result arguments in this text:

- The middle three arguments for the `select` function (Section 6.3).
- The length argument for the `getsockopt` function (Section 7.2).
- The `msg_namelen` and `msg_controllen` members of the `msghdr` structure, when used with `recvmsg` (Section 13.5).
- The `ifc_len` member of the `ifconf` structure (Figure 16.2).
- The first of the two length arguments for the `sysctl` function (Section 17.4).

3.4 Byte Ordering Functions

Consider a 16-bit integer that is made up of 2 bytes. There are two ways to store the 2 bytes in memory: with the low-order byte at the starting address, known as *little-endian* byte order, or with the high-order byte at the starting address, known as *big-endian* byte order. We show these two formats in Figure 3.8.

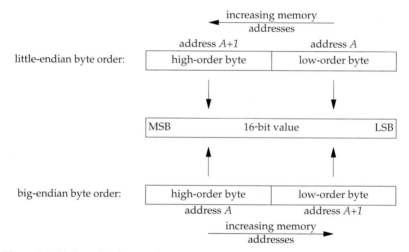

Figure 3.8 Little-endian byte order and big-endian byte order for a 16-bit integer.

In this figure we show increasing memory addresses going from right to left in the top, and from left to right in the bottom. We also show the *MSB* (most significant bit) as the leftmost bit of the 16-bit value and the *LSB* (least significant bit) as the rightmost bit.

> The terms "little endian" and "big endian" indicate which end of the multibyte value, the little end or the big end, is stored at the starting address of the value.

Unfortunately there is no standard between these two byte orderings and we encounter systems that use both formats. We refer to the byte ordering used by a given system as the *host byte order*. The program shown in Figure 3.9 prints the host byte order.

—————————————————————————————————— *intro/byteorder.c*

```
 1 #include    "unp.h"

 2 int
 3 main(int argc, char **argv)
 4 {
 5     union {
 6         short   s;
 7         char    c[sizeof(short)];
 8     } un;

 9     un.s = 0x0102;
10     printf("%s: ", CPU_VENDOR_OS);
11     if (sizeof(short) == 2) {
12         if (un.c[0] == 1 && un.c[1] == 2)
13             printf("big-endian\n");
14         else if (un.c[0] == 2 && un.c[1] == 1)
15             printf("little-endian\n");
16         else
17             printf("unknown\n");
18     } else
19         printf("sizeof(short) = %d\n", sizeof(short));

20     exit(0);
21 }
```
—————————————————————————————————— *intro/byteorder.c*

Figure 3.9 Program to determine host byte order.

We store the 2-byte value `0x0102` into the short integer and then look at the two consecutive bytes `c[0]` (the address *A* in Figure 3.8) and `c[1]` (the address *A+1* in Figure 3.8) to determine the byte order.

The string `CPU_VENDOR_OS` is determined by the GNU `autoconf` program when the software in this book is configured, and it identifies the CPU type, vendor, and operating system release. We show some examples here in the output from this program when run on the various systems in Figure 1.16.

```
aix % byteorder
powerpc-ibm-aix4.2.0.0: big-endian

alpha % byteorder
alpha-dec-osf4.0: little-endian

bsdi % byteorder
i386-pc-bsdi3.0: little-endian

gemini % byteorder
sparc-sun-sunos4.1.4: big-endian

hpux % byteorder
hppa1.1-hp-hpux10.30: big-endian

linux % byteorder
i586-pc-linux-gnu: little-endian

solaris % byteorder
sparc-sun-solaris2.5.1: big-endian
```

```
unixware % byteorder
i386-univel-sysv4.2MP: little-endian
```

We have talked about the byte ordering of a 16-bit integer, and obviously the same discussion applies to a 32-bit integer.

> There are systems that can change between little-endian and big-endian byte ordering ([Dewar and Smosna 1990]), either when the system is reset (MIPS 2000), or at any point while a program is running (Intel i860).

We must deal with the byte ordering differences as network programmers because networking protocols must specify a *network byte order*. For example, in a TCP segment there is a 16-bit port number and a 32-bit IPv4 address. The sending protocol stack and the receiving protocol stack must agree on the order in which the bytes of these multibyte fields are transmitted. The Internet protocols use big-endian byte ordering for these multibyte integers.

In theory an implementation could store the fields in a socket address structure in host byte order and then convert to and from the network byte order when moving the fields to and from the protocol headers, saving us from having to worry about this detail. But both history and Posix.1g specify that certain fields in the socket address structures be maintained in network byte order. Our concern is therefore converting between the host byte order and the network byte order. We use the following four functions to convert between these two byte orders.

```
#include <netinet/in.h>

uint16_t htons(uint16_t host16bitvalue);

uint32_t htonl(uint32_t host32bitvalue);

                                          Both return: value in network byte order

uint16_t ntohs(uint16_t net16bitvalue);

uint32_t ntohl(uint32_t net32bitvalue);

                                            Both return: value in host byte order
```

In the names of these functions h stands for *host*, n stands for *network*, s stands for *short*, and l stands for *long*. The terms *short* and *long* are historical artifacts from the Digital VAX implementation of 4.2BSD. We should instead think of s as a 16-bit value (such as a TCP or UDP port number) and l as a 32-bit value (such as an IPv4 address). Indeed, on the 64-bit Digital Alpha, a long integer occupies 64 bits, yet the htonl and ntohl functions operate on 32-bit values.

When using these functions we do not care about the actual values (big endian or little endian) for the host byte order and the network byte order. What we must do is be certain to call the appropriate function to convert a given value between the host and network byte order. On those systems that have the same byte ordering as the Internet protocols (big endian), these four functions are usually defined as null macros.

We talk more about the byte ordering problem, with respect to the data contained in a network packet, as opposed to the fields in the protocol headers, in Section 5.18 and Exercise 5.8.

We have not defined the term *byte*. We use the term to mean an 8-bit quantity since almost all current computer systems use 8-bit bytes. Most Internet standards use the term *octet* instead of byte to mean an 8-bit quantity. This started in the early days of TCP/IP because much of the early work was done on systems such as the DEC-10, which did not use 8-bit bytes.

> A common network programming error in the 1980s was to develop code on Sun workstations (big-endian Motorola 68000s) and forget to call any of these four functions. The code worked fine on these workstations but would not work when ported to little-endian machines (such as VAXes).

3.5 Byte Manipulation Functions

There are two groups of functions that operate on multibyte fields, without interpreting the data, and without assuming that the data is a null-terminated C string. We need these types of functions when dealing with socket address structures, because we need to manipulate fields such as IP addresses, which can contain bytes of 0, but these fields are not C character strings. The functions beginning with str (for string), defined by including the <string.h> header, deal with null-terminated C character strings.

The first group of functions, whose names begin with b (for byte), are from 4.2BSD and are still provided by almost any system that supports the socket functions. The second group of functions, whose names begin with mem (for memory), are from the ANSI C standard and are provided with any system that supports an ANSI C library.

We first show the Berkeley-derived functions, although the only one of these that we use in this text is bzero. (We use it because it has only two arguments and is easier to remember than the three-argument memset function, as explained on p. 8.) The other two functions, bcopy and bcmp, you may encounter in existing applications.

```
#include <strings.h>

void bzero(void *dest, size_t nbytes);

void bcopy(const void *src, void *dest, size_t nbytes);

int bcmp(const void *ptr1, const void *ptr2, size_t nbytes);
```
                                                    Returns: 0 if equal, nonzero if unequal

> This is our first encounter with the ANSI C const qualifier. In the three uses here it indicates that what is pointed to by the pointer with this qualification, *src*, *ptr1*, and *ptr2*, is not modified by the function. Worded another way, the memory pointed to by the const pointer is read but not modified by the function.

bzero sets the specified number of bytes to 0 in the destination. We often use this function to initialize a socket address structure to 0. bcopy moves the specified number of bytes from the source to the destination. bcmp compares two arbitrary byte strings. The return value is zero if the two byte strings are identical; otherwise it is nonzero.

The following functions are the ANSI C functions:

```
#include <string.h>

void *memset(void *dest, int c, size_t len);

void *memcpy(void *dest, const void *src, size_t nbytes);

int memcmp(const void *ptr1, const void *ptr2, size_t nbytes);
```

Returns: 0 if equal, <0 or >0 if unequal (see text)

memset sets the specified number of bytes to the value *c* in the destination. memcpy is similar to bcopy but the order of the two pointer arguments is swapped. bcopy correctly handles overlapping fields, while the behavior of memcpy is undefined if the source and destination overlap. The ANSI C memmove function must be used when the fields overlap (Exercise 30.3).

> One way to remember the order of the two pointers for memcpy is to remember that they are written in the same left-to-right order as an assignment statement in C:
>
> *dest* = *src*;
>
> One way to remember the order of the final two arguments to memset is to realize that all of the ANSI C mem*XXX* functions require a length argument, and it is always the final argument.

memcmp compares two arbitrary byte strings and returns 0 if they are identical. If not identical, the return value is either greater than 0 or less than 0, depending whether the first unequal byte pointed to by *ptr1* is greater than or less than the corresponding byte pointed to by *ptr2*. The comparison is done assuming the two unequal bytes are unsigned chars.

3.6   `inet_aton`, `inet_addr`, and `inet_ntoa` Functions

There are two groups of address conversion functions that we describe in this section and the next. They convert Internet addresses between ASCII strings (what humans prefer to use) and network byte ordered binary values (values that are stored in socket address structures).

1. inet_aton, inet_ntoa, and inet_addr convert an IPv4 address between a dotted-decimal string (e.g., "206.62.226.33") and its 32-bit network byte ordered binary value. You will probably encounter these functions in lots of existing code.

2. The newer functions inet_pton and inet_ntop handle both IPv4 and IPv6 addresses. We describe these two functions in the next section and use them throughout the text.

```
#include <arpa/inet.h>

int inet_aton(const char *strptr, struct in_addr *addrptr);
```
                                                 Returns: 1 if string was valid, 0 on error

```
in_addr_t inet_addr(const char *strptr);
```
                   Returns: 32-bit binary network byte ordered IPv4 address; INADDR_NONE if error

```
char *inet_ntoa(struct in_addr inaddr);
```
                                                 Returns: pointer to dotted-decimal string

The first of these, inet_aton, converts the C character string pointed to by *strptr* into its 32-bit binary network byte ordered value, which is stored through the pointer *addrptr*. If successful, 1 is returned; otherwise 0 is returned.

> An undocumented feature of inet_aton is that if *addrptr* is a null pointer, the function still performs its validation of the input string but does not store any result.

inet_addr does the same conversion, returning the 32-bit binary network byte ordered value as the return value. The problem with this function is that all 2^{32} possible binary values are valid IP addresses (0.0.0.0 through 255.255.255.255), but the function returns the constant INADDR_NONE (typically 32 one-bits) on an error. This means the dotted-decimal string 255.255.255.255 (the IPv4 limited broadcast address, Section 18.2) cannot be handled by this function, since its binary value appears to indicate failure of the function.

> Many older versions of Ping output the error "unknown host" if we try execute ping 255.255.255.255. The reason for this incorrect error is that inet_addr appears to fail, so it tries to look up the dotted-decimal string as a hostname, which fails.

> Another potential problem with inet_addr is that some manual pages state that it returns −1 on an error, instead of INADDR_NONE. This can lead to problems, depending on the C compiler, when comparing the return value of the function (an unsigned value) to a negative constant.

Today inet_addr is deprecated and any new code should use inet_aton instead. Better still is to use the newer functions described in the next section, which handle both IPv4 and IPv6.

The inet_ntoa function converts a 32-bit binary network byte ordered IPv4 address into its corresponding dotted-decimal string. The string pointed to by the return value of the function resides in static memory. This means the function is not reentrant, which we discuss in Section 11.14. Finally, notice that this function takes a structure as its argument, not a pointer to a structure.

Functions that take actual structures as arguments are rare. It is more common to pass a pointer to the structure.

3.7 `inet_pton` and `inet_ntop` Functions

These two functions are new with IPv6 and work with both IPv4 and IPv6 addresses. We use these two functions throughout the text. The letters p and n stand for *presentation* and *numeric*. The presentation format for an address is often an ASCII string and the numeric format is the binary value that goes into a socket address structure.

```
#include   <arpa/inet.h>

int inet_pton(int family, const char *strptr, void *addrptr);
```

Returns: 1 if OK, 0 if input not a valid presentation format, −1 on error

```
const char *inet_ntop(int family, const void *addrptr, char *strptr, size_t len);
```

Returns: pointer to result if OK, NULL on error

The *family* argument for both functions is either AF_INET or AF_INET6. If *family* is not supported, both functions return an error with errno set to EAFNOSUPPORT.

The first function tries to convert the string pointed to by *strptr*, storing the binary result through the pointer *addrptr*. If successful, the return value is 1. If the input string is not a valid presentation format for the specified *family*, 0 is returned.

inet_ntop does the reverse conversion, from numeric (*addrptr*) to presentation (*strptr*). The *len* argument is the size of the destination, to prevent the function from overflowing the caller's buffer. To help specify this size, the following two definitions are defined by including the <netinet/in.h> header:

```
#define   INET_ADDRSTRLEN    16     /* for IPv4 dotted-decimal */
#define   INET6_ADDRSTRLEN   46     /* for IPv6 hex string */
```

If *len* is too small to hold the resulting presentation format, including the terminating null, a null pointer is returned and errno is set to ENOSPC.

The *strptr* argument to inet_ntop cannot be a null pointer. The caller must allocate memory for the destination and specify its size. On success this pointer is the return value of the function.

Figure 3.10 summarizes the five functions that we have described in this section and the previous section.

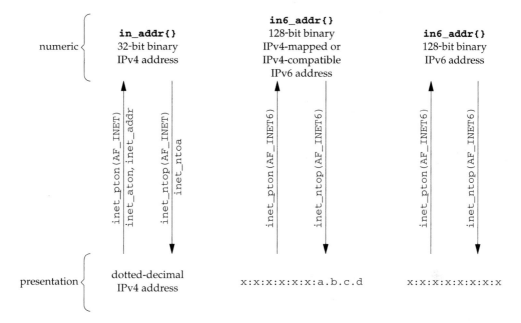

Figure 3.10 Summary of address conversion functions.

Example

Even if your system does not yet include support for IPv6, you can start using these newer functions by replacing calls of the form

```
foo.sin_addr.s_addr = inet_addr(cp);
```

with

```
inet_pton(AF_INET, cp, &foo.sin_addr);
```

and replacing calls of the form

```
ptr = inet_ntoa(foo.sin_addr);
```

with

```
char  str[INET_ADDRSTRLEN];
ptr = inet_ntop(AF_INET, &foo.sin_addr, str, sizeof(str));
```

Figure 3.11 shows a simple definition of inet_pton that supports only IPv4. Similarly, Figure 3.12 shows a simple version of inet_ntop that supports only IPv4.

libfree/inet_pton_ipv4.c

```
10 int
11 inet_pton(int family, const char *strptr, void *addrptr)
12 {
13     if (family == AF_INET) {
14         struct in_addr in_val;

15         if (inet_aton(strptr, &in_val)) {
16             memcpy(addrptr, &in_val, sizeof(struct in_addr));
17             return (1);
18         }
19         return (0);
20     }
21     errno = EAFNOSUPPORT;
22     return (-1);
23 }
```

libfree/inet_pton_ipv4.c

Figure 3.11 Simple version of inet_pton that supports only IPv4.

libfree/inet_ntop_ipv4.c

```
 8 const char *
 9 inet_ntop(int family, const void *addrptr, char *strptr, size_t len)
10 {
11     const u_char *p = (const u_char *) addrptr;

12     if (family == AF_INET) {
13         char    temp[INET_ADDRSTRLEN];

14         snprintf(temp, sizeof(temp), "%d.%d.%d.%d",
15                  p[0], p[1], p[2], p[3]);
16         if (strlen(temp) >= len) {
17             errno = ENOSPC;
18             return (NULL);
19         }
20         strcpy(strptr, temp);
21         return (strptr);
22     }
23     errno = EAFNOSUPPORT;
24     return (NULL);
25 }
```

libfree/inet_ntop_ipv4.c

Figure 3.12 Simple version of inet_ntop that supports only IPv4.

3.8   sock_ntop and Related Functions

A basic problem with inet_ntop is that it requires the caller to pass a pointer to a binary address. This address is normally contained in a socket address structure, requiring the caller to know the format of the structure and the address family. That is, to use it we must write code of the form

```
struct sockaddr_in    addr;

inet_ntop(AF_INET, &addr.sin_addr, str, sizeof(str));
```

for IPv4, or

```
struct sockaddr_in6    addr6;

inet_ntop(AF_INET6, &addr6.sin6_addr, str, sizeof(str));
```

for IPv6. This makes our code protocol dependent.

To solve this we will write our own function named sock_ntop that takes a pointer to a socket address structure, looks inside the structure, and calls the appropriate function to return the presentation format of the address.

```
#include "unp.h"

char *sock_ntop(const struct sockaddr *sockaddr, socklen_t addrlen);

                                        Returns: nonnull pointer if OK, NULL on error
```

> This is the notation we use for functions of our own that we use throughout the book that are not standard system functions: the box around the function prototype and return value is dashed. The header that is included at the beginning is usually our unp.h header.

sockaddr points to a socket address structure whose length is *addrlen*. The function uses its own static buffer to hold the result and a pointer to this buffer is the return value.

> Notice that using static storage for the result prevents the function from being *reentrant* or *thread-safe*. We talk more about this in Section 11.14. We make this design decision for this function to allow us to easily call it from the simple examples in the book.

The presentation format is the dotted-decimal form of an IPv4 address or the hex string form of an IPv6 address, followed by a terminator (we use a period, similar to netstat), followed by the decimal port number, followed by a null character. Hence the buffer size must be at least INET_ADDRSTRLEN plus 5 bytes for IPv4 ($16 + 5 = 21$), or INET6_ADDRSTRLEN plus 5 bytes for IPv6 ($46 + 5 = 51$).

We show the source code for only the AF_INET case in Figure 3.13.

```
                                                                  ─────── lib/sock_ntop.c
 5 char *
 6 sock_ntop(const struct sockaddr *sa, socklen_t salen)
 7 {
 8     char    portstr[7];
 9     static char str[128];         /* Unix domain is largest */

10     switch (sa->sa_family) {
11     case AF_INET:{
12             struct sockaddr_in *sin = (struct sockaddr_in *) sa;

13             if (inet_ntop(AF_INET, &sin->sin_addr, str, sizeof(str)) == NULL)
14                 return (NULL);
15             if (ntohs(sin->sin_port) != 0) {
16                 snprintf(portstr, sizeof(portstr), ".%d", ntohs(sin->sin_port));
17                 strcat(str, portstr);
18             }
19             return (str);
20         }
                                                                  ─────── lib/sock_ntop.c
```

Figure 3.13 Our sock_ntop function.

There are a few other functions that we define to operate on socket address structures, and these will simplify the portability of our code between IPv4 and IPv6.

```
#include "unp.h"

int sock_bind_wild(int sockfd, int family);

                                                     Returns: 0 if OK, −1 on error

int sock_cmp_addr(const struct sockaddr *sockaddr1,
                  const struct sockaddr *sockaddr2, socklen_t addrlen);

                      Returns: 0 if the addresses are of the same family and equal, else nonzero

int sock_cmp_port(const struct sockaddr *sockaddr1,
                  const struct sockaddr *sockaddr2, socklen_t addrlen);

              Returns: 0 if the addresses are of the same family and the ports are equal, else nonzero

int sock_get_port(const struct sockaddr *sockaddr, socklen_t addrlen);

                              Returns: nonnegative port number for IPv4 or IPv6 address, else −1

char *sock_ntop_host(const struct sockaddr *sockaddr, socklen_t addrlen);

                                           Returns: nonnull pointer if OK, NULL on error

void sock_set_addr(const struct sockaddr *sockaddr, socklen_t addrlen, void *ptr);

void sock_set_port(const struct sockaddr *sockaddr, socklen_t addrlen, int port);

void sock_set_wild(struct sockaddr *sockaddr, socklen_t addrlen);
```

sock_bind_wild binds the wildcard address and an ephemeral port to a socket. sock_cmp_addr compares the address portion of two socket address structures and sock_cmp_port compares the port number of two socket address structures. sock_get_port returns just the port number and sock_ntop_host converts just the host portion of a socket address structure to presentation format (not the port number). sock_set_addr sets just the address portion of a socket address structure to the value pointed to by *ptr* and sock_set_port sets just the port number of a socket address structure. sock_set_wild sets the address portion of a socket address structure to the wildcard. As with all of the functions in the text, we provide a wrapper function whose name begins with S for all of these functions that return other than void and normally call the wrapper function from our programs. We do not show the source code for all these functions, but it is freely available (see the Preface).

3.9 `readn`, `writen`, and `readline` Functions

Stream sockets (e.g., TCP sockets) exhibit a behavior with the read and write functions that differs from normal file I/O. A read or write on a stream socket might input or output fewer bytes than requested, but this is not an error condition. The reason is that buffer limits might be reached for the socket in the kernel. All that is required is for the caller to invoke the read or write function again, to input or output the remaining bytes. (Some versions of Unix also exhibit this behavior when writing more than 4096 bytes to a pipe.) This scenario is always a possibility on a stream socket with read, but is normally seen with write only if the socket is nonblocking. Nevertheless, we always call our writen function instead of write, in case the implementation returns a short count.

We provide the following three functions that we use whenever we read from or write to a stream socket.

```
#include "unp.h"

ssize_t readn(int filedes, void *buff, size_t nbytes);

ssize_t writen(int filedes, const void *buff, size_t nbytes);

ssize_t readline(int filedes, void *buff, size_t maxlen);

                          All return: number of bytes read or written, –1 on error
```

Figure 3.14 shows the readn function. Figure 3.15 shows the writen function, and Figure 3.16 shows the readline function.

——————————————————————————— lib/readn.c

```
1 #include    "unp.h"

2 ssize_t                              /* Read "n" bytes from a descriptor. */
3 readn(int fd, void *vptr, size_t n)
4 {
5     size_t  nleft;
6     ssize_t nread;
7     char    *ptr;

8     ptr = vptr;
9     nleft = n;
10    while (nleft > 0) {
11        if ( (nread = read(fd, ptr, nleft)) < 0) {
12            if (errno == EINTR)
13                nread = 0;      /* and call read() again */
14            else
15                return (-1);
16        } else if (nread == 0)
17            break;              /* EOF */

18        nleft -= nread;
19        ptr += nread;
20    }
21    return (n - nleft);         /* return >= 0 */
22 }
```

——————————————————————————— lib/readn.c

Figure 3.14   readn function: read *n* bytes from a descriptor.

——————————————————————————— lib/writen.c

```
1 #include    "unp.h"

2 ssize_t                              /* Write "n" bytes to a descriptor. */
3 writen(int fd, const void *vptr, size_t n)
4 {
5     size_t  nleft;
6     ssize_t nwritten;
7     const char *ptr;

8     ptr = vptr;
9     nleft = n;
10    while (nleft > 0) {
11        if ( (nwritten = write(fd, ptr, nleft)) <= 0) {
12            if (errno == EINTR)
13                nwritten = 0;   /* and call write() again */
14            else
15                return (-1);    /* error */
16        }
17        nleft -= nwritten;
18        ptr += nwritten;
19    }
20    return (n);
21 }
```

——————————————————————————— lib/writen.c

Figure 3.15   writen function: write *n* bytes to a descriptor.

—————————————————————————— test/readline1.c

```
 1 #include     "unp.h"

 2 ssize_t
 3 readline(int fd, void *vptr, size_t maxlen)
 4 {
 5     ssize_t n, rc;
 6     char    c, *ptr;

 7     ptr = vptr;
 8     for (n = 1; n < maxlen; n++) {
 9       again:
10         if ( (rc = read(fd, &c, 1)) == 1) {
11             *ptr++ = c;
12             if (c == '\n')
13                 break;          /* newline is stored, like fgets() */
14         } else if (rc == 0) {
15             if (n == 1)
16                 return (0);     /* EOF, no data read */
17             else
18                 break;          /* EOF, some data was read */
19         } else {
20             if (errno == EINTR)
21                 goto again;
22             return (-1);        /* error, errno set by read() */
23         }
24     }

25     *ptr = 0;                   /* null terminate like fgets() */
26     return (n);
27 }
```

—————————————————————————— test/readline1.c

Figure 3.16 readline function: read a text line from a descriptor, 1 byte at a time.

Our three functions look for the error EINTR (the system call was interrupted by a caught signal, which we discuss in more detail in Section 5.9) and continue reading or writing if the error occurs. We handle the error here, instead of forcing the caller to call readn or writen again, since the purpose of these three functions is to prevent the caller from having to handle a short count.

In Section 13.3 we mention that the MSG_WAITALL flag can be used with the recv function to replace the need for a separate readn function.

Note that our readline function calls the system's read function once for every byte of data. This is inefficient, as shown in Section 3.9 of APUE. What we would like to do is buffer the data by calling read to obtain as much data as we can and then examine the buffer 1 byte at a time. One way to do this is to use the standard I/O library, as we describe in Section 13.8.

Figure 3.17 shows a faster version of the readline function, which reads up to MAXLINE bytes at a time and then returns one character at a time.

```
 1 #include     "unp.h"

 2 static ssize_t
 3 my_read(int fd, char *ptr)
 4 {
 5     static int read_cnt = 0;
 6     static char *read_ptr;
 7     static char read_buf[MAXLINE];

 8     if (read_cnt <= 0) {
 9       again:
10         if ( (read_cnt = read(fd, read_buf, sizeof(read_buf))) < 0) {
11             if (errno == EINTR)
12                 goto again;
13             return (-1);
14         } else if (read_cnt == 0)
15             return (0);
16         read_ptr = read_buf;
17     }
18     read_cnt--;
19     *ptr = *read_ptr++;
20     return (1);
21 }

22 ssize_t
23 readline(int fd, void *vptr, size_t maxlen)
24 {
25     int     n, rc;
26     char    c, *ptr;

27     ptr = vptr;
28     for (n = 1; n < maxlen; n++) {
29         if ( (rc = my_read(fd, &c)) == 1) {
30             *ptr++ = c;
31             if (c == '\n')
32                 break;          /* newline is stored, like fgets() */
33         } else if (rc == 0) {
34             if (n == 1)
35                 return (0);     /* EOF, no data read */
36             else
37                 break;          /* EOF, some data was read */
38         } else
39             return (-1);        /* error, errno set by read() */
40     }

41     *ptr = 0;                   /* null terminate like fgets() */
42     return (n);
43 }
```

Figure 3.17 Better version of readline function.

2-21   The internal function `my_read` reads up to `MAXLINE` characters at a time and then returns them, one at a time.

29   The only change to the `readline` function itself is to call `my_read` instead of `read`.

Making this small change to our `readline` function makes a big difference. If we measure the time required by the old and new versions to read a 2781-line file (135,816 bytes) the *clock times* are 8.8 seconds for the old version and 0.3 seconds for the new version. Almost all of the difference is in the time spent within the kernel, the *system time*, as the old version performs 135,816 system calls while the new version performs only 34 system calls (135,816 divided by `MAXLINE`, which is 4096).

> Unfortunately by using `static` variables in `my_read` to maintain the state information across successive calls, the function is no longer *reentrant* or *thread-safe*. We discuss this in Sections 11.14 and 23.5. We develop a thread-safe version using thread-specific data in Figure 23.11.

3.10 `isfdtype` Function

There are times when we need to test a descriptor to see if it is of a specified type. Historically this has been done by calling the Posix.1 `fstat` function and then testing the returned `st_mode` value using one of the `S_ISxxx` macros. (This is discussed on pp. 73–76 of APUE.) Many implementations, but not all, define the `S_ISSOCK` macro that tests whether or not a descriptor is a socket. Since there are some implementations that cannot tell whether a descriptor is a socket based on just the information returned by the `fstat` function, Posix.1g provides the new `isfdtype` function.

```
#include <sys/stat.h>

int isfdtype(int sockfd, int fdtype);
```
                                  Returns: 1 if descriptor of specified type, 0 if not, −1 on error

To test for a socket, *fdtype* is `S_IFSOCK`. One use for this function is in a program that is `exec`ed by another program (Section 4.7) to test whether an expected descriptor is really a socket.

Figure 3.18 shows a sample implementation of this function, assuming that the implementation supports the `S_IFSOCK` mode returned by `fstat`.

```
                                                                          ──── lib/isfdtype.c
 1 #include    "unp.h"

 2 #ifndef S_IFSOCK
 3 #error S_IFSOCK not defined
 4 #endif

 5 int
 6 isfdtype(int fd, int fdtype)
 7 {
 8     struct stat buf;

 9     if (fstat(fd, &buf) < 0)
10         return (-1);

11     if ((buf.st_mode & S_IFMT) == fdtype)
12         return (1);
13     else
14         return (0);
15 }
                                                                          ──── lib/isfdtype.c
```

Figure 3.18 Implementation of `isfdtype` using `fstat`.

There are numerous other S_IF*xxx* constants defined by including the
<sys/stat.h> header and our implementation allows them. Posix.1g, however, only
specifies that this function works when *fdtype* is S_IFSOCK.

3.11 Summary

Socket address structures are an integral part of every network program. We allocate
them, fill them in, and pass pointers to them to the various socket functions. Sometimes
we pass a pointer to one of these structures to the socket function and it fills in the contents. We always pass these structures by reference (that is we pass a pointer to the
structure, not the structure itself) and always pass the size of the structure as another
argument. When the socket function fills in the structure, the length is also passed by
reference, so that its value can be updated by the function, and we call these
value–result arguments.

Socket address structures are self-defining because they always begin with a field
(the "family") that identifies the address family contained in the structure. Newer
implementations that support variable-length socket address structures also contain a
length field at the beginning, which contains the length of the entire structure.

The two functions that convert IP addresses between presentation format (what we
write, such as ASCII characters) and numerical format (what goes into a socket address
structure) are inet_pton and inet_ntop. Although we will use these two functions
in the coming chapters, they are protocol dependent. A better technique is to manipulate socket address structures as opaque objects, knowing just the pointer to the structure and its size, and we developed a set of sock_ functions that help make our
programs protocol independent. We complete the development of our protocol-
independent tools in Chapter 11 with the getaddrinfo and getnameinfo functions.

TCP sockets provide a byte stream to the application: there are no record markers. The return value from a `read` can be less than what we asked for, but this does not indicate an error. To help read and write a byte stream we developed three functions, `readn`, `writen`, and `readline`, which we use throughout the text.

Exercises

3.1   Why must value–result arguments such as the length of a socket address structure be passed by reference?

3.2   Why do the `readn` and `writen` functions both copy the `void*` pointer into a `char*` pointer?

3.3   The `inet_ntoa` and `inet_addr` functions have traditionally been liberal in what they accept as a dotted-decimal IPv4 address string: allowing from one to four numbers separated by decimal points, and allowing a leading `0x` to specify a hexadecimal number, or a leading 0 to specify an octal number. (Try `telnet 0xe` to see this behavior.) `inet_pton` is much stricter with IPv4 address and requires exactly four numbers separated by three decimal points, with each number being a decimal number between 0 and 255. `inet_pton` does not allow a dotted-decimal number to be specified when the address family is `AF_INET6`, although one could argue that these should be allowed and the return value is then the IPv4-mapped IPv6 address for the dotted-decimal string (Figure A.10). Write a new function named `inet_pton_loose` that handles these scenarios: if the address family is `AF_INET` and `inet_pton` returns 0, call `inet_aton` and see if it succeeds. Similarly, if the address family is `AF_INET6` and `inet_pton` returns 0, call `inet_aton` and if it succeeds, return the IPv4-mapped IPv6 address.

4

Elementary TCP Sockets

4.1 Introduction

This chapter describes the elementary socket functions required to write a complete TCP client and server. We first describe all of the elementary socket functions that we will be using and then develop the client and server in the next chapter. We will work with this client and server throughout the text, enhancing it many times (Figures 1.12 and 1.13).

We also describe concurrent servers, a common Unix technique for providing concurrency when numerous clients are connected to the same server at the same time. Each client connection causes the server to `fork` a new process just for that client. In this chapter we consider only the one-*process*-per-client model using `fork` but consider a different one-*thread*-per-client model when we describe threads in Chapter 23.

Figure 4.1 shows a time line of the typical scenario that takes place between a TCP client and server. First the server is started, then sometime later a client is started that connects to the server. We assume that the client sends a request to the server, the server processes the request, and the server sends back a reply to the client. This continues until the client closes its end of the connection, which sends an end-of-file notification to the server. The server then closes its end of the connection and either terminates or waits for a new client connection.

4.2 `socket` Function

To perform network I/O, the first thing a process must do is call the `socket` function, specifying the type of communication protocol desired (TCP using IPv4, UDP using IPv6, Unix domain stream protocol, etc.).

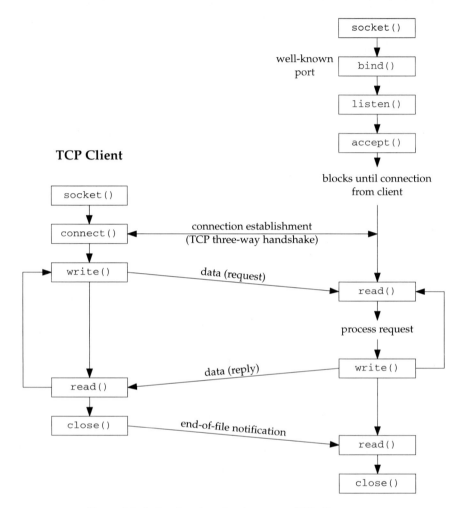

Figure 4.1 Socket functions for elementary TCP client–server.

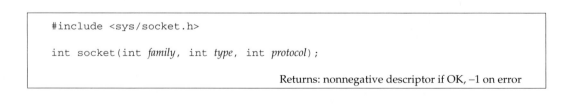

The *family* specifies the protocol family and is one of the constants shown in Figure 4.2. The socket *type* is one of the constants shown in Figure 4.3. Normally the *protocol* argument to the socket function is set to 0 except for raw sockets. We will discuss these in Chapter 25.

Not all combinations of socket *family* and *type* are valid. Figure 4.4 shows the valid combinations, along with the actual protocol that is selected by the pair. The boxes marked "Yes" are valid but do not have handy acronyms. The blank boxes are not supported.

family	Description
AF_INET	IPv4 protocols
AF_INET6	IPv6 protocols
AF_LOCAL	Unix domain protocols (Chapter 14)
AF_ROUTE	Routing sockets (Chapter 17)
AF_KEY	Key socket

Figure 4.2 Protocol *family* constants for socket function.

type	Description
SOCK_STREAM	stream socket
SOCK_DGRAM	datagram socket
SOCK_RAW	raw socket

Figure 4.3 *type* of socket for socket function.

	AF_INET	AF_INET6	AF_LOCAL	AF_ROUTE	AF_KEY
SOCK_STREAM	TCP	TCP	Yes		
SOCK_DGRAM	UDP	UDP	Yes		
SOCK_RAW	IPv4	IPv6		Yes	Yes

Figure 4.4 Combinations of *family* and *type* for the socket function.

You may also encounter the corresponding PF_*xxx* constant as the first argument to socket. We say more about this at the end of this section.

We note that you may encounter AF_UNIX (the historical Unix name) instead of AF_LOCAL (the Posix.1g name), and we say more about this in Chapter 14.

There are other values for the *family* and *type* arguments. For example, 4.4BSD supports both AF_NS (the Xerox NS protocols, often called XNS) and AF_ISO (the OSI protocols). But few people use either of these protocols today. Similarly, the *type* of SOCK_SEQPACKET, a sequenced-packet socket, is implemented by both the Xerox NS protocols and the OSI protocols. But TCP is a byte stream and supports only SOCK_STREAM sockets.

Linux supports a new socket type, SOCK_PACKET, that provides access to the datalink, similar to BPF and DLPI in Figure 2.1. We say more about this in Chapter 26.

The key socket, `AF_KEY`, is new. IPv6 requires support for cryptographic security and many systems will probably support this for IPv4 too. Similar to the way that a routing socket (`AF_ROUTE`) is an interface to the kernel's routing table, the key socket is an interface into the kernel's key table. Preliminary documentation on this family is in [McDonald, Phan, and Atkinson 1996] and [McDonald, Metz, and Phan 1997].

On success the `socket` function returns a small nonnegative integer value, similar to a file descriptor. We call this a *socket descriptor*, or a *sockfd*. To obtain this socket descriptor, all we have specified is a protocol family (IPv4, IPv6, or Unix) and the socket type (stream, datagram, or raw). We have not yet specified either the local protocol address or the foreign protocol address.

AF_*xxx* **versus PF_***xxx*

The `AF_` prefix stands for "address family" and the `PF_` prefix stands for "protocol family." Historically the intent was that a single protocol family might support multiple address families and that the `PF_` value was used to create the socket and the `AF_` value was used in socket address structures. But in actuality, a protocol family supporting multiple address families has never been supported and the `<sys/socket.h>` header defines the `PF_` value for a given protocol to be equal to the `AF_` value for that protocol. While there is no guarantee that this equality between the two will always be true, should anyone change this for existing protocols, lots of existing code would break. To conform to existing coding practice, we use only the `AF_` constants in this text, although you may encounter the `PF_` value, mainly in calls to `socket`.

Looking at 137 programs that call `socket` in the BSD/OS 2.1 release shows 143 calls that specify the `AF_` value and only 8 that specify the `PF_` value.

Historically, the reason for the similar sets of constants with the `AF_` and `PF_` prefixes goes back to 4.1cBSD [Lanciani 1996] and a version of the `socket` function that predates the one we are describing (which appeared with 4.2BSD). The 4.1cBSD version of `socket` took four arguments, one of which was a pointer to a `sockproto` structure. The first member of this structure was named `sp_family` and its value was one of the `PF_` values. The second member, `sp_protocol`, was a protocol number, similar to the third argument to `socket` today. Specifying this structure was the only way to specify the protocol family. Therefore, in this early system the `PF_` values were used as structure tags to specify the protocol family in the `sockproto` structure, and the `AF_` values were used as structure tags to specify the address family in the socket address structures. The `sockproto` structure is still in 4.4BSD (pp. 626–627 of TCPv2) but is only used internally by the kernel. The original definition had the comment "protocol family" for the `sp_family` member, but this has been changed to "address family" in the 4.4BSD source code.

To confuse this difference between the `AF_` and `PF_` constants even more, the Berkeley kernel data structure that contains the value that is compared to the first argument to `socket` (the `dom_family` member of the `domain` structure, p. 187 of TCPv2) has the comment that it contains an `AF_` value. But some of the `domain` structures within the kernel are initialized to the corresponding `AF_` value (p. 192 of TCPv2) while others are initialized to the `PF_` value (p. 646 of TCPv2 and p. 229 of TCPv3).

As another historical note, the 4.2BSD manual page for `socket`, dated July 1983, calls its first argument *af* and lists the possible values as the `AF_` constants.

Finally, we note that Posix.1g specifies the first argument to socket be a PF_ value, and the AF_ value be used for socket address structure. But it then defines only one family value in the addrinfo structure (Section 11.2), intended for use in either a call to socket or in a socket address structure!

4.3   connect **Function**

The connect function is used by a TCP client to establish a connection with a TCP server.

```
#include <sys/socket.h>

int connect(int sockfd, const struct sockaddr *servaddr, socklen_t addrlen);
```
                                                              Returns: 0 if OK, −1 on error

sockfd is a socket descriptor that was returned by the socket function. The second and third arguments are a pointer to a socket address structure, and its size, as described in Section 3.3. The socket address structure must contain the IP address and port number of the server. We saw an example of this function in Figure 1.5.

The client does not have to call bind (which we describe in the next section) before calling connect: the kernel will choose both an ephemeral port and the source IP address if necessary.

In the case of a TCP socket, the connect function initiates TCP's three-way handshake (Section 2.5). The function returns only when the connection is established or an error occurs. There are several different error returns possible.

1. If the client TCP receives no response to its SYN segment, ETIMEDOUT is returned. 4.4BSD, for example, sends one SYN when connect is called, another 6 seconds later, and another 24 seconds later (p. 828 of TCPv2). If no response is received after a total of 75 seconds, the error is returned.

   Some systems provide administrative control over this timeout; see Appendix E of TCPv1.

2. If the server's response to the client's SYN is an RST, this indicates that no process is waiting for connections on the server host at the port that we specified (i.e., the server process is probably not running). This is a *hard error* and the error ECONNREFUSED is returned to the client as soon as the RST is received.

   An RST, meaning "reset," is a type of TCP segment that is sent by TCP when something is wrong. Three conditions that generate an RST are when a SYN arrives for a port that has no listening server (what we just described), when TCP wants to abort an existing connection, and when TCP receives a segment for a connection that does not exist. (TCPv1 pp. 246−250 contains additional information.)

3. If the client's SYN elicits an ICMP destination unreachable from some intermediate router, this is considered a *soft error*. The client kernel saves the message

but keeps sending SYNs with the same time between each SYN as in the first scenario. But if no response is received after some fixed amount of time (75 seconds for 4.4BSD), the saved ICMP error is returned to the process as either EHOSTUNREACH or ENETUNREACH.

> Many earlier systems, such as 4.2BSD, incorrectly aborted the connection establishment attempt when the ICMP destination unreachable was received. This is wrong because this ICMP error can indicate a transient condition. For example, it could be that the condition is caused by a routing problem that will be corrected in 15 seconds.
>
> Notice that ENETUNREACH is not listed in Figure A.15, even when the error indicates that the destination network is unreachable. Network unreachables are considered obsolete, and even if 4.4BSD receives one, EHOSTUNREACH is returned to the application.

We see these different error conditions with our simple client from Figure 1.5. We first specify the local host (127.0.0.1), which is running the daytime server and see the normal output.

```
solaris % daytimetcpcli 127.0.0.1
Tue Jan 16 16:45:07 1996
```

To see a different format for the returned reply, we specify the local Cisco router (Figure 1.16).

```
solaris % daytimetcpcli 206.62.226.62
Tuesday, May 7, 1996 11:01:33-MST
```

Next we specify an IP address that is on the local subnet (206.62.226) but the host ID (55) is nonexistent. That is, there does not exist a host on the subnet with a host ID of 55, so when the client host sends out ARP requests (asking for that host to respond with its hardware address), it will never receive an ARP reply.

```
solaris % daytimetcpcli 206.62.226.55
connect error: Connection timed out
```

We only get the error after the `connect` times out (which we said was 3 minutes with Solaris 2.5). Notice that our `err_sys` function prints the human-readable string associated with the `ETIMEDOUT` error.

Our next example is to the host `gateway`, which is a Cisco router, that is not running a daytime server.

```
solaris % daytimetcpcli 140.252.1.4
connect error: Connection refused
```

The server responds immediately with an RST.

Our final example specifies an IP address that is not reachable on the Internet. If we watch the packets with `tcpdump`, we see that a router six hops away returns an ICMP host unreachable error.

```
solaris % daytimetcpcli 192.3.4.5
connect error: No route to host
```

As with the `ETIMEDOUT` error, in this example the `connect` returns the `EHOSTUNREACH` error only after waiting its specified amount of time.

In terms of the TCP state transition diagram (Figure 2.4), `connect` moves from the CLOSED state (the state in which a socket begins when it is created by the `socket` function) to the SYN_SENT state and then, on success, to the ESTABLISHED state. If the `connect` fails, the socket is no longer usable and must be closed. We cannot call `connect` again on the socket. In Figure 11.6 we will see that when we call `connect` in a loop, trying each IP address for a given host until one works, each time `connect` fails we must `close` the socket descriptor and call `socket` again.

4.4 `bind` **Function**

The `bind` function assigns a local protocol address to a socket. With the Internet protocols the protocol address is the combination of either a 32-bit IPv4 address or a 128-bit IPv6 address, along with a 16-bit TCP or UDP port number.

```
#include <sys/socket.h>

int bind(int sockfd, const struct sockaddr *myaddr, socklen_t addrlen);
```
                                                               Returns: 0 if OK, −1 on error

> Historically the manual page description of `bind` has said "bind assigns a name to an unnamed socket." The use of the term "name" is confusing and gives the connotation of domain names (Chapter 9) such as `foo.bar.com`. The `bind` function has nothing to do with names. `bind` assigns a protocol address to a socket, and what that protocol address means depends on the protocol.

The second argument is a pointer to a protocol-specific address and the third argument is the size of this address structure. With TCP, calling `bind` lets us specify a port number, an IP address, both, or neither.

- Servers bind their well-known port when they start. We saw this in Figure 1.9. If a TCP client or server does not do this, the kernel chooses an ephemeral port for the socket when either `connect` or `listen` is called. It is normal for a TCP client to let the kernel choose an ephemeral port, unless the application requires a reserved port (Figure 2.6), but it is rare for a TCP server to let the kernel choose an ephemeral port, since servers are known by their well-known port.

  > Exceptions to this rule are RPC (Remote Procedure Call) servers. They normally let the kernel choose an ephemeral port for their listening socket since this port is then registered with the RPC port mapper. Clients have to contact the port mapper to obtain the ephemeral port before they can `connect` to the server. This also applies to RPC servers using UDP.

- A process can `bind` a specific IP address to its socket. The IP address must belong to an interface on the host. For a TCP client, this assigns the source IP address that will be used for IP datagrams sent on the socket. For a TCP server, this restricts the socket to receive incoming client connections destined only to that IP address.

Normally a TCP client does not `bind` an IP address to its socket. The kernel then chooses the source IP address when the socket is connected, based on the outgoing interface that is used, which in turn is based on the route required to reach the server (p. 737 of TCPv2).

If a TCP server does not bind an IP address to its socket, the kernel uses the destination IP address of the client's SYN as the server's source IP address (p. 943 of TCPv2).

As we said, calling `bind` lets us specify the IP address, the port, both, or neither. Figure 4.5 summarizes the values to which we set the `sin_addr` and `sin_port`, or the `sin6_addr` and `sin6_port`, depending on the desired result.

Process specifies		Result
IP address	port	
wildcard	0	kernel chooses IP address and port
wildcard	nonzero	kernel chooses IP address, process specifies port
local IP address	0	process specifies IP address, kernel chooses port
local IP address	nonzero	process specifies IP address and port

Figure 4.5   Result when specifying IP address and/or port number to `bind`.

If we specify a port number of 0, the kernel chooses an ephemeral port when `bind` is called. But if we specify a wildcard IP address, the kernel does not choose the local IP address until either the socket is connected (TCP) or until a datagram is sent on the socket (UDP).

With IPv4 the *wildcard* address is specified by the constant `INADDR_ANY`, whose value is normally 0. This tells the kernel to choose the IP address. We saw the use of this in Figure 1.9 with the assignment

```
struct sockaddr_in   servaddr;

servaddr.sin_addr.s_addr = htonl(INADDR_ANY);    /* wildcard */
```

While this works with IPv4, where an IP address is a 32-bit value that can be represented as a simple numeric constant (0 in this case), we cannot use this technique with IPv6, since the 128-bit IPv6 address is stored in a structure. (In C we cannot represent a constant structure on the right-hand side of an assignment.) To solve this problem, we write

```
struct sockaddr_in6   serv;

serv.sin6_addr = in6addr_any;    /* wildcard */
```

The system allocates and initializes the `in6addr_any` variable to the constant `IN6ADDR_ANY_INIT`. The `<netinet/in.h>` header contains the `extern` declaration for `in6addr_any`.

The value of `INADDR_ANY` (0) is the same in either network or host byte order, so the use of `htonl` is not really required. But since all the `INADDR_` constants defined by the `<netinet/in.h>` header are defined in host byte order, we should use `htonl` with any of these constants.

If we tell the kernel to choose an ephemeral port number for our socket, notice that `bind` does not return the chosen value. Indeed, it cannot return this value since the second argument to `bind` has the `const` qualifier. To obtain the value of the ephemeral port assigned by the kernel we must call `getsockname` to return the protocol address.

A common example of a process binding a nonwildcard IP address to a socket is on a host that provides Web servers to multiple organizations (Section 14.2 of TCPv3). First, each organization has its own domain name, such as www.*organization*.com. Next, each organization's domain name maps into a different IP address, but typically on the same subnet. For example, if the subnet is 198.69.10, the first organization's IP address could be 198.69.10.128, the next 198.69.10.129, and so on. All of these IP addresses are then *aliased* onto a single network interface (using the `alias` option of the `ifconfig` command on 4.4BSD, for example) so that the IP layer will accept incoming datagrams destined for any of the aliased addresses. Finally, one copy of the HTTP server is started for each organization and each copy `binds` only the IP address for that organization.

> An alternative technique is to run a single server that binds the wildcard address. When a connection arrives, the server calls `getsockname` to obtain the destination IP address from the client, which in our discussion above could be 198.69.10.128, 198.69.10.129, and so on. The server then handles the client request based on the IP address to which the connection was issued.
>
> One advantage in binding a nonwildcard IP address is that the demultiplexing of a given destination IP address to a given server process is then done by the kernel.
>
> We must be careful to distinguish between the interface on which a packet arrives versus the destination IP address of that packet. In Section 8.8 we talk about the weak end system model and the strong end system model. Most implementations employ the former, meaning it is OK for a packet to arrive with a destination IP address that identifies an interface other than the interface on which the packet arrives. (This assumes a multihomed host.) Binding a nonwildcard IP address restricts the datagrams that will be delivered to the socket based only on the destination IP address. It says nothing about the arriving interface, unless the host employs the strong end system model.

A common error from `bind` is `EADDRINUSE` ("Address already in use"). We say more about this in Section 7.5 when we talk about the `SO_REUSEADDR` and `SO_REUSEPORT` socket options.

4.5   `listen` Function

The `listen` function is called only by a TCP server and it performs two actions.

1. When a socket is created by the `socket` function, it is assumed to be an active socket, that is, a client socket that will issue a `connect`. The `listen` function converts an unconnected socket into a passive socket, indicating that the kernel should accept incoming connection requests directed to this socket. In terms of the TCP state transition diagram (Figure 2.4) the call to `listen` moves the socket from the CLOSED state to the LISTEN state.

2. The second argument to this function specifies the maximum number of connections that the kernel should queue for this socket.

```
#include <sys/socket.h>

int listen(int sockfd, int backlog);
```

Returns: 0 if OK, −1 on error

This function is normally called after both the `socket` and `bind` functions and must be called before calling the `accept` function.

To understand the *backlog* argument we must realize that for a given listening socket, the kernel maintains two queues:

1. An *incomplete connection queue*, which contains an entry for each SYN that has arrived from a client for which the server is awaiting completion of the TCP three-way handshake. These sockets are in the SYN_RCVD state (Figure 2.4).

2. A *completed connection queue*, which contains an entry for each client with whom the TCP three-way handshake has completed. These sockets are in the ESTAB-LISHED state (Figure 2.4).

Figure 4.6 depicts these two queues for a given listening socket.

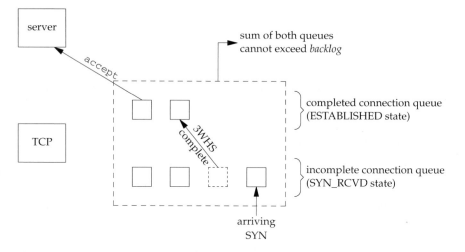

Figure 4.6   The two queues maintained by TCP for a listening socket.

Figure 4.7 depicts the packets exchanged during the connection establishment with these two queues.

When a SYN arrives from a client, TCP creates a new entry on the incomplete queue and then responds with the second segment of the three-way handshake: the server's SYN with an ACK of the client's SYN (Section 2.5). This entry will remain on the

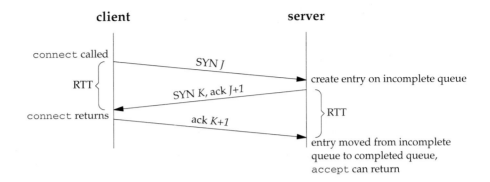

Figure 4.7   TCP three-way handshake and the two queues for a listening socket.

incomplete queue until the third segment of the three-way handshake arrives (the client's ACK of the server's SYN), or until the entry times out. (Berkeley-derived implementations have a timeout of 75 seconds for these incomplete entries.) If the three-way handshake completes normally, the entry moves from the incomplete queue to the end of the completed queue. When the process calls accept, which we describe in the next section, the first entry on the completed queue is returned to the process or, if the queue is empty, the process is put to sleep until an entry is placed onto the completed queue.

There are several points to consider about the handling of these two queues.

- The *backlog* argument to the listen function has historically specified the maximum value for the sum of both queues.

  > There has never been a formal definition of what the *backlog* means. The 4.2BSD manual page says that it "defines the maximum length the queue of pending connections may grow to." Many manual pages and even Posix.1g copy this definition verbatim, but this definition does not say whether a pending connection is one in the SYN_RCVD state, one in the ESTAB-LISHED state that has not yet been accepted, or either. The historical definition in this bullet is the Berkeley implementation, dating back to 4.2BSD, and copied by many others.

- Berkeley-derived implementations add a fudge factor to the *backlog* that we specify: it is multiplied by 1.5 (p. 257 of TCPv1 and p. 462 of TCPv2). For example, the commonly specified *backlog* of 5 really allows up to eight queued entries on these systems, as we show in Figure 4.10.

  > The reason for adding this fudge factor appears lost in history [Joy 1994]. But if we consider the *backlog* as specifying the maximum number of completed connections that the kernel will queue for a socket ([Borman 1997c], as discussed shortly), then the reason for the fudge factor is to take into account incomplete connections on the queue.

- Do not specify a *backlog* of 0, as different implementations interpret this differently (Figure 4.10). Some implementations allow one queued connection, while others do not allow any queued connections. If you do not want any clients connecting to your listening socket, then close the listening socket.

- Assuming the three-way handshake completes normally (i.e., no lost segments and no retransmissions), an entry remains on the incomplete connection queue for one round-trip time (RTT), whatever that value happens to be between this particular client and the server. Section 14.4 of TCPv3 shows that for one Web server the median RTT between many clients and the server was 187 ms. (The median is often used for this statistic, since a few large values can noticeably skew the mean.)

- Historically, sample code always shows a *backlog* of 5, as that was the maximum value supported by 4.2BSD. This was adequate in the 1980s when busy servers would handle only a few hundred connections per day. But with the growth of the World Wide Web (WWW), where busy servers handle millions of connections per day, this small number is completely inadequate (pp. 187–192 of TCPv3). Busy HTTP servers must specify a much larger *backlog*, and newer kernels must support larger values.

  Many current systems allow the administrator to modify the maximum value for the *backlog*.

- A problem is: what value should the application specify for the *backlog*, since 5 is often inadequate? There is no easy answer for this. HTTP servers now specify a larger value, but if the value specified is a constant in the source code to increase the constant requires recompiling the server. Another method is to assume some default but allow a command-line option or an environment variable to override the default. It is always OK to specify a value that is larger than supported by the kernel, as the kernel should silently truncate the value to the maximum value that it supports, without returning an error (p. 456 of TCPv2).

We can provide a simple solution to this problem by modifying our wrapper function for the `listen` function. Figure 4.8 shows the actual code. We allow the environment variable `LISTENQ` to override the value specified by the caller.

—— *lib/wrapsock.c*
```
74 void
75 Listen(int fd, int backlog)
76 {
77     char    *ptr;

78         /* can override 2nd argument with environment variable */
79     if ( (ptr = getenv("LISTENQ")) != NULL)
80         backlog = atoi(ptr);

81     if (listen(fd, backlog) < 0)
82         err_sys("listen error");
83 }
```
—— *lib/wrapsock.c*

Figure 4.8 Wrapper function for `listen` that allows an environment variable to specify *backlog*.

- Manuals and books have historically said that the reason for queueing a fixed number of connections is to handle the case of the server process being busy between successive calls to `accept`. This implies that of the two queues, the completed queue should normally have more entries than the incomplete queue. Again, busy

Web servers have shown that this is false. The reason for specifying a large *backlog* is because the incomplete connection queue can grow as client SYNs arrive, waiting for completion of the three-way handshake.

Figure 4.9 shows the actual number of entries on each queue measured on a moderately busy Web server. These values were obtained by sampling these two counters for a listening HTTP socket approximately every 84 ms for 2 hours during the middle of a weekday.

#entries on queue	Incomplete queue	Complete queue
0	3,033	90,358
1	7,158	107
2	10,551	59
3	12,960	52
4	11,949	38
5	9,836	27
6	7,754	31
7	6,165	22
8	4,829	30
9	3,687	35
10	2,674	30
11	1,893	25
12	1,431	29
13	1,083	25
14	1,065	49
15	980	7
16	784	
17	696	
18	514	
19	382	
20	294	
21	248	
22	161	
23	152	
24	121	
25	77	
26	48	
27	33	
28	79	
29	78	
30	90	
31	70	
32	29	
33	16	
34	4	
	90,924	90,924

Figure 4.9   Number of entries on incomplete and completed connection queues.

The completed connection queue was empty 99.4% of the time, but there were periods when this queue was not empty. The system on which this server was running

(BSD/OS 2.0.1) had a maximum backlog of 64, although the values shown do not appear to have reached this limit.

- If the queues are full when a client SYN arrives, TCP ignores the arriving SYN (pp. 930−931 of TCPv2), it does not send an RST. This is because the condition is considered temporary, and the client TCP will retransmit its SYN, hopefully finding room on the queue in the near future. If the server TCP were to send an RST, the client's connect would immediately return an error, forcing the application to handle this condition, instead of letting TCP's normal retransmission take over. Also, the client could not differentiate between an RST in response to a SYN meaning "there is no server at this port" versus "there is a server at this port but its queues are full."

  > Posix.1g allows either behavior: ignoring the new SYN or responding to the new SYN with an RST. Historically, all Berkeley-derived implementations have ignored the new SYN.

- Data that arrives after the three-way handshake completes, but before the server calls accept, should be queued by the server TCP, up to the size of the connected socket's receive buffer.

Figure 4.10 shows the actual number of queued connections provided for different values of the *backlog* argument for the various operating systems in Figure 1.16. For nine different operating systems there are six distinct columns, showing the variety of interpretations about what the backlog means!

		Maximum actual number of queued connections				
backlog	AIX 4.2, BSD/OS 3.0	DUnix 4.0, Linux 2.0.27, UWare 2.1.2	HP-UX 10.30	SunOS 4.1.4	Solaris 2.5.1	Solaris 2.6
0	1	0	1	1	1	1
1	2	1	1	2	2	3
2	4	2	3	4	3	4
3	5	3	4	5	4	6
4	7	4	6	7	5	7
5	8	5	7	8	6	9
6	10	6	9	8	7	10
7	11	7	10	8	8	12
8	13	8	12	8	9	13
9	14	9	13	8	10	15
10	16	10	15	8	11	16
11	17	11	16	8	12	18
12	19	12	18	8	13	19
13	20	13	18	8	14	21
14	22	14	19	8	15	22

Figure 4.10 Actual number of queued connections for values of *backlog*.

AIX, BSD/OS, and SunOS 4 have the traditional Berkeley algorithm, although the latter does not allow the *backlog* to go above 5. HP-UX and Solaris 2.6 add a different fudge factor to the *backlog*. Digital Unix, Linux, and UnixWare interpret the *backlog* literally, and Solaris 2.5.1 just adds one to the *backlog*.

> Linux allowed an unlimited number of connections for a *backlog* of 0, indicating a bug.

> The program to measure these values is shown in the solution for Exercise 14.5.

> As we said, historically the backlog has specified the maximum value for the sum of both queues. During 1996 a new type of attack was launched on the Internet, called *SYN flooding* [CERT 1996b]. The hacker writes a program to send SYNs at a high rate to the victim, filling the incomplete connection queue for one or more TCP ports. (We use the term *hacker* to mean the attacker, as described in the Preface of [Cheswick and Bellovin 1994].) Additionally the source IP address of each SYN is set to a random number (this is called *IP spoofing*) so that the server's SYN/ACK goes nowhere. This also prevents the server from knowing the real IP address of the hacker. By filling the incomplete queue with bogus SYNs, legitimate SYNs are not queued, providing a *denial of service* to legitimate clients. There are two commonly used methods of handling these attacks, summarized in [Borman 1997c]. But what is most interesting in this note is revisiting what the listen backlog really means. It should specify the maximum number of *completed* connections for a given socket that the kernel will queue. The purpose of having a limit on these completed connections is to stop the kernel from accepting new connection requests for a given socket when the application is not accepting them (for whatever reason). If a system implements this interpretation, as does BSD/OS 3.0, then the application need not specify huge *backlog* values just because the server handles lots of client requests (e.g., a busy Web server) or to provide protection against SYN flooding. The kernel handles lots of incomplete connections, regardless of whether they are legitimate or from a hacker. But even with this interpretation, we can see in Figure 4.9 that scenarios do occur when the completed connection queue accumulates entries (up to 15 in this figure), where the traditional value of 5 is inadequate.

4.6   accept Function

accept is called by a TCP server to return the next completed connection from the front of the completed connection queue (Figure 4.6). If the completed connection queue is empty, the process is put to sleep (assuming the default of a blocking socket).

```
#include <sys/socket.h>

int accept(int sockfd, struct sockaddr *cliaddr, socklen_t *addrlen);
```
                                        Returns: nonnegative descriptor if OK, –1 on error

The *cliaddr* and *addrlen* arguments are used to return the protocol address of the connected peer process (the client). *addrlen* is a value–result argument (Section 3.3): before the call, we set the integer value pointed to by *addrlen* to the size of the socket address structure pointed to by *cliaddr*, and on return this integer value contains the actual number of bytes stored by the kernel in the socket address structure.

If accept is successful, its return value is a brand new descriptor that was automatically created by the kernel. This new descriptor refers to the TCP connection with the client. When discussing accept we call the first argument to accept the *listening socket* (the descriptor created by socket and then used as the first argument to both bind and listen), and we call the return value from accept the *connected socket*. It is important to differentiate between these two sockets. A given server normally creates only one listening socket, which then exists for the lifetime of the server. The kernel then creates one connected socket for each client connection that is accepted (i.e., for which the TCP three-way handshake completes). When the server is finished serving a given client, the connected socket is closed.

This function returns up to three values: an integer return code that is either a new socket descriptor or an error indication, the protocol address of the client process (through the *cliaddr* pointer), and the size of this address (through the *addrlen* pointer). If we are not interested in having the protocol address of the client returned, we set both *cliaddr* and *addrlen* to null pointers.

Figure 1.9 shows these points. The connected socket is closed each time through the loop, but the listening socket remains open for the life of the server. We also see that the second and third arguments to accept are null pointers, since we were not interested in the identity of the client.

Example: Value–Result Arguments

We will now show how to handle the value–result argument to accept by modifying the code from Figure 1.9 to print the IP address and port of the client. We show this in Figure 4.11.

New declarations

7-8   We define two new variables: len, which will be a value–result variable, and cliaddr, which will contain the client's protocol address.

Accept connection and print client's address

19-23   We initialize len to the size of the socket address structure and pass a pointer to the cliaddr structure and a pointer to len as the second and third arguments to accept. We call inet_ntop (Section 3.7) to convert the 32-bit IP address in the socket address structure into a dotted-decimal ASCII string and call ntohs (Section 3.4) to convert the 16-bit port number from network byte order to host byte order.

> Calling sock_ntop instead of inet_ntop would make our server more protocol independent, but this server is already dependent on IPv4. We show a protocol-independent version of this server in Figure 11.9.

If we run our new server and then run our client on the same host, connecting to our server twice in a row, we have the following output from the client:

```
solaris % daytimetcpcli 127.0.0.1
Wed Jan 17 15:42:35 1996
solaris % daytimetcpcli 206.62.226.33
Wed Jan 17 15:42:53 1996
```

We first specify the server's IP address as the loopback address (127.0.0.1) and then as its own IP address (206.62.226.33). Here is the corresponding server output.

intro/daytimetcpsrv1.c

```
 1 #include     "unp.h"
 2 #include     <time.h>

 3 int
 4 main(int argc, char **argv)
 5 {
 6     int      listenfd, connfd;
 7     socklen_t len;
 8     struct sockaddr_in servaddr, cliaddr;
 9     char     buff[MAXLINE];
10     time_t   ticks;

11     listenfd = Socket(AF_INET, SOCK_STREAM, 0);

12     bzero(&servaddr, sizeof(servaddr));
13     servaddr.sin_family = AF_INET;
14     servaddr.sin_addr.s_addr = htonl(INADDR_ANY);
15     servaddr.sin_port = htons(13);   /* daytime server */

16     Bind(listenfd, (SA *) &servaddr, sizeof(servaddr));

17     Listen(listenfd, LISTENQ);

18     for ( ; ; ) {
19         len = sizeof(cliaddr);
20         connfd = Accept(listenfd, (SA *) &cliaddr, &len);
21         printf("connection from %s, port %d\n",
22                 Inet_ntop(AF_INET, &cliaddr.sin_addr, buff, sizeof(buff)),
23                 ntohs(cliaddr.sin_port));

24         ticks = time(NULL);
25         snprintf(buff, sizeof(buff), "%.24s\r\n", ctime(&ticks));
26         Write(connfd, buff, strlen(buff));

27         Close(connfd);
28     }
29 }
```

intro/daytimetcpsrv1.c

Figure 4.11 Daytime server that prints client IP address and port.

```
solaris # daytimetcpsrv1
connection from 127.0.0.1, port 33188
connection from 206.62.226.33, port 33189
```

Notice what happens with the client's IP address. Since our daytime client (Figure 1.5) does not call bind, we said in Section 4.4 that the kernel chooses the source IP address based on the outgoing interface that is used. In the first case the kernel sets the source IP address to the loopback address and in the second case it sets the address to the IP address of the Ethernet interface. We can also see in this example that the ephemeral port chosen by the Solaris kernel is 33188, and then 33189 (recall Figure 2.6).

As a final point, our shell prompt for the server script changes to the pound sign (#), the commonly used prompt for the superuser. Our server must run with superuser privileges to `bind` the reserved port of 13. If we do not have superuser privileges, the call to `bind` fails:

```
solaris % daytimetcpsrv1
bind error: Permission denied
```

4.7   `fork` and `exec` Functions

Before describing how to write a concurrent server in the next section we must describe the Unix `fork` function. This function is the only way in Unix to create a new process.

```
#include <unistd.h>

pid_t fork(void);
```
                                    Returns: 0 in child, process ID of child in parent, −1 on error

If you have never seen this function before, the hard part in understanding `fork` is that it is called *once* but it returns *twice*. It returns once in the calling process (called the parent) with a return value that is the process ID of the newly created process (the child). It also returns once in the child, with a return value of 0. Hence the return value tells the process whether it is the parent or the child.

The reason `fork` returns 0 in the child, instead of the parent's process ID, is because a child has only one parent and it can always obtain the parent's process ID by calling `getppid`. A parent, on the other hand, can have any number of children, and there is no way to obtain the process IDs of its children. If the parent wants to keep track of the process IDs of all its children, it must record the return values from `fork`.

All descriptors open in the parent before the call to `fork` are shared with the child after `fork` returns. We will see this feature used by network servers: the parent calls `accept` and then calls `fork`. The connected socket is then shared between the parent and child. Normally the child then reads and writes the connected socket and the parent closes the connected socket.

There are two typical uses of `fork`.

1. A process makes a copy of itself so that one copy can handle one operation while the other copy does another task. This is typical for network servers. We will see many examples of this later in the text.

2. A process wants to execute another program. Since the only way to create a new process is by calling `fork`, the process first calls `fork` to make a copy of itself, and then one of the copies (typically the child process) calls `exec` (described next) to replace itself with the new program. This is typical for programs such as shells.

The only way in which an executable program file on disk is executed by Unix is for an existing process to call one of the six `exec` functions. (We often refer generically to "the exec function" when it does not matter which of the six is called.) exec replaces the current process image with the new program file and this new program normally starts at the main function. The process ID does not change. We refer to the process that calls exec as the *calling process* and the newly executed program as the *new program*.

> Older manuals and books incorrectly refer to the new program as the *new process*, which is wrong, because a new process is not created.

The difference in the six exec functions is (a) whether the program file to execute is specified by a *filename* or a *pathname*, (b) whether the arguments to the new program are listed one by one or referenced through an array of pointers, and (c) whether the environment of the calling process is passed to the new program or whether a new environment is specified.

```
#include <unistd.h>

int execl(const char *pathname, const char *arg0, ... /* (char *) 0 */ );

int execv(const char *pathname, char *const argv[]);

int execle(const char *pathname, const char *arg0, ...
            /* (char *) 0, char *const envp[] */ );

int execve(const char *pathname, char *const argv[], char *const envp[]);

int execlp(const char *filename, const char *arg0, ... /* (char *) 0 */ );

int execvp(const char *filename, char *const argv[]);
```
                                            All six return: −1 on error, no return on success

These functions return to the caller only if an error occurs. Otherwise control passes to the start of the new program, normally the main function.

The relationship among these six functions is shown in Figure 4.12. Normally only execve is a system call within the kernel and the other five are library functions that call execve.

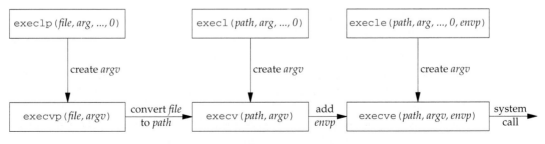

Figure 4.12 Relationship among the six exec functions.

Note the following differences among these six functions:

1. The three functions in the top row specify each argument string as a separate argument to the exec function, with a null pointer terminating the variable number of arguments. The three functions in the second row have an *argv* array, containing the pointers to the argument strings. This *argv* array must contain a null pointer to specify its end, since a count is not specified.

2. The two functions in the left column specify a *filename* argument. This is converted into a *pathname* using the current PATH environment variable. If the *filename* argument to execlp or execvp contains a slash (/) anywhere in the string, the PATH variable is not used. The four functions in the right two columns specify a fully qualified *pathname* argument.

3. The four functions in the left two columns do not specify an explicit environment pointer. Instead the current value of the external variable environ is used for building an environment list that is passed to the new program. The two functions in the right column specify an explicit environment list. The *envp* array of pointers must be terminated by a null pointer.

Descriptors open in the process before calling exec normally remain open across the exec. We use the qualifier "normally" because this can be disabled using fcntl to set the FD_CLOEXEC descriptor flag. The inetd server uses this feature, as we describe in Section 12.5.

4.8   Concurrent Servers

The server in Figure 4.11 is an *iterative server*. For something as simple as a daytime server, this is fine. But when the client request can take longer to service, we do not want to tie up a single server with one client; we want to handle multiple clients at the same time. The simplest way to write a *concurrent server* under Unix is to fork a child process to handle each client. Figure 4.13 shows the outline for a typical concurrent server.

When a connection is established, accept returns, the server calls fork, and then the child process services the client (on connfd, the connected socket) and the parent process waits for another connection (on listenfd, the listening socket). The parent closes the connected socket since the child handles this new client.

In Figure 4.13 we assume that the function doit does whatever is required to service the client. When this function returns, we explicitly close the connected socket in the child. This is not required since the next statement calls exit, and part of process termination is closing all open descriptors by the kernel. Whether to include this explicit call to close or not is a matter of personal programming taste.

We said in Section 2.5 that calling close on a TCP socket causes a FIN to be sent, followed by the normal TCP connection termination sequence. Why doesn't the close of connfd in Figure 4.13 by the parent terminate its connection with the client? To understand what's happening we must understand that every file or socket has a reference count. The reference count is maintained in the file table (pp. 58–59 of APUE). This is a count of the number of descriptors that are currently open that refer to this file

```
pid_t  pid;
int    listenfd, connfd;

listenfd = Socket( ... );

    /* fill in sockaddr_in{} with server's well-known port */
Bind(listenfd, ... );
Listen(listenfd, LISTENQ);

for ( ; ; ) {
    connfd = Accept(listenfd, ... );        /* probably blocks */

    if ( (pid = Fork()) == 0) {
        Close(listenfd);    /* child closes listening socket */
        doit(connfd);       /* process the request */
        Close(connfd);      /* done with this client */
        exit(0);            /* child terminates */
    }

    Close(connfd);          /* parent closes connected socket */
}
```

Figure 4.13 Outline for typical concurrent server.

or socket. In Figure 4.13, after `socket` returns, the file table associated with `listenfd` has a reference count of 1. After `accept` returns, the file table associated with `connfd` has a reference count of 1. But after `fork` returns, both descriptors are shared (i.e., duplicated) between the parent and child, so the file tables associated with both sockets now have a reference count of 2. Therefore, when the parent closes `connfd`, it just decrements the reference count from 2 to 1 and that is all. A real close on the descriptor does not take place until the reference count reaches 0. This will occur at some time later when the child closes `connfd`.

We can also visualize the sockets and the connection that occurs in Figure 4.13 as follows. First, Figure 4.14 shows the status of the client and server while the server is blocked in the call to `accept` and the connection request arrives from the client.

Figure 4.14 Status of client–server before call to `accept`.

Immediately after `accept` returns we have the scenario shown in Figure 4.15. The connection is accepted by the kernel and a new socket, `connfd`, is created. This is a connected socket and data can now be read and written across the connection.

The next step in the concurrent server is to call `fork`. Figure 4.16 shows the status after `fork` returns.

Figure 4.15 Status of client–server after return from accept.

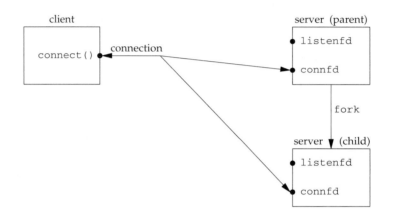

Figure 4.16 Status of client–server after fork returns.

Notice that both descriptors, listenfd and connfd, are shared (duplicated) between the parent and child.

The next step is for the parent to close the connected socket and the child to close the listening socket. This is shown in Figure 4.17.

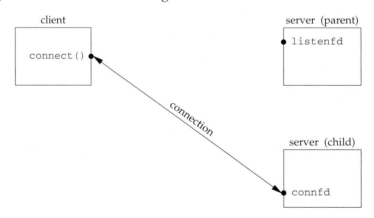

Figure 4.17 Status of client–server after parent and child close appropriate sockets.

This is the desired final state of the sockets. The child is handling the connection with the client and the parent can call accept again on the listening socket, to handle the next client connection.

4.9   `close` Function

The normal Unix `close` function is also used to close a socket and terminate a TCP connection.

```
#include <unistd.h>

int close(int sockfd);
```
                                                        Returns: 0 if OK, –1 on error

The default action of `close` with a TCP socket is to mark the socket as closed and return to the process immediately. The socket descriptor is no longer usable by the process: it cannot be used as an argument to `read` or `write`. But TCP will try to send any data that is already queued to be sent to the other end, and after this occurs the normal TCP connection termination sequence takes place (Section 2.5).

In Section 7.5 we describe the `SO_LINGER` socket option which lets us change this default action with a TCP socket. In this section we also describe what a TCP application must do to be guaranteed that the peer application has received any outstanding data.

Descriptor Reference Counts

At the end of Section 4.8 we mentioned that when the parent process in our concurrent server `close`s the connected socket, this just decrements the reference count for the descriptor. Since the reference count was still greater than 0, this call to `close` did not initiate TCP's four-packet connection termination sequence. This is the behavior we want with our concurrent server with the connected socket that is shared between the parent and child.

If we really want to send a FIN on a TCP connection, the `shutdown` function can be used (Section 6.6) instead of `close`. We describe the motivation for this in Section 6.5.

We must also be aware of what happens in our concurrent server if the parent does not call `close` for each connected socket returned by `accept`. First, the parent will eventually run out of descriptors, as there is usually a limit to the number of open descriptors that any process can have open at any time. But more importantly, none of the client connections will be terminated. When the child closes the connected socket, its reference count will go from 2 to 1 and it will remain at 1 since the parent never `close`s the connected socket. This will prevent TCP's connection termination sequence from occurring, and the connection remains open.

4.10   `getsockname` and `getpeername` Functions

These two functions return either the local protocol address associated with a socket (`getsockname`) or the foreign protocol address associated with a socket (`getpeername`).

```
#include <sys/socket.h>

int getsockname(int sockfd, struct sockaddr *localaddr, socklen_t *addrlen);

int getpeername(int sockfd, struct sockaddr *peeraddr, socklen_t *addrlen);
```

Both return: 0 if OK, −1 on error

Notice that the final argument for both functions is a value–result argument. That is, both functions fill in the socket address structure pointed to by *localaddr* or *peeraddr*.

> We mentioned with our discussion of bind that the term "name" is misleading. These two functions return the protocol address associated with one of the two ends of a network connection, which for IPv4 and IPv6 is the combination of an IP address and port number. These functions have nothing to do with domain names (Chapter 9).

These two functions are required for the following reasons:

- After `connect` successfully returns in a TCP client that does not call `bind`, `getsockname` returns the local IP address and local port number assigned to the connection by the kernel.

- After calling `bind` with a port number of 0 (telling the kernel to choose the local port number), `getsockname` returns the local port number that was assigned.

- `getsockname` can be called to obtain the address family of a socket, as we show in Figure 4.19.

- In a TCP server that `bind`s the wildcard IP address (Figure 1.9), once a connection is established with a client (`accept` returns successfully), the server can call `getsockname` to obtain the local IP address assigned to the connection. The socket descriptor argument in this call must be that of the connected socket, and not the listening socket.

- When a server is `exec`ed by the process that calls `accept`, the only way the server can obtain the identity of the client is to call `getpeername`. This is what happens whenever `inetd` (Section 12.5) `fork`s and `exec`s a TCP server. Figure 4.18 shows this scenario. `inetd` calls `accept` (top left box) and two values are returned: the connected socket descriptor, `connfd`, is the return value of the function, and the small box we label "peer's address" (an Internet socket address structure) contains the IP address and port number of the client. `fork` is called and a child of `inetd` is created. Since the child starts with a copy of the parent's memory image, the socket address structure is available to the child, as is the connected socket descriptor (since the descriptors are shared between the parent and child). But when the child `exec`s the real server (say the Telnet server that we show), the memory image of the child is replaced with the new program file for the Telnet server (i.e., the socket address structure containing the peer's address is lost), but the connected socket descriptor remains open across the `exec`. One of the first function calls performed by the Telnet server is `getpeername` to obtain the IP address and port number of the client.

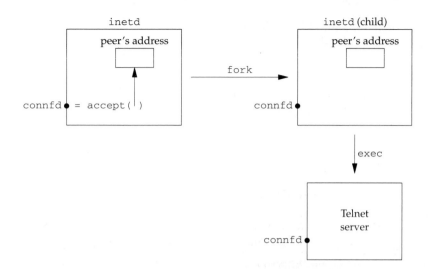

Figure 4.18 Example of inetd spawning a server.

Obviously the Telnet server in this final example must know the value of connfd when it starts. There are two common ways to do this. First, the process calling exec can format the descriptor number as a character string and pass it as a command-line argument to the newly execed program. Alternately a convention can be established that a certain descriptor is always set to the connected socket before calling exec. The latter is what inetd does, always setting descriptors 0, 1, and 2 to be the connected socket.

Example: Obtaining the Address Family of a Socket

The sockfd_to_family function shown in Figure 4.19 returns the address family of a socket.

——— lib/sockfd_to_family.c

```
 1 #include    "unp.h"

 2 int
 3 sockfd_to_family(int sockfd)
 4 {
 5     union {
 6         struct sockaddr sa;
 7         char    data[MAXSOCKADDR];
 8     } un;
 9     socklen_t len;

10     len = MAXSOCKADDR;
11     if (getsockname(sockfd, (SA *) un.data, &len) < 0)
12         return (-1);
13     return (un.sa.sa_family);
14 }
```

——— lib/sockfd_to_family.c

Figure 4.19 Return the address family of a socket.

Allocate room for largest socket address structure

5-8   Since we do not know what type of socket address structure to allocate, we use the constant MAXSOCKADDR in our unp.h header, which is the size in bytes of the largest socket address structure. We define a char array of this size within a union that includes a generic socket address structure.

Call getsockname

10-13   We call getsockname and return the address family.

Since Posix.1g allows a call to getsockname on an unbound socket, this function should work for any open socket descriptor.

4.11 Summary

All clients and servers begin with a call to socket, returning a socket descriptor. Clients then call connect, while servers call bind, listen, and accept. Sockets are normally closed with the standard close function, although we will see another way to do this with the shutdown function (Section 6.6) and we will also examine the effect of the SO_LINGER socket option (Section 7.5).

Most TCP servers are concurrent with the server calling fork for every client connection that it handles. We will see that most UDP servers are iterative. While these two models have been used successfully for many years, in Chapter 27 we will look at other server design options, using threads and processes.

Exercises

4.1   In Section 4.4 we stated that the INADDR_ constants defined by the <netinet/in.h> header are in host byte order. How can we tell this?

4.2   Modify Figure 1.5 to call getsockname after connect returns success. Print the local IP address and local port assigned to the TCP socket using sock_ntop. In what range (Figure 2.6) are your system's ephemeral ports?

4.3   In a concurrent server assume the child runs first after the call to fork. The child then completes the service of the client before the call to fork returns to the parent. What happens in the two calls to close in Figure 4.13?

4.4   In Figure 4.11 first change the server's port from 13 to 9999 (so that we do not need superuser privileges to start the program). Remove the call to listen. What happens?

4.5   Continue the previous exercise. Remove the call to bind, but allow the call to listen. What happens?

5

TCP Client–Server Example

5.1   Introduction

We now use the elementary functions from the previous chapter to write a complete TCP client–server example. Our simple example is an echo server that performs the following steps:

1. The client reads a line of text from its standard input and writes the line to the server.

2. The server reads the line from its network input and echoes the line back to the client.

3. The client reads the echoed line and prints it on its standard output.

Figure 5.1 depicts this simple client–server along with the functions used for input and output.

Figure 5.1 Simple echo client and server.

We show two arrows between the client and server but this is one full-duplex TCP connection. The fgets and fputs functions are from the standard I/O library and the writen and readline functions are shown in Section 3.9.

While we develop our own implementation of an echo server, most TCP/IP implementations provide such a server, using both TCP and UDP (Section 2.10). We will also use this server with our own client.

A client–server that echoes input lines is a valid, yet simple, example of a network application. All the basic steps required to implement any client–server are illustrated by this example. To expand this example into your own application all you need to do is change what the server does with the input it receives from its clients.

Besides running our client and server in its normal mode (type in a line and watch it echo) we examine lots of boundary conditions for this example: what happens when the client and server are started; what happens when the client terminates normally; what happens to the client if the server process terminates before the client is done; what happens to the client if the server host crashes; and so on. By looking at all these scenarios and understanding what happens at the network level, and how this appears to the sockets API, we will understand more about what goes on at these levels and how to code our applications to handle these scenarios.

In all these examples, we have "hard-coded" protocol-specific constants such as addresses and ports. There are two reasons for this. First, we need to understand exactly what needs to be stored in the protocol-specific address structures. Second, we have not yet covered the library functions that make this more portable. These functions are covered in Chapters 9 and 11.

We note now that we will make many changes to both the client and server in successive chapters as we learn more about network programming (Figures 1.12 and 1.13).

5.2 TCP Echo Server: `main` Function

Our TCP client and server follow the flow of functions that we diagramed in Figure 4.1. We show the concurrent server program in Figure 5.2.

Create socket, bind server's well-known port

9–15   A TCP socket is created. An Internet socket address structure is filled in with the wildcard address (INADDR_ANY) and the server's well-known port (SERV_PORT, which is defined as 9877 in our unp.h header). Binding the wildcard address tells the system that we will accept a connection destined for any local interface, in case the system is multihomed. Our choice of the TCP port number is based on Figure 2.6. It should be greater than 1023 (we do not need a reserved port), greater than 5000 (to avoid conflict with the ephemeral ports allocated by many Berkeley-derived implementations), less than 49152 (to avoid conflict with the "correct" range of ephemeral ports), and should not conflict with any registered port. The socket is converted into a listening socket by listen.

Wait for client connection to complete

17–18   The server blocks in the call to accept, waiting for a client connection to complete.

Concurrent server

19–24   For each client, fork spawns a child, and the child handles the new client. As we discussed in Section 4.8, the child closes the listening socket and the parent closes the connected socket. The child then calls str_echo (Figure 5.3) to handle the client.

tcpcliserv/tcpserv01.c

```
 1 #include    "unp.h"

 2 int
 3 main(int argc, char **argv)
 4 {
 5     int     listenfd, connfd;
 6     pid_t   childpid;
 7     socklen_t clilen;
 8     struct sockaddr_in cliaddr, servaddr;

 9     listenfd = Socket(AF_INET, SOCK_STREAM, 0);

10     bzero(&servaddr, sizeof(servaddr));
11     servaddr.sin_family = AF_INET;
12     servaddr.sin_addr.s_addr = htonl(INADDR_ANY);
13     servaddr.sin_port = htons(SERV_PORT);

14     Bind(listenfd, (SA *) &servaddr, sizeof(servaddr));

15     Listen(listenfd, LISTENQ);

16     for ( ; ; ) {
17         clilen = sizeof(cliaddr);
18         connfd = Accept(listenfd, (SA *) &cliaddr, &clilen);

19         if ( (childpid = Fork()) == 0) {      /* child process */
20             Close(listenfd);    /* close listening socket */
21             str_echo(connfd);   /* process the request */
22             exit(0);
23         }
24         Close(connfd);               /* parent closes connected socket */
25     }
26 }
```

tcpcliserv/tcpserv01.c

Figure 5.2 TCP echo server.

5.3 TCP Echo Server: `str_echo` Function

The function `str_echo`, shown in Figure 5.3, performs the server processing for each client: reading the lines from the client and echoing them back to the client.

Read a line and echo the line

7–11 `readline` reads the next line from the socket and the line is echoed back to the client by `writen`. If the client closes the connection (the normal scenario), the receipt of the client's FIN causes the child's `readline` to return 0. This causes the `str_echo` function to return, which terminates the child in Figure 5.2.

5.4 TCP Echo Client: `main` Function

Figure 5.4 shows the TCP client `main` function.

————————————————————————————— lib/str_echo.c

```
1 #include    "unp.h"

2 void
3 str_echo(int sockfd)
4 {
5     ssize_t n;
6     char    line[MAXLINE];

7     for ( ; ; ) {
8         if ( (n = Readline(sockfd, line, MAXLINE)) == 0)
9             return;                 /* connection closed by other end */

10        Writen(sockfd, line, n);
11    }
12 }
```

————————————————————————————— lib/str_echo.c

Figure 5.3 str_echo function: echo lines on a socket.

————————————————————————————— tcpcliserv/tcpcli01.c

```
1 #include    "unp.h"

2 int
3 main(int argc, char **argv)
4 {
5     int     sockfd;
6     struct sockaddr_in servaddr;

7     if (argc != 2)
8         err_quit("usage: tcpcli <IPaddress>");

9     sockfd = Socket(AF_INET, SOCK_STREAM, 0);

10    bzero(&servaddr, sizeof(servaddr));
11    servaddr.sin_family = AF_INET;
12    servaddr.sin_port = htons(SERV_PORT);
13    Inet_pton(AF_INET, argv[1], &servaddr.sin_addr);

14    Connect(sockfd, (SA *) &servaddr, sizeof(servaddr));

15    str_cli(stdin, sockfd);     /* do it all */

16    exit(0);
17 }
```

————————————————————————————— tcpcliserv/tcpcli01.c

Figure 5.4 TCP echo client.

Create socket, fill in Internet socket address structure

9–13 A TCP socket is created and an Internet socket address structure is filled in with the server's IP address and port number. We take the server's IP address from the command-line argument and the server's well-known port (SERV_PORT) is from our unp.h header.

Connect to server

14–15 connect establishes the connection with the server. The function str_cli (Figure 5.5) then handles the rest of the client processing.

5.5   TCP Echo Client: `str_cli` Function

This function, shown in Figure 5.5, handles the client processing loop: read a line of text from standard input, write it to the server, read back the server's echo of the line, and output the echoed line to standard output.

—— *lib/str_cli.c*

```
 1 #include    "unp.h"

 2 void
 3 str_cli(FILE *fp, int sockfd)
 4 {
 5     char    sendline[MAXLINE], recvline[MAXLINE];

 6     while (Fgets(sendline, MAXLINE, fp) != NULL) {

 7         Writen(sockfd, sendline, strlen(sendline));

 8         if (Readline(sockfd, recvline, MAXLINE) == 0)
 9             err_quit("str_cli: server terminated prematurely");

10         Fputs(recvline, stdout);
11     }
12 }
```
—— *lib/str_cli.c*

Figure 5.5 `str_cli` function: client processing loop.

Read a line, write to server

6-7   `fgets` reads a line of text and `writen` sends the line to the server.

Read echoed line from server, write to standard output

8-10   `readline` reads the line echoed back from the server and `fputs` writes it to the standard output.

Return to `main`

11-12   The loop terminates when `fgets` returns a null pointer, which occurs when it encounters either an end-of-file or an error. Our `Fgets` wrapper function checks for an error and aborts if one occurs, so `Fgets` returns a null pointer only when an end-of-file is encountered.

5.6   Normal Startup

Although our TCP example is small (about 150 lines of code for the two `main` functions, `str_echo`, `str_cli`, `readline`, and `writen`), it is essential that we understand how the client and server start, how they end, and most importantly, what happens when something goes wrong: the client host crashes, the client process crashes, network connectivity is lost, and so on. Only by understanding these boundary conditions, and their interaction with the TCP/IP protocols, can we write robust clients and servers that can handle these conditions.

We first start the server in the background on the host `bsdi`.

```
bsdi % tcpserv01 &
[1]     21130
```

When the server starts, it calls `socket`, `bind`, `listen`, and `accept`, blocking in the call to `accept`. (We have not started the client yet.) Before starting the client, we run the `netstat` program to verify the state of the server's listening socket.

```
bsdi % netstat -a
Proto Recv-Q Send-Q  Local Address      Foreign Address      (state)
tcp        0      0  *.9877             *.*                  LISTEN
```

Here we show only the first line of output (the heading), and the line that we are interested in. This command shows the status of *all* sockets on the system, which can be lots of output. We must specify the -a flag to see listening sockets.

The output is what we expect. A socket is in the LISTEN state with a wildcard for the local IP address and a local port of 9877. `netstat` prints an asterisk for an IP address of 0 (INADDR_ANY, the wildcard) or for a port of 0.

We then start the client on the same host, specifying the server's IP address of 127.0.0.1. We could have also specified this address as 206.62.226.35 (Figure 1.16).

```
bsdi % tcpcli01 127.0.0.1
```

The client calls `socket` and `connect`, the latter causing TCP's three-way handshake to take place. When the three-way handshake completes, `connect` returns in the client and `accept` returns in the server. The connection is established. The following steps then take place:

1. The client calls `str_cli`, which will block in the call to `fgets`, because we have not typed a line of input yet.

2. When `accept` returns in the server, it calls `fork` and the child calls `str_echo`. This function calls `readline`, which calls `read`, which blocks, waiting for a line to be sent from the client.

3. The server parent, on the other hand, calls `accept` again, and blocks, waiting for the next client connection.

We have three processes, and all three are asleep (blocked): client, server parent, and server child.

> When the three-way handshake completes, we purposely list the client step first, and then the server steps. The reason can be seen in Figure 2.5: `connect` returns when the second segment of the handshake is received by the client but `accept` does not return until the third segment of the handshake is received by the server, one-half of a round-trip time after `connect` returns.

We purposely run the client and server on the same host, because this is the easiest way to experiment with client–server applications. Since we are running the client and server on the same host, `netstat` now shows two additional lines of output, corresponding to the TCP connection.

```
bsdi % netstat -a
Proto Recv-Q Send-Q  Local Address        Foreign Address      (state)
tcp        0      0  localhost.9877       localhost.1052       ESTABLISHED
tcp        0      0  localhost.1052       localhost.9877       ESTABLISHED
tcp        0      0  *.9877               *.*                  LISTEN
```

The first of the ESTABLISHED lines corresponds to the server child's socket, since the local port is 9877. The second of the ESTABLISHED lines is the client's socket, since the local port is 1052. If we were running the client and server on different hosts, the client host would display only the client's socket, and the server host would display only the two server sockets.

We can also use the `ps` command to check the status and relationship of these processes.

```
bsdi % ps -l
   PID   PPID   WCHAN   STAT  TT       TIME COMMAND
 19130  19129   wait    Is    p1    0:04.99 -ksh (ksh)
 21130  19130   netcon  I     p1    0:00.06 tcpserv01
 21131  19130   ttyin   I+    p1    0:00.09 tcpcli01 127.0.0.1
 21132  21130   netio   I     p1    0:00.01 tcpserv01
 21134  21133   wait    Ss    p2    0:03.50 -ksh (ksh)
 21149  21134   -       R+    p2    0:00.05 ps -l
```

(We have removed several columns of output that do not affect this discussion.) In this output we ran the client and server from the same window (p1, which stands for pseudo-terminal number 1) and ran the `ps` command from another (p2). The PID and PPID columns show the parent and child relationships. We can tell that the first `tcpserv01` line is the parent and the second `tcpserv01` line is the child since the PPID of the child is the parent's PID. Also the PPID of the parent is the shell (`ksh`).

The STAT column for all three of our network processes is "I" meaning the process is idle (i.e., asleep). The plus sign at the end of two of the STAT columns indicates that the process is in the foreground process group of its control terminal. If the process is asleep, the WCHAN column specifies the condition. 4.4BSD prints `netcon` if the process is blocked in either `accept` or `connect`, `netio` if the process is blocked on socket input or output, and `ttyin` if the process is blocked on terminal I/O. The WCHAN values for our three network processes make sense.

5.7   Normal Termination

At this point the connection is established and whatever we type to the client is echoed back.

```
bsdi % tcpcli01 127.0.0.1          we showed this line earlier
hello, world                       we now type this
hello, world                       and the line is echoed
good bye
good bye
^D                                 Control-D is our terminal EOF character
```

We type in two lines, each one is echoed, and then we type our terminal EOF character (Control-D) which terminates the client. If we immediately execute `netstat` we have

```
bsdi % netstat -a | grep 9877
tcp        0        0  localhost.1052     localhost.9877      TIME_WAIT
tcp        0        0  *.9877             *.*                 LISTEN
```

The client's side of the connection (since the local port is 1052) enters the TIME_WAIT state (Section 2.6), and the listening server is still waiting for another client connection. (This time we pipe the output of `netstat` into `grep`, printing only the lines with our server's well-known port. But doing this also removes the heading line.)

We can follow through the steps involved in the normal termination of our client and server.

1. When we type our EOF character, `fgets` returns a null pointer and the function `str_cli` (Figure 5.5) returns.

2. When `str_cli` returns to the client `main` function (Figure 5.4), the latter terminates by calling `exit`.

3. Part of process termination is the closing of all open descriptors, so the client socket is closed by the kernel. This sends a FIN to the server, to which the server TCP responds with an ACK. This is the first half of the TCP connection termination sequence. At this point the server socket is in the CLOSE_WAIT state and the client socket is in the FIN_WAIT_1 state (Figure 2.5).

4. When the server TCP receives the FIN, the server child is blocked in a call to `readline` (Figure 5.3), and `readline` then returns 0. This causes the `str_echo` function to return to the server child `main`.

5. The server child terminates by calling `exit` (Figure 5.2).

6. All open descriptors in the server child are closed. Closing the connected socket by the child causes the final two segments of the TCP connection termination to take place: a FIN from the server to the client, and an ACK from the client (Figure 2.5). At this point the connection is completely terminated. The client socket enters the TIME_WAIT state.

7. Another part of process termination is for the SIGCHLD signal to be sent to the parent when the server child terminates. That occurs in this example, but we do not catch the signal in our code, and the default action of this signal is to be ignored. The child enters the zombie state. We can verify this with the `ps` command.

```
bsdi % ps
  PID  TT  STAT      TIME COMMAND
19130  p1  Ss     0:05.08 -ksh (ksh)
21130  p1  I      0:00.06 tcpserv01
21132  p1  Z      0:00.00 (tcpserv01)
21167  p1  R+     0:00.10 ps
```

The STAT of the child is now Z (for zombie).

We need to clean up our zombie processes and doing this requires dealing with Unix signals. In the next section we give an overview of signal handling and the following section continues our example.

5.8 Posix Signal Handling

A *signal* is a notification to a process that an event has occurred. Signals are sometimes called *software interrupts*. Signals usually occur *asynchronously*. By this we mean that the process doesn't know ahead of time exactly when a signal will occur.

Signals can be sent

- by one process to another process (or to itself),
- by the kernel to a process.

The `SIGCHLD` signal that we described at the end of the previous section is one that is sent by the kernel whenever a process terminates, to the parent of the terminating process.

Every signal has a *disposition*, which is also called the *action* associated with the signal. We set the disposition of a signal by calling the `sigaction` function (described shortly) and we have three choices for the disposition.

1. We can provide a function that is called whenever a specific signal occurs. This function is called a *signal handler* and this action is called *catching* the signal. The two signals `SIGKILL` and `SIGSTOP` cannot be caught. Our function is called with a single integer argument that is the signal number and the function returns nothing. Its function prototype is therefore

   ```
   void handler(int signo);
   ```

   For most signals, calling `sigaction` and specifying a function to be called when the signal occurs is all that is required to catch a signal. But we will see later that a few signals, `SIGIO`, `SIGPOLL`, and `SIGURG`, all require additional actions on the part of the process to catch the signal.

2. We can *ignore* a signal by setting its disposition to `SIG_IGN`. The two signals `SIGKILL` and `SIGSTOP` cannot be ignored.

3. We can set the *default* disposition for a signal by setting its disposition to `SIG_DFL`. The default is normally to terminate a process on the receipt of a signal, with certain signals also generating a core image of the process in its current working directory. There are a few signals whose default disposition is to be ignored: `SIGCHLD` and `SIGURG` (sent on the arrival of out-of-band data, Chapter 21) are two that we encounter in this text that are ignored by default.

`signal` Function

The Posix way to establish the disposition of a signal is to call the `sigaction` function. This gets complicated, however, as one argument to the function is a structure that we must allocate and fill in. An easier way to set the disposition for a signal is to call the signal function. The first argument is the signal name and the second argument is either a pointer to a function or one of the constants SIG_IGN or SIG_DFL. But signal is a historical function that predates Posix.1 and different implementations provide different signal semantics when it is called, providing backward compatibility, whereas Posix explicitly spells out the semantics when sigaction is called. The solution is to define our own function named signal that just calls the Posix sigaction function. This provides a simple interface with the desired Posix semantics. We include this function in our own library, along with our err_XXX functions and our wrapper functions, for example, that we specify when building any of our programs in this text. This function is shown in Figure 5.6.

lib/signal.c

```
 1 #include    "unp.h"

 2 Sigfunc *
 3 signal(int signo, Sigfunc *func)
 4 {
 5     struct sigaction act, oact;

 6     act.sa_handler = func;
 7     sigemptyset(&act.sa_mask);
 8     act.sa_flags = 0;
 9     if (signo == SIGALRM) {
10 #ifdef  SA_INTERRUPT
11         act.sa_flags |= SA_INTERRUPT;    /* SunOS 4.x */
12 #endif
13     } else {
14 #ifdef  SA_RESTART
15         act.sa_flags |= SA_RESTART;    /* SVR4, 4.4BSD */
16 #endif
17     }
18     if (sigaction(signo, &act, &oact) < 0)
19         return (SIG_ERR);
20     return (oact.sa_handler);
21 }
```

lib/signal.c

Figure 5.6 signal function that calls the Posix sigaction function.

Simplify function prototype using `typedef`

2–3   The normal function prototype for signal is complicated by the level of nested parentheses:

    void (*signal(int *signo*, void (**func*)(int)))(int);

To simplify this we define the Sigfunc type in our unp.h header as

    typedef void Sigfunc(int);

stating that signal handlers are functions with an integer argument and the function returns nothing (void). The function prototype is then

    Sigfunc *signal(int *signo*, Sigfunc *func*);

A pointer to a signal handling function is the second argument to the function, as well as the return value from the function.

Set handler

6   The sa_handler member of the sigaction structure is set to the *func* argument.

Set signal mask for handler

7   Posix allows us to specify a set of signals that will be *blocked* when our signal handler is called. Any signal that is blocked cannot be *delivered* to the process. We set the sa_mask member to the empty set, which means that no additional signals are blocked while our signal handler is running. Posix guarantees that the signal being caught is always blocked while its handler is executing.

Set SA_RESTART flag

8–17   An optional flag is SA_RESTART and if set, a system call interrupted by this signal will be automatically restarted by the kernel. (We talk more about interrupted system calls in the next section when we continue our example.) If the signal being caught is not SIGALRM, we specify the SA_RESTART flag, if defined. (The reason for making a special case for SIGALRM is that the purpose of generating this signal is normally to place a timeout on an I/O operation, as we show in Section 13.2, in which case we want the blocked system call to be interrupted by the signal.) Older systems, notably SunOS 4.x, automatically restart an interrupted system call by default and then define the complement of this flag as SA_INTERRUPT. If this flag is defined, we set it if the signal being caught is SIGALRM.

Call sigaction

18–20   We call sigaction and then return the old action for the signal as the return value of the signal function.

Throughout this text we use the signal function from Figure 5.6.

Posix Signal Semantics

We summarize the following points about signal handling on a Posix-compliant system.

- Once a signal handler is installed, it remains installed. (Older systems removed the signal handler each time it was executed.)

- While a signal handler is executing, the signal being delivered is blocked. Furthermore any additional signals that were specified in the sa_mask signal set passed to sigaction when the handler was installed are also blocked. In Figure 5.6 we set sa_mask to the empty set, meaning no additional signals are blocked other than the signal being caught.

- If a signal is generated one or more times while it is blocked, it is normally delivered only one time after the signal is unblocked. That is, by default Unix signals are not *queued*. We will see an example of this in the next section. The Posix realtime standard, 1003.1b, defines a set of reliable signals that are queued, but we do not use them in this text.

- It is possible to selectively block and unblock a set of signals using the sigprocmask function. This lets us protect a critical region of code by preventing certain signals from being caught while that region of code is executing.

5.9   Handling SIGCHLD Signals

The purpose of the zombie state is to maintain information about the child for the parent to fetch at some later time. This information includes the process ID of the child, its termination status, and information on the resource utilization of the child (CPU time, memory, etc.). If a process terminates, and that process has children in the zombie state, the parent process ID of all the zombie children is set to 1 (the init process), which will inherit the children and clean them up (i.e., init will wait for them, which removes the zombie). Some Unix systems show the COMMAND column for a zombie process as <defunct>.

Handling Zombies

Obviously we do not want to leave zombies around. They take up space in the kernel and eventually we can run out of processes. Whenever we fork children, we must wait for them to prevent them from becoming zombies. To do this we establish a signal handler to catch SIGCHLD and within the handler we call wait. (We describe the wait and waitpid functions in Section 5.10.) We establish the signal handler by adding the function call

```
Signal(SIGCHLD, sig_chld);
```

in Figure 5.2, after the call to listen. (It must be done sometime before we fork the first child and need be done only once.) We then define the signal handler, the function sig_chld, which we show in Figure 5.7.

————————————————————————————————— *tcpcliserv/sigchldwait.c*
```
 1 #include     "unp.h"

 2 void
 3 sig_chld(int signo)
 4 {
 5     pid_t   pid;
 6     int     stat;

 7     pid = wait(&stat);
 8     printf("child %d terminated\n", pid);
 9     return;
10 }
```
————————————————————————————————— *tcpcliserv/sigchldwait.c*

Figure 5.7   Version of SIGCHLD signal handler that calls wait.

Warning: Calling standard I/O functions such as printf in a signal handler is not recommended, for reasons that we discuss in Section 11.14. We call printf here as a diagnostic tool to see when the child terminates.

Under System V and Unix 98 the child of a process does not become a zombie if the process sets the disposition of SIGCHLD to SIG_IGN. Unfortunately this works only under System V and Unix 98. Posix.1 explicitly states that this behavior is unspecified. The portable way to handle zombies is to catch SIGCHLD and call wait or waitpid.

If we compile this program—Figure 5.2, with the call to Signal, with our sig_chld handler—under Solaris 2.5 and use the signal function from the system library (not our version from Figure 5.6), we have the following:

```
solaris % tcpserv02 &                        start server in background
[2]      16939
solaris % tcpcli01 127.0.0.1                  then client in foreground
hi there                                      we type this
hi there                                      and this is echoed
^D                                            we type our EOF character
child 16942 terminated                        output by printf in signal handler
accept error: Interrupted system call         but main function aborts
```

The sequence of steps is as follows:

1. We terminate the client by typing our EOF character. The client TCP sends a FIN to the server and the server responds with an ACK.

2. The receipt of the FIN delivers an EOF to the child's pending readline. The child terminates.

3. The parent is blocked in its call to accept when the SIGCHLD signal is delivered. The sig_chld function executes (our signal handler), wait fetches the child's PID and termination status, and printf is called from the signal handler. The signal handler returns.

4. Since the signal was caught by the parent while the parent was blocked in a slow system call (accept), the kernel causes the accept to return an error of EINTR (interrupted system call). The parent does not handle this error (Figure 5.2), so it aborts.

The purpose of this example is to show that when writing network programs that catch signals, we must be cognizant of interrupted system calls, and we must handle them. In this specific example, running under Solaris 2.5, the signal function provided in the standard C library does not cause an interrupted system call to be automatically restarted by the kernel. That is, the SA_RESTART flag that we set in Figure 5.6 is not set by the signal function in the system library. Some other systems automatically restart the interrupted system call. If we run the same example under 4.4BSD, using its library version of the signal function, the kernel restarts the interrupted system call and accept does not return an error. To handle this potential problem between different operating systems is one reason we define our own version of the signal function that we use throughout the text (Figure 5.6).

We always code an explicit return in our signal handlers (Figure 5.7), even though falling off the end of the function does the same thing for a function returning void. This provides a warning that the return may interrupt a system call.

Handling Interrupted System Calls

We used the term *slow system call* to describe `accept` and we use this term for any system call that can block forever. That is, the system call need never return. Most networking functions falls into this category. For example, there is no guarantee that a server's call to `accept` will ever return, if there are no clients that will connect to the server. Similarly our server's call to `read` (through `readline`) in Figure 5.3 will never return if the client never sends a line for the server to echo. Other examples of slow system calls are reads and writes of pipes and terminal devices. A notable exception is disk I/O, which usually returns to the caller (assuming no catastrophic hardware failure).

The basic rule that applies here is that when a process is blocked in a slow system call *and* the process catches a signal *and* the signal handler returns, the system call *can* return an error of EINTR. *Some* kernels automatically restart *some* interrupted system calls. For portability when we write a program that catches signals (most concurrent servers catch SIGCHLD), we must be prepared for slow system calls to return EINTR. Portability problems are caused by the qualifiers "can" and "some" used earlier and the fact that support for the Posix SA_RESTART flag is optional. Even if the implementation supports the SA_RESTART flag, not all interrupted system calls may automatically be restarted. Most Berkeley-derived implementations, for example, never automatically restart `select` and some of these implementations never restart `accept` or `recvfrom`.

To handle an interrupted `accept` we change the call to `accept` in Figure 5.2, the beginning of the `for` loop, to the following:

```
for ( ; ; ) {
    clilen = sizeof(cliaddr);
    if ( (connfd = accept(listenfd, (SA) &cliaddr, &clilen)) < 0) {
        if (errno == EINTR)
            continue;        /* back to for() */
        else
            err_sys("accept error");
    }
}
```

Notice that we call `accept` and not our wrapper function `Accept`, since we must handle the failure of the function ourself.

What we are doing in this piece of code is restarting the interrupted system call ourself. This is fine for `accept` along with the functions such as `read`, `write`, `select`, and `open`. But there is one function that we cannot restart ourself: `connect`. If this function returns EINTR, we cannot call it again, as doing so will return an immediate error. When `connect` is interrupted by a caught signal that is not automatically restarted, we must call `select` to wait for the connection to complete, as we describe in Section 15.3.

5.10 `wait` and `waitpid` Functions

In Figure 5.7 we called the `wait` function to handle the terminated child.

```
#include <sys/wait.h>

pid_t wait(int *statloc);

pid_t waitpid(pid_t pid, int *statloc, int options);
```
Both return: process ID if OK, 0, or −1 on error

wait and waitpid both return two values: the return value of the function is the process ID of the terminated child, and the termination status of the child (an integer) is
returned through the *statloc* pointer. There are three macros that we can call that examine the termination status and tell us if the child terminated normally, was killed by a
signal, or is just job-control stopped. Additional macros let us then fetch the exit status
of the child, or the value of the signal that killed the child, or the value of the job-control
signal that stopped the child. We use the WIFEXITED and WEXITSTATUS macros in
Figure 14.10.

    If there are no terminated children for the process calling wait, but the process has
one or more children that are still executing, then wait blocks until the first of the existing children terminate.

    waitpid gives us more control over which process to wait for and whether or not
to block. First, the *pid* argument lets us specify the process ID that we want to wait for.
A value of −1 says to wait for the first of our children to terminate. (There are other
options, dealing with process group IDs, but we do not need them in this tex .) The
options argument lets us specify additional options. The most common option is
WNOHANG. This tells the kernel not to block if there are no terminated children; it blocks
only if there are children still executing.

Difference between wait and waitpid

We now want to illustrate the difference between the wait and waitpid functions,
when used to clean up terminated children. To do this we modify our TCP client as
shown in Figure 5.9. The client establishes five connections with the server and then
uses only the first one (sockfd[0]) in the call to str_cli. The purpose of establishing multiple connections is to spawn multiple children from the concurrent server, as
shown in Figure 5.8.

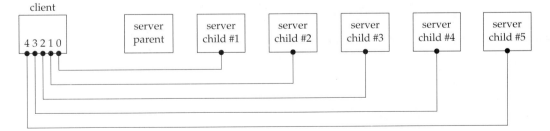

Figure 5.8 Client with five established connections to same concurrent server.

tcpcliserv/tcpcli04.c

```
1 #include     "unp.h"

2 int
3 main(int argc, char **argv)
4 {
5     int    i, sockfd[5];
6     struct sockaddr_in servaddr;

7     if (argc != 2)
8         err_quit("usage: tcpcli <IPaddress>");

9     for (i = 0; i < 5; i++) {
10         sockfd[i] = Socket(AF_INET, SOCK_STREAM, 0);

11         bzero(&servaddr, sizeof(servaddr));
12         servaddr.sin_family = AF_INET;
13         servaddr.sin_port = htons(SERV_PORT);
14         Inet_pton(AF_INET, argv[1], &servaddr.sin_addr);

15         Connect(sockfd[i], (SA *) &servaddr, sizeof(servaddr));
16     }

17     str_cli(stdin, sockfd[0]);   /* do it all */

18     exit(0);
19 }
```

tcpcliserv/tcpcli04.c

Figure 5.9 TCP client that establishes five connections with server.

When the client terminates, all open descriptors are closed automatically by the kernel (we do not call `close`, only `exit`), and all five connections are terminated at about the same time. This causes five FINs to be sent, one on each connection, which in turn causes all five server children to terminate at about the same time. This causes five `SIGCHLD` signals to be delivered to the parent at about the same time, which we show in Figure 5.10.

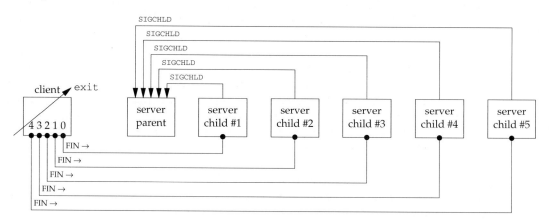

Figure 5.10 Client terminates, closing all five connections, terminating all five children.

It is this delivery of multiple occurrences of the same signal that causes the problem we are about to see.

We first run the server in the background and then our new client. Our server is Figure 5.2, modified to call `signal` to establish Figure 5.7 as a signal handler for SIGCHLD.

```
bsdi % tcpserv03 &
[1]      21282
bsdi % tcpcli04 206.62.226.35
hello                              we type this
hello                             and it is echoed
^D                                we then type our EOF character
child 21288 terminated            output by server
```

The first thing we notice is that only one `printf` is output, when we expect all five children to have terminated. If we execute `ps`, we see that the other four children still exist as zombies.

```
    PID   TT   STAT      TIME  COMMAND
  21282   p1   S      0:00.09  tcpserv03
  21284   p1   Z      0:00.00  (tcpserv03)
  21285   p1   Z      0:00.00  (tcpserv03)
  21286   p1   Z      0:00.00  (tcpserv03)
  21287   p1   Z      0:00.00  (tcpserv03)
```

Establishing a signal handler and calling `wait` from that handler are insufficient for preventing zombies. The problem is that all five signals are generated before the signal handler is executed, and the signal handler is executed only one time because Unix signals are normally not *queued*. Furthermore this problem is nondeterministic. In the example we just ran, with the client and server on the same host, the signal handler is executed once, leaving four zombies. But if we run the client and server on different hosts, the signal handler is normally executed two times: once as a result of the first signal being generated, and since the other four signals occur while the signal handler is executing, the handler is called only one more time. This leaves three zombies. But sometimes, probably dependent on the timing of the FINs arriving at the server host, the signal handler is executed three or even four times.

The correct solution is to call `waitpid` instead of `wait`. Figure 5.11 shows the version of our `sig_chld` function that handles SIGCHLD correctly. This version works because we call `waitpid` within a loop, fetching the status of any of our children that have terminated. We must specify the WNOHANG option: this tells `waitpid` not to block if there exist running children that have not yet terminated. In Figure 5.7 we cannot call `wait` in a loop, because there is no way to prevent `wait` from blocking if there exist running children that have not yet terminated.

Figure 5.12 shows the final version of our server. It correctly handles a return of EINTR from `accept` and it establishes a signal handler (Figure 5.11) that calls `waitpid` for all terminated children.

```
                                                              ───────── tcpcliserv/sigchldwaitpid.c
 1 #include    "unp.h"

 2 void
 3 sig_chld(int signo)
 4 {
 5     pid_t   pid;
 6     int     stat;

 7     while ( (pid = waitpid(-1, &stat, WNOHANG)) > 0)
 8         printf("child %d terminated\n", pid);
 9     return;
10 }
                                                              ───────── tcpcliserv/sigchldwaitpid.c
```

Figure 5.11 Final (correct) version of `sig_chld` function that calls `waitpid`.

```
                                                              ───────── tcpcliserv/tcpserv04.c
 1 #include    "unp.h"

 2 int
 3 main(int argc, char **argv)
 4 {
 5     int     listenfd, connfd;
 6     pid_t   childpid;
 7     socklen_t clilen;
 8     struct sockaddr_in cliaddr, servaddr;
 9     void    sig_chld(int);

10     listenfd = Socket(AF_INET, SOCK_STREAM, 0);

11     bzero(&servaddr, sizeof(servaddr));
12     servaddr.sin_family = AF_INET;
13     servaddr.sin_addr.s_addr = htonl(INADDR_ANY);
14     servaddr.sin_port = htons(SERV_PORT);

15     Bind(listenfd, (SA *) &servaddr, sizeof(servaddr));

16     Listen(listenfd, LISTENQ);

17     Signal(SIGCHLD, sig_chld);  /* must call waitpid() */

18     for ( ; ; ) {
19         clilen = sizeof(cliaddr);
20         if ( (connfd = accept(listenfd, (SA *) &cliaddr, &clilen)) < 0) {
21             if (errno == EINTR)
22                 continue;       /* back to for() */
23             else
24                 err_sys("accept error");
25         }
26         if ( (childpid = Fork()) == 0) {     /* child process */
27             Close(listenfd);   /* close listening socket */
28             str_echo(connfd);  /* process the request */
29             exit(0);
30         }
31         Close(connfd);                /* parent closes connected socket */
32     }
33 }
                                                              ───────── tcpcliserv/tcpserv04.c
```

Figure 5.12 Final (correct) version of TCP server that handles an error of `EINTR` from `accept`.

The purpose of this section has been to demonstrate three scenarios that we can encounter with network programming.

1. We must catch the SIGCHLD signal when forking child processes.
2. We must handle interrupted system calls when we catch signals.
3. A SIGCHLD handler must be coded correctly using waitpid to prevent any zombies from being left around.

The final version of our TCP server (Figure 5.12) along with the SIGCHLD handler in Figure 5.11 handles all three scenarios.

5.11 Connection Abort before accept Returns

There is another condition, similar to the interrupted system call example in the previous section, that can cause accept to return a nonfatal error, in which case we should just call accept again. The sequence of packets shown in Figure 5.13 has been seen on busy servers (typically busy Web servers).

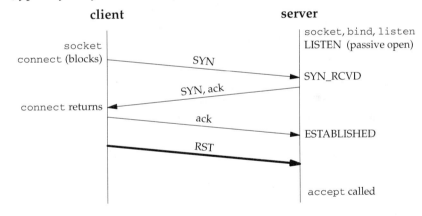

Figure 5.13 Receiving an RST for an ESTABLISHED connection before accept is called.

The three-way handshake completes, the connection is established, and then the client TCP sends an RST (reset). On the server side the connection is queued by its TCP, waiting for the server process to call accept when the RST arrives. Some time later the server process calls accept.

> An easy way to simulate this scenario is to start the server, have it call socket, bind, and listen, and then go to sleep for a short period of time before calling accept. While the server process is asleep, start the client, have it call socket and connect. As soon as connect returns, set the SO_LINGER socket option to generate the RST (which we describe in Section 7.5 and show an example of in Figure 15.21) and terminate.

Unfortunately, what happens to the aborted connection is implementation dependent. Berkeley-derived implementations handle the aborted connection completely within the kernel, and the server process never sees it. Most SVR4 implementations, however, return an error to the process as the return from accept, and the error depends on the implementation. These SVR4 implementations return an errno of EPROTO ("protocol error"), but Posix.1g specifies that the return must be ECONNABORTED ("software caused connection abort") instead. The reason for the Posix.1g change is that EPROTO is also returned when some fatal protocol-related events occur on the streams subsystem. Returning the same error for the nonfatal abort of an established connection by the client makes it impossible for the server to know whether to call accept again or not. In the case of the ECONNABORTED error, the server can ignore the error and just call accept again.

> Solaris 2.6 implements the Posix.1g change.
>
> The steps involved in Berkeley-derived kernels that never pass this error to the process can be followed in TCPv2. The RST is processed on p. 964, causing tcp_close to be called. This function calls in_pcbdetach on p. 897, which in turn calls sofree on p. 719. sofree (p. 473) finds that the socket being aborted is still on the listening socket's completed connection queue and removes the socket from the queue and frees the socket. When the server gets around to calling accept, it will never know that a connection that had completed has since been removed from the queue.

We return to these aborted connections in Section 15.6 and see how they can present a problem when combined with select and a listening socket in the normal blocking mode.

5.12 Termination of Server Process

We now start our client–server and then kill the server child process. This simulates the crashing of the server process, so we can see what happens to the client. (We must be careful to distinguish between the crashing of the server *process*, which we are about to describe, and the crashing of the server *host*, which we describe in Section 5.14.) The following steps take place:

1. We start the server and client on different hosts and type one line to the client to verify that all is OK. That line is echoed normally by the server child.

2. We find the process ID of the server child and kill it. As part of process termination all open descriptors in the child are closed. This causes a FIN to be sent to the client, and the client TCP responds with an ACK. This is the first half of the TCP connection termination.

3. The SIGCHLD signal is sent to the server parent and handled correctly (Figure 5.12).

4. Nothing happens at the client. The client TCP receives the FIN from the server TCP, and responds with an ACK, but the problem is that the client process is blocked in the call to fgets waiting for a line from the terminal.

5. Running `netstat` at this point from another window on the client shows the state of the client socket.

    ```
    solaris % netstat | grep 9877
    Local Address    Remote Address   Swind Send-Q Rwind Recv-Q  State
    solaris.34673    bsdi.9877         8760      0  8760      0  CLOSE_WAIT
    ```

    (This is the first time we have shown the `netstat` output from Solaris so we have added the heading line. The format is slightly different from the BSD output, but the information is similar.) We also run `netstat` from another window on the server:

    ```
    bsdi % netstat | grep 9877
    tcp      0     0  bsdi.9877      solaris.34673      FIN_WAIT_2
    ```

    From Figure 2.4 we see that half of the TCP connection termination sequence has taken place.

6. We can still type a line of input to the client. Here is what happens at the client starting from step 1.

    ```
    solaris % tcpcli01 206.62.226.35     start client
    hello                                the first line that we type
    hello                                it is echoed correctly
                                         here we kill the server child on the server host
    another line                         we then type a second line to the client
    str_cli: server terminated prematurely
    ```

    When we type "another line", `str_cli` calls `writen` and the client TCP sends the data to the server. This is allowed by TCP because the receipt of the FIN by the client TCP only indicates that the server process has closed its end of the connection and will not be sending any more data. The receipt of the FIN does *not* tell the client TCP that the server process has terminated (which in this case it has). We cover this again in Section 6.6 when we talk about TCP's half-close.

    When the server TCP receives the data from the client, it responds with an RST since the process that had that socket open has terminated. We can verify that the RST is sent by watching the packets with `tcpdump`.

7. But the client process will not see the RST because it calls `readline` immediately after the call to `writen` and `readline` returns 0 (end-of-file) immediately because of the FIN that was received in step 2. Our client is not expecting to receive an end-of-file at this point (Figure 5.5) so it quits with the error message "server terminated prematurely."

8. When the client terminates (by calling `err_quit` in Figure 5.5), all its open descriptors are closed.

> What we have described also depends on the timing of the example. When we run the client and server on different hosts, as we just described, it takes a few milliseconds for the data to be sent from the client to the server (the "another line") and the server's RST to be received by the client. That is why the client's call to `readline` returns 0 because the FIN that was received earlier is ready to be read. But if we run the client and server on the same host, or if we were

to put a slight pause in the client before its call to readline, then the received RST takes precedence over the FIN that was received earlier. This would cause readline to return an error and errno would contain ECONNRESET ("Connection reset by peer").

The problem in this example is that the client is blocked in the call to fgets when the FIN arrives on the socket. The client is really working with two descriptors—the socket and the user input—and instead of blocking on input from only one of the two sources (as str_cli is currently coded), it should block on input from either source. Indeed, this is one purpose of the select and poll functions, which we describe in Chapter 6. When we recode the str_cli function in Section 6.4, as soon as we kill the server child, the client is notified of the received FIN.

5.13 SIGPIPE Signal

What happens if the client ignores the error return from readline and writes more data to the server? This can happen, for example, if the client needs to perform two writes to the server before reading anything back, with the first write eliciting the RST.

The rule that applies is: when a process writes to a socket that has received an RST, the SIGPIPE signal is sent to the process. The default action of this signal is to terminate the process so the process must catch the signal to avoid being involuntarily terminated.

If the process either catches the signal and returns from the signal handler, or ignores the signal, the write operation returns EPIPE.

A frequently asked question (FAQ) on Usenet is how to obtain this signal on the first write, and not the second. This is not possible. Following our discussion above, the first write elicits the RST and the second write elicits the signal. It is OK to write to a socket that has received a FIN, but it is an error to write to a socket that has received an RST.

To see what happens with SIGPIPE we modify our client as shown in Figure 5.14.

                                                            ———————— tcpcliserv/str_cli11.c
```
 1 #include    "unp.h"

 2 void
 3 str_cli(FILE *fp, int sockfd)
 4 {
 5     char    sendline[MAXLINE], recvline[MAXLINE];

 6     while (Fgets(sendline, MAXLINE, fp) != NULL) {

 7         Writen(sockfd, sendline, 1);
 8         sleep(1);
 9         Writen(sockfd, sendline + 1, strlen(sendline) - 1);

10         if (Readline(sockfd, recvline, MAXLINE) == 0)
11             err_quit("str_cli: server terminated prematurely");

12         Fputs(recvline, stdout);
13     }
14 }
```
                                                            ———————— tcpcliserv/str_cli11.c
Figure 5.14 str_cli that calls writen twice.

7-9   All we have changed is to call `writen` two times: the first time the first byte of data is written to the socket, followed by a pause of 1 second, followed by the remainder of the line. The intent is for the first `writen` to elicit the RST and then for the second `writen` to generate `SIGPIPE`.

If we run the client on our BSD/OS host, we get:

```
bsdi % tcpcli11 206.62.226.34
hi there                          we type this line
hi there                          this is echoed by the server
                                  here we kill the server child
bye                               then we type this line
bsdi % echo $?                    what is the KornShell's return value of last command?
269                               269 = 256 + 13
bsdi % grep SIGPIPE /usr/include/sys/signal.h
#define SIGPIPE 13       /* write on a pipe with no one to read it */
```

We start the client, type in one line, see that line echoed correctly, and then terminate the server child on the server host. We then type another line ("bye") but nothing is echoed and we just get a shell prompt. Since the default action of `SIGPIPE` is to terminate the process without generating a `core` file, nothing is printed by the KornShell. This is the problem with programs terminated by `SIGPIPE`: normally nothing is output even by the shell to indicate what has happened.

We must execute `echo $?` to print the shell's return value, which is 269. We then print the numeric value of the constant `SIGPIPE` and see that the KornShell's return value is 256 plus the signal number. But if we execute this program under Digital Unix 4.0, Solaris 2.5, or UnixWare 2.1.2, the KornShell's return value is 141, or 128 plus 13.

> The 11/16/88 version of the KornShell returned 128 plus the signal number, while newer versions return 256 plus the signal number. All that Posix.2 specifies is that the return value be greater than 128. Other shells may return different values.

The recommended way to handle `SIGPIPE` depends on what the application wants to do when this occurs. If there is nothing special to do, then setting the signal disposition to `SIG_IGN` is easy, assuming that subsequent output operations will catch the error of `EPIPE` and terminate. If special actions are needed when the signal occurs (writing to a log file perhaps), then the signal should be caught and any desired actions can be performed in the signal handler. Be aware, however, that if multiple sockets are in use, the delivery of the signal does not tell us which socket encountered the error. If we need to know which `write` caused the error, then we must either ignore the signal or return from the signal handler and handle `EPIPE` from the `write`.

5.14 Crashing of Server Host

Our next scenario is to see what happens when the server host crashes. To simulate this we must run the client and server on different hosts. We then start the server, start the client, type in a line to the client to verify that the connection is up, disconnect the server host from the network, and type in another line at the client. This also covers the scenario of the server host being unreachable when the client sends data (i.e., some intermediate router is down after the connection has been established).

The following steps take place:

1. When the server host crashes, nothing is sent out on the existing network connections. That is, we are assuming the host crashes, and is not shut down by an operator (which we cover in Section 5.16).

2. We type a line of input to the client, it is written by `writen` (Figure 5.5), and is sent by the client TCP as a data segment. The client then blocks in the call to `readline`, waiting for the echoed reply.

3. If we watch the network with `tcpdump`, we will see the client TCP continually retransmits the data segment, trying to receive an ACK from the server. Section 25.11 of TCPv2 shows a typical pattern for TCP retransmissions: Berkeley-derived implementations retransmit the data segment 12 times, waiting for around 9 minutes before giving up. When the client TCP finally gives up (assuming the server host has not been rebooted during this time, or if the server host has not crashed but was unreachable on the network, assuming the host was still unreachable), an error is returned to the client process. Since the client is blocked in the call to `readline`, it returns an error. Assuming the server host had crashed and there were no responses at all to the client's data segments, the error is `ETIMEDOUT`. But if some intermediate router determined that the server host was unreachable and responded with an ICMP destination unreachable message, the error is either `EHOSTUNREACH` or `ENETUNREACH`.

Although our client discovers (eventually) that the peer is down or unreachable, there are times when we want to detect this quicker than having to wait 9 minutes. The solution is to place a timeout on the call to `readline`, which we discuss in Section 13.2.

The scenario that we just discussed detects that the server host has crashed only when we send data to that host. If we want to detect the crashing of the server host even if we are not actively sending it data, another technique is required. We discuss the `SO_KEEPALIVE` socket option in Section 7.5 and some client–server heartbeat functions in Section 21.5.

5.15 Crashing and Rebooting of Server Host

In this scenario we establish the connection between the client and server and then assume the server host crashes and reboots. In the previous section the server host was still down when we sent it data. Here we will let the server host reboot before sending it data. The easiest way to simulate this is to establish the connection, disconnect the server from the network, shut down the server host and then reboot it, and then reconnect the server host to the network. We do not want the client to see the server host shut down (which we cover in Section 5.16).

As stated in the previous section, if the client is not actively sending data to the server when the server host crashes, the client is not aware that the server host has crashed. (This assumes we are not using the `SO_KEEPALIVE` socket option.) The following steps take place:

1. We start the server and then the client. We type a line to verify that the connection is established.

2. The server host crashes and reboots.

3. We type a line of input to the client, which is sent as a TCP data segment to the server host

4. When the server host reboots after crashing, its TCP loses all information about connections that existed before the crash. Therefore the server TCP responds to the received data segment from the client with an RST.

5. Our client is blocked in the call to `readline` when the RST is received, causing `readline` to return the error ECONNRESET.

If it is important for our client to detect the crashing of the server host, even if the client is not actively sending data, then some other technique (such as the SO_KEEPALIVE socket option or some client–server heartbeat functions) is required.

5.16 Shutdown of Server Host

The previous two sections discussed the crashing of the server host, or the server host being unreachable across the network. We now consider what happens if the server host is shut down by an operator while our server process is running on that host.

When a Unix system is shut down, the `init` process normally sends the SIGTERM signal to all processes (we can catch this signal), waits some fixed amount of time (often between 5 and 20 seconds), and then sends the SIGKILL signal (which we cannot catch) to any processes still running. This gives all running processes a short amount of time to clean up and terminate. If we do not catch SIGTERM and terminate, our server will be terminated by the SIGKILL signal. When the process terminates, all open descriptors are closed, and we then follow the same sequence of steps discussed in Section 5.12. As we stated there, we must use the `select` or `poll` function in our client to have the client detect the termination of the server process as soon as it occurs.

5.17 Summary of TCP Example

Before any TCP client and server can communicate with each other, each end must specify the socket pair for the connection: the local IP address, local port, foreign IP address, and foreign port. In Figure 5.15 we show these four values as bullets. This figure is from the client's perspective. The foreign IP address and foreign port must be specified by the client in the call to `connect`. The two local values are normally chosen by the kernel as part of the `connect` function. The client has the option of specifying either or both of the local values, by calling `bind` before `connect`, but this is not common.

As we mentioned in Section 4.10, the client can obtain the two local values chosen by the kernel by calling `getsockname` after the connection is established.

Figure 5.16 shows the same four values, but from the server's perspective.

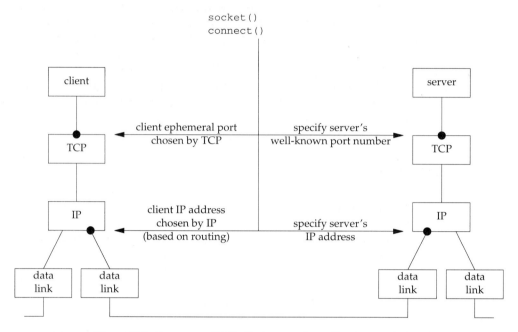

Figure 5.15 Summary of TCP client–server from client's perspective.

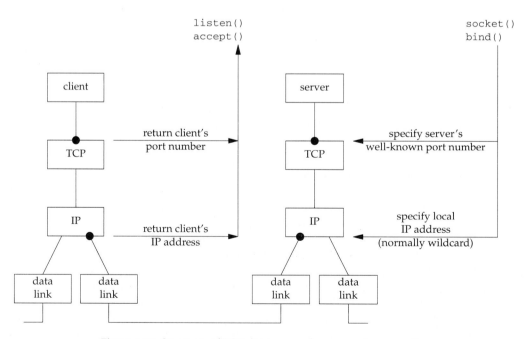

Figure 5.16 Summary of TCP client–server from server's perspective.

The local port (the server's well-known port) is specified by `bind`. Normally the server also specifies the wildcard IP address in this call, although the server can restrict itself to receiving connections destined for one particular local interface by binding a nonwildcard IP address. If the server binds the wildcard IP address on a multihomed host, it can determine the local IP address by calling `getsockname` after the connection is established (Section 4.10). The two foreign values are returned to the server by `accept`. As we mentioned in Section 4.10, if another program is `exec`ed by the server that calls `accept`, that program can call `getpeername` to determine the client's IP address and port, if necessary.

5.18 Data Format

In our example the server never examines the request that it receives from the client. The server just reads all the data up through and including the newline and sends it back to the client, looking for only the newline. This is an exception, not the rule, and normally we must worry about the format of the data exchanged between the client and server.

Example: Passing Text Strings between Client and Server

Let's modify our server so that it still reads a line of text from the client, but the server now expects that line to contain two integers separated by white space, and the server returns the sum of those two integers. Our client and server `main` functions remain the same, as does our `str_cli` function. All that changes is our `str_echo` function, which we show in Figure 5.17.

tcpcliserv/str_echo08.c

```
 1 #include     "unp.h"

 2 void
 3 str_echo(int sockfd)
 4 {
 5     long    arg1, arg2;
 6     ssize_t n;
 7     char    line[MAXLINE];

 8     for ( ; ; ) {
 9         if ( (n = Readline(sockfd, line, MAXLINE)) == 0)
10             return;              /* connection closed by other end */

11         if (sscanf(line, "%ld%ld", &arg1, &arg2) == 2)
12             snprintf(line, sizeof(line), "%ld\n", arg1 + arg2);
13         else
14             snprintf(line, sizeof(line), "input error\n");

15         n = strlen(line);
16         Writen(sockfd, line, n);
17     }
18 }
```

tcpcliserv/str_echo08.c

Figure 5.17 `str_echo` function that adds two numbers.

11-14   We call `sscanf` to convert the two arguments from text strings to long integers, and
then `snprintf` to convert the result into a text string.

This new client and server work fine, regardless of the byte ordering of the client
and server hosts.

Example: Passing Binary Structures between Client and Server

We now modify our client and server to pass binary values across the socket, instead of
text strings. We will see that this does not work when the client and server are run on
hosts with different byte orders, or on hosts that do not agree on the size of a long integer (Figure 1.17).

Our client and server `main` functions do not change. We define one structure for
the two arguments, another structure for the result, and place both definitions in our
`sum.h` header, shown in Figure 5.18. Figure 5.19 shows the `str_cli` function.

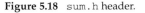
── *tcpcliserv/sum.h*

```
1 struct args {
2     long    arg1;
3     long    arg2;
4 };

5 struct result {
6     long    sum;
7 };
```
── *tcpcliserv/sum.h*

Figure 5.18 `sum.h` header.

── *tcpcliserv/str_cli09.c*

```
 1 #include    "unp.h"
 2 #include    "sum.h"

 3 void
 4 str_cli(FILE *fp, int sockfd)
 5 {
 6     char    sendline[MAXLINE];
 7     struct args args;
 8     struct result result;

 9     while (Fgets(sendline, MAXLINE, fp) != NULL) {
10         if (sscanf(sendline, "%ld%ld", &args.arg1, &args.arg2) != 2) {
11             printf("invalid input: %s", sendline);
12             continue;
13         }
14         Writen(sockfd, &args, sizeof(args));

15         if (Readn(sockfd, &result, sizeof(result)) == 0)
16             err_quit("str_cli: server terminated prematurely");

17         printf("%ld\n", result.sum);
18     }
19 }
```
── *tcpcliserv/str_cli09.c*

Figure 5.19 `str_cli` function that sends two binary integers to server.

10-14   sscanf converts the two arguments from text strings to binary and we call `writen` to send the structure to the server.

15-17   We call `readn` to read the reply, and print the result using `printf`.
           Figure 5.20 shows our `str_echo` function.

―― *tcpcliserv/str_echo09.c*
```
 1 #include    "unp.h"
 2 #include    "sum.h"

 3 void
 4 str_echo(int sockfd)
 5 {
 6     ssize_t n;
 7     struct args args;
 8     struct result result;

 9     for ( ; ; ) {
10         if ( (n = Readn(sockfd, &args, sizeof(args))) == 0)
11             return;               /* connection closed by other end */

12         result.sum = args.arg1 + args.arg2;
13         Writen(sockfd, &result, sizeof(result));
14     }
15 }
```
―― *tcpcliserv/str_echo09.c*

Figure 5.20   `str_echo` function that adds two binary integers.

9-14   We read the arguments by calling `readn`, calculate and store the sum, and call `writen` to send back the result structure.

If we run the client and server on two machines of the same architecture, say `solaris` and `sunos5` in Figure 1.16, everything works fine. Here is the client interaction:

```
sunos5 % tcpcli09 206.62.226.33
11 22                               we type this
33                                  and this is the server's reply
-11 -44
-55
```

But when the client and server are on two machines of different architectures (the server on the big-endian Sparc system `solaris` and the client on the little-endian Intel system `bsdi`) it does not work.

```
bsdi % tcpcli09 206.62.226.33
1 2                                 we type this
3                                   and it works
-22 -77                             then we type this
-16777314                           and it does not work
```

The problem is that the two binary integers are sent across the socket in little-endian format by the client, but interpreted as big-endian integers by the server. We see that it appears to work for positive integers but fails for negative integers (see Exercise 5.8). There are really three potential problems with this example.

1. Different implementations store binary numbers in different formats. The most common formats are big endian and little endian, as we described in Section 3.4.

2. Different implementations can store the same C datatype differently. For example, most 32-bit Unix systems use 32 bits for a `long` but 64-bit systems typically use 64 bits for the same datatype (Figure 1.17). There is no guarantee that a `short`, `int`, or `long` is of any certain size.

3. Different implementations pack structures differently, depending on the number of bits used for the various datatypes and the alignment restrictions of the machine. Therefore it is never wise to send binary structures across a socket.

There are two common solutions to this data format problem.

1. Pass all the numeric data as text strings. This is what we did in Figure 5.17. This assumes that both hosts have the same character set.

2. Explicitly define the binary formats of the supported datatypes (number of bits, big or little endian) and pass all data between the client and server in this format. Remote procedure call (RPC) packages normally use this technique. RFC 1832 [Srinivasan 1995] describes the *External Data Representation* (XDR) standard that is used with the Sun RPC package.

5.19 Summary

The first version of our echo client–server totaled about 150 lines (including the `readline` and `writen` functions), yet provided lots of details to examine. The first problem we encountered was zombie children and we caught the SIGCHLD signal to handle this. Our signal handler then called `waitpid` and we demonstrated that we must call this function instead of the older `wait` function, since Unix signals are not queued. This led us into some of the details of Posix signal handling, and additional information on this topic is provided in Chapter 10 of APUE.

The next problem we encountered was the client not being notified when the server process terminated. We saw that our client's TCP was notified, but we did not receive that notification since we were blocked waiting for user input. We will use the `select` or `poll` function in Chapter 6 to handle this scenario, by waiting for any one of multiple descriptors to be ready, instead of blocking on a single descriptor.

We also discovered that if the server host crashes, we do not detect this until the client sends data to the server. Some applications must be made aware of this fact sooner and in Section 7.5 we look at the SO_KEEPALIVE socket option, and in Section 21.5 we develop a set of client–server heartbeat functions.

Our simple example exchanged lines of text, which was OK since the server never looked at the lines that it echoed. Sending numerical data between the client and server can lead to a new set of problems, as shown.

Exercises

5.1 Build the TCP server from Figures 5.2 and 5.3 and the TCP client from Figures 5.4 and 5.5. Start the server and then start the client. Type in a few lines to verify that the client and server work. Terminate the client by typing your end-of-file character and note the time. Use netstat on the client host to verify that the client's end of the connection goes through the TIME_WAIT state. Execute netstat every 5 seconds or so to see when the TIME_WAIT state ends. What is the MSL for this implementation?

5.2 What happens with our echo client–server if we run the client and redirect standard input to a binary file?

5.3 What is the difference between our echo client–server and using the Telnet client to communicate with our echo server?

5.4 In our example in Section 5.12 we verified that the first two segments of the connection termination are sent (the FIN from the server that is then ACKed by the client) by looking at the socket states using netstat. Are the final two segments exchanged (a FIN from client that is ACKed by the server)? If so, when, and if not, why?

5.5 What happens in the example outlined in Section 5.14 if between steps 2 and 3 we restart our server application on the server host?

5.6 To verify what we claimed happens with SIGPIPE in Section 5.13, modify Figure 5.4 as follows. Write a signal handler for SIGPIPE that just prints a message and returns. Establish this signal handler before calling connect. Change the server's port number to 13, the daytime server. When the connection is established, sleep for 2 seconds, write a few bytes to the socket, sleep for another 2 seconds, and write a few more bytes to the socket. Run the program. What happens?

5.7 What happens in Figure 5.15 if the IP address of the server host that is specified by the client in its call to connect is the IP address associated with the rightmost datalink on the server, instead of the IP address associated with the leftmost datalink on the server?

5.8 In our example output from Figure 5.20 when the client and server were on different endian systems, the example worked for small positive numbers, but not for small negative numbers. Why? (*Hint*: Draw a picture of the values exchanged across the socket, similar to Figure 3.8.)

5.9 In our example in Figures 5.19 and 5.20 can we solve the byte ordering problem by having the client convert the two arguments into network byte order using htonl, having the server then call ntohl on each argument before doing the addition, and then doing a similar conversion on the result?

5.10 What happens in Figures 5.19 and 5.20 if the client is on a Sparc that stores a long in 32 bits, but the server is on a Digital Alpha that stores a long in 64 bits? Does this change if the client and server are swapped between these two hosts?

5.11 In Figure 5.15 we say that the client IP address is chosen by IP, based on routing. What does this mean?

6

I/O Multiplexing: The
`select` *and* `poll` *Functions*

6.1   Introduction

We saw in Section 5.12 that our TCP client is handling two inputs at the same time: standard input and a TCP socket. The problem we encountered was when the client was blocked in a call to `read` (by calling our `readline` function), and the server process was killed. The server TCP correctly sends a FIN to the client TCP, but since the client process is blocked reading from standard input, it never sees the end-of-file until it reads from the socket (possibly much later in time). What we need is the capability to tell the kernel that we want to be notified if one or more I/O conditions are ready (i.e., input is ready to be read, or the descriptor is capable of taking more output). This capability is called *I/O multiplexing* and is provided by the `select` and `poll` functions. We also cover a newer Posix.1g variation of the former, called `pselect`.

I/O multiplexing is typically used in networking applications in the following scenarios:

- When a client is handling multiple descriptors (normally interactive input and a network socket), I/O multiplexing should be used. This is the scenario we described in the previous paragraph.

- It is possible, but rare, for a client to handle multiple sockets at the same time. We show an example of this using `select` in Section 15.5 in the context of a Web client.

- If a TCP server handles both a listening socket and its connected sockets, I/O multiplexing is normally used as we show in Section 6.8.

- If a server handles both TCP and UDP, I/O multiplexing is normally used. We show an example of this in Section 8.15.

143

- If a server handles multiple services and perhaps multiple protocols (e.g., the `inetd` daemon that we describe in Section 12.5), I/O multiplexing is normally used.

I/O multiplexing is not limited to network programming. Any nontrivial application often finds a need to use this technique.

6.2   I/O Models

Before describing `select` and `poll` we need to step back and look at the bigger picture, examining the basic differences in the five I/O models that are available to us under Unix:

- blocking I/O,
- nonblocking I/O,
- I/O multiplexing (`select` and `poll`),
- signal driven I/O (`SIGIO`), and
- asynchronous I/O (the Posix.1 `aio_` functions).

You may want to skim this section on your first reading and then refer back to it as you encounter the different I/O models described in more detail in later chapters.

As we show in all the examples in this section, there are normally two distinct phases for an input operation:

1. waiting for the data to be ready, and
2. copying the data from the kernel to the process.

For an input operation on a socket the first step normally involves waiting for data to arrive on the network. When the packet arrives, it is copied into a buffer within the kernel. The second step is copying this data from the kernel's buffer into our application buffer.

Blocking I/O Model

The most prevalent model for I/O is the *blocking I/O model*, which we have used for all our examples so far in the text. By default, all sockets are blocking. Using a datagram socket for our examples we have the scenario shown in Figure 6.1.

We use UDP for this example, instead of TCP, because with UDP the concept of data being "ready" to read is simple: either an entire datagram has been received or not. With TCP it gets more complicated, as additional variables, such as the socket's low-water mark, come into play.

In the examples in this section we also refer to `recvfrom` as a system call, because we are differentiating between our application and the kernel. Regardless of how `recvfrom` is implemented (as a system call on a Berkeley-derived kernel, or as a function that invokes the `getmsg` system call on a System V kernel), there is normally a

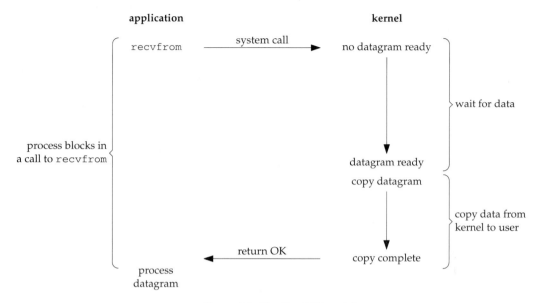

Figure 6.1 Blocking I/O model.

switch from running in the application to running in the kernel, followed at some time later by a return to the application.

In Figure 6.1 the process calls recvfrom and the system call does not return until the datagram arrives and is copied into our application buffer, or an error occurs. The most common error is the system call being interrupted by a signal, as we described in Section 5.9. We say that our process is *blocked* the entire time from when it calls recvfrom until it returns. When recvfrom returns OK, our application processes the datagram.

Nonblocking I/O Model

When we set a socket nonblocking, we are telling the kernel "when an I/O operation that I request cannot be completed without putting the process to sleep, do not put the process to sleep but return an error instead." We describe nonblocking I/O in Chapter 15 but show a summary in Figure 6.2 for the example we are considering.

The first three times that we call recvfrom, there is no data to return, so the kernel immediately returns an error of EWOULDBLOCK instead. The fourth time we call recvfrom a datagram is ready, it is copied into our application buffer, and recvfrom returns OK. We then process the data.

When an application sits in a loop calling recvfrom on a nonblocking descriptor like this, it is called *polling*. The application is continually polling the kernel to see if some operation is ready. This is often a waste of CPU time, but this model is occasionally encountered, normally on systems dedicated to one function.

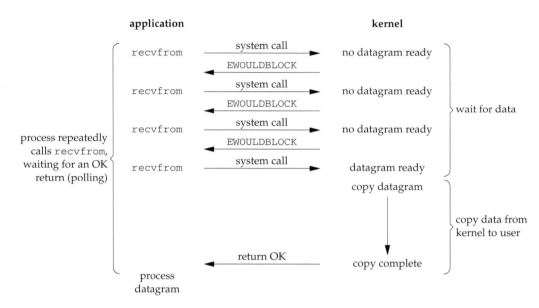

Figure 6.2 Nonblocking I/O model.

I/O Multiplexing Model

With *I/O multiplexing*, we call `select` or `poll` and block in one of these two system calls, instead of blocking in the actual I/O system call. Figure 6.3 is a summary of the I/O multiplexing model.

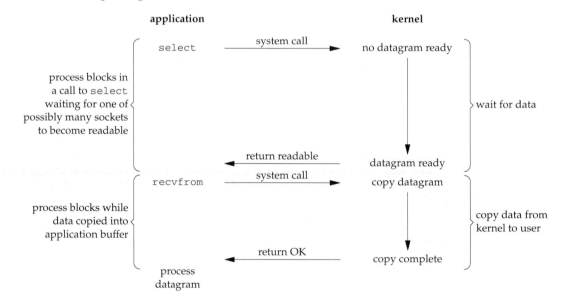

Figure 6.3 I/O multiplexing model.

We block in a call to `select`, waiting for the datagram socket to be readable. When `select` returns that the socket is readable, we then call `recvfrom` to copy the datagram into our application buffer.

Comparing Figure 6.3 to Figure 6.1, there does not appear to be any advantage, and in fact there is a slight disadvantage because using `select` requires two system calls instead of one. But the advantage in using `select`, which we will see later in this chapter, is that we can wait for more than one descriptor to be ready.

Signal Driven I/O Model

We can also use signals, telling the kernel to notify us with the `SIGIO` signal when the descriptor is ready. We call this *signal driven I/O* and show a summary of it in Figure 6.4.

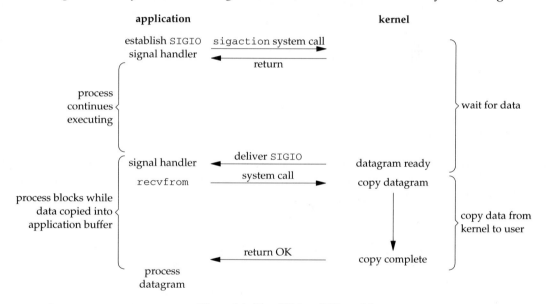

Figure 6.4 Signal Driven I/O model.

We first enable the socket for signal driven I/O (as we describe in Section 22.2) and install a signal handler using the `sigaction` system call. The return from this system call is immediate and our process continues; it is not blocked. When the datagram is ready to be read, the `SIGIO` signal is generated for our process. We can either read the datagram from the signal handler by calling `recvfrom` and then notify the main loop that the data is ready to be processed (this is what we do in Section 22.3), or we can notify the main loop and let it read the datagram.

Regardless of how we handle the signal, the advantage in this model is that we are not blocked while waiting for the datagram to arrive. The main loop can continue executing and just wait to be notified by the signal handler that either the data is ready to process or that the datagram is ready to be read.

Asynchronous I/O Model

Asynchronous I/O is new with the 1993 edition of Posix.1 (the "realtime" extensions). We tell the kernel to start the operation and to notify us when the entire operation (including the copy of the data from the kernel to our buffer) is complete. We do not discuss it in this book because it is not yet widespread. The main difference between this model and the signal driven I/O model in the previous section is that with signal driven I/O the kernel tells us when an I/O operation can be *initiated*, but with asynchronous I/O the kernel tells us when an I/O operation is *complete*. We show an example in Figure 6.5.

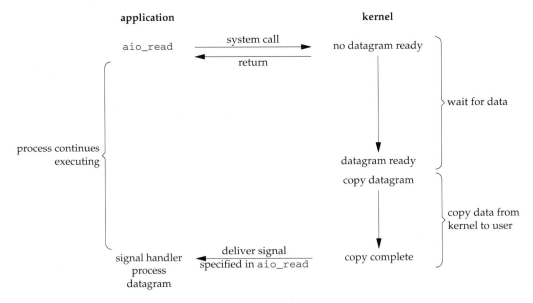

Figure 6.5 Asynchronous I/O model.

We call `aio_read` (the Posix asynchronous I/O functions begin with `aio_` or `lio_`) and pass the kernel the descriptor, buffer pointer, buffer size (the same three arguments for `read`), file offset (similar to `lseek`), and how to notify us when the entire operation is complete. This system call returns immediately and our process is not blocked waiting for the I/O to complete. We assume in this example that we ask the kernel to generate some signal when the operation is complete. This signal is not generated until the data has been copied into our application buffer, which is different from the signal driven I/O model.

> As of this writing, few systems support Posix.1 asynchronous I/O. We are not certain, for example, if systems will support it for sockets. Our use of it here is as an example to compare against the signal driven I/O model.

Comparison of the I/O Models

Figure 6.6 is a comparison of the five different I/O models. This shows that the main difference between the first four models is the first phase, as the second phase in the first four models is the same: the process is blocked in a call to `recvfrom` while the data is copied from the kernel to the caller's buffer. Asynchronous I/O, however, handles both phases and is different from the first four.

blocking	nonblocking	I/O multiplexing	signal-driven I/O	asynchronous I/O	
initiate	check	check		initiate	⎫
	check				
	check				wait for data
	check	blocked			
	check				
	check				
blocked	check				
	check				
	check	ready	notification		⎬
		initiate	initiate		
	blocked	blocked	blocked		copy data from kernel to user
complete	complete	complete	complete	notification	⎭

1st phase handled differently,
2nd phase handled the same
(blocked in call to `recvfrom`)

handles both
phases

Figure 6.6 Comparison of the five I/O models.

Synchronous I/O versus Asynchronous I/O

Posix.1 defines these two terms as follows:

- A *synchronous I/O operation* causes the requesting process to be blocked until that I/O operation completes.
- An *asynchronous I/O operation* does not cause the requesting process to be blocked.

Using these definitions the first four I/O models—blocking, nonblocking, I/O multiplexing, and signal-driven I/O—are all synchronous because the actual I/O operation (`recvfrom`) blocks the process. Only the asynchronous I/O model matches the asynchronous I/O definition.

6.3   `select` Function

This function allows the process to instruct the kernel to wait for any one of multiple events to occur and to wake up the process only when one or more of these events occurs or when a specified amount of time has passed.

As an example, we can call `select` and tell the kernel to return only when

- any of the descriptors in the set {1, 4, 5} are ready for reading, or
- any of the descriptors in the set {2, 7} are ready for writing, or
- any of the descriptors in the set {1, 4} have an exception condition pending, or
- after 10.2 seconds have elapsed.

That is, we tell the kernel what descriptors we are interested in (for reading, writing, or an exception condition) and how long to wait. The descriptors in which we are interested are not restricted to sockets: any descriptor can be tested using `select`.

> Berkeley-derived implementations have always allowed I/O multiplexing with any descriptor. SVR3 originally limited I/O multiplexing to descriptors that were streams devices (Chapter 33), but this limitation was removed with SVR4.

```
#include <sys/select.h>
#include <sys/time.h>

int select(int maxfdp1, fd_set *readset, fd_set *writeset, fd_set *exceptset,
           const struct timeval *timeout);
```

                                    Returns: positive count of ready descriptors, 0 on timeout, −1 on error

We start our description of this function with its final argument, which tells the kernel how long to wait for one of the specified descriptors to become ready. A `timeval` structure specifies the number of seconds and microseconds.

```
struct timeval {
  long    tv_sec;       /* seconds */
  long    tv_usec;      /* microseconds */
};
```

There are three possibilities.

1. Wait forever: return only when one of the specified descriptors is ready for I/O. For this, we specify the *timeout* argument as a null pointer.

2. Wait up to a fixed amount of time: return when one of the specified descriptors is ready for I/O, but do not wait beyond the number of seconds and microseconds specified in the `timeval` structure pointed to by the *timeout* argument.

3. Do not wait at all: return immediately after checking the descriptors. This is called *polling*. To specify this, the *timeout* argument must point to a `timeval`

structure, and the timer value (the number of seconds and microseconds specified by the structure) must be 0.

The wait in the first two scenarios is normally interrupted if the process catches a signal and returns from the signal handler.

> Berkeley-derived kernels never automatically restart select (p. 527 of TCPv2), while SVR4 will if the SA_RESTART flag is specified when the signal handler is installed. This means that for portability we must be prepared for select to return an error of EINTR if we are catching signals.

Although the timeval structure lets us specify a resolution in microseconds, the actual resolution supported by the kernel is often more coarse. For example, many Unix kernels round the timeout value up to a multiple of 10 ms. There is also a scheduling latency involved, meaning it takes some time after the timer expires before the kernel schedules this process to run.

The const qualifier on the *timeout* argument means it is not modified by select on return. For example, if we specify a time limit of 10 seconds, and select returns before the timer expires, with one or more of the descriptors ready or with an error of EINTR, the timeval structure is not updated with the number of seconds remaining when the function returns. If we wish to know this value, we must obtain the system time before calling select, and then again when it returns, and subtract the two.

> Current Linux systems modify the timeval structure. Therefore for portability, assume the timeval structure is undefined upon return, and initialize it before each call to select. Posix.1g specifies the const qualifier.

The three middle arguments *readset*, *writeset*, and *exceptset* specify the descriptors that we want the kernel to test for reading, writing, and exception conditions. There are only two exception conditions currently supported.

1. The arrival of out-of-band data for a socket. We describe this in more detail in Chapter 21.

2. The presence of control status information to be read from the master side of a pseudo terminal that has been put into packet mode. We do not talk about pseudo terminals in this volume.

A design problem is how to specify one or more descriptor values for each of these three arguments. select uses *descriptor sets*, typically an array of integers, with each bit in each integer corresponding to a descriptor. For example, using 32-bit integers, the first element of the array corresponds to descriptors 0 through 31, the second element of the array corresponds to descriptors 32 through 63, and so on. All the implementation details are irrelevant to the application and are hidden in the fd_set datatype and the following four macros:

```
void FD_ZERO(fd_set *fdset);          /* clear all bits in fdset */
void FD_SET(int fd, fd_set *fdset);   /* turn on the bit for fd in fdset */
void FD_CLR(int fd, fd_set *fdset);   /* turn off the bit for fd in fdset */
int  FD_ISSET(int fd, fd_set *fdset); /* is the bit for fd on in fdset ? */
```

We allocate a descriptor set of the `fd_set` datatype, we set and test the bits in the set using these macros, and we can also assign it to another descriptor set across an equals sign in C.

> What we are describing, an array of integers using one bit per descriptor, is just one possible way to implement `select`. Nevertheless, it is common to refer to the individual descriptors within a descriptor set as *bits*, as in "turn on the bit for the listening descriptor in the read set."
>
> We will see in Section 6.10 that the `poll` function uses a completely different representation: a variable-length array of structures with one structure per descriptor.

For example, to define a variable of type `fd_set` and then turn on the bits for descriptors 1, 4, and 5, we write

```
fd_set  rset;

FD_ZERO(&rset);      /* initialize the set: all bits off */
FD_SET(1, &rset);    /* turn on bit for fd 1 */
FD_SET(4, &rset);    /* turn on bit for fd 4 */
FD_SET(5, &rset);    /* turn on bit for fd 5 */
```

It is important to initialize the set, since unpredictable results can occur if the set is allocated as an automatic variable and not initialized.

Any of the middle three arguments to `select`, *readset*, *writeset*, or *exceptset*, can be specified as a null pointer, if we are not interested in that condition. Indeed, if all three pointers are null, then we have a higher precision timer than the normal Unix `sleep` function (which sleeps for multiples of a second). The `poll` function provides similar functionality. Figures C.9 and C.10 of APUE show a `sleep_us` function implemented using both `select` and `poll` that sleeps for multiples of a microsecond.

The *maxfdp1* argument specifies the number of descriptors to be tested. Its value is the maximum descriptor to be tested, plus one (hence our name of *maxfdp1*). The descriptors 0, 1, 2, up through and including *maxfdp1–1* are tested.

The constant `FD_SETSIZE`, defined by including `<sys/select.h>`, is the number of descriptors in the `fd_set` datatype. Its value is often 1024, but few programs use that many descriptors. The *maxfdp1* argument forces us to calculate the largest descriptor that we are interested in and then tell the kernel this value. For example, given the previous code that turns on the indicators for descriptors 1, 4, and 5, *maxfdp1* value is 6. The reason it is 6 and not 5 is that we are specifying the number of descriptors, not the largest value, and descriptors start at 0.

> The reason this argument exists along with the burden of calculating its value is purely for efficiency. Although each `fd_set` has room for many descriptors, typically 1024, this is much more than the number used by a typical process. The kernel gains efficiency by not copying unneeded portions of the descriptor set between the process and the kernel, and by not testing bits that are always 0 (Section 16.13 of TCPv2).

`select` modifies the descriptor sets pointed to by the *readset*, *writeset*, and *exceptset* pointers. These three arguments are value–result arguments. When we call the function, we specify the values of the descriptors that we are interested in and on return the result indicates which descriptors are ready. We use the `FD_ISSET` macro on return to test a specific descriptor in an `fd_set` structure. Any descriptor that is not ready on return will have its corresponding bit cleared in the descriptor set. To handle this we turn on all the bits in which we are interested in all the descriptor sets each time we call `select`.

> The two most common programming errors when using `select` are to forget to add one to the largest descriptor number and to forget that the descriptors sets are value–result. The second error results in `select` being called with a bit set to 0 in the descriptor set, when we think that bit is 1. The author also wasted 2 hours debugging an example for this text that uses `select` by forgetting to add one to the first argument.

The return value from this function indicates the total number of bits that are ready across all the descriptor sets. If the timer value expires before any of the descriptors are ready, a value of 0 is returned. A return value of −1 indicates an error (which can happen, for example, if the function is interrupted by a caught signal).

> Early releases of SVR4 had a bug in their implementation of `select`: if the same bit was on in multiple sets, say a descriptor was ready for both reading and writing, it was counted only once. Current releases fix this bug.

Under What Conditions Is a Descriptor Ready?

We have been talking about waiting for a descriptor to become ready for I/O (reading or writing) or to have an exception condition pending on it (out-of-band data). While readability and writability are obvious for descriptors such as regular files, we must be more specific about the conditions that cause `select` to return "ready" for sockets (Figure 16.52 of TCPv2).

1. A socket is ready for reading if any of the following four conditions is true:

    a. The number of bytes of data in the socket receive buffer is greater than or equal to the current size of the low-water mark for the socket receive buffer. A read operation on the socket will not block and will return a value greater than 0 (i.e., the data that is ready to be read). We can set this low-water mark using the `SO_RCVLOWAT` socket option. It defaults to 1 for TCP and UDP sockets.

    b. The read-half of the connection is closed (i.e., a TCP connection that has received a FIN). A read operation on the socket will not block and will return 0 (i.e., end-of-file).

    c. The socket is a listening socket and the number of completed connections is nonzero. An `accept` on the listening socket will normally not block, although we describe a timing condition in Section 15.6 under which the `accept` can block.

    d. A socket error is pending. A read operation on the socket will not block and will return an error (−1) with `errno` set to the specific error condition. These *pending errors* can also be fetched and cleared by calling `getsockopt` specifying the `SO_ERROR` socket option.

2. A socket is ready for writing if any of the following three conditions is true:

   a. The number of bytes of available space in the socket send buffer is greater than or equal to the current size of the low-water mark for the socket send buffer *and* either (i) the socket is connected, or (ii) the socket does not require a connection (e.g., UDP). This means that if we set the socket nonblocking (Chapter 15), a write operation will not block and will return a positive value (e.g., the number of bytes accepted by the transport layer). We can set this low-water mark using the `SO_SNDLOWAT` socket option. This low-water mark normally defaults to 2048 for TCP and UDP sockets.

   b. The write-half of the connection is closed. A write operation on the socket will generate `SIGPIPE` (Section 5.12).

   c. A socket error is pending. A write operation on the socket will not block and will return an error (–1) with `errno` set to the specific error condition. These *pending errors* can also be fetched and cleared by calling `getsockopt` for the `SO_ERROR` socket option.

3. A socket has an exception condition pending if there exists out-of-band data for the socket or the socket is still at the out-of-band mark. (We describe out-of-band data in Chapter 21.)

> Our definitions of "readable" and "writable" are taken directly from the kernel's `soreadable` and `sowriteable` macros on pp. 530–531 of TCPv2. Similarly our definition of the "exception condition" for a socket is from the `soo_select` function on these same pages.

Notice that when an error occurs on a socket it is marked as both readable and writable by `select`.

The purpose of the receive and send low-water marks is to give the application control over how much data must be available for reading or how much space must be available for writing before `select` returns readable or writable. For example, if we know that our application has nothing productive to do unless at least 64 bytes of data are present, we can set the receive low-water mark to 64 to prevent `select` from waking us up if less than 64 bytes are ready for reading.

As long as the send low-water mark for a UDP socket is less than the send buffer size (which should always be the default relationship), the UDP socket is always writable, since a connection is not required.

Figure 6.7 summarizes the conditions just described that cause a socket to be ready for `select`.

Maximum Number of Descriptors for `select`?

We said earlier that most applications do not use lots of descriptors. It is rare, for example, to find an application that uses hundreds of descriptors. But these applications do exist, and they often use `select` to multiplex the descriptors. When `select` was originally designed, the operating system normally had an upper limit on the maximum number of descriptors per process (the 4.2BSD limit was 31), and `select` just used this same limit. But current versions of Unix allow for an unlimited number of descriptors

Condition	readable?	writable?	exception?
data to read read-half of the connection closed new connection ready for listening socket	• • •		
space available for writing write-half of the connection closed		• •	
pending error	•	•	
TCP out-of-band data			•

Figure 6.7 Summary of conditions that cause a socket to be ready for select.

per process (often limited only by the amount of memory and any administrative limits), so the question is: how does this affect select?

Many implementations have declarations similar to the following, which are taken from the 4.4BSD <sys/types.h> header:

```
/*
 * Select uses bitmasks of file descriptors in longs.  These macros
 * manipulate such bit fields (the filesystem macros use chars).
 * FD_SETSIZE may be defined by the user, but the default here should
 * be enough for most uses.
 */
#ifndef FD_SETSIZE
#define FD_SETSIZE      256
#endif
```

This makes us think that we can just #define FD_SETSIZE to some larger value before including this header to increase the size of the descriptor sets used by select. Unfortunately, this normally does not work.

> To see what is wrong, notice that Figure 16.53 of TCPv2 declares three descriptor sets within the kernel and also uses the kernel's definition of FD_SETSIZE as the upper limit. The only way to increase the size of the descriptor sets is to increase the value of FD_SETSIZE and then recompile the kernel. Changing the value without recompiling the kernel is inadequate.

Some vendors are changing their implementation of select to allow the process to define FD_SETSIZE to a larger than default value. BSD/OS has changed the kernel implementation to allow larger descriptor sets, and it also provides four new FD_*xxx* macros to dynamically allocate and manipulate these larger sets. From a portability standpoint, however, beware of using large descriptor sets.

6.4 str_cli Function (Revisited)

We can now rewrite our str_cli function from Section 5.5, this time using select, so we are notified as soon as the server process terminates. The problem with that earlier version was that we could be blocked in the call to fgets when something happened on the socket. Our new version blocks in a call to select instead, waiting for either standard input or the socket to be readable. Figure 6.8 shows the various conditions that are handled by our call to `select`.

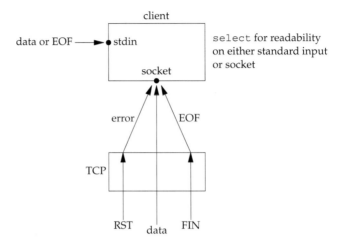

Figure 6.8 Conditions handled by `select` in `strcli`.

Three conditions are handled with the socket.

1. If the peer TCP sends data, the socket becomes readable and `read` returns greater than 0 (i.e., the number of bytes of data).

2. If the peer TCP sends a FIN (the peer process terminates), the socket becomes readable and `read` returns 0 (end-of-file).

3. If the peer TCP sends an RST (the peer host has crashed and rebooted), the socket becomes readable and `read` returns −1 and `errno` contains the specific error code.

Figure 6.9 shows the source code for this new version.

Call `select`

8–13   We only need one descriptor set—to check for readability. This set is initialized by `FD_ZERO` and then two bits are turned on using `FD_SET`: the bit corresponding to the standard I/O file pointer `fp` and the bit corresponding to the socket `sockfd`. The function `fileno` converts a standard I/O file pointer into its corresponding descriptor. `select` (and `poll`) work only with descriptors.

   `select` is called after calculating the maximum of the two descriptors. In the call the write-set pointer and the exception-set pointer are both null pointers. The final argument (the time limit) is also a null pointer since we want the call to block until something is ready.

Handle readable socket

14–18   If, on return from `select`, the socket is readable, the echoed line is read with `readline` and output by `fputs`.

select/strcliselect01.c

```
 1 #include     "unp.h"

 2 void
 3 str_cli(FILE *fp, int sockfd)
 4 {
 5     int     maxfdp1;
 6     fd_set  rset;
 7     char    sendline[MAXLINE], recvline[MAXLINE];

 8     FD_ZERO(&rset);
 9     for ( ; ; ) {
10         FD_SET(fileno(fp), &rset);
11         FD_SET(sockfd, &rset);
12         maxfdp1 = max(fileno(fp), sockfd) + 1;
13         Select(maxfdp1, &rset, NULL, NULL, NULL);

14         if (FD_ISSET(sockfd, &rset)) {  /* socket is readable */
15             if (Readline(sockfd, recvline, MAXLINE) == 0)
16                 err_quit("str_cli: server terminated prematurely");
17             Fputs(recvline, stdout);
18         }
19         if (FD_ISSET(fileno(fp), &rset)) { /* input is readable */
20             if (Fgets(sendline, MAXLINE, fp) == NULL)
21                 return;             /* all done */
22             Writen(sockfd, sendline, strlen(sendline));
23         }
24     }
25 }
```

select/strcliselect01.c

Figure 6.9 Implementation of `str_cli` function using `select`.

Handle readable input

19–23   If the standard input is readable, a line is read by `fgets` and written to the socket using `writen`.

Notice that the same four I/O functions are used as in Figure 5.5: `fgets`, `writen`, `readline`, and `fputs`, but the order of flow within the function has changed. Instead of the function flow being driven by the call to `fgets`, it is now driven by the call to `select`. With only a few additional lines of code in Figure 6.9, compared to Figure 5.5, we have added greatly to the robustness of our client.

6.5   Batch Input

Unfortunately, our `str_cli` function is still not correct. First lets go back to our original version, Figure 5.5. It operates in a stop-and-wait mode, which is fine for interactive use: it sends a line to the server and then waits for the reply. This amount of time is one RTT (round-trip time) plus the server's processing time (which is close to 0 for a simple echo server). We can therefore estimate how long it will take for a given number of lines to be echoed, if we know the RTT between the client and server.

The Ping program is an easy way to measure RTTs. If we run Ping to the host `connix.com` from our host `solaris`, the average RTT over 30 measurements is 175 ms. Page 89 of TCPv1 shows that these Ping measurements are for an IP datagram whose length is 84 bytes. If we take the first 2000 lines of the Solaris 2.5 `termcap` file, the resulting file size is 98,349 bytes, for an average of 49 bytes per line. If we add the sizes of the IP header (20 bytes) and the TCP header (20), the average TCP segment will be about 89 bytes, nearly the same as the Ping packet sizes. We can therefore estimate that the total clock time will be around 350 seconds for 2000 lines ($2000 \times 0.175sec$). If we run our TCP echo client from Chapter 5, the actual time is about 354 seconds, which is very close to our estimate.

If we consider the network between the client and server as a full-duplex pipe, with requests going from the client to server, and replies in the reverse direction, then Figure 6.10 shows our stop-and-wait mode.

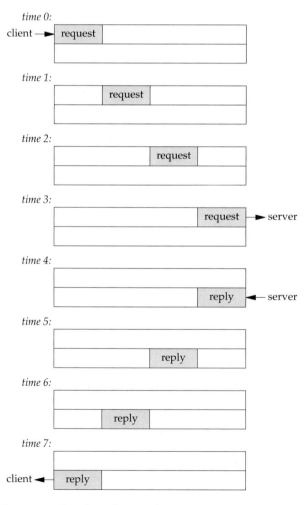

Figure 6.10   Time line of stop-and-wait mode: interactive input.

The request is sent by the client at time 0 and we assume an RTT of 8 units of time. The reply sent at time 4 is received at time 7. We also assume that there is no server processing time and that the size of the request is the same as the reply. We show only the data packets between the client and server, ignoring the TCP acknowledgments that are also going across the network.

But since there is a delay between sending a packet and that packet arriving at the other end of the pipe, and since the pipe is full-duplex, in this example we are only using one-eighth of the pipe capacity. This stop-and-wait mode is fine for interactive input, but since our client reads from standard input and writes to standard output, and since it is trivial under the Unix shells to redirect the input and output, we can easily run our client in a batch mode. When we redirect the input and output, however, the resulting output file is always smaller than the input file (and they should be identical for an echo server).

To see what's happening, realize that in a batch mode we can keep sending requests as fast as the network can accept them. The server processes them and sends back the replies at the same rate. This leads to the full pipe at time 7, as shown in Figure 6.11.

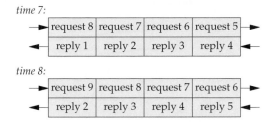

Figure 6.11 Filling the pipe between the client and server: batch mode.

Here we assume that after sending the first request, we immediately send another, and another. We also assume that we can keep sending them as fast as the network can accept them, along with processing the replies as fast as the network supplies them.

> There are numerous subtleties dealing with TCP's bulk data flow that we are ignoring here, such as its slow start algorithm, which limits the rate at which data is sent on a new or idle connection, and the returning ACKs. These are all covered in Chapter 20 of TCPv1.

To see the problem with our revised `str_cli` function in Figure 6.9, assume that the input file contains only nine lines. The last line is sent at time 8, as shown in Figure 6.11. But we cannot close the connection after writing this request, because there are still other requests and replies in the pipe. The cause of the problem is our handling of an end-of-file on input: the function returns to the `main` function, which then terminates. But in a batch mode, an end-of-file on the input does not imply that we have finished reading from the socket: there might still be requests on the way to the server, or replies on the way back from the server.

What we need is a way to close one-half of the TCP connection. That is, we want to send a FIN to the server, telling it we have finished sending data, but leave the socket descriptor open for reading. This is done with the `shutdown` function, described in the next section.

6.6   `shutdown` Function

The normal way to terminate a network connection is to call the `close` function. But there are two limitations with `close` that can be avoided with `shutdown`.

1. `close` decrements the descriptor's reference count and closes the socket only if the count reaches 0. We talked about this in Section 4.8. With `shutdown` we can initiate TCP's normal connection termination sequence (the four segments beginning with a FIN in Figure 2.5) regardless of the reference count.

2. `close` terminates both directions of data transfer, reading and writing. Since a TCP connection is full-duplex, there are times when we want to tell the other end that we have finished sending, even though that end might have more data to send us. This is the scenario we encountered in the previous section with batch input to our `str_cli` function. Figure 6.12 shows the typical function calls in this scenario.

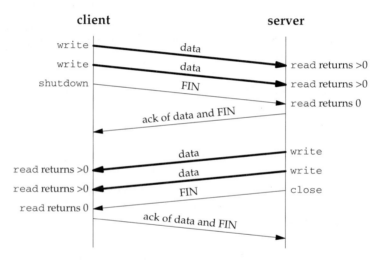

Figure 6.12 Calling `shutdown` to close half of a TCP connection.

```
#include <sys/socket.h>

int shutdown(int sockfd, int howto);
```

Returns: 0 if OK, −1 on error

The action of the function depends on the value of the *howto* argument.

SHUT_RD   The read-half of the connection is closed: no more data can be received on the socket and any data currently in the socket receive buffer is discarded. The process can no longer issue any of the read functions on the socket. Any data received after this call for a TCP socket is acknowledged and then silently discarded.

> By default, everything written to a routing socket (Chapter 17) loops back as possible input to all routing sockets on the host. Some programs call shutdown with a second argument of SHUT_RD to prevent the loopback copy. An alternative way to prevent this loopback copy is to clear the SO_USELOOPBACK socket option.

SHUT_WR   The write-half of the connection is closed. In the case of TCP, this is called a *half-close* (Section 18.5 of TCPv1). Any data currently in the socket send buffer will be sent, followed by TCP's normal connection termination sequence. As we mentioned earlier, this closing of the write-half is done regardless whether or not the socket descriptor's reference count is currently greater than 0. The process can no longer issue any of the write functions on the socket.

SHUT_RDWR   The read-half and the write-half of the connection are both closed. This is equivalent to calling shutdown twice: first with SHUT_RD and then with SHUT_WR.

Figure 7.10 summarizes the different possibilities available to the process by calling shutdown and close. The operation of close depends on the value of the SO_LINGER socket option.

> The three SHUT_*xxx* names are new with Posix.1g. Typical values for the *howto* argument that you will encounter will be 0 (close the read-half), 1 (close the write-half), and 2 (close the read-half and the write-half).

6.7   str_cli Function (Revisited Again)

Figure 6.13 shows our revised (and correct) version of the str_cli function. This version uses select and shutdown. The former notifies us as soon as the server closes its end of the connection and the latter lets us handle batch input correctly.

5–8   stdineof is a new flag that is initialized to 0. As long as this flag is 0, each time around the main loop we select on standard input for readability.

16–24   When we read the end-of-file on the socket, if we have already encountered an end-of-file on standard input, this is the normal termination and the function returns. But if we have not yet encountered an end-of-file on standard input, the server process has prematurely terminated.

25–33   When we encounter the end-of-file on standard input, our new flag stdineof is set and we call shutdown with a second argument of SHUT_WR to send the FIN.

If we measure our TCP client using the str_cli function from Figure 6.13 using the same 2000-line file, the clock time is now about 12.3 seconds, about 30 times faster than the stop-and-wait version.

── select/strcliselect02.c
```
1 #include    "unp.h"

2 void
3 str_cli(FILE *fp, int sockfd)
4 {
5     int     maxfdp1, stdineof;
6     fd_set  rset;
7     char    sendline[MAXLINE], recvline[MAXLINE];

8     stdineof = 0;
9     FD_ZERO(&rset);
10    for ( ; ; ) {
11        if (stdineof == 0)
12            FD_SET(fileno(fp), &rset);
13        FD_SET(sockfd, &rset);
14        maxfdp1 = max(fileno(fp), sockfd) + 1;
15        Select(maxfdp1, &rset, NULL, NULL, NULL);

16        if (FD_ISSET(sockfd, &rset)) {  /* socket is readable */
17            if (Readline(sockfd, recvline, MAXLINE) == 0) {
18                if (stdineof == 1)
19                    return;      /* normal termination */
20                else
21                    err_quit("str_cli: server terminated prematurely");
22            }
23            Fputs(recvline, stdout);
24        }
25        if (FD_ISSET(fileno(fp), &rset)) {  /* input is readable */
26            if (Fgets(sendline, MAXLINE, fp) == NULL) {
27                stdineof = 1;
28                Shutdown(sockfd, SHUT_WR);  /* send FIN */
29                FD_CLR(fileno(fp), &rset);
30                continue;
31            }
32            Written(sockfd, sendline, strlen(sendline));
33        }
34    }
35 }
```
── select/strcliselect02.c

Figure 6.13 `str_cli` function using `select` that handles end-of-file correctly.

We are not finished with our `str_cli` function. We develop a version using non-blocking I/O in Section 15.2, and a version using threads in Section 23.3.

6.8 TCP Echo Server (Revisited)

We can revisit our TCP echo server from Sections 5.2 and 5.3 and rewrite the server as a single process that uses `select` to handle any number of clients, instead of `forking` one child per client. Before showing the code, let's look at the data structures that we will use to keep track of the clients. Figure 6.14 shows the state of the server before the first client has established a connection.

Figure 6.14 TCP server before first client has established a connection.

The server has a single listening descriptor, which we show as a bullet.

The server maintains only a read descriptor set, which we show in Figure 6.15. We assume that the server is started in the foreground, so descriptors 0, 1, and 2 are set to standard input, output, and error. Therefore the first available descriptor for the listening socket is 3. We also show an array of integers named `client` that contains the connected socket descriptor for each client. All elements in this array are initialized to −1.

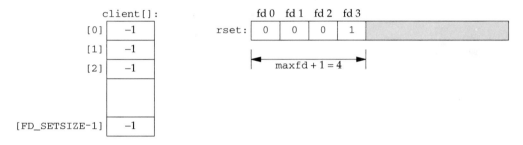

Figure 6.15 Data structures for TCP server with just listening socket.

The only nonzero entry in the descriptor set is the entry for the listening socket and the first argument to `select` will be 4.

When the first client establishes a connection with our server, the listening descriptor becomes readable and our server calls `accept`. The new connected descriptor returned by `accept` will be 4, given the assumptions of this example. Figure 6.16 shows the connection from the client to the server.

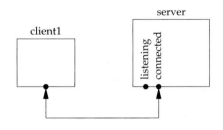

Figure 6.16 TCP server after first client establishes connection.

From this point on our server must remember the new connected socket in its `client` array, and the connected socket must be added to the descriptor set. These updated data structures are shown in Figure 6.17.

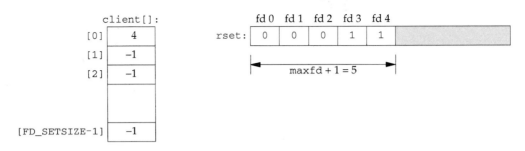

Figure 6.17 Data structures after first client connection is established.

Some time later a second client establishes a connection and we have the scenario shown in Figure 6.18.

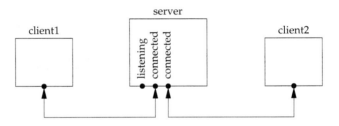

Figure 6.18 TCP server after second client connection is established.

The new connected socket (which we assume is 5) must be remembered, giving the data structures shown in Figure 6.19.

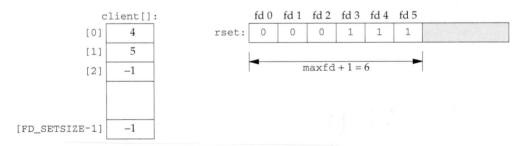

Figure 6.19 Data structures after second client connection is established.

Next we assume the first client terminates its connection. The client TCP sends a FIN, which makes descriptor 4 in the server readable. When our server reads this connected socket, `readline` returns 0. We then close this socket and update our data structures accordingly. The value of `client[0]` is set to −1 and descriptor 4 in the descriptor set is set to 0. This is shown in Figure 6.20. Notice that the value of `maxfd` does not change.

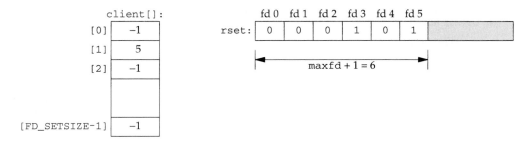

Figure 6.20 Data structures after first client terminates its connection.

In summary, as clients arrive we record their connected socket descriptor in the first available entry in the `client` array (i.e., the first entry with a value of −1). We must also add the connected socket to the read descriptor set. The variable `maxi` is the highest index in the `client` array that is currently in use and the variable `maxfd` (plus one) is the current value of the first argument to `select`. The only limit on the number of clients that this server can handle is the minimum of the two values `FD_SETSIZE` and the maximum number of descriptors allowed for this process by the kernel (which we talked about at the end of Section 6.3).

Figure 6.21 shows the first half of this version of the server.

tcpcliserv/tcpservselect01.c

```
 1 #include     "unp.h"

 2 int
 3 main(int argc, char **argv)
 4 {
 5     int     i, maxi, maxfd, listenfd, connfd, sockfd;
 6     int     nready, client[FD_SETSIZE];
 7     ssize_t n;
 8     fd_set  rset, allset;
 9     char    line[MAXLINE];
10     socklen_t clilen;
11     struct sockaddr_in cliaddr, servaddr;

12     listenfd = Socket(AF_INET, SOCK_STREAM, 0);

13     bzero(&servaddr, sizeof(servaddr));
14     servaddr.sin_family = AF_INET;
15     servaddr.sin_addr.s_addr = htonl(INADDR_ANY);
16     servaddr.sin_port = htons(SERV_PORT);

17     Bind(listenfd, (SA *) &servaddr, sizeof(servaddr));

18     Listen(listenfd, LISTENQ);

19     maxfd = listenfd;          /* initialize */
20     maxi = -1;                 /* index into client[] array */
21     for (i = 0; i < FD_SETSIZE; i++)
22         client[i] = -1;        /* -1 indicates available entry */
23     FD_ZERO(&allset);
24     FD_SET(listenfd, &allset);
```

tcpcliserv/tcpservselect01.c

Figure 6.21 TCP server using a single process and `select`: initialization.

Create listening socket and initialize for `select`

12–24   The steps to create the listening socket are the same as seen earlier: `socket`, `bind`, and `listen`. We initialize our data structures given that the only descriptor that we will `select` on initially is the listening socket.

The last half of the function is shown in Figure 6.22

———————————————————— tcpcliserv/tcpservselect01.c

```
25      for ( ; ; ) {
26          rset = allset;              /* structure assignment */
27          nready = Select(maxfd + 1, &rset, NULL, NULL, NULL);

28          if (FD_ISSET(listenfd, &rset)) {     /* new client connection */
29              clilen = sizeof(cliaddr);
30              connfd = Accept(listenfd, (SA *) &cliaddr, &clilen);

31              for (i = 0; i < FD_SETSIZE; i++)
32                  if (client[i] < 0) {
33                      client[i] = connfd;      /* save descriptor */
34                      break;
35                  }
36              if (i == FD_SETSIZE)
37                  err_quit("too many clients");

38              FD_SET(connfd, &allset);     /* add new descriptor to set */
39              if (connfd > maxfd)
40                  maxfd = connfd; /* for select */
41              if (i > maxi)
42                  maxi = i;          /* max index in client[] array */

43              if (--nready <= 0)
44                  continue;          /* no more readable descriptors */
45          }
46          for (i = 0; i <= maxi; i++) {    /* check all clients for data */
47              if ( (sockfd = client[i]) < 0)
48                  continue;
49              if (FD_ISSET(sockfd, &rset)) {
50                  if ( (n = Readline(sockfd, line, MAXLINE)) == 0) {
51                          /* connection closed by client */
52                      Close(sockfd);
53                      FD_CLR(sockfd, &allset);
54                      client[i] = -1;
55                  } else
56                      Writen(sockfd, line, n);

57                  if (--nready <= 0)
58                      break;       /* no more readable descriptors */
59              }
60          }
61      }
62  }
```

———————————————————— tcpcliserv/tcpservselect01.c

Figure 6.22 TCP server using a single process and `select`: loop.

Block in `select`

26-27   `select` waits for something to happen: either the establishment of a new client connection or the arrival of data, a FIN, or an RST on an existing connection.

`accept` new connections

28-45   If the listening socket is readable, a new connection has been established. We call `accept` and update our data structures accordingly. We use the first unused entry in the `client` array to record the connected socket. The number of ready descriptors is decremented, and if it is 0, we can avoid the next `for` loop. This lets us use the return value from `select` to avoid checking descriptors that are not ready.

Check existing connections

46-60   A test is made for each existing client connection as to whether or not its descriptor is in the descriptor set returned by `select`. If so, a line is read from the client and echoed back to the client. If the client closes the connection, `readline` returns 0 and we update our data structures accordingly.

We never decrement the value of `maxi` but could check for this possibility each time a client closes its connection.

This server is more complicated than the one shown in Figures 5.2 and 5.3, but it avoids all the overhead of creating a new process for each client and it is a nice example of `select`. Nevertheless, in Section 15.6 we will describe a problem with this server that is easily fixed by making the listening socket nonblocking and then checking for, and ignoring, a few errors from `accept`.

Denial of Service Attacks

Unfortunately there is a problem with the server that we just showed. Consider what happens if a malicious client connects to the server, sends 1 byte of data (other than a newline), and then goes to sleep. The server will call `readline`, which will read the single byte of data from the client and then block in the next call to `read`, waiting for more data from this client. The server is then blocked ("hung" may be a better term) by this one client and will not service any other clients (either new client connections or existing client's data) until the malicious client either sends a newline or terminates.

The basic concept here is that when a server is handling multiple clients the server can *never* block in a function call related to a single client. Doing so can hang the server and deny service to all other clients. This is called a *denial of service* attack. It does something to the server that prevents it from servicing other legitimate clients. Possible solutions are to (a) use nonblocking I/O (Chapter 15), (b) have each client serviced by a separate thread of control (e.g., either spawn a process or a thread to service each client), or (c) place a timeout on the I/O operations (Section 13.2).

6.9   pselect Function

The pselect function was invented by Posix.1g.

```
#include <sys/select.h>
#include <signal.h>
#include <time.h>

int pselect(int maxfdp1, fd_set *readset, fd_set *writeset, fd_set *exceptset,
            const struct timespec *timeout, const sigset_t *sigmask);
```

Returns: count of ready descriptors, 0 on timeout, −1 on error

pselect contains two changes from the normal select function.

1. pselect uses the timespec structure, an invention of the Posix.1b realtime standard, instead of the timeval structure.

   ```
   struct timespec {
     time_t tv_sec;      /* seconds */
     long   tv_nsec;     /* nanoseconds */
   };
   ```

   The difference in these two structures is with the second member: the tv_nsec member of the newer structure specifies nanoseconds, whereas the tv_usec member of the older structure specifies microseconds.

2. pselect adds a sixth argument: a pointer to a signal mask. This allows the program to disable the delivery of certain signals, test some global variables that are set by the handlers for these now-disabled signals, and then call pselect, telling it to reset the signal mask.

With regard to the second point, consider the following example (discussed on pp. 308–309 of APUE). Our program's signal handler for SIGINT just sets the global intr_flag and returns. If our process is blocked in a call to select, the return from the signal handler causes the function to return with errno set to EINTR. But when select is called, the code looks like the following:

```
if (intr_flag)
    handle_intr();      /* handle the signal */
if ( (nready = select( ... )) < 0) {
    if (errno == EINTR) {
        if (intr_flag)
            handle_intr();
    }
    ...
}
```

The problem is that between the test of intr_flag and the call to select, if the signal occurs, it will be lost if select blocks forever. With pselect we can now code this example reliably as

```
sigset_t  newmask, oldmask, zeromask;

sigemptyset(&zeromask);
sigemptyset(&newmask);
sigaddset(&newmask, SIGINT);

sigprocmask(SIG_BLOCK, &newmask, &oldmask); /* block SIGINT */
if (intr_flag)
    handle_intr();     /* handle the signal */
if ( (nready = pselect( ... , &zeromask)) < 0) {
    if (errno == EINTR) {
        if (intr_flag)
            handle_intr();
    }
    ...
}
```

Before testing the intr_flag variable we block SIGINT. When pselect is called, it replaces the signal mask of the process with an empty set (i.e., zeromask) and then checks the descriptors, possibly going to sleep. But when pselect returns, the signal mask of the process is reset to its value before pselect was called (i.e., SIGINT is blocked).

We say more about pselect and show an example of it in Section 18.5. We use pselect in Figure 18.7 and show a simple, albeit incorrect, implementation of pselect in Figure 18.8.

> There is one other slight difference between the two select functions. The first member of the timeval structure is a signed long integer while the first member of the timespec structure is a time_t. The signed long in the former should also be a time_t but was not changed retroactively, to avoid breaking existing code. The brand new function, however, could make this change.

6.10 poll Function

The poll function originated with SVR3 and was originally limited to streams devices (Chapter 33). SVR4 removed this limitation, allowing poll to work with any descriptor. poll provides functionality that is similar to select, but poll provides additional information when dealing with streams devices.

```
#include <poll.h>

int poll(struct pollfd *fdarray, unsigned long nfds, int timeout);
```
                                    Returns: count of ready descriptors, 0 on timeout, −1 on error

The first argument is a pointer to the first element of an array of structures. Each element of the array is a pollfd structure that specifies the conditions to be tested for a given descriptor fd.

```
struct pollfd {
  int    fd;       /* descriptor to check */
  short  events;   /* events of interest on fd */
  short  revents;  /* events that occurred on fd */
};
```

The conditions to be tested are specified by the `events` member, and the function returns the status for that descriptor in the corresponding `revents` member. (Having two variables per descriptor, one a value and one a result, avoids value–result arguments. Recall that the middle three arguments for `select` are value–result.) Each of these two members is composed of one or more bits that specify a certain condition. Figure 6.23 shows the constants used to specify the `events` flag and to test the `revents` flag against.

Constant	Input to *events* ?	Result from *revents* ?	Description
POLLIN	•	•	normal or priority band data can be read
POLLRDNORM	•	•	normal data can be read
POLLRDBAND	•	•	priority band data can be read
POLLPRI	•	•	high-priority data can be read
POLLOUT	•	•	normal data can be written
POLLWRNORM	•	•	normal data can be written
POLLWRBAND	•	•	priority band data can be written
POLLERR		•	an error has occurred
POLLHUP		•	hangup has occurred
POLLNVAL		•	descriptor is not an open file

Figure 6.23 Input *events* and returned *revents* for `poll`.

We have divided this figure into three sections: the first four constants deal with input, the next three deal with output, and the final three deal with errors. Notice that the final three cannot be set in `events` but are always returned in `revents` when the corresponding condition exists.

There are three classes of data identified by `poll`: *normal*, *priority band*, and *high priority*. These terms come from the streams-based implementations (Figure 33.5).

> POLLIN can be defined as the logical OR of `POLLRDNORM` and `POLLRDBAND`. The `POLLIN` constant exists from SVR3 implementations that predated the priority bands in SVR4, so the constant remains for backward compatibility. Similarly, `POLLOUT` is equivalent to `POLLWRNORM`, with the former predating the latter.

With regard to TCP and UDP sockets, the following conditions cause `poll` to return the specified *revent*. Unfortunately, Posix.1g leaves many holes (i.e., optional ways to return the same condition) in its definition of `poll`.

- All regular TCP data and all UDP data is considered normal.
- TCP's out-of-band data (Chapter 21) is considered priority band.
- When the read-half of a TCP connection is closed (e.g., a FIN is received), this is also considered normal data and a subsequent read operation will return 0.

- The presence of an error for a TCP connection can be considered either normal data or an error (POLLERR). In either case, a subsequent read will return –1 with errno set to the appropriate value. This handles conditions such as the receipt of an RST or a timeout.

- The availability of a new connection on a listening socket can be considered either normal data or priority data. Most implementations consider this normal data.

The number of elements in the array of structures is specified by the *nfds* argument.

> Historically this argument has been an unsigned long, which seems excessive. An unsigned int would be adequate. Unix 98 defines a new datatype for this argument: nfds_t.

The *timeout* argument specifies how long the function is to wait before returning. A positive value specifies the number of milliseconds to wait. Figure 6.24 shows the possible values for the *timeout* argument.

timeout value	Description
INFTIM	wait forever
0	return immediately, do not block
> 0	wait specified number of milliseconds

Figure 6.24 *timeout* values for poll.

The constant INFTIM is defined to be a negative value. If the system does not provide a timer with millisecond accuracy, the value is rounded up to the nearest supported value.

> Posix.1g requires that INFTIM be defined by including <poll.h>, but many systems still define it in <sys/stropts.h>.

> As with select, any timeout set for poll is limited by the implementation's clock resolution (often 10 ms).

The return value from poll is –1 if an error occurred, 0 if no descriptors are ready before the timer expires, otherwise it is the number of descriptors that have a nonzero revents member.

If we are no longer interested in a particular descriptor, we just set the fd member of the pollfd structure to a negative value. Then the events member is ignored and the revents member is set to 0 on return.

Recall our discussion at the end of Section 6.3 about FD_SETSIZE and the maximum number of descriptors per descriptor set versus the maximum number of descriptors per process. We do not have that problem with poll since it is the caller's responsibility to allocate an array of pollfd structures and then tell the kernel the number of elements in the array. There is no fixed-size datatype similar to fd_set that the kernel knows about.

Posix.1g requires both `select` and `poll`. But from a portability perspective today, more systems support `select` than support `poll`. Also, Posix.1g defines `pselect`, an enhanced version of `select` that handles signal blocking and provides increased time resolution but defines nothing similar for `poll`.

6.11   TCP Echo Server (Revisited Again)

We now redo our TCP echo server from Section 6.8 using `poll` instead of `select`. In the previous version using `select` we had to allocate a `client` array along with a descriptor set named `rset` (Figure 6.15). With `poll` we must allocate an array of `pollfd` structures so we use it to maintain the client information, instead of allocating another array. We handle the `fd` member of this array the same way we handled the `client` array in Figure 6.15: a value of −1 means the entry is not in use; otherwise it is the descriptor value. Recall from the previous section that any entry in the array of `pollfd` structures passed to `poll` with a negative value for the `fd` member is just ignored.

Figure 6.25 shows the first half of our server.

———————————————————————————— *tcpcliserv/tcpservpoll01.c*

```
 1 #include    "unp.h"
 2 #include    <limits.h>            /* for OPEN_MAX */

 3 int
 4 main(int argc, char **argv)
 5 {
 6     int     i, maxi, listenfd, connfd, sockfd;
 7     int     nready;
 8     ssize_t n;
 9     char    line[MAXLINE];
10     socklen_t clilen;
11     struct pollfd client[OPEN_MAX];
12     struct sockaddr_in cliaddr, servaddr;

13     listenfd = Socket(AF_INET, SOCK_STREAM, 0);

14     bzero(&servaddr, sizeof(servaddr));
15     servaddr.sin_family = AF_INET;
16     servaddr.sin_addr.s_addr = htonl(INADDR_ANY);
17     servaddr.sin_port = htons(SERV_PORT);

18     Bind(listenfd, (SA *) &servaddr, sizeof(servaddr));

19     Listen(listenfd, LISTENQ);

20     client[0].fd = listenfd;
21     client[0].events = POLLRDNORM;
22     for (i = 1; i < OPEN_MAX; i++)
23         client[i].fd = -1;        /* -1 indicates available entry */
24     maxi = 0;                     /* max index into client[] array */
```

———————————————————————————— *tcpcliserv/tcpservpoll01.c*

Figure 6.25   First half of TCP server using `poll`.

Allocate array of `pollfd` structures

11   We declare OPEN_MAX elements in our array of pollfd structures. Determining the maximum number of descriptors that a process can have open at any one time is hard. We encounter this problem again in Figure 12.4. One way is to call the Posix.1 sysconf function with an argument of _SC_OPEN_MAX (as described on pp. 42–44 of APUE) and then dynamically allocate an array of the appropriate size. But one of the possible returns from sysconf is "indeterminate," meaning we still have to guess a value. Here we just use the Posix.1 OPEN_MAX constant.

Initialize

20-24   We use the first entry in the client array for the listening socket, and set the descriptor for the remaining entries to −1. We also set the POLLRDNORM event for this descriptor, to be notified by poll when a new connection is ready to be accepted. The variable maxi contains the largest index of the client array currently in use.

The second half of our function is shown in Figure 6.26.

Call `poll`; check for new connection

26-42   We call poll to wait for either a new connection or data on an existing connection. When a new connection is accepted, we find the first available entry in the client array by looking for the first one with a negative descriptor. Notice that we start the search with the index of 1, since client[0] is used for the listening socket. When an available entry is found, we save the descriptor and set the POLLRDNORM event.

Check for data on an existing connection

43-63   The two return events that we check for are POLLRDNORM and POLLERR. The second of these we did not set in the event member, because it is always returned when the condition is true. The reason we check for POLLERR is because some implementations return this event when an RST is received for a connection, while others just return POLLRDNORM. In either case we call readline and if an error has occurred, it will return an error. When an existing connection is terminated by the client, we just set the fd member to −1.

```
                                                      ——— tcpcliserv/tcpservpoll01.c
25      for ( ; ; ) {
26          nready = Poll(client, maxi + 1, INFTIM);

27          if (client[0].revents & POLLRDNORM) {   /* new client connection */
28              clilen = sizeof(cliaddr);
29              connfd = Accept(listenfd, (SA *) &cliaddr, &clilen);

30              for (i = 1; i < OPEN_MAX; i++)
31                  if (client[i].fd < 0) {
32                      client[i].fd = connfd;  /* save descriptor */
33                      break;
34                  }
35              if (i == OPEN_MAX)
36                  err_quit("too many clients");

37              client[i].events = POLLRDNORM;
38              if (i > maxi)
39                  maxi = i;        /* max index in client[] array */

40              if (--nready <= 0)
41                  continue;        /* no more readable descriptors */
42          }
43          for (i = 1; i <= maxi; i++) {   /* check all clients for data */
44              if ( (sockfd = client[i].fd) < 0)
45                  continue;
46              if (client[i].revents & (POLLRDNORM | POLLERR)) {
47                  if ( (n = readline(sockfd, line, MAXLINE)) < 0) {
48                      if (errno == ECONNRESET) {
49                              /* connection reset by client */
50                          Close(sockfd);
51                          client[i].fd = -1;
52                      } else
53                          err_sys("readline error");
54                  } else if (n == 0) {
55                          /* connection closed by client */
56                      Close(sockfd);
57                      client[i].fd = -1;
58                  } else
59                      Writen(sockfd, line, n);

60                  if (--nready <= 0)
61                      break;       /* no more readable descriptors */
62              }
63          }
64      }
65  }
                                                      ——— tcpcliserv/tcpservpoll01.c
```

Figure 6.26 Second half of TCP server using poll.

6.12 Summary

There are five different models for I/O provided by Unix:

- blocking,
- nonblocking,
- I/O multiplexing,
- signal-driven I/O, and
- asynchronous I/O.

The default is blocking I/O, which is also the most commonly used. We cover non-blocking I/O and signal-driven I/O in later chapters and have covered I/O multiplexing in this chapter. True asynchronous I/O is defined by Posix.1, but few implementations exist.

The most commonly used function for I/O multiplexing is `select`. We tell the function what descriptors we are interested in (for reading, writing, and exceptions), the maximum amount of time to wait, the maximum descriptor number (plus one). Most calls to `select` specify readability, and we noted that the only exception condition when dealing with sockets is the arrival of out-of-band data (Chapter 21). Since `select` provides a time limit on how long the function blocks, we will use this feature in Figure 13.3 to place a time limit on an input operation.

We used our echo client in a batch mode using `select` and discovered that even though the end of the user input is encountered, data can still be in the pipe to or from the server. To handle this scenario requires the `shutdown` function, and it lets us take advantage of TCP's half-close feature.

Posix.1g defines the new function `pselect`, which increases the time precision from microseconds to nanoseconds and takes a new argument that is a pointer to a signal set. This lets us avoid race conditions when signals are being caught and we talk more about this in Section 18.5.

The `poll` function from System V provides functionality similar to `select` and provides additional information on streams devices. Posix.1g requires both `select` and `poll`, but the former is used more often.

Exercises

6.1   We said that a descriptor set can be assigned to another descriptor set across an equals sign in C. How is this done if a descriptor set is an array of integers? (*Hint*: Look at your system's `<sys/select.h>` or `<sys/types.h>` header.)

6.2   When describing the conditions for which `select` returns "writable" in Section 6.3, why did we need the qualifier that the socket had to be nonblocking in order for a write operation to return a positive value?

6.3 What happens in Figure 6.9 if we prepend the word `else` before the word `if` on line 19?

6.4 In our example in Figure 6.21 add code to allow the server to be able to use as many descriptors as currently allowed by the kernel. (*Hint*: Look at the `setrlimit` function.)

6.5 Let's see what happens when the second argument to `shutdown` is `SHUT_RD`. Start with the TCP client in Figure 5.4 and make the following changes: change the port number from `SERV_PORT` to 19, the `chargen` server (Figure 2.13); replace the call to `str_cli` with a call to the `pause` function. Run this program specifying the IP address of a local host that runs the `chargen` server. Watch the packets with a tool such as `tcpdump` (Section C.5). What happens?

6.6 Why would an application call `shutdown` with an argument of `SHUT_RDWR`, instead of just calling `close`?

6.7 What happens in Figure 6.22 when the client sends an RST to terminate the connection?

6.8 Recode Figure 6.25 to call `sysconf` to determine the maximum number of descriptors and allocate the `client` array accordingly.

7

Socket Options

7.1 Introduction

There are various ways to get and set the options that affect a socket:

- the `getsockopt` and `setsockopt` functions,
- the `fcntl` function, and
- the `ioctl` function.

This chapter starts by covering the `setsockopt` and `getsockopt` functions, followed by an example that prints the default value of all the options, followed by a detailed description of all of the socket options. We divide the detailed descriptions into the following categories: generic, IPv4, IPv6, and TCP. This detailed coverage can be skipped during a first reading of this chapter, and the individual sections referred to when needed. A few options are discussed in detail in a later chapter, such as the IPv4 and IPv6 multicasting options, which we describe with multicasting in Section 19.5.

We also describe the `fcntl` function, because it is the Posix way to set a socket for nonblocking I/O, signal-driven I/O, and to set the owner of a socket. We save the `ioctl` function for Chapter 16.

7.2   `getsockopt` and `setsockopt` Functions

These two functions apply only to sockets.

```
#include <sys/socket.h>

int getsockopt(int sockfd, int level, int optname, void *optval, socklen_t *optlen);

int setsockopt(int sockfd, int level, int optname, const void *optval,
               socklen_t optlen);
```
Both return: 0 if OK, −1 on error

sockfd must refer to an open socket descriptor. The *level* specifies the code in the system to interpret the option: the general socket code, or some protocol-specific code (e.g., IPv4, IPv6, or TCP).

optval is a pointer to a variable from which the new value of the option is fetched by `setsockopt`, or into which the current value of the option is stored by `getsockopt`. The size of this variable is specified by the final argument, as a value for `setsockopt` and as a value–result for `getsockopt`.

Figure 7.1 summarizes the options that can be queried by `getsockopt` or set by `setsockopt`. The "Datatype" column shows the datatype of what the *optval* pointer must point to for each option. We use the notation of two braces to indicate a structure, as in `linger{}` to mean a `struct linger`.

There are two basic types of options: binary options that enable or disable a certain feature (flags), and options that fetch and return specific values that we can either set or examine (values). The column labeled "Flag" specifies if the option is a flag option. When calling `getsockopt` for these flag options, *optval* is an integer. The value returned in *optval* is zero if the option is disabled, or nonzero if the option is enabled. Similarly, `setsockopt` requires a nonzero *optval* to turn the option on, and a zero value to turn the option off. If the "Flag" column does not contain a "•" then the option is used to pass a value of the specified datatype between the user process and the system.

Following sections of this chapter give additional details on the options that affect a socket.

7.3   Checking If an Option Is Supported and Obtaining the Default

We now write a program to check whether most of the options defined in Figure 7.1 are supported, and if so, print their default value. Figure 7.2 contains the declarations for our program.

level	optname	get	set	Description	Flag	Datatype
SOL_SOCKET	SO_BROADCAST	•	•	permit sending of broadcast datagrams	•	int
	SO_DEBUG	•	•	enable debug tracing	•	int
	SO_DONTROUTE	•	•	bypass routing table lookup	•	int
	SO_ERROR	•		get pending error and clear		int
	SO_KEEPALIVE	•	•	periodically test if connection still alive	•	int
	SO_LINGER	•	•	linger on close if data to send		linger{}
	SO_OOBINLINE	•	•	leave received out-of-band data inline	•	int
	SO_RCVBUF	•	•	receive buffer size		int
	SO_SNDBUF	•	•	send buffer size		int
	SO_RCVLOWAT	•	•	receive buffer low-water mark		int
	SO_SNDLOWAT	•	•	send buffer low-water mark		int
	SO_RCVTIMEO	•	•	receive timeout		timeval{}
	SO_SNDTIMEO	•	•	send timeout		timeval{}
	SO_REUSEADDR	•	•	allow local address reuse	•	int
	SO_REUSEPORT	•	•	allow local address reuse	•	int
	SO_TYPE	•		get socket type		int
	SO_USELOOPBACK	•	•	routing socket gets copy of what it sends	•	int
IPPROTO_IP	IP_HDRINCL	•	•	IP header included with data	•	int
	IP_OPTIONS	•	•	IP header options		(see text)
	IP_RECVDSTADDR	•	•	return destination IP address	•	int
	IP_RECVIF	•	•	return received interface index	•	int
	IP_TOS	•	•	type-of-service and precedence		int
	IP_TTL	•	•	time-to-live		int
	IP_MULTICAST_IF	•	•	specify outgoing interface		in_addr{}
	IP_MULTICAST_TTL	•	•	specify outgoing TTL		u_char
	IP_MULTICAST_LOOP	•	•	specify loopback		u_char
	IP_ADD_MEMBERSHIP		•	join a multicast group		ip_mreq{}
	IP_DROP_MEMBERSHIP		•	leave a multicast group		ip_mreq{}
IPPROTO_ICMPV6	ICMP6_FILTER	•	•	specify ICMPv6 message types to pass		icmp6_filter{}
IPPROTO_IPV6	IPV6_ADDRFORM	•	•	change address format of socket		int
	IPV6_CHECKSUM	•	•	offset of checksum field for raw sockets		int
	IPV6_DSTOPTS	•	•	receive destination options	•	int
	IPV6_HOPLIMIT	•	•	receive unicast hop limit	•	int
	IPV6_HOPOPTS	•	•	receive hop-by-hop options	•	int
	IPV6_NEXTHOP	•	•	specify next-hop address	•	sockaddr{}
	IPV6_PKTINFO	•	•	receive packet information	•	int
	IPV6_PKTOPTIONS	•	•	specify packet options		(see text)
	IPV6_RTHDR	•	•	receive source route	•	int
	IPV6_UNICAST_HOPS	•	•	default unicast hop limit		int
	IPV6_MULTICAST_IF	•	•	specify outgoing interface		in6_addr{}
	IPV6_MULTICAST_HOPS	•	•	specify outgoing hop limit		u_int
	IPV6_MULTICAST_LOOP	•	•	specify loopback	•	u_int
	IPV6_ADD_MEMBERSHIP		•	join a multicast group		ipv6_mreq{}
	IPV6_DROP_MEMBERSHIP		•	leave a multicast group		ipv6_mreq{}
IPPROTO_TCP	TCP_KEEPALIVE	•	•	seconds between keepalive probes		int
	TCP_MAXRT	•	•	TCP maximum retransmit time		int
	TCP_MAXSEG	•	•	TCP maximum segment size		int
	TCP_NODELAY	•	•	disable Nagle algorithm	•	int
	TCP_STDURG	•	•	interpretation of urgent pointer	•	int

Figure 7.1 Summary of socket options for getsockopt and setsockopt.

——— sockopt/checkopts.c

```
 1 #include      "unp.h"
 2 #include      <netinet/tcp.h>      /* for TCP_xxx defines */

 3 union val {
 4   int             i_val;
 5   long            l_val;
 6   char            c_val[10];
 7   struct linger   linger_val;
 8   struct timeval  timeval_val;
 9 } val;

10 static char *sock_str_flag(union val *, int);
11 static char *sock_str_int(union val *, int);
12 static char *sock_str_linger(union val *, int);
13 static char *sock_str_timeval(union val *, int);

14 struct sock_opts {
15   char     *opt_str;
16   int       opt_level;
17   int       opt_name;
18   char     *(*opt_val_str)(union val *, int);
19 } sock_opts[] = {
20     "SO_BROADCAST",     SOL_SOCKET, SO_BROADCAST,     sock_str_flag,
21     "SO_DEBUG",         SOL_SOCKET, SO_DEBUG,         sock_str_flag,
22     "SO_DONTROUTE",     SOL_SOCKET, SO_DONTROUTE,     sock_str_flag,
23     "SO_ERROR",         SOL_SOCKET, SO_ERROR,         sock_str_int,
24     "SO_KEEPALIVE",     SOL_SOCKET, SO_KEEPALIVE,     sock_str_flag,
25     "SO_LINGER",        SOL_SOCKET, SO_LINGER,        sock_str_linger,
26     "SO_OOBINLINE",     SOL_SOCKET, SO_OOBINLINE,     sock_str_flag,
27     "SO_RCVBUF",        SOL_SOCKET, SO_RCVBUF,        sock_str_int,
28     "SO_SNDBUF",        SOL_SOCKET, SO_SNDBUF,        sock_str_int,
29     "SO_RCVLOWAT",      SOL_SOCKET, SO_RCVLOWAT,      sock_str_int,
30     "SO_SNDLOWAT",      SOL_SOCKET, SO_SNDLOWAT,      sock_str_int,
31     "SO_RCVTIMEO",      SOL_SOCKET, SO_RCVTIMEO,      sock_str_timeval,
32     "SO_SNDTIMEO",      SOL_SOCKET, SO_SNDTIMEO,      sock_str_timeval,
33     "SO_REUSEADDR",     SOL_SOCKET, SO_REUSEADDR,     sock_str_flag,
34 #ifdef  SO_REUSEPORT
35     "SO_REUSEPORT",     SOL_SOCKET, SO_REUSEPORT,     sock_str_flag,
36 #else
37     "SO_REUSEPORT",     0,          0,                NULL,
38 #endif
39     "SO_TYPE",          SOL_SOCKET, SO_TYPE,          sock_str_int,
40     "SO_USELOOPBACK",   SOL_SOCKET, SO_USELOOPBACK,   sock_str_flag,
41     "IP_TOS",           IPPROTO_IP, IP_TOS,           sock_str_int,
42     "IP_TTL",           IPPROTO_IP, IP_TTL,           sock_str_int,
43     "TCP_MAXSEG",       IPPROTO_TCP,TCP_MAXSEG,       sock_str_int,
44     "TCP_NODELAY",      IPPROTO_TCP,TCP_NODELAY,      sock_str_flag,
45     NULL,               0,          0,                NULL
46 };
```

——— sockopt/checkopts.c

Figure 7.2 Declarations for our program to check the socket options.

Declare `union` of possible values

3-9   Our `union` contains one member for each possible return value from `getsockopt`.

Define function prototypes

10-13   We define function prototypes for four functions that are called to print the value for a given socket option.

Define structure and initialize array

14-46   Our `sock_opts` structure contains all the information necessary to call `getsockopt` for each socket option and then print its current value. The final member, `opt_val_str`, is a pointer to one of our four functions that will print the option value. We allocate and initialize an array of these structures, one element for each socket option.

> Not all implementations support all socket options. The way to determine if a given option is supported is to use an `#ifdef` or a `#if defined`, as we show for `SO_REUSEPORT`. For completeness *every* element of the array should be compiled similar to what we show for `SO_REUSEPORT`, but we omit these because the `#ifdef`s just lengthen the code that we show and add nothing to the discussion.

Figure 7.3 shows our `main` function.

——————————————————————————————— sockopt/checkopts.c
```
47 int
48 main(int argc, char **argv)
49 {
50     int     fd, len;
51     struct sock_opts *ptr;

52     fd = Socket(AF_INET, SOCK_STREAM, 0);

53     for (ptr = sock_opts; ptr->opt_str != NULL; ptr++) {
54         printf("%s: ", ptr->opt_str);
55         if (ptr->opt_val_str == NULL)
56             printf("(undefined)\n");
57         else {
58             len = sizeof(val);
59             if (getsockopt(fd, ptr->opt_level, ptr->opt_name,
60                            &val, &len) == -1) {
61                 err_ret("getsockopt error");
62             } else {
63                 printf("default = %s\n", (*ptr->opt_val_str) (&val, len));
64             }
65         }
66     }
67     exit(0);
68 }
```
——————————————————————————————— sockopt/checkopts.c

Figure 7.3 `main` function to check all socket options.

Create TCP socket, go through all options

52–56   We create a TCP socket and then go through all elements in our array. If the `opt_val_str` pointer is null, the option is not defined by the implementation (which we showed is possible for `SO_REUSEPORT`).

Call `getsockopt`

57–61   We call `getsockopt` but do not terminate if an error is returned. Many implementations define some of the socket option names even though they do not support the option. Unsupported options should elicit an error of `ENOPROTOOPT`.

Print option's default value

62–63   If `getsockopt` returns success, we call our function to convert the option value to a string, and print the string.

In Figure 7.2 we showed four function prototypes, one for each type of option value that is returned. Figure 7.4 shows one of these four functions, `sock_str_flag`, which prints the value of a flag option. The other three functions are similar.

```
                                                                     ———— sockopt/checkopts.c
69 static char strres[128];

70 static char *
71 sock_str_flag(union val *ptr, int len)
72 {
73     if (len != sizeof(int))
74         snprintf(strres, sizeof(strres), "size (%d) not sizeof(int)", len);
75     else
76         snprintf(strres, sizeof(strres),
77                 "%s", (ptr->i_val == 0) ? "off" : "on");
78     return(strres);

79 }
                                                                     ———— sockopt/checkopts.c
```

Figure 7.4 `sock_str_flag` function: convert flag option to a string.

73–78   Recall that the final argument to `getsockopt` is a value–result argument. The first check we make is that the size of the value returned by `getsockopt` is the expected size. The string returned is `off` or `on`, depending whether the value of the flag option is 0 or nonzero, respectively.

Running this program under AIX 4.2 gives the following output:

```
aix % checkopts
SO_BROADCAST: default = off
SO_DEBUG: default = off
SO_DONTROUTE: default = off
SO_ERROR: default = 0
SO_KEEPALIVE: default = off
SO_LINGER: default = l_onoff = 0, l_linger = 0
SO_OOBINLINE: default = off
SO_RCVBUF: default = 16384
SO_SNDBUF: default = 16384
```

```
SO_RCVLOWAT: default = 1
SO_SNDLOWAT: default = 4096
SO_RCVTIMEO: default = 0 sec, 0 usec
SO_SNDTIMEO: default = 0 sec, 0 usec
SO_REUSEADDR: default = off
SO_REUSEPORT: (undefined)
SO_TYPE: default = 1
SO_USELOOPBACK: default = off
IP_TOS: default = 0
IP_TTL: default = 60
TCP_MAXSEG: default = 512
TCP_NODELAY: default = off
```

The value of 1 returned for the SO_TYPE option corresponds to SOCK_STREAM for this implementation.

7.4   Socket States

For some socket options there are timing considerations about when to set or fetch the option versus the state of the socket. We mention these with the affected options.

The following socket options are inherited by a connected TCP socket from the listening socket (pp. 462–463 of TCPv2): SO_DEBUG, SO_DONTROUTE, SO_KEEPALIVE, SO_LINGER, SO_OOBINLINE, SO_RCVBUF, and SO_SNDBUF. This is important with TCP because the connected socket is not returned to a server by accept until the three-way handshake is completed by the TCP layer. If we want to ensure that one of these socket options is set for the connected socket when the three-way handshake completes, we must set that option for the listening socket.

7.5   Generic Socket Options

We start with a discussion of the generic socket options. These options are protocol independent (that is, they are handled by the protocol-independent code within the kernel, not by one particular protocol module such as IPv4), but some of the options apply to only certain types of sockets. For example, even though the SO_BROADCAST socket option is called "generic," it applies only to datagram sockets.

SO_BROADCAST Socket Option

This option enables or disables the ability of the process to send broadcast messages. Broadcasting is supported for only datagram sockets and only on networks that support the concept of a broadcast message (e.g., Ethernet, token ring, etc.). You cannot broadcast on a point-to-point link. We talk more about broadcasting in Chapter 18.

Since an application must set this socket option before sending a broadcast datagram, it prevents a process from sending a broadcast when the application was never designed to broadcast. For example, a UDP application might take the destination IP address as a command-line argument, but the application never intended for a user to type in a broadcast address. Rather than forcing the application to try to determine if a given address is a broadcast address or not, the test is in the kernel: if the destination address is a broadcast address and this socket option is not set, EACCES is returned (p. 233 of TCPv2).

SO_DEBUG Socket Option

This option is supported only by TCP. When enabled for a TCP socket, the kernel keeps track of detailed information about all the packets sent or received by TCP for the socket. These are kept in a circular buffer within the kernel that can be examined with the trpt program. Pages 916–920 of TCPv2 provide additional details and an example that uses this option.

SO_DONTROUTE Socket Option

This option specifies that outgoing packets are to bypass the normal routing mechanisms of the underlying protocol. For example, with IPv4, the packet is directed to the appropriate local interface, as specified by the network and subnet portions of the destination address. If the local interface cannot be determined from the destination address (e.g., the destination is not on the other end of a point-to-point link, or not on a shared network), ENETUNREACH is returned.

The equivalent of this option can also be applied to individual datagrams using the MSG_DONTROUTE flag with the send, sendto, or sendmsg functions.

This option is often used by the routing daemons (routed and gated) to bypass the routing table (in case the routing table is incorrect) and force a packet to be sent out a particular interface.

SO_ERROR Socket Option

When an error occurs on a socket, the protocol module in a Berkeley-derived kernel sets a variable named so_error for that socket to one of the standard Unix E*xxx* values. This is called the *pending error* for the socket. The process can be immediately notified of the error in one of two ways.

1. If the process is blocked in a call to select on the socket (Section 6.3), for either readability or writability, select returns with either or both conditions set.

2. If the process is using signal-driven I/O (Chapter 22), the SIGIO signal is generated for either the process or the process group.

The process can then obtain the value of so_error by fetching the SO_ERROR socket option. The integer value returned by getsockopt is the pending error for the socket. The value of so_error is then reset to 0 by the kernel (p. 547 of TCPv2).

If so_error is nonzero when the process calls read and there is no data to return, read returns −1 with errno set to the value of so_error (p. 516 of TCPv2). The value of `so_error` is then reset to 0. If there is data queued for the socket, that data is returned by `read` instead of the error condition. If `so_error` is nonzero when the process calls `write`, −1 is returned with `errno` set to the value of `so_error` (p. 495 of TCPv2) and `so_error` is reset to 0.

> There is a bug in the code shown on p. 495 of TCPv2, in that `so_error` is not reset to 0. This has been fixed in the BSD/OS release. Anytime the pending error for a socket is returned, it must be reset to 0.

This is the first socket option that we have encountered that can be fetched but cannot be set.

`SO_KEEPALIVE` Socket Option

When the keepalive option is set for a TCP socket and no data has been exchanged across the socket in either direction for 2 hours, TCP automatically sends a *keepalive probe* to the peer. This probe is a TCP segment to which the peer must respond. One of three scenarios results.

1. The peer responds with the expected ACK. The application is not notified (since everything is OK). TCP will send another probe following another 2 hours of inactivity.

2. The peer responds with an RST, which tells the local TCP that the peer host has crashed and rebooted. The socket's pending error is set to `ECONNRESET` and the socket is closed.

3. There is no response from the peer to the keepalive probe. Berkeley-derived TCPs send eight additional probes, 75 seconds apart, trying to elicit a response. TCP will give up if there is no response within 11 minutes and 15 seconds after sending the first probe. If there is no response at all to TCP's keepalive probes, the socket's pending error is set to `ETIMEDOUT` and the socket is closed. But if the socket receives an ICMP error in response to one of the keepalive probes, the corresponding error (Figures A.15 and A.16) is returned instead (and the socket is still closed). A common ICMP error in this scenario is "host unreachable," indicating that the peer host has not crashed but is just unreachable, in which case the pending error is set to `EHOSTUNREACH`.

Chapter 23 of TCPv1 and pp. 828–831 of TCPv2 contain additional details on the keepalive option.

Undoubtedly the most common question regarding this option is whether the timing parameters can be modified (usually to reduce the 2-hour period of inactivity to some shorter value). We describe the new Posix.1g `TCP_KEEPALIVE` option in Section 7.9, but this is not widely implemented. Appendix E of TCPv1 discusses how to change these timing parameters for various kernels, but be aware that most kernels maintain these parameters on a per-kernel basis, not on a per-socket basis, so changing the inactivity period from 2 hours to 15 minutes, for example, will affect *all* sockets on the host that enable this option.

The purpose of this option is to detect if the peer *host* crashes. If the peer *process* crashes, its TCP will send a FIN across the connection, which we can easily detect with `select`. (This was why we used `select` in Section 6.4.) Also realize that if there is no response to any of the keepalive probes (scenario 3), we are not guaranteed that the peer host has crashed, and TCP may well terminate a valid connection. It could be that some intermediate router has crashed for 15 minutes, and that period of time just happens to completely overlap our host's 11-minute and 15-second keepalive probe period.

This option is normally used by servers, although clients can also use the option. Servers use the option because they spend most of their time blocked waiting for input across the TCP connection, that is, waiting for a client request. But if the client host crashes, the server process will never know about it, and the server will continually wait for input that can never arrive. This is called a *half-open connection*. The keepalive option will detect these half-open connections and terminate them.

> Most Rlogin and Telnet servers set this option to terminate the connection if the interactive client hangs up the phone line or powers off the terminal (for example) without logging out.

> Some servers, notably FTP servers, provide an application timeout, often on the order of minutes. This is done by the application itself, normally around a call to `read`, reading the next client command. This timeout does not involve this socket option.

Figure 7.5 summarizes the various methods that we have to detect when something happens on the other end of a TCP connection. When we say "using `select` for readability" we mean calling `select` to test whether the socket is readable.

Scenario	Peer process crashes	Peer host crashes	Peer host is unreachable
Our TCP is actively sending data	Peer TCP sends a FIN, which we can detect immediately using `select` for readability. If TCP sends another segment, peer TCP responds with RST. If TCP sends yet another segment, our TCP sends us `SIGPIPE`.	Our TCP will time out and our socket's pending error is set to `ETIMEDOUT`.	Our TCP will time out and our socket's pending error is set to `EHOSTUNREACH`.
Our TCP is actively receiving data	Peer TCP will send a FIN, which we will read as a (possibly premature) end-of-file.	We will stop receiving data.	We will stop receiving data.
Connection is idle, keepalive set	Peer TCP sends a FIN, which we can detect immediately using `select` for readability.	Nine keepalive probes are sent after 2 hours of inactivity and then our socket's pending error is set to `ETIMEDOUT`.	Nine keepalive probes are sent after 2 hours of inactivity and then our socket's pending error is set to `EHOSTUNREACH`.
Connection is idle, keepalive not set	Peer TCP sends a FIN, which we can detect immediately using `select` for readability.	(Nothing.)	(Nothing.)

Figure 7.5 Ways to detect various TCP conditions.

SO_LINGER **Socket Option**

This option specifies how the close function operates for a connection-oriented proto-col (e.g., for TCP but not for UDP). By default, close returns immediately, but if there is any data still remaining in the socket send buffer, the system will try to deliver the data to the peer.

The SO_LINGER socket option lets us change this default. This option requires the following structure to be passed between the user process and the kernel. It is defined by including <sys/socket.h>.

```
struct linger {
    int    l_onoff;    /* 0=off, nonzero=on */
    int    l_linger;   /* linger time, Posix.1g specifies units as seconds */
};
```

Calling setsockopt leads to one of the following three scenarios depending on the values of the two structure members.

1. If l_onoff is 0, the option is turned off. The value of l_linger is ignored and the previously discussed TCP default applies: close returns immediately.

2. If l_onoff is nonzero and l_linger is 0, TCP aborts the connection when it is closed (pp. 1019–1020 of TCPv2). That is, TCP discards any data still remaining in the socket send buffer and sends an RST to the peer, not the normal four-packet connection termination sequence (Section 2.5). We show an example of this in Figure 15.21. This avoids TCP's TIME_WAIT state, but in doing so leaves open the possibility of another incarnation of this connection being created within 2MSL seconds and having old duplicate segments from the just-terminated connection being incorrectly delivered to the new incarnation (Section 2.6).

    > Some implementations, notably Solaris 2.x where x ≤ 5, do not implement this feature of the SO_LINGER option.

    > Occasional Usenet postings advocate the use of this feature just to avoid the TIME_WAIT state and to be able to restart a listening server even if connections are still in use with the server's well-known port. This should not be done and could lead to data corruption, as detailed in RFC 1337 [Braden 1992a]. Instead, the SO_REUSEADDR socket option should always be used in the server before the call to bind, as we describe shortly. The TIME_WAIT state is our friend and is there to help us (i.e., to let old duplicate segments expire in the network). Instead of trying to avoid the state, we should understand it (Section 2.6).

3. If l_onoff is nonzero and l_linger is nonzero, then the kernel will *linger* when the socket is closed (p. 472 of TCPv2). That is, if there is any data still remaining in the socket send buffer, the process is put to sleep until either (a) all the data is sent and acknowledged by the peer TCP, or (b) the linger time expires. If the socket has been set nonblocking (Chapter 15), it will not wait for the close to complete, even if the linger time is nonzero.

When using this feature of the SO_LINGER option it is important for the application to check the return value from close, because if the linger time expires before the remaining data is sent and acknowledged, close returns EWOULDBLOCK and any remaining data in the send buffer is discarded.

> Unfortunately the interpretation of a nonzero l_linger member in the third case is implementation dependent. 4.4BSD assumes the units are clock ticks (one-hundreds of a second) but Posix.1g specifies the units as seconds. Another problem with existing Berkeley-derived implementations is that the l_linger member (an int) is copied into a kernel variable (so_linger) that is a 16-bit signed integer, limiting the linger time to 32767 clock ticks, or 32.767 seconds.

We now need to see exactly when a close on a socket returns, given the various scenarios that we have looked at. We assume that the client writes data to the socket and then calls close. Figure 7.6 shows the default situation.

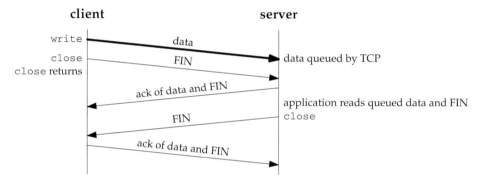

Figure 7.6 Default operation of close: it returns immediately.

We assume that when the client's data arrives, the server is temporarily busy, so the data is added to the socket receive buffer by its TCP. Similarly the next segment, the client's FIN, is also added to the socket receive buffer (in whatever manner the implementation records that a FIN has been received on the connection). But by default the client's close returns immediately. As we show in this scenario, the client's close can return before the server reads the remaining data in its socket receive buffer. It is possible for the server host to crash before the server application reads this remaining data, and the client application will never know.

The client can set the SO_LINGER socket option, specifying some positive linger time. When this occurs, the client's close does not return until all the client's data and its FIN have been acknowledged by the server TCP. We show this in Figure 7.7. But we still have the same problem as in Figure 7.6: the server host can crash before the server application reads its remaining data, and the client application will never know.

The basic principle here is that a successful return from close, with the SO_LINGER socket option set, only tells us that the data we sent (and our FIN) have been acknowledged by the peer TCP. This does *not* tell us whether the peer application

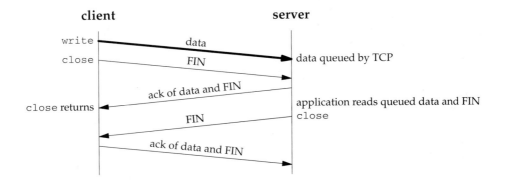

Figure 7.7   `close` with `SO_LINGER` socket option set and `l_linger` a positive value.

has read the data. If we do not set the `SO_LINGER` socket option, we do not know whether the peer TCP has acknowledged the data.

One way for the client to know that the server has read its data is to call `shutdown` (with a second argument of `SHUT_WR`) instead of `close` and wait for the peer to `close` its end of the connection. We show this scenario in Figure 7.8.

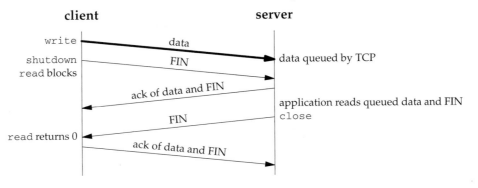

Figure 7.8   Using `shutdown` to know that peer has received our data.

Comparing this figure to Figures 7.6 and 7.7 we see that when we close our end of the connection, depending on the function called (`close` or `shutdown`) and whether the `SO_LINGER` socket option is set, the return can occur at three different times:

1. `close` returns immediately, without waiting at all (the default; Figure 7.6),

2. `close` lingers until the ACK of our FIN is received (Figure 7.7), or

3. `shutdown` followed by a `read` waits until we receive the peer's FIN (Figure 7.8).

Another way to know that the peer application has read our data is to use an *application-level acknowledgment* or *application ACK*. For example, the client sends its data to the server and then calls `read` for 1 byte of data:

```
char  ack;

Write(sockfd, data, nbytes);      /* data from client to server */
n = Read(sockfd, &ack, 1);        /* wait for application-level ACK */
```

The server reads the data from the client and then sends back the 1-byte application-level ACK:

```
nbytes = Read(sockfd, buff, sizeof(buff));  /* data from client */
        /* server verifies it received the correct
           amount of data from the client */
Write(sockfd, "", 1);             /* server's ACK back to client */
```

We are guaranteed that when the `read` in the client returns, the server process has read the data that we sent. (This assumes that either the server knows how much data the client is sending, or there is some application-defined end-of-record marker, which we do not show here.) Here the application-level ACK is a byte of 0, but the contents of this byte could be used to signal other conditions from the server to the client. Figure 7.9 shows the possible packet exchange.

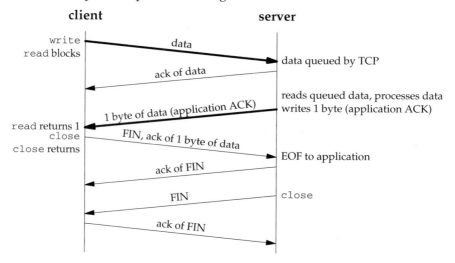

Figure 7.9 Application ACK.

Figure 7.10 summarizes the two possible calls to `shutdown` and the three possible calls to `close`, and the effect on a TCP socket.

Function	Description
`shutdown, SHUT_RD`	No more receives can be issued on socket; process can still send on socket; socket receive buffer discarded; any further data received is discarded by TCP (Exercise 6.5); no effect on socket send buffer.
`shutdown, SHUT_WR`	No more sends can be issued on socket; process can still receive on socket; contents of socket send buffer sent to other end, followed by normal TCP connection termination (FIN); no effect on socket receive buffer.
`close, l_onoff = 0` (default)	No more receives or sends can be issued on socket; contents of socket send buffer sent to other end. If descriptor reference count becomes 0: normal TCP connection termination (FIN) sent following data in send buffer and socket receive buffer discarded.
`close, l_onoff = 1` `l_linger = 0`	No more receives or sends can be issued on socket. If descriptor reference count becomes 0: RST sent to other end, connection state set to CLOSED (no TIME_WAIT state), socket send buffer and socket receive buffer discarded.
`close, l_onoff = 1` `l_linger != 0`	No more receives or sends can be issued on socket; contents of socket send buffer sent to other end. If descriptor reference count becomes 0: normal TCP connection termination (FIN) sent following data in send buffer, socket receive buffer discarded, and if linger time expires before connection CLOSED, `close` returns EWOULDBLOCK.

Figure 7.10 Summary of `shutdown` and `SO_LINGER` scenarios.

`SO_OOBINLINE` Socket Option

When this option is set, out-of-band data will be placed in the normal input queue (i.e., inline). When this occurs, the `MSG_OOB` flag to the receive functions cannot be used to read the out-of-band data. We discuss out-of-band data in more detail in Chapter 21.

`SO_RCVBUF` and `SO_SNDBUF` Socket Options

Every socket has a send buffer and a receive buffer. We described the operation of the send buffers with TCP and UDP in Figures 2.11 and 2.12.

The receive buffers are used by TCP and UDP to hold received data until it is read by the application. With TCP, the available room in the socket receive buffer is the window that TCP advertises to the other end. The TCP socket receive buffer cannot overflow because the peer is not allowed to send data beyond the advertised window. This is TCP's flow control and if the peer ignores the advertised window and sends data beyond the window, the receiving TCP discards it. With UDP, however, when a datagram arrives that will not fit in the socket receive buffer, that datagram is discarded. Recall that UDP has no flow control: it is easy for a fast sender to overwhelm a slower receiver, causing datagrams to be discarded by the receiver's UDP, as we show in Section 8.13.

These two socket options let us change the default sizes. The default values differ widely between implementations. Older Berkeley-derived implementations would default the TCP send and receive buffers to 4096 bytes, but newer systems use larger values, anywhere from 8192 to 61440 bytes. The UDP send buffer size often defaults to a value around 9000 bytes if the host supports NFS, and the UDP receive buffer size often defaults to a value around 40000 bytes.

When setting the size of the TCP socket receive buffer, the ordering of the function calls is important. This is because of TCP's window scale option (Section 2.5), which is exchanged with the peer on the SYN segments when the connection is established. For a client, this means the SO_RCVBUF socket option must be set before calling connect. For a server, this means the socket option must be set for the listening socket before calling listen. Setting this option for the connected socket will have no effect whatsoever on the possible window scale option because accept does not return with the connected socket until TCP's three-way handshake is complete. That is why this option must be set for the listening socket. (The sizes of the socket buffers are always inherited from the listening socket by the newly created connected socket: pp. 462–463 of TCPv2.)

The TCP socket buffer sizes should be at least three times the MSS for the connection. If we are dealing with unidirectional data transfer, such as a file transfer in one direction, when we say "socket buffer sizes" we mean the socket send buffer size on the sending host and the socket receive buffer size on the receiving host. For bidirectional data transfer, we mean both socket buffer sizes on the sender and both socket buffer sizes on the receiver. With typical default buffer sizes of 8192 bytes or larger, and a typical MSS of 512 or 1460, this requirement is normally met. The problem has been seen on networks with large MTUs, which then provide a larger than normal MSS (e.g., ATM networks with an MTU of 9188 as described in [Comer and Lin 1994]).

The TCP socket buffer sizes should also be an even multiple of the MSS for the connection. Some implementations handle this detail for the application, rounding up the socket buffer size after the connection is established (p. 902 of TCPv2). This is another reason to set these two socket options before establishing a connection. For example, using the default 4.4BSD sizes of 8192 and assuming an Ethernet with an MSS of 1460, both socket buffers are rounded up to 8760 (6 × 1460) when the connection is established.

Another consideration in setting the socket buffer sizes deals with performance. Figure 7.11 shows a TCP connection between two endpoints (which we call a *pipe*) with a capacity of eight segments.

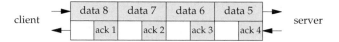

Figure 7.11 TCP connection (pipe) with a capacity of eight segments.

We show four data segments on the top, and four ACKs on the bottom. Even though there are only four segments of data in the pipe, the client must have a send buffer capacity of at least eight segments, because the client TCP must keep a copy of each segment until the ACK is received from the server.

> We are ignoring some details here. First, TCP's slow start algorithm limits the rate at which segments are initially sent on an idle connection. Next, TCP often acknowledges every other segment, not every segment as we show. All these details are covered in Chapters 20 and 24 of TCPv1.

What is important to understand is the concept of the full-duplex pipe, its capacity, and how that relates to the socket buffer sizes on both ends of the connection. The capacity of the pipe is called the *bandwidth-delay product* and we calculate this by multiplying the bandwidth (in bits/sec) times the RTT (round-trip time, in seconds), converting the result from bits to bytes. The RTT is easily measured with the Ping program. The bandwidth is the value corresponding to the slowest link between the two endpoints and must somehow be known. For example, a T1 line (1,536,000 bits/sec) with an RTT of 60 ms gives a bandwidth-delay product of 11,520 bytes. If the socket buffer sizes are less than this, the pipe will not stay full, and the performance will be less than expected. Large socket buffers are required when the bandwidth gets faster (e.g., T3 lines at 45 Mbits/sec) or when the RTT gets large (e.g., satellite links with an RTT around 500 ms). When the bandwidth-delay product exceeds TCP's maximum normal window size (65535 bytes), both endpoints also need the TCP *long fat pipe* options that we mentioned in Section 2.5.

> Most implementations have an upper limit for the sizes of the socket send and receive buffers, and sometimes this limit can be modified by the administrator. Older Berkeley-derived implementations had a hard upper limit of around 52,000 bytes, but newer implementations have a default limit of 256,000 bytes or more, and this can usually be increased by the administrator. Unfortunately there is no simple way for an application to determine this limit. Posix.1 defines the fpathconf function, which most implementations support, and Posix.1g defines a new constant that can be used as the second argument to this function, _PC_SOCK_MAXBUF, which returns the maximum size of the socket buffers.

SO_RCVLOWAT and SO_SNDLOWAT Socket Options

Every socket also has a receive low-water mark and a send low-water mark. These are used by the select function, as we described in Section 6.3. These two socket options let us change these two low-water marks.

The receive low-water mark is the amount of data that must be in the socket receive buffer for select to return "readable." It defaults to 1 for a TCP and UDP sockets. The send low-water mark is the amount of available space that must exist in the socket send buffer for select to return "writable." This low-water mark normally defaults to 2048 for TCP sockets. With UDP the low-water mark is used, as we described in Section 6.3, but since the number of bytes of available space in the send buffer for a UDP socket never changes (since UDP does not keep a copy of the datagrams sent by the application), as long as the UDP socket send buffer size is greater than the socket's low-water mark, the UDP socket is always writable. Recall from Figure 2.12 that UDP does not have a send buffer it has only a send buffer size.

> Posix.1g does not require support for these two socket options.

SO_RCVTIMEO and SO_SNDTIMEO Socket Options

These two socket options allow us to place a timeout on socket receives and sends. Notice that the argument to the two sockopt functions is a pointer to a timeval structure, the same one used with select (Section 6.3). This lets us specify the timeouts in seconds and microseconds. We disable a timeout by setting its value to 0 seconds and 0 microseconds. Both timeouts are disabled by default.

The receive timeout affects the five input functions: `read`, `readv`, `recv`, `recvfrom`, and `recvmsg`. The send timeout affects the five output functions: `write`, `writev`, `send`, `sendto`, and `sendmsg`. We talk more about socket timeouts in Section 13.2.

> These two socket options and the concept of inherent timeouts on socket receives and sends were added with 4.3BSD Reno. Posix.1g does not require support for these two socket options.
>
> In Berkeley-derived implementations these two values really implement an inactivity timer and not an absolute timer on the read or write system call. Pages 496 and 516 ot TCPv2 talk about this in more detail.

SO_REUSEADDR and SO_REUSEPORT Socket Options

The SO_REUSEADDR socket option serves four different purposes.

1. SO_REUSEADDR allows a listening server to start and `bind` its well-known port even if previously established connections exist that use this port as their local port. This condition is typically encountered as follows:

    (a) A listening server is started.

    (b) A connection request arrives and a child process is spawned to handle that client.

    (c) The listening server terminates but the child continues to service the client on the existing connection.

    (d) The listening server is restarted.

    By default, when the listening server is restarted in (d) by calling `socket`, `bind`, and `listen`, the call to `bind` fails because the listening server is trying to bind a port that is part of an existing connection (the one being handled by the previously spawned child). But if the server sets the SO_REUSEADDR socket option between the calls to `socket` and `bind`, the latter function will succeed. *All* TCP servers should specify this socket option to allow the server to be restarted in this situation.

    > This scenario is one of the most frequently asked questions on Usenet.

2. SO_REUSEADDR allows multiple instances of the same server to be started on the same port, as long as each instance binds a different local IP address. This is common for a site hosting multiple HTTP servers using the IP alias technique (Section A.4). Assume the local host's primary IP address is 198.69.10.2 but it has two aliases of 198.69.10.128 and 198.69.10.129. Three HTTP servers are started. The first HTTP server would call `bind` with a local IP address of 198.69.10.128 and a local port of 80 (the well-known port for HTTP). The second

server would `bind` 198.69.10.129 and port 80. But this second call to `bind` fails unless `SO_REUSEADDR` is set before the call. The third server would call `bind` with the wildcard as the local IP address and a local port of 80. Again, `SO_REUSEADDR` is required for this final call to succeed. Assuming `SO_REUSEADDR` is set and the three servers are started, incoming TCP connection requests with a destination IP address of 198.69.10.128 and a destination port of 80 are delivered to the first server, incoming requests with a destination IP address of 198.69.10.129 and a destination port of 80 are delivered to the second server, and all other TCP connection requests with a destination port of 80 are delivered to the third server. This final server handles requests destined for 198.69.10.2 in addition to any other IP aliases that the host may have configured. The wildcard means "everything that doesn't have a better (more specific) match." Note that this scenario of allowing multiple servers for a given service is handled automatically if the server always sets the `SO_REUSEADDR` socket option (as we recommend).

With TCP we are never able to start multiple servers that `bind` the same IP address and the same port: a *completely duplicate binding*. That is, we cannot start one server that binds 198.69.10.2 port 80 and start another that also binds 198.69.10.2 port 80, even if we set the `SO_REUSEADDR` socket option for the second server.

3. `SO_REUSEADDR` allows a single process to bind the same port to multiple sockets, as long as each bind specifies a different local IP address. This is common for UDP servers that need to know the destination IP address of client requests on systems that do not provide the `IP_RECVDSTADDR` socket option, and we develop an example using this technique in Section 19.11. This technique is normally not used with TCP servers since a TCP server can always determine the destination IP address by calling `getsockname` after the connection is established.

4. `SO_REUSEADDR` allows *completely duplicate bindings*: a `bind` of an IP address and port, when that same IP address and port are already bound to another socket. Normally this feature is supported only on systems that support multicasting, when that system does not support the `SO_REUSEPORT` socket option (which we describe shortly), and only for UDP sockets (multicasting does not work with TCP).

    This feature is used with multicasting to allow the same application to be run multiple times on the same host. When a UDP datagram is received for one of these multiply bound sockets, the rule is that if the datagram is destined for either a broadcast address or a multicast address, one copy of the datagram is delivered to each matching socket. But if the datagram is destined for a unicast address, the datagram is delivered to only one socket. If, in the case of a unicast datagram, there are multiple sockets that match the datagram, which one of the sockets will receive the datagram is implementation dependent. Pages 777–779 of TCPv2 talks more about this feature. We talk more about broadcasting and multicasting in Chapters 18 and 19.

Exercises 7.5 and 7.6 show some examples of this socket option.

4.4BSD introduced the SO_REUSEPORT socket option when support for multicasting was added. Instead of overloading SO_REUSEADDR with the desired multicast semantics that allow completely duplicate bindings, this new socket option was introduced with the following semantics:

1. This option allows completely duplicate bindings but only if each socket that wants to bind the same IP address and port specify this socket option.

2. SO_REUSEADDR is considered equivalent to SO_REUSEPORT if the IP address being bound is a multicast address (p. 731 of TCPv2).

The problem with this socket option is that not all systems support it, and on those that do not support the option but do support multicasting, SO_REUSEADDR is used instead of SO_REUSEPORT to allow completely duplicate bindings when it makes sense (i.e., a UDP server that can be run multiple times on the same host at the same time and that expects to receive either broadcast or multicast datagrams).

We can summarize our discussion of these socket options with the following recommendations:

1. Set the SO_REUSEADDR socket option before calling bind in all TCP servers.

2. When writing a multicast application that can be run multiple times on the same host at the same time, set the SO_REUSEADDR socket option and bind the group's multicast address as the local IP address.

Chapter 22 of TCPv2 talks about these two socket options in more detail.

There is a potential security problem with SO_REUSEADDR. If a socket exists that is bound to, say, the wildcard address and port 5555, if we specify SO_REUSEADDR, we can bind that same port to a different IP address, say the primary IP address of the host. Any future datagrams that arrive destined to port 5555 and the IP address that we bound to our socket are delivered to our socket, not to the other socket bound to the wildcard address. These could be TCP SYN segments or UDP datagrams. (Exercise 11.3 shows this feature with UDP.) For most well-known services, HTTP, FTP, and Telnet, for example, this is not a problem because these servers all bind a reserved port. Hence, any process that comes along later and tries to bind a more-specific instance of that port (i.e., steal the port) requires superuser privileges. NFS, however, can be a problem, since its normal port (2049) is not reserved.

> One underlying problem with the sockets API is that the setting of the socket pair is done with two function calls (bind and connect), instead of one. [Torek 1994] proposes a single function that solves this problem:
>
> ```
> int bind_connect_listen(int sockfd,
>                         const struct sockaddr *laddr, int laddrlen,
>                         const struct sockaddr *faddr, int faddrlen,
>                         int listen);
> ```
>
> *laddr* specifies the local IP address and local port, *faddr* specifies the foreign IP address and foreign port, and *listen* specifies a client (0) or a server (nonzero; same as the backlog argument to

listen). Then bind would be a library function that calls this function with *faddr* a null pointer and *faddrlen* 0, and connect would be a library function that calls this function with *laddr* a null pointer and *laddrlen* 0. There are a few applications, notably FTP, that need to specify both the local pair and the foreign pair, and they could call bind_connect_listen directly. With such a function, the need for SO_REUSEADDR disappears, other than for multicast UDP servers that explicitly need to allow completely duplicate bindings of the same IP address and port. Another benefit of this new function is that a TCP server could restrict itself to servicing connection requests that arrive from one specific IP address and port, something which RFC 793 [Postel 1981c] specifies but is impossible with the existing sockets API.

A similar proposal for a function named set_addresses was made in 1993 to the Posix 1003.12 working group by Keith Sklower. The proposal was, however, rejected.

SO_TYPE Socket Option

This option returns the socket type. The integer value returned is a value such as SOCK_STREAM or SOCK_DGRAM. This option is typically used by a process that inherits a socket when it is started.

SO_USELOOPBACK Socket Option

This option applies only to sockets in the routing domain (AF_ROUTE). This option defaults on for these sockets (the only one of the SO_*xxx* socket options that defaults on instead of off). When this option is enabled, the socket receives a copy of everything sent on the socket.

> Another way to disable these loopback copies is to call shutdown with a second argument of SHUT_RD.

7.6   IPv4 Socket Options

These socket options are processed by IPv4 and have a *level* of IPPROTO_IP. We defer discussion of the five multicasting socket options until Section 19.5.

> All of the socket options that we describe in this section are specified by Posix.1g, with the exception of IP_RECVIF.

IP_HDRINCL

If this option is set for a raw IP socket (Chapter 25), we must build our own IP header for all the datagrams that we send on the raw socket. Normally the kernel builds the IP header for datagrams sent on a raw socket, but there are some applications (noticeably Traceroute) that build their own IP header to override values that IP would place into certain header fields.

When this option is set, we build a complete IP header, with the following exceptions:

- IP always calculates and stores the IP header checksum.

- If we set the IP identification field to 0, the kernel will set the field.

- If the source IP address is INADDR_ANY, IP sets it to the primary IP address of the outgoing interface.

- How to set IP options is implementation dependent. Some implementations take any IP options that were set using the IP_OPTIONS socket option and append these to the header that we build, while others require our header to also contain any desired IP options.

We show an example of this option in Section 26.6. Pages 1056–1057 of TCPv2 provide additional details on this socket option.

IP_OPTIONS Socket Option

Setting this option allows us to set IP options in the IPv4 header. This requires intimate knowledge of the format of the IP options in the IP header. We discuss this option with regard to IPv4 source routes in Section 24.3.

IP_RECVDSTADDR

This socket option causes the destination IP address of a received UDP datagram to be returned as ancillary data by recvmsg. We show an example of this option in Section 20.2.

IP_RECVIF

This socket option causes the index of the interface on which a UDP datagram is received to be returned as ancillary data by recvmsg. We show an example of this option in Section 20.2.

> This is a new socket option that was developed by Bill Fenner for FreeBSD and NetBSD for the DARTNet testbed [Fenner 1997]. This is an experimental research network used for testing new protocols and applications. The socket option was supposed to be in 4.4BSD, but never made it into the release. The author took the FreeBSD implementation and added it to BSD/OS 3.0.

IP_TOS

This option lets us set the type-of-service field (Figure A.1) in the IP header for a TCP or UDP socket. If we call getsockopt for this option, the current value that would be placed into the TOS field in the IP header (which defaults to 0) is returned. There is no way to fetch the value from a received IP datagram.

We can set the TOS to one of the constants shown in Figure 7.12, which are defined by including <netinet/ip.h>.

Constant	Description
`IPTOS_LOWDELAY`	minimize delay
`IPTOS_THROUGHPUT`	maximize throughput
`IPTOS_RELIABILITY`	maximize reliability
`IPTOS_LOWCOST`	minimize cost

Figure 7.12 IPv4 type-of-service constants.

RFC 1349 [Almquist 1992] contains a detailed description of the TOS field and how this field should be set for the standard Internet applications. For example, Telnet and Rlogin should specify `IPTOS_LOWDELAY` while the data portion of an FTP transfer should specify `IPTOS_THROUGHPUT`.

IP_TTL

With this option we can set and fetch the default TTL (time-to-live field, Figure A.1) that the system will use for a given socket. 4.4BSD, for example, uses the default of 64 for both TCP and UDP sockets (which is specified in RFC 1700 [Reynolds and Postel 1994]), and 255 for raw sockets. As with the TOS field, calling `getsockopt` returns the default value of the field that the system will use in outgoing datagrams—there is no way to obtain the value from a received datagram. We set this socket option with our Traceroute program in Figure 25.18.

7.7   ICMPv6 Socket Option

This socket option is processed by ICMPv6 and has a *level* of `IPPROTO_ICMPV6`.

ICMP6_FILTER

This option lets us fetch and set an `icmp6_filter` structure that specifies which of the 256 possible ICMPv6 message types are passed to the process on a raw socket. We discuss this option in Section 25.4.

7.8   IPv6 Socket Options

These socket options are processed by IPv6 and have a *level* of `IPPROTO_IPV6`. We defer discussion of the five multicasting socket options until Section 19.5. We note that many of these options make use of *ancillary data* with the `recvmsg` function, and we describe this in Section 13.6. All the IPv6 socket options are defined in RFC 2133 [Gilligan et al. 1997] and [Stevens and Thomas 1997].

Posix.1g says nothing about IPv6.

IPV6_ADDRFORM

This option allows a socket to be converted from IPv4 to IPv6 or vice versa. We describe this option in Section 10.5.

IPV6_CHECKSUM

This socket option specifies the byte offset into the user data of where the checksum field is located. If this value is nonnegative, the kernel will (1) compute and store a checksum for all outgoing packets, and (2) verify the received checksum on input, discarding packets with an invalid checksum. This option affects all IPv6 raw sockets other than ICMPv6 raw sockets. (The kernel always calculates and stores the checksum for ICMPv6 raw sockets.) If a value of −1 is specified (the default), the kernel will not calculate and store the checksum for outgoing packets on this raw socket and will not verify the checksum for received packets.

> All protocols that use IPv6 should have a checksum in their own protocol header. These checksums include a pseudoheader (RFC 1883 [Deering and Hinden 1995]) that includes the source IPv6 address as part of the checksum (which differs from all the other protocols that are normally implemented using a raw socket with IPv4). Rather than forcing the application using the raw socket to perform source address selection, the kernel will do this and then calculate and store the checksum incorporating the standard IPv6 pseudoheader.

IPV6_DSTOPTS

Setting this option specifies that any received IPv6 destination options are to be returned as ancillary data by `recvmsg`. This option defaults off. We describe the functions that are used to build and process these options in Section 24.5.

IPV6_HOPLIMIT

Setting this option specifies that the received hop limit field be returned as ancillary data by `recvmsg`. This option defaults off. We describe this option in Section 20.8.

> There is no way with IPv4 to obtain the received time-to-live field.

IPV6_HOPOPTS

Setting this option specifies that any received IPv6 hop-by-hop options are to be returned as ancillary data by `recvmsg`. This option defaults off. We describe the functions that are used to build and process these options in Section 24.5.

IPV6_NEXTHOP

This is not a socket option but the type of an ancillary data object that can be specified to `sendmsg`. This object specifies the next-hop address for a datagram as a socket address structure. We say more about this feature in Section 20.8.

IPV6_PKTINFO

Setting this option specifies that the following two pieces of information about a received IPv6 datagram are to be returned as ancillary data by `recvmsg`: the destination IPv6 address and the arriving interface index. We describe this option in Section 20.8.

IPV6_PKTOPTIONS

Most of the IPv6 socket options assume a UDP socket with the information being passed between the kernel and the application using ancillary data with `recvmsg` and `sendmsg`. A TCP socket fetches and stores these values using the `IPV6_PKTOPTIONS` socket option.

The buffer pointed to by `getsockopt` and `setsockopt` contains the same information as would be passed using ancillary data using either `recvmsg` or `sendmsg`. We discuss this option in Section 24.7.

IPV6_RTHDR

Setting this option specifies that a received IPv6 routing header is to be returned as ancillary data by `recvmsg`. This option defaults off. We describe the functions that are used to build and process an IPv6 routing header in Section 24.6.

IPV6_UNICAST_HOPS

This IPv6 option is similar to the IPv4 `IP_TTL` socket option. Setting the socket option specifies the default hop limit for outgoing datagrams sent on the socket, while fetching the socket option returns the value for the hop limit that the kernel will use for the socket. To obtain the actual hop limit field from a received IPv6 datagram requires using the `IPV6_HOPLIMIT` socket option. We set this socket option with our Traceroute program in Figure 25.18.

7.9   TCP Socket Options

There are five socket options for TCP, but three are new with Posix.1g and not widely supported. We specify the *level* as `IPPROTO_TCP`.

TCP_KEEPALIVE Socket Option

This option is new with Posix.1g. It specifies the idle time in seconds for the connection before TCP starts sending keepalive probes. The default value must be at least 7200 seconds, which is 2 hours. This option is effective only when the `SO_KEEPALIVE` socket option is enabled.

`TCP_MAXRT` Socket Option

This option is new with Posix.1g. It specifies the amount of time in seconds before a connection is broken once TCP starts retransmitting data. A value of 0 means to use the system default, and a value of −1 means to retransmit forever. If a positive value is specified, it may be rounded up to the implementation's next retransmission time.

`TCP_MAXSEG` Socket Option

This socket option allows us to fetch or set the *maximum segment size* (MSS) for a TCP connection. The value returned is the maximum amount of data that our TCP will send to the other end; often it is the MSS announced by the other end with its SYN, unless our TCP chooses to use a smaller value than the peer's announced MSS. If this value is fetched before the socket is connected, the value returned is the default value that will be used if an MSS option is not received from the other end. Also be aware that a value smaller than the returned value can actually be used for the connection if the timestamp option, for example, is in use because this option occupies 12 bytes of TCP options in each segment.

The maximum amount of data that our TCP will send per segment can also change during the life of a connection if TCP supports path MTU discovery. If the route to the peer changes, this value can go up or down.

We note in Figure 7.1 that this socket option can also be set by the application. Before 4.4BSD this was not possible: it was a read-only option. 4.4BSD limits the application to *decreasing* the value: we cannot increase the value (p. 1023 of TCPv2). Since this option controls the amount of data that TCP sends per segment, it makes sense to forbid the application from increasing the value. Once the connection is established, this value is the MSS option that was announced by the peer, and we cannot exceed that value. Our TCP, however, can always send less than the peer's announced MSS.

`TCP_NODELAY` Socket Option

If set, this option disables TCP's *Nagle algorithm* (Section 19.4 of TCPv1 and pp. 858−859 of TCPv2). By default this algorithm is enabled.

The purpose of the Nagle algorithm is to reduce the number of small packets on a WAN. The algorithm states that if a given connection has outstanding data (that is, data that our TCP has sent, and for which it is currently awaiting an acknowledgment), then no small packets will be sent on the connection until the existing data is acknowledged. The definition of a "small" packet is any packet smaller than the MSS. TCP will always send a full-sized packet if possible; the purpose of the Nagle algorithm is to prevent a connection from having multiple small packets outstanding at any time.

The two common generators of small packets are the Rlogin and Telnet clients, since they normally send each keystroke as a separate packet. On a fast LAN we normally do not notice the Nagle algorithm with these clients, because the time required for a small packet to be acknowledged is typically a few milliseconds, far less than the time between two successive characters that we type. But on a WAN, where it can take a second for a small packet to be acknowledged, we can notice a delay in the character echoing, and this delay is often exaggerated by the Nagle algorithm.

Consider the following example. We type the six-character string "hello!" to either the Rlogin or Telnet client, with exactly 250 ms between each character. The RTT to the server is 600 ms and the server immediately sends back the echo of the character. We assume the ACK of the client's character is sent back to the client along with the character echo and we ignore the ACKs that the client sends for the server's echo. (We talk about delayed ACKs shortly.) Assuming the Nagle algorithm is disabled, we have the 12 packets shown in Figure 7.13.

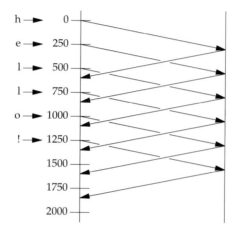

Figure 7.13   Six characters echoed by server with Nagle algorithm disabled.

Each character is sent in a packet by itself: the data segments from the left to right, and the ACKs from the right to left.

But if the Nagle algorithm is enabled (the default), we have the six packets shown in Figure 7.14. The first character is sent as a packet by itself, but the next two characters are not sent, since the connection has a small packet outstanding. At time 600, when the ACK of the first packet is received, along with the echo of the first character, these two characters are sent. Until this packet is ACKed at time 1200, no more small packets are sent.

The Nagle algorithm often interacts with another TCP algorithm: the *delayed ACK* algorithm. This algorithm causes TCP to not send an ACK immediately when it receives data; instead TCP will wait some small amount of time (typically 50–200 ms) and only then send the ACK. The hope is that in this small amount of time there will be data to send back to the peer, and the ACK can piggyback with the data, saving one TCP segment. This is normally the case with the Rlogin and Telnet clients, because the servers typically echo each character sent by the client, so the ACK of the client's character piggybacks with the server's echo of that character.

The problem is with other clients whose servers do not generate traffic in the reverse direction on which ACKs can piggyback. These clients can detect noticeable

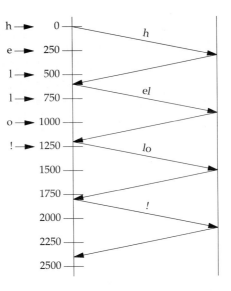

Figure 7.14   Six characters echoed by server with Nagle algorithm enabled.

delays because the client TCP will not send any data to the server until the server's delayed-ACK timer expires. These clients need a way to disable the Nagle algorithm, hence the TCP_NODELAY option.

Another type of client that interacts badly with the Nagle algorithm and TCP's delayed ACKs is a client that sends a single logical request to its server in small pieces. For example, assume a client sends a 400-byte request to its server, but this is a 4-byte request type followed by 396 bytes of request data. If the client performs a 4-byte write followed by a 396-byte write, the second write will not be sent by the client TCP until the server TCP acknowledges the 4-byte write. Also, since the server application cannot operate on the 4 bytes of data until it receives the remaining 396 bytes of data, the server TCP will delay the ACK of the 4 bytes of data (i.e., there will not be any data from the server to the client on which to piggyback the ACK). There are three ways to fix this type of client.

1. Use writev (Section 13.4) instead of two calls to write. A single call to writev ends up with one call to TCP output, instead of two calls, resulting in one TCP segment for our example. This is the preferred solution.

2. Copy the 4 bytes of data and the 396 bytes of data into a single buffer and call write once for this buffer.

3. Set the TCP_NODELAY socket option and continue to call write two times. This is the least desirable solution.

Exercises 7.8 and 7.9 continue this example.

TCP_STDURG **Socket Option**

This option is new with Posix.1g and it affects the interpretation of TCP's urgent pointer (which we encounter with out-of-band data in Chapter 21). There are two possible interpretations about where TCP's urgent pointer points (pp. 292–293 of TCPv1). By default the urgent pointer points to the data byte following the byte sent with the MSG_OOB flag. This is how almost all implementations interoperate today. But if this socket option is set nonzero, the urgent pointer will point to the data byte sent with the MSG_OOB flag.

> This socket option should never need to be set, and it is questionable why Posix.1g even defines it.

7.10 fcntl **Function**

fcntl stands for "file control" and this function performs various descriptor control operations. Before describing the function, and how it affects a socket, we need to look at the bigger picture. Figure 7.15 summarizes the different operations performed by fcntl, ioctl, and routing sockets.

Operation	fcntl	ioctl	Routing socket	Posix.1g
set socket for nonblocking I/O	F_SETFL, O_NONBLOCK	FIONBIO		fcntl
set socket for signal-driven I/O	F_SETFL, O_ASYNC	FIOASYNC		fcntl
set socket owner	F_SETOWN	SIOCSPGRP or FIOSETOWN		fcntl
get socket owner	F_GETOWN	SIOCGPGRP or FIOGETOWN		fcntl
get #bytes in socket receive buffer		FIONREAD		
test for socket at out-of-band mark		SIOCATMARK		sockatmark
obtain interface list		SIOCGIFCONF	sysctl	
interface operations		SIOC[GS]IF*xxx*		
ARP cache operations		SIOC*x*ARP	RTM_*xxx*	
routing table operations		SIOC*xxx*RT	RTM_*xxx*	

Figure 7.15 Summary of fcntl, ioctl, and routing socket operations.

The first six operations can be applied to sockets by any process, while many of the latter four (interface, ARP, and routing table) are issued by administrative programs such as ifconfig and route. We talk more about the various ioctl operations in Chapter 16 and routing sockets in Chapter 17.

There are multiple ways to perform the first four operations, but we note in the final column that Posix.1g specifies that fcntl is the preferred way. We also note that Posix.1g provides the sockatmark function (Section 21.3) as the preferred way to test for the out-of-band mark. The remaining operations, with a blank final column, have not been standardized by Posix.

We also note that the first two operations, setting a socket for nonblocking I/O and for signal-driven I/O, have been set historically using the FNDELAY and FASYNC commands with fcntl. Posix defines the O_*xxx* constants.

The fcntl function provides the following features related to network programming:

- Nonblocking I/O. We can set the O_NONBLOCK file status flag using the F_SETFL command to set a socket nonblocking. We describe nonblocking I/O in Chapter 15.

- Signal-driven I/O. We can set the O_ASYNC file status flag using the F_SETFL command which causes the SIGIO signal to be generated when the status of a socket changes. We discuss this in Chapter 22.

    This flag is new with Posix.1g.

- The F_SETOWN command lets us set the socket owner (the process ID or process group ID) to receive the SIGIO and SIGURG signals. The former signal is generated when signal-driven I/O is enabled for a socket (Chapter 22) and the latter is generated when new out-of-band data arrives for a socket (Chapter 21). The F_GETOWN command returns the current owner of the socket.

    The term "socket owner" is new with Posix.1g. Historically Berkeley-derived implementations have called this "the process group ID of the socket" because the variable that stores this ID is the so_pgid member of the socket structure (p. 438 of TCPv2).

```
#include <fcntl.h>

int fcntl(int fd, int cmd, ... /* int arg */ );
```
                                                    Returns: depends on *cmd* if OK, −1 on error

Each descriptor (including a socket) has a set of file flags that are fetched with the F_GETFL command and set with the F_SETFL command. The two flags that affect a socket are

```
O_NONBLOCK   nonblocking I/O
O_ASYNC      signal-driven I/O notification
```

We describe both of these features in more detail later. For now we note that typical code to enable nonblocking I/O, using fcntl, would be:

```
int     flags;

    /* Set socket nonblocking */
if ( (flags = fcntl(fd, F_GETFL, 0)) < 0)
    err_sys("F_GETFL error");
flags |= O_NONBLOCK;
if (fcntl(fd, F_SETFL, flags) < 0)
    err_sys("F_SETFL error");
```

Beware of code that you may encounter that simply sets the desired flag:

```
    /* Wrong way to set socket nonblocking */
if (fcntl(fd, F_SETFL, O_NONBLOCK) < 0)
    err_sys("F_SETFL error");
```

While this sets the nonblocking flag, it also clears all the other file status flags. The only correct way to set one of the file status flags is to fetch the current flags, logically OR in the new flag, and then set the flags.

The following code turns off the nonblocking flag, assuming flags was set by the call to fcntl shown above:

```
flags &= ~O_NONBLOCK;
if (fcntl(fd, F_SETFL, flags) < 0)
    err_sys("F_SETFL error");
```

The two signals SIGIO and SIGURG are different from other signals in that these two are generated for a socket only if the socket has been assigned an owner with the F_SETOWN command. The integer *arg* value for the F_SETOWN command can be either a positive integer, specifying the process ID to receive the signal, or a negative integer whose absolute value is the process group ID to receive the signal. The F_GETOWN command returns the socket owner as the return value from the fcntl function, either the process ID (a positive return value) or the process group ID (a negative value other than −1). The difference between specifying a process or a process group to receive the signal is that the former causes only a single process to receive the signal, while the latter causes all processes in the process group (perhaps more than one) to receive the signal.

> SVR4 only allows the socket owner to be set to a process ID and not to a process group ID.

When a new socket is created by socket, it has no owner. But when a new socket is created from a listening socket, the socket owner is inherited from the listening socket by the connected socket (as are many socket options, pp. 462−463 of TCPv2).

7.11 Summary

Socket options run the gamut from the very general (SO_ERROR) to the very specific (IP header options). The most commonly used options that we might encounter are SO_KEEPALIVE, SO_RCVBUF, SO_SNDBUF, and SO_REUSEADDR. The latter should always be set for a TCP server before it calls bind (Figure 11.8). The SO_BROADCAST option and the 10 multicast socket options are only for applications that broadcast or multicast, respectively.

The SO_KEEPALIVE socket option is set by many TCP servers and automatically terminates a half-open connection. The nice feature of this option is that it is handled by the TCP layer, without requiring an application-level inactivity timer, but its downside is that it cannot tell the difference between a crashed client and a temporary loss of connectivity to the client.

The SO_LINGER socket option gives us more control over when close returns and also lets us force an RST to be sent instead of TCP's four-packet connection termination sequence. We must be careful sending RSTs, because this avoids TCP's TIME_WAIT state. There are also instances where this socket option does not provide the information that we need, in which case an application-level ACK is required.

Every TCP socket has a send buffer and a receive buffer, and every UDP socket has a receive buffer. The SO_SNDBUF and SO_RCVBUF socket options let us change the sizes of these buffers. The most common use of these options is for bulk data transfer across long fat pipes: TCP connections with either a high bandwidth or a long delay, often using the RFC 1323 extensions. UDP sockets, on the other hand, might want to increase the size of the receive buffer to allow the kernel to queue more datagrams if the application is busy.

Exercises

7.1   Write a program that prints the default TCP and UDP send and receive buffer sizes and run it on the systems to which you have access.

7.2   Modify Figure 1.5 as follows. Before calling connect, call getsockopt to obtain the socket receive buffer size and the MSS. Print both values. After connect returns success, fetch these same two socket options and print their values. Have the values changed? Why? Run the program connecting to a server on your local network and also run the program connecting to a server on a remote network. Does the MSS change? Why? You should also run the program on any different hosts to which you have access.

7.3   Start with our TCP server from Figures 5.2 and 5.3 and our TCP client from Figures 5.4 and 5.5. Modify the client main function to set the SO_LINGER socket option before calling exit, setting l_onoff to 1 and l_linger to 0. Start the server and then start the client. Type in a line or two at the client to verify the operation, and then terminate the client by entering your end-of-file character. What happens? After you terminate the client, run netstat on the client host and see if the socket goes through the TIME_WAIT state.

7.4   Assume two TCP clients start at about the same time. Both set the SO_REUSEADDR socket option and then call bind with the same local IP address and the same local port (say 1500). But one client connects to 198.69.10.2 port 7000 and the second connects to 198.69.10.2 (same peer IP address) but port 8000. Describe the race condition that occurs.

7.5   Obtain the source code for the examples in this book (see the Preface) and compile the sock program (Section C.3). First classify your host as (1) no multicast support, (2) multicast support but SO_REUSEPORT not provided, or (3) multicast support and SO_REUSEPORT provided. Try to start multiple instances of the sock program as a TCP server (-s command-line option) on the same port, binding the wildcard address, one of your host's interface addresses, and the loopback address. Do you need to specify the SO_REUSEADDR option (the -A command-line option)? Use netstat to see the listening sockets.

7.6   Continue the previous example, but start a UDP server (-u command-line option) and try to start two instances, both binding the same local IP address and port. If your implementation supports SO_REUSEPORT, try using it (-T command-line option).

7.7   Many versions of the Ping program have a -d flag to enable the SO_DEBUG socket option. What does this do?

7.8   Continuing the example at the end of our discussion of the `TCP_NODELAY` socket option, assume that a client performs two `write`s: the first of 4 bytes and the second of 396 bytes. Also assume that the server's delayed-ACK time is 100 ms, the RTT between the client and server is 100 ms, and the server's processing time for the client's request is 50 ms. Draw a time line that shows the interaction of the Nagle algorithm with delayed-ACKs.

7.9   Redo the previous exercise, assuming the `TCP_NODELAY` socket option is set.

7.10 Redo Exercise 7.8 assuming the process calls `writev` one time, for both the 4-byte buffer and the 396-byte buffer.

7.11 Read RFC 1122 [Braden 1989] to determine the recommended interval for delayed ACKs.

7.12 Where does our server in Figures 5.2 and 5.3 spend most of its time? If the server sets the `SO_KEEPALIVE` socket option, there is no data being exchanged across the connection, and the client host crashes and does not reboot, what happens?

7.13 Where does our client in Figures 5.4 and 5.5 spend most of its time? If the client sets the `SO_KEEPALIVE` socket option, there is no data being exchanged across the connection, and the server host crashes and does not reboot, what happens?

7.14 Where does our client in Figures 5.4 and 6.13 spend most of its time? If the client sets the `SO_KEEPALIVE` socket option, there is no data being exchanged across the connection, and the server host crashes and does not reboot, what happens?

7.15 Assume both a client and server set the `SO_KEEPALIVE` socket option. Connectivity is maintained between the two peers but there is no application data exchanged across the connection. When the keepalive timer expires every 2 hours, how many TCP segments are exchanged across the connection?

7.16 Almost all implementations define the constant `SO_ACCEPTCON` in the `<sys/socket.h>` header, but we have not described this option. Read [Lanciani 1996] to find out why this option exists.

8

Elementary UDP Sockets

8.1 Introduction

There are some fundamental differences between applications written using TCP versus those that use UDP. These are because of the differences in the two transport layers: UDP is a connectionless, unreliable, datagram protocol, quite unlike the connection-oriented, reliable byte stream provided by TCP. Nevertheless, there are instances when it makes sense to use UDP instead of TCP and we go over this design choice in Section 20.4. Some popular applications are built using UDP: DNS (the Domain Name System), NFS (the Network File System), and SNMP (Simple Network Management Protocol), for example.

Figure 8.1 shows the function calls for a typical UDP client–server. The client does not establish a connection with the server. Instead, the client just sends a datagram to the server using the sendto function (described in the next section), which requires the address of the destination (the server) as a parameter. Similarly, the server does not accept a connection from a client. Instead, the server just calls the recvfrom function, which waits until data arrives from some client. recvfrom returns the protocol address of the client, along with the datagram, so the server can send a response to the correct client.

Figure 8.1 shows a time line of the typical scenario that takes place for a UDP client–server exchange. We can compare this to the typical TCP exchange, Figure 4.1.

In this chapter we describe the new functions that we use with UDP sockets, recvfrom and sendto, and redo our echo client–server to use UDP. We also describe the use of the connect function with a UDP socket, and the concept of asynchronous errors.

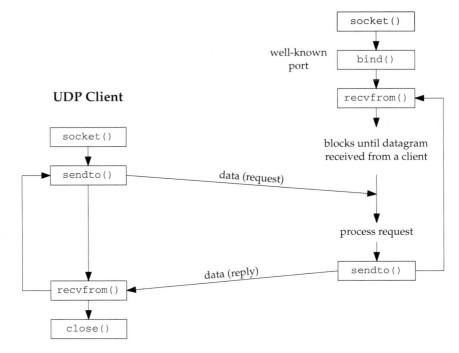

Figure 8.1   Socket functions for UDP client–server.

8.2   `recvfrom` and `sendto` Functions

These two functions are similar to the standard `read` and `write` functions, but three additional arguments are required.

```
#include <sys/socket.h>

ssize_t recvfrom(int sockfd, void *buff, size_t nbytes, int flags,
                 struct sockaddr *from, socklen_t *addrlen);

ssize_t sendto(int sockfd, const void *buff, size_t nbytes, int flags,
               const struct sockaddr *to, socklen_t addrlen);
```
                                   Both return: number of bytes read or written if OK, −1 on error

The first three arguments, *sockfd*, *buff*, and *nbytes*, are identical to the first three arguments for `read` and `write`: descriptor, pointer to buffer to read into or write from, and number of bytes to read or write.

We describe the *flags* argument in Chapter 13 when we discuss the `recv`, `send`, `recvmsg`, and `sendmsg` functions, since we do not need them with our simple UDP client–server example in this chapter. For now we always set the *flags* to 0.

The *to* argument for `sendto` is a socket address structure containing the protocol address (e.g., IP address and port number) of where the data is to be sent. The size of this socket address structure is specified by *addrlen*. The `recvfrom` function fills in the socket address structure pointed to by *from* with the protocol address of who sent the datagram. The number of bytes stored in this socket address structure is also returned to the caller in the integer pointed to by *addrlen*. Note that the final argument to `sendto` is an integer value, while the final argument to `recvfrom` is a pointer to an integer value (a value–result argument).

The final two arguments to `recvfrom` are similar to the final two arguments to `accept`: the contents of the socket address structure upon return tell us who sent the datagram (in the case of UDP) or who initiated the connection (in the case of TCP). The final two arguments to `sendto` are similar to the final two arguments to `connect`: we fill in the socket address structure with the protocol address of where to send the datagram (in the case of UDP) or with whom to establish a connection (in the case of TCP).

Both functions return the length of the data that was read or written as the value of the function. In the typical use of `recvfrom`, with a datagram protocol, the return value is the amount of user data in the datagram that was received.

Writing a datagram of length 0 is OK. In the case of UDP, this results in an IP datagram containing an IP header (normally 20 bytes for IPv4 and 40 bytes for IPv6), an 8-byte UDP header, and no data. This also means that a return value of 0 from `recvfrom` is OK for a datagram protocol: it does not mean that the peer has closed the connection, as does a return value of 0 from `read` on a TCP socket. Since UDP is connectionless, there is no such thing as closing a UDP connection.

If the *from* argument to `recvfrom` is a null pointer, then the corresponding length argument (*addrlen*) must also be a null pointer, and this indicates that we are not interested in knowing the protocol address of who sent us data.

Both `recvfrom` and `sendto` can be used with TCP, although there is normally no reason to do so.

> T/TCP, TCP for Transactions, uses `sendto` as we describe in Section 13.9.

8.3 UDP Echo Server: `main` Function

We now redo our simple echo client–server from Chapter 5 using UDP. Our UDP client and server programs follow the function call flow that we diagramed in Figure 8.1. Figure 8.2 depicts the functions that are used. Figure 8.3 shows the server `main` function.

Figure 8.2 Simple echo client–server using UDP.

---
udpcliserv/ucpserv01.c

```
1 #include     "unp.h"

2 int
3 main(int argc, char **argv)
4 {
5     int     sockfd;
6     struct sockaddr_in servaddr, cliaddr;

7     sockfd = Socket(AF_INET, SOCK_DGRAM, 0);

8     bzero(&servaddr, sizeof(servaddr));
9     servaddr.sin_family = AF_INET;
10    servaddr.sin_addr.s_addr = htonl(INADDR_ANY);
11    servaddr.sin_port = htons(SERV_PORT);

12    Bind(sockfd, (SA *) &servaddr, sizeof(servaddr));

13    dg_echo(sockfd, (SA *) &cliaddr, sizeof(cliaddr));
14 }
```
udpcliserv/ucpserv01.c

Figure 8.3   UDP echo server.

Create UDP socket, bind server's well-known port

7–12   We create a UDP socket by specifying the second argument to socket as SOCK_DGRAM (a datagram socket in the IPv4 protocol). As with the TCP server example, the IPv4 address for the bind is specified as INADDR_ANY and the server's well-known port is the constant SERV_PORT from the unp.h header.

13   The function dg_echo is then called to perform the server processing.

8.4   UDP Echo Server: `dg_echo` Function

Figure 8.4 shows the dg_echo function.

---
lib/dg_echo.c

```
1 #include     "unp.h"

2 void
3 dg_echo(int sockfd, SA *pcliaddr, socklen_t clilen)
4 {
5     int     n;
6     socklen_t len;
7     char    mesg[MAXLINE];

8     for ( ; ; ) {
9         len = clilen;
10        n = Recvfrom(sockfd, mesg, MAXLINE, 0, pcliaddr, &len);

11        Sendto(sockfd, mesg, n, 0, pcliaddr, len);
12    }
13 }
```
lib/dg_echo.c

Figure 8.4   dg_echo function: echo lines on a datagram socket.

Read datagram, echo back to sender

8-12   This function is a simple loop that reads the next datagram arriving at the server's port using recvfrom and sends it back using sendto.

Despite the simplicity of this function, there are numerous details to consider. First, this function never terminates. Since UDP is a connectionless protocol, there is nothing like an end-of-file as we have with TCP.

Next, this function provides an *iterative server*, not a concurrent server as we had with TCP. There is no call to fork, so a single server process handles any and all clients. In general, most TCP servers are concurrent and most UDP servers are iterative.

There is implied queueing taking place in the UDP layer for this socket. Indeed, each UDP socket has a receive buffer and each datagram that arrives for this socket is placed in that socket receive buffer. When the process calls recvfrom, the next datagram from the buffer is returned to the process in a FIFO (first-in, first-out) order. This way, if multiple datagrams arrive for the socket, before the process can read what's already queued for the socket, the arriving datagrams are just added to the socket receive buffer. But this buffer has a limited size. We discussed this size, and how to increase it, with the SO_RCVBUF socket option in Section 7.5.

Figure 8.5 summarizes our TCP client–server from Chapter 5 when two clients establish connections with the server.

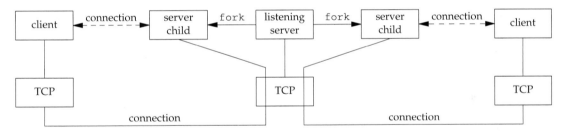

Figure 8.5 Summary of TCP client–server with two clients.

There are two connected sockets and each of the two connected sockets on the server host has its own socket receive buffer.

Figure 8.6 shows the scenario when two clients send datagrams to our UDP server.

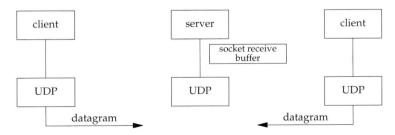

Figure 8.6 Summary of UDP client–server with two clients.

There is only one server process and it has a single socket on which it receives all arriving datagrams and sends all responses. That socket has a receive buffer into which all arriving datagrams are placed.

The `main` function in Figure 8.3 is *protocol dependent* (it creates a socket of protocol `AF_INET` and allocates and initializes an IPv4 socket address structure), but the `dg_echo` function is *protocol independent*. The reason `dg_echo` is protocol independent is because the caller (the `main` function in our case) must allocate a socket address structure of the correct size, and a pointer to this structure, along with its size, are passed as arguments to `dg_echo`. The function `dg_echo` never looks inside this protocol-dependent structure: it simply passes a pointer to the structure to `recvfrom` and `sendto`. It is `recvfrom` that fills in this structure with the IP address and port number of the client, and since the same pointer (`pcliaddr`) is then passed to `sendto` as the destination address, this is how the datagram is echoed back to the client that sent the datagram.

8.5   UDP Echo Client: `main` Function

The UDP client `main` function is shown in Figure 8.7.

—————————————————————————— udpcliserv/udpcli01.c

```
 1 #include     "unp.h"

 2 int
 3 main(int argc, char **argv)
 4 {
 5     int       sockfd;
 6     struct sockaddr_in servaddr;

 7     if (argc != 2)
 8         err_quit("usage: udpcli <IPaddress>");

 9     bzero(&servaddr, sizeof(servaddr));
10     servaddr.sin_family = AF_INET;
11     servaddr.sin_port = htons(SERV_PORT);
12     Inet_pton(AF_INET, argv[1], &servaddr.sin_addr);

13     sockfd = Socket(AF_INET, SOCK_DGRAM, 0);

14     dg_cli(stdin, sockfd, (SA *) &servaddr, sizeof(servaddr));

15     exit(0);
16 }
```

—————————————————————————— udpcliserv/udpcli01.c

Figure 8.7 UDP echo client.

Fill in socket address structure with server's address

9–12   An IPv4 socket address structure is filled in with the IP address and port number of the server. This structure will be passed to `dg_cli`, specifying where to send the datagrams.

13–14   A UDP socket is created and the function `dg_cli` is called.

8.6   UDP Echo Client: `dg_cli` Function

Figure 8.8 shows the function `dg_cli`, which performs most of the client processing.

———————————————————————————————— *lib/dg_cli.c*
```
 1 #include    "unp.h"

 2 void
 3 dg_cli(FILE *fp, int sockfd, const SA *pservaddr, socklen_t servlen)
 4 {
 5     int     n;
 6     char    sendline[MAXLINE], recvline[MAXLINE + 1];

 7     while (Fgets(sendline, MAXLINE, fp) != NULL) {

 8         Sendto(sockfd, sendline, strlen(sendline), 0, pservaddr, servlen);

 9         n = Recvfrom(sockfd, recvline, MAXLINE, 0, NULL, NULL);

10         recvline[n] = 0;          /* null terminate */
11         Fputs(recvline, stdout);
12     }
13 }
```
———————————————————————————————— *lib/dg_cli.c*

Figure 8.8 `dg_cli` function: client processing loop.

7–12   There are four steps in the client processing loop: read a line from standard input using `fgets`, send the line to the server using `sendto`, read back the server's echo using `recvfrom`, and print the echoed line to standard output using `fputs`.

Our client has not asked the kernel to assign an ephemeral port to its socket. (With a TCP client we said the call to `connect` is where this takes place.) With a UDP socket, the first time the process calls `sendto`, if the socket has not yet had a local port bound to it, that is when an ephemeral port is chosen by the kernel for the socket. As with TCP, the client can call `bind` explicitly, but this is rarely done.

Notice that the call to `recvfrom` specifies a null pointer as the fifth and sixth arguments. This tells the kernel that we are not interested in knowing who sent the reply. There is a risk that any process, on either the same host or some other host, can send a datagram to the client's IP address and port, and that datagram will be read by the client who will think it is the server's reply. We will address this in Section 8.8.

As with the server function `dg_echo`, the client function `dg_cli` is protocol independent, but the client `main` function is protocol dependent. The `main` function allocates and initializes a socket address structure of some protocol type and then passes a pointer to this structure along with its size to `dg_cli`.

8.7   Lost Datagrams

Our UDP client–server example is not reliable. If a client datagram is lost (say it is discarded by some router between the client and server), the client will block forever in its call to `recvfrom` in the function `dg_cli`, waiting for a server reply that will never arrive. Similarly, if the client datagram arrives at the server but the server's reply is lost, the client will again block forever in its call to `recvfrom`. The only way to prevent this is to place a timeout on the client's call to `recvfrom`. We discuss this in Section 13.2.

Just placing a timeout on the `recvfrom` is not the entire solution. For example, if we do time out, we cannot tell whether our datagram never made it to the server, or if the server's reply never made it back. It the client's request were something like "transfer a certain amount of money from account A to account B" (instead of our simple echo server), it makes a big difference whether the request is lost or whether the reply is lost. We talk more about adding reliability to a UDP client–server in Section 20.5.

8.8   Verifying Received Response

At the end of Section 8.6 we mentioned that any process that knows the client's ephemeral port number could send datagrams to our client, and these will be intermixed with the normal server replies. What we can do is change the call to `recvfrom` in Figure 8.8 to return the IP address and port of who sent the reply and ignore any received datagrams that are not from the server to whom we sent the datagram. There are a few pitfalls with this, however, as we will see.

First, we change the client `main` function (Figure 8.7) to use the standard echo server (Figure 2.13). We just replace the assignment

```
servaddr.sin_port = htons(SERV_PORT);
```

with

```
servaddr.sin_port = htons(7);
```

We do this so we can use any host running the standard echo server with our client.

We then recode the `dg_cli` function to allocate another socket address structure to hold the structure returned by `recvfrom`. We show this in Figure 8.9.

Allocate another socket address structure

9   We allocate another socket address structure by calling `malloc`. Notice that the `dg_cli` function is still protocol independent; as we do not care what type of socket address structure we are dealing with, we use only its size in the call to `malloc`.

Compare returned address

12–18   In the call to `recvfrom` we tell the kernel to return the address of the sender of the datagram. We first compare the length returned by `recvfrom` in the value–result argument and then compare the socket address structures themselves using `memcmp`.

This new version of our client works fine if the server is on a host with just a single IP address. But this program can fail if the server is multihomed. We run this program to our host `bsdi`, which has two interfaces and two IP addresses.

```
solaris % host bsdi
bsdi.kohala.com has address 206.62.226.35
bsdi.kohala.com has address 206.62.226.66
```

```
                                                              ─── udpcliserv/dgcliaddr.c
 1 #include     "unp.h"

 2 void
 3 dg_cli(FILE *fp, int sockfd, const SA *pservaddr, socklen_t servlen)
 4 {
 5     int     n;
 6     char    sendline[MAXLINE], recvline[MAXLINE + 1];
 7     socklen_t len;
 8     struct sockaddr *preply_addr;

 9     preply_addr = Malloc(servlen);

10     while (Fgets(sendline, MAXLINE, fp) != NULL) {

11         Sendto(sockfd, sendline, strlen(sendline), 0, pservaddr, servlen);

12         len = servlen;
13         n = Recvfrom(sockfd, recvline, MAXLINE, 0, preply_addr, &len);
14         if (len != servlen || memcmp(pservaddr, preply_addr, len) != 0) {
15             printf("reply from %s (ignored)\n",
16                     Sock_ntop(preply_addr, len));
17             continue;
18         }
19         recvline[n] = 0;          /* null terminate */
20         Fputs(recvline, stdout);
21     }
22 }
                                                              ─── udpcliserv/dgcliaddr.c
```

Figure 8.9 Version of `dg_cli` that verifies returned socket address.

```
solaris % udpcli02 206.62.226.66
hello
reply from 206.62.226.35.7 (ignored)
goodbye
reply from 206.62.226.35.7 (ignored)
```

From Figure 1.16 we see that we specified the IP address that does not share the same subnet as the client.

> This is normally allowed. Most IP implementations accept an arriving IP datagram that is destined for *any* of the host's IP addresses, regardless of the interface on which the datagram arrives (pp. 217–219 of TCPv2). RFC 1122 [Braden 1989] calls this the *weak end system model*. If a system were to implement what this RFC calls the *strong end system model*, it would accept an arriving datagram only if that datagram arrives on the interface to which it is addressed.

The IP address returned by `recvfrom` (the source IP address of the UDP datagram) is not the IP address to which we sent the datagram. When the server sends its reply, the destination IP address is 206.62.226.33. The routing function within the kernel on `bsdi` chooses 206.62.226.35 as the outgoing interface. Since the server has not bound an IP address to its socket (the server has bound the wildcard address to its socket, something we can verify by running `netstat` on `bsdi`), the kernel chooses the source address for the IP datagram. It is chosen to be the primary IP address of the outgoing interface (pp. 232–233 of TCPv2). Also, since it is the primary IP address of the interface, if we send our datagram to a nonprimary IP address of the interface (i.e., an alias), this will also cause our test in Figure 8.9 to fail.

One solution is for the client to verify the responding host's domain name instead of its IP address by looking up the server's name in the DNS (Chapter 9), given the IP address returned by `recvfrom`. Another solution is for the UDP server to create one socket for every IP address that is configured on the host, `bind` that IP address to the socket, use `select` across all these sockets (waiting for any one to become readable), and then reply from the socket that is readable. Since the socket used for the reply was bound to the IP address that was the destination address of the client's request (or the datagram would not have been delivered to the socket), this guarantees that the source address of the reply is the same as the destination address of the request. We show examples of this in Sections 19.11 and 20.6.

> On a multihomed Solaris system, the source IP address for the server's reply is the destination IP address of the client's request. The scenario described in this section is for Berkeley-derived implementations that choose the source IP address based on the outgoing interface.

8.9 Server Not Running

The next scenario to examine is if we start the client without starting the server. If we do so and type in a single line to the client, nothing happens. The client blocks forever in its call to `recvfrom`, waiting for a server reply that will never appear. But this is an example where we need to understand more about the underlying protocols to understand what is happening to our networking application.

First we start `tcpdump` on the host `bsdi` and then we start the client on the same host, specifying the host `solaris` as the server host. We then type a single line, but the line is not echoed.

```
bsdi % udpcli01 206.62.226.33
hello, world                        we type this line
                                    but nothing is echoed back
```

Figure 8.10 shows the `tcpdump` output.

```
1  0.0                 arp who-has solaris tell bsdi
2  0.002526 (0.0025)   arp reply solaris is-at 8:0:20:78:e3:e3

3  0.002932 (0.0004)   bsdi.1105 > solaris.9877: udp 13
4  0.006932 (0.0040)   solaris > bsdi: icmp: solaris udp port 9877 unreachable
```

Figure 8.10 `tcpdump` output when server process not started on server host.

First we notice that an ARP request and reply are needed before the client host can send the UDP datagram to the server host. (We left this exchange in the output to reiterate the potential for an ARP request–reply before an IP datagram can be sent to another host or router on the local network.)

In line 3 we see the client datagram sent but the server host responds in line 4 with an ICMP port unreachable. (The length of 13 accounts for the 12 characters and the newline.) This ICMP error, however, is not returned to the client process, for reasons that we describe shortly. Instead, the client blocks forever in the call to `recvfrom` in Figure 8.8. We also note that ICMPv6 has a "port unreachable" error, similar to ICMPv4 (Figures A.15 and A.16), so the results described here are similar for IPv6.

We call this ICMP error an *asynchronous error*. The error was caused by the `sendto`, but `sendto` returned OK. Recall from Section 2.9 that an OK return from a UDP output operation only means there was room for the resulting IP datagram on the interface output queue. The ICMP error is not returned until later (4 ms later in Figure 8.10), which is why it is called asynchronous.

The basic rule is that asynchronous errors are not returned for UDP sockets unless the socket has been connected. We describe how to call `connect` for a UDP socket in Section 8.11. Why this design decision was made when sockets were first implemented is rarely understood. (The implementation implications are discussed on pp. 748–749 of TCPv2.) Consider a UDP client that sends three datagrams in a row to three different servers (i.e., three different IP addresses) on a single UDP socket. The client then enters a loop that calls `recvfrom` to read the replies. Two of the datagrams are correctly delivered (that is, the server was running on two of the three hosts) but the third host was not running the server. This third host responds with an ICMP port unreachable. This ICMP error message contains the IP header and the UDP header of the datagram that caused the error. (ICMPv4 and ICMPv6 error messages always contain the IP header and all of the UDP header or part of the TCP header to allow the receiver of the ICMP error to determine which socket caused the error. We show this in Figures 25.20 and 25.21.) The client that sent the three datagrams needs to know the destination of the datagram that caused the error to distinguish which of the three datagrams caused the error. But how can the kernel return this information to the process? The only piece of information that `recvfrom` can return is an `errno` value; `recvfrom` has no way of returning the destination IP address and destination UDP port number of the datagram in error. The decision was made, therefore, that these asynchronous errors are returned to the process only if the process has connected the UDP socket to exactly one peer.

> Linux returns most ICMP destination unreachable errors even for an unconnected socket, as long as the `SO_BSDCOMPAT` socket option is not enabled. All the destination unreachable errors from Figure A.15 are returned, other than codes 0, 1, 4, 5, 11, and 12.

> The XTI interface provides a way of returning this additional information to the process: the `t_rcvuderr` can return this information (Section 31.4). Unfortunately, many XTI implementations do not return this information.

> We return to this problem of asynchronous errors with a UDP socket in Section 25.7 and show an easy way to obtain these errors on an unconnected socket using a daemon of our own.

8.10 Summary of UDP example

Figure 8.11 shows as bullets the four values that must be specified or chosen when the client sends a UDP datagram.

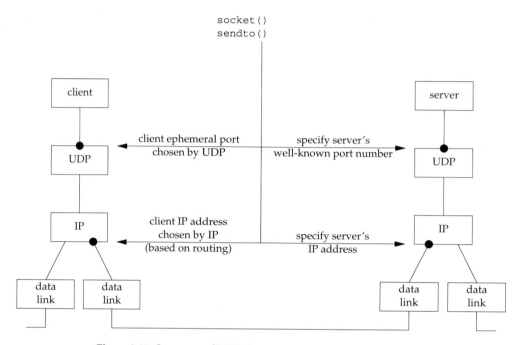

Figure 8.11 Summary of UDP client–server from client's perspective.

The client must specify the server's IP address and port number for the call to sendto. Normally the client's IP address and port are chosen automatically by the kernel, although we mentioned that the client can call bind if it so chooses. If these two values for the client are chosen by the kernel, we also mentioned that the client ephemeral port is chosen once, on the first sendto, and then never changes. The client's IP address, however, can change for every UDP datagram that the client sends, assuming the client does not bind a specific IP address to the socket. The reason is shown in Figure 8.11: if the client host is multihomed, the client could alternate between two destinations, one going out the datalink on the left, and the other going out the datalink on the right. In this worst case scenario, the client's IP address, as chosen by the kernel based on the outgoing datalink, would change for every datagram.

What happens if the client binds an IP address to its socket, but the kernel decides that an outgoing datagram must be sent out some other datalink? In this case the IP datagram will contain a source IP address that is different from the IP address of the outgoing datalink. (See Exercise 8.6.)

Figure 8.12 shows the same four values, but from the server's perspective.

There are four pieces of information that a server might want to know from an IP datagram that arrives: the source IP address, destination IP addresses, source port number, and destination port number. Figure 8.13 shows the function calls that return this information for a TCP server and a UDP server.

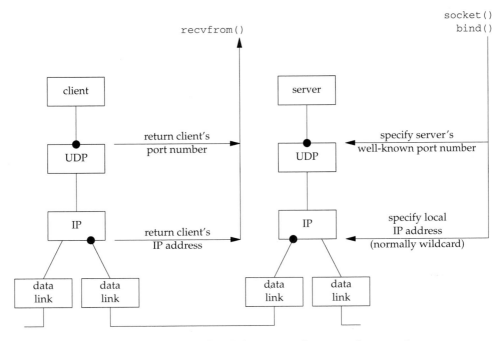

Figure 8.12 Summary of UDP client–server from server's perspective.

From client's IP datagram	TCP server	UDP server
source IP address	accept	recvfrom
source port number	accept	recvfrom
destination IP address	getsockname	recvmsg
destination port number	getsockname	getsockname

Figure 8.13 Information available to server from arriving IP datagram.

A TCP server always has easy access to all four pieces of information for a connected socket, and these four values remain constant for the lifetime of a connection. With a UDP socket, however, the destination IP address can only be obtained by setting the IP_RECVDSTADDR socket option for IPv4 or the IPV6_PKTINFO socket option for IPv6 and then calling recvmsg instead of recvfrom. Since UDP is connectionless, the destination IP address can change for each datagram that is sent to the server. A UDP server can also receive datagrams destined for one of the host's broadcast addresses or for a multicast address, as we discuss in Chapters 18 and 19. We will show how to determine the destination address of a UDP datagram in Section 20.2, after we cover the recvmsg function.

8.11 `connect` Function with UDP

We mentioned at the end of Section 8.9 that asynchronous errors are not returned on UDP sockets unless the socket has been connected. Indeed, we are able to call `connect` (Section 4.3) for a UDP socket. But this does not result in anything like a TCP connection: there is no three-way handshake. Instead, the kernel just records the IP address and port number of the peer, which are contained in the socket address structure passed to `connect`, and returns immediately to the calling process.

> Overloading the `connect` function with this capability for UDP sockets is confusing. If the convention that `sockname` is the local protocol address and `peername` is the foreign protocol address is used, then a better name would have been `setpeername`. Similarly, a better name for the `bind` function would be `setsockname`.

With this capability we must now distinguish between

- an *unconnected UDP socket*, the default when we create a UDP socket, and
- a *connected UDP socket*, the result of calling `connect` on a UDP socket.

With a connected UDP socket three things change, compared to the default unconnected UDP socket.

1. We can no longer specify the destination IP address and port for an output operation. That is, we do not use `sendto` but use `write` or `send` instead. Anything written to a connected UDP socket is automatically sent to the protocol address (e.g., IP address and port) specified by the `connect`.

   > Similar to TCP, we can call `sendto` for a connected UDP socket, but we cannot specify a destination address. The fifth argument to `sendto` (the pointer to the socket address structure) must be a null pointer, and the sixth argument (the size of the socket address structure) should be 0. Posix.1g specifies that when the fifth argument is a null pointer, the sixth argument is ignored.

2. We do not use `recvfrom` but use `read` or `recv` instead. The only datagrams returned by the kernel for an input operation on a connected UDP socket are those arriving from the protocol address specified in the `connect`. Datagrams destined to the connected UDP socket's local protocol address (e.g., IP address and port) but arriving from a protocol address other than the one to which the socket was `connected`, are not passed to the connected socket. This limits a connected UDP socket to exchanging datagrams with one and only one peer.

   > Technically, a connected UDP socket exchanges datagrams with only one IP address, because it is possible to `connect` to a multicast or broadcast address.

3. Asynchronous errors are returned to the process for a connected UDP socket. The corollary, as we previously described, is that an unconnected UDP socket does not receive any asynchronous errors.

Figure 8.14 summarizes the first point in the list with respect to 4.4BSD.

Type of socket	write or send	sendto that does not specify a destination	sendto that specifies a destination
TCP socket	OK	OK	EISCONN
UDP socket, connected	OK	OK	EISCONN
UDP socket, unconnected	EDESTADDRREQ	EDESTADDRREQ	OK

Figure 8.14 TCP and UDP sockets: can a destination protocol address be specified?

Posix.1g specifies that an output operation that does not specify a destination address on an unconnected UDP socket should return ENOTCONN, not EDESTADDRREQ.

Solaris 2.5 allows a sendto that specifies a destination address for a connected UDP socket. Posix.1g specifies that EISCONN should be returned instead.

Figure 8.15 summarizes the three points that we made about a connected UDP socket.

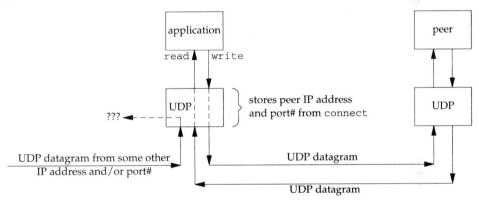

Figure 8.15 Connected UDP socket.

The application calls connect, specifying the IP address and port number of its peer. It then uses read and write to exchange data with the peer.

Datagrams arriving from any other IP address or port (which we show as "???" in Figure 8.15) are not passed to the connected socket because either the source IP address or source UDP port does not match the protocol address to which the socket is connected. These datagrams could be delivered to some other UDP socket on the host. If there is no other matching socket for the arriving datagram, UDP will discard it and generate an ICMP port unreachable error.

In summary we can say that a UDP client or server can call connect only if that process uses the UDP socket to communicate with exactly one peer. Normally it is a UDP client that calls connect, but there are applications in which the UDP server communicates with a single client for a long duration (e.g., TFTP), and in this case both the client and server can call connect.

The DNS provides another example, as shown in Figure 8.16.

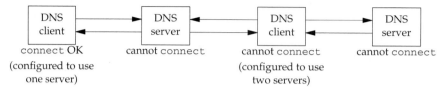

Figure 8.16   Example of DNS clients and servers and the `connect` function.

A DNS client can be configured to use one or more servers, normally by listing the IP addresses of the server in the file `/etc/resolv.conf`. If a single server is listed (the leftmost box in the figure), the client can call `connect`, but if multiple servers are listed (the second box from the right in the figure), the client cannot call `connect`. Also, a DNS server normally handles any client's request, so the servers cannot call `connect`.

Calling `connect` Multiple Times for a UDP Socket

A process with a connected UDP socket can call `connect` again for that socket, to either

- specify a new IP address and port, or to
- unconnect the socket.

The first case, specifying a new peer for a connected UDP socket, differs from the use of `connect` with a TCP socket: `connect` can be called only one time for a TCP socket.

To unconnect a UDP socket we call `connect` but set the family member of the socket address structure (`sin_family` for IPv4 or `sin6_family` for IPv6) to `AF_UNSPEC`. This might return an error of `EAFNOSUPPORT` (p. 736 of TCPv2) but that is OK. It is the process of calling `connect` on an already connected UDP socket that causes the socket to become unconnected (pp. 787–788 of TCPv2).

> The BSD manual page for `connect` has traditionally said "Datagram sockets may dissolve the association by connecting to an invalid address, such as the null address." Unfortunately the manual page never defines what a "null address" is, and doesn't mention that an error results (which is OK). Posix.1g explicitly states that the address family must be set to `AF_UNSPEC` but then waffles by saying that this call to `connect` may or may not return the error of `EAFNOSUPPORT`.

Performance

When an application calls `sendto` on an unconnected UDP socket, Berkeley-derived kernels temporarily connect the socket, send the datagram, and then unconnect the socket (pp. 762–763 of TCPv2). Calling `sendto` for two datagrams on an unconnected UDP socket then involves the following six steps by the kernel:

- connect the socket,
- output the first datagram,
- unconnect the socket,

  • connect the socket,
  • output the second datagram, and
  • unconnect the socket.

> Another consideration is the number of searches of the routing table. The first temporary con-
> nect searches the routing table for the destination IP address and saves (caches) that informa-
> tion. The second temporary connect notices that the destination address equals the destination
> of the cached routing table information (we are assuming two sendtos to the same destina-
> tion) and need not search the routing table again (pp. 737–738 of TCPv2).

When the application knows it will be sending multiple datagrams to the same
peer, it is more efficient to connect the socket explicitly. Calling connect and then calling write two times now involves the following steps by the kernel:

  • connect the socket,
  • output first datagram, and
  • output second datagram.

In this case the kernel copies only the socket address structure containing the destination IP address and port one time, versus two times when sendto is called twice. [Par-
tridge and Pink 1993] note that the temporary connecting of an unconnected UDP
socket accounts for nearly one-third of the cost of each UDP transmission.

8.12 dg_cli Function (Revisited)

We now return to the dg_cli function from Figure 8.8 and recode it to call connect.
Figure 8.17 shows the new function.

———————————————————————————— udpcliserv/dgcliconnect.c
```
 1 #include    "unp.h"

 2 void
 3 dg_cli(FILE *fp, int sockfd, const SA *pservaddr, socklen_t servlen)
 4 {
 5     int     n;
 6     char    sendline[MAXLINE], recvline[MAXLINE + 1];

 7     Connect(sockfd, (SA *) pservaddr, servlen);

 8     while (Fgets(sendline, MAXLINE, fp) != NULL) {

 9         Write(sockfd, sendline, strlen(sendline));

10         n = Read(sockfd, recvline, MAXLINE);

11         recvline[n] = 0;          /* null terminate */
12         Fputs(recvline, stdout);
13     }
14 }
```
———————————————————————————— udpcliserv/dgcliconnect.c

Figure 8.17 dg_cli function that calls connect.

The changes are the new call to connect and replacing the calls to sendto and recvfrom with calls to write and read. This function is still protocol independent since it doesn't look inside the socket address structure that is passed to connect. Our client main function, Figure 8.7, remains the same.

If we run this program on the host bsdi, specifying the IP address of the host solaris (which is not running our server on port 9877), we have the following output:

```
bsdi % udpcli04 206.62.226.33
hello, world
read error: Connection refused
```

The first point we notice is that we do *not* receive the error when we start the client process. The error occurs only after we send the first datagram to the server. It is sending this datagram that elicits the ICMP error from the server host. But when a TCP client calls connect, specifying a server host that is not running the server process, connect returns the error because the call to connect causes the first packet of TCP's three-way handshake to be sent, and it is this packet that elicits the RST from the server TCP (Section 4.3).

Figure 8.18 shows the tcpdump output.

```
bsdi % tcpdump
 1  0.0                        bsdi.1318 > solaris.9877: udp 13
 2  0.000628 ( 0.0006)         solaris > bsdi: icmp: solaris udp port 9877 unreachable
```

Figure 8.18   tcpdump output when running Figure 8.17.

We also see in Figure A.15 that this ICMP error is mapped by the kernel into the error ECONNREFUSED, which corresponds to the message string output by our err_sys function: "Connection refused."

> Unfortunately, not all kernels return ICMP messages to a connected UDP socket, as we have shown in this section. Normally Berkeley-derived kernels return the error, while System V kernels do not. For example, if we run the same client on a Solaris 2.4 host and connect to a host that is not running our server, we can watch with tcpdump and verify that the ICMP port unreachable error is returned by the server host, but the client's call to read never returns. This bug was fixed in Solaris 2.5. UnixWare does not return the error while AIX, Digital Unix, HP-UX, and Linux all return the error.

8.13 Lack of Flow Control with UDP

We now examine the effect of UDP not having any flow control. First we modify our dg_cli function to send a fixed number of datagrams. It no longer reads from standard input. Figure 8.19 shows the new version. This function writes 2000 1400-byte UDP datagrams to the server.

We then modify the server to receive the datagrams and count the number received. This server no longer echoes the datagrams back to the client. Figure 8.20 shows the new dg_echo function. When we terminate the server with our terminal interrupt key (SIGINT), it prints the number of received datagrams and terminates.

udpcliserv/dgcliloop1.c

```
 1 #include    "unp.h"

 2 #define NDG     2000          /* #datagrams to send */
 3 #define DGLEN   1400          /* length of each datagram */

 4 void
 5 dg_cli(FILE *fp, int sockfd, const SA *pservaddr, socklen_t servlen)
 6 {
 7     int     i;
 8     char    sendline[MAXLINE];

 9     for (i = 0; i < NDG; i++) {
10         Sendto(sockfd, sendline, DGLEN, 0, pservaddr, servlen);
11     }
12 }
```

udpcliserv/dgcliloop1.c

Figure 8.19 `dg_cli` function that writes a fixed number of datagrams to server.

udpcliserv/dgecholoop1.c

```
 1 #include    "unp.h"

 2 static void recvfrom_int(int);
 3 static int count;

 4 void
 5 dg_echo(int sockfd, SA *pcliaddr, socklen_t clilen)
 6 {
 7     socklen_t len;
 8     char    mesg[MAXLINE];

 9     Signal(SIGINT, recvfrom_int);

10     for ( ; ; ) {
11         len = clilen;
12         Recvfrom(sockfd, mesg, MAXLINE, 0, pcliaddr, &len);

13         count++;
14     }
15 }

16 static void
17 recvfrom_int(int signo)
18 {
19     printf("\nreceived %d datagrams\n", count);
20     exit(0);
21 }
```

udpcliserv/dgecholoop1.c

Figure 8.20 `dg_echo` function that counts received datagrams.

We now run the server on the host `bsdi`, which was a slow 80386. We run the client on the much faster SparcStation 4. Additionally, we run `netstat -s` on the server, both before and after, as the statistics that are output tell us how many datagrams were lost. Figure 8.21 shows the output on the server.

```
bsdi % netstat -s | tail
udp:    80300 datagrams received
        0 with incomplete header
        0 with bad data length field
        0 with bad checksum
        12 dropped due to no socket
        77725 broadcast/multicast datagrams dropped due to no socket
        1970 dropped due to full socket buffers
        593 delivered
        70592 datagrams output
bsdi % udpserv06                      start our server
                                      we run the client here
^?                                    type our interrupt key after client is finished
received 82 datagrams
bsdi % netstat -s | tail
udp:    82294 datagrams received
        0 with incomplete header
        0 with bad data length field
        0 with bad checksum
        12 dropped due to no socket
        77725 broadcast/multicast datagrams dropped due to no socket
        3882 dropped due to full socket buffers
        675 delivered
        70592 datagrams output
```

Figure 8.21 Output on server host.

The client sent 2000 datagrams, but the server application received only 82 of these, for a 96% loss rate. There is *no* indication whatsoever to the server application or to the client application that these datagrams are lost. As we have said, UDP has no flow control and it is unreliable. It is trivial, as we have shown, for a UDP sender to overrun the receiver.

If we look at the netstat output, the total number of datagrams received by the server host (not the server application) is 1994 (82294 − 80300). Six datagrams were never received by the interface, either because the interface's buffers were full or they could have been discarded by the sending host. The counter "dropped due to full socket buffers" indicates how many datagrams were received by UDP but were discarded because the receiving socket's receive queue was full (p. 775 of TCPv2). This value is 1912 (3882 − 1970), which when added to the counter output by the application (82) equals the 1994 datagrams that the host received. Unfortunately, the netstat counter of the number dropped due to full socket buffer is systemwide. There is no way to determine which applications (e.g., which UDP ports) are affected.

> Notice that 97% of all the received UDP datagrams (77725 ÷ 80300) on this particular host are broadcast or multicast datagrams that are then discarded because there is no application with a socket bound to the destination port. We return to this phenomenon when we talk about broadcasting in Chapter 18.

The number of datagrams received by the server in this example is nondeterministic. It depends on many factors, such as the network load, the processing load on the client host, and the processing load on the server host. If we run this example five more times the count of received datagrams is 37, 108, 30, 108, and 114.

If we run the same client and server, but this time with the client on the slow 80386 and the server on the faster SparcStation, no datagrams are lost.

```
solaris % udpserv06
^?                                     type our interrupt key after client is finished
received 2000 datagrams
```

If we run `netstat -s` under Solaris, the output format differs from the classical Berkeley output shown in Figure 8.21. The Solaris format mimics the SNMP counters (Simple Network Management Protocol, described in Chapter 25 of TCPv1). The `netstat` counter `udpInDatagrams`, the number of UDP datagrams delivered to user processes, is 139 before and 2139 after, accounting for all 2000 datagrams. The counter `udpInOverflows`, which is not an official SNMP counter, counts the number of received UDP datagrams that are discarded because the receiving socket's receive queue has no room. Its value is 0 both before and after, as we expect.

UDP Socket Receive Buffer

The number of UDP datagrams that are queued by UDP for a given socket is limited by the size of that socket's receive buffer. We can change this with the SO_RCVBUF socket option, as we described in Section 7.5. The default size of the UDP socket receive buffer under BSD/OS is 41,600 bytes, which allows room for only 29 of our 1400-byte datagrams. If we increase the size of the socket receive buffer, we expect the server to receive additional datagrams. Figure 8.22 shows a modification to the dg_echo function from Figure 8.20 that sets the socket receive buffer to 240 Kbytes. If we run this server five times on the 80386 and the client on the SparcStation 4, the count of received datagrams is 115, 168, 179, 145, and 133. While this is slightly better than the earlier example with the default socket receive buffer, it is no panacea.

> Why do we set the receive socket buffer size to 240 × 1024 in Figure 8.22? The maximum size of a socket receive buffer in BSD/OS 2.1 defaults to 262,144 bytes (256 × 1024) but due to the buffer allocation policy (described in Chapter 2 of TCPv2) the actual limit is 246,723 bytes. Many earlier systems based on 4.3BSD restricted the size of a socket buffer to around 52,000 bytes.

8.14 Determining Outgoing Interface with UDP

A connected UDP socket can also be used to determine the outgoing interface that will be used to a particular destination. This is because of a side effect of the connect function when applied to a UDP socket: the kernel chooses the local IP address (assuming the process has not already called bind to explicitly assign this). This local IP address is chosen by searching the routing table for the destination IP address, and then using the primary IP address for the resulting interface.

———————————————————————————— udpcliserv/dgecholoop2.c

```
 1 #include     "unp.h"

 2 static void recvfrom_int(int);
 3 static int count;

 4 void
 5 dg_echo(int sockfd, SA *pcliaddr, socklen_t clilen)
 6 {
 7     int     n;
 8     socklen_t len;
 9     char    mesg[MAXLINE];

10     Signal(SIGINT, recvfrom_int);

11     n = 240 * 1024;
12     Setsockopt(sockfd, SOL_SOCKET, SO_RCVBUF, &n, sizeof(n));

13     for ( ; ; ) {
14         len = clilen;
15         Recvfrom(sockfd, mesg, MAXLINE, 0, pcliaddr, &len);

16         count++;
17     }
18 }

19 static void
20 recvfrom_int(int signo)
21 {
22     printf("\nreceived %d datagrams\n", count);
23     exit(0);
24 }
```

———————————————————————————— udpcliserv/dgecholoop2.c

Figure 8.22 dg_echo function that increases the size of the socket receive queue.

Figure 8.23 shows a simple UDP program that connects to a specified IP address and then calls getsockname, printing the local IP address and port.

If we run the program on the multihomed host bsdi, we have the following output:

```
bsdi % udpcli09 206.62.226.42
local address 206.62.226.35.1331

bsdi % udpcli09 206.62.226.65
local address 206.62.226.66.1332

bsdi % udpcli09 127.0.0.1
local address 127.0.0.1.1335
```

We see from Figure 1.16 that the first two times we run the program the command-line argument is an IP address on a different Ethernet. The kernel assigns the local IP address to the primary address of the interface on that Ethernet. That is, the .42 host is on the top Ethernet so the outgoing interface address has the .35 address. The .65 host is on the lower Ethernet so the outgoing interface has the .66 address. Calling connect on a UDP socket does not send anything to that host; it is entirely a local operation that saves the peer's IP address and port. We also see that calling connect on an unbound UDP socket also assigns an ephemeral port to the socket.

udpcliserv/udpcli09.c

```
 1 #include    "unp.h"

 2 int
 3 main(int argc, char **argv)
 4 {
 5     int     sockfd;
 6     socklen_t len;
 7     struct sockaddr_in cliaddr, servaddr;

 8     if (argc != 2)
 9         err_quit("usage: udpcli <IPaddress>");

10     sockfd = Socket(AF_INET, SOCK_DGRAM, 0);

11     bzero(&servaddr, sizeof(servaddr));
12     servaddr.sin_family = AF_INET;
13     servaddr.sin_port = htons(SERV_PORT);
14     Inet_pton(AF_INET, argv[1], &servaddr.sin_addr);

15     Connect(sockfd, (SA *) &servaddr, sizeof(servaddr));

16     len = sizeof(cliaddr);
17     Getsockname(sockfd, (SA *) &cliaddr, &len);
18     printf("local address %s\n", Sock_ntop((SA *) &cliaddr, len));

19     exit(0);
20 }
```

udpcliserv/udpcli09.c

Figure 8.23 UDP program that uses `connect` to determine outgoing interface.

Unfortunately this technique does not work on all implementations, notably SVR4-derived kernels. For example this does not work on HP-UX, Solaris 2.5, and UnixWare, but it works on AIX, Digital Unix, Linux, and Solaris 2.6.

8.15 TCP and UDP Echo Server Using `select`

We now combine our concurrent TCP echo server from Chapter 5 with our iterative UDP echo server from this chapter into a single server that uses `select` to multiplex a TCP and UDP socket. Figure 8.24 is the first half of this server.

Create listening TCP socket

14-22   A listening TCP socket is created that is bound to the server's well-known port. We set the `SO_REUSEADDR` socket option in case connections exist on this port.

Create UDP socket

23-29   A UDP socket is also created and bound to the same port. Even though the same port is used for the TCP and UDP sockets, there is no need to set the `SO_REUSEADDR` socket option before this call to `bind`, because TCP ports are independent of UDP ports.

Figure 8.25 shows the second half of our server.

—————————————————————————————— udpcliserv/udpservselect01.c

```
 1 #include     "unp.h"

 2 int
 3 main(int argc, char **argv)
 4 {
 5     int     listenfd, connfd, udpfd, nready, maxfdp1;
 6     char    mesg[MAXLINE];
 7     pid_t   childpid;
 8     fd_set  rset;
 9     ssize_t n;
10     socklen_t len;
11     const int on = 1;
12     struct sockaddr_in cliaddr, servaddr;
13     void    sig_chld(int);

14         /* create listening TCP socket */
15     listenfd = Socket(AF_INET, SOCK_STREAM, 0);

16     bzero(&servaddr, sizeof(servaddr));
17     servaddr.sin_family = AF_INET;
18     servaddr.sin_addr.s_addr = htonl(INADDR_ANY);
19     servaddr.sin_port = htons(SERV_PORT);

20     Setsockopt(listenfd, SOL_SOCKET, SO_REUSEADDR, &on, sizeof(on));
21     Bind(listenfd, (SA *) &servaddr, sizeof(servaddr));

22     Listen(listenfd, LISTENQ);

23         /* create UDP socket */
24     udpfd = Socket(AF_INET, SOCK_DGRAM, 0);

25     bzero(&servaddr, sizeof(servaddr));
26     servaddr.sin_family = AF_INET;
27     servaddr.sin_addr.s_addr = htonl(INADDR_ANY);
28     servaddr.sin_port = htons(SERV_PORT);

29     Bind(udpfd, (SA *) &servaddr, sizeof(servaddr));
```

—————————————————————————————— udpcliserv/udpservselect01.c

Figure 8.24 First half of echo server that handles TCP and UDP using select.

Establish signal handler for SIGCHLD

30   A signal handler is established for SIGCHLD because TCP connections will be handled by a child process. We showed this signal handler in Figure 5.11.

Prepare for select

31–32   We initialize a descriptor set for select and calculate the maximum of the two descriptors for which we will wait.

Call select

34–41   We call select waiting only for readability on the listening TCP socket or readability on the UDP socket. Since our sig_chld handler can interrupt our call to select, we handle an error of EINTR.

————————————————————————— udpcliserv/udpservselect01.c
```
30      Signal(SIGCHLD, sig_chld);  /* must call waitpid() */

31      FD_ZERO(&rset);
32      maxfdp1 = max(listenfd, udpfd) + 1;
33      for ( ; ; ) {
34          FD_SET(listenfd, &rset);
35          FD_SET(udpfd, &rset);
36          if ( (nready = select(maxfdp1, &rset, NULL, NULL, NULL)) < 0) {
37              if (errno == EINTR)
38                  continue;          /* back to for() */
39              else
40                  err_sys("select error");
41          }
42          if (FD_ISSET(listenfd, &rset)) {
43              len = sizeof(cliaddr);
44              connfd = Accept(listenfd, (SA *) &cliaddr, &len);

45              if ( (childpid = Fork()) == 0) {     /* child process */
46                  Close(listenfd);    /* close listening socket */
47                  str_echo(connfd);   /* process the request */
48                  exit(0);
49              }
50              Close(connfd);          /* parent closes connected socket */
51          }
52          if (FD_ISSET(udpfd, &rset)) {
53              len = sizeof(cliaddr);
54              n = Recvfrom(udpfd, mesg, MAXLINE, 0, (SA *) &cliaddr, &len);

55              Sendto(udpfd, mesg, n, 0, (SA *) &cliaddr, len);
56          }
57      }
58  }
```
————————————————————————— udpcliserv/udpservselect01.c

Figure 8.25 Second half of echo server that handles TCP and UDP using `select`.

Handle new client connection

42–51   We `accept` a new client connection when the listening TCP socket is readable, `fork` a child, and call our `str_echo` function in the child. This is the same sequence of steps that we used in Chapter 5.

Handle arrival of datagram

52–57   If the UDP socket is readable, a datagram has arrived. We read it with `recvfrom` and send it back to the client with `sendto`.

8.16 Summary

Converting our echo client–server to use UDP instead of TCP was simple. But lots of features provided by TCP are missing: detecting lost packets and retransmitting, verifying responses as being from the correct peer, and the like. We return to this topic in Section 20.5 and see what it takes to add some reliability to a UDP application.

UDP sockets can generate asynchronous errors, that is, errors that are reported some time after the packet was sent. TCP sockets always report these errors to the application, but with UDP the socket must be connected to receive these errors.

UDP has no flow control, and this is easy to demonstrate. Normally this is not a problem, because many UDP applications are built using a request–reply model, and not for transferring bulk data.

There are still more points to consider when writing UDP applications, but we save these until Chapter 20, after covering the interface functions, broadcasting, and multicasting.

Exercises

8.1 We have two applications, one using TCP and the other using UDP. 4096 bytes are in the receive buffer for the TCP socket and two 2048-byte datagrams are in the receive buffer for the UDP socket. The TCP application calls `read` with a third argument of 4096 and the UDP application calls `recvfrom` with a third argument of 4096. Is there any difference?

8.2 What happens in Figure 8.4 if we replace the final argument to `sendto` (which we show as `len`) with `clilen`?

8.3 Compile and run the UDP server in Figures 8.3 and 8.4 and then the UDP client in Figures 8.7 and 8.8. Verify that the client and server work together.

8.4 Run the `ping` program in one window, specifying the `-i 60` option (send one packet every 60 seconds; some systems use `-I` instead of `-i`), the `-v` option (print all received ICMP errors), and specifying the loopback address (normally 127.0.0.1). We will use this program to see the ICMP port unreachable returned by the server host. Then run our client from the previous exercise in another window, specifying the IP address of some host that is not running the server. What happens?

8.5 We said with Figure 8.5 that each connected TCP socket has its own socket receive buffer. What about the listening socket; do you think it has its own socket receive buffer?

8.6 Use the `sock` program (Section C.3) and a tool such as `tcpdump` (Section C.5) to test what we claimed in Section 8.10: if the client `binds` an IP address to it socket but sends a datagram that goes out some other interface, the resulting IP datagram still contains the IP address that was bound to the socket, even though this does not correspond to the outgoing interface.

8.7 Compile the programs from Section 8.13 and run the client and server on different hosts. Put a `printf` in the client each time a datagram is written to the socket. Does this change the percentage of received packets? Why? Put a `printf` in the server each time a datagram is read from the socket. Does this change the percentage of received packets? Why?

8.8 What is the largest length that we can pass to `sendto` for a UDP/IPv4 socket, that is, what is the largest amount of data that can fit into a UDP/IPv4 datagram? What changes with UDP/IPv6?

Modify Figure 8.8 to send one maximum size UDP datagram, read it back, and print the number of bytes returned by `recvfrom`.

9

Elementary Name and Address Conversions

9.1 Introduction

All the examples so far in this text have used numeric addresses for the hosts (e.g., 206.6.226.33) and numeric port numbers to identify the servers (e.g., port 13 for the standard daytime server and port 9877 for our echo server). We should, however, use names instead of numbers for numerous reasons: names are easier to remember, the numeric address can change but the name can remain the same, and with the move to IPv6 numeric addresses become much longer making it much more error prone to enter an address by hand. This chapter describes the functions that convert between names and numeric values: `gethostbyname` and `gethostbyaddr` to convert between hostnames and IP addresses, and `getservbyname` and `getservbyport` to convert between service names and port numbers.

The hostname functions have recently been enhanced to work with IPv6, in addition to IPv4, and we also describe these changes. This is the beginning of our move toward protocol independence, which we continue in Chapter 11. Indeed, Chapter 11 takes the functions that we describe in this chapter and develops numerous functions that can make our applications protocol independent.

9.2 Domain Name System

The *Domain Name System*, or DNS, is used primarily to map between hostnames and IP addresses. A hostname can be either a *simple name* , such as `solaris` or `bsdi`, or a *fully qualified domain name* (FQDN) such as `solaris.kohala.com`.

> Technically, an FQDN is also called an *absolute name* and must end with a period, but users often omit the ending period.

In this section we cover only the basics of the DNS that we need for network programming. Readers interested in additional details should consult Chapter 14 of TCPv1 and [Albitz and Liu 1997]. The additions required for IPv6 are in RFC 1886 [Thomson and Huitema 1995].

Resource Records

Entries in the DNS are known as *resource records* (RRs). There are only a few types of RRs that affect us.

A   An A record maps a hostname into a 32-bit IPv4 address. For example, here are the four DNS records for the host `solaris` in the `kohala.com` domain, the first of which is an A record:

```
solaris   IN   A      206.62.226.33
          IN   AAAA   5f1b:df00:ce3e:e200:0020:0800:2078:e3e3
          IN   MX     5  solaris.kohala.com.
          IN   MX     10 mailhost.kohala.com.
```

AAAA   A AAAA record, called a "quad A" record, maps a hostname into a 128-bit IPv6 address. The term "quad A" was chosen because a 128-bit address is four times larger than a 32-bit address.

PTR   PTR records (called "pointer records") map IP addresses into hostnames. For an IPv4 address the 4 bytes of the 32-bit address are reversed, each byte is converted to its decimal ASCII value (0–255), and `in-addr.arpa` is then appended. The resulting string is used in the PTR query.

For an IPv6 address the 32 4-bit nibbles of the 128-bit address are reversed, each nibble is converted to its corresponding hexadecimal ASCII value (0-9a-f), and `ip6.int` is appended.

For example, the two PTR records for our host `solaris` would be `33.226.62.206.in-addr.arpa` and `3.e.3.e.8.7.0.2.0.0.8.0.0.2.0.0.0.0.2.e.e.3.e.c.0.0.f.d.b.1.f.5.ip6.int`.

MX   An MX record specifies a host to act as a "mail exchanger" for the specified host. In the example for the host `solaris` above, two MX records are provided. The first has a preference value of 5 and the second has a preference value of 10. When multiple MX records exist, they are used in order of preference, starting with the smallest value.

> We do not use MX records in this text, but we mention them because they are used extensively in the real world.

CNAME   CNAME stands for "canonical name." A common use is to assign CNAME records for common services, such as `ftp` and `www`. If people use these service names, instead of the actual hostname, it is transparent if the service is moved to another host. For example, the following could be CNAMEs for our host `bsdi`:

```
ftp       IN   CNAME  bsdi.kohala.com.
www       IN   CNAME  bsdi.kohala.com.
mailhost  IN   CNAME  bsdi.kohala.com.
```

It is too early in the deployment of IPv6 to know what conventions administrators will use for hosts that support both IPv4 and IPv6. In our example earlier in this section we specified both an A record and a AAAA record for our host `solaris`. Some administrators place all AAAA records into their own subdomain, often named `ipv6`. For example the hostname associated with the AAAA record would then be `solaris.ipv6.kohala.com`. Sometimes this is done because the administrator of the dual-stack host does not have domain name responsibility for the entire domain but obtains responsibility for the separate `ipv6` subdomain.

Instead, the author places both the A record and the AAAA record under the host's normal name (as shown earlier) and creates another RR whose name ends in `-4` containing the A record, another RR whose name ends in `-6` containing the AAAA record, and another RR whose name ends in `-611` containing a AAAA record with the host's link-local address (which is sometimes handy for debugging purposes). All the records for another of our hosts are then

```
aix-4     IN   A      206.62.226.43
aix       IN   A      206.62.226.43
          IN   MX     5  aix.kohala.com.
          IN   MX     10 mailhost.kohala.com.
          IN   AAAA   5f1b:df00:ce3e:e200:0020:0800:5afc:2b36
aix-6     IN   AAAA   5f1b:df00:ce3e:e200:0020:0800:5afc:2b36
aix-611   IN   AAAA                        fe80::0800:5afc:2b36
```

This gives us additional control over the protocol chosen by some applications, as we will see in the next chapter.

Resolvers and Name Servers

Organizations run one or more *name servers*, often the program known as BIND (Berkeley Internet Name Domain). Applications such as the clients and servers that we are writing in this text contact a DNS server by calling functions in a library known as the *resolver*. The common resolver functions are `gethostbyname` and `gethostbyaddr`, both of which are described in this chapter. The former maps a hostname into its IP addresses, and the latter does the reverse mapping.

Figure 9.1 shows a typical arrangement of applications, resolvers, and name servers. We write the application code. The resolver code is contained in a system library and is link-edited into the application when the application is built. The application code calls the resolver code using normal function calls, typically calling the functions `gethostbyname` and `gethostbyaddr`.

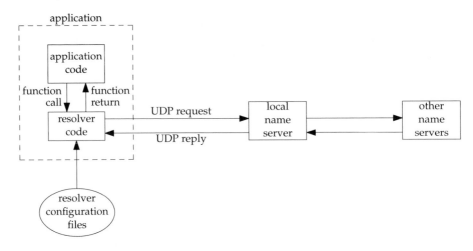

Figure 9.1 Typical arrangement of clients, resolvers, and name servers.

The resolver code reads its system-dependent configuration files to determine the location of the organization's name servers. (We use the plural "name servers" because most organizations run multiple name servers, even though we show only one local server in the figure.) The file `/etc/resolv.conf` normally contains the IP addresses of the local name servers.

The resolver sends the query to the local name server using UDP. If the local name server does not know the answer, it will normally query other name servers across the Internet, also using UDP.

DNS Alternatives

It is possible to obtain the name and address information without using the DNS and common alternatives are static hosts files (normally the file `/etc/hosts` as we describe in Figure 9.9) or NIS (Network Information System). Unfortunately it is implementation dependent how an administrator configures a host to use the different types of name service. Solaris 2.x and HP-UX 10.30 use the file `/etc/nsswitch.conf`, Digital Unix uses the file `/etc/svc.conf`, and AIX uses the file `/etc/netsvc.conf`. BIND 8.1 supplies its own version named IRS (Information Retrieval Service) that uses the file `/etc/irs.conf`. If a name server is to be used for hostname lookups, then all these systems use the file `/etc/resolv.conf` to specify the IP addresses of the name servers. Fortunately, these differences are normally hidden to the application programmer, so we just call the resolver functions such as `gethostbyname` and `gethostbyaddr`.

9.3   `gethostbyname` Function

Host computers are normally known by human-readable names. All the examples that we have shown so far in this book have intentionally used IP addresses instead of names, so we know exactly what goes into the socket address structures, for functions such as `connect` and `sendto`, and what is returned by functions such as `accept` and `recvfrom`. But most applications should deal with names and not addresses. This is especially true as we move to IPv6, since IPv6 addresses (hex strings) are much longer than IPv4 dotted-decimal numbers. (The example AAAA record and `ip6.int` PTR record in the previous section should make this obvious.)

The most basic function that looks up a hostname is `gethostbyname`. If successful, it returns a pointer to a `hostent` structure that contains all the IPv4 addresses or all the IPv6 addresses for the host.

```
#include <netdb.h>

struct hostent *gethostbyname(const char *hostname);
```
                                   Returns: nonnull pointer if OK, NULL on error with h_errno set

The nonnull pointer returned by this function points to the following `hostent` structure:

```
struct hostent {
  char   *h_name;      /* official (canonical) name of host */
  char  **h_aliases;   /* pointer to array of pointers to alias names */
  int     h_addrtype;  /* host address type: AF_INET or AF_INET6 */
  int     h_length;    /* length of address: 4 or 16 */
  char  **h_addr_list; /* ptr to array of ptrs with IPv4 or IPv6 addrs */
};

#define h_addr  h_addr_list[0]  /* first address in list */
```

In terms of the DNS, `gethostbyname` performs a query for an A record or for a AAAA record. This function can return either IPv4 addresses or IPv6 addresses. We summarize in Figure 9.5 the conditions under which it returns these two types of addresses.

> The definition of h_addr is for backward compatibility and new code should not use h_addr. 4.2BSD did not have the h_addr_list member, having a char *h_addr that pointed only to one IP address.

Figure 9.2 shows the arrangement of the `hostent` structure and the information that it points to assuming the hostname that is looked up has two alias names and three IPv4 addresses. Of these fields, the official hostname and all of the aliases are null-terminated C strings.

The returned h_name is called the *canonical* name of the host. For example, given the CNAME records shown in the previous section, the canonical name of the host `ftp.kohala.com` would be `bsdi.kohala.com`. Also, if we call `gethostbyname` from the host `solaris` with an unqualified hostname, say `solaris`, the FQDN (`solaris.kohala.com`) is returned as the canonical name.

When IPv6 addresses are returned, the h_addrtype member of the `hostent` structure is set to `AF_INET6` and the h_length member is set to 16. Figure 9.3 shows these changes, with the shaded fields having changed from Figure 9.2.

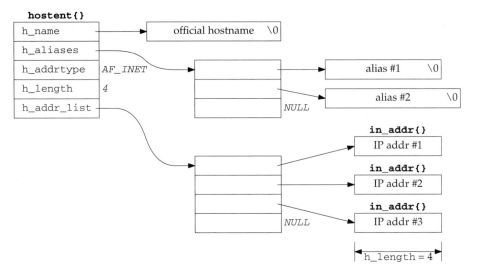

Figure 9.2 hostent structure and the information it contains.

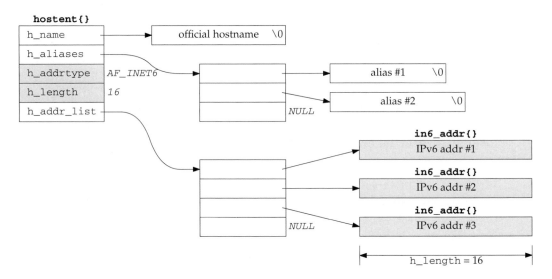

Figure 9.3 Changes in information returned in hostent structure with IPv6 addresses.

Recent versions of gethostbyname, starting around BIND release 4.9.2, allow the *hostname* argument to be a dotted-decimal string. That is, a call of the form

```
hptr = gethostbyname("206.62.226.33");
```

will work. This code was added because the Rlogin client accepts only a hostname, calling gethostbyname, and will not accept a dotted-decimal string [Vixie 1996].

gethostbyname differs from the other socket functions that we have described in that it does not set errno when an error occurs. Instead, it sets the global integer h_errno to one of the following constants defined by including <netdb.h>:

- HOST_NOT_FOUND
- TRY_AGAIN
- NO_RECOVERY
- NO_DATA (identical to NO_ADDRESS)

The NO_DATA error means the specified name is valid, but it does not have either an A record or a AAAA record. An example of this is a hostname with only an MX record.

Current releases of BIND provide the function hstrerror that takes an h_errno value as its only argument and returns a const char * pointer to a description of the error. We show some examples of the strings returned by this function in the next example.

Example

Figure 9.4 shows a simple program that calls gethostbyname for any number of command-line arguments and prints all the returned information.

8-14   gethostbyname is called for each command-line argument.

15-17   The official hostname is output followed by the list of alias names.

20-22   For this program to support both IPv4 and IPv6 addresses we allow the returned address type to be either AF_INET or AF_INET6. But we do not allow the latter unless it is defined (i.e., the host supports IPv6).

23-26   pptr points to the array of pointers to the individual addresses. For each address we call inet_ntop and print the returned string. Note that inet_ntop handles both IPv4 and IPv6 addresses, based on its first argument. Also notice that we defined str of length INET6_ADDRSTRLEN, which we said in Section 3.7 is large enough for the longest possible IPv6 address string. In our unp.h file we define this constant, even if the host does not support IPv6, so that we can always count on it being defined (avoiding yet another #ifdef within our code).

We first execute the program with the name of our host solaris, which has just one IPv4 address.

```
solaris % hostent solaris
official hostname: solaris.kohala.com
        address: 206.62.226.33
```

Notice that the official hostname is the FQDN. Also notice that even though this host has an IPv6 address, only the IPv4 address is returned. Next is a host with multiple IPv4 addresses.

```
solaris % hostent gemini.tuc.noao.edu
official hostname: gemini.tuc.noao.edu
        address: 140.252.1.11
        address: 140.252.3.54
        address: 140.252.4.54
        address: 140.252.8.54
```

——— names/hostent.c

```
 1 #include    "unp.h"

 2 int
 3 main(int argc, char **argv)
 4 {
 5     char    *ptr, **pptr;
 6     char    str[INET6_ADDRSTRLEN];
 7     struct hostent *hptr;

 8     while (--argc > 0) {
 9         ptr = *++argv;
10         if ( (hptr = gethostbyname(ptr)) == NULL) {
11             err_msg("gethostbyname error for host: %s: %s",
12                     ptr, hstrerror(h_errno));
13             continue;
14         }
15         printf("official hostname: %s\n", hptr->h_name);

16         for (pptr = hptr->h_aliases; *pptr != NULL; pptr++)
17             printf("\talias: %s\n", *pptr);

18         switch (hptr->h_addrtype) {
19         case AF_INET:
20 #ifdef  AF_INET6
21         case AF_INET6:
22 #endif
23             pptr = hptr->h_addr_list;
24             for ( ; *pptr != NULL; pptr++)
25                 printf("\taddress: %s\n",
26                         Inet_ntop(hptr->h_addrtype, *pptr, str, sizeof(str)));
27             break;

28         default:
29             err_ret("unknown address type");
30             break;
31         }
32     }
33     exit(0);
34 }
```

——— names/hostent.c

Figure 9.4 Call `gethostbyname` and print returned information.

Next is a name that we showed in Section 9.2 as having a CNAME record.

```
solaris % hostent www
official hostname: bsdi.kohala.com
        alias: www.kohala.com
        address: 206.62.226.35
```

As expected, the official hostname differs from our command-line argument.

To see the error strings returned by the `hstrerror` function we first specify a non-existent hostname, and then a name that has only an MX record.

```
solaris % hostent nosuchname
gethostbyname error for host: nosuchname: Unknown host

solaris % hostent uunet.uu.net
gethostbyname error for host: uunet.uu.net: No address associated with name
```

9.4 `RES_USE_INET6` **Resolver Option**

Newer releases of BIND (4.9.4 and later) provide a resolver option named RES_USE_INET6 that we can set in three different ways. We can use this option to tell the resolver that we want IPv6 addresses returned by gethostbyname, instead of IPv4 addresses.

1. An application can set this option itself by first calling the resolver's res_init function and then enabling the option:

    ```
    #include <resolv.h>

    res_init();
    _res.options |= RES_USE_INET6;
    ```

    This must be done before the first call to gethostbyname or gethostbyaddr. The effect of this option is only on the application that sets the option.

2. If the environment variable RES_OPTIONS contains the string inet6, the option is enabled. The effect of this option depends on the scope of the environment variable. If we set it in our .profile file for example (assuming a Korn-Shell) with the export attribute, as in

    ```
    export RES_OPTIONS=inet6
    ```

    then it affects every program that we run from our login shell. But if we just set the variable on a command line (as we show shortly), then it affects only that command.

3. The resolver configuration file (normally /etc/resolv.conf) can contain the line

    ```
    options inet6
    ```

    Be aware, however, that setting this option in the resolver configuration file affects *all* applications on the host that call the resolver functions. Therefore this technique should not be used until all applications on the host are capable of handling IPv6 addresses returned in a hostent structure.

The first method sets the option on a per-application basis, the second method on a per-user basis, and the third method on a per-system basis.

We now run our example program from Figure 9.4 setting the environment variable RES_OPTIONS to the value inet6.

```
solaris % RES_OPTIONS=inet6 hostent solaris    a name with a AAAA record
official hostname: solaris.kohala.com
        address: 5f1b:df00:ce3e:e200:20:800:2078:e3e3

solaris % RES_OPTIONS=inet6 hostent bsdi    a name without a AAAA record
official hostname: bsdi.kohala.com
        address: ::ffff:206.62.226.35
        address: ::ffff:206.62.226.66
```

The first time we execute our program it returns the IPv6 address of the host (recall its AAAA record in Section 9.2). The second time we execute our program we specify a hostname that does not have a AAAA record. Still IPv6 addresses are returned: the IPv4-mapped IPv6 addresses (Section A.5).

We talk more about the IPv6 support in the resolver in the next two sections.

9.5   `gethostbyname2` Function and IPv6 Support

When support for IPv6 was added to BIND 4.9.4, the function `gethostbyname2` was added, which has two arguments, allowing us to specify the address family.

```
#include <netdb.h>

struct hostent *gethostbyname2(const char *hostname, int family);
```
                    Returns: nonnull pointer if OK, NULL on error with h_errno set

The return value is the same as with `gethostbyname`, a pointer to a `hostent` structure, and this structure remains the same. The logic of the function depends on the `family` argument and on the `RES_USE_INET6` resolver option (which we mentioned at the end of the previous section).

Before describing the details, Figure 9.5 summarizes the operation of `gethostbyname` and `gethostbyname2` with regard to the new `RES_USE_INET6` option. We show in a bolder font the values that can change:

- whether the `RES_USE_INET6` option is **off** or **on**,
- whether the second argument to `gethostbyname2` is **AF_INET** or **AF_INET6**,
- whether the resolver searches for **A** records or **AAAA** records, and
- whether the returned addresses are of length **4** or **16**.

The operation of `gethostbyname2` is as follows:

- If the *family* argument is AF_INET, a query is made for A records. If unsuccessful, the function returns a null pointer. If successful, the type and size of the returned addresses depends on the new `RES_USE_INET6` resolver option: if the option is not set (the default), IPv4 addresses are returned and the `h_length` member of the `hostent` structure will be 4; if the option is set, IPv4-mapped IPv6 addresses are returned and the `h_length` member of the `hostent` structure will be 16.

	RES_USE_INET6 option	
	off	on
gethostbyname (*host*)	Search for **A** records. If found, return IPv4 addresses (h_length = **4**). Else error. This provides backward compatibility for all existing IPv4 applications.	Search for **AAAA** records. If found, return IPv6 addresses (h_length = **16**). Else search for **A** records. If found, return IPv4-mapped IPv6 addresses (h_length = **16**). Else error.
gethostbyname2 (*host*, **AF_INET**)	Search for **A** records. If found, return IPv4 addresses (h_length = **4**). Else error.	Search for **A** records. If found, return IPv4-mapped IPv6 addresses (h_length = **16**). Else error.
gethostbyname2 (*host*, **AF_INET6**)	Search for **AAAA** records. If found, return IPv6 addresses (h_length = **16**). Else error.	Search for **AAAA** records. If found, return IPv6 addresses (h_length = **16**). Else error.

Figure 9.5 gethostbyname and gethostbyname2 with resolver RES_USE_INET6 option.

- If the *family* argument is AF_INET6, a query is made for AAAA records. If successful, IPv6 addresses are returned and the h_length member of the hostent structure will be 16; otherwise the function returns a null pointer.

This function can be used if the application wants to force a search for one specific type of address, either IPv4 or IPv6. But it is more common for applications to call gethostbyname, and newer versions of this function can return either IPv4 or IPv6 addresses.

One way to describe the actions of gethostbyname and the RES_USE_INET6 option is to look at its source code, which we show in Figure 9.6.

If the resolver has not yet been initialized (the RES_INIT flag is not set), res_init is called. This initialization function examines and processes the RES_OPTIONS environment variable. If this variable contains the string inet6 or if the resolver configuration file contains the options inet6 line, then the flag RES_USE_INET6 is set by res_init. The res_init function is normally called automatically by gethostbyname (as we show here) the first time it is called by the application, or by gethostbyaddr. Alternately, we showed that the application can also call res_init and then set the RES_USE_INET6 flag explicitly.

If the RES_USE_INET6 option is *not* set, the last line of the function is executed and gethostbyname2 is called with an address family argument of AF_INET. We saw in Figure 9.5 that this call searches for only A records. This provides backward compatibility for all existing applications.

If the RES_USE_INET6 option is enabled, gethostbyname2 is called with an address family argument of AF_INET6 to search for AAAA records (Figure 9.5). If this succeeds, gethostbyname returns. If this fails, gethostbyname2 is called with an address family argument of AF_INET to search for A records. If this succeeds, what is

```
struct hostent *
gethostbyname(const char *name)
{
    struct hostent *hp;

    if ((_res.options & RES_INIT) == 0 && res_init() == -1) {
            h_errno = NETDB_INTERNAL;
            return (NULL);
    }

    if (_res.options & RES_USE_INET6) {
        hp = gethostbyname2(name, AF_INET6);
        if (hp)
            return (hp);
    }
    return (gethostbyname2(name, AF_INET));
}
```

Figure 9.6 gethostbyname function and IPv6 support.

not apparent in Figure 9.6 is that these 4-byte addresses are automatically mapped into 16-byte IPv4-mapped IPv6 addresses.

In summary, when the RES_USE_INET6 option is enabled and the application calls gethostbyname, the application is telling the resolver "I want only IPv6 addresses returned, period. Search for AAAA records first, but if none are found then search for A records and if they are found, return the addresses as IPv4-mapped IPv6 addresses."

9.6 **gethostbyaddr Function**

The function gethostbyaddr takes a binary IP address and tries to find the hostname corresponding to that address. This is the reverse of gethostbyname.

```
#include <netdb.h>

struct hostent *gethostbyaddr(const char *addr, size_t len, int family);
```
                                   Returns: nonnull pointer if OK, NULL on error with h_errno set

This function returns a pointer to the same hostent structure that we described with gethostbyname. The field of interest in this structure is normally h_name, the canonical hostname.

The *addr* argument is not a char* but is really a pointer to an in_addr or in6_addr structure containing the IPv4 or IPv6 address. *len* is the size of this structure: 4 for an IPv4 addresses, or 16 for an IPv6 address. The *family* argument is either AF_INET or AF_INET6.

In terms of the DNS, gethostbyaddr queries a name server for a PTR record in the in-addr.arpa domain for an IPv4 address, or a PTR record in the ip6.int domain for an IPv6 address.

`gethostbyaddr` Function and IPv6 Support

`gethostbyaddr` has always had an address family argument, so when IPv6 support was added to BIND there was no need to invent another function (similar to `gethostbyname2`). But there are a few differences with `gethostbyaddr` when the argument is an IPv6 address. The following three tests are applied in the order listed:

1. If the *family* is `AF_INET6`, the *len* is 16, and the address is an IPv4-mapped IPv6 address, then the low-order 32 bits of the address (the IPv4 portion) are looked up in the `in-addr.arpa` domain.

2. If the *family* is `AF_INET6`, the *len* is 16, and the address is an IPv4-compatible IPv6 address, then the low-order 32 bits of the address (the IPv4 portion) are looked up in the `in-addr.arpa` domain.

3. If an IPv4 address was looked up (either the `family` argument was `AF_INET` or one of the two cases above were true) and the `RES_USE_INET6` resolver option is set, then the one returned address (a copy of the *addr* argument) is converted to an IPv4-mapped address: `h_addrtype` is `AF_INET6` and `h_length` is 16.

The third point is usually of little importance because few applications examine the IP address returned by `gethostbyaddr`, since it is just a copy of the argument. Applications normally call this function to examine the `h_name` member of the returned `hostent` structure (and possibly the aliases too).

9.7 `uname` Function

The `uname` function returns the name of the current host. This function is not part of the resolver library, but we cover it here because it is often used along with `gethostbyname` to determine the local host's IP addresses.

```
#include <sys/utsname.h>

int uname(struct utsname *name);
```
Returns: nonnegative value if OK, –1 on error

This function fills in a `utsname` structure whose address is passed by the caller:

```
#define _UTS_NAMESIZE   16
#define _UTS_NODESIZE   256

struct utsname {
  char   sysname[_UTS_NAMESIZE];   /* name of this operating system */
  char   nodename[_UTS_NODESIZE];  /* name of this node */
  char   release[_UTS_NAMESIZE];   /* O.S. release level */
  char   version[_UTS_NAMESIZE];   /* O.S. version level */
  char   machine[_UTS_NAMESIZE];   /* hardware type */
};
```

Unfortunately all that Posix.1 specifies is the names of the five structure members that we show, and that each array is a null-terminated array of characters. Nothing is said about the size of each array or its contents. The sizes that we show are from 4.4BSD. Other operating systems use different sizes.

The most important omission, from our network programming perspective, is a definition of the size and contents of the `nodename` array. Some systems store only the hostname in this array (e.g., `gemini`) while others store the FQDN (e.g., `gemini.tuc.noao.edu`). On some operating systems, such as Solaris 2.x, it can contain either, depending on how the operating system was installed by the administrator.

Example: Determine Local Host's IP addresses

To determine the local host's IP addresses we call `uname` to obtain the host's name, and then `gethostbyname` to obtain all of its IP addresses. The `my_addrs` function shown in Figure 9.7 performs these steps.

———————————————————————————————————— lib/my_addrs.c

```
 1 #include      "unp.h"
 2 #include      <sys/utsname.h>

 3 char **
 4 my_addrs(int *addrtype)
 5 {
 6     struct hostent *hptr;
 7     struct utsname myname;

 8     if (uname(&myname) < 0)
 9         return (NULL);

10     if ( (hptr = gethostbyname(myname.nodename)) == NULL)
11         return (NULL);

12     *addrtype = hptr->h_addrtype;
13     return (hptr->h_addr_list);
14 }
```

———————————————————————————————————— lib/my_addrs.c

Figure 9.7 Function to return all of a host's IP addresses.

The return value of the function is the `h_addr_list` member of the `hostent` structure, the array of pointers to the IP addresses. We also return the address family through the pointer argument.

Another way to determine the local host's IP addresses is with the `SIOCGIFCONF` command of `ioctl`. We discuss this in Chapter 16.

9.8   `gethostname` Function

The `gethostname` function also returns the name of the current host.

```
#include <unistd.h>

int gethostname(char *name, size_t namelen);
```

                                                        Returns: 0 if OK, −1 on error

name is a pointer to where the hostname is stored, and *namelen* is the size of this array. If there is room, the hostname is null terminated. The maximum size of the hostname is normally the MAXHOSTNAMELEN constant that is defined by including the <sys/param.h> header.

> Historically uname was defined by System V and gethostname by Berkeley. Posix.1 specifies uname but Unix 98 requires both.

9.9   getservbyname and getservbyport Functions

Services, like hosts, are often known by names too. If we refer to a service in our code by its name, instead of by its port number, and if the mapping from the name to port number is contained in a file (normally /etc/services), then if the port number changes, all we need modify is one line in the /etc/services file, instead of having to recompile the applications. The next function, getservbyname, looks up a service given its name.

```
#include <netdb.h>

struct servent *getservbyname(const char *servname, const char *protoname);
```

                                              Returns: nonnull pointer if OK, NULL on error

This function returns a pointer to the following structure:

```
struct servent {
  char   *s_name;      /* official service name */
  char   **s_aliases;  /* alias list */
  int     s_port;      /* port number, network-byte order */
  char   *s_proto;     /* protocol to use */
};
```

The service name *servname* must be specified. If a protocol is also specified (if *protoname* is a nonnull pointer), then the entry must also have a matching protocol. Some Internet services are provided using either TCP or UDP (for example, the DNS and all the services in Figure 2.13), while others support only a single protocol (FTP requires TCP.) If *protoname* is not specified and the service supports multiple protocols, it is implementation dependent which port number is returned. Normally this does not matter, because services that support multiple protocols often use the same TCP and UDP port number, but this is not guaranteed.

The main field of interest in the servent structure is the port number. Since the port number is returned in network-byte order, we must not call htons when storing this into a socket address structure.

Typical calls to this function could be

```
struct servent  *sptr;

sptr = getservbyname("domain", "udp"); /* DNS using UDP */
sptr = getservbyname("ftp", "tcp");    /* FTP using TCP */
sptr = getservbyname("ftp", NULL);     /* FTP using TCP */
sptr = getservbyname("ftp", "udp");    /* this call will fail */
```

Since FTP supports only TCP, the second and third calls are the same, and the fourth call will fail. Typical lines from the /etc/services file are

```
solaris % grep -e ftp -e domain /etc/services
ftp-data        20/tcp
ftp             21/tcp
domain          53/udp
domain          53/tcp
tftp            69/udp
```

The next function, getservbyport, looks up a service given its port number and an optional protocol.

```
#include <netdb.h>

struct servent *getservbyport(int port, const char *protname);
```

                                          Returns: nonnull pointer if OK, NULL on error

The *port* value must be network byte ordered. Typical calls to this function could be

```
struct servent  *sptr;

sptr = getservbyport(htons(53), "udp");  /* DNS using UDP */
sptr = getservbyport(htons(21), "tcp");  /* FTP using TCP */
sptr = getservbyport(htons(21), NULL);   /* FTP using TCP */
sptr = getservbyport(htons(21), "udp");  /* this call will fail */
```

The last call fails because there is no service that uses port 21 with UDP.

Be aware that a few port numbers are used with TCP for one service, but the same port number is used with UDP for a totally different service. For example,

```
solaris % grep 514 /etc/services
shell           514/tcp
syslog          514/udp
```

shows that port 514 is used by the rsh command with TCP but with the syslog daemon with UDP. Ports 512–514 have this property.

Example: Using `gethostbyname` and `getservbyname`

We can now modify our TCP daytime client from Figure 1.5 to use gethostbyname and getservbyname and take two command-line arguments: a hostname and a service name. Figure 9.8 shows our program. This program also shows the desired behavior of attempting to connect to all the IP addresses for a multihomed server, until one succeeds or all the addresses have been tried.

names/daytimetcpcli1.c

```
 1 #include     "unp.h"

 2 int
 3 main(int argc, char **argv)
 4 {
 5     int     sockfd, n;
 6     char    recvline[MAXLINE + 1];
 7     struct sockaddr_in servaddr;
 3     struct in_addr **pptr;
 9     struct hostent *hp;
10     struct servent *sp;

11     if (argc != 3)
12         err_quit("usage: daytimetcpcli1 <hostname> <service>");

13     if ( (hp = gethostbyname(argv[1])) == NULL)
14         err_quit("hostname error for %s: %s", argv[1], hstrerror(h_errno));

15     if ( (sp = getservbyname(argv[2], "tcp")) == NULL)
16         err_quit("getservbyname error for %s", argv[2]);

17     pptr = (struct in_addr **) hp->h_addr_list;
18     for ( ; *pptr != NULL; pptr++) {
19         sockfd = Socket(AF_INET, SOCK_STREAM, 0);

20         bzero(&servaddr, sizeof(servaddr));
21         servaddr.sin_family = AF_INET;
22         servaddr.sin_port = sp->s_port;
23         memcpy(&servaddr.sin_addr, *pptr, sizeof(struct in_addr));
24         printf("trying %s\n",
25                 Sock_ntop((SA *) &servaddr, sizeof(servaddr)));

26         if (connect(sockfd, (SA *) &servaddr, sizeof(servaddr)) == 0)
27             break;                /* success */
28         err_ret("connect error");
29         close(sockfd);
30     }
31     if (*pptr == NULL)
32         err_quit("unable to connect");

33     while ( (n = Read(sockfd, recvline, MAXLINE)) > 0) {
34         recvline[n] = 0;          /* null terminate */
35         Fputs(recvline, stdout);
36     }
37     exit(0);
38 }
```

names/daytimetcpcli1.c

Figure 9.8 Our daytime client that uses gethostbyname and getservbyname.

Call gethostbyname and getservbyname

13-16   The first command-line argument is a hostname, which we pass as an argument to gethostbyname and the second is a service name, which we pass as an argument to getservbyname. Our code assumes TCP, and that is what we code as the second argument to getservbyname.

Try each server address

18-25   We now code the calls to socket and connect in a loop that is executed for every server address until a connect succeeds or the list of IP addresses is exhausted. After calling socket, we fill in an Internet socket address structure with the IP address and port of the server. While we could move the call to bzero and the subsequent two assignments out of the loop, for efficiency, the code is easier to read as shown. Establishing the connection with the server is rarely the performance bottleneck of a network client.

Call connect

26-30   connect is called, and if it succeeds, break terminates the loop. If the connection establishment fails, we print an error and close the socket. Recall that a descriptor that fails a call to connect must be closed and is no longer usable.

Check for failure

31-32   If the loop terminates because no call to connect succeeded, the program terminates.

Read server's reply

33-37   Otherwise we read the server's response, terminating when the server closes the connection.

If we run this program specifying one of our hosts that is running the daytime server we get the expected output:

```
solaris % daytimetcpcli1 aix daytime
trying 206.62.226.35.13
Thu May 22 19:28:11 1997
```

What is more interesting is to run the program to a multihomed router that is not running the daytime server:

```
solaris % daytimetcpcli1 gateway.tuc.noao.edu daytime
trying 140.252.1.4.13
connect error: Connection refused
trying 140.252.101.4.13
connect error: Connection refused
trying 140.252.102.1.13
connect error: Connection refused
trying 140.252.104.1.13
connect error: Connection refused
trying 140.252.3.6.13
connect error: Connection refused
trying 140.252.4.100.13
connect error: Connection refused
unable to connect
```

9.10 Other Networking Information

Our focus in this chapter has been on hostnames and IP addresses and service names and their port numbers. But looking at the bigger picture, there are four types of information (related to networking) that an application might want to look up: hosts, networks, protocols, and services. Most lookups are for hosts (gethostbyname and gethostbyaddr), with a smaller number for services (getservbyname and getservbyaddr), and an even smaller number for networks and protocols.

All four types of information can be stored in a file and three functions are defined for each of the four types:

1. A getXXXent function that reads the next entry in the file, opening the file if necessary.

2. A setXXXent function that opens (if not already open) and rewinds the file.

3. A endXXXent function that closes the file.

Each of the four types of information defines its own structure, and these definitions are defined by including the <netdb.h> header: the hostent, netent, protoent, and servent structures.

In addition to the three get, set, and end functions, which allow sequential processing of the file, each of the four types of information provides some *keyed lookup* functions. These functions go through the file sequentially (calling the getXXXent function to read each line) but instead of returning each line to the caller, these functions look for an entry that matches an argument. These keyed lookup functions have names of the form getXXXbyYYY. For example, the two keyed lookup functions for the host information are gethostbyname (look for an entry that matches a hostname) and gethostbyaddr (look for an entry that matches an IP address). Figure 9.9 summarizes this information.

Information	Data file	Structure	Keyed lookup functions	
hosts	/etc/hosts	hostent	gethostbyaddr,	gethostbyname
networks	/etc/networks	netent	getnetbyaddr,	getnetbyname
protocols	/etc/protocols	protoent	getprotobyname,	getprotobynumber
services	/etc/services	servent	getservbyname,	getservbyport

Figure 9.9 Four types of network-related information.

How does this apply when the DNS is being used? First, only the host and network information is available through the DNS. The protocol and service information is always read from the corresponding file. We mentioned earlier in this chapter (with Figure 9.1) that different implementations use different ways for the administrator to specify whether to use the DNS or a file for the host and network information.

Second, if the DNS is being used for the host and network information, then only the keyed lookup functions make sense. You cannot, for example, use `gethostent` and expect to sequence through all entries in the DNS! If `gethostent` is called, it reads only the hosts file and avoids the DNS.

> Although the network information can be made available through the DNS, few people set this up. Pages 346–348 of [Albitz and Liu 1997] describe this feature. Typically, however, administrators build and maintain an `/etc/networks` file and it is used instead of the DNS. The `netstat` program with the `-i` option uses this file, if present, and prints the name for each network.

9.11 Summary

The set of functions that an application calls to convert a hostname into an IP address and vice versa is called the resolver. The two functions `gethostbyname` and `gethostbyaddr` are the common entry points. With the move to IPv6 the `hostent` structure filled in by these two functions remains the same, but some of the information within this structure changes. A new function, `gethostbyname2`, and a new resolver option, `RES_USE_INET6`, are also needed for IPv6 support.

The commonly used function dealing with service names and port numbers is `getservbyname`, which takes a service name and returns a structure containing the port number. This mapping is normally contained in a text file. Additional functions exist to map protocol names into protocol numbers, and network names into network numbers, but these are rarely used.

Another alternative that we have not mentioned is calling the resolver functions directly, instead of using `gethostbyname` and `gethostbyaddr`. One program that invokes the DNS this way is `sendmail` to search for an MX record, something that the `gethostbyXXX` functions cannot do. The resolver functions have names that begin with `res_` and the `res_init` function that we described in Section 9.3 is an example. A description of these functions and an example program that calls them is in Chapter 14 of [Albitz and Liu 1997] and typing `man resolver` should display the manual pages for these functions.

We continue the topic of name and address conversions in Chapter 11 when we look at a protocol-independent interface to `gethostbyname` and `gethostbyaddr`: the `getaddrinfo` and `getnameinfo` functions. These two new functions were designed to work with IPv4 and IPv6, but we first need to look at some interoperability aspects of IPv4 and IPv6 in the next chapter, before discussing the newer functions.

Exercises

9.1   Modify the program in Figure 9.4 to call `gethostbyaddr` for each returned address, and then print the h_name that is returned. First run the program specifying a hostname with just one IP address and then run the program specifying a hostname that has more than one IP address. What happens?

9.2   Fix the problem shown in the preceding exercise.

9.3   Modify Figure 9.7 to call `gethostname` instead of `uname`. Write a `main` function to call `my_addrs` and then print the IP addresses.

9.4   In Figure 9.8 what can happen if we change the third argument to `memcpy` (when filling in the socket address structure) to be `hp->h_length`? (*Hint*: Consider what happens if we set `RES_OPTIONS=inet6` when executing the program and specify a hostname that has an IPv6 address.)

9.5   Run Figure 9.8 specifying a service name of `chargen`.

9.6   Run Figure 9.8 specifying a dotted-decimal IP address as the hostname. Does your resolver allow this? Modify Figure 9.8 to allow a dotted-decimal IP address as the hostname and to allow a decimal port number string as the service name. In testing the IP address for either a dotted-decimal string or a hostname, in what order should these two tests be performed?

9.7   Modify Figure 9.8 to work with either IPv4 of IPv6.

9.8   Modify Figure 8.9 to query the DNS and compare the returned IP address with all of the destination host's IP addresses. That is, call `gethostbyaddr` using the IP address returned by `recvfrom`, followed by `gethostbyname` to find all the IP addresses for the host.

Part 3

Advanced Sockets

10

IPv4 and IPv6 Interoperability

10.1 Introduction

Over the coming years there will probably be a gradual transition of the Internet from IPv4 to IPv6. During this transition phase it is important that existing IPv4 applications continue to work with newer IPv6 applications. For example, a vendor cannot provide a Telnet client that works only with IPv6 Telnet servers but must provide one that works with IPv4 servers and one that works with IPv6 servers. Better yet would be one IPv6 Telnet client that can work with both IPv4 and IPv6 servers, along with one Telnet server that can work with both IPv4 and IPv6 clients. We will see how this is done in this chapter.

We assume throughout this chapter that the hosts are running *dual stacks*, that is both an IPv4 protocol stack and an IPv6 protocol stack. Our example in Figure 2.1 is a dual-stack host. Hosts and routers will probably run like this for many years into the transition to IPv6. At some point many systems will be able to turn off their IPv4 stack, but only time will tell when (and if) that will occur.

In this chapter we discuss how IPv4 applications and IPv6 applications can communicate with each other. There are four combinations of clients and servers using either IPv4 or IPv6 and we show these in Figure 10.1.

	IPv4 server	IPv6 server
IPv4 client	Almost all existing clients and servers.	Discussed in Section 10.2.
IPv6 client	Discussed in Section 10.3.	Simple modifications to most existing clients and servers (e.g., Figure 1.5 to Figure 1.6).

Figure 10.1 Combinations of clients and servers using IPv4 or IPv6.

We will not say much more about the two scenarios where the client and server use the same protocol. The interesting cases are when the client and server use different protocols.

10.2 IPv4 Client, IPv6 Server

A general property of a dual-stack host is that IPv6 servers can handle both IPv4 and IPv6 clients. This is done using IPv4-mapped IPv6 addresses (Figure A.10). Figure 10.2 shows an example of this.

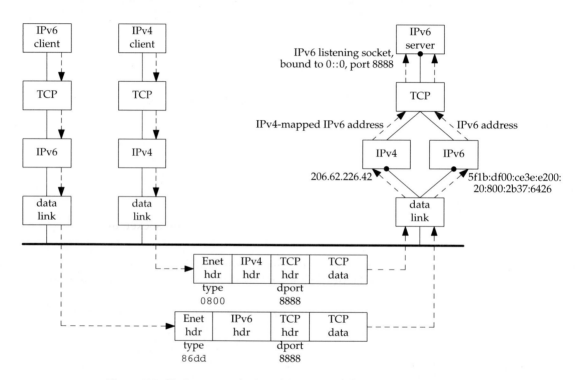

Figure 10.2   IPv6 server on dual-stack host serving IPv4 and IPv6 clients.

We have an IPv4 client and an IPv6 client on the left. The server on the right is written using IPv6 and it is running on a dual-stack host. The server has created an IPv6 listening TCP socket that is bound to the IPv6 wildcard address and TCP port 8888.

We assume the clients and server are on the same Ethernet. They could also be connected by routers, as long as all the routers support IPv4 and IPv6, but that adds nothing to this discussion. Section B.3 discusses a different case where IPv6 clients and servers are connected by IPv4-only routers.

We assume both clients send SYN segments to establish a connection with the server. The IPv4 client host will send the SYN in an IPv4 datagram and the IPv6 client host will send the SYN in an IPv6 datagram. The TCP segment from the IPv4 client appears on the wire as an Ethernet header followed by an IPv4 header, a TCP header, and the TCP data. The Ethernet header contains a type field of `0x0800`, which identifies the frame as an IPv4 frame. The TCP header contains the destination port of 8888. (Appendix A talks more about the formats and contents of these headers.) The destination IP address in the IPv4 header, which we do not show, would be 206.62.226.42.

The TCP segment from the IPv6 client appears on the wire as an Ethernet header followed by an IPv6 header, a TCP header, and the TCP data. The Ethernet header contains a type field of `0x86dd`, which identifies the frame as an IPv6 frame. The TCP header has the same format as the TCP header in the IPv4 packet and contains the destination port of 8888. The destination IP address in the IPv6 header, which we do not show, would be `5f1b:df00:ce3e:e200:20:800:2b37:6426`.

The receiving datalink looks at the Ethernet type field and passes each frame to the appropriate IP module. The IPv4 module, probably in conjunction with the TCP module, detects that the destination socket is an IPv6 socket, and the source IPv4 address in the IPv4 header is converted into the equivalent IPv4-mapped IPv6 address. That mapped address is returned to the IPv6 socket as the client's IPv6 address when `accept` returns to the server with the IPv4 client connection. All remaining datagrams for this connection are IPv4 datagrams.

When `accept` returns to the server with the IPv6 client connection, the client's IPv6 address does not change from whatever source address appears in the IPv6 header. All remaining datagrams for this connection are IPv6 datagrams.

We can summarize the steps that allow an IPv4 TCP client to communicate with an IPv6 server.

1. The IPv6 server starts, creates an IPv6 listening socket, and we assume it `binds` the wildcard address to the socket.

2. The IPv4 client calls `gethostbyname` and finds an A record for the server (Figure 9.5). The server host will have both an A record and a AAAA record, since it supports both protocols but the IPv4 client asks for only an A record.

3. The client calls `connect` and the client's host sends an IPv4 SYN to the server.

4. The server host receives the IPv4 SYN directed to the IPv6 listening socket, sets a flag indicating that this connection is using IPv4-mapped IPv6 addresses, and responds with an IPv4 SYN/ACK. When the connection is established, the address returned to the server by `accept` is the IPv4-mapped IPv6 address.

5. All communication between this client and server takes place using IPv4 datagrams.

6. Unless the server explicitly checks whether this IPv6 address is an IPv4-mapped IPv6 address (using the `IN6_IS_ADDR_V4MAPPED` macro described in Section 10.4), the server never knows that it is communicating with an IPv4 client. The dual protocol stack handles this detail. Similarly, the IPv4 client has no idea that it is communicating with an IPv6 server.

An underlying assumption in this scenario is that the dual-stack server host has both an IPv4 address and an IPv6 address. This will work until all the IPv4 addresses are taken.

The scenario is similar for an IPv6 UDP server, but the address format can change for each datagram. For example, if the IPv6 server receives a datagram from an IPv4 client, the address returned by `recvfrom` will be the client's IPv4-mapped IPv6 address. The server responds to this client's request by calling `sendto` with the IPv4-mapped IPv6 address as the destination. This address format tells the kernel to send an IPv4 datagram to the client. But the next datagram received for the server could be an IPv6 datagram, and `recvfrom` will return the IPv6 address. If the server responds, the kernel will generate an IPv6 datagram.

Figure 10.3 summarizes how a received IPv4 or IPv6 datagram is processed, depending on the type of the receiving socket, for TCP and UDP, assuming a dual-stack host.

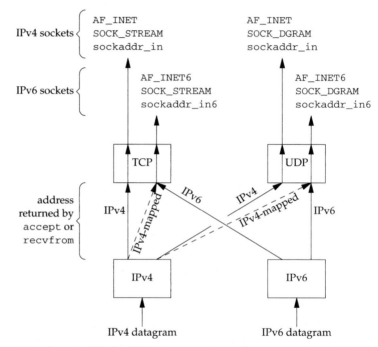

Figure 10.3 Processing of received IPv4 or IPv6 datagrams, depending on type of receiving socket.

- If an IPv4 datagram is received for an IPv4 socket, nothing special is done. These are the two arrows labeled "IPv4" in the figure, one to TCP and one to UDP. IPv4 datagrams are exchanged between the client and server.

- If an IPv6 datagram is received for an IPv6 socket, nothing special is done. These are the two arrows labeled "IPv6" in the figure, one to TCP and one to UDP. IPv6 datagrams are exchanged between the client and server.

- But when an IPv4 datagram is received for an IPv6 socket, the kernel returns the corresponding IPv4-mapped IPv6 address as the address returned by `accept` (TCP) or `recvfrom` (UDP). These are the two dashed arrows in the figure. This mapping is possible because an IPv4 address can always be represented as an

IPv6 address. IPv4 datagrams are exchanged between the client and server.

* The converse of the previous bullet is false: in general an IPv6 address cannot be represented as an IPv4 address; therefore there are no arrows from the IPv6 protocol box to the two IPv4 sockets.

Most dual-stack hosts should use the following rules in dealing with listening sockets:

1. A listening IPv4 socket can accept incoming connections from only IPv4 clients.

2. If a server has a listening IPv6 socket that has bound the wildcard address, that socket can accept incoming connections from either IPv4 clients or IPv6 clients. For a connection from an IPv4 client the server's local address for the connection will be the corresponding IPv4-mapped IPv6 address.

3. If a server has a listening IPv6 socket that has bound an IPv6 address other than an IPv4-mapped IPv6 address, that socket can accept incoming connections from IPv6 clients only.

10.3 IPv6 Client, IPv4 Server

We now swap the protocols used by the client and server from the example in the previous section. First consider an IPv6 TCP client running on a dual-stack host.

1. An IPv4 server starts on an IPv4-only host and creates an IPv4 listening socket.

2. The IPv6 client starts, calls `gethostbyname` asking for only IPv6 addresses (it enables the `RES_USE_INET6` option). Since the IPv4-only server host has only A records, we see from Figure 9.5 that an IPv4-mapped IPv6 address is returned to the client.

3. The IPv6 client calls `connect` with the IPv4-mapped IPv6 address in the IPv6 socket address structure. The kernel detects the mapped address and automatically sends an IPv4 SYN to the server.

4. The server responds with an IPv4 SYN/ACK, and the connection is established using IPv4 datagrams.

We can summarize this scenario in Figure 10.4.

* If an IPv4 TCP client calls `connect` specifying an IPv4 address, or if an IPv4 UDP client calls `sendto` specifying an IPv4 address, nothing special is done. These are the two arrows labeled "IPv4" in the figure.

* If an IPv6 TCP client calls `connect` specifying an IPv6 address, or if an IPv6 UDP client calls `sendto` specifying an IPv6 address, nothing special is done. These are the two arrow labeled "IPv6" in the figure.

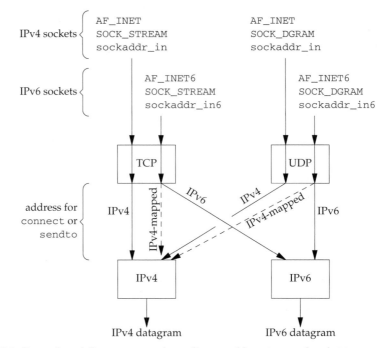

Figure 10.4 Processing of client requests, depending on address type and socket type.

- If an IPv6 TCP client specifies an IPv4-mapped IPv6 address to `connect` or if an IPv6 UDP client specifies an IPv4-mapped IPv6 address to `sendto`, the kernel detects the mapped address and causes an IPv4 datagram to be sent, instead of an IPv6 datagram. These are the two dashed arrows in the figure.

- An IPv4 client cannot specify an IPv6 address to either `connect` or `sendto` because a 16-byte IPv6 address does not fit in the 4-byte `in_addr` structure within the IPv4 `sockaddr_in` structure. Therefore there are no arrows from the IPv4 clients to the IPv6 protocol box in the figure.

In the previous section (an IPv4 datagram arriving for an IPv6 server socket) the conversion of the received address to the IPv4-mapped IPv6 address is done by the kernel and returned transparently to the application by `accept` or `recvfrom`. In this section (an IPv4 datagram needing to be sent on an IPv6 socket) the conversion of the IPv4 address to the IPv4-mapped IPv6 address is done by the resolver according to the rules in Figure 9.5, and the mapped address is then passed transparently by the application to `connect` or `sendto`.

Summary of Interoperability

Figure 10.5 summarizes this section and the previous section and the combinations of clients and servers.

	IPv4 server IPv4-only host (A only)	IPv6 server IPv6-only host (AAAA only)	IPv4 server dual-stack host (A and AAAA)	IPv6 server dual-stack host (A and AAAA)
IPv4 client, IPv4-only host	IPv4	(no)	IPv4	IPv4
IPv6 client, IPv6-only host	(no)	IPv6	(no)	IPv6
IPv4 client, dual-stack host	IPv4	(no)	IPv4	IPv4
IPv6 client, dual-stack host	IPv4	IPv6	(no*)	IPv6

Figure 10.5 Summary of interoperability between IPv4 and IPv6 clients and servers.

Each box contains "IPv4" or "IPv6" if the combination is OK, indicating which protocol is used, or "(no)" if the combination is invalid. The third column on the final row is marked with an asterisk because interoperability depends on the address chosen by the client. Choosing the AAAA record and sending an IPv6 datagram will not work. But choosing the A record, which is returned to the client as an IPv4-mapped IPv6 address, causes an IPv4 datagram to be sent, which will work.

Although it appears that one-fourth of the table will not interoperate, in the real world for the foreseeable future, most implementations of IPv6 will be on dual-stack hosts and will not be IPv6-only implementations. If we then remove the second row and second column, all of the "(no)" entries disappear and the only problem is the entry with the asterisk.

10.4   IPv6 Address Testing Macros

There are a small class of IPv6 applications that must know whether they are talking to an IPv4 peer. These applications need to know if the peer's address is an IPv4-mapped IPv6 address. Twelve macros are defined to test an IPv6 address for certain properties.

```
#include <netinet/in.h>

int IN6_IS_ADDR_UNSPECIFIED(const struct in6_addr *aptr);
int IN6_IS_ADDR_LOOPBACK(const struct in6_addr *aptr);
int IN6_IS_ADDR_MULTICAST(const struct in6_addr *aptr);
int IN6_IS_ADDR_LINKLOCAL(const struct in6_addr *aptr);
int IN6_IS_ADDR_SITELOCAL(const struct in6_addr *aptr);
int IN6_IS_ADDR_V4MAPPED(const struct in6_addr *aptr);
int IN6_IS_ADDR_V4COMPAT(const struct in6_addr *aptr);


int IN6_IS_ADDR_MC_NODELOCAL(const struct in6_addr *aptr);
int IN6_IS_ADDR_MC_LINKLOCAL(const struct in6_addr *aptr);
int IN6_IS_ADDR_MC_SITELOCAL(const struct in6_addr *aptr);
int IN6_IS_ADDR_MC_ORGLOCAL(const struct in6_addr *aptr);
int IN6_IS_ADDR_MC_GLOBAL(const struct in6_addr *aptr);
```

                    All return: nonzero if IPv6 address is of specified type, 0 otherwise

The first seven macros test the basic type of IPv6 address. We show these various address types in Section A.5. The final five macros test the scope of an IPv6 multicast address (Section 19.2).

An IPv6 client could call the `IN6_IS_ADDR_V4MAPPED` macro to test the IPv6 address returned by the resolver. An IPv6 server could call this function to test the IPv6 address returned by `accept` or `recvfrom`.

As an example of an application that needs this macro, consider FTP and its PORT command. If we start an FTP client, log in to an FTP server, and issue an FTP `dir` command, the FTP client sends a PORT command to the FTP server across the control connection. This tells the server the client's IP address and port to which the server then creates a data connection. (Chapter 27 of TCPv1 contains all the details on the FTP application protocol.) But an IPv6 FTP client must know whether the server is an IPv4 server or an IPv6 server, because the former requires a command of the form "PORT *a1,a2,a3,a4,p1,p2*" where the first four numbers (each between 0 and 255) form the 4-byte IPv4 address and the last two numbers form the 2-byte port number. An IPv6 server, however, requires an LPORT command (documented in RFC 1639 [Piscitello 1994]) containing 21 numbers. Exercise 10.1 gives an example of both commands.

10.5 `IPV6_ADDRFORM` Socket Option

The `IPV6_ADDRFORM` socket option can change a socket from one type to another, subject to the following restrictions:

1. An IPv4 socket can always be changed to an IPv6 socket. Any IPv4 addresses already associated with the socket are converted to IPv4-mapped IPv6 addresses.

2. An IPv6 socket can be changed to an IPv4 socket only if any addresses already associated with the socket are IPv4-mapped IPv6 addresses.

The reason for wanting to change the address format of a socket is that descriptors can be passed between processes easily under Unix. The most common way is across an `exec`, but we will see how a descriptor can be passed between related processes in Section 14.7 and between unrelated processes in Section 25.7.

As an example, consider a process that creates a listening IPv4 socket and then accepts a connection from an IPv4 client. This server then calls `fork` and `exec`, starting a new program to handle the client. Assume that the convention with this application is that the connected socket is passed to the new program as standard input, standard output, and standard error (this is similar to what `inetd` does, Section 12.5). We could have the pseudocode shown in Figure 10.6. The only difference from our concurrent server in Section 4.8 is duplicating the connected socket to the agreed on descriptors and then calling `exec`.

But the program that is `exec`ed expects an IPv6 socket. We can use the `IPV6_ADDRFORM` socket option to convert the socket's address format, as shown in Figure 10.7.

```
int                 listenfd, connfd;
socklen_t           clilen;
struct sockaddr_in  serv, cli;                      /* IPv4 structs */

listenfd = Socket(AF_INET, SOCK_STREAM, 0);     /* IPv4 socket */

/* fill in serv{} with well-known port */
Bind(listenfd, &serv, sizeof(serv));
Listen(listenfd, LISTENQ);

for ( ; ; ) {
    clilen = sizeof(cli);
    connfd = Accept(listenfd, &cli, &clilen);

    if (Fork() == 0) {
        Close(listenfd);               /* child */
        Dup2(connfd, STDIN_FILENO);
        Dup2(connfd, STDOUT_FILENO);
        Dup2(connfd, STDERR_FILENO);
        Close(connfd);
        Exec( ... );    /* start new program */
    }
    Close(connfd);      /* parent */
}
```

Figure 10.6 Server that accepts incoming connection and execs new program.

```
int                 af;
socklen_t           clilen;
struct sockaddr_in6 cli;        /* IPv6 struct */
struct hostent      *ptr;

af = AF_INET6;
Setsockopt(STDIN_FILENO, IPPROTO_IPV6, IPV6_ADDRFORM, &af, sizeof(af));

clilen = sizeof(cli);
Getpeername(0, &cli, &clilen);

ptr = gethostbyaddr(&cli.sin6_addr, 16, AF_INET6);
```

Figure 10.7 Converting an IPv4 socket to an IPv6 socket.

The call to setsockopt changes the address format of the socket from IPv4 to IPv6, and the call to getpeername will return an IPv4-mapped IPv6 address, assuming the socket was an IPv4 socket. But if this program is execed with an IPv6 socket on standard input, the call to setsockopt does nothing, as the address format is already IPv6.

One scenario where this socket option can be used is when the program that accepts the incoming IPv4 connection is provided by someone else (i.e., we do not have the source code to modify the program to use IPv6, or better still to be protocol independent), but our program that is execed handles IPv6.

If getsockopt is called for IPV6_ADDRFORM, the returned value is either AF_INET or AF_INET6, depending on the address format of the socket. The second argument to `getsockopt` or `setsockopt` can be either `IPPROTO_IP` or `IPPROTO_IPV6`.

10.6 Source Code Portability

Most existing network applications are written assuming IPv4. `sockaddr_in` structures are allocated and filled in and the calls to `socket` specify `AF_INET` as the first argument. We saw in the conversion from Figure 1.5 to Figure 1.6 that these IPv4 applications can be converted to use IPv6 without too much effort. Many of the changes that we showed could be done automatically using some editing scripts. Programs that are more dependent on IPv4, using features such as multicasting, IP options, or raw sockets, will take more work to convert.

If we convert an application to use IPv6 and distribute it in source code, we now have to worry whether or not the recipient's system supports IPv6. The typical way to handle this is with `#ifdefs` throughout the code, using IPv6 when possible (since we have seen in this chapter that an IPv6 client can still communicate with IPv4 servers, and vice versa). The problem with this approach is that the code becomes littered with `#ifdefs` very quickly, and harder to follow and maintain.

A better approach is to look upon the move to IPv6 as a chance to make the program protocol independent. The first step is to remove calls to `gethostbyname` and `gethostbyaddr` and use the `getaddrinfo` and `getnameinfo` functions that we describe in the next chapter. This lets us deal with socket address structures as opaque objects, referenced by a pointer and size, which is exactly what the basic socket functions do: `bind`, `connect`, `recvfrom`, and so on. Our `sock_XXX` functions from Section 3.8 can help manipulate these, independent of IPv4 or IPv6. Obviously these functions contain `#ifdefs` to handle IPv4 and IPv6, but hiding all of this protocol dependency in a few library functions makes our code simpler. We develop a set of `mcast_XXX` functions in Section 19.6 that can make multicast applications independent of IPv4 or IPv6.

Another point to consider is what happens if we compile our source code on a system that supports both IPv4 and IPv6, distribute either executable code or object files (but not the source code), and someone runs our application on a system that does not support IPv6. There is a chance that the local name server supports AAAA records and returns both AAAA records and A records for some peer with which our application tries to connect. If our application, which is IPv6-capable, calls `socket` to create an IPv6 socket, it will fail if the host does not support IPv6. We handle this in the functions described in the next chapter by ignoring the error from `socket` and trying the next address on the list returned by the name server. Assuming the peer has an A record, and that the name server returns the A record in addition to any AAAA records, the creation of an IPv4 socket will succeed. This is the type of functionality that belongs in a library function, and not in the source code of every application.

10.7 Summary

An IPv6 server on a dual-stack host can service both IPv4 clients and IPv6 clients. An IPv4 client still sends IPv4 datagrams to the server, but the server's protocol stack converts the client's address into an IPv4-mapped IPv6 address, since the IPv6 server is dealing with IPv6 socket address structures.

Similarly an IPv6 client on a dual-stack host can communicate with an IPv4 server. The client's resolver will return IPv4-mapped IPv6 addresses for all of the server's A records, and calling connect for one of these addresses results in the dual-stack sending an IPv4 SYN segment. Only a few special clients and servers need to know the protocol being used by the peer (e.g., FTP) and the IN6_IS_ADDR_V4MAPPED can be used to see if the peer is using IPv4. The IPV6_ADDRFORM socket option can be used by a program that expects one type of socket (normally an IPv6 socket).

Exercises

10.1 Start an IPv6 FTP client on a dual-stack host running IPv4 and IPv6. Connect to an IPv4 FTP server, issue the debug command, and then the dir command. Then perform the same operations but to an IPv6 server, and compare the PORT commands issued as a result of the dir commands.

10.2 Write a program that requires one command-line argument that is an IPv4 dotted-decimal address. Create an IPv4 TCP socket and bind this address to the socket along with some port, say 8888. Call listen and then pause. Write a similar program that takes an IPv6 hex string as the command-line argument and creates a listening IPv6 TCP socket. Start the IPv4 program, specifying the wildcard address as the argument. Then go to another window and start the IPv6 program, specifying the IPv6 wildcard address as the argument. Can you start the IPv6 program, since the IPv4 program has already bound that port? Does the SO_REUSEADDR socket option make a difference? What if you start the IPv6 program first, and then try to start the IPv4 program?

11

Advanced Name and Address Conversions

11.1 Introduction

The two functions described in Chapter 9, `gethostbyname` and `gethostbyaddr`, are protocol dependent. When using the former, we must know which member of the socket address structure to move the result into (e.g., the `sin_addr` member for IPv4 or the `sin6_addr` member for IPv6), and when calling the latter, we must know which member contains the binary address. This chapter begins with the new Posix.1g `getaddrinfo` function that provides protocol independence for our applications. We cover its complement, `getnameinfo`, later in the chapter.

We then use this function and develop six functions of our own that handle the typical scenarios for TCP and UDP clients and servers. We use these functions throughout the remainder of the text instead of calling `getaddrinfo` directly.

The functions `gethostbyname` and `gethostbyaddr` are also nice examples of functions that are nonreentrant. We show why this is so and describe some replacement functions that avoid this problem. Reentrancy is a problem that we come back to in Chapter 23, but we are able to show and explain the problem now, without having to understand the details of threads.

We finish the chapter showing our complete implementation of `getaddrinfo`. This lets us understand more about the function: how it operates, what it returns, and its interaction with IPv4 and IPv6.

11.2 `getaddrinfo` Function

The `getaddrinfo` function hides all of the protocol dependencies in the library function, which is where they belong. The application deals only with the socket address structures that are filled in by `getaddrinfo`. This function is defined in Posix.1g.

The Posix.1g definition of this function comes from an earlier proposal by Keith Sklower for a function named `getconninfo`. This function was the result of discussions with Eric Allman, William Durst, Michael Karels, and Steven Wise and from an early implementation written by Eric Allman. The observation that specifying a hostname and a service name would suffice for connecting to a service independent of protocol details was made by Marshall Rose in a proposal to X/Open.

```
#include <netdb.h>

int getaddrinfo(const char *hostname, const char *service,
                const struct addrinfo *hints, struct addrinfo **result);
```

Returns: 0 if OK, nonzero on error (see Figure 11.3)

This function returns, through the *result* pointer, a pointer to a linked list of `addrinfo` structures, which is defined by including `<netdb.h>`:

```
struct addrinfo {
    int     ai_flags;          /* AI_PASSIVE, AI_CANONNAME */
    int     ai_family;         /* AF_xxx */
    int     ai_socktype;       /* SOCK_xxx */
    int     ai_protocol;       /* 0 or IPPROTO_xxx for IPv4 and IPv6 */
    size_t  ai_addrlen;        /* length of ai_addr */
    char    *ai_canonname;     /* ptr to canonical name for host */
    struct sockaddr  *ai_addr; /* ptr to socket address structure */
    struct addrinfo  *ai_next; /* ptr to next structure in linked list */
};
```

The *hostname* is either a hostname or an address string (dotted-decimal for IPv4 or a hex string for IPv6). The *service* is either a service name or a decimal port number string. (Recall our solution to Exercise 9.6 where we allowed an address string for the host or a port number string for the service.)

hints is either a null pointer or a pointer to an `addrinfo` structure that the caller fills in with hints about the types of information that the caller wants returned. For example, if the specified service is provided for both TCP and UDP (e.g., the domain service, which refers to a DNS server), the caller can set the `ai_socktype` member of the *hints* structure to `SOCK_DGRAM`. The only information returned will be for datagram sockets.

The members of the *hints* structure that can be set by the caller are:

- `ai_flags` (`AI_PASSIVE`, `AI_CANONNAME`),
- `ai_family` (an `AF_xxx` value),
- `ai_socktype` (a `SOCK_xxx` value), and
- `ai_protocol`.

The `AI_PASSIVE` flag indicates that the socket will be used for a passive open, and the `AI_CANONNAME` flag tells the function to return the canonical name of the host.

If the *hints* argument is a null pointer, the function assumes a value of 0 for `ai_flags`, `ai_socktype`, and `ai_protocol`, and a value of `AF_UNSPEC` for `ai_family`.

If the function returns success (0), the variable pointed to by the *result* argument is filled in with a pointer to a linked list of `addrinfo` structures, linked through the `ai_next` pointer. There are two ways that multiple structures can be returned.

1. If there are multiple addresses associated with the *hostname*, one structure is returned for each address that is usable with the requested address family (the `ai_family` hint, if specified).

2. If the service is provided for multiple socket types, one structure can be returned for each socket type, depending on the `ai_socktype` hint.

For example, if no hints are provided and if the `domain` service is looked up for a host with two IP addresses, four `addrinfo` structures are returned:

- one for the first IP address and a socket type of `SOCK_STREAM`,
- one for the first IP address and a socket type of `SOCK_DGRAM`,
- one for the second IP address and a socket type of `SOCK_STREAM`, and
- one for the second IP address and a socket type of `SOCK_DGRAM`.

We show a picture of this example in Figure 11.1. There is no guaranteed order of the structures when multiple items are returned; that is, we cannot assume that TCP services are returned before UDP services.

> Although not guaranteed, an implementation should return the IP addresses in the same order as they are returned by the DNS. For example, many DNS servers sort the returned addresses so that if the host sending the query and the name server are on the same network, then addresses on that shared network are returned first. Also, newer versions of BIND allow the resolver to specify an address sorting order in the `/etc/resolv.conf` file.

The information returned in the `addrinfo` structures is ready for a call to `socket` and then either a call to `connect`, or `sendto` (for a client) or `bind` (for a server). The arguments to `socket` are the members `ai_family`, `ai_socktype`, and `ai_protocol`. The second and third arguments to either `connect` or `bind` are `ai_addr` (a pointer to a socket address structure of the appropriate type, filled in by `getaddrinfo`) and `ai_addrlen` (the length of this socket address structure).

If the `AI_CANONNAME` flag is set in the *hints* structure, the `ai_canonname` member of the first returned structure points to the canonical name of the host. In terms of the DNS this is normally the FQDN.

Figure 11.1 shows the returned information if we execute

```
struct addrinfo     hints, *res;

bzero(&hints, sizeof(hints));
hints.ai_flags = AI_CANONNAME;
hints.ai_family = AF_INET;

getaddrinfo("bsdi", "domain", &hints, &res);
```

In this figure everything other than the `res` variable is dynamically allocated memory (e.g., from `malloc`). We assume that the canonical name of the host `bsdi` is `bsdi.kohala.com` and that this host has two IPv4 addresses in the DNS (Figure 1.16).

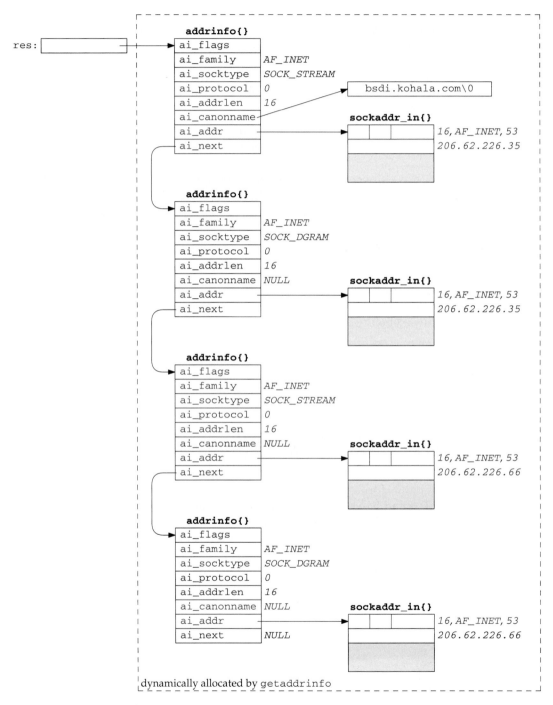

Figure 11.1 Example of information returned by getaddrinfo.

Port 53 is for the `domain` service, and realize that this port number will be in network byte order in the socket address structures. We also show the returned `ai_protocol` values as 0 since the combination of the `ai_family` and `ai_socktype` completely specifies the protocol for TCP and UDP. It would also be OK for `getaddrinfo` to return an `ai_protocol` of `IPPROTO_TCP` for the two `SOCK_STREAM` structures, and an `ai_protocol` of `IPPROTO_UDP` for the two `SOCK_DGRAM` structures.

Figure 11.2 summarizes the number of `addrinfo` structures returned for each address that is being returned, based on the specified service name (which can be a decimal port number) and any `ai_socktype` hint.

ai_socktype hint	Service is a name, service provided by:			Service is a port number
	TCP only	UDP only	TCP and UDP	
0	1	1	2	2
SOCK_STREAM	1	error	1	1
SOCK_DGRAM	error	1	1	1

Figure 11.2 Number of `addrinfo` structures returned per IP address.

Multiple `addrinfo` structures are returned for each IP address only when no `ai_socktype` hint is provided and either the service name is supported by TCP and UDP (as indicated in the `/etc/services` file) or a port number is specified.

If we enumerated all 64 possible inputs to `getaddrinfo` (there are six input variables), many would be invalid and some make little sense. Instead we will look at the common cases.

- Specify the *hostname* and *service*. This is normal for a TCP or UDP client. On return a TCP client loops through all returned IP addresses, calling `socket` and `connect` for each one, until the connection succeeds or until all addresses have been tried. We show an example of this with our `tcp_connect` function in Figure 11.6.

  For a UDP client, the socket address structure filled in by `getaddrinfo` would be used in a call to `sendto` or `connect`. If the client can tell that the first address doesn't appear to work (either an error on a connected UDP socket or a timeout on an unconnected socket), additional addresses can be tried.

  If the client knows it handles only one type of socket (e.g., Telnet and FTP clients handle only TCP, TFTP clients handle only UDP), then the `ai_socktype` member of the *hints* structure should be specified as either `SOCK_STREAM` or `SOCK_DGRAM`.

- A typical server specifies *service* but not the *hostname*, and specifies the `AI_PASSIVE` flag in the *hints* structure. The socket address structures returned should contain an IP address of `INADDR_ANY` (for IPv4) or `IN6ADDR_ANY_INIT` (for IPv6). A TCP server then calls `socket`, `bind`, and `listen`. If the server wants to `malloc` another socket address structure to obtain the client's address from `accept`, the returned `ai_addrlen` value specifies this size.

A UDP server would call socket, bind, and then recvfrom. If the server wants to malloc another socket address structure to obtain the client's address from recvfrom, the returned ai_addrlen value specifies this size.

As with the typical client code, if the server knows it only handles one type of socket, the ai_socktype member of the *hints* structure should be set to either SOCK_STREAM or SOCK_DGRAM. This avoids having multiple structures returned, possibly with the wrong ai_socktype value.

- The TCP servers that we have shown so far create one listening socket, and the UDP servers create one datagram socket. That is what we assume in the previous item. An alternate server design is for the server to handle multiple sockets using select. In this scenario the server would go through the entire list of structures returned by getaddrinfo, create one socket per structure, and use select.

> The problem with this technique is that one reason for getaddrinfo returning multiple structures is when a service can be handled by IPv4 and IPv6 (Figure 11.4). But these two protocols are not completely independent, as we saw in Section 10.2. That is, if we create a listening IPv6 socket for a given port, there is no need to also create a listening IPv4 socket for that same port, because connections arriving from IPv4 clients are automatically handled by the protocol stack and by the IPv6 listening socket.

Despite the fact that getaddrinfo is "better" than the gethostbyname and getservbyname functions (it makes it easier to write protocol-independent code, one function handles both the hostname and the service, and all the returned information is dynamically allocated, not statically allocated), it is still not as easy to use as it could be. The problem is that we must allocate a *hints* structure, initialize it to 0, fill in the desired fields, call getaddrinfo, and then traverse a linked list trying each one. In the next sections we provide some simpler interfaces for the typical TCP and UDP clients and servers that we write in the remainder of this text.

getaddrinfo solves the problem of converting hostnames and service names into socket address structures. In Section 11.13 we describe the reverse function, getnameinfo, which converts socket address structures into hostnames and service names. In Section 11.16 we provide an implementation of getaddrinfo, getnameinfo, and freeaddrinfo.

11.3 gai_strerror Function

The nonzero error return values from getaddrinfo have the names and meanings shown in Figure 11.3. The function gai_strerror takes one of these values as an argument and returns a pointer to the corresponding error string.

```
#include <netdb.h>

char *gai_strerror(int error);
```
                                    Returns: pointer to string describing error message

Constant	Description
EAI_ADDRFAMILY	address family for *hostname* not supported
EAI_AGAIN	temporary failure in name resolution
EAI_BADFLAGS	invalid value for ai_flags
EAI_FAIL	nonrecoverable failure in name resolution
EAI_FAMILY	ai_family not supported
EAI_MEMORY	memory allocation failure
EAI_NODATA	no address associated with *hostname*
EAI_NONAME	*hostname* nor *service* provided, or not known
EAI_SERVICE	*service* not supported for ai_socktype
EAI_SOCKTYPE	ai_socktype not supported
EAI_SYSTEM	system error returned in errno

Figure 11.3 Nonzero error return constants from getaddrinfo.

11.4 `freeaddrinfo` Function

All of the storage returned by getaddrinfo, the addrinfo structures, the ai_addr structures, and the ai_canonname string are obtained dynamically from malloc. This storage is returned by calling freeaddrinfo.

```
#include <netdb.h>

void freeaddrinfo(struct addrinfo *ai);
```

ai should point to the first of the addrinfo structures returned by getaddrinfo. All the structures in the linked list are freed, along with any dynamic storage pointed to by those structures (e.g., socket address structures and canonical hostnames).

Assume we call getaddrinfo, traverse the linked list of addrinfo structures, and find the desired structure. If we then try to save a copy of the information by copying just the addrinfo structure and then call freeaddrinfo, we have a lurking bug. The reason is that the addrinfo structure itself points to dynamically allocated memory (for the socket address structure and possibly the canonical name) and memory pointed to by our saved structure is returned to the system when freeaddrinfo is called and can be used for something else.

> Making a copy of just the addrinfo structure and not the structures that it in turn points to is called a *shallow copy*. Copying the addrinfo structure and all the structures that it points to is called a *deep copy*.

11.5 `getaddrinfo` Function: IPv6 and Unix Domain

Although Posix.1g defines the getaddrinfo function, it says nothing about IPv6 at all. The interaction between this function, the resolver (especially the RES_USE_INET6 option; recall Figure 9.5), and IPv6 is nontrivial. We note the following points before summarizing these interactions in Figure 11.4.

- `getaddrinfo` is dealing with two different inputs: what type of socket address structure does the caller want back and what type of records should be searched for in the DNS.

- The address family in the hints structure provided by the caller specifies the type of socket address structure that the caller expects to be returned. If the caller specifies `AF_INET`, the function must not return any `sockaddr_in6` structures and if the caller specifies `AF_INET6`, the function must not return any `sockaddr_in` structures.

- Posix.1g says that specifying `AF_UNSPEC` shall return addresses that can be used with *any* protocol family that can be used with the hostname and service name. This implies that if a host has both AAAA records and A records, the AAAA records are returned as `sockaddr_in6` structures and the A records are returned as `sockaddr_in` structures. It makes no sense to also return the A records as IPv4-mapped IPv6 addresses in `sockaddr_in6` structures as no additional information is being returned: these addresses are already being returned in `sockaddr_in` structures.

- This statement in Posix.1g also implies that if the `AI_PASSIVE` flag is specified without a hostname, then the IPv6 wildcard address (`IN6ADDR_ANY_INIT` or `0::0`) should be returned as a `sockaddr_in6` structure along with the IPv4 wildcard address (`INADDR_ANY` or 0.0.0.0), returned as a `sockaddr_in` structure. It also makes sense to return the IPv6 wildcard address first because we saw in Section 10.2 that an IPv6 server socket can handle both IPv6 and IPv4 clients on a dual-stack host.

- The resolver's `RES_USE_INET6` option along with which function is called (`gethostbyname` or `gethostbyname2`) dictates the type of records that are searched for in the DNS (A or AAAA) and what type of addresses are returned (IPv4, IPv6, or IPv4-mapped IPv6). We summarized this in Figure 9.5.

- The hostname can also be either an IPv6 hex string or an IPv4 dotted-decimal string. The validity of this string depends on the address family specified by the caller. An IPv6 hex string is not acceptable if `AF_INET` is specified, and an IPv4 dotted-decimal string is not acceptable if `AF_INET6` is specified. But either is acceptable if `AF_UNSPEC` is specified, and the appropriate type of socket address structure is returned.

> One could argue that if `AF_INET6` is specified, then a dotted-decimal string should be returned as an IPv4-mapped IPv6 address in a `sockaddr_in6` structure. But another way to obtain this result is to prefix the dotted-decimal string with `0::ffff:`.

Figure 11.4 summarizes how we expect `getaddrinfo` to handle IPv4 and IPv6 addresses. The "result" column is what we want returned to the caller, given the variables in the first three columns. The "action" column is how we obtain this result and we show the code that performs this action in our implementation of `getaddrinfo` in Section 11.16.

Hostname specified by caller	Address family specified by caller	Hostname string contains	Result	Action
nonnull hostname string; active or passive	AF_UNSPEC	hostname	all AAAA records returned as sockaddr_in6{}s *and* all A records returned as sockaddr_in{}s	two DNS searches (note 1): gethostbyname2(AF_INET6) with RES_USE_INET6 off gethostbyname2(AF_INET) with RES_USE_INET6 off
		hex string	one sockaddr_in6{}	inet_pton(AF_INET6)
		dotted decimal	one sockaddr_in{}	inet_pton(AF_INET)
	AF_INET6	hostname	all AAAA records returned as sockaddr_in6{}s, *else* all A records returned as IPv4-mapped IPv6 as sockaddr_in6{}s	gethostbyname() with RES_USE_INET6 on (note 2)
		hex string	one sockaddr_in6{}	inet_pton(AF_INET6)
		dotted decimal	error: EAI_ADDRFAMILY	
	AF_INET	hostname	all A records returned as sockaddr_in{}s	gethostbyname() with RES_USE_INET6 off
		hex string	error: EAI_ADDRFAMILY	
		dotted decimal	one sockaddr_in{}	inet_pton(AF_INET)
null hostname string; passive	AF_UNSPEC	implied 0::0 implied 0.0.0.0	one sockaddr_in6{} and one sockaddr_in{}	inet_pton(AF_INET6) inet_pton(AF_INET)
	AF_INET6	implied 0::0	one sockaddr_in6{}	inet_pton(AF_INET6)
	AF_INET	implied 0.0.0.0	one sockaddr_in{}	inet_pton(AF_INET)
null hostname string; active	AF_UNSPEC	implied 0::1 implied 127.0.0.1	one sockaddr_in6{} and one sockaddr_in{}	inet_pton(AF_INET6) inet_pton(AF_INET)
	AF_INET6	implied 0::1	one sockaddr_in6{}	inet_pton(AF_INET6)
	AF_INET	implied 127.0.0.1	one sockaddr_in{}	inet_pton(AF_INET)

Figure 11.4 Summary of getaddrinfo and its actions and results.

Note 1 is that when the two DNS searches are performed, either can fail (i.e., find no records of the desired type for the hostname) but at least one must succeed. But if both searches succeed (the hostname has both AAAA and A records), then both types of socket address structures are returned.

Note 2 is that this DNS search must succeed, or an error is returned. But since the RES_USE_INET6 option is enabled, gethostbyname first looks for the AAAA records, and if nothing is found, then looks for A records (Figure 9.6).

The setting and clearing of the resolver's RES_USE_INET6 option with the scenarios in notes 1 and 2 is to force the desired DNS search, given the rules in Figure 9.5.

We note that Figure 11.4 specifies only how getaddrinfo handles IPv4 and IPv6; that is, the number of addresses returned to the caller. The actual number of addrinfo structures returned to the caller also depends on the socket type specified and the service name, as summarized earlier in Figure 11.2.

Posix.1g says nothing specific about `getaddrinfo` and Unix domain sockets (which we describe in detail in Chapter 14). Nevertheless, adding support for Unix domain sockets to our implementation of `getaddrinfo` and testing applications with these protocols is a good test for protocol independence.

Our implementation makes the following assumption: if the hostname argument for `getaddrinfo` is either `/local` or `/unix` and the service name argument is an absolute pathname (one that begins with a slash), Unix domain socket structures are returned. Valid DNS hostnames cannot contain a slash and no existing IANA service names begin with a slash (Exercise 11.5). The socket address structures returned contain this absolute pathname, ready for a call to either `bind` or `connect`. If the caller specifies the `AI_CANONNAME` flag, the host's name (Section 9.7) is returned as the canonical name.

11.6 `getaddrinfo` Function: Examples

We will now show some examples of `getaddrinfo` using a test program that lets us enter all the parameters: the hostname, service name, address family, socket type, and the `AI_CANONNAME` and `AI_PASSIVE` flags. (We do not show this test program, as it is about 350 lines of uninteresting code. It is provided with the source code for the book, as described in the Preface.) The test program outputs information on the variable number of `addrinfo` structures that are returned, showing the arguments for a call to `socket` and the address in each socket address structure.

We first show the same example as in Figure 11.1.

```
solaris % testga  -f inet  -c  -h bsdi  -s domain

socket(AF_INET, SOCK_STREAM, 0), ai_canonname = bsdi.kohala.com
        address: 206.62.226.35.53

socket(AF_INET, SOCK_DGRAM, 0)
        address: 206.62.226.35.53

socket(AF_INET, SOCK_STREAM, 0)
        address: 206.62.226.66.53

socket(AF_INET, SOCK_DGRAM, 0)
        address: 206.62.226.66.53
```

The `-f inet` option specifies the address family, `-c` says to return the canonical name, `-h bsdi` specifies the hostname, and `-s domain` specifies the service name.

The common client scenario is to specify the address family, the socket type (the `-t` option), the hostname, and the service name. The following example shows this, for a multihomed host with six IPv4 addresses.

```
solaris % testga  -f inet  -t stream  -h gateway.tuc.noao.edu  -s daytime

socket(AF_INET, SOCK_STREAM, 0)
        address: 140.252.101.4.13

socket(AF_INET, SOCK_STREAM, 0)
        address: 140.252.102.1.13
```

```
socket(AF_INET, SOCK_STREAM, 0)
        address: 140.252.104.1.13

socket(AF_INET, SOCK_STREAM, 0)
        address: 140.252.3.6.13

socket(AF_INET, SOCK_STREAM, 0)
        address: 140.252.4.100.13

socket(AF_INET, SOCK_STREAM, 0)
        address: 140.252.1.4.13
```

Next we specify our host `alpha`, which has both a AAAA record and an A record, without specifying the address family, and a service name of `ftp`, which is provided by TCP only.

```
solaris % testga  -h alpha  -s ftp

socket(AF_INET6, SOCK_STREAM, 0)
        address: 5f1b:df00:ce3e:e200:20:800:2b37:6426.21

socket(AF_INET, SOCK_STREAM, 0)
        address: 206.62.226.42.21
```

Since we did not specify the address family, and since we ran this example on a host that supports both IPv4 and IPv6, two structures are returned: one for IPv6 and one for IPv4.

Next we specify the `AI_PASSIVE` flag (the `-p` option), do not specify an address family, do not specify a hostname (implying the wildcard address), specify a port number of 8888, and do not specify a socket type.

```
solaris % testga  -p  -s 8888

socket(AF_INET6, SOCK_STREAM, 0)
        address: ::.8888

socket(AF_INET6, SOCK_DGRAM, 0)
        address: ::.8888

socket(AF_INET, SOCK_STREAM, 0)
        address: 0.0.0.0.8888

socket(AF_INET, SOCK_DGRAM, 0)
        address: 0.0.0.0.8888
```

Four structures are returned. Since we ran this on a host that supports IPv6 and IPv4, without specifying an address family, `getaddrinfo` returns the IPv6 wildcard address and the IPv4 wildcard address. Since we specified a port number without a socket type, `getaddrinfo` returns one structure for each address specifying TCP and another structure for each address specifying UDP. The two IPv6 structures are returned before the two IPv4 structures, because we saw in Chapter 10 that an IPv6 client or server on a dual-stack host can communicate with either IPv6 or IPv4 peers.

As an example of Unix domain sockets, we specify `/local` as the hostname and `/tmp/test.1` as the service name.

```
        solaris % testga  -c  -p  -h /local  -s /tmp/test.1

    socket(AF_LOCAL, SOCK_STREAM, 0), ai_canonname = solaris.kohala.com
            address: /tmp/test.1

    socket(AF_LOCAL, SOCK_DGRAM, 0)
            address: /tmp/test.1
```

Since we do not specify the socket type, two structures are returned: the first for a
stream socket and the second for a datagram socket.

11.7 `host_serv` Function

Our first interface to `getaddrinfo` does not require the caller to allocate a hints structure and fill it in. Instead, the two fields of interest, the address family and the socket
type, are arguments to our `host_serv` function.

```
#include "unp.h"

struct addrinfo *host_serv(const char *hostname, const char *service,
                           int family, int socktype);

                              Returns: pointer to addrinfo structure if OK, NULL on error
```

Figure 11.5 shows the source code for this function.

―――――――――――――――――――――――――――――――――――――― *lib/host_serv.c*
```
 1 #include     "unp.h"

 2 struct addrinfo *
 3 host_serv(const char *host, const char *serv, int family, int socktype)
 4 {
 5     int     n;
 6     struct addrinfo hints, *res;

 7     bzero(&hints, sizeof(struct addrinfo));
 8     hints.ai_flags = AI_CANONNAME;  /* always return canonical name */
 9     hints.ai_family = family;    /* AF_UNSPEC, AF_INET, AF_INET6, etc. */
10     hints.ai_socktype = socktype;   /* 0, SOCK_STREAM, SOCK_DGRAM, etc. */

11     if ( (n = getaddrinfo(host, serv, &hints, &res)) != 0)
12         return (NULL);

13     return (res);               /* return pointer to first on linked list */
14 }
```
―――――――――――――――――――――――――――――――――――――― *lib/host_serv.c*

Figure 11.5 `host_serv` function.

7-13   The function initializes a hints structure, calls `getaddrinfo`, and returns a null
pointer if an error occurs.

We call this function from Figure 15.17 when we want to use `getaddrinfo` to
obtain the host and service information, but we want to establish the connection ourself.

11.8 `tcp_connect` Function

We now write two functions that use `getaddrinfo` to handle most scenarios for the TCP clients and servers that we write. The first function, `tcp_connect`, performs the normal client steps: create a TCP socket and connect to a server.

```
#include "unp.h"

int tcp_connect(const char *hostname, const char *service);
```
                                                Returns: connected socket descriptor if OK, no return on error

Figure 11.6 shows the source code.

─── *lib/tcp_connect.c*
```
 1 #include     "unp.h"

 2 int
 3 tcp_connect(const char *host, const char *serv)
 4 {
 5     int     sockfd, n;
 6     struct addrinfo hints, *res, *ressave;

 7     bzero(&hints, sizeof(struct addrinfo));
 8     hints.ai_family = AF_UNSPEC;
 9     hints.ai_socktype = SOCK_STREAM;

10     if ( (n = getaddrinfo(host, serv, &hints, &res)) != 0)
11         err_quit("tcp_connect error for %s, %s: %s",
12                 host, serv, gai_strerror(n));
13     ressave = res;

14     do {
15         sockfd = socket(res->ai_family, res->ai_socktype, res->ai_protocol);
16         if (sockfd < 0)
17             continue;          /* ignore this one */

18         if (connect(sockfd, res->ai_addr, res->ai_addrlen) == 0)
19             break;             /* success */

20         Close(sockfd);         /* ignore this one */
21     } while ( (res = res->ai_next) != NULL);

22     if (res == NULL)          /* errno set from final connect() */
23         err_sys("tcp_connect error for %s, %s", host, serv);

24     freeaddrinfo(ressave);

25     return (sockfd);
26 }
```
─── *lib/tcp_connect.c*

Figure 11.6 `tcp_connect` function: perform normal client steps.

Call `getaddrinfo`

7–13   `getaddrinfo` is called once and we specify the address family as `AF_UNSPEC` and the socket type as `SOCK_STREAM`.

Try each `addrinfo` structure until success or end of list

14–25   Each returned IP address is then tried: `socket` and `connect` are called. It is not a fatal error for `socket` to fail, as this could happen if an IPv6 address were returned but the host kernel does not support IPv6. If `connect` succeeds, a `break` is made out of the loop. Otherwise, when all the addresses have been tried, the loop also terminates. `freeaddrinfo` returns all the dynamic memory.

This function (and our other functions that provide a simpler interface to `getaddrinfo` in the following sections) terminates if either `getaddrinfo` fails, or if no call to `connect` succeeds. The only return is upon success. It would be hard to return an error code (one of the `EAI_xxx` constants) without adding another argument. This means that our wrapper function is trivial:

```
int
Tcp_connect(const char *host, const char *serv)
{
    return(tcp_connect(host, serv));
}
```

Nevertheless, we still call our wrapper function, instead of `tcp_connect`, to maintain consistency with the remainder of the text.

> The problem with the return value is that descriptors are nonnegative but we do not know whether the `EAI_xxx` values are positive or negative. If these values were positive, we could return the negative of these values if `getaddrinfo` fails, but we also have to return some other negative value to indicate that all the structures were tried without success.

Example: Daytime Client

Figure 11.7 shows our daytime client from Figure 1.5 recoded to use `tcp_connect`.

Command-line arguments

9–10   We now require a second command-line argument to specify either the service name or the port number, which allows our program to connect to other ports.

Connect to server

11   All of the socket code for this client is now performed by `tcp_connect`.

Print server's address

12–15   We call `getpeername` to fetch the server's protocol address and print it. We do this to verify the protocol being used in the examples we are about to show.

Note that `tcp_connect` does not return the size of the socket address structure that was used for the `connect`. We could have added a pointer argument to return this value, but one design goal for this function was to reduce the number of arguments, compared to `getaddrinfo`. What we do instead is define the constant `MAXSOCKADDR` in our `unp.h` header to be the size of the largest socket address structure. This is normally the size of a Unix domain socket address structure (Section 14.2), just over 100 bytes. We allocate room for a structure of this size and this is what `getpeername` fills in.

———————————————————————— names/daytimetcpcli.c

```
 1 #include    "unp.h"

 2 int
 3 main(int argc, char **argv)
 4 {
 5     int     sockfd, n;
 6     char    recvline[MAXLINE + 1];
 7     socklen_t len;
 8     struct sockaddr *sa;

 9     if (argc != 3)
10         err_quit("usage: daytimetcpcli <hostname/IPaddress> <service/port#>");

11     sockfd = Tcp_connect(argv[1], argv[2]);

12     sa = Malloc(MAXSOCKADDR);
13     len = MAXSOCKADDR;
14     Getpeername(sockfd, sa, &len);
15     printf("connected to %s\n", Sock_ntop_host(sa, len));

16     while ( (n = Read(sockfd, recvline, MAXLINE)) > 0) {
17         recvline[n] = 0;           /* null terminate */
18         Fputs(recvline, stdout);
19     }
20     exit(0);
21 }
```

———————————————————————— names/daytimetcpcli.c

Figure 11.7 Daytime client recoded to use `getaddrinfo`.

We call `malloc` for this structure, instead of allocating it as

```
    char   sockaddr[MAXSOCKADDR];
```

for alignment reasons. `malloc` always returns a pointer with the strictest alignment required by the system, while a `char` array could be allocated on an odd-byte boundary, which could be a problem for the IP address or port number fields in the socket address structure. Another way to handle this potential alignment problem was shown in Figure 4.19 using a `union`.

This version of our client works with both IPv4 and IPv6, while the version in Figure 1.5 worked only with IPv4 and the version in Figure 1.6 worked only with IPv6. You should also compare our new version with Figure E.14, which we coded to use `gethostbyname` and `getservbyname` to support both IPv4 and IPv6.

We first specify the name of a host that supports only IPv4.

```
solaris % daytimetcpcli bsdi daytime
connected to 206.62.226.35
Fri May 30 12:33:32 1997
```

Next we specify the name of a host that supports both IPv4 and IPv6.

```
solaris % daytimetcpcli aix daytime
connected to 5f1b:df00:ce3e:e200:20:800:5afc:2b36
Fri May 30 12:43:43 1997
```

The IPv6 address is used because the host has both a AAAA record and an A record, and as noted in Figure 11.4, since `tcp_connect` sets the address family to `AF_UNSPEC`, AAAA records are searched for first, and only if this fails is a search made for an A record.

In the next example we force the use of the IPv4 address by specifying the hostname with our -4 suffix, which we noted in Section 9.2 is our convention for the hostname with only A records.

```
solaris % daytimetcpcli aix-4 daytime
connected to 206.62.226.43
Fri May 30 12:43:48 1997
```

11.9 `tcp_listen` Function

Our next function, `tcp_listen`, performs the normal TCP server steps: create a TCP socket, `bind` the server's well-known port, and allow incoming connection requests to be accepted. Figure 11.8 shows the source code.

```
#include "unp.h"

int tcp_listen(const char *hostname, const char *service, socklen_t *lenptr);

                              Returns: connected socket descriptor if OK, no return on error
```

Call `getaddrinfo`

8-15   We initialize an `addrinfo` structure with our hints: `AI_PASSIVE`, since this function is for a server, `AF_UNSPEC` for the address family, and `SOCK_STREAM`. Recall from Figure 11.4 that if a hostname is not specified (which is common for a server that wants to bind the wildcard address), the `AI_PASSIVE` and `AF_UNSPEC` hints will cause two socket address structures to be returned: the first for IPv6 and the next for IPv4 (assuming a dual-stack host).

Create socket and bind address

16-24   The `socket` and `bind` functions are called. If either call fails we just ignore this `addrinfo` structure and move on to the next one. As stated in Section 7.5, we always set the `SO_REUSEADDR` socket option for a TCP server.

Check for failure

25-26   If all the calls to `socket` and `bind` failed, we print an error and terminate. As with our `tcp_connect` function in the previous section, we do not try to return an error from this function.

27   The socket is turned into a listening socket by `listen`.

Return size of socket address structure

28-31   If the *addrlenp* argument is nonnull, we return the size of the protocol addresses through this pointer. This allows the caller to allocate memory for a socket address structure to obtain the client's protocol address from `accept`. (See Exercise 11.1 also.)

——————————————————————————— lib/tcp_listen.c

```
 1 #include    "unp.h"

 2 int
 3 tcp_listen(const char *host, const char *serv, socklen_t *addrlenp)
 4 {
 5     int     listenfd, n;
 6     const int on = 1;
 7     struct addrinfo hints, *res, *ressave;

 8     bzero(&hints, sizeof(struct addrinfo));
 9     hints.ai_flags = AI_PASSIVE;
10     hints.ai_family = AF_UNSPEC;
11     hints.ai_socktype = SOCK_STREAM;

12     if ( (n = getaddrinfo(host, serv, &hints, &res)) != 0)
13         err_quit("tcp_listen error for %s, %s: %s",
14                 host, serv, gai_strerror(n));
15     ressave = res;

16     do {
17         listenfd = socket(res->ai_family, res->ai_socktype, res->ai_protocol);
18         if (listenfd < 0)
19             continue;           /* error, try next one */

20         Setsockopt(listenfd, SOL_SOCKET, SO_REUSEADDR, &on, sizeof(on));
21         if (bind(listenfd, res->ai_addr, res->ai_addrlen) == 0)
22             break;              /* success */

23         Close(listenfd);        /* bind error, close and try next one */
24     } while ( (res = res->ai_next) != NULL);

25     if (res == NULL)            /* errno from final socket() or bind() */
26         err_sys("tcp_listen error for %s, %s", host, serv);

27     Listen(listenfd, LISTENQ);

28     if (addrlenp)
29         *addrlenp = res->ai_addrlen;     /* return size of protocol address */

30     freeaddrinfo(ressave);

31     return (listenfd);
32 }
```

——————————————————————————— lib/tcp_listen.c

Figure 11.8 tcp_listen function: perform normal server steps.

Example: Daytime Server

Figure 11.9 shows our daytime server from Figure 4.11 recoded to use tcp_listen.

Require service name or port number as command-line argument

11–12   We require a command-line argument to specify either the service name or the port number. This makes it easier to test our server, since binding port 13 for the daytime server requires superuser privileges.

```
                                                              ─── names/daytimetcpsrv1.c
 1 #include    "unp.h"
 2 #include    <time.h>

 3 int
 4 main(int argc, char **argv)
 5 {
 6     int      listenfd, connfd;
 7     socklen_t addrlen, len;
 8     char     buff[MAXLINE];
 9     time_t   ticks;
10     struct sockaddr *cliaddr;

11     if (argc != 2)
12         err_quit("usage: daytimetcpsrv1 <service or port#>");

13     listenfd = Tcp_listen(NULL, argv[1], &addrlen);

14     cliaddr = Malloc(addrlen);

15     for ( ; ; ) {
16         len = addrlen;
17         connfd = Accept(listenfd, cliaddr, &len);
18         printf("connection from %s\n", Sock_ntop(cliaddr, len));

19         ticks = time(NULL);
20         snprintf(buff, sizeof(buff), "%.24s\r\n", ctime(&ticks));
21         Write(connfd, buff, strlen(buff));

22         Close(connfd);
23     }
24 }
                                                              ─── names/daytimetcpsrv1.c
```

Figure 11.9 Daytime server recoded to use `getaddrinfo`.

Create listening socket

13–14   `tcp_listen` creates the listening socket and `malloc` allocates a buffer to hold the client's address.

Server loop

15–23   `accept` waits for each client connection. We print the client address by calling `sock_ntop`. In the case of either IPv4 or IPv6, this function prints the IP address and port number. We could use the function `getnameinfo` (described in Section 11.13) to try to obtain the hostname of the client, but that involves a PTR query in the DNS, which can take some time, especially if the PTR query fails. Section 14.8 of TCPv3 notes that on a busy Web server almost 25% of all clients connecting to that server did not have PTR records in the DNS. Since we do not want a server (especially an iterative server) to wait seconds for a PTR query, we just print the IP address and port.

Example: Daytime Server with Protocol Specification

There is a slight problem with Figure 11.9: the first argument to `tcp_listen` is a null pointer, which combined with the address family of AF_UNSPEC that `tcp_listen` specifies might cause getaddrinfo to return a socket address structure with an address family other than what is desired. For example, the first socket address structure returned will be for IPv6 on a dual-stack host (Figure 11.4) but we might want our server to handle only IPv4.

Clients do not have this problem, since the client must always specify either an IP address or a hostname. Client applications normally allow the user to enter this as a command-line argument. This gives us the opportunity to specify a hostname that is associated with a particular type of IP address (recall our -4 and -6 hostnames in Section 9.2), or to specify either an IPv4 dotted-decimal string (forcing IPv4) or an IPv6 hex string (forcing IPv6).

But there is a simple technique for servers that lets us force a given protocol upon a server, either IPv4 or IPv6: allow the user to enter either an IP address or a hostname as a command-line argument to the program and pass this to getaddrinfo. In the case of an IP address, an IPv4 dotted-decimal string differs from an IPv6 hex string. The following calls to inet_pton either fail or succeed, as indicated.

```
inet_pton(AF_INET,  "0.0.0.0", &foo);      /* succeeds */
inet_pton(AF_INET,  "0::0",    &foo);      /* fails */
inet_pton(AF_INET6, "0.0.0.0", &foo);      /* fails */
inet_pton(AF_INET6, "0::0",    &foo);      /* succeeds */
```

Therefore, if we change our servers to accept an optional argument, then if we enter

```
% server
```

it defaults to IPv6 on a dual-stack host, but entering

```
% server 0.0.0.0
```

explicitly specifies IPv4 and

```
% server 0::0
```

explicitly specifies IPv6.

Figure 11.10 shows this final version of our daytime server.

Handle command-line arguments

11-16   The only change from Figure 11.9 is the handling of the command-line arguments, allowing the user to specify either a hostname or an IP address for the server to bind, in addition to a service name or port.

We first start this server with an IPv4 socket and then connect to the server from clients on two other hosts on the local subnet.

```
solaris % daytimetcpsrv2 0.0.0.0 9999
connection from 206.62.226.36.32789
connection from 206.62.226.35.1389
```

But now we start the server with an IPv6 socket.

```
solaris % daytimetcpsrv2 0::0 9999
connection from 5f1b:df00:ce3e:e200:20:800:2003:f642.32799
connection from 5f1b:df00:ce3e:e200:20:800:2b37:6426.1026
```

—— names/daytimetcpsrv2.c

```
 1 #include     "unp.h"
 2 #include     <time.h>

 3 int
 4 main(int argc, char **argv)
 5 {
 6     int     listenfd, connfd;
 7     socklen_t addrlen, len;
 8     struct sockaddr *cliaddr;
 9     char     buff[MAXLINE];
10     time_t  ticks;

11     if (argc == 2)
12         listenfd = Tcp_listen(NULL, argv[1], &addrlen);
13     else if (argc == 3)
14         listenfd = Tcp_listen(argv[1], argv[2], &addrlen);
15     else
16         err_quit("usage: daytimetcpsrv2 [ <host> ] <service or port>");

17     cliaddr = Malloc(addrlen);

18     for ( ; ; ) {
19         len = addrlen;
20         connfd = Accept(listenfd, cliaddr, &len);
21         printf("connection from %s\n", Sock_ntop(cliaddr, len));

22         ticks = time(NULL);
23         snprintf(buff, sizeof(buff), "%.24s\r\n", ctime(&ticks));
24         Write(connfd, buff, strlen(buff));

25         Close(connfd);
26     }
27 }
```

—— names/daytimetcpsrv2.c

Figure 11.10 Protocol-independent daytime server that uses `getaddrinfo`.

```
connection from ::ffff:206.62.226.36.32792
connection from ::ffff:206.62.226.35.1390
```

The first connection is from the host `sunos5` using IPv6 and the second is from the host `alpha` using IPv6. The next two connections are from the hosts `sunos5` and `bsdi`, but using IPv4, not IPv6. We can tell this because the client's addresses returned by `accept` are both IPv4-mapped IPv6 addresses.

What we have just shown is that an IPv6 server running on a dual-stack host can handle either IPv4 or IPv6 clients. The IPv4 client addresses are passed to the IPv6 server as IPv4-mapped IPv6 address, as we discussed in Section 10.2.

This server, along with the client in Figure 11.7, also work with Unix domain sockets (Chapter 14) since our implementation of `getaddrinfo` in Section 11.16 supports Unix domain sockets. For example, we start the server as

```
solaris % daytimetcpsrv2 /local /tmp/rendezvous
```

where the pathname /tmp/rendezvous is an arbitrary pathname we choose for the server to bind and to which the client connects. We then start the client on the same host, specifying /local as the hostname and /tmp/rendezvous as the service name.

```
solaris % daytimetcpcli /tmp/rendezvous 0
connected to /tmp/rendezvous
Fri May 30 16:31:37 1997
```

11.10 udp_client Function

Our functions that provide a simpler interface to getaddrinfo change with UDP because we provide one client function that creates an unconnected UDP socket, and another in the next section that creates a connected UDP socket.

```
#include "unp.h"

int udp_client(const char *hostname, const char *service,
               void **saptr, socklen_t *lenp);

                              Returns: unconnected socket descriptor if OK, no return on error
```

This function creates an unconnected UDP socket, returning three items. First, the return value is the socket descriptor. Second, *saptr* is the address of a pointer (declared by the caller) to a socket address structure (allocated dynamically by udp_client) and in that structure the function stores the destination IP address and port for future calls to sendto. The size of that socket address structure is returned in the variable pointed to by *lenp*. This final argument cannot be a null pointer (as we allowed for the final argument to tcp_listen) because the length of the socket address structure is required in any calls to sendto and recvfrom.

> saptr should be declared as struct sockaddr **. We use the void ** datatype because we define another version of this function that uses XTI in Section 31.3 and it uses this argument to contain the address of a pointer to a different type of structure. This means our calls to this function must contain the cast (void **).

Figure 11.11 shows the source code for this function.

getaddrinfo converts the *hostname* and *service* arguments. A datagram socket is created. Memory is allocated for one socket address structure and the socket address structure corresponding to the socket that was created is copied into the memory.

Example: Protocol-Independent Daytime Client

We now recode our daytime client from Figure 11.7 to use UDP and our udp_client function. Figure 11.12 shows the protocol-independent source code.

11–16   We call our udp_client function and then print the IP address and port of the server to which we will send the UDP datagram. We send a 1-byte datagram and then read and print the reply.

—— *lib/udp_client.c*

```
 1 #include    "unp.h"

 2 int
 3 udp_client(const char *host, const char *serv, void **saptr, socklen_t *lenp)
 4 {
 5     int      sockfd, n;
 6     struct addrinfo hints, *res, *ressave;

 7     bzero(&hints, sizeof(struct addrinfo));
 8     hints.ai_family = AF_UNSPEC;
 9     hints.ai_socktype = SOCK_DGRAM;

10     if ( (n = getaddrinfo(host, serv, &hints, &res)) != 0)
11         err_quit("udp_client error for %s, %s: %s",
12                 host, serv, gai_strerror(n));
13     ressave = res;

14     do {
15         sockfd = socket(res->ai_family, res->ai_socktype, res->ai_protocol);
16         if (sockfd >= 0)
17             break;                  /* success */
18     } while ( (res = res->ai_next) != NULL);

19     if (res == NULL)                /* errno set from final socket() */
20         err_sys("udp_client error for %s, %s", host, serv);

21     *saptr = Malloc(res->ai_addrlen);
22     memcpy(*saptr, res->ai_addr, res->ai_addrlen);
23     *lenp = res->ai_addrlen;

24     freeaddrinfo(ressave);

25     return (sockfd);
26 }
```

—— *lib/udp_client.c*

Figure 11.11 udp_client function: create an unconnected UDP socket.

> We need to send only a 0-byte UDP datagram, as what triggers the daytime server's response is just the arrival of a datagram, regardless of its length and contents. But many SVR4 implementations do not allow a 0-length UDP datagram.

We run our client specifying a hostname that has a AAAA record and an A record. Since the structure with the AAAA record is returned first by getaddrinfo, an IPv6 socket is created.

```
solaris % daytimeudpcli1 aix daytime
sending to 5f1b:df00:ce3e:e200:20:800:5afc:2b36
Sat May 31 08:13:34 1997
```

Next we specify the dotted-decimal address of the same host, resulting in an IPv4 socket.

```
solaris % daytimeudpcli1 206.62.226.43 daytime
sending to 206.62.226.43
Sat May 31 08:14:02 1997
```

names/daytimeudpcli1.c

```
 1 #include    "unp.h"

 2 int
 3 main(int argc, char **argv)
 4 {
 5     int     sockfd, n;
 6     char    recvline[MAXLINE + 1];
 7     socklen_t salen;
 8     struct sockaddr *sa;

 9     if (argc != 3)
10         err_quit("usage: daytimeudpcli1 <hostname/IPaddress> <service/port#>");

11     sockfd = Udp_client(argv[1], argv[2], (void **) &sa, &salen);

12     printf("sending to %s\n", Sock_ntop_host(sa, salen));

13     Sendto(sockfd, "", 1, 0, sa, salen);      /* send 1-byte datagram */

14     n = Recvfrom(sockfd, recvline, MAXLINE, 0, NULL, NULL);
15     recvline[n] = 0;                /* null terminate */
16     Fputs(recvline, stdout);

17     exit(0);
18 }
```

names/daytimeudpcli1.c

Figure 11.12 UDP daytime client using our udp_client function.

11.11 udp_connect Function

Our udp_connect function creates a connected UDP socket.

```
#include "unp.h"

int udp_connect(const char *hostname, const char *service);

                        Returns: connected socket descriptor if OK, no return on error
```

With a connected UDP socket the final two arguments required by udp_client are no longer needed. The caller can call write instead of sendto, so our function need not return a socket address structure and its length.

Figure 11.13 shows the source code.

This function is nearly identical to tcp_connect. One difference, however, is that the call to connect with a UDP socket does not send anything to the peer. If something is wrong (the peer is unreachable or there is no server at the specified port), the caller does not discover that until it sends a datagram to the peer.

lib/udp_connect.c

```
 1 #include    "unp.h"

 2 int
 3 udp_connect(const char *host, const char *serv)
 4 {
 5     int     sockfd, n;
 6     struct addrinfo hints, *res, *ressave;

 7     bzero(&hints, sizeof(struct addrinfo));
 8     hints.ai_family = AF_UNSPEC;
 9     hints.ai_socktype = SOCK_DGRAM;

10     if ( (n = getaddrinfo(host, serv, &hints, &res)) != 0)
11         err_quit("udp_connect error for %s, %s: %s",
12                 host, serv, gai_strerror(n));
13     ressave = res;

14     do {
15         sockfd = socket(res->ai_family, res->ai_socktype, res->ai_protocol);
16         if (sockfd < 0)
17             continue;             /* ignore this one */

18         if (connect(sockfd, res->ai_addr, res->ai_addrlen) == 0)
19             break;                /* success */

20         Close(sockfd);            /* ignore this one */
21     } while ( (res = res->ai_next) != NULL);

22     if (res == NULL)              /* errno set from final connect() */
23         err_sys("udp_connect error for %s, %s", host, serv);

24     freeaddrinfo(ressave);

25     return (sockfd);
26 }
```

lib/udp_connect.c

Figure 11.13 udp_connect function: create a connected UDP socket.

11.12 `udp_server` Function

Our final UDP function that provides a simpler interface to `getaddrinfo` is `udp_server`.

```
#include "unp.h"

int udp_server(const char *hostname, const char *service, socklen_t *lenptr);

                              Returns: unconnected socket descriptor if OK, no return on error
```

The arguments are the same as for `tcp_listen`: an optional *hostname*, a required *service* (so its port number can be bound), and an optional pointer to a variable in which the size of the socket address structure is returned.

Figure 11.14 shows the source code.

lib/udp_server.c
```
 1 #include    "unp.h"

 2 int
 3 udp_server(const char *host, const char *serv, socklen_t *addrlenp)
 4 {
 5     int     sockfd, n;
 6     struct addrinfo hints, *res, *ressave;

 7     bzero(&hints, sizeof(struct addrinfo));
 8     hints.ai_flags = AI_PASSIVE;
 9     hints.ai_family = AF_UNSPEC;
10     hints.ai_socktype = SOCK_DGRAM;

11     if ( (n = getaddrinfo(host, serv, &hints, &res)) != 0)
12         err_quit("udp_server error for %s, %s: %s",
13                 host, serv, gai_strerror(n));
14     ressave = res;

15     do {
16         sockfd = socket(res->ai_family, res->ai_socktype, res->ai_protocol);
17         if (sockfd < 0)
18             continue;           /* error, try next one */

19         if (bind(sockfd, res->ai_addr, res->ai_addrlen) == 0)
20             break;              /* success */

21         Close(sockfd);          /* bind error, close and try next one */
22     } while ( (res = res->ai_next) != NULL);

23     if (res == NULL)            /* errno from final socket() or bind() */
24         err_sys("udp_server error for %s, %s", host, serv);

25     if (addrlenp)
26         *addrlenp = res->ai_addrlen;    /* return size of protocol address */

27     freeaddrinfo(ressave);

28     return (sockfd);
29 }
```
lib/udp_server.c

Figure 11.14 udp_server function: create an unconnected socket for a UDP server.

This function is nearly identical to `tcp_listen`, but without the call to `listen`. We set the address family to `AF_UNSPEC` but the caller can use the same technique that we described with Figure 11.10 to force a particular protocol (IPv4 or IPv6).

We do not set the `SO_REUSEADDR` socket option for the UDP socket because this socket option can allow multiple sockets to bind the same UDP port on hosts that support multicasting, as we described in Section 7.5. Since there is nothing like TCP's TIME_WAIT state for a UDP socket, there is no need to set this socket option when the server is started.

Example: Protocol-Independent Daytime Server

Figure 11.15 shows our daytime server, modified from Figure 11.10 to use UDP.

── names/daytimeudpsrv2.c

```
 1 #include    "unp.h"
 2 #include    <time.h>

 3 int
 4 main(int argc, char **argv)
 5 {
 6     int     sockfd;
 7     ssize_t n;
 8     char    buff[MAXLINE];
 9     time_t  ticks;
10     socklen_t addrlen, len;
11     struct sockaddr *cliaddr;

12     if (argc == 2)
13         sockfd = Udp_server(NULL, argv[1], &addrlen);
14     else if (argc == 3)
15         sockfd = Udp_server(argv[1], argv[2], &addrlen);
16     else
17         err_quit("usage: daytimeudpsrv [ <host> ] <service or port>");

18     cliaddr = Malloc(addrlen);

19     for ( ; ; ) {
20         len = addrlen;
21         n = Recvfrom(sockfd, buff, MAXLINE, 0, cliaddr, &len);
22         printf("datagram from %s\n", Sock_ntop(cliaddr, len));

23         ticks = time(NULL);
24         snprintf(buff, sizeof(buff), "%.24s\r\n", ctime(&ticks));
25         Sendto(sockfd, buff, strlen(buff), 0, cliaddr, len);
26     }
27 }
```

── names/daytimeudpsrv2.c

Figure 11.15 Protocol independent UDP daytime server.

11.13 `getnameinfo` Function

This function is the complement of `getaddrinfo`: it takes a socket address and returns a character string describing the host and another character string describing the service. This function provides this information in a protocol-independent fashion; that is, the caller does not care what type of protocol address is contained in the socket address structure, as that detail is handled by the function.

```
#include <netdb.h>

int getnameinfo(const struct sockaddr *sockaddr, socklen_t addrlen,
                char *host, size_t hostlen,
                char *serv, size_t servlen, int flags);
```

Returns: 0 if OK, −1 on error

sockaddr points to the socket address structure containing the protocol address to be converted into a human-readable string, and *addrlen* is the length of this structure. This structure and its length are normally returned by either accept, recvfrom, getsockname, or getpeername.

The caller allocates space for the two human-readable strings: *host* and *hostlen* specify the host string, and *serv* and *servlen* specify the service string. If the caller does not want the host string returned, a *hostlen* of 0 is specified. Similarly a *servlen* of 0 specifies not to return information on the service. To help allocate arrays to hold these two strings, the constants shown in Figure 11.16 are defined by including the <netdb.h> header.

Constant	Description	Value
NI_MAXHOST	maximum size of returned host string	1025
NI_MAXSERV	maximum size of returned service string	32

Figure 11.16 Constants for returned string sizes from getnameinfo.

The difference between sock_ntop and getnameinfo is that the former does not involve the DNS and just returns a printable version of the IP address and port number. The latter normally tries to obtain a name for both the host and service.

Figure 11.17 shows the five *flags* that can be specified to change the operation of getnameinfo.

Constant	Description
NI_DGRAM	datagram service
NI_NAMEREQD	return an error if name cannot be resolved from address
NI_NOFQDN	return only hostname portion of FQDN
NI_NUMERICHOST	return numeric string for hostname
NI_NUMERICSERV	return numeric string for service name

Figure 11.17 *flags* for getnameinfo.

NI_DGRAM should be specified when the caller knows it is dealing with a datagram socket. The reason is that given only the IP address and port number in the socket address structure, getnameinfo cannot determine the protocol (TCP or UDP). There exist a few port numbers that are used for one service with TCP and a completely different service with UDP. An example is port 514, which is the rsh service with TCP, but the syslog service with UDP.

NI_NAMEREQD causes an error to be returned if the hostname cannot be resolved using the DNS. This can be used by servers that require the client's IP address be mapped into a hostname. These servers then take this returned hostname and call gethostbyname and verify that one of the returned addresses is the address in the socket address structure.

NI_NOFQDN causes the returned hostname to be truncated at the first period. For example, if the IP address in the socket address structure were 206.62.226.42, gethostbyaddr would return a name of alpha.kohala.com. But if this flag is specified to getnameinfo, it returns the hostname as just alpha.

NI_NUMERICHOST tells getnameinfo not to call the DNS (which can take time). Instead the numeric representation of the IP address is returned, probably by calling inet_ntop. Similarly the NI_NUMERICSERV specifies that the decimal port number is to be returned, instead of looking up the service name. Servers should normally specify NI_NUMERICSERV because the client port numbers normally have no associated service name—they are ephemeral ports.

The logical OR of multiple flags can be specified if they make sense together (e.g., NI_DGRAM and NI_NUMERICHOST), while other combinations make no sense (e.g., NI_NAMEREQD and NI_NUMERICHOST).

getnameinfo was overlooked by Posix.1g but is specified in RFC 2133 [Gilligan et al. 1997].

11.14 Reentrant Functions

The gethostbyname function from Section 9.3 presents an interesting problem that we have not yet examined in the text: it is not *reentrant*. We will encounter this problem in general when we deal with threads in Chapter 23, but it is interesting to examine the problem now (without having to deal with the concept of threads) and to see how to fix it.

First let us look at how the function works. If we look at its source code (which is easy since the source code for the entire BIND release is publicly available), we see that one file contains both gethostbyname and gethostbyaddr, and the file has the following general outline:

```
static struct hostent  host;    /* result stored here */

struct hostent *
gethostbyname(const char *hostname)
{
    return(gethostbyname2(hostname, family));  /* Figure 9.6 */
}

struct hostent *
gethostbyname2(const char *hostname, int family)
{
    /* call DNS functions for A or AAAA query */

    /* fill in host structure */

    return(&host);
}

struct hostent *
gethostbyaddr(const char *addr, size_t len, int family)
{
    /* call DNS functions for PTR query in in-addr.arpa domain */

    /* fill in host structure */

    return(&host);
}
```

We highlight the `static` storage class specifier of the result structure, because that is the basic problem. The fact that these three functions share a single `host` variable presents yet another problem that we discussed in Exercise 9.1. (Recall from Figure 9.6 that `gethostbyname2` is new with the IPv6 support in BIND 4.9.4. We will ignore the fact that `gethostbyname2` is involved when we call `gethostbyname`, as that doesn't affect this discussion.)

The reentrancy problem can occur in a normal Unix process that calls `gethostbyname` or `gethostbyaddr` from both the main flow of control and from a signal handler. When the signal handler is called (say it is a `SIGALRM` signal that is generated once a second), the main flow of control of the process is temporarily stopped and the signal handling function is called. Consider the following.

```
main()
{
    struct hostent   *hptr;

    ...
    signal(SIGALRM, sig_alrm);

    ...
    hptr = gethostbyname( ... );
    ...
}

void
sig_alrm(int signo)
{
    struct hostent   *hptr;

    ...
    hptr = gethostbyname( ... );
    ...
}
```

If the main flow of control is in the middle of `gethostbyname` when it is temporarily stopped (say the function has filled in the `host` variable and is about to return), and the signal handler then calls `gethostbyname`, since only one copy of the variable `host` exists in the process, it is reused. This overwrites the values that were calculated for the call from the main flow of control with the values calculated for the call from the signal handler.

If we look at the name and address conversion functions presented in this chapter and Chapter 9, along with the `inet_XXX` functions from Chapter 4, we note the following:

- Historically, `gethostbyname`, `gethostbyname2`, `gethostbyaddr`, `getservbyname`, and `getservbyport` are not reentrant because all return a pointer to a static structure.

  Some implementations that support threads (Solaris 2.x) provide reentrant versions of these four functions with names ending with the `_r` suffix, which we describe in the next section.

Alternately, some implementations that support threads (Digital Unix 4.0 and HP-UX 10.30) provide reentrant versions of these functions using thread-specific data.

- `inet_pton` and `inet_ntop` are always reentrant.
- Historically `inet_ntoa` is not reentrant but some implementations that support threads provide a reentrant version that uses thread-specific data.
- `getaddrinfo` is reentrant only if it calls reentrant functions itself; that is, if it calls reentrant versions of `gethostbyname` for the hostname, and `getservbyname` for the service name. One reason that all the memory for the results is dynamically allocated is to allow it to be reentrant.
- `getnameinfo` is reentrant only if it calls reentrant functions itself; that is, if it calls reentrant versions of `gethostbyaddr` to obtain the hostname, and `getservbyport` to obtain the service name. Notice that both result strings (for the hostname and the service name) are allocated by the caller, to allow this reentrancy.

A similar problem occurs with the variable `errno`. Historically there has been a single copy of this integer variable per process. If the process makes a system call that returns an error, an integer error code is stored into this variable. For example, when the function named `close` in the standard C library is called, it might execute something like the following pseudocode:

- put the argument to the system call (an integer descriptor) into a register
- put a value in another register indicating the `close` system call is being called
- invoke the system call (switch to the kernel with a special instruction)
- test the value of a register to see if an error occurred
- if no error, `return(0)`
- store the value of some other register into `errno`
- `return(-1)`

First notice that if an error does not occur, the value of `errno` is not changed. That is why we cannot look at the value of `errno` unless we know that an error has occurred (normally indicated by the function returning –1).

Assume the program tests the return value of the `close` function and then prints the value of `errno` if an error occurred, as in the following:

```
if (close(fd) < 0) {
    fprintf(stderr, "close error, errno = %d\n", errno)
    exit(1);
}
```

There is a small window of time between the storing of the error code into `errno` when the system call returns, and the printing of this value by the program, during which another thread of execution within this process (i.e., a signal handler) can change the value of `errno`. For example, if, when the signal handler is called, the main flow of control is between the `close` and the `fprintf` and the signal handler calls some other system call that returns an error (say `write`), then the `errno` value stored from the write system call overwrites the value stored by the close system call.

In looking at these two problems with regard to signal handlers, one solution to the problem with gethostbyname (returning a pointer to a static variable) is to *not* call nonreentrant functions from a signal handler. The problem with errno (a single global variable that can be changed by the signal handler) can be avoided by coding the signal handler to save and restore the value of errno in the signal handler, as follows:

```
void
sig_alrm(int signo)
{
    int  errno_save;

    errno_save = errno;         /* save its value on entry *
    if (write( ... ) != nbytes)
        fprintf(stderr, "write error, errno = %d\n", errno);
    errno = errno_save;         /* restore its value on return */
}
```

In this example code we also call fprintf, a standard I/O function, from the signal handler. This is yet another reentrancy problem because many versions of the standard I/O library are nonreentrant: standard I/O functions should not be called from signal handlers.

We revisit this problem of reentrancy in Chapter 23 and we will see how threads handle the problem of the errno variable. The next section describes some reentrant versions of the hostname functions.

11.15 gethostbyname_r and gethostbyaddr_r Functions

There are two ways to make a nonreentrant function such as gethostbyname reentrant.

1. Instead of filling in and returning a static structure, the caller allocates the structure and the reentrant function fills in the caller's structure. This is the technique used in going from the nonreentrant gethostbyname to the reentrant gethostbyname_r. But this solution gets more complicated because not only must the caller provide the hostent structure to fill in, but this structure also points to other information: the canonical name, the array of alias pointers, the alias strings, the array of address pointers, and the addresses (e.g., Figure 9.2). The caller must provide one large buffer that is used for this additional information and the hostent structure that is filled in then contains numerous pointers into this other buffer. This adds at least three arguments to the function: a pointer to the hostent structure to fill in, a pointer to the buffer to use for all the other information, and the size of this buffer. A fourth additional argument is also required, a pointer to an integer in which an error code can be stored, since the global integer h_errno can no longer be used. (The global integer h_errno presents the same reentrancy problem that we described with errno.)

   This technique is also used by getnameinfo and inet_ntop.

2. The reentrant function calls `malloc` and dynamically allocates the memory. This is the technique used by `getaddrinfo`. The problem with this approach is that the application calling this function must also call `freeaddrinfo` to free the dynamic memory. If the free function is not called, a *memory leak* occurs: each time the process calls the function that allocates the memory, the memory use of the process increases. If the process runs for a long time (a common trait of network servers), the memory usage just grows and grows over time.

We now discuss the Solaris 2.x reentrant functions for name-to-address and address-to-name resolution.

```
#include <netdb.h>

struct hostent *gethostbyname_r(const char *hostname,
                                struct hostent *result,
                                char *buf, int buflen, int *h_errnop);

struct hostent *gethostbyaddr_r(const char *addr, int len, int type,
                                struct hostent *result,
                                char *buf, int buflen, int *h_errnop);
```

Both return: nonnull pointer if OK, NULL on error

Four additional arguments are required for each function. *result* is a `hostent` structure allocated by the caller which is filled in by the function. On success this pointer is also the return value of the function.

buf is a buffer allocated by the caller and *buflen* is its size. This buffer will contain the canonical hostname, the alias pointers, the alias strings, the address pointers, and the actual addresses. All the pointers in the structure pointed to by *result* point into this buffer. How big should this buffer be? Unfortunately all that most manual pages say is something vague like "The buffer must be large enough to hold all of the data associated with the host entry." Current implementations of `gethostbyname` can return up to 35 alias pointers, 35 address pointers, and internally use an 8192-byte buffer to hold the alias names and addresses. So a buffer size of 8192 bytes should be adequate.

If an error occurs, the error code is returned through the *h_errnop* pointer, and not through the global `h_errno`.

> Unfortunately this problem of reentrancy is even worse than it appears. First, there is no standard regarding reentrancy and `gethostbyname` and `gethostbyaddr`. Posix.1g specifies both functions but says nothing about thread safety. Unix 98 just says that these two functions need not be thread-safe.
>
> Second, there is no standard for the _r functions. What we have shown in this section (for example purposes) are two of the _r functions provided by Solaris 2.x. But Digital Unix 4.0 and HP-UX 10.30 have versions of these functions with different arguments. The first two arguments for `gethostbyname_r` are the same as the Solaris version, but the remaining three arguments for the Solaris version are combined into a new `hostent_data` structure (which must be allocated by the caller), and a pointer to this structure is the third and final argument. The normal functions `gethostbyname` and `gethostbyaddr` in Digital Unix 4.0 and HP-UX

10.30 are reentrant, by using thread-specific data (Section 23.5). An interesting history of the development of the Solaris 2.x _r functions is in [Maslen 1997].

Lastly, while a reentrant version of `gethostbyname` may provide safety from different threads calling it at the same time, this says nothing about the reentrancy of the underlying resolver functions. As of this writing, the resolver functions in BIND are not reentrant.

11.16 Implementation of `getaddrinfo` and `getnameinfo` Functions

We now look at an implementation of `getaddrinfo` and `getnameinfo`. Developing an implementation of the former will let us look at how it operates in more detail. Our implementation also supports Unix domain sockets, as we mentioned in Section 11.5.

> Note: All of the appropriate portions of the code that we look at in this section that are dependent on IPv4, IPv6, or Unix domain support, are bounded by an `#ifdef` and `#endif` of the appropriate constant: IPV4, IPV6, or UNIXDOMAIN. This allows the code to be compiled on a system that supports any combination of these three protocols. But we have removed all these preprocessor statements from the code that we show because they add nothing to our discussion and make the code harder to follow.
>
> We also note that we do not cover Unix domain sockets in detail until Chapter 14.

Figure 11.18 shows the functions that are called by `getaddrinfo`. All begin with the `ga_` prefix.

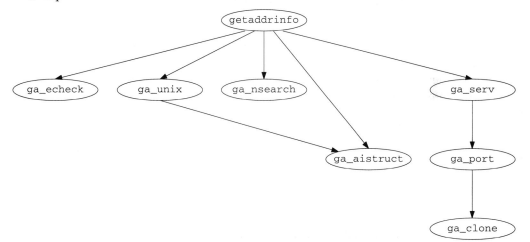

Figure 11.18 Functions called by our implementation of `getaddrinfo`.

The first file is our `gai_hdr.h` header, shown in Figure 11.19, which is included by all our source files.

We include our normal `unp.h` header and one additional header. We will see the use of our `AI_CLONE` flag and our `search` structure shortly. The remainder of the header defines the function prototypes for the various functions we show in this section.

libgai/gai_hdr.c

```
 1 #include    "unp.h"
 2 #include    <ctype.h>          /* isxdigit(), etc. */

 3          /* following internal flag cannot overlap with other AI_xxx flags */
 4 #define AI_CLONE         4       /* clone this entry for other socket types */

 5 struct search {
 6     const char *host;          /* hostname or address string */
 7     int     family;            /* AF_xxx */
 8 };

 9              /* function prototypes for our own internal functions */
10 int     ga_aistruct(struct addrinfo ***, const struct addrinfo *,
11                     const void *, int);
12 struct addrinfo *ga_clone(struct addrinfo *);
13 int     ga_echeck(const char *, const char *, int, int, int, int);
14 int     ga_nsearch(const char *, const struct addrinfo *, struct search *);
15 int     ga_port(struct addrinfo *, int, int);
16 int     ga_serv(struct addrinfo *, const struct addrinfo *, const char *);
17 int     ga_unix(const char *, struct addrinfo *, struct addrinfo **);

18 int     gn_ipv46(char *, size_t, char *, size_t, void *, size_t,
19                  int, int, int);
```

libgai/gai_hdr.c

Figure 11.19 gai_hdr.h header.

Figure 11.20 shows the first part of the getaddrinfo function.

Define error macro

13–17   At more than a dozen points throughout this function if we encounter an error, we want to free all the memory that we have allocated and return the appropriate return code. To simplify the code we define this macro that stores the return code in the variable error and branches to the label bad at the end of the function (Figure 11.26).

Initialize automatic variables

18–20   Some automatic variables are initialized. We describe the aihead and aipnext pointers in Figure 11.34.

Copy caller's hints structure

21–25   If the caller provides a *hints* structure, we copy it into our own local variable, so we can modify it later. Otherwise we start with a structure that is all zero, other than ai_family, which is initialized to AF_UNSPEC. The latter is normally defined to be 0, but this is not required by Posix.1g.

Check arguments

26–29   We call our ga_echeck function, shown in Figure 11.39, to validate some of the arguments.

Check for Unix domain pathname

30–34   If the hostname is either /local or /unix and the service name begins with a slash, we process this argument as a Unix domain pathname. Our function ga_unix (Figure 11.33) completely processes the pathname.

libgai/getaddrinfo.c
```
 1 #include    "gai_hdr.h"
 2 #include    <arpa/nameser.h>    /* needed for <resolv.h> */
 3 #include    <resolv.h>          /* res_init, _res */

 4 int
 5 getaddrinfo(const char *hostname, const char *servname,
 6             const struct addrinfo *hintsp, struct addrinfo **result)
 7 {
 8     int     rc, error, nsearch;
 9     char    **ap, *canon;
10     struct hostent *hptr;
11     struct search search[3], *sptr;
12     struct addrinfo hints, *aihead, **aipnext;

13     /*
14      * If we encounter an error we want to free() any dynamic memory
15      * that we've allocated.  This is our hack to simplify the code.
16      */
17 #define error(e) { error = (e); goto bad; }

18     aihead = NULL;              /* initialize automatic variables */
19     aipnext = &aihead;
20     canon = NULL;

21     if (hintsp == NULL) {
22         bzero(&hints, sizeof(hints));
23         hints.ai_family = AF_UNSPEC;
24     } else
25         hints = *hintsp;        /* struct copy */

26         /* first some basic error checking */
27     if ( (rc = ga_echeck(hostname, servname, hints.ai_flags, hints.ai_family,
28                     hints.ai_socktype, hints.ai_protocol)) != 0)
29         error(rc);

30         /* special case Unix domain first */
31     if (hostname != NULL &&
32       (strcmp(hostname, "/local") == 0 || strcmp(hostname, "/unix") == 0) &&
33         (servname != NULL && servname[0] == '/'))
34         return (ga_unix(servname, &hints, result));
```
libgai/getaddrinfo.c

Figure 11.20 getaddrinfo function: first part, initialization.

The remainder of our getaddrinfo function (which continues in Figure 11.24) deals with IPv4 and IPv6 sockets. Our function ga_nsearch, the first part of which is shown in Figure 11.21, calculates the number of times that we look up a hostname. If the caller specifies an address family of AF_INET or AF_INET6, then we look up the hostname only one time. But if the address family is unspecified, AF_UNSPEC, then we do two lookups: once for an IPv6 hostname, and again for an IPv4 hostname. We show the function in three parts:

- no hostname and AI_PASSIVE specified,
- no hostname and AI_PASSIVE not specified (i.e., active), and
- hostname specified.

These three parts correspond to the three major portions of Figure 11.4.

—— *libgai/ga_nsearch.c*

```
 6 int
 7 ga_nsearch(const char *hostname, const struct addrinfo *hintsp,
 8            struct search *search)
 9 {
10     int     nsearch = 0;

11     if (hostname == NULL || hostname[0] == '\0') {
12         if (hintsp->ai_flags & AI_PASSIVE) {
13             /* no hostname and AI_PASSIVE: implies wildcard bind */
14             switch (hintsp->ai_family) {
15             case AF_INET:
16                 search[nsearch].host = "0.0.0.0";
17                 search[nsearch].family = AF_INET;
18                 nsearch++;
19                 break;
20             case AF_INET6:
21                 search[nsearch].host = "0::0";
22                 search[nsearch].family = AF_INET6;
23                 nsearch++;
24                 break;
25             case AF_UNSPEC:
26                 search[nsearch].host = "0::0";   /* IPv6 first, then IPv4 */
27                 search[nsearch].family = AF_INET6;
28                 nsearch++;
29                 search[nsearch].host = "0.0.0.0";
30                 search[nsearch].family = AF_INET;
31                 nsearch++;
32                 break;
33             }
```
—— *libgai/ga_nsearch.c*

Figure 11.21 ga_nsearch function: no hostname and passive.

No hostname and passive socket

11-33   If the caller does not specify a hostname and specifies AI_PASSIVE, we return information to create one or more passive sockets that will bind the wildcard address. A switch is made based on the address family: an IPv4 socket needs to bind 0.0.0.0 (INADDR_ANY), and an IPv6 socket needs to bind 0::0 (IN6ADDR_ANY_INIT). If the family is AF_UNSPEC, we must return information to create two sockets: the first one for IPv6 and the second for IPv4. The reason for the ordering of IPv6 first, and then IPv4 is because an IPv6 socket on a dual-stack host can handle both IPv6 and IPv4 clients. In this scenario, if the caller creates only one socket from the returned list of addrinfo structures, it should be the IPv6 socket.

This function creates an array of search structures (Figure 11.19) with each entry specifying the hostname to look up and the address family. The pointer to the caller's array of search structures is the last argument to this function. The return value is the number of these structures that are created, and this will always be one or two.

The next part of this function, shown in Figure 11.22, handles the case of no hostname and `AI_PASSIVE` not set. This implies that the caller wants to create an active socket to the local host.

```
                                                            ─ libgai/ga_nsearch.c
34          } else {
35                  /* no host and not AI_PASSIVE: connect to local host */
36              switch (hintsp->ai_family) {
37              case AF_INET:
38                  search[nsearch].host = "localhost";      /* 127.0.0.1 */
39                  search[nsearch].family = AF_INET;
40                  nsearch++;
41                  break;
42              case AF_INET6:
43                  search[nsearch].host = "0::1";
44                  search[nsearch].family = AF_INET6;
45                  nsearch++;
46                  break;
47              case AF_UNSPEC:
48                  search[nsearch].host = "0::1";  /* IPv6 first, then IPv4 */
49                  search[nsearch].family = AF_INET6;
50                  nsearch++;
51                  search[nsearch].host = "localhost";
52                  search[nsearch].family = AF_INET;
53                  nsearch++;
54                  break;
55              }
56          }
                                                            ─ libgai/ga_nsearch.c
```

Figure 11.22 `ga_nsearch` function: no hostname and not passive.

34–56   For IPv4 we assume the hostname `localhost` will return the loopback address, normally 127.0.0.1. There is no common hostname for the local host with IPv6, so we return the loopback address of `0::1`. As with the passive case, if no address family is specified we return two structures: first one for IPv6 and then one for IPv4.

Figure 11.23 shows the final part of this function, the `else` clause of the original `if` statement. This code is executed when a hostname is specified.

57–82   The `AI_PASSIVE` flag does not matter in this scenario; the hostname needs to be looked up. If the caller creates a passive socket, then the resulting socket address structure will be used in a call to `bind`, but if the caller creates an active socket, the socket address structure will be used in a call to `connect`. We create one or two `search` structures: one if the address family is specified and two if it is not specified. As with the previous two scenarios, if two structures are returned, the first is for IPv6 and the second for IPv4.

We now return to our `getaddrinfo` function, in Figure 11.24, which starts with a call to `ga_nsearch`.

libgai/ga_nsearch.c

```
57    } else {                         /* host is specified */
58        switch (hintsp->ai_family) {
59        case AF_INET:
60            search[nsearch].host = hostname;
61            search[nsearch].family = AF_INET;
62            nsearch++;
63            break;
64        case AF_INET6:
65            search[nsearch].host = hostname;
66            search[nsearch].family = AF_INET6;
67            nsearch++;
68            break;
69        case AF_UNSPEC:
70            search[nsearch].host = hostname;
71            search[nsearch].family = AF_INET6;   /* IPv6 first */
72            nsearch++;
73            search[nsearch].host = hostname;
74            search[nsearch].family = AF_INET;    /* then IPv4 */
75            nsearch++;
76            break;
77        }
78    }
79    if (nsearch < 1 || nsearch > 2)
80        err_quit("nsearch = %d", nsearch);
81    return (nsearch);
82 }
```

libgai/ga_nsearch.c

Figure 11.23 ga_nsearch function: hostname specified.

Call ga_nsearch

36   We call our ga_nsearch function, filling in our search array, and returning the number of structures in the array: one or two.

Loop through all the search structures

37   We loop through each search structure that was created by ga_nsearch.

Check for IPv4 dotted-decimal string

39–44   If the first character of the hostname is a digit, we check whether or not the hostname is really a dotted-decimal string. We call inet_pton to do this check and conversion. If it succeeds but the caller specifies an address family other than AF_INET, this is an error.

45–46   We check that the family of the search structure is also AF_INET, but a mismatch here only causes this search structure to be ignored. This scenario can happen, for example, if the caller specifies a hostname of 192.3.4.5 but no address family. ga_nsearch creates two search structures: one for IPv6 and one for IPv4. The first time through the for loop the call to inet_pton succeeds, but since the family of the search structure is AF_INET6, we want to ignore this structure, and not generate an error.

libgai/getaddrinfo.c

```
35          /* remainder of function for IPv4/IPv6 */
36      nsearch = ga_nsearch(hostname, &hints, &search[0]);
37      for (sptr = &search[0]; sptr < &search[nsearch]; sptr++) {
38              /* check for an IPv4 dotted-decimal string */
39          if (isdigit(sptr->host[0])) {
40              struct in_addr inaddr;

41              if (inet_pton(AF_INET, sptr->host, &inaddr) == 1) {
42                  if (hints.ai_family != AF_UNSPEC &&
43                      hints.ai_family != AF_INET)
44                      error(EAI_ADDRFAMILY);
45                  if (sptr->family != AF_INET)
46                      continue;     /* ignore */
47                  rc = ga_aistruct(&aipnext, &hints, &inaddr, AF_INET);
48                  if (rc != 0)
49                      error(rc);
50                  continue;
51              }
52          }
53              /* check for an IPv6 hex string */
54          if ((isxdigit(sptr->host[0]) || sptr->host[0] == ':') &&
55              (strchr(sptr->host, ':') != NULL)) {
56              struct in6_addr in6addr;

57              if (inet_pton(AF_INET6, sptr->host, &in6addr) == 1) {
58                  if (hints.ai_family != AF_UNSPEC &&
59                      hints.ai_family != AF_INET6)
60                      error(EAI_ADDRFAMILY);
61                  if (sptr->family != AF_INET6)
62                      continue;     /* ignore */
63                  rc = ga_aistruct(&aipnext, &hints, &in6addr, AF_INET6);
64                  if (rc != 0)
65                      error(rc);
66                  continue;
67              }
68          }
```

libgai/getaddrinfo.c

Figure 11.24 getaddrinfo function: check for IPv4 or IPv6 address string.

Create addrinfo structure

47–52   Our function ga_aistruct creates an addrinfo structure and adds it to the linked list that is being built (the aipnext pointer).

Check for IPv6 address string

53–60   If the first character of the hostname is either a hexadecimal digit or a colon and the string contains a colon, we check whether the hostname is an IPv6 address string by calling inet_pton. If it succeeds but the caller specifies an address family other than AF_INET6, this is an error.

61–62   We check that the family of the search structure is also AF_INET6, but a mismatch here only causes this search structure to be ignored.

Create `addrinfo` structure

63–68   Our function `ga_aistruct` creates an `addrinfo` structure and adds it to the linked list that is being built.

The first two tests in the loop (Figure 11.24) handle an IPv4 dotted-decimal string or an IPv6 address string. The remainder of the loop, shown in Figure 11.25, looks up the hostname by calling either `gethostbyname` or `gethostbyname2`.

Initialize resolver first time

70–71   We call the resolver's `res_init` function if it has not been called before.

Call `gethostbyname2` if two searches are being performed

72–74   If `nsearch` is 2, then we are going through the `for` loop twice: once for IPv6 and again for IPv4. If the hostname argument has an address in only one of the two families, we want to return only that address. For example, our host `solaris` in Section 9.2 has a AAAA record and an A record in the DNS. The first time around the loop we want to find the AAAA record, and the second time the A record. But if the hostname has only an A record, we do not want to process that record the first time around the loop when the `family` member of the `search` structure is `AF_INET6`. That is, since we know that we will be searching for an A record for this host, do not search for a AAAA record using `gethostbyname` and possibly return the IPv4-mapped IPv6 address corresponding to the A record. Looking at Figure 9.5 the way to search for only A records when the family is `AF_INET` and to search for only AAAA records when the family is `AF_INET6` is to call `gethostbyname2` instead of `gethostbyname`, with the `RES_USE_INET6` option off.

Call `gethostbyname` if one search is being performed

75–81   If only one search is being performed, we call `gethostbyname` with the `RES_USE_INET6` option set if the family is `AF_INET6` or the option cleared if the family is `AF_INET`. For example, if the caller specifies a hostname that has only an A record, but specifies a family of `AF_INET6`, we want to return the IPv4-mapped IPv6 address.

Handle resolver failure

82–97   If the call to the resolver failed, but `nsearch` is two, this is not an error, as one of the passes through the loop may succeed. (We check at the end of the loop that at least one `addrinfo` structure is being returned.) But if this was the only call to the resolver we return an error corresponding to the resolver's `h_errno`.

Check for address family mismatch

98–100   If the caller specifies an address family, but the family returned by the resolver differs, this is an error.

Save canonical name

101–106   If the caller specifies a hostname and the `AI_CANONNAME` flag, we save the first canonical name returned by the resolver. (Recall from Figure 11.22 that we call the resolver for the name `localhost` even of the caller does not specify a hostname.) We duplicate the string returned by the resolver and save its pointer in `canon`.

libgai/getaddrinfo.c

```
69                  /* remainder of for() to look up hostname */
70          if ((_res.options & RES_INIT) == 0)
71              res_init();            /* need this to set _res.options */

72          if (nsearch == 2) {
73              _res.options &= ~RES_USE_INET6;
74              hptr = gethostbyname2(sptr->host, sptr->family);
75          } else {
76              if (sptr->family == AF_INET6)
77                  _res.options |= RES_USE_INET6;
78              else
79                  _res.options &= ~RES_USE_INET6;
80              hptr = gethostbyname(sptr->host);
81          }
82          if (hptr == NULL) {
83              if (nsearch == 2)
84                  continue;          /* failure OK if multiple searches */

85              switch (h_errno) {
86              case HOST_NOT_FOUND:
87                  error(EAI_NONAME);
88              case TRY_AGAIN:
89                  error(EAI_AGAIN);
90              case NO_RECOVERY:
91                  error(EAI_FAIL);
92              case NO_DATA:
93                  error(EAI_NODATA);
94              default:
95                  error(EAI_NONAME);
96              }
97          }
98              /* check for address family mismatch if one specified */
99          if (hints.ai_family != AF_UNSPEC && hints.ai_family != hptr->h_addrtype)
100             error(EAI_ADDRFAMILY);

101             /* save canonical name first time */
102         if (hostname != NULL && hostname[0] != '\0' &&
103             (hints.ai_flags & AI_CANONNAME) && canon == NULL) {
104             if ( (canon = strdup(hptr->h_name)) == NULL)
105                 error(EAI_MEMORY);
106         }
107             /* create one addrinfo{} for each returned address */
108         for (ap = hptr->h_addr_list; *ap != NULL; ap++) {
109             rc = ga_aistruct(&aipnext, &hints, *ap, hptr->h_addrtype);
110             if (rc != 0)
111                 error(rc);
112         }
113     }
114     if (aihead == NULL)
115         error(EAI_NONAME);         /* nothing found */
```

libgai/getaddrinfo.c

Figure 11.25 `getaddrinfo` function: lookup hostname.

Create one `addrinfo` structure per address

107-112   For each address returned by the resolver in the `h_addr_list` array, we call our `ga_aistruct` function to create an `addrinfo` structure and append it to the linked list of structures being created.

Check for no matches

114-115   If the head of the linked list of `addrinfo` structures is still a null pointer, all iterations through the `for` loop failed.

Figure 11.26 shows the final part of the `getaddrinfo` function.

libgai/getaddrinfo.c
```
116            /* return canonical name */
117     if (hostname != NULL && hostname[0] != '\0' &&
118         hints.ai_flags & AI_CANONNAME) {
119         if (canon != NULL)
120             aihead->ai_canonname = canon;    /* strdup'ed earlier */
121         else {
122             if ( (aihead->ai_canonname = strdup(search[0].host)) == NULL)
123                 error(EAI_MEMORY);
124         }
125     }
126         /* now process the service name */
127     if (servname != NULL && servname[0] != '\0') {
128         if ( (rc = ga_serv(aihead, &hints, servname)) != 0)
129             error(rc);
130     }
131     *result = aihead;           /* pointer to first structure in linked list */
132     return (0);

133  bad:
134     freeaddrinfo(aihead);       /* free any alloc'ed memory */
135     return (error);
136 }
```
libgai/getaddrinfo.c

Figure 11.26 `getaddrinfo` function: process service name.

Return canonical name

116-125   If the caller specifies a hostname and the `AI_CANONNAME` flag, and if we saved a copy to the canonical name in our `canon` pointer, that pointer is returned in the `ai_canonname` member of the first `addrinfo` structure. If no canonical name was found by the resolver (perhaps the hostname was an address string), then a copy of the hostname argument is returned instead.

Process service name

126-130   If the caller specifies a service name, it is now processed by calling our `ga_serv` function.

Return pointer to linked list

131-132   The pointer to the head of the linked list of `addrinfo` structures that have been created is returned, along with a function return value of 0.

Error return

133–135   If an error was encountered, `freeaddrinfo` is called to free all the memory that was allocated, and the return value is the EAI_*xxx* value.

Our `ga_serv` function, which was called from Figure 11.26 to process the service name argument, is shown in Figure 11.27.

Check for port number string

12–27   If the first character of the service name is a digit, we assume the service name is a port number and call `atoi` to convert it to binary. If the caller specifies a socket type (SOCK_STREAM or SOCK_DGRAM), then our `ga_port` function is called once for that socket type. But if no socket type is specified, our `ga_port` function is called twice, once for TCP and once for UDP. (Recall Figure 11.2.)

Try `getservbyname` for TCP

28–36   If no socket type is specified, or a TCP socket is specified, `getservbyname` is called with a second argument of `"tcp"`. If this succeeds, our `ga_port` function is called. If this call fails, that is OK, as the service name could be valid for UDP. We keep a counter of the number of times that `ga_port` returns success and return an error only if this is 0 at the end of the function.

Try `getservbyname` for UDP

37–44   If no socket type is specified, or a UDP socket is specified, we call `getservbyname` with a second argument of `"udp"`. If this succeeds, we call our `ga_port` function.

Check for error

45–51   If our `nfound` counter is nonzero, we had success. Otherwise an error is returned.

Our `ga_port` function, which we show in Figure 11.28, was called from Figure 11.27 each time a port number was found.

Loop through all `addrinfo` structures

33   We loop through all the `addrinfo` structures that were created by the calls to `ga_aistruct` in Figures 11.24 and 11.25. The AI_CLONE flag is always set by `ga_aistruct` when no socket type is specified by the caller. That is an indication that this `addrinfo` structure might need to be cloned for both TCP and UDP.

Check `AI_CLONE` flag

34–42   If the AI_CLONE flag is set and if the socket type is nonzero, another `addrinfo` structure is cloned from this one by our `ga_clone` function. We show an example of this shortly.

Set port number in socket address structure

44–47   The port number in the socket address structure is set and our counter `nfound` is incremented.

libgai/ga_serv.c

```
 5 int
 6 ga_serv(struct addrinfo *aihead, const struct addrinfo *hintsp,
 7         const char *serv)
 8 {
 9     int      port, rc, nfound;
10     struct servent *sptr;

11     nfound = 0;
12     if (isdigit(serv[0])) {       /* check for port number string first */
13         port = htons(atoi(serv));
14         if (hintsp->ai_socktype) {
15               /* caller specifies socket type */
16             if ( (rc = ga_port(aihead, port, hintsp->ai_socktype)) < 0)
17                 return (EAI_MEMORY);
18             nfound += rc;
19         } else {
20               /* caller does not specify socket type */
21             if ( (rc = ga_port(aihead, port, SOCK_STREAM)) < 0)
22                 return (EAI_MEMORY);
23             nfound += rc;
24             if ( (rc = ga_port(aihead, port, SOCK_DGRAM)) < 0)
25                 return (EAI_MEMORY);
26             nfound += rc;
27         }
28     } else {
29             /* try service name, TCP then UDP */
30         if (hintsp->ai_socktype == 0 || hintsp->ai_socktype == SOCK_STREAM) {
31             if ( (sptr = getservbyname(serv, "tcp")) != NULL) {
32                 if ( (rc = ga_port(aihead, sptr->s_port, SOCK_STREAM)) < 0)
33                     return (EAI_MEMORY);
34                 nfound += rc;
35             }
36         }
37         if (hintsp->ai_socktype == 0 || hintsp->ai_socktype == SOCK_DGRAM) {
38             if ( (sptr = getservbyname(serv, "udp")) != NULL) {
39                 if ( (rc = ga_port(aihead, sptr->s_port, SOCK_DGRAM)) < 0)
40                     return (EAI_MEMORY);
41                 nfound += rc;
42             }
43         }
44     }

45     if (nfound == 0) {
46         if (hintsp->ai_socktype == 0)
47             return (EAI_NONAME);    /* all calls to getservbyname() failed */
48         else
49             return (EAI_SERVICE);   /* service not supported for socket type */
50     }
51     return (0);
52 }
```

libgai/ga_serv.c

Figure 11.27 ga_serv function.

libgai/ga_port.c

```
27 int
28 ga_port(struct addrinfo *aihead, int port, int socktype)
29         /* port must be in network byte order */
30 {
31     int     nfound = 0;
32     struct addrinfo *ai;

33     for (ai = aihead; ai != NULL; ai = ai->ai_next) {
34         if (ai->ai_flags & AI_CLONE) {
35             if (ai->ai_socktype != 0) {
36                 if ( (ai = ga_clone(ai)) == NULL)
37                     return (-1);    /* memory allocation error */
38                 /* ai points to newly cloned entry, which is what we want */
39             }
40         } else if (ai->ai_socktype != socktype)
41             continue;              /* ignore if mismatch on socket type */

42         ai->ai_socktype = socktype;

43         switch (ai->ai_family) {
44         case AF_INET:
45             ((struct sockaddr_in *) ai->ai_addr)->sin_port = port;
46             nfound++;
47             break;
48         case AF_INET6:
49             ((struct sockaddr_in6 *) ai->ai_addr)->sin6_port = port;
50             nfound++;
51             break;
52         }
53     }
54     return (nfound);
55 }
```

libgai/ga_port.c

Figure 11.28 `ga_port` function.

Consider an example. In Figure 11.1 we assumed a call to `getaddrinfo` for a host with two IP addresses, a service name of `domain` (port 53 for both TCP and UDP), and no specification of the socket type. The loop in our `getaddrinfo` function (Figure 11.25) creates two `addrinfo` structures, one for each IP address returned by `gethostbyname`. The `AI_CLONE` flag is also set in each structure, because no socket type is specified. We show the resulting linked list in Figure 11.29.

`ga_serv` is called from Figure 11.26. Since the `domain` service name is valid for both TCP and UDP, `getservbyname` is called two times, and `ga_port` is called two times: first with a final argument of `SOCK_STREAM` and again with a final argument of `SOCK_DGRAM`. The first time `ga_port` is called it starts with the linked list shown in Figure 11.29. In Figure 11.28 the `AI_CLONE` flag is set for both structures, but the socket type is 0. Therefore all that happens to each `addrinfo` structure the first time `ga_port` is called is to set the `ai_socktype` member to `SOCK_STREAM` and the port number in the socket address structure to 53. The `AI_CLONE` flag remains set. This gives us the linked list shown in Figure 11.30.

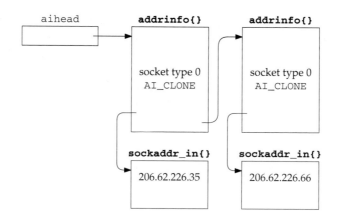

Figure 11.29 addrinfo structures when ga_port is called first time.

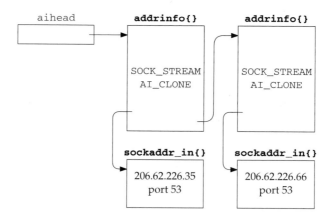

Figure 11.30 addrinfo structures after first call to ga_port.

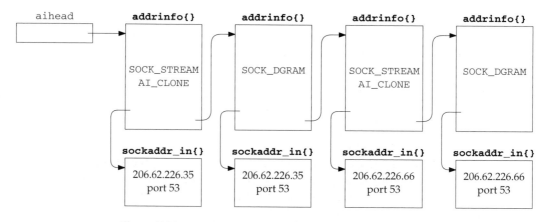

Figure 11.31 addrinfo structures after second call to ga_port.

But the second time `ga_port` is called (with a final argument of SOCK_DGRAM), since the AI_CLONE flag is set and the socket type is not 0, `ga_clone` is called for each `addrinfo` structure. The `ai_socktype` member in each of the newly cloned structures is set to SOCK_DGRAM and we end up with the linked list shown in Figure 11.31. In this figure the second `addrinfo` structure and its socket address structure are cloned from the first set of structures, and the fourth `addrinfo` structure and its socket address structure are cloned from the third set of structures.

Figure 11.32 shows our `ga_clone` function, which was called from Figure 11.28 to clone a new `addrinfo` structure and its socket address structure from an existing set of structures.

———————————— libgai/ga_clone.c

```
 5 struct addrinfo *
 6 ga_clone(struct addrinfo *ai)
 7 {
 8     struct addrinfo *new;

 9     if ( (new = calloc(1, sizeof(struct addrinfo))) == NULL)
10             return (NULL);

11     new->ai_next = ai->ai_next;
12     ai->ai_next = new;

13     new->ai_flags = 0;            /* make sure AI_CLONE is off */
14     new->ai_family = ai->ai_family;
15     new->ai_socktype = ai->ai_socktype;
16     new->ai_protocol = ai->ai_protocol;
17     new->ai_canonname = NULL;
18     new->ai_addrlen = ai->ai_addrlen;
19     if ( (new->ai_addr = malloc(ai->ai_addrlen)) == NULL)
20         return (NULL);
21     memcpy(new->ai_addr, ai->ai_addr, ai->ai_addrlen);

22     return (new);
23 }
```

———————————————————————— libgai/ga_clone.c

Figure 11.32 `ga_clone` function.

Allocate `addrinfo` structure and insert into linked list

9–12   A new `addrinfo` structure is allocated and its `ai_next` pointer is set to the `ai_next` pointer of the entry being cloned (i.e., what will be the previous entry on the list). The next pointer of the entry being cloned becomes the new structure just allocated.

Initialize from cloned entry

13–22   All the fields in the new `addrinfo` structure are copied from the entry being cloned with the exception of `ai_flags`, which is set to 0, and `ai_canonname`, which is set to a null pointer. A pointer to the newly created structure is the return value of the function.

Our `ga_unix` function, which we shown in Figure 11.33, was called from Figure 11.20 to completely process a Unix domain pathname.

```
                                                                  libgai/ga_unix.c
 3 int
 4 ga_unix(const char *path, struct addrinfo *hintsp, struct addrinfo **result)
 5 {
 6     int     rc;
 7     struct addrinfo *aihead, **aipnext;

 8     aihead = NULL;
 9     aipnext = &aihead;

10     if (hintsp->ai_family != AF_UNSPEC && hintsp->ai_family != AF_LOCAL)
11         return (EAI_ADDRFAMILY);

12     if (hintsp->ai_socktype == 0) {
13             /* no socket type specified: return stream then dgram */
14         hintsp->ai_socktype = SOCK_STREAM;
15         if ( (rc = ga_aistruct(&aipnext, hintsp, path, AF_LOCAL)) != 0)
16             return (rc);
17         hintsp->ai_socktype = SOCK_DGRAM;
18     }
19     if ( (rc = ga_aistruct(&aipnext, hintsp, path, AF_LOCAL)) != 0)
20         return (rc);

21     if (hintsp->ai_flags & AI_CANONNAME) {
22         struct utsname myname;

23         if (uname(&myname) < 0)
24             return (EAI_SYSTEM);
25         if ( (aihead->ai_canonname = strdup(myname.nodename)) == NULL)
26             return (EAI_MEMORY);
27     }
28     *result = aihead;              /* pointer to first structure in linked list */
29     return (0);
30 }
                                                                  libgai/ga_unix.c
```

Figure 11.33 `ga_unix` function.

`ga_aistruct` creates structures

10-20 If a socket type is not specified, we call our `ga_aistruct` function twice to create two `addrinfo` structures: one with a socket type of `SOCK_STREAM` and another with a socket type of `SOCK_DGRAM`. But if the caller specifies a nonzero socket type, our `ga_aistruct` function is called only once, creating one `addrinfo` structure with that socket type.

Return canonical name

21-27 If the `AI_CANONNAME` flag was specified by the caller, we call `uname` to obtain the system name and return the `nodename` member (Section 9.7) as the canonical name.

We explain the `aihead` and `aipnext` pointers with the `ga_aistruct` function, which we describe next.

Our `ga_aistruct` function was called from Figures 11.24 and 11.25 to create an addrinfo structure for an IPv4 or IPv6 address, and from Figure 11.33 to create an addrinfo structure for a Unix domain socket. We show the first part of the function in Figure 11.34.

————————————————————————————————— libgai/ga_aistruct.c
```
 5 int
 6 ga_aistruct(struct addrinfo ***paipnext, const struct addrinfo *hintsp,
 7             const void *addr, int family)
 8 {
 9     struct addrinfo *ai;

10     if ( (ai = calloc(1, sizeof(struct addrinfo))) == NULL)
11             return (EAI_MEMORY);
12     ai->ai_next = NULL;
13     ai->ai_canonname = NULL;
14     **paipnext = ai;
15     *paipnext = &ai->ai_next;

16     if ( (ai->ai_socktype = hintsp->ai_socktype) == 0)
17         ai->ai_flags |= AI_CLONE;

18     ai->ai_protocol = hintsp->ai_protocol;
```
————————————————————————————————— libgai/ga_aistruct.c

Figure 11.34 `ga_aistruct` function: first part.

Allocate `addrinfo` structure and add to linked list

10–15   An addrinfo structure is allocated and added to the linked list being built. Two pointers are used to build the linked list: `aihead` and `aipnext`. Both were allocated and initialized in Figure 11.20 for an IPv4 or an IPv6 socket, or in Figure 11.33 for a Unix domain socket. `aihead` is initialized to a null pointer and `aipnext` is initialized to point to `aihead`. We show this in Figure 11.35.

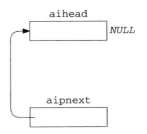

Figure 11.35 Initialization of linked list pointers.

`aihead` always points to the first addrinfo structure on the linked list (therefore its datatype is `struct addrinfo *`). `aipnext` normally points to the `ai_next` member of the last structure on the linked list (therefore its datatype is `struct addrinfo **`). We use the qualifier "normally" with regard to `aipnext` because upon initialization it really points to `aihead`, but after the first structure is allocated and placed onto the list, it always points to the `ai_next` member.

Returning to our `ga_aistruct` function, after a new structure is allocated the two statements

```
**paipnext = ai;
*paipnext = &ai->ai_next;
```

are executed. The first statement sets the `ai_next` pointer of the last structure on the list (or `aihead` if this new structure is the first on the list) to point to the newly allocated structure, and the second statement sets `aipnext` to point to the `ai_next` member of the newly allocated structure. The extra level of indirection is needed in both statements because the address of `aipnext` is an argument to the function (see Exercise 11.4). When the first structure is added to the list, we have the data structures shown in Figure 11.36.

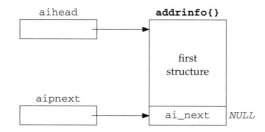

Figure 11.36   Linked list after first structure added.

When our `ga_aistruct` function is called the next time to allocate a second structure and add it to the list, we have the data structures shown in Figure 11.37.

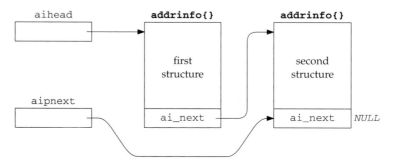

Figure 11.37   Linked list after second structure added.

Set socket type

16–17   The `ai_socktype` member is set to the socket type provided by the caller and if this is 0, the `AI_CLONE` flag is set.

Figure 11.38 shows the second part of the function: a `switch` with one `case` per address family to allocate a socket address structure and initialize it.

libgai/ga_aistruct.c

```
19      switch ((ai->ai_family = family)) {
20      case AF_INET:{
21              struct sockaddr_in *sinptr;

22                  /* allocate sockaddr_in{} and fill in all but port */
23              if ( (sinptr = calloc(1, sizeof(struct sockaddr_in))) == NULL)
24                      return (EAI_MEMORY);
25 #ifdef  HAVE_SOCKADDR_SA_LEN
26              sinptr->sin_len = sizeof(struct sockaddr_in);
27 #endif
28              sinptr->sin_family = AF_INET;
29              memcpy(&sinptr->sin_addr, addr, sizeof(struct in_addr));
30              ai->ai_addr = (struct sockaddr *) sinptr;
31              ai->ai_addrlen = sizeof(struct sockaddr_in);
32              break;
33          }
34      case AF_INET6:{
35              struct sockaddr_in6 *sin6ptr;

36                  /* allocate sockaddr_in6{} and fill in all but port */
37              if ( (sin6ptr = calloc(1, sizeof(struct sockaddr_in6))) == NULL)
38                      return (EAI_MEMORY);
39 #ifdef  HAVE_SOCKADDR_SA_LEN
40              sin6ptr->sin6_len = sizeof(struct sockaddr_in6);
41 #endif
42              sin6ptr->sin6_family = AF_INET6;
43              memcpy(&sin6ptr->sin6_addr, addr, sizeof(struct in6_addr));
44              ai->ai_addr = (struct sockaddr *) sin6ptr;
45              ai->ai_addrlen = sizeof(struct sockaddr_in6);
46              break;
47          }
48      case AF_LOCAL:{
49              struct sockaddr_un *unp;

50                  /* allocate sockaddr_un{} and fill in */
51              if (strlen(addr) >= sizeof(unp->sun_path))
52                  return(EAI_SERVICE);
53              if ( (unp = calloc(1, sizeof(struct sockaddr_un))) == NULL)
54                  return(EAI_MEMORY);

55              unp->sun_family = AF_LOCAL;
56              strcpy(unp->sun_path, addr);
57 #ifdef  HAVE_SOCKADDR_SA_LEN
58              unp->sun_len = SUN_LEN(unp);
59 #endif
60              ai->ai_addr = (struct sockaddr *) unp;
61              ai->ai_addrlen = sizeof(struct sockaddr_un);
62              if (hintsp->ai_flags & AI_PASSIVE)
63                  unlink(unp->sun_path);  /* OK if this fails */
64              break;
65          }
66      }
67      return (0);
68 }
```

libgai/ga_aistruct.c

Figure 11.38 ga_aistruct function: second part.

Allocate IPv4 socket address structure and initialize

20-33   A `sockaddr_in` structure is allocated and the `ai_addr` pointer in the `addrinfo` structure is set to point to it. The IP address, address family, and length members of the socket address structure are all initialized. The port number is not initialized until `ga_serv` is called, which in turn calls `ga_port`.

Allocate IPv6 socket address structure and initialize

34-47   A `sockaddr_in6` structure is allocated and initialized, similar to the IPv4 case.

Allocate Unix domain socket address structure and initialize

48-65   A `sockaddr_un` structure is allocated and initialized. The address is a pathname and if the `AI_PASSIVE` flag was specified by the caller, we try to `unlink` the pathname to prevent an error return when the caller calls `bind`. But it is not an error if the `unlink` fails.

Our `ga_echeck` function, which we show in Figure 11.39, was called from Figure 11.20 to perform some initial error checking on the caller's arguments.

libgai/ga_echeck.c

```
 5 int
 6 ga_echeck(const char *hostname, const char *servname,
 7           int flags, int family, int socktype, int protocol)
 8 {
 9     if (flags & ~(AI_PASSIVE | AI_CANONNAME))
10         return (EAI_BADFLAGS);   /* unknown flag bits */

11     if (hostname == NULL || hostname[0] == '\0') {
12         if (servname == NULL || servname[0] == '\0')
13             return (EAI_NONAME);    /* host or service must be specified */
14     }
15     switch (family) {
16     case AF_UNSPEC:
17         break;
18     case AF_INET:
19         if (socktype != 0 &&
20             (socktype != SOCK_STREAM &&
21              socktype != SOCK_DGRAM &&
22              socktype != SOCK_RAW))
23             return (EAI_SOCKTYPE);   /* invalid socket type */
24         break;
25     case AF_INET6:
26         if (socktype != 0 &&
27             (socktype != SOCK_STREAM &&
28              socktype != SOCK_DGRAM &&
29              socktype != SOCK_RAW))
30             return (EAI_SOCKTYPE);   /* invalid socket type */
31         break;
32     case AF_LOCAL:
33         if (socktype != 0 &&
34             (socktype != SOCK_STREAM &&
35              socktype != SOCK_DGRAM))
36             return (EAI_SOCKTYPE);   /* invalid socket type */
37         break;
```

```
38      default:
39          return (EAI_FAMILY);    /* unknown protocol family */
40      }
41      return (0);
42  }
```
————————————————————————————————— libgai/ga_echeck.c

Figure 11.39 ga_echeck function.

9–14   The flags are verified and either a hostname or a service name must be specified.

15–41   Depending on the address family, only certain types of sockets are supported, and this verifies the socket type.

We do not check the caller's ai_protocol hint, if any, as few applications specify this value (which becomes the third argument to socket). Should an invalid combination be specified, such as a socket type of SOCK_DGRAM and a protocol of IPPROTO_TCP, the protocol hint is returned to the caller in Figure 11.34 and if the caller uses this value in a call to socket, an error of EPROTONOSUPPORT will be returned.

We have finished with the getaddrinfo function, and all the internal functions that it calls. Figure 11.40 shows the freeaddrinfo function, which releases all the memory in the linked list. We called this function from Figure 11.26 if an error occurred, and the user also calls it to release a linked list of structures.

————————————————————————————————— libgai/freeaddrinfo.c
```
1  #include    "gai_hdr.h"

2  void
3  freeaddrinfo(struct addrinfo *aihead)
4  {
5      struct addrinfo *ai, *ainext;

6      for (ai = aihead; ai != NULL; ai = ainext) {
7          if (ai->ai_addr != NULL)
8              free(ai->ai_addr);  /* socket address structure */

9          if (ai->ai_canonname != NULL)
10             free(ai->ai_canonname);

11         ainext = ai->ai_next;   /* can't fetch ai_next after free() */
12         free(ai);               /* the addrinfo{} itself */
13     }
14 }
```
————————————————————————————————— libgai/freeaddrinfo.c

Figure 11.40 freeaddrinfo function: first part.

6–13   The linked list of addrinfo structures is traversed. If a socket address structure has been allocated, it is freed. If a canonical name string has been allocated, it is freed. Finally, the addrinfo structure itself is freed. We must be careful to save the contents of the structure's ai_next pointer before freeing the structure, as we cannot reference the structure after free returns.

Figure 11.41 shows our implementation of the getnameinfo function. It consists of a switch statement with one case per address family.

libgai/getnameinfo.c

```
2 int
3 getnameinfo(const struct sockaddr *sa, socklen_t salen,
4             char *host, size_t hostlen,
5             char *serv, size_t servlen, int flags)
6 {
7     switch (sa->sa_family) {
8     case AF_INET:{
9             struct sockaddr_in *sain = (struct sockaddr_in *) sa;

10            return (gn_ipv46(host, hostlen, serv, servlen,
11                           &sain->sin_addr, sizeof(struct in_addr),
12                           AF_INET, sain->sin_port, flags));
13        }

14    case AF_INET6:{
15            struct sockaddr_in6 *sain = (struct sockaddr_in6 *) sa;

16            return (gn_ipv46(host, hostlen, serv, servlen,
17                           &sain->sin6_addr, sizeof(struct in6_addr),
18                           AF_INET6, sain->sin6_port, flags));
19        }

20    case AF_LOCAL:{
21            struct sockaddr_un *un = (struct sockaddr_un *) sa;

22            if (hostlen > 0)
23                snprintf(host, hostlen, "%s", "/local");
24            if (servlen > 0)
25                snprintf(serv, servlen, "%s", un->sun_path);
26            return (0);
27        }

28    default:
29        return (1);
30    }
31 }
```

libgai/getnameinfo.c

Figure 11.41 getnameinfo function.

Handle IPv4 and IPv6 socket address structures

8–19   We call our gn_ipv46 function (shown next) to handle IPv4 and IPv6 socket address structures.

Handle Unix domain socket address structures

20–27   For a Unix domain socket address structure we return /local as the hostname and the pathname that is bound to the socket as the service name. If no pathname is bound to the socket, then the returned service name will be a null string.

We return the hostname and service name using `snprintf` instead of `strncpy`. If we used the latter we could write

```
strncpy(host, "/local", hostlen);
```

While this guarantees that we do not overflow the caller's buffer, if `hostlen` is less than or equal to 6, then the caller's buffer will not be null terminated. But we are writing a library routine and we should always return a null-terminated string if that is what the caller expects. This could cause problems for the caller at a later time in the program. Therefore we should always write

```
strncpy(host, "/local", hostlen-1);
host[hostlen-1] = '\0';
```

which guarantees that we do not overwrite the caller's buffer and that the result is null terminated. We use `snprintf` instead of these two statements, since it will not overflow the destination and it guarantees that the destination is null terminated. An alternate design would be to define our own library function that calls `strncpy` and null terminates the result, but calling the existing `snprintf` seems simpler.

Figure 11.42 is our `gn_ipv46` function, which handles IPv4 and IPv6 socket address structures for `getnameinfo`.

Return hostname

12–23   If the `NI_NUMERICHOST` flag is specified, we call `inet_ntop` to return the presentation format of the IP address; otherwise `gethostbyaddr` searches for the hostname corresponding to the IP address. If `gethostbyaddr` succeeds and the `NI_NOFQDN` (no fully qualified domain name) flag is specified, the hostname is terminated at the first period in the name.

Handle failure of `gethostbyaddr`

24–29   If `gethostbyaddr` fails (which, unfortunately is all too common given the number of misconfigured DNS servers on the Internet; see Section 14.8 of TCPv3) and the `NI_NAMEREQD` flag was specified, an error is returned. Otherwise the address string corresponding to the IP address is formed by `inet_ntop`.

Return service string

32–42   If the `NI_NUMERICSERV` flag is specified, just the decimal port number is returned. Otherwise `getservbyport` is called. The final argument is a null pointer unless the `NI_DGRAM` flag is specified. If `getservbyport` fails, the decimal port number is returned instead.

libgai/gn_ipv46.c

```
 5 int
 6 gn_ipv46(char *host, size_t hostlen, char *serv, size_t servlen,
 7          void *aptr, size_t alen, int family, int port, int flags)
 8 {
 9     char    *ptr;
10     struct hostent *hptr;
11     struct servent *sptr;

12     if (hostlen > 0) {
13         if (flags & NI_NUMERICHOST) {
14             if (inet_ntop(family, aptr, host, hostlen) == NULL)
15                 return (1);
16         } else {
17             hptr = gethostbyaddr(aptr, alen, family);
18             if (hptr != NULL && hptr->h_name != NULL) {
19                 if (flags & NI_NOFQDN) {
20                     if ( (ptr = strchr(hptr->h_name, '.')) != NULL)
21                         *ptr = 0;    /* overwrite first dot */
22                 }
23                 snprintf(host, hostlen, "%s", hptr->h_name);
24             } else {
25                 if (flags & NI_NAMEREQD)
26                     return (1);
27                 if (inet_ntop(family, aptr, host, hostlen) == NULL)
28                     return (1);
29             }
30         }
31     }
32     if (servlen > 0) {
33         if (flags & NI_NUMERICSERV) {
34             snprintf(serv, servlen, "%d", ntohs(port));
35         } else {
36             sptr = getservbyport(port, (flags & NI_DGRAM) ? "udp" : NULL);
37             if (sptr != NULL && sptr->s_name != NULL)
38                 snprintf(serv, servlen, "%s", sptr->s_name);
39             else
40                 snprintf(serv, servlen, "%d", ntohs(port));
41         }
42     }
43     return (0);
44 }
```

libgai/gn_ipv46.c

Figure 11.42 gn_ipv46 function: handle IPv4 and IPv6 socket address structures.

11.17 Summary

getaddrinfo is a useful function that lets us write protocol-independent code. But calling it directly takes a few steps, and there are still repetitive details that must be handled for different scenarios: go through all the returned structures, ignore error returns from socket, set the SO_REUSEADDR socket option for TCP servers, and the like. We simplify all these details with our five functions tcp_connect, tcp_listen, `udp_client`, `udp_connect`, and `udp_server`. We showed the use of these functions in writing protocol-independent versions of our TCP and UDP daytime clients and daytime servers.

`gethostbyname` and `gethostbyaddr` are also examples of functions that are not normally reentrant. The two functions share a static result structure to which both return a pointer. We encounter this problem of reentrancy again with threads in Chapter 23 and discuss ways around the problem. We discussed the `_r` versions of these two functions that some vendors provide, which is one solution, but it requires a change in all the applications that call the functions.

Exercises

11.1   In Figure 11.8 the caller must pass a pointer to an integer to obtain the size of the protocol address. If the caller does not do this (i.e., passes a null pointer as the final argument), how can the caller still obtain the actual size of the protocol's addresses?

11.2   Modify Figure 11.10 to call `getnameinfo` instead of `sock_ntop`. What flags should you pass to `getnameinfo`?

11.3   In Section 7.5 we discussed port stealing with the `SO_REUSEADDR` socket option. To see how this works, build the protocol-independent UDP daytime server in Figure 11.15. Start one instance of the server in one window, binding the wildcard address and some port of your choosing. Start a client in another window and verify that this server is handling the client (note the `printf` in the server). Then start another instance of the server in another window, this time binding one of the host's unicast addresses and the same port as the first server. What problem do you immediately encounter? Fix this problem and restart this second server. Start a client, send a datagram, and verify that the second server has stolen the port from the first server. If possible, start the second server again, from a different login account from the first server, to see if the stealing still succeeds, because some vendors will not allow the second bind unless the user ID is the same as that of the process that has already bound the port.

11.4   When discussing Figure 11.34 we noted that the address of `aipnext` is an argument to the `ga_aistruct` function, necessitating an extra level of indirection when referencing the variable. Why do we not make `aipnext` a global variable, instead of passing its address as an argument?

11.5   In our discussion of Unix domain at the end of Section 11.5 we mentioned that none of the IANA service names begin with a slash. Do any of these service names contain a slash?

11.6   At the end of Section 2.10 we showed two `telnet` examples: to the `daytime` server and to the `echo` server . Knowing that a client goes through the two steps `gethostbyname` and `connect`, which lines output by the client indicate which steps?

11.7   `gethostbyaddr` can take a long time (up to 80 seconds) to return an error if a hostname cannot be found for an IP address. Write a new function named `getnameinfo_timeo` that takes an additional integer argument specifying the maximum number of seconds to wait for a reply. If the timer expires and the `NI_NAMEREQD` flag is not specified, just call `inet_ntop` and return an address string.

12

Daemon Processes
and `inetd` *Superserver*

12.1 Introduction

A *daemon* is a process that runs in the background and is independent of control from all terminals. Unix systems typically have many processes that are daemons (on the order or 20 to 50), running in the background, performing different administrative tasks.

The reason for wanting independence from all terminals is in case the daemon is started from a terminal (as opposed to starting from an initialization script). We want to be able to use that terminal for other tasks at a later time. For example, if we start the daemon from a terminal, log off the terminal, and someone else logs in on the terminal, we do not want any daemon error messages appearing during the next user's terminal session. Similarly, signals generated from terminal keys (e.g., the interrupt signal) must not affect any daemons that were started from that terminal earlier. While it is easy to run our server in the background (by ending the shell command line with an ampersand), we should have our program put itself in the background automatically and we also need to make it independent of any terminal.

There are numerous ways to start a daemon:

1. During system startup many daemons are started by the system initialization scripts. These scripts are often in the directory /etc or in a directory whose name begins with /etc/rc, but their location and contents are implementation dependent. Daemons started by these scripts begin with superuser privileges.

   A few network servers are often started from these scripts: the `inetd` superserver (our next item), a Web server, and a mail server (often `sendmail`). The `syslogd` daemon that we describe in Section 12.2 is normally started by one of these scripts.

2. Many network servers are started by the `inetd` superserver, which we describe later in this chapter. `inetd` itself is started from one of the scripts in step 1. `inetd` listens for network requests (Telnet, FTP, etc.) and when a request arrives, it invokes the actual server (Telnet server, FTP server, etc.).

3. The execution of programs on a regular basis is performed by the `cron` daemon, and programs that it invokes run as daemons. The `cron` daemon itself is started in step 1 during system startup.

4. The execution of a program at one time in the future is specified by the `at` command. The `cron` daemon normally initiates these programs when their time arrives, so these programs run as daemons.

5. Daemons can be started from user terminals, either in the foreground or in the background. This is often done when testing a daemon, or restarting a daemon that was terminated for some reason.

Since a daemon does not have a controlling terminal, it needs some way to output messages when something happens, either normal informational messages, or emergency messages that need to be handled by an administrator. The `syslog` function is the standard way to output these messages, and it sends the messages to the `syslogd` daemon.

12.2 `syslogd` Daemon

Unix systems normally start a daemon named `syslogd` from one of the system initializations scripts, and it runs as long as the system is up. Berkeley-derived implementations of `syslogd` perform the following actions upon startup:

1. The configuration file, normally `/etc/syslog.conf`, is read, specifying what to do with each type of log message that the daemon can receive. These messages can be appended to a file (a special case of which is the file `/dev/console`, which writes the message to the console), written to a specific user (if that user is logged in), or forwarded to the `syslogd` daemon on another host.

2. A Unix domain socket is created and bound to the pathname `/var/run/log` (`/dev/log` on some systems).

3. A UDP socket is created and bound to port 514 (the `syslog` service).

4. The pathname `/dev/klog` is opened. Any error messages from within the kernel appear as input on this device.

The `syslogd` daemon then runs in an infinite loop that calls `select`, waiting for any one of its three descriptors (from steps 2, 3, and 4) to be readable, reads the log message, and does what the configuration file says to do with that message. If the daemon receives the SIGHUP signal, it rereads its configuration file.

We could send log messages to the `syslogd` daemon from our daemons by creating a Unix domain datagram socket and sending our messages to the pathname that the daemon has bound, but an easier interface is the `syslog` function that we describe in the next section. Alternately we could create a UDP socket and send our log messages to the loopback address and port 514.

> Newer implementations disable the creation of the UDP socket unless specified by the administrator, as allowing anyone to send UDP datagrams to this port (possible filling its socket receive buffer) might prevent legitimate log messages from being received.

> Differences exist between the various implementations of `syslogd`. For example, Unix domain sockets are used by Berkeley-derived implementations but System V implementations use a streams log driver. Different Berkeley-derived implementations use different pathnames for the Unix domain socket. We can ignore all these details if we use the `syslog` function.

12.3 `syslog` Function

Since a daemon does not have a controlling terminal, it cannot just `fprintf` to `stderr`. The common technique for logging messages from a daemon is to call the `syslog` function.

```
#include <syslog.h>

void syslog(int priority, const char *message, ... );
```

> Although this function was originally developed for BSD systems, it is provided by most Unix vendors today. Posix says nothing about `syslog` but it is required by Unix 98.

The *priority* argument is a combination of a *level* and a *facility*, which we show in Figures 12.1 and 12.2. The *message* is like a format string to `printf`, with the addition of a `%m` specification, which is replaced with the error message corresponding to the current value of `errno`. A newline can appear at the end of the *message* but is not mandatory.

Log messages have a *level* between 0 and 7, which we show in Figure 12.1. These are ordered values. If no *level* is specified by the sender, `LOG_NOTICE` is the default.

level	Value	Description
LOG_EMERG	0	system is unusable (highest priority)
LOG_ALERT	1	action must be taken immediately
LOG_CRIT	2	critical conditions
LOG_ERR	3	error conditions
LOG_WARNING	4	warning conditions
LOG_NOTICE	5	normal but significant condition (default)
LOG_INFO	6	informational
LOG_DEBUG	7	debug-level messages (lowest priority)

Figure 12.1 *level* of log messages.

Log messages also contain a *facility* to identify the type of process sending the message. We show the different values in Figure 12.2. If no *facility* is specified, LOG_USER is the default.

facility	Description
LOG_AUTH	security/authorization messages
LOG_AUTHPRIV	security/authorization messages (private)
LOG_CRON	cron daemon
LOG_DAEMON	system daemons
LOG_FTP	FTP daemon
LOG_KERN	kernel messages
LOG_LOCAL0	local use
LOG_LOCAL1	local use
LOG_LOCAL2	local use
LOG_LOCAL3	local use
LOG_LOCAL4	local use
LOG_LOCAL5	local use
LOG_LOCAL6	local use
LOG_LOCAL7	local use
LOG_LPR	line printer system
LOG_MAIL	mail system
LOG_NEWS	network news system
LOG_SYSLOG	messages generated internally by syslogd
LOG_USER	random user-level messages (default)
LOG_UUCP	UUCP system

Figure 12.2 *facility* of log messages.

For example, the following call could be issued by a daemon when a call to the rename function unexpectedly fails:

```
syslog(LOG_INFO|LOG_LOCAL2, "rename(%s, %s): %m", file1, file2);
```

The purpose of the *facility* and *level* is to allow all messages from a given facility to be handled the same in the /etc/syslog.conf file, or to allow all messages of a given level to be handled the same. For example, the configuration file could contain the lines

```
kern.*              /dev/console
local7.debug        /var/log/cisco.log
```

to specify that all kernel messages get logged to the console, and all debug messages from the local7 facility get appended to the file /var/log/cisco.log.

When the application calls syslog the first time, it creates a Unix domain datagram socket and then calls connect to the well-known pathname of the socket created by the syslogd daemon (e.g., /var/run/log). This socket remains open until the process terminates. Alternately, the process can call openlog and closelog.

```
#include <syslog.h>

void openlog(const char *ident, int options, int facility);

void closelog(void);
```

openlog can be called before the first call to syslog and closelog can be called when the application is finished sending log messages.

ident is a string that will be prepended to each log message by syslog. Often this is the program name.

The *options* argument is formed as the logical OR of one or more of the constants in Figure 12.3.

options	Description
LOG_CONS	log to console if cannot send to syslogd daemon
LOG_NDELAY	do not delay open, create socket now
LOG_PERROR	log to standard error as well as sending to syslogd daemon
LOG_PID	log the process ID with each message

Figure 12.3 *options* for openlog.

Normally the Unix domain socket is not created when openlog is called. Instead it will be opened upon the first call to syslog. The LOG_NDELAY option causes the socket to be created when openlog is called.

The *facility* argument to openlog specifies a default facility for any subsequent calls to syslog that do not specify a facility. Some daemons call openlog and specify the facility (which normally does not change for a given daemon) and then specify only the *level* in each call to syslog (since the *level* can change depending on the error).

Log messages can also be generated by the logger command. This can be used from within shell scripts, for example, to send messages to syslogd.

12.4 `daemon_init` Function

Figure 12.4 shows a function named daemon_init that we can call (normally from a server) to daemonize the process.

fork

10-11   We first call fork and then the parent terminates and the child continues. If the process was started as a shell command in the foreground, when the parent terminates the shell thinks the command is done. This automatically runs the process in the background. Also, the child inherits the process group ID from the parent but gets its own process ID. This guarantees that the child is not a process group leader, which is required for the next call to setsid.

setsid

12-13   setsid is a Posix.1 function that creates a new session. (Chapter 9 of APUE talks about process relationships and sessions in detail.) The process becomes the session leader of the new session, becomes the process group leader of a new process group, and has no controlling terminal.

Ignore `SIGHUP` and `fork` again

14-16   We ignore the SIGHUP signal and call fork again. When this function returns, the parent is really the first child, and it terminates, leaving the second child running. The

——— *daemon_init.c*

```
 1 #include    "unp.h"
 2 #include    <syslog.h>

 3 #define MAXFD    64

 4 extern int daemon_proc;        /* defined in error.c */

 5 void
 6 daemon_init(const char *pname, int facility)
 7 {
 8     int     i;
 9     pid_t   pid;

10     if ( (pid = Fork()) != 0)
11         exit(0);               /* parent terminates */

12         /* 1st child continues */
13     setsid();                  /* become session leader */

14     Signal(SIGHUP, SIG_IGN);
15     if ( (pid = Fork()) != 0)
16         exit(0);               /* 1st child terminates */

17         /* 2nd child continues */
18     daemon_proc = 1;           /* for our err_XXX() functions */

19     chdir("/");                /* change working directory */

20     umask(0);                  /* clear our file mode creation mask */

21     for (i = 0; i < MAXFD; i++)
22         close(i);

23     openlog(pname, LOG_PID, facility);
24 }
```

——— *daemon_init.c*

Figure 12.4 daemon_init function: daemonize the process.

purpose of this second fork is to guarantee that the daemon cannot automatically acquire a controlling terminal should it open a terminal device in the future. Under SVR4, when a session leader without a controlling terminal opens a terminal device (that is not currently some other session's controlling terminal), the terminal becomes the controlling terminal of the session leader. But by calling fork a second time we guarantee that the second child is no longer a session leader, so it cannot acquire a controlling terminal. We must ignore SIGHUP because when the session leader terminates (the first child), all processes in the session (our second child) are sent the SIGHUP signal.

Set flag for error functions

17–18   We set the global daemon_proc nonzero. This external is defined by our err_*XXX* functions (Section D.4) and when its value is nonzero, this tells them to call syslog instead of doing an fprintf to standard error. This saves us from having to go through all our code and call one of our error functions if the server is not being run as a daemon (i.e., when we are testing the server) but call syslog if it is being run as a daemon.

Change working directory and clear file mode creation mask

19-20   We change the working directory to the root directory, although some daemons might have a reason to change to some other directory. For example, a printer daemon might change to the printer's spool directory, where it does all its work. Should the daemon ever generate a core file, that file is generated in the current working directory. Another reason to change the working directory is that the daemon could have been started anywhere in the filesystem, and if it remains there, that filesystem cannot be unmounted. The file mode creation mask is reset to 0 so that if the daemon creates its own files, permission bits in the inherited file mode creation mask do not affect the permission bits of the new files.

Close any open descriptors

21-22   We close any open descriptors that are inherited from the process that executed the daemon (normally a shell). The problem is determining the highest descriptor in use: there is no Unix function that provides this value. There are ways to determine the maximum number of descriptors that the process can open, but even this gets complicated (see p. 43 of APUE) because the limit can be infinite. Our solution is to close the first 64 descriptors, even though most of these are probably not open.

Some daemons open /dev/null for reading and writing and duplicate the descriptor to standard input, standard output, and standard error. This guarantees that these common descriptors are open, and a read from any of these descriptors returns 0 (end-of-file) and the kernel just discards anything written to any of these three descriptors. The reason for opening these descriptors is so that any library function called by the daemon that assumes it can read from standard input, or write to either standard output or standard error, will not fail. Alternately, some daemons open a log file that they will write to while running and duplicate its descriptor to standard output and standard error.

Use syslogd for errors

23   openlog is called. The first argument is from the caller and is normally the name of the program (e.g., argv[0]). We specify that the process ID should be added to each log message. The *facility* is also specified by the caller, as one of the values from Figure 12.2, or 0 if the default of LOG_USER is OK.

We note that since a daemon runs without a controlling terminal it should never receive the SIGHUP signal from the kernel. Therefore many daemons use this signal as a notification from the administrator that the daemon's configuration file has changed, and the daemon should reread the file. Two other signals that a daemon should never receive are SIGINT and SIGWINCH, and these can also be used to notify a daemon of some change.

Example: Daytime Server as a Daemon

Figure 12.5 is a modification of our protocol-independent daytime server from Figure 11.10 that calls our `daemon_init` function to run as a daemon.

——— *inetd/daytimetcpsrv2.c*

```
 1 #include    "unp.h"
 2 #include    <time.h>

 3 int
 4 main(int argc, char **argv)
 5 {
 6     int     listenfd, connfd;
 7     socklen_t addrlen, len;
 8     struct sockaddr *cliaddr;
 9     char    buff[MAXLINE];
10     time_t  ticks;

11     daemon_init(argv[0], 0);

12     if (argc == 2)
13         listenfd = Tcp_listen(NULL, argv[1], &addrlen);
14     else if (argc == 3)
15         listenfd = Tcp_listen(argv[1], argv[2], &addrlen);
16     else
17         err_quit("usage: daytimetcpsrv2 [ <host> ] <service or port>");

18     cliaddr = Malloc(addrlen);

19     for ( ; ; ) {
20         len = addrlen;
21         connfd = Accept(listenfd, cliaddr, &len);
22         err_msg("connection from %s", Sock_ntop(cliaddr, len));

23         ticks = time(NULL);
24         snprintf(buff, sizeof(buff), "%.24s\r\n", ctime(&ticks));
25         Write(connfd, buff, strlen(buff));

26         Close(connfd);
27     }
28 }
```

——— *inetd/daytimetcpsrv2.c*

Figure 12.5 Protocol-independent daytime server that runs as a daemon.

There are only two changes: we call our `daemon_init` function as soon as the program starts, and we call our `err_msg` function, instead of `printf`, to print the client's IP address and port. Indeed, if we want our programs to be able to run as a daemon, we must avoid calling the `printf` and `fprintf` functions and use our `err_msg` function instead.

If we run this program on our host `solaris` and then check the `/var/adm/messages` file (where we send all `LOG_USER` messages) after connecting from our host `bsdi`, we have:

```
Jun  4 15:15:33 solaris.kohala.com daytimetcpsrv2[14882]:
connection from ::ffff:206.62.226.35.3356
```

(We have wrapped the one long line.) The date and time are prefixed automatically by the `syslogd` daemon.

12.5 `inetd` Daemon

On a typical Unix system there could be many servers in existence, just waiting for a client request to arrive. Examples are FTP, Telnet, Rlogin, TFTP, and so on. With systems before 4.3BSD, each of these services had a process associated with it. This process was started at boot time from the file `/etc/rc`, and each process did nearly identical startup tasks: create a socket, `bind` the server's well-known port to the socket, wait for a connection (if TCP) or a datagram (if UDP), and then `fork`. The child process serviced the client and the parent waited for the next client request. There are two problems with this model.

1. All these daemons contained nearly identical startup code, first with respect to socket creation, and also with respect to becoming a daemon process (similar to our `daemon_init` function).

2. Each daemon took a slot in the process table, but each daemon was asleep most of the time.

The 4.3BSD release simplified this by providing an Internet *superserver*: the `inetd` daemon. This daemon can be used by servers that use either TCP or UDP. It does not handle other protocols, such as Unix domain sockets. This daemon fixes the two problems just mentioned.

1. It simplifies writing daemon processes, since most of the startup details are handled by `inetd`. This obviates the need for each server to call our `daemon_init` function.

2. It allows a single process (`inetd`) to be waiting for incoming client requests for multiple services, instead of one process for each service. This reduces the total number of processes in the system.

The `inetd` process establishes itself as a daemon using the techniques that we described with our `daemon_init` function. It then reads and processes its configuration file, typically `/etc/inetd.conf`. This file specifies the services that the superserver is to handle, and what to do when a service request arrives. Each line contains the fields shown in Figure 12.6. Some sample lines are:

```
ftp       stream  tcp  nowait  root    /usr/bin/ftpd     ftpd -l
telnet    stream  tcp  nowait  root    /usr/bin/telnetd  telnetd
login     stream  tcp  nowait  root    /usr/bin/rlogind  rlogind -s
tftp      dgram   udp  wait    nobody  /usr/bin/tftpd    tftpd -s /tftpboot
```

The actual name of the server is always passed as the first argument to a program when it is `execed`.

Field	Description
service-name	must be in `/etc/services`
socket-type	`stream` (TCP) or `dgram` (UDP)
protocol	must be in `/etc/protocols`: either `tcp` or `udp`
wait-flag	normally `nowait` for TCP or `wait` for UDP
login-name	from `/etc/passwd`: typically `root`
server-program	full pathname to `exec`
server-program-arguments	arguments for `exec`

Figure 12.6   Fields in `inetd.conf` file.

This figure and the sample lines are just examples. Most vendors have added their own features to `inetd`. Examples are the ability to handle remote procedure call (RPC) servers, in addition to TCP and UDP servers, and the ability to handle protocols other than TCP and UDP. Also, the pathname to `exec` and the command-line arguments to the server obviously depend on the implementation.

The interaction of IPv6 with `/etc/inetd.conf` depends on the vendor. Some use a *protocol* of `tcp6` or `udp6` to indicate that an IPv6 socket should be created for the server.

A picture of what the `inetd` daemon does is shown in Figure 12.7.

1. On startup it reads the `/etc/inetd.conf` file and creates a socket of the appropriate type (stream or datagram) for all the services specified in the file. The maximum number of servers that `inetd` can handle depends on the maximum number of descriptors that `inetd` can create. Each new socket is added to a descriptor set that will be used in a call to `select`.

2. `bind` is called for the socket, specifying the well-known port for the server and the wildcard IP address. This TCP or UDP port number is obtained by calling `getservbyname` with the *service-name* and the *protocol* fields from the configuration file as arguments.

3. For TCP sockets, `listen` is called, so that incoming connection requests are accepted. This step is not done for datagram sockets.

4. After all the sockets are created, `select` is called to wait for any of the sockets to become readable. Recall from Section 6.3 that a TCP socket becomes readable when a new connection is ready to be `accepted` and a UDP socket becomes readable when a datagram arrives. `inetd` spends most of its time blocked in this call to `select`, waiting for a socket to be readable.

5. When `select` returns that a socket is readable, if the socket is a TCP socket, `accept` is called to accept the new connection.

6. The `inetd` daemon `forks` and the child process handles the service request. This is similar to a standard concurrent server (Section 4.8).

    The child closes all descriptors other than the socket descriptor that it is handling: the new connected socket returned by `accept` for a TCP server, or the original UDP socket.

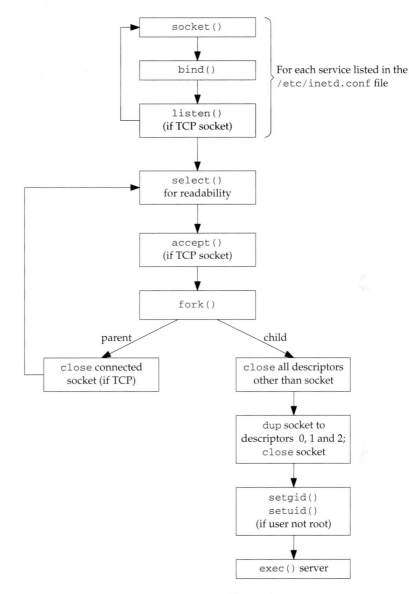

Figure 12.7 Steps performed by inetd.

The child calls dup2 three times, duplicating the socket onto descriptors 0, 1, and 2 (standard input, standard output, and standard error). The original socket descriptor is then closed. By doing this, the only descriptors that are open in the child are 0, 1, and 2. If the child reads from standard input, it is reading from the socket and anything it writes to standard output or standard error is written to the socket.

The child calls `getpwnam` to get the password file entry for the *login-name* specified in the configuration file. If this field is not `root`, then the child becomes the specified user by executing the `setgid` and `setuid` function calls. (Since the `inetd` process is executing with a user ID of 0, the child process inherits this user ID across the `fork`, so it is able to become any user that it chooses.)

The child process now does an `exec` to execute the appropriate *server-program* to handle the request, passing the arguments specified in the configuration file.

7. If the socket is a stream socket, the parent process must close the connected socket (like our standard concurrent server). The parent calls `select` again, waiting for the next socket to become readable.

If we look in more detail at the descriptor handling that is taking place, Figure 12.8 shows the descriptors in `inetd` when a new connection request arrives from an FTP client.

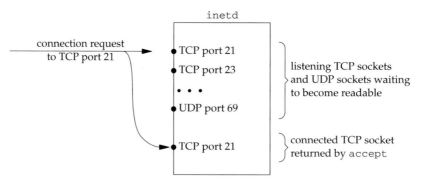

Figure 12.8   `inetd` descriptors when connection request arrives for TCP port 21.

The connection request is directed to TCP port 21, but a new connected socket is created by `accept`.

Figure 12.9 shows the descriptors in the child, after the call to `fork`, after the child has closed all the descriptors other than the connected socket.

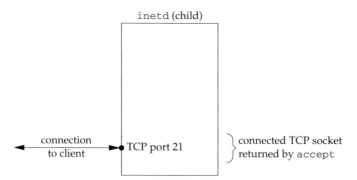

Figure 12.9   `inetd` descriptors in child.

The next step is for the child to duplicate the connected socket to descriptors 0, 1, and 2 and then close the connected socket. This gives us the descriptors shown in Figure 12.10.

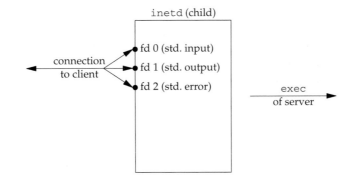

Figure 12.10   inetd descriptors after dup2.

The child then calls exec, and recall from Section 4.7 that all descriptors normally remain open across an exec, so the real server that is execed uses any of the descriptors 0, 1, or 2 to communicate with the client. These should be the only descriptors open in the server.

The scenario we have described handles the case where the configuration file specifies nowait for the server. This is typical for all TCP services and it means that inetd need not wait for its child to terminate before accepting another connection for that service. If another connection request arrives for the same service, it is returned to the parent process as soon as it calls select again. Steps 4, 5, and 6 listed earlier are executed again, and another child process handles this new request.

Specifying the wait flag for a datagram service changes the steps done by the parent process. This flag says that inetd must wait for its child to terminate before selecting on this UDP socket again. The following changes occur:

1. When fork returns in the parent, the parent saves the process ID of the child. This allows the parent to know when this specific child process terminates, by looking at the value returned by waitpid.

2. The parent disables the socket from future selects by using the FD_CLR macro to turn off the bit in its descriptor set. This means that the child process takes over the socket until it terminates.

3. When the child terminates, the parent is notified by a SIGCHLD signal, and the parent's signal handler obtains the process ID of the terminating child. It reenables select for the corresponding socket by turning on the bit in its descriptor set for this socket.

The reason that a datagram server must take over the socket until it terminates, preventing inetd from selecting on that socket for readability (awaiting another client datagram) is because there is only one socket for a datagram server, unlike a TCP server that has a listening socket and one connected socket per client. If `inetd` did not turn off readability for the datagram socket, and say the parent (`inetd`) executed before the child, then the datagram from the client would still be in the socket receive buffer, causing `select` to return readable again, causing `inetd` to `fork` another (unneeded) child. `inetd` must ignore the datagram socket until it knows that the child has read the datagram from the socket receive queue. The way that `inetd` knows when that child is finished with the socket is by receiving `SIGCHLD`, indicating that the child has terminated. We show an example of this in Section 20.7.

The five standard Internet services that we described in Figure 2.13 are handled internally by `inetd`. (See Exercise 12.2.)

Since `inetd` is the process that calls `accept` for a TCP server, the actual server that is invoked by `inetd` normally calls `getpeername` to obtain the IP address and port number of the client. Recall Figure 4.18 where we showed that after a `fork` and an `exec` (which is what `inetd` does) the only way for the actual server to obtain the identify of the client is to call `getpeername`.

`inetd` is normally not used for high-volume servers, notably mail and Web servers. `sendmail`, for example, is normally run as a standard concurrent server, as we described in Section 4.8. In this mode the process control cost for each client connection is just a `fork`, while the cost for a TCP server invoked by `inetd` is a `fork` and an `exec`. Web servers use a variety of techniques to minimize the process control overhead for each client connection, as we discuss in Chapter 27.

12.6 `daemon_inetd` Function

Figure 12.11 shows a function named `daemon_inetd` that we can call from a server that we know is invoked by `inetd`.

─── *daemon_inetd.c*

```
1 #include    "unp.h"
2 #include    <syslog.h>

3 extern int daemon_proc;         /* defined in error.c */

4 void
5 daemon_inetd(const char *pname, int facility)
6 {
7     daemon_proc = 1;               /* for our err_XXX() functions */
8     openlog(pname, LOG_PID, facility);
9 }
```
─── *daemon_inetd.c*

Figure 12.11 `daemon_inetd` function: daemonize process run by `inetd`.

This function is trivial, compared to `daemon_init`, because all of the daemonization steps are performed by `inetd` when it starts. All that we do is set the `daemon_proc` flag for our error functions (Figure D.4) and call `openlog`, with the same arguments as the call in Figure 12.4.

Example: Daytime Server as a Daemon Invoked by `inetd`

Figure 12.12 is a modification of our daytime server from Figure 12.5 that can be invoked by `inetd`.

————————————————————————————— inetd/daytimetcpsrv3.c
```
 1 #include    "unp.h"
 2 #include    <time.h>

 3 int
 4 main(int argc, char **argv)
 5 {
 6     socklen_t len;
 7     struct sockaddr *cliaddr;
 8     char    buff[MAXLINE];
 9     time_t  ticks;

10     daemon_inetd(argv[0], 0);

11     cliaddr = Malloc(MAXSOCKADDR);
12     len = MAXSOCKADDR;
13     Getpeername(0, cliaddr, &len);
14     err_msg("connection from %s", Sock_ntop(cliaddr, len));

15     ticks = time(NULL);
16     snprintf(buff, sizeof(buff), "%.24s\r\n", ctime(&ticks));
17     Write(0, buff, strlen(buff));

18     Close(0);                       /* close TCP connection */
19     exit(0);
20 }
```
————————————————————————————— inetd/daytimetcpsrv3.c

Figure 12.12 Protocol-independent daytime server that can be invoked by `inetd`.

There are two major changes in this program. First, all the socket creation code is gone: the calls to `tcp_listen` and to `accept`. Those steps are done by `inetd` and we reference the TCP connection using descriptor 0 (standard input). Second, the infinite `for` loop is gone, because we are invoked once per client connection. After servicing this client we terminate.

Call `getpeername`

11–14   Since we do not call `tcp_listen`, we do not know the size of the socket address structure that it returns, and since we do not call `accept`, we do not know the client's protocol address. Therefore we allocate a buffer for the socket address structure using our `MAXSOCKADDR` constant and call `getpeername` with descriptor 0 as the first argument.

To run this example on our BSD/OS system, we first assign the service a name and port, adding the following line to `/etc/services`:

```
    mydaytime    9999/tcp
```

We then add a line to `/etc/inetd.conf`:

```
mydaytime  stream  tcp  nowait  rstevens
          /usr/home/rstevens/daytimetcpsrv3  daytimetcpsrv3
```

(We have wrapped the long line.) We place the executable in the specified file and send the SIGHUP signal to inetd, telling it to reread its configuration file. The next step is to execute netstat to verify that a listening socket has been created on TCP port 9999:

```
bsdi % netstat -na | grep 9999
tcp      0    0     *.9999          *.*              LISTEN
```

We then invoke the server from another host:

```
alpha % telnet bsdi 9999
Trying 206.62.226.35...
Connected to bsdi.
Escape character is '^]'.
Thu Jun  5 11:13:50 1997
Connection closed by foreign host.
```

The /var/log/messages file (where we have directed the LOG_USER facility messages to be logged in our /etc/syslog.conf file) contains the entry

```
Jun  5 11:13:50 bsdi daytimetcpsrv3[28724]: connection from 206.62.226.42.1042
```

12.7 Summary

Daemons are processes that run in the background independent of control from all terminals. Many network servers run as daemons. All output from a daemon is normally sent to the syslogd daemon by calling the syslog function. The administrator then has complete control over what happens to these messages, based on the daemon that sent the message and the severity of the message.

To start an arbitrary program and have it run as a daemon requires a few steps: call fork to run in the background, call setsid to create a new Posix.1 session and become the session leader, fork again to avoid obtaining a new controlling terminal, change the working directory and the file mode creation mask, and close all unneeded files. Our daemon_init function handles all these details.

Many Unix servers are started by the inetd daemon. It handles all of the required daemonization steps and when the actual server is started, the socket is open on standard input, standard output, and standard error. This lets us omit the calls to socket, bind, listen, and accept, since all these steps are handled by inetd.

Exercises

12.1 What happens in Figure 12.5 if we wait to call daemon_init until the command-line arguments have been processed, so that the call to err_quit appears before the program becomes a daemon?

12.2 For the five services handled internally by `inetd` (Figure 2.13), considering the TCP version and the UDP version of each service, which of the 10 servers do you think are implemented with a call to `fork`, and which do not require a `fork`?

12.3 What happens if we create a UDP socket, bind port 7 to the socket (the standard `echo` server in Figure 2.13), and send a UDP datagram to a `chargen` server?

12.4 The Solaris 2.x manual page for `inetd` describes a `-t` flag that causes `inetd` to call `syslog` (with a facility of `LOG_DAEMON` and a level of `LOG_NOTICE`) to log the client's IP address and port for any TCP service that `inetd` handles. How does `inetd` obtain this information?

This manual page also says that `inetd` cannot do this for a UDP service. Why?

Is there a way around this limitation for UDP services?

13

Advanced I/O Functions

13.1 Introduction

This chapter covers a variety of functions and techniques that we lump into the category of "advanced I/O." First is setting a timeout on an I/O operation, which can be done in three different ways.

Next are three more variations on the `read` and `write` functions: `recv` and `send`, which allow a fourth argument that contains flags from the process to the kernel, `readv` and `writev`, which lets us specify a vector of buffers to input into or output from, and `recvmsg` and `sendmsg`, which combine all the features from the other I/O functions along with the new capability of receiving and sending ancillary data.

We also consider how to determine how much data is in the socket receive buffer and how to use the C standard I/O library with sockets. We finish the chapter with a brief look at T/TCP, TCP for Transactions, which can avoid the three-way handshake.

13.2 Socket Timeouts

There are three ways to place a timeout on an I/O operation involving a socket.

1. Call `alarm`, which generates the `SIGALRM` signal when the specified time has expired. This involves signal handling, which can differ from one implementation to the next, and it may interfere with other existing calls to `alarm` in the process.

2. Block waiting for I/O in `select`, which has a time limit built in, instead of blocking in a call to `read` or `write`.

3. Use the newer SO_RCVTIMEO and SO_SNDTIMEO socket options. The problem with this approach is that not all implementations support these two socket options.

All three techniques work with input and output operations (e.g., read, write, and the other variations such as recvfrom and sendto) but we would also like a technique that we can use with connect, since a TCP connect can take a long time to time out (typically 75 seconds). select can be used to place a timeout on connect only when the socket is in a nonblocking mode (which we show in Section 15.3), and the two socket options do not work with connect. We also note that the first two techniques work with any descriptor while the third technique works only with socket descriptors.

We now show examples of all three techniques.

connect with a Timeout Using SIGALRM

Figure 13.1 shows our function connect_timeo that calls connect with a upper limit specified by the caller. The first three arguments are the three required by connect and the fourth argument is the number of seconds to wait.

lib/connect_timeo.c

```
 1 #include    "unp.h"

 2 static void connect_alarm(int);

 3 int
 4 connect_timeo(int sockfd, const SA *saptr, socklen_t salen, int nsec)
 5 {
 6     Sigfunc *sigfunc;
 7     int     n;

 8     sigfunc = Signal(SIGALRM, connect_alarm);
 9     if (alarm(nsec) != 0)
10         err_msg("connect_timeo: alarm was already set");

11     if ( (n = connect(sockfd, (struct sockaddr *) saptr, salen)) < 0) {
12         close(sockfd);
13         if (errno == EINTR)
14             errno = ETIMEDOUT;
15     }
16     alarm(0);                   /* turn off the alarm */
17     Signal(SIGALRM, sigfunc);   /* restore previous signal handler */

18     return (n);
19 }

20 static void
21 connect_alarm(int signo)
22 {
23     return;                     /* just interrupt the connect() */
24 }
```

lib/connect_timeo.c

Figure 13.1 connect with a timeout.

Establish signal handler

8   A signal handler is established for SIGALRM. The current signal handler (if any) is saved, so we can restore it at the end of the function.

Set alarm

9-10   The alarm clock for the process is set to the number of seconds specified by the caller. The return value from alarm is the number of seconds currently remaining in the alarm clock for the process (if one has already been set by the process) or 0 (if there is no current alarm). In the former case we print a warning message, since we are wiping out that previously set alarm. (See Exercise 13.2.)

Call connect

11-16   connect is called and if the function is interrupted (EINTR), we set the errno value to ETIMEDOUT instead. The socket is closed to prevent the three-way handshake from continuing.

Turn off alarm and restore any previous signal handler

17-18   The alarm is turned off by setting it to 0 and the previous signal handler (if any) is restored.

Handle SIGALRM

20-24   The signal handler just returns, assuming this return will interrupt the pending connect, causing connect to return an error of EINTR. Recall our signal function (Figure 5.6) that does not set the SA_RESTART flag when the signal being caught is SIGALRM.

     One point to make with this example is that we can always reduce the timeout period for a connect using this technique, but we cannot extend the kernel's existing timeout. That is, on a Berkeley-derived kernel the timeout for a connect is normally 75 seconds. We can specify a smaller value for our function, say 10, but if we specify a larger value, say 80, the connect itself will still time out after 75 seconds.

     Another point with this example is that we use the interruptibility of the system call (connect) to return before the kernel's time limit expires. This is fine when we perform the system call and can handle the EINTR error return. But in Section 26.6 we encounter a library function that performs the system call, and the library function reissues the system call when EINTR is returned. We can still use SIGALRM in this scenario, but we will see in Figure 26.10 that we also have to use sigsetjmp and siglongjmp to get around the library's ignoring of EINTR.

recvfrom with a Timeout Using SIGALRM

     Figure 13.2 is a redo of our dg_cli function from Figure 8.8, but with a call to alarm to interrupt the recvfrom if a reply is not received within 5 seconds.

Handle timeout from recvfrom

8-22   We establish a signal handler for SIGALRM and then call alarm for a 5-second timeout before each call to recvfrom. If recvfrom is interrupted by our signal handler, we

```
                                                              ──── advio/dgclitimeo3.c
 1 #include    "unp.h"

 2 static void sig_alrm(int);

 3 void
 4 dg_cli(FILE *fp, int sockfd, const SA *pservaddr, socklen_t servlen)
 5 {
 6     int     n;
 7     char    sendline[MAXLINE], recvline[MAXLINE + 1];

 8     Signal(SIGALRM, sig_alrm);

 9     while (Fgets(sendline, MAXLINE, fp) != NULL) {

10         Sendto(sockfd, sendline, strlen(sendline), 0, pservaddr, servlen);

11         alarm(5);
12         if ( (n = recvfrom(sockfd, recvline, MAXLINE, 0, NULL, NULL)) < 0) {
13             if (errno == EINTR)
14                 fprintf(stderr, "socket timeout\n");
15             else
16                 err_sys("recvfrom error");
17         } else {
18             alarm(0);
19             recvline[n] = 0;     /* null terminate */
20             Fputs(recvline, stdout);
21         }
22     }
23 }

24 static void
25 sig_alrm(int signo)
26 {
27     return;                        /* just interrupt the recvfrom() */
28 }
```
──── advio/dgclitimeo3.c

Figure 13.2 dg_cli function with alarm to timeout recvfrom.

print a message and continue. If a line is read from the server, we turn off the pending
alarm and print the reply.

SIGALRM signal handler

24–28   Our signal handler just returns, to interrupt the blocked recvfrom.

This example works correctly because we are reading only one reply each time we
establish an alarm. In Section 18.4 we use the same technique but since we are reading
multiple replies for a given alarm, a race condition exists that we must handle.

recvfrom with a Timeout Using select

We demonstrate the second technique for setting a timeout (using select) in Figure 13.3. It shows our function named readable_timeo that waits up to a specified
number of seconds for a descriptor to become readable.

```
                                                              ─── lib/readable_timeo.c
 1 #include    "unp.h"

 2 int
 3 readable_timeo(int fd, int sec)
 4 {
 5      fd_set  rset;
 6      struct timeval tv;

 7      FD_ZERO(&rset);
 8      FD_SET(fd, &rset);

 9      tv.tv_sec = sec;
10      tv.tv_usec = 0;

11      return (select(fd + 1, &rset, NULL, NULL, &tv));
12          /* > 0 if descriptor is readable */
13 }
                                                              ─── lib/readable_timeo.c
```

Figure 13.3 `readable_timeo` function: wait for a descriptor to become readable.

Prepare arguments for `select`

7–10   The bit corresponding to the descriptor is turned on in the read descriptor set. A `timeval` structure is set to the number of seconds that the caller wants to wait.

Block in `select`

11–12   `select` then waits for the descriptor to become readable, or for the timeout to expire. The return value of this function is the return value of `select`: −1 on an error, 0 if a timeout occurs, or a positive value specifying the number of ready descriptors.

This function does not perform the read operation; it just waits for the descriptor to be ready for reading. Therefore this function can be used with any type of socket: TCP or UDP.

It is trivial to create a similar function named `writable_timeo` that waits for a descriptor to become writable.

We use this function in Figure 13.4, which is a redo of our `dg_cli` function from Figure 8.8. This new version calls `recvfrom` only when our `readable_timeo` function returns a positive value.

We do not block in the call to `recvfrom` until the function `readable_timeo` tells us that the descriptor is readable. This guarantees that `recvfrom` will not block.

`recvfrom` with a Timeout Using the `SO_RCVTIMEO` Socket Option

Our final example demonstrates the `SO_RCVTIMEO` socket option. We set this option once for a descriptor, specifying the timeout value, and this timeout then applies to all read operations on that descriptor. The nice thing about this method is that we set the option only once, compared to the previous two methods which required doing something before every operation on which we want to place a time limit. But this socket option applies only to read operations, and the similar option `SO_SNDTIMEO` applies

————————————————————————————————————— advio/dgclitimeo1.c

```
 1 #include    "unp.h"

 2 void
 3 dg_cli(FILE *fp, int sockfd, const SA *pservaddr, socklen_t servlen)
 4 {
 5     int     n;
 6     char    sendline[MAXLINE], recvline[MAXLINE + 1];

 7     while (Fgets(sendline, MAXLINE, fp) != NULL) {

 8         Sendto(sockfd, sendline, strlen(sendline), 0, pservaddr, servlen);

 9         if (Readable_timeo(sockfd, 5) == 0) {
10             fprintf(stderr, "socket timeout\n");
11         } else {
12             n = Recvfrom(sockfd, recvline, MAXLINE, 0, NULL, NULL);
13             recvline[n] = 0;      /* null terminate */
14             Fputs(recvline, stdout);
15         }
16     }
17 }
```

————————————————————————————————————— advio/dgclitimeo1.c

Figure 13.4 `dg_cli` function that calls `readable_timeo` to set a timeout.

only to write operations: neither socket option can be used to set a timeout for a `connect`.

Figure 13.5 shows another version of our `dg_cli` function that uses the SO_RCVTIMEO socket option.

Set socket option

8–10   The fourth argument to `setsockopt` is a pointer to a `timeval` structure that is filled in with the desired timeout.

Test for timeout

15–17   If the I/O operation times out, the function (`recvfrom` in this case) returns EWOULDBLOCK.

13.3 `recv` and `send` Functions

These two functions are similar to the standard `read` and `write` functions, but one additional argument is required.

```
#include <sys/socket.h>

ssize_t recv(int sockfd, void *buff, size_t nbytes, int flags);

ssize_t send(int sockfd, const void *buff, size_t nbytes, int flags);
                                    Both return: number of bytes read or written if OK, −1 on error
```

advio/dgclitimeo2.c

```
 1 #include    "unp.h"

 2 void
 3 dg_cli(FILE *fp, int sockfd, const SA *pservaddr, socklen_t servlen)
 4 {
 5     int     n;
 6     char    sendline[MAXLINE], recvline[MAXLINE + 1];
 7     struct timeval tv;

 8     tv.tv_sec = 5;
 9     tv.tv_usec = 0;
10     Setsockopt(sockfd, SOL_SOCKET, SO_RCVTIMEO, &tv, sizeof(tv));

11     while (Fgets(sendline, MAXLINE, fp) != NULL) {

12         Sendto(sockfd, sendline, strlen(sendline), 0, pservaddr, servlen);

13         n = recvfrom(sockfd, recvline, MAXLINE, 0, NULL, NULL);
14         if (n < 0) {
15             if (errno == EWOULDBLOCK) {
16                 fprintf(stderr, "socket timeout\n");
17                 continue;
18             } else
19                 err_sys("recvfrom error");
20         }
21         recvline[n] = 0;          /* null terminate */
22         Fputs(recvline, stdout);
23     }
24 }
```

advio/dgclitimeo2.c

Figure 13.5 dg_cli function that uses the SO_RCVTIMEO socket option to set a timeout.

The first three arguments to recv and send are the same as the first three arguments to read and write. The *flags* argument is either 0, or is formed by logically OR'ing one or more of the constants shown in Figure 13.6.

flags	Description	recv	send
MSG_DONTROUTE	bypass routing table lookup		•
MSG_DONTWAIT	only this operation is nonblocking	•	•
MSG_OOB	send or receive out-of-band data	•	•
MSG_PEEK	peek at incoming message	•	
MSG_WAITALL	wait for all the data	•	

Figure 13.6 *flags* for I/O functions.

MSG_DONTROUTE   This flag tells the kernel that the destination is on a locally attached network and not to perform a lookup of the routing table. We provided additional information on this feature with the SO_DONTROUTE socket option (Section 7.5). This feature can be enabled for a single output operation with the MSG_DONTROUTE flag, or enabled for all output operations for a given socket using the socket option.

MSG_DONTWAIT   This flag specifies nonblocking for a single I/O operation, without having to turn on the nonblocking flag for the socket, perform the I/O operation, and then turn off the nonblocking flag. We describe nonblocking I/O in Chapter 15 along with turning the nonblocking flag on and off for all I/O operations on a socket.

> This flag is new with Net/3 and might not be supported on all systems.

MSG_OOB   With send, this flag specifies that out-of-band data is being sent. With TCP only 1 byte should be sent as out-of-band data, as we describe in Chapter 21. With recv, this flag specifies that out-of-band data is to be read instead of normal data.

MSG_PEEK   This flag lets us look at the data that is available to be read, without having the system discard the data after the recv or recvfrom returns. We talk more about this in Section 13.7.

MSG_WAITALL   This flag was introduced with 4.3BSD Reno. It tells the kernel not to return from a read operation until the requested number of bytes have been read. If the system supports this flag, we can then omit the readn function (Figure 3.14) and replace it with the macro

```
#define  readn(fd, ptr, n)  recv(fd, ptr, n, MSG_WAITALL)
```

Even if we specify MSG_WAITALL, the function can still return fewer than the requested number of bytes if (a) a signal is caught, (b) the connection is terminated, or (c) an error is pending for the socket.

There are additional flags used by other protocols, but not TCP/IP. For example, the OSI transport layer is record based (not a byte stream such as TCP) and supports the MSG_EOR flag for output operations to specify the end of a logical record. T/TCP (TCP for transactions, described in Section 13.9) supports a new MSG_EOF flag to combine an output operation with the sending of a FIN.

There is a fundamental design problem with the *flags* argument: it is passed by value; it is not a value–result argument. Therefore it can be used only to pass flags from the process to the kernel. The kernel cannot pass back flags to the process. This is not a problem with TCP/IP, because it is rare to need to pass flags back to the process from the kernel. But when the OSI protocols were added to 4.3BSD Reno, the need arose to return MSG_EOR to the process with an input operation. The decision was made with

4.3BSD Reno to leave the arguments to the commonly used input functions (`recv` and `recvfrom`) as is and change the `msghdr` structure that is used with `recvmsg` and `sendmsg`. We will see in Section 13.5 that an integer `msg_flags` member was added to this structure, and since the structure is passed by reference, the kernel can modify these flags on return. This also means that if a process needs to have the flags updated by the kernel, the process must call `recvmsg` instead of either `recv` or `recvfrom`.

13.4 `readv` and `writev` Functions

These two functions are similar to `read` and `write`, but `readv` and `writev` let us read into or write from one or more buffers with a single function call. These operations are called *scatter read* (since the input data is scattered into multiple application buffers) and *gather write* (since multiple buffers are gathered for a single output operation).

```
#include <sys/uio.h>

ssize_t readv(int filedes, const struct iovec *iov, int iovcnt);

ssize_t writev(int filedes, const struct iovec *iov, int iovcnt);
```
                                    Both return: number of bytes read or written, −1 on error

The second argument to both functions is a pointer to an array of `iovec` structures, which is defined by including the `<sys/uio.h>` header:

```
struct iovec {
  void   *iov_base;   /* starting address of buffer */
  size_t  iov_len;    /* size of buffer */
};
```

> The `readv` and `writev` functions have not yet been standardized by Posix. But the `iovec` structure is also used with the `recvmsg` and `sendmsg` functions (Section 13.5) and this structure is standardized by Posix.1g. The datatypes shown for the members of the `iovec` structure are those specified by Posix.1g. You may encounter implementations that define `iov_base` to be a `char *`, and `iov_len` to be an `int`.

There is some limit to the number of elements in the array of `iovec` structures that an implementation allows. 4.4BSD, for example, allows up to 1024 while Solaris 2.5 has a limit of 16. Posix.1g requires that the constant `IOV_MAX` be defined by including the `<sys/uio.h>` header and that its value be at least 16.

The `readv` and `writev` functions can be used with any descriptor, not just sockets. Also, `writev` is an atomic operation. For a record-based protocol such as UDP, one call to `writev` generates a single UDP datagram.

We mentioned one use of `writev` with the `TCP_NODELAY` socket option in Section 7.9. We said that a `write` of 4 bytes followed by a `write` of 396 bytes could invoke the Nagle algorithm and a preferred solution is to call `writev` for the two buffers.

13.5 `recvmsg` and `sendmsg` Functions

These two functions are the most general of all the I/O functions. Indeed, we could replace all calls to `read`, `readv`, `recv`, and `recvfrom` with calls to `recvmsg`. Similarly all calls to the various output functions could be replaced with calls to `sendmsg`.

```
#include <sys/socket.h>

ssize_t recvmsg(int sockfd, struct msghdr *msg, int flags);

ssize_t sendmsg(int sockfd, struct msghdr *msg, int flags);
```

Both return: number of bytes read or written if OK, −1 on error

Both functions package most of the arguments into a `msghdr` structure:

```
struct msghdr {
  void          *msg_name;        /* protocol address */
  socklen_t      msg_namelen;     /* size of protocol address */
  struct iovec  *msg_iov;         /* scatter/gather array */
  size_t         msg_iovlen;      /* # elements in msg_iov */
  void          *msg_control;     /* ancillary data; must be aligned for
                                     a cmsghdr structure */
  socklen_t      msg_controllen;  /* length of ancillary data */
  int            msg_flags;       /* flags returned by recvmsg() */
};
```

> The `msghdr` structure that we show originated with 4.3BSD Reno and is the one specified in Posix.1g. Some systems (Solaris 2.5) still use an older `msghdr` structure that originated with 4.2BSD. This older structure does not have the `msg_flags` member and the `msg_control` and `msg_controllen` members are named `msg_accrights` and `msg_accrightslen`. The only form of ancillary data supported by these older systems is the passing of file descriptors (called access rights). 4.3BSD Reno added more forms of ancillary data when the OSI protocols were added and therefore generalized the structure member names.

The `msg_name` and `msg_namelen` members are used when the socket is not connected (e.g., an unconnected UDP socket). They are similar to the fifth and sixth arguments to `recvfrom` and `sendto`: `msg_name` points to a socket address structure in which the caller stores the destination's protocol address for `sendmsg`, or in which `recvmsg` stores the sender's protocol address. If a protocol address does not need to be specified (e.g., a TCP socket or a connected UDP socket), `msg_name` should be set to a null pointer. `msg_namelen` is a value for `sendmsg` but a value–result for `recvmsg`.

The `msg_iov` and `msg_iovlen` members specify the array of input or output buffers (the array of `iovec` structures), similar to the second and third arguments for `readv` or `writev`.

The `msg_control` and `msg_controllen` members specify the location and size of the optional ancillary data. `msg_controllen` is a value–result argument for `recvmsg`. We describe ancillary data in Section 13.6.

With `recvmsg` and `sendmsg` we must distinguish between two flag variables: the *flags* argument, which is passed by value, and the `msg_flags` member of the `msghdr` structure, which is passed by reference (since the address of the structure is passed to the function).

- The msg_flags member is used only by recvmsg. When recvmsg is called, the *flags* argument is copied into the msg_flags member (p. 502 of TCPv2) and this value is used by the kernel to drive its receive processing. This value is then updated based on the result of recvmsg.

- The msg_flags member is ignored by sendmsg because this function uses the *flags* argument to drive its output processing. This means if we want to set the MSG_DONTWAIT flag in a call to sendmsg, we set the *flags* argument to this value; setting the msg_flags member to this value has no effect.

Figure 13.7 summarizes which flags are examined by the kernel for both the input and output functions, and which of the msg_flags might be returned by recvmsg. There is no column for sendmsg msg_flags because we mentioned that it is not used.

Flag	Examined by: send *flags* sendto *flags* sendmsg *flags*	Examined by: recv *flags* recvfrom *flags* recvmsg *flags*	Returned by: recvmsg msg_flags
MSG_DONTROUTE	•		
MSG_DONTWAIT	•	•	
MSG_PEEK		•	
MSG_WAITALL		•	
MSG_EOR	•		•
MSG_OOB	•	•	•
MSG_BCAST			•
MSG_MCAST			•
MSG_TRUNC			•
MSG_CTRUNC			•

Figure 13.7 Summary of input and output flags by various I/O functions.

The first four flags are only examined and never returned, the next two are both examined and returned, and the last four are only returned. The following comments apply to the six flags that are returned by recvmsg:

MSG_BCAST   This flag is new with BSD/OS and is returned if the datagram was received as a link-layer broadcast or with a destination IP address that is a broadcast address. This flag is a better way of determining if a UDP datagram was sent to a broadcast address, compared to the IP_RECVDSTADDR socket option.

MSG_MCAST   This flag is new with BSD/OS and is returned if the datagram was received as a link-layer multicast.

MSG_TRUNC   This flag is returned if the datagram was truncated: the kernel
                   has more data to return than the process has allocated room for
                   (the sum of all the `iov_len` members). We discuss this more in
                   Section 20.3.

MSG_CTRUNC   This flag is returned if the ancillary data was truncated: the ker-
                   nel has more ancillary data to return than the process has allo-
                   cated room for (`msg_controllen`).

MSG_EOR   This flag is cleared if the returned data does not end a logical
                   record, or the flag is turned on if the returned data ends a logical
                   record. TCP does *not* use this flag, since it is a byte-stream
                   protocol.

MSG_OOB   This flag is *never* returned for TCP out-of-band data. This flag is
                   returned by other protocol suites (e.g., the OSI protocols).

Implementations might return some of the input *flags* in the `msg_flags` member, so we
should examine only those flag values that we are interested in (e.g., the last six in Figure 13.7).

Figure 13.8 shows a `msghdr` structure and the various information that it points to.
We assume in this figure that the process is about to call `recvmsg` for a UDP socket.

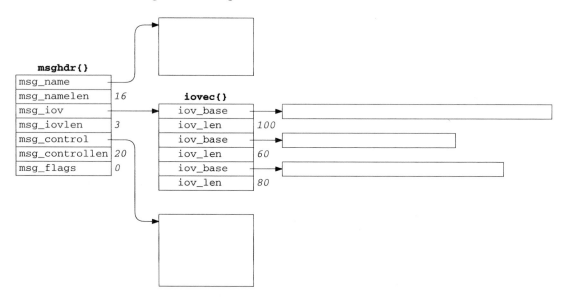

Figure 13.8 Data structures when `recvmsg` is called for a UDP socket.

Sixteen bytes are allocated for the protocol address and 20 bytes are allocated for the
ancillary data. An array of three `iovec` structures is initialized: the first specifies a
100-byte buffer, the second a 60-byte buffer, and the third an 80-byte buffer. We also

assume that the IP_RECVDSTADDR socket option has been set for the socket, to receive the destination IP address from the UDP datagram.

We then assume that a 170-byte UDP datagram arrives from 198.69.10.2, port 2000, destined for our UDP socket with a destination IP address of 206.62.226.35. Figure 13.9 shows all the information in the msghdr structure when recvmsg returns.

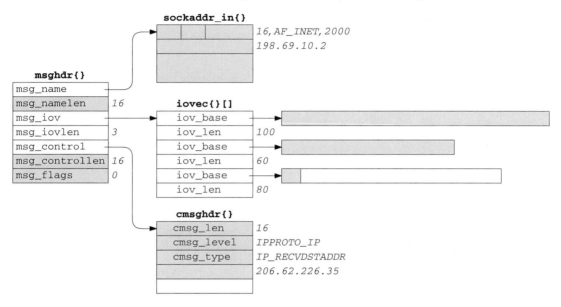

Figure 13.9 Update of Figure 13.8 when recvmsg returns.

The shaded fields are modified by recvmsg. The following items have changed from Figure 13.8 to Figure 13.9:

- The buffer pointed to by msg_name has been filled in as an Internet socket address structure containing the source IP address and source UDP port from the received datagram.

- msg_namelen, a value–result argument, is updated with the amount of data stored in msg_name. Nothing changes since its value before the call was 16 and its value when recvmsg returns is also 16.

- The first 100 bytes of data are stored in the first buffer, the next 60 bytes are stored in the second buffer, and the final 10 bytes are stored in the third buffer. The last 70 bytes of the final buffer are not modified. The return value of the recvmsg function is the size of the datagram, 170.

- The buffer pointed to by msg_control is filled in as a cmsghdr structure. (We say more about ancillary data in Section 13.6 and more about this particular socket option in Section 20.2.) The cmsg_len is 16, cmsg_level is IPPROTO_IP, cmsg_type is IP_RECVDSTADDR, and the next 4 bytes contain the destination IP address from the received UDP datagram. The final 4 bytes of the 20-byte buffer that we supplied to hold the ancillary data are not modified.

- The `msg_controllen` member is updated with the actual amount of ancillary data that was stored; it is also a value–result argument and its result on return is 16.

- The `msg_flags` member is updated by `recvmsg` but there are no flags to return to the process.

Figure 13.10 summarizes the differences between the five groups of I/O functions that we have described.

Function	Any descriptor	Only socket descriptor	Single read/write buffer	Scatter/ gather read/write	Optional flags	Optional peer address	Optional control information
`read, write`	•		•				
`readv, writev`	•			•			
`recv, send`		•	•		•		
`recvfrom, sendto`		•	•		•	•	
`recvmsg, sendmsg`		•		•	•	•	•

Figure 13.10 Comparison of the five groups of I/O functions.

13.6 Ancillary Data

Ancillary data can be sent and received using the `msg_control` and `msg_controllen` members of the `msghdr` structure with the `sendmsg` and `recvmsg` functions. Another term for ancillary data is *control information*. In this section we describe the concept and show the structure and macros that are used to build and process ancillary data, but we save the code examples for later chapters that describe the actual uses of ancillary data.

Figure 13.11 is a summary of the various uses of ancillary data that we cover in this text.

Protocol	cmsg_level	cmsg_type	Description
IPv4	IPPROTO_IP	IP_RECVDSTADDR IP_RECVIF	receive destination address with UDP datagram receive interface index with UDP datagram
IPv6	IPPROTO_IPV6	IPV6_DSTOPTS IPV6_HOPLIMIT IPV6_HOPOPTS IPV6_NEXTHOP IPV6_PKTINFO IPV6_RTHDR	specify/receive destination options specify/receive hop limit specify/receive hop-by-hop options specify next-hop address specify/receive packet information specify/receive routing header
Unix domain	SOL_SOCKET	SCM_RIGHTS SCM_CREDS	send/receive descriptors send/receive user credentials

Figure 13.11 Summary of uses for ancillary data.

The OSI protocol suite also uses ancillary data for various purposes that we do not discuss in this text.

Ancillary data consists of one or more *ancillary data objects*, each one beginning with a cmsghdr structure, defined by including <sys/socket.h>:

```
struct cmsghdr {
   socklen_t   cmsg_len;    /* length in bytes, including this structure */
   int         cmsg_level; /* originating protocol */
   int         cmsg_type;  /* protocol-specific type */
       /* followed by unsigned char cmsg_data[] */
};
```

We have already seen this structure in Figure 13.9, when used with the IP_RECVDSTADDR socket option to return the destination IP address of a received UDP datagram. The ancillary data pointed to by msg_control must be suitably aligned for a cmsghdr structure . We show one way to do this in Figure 14.11.

Figure 13.12 shows an example of two ancillary data objects in the control buffer.

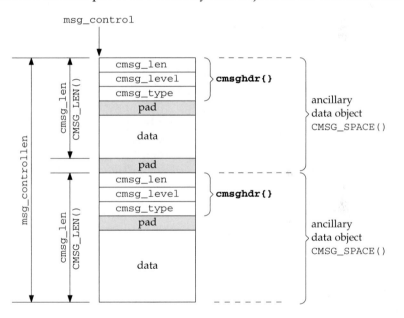

Figure 13.12 Ancillary data containing two ancillary data objects.

msg_control points to the first ancillary data object and the total length of the ancillary data is specified by msg_controllen. Each object is preceded by a cmsghdr structure that describes the object. There can be padding between the cmsg_type member and the actual data, and there can also be padding at the end of the data, before the next ancillary data object. The five CMSG_*xxx* macros that we describe shortly account for this possible padding.

Not all implementations support multiple ancillary data objects in the control buffer.

Figure 13.13 shows the format of the `cmsghdr` structure when used with a Unix domain socket for descriptor passing (Section 14.7) or credential passing (Section 14.8).

<table>
<tr><td colspan="2">cmsghdr{}</td><td></td><td colspan="2">cmsghdr{}</td></tr>
<tr><td>cmsg_len</td><td>16</td><td></td><td>cmsg_len</td><td>112</td></tr>
<tr><td>cmsg_level</td><td>SOL_SOCKET</td><td></td><td>cmsg_level</td><td>SOL_SOCKET</td></tr>
<tr><td>cmsg_type</td><td>SCM_RIGHTS</td><td></td><td>cmsg_type</td><td>SCM_CREDS</td></tr>
<tr><td>descriptor</td><td></td><td></td><td>fcred{}</td><td></td></tr>
</table>

Figure 13.13   `cmsghdr` structure when used with Unix domain sockets.

In this figure we assume each of the three members of the `cmsghdr` structure occupies 4 bytes and there is no padding between the `cmsghdr` structure and the actual data. When descriptors are passed, the contents of the `cmsg_data` array are the actual descriptor values. In this figure we show only one descriptor being passed, but in general more than one can be passed (in which case the `cmsg_len` value will be 12 plus 4 times the number of descriptors, assuming each descriptor occupies 4 bytes).

Since the ancillary data returned by `recvmsg` can contain any number of ancillary data objects and to hide the possible padding from the application, the following five macros are defined by including the `<sys/socket.h>` header to simplify the processing of the ancillary data.

```
#include <sys/socket.h>
#include <sys/param.h>    /* for ALIGN macro on many implementations */

struct cmsghdr *CMSG_FIRSTHDR(struct msghdr *mhdrptr);

               Returns: pointer to first cmsghdr structure or NULL if no ancillary data

struct cmsghdr *CMSG_NXTHDR(struct msghdr *mhdrptr, struct cmsghdr *cmsgptr);

          Returns: pointer to next cmsghdr structure or NULL if no more ancillary data objects

unsigned char *CMSG_DATA(struct cmsghdr *cmsgptr);

               Returns: pointer to first byte of data associated with cmsghdr structure

unsigned int CMSG_LEN(unsigned int length);

               Returns: value to store in cmsg_len given the amount of data

unsigned int CMSG_SPACE(unsigned int length);

               Returns: total size of an ancillary data object given the amount of data
```

Posix.1g defines the first three macros, [Stevens and Thomas 1997] define the last two.

These macros would be used in the following pseudocode:

```
struct msghdr    msg;
struct cmsghdr   *cmsgptr;

/* fill in msg structure */

/* call recvmsg() */

for (cmsgptr = CMSG_FIRSTHDR(&msg); cmsgptr != NULL;
     cmsgptr = CMSG_NXTHDR(&msg, cmsgptr)) {
    if (cmsgptr->cmsg_level == ... &&
        cmsgptr->cmsg_type == ... ) {
        u_char  *ptr;

        ptr = CMSG_DATA(cmsgptr);
        /* process data pointed to by ptr */
    }
}
```

CMSG_FIRSTHDR returns a pointer to the first ancillary data object, or a null pointer if there is no ancillary data in the msghdr structure (either msg_control is a null pointer, or cmsg_len is less than the size of a cmsghdr structure). CMSG_NXTHDR returns a null pointer when there is no another ancillary data object in the control buffer.

> Many existing implementations of CMSG_FIRSTHDR never look at msg_controllen and just return the value of cmsg_control. In Figure 20.2 we test the value of msg_controllen before calling this macro.

The difference between CMSG_LEN and CMSG_SPACE is that the former does not account for any padding following the data portion of the ancillary data object and is therefore the value to store in cmsg_len, while the latter accounts for the padding at the end and is therefore the value to use if dynamically allocating space the ancillary data object.

13.7 How Much Data Is Queued?

There are times when we want to see how much data is queued to be read on a socket, without reading the data. Three techniques are available.

1. If the goal is not to block in the kernel because we have something else to do when nothing is ready to be read, nonblocking I/O can be used. We describe this in Chapter 15.

2. If we want to examine the data but still leave it on the receive queue for some other part of our process to read, we can use the MSG_PEEK flag (Figure 13.6). If we want to do this, but we are not sure that something is ready to be read, we can combine this flag with a nonblocking socket or combine this flag with the MSG_DONTWAIT flag.

Be aware that the amount of data on the receive queue can change between two successive calls to `recv` for a stream socket. For example, assume we call `recv` for a TCP socket specifying a buffer length of 1024 along with the `MSG_PEEK` flag, and the return value is 100. If we then call `recv` again, it is possible for more than 100 bytes to be returned (assuming we specify a buffer length greater than 100), because more data can be received by TCP between our two calls.

In the case of a UDP socket with a datagram on the receive queue, if we call `recvfrom` specifying `MSG_PEEK`, followed by another call without specifying `MSG_PEEK`, the return values from both calls (the datagram size, its contents, and the sender's address) will be the same, even if additional datagrams are added to the socket receive buffer between the two calls. (We are assuming, of course, that some other process is not sharing the same descriptor and reading from this socket at the same time.)

3. Some implementations support the `FIONREAD` command of `ioctl`. The third argument to `ioctl` is a pointer to an integer, and the value returned in that integer is the current number of bytes on the socket's receive queue (p. 553 of TCPv2). This value is the total number of bytes queued, which for a UDP socket includes all queued datagrams. Also be aware that the count returned for a UDP socket by Berkeley-derived implementations includes the space required for the socket address structure containing the sender's IP address and port for each datagram (16 bytes for IPv4; 24 bytes for IPv6).

13.8 Sockets and Standard I/O

In all our examples so far we have used what is sometimes called *Unix I/O*, the `read` and `write` functions and their variants (`recv`, `send`, etc.). These functions work with *descriptors* and are normally implemented as system calls within the Unix kernel.

Another method of performing I/O is the *standard I/O library*. It is specified by the ANSI C standard and is intended to be portable to non-Unix systems that support ANSI C. The standard I/O library handles some of the details that we must worry about ourselves when using the Unix I/O functions, such as automatically buffering the input and output streams. Unfortunately its handling of a stream's buffering can present a new set of problems that we must worry about. Chapter 5 of APUE covers the standard I/O library in detail and [Plauger 1992] presents and discusses a complete implementation of the standard I/O library.

> The term *stream* is used with the standard I/O library, as in "we open an input stream" or "we flush the output stream." Do not confuse this with the System V streams subsystem, which we discuss in Chapter 33.

The standard I/O library can be used with sockets, but there are a few items to consider.

• A standard I/O stream can be created from any descriptor by calling the `fdopen` function. Similarly, given a standard I/O stream, we can obtain the corresponding descriptor by calling `fileno`. Our first encounter with `fileno` was in Figure 6.9 when we wanted to call `select` on a standard I/O stream. `select` works only with descriptors, so we had to obtain the descriptor for the standard I/O stream.

- TCP and UDP sockets are full-duplex. Standard I/O streams can also be full-duplex: we just open the stream with a type of `r+`, which means read–write. But on such a stream an output function cannot be followed by an input function without an intervening call to `fflush`, `fseek`, `fsetpos`, or `rewind`. Similarly, an input function cannot be followed by an output function without an intervening call to `fseek`, `fsetpos`, or `rewind`, unless the input function encounters an end-of-file. The problem with these latter three functions is that they all call `lseek`, which fails on a socket.

- The easiest way to handle this read–write problem is to open two standard I/O streams for a given socket: one for reading, and one for writing.

Example: `str_echo` Function Using Standard I/O

We now redo our TCP echo server (Figure 5.3) to use standard I/O instead of `readline` and `writen`. Figure 13.14 is a version of our `str_echo` function that uses standard I/O. (This version has a problem that we describe shortly.)

```
                                                          ───────── advio/str_echo_stdio02.c
 1 #include    "unp.h"

 2 void
 3 str_echo(int sockfd)
 4 {
 5     char    line[MAXLINE];
 6     FILE    *fpin, *fpout;

 7     fpin = Fdopen(sockfd, "r");
 8     fpout = Fdopen(sockfd, "w");

 9     for ( ; ; ) {
10         if (Fgets(line, MAXLINE, fpin) == NULL)
11             return;               /* connection closed by other end */

12         Fputs(line, fpout);
13     }
14 }
                                                          ───────── advio/str_echo_stdio02.c
```

Figure 13.14 `str_echo` function recoded to use standard I/O.

Convert descriptor into input stream and output stream

7–13   Two standard I/O streams are created by `fdopen`: one for input and one for output. The calls to `readline` and `writen` are replaced with calls to `fgets` and `fputs`.

If we run our server with this version of `str_echo` and then run our client, we see the following.

```
solaris % tcpcli02 206.62.226.33
hello, world                           we type this line, but nothing echoed
and hi                                 and this one, still no echo
hello??                                and this one, still no echo
^D                                     and our end-of-file character
hello, world                           and then the three echoed lines are output
and hi
hello??
```

There is a buffering problem here because nothing is echoed by the server until we enter our end-of-file character. The following steps are taking place:

- We type the first line of input and it is sent to the server.

- The server reads the line with `fgets` and echoes it with `fputs`.

- But the server's standard I/O stream is *fully buffered* by the standard I/O library. This means the library copies the echoed line into its standard I/O buffer for this stream but does not write the buffer to the descriptor, because the buffer is not full.

- We type the second line of input and it is sent to the server.

- The server reads the line with `fgets` and echoes it with `fputs`.

- Again, the server's standard I/O library just copies the line into its buffer but does not write the buffer because it still is not full.

- The same scenario happens with the third line of input that we enter.

- We type our end-of-file character, and our `str_cli` function (Figure 6.13) calls `shutdown`, sending a FIN to the server.

- The server TCP receives the FIN, which `fgets` reads, causing `fgets` to return a null pointer.

- The `str_echo` function returns to the server `main` function (Figure 5.12) and the child terminates by calling `exit`.

- The C library function `exit` calls the standard I/O cleanup function (pp. 162–164 of APUE) and the output buffer that was partially filled by our calls to `fputs` is now output.

- The server child process then terminates, causing its connected socket to be closed, sending a FIN to the client, completing the TCP four-packet termination sequence.

- The three echoed lines are received by our `str_cli` function and output.

- `str_cli` then receives an end-of-file on its socket, and the client terminates.

The problem here is the buffering performed automatically by the standard I/O library on the server. There are three types of buffering performed by the standard I/O library.

1. *Fully buffered* means that I/O takes place only when the buffer is full, the process explicitly calls `fflush`, or the process terminates by calling `exit`. A common size for the standard I/O buffer is 8192 bytes.

2. *Line buffered* means that I/O takes place when a newline is encountered, when the process calls `fflush`, or when the process terminates by calling `exit`.

3. *Unbuffered* means that I/O takes place each time a standard I/O output function is called.

Most Unix implementations of the standard I/O library use the following rules:

- Standard error is always unbuffered.

- Standard input and standard output are fully buffered, unless they refer to a terminal device, in which case they are line buffered.

- All other streams are fully buffered unless they refer to a terminal device, in which case they are line buffered.

Since a socket is not a terminal device, the problem seen with our `str_echo` function in Figure 13.14 is that the output stream (`fpout`) is fully buffered. There are two solutions: we can force the output stream to be line buffered by calling `setvbuf`, or we can force each echoed line to be output by calling `fflush` after each call to `fputs`. Applying either of these changes corrects the behavior of our `str_echo` function.

> Another solution is to avoid the standard I/O library altogether and use the `sfio` library. It is described in [Korn and Vo 1991] and the source code is publicly available.

> Be aware that some implementations of the standard I/O library still have a problem with descriptors greater than 255. This can be a problem with network servers that handle lots of descriptors. Check the definition of the `FILE` structure in your `<stdio.h>` header to see what type of variable holds the descriptor.

13.9 T/TCP: TCP for Transactions

T/TCP is a slight modification to TCP that can avoid the three-way handshake between hosts that have communicated with each other recently. T/TCP is described in detail in TCPv3, RFC 1379 [Braden 1992b], and RFC 1644 [Braden 1994].

> The most widespread implementation of T/TCP is in FreeBSD.

T/TCP can combine the SYN, FIN, and data into a single segment, assuming the size of the data is less than the MSS. We show this in Figure 13.15. The first segment is the client's SYN, FIN, and data, generated by one call to `sendto`. This combines the functionality of `connect`, `write`, and `shutdown`. The server does the normal steps of `socket`, `bind`, `listen`, and `accept`, the latter returning when the client's segment arrives. The server sends its reply with `send` and closes the socket. This causes the server's SYN, FIN, and reply to be sent to the client. If we compare this to Figure 2.5, we see that not only are fewer segments required in the network (three for T/TCP, 10 for TCP, and two for UDP), but the time that it takes for the client to initiate the connection, send a request, and read the reply has been decreased by one RTT.

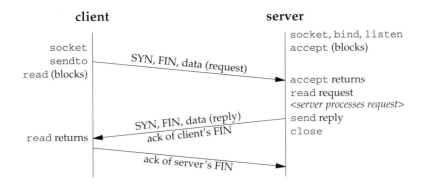

Figure 13.15 Time line of minimal T/TCP transaction.

The benefit of T/TCP is that all the reliability of TCP is retained (sequence numbers, timeouts, retransmissions, and the like), unlike a UDP solution, which pushes the reliability into the application. T/TCP also maintains TCP's slow start and congestion avoidance, features that are often missing from UDP applications.

> We are ignoring some details here, all of which are covered in TCPv3. For example, the first time this client talks to this server the three-way handshake is required. But this can be avoided in the future as long as some cached information on both ends does not expire, and as long as neither end crashes and reboots. The three segments shown form the minimum request–reply exchange. Additional segments are required if either the request or the reply do not fit into one segment. The term "transaction" means a client request and the server's reply. Common examples are a DNS request and the server's reply, and an HTTP request and the server's reply. The term is not being used to refer to a two-phase commit protocol.

A few changes are made to the sockets API to handle T/TCP. We note that on a system providing T/TCP no changes need be made to any TCP applications, unless the features of T/TCP are desired. All existing TCP applications continue to work using the sockets API that we have already described.

- A client calls `sendto` to combine the connection establishment with the sending of data. This replaces the separate calls to `connect` and `write`. The server's protocol address is now passed to `sendto`, instead of `connect`.

- A new output flag, `MSG_EOF` is provided (Figure 13.6) to indicate that no more data will be sent on this socket. This allows us to combine an output operation (`send` or `sendto`) with a `shutdown`. Specifying this flag with a `sendto` that also specifies the server's address is the way that a segment is sent containing a SYN, FIN, and data. Also note in Figure 13.15 that the server sends its reply using `send` and not `write`. The reason is to specify `MSG_EOF` to send the FIN with the reply. (Do not confuse this new flag with the existing `MSG_EOR` flag, which indicates the end-of-record for record-oriented protocols.)

- A new socket option, `TCP_NOPUSH` is defined with a *level* of `IPPROTO_TCP`. When this option is enabled, it prevents TCP from sending a segment just to empty the socket send buffer. Clients should set this option when sending a request with a single `sendto`, if the request exceeds the MSS, as it may reduce the number of segments sent. Pages 47–49 of TCPv3 talk about this new socket option in more detail.

- A client that wants to establish a connection with a server and send a request using T/TCP should call `socket`, `setsockopt` (to enable the `TCP_NOPUSH` option), and `sendto` (specifying `MSG_EOF` if only one request is to be sent). If `setsockopt` fails with an error of `ENOPROTOOPT` or if `sendto` fails with an error of `ENOTCONN`, then the host does not support T/TCP. In this case the client just calls `connect` and `write`, possibly followed by `shutdown` (if only one request is to be sent).

- The only change required by a server is to call `send` with the `MSG_EOF` flag to send a reply, instead of `write`, if the server wants to send a FIN with the reply.

- Compile-time tests for T/TCP can use `#ifdef MSG_EOF`.

Appendix B of TCPv3 contains example T/TCP client and server code.

13.10 Summary

There are three way to set a time limit on a socket operation:

- use the `alarm` function and the `SIGALRM` function,
- use the time limit that is provided by `select`, and
- use the newer `SO_RCVTIMEO` and `SO_SNDTIMEO` socket options.

The first is easy to use but involves signal handling and as we see in Section 18.5 can lead to race conditions. Using `select` means that we block in this function, with its provided time limit, instead of blocking in a call to `read`, `write`, or `connect`. The third alternative, the new socket options, is also easy to use but not provided by all implementations.

`recvmsg` and `sendmsg` are the most general of the five groups of I/O functions that are provided. They combine the ability to specify an MSG_*xxx* flag (from `recv` and `send`), with the ability to return or specify the peer's protocol address (from `recvfrom` and `sendto`), with the ability to use multiple buffers (from `readv` and `writev`), along with two new features: returning flags to the application and receiving or sending ancillary data.

We describe 10 different forms of ancillary data in the text, six of which are new with IPv6. Ancillary data consists of one or more ancillary data objects, each object preceded by a `cmsghdr` structure specifying its length, protocol level, and type of data. Five functions beginning with `CMSG_` are used to build and parse ancillary data.

Sockets can be used with the C standard I/O library, but doing this adds another level of buffering to that already being performed by TCP. Indeed, a lack of understanding of the buffering performed by the standard I/O library is the most common problem with the library. Since a socket is not a terminal device, the common solution to this potential problem is to set the standard I/O stream unbuffered.

T/TCP is a simple enhancement to TCP that can avoid the three-way handshake, allowing a faster response by a server to a client's query, if that client and server have communicated recently. From a programming perspective a client takes advantage of T/TCP by calling `sendto` instead of normal sequence of `connect`, `write`, and `shutdown`.

Exercises

13.1   What happens in Figure 13.1 when we reset the signal handler, if the process has not established a handler for `SIGALRM`?

13.2   In Figure 13.1 we print a warning if the process already has an `alarm` timer set. Modify the function to reset this `alarm` for the process after the `connect`, before the function returns.

13.3   Modify Figure 11.7 as follows: before calling `read`, call `recv` specifying `MSG_PEEK`. When this returns, call `ioctl` with a command of `FIONREAD` and print the number of bytes queued on the socket's receive buffer. Then call `read` to actually read the data.

13.4   What happens to the data in a standard I/O buffer that has not yet been output if the process falls off the end of the `main` function instead of calling `exit`?

13.5   Apply each of the two changes described following Figure 13.14 and verify that each one corrects the buffering problem.

14

Unix Domain Protocols

14.1 Introduction

The Unix domain protocols are not an actual protocol suite, but a way of performing client–server communication on a single host using the same API that is used for clients and servers on different hosts: sockets or XTI. The Unix domain protocols are an alternative to the IPC methods described in Volume 2 of this series, when the client and server are on the same host. Details on the actual implementation of Unix domain sockets in a Berkeley-derived kernel are provided in Part 3 of TCPv3.

Two types of sockets are provided in the Unix domain: stream sockets (similar to TCP) and datagram sockets (similar to UDP). Even though a raw socket is also provided, its semantics have never been documented, it is not used by any program that the author is aware of, and it is not defined by Posix.1g.

Unix domain sockets are used for three reasons.

1. On Berkeley-derived implementations Unix domain sockets are often twice as fast as a TCP socket, when both peers are on the same host (pp. 223–224 of TCPv3). One application takes advantage of this: the X Window System. When an X11 client starts and opens a connection to the X11 server, the client checks the value of the DISPLAY environment variable, which specifies the server's hostname, window, and screen. If the server is on the same host as the client, the client opens a Unix domain stream connection to the server; otherwise the client opens a TCP connection to the server.

2. Unix domain sockets are used when passing descriptors between processes on the same host. We provide a complete example of this in Section 14.7.

3. Newer implementations of Unix domain sockets provide the client's credentials (user ID and group IDs) to the server, which can provide additional security checking. We describe this in Section 14.8.

The protocol addresses used to identify clients and servers in the Unix domain are pathnames within the normal filesystem. Recall that IPv4 uses a combination of 32-bit addresses and 16-bit port numbers for its protocol addresses, and IPv6 uses a combination of 128-bit addresses and 16-bit port numbers for its protocol addresses. These pathnames are not normal Unix files: we cannot read from or write to these files except from a program that has associated the pathname with a Unix domain socket.

14.2 Unix Domain Socket Address Structure

Figure 14.1 shows the Unix domain socket address structure, defined by including the `<sys/un.h>` header.

```
struct sockaddr_un {
  uint8_t       sun_len;
  sa_family_t   sun_family;     /* AF_LOCAL */
  char          sun_path[104];  /* null-terminated pathname */
};
```

Figure 14.1 Unix domain socket address structure: `sockaddr_un`.

> Earlier BSD releases defined the size of the `sun_path` array as 108 bytes, not the 104 that we show in this figure. Posix.1g requires only that its size be at least 100 bytes. The reason for these limits is an implementation artifact dating back to 4.2BSD requiring that this structure fit in a 128-byte mbuf (a kernel memory buffer).

The pathname stored in the `sun_path` array must be null terminated. The macro `SUN_LEN` is provided and it takes a pointer to a `sockaddr_un` structure and returns the length of the structure, including the number of nonnull bytes in the pathname. The unspecified address is indicated by a null string as the pathname, that is, a structure with `sun_path[0]` equal to 0. This is the Unix domain equivalent of the IPv4 `INADDR_ANY` constant and the IPv6 `IN6ADDR_ANY_INIT` constant.

> Posix.1g renames the Unix domain protocols as "local IPC," to remove the dependence of the Unix operating system. The historical constant `AF_UNIX` becomes `AF_LOCAL`. Nevertheless, we still use the term "Unix domain" as that has become its de facto name, regardless of the underlying operating system. Also, even with Posix.1g attempting to make these operating system independent, the socket address structure still retains the _un suffix!

Example: `bind` of Unix Domain Socket

The program in Figure 14.2 creates a Unix domain socket, `bind`s a pathname to it, and then calls `getsockname` and prints the bound pathname.

unixdomain/unixbind.c

```
 1 #include      "unp.h"

 2 int
 3 main(int argc, char **argv)
 4 {
 5     int      sockfd;
 6     socklen_t len;
 7     struct sockaddr_un addr1, addr2;

 8     if (argc != 2)
 9         err_quit("usage: unixbind <pathname>");

10     sockfd = Socket(AF_LOCAL, SOCK_STREAM, 0);

11     unlink(argv[1]);               /* OK if this fails */

12     bzero(&addr1, sizeof(addr1));
13     addr1.sun_family = AF_LOCAL;
14     strncpy(addr1.sun_path, argv[1], sizeof(addr1.sun_path) - 1);
15     Bind(sockfd, (SA *) &addr1, SUN_LEN(&addr1));

16     len = sizeof(addr2);
17     Getsockname(sockfd, (SA *) &addr2, &len);
18     printf("bound name = %s, returned len = %d\n", addr2.sun_path, len);

19     exit(0);
20 }
```

unixdomain/unixbind.c

Figure 14.2 bind of a pathname to a Unix domain socket.

Remove pathname first

11   The pathname to bind to the socket is the command-line argument. But the bind will fail if the pathname already exists in the filesystem. Therefore we call unlink to delete the pathname, in case it already exists. If it does not exist, unlink returns an error, which we ignore.

bind and then getsockname

12–18   We copy the command-line argument using strncpy, to avoid overflowing the structure if the pathname is too long. Since we initialize the structure to 0 and then subtract one from the size of the sun_path array, we know the pathname is null terminated. bind is called and we use the macro SUN_LEN to calculate the length argument for the function. We then call getsockname to fetch the name that was just bound and print the result.

   If we run this program under BSD/OS we have the following results:

```
bsdi % umask                                        first print our umask value
0002                                                shells print this value in octal
bsdi % unixbind /tmp/foo.bar
bound name = /tmp/foo.bar, returned len = 14
bsdi % unixbind /tmp/foo.bar                        run it again
bound name = /tmp/foo.bar, returned len = 14
bsdi % ls -l /tmp/foo.bar
srwxrwxrwx  1 rstevens  wheel   0 May 20 11:02 /tmp/foo.bar
bsdi % ls -lF /tmp/foo.bar
srwxrwxrwx  1 rstevens  wheel   0 May 20 11:02 /tmp/foo.bar=
```

We first print our umask value, because Posix.1g specifies that the file access permissions of the resulting pathname be modified by this value. Our value of 2 turns off the other-write bit (sometimes called world-write). We then run the program and see that the length returned by getsockname is 14: 1 byte for the sun_len member, 1 byte for the sun_family member, and 12 bytes for the actual pathname (excluding the terminating null byte). This is an example of a value–result argument whose result when the function returns differs from its value when the function was called. We can output the pathname using the %s format of printf because the pathname is null terminated in the sun_path member. We then run the program again, to verify that calling unlink removes the pathname.

We run ls -l to see the file permissions and the file type. Under 4.4BSD the file type is a socket, which is printed as s. We also notice that all nine permission bits are on, as 4.4BSD does not modify this default with our umask value. Finally we run ls again, with the -F option, which causes 4.4BSD to append an equals sign to the pathname.

> Posix.2 knows nothing about sockets and only specifies that the -F option print a slash for a directory, an asterisk for an executable file, and a vertical bar for a FIFO.

We now run the same program under Solaris 2.5.

```
solaris % umask
02
solaris % unixbind /tmp/foo.bar
bound name = /tmp/foo.bar, returned len = 110
solaris % unixbind /tmp/foo.bar
bound name = /tmp/foo.bar, returned len = 110
solaris % ls -1F /tmp/foo.bar
p---------   1 rstevens other1          0 May 20 11:36 /tmp/foo.bar|
```

The first difference is that the length returned by getsockname is 110, the total size of the Solaris sockaddr_un structure. This is OK, since the pathname is null terminated in the sun_path member. We also notice that the default file permissions are 0: all read, write, and execute permissions are turned off. Since all the permission bits are off, we cannot tell whether our umask value was used or not. Finally we notice that ls -l indicates that the pathname is a FIFO, which is how all Unix domain sockets appear under SVR4, and the -F option prints the vertical bar for a FIFO.

14.3 socketpair Function

The socketpair function creates two sockets that are then connected together. This function applies to only Unix domain sockets.

```
#include <sys/socket.h>

int socketpair(int family, int type, int protocol, int sockfd[2]);
```

Returns: nonzero if OK, −1 on error

The *family* must be AF_LOCAL and the *protocol* must be 0. The *type*, however, can be either SOCK_STREAM or SOCK_DGRAM. The two socket descriptors that are created are returned as *sockfd[0]* and *sockfd[1]*.

> This function is similar to the Unix pipe function: two descriptors are returned, and each descriptor is connected to the other. Indeed, Berkeley-derived implementations implement pipe by performing the same internal operations as socketpair (pp. 253–254 of TCPv3).

The two created sockets are unnamed; that is, there is no implicit bind involved.

The result of socketpair with a *type* of SOCK_STREAM is called a *stream pipe*. It is similar to a regular Unix pipe (created by the pipe function), but a stream pipe is *full-duplex*; that is, both descriptors can be read and written. We show a picture of a stream pipe created by socketpair in Figure 14.7.

> Posix.1 does not require full-duplex pipes. On SVR4 pipe returns two full-duplex descriptors, while Berkeley-derived kernels traditionally return two half-duplex descriptors (Figure 17.31 of TCPv3).

14.4 Socket Functions

There are several differences and restrictions in the socket functions when using Unix domain sockets. We list the Posix.1g requirements when applicable, and note that not all implementations are currently at this level.

1. The default file access permissions for a pathname created by bind should be 0777 (read, write, and execute by user, group, and other), modified by the current umask value.

2. The pathname associated with a Unix domain socket should be an absolute pathname, not a relative pathname. The reason to avoid the latter is that its resolution depends on the current working directory of the caller. That is, if the server binds a relative pathname, then the client must be in the same directory as the server (or must know this directory) for the client's call to either connect or sendto to succeed.

   > Posix.1g says that binding a relative pathname to a Unix domain socket gives unpredictable results.

3. The pathname specified in a call to connect must be a pathname that is currently bound to an open Unix domain socket of the same type (stream or datagram). Errors occur if (a) the pathname exists but is not a socket, (b) the pathname exists and is a socket but no open socket descriptor is associated with the pathname, or (c) the pathname exists and is an open socket but is of the wrong type (that is, a Unix domain stream socket cannot connect to a pathname associated with a Unix domain datagram socket, and vice versa).

4. The permission testing associated with the connect of a Unix domain socket is the same as if open had been called for write-only access to the pathname.

5. Unix domain stream sockets are similar to TCP sockets: they provide a byte stream interface to the process with no record boundaries.

6. If a call to `connect` for a Unix domain stream socket finds that the listening socket's queue is full (Section 4.5), `ECONNREFUSED` is returned immediately. This differs from TCP: the TCP listener ignores an arriving SYN if the socket's queue is full, and the TCP connector retries by sending the SYN several times.

7. Unix domain datagram sockets are similar to UDP sockets: they provide an unreliable datagram service that preserves record boundaries.

8. Unlike UDP sockets, sending a datagram on an unbound Unix domain datagram socket does not bind a pathname to the socket. (Recall that sending a UDP datagram on an unbound UDP socket causes an ephemeral port to be bound to the socket.) This means the receiver of the datagram will be unable to send a reply unless the sender has bound a pathname to its socket. Similarly, unlike TCP and UDP, calling `connect` for a Unix domain socket does not bind a pathname to the socket.

14.5 Unix Domain Stream Client–Server

We now recode our TCP echo client–server from Chapter 5 to use Unix domain sockets. Figure 14.3 shows the server, which is a modification of Figure 5.12 to use the Unix domain stream protocol instead of TCP.

8   The datatype of the two socket address structure is now `sockaddr_un`.

10   The first argument to `socket` is `AF_LOCAL` to create a Unix domain stream socket.

11–15   The constant `UNIXSTR_PATH` is defined in `unp.h` to be `/tmp/unix.str`. We first `unlink` the pathname, in case it exists from an earlier run of the server, and then initialize the socket address structure before calling `bind`. An error from `unlink` is OK.

Notice that this call to `bind` differs from the call in Figure 14.2. Here we specify the size of the socket address structure (the third argument) as the total size of the `sockaddr_un` structure, not just the number of bytes occupied by the pathname. Both lengths are valid, since the pathname must be null terminated.

The remainder of the function is the same as Figure 5.12. The same `str_echo` function is used (Figure 5.3).

Figure 14.4 (p. 380) is the Unix domain stream protocol echo client. It is a modification of Figure 5.4.

6   The socket address structure to contain the server's address is now a `sockaddr_un` structure.

7   The first argument to `socket` is `AF_LOCAL`.

8–10   The code to fill in the socket address structure is identical to the code shown for the server: initialize the structure to 0, set the family to `AF_LOCAL`, and copy the pathname into the `sun_path` member.

12   The function `str_cli` is the same as earlier (Figure 6.13 was the last version that we developed).

——————————————————————————————————— unixdomain/unixstrserv01.c

```
 1 #include    "unp.h"

 2 int
 3 main(int argc, char **argv)
 4 {
 5     int     listenfd, connfd;
 6     pid_t   childpid;
 7     socklen_t clilen;
 8     struct sockaddr_un cliaddr, servaddr;
 9     void    sig_chld(int);

10     listenfd = Socket(AF_LOCAL, SOCK_STREAM, 0);

11     unlink(UNIXSTR_PATH);
12     bzero(&servaddr, sizeof(servaddr));
13     servaddr.sun_family = AF_LOCAL;
14     strcpy(servaddr.sun_path, UNIXSTR_PATH);

15     Bind(listenfd, (SA *) &servaddr, sizeof(servaddr));

16     Listen(listenfd, LISTENQ);

17     Signal(SIGCHLD, sig_chld);

18     for ( ; ; ) {
19         clilen = sizeof(cliaddr);
20         if ( (connfd = accept(listenfd, (SA *) &cliaddr, &clilen)) < 0) {
21             if (errno == EINTR)
22                 continue;        /* back to for() */
23             else
24                 err_sys("accept error");
25         }
26         if ( (childpid = Fork()) == 0) {      /* child process */
27             Close(listenfd);    /* close listening socket */
28             str_echo(connfd);   /* process the request */
29             exit(0);
30         }
31         Close(connfd);              /* parent closes connected socket */
32     }
33 }
```

——————————————————————————————————— unixdomain/unixstrserv01.c

Figure 14.3 Unix domain stream protocol echo server.

14.6 Unix Domain Datagram Client–Server

We now recode our UDP client–server from Sections 8.3 and 8.5 to use Unix domain datagram sockets. Figure 14.5 shows the server, which is a modification of Figure 8.3.

unixdomain/unixstrcli01.c

```
1 #include    "unp.h"

2 int
3 main(int argc, char **argv)
4 {
5     int     sockfd;
6     struct sockaddr_un servaddr;

7     sockfd = Socket(AF_LOCAL, SOCK_STREAM, 0);

8     bzero(&servaddr, sizeof(servaddr));
9     servaddr.sun_family = AF_LOCAL;
10    strcpy(servaddr.sun_path, UNIXSTR_PATH);

11    Connect(sockfd, (SA *) &servaddr, sizeof(servaddr));

12    str_cli(stdin, sockfd);     /* do it all */

13    exit(0);
14 }
```

unixdomain/unixstrcli01.c

Figure 14.4 Unix domain stream protocol echo client.

unixdomain/unixdgserv01.c

```
1 #include    "unp.h"

2 int
3 main(int argc, char **argv)
4 {
5     int     sockfd;
6     struct sockaddr_un servaddr, cliaddr;

7     sockfd = Socket(AF_LOCAL, SOCK_DGRAM, 0);

8     unlink(UNIXDG_PATH);
9     bzero(&servaddr, sizeof(servaddr));
10    servaddr.sun_family = AF_LOCAL;
11    strcpy(servaddr.sun_path, UNIXDG_PATH);

12    Bind(sockfd, (SA *) &servaddr, sizeof(servaddr));

13    dg_echo(sockfd, (SA *) &cliaddr, sizeof(cliaddr));
14 }
```

unixdomain/unixdgserv01.c

Figure 14.5 Unix domain datagram protocol echo server.

6   The datatype of the two socket address structures is now `sockaddr_un`.

7   The first argument to `socket` is `AF_LOCAL` to create a Unix domain datagram socket.

8–12   The constant `UNIXDG_PATH` is defined in `unp.h` to be `/tmp/unix.dg`. We first `unlink` the pathname, in case it exists from an earlier run of the server, and then initialize the socket address structure before calling `bind`. An error from `unlink` is OK.

13   The same `dg_echo` function is used (Figure 8.4).

Figure 14.6 is the Unix domain datagram protocol echo client. It is a modification of Figure 8.7.

————————————————————————— unixdomain/unixdgcli01.c
```
1 #include    "unp.h"

2 int
3 main(int argc, char **argv)
4 {
5      int    sockfd;
6      struct sockaddr_un cliaddr, servaddr;

7      sockfd = Socket(AF_LOCAL, SOCK_DGRAM, 0);

8      bzero(&cliaddr, sizeof(cliaddr));    /* bind an address for us */
9      cliaddr.sun_family = AF_LOCAL;
10     strcpy(cliaddr.sun_path, tmpnam(NULL));

11     Bind(sockfd, (SA *) &cliaddr, sizeof(cliaddr));

12     bzero(&servaddr, sizeof(servaddr));     /* fill in server's address */
13     servaddr.sun_family = AF_LOCAL;
14     strcpy(servaddr.sun_path, UNIXDG_PATH);

15     dg_cli(stdin, sockfd, (SA *) &servaddr, sizeof(servaddr));

16     exit(0);
17 }
```
————————————————————————— unixdomain/unixdgcli01.c

Figure 14.6 Unix domain datagram protocol echo client.

6   The socket address structure to contain the server's address is now a `sockaddr_un` structure. We also allocate one of these structures to contain the client's address, which we talk about shortly.

7   The first argument to `socket` is `AF_LOCAL`.

8–11   Unlike our UDP client, when using the Unix domain datagram protocol we must explicitly `bind` a pathname to our socket, so that the server has a pathname to which it can send its reply. We call `tmpnam` to assign a unique pathname that we then `bind` to our socket. Recall from Section 14.4 that sending a datagram on an unbound Unix domain datagram socket does not implicitly bind a pathname to the socket. Therefore if we omit this step, the server's call to `recvfrom` in the `dg_echo` function returns a null pathname, which then causes an error when the server calls `sendto`.

12–14 The code to fill in the socket address structure with the server's well-known pathname is identical to the code shown earlier for the server.

15   The function `dg_cli` is the same as earlier (Figure 8.8).

14.7 Passing Descriptors

When we think of passing an open descriptor from one process to another, we normally think of either

1. a child sharing all the open descriptors with the parent after a call to `fork`, or

2. all descriptors normally remaining open when `exec` is called.

In the first example the process opens a descriptor, calls `fork`, and then the parent closes the descriptor, letting the child handle the descriptor. This passes an open descriptor from the parent to the child. But we would also like the ability for the child to open a descriptor and pass it back to the parent.

Current Unix systems provide a way to pass any open descriptor from one process to any other process. That is, there is no need for the processes to be related, such as a parent and its child. The technique requires us to first establish a Unix domain socket between the two processes and then use `sendmsg` to send a special message across the Unix domain socket. This message is handled specially by the kernel, passing the open descriptor from the sender to the receiver.

> The black magic performed by the 4.4BSD kernel in passing an open descriptor across a Unix domain socket is described in detail in Chapter 18 of TCPv3.

> SVR4 uses a different technique within the kernel to pass an open descriptor, the `I_SENDFD` and `I_RECVFD ioctl` commands, described in Section 15.5.1 of APUE. But the process can still access this kernel feature using a Unix domain socket. In this text we describe the use of Unix domain sockets to pass open descriptors, since this is the most portable programming technique: it works under both Berkeley-derived kernels and SVR4, whereas using the `I_SENDFD` and `I_RECVFD ioctl`s works only under SVR4.

> The 4.4BSD technique allows multiple descriptors to be passed with a single `sendmsg`, whereas the SVR4 technique passes only a single descriptor at a time. All our examples pass one descriptor at a time.

The steps involved in passing a descriptor between two processes are then:

1. Create a Unix domain socket, either a stream socket or a datagram socket.

   If the goal is to `fork` a child, have the child open the descriptor and pass the descriptor back to the parent; the parent can call `socketpair` to create a stream pipe that can be used to exchange the descriptor.

   If the processes are unrelated, then the server must create a Unix domain stream socket, `bind` a pathname to it, allowing the client to `connect` to that socket. The client can then send a request to the server to open some descriptor, and the server can pass back the descriptor across the Unix domain socket. Alternately, a Unix domain datagram socket can also be used between the client and server, but there is little advantage in doing this, and the possibility exists for a datagram to be discarded. We will use a stream socket between the client and server in our example later in this section.

2. One process opens a descriptor by calling any of the Unix functions that returns a descriptor: `open`, `pipe`, `mkfifo`, `socket`, or `accept`, for example. *Any* type of descriptor can be passed from one process to another, which is why we call the technique "descriptor passing" and not "file descriptor passing."

3. The sending process builds a msghdr structure (Section 13.5) containing the descriptor to be passed. Posix.1g specifies that the descriptor be sent as ancillary data (the msg_control member of the msghdr structure, Section 13.6), but older implementations use the msg_accrights member. The sending process calls sendmsg to send the descriptor across the Unix domain socket from step 1. At this point we say that the descriptor is "in flight." Even if the sending process closes the descriptor, after calling sendmsg, but before the receiving process calls recvmsg (in the next step), the descriptor remains open for the receiving process. Sending a descriptor increments the descriptor's reference count by one.

4. The receiving process calls recvmsg to receive the descriptor on the Unix domain socket from step 1. It is normal for the descriptor number in the receiving process to differ from the descriptor number in the sending process, but that is OK. Passing a descriptor is not passing a descriptor number, but involves creating a new descriptor in the receiving process that refers to the same file table entry within the kernel as the descriptor that was sent by the sending process.

The client and server must have some application protocol so that the receiver of the descriptor knows when to expect it. If the receiver calls recvmsg without allocating room to receive the descriptor, and a descriptor was passed and is ready to be read, the descriptor that was being passed is closed (p. 518 of TCPv2). Also, the MSG_PEEK flag should be avoided with recvmsg if a descriptor is expected, as the result is unpredictable.

Descriptor Passing Example

We now provide an example of descriptor passing. We will write a program named mycat that takes a pathname as a command-line argument, opens the file, and copies it to standard output. But instead of calling the normal Unix open function, we call our own function named my_open. This function creates a stream pipe and calls fork and exec to initiate another program that opens the desired file. This program must then pass the open descriptor back to the parent across the stream pipe.

Figure 14.7 shows the first step: our mycat program after creating a stream pipe by calling socketpair. We designate the two descriptors returned by socketpair as [0] and [1].

Figure 14.7 mycat program after creating stream pipe using socketpair.

The process then calls fork and the child calls exec to execute the openfile program. The parent closes the [1] descriptor and the child closes the [0] descriptor.

(There is no difference in either end of the stream pipe. The child could close [1] and the parent could close [0].) This gives us the arrangement shown in Figure 14.8.

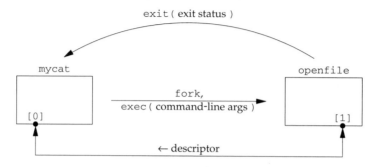

Figure 14.8 mycat program after invoking openfile program.

The parent must pass three pieces of information to the openfile program: (1) the pathname of the file to open, (2) the open mode (read-only, read–write, or write-only), and (3) the descriptor number corresponding to its end of the stream pipe (what we show as [1]). We choose to pass these three items as command-line arguments in the call to exec. An alternative method is to send these three items as data across the stream pipe. The openfile program sends back the open descriptor across the stream pipe and terminates. The exit status of the program tells the parent whether the file could be opened, and if not, what type of error occurred.

The advantage in executing another program to open the file is that the program could be set-user-ID to root, allowing it to open files that we normally do not have permission to open. This program could extend the concept of normal Unix permissions (user, group, and other) to any form of access checking that it desires.

We begin with the mycat program, shown in Figure 14.9.

—————————————————————————————————— unixdomain/mycat.c

```
 1 #include     "unp.h"

 2 int     my_open(const char *, int);

 3 int
 4 main(int argc, char **argv)
 5 {
 6     int     fd, n;
 7     char    buff[BUFFSIZE];

 8     if (argc != 2)
 9         err_quit("usage: mycat <pathname>");

10     if ( (fd = my_open(argv[1], O_RDONLY)) < 0)
11         err_sys("cannot open %s", argv[1]);

12     while ( (n = Read(fd, buff, BUFFSIZE)) > 0)
13         Write(STDOUT_FILENO, buff, n);
```

```
14        exit(0);
15 }
```
————————————————————————————————— *unixdomain/mycat.c*

Figure 14.9 `mycat` program: copy a file to standard output.

If we replace the call to `my_open` with a call to `open`, this simple program just copies a file to standard output.

The function `my_open`, shown in Figure 14.10 is intended to look like the normal Unix `open` function to its caller. It takes two arguments, a pathname and an open mode (such as `O_RDONLY` to mean read-only), opens the file, and returns a descriptor.

————————————————————————————————— *unixdomain/myopen.c*
```
 1 #include    "unp.h"

 2 int
 3 my_open(const char *pathname, int mode)
 4 {
 5     int     fd, sockfd[2], status;
 6     pid_t   childpid;
 7     char    c, argsockfd[10], argmode[10];

 8     Socketpair(AF_LOCAL, SOCK_STREAM, 0, sockfd);

 9     if ( (childpid = Fork()) == 0) {       /* child process */
10         Close(sockfd[0]);
11         snprintf(argsockfd, sizeof(argsockfd), "%d", sockfd[1]);
12         snprintf(argmode, sizeof(argmode), "%d", mode);
13         execl("./openfile", "openfile", argsockfd, pathname, argmode,
14               (char *) NULL);
15         err_sys("execl error");
16     }
17     /* parent process - wait for the child to terminate */
18     Close(sockfd[1]);                  /* close the end we don't use */

19     Waitpid(childpid, &status, 0);
20     if (WIFEXITED(status) == 0)
21         err_quit("child did not terminate");
22     if ( (status = WEXITSTATUS(status)) == 0)
23         Read_fd(sockfd[0], &c, 1, &fd);
24     else {
25         errno = status;           /* set errno value from child's status */
26         fd = -1;
27     }

28     Close(sockfd[0]);
29     return (fd);
30 }
```
————————————————————————————————— *unixdomain/myopen.c*

Figure 14.10 `my_open` function: open a file and return a descriptor.

Create stream pipe

8   `socketpair` creates a stream pipe. Two descriptors are returned: `sockfd[0]` and `sockfd[1]`. This is the state that we show in Figure 14.7.

fork and exec

9–16   `fork` is called and the child then closes one end of the stream pipe. The descriptor number of the other end of the stream pipe is formatted into the `argsockfd` array and the open mode is formatted into the `argmode` array. We call `snprintf` are because the arguments to exec must be character strings. The `openfile` program is executed. The `execl` function should not return unless it encounters an error. On success the `main` function of the `openfile` program starts executing.

Parent waits for child

17–22   The parent closes the other end of the stream pipe and calls `waitpid` to wait for the child to terminate. The termination status of the child is returned in the variable `status` and we first verify that the program terminated normally (i.e., it was not terminated by a signal). The `WEXITSTATUS` macro then converts the termination status into the exit status, whose value will be between 0 and 255. We will see shortly that if the `openfile` program encounters an error opening the requested file, it terminates with the corresponding `errno` value as its exit status.

Receive descriptor

23   Our function `read_fd`, shown next, receives the descriptor on the stream pipe. In addition to the descriptor, we read 1 byte of data, but do nothing with the data.

> When sending and receiving a descriptor across a stream pipe, we always send at least 1 byte of data, even if the receiver does nothing with the data. Otherwise the receiver cannot tell whether a return value of 0 from `read_fd` means "no data (but possibly a descriptor)" or "end-of-file."

Figure 14.11 shows the `read_fd` function, which calls `recvmsg` to receive data and a descriptor on a Unix domain socket. The first three arguments to this function are the same as for the `read` function, with a fourth argument being a pointer to an integer that will contain the received descriptor on return.

9–26   This function must deal with two versions of `recvmsg`: those with the `msg_control` member and those with the `msg_accrights` member. Our `config.h` header (Figure D.2) defines the constant `HAVE_MSGHDR_MSG_CONTROL` if the `msg_control` version is supported.

Make certain `msg_control` is suitably aligned

10–13   The `msg_control` buffer must be suitably aligned for a `cmsghdr` structure. Simply allocating a `char` array is inadequate. Here we declare a `union` of a `cmsghdr` structure with the character array, which guarantees that the array is suitably aligned. Another technique is to call `malloc` but that would require freeing the memory before the function returns.

27–45   `recvmsg` is called. If ancillary data is returned, the format is as shown in Figure 13.13. We verify that the length, level, and type are correct, then fetch the newly created descriptor, and return it through the caller's `recvfd` pointer. `CMSG_DATA` returns the pointer to the `cmsg_data` member of the ancillary data object as an `unsigned char` pointer. We cast this to an `int` pointer and fetch the integer descriptor that is pointed to.

lib/read_fd.c

```
 1 #include    "unp.h"

 2 ssize_t
 3 read_fd(int fd, void *ptr, size_t nbytes, int *recvfd)
 4 {
 5     struct msghdr msg;
 6     struct iovec iov[1];
 7     ssize_t n;
 8     int     newfd;

 9 #ifdef  HAVE_MSGHDR_MSG_CONTROL
10     union {
11         struct cmsghdr cm;
12         char    control[CMSG_SPACE(sizeof(int))];
13     } control_un;
14     struct cmsghdr *cmptr;

15     msg.msg_control = control_un.control;
16     msg.msg_controllen = sizeof(control_un.control);
17 #else
18     msg.msg_accrights = (caddr_t) & newfd;
19     msg.msg_accrightslen = sizeof(int);
20 #endif

21     msg.msg_name = NULL;
22     msg.msg_namelen = 0;

23     iov[0].iov_base = ptr;
24     iov[0].iov_len = nbytes;
25     msg.msg_iov = iov;
26     msg.msg_iovlen = 1;

27     if ( (n = recvmsg(fd, &msg, 0)) <= 0)
28         return (n);

29 #ifdef  HAVE_MSGHDR_MSG_CONTROL
30     if ( (cmptr = CMSG_FIRSTHDR(&msg)) != NULL &&
31         cmptr->cmsg_len == CMSG_LEN(sizeof(int))) {
32         if (cmptr->cmsg_level != SOL_SOCKET)
33             err_quit("control level != SOL_SOCKET");
34         if (cmptr->cmsg_type != SCM_RIGHTS)
35             err_quit("control type != SCM_RIGHTS");
36         *recvfd = *((int *) CMSG_DATA(cmptr));
37     } else
38         *recvfd = -1;           /* descriptor was not passed */
39 #else
40     if (msg.msg_accrightslen == sizeof(int))
41         *recvfd = newfd;
42     else
43         *recvfd = -1;       /* descriptor was not passed */

44 #endif

45     return (n);
46 }
```

lib/read_fd.c

Figure 14.11 read_fd function: receive data and a descriptor.

If the older `msg_accrights` member is supported, the length should be the size of an integer and the newly created descriptor is returned through the caller's `recvfd` pointer.

Figure 14.12 shows the `openfile` program. It takes the three command-line arguments that must be passed and calls the normal `open` function.

———————————————————————————————————— *unixdomain/openfile.c*

```
 1 #include     "unp.h"

 2 int
 3 main(int argc, char **argv)
 4 {
 5     int     fd;
 6     ssize_t n;

 7     if (argc != 4)
 8         err_quit("openfile <sockfd#> <filename> <mode>");

 9     if ( (fd = open(argv[2], atoi(argv[3]))) < 0)
10         exit((errno > 0) ? errno : 255);

11     if ( (n = write_fd(atoi(argv[1]), "", 1, fd)) < 0)
12         exit((errno > 0) ? errno : 255);

13     exit(0);
14 }
```

———————————————————————————————————— *unixdomain/openfile.c*

Figure 14.12 `openfile` function: open a file and pass back the descriptor.

Command-line arguments

7–12   Since two of the three command-line arguments were formatted into character strings by `my_open`, two are converted back into integers using `atoi`.

open the file

9–10   The file is opened by calling `open`. If an error is encountered, the `errno` value corresponding to the `open` error is returned as the exit status of the process.

Pass back descriptor

11–12   The descriptor is passed back by `write_fd`, which we show next. This process then terminates, but recall that earlier in the chapter we said that it is OK for the sending process to close the descriptor that was passed (which happens when we call `exit`) because the kernel knows that the descriptor is in flight, and keeps it open for the receiving process.

> The exit status must be between 0 and 255. The highest `errno` value is around 150. An alternate technique that doesn't require the `errno` values to be less than 256 would be to pass back an error indication as normal data in the call to `sendmsg`.

Figure 14.13 shows the final function, `write_fd`, which calls `sendmsg` to send a descriptor (and optional data, which we do not use) across a Unix domain socket.

———————————————————————————————— lib/write_fd.c

```
 1 #include     "unp.h"

 2 ssize_t
 3 write_fd(int fd, void *ptr, size_t nbytes, int sendfd)
 4 {
 5     struct msghdr msg;
 6     struct iovec iov[1];

 7 #ifdef  HAVE_MSGHDR_MSG_CONTROL
 8     union {
 9         struct cmsghdr cm;
10         char    control[CMSG_SPACE(sizeof(int))];
11     } control_un;
12     struct cmsghdr *cmptr;

13     msg.msg_control = control_un.control;
14     msg.msg_controllen = sizeof(control_un.control);

15     cmptr = CMSG_FIRSTHDR(&msg);
16     cmptr->cmsg_len = CMSG_LEN(sizeof(int));
17     cmptr->cmsg_level = SOL_SOCKET;
18     cmptr->cmsg_type = SCM_RIGHTS;
19     *((int *) CMSG_DATA(cmptr)) = sendfd;
20 #else
21     msg.msg_accrights = (caddr_t) & sendfd;
22     msg.msg_accrightslen = sizeof(int);
23 #endif

24     msg.msg_name = NULL;
25     msg.msg_namelen = 0;

26     iov[0].iov_base = ptr;
27     iov[0].iov_len = nbytes;
28     msg.msg_iov = iov;
29     msg.msg_iovlen = 1;

30     return (sendmsg(fd, &msg, 0));
31 }
```

———————————————————————————————— lib/write_fd.c

Figure 14.13 `write_fd` function: pass a descriptor by calling `sendmsg`.

As with `read_fd`, this function must deal with either ancillary data or the older access rights. In either case the `msghdr` structure is initialized and then `sendmsg` is called.

We show an example of descriptor passing in Section 25.7 that involves unrelated processes and an example in Section 27.9 that involves related processes. We will use the `read_fd` and `write_fd` functions that we just described.

14.8 Receiving Sender Credentials

In Figure 13.13 we showed another type of data that can be passed along a Unix domain socket as ancillary data: user credentials via the `fcred` structure, which is defined by including the `<sys/ucred.h>` header.

```
struct fcred {
  uid_t  fc_ruid;                 /* real user ID */
  gid_t  fc_rgid;                 /* real group ID */
  char   fc_login[MAXLOGNAME];    /* setlogin() name */
  uid_t  fc_uid;                  /* effective user ID */
  short  fc_ngroups;              /* number of groups */
  gid_t  fc_groups[NGROUPS];      /* supplementary group IDs */
};
#define fc_gid   fc_groups[0]     /* effective group ID */
```

Normally `MAXLOGNAME` is 16, and `NGROUPS` is also 16. `fc_ngroups` is always at least 1, with the first element of the array the effective group ID.

> This structure is actually defined as a `ucred` structure within the `fcred` structure, with `#defined` names to make it appear as a single structure. We show the "logical" definition of the structure.

> This feature is new with BSD/OS 2.1. We describe it, even thought it is not widespread, because it is an important, yet simple, addition to the Unix domain protocols. When a client and server communicate using these protocols, the server often needs a way to know exactly who the client is, to validate that the client has permission to ask for the service being requested.

This information is always available on a Unix domain socket, subject to the following conditions:

- The credentials are sent as ancillary data when data is sent on the Unix domain socket, but only if the receiver of the data has enabled the `LOCAL_CREDS` socket option. The *level* for this option (Section 7.2) is 0.

- On a datagram socket, the credentials accompany every datagram. On a stream socket, the credentials are sent only once, the first time data is sent.

- Credentials cannot be sent along with a descriptor. That is, only one of the two types of ancillary data can be sent with a given message.

> This is a limitation of the BSD/OS implementation. In general, we should be able to pass multiple types of ancillary data in a single call to `sendmsg`, since each ancillary data object has its own type and length (Figure 13.12).

- Users are not able to forge credentials. That is, when ancillary data is sent on a Unix domain socket, the kernel verifies that the ancillary data is not of level `SOL_SOCKET` and not of type `SCM_CREDS`. If the sender tries to forge its own credentials, the ancillary data is discarded by the kernel.

One point that we did not mention in the previous section is that when a descriptor is received under SVR4 (using `ioctl` with the `I_RECVFD` command), the kernel also passes the sender's credentials to the receiving process: a `strrecvfd` structure containing the newly created descriptor, the effective user ID, and the effective group ID. This is a form of credential passing that takes place every time a descriptor is passed. Additionally, when client–server connections are created under SVR4 using the `connld` streams module (similar to the creation of a new socket by `accept` on a Unix domain socket), the new descriptor is passed along with a `strrecvfd` structure containing the client's credentials. Under SVR4 we are not able to access these credentials using Unix domain sockets. (Section 15.5.1 of APUE details the use of the SVR4 `connld` streams module.) If a Berkeley-derived implementation does not support the new credential passing that we describe in this section, there is no guaranteed way for a Unix domain server to obtain the client's credentials. Section 15.5.2 of APUE details one work-around to obtain this information, but user credentials should always be supplied by the kernel.

Example

As an example of credential passing, we modify our Unix domain stream server to ask for the client's credentials. Figure 14.14 shows a new function, `read_cred`, that is similar to `read` but also returns an `fcred` structure containing the sender's credentials.

4–5   The first three arguments are identical to `read`, with the fourth argument being a pointer to an `fcred` structure that will be filled in. The format of the returned ancillary data is shown in Figure 13.13.

27–37   If credentials were returned, the length, level, and type of the ancillary data are verified, and the resulting structure copied back to the caller. If no credentials were returned, we set the structure to 0. Since the number of groups (`fc_ngroups`) is always one or more, its value of 0 indicates to the caller that no credentials were returned by the kernel.

The `main` function for our echo server, Figure 14.3, is unchanged. Figure 14.15 (p. 393) shows the new version of the `str_echo` function, modified from Figure 5.3. This function is called by the child after the parent has accepted a new client connection and called `fork`.

12   The `LOCAL_CREDS` socket option is enabled for the connected socket.

13–14   Our function `read_cred` is called the first time. We specify a length of 0 as we do not want any data; we want only the ancillary data.

17–27   If credentials were returned, they are printed.

28–32   The remainder of the loop is unchanged. This code reads lines from the client and writes them back to the client.

Our client from Figure 14.4 is unchanged.

—————————————————————————————————— unixdomain/readcred.c

```
 1 #include     "unp.h"
 2 #include     <sys/param.h>
 3 #include     <sys/ucred.h>

 4 ssize_t
 5 read_cred(int fd, void *ptr, size_t nbytes, struct fcred *fcredptr)
 6 {
 7     struct msghdr msg;
 8     struct iovec iov[1];
 9     ssize_t n;

10     union {
11         struct cmsghdr cm;
12         char    control[CMSG_SPACE(sizeof(struct fcred))];
13     } control_un;
14     struct cmsghdr *cmptr;

15     msg.msg_control = control_un.control;
16     msg.msg_controllen = sizeof(control_un.control);

17     msg.msg_name = NULL;
18     msg.msg_namelen = 0;

19     iov[0].iov_base = ptr;
20     iov[0].iov_len = nbytes;
21     msg.msg_iov = iov;
22     msg.msg_iovlen = 1;

23     if ( (n = recvmsg(fd, &msg, 0)) < 0)
24         return (n);
25     if (fcredptr) {
26         if (msg.msg_controllen > sizeof(struct cmsghdr)) {
27             cmptr = CMSG_FIRSTHDR(&msg);

28             if (cmptr->cmsg_len != CMSG_LEN(sizeof(struct fcred)))
29                 err_quit("control length = %d", cmptr->cmsg_len);
30             if (cmptr->cmsg_level != SOL_SOCKET)
31                 err_quit("control level != SOL_SOCKET");
32             if (cmptr->cmsg_type != SCM_CREDS)
33                 err_quit("control type != SCM_CREDS");
34             memcpy(fcredptr, CMSG_DATA(cmptr), sizeof(struct fcred));
35         } else
36             bzero(fcredptr, sizeof(struct fcred)); /* none returned */
37     }

38     return (n);
39 }
```

—————————————————————————————————— unixdomain/readcred.c

Figure 14.14 read_cred function: read and return sender's credentials.

—— unixdomain/strecho.c

```
 1 #include    "unp.h"
 2 #include    <sys/param.h>
 3 #include    <sys/ucred.h>

 4 ssize_t read_cred(int, void *, size_t, struct fcred *);

 5 void
 6 str_echo(int sockfd)
 7 {
 8     ssize_t n;
 9     const int on = 1;
10     char    line[MAXLINE];
11     struct fcred cred;

12     Setsockopt(sockfd, 0, LOCAL_CREDS, &on, sizeof(on));

13     if ( (n = read_cred(sockfd, NULL, 0, &cred)) < 0)
14         err_sys("read_cred error");
15     if (cred.fc_ngroups == 0)
16         printf("(no credentials returned)\n");
17     else {
18         printf("real user ID = %d\n", cred.fc_ruid);
19         printf("real group ID = %d\n", cred.fc_rgid);
20         printf("login name = %-*s\n", MAXLOGNAME, cred.fc_login);
21         printf("effective user ID = %d\n", cred.fc_uid);
22         printf("effective group ID = %d\n", cred.fc_gid);
23         printf("%d supplementary groups:", cred.fc_ngroups - 1);
24         for (n = 1; n < cred.fc_ngroups; n++)   /* [0] is the egid */
25             printf(" %d", cred.fc_groups[n]);
26         printf("\n");
27     }

28     for ( ; ; ) {
29         if ( (n = Readline(sockfd, line, MAXLINE)) == 0)
30             return;                 /* connection closed by other end */

31         Writen(sockfd, line, n);
32     }
33 }
```

—— unixdomain/strecho.c

Figure 14.15 `str_echo` function that asks for client's credentials.

If we run the server in one window, and the client in another, here is the output from the server after running the client one time.

```
bsdi % unixstrserv02
real user ID = 482
real group ID = 52
login name = rstevens
effective user ID = 482
effective group ID = 52
7 supplementary groups: 20 0 1 2 3 5 7
```

This information is output only after the client has sent the first line for the server to echo, because we noted earlier that the credentials are sent by the kernel on a stream socket the first time data is sent on the socket (not when the connection is established). This differs from the SVR4 technique mentioned earlier, where the credentials are sent with the descriptor when the newly created descriptor is returned (which would be the equivalent of `accept` returning for the Unix domain socket).

14.9 Summary

Unix domain sockets are an alternative to IPC when the client and server are on the same host. The advantage in using Unix domain sockets over some form of IPC is that the API is nearly identical to a networked client–server. The advantage in using Unix domain sockets over TCP, when the client and server are on the same host, is the increased performance of Unix domain sockets over TCP on many implementations.

We modified our TCP and UDP echo client and echo servers to use the Unix domain protocols and the only major difference was having to `bind` a pathname to the UDP client's socket, so that the UDP server has somewhere to send the replies. Our code in Sections 14.5 and 14.6 manipulated the Unix domain socket address structures directly, but a better approach is to use the `tcp_XXX` and `udp_XXX` functions from Chapter 11, since our implementation of `getaddrinfo` supports Unix domain sockets.

Descriptor passing is a powerful technique between clients and servers on the same host and it takes place across a Unix domain socket. We showed an example in Section 14.7 that passed a descriptor from a child back to the parent. In Section 25.7 we show an example in which the client and server are unrelated, and in Section 27.9 we show another example that passes a descriptor from a parent to a child.

Exercises

14.1   What happens if a Unix domain server calls `unlink` after calling `bind`?

14.2   What happens if a Unix domain server does not `unlink` its well-known pathname when it terminates, and a client tries to `connect` to the server sometime after the server terminates?

14.3   Compile Figures 11.12 and 11.15, our protocol-independent UDP daytime client and server, and run them specifying a Unix domain socket (Section 11.6). What happens? How can you fix this?

14.4   Start with Figure 11.7 and modify it to call `sleep(5)` after the peer's protocol address is printed, and to also print the number of bytes returned by `read` each time `read` returns a positive value. Start with Figure 11.10 and modify it to call `write` for each byte of the result that is sent to the client. (We discussed similar modifications in the solution to Exercise 1.5.) Run the client and server on the same host using TCP. How many bytes are `read` by the client?

Run the client and server on the same host using a Unix domain socket. Does anything change?

Now call `send` instead of `write` in the server and specify the `MSG_EOR` flag. (You need a Berkeley-derived implementation to finish this exercise.) Run the client and server on the same host using a Unix domain socket. Does anything change?

14.5   Write a program to determine the values shown in Figure 4.10. One approach is to create a stream pipe and then `fork` into a parent and child. The parent enters a `for` loop, incrementing the backlog from 0 through 14. Each time through the loop the parent first writes the value of the backlog to the stream pipe. The child reads this value, creates a listening socket bound to the loopback address, and sets the backlog to that value. The child then writes to the stream pipe, just to tell the parent that it is ready. The parent then tries to establish as many connections as possible, but with an `alarm` set to 2 seconds, because the call to `connect` that hits the backlog limit will block, resending the SYN. The child never calls `accept`, to let the kernel queue the connections from the parent. When the parent's `alarm` expires, it knows from the loop counter which `connect` hit the backlog limit. The parent then closes its sockets and writes the next new backlog value to the stream pipe for the child. When the child reads this next value it closes its listening socket and creates a new listening socket, starting the procedure again.

14.6   Verify that omitting the call to `bind` in Figure 14.6 causes an error in the server.

15

Nonblocking I/O

15.1 Introduction

By default, sockets are blocking. This means that when we issue a socket call that cannot be completed immediately, our process is put to sleep, waiting for the condition to be true. We can divide the socket calls that may block into four categories.

1. Input operations: the `read`, `readv`, `recv`, `recvfrom`, and `recvmsg` functions. If we call one of these input functions for a blocking TCP socket (the default), and there is no data available in the socket receive buffer, we are put to sleep until some data arrives. Since TCP is a byte stream, we will be awakened when "some" data arrives: it could be a single byte of data, or it could be a full TCP segment of data. If we want to wait until some fixed amount of data is available, we can call our own function `readn` (Figure 3.14) or specify the `MSG_WAITALL` flag (Figure 13.6).

   Since UDP is a datagram protocol, if the socket receive buffer is empty for a blocking UDP socket, we are put to sleep until a UDP datagram arrives.

   With a nonblocking socket, if the input operation cannot be satisfied (at least 1 byte of data for a TCP socket or a complete datagram for a UDP socket), return is made immediately with an error of `EWOULDBLOCK`.

2. Output operations: the `write`, `writev`, `send`, `sendto`, and `sendmsg` functions. For a TCP socket we said in Section 2.9 that the kernel copies data from the application's buffer into the socket send buffer. If there is no room in the socket send buffer for a blocking socket, the process is put to sleep until there is room.

With a nonblocking TCP socket, if there is no room at all in the socket send buffer, return is made immediately with an error of `EWOULDBLOCK`. If there is some room in the socket send buffer, the return value will be the number of bytes that the kernel was able to copy into the buffer. (This is called a *short count*.)

We also said in Section 2.9 that there is no actual UDP socket send buffer. The kernel just copies the application data and moves it down the stack, prepending the UDP and IP headers. Therefore an output operation on a blocking UDP socket (the default) should never block.

3. Accepting incoming connections: the `accept` function. If `accept` is called for a blocking socket and a new connection is not available, the process is put to sleep.

   If `accept` is called for a nonblocking socket and a new connection is not available, the error `EWOULDBLOCK` is returned instead.

4. Initiating outgoing connections: the `connect` function for TCP. (Recall that `connect` can be used with UDP but it does not cause a "real" connection to be established; it just causes the kernel to store the peer's IP address and port number.) We showed in Section 2.5 that the establishment of a TCP connection involves a three-way handshake and the `connect` function does not return until the client receives the ACK of its SYN. This means that a TCP `connect` always blocks the calling process for at least the round-trip time (RTT) to the server.

   If `connect` is called for a nonblocking TCP socket and the connection cannot be established immediately, the connection establishment is initiated (e.g., the first packet of TCP's three-way handshake is sent) but the error `EINPROGRESS` is returned. Notice that this error differs from the error returned in the previous three scenarios. Also notice that some connections can be established immediately, normally when the server is on the same host as the client, so even with a nonblocking `connect` we must be prepared for `connect` to return OK. We show an example of a nonblocking `connect` in Section 15.3.

   > Traditionally, System V has returned the error `EAGAIN` for a nonblocking I/O operation that cannot be satisfied while Berkeley-derived implementations have returned the error `EWOULDBLOCK`. To confuse things even more, Posix.1 specifies that `EAGAIN` is used while Posix.1g specifies that `EWOULDBLOCK` is used. Fortunately, most current systems (including SVR4 and 4.4BSD) define these two error codes to be the same (check your system's `<sys/errno.h>` header), so it doesn't matter which one we use. In this text we use `EWOULDBLOCK`, as specified by Posix.1g.

Section 6.2 summarized the different models available for I/O and compares nonblocking I/O to other models. In this section we provide examples of all four types of operations, and develop a new type of client, similar to a Web client, that initiates multiple TCP connections at the same time, using a nonblocking `connect`.

15.2 Nonblocking Reads and Writes: `str_cli` Function (Revisited)

We return once again to our `str_cli` function, which we have discussed in Sections 5.5 and 6.4. The latter version, which uses `select`, still uses blocking I/O. For example, if a line is available on standard input, we read it with `fgets` and then send it to the server with `writen`. But the call to `writen` can block, if the socket send buffer is full. While we are blocked in the call to `writen`, data could be available for reading from the socket receive buffer. Similarly, if a line of input is available from the socket we can block in the subsequent call to `fputs`, if standard output is slower than the network. Our goal in this section is to develop a version of this function that uses nonblocking I/O. This prevents us from blocking while we could be doing something productive.

Unfortunately the addition of nonblocking I/O complicates the function's buffer management noticeably, so we will present the function in pieces. We also change our handling of standard input and standard output to use `read` and `write` directly, instead of using standard I/O. This avoids using standard I/O with nonblocking descriptors, a recipe for disaster.

We maintain two buffers: `to` contains data going from standard input to the server, and `fr` contains data arriving from the server going to standard output. Figure 15.1 shows the arrangement of the `to` buffer and the pointers into the buffer.

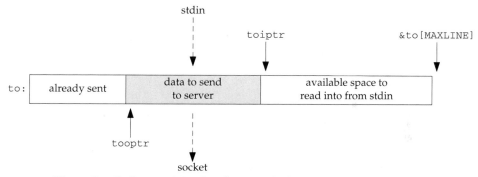

Figure 15.1 Buffer containing data from standard input going to the socket.

The pointer `toiptr` points to the next byte into which data can be read from standard input. `tooptr` points to the next byte that must be written to the socket. There are `toiptr` minus `tooptr` bytes to be written to the socket. The number of bytes that can be read from standard input is `&to[MAXLINE]` minus `toiptr`. As soon as `tooptr` reaches `toiptr`, both pointers are reset to the beginning of the buffer.

Figure 15.2 shows the corresponding arrangement of the `fr` buffer.

Figure 15.3 shows the first part of the function.

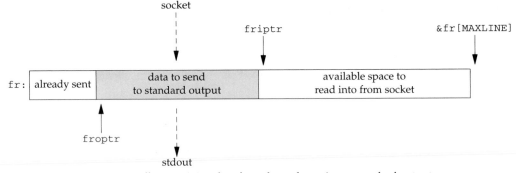

Figure 15.2 Buffer containing data from the socket going to standard output.

nonblock/strclinonb.c

```
 1 #include    "unp.h"

 2 void
 3 str_cli(FILE *fp, int sockfd)
 4 {
 5     int    maxfdp1, val, stdineof;
 6     ssize_t n, nwritten;
 7     fd_set  rset, wset;
 8     char    to[MAXLINE], fr[MAXLINE];
 9     char   *toiptr, *tooptr, *friptr, *froptr;

10     val = Fcntl(sockfd, F_GETFL, 0);
11     Fcntl(sockfd, F_SETFL, val | O_NONBLOCK);

12     val = Fcntl(STDIN_FILENO, F_GETFL, 0);
13     Fcntl(STDIN_FILENO, F_SETFL, val | O_NONBLOCK);

14     val = Fcntl(STDOUT_FILENO, F_GETFL, 0);
15     Fcntl(STDOUT_FILENO, F_SETFL, val | O_NONBLOCK);

16     toiptr = tooptr = to;       /* initialize buffer pointers */
17     friptr = froptr = fr;
18     stdineof = 0;

19     maxfdp1 = max(max(STDIN_FILENO, STDOUT_FILENO), sockfd) + 1;
20     for ( ; ; ) {
21         FD_ZERO(&rset);
22         FD_ZERO(&wset);
23         if (stdineof == 0 && toiptr < &to[MAXLINE])
24             FD_SET(STDIN_FILENO, &rset);    /* read from stdin */
25         if (friptr < &fr[MAXLINE])
26             FD_SET(sockfd, &rset);  /* read from socket */
27         if (tooptr != toiptr)
28             FD_SET(sockfd, &wset);  /* data to write to socket */
29         if (froptr != friptr)
30             FD_SET(STDOUT_FILENO, &wset);   /* data to write to stdout */

31         Select(maxfdp1, &rset, &wset, NULL, NULL);
```

nonblock/strclinonb.c

Figure 15.3 str_cli function: first part, initialize and call select.

Set descriptors nonblocking

10-15   All three descriptors are set nonblocking using `fcntl`: the socket to and from the server, standard input, and standard output.

Initialize buffer pointers

16-19   The pointers into the two buffers are initialized and the maximum descriptor plus one is calculated that will be used as the first argument for `select`.

Main loop: prepare to call `select`

20   As with the previous version of this function, Figure 6.13, the main loop of the function is a call to `select` followed by individual tests of the various conditions that we are interested in.

Specify descriptors that we are interested in

21-30   Both descriptor sets are set to 0 and then up to 2 bits are turned on in each set. If we have not yet read an end-of-file on standard input, and there is room for at least 1 byte of data in the `to` buffer, the bit corresponding to standard input is turned on in the read set. If there is room for at least 1 byte of data in the `fr` buffer, the bit corresponding to the socket is turned on in the read set. If there is data to write to the socket in the `to` buffer, the bit corresponding to the socket is turned on in the write set. Finally, if there is data in the `fr` buffer to send to standard output, the bit corresponding to standard output is turned on in the write set.

Call `select`

31   `select` is called, waiting for any one of the four possible conditions to be true. We do not specify a timeout for this function.

    The next part of the function is shown in Figure 15.4. This code contains the first two tests (of four) that are made after `select` returns.

`read` from standard input

32-33   If standard input is readable, we call `read`. The third argument is the amount of available space in the `to` buffer.

Handle nonblocking error

34-35   If an error occurs and it is `EWOULDBLOCK`, nothing happens. Normally this condition "should not happen," that is, `select` telling us that the descriptor is readable and `read` returning `EWOULDBLOCK`, but we handle it nevertheless.

`read` returns end-of-file

36-40   If `read` returns 0 we are finished with the standard input. Our flag `stdineof` is set. If there is no more data in the `to` buffer to send (`tooptr` equals `to`), `shutdown` sends a FIN to the server. If there is still data in the `to` buffer to send, the FIN cannot be sent until the buffer is written to the socket.

> We output a line to standard error noting the end-of-file, along with the current time, and we show how we use this output after describing this function. Similar calls to `fprintf` are throughout this function.

nonblock/strclinonb.c

```
32              if (FD_ISSET(STDIN_FILENO, &rset)) {
33                  if ( (n = read(STDIN_FILENO, toiptr, &to[MAXLINE] - toiptr)) < 0) {
34                      if (errno != EWOULDBLOCK)
35                          err_sys("read error on stdin");

36                  } else if (n == 0) {
37                      fprintf(stderr, "%s: EOF on stdin\n", gf_time());
38                      stdineof = 1;    /* all done with stdin */
39                      if (tooptr == to)
40                          Shutdown(sockfd, SHUT_WR);   /* send FIN */

41                  } else {
42                      fprintf(stderr, "%s: read %d bytes from stdin\n", gf_time(), n);
43                      toiptr += n;     /* # just read */
44                      FD_SET(sockfd, &wset);   /* try and write to socket below */
45                  }
46              }
47              if (FD_ISSET(sockfd, &rset)) {
48                  if ( (n = read(sockfd, friptr, &fr[MAXLINE] - friptr)) < 0) {
49                      if (errno != EWOULDBLOCK)
50                          err_sys("read error on socket");

51                  } else if (n == 0) {
52                      fprintf(stderr, "%s: EOF on socket\n", gf_time());
53                      if (stdineof)
54                          return;      /* normal termination */
55                      else
56                          err_quit("str_cli: server terminated prematurely");

57                  } else {
58                      fprintf(stderr, "%s: read %d bytes from socket\n",
59                              gf_time(), n);
60                      friptr += n;     /* # just read */
61                      FD_SET(STDOUT_FILENO, &wset);   /* try and write below */
62                  }
63              }
```

nonblock/strclinonb.c

Figure 15.4 `str_cli` function: second part, read from standard input or socket.

read returns data

41–45   When `read` returns data, we increment `toiptr` accordingly. We also turn on the bit corresponding to the socket in the write set, to cause the test for this bit to be true later in the loop, causing a `write` to be attempted to the socket.

> This is one of the hard design decisions when writing code. We have a few alternatives here. Instead of setting the bit in the write set, we could do nothing, in which case `select` will test for writability of the socket the next time it is called. But this requires another loop around and another call to `select` when we already know that we have data to write to the socket. Another choice is to duplicate the code that writes to the socket here, but this seems wasteful and a potential source for an error (in case there is a bug in that piece of duplicated code, and we fix it in one location but not the other). Lastly, we could create a function that writes to the socket and call that function instead of duplicating the code, but that function needs to share

three of the local variables with `str_cli`, which would necessitate making these variables global. The choice made is the author's (biased) view about which alternative is best.

read from socket

47–63   These lines of code are similar to the `if` statement we just described when standard input is readable. If `read` returns `EWOULDBLOCK`, nothing happens. If we encounter an end-of-file from the server, this is OK if we have already encountered an end-of-file on the standard input, but it is not expected otherwise. If `read` returns some data, `friptr` is incremented and the bit for standard output is turned on in the write descriptor set, to try to write the data in the next part of the function.

Figure 15.5 shows the final portion of the function.

———————————————————————— nonblock/strclinonb.c

```
64          if (FD_ISSET(STDOUT_FILENO, &wset) && ((n = friptr - froptr) > 0)) {
65              if ( (nwritten = write(STDOUT_FILENO, froptr, n)) < 0) {
66                  if (errno != EWOULDBLOCK)
67                      err_sys("write error to stdout");

68              } else {
69                  fprintf(stderr, "%s: wrote %d bytes to stdout\n",
70                          gf_time(), nwritten);
71                  froptr += nwritten;      /* # just written */
72                  if (froptr == friptr)
73                      froptr = friptr = fr;   /* back to beginning of buffer */
74              }
75          }
76          if (FD_ISSET(sockfd, &wset) && ((n = toiptr - tooptr) > 0)) {
77              if ( (nwritten = write(sockfd, tooptr, n)) < 0) {
78                  if (errno != EWOULDBLOCK)
79                      err_sys("write error to socket");
80              } else {
81                  fprintf(stderr, "%s: wrote %d bytes to socket\n",
82                          gf_time(), nwritten);
83                  tooptr += nwritten;      /* # just written */
84                  if (tooptr == toiptr) {
85                      toiptr = tooptr = to;   /* back to beginning of buffer */
86                      if (stdineof)
87                          Shutdown(sockfd, SHUT_WR);  /* send FIN */
88                  }
89              }
90          }
91      }
92  }
```

———————————————————————— nonblock/strclinonb.c

Figure 15.5 `str_cli` function: third part, write to standard output or socket.

write to standard output

64–67   If standard output is writable and the number of bytes to write is greater than 0, `write` is called. If `EWOULDBLOCK` is returned, nothing happens. Notice that this condition is entirely possible, because the code at the end of the previous part of this function turns on the bit for standard output in the write set, without knowing whether the `write` will succeed or not.

`write` **OK**

68–74   If the `write` is successful, `froptr` is incremented by the number of bytes written. If the output pointer has caught up with the input pointer, both pointers are reset to point to the beginning of the buffer.

`write` **to socket**

76–90   This section of code is similar to the code we just described for writing to the standard output. The one difference is that when the output pointer catches up with the input pointer, not only are both pointers reset to the beginning of the buffer, but if we have encountered an end-of-file on standard input, the FIN can now be sent to the server.

We now examine the operation of this function and the overlapping of the non-blocking I/O. Figure 15.6 shows our `gf_time` function that is called from our `str_cli` function.

---
lib/gf_time.c

```
 1 #include     "unp.h"
 2 #include     <time.h>

 3 char *
 4 gf_time(void)
 5 {
 6     struct timeval tv;
 7     static char str[30];
 8     char    *ptr;

 9     if (gettimeofday(&tv, NULL) < 0)
10         err_sys("gettimeofday error");

11     ptr = ctime(&tv.tv_sec);
12     strcpy(str, &ptr[11]);
13     /* Fri Sep 13 00:00:00 1986\n\0 */
14     /* 0123456789012345678901234 5  */
15     snprintf(str + 8, sizeof(str) - 8, ".%06ld", tv.tv_usec);

16     return (str);
17 }
```

lib/gf_time.c

Figure 15.6   `gf_time` function: return pointer to time string.

This function returns a string containing the current time, including microseconds, in the format

```
12:34:56.123456
```

This is intentionally in the same format as the timestamps output by `tcpdump`. Also notice that all the calls to `fprintf` in our `str_cli` function write to standard error, allowing us to separate standard output (the lines echoed by the server) from our diagnostic output. We can then run our client and `tcpdump` and take this diagnostic output along with the tcpdump output and sort the two outputs together, ordered by the time. This lets us see what happens in our program and correlate it with the corresponding TCP action.

For example, we first run tcpdump on our host solaris, capturing only TCP segments to or from port 7 (the echo server), saving the output in the file named tcpd.

```
solaris % tcpdump -w tcpd tcp and port 7
```

We then run our TCP client on this host, specifying the server on the host bsdi.

```
solaris % tcpcli01 206.62.226.35 < 2000.lines > out 2> diag
```

Standard input is the file 2000.lines, the same file we used with Figure 6.13. Standard output is sent to the file out, and standard error is sent to the file diag. On completion we run

```
solaris % diff 2000.lines out
```

to verify that the echoed lines are identical to the input lines. Finally we terminate tcpdump with our interrupt key and then print the tcpdump records, sorting these records with the diagnostic output from the client. Figure 15.7 shows the first part of this result.

```
solaris % tcpdump -r tcpd -N | sort diag
10:18:34.486392 solaris.33621 > bsdi.echo: S 1802738644:1802738644(0)
                                            win 8760 <mss 1460>
10:18:34.488278 bsdi.echo > solaris.33621: S 3212986316:3212986316(0)
                                            ack 1802738645 win 8760 <mss 1460>
10:18:34.488490 solaris.33621 > bsdi.echo: . ack 1 win 8760

10:18:34.491482: read 4096 bytes from stdin
10:18:34.518663 solaris.33621 > bsdi.echo: P 1:1461(1460) ack 1 win 8760
10:18:34.519016: wrote 4096 bytes to socket
10:18:34.528529 bsdi.echo > solaris.33621: P 1:1461(1460) ack 1461 win 8760
10:18:34.528785 solaris.33621 > bsdi.echo: . 1461:2921(1460) ack 1461 win 8760
10:18:34.528900 solaris.33621 > bsdi.echo: P 2921:4097(1176) ack 1461 win 8760
10:18:34.528958 solaris.33621 > bsdi.echo: . ack 1461 win 8760
10:18:34.536193 bsdi.echo > solaris.33621: . 1461:2921(1460) ack 4097 win 8760
10:18:34.536697 bsdi.echo > solaris.33621: P 2921:3509(588) ack 4097 win 8760
10:18:34.544636: read 4096 bytes from stdin
10:18:34.568505: read 3508 bytes from socket
10:18:34.580373 solaris.33621 > bsdi.echo: . ack 3509 win 8760
10:18:34.582244 bsdi.echo > solaris.33621: P 3509:4097(588) ack 4097 win 8760
10:18:34.593354: wrote 3508 bytes to stdout
10:18:34.617272 solaris.33621 > bsdi.echo: P 4097:5557(1460) ack 4097 win 8760
10:18:34.617610 solaris.33621 > bsdi.echo: P 5557:7017(1460) ack 4097 win 8760
10:18:34.617908 solaris.33621 > bsdi.echo: P 7017:8193(1176) ack 4097 win 8760
10:18:34.618062: wrote 4096 bytes to socket
10:18:34.623310 bsdi.echo > solaris.33621: . ack 8193 win 8760
10:18:34.626129 bsdi.echo > solaris.33621: . 4097:5557(1460) ack 8193 win 8760
10:18:34.626339 solaris.33621 > bsdi.echo: . ack 5557 win 8760
10:18:34.626611 bsdi.echo > solaris.33621: P 5557:6145(588) ack 8193 win 8760
10:18:34.628396 bsdi.echo > solaris.33621: . 6145:7605(1460) ack 8193 win 8760
10:18:34.643524: read 4096 bytes from stdin
10:18:34.667305: read 2636 bytes from socket
```

```
10:18:34.670324 solaris.33621 > bsdi.echo: . ack 7605 win 8760
10:18:34.672221 bsdi.echo > solaris.33621: P 7605:8193(588) ack 8193 win 8760
10:18:34.691039: wrote 2636 bytes to stdout
```

Figure 15.7 Sorted output from `tcpdump` and diagnostic output.

We have wrapped the long lines containing the SYNs and we have also removed the `(DF)` notations from the Solaris segments, denoting that it sets the don't-fragment bit (path MTU discovery). The `-N` option to `tcpdump` prints only the host portion (`solaris`) of the fully qualified domain name (`solaris.kohala.com`).

Using this output we can draw a time line of what's happening. We show this in Figure 15.8 with time increasing down the page.

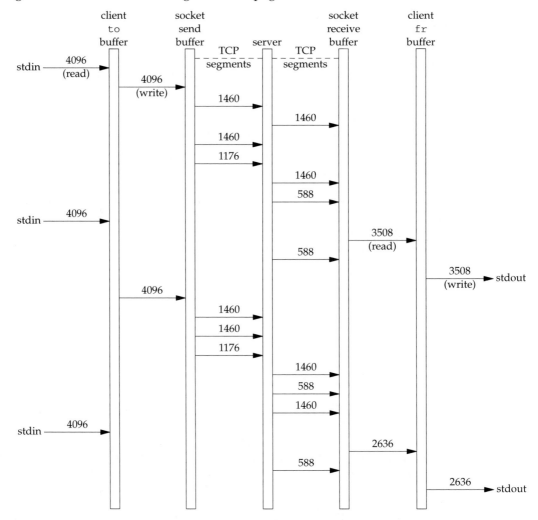

Figure 15.8 Time line of nonblocking example.

In this figure we do not show the ACK segments. Also realize that when the program outputs "wrote N bytes to stdout," the `write` has returned, possibly causing TCP to send one or more segments of data.

What we can see from this time line are the dynamics of a client–server exchange. Using nonblocking I/O lets the program take advantage of these dynamics, reading or writing when the operation can take place. We let the kernel tell us when an I/O operation can occur by using the `select` function.

We can time our nonblocking version using the same 2000-line file and the same server (a 175-ms RTT from the client) as in Section 6.7. The clock time is now 6.9 seconds, compared to 12.3 seconds for the version in Section 6.7. Therefore nonblocking I/O reduces the overall time for this example that sends a file to the server.

A Simpler Version of `str_cli`

The nonblocking version of `str_cli` that we just showed is nontrivial: about 135 lines of code, compared to 40 lines for the version using `select` with blocking I/O in Figure 6.13, and 20 lines for our original stop-and-wait version (Figure 5.5). We know that doubling the size of the code from 20 to 40 lines was worth the effort, because the speed increased by almost a factor of 30 in a batch mode and using `select` with blocking descriptors was not overly complicated. But is it worth the effort to code an application using nonblocking I/O, given the complexity of the resulting code? The answer is no. Whenever we find the need to use nonblocking I/O, it will usually be simpler to split the application into either processes (using `fork`) or threads (Chapter 23).

Figure 15.10 is yet another version of our `str_cli` function, with the function dividing itself into two processes using `fork`.

The function immediately calls `fork` to split into a parent and child. The child copies lines from the server to standard output and the parent copies lines from standard input to the server, as shown in Figure 15.9.

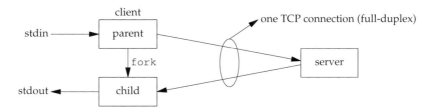

Figure 15.9 `str_cli` function using two processes.

We explicitly note that the TCP connection is full-duplex and that the parent and child are sharing the same socket descriptor: the parent writes to the socket and the child reads from the socket. There is only one socket, one socket receive buffer, and one socket send buffer, but this socket is referenced by two descriptors: one in the parent and one in the child.

We again need to worry about the termination sequence. Normal termination occurs when the end-of-file on standard input is encountered. The parent reads this

—————————————————————————————— nonblock/strclifork.c
```
 1 #include      "unp.h"

 2 void
 3 str_cli(FILE *fp, int sockfd)
 4 {
 5     pid_t   pid;
 6     char    sendline[MAXLINE], recvline[MAXLINE];

 7     if ( (pid = Fork()) == 0) {   /* child: server -> stdout */
 8         while (Readline(sockfd, recvline, MAXLINE) > 0)
 9             Fputs(recvline, stdout);

10         kill(getppid(), SIGTERM);   /* in case parent still running */
11         exit(0);
12     }
13     /* parent: stdin -> server */
14     while (Fgets(sendline, MAXLINE, fp) != NULL)
15         Writen(sockfd, sendline, strlen(sendline));

16     Shutdown(sockfd, SHUT_WR);   /* EOF on stdin, send FIN */
17     pause();
18     return;
19 }
```
—————————————————————————————— nonblock/strclifork.c

Figure 15.10   Version of str_cli function that uses fork.

end-of-file and calls shutdown to send a FIN. (The parent cannot call close. See Exercise 15.1.) But when this happens, the child needs to continue copying from the server to the standard output, until it reads an end-of-file on the socket.

It is also possible for the server process to terminate prematurely (Section 5.12), and if this occurs, the child will read an end-of-file on the socket. If this happens the child must tell the parent to stop copying from the standard input to the socket (see Exercise 15.2). In Figure 15.10 the child sends the SIGTERM signal to the parent, in case the parent is still running (see Exercise 15.3). Another way to handle this would be for the child to terminate, and have the parent catch SIGCHLD, if the parent is still running.

The parent calls pause when it has finished copying, which puts it to sleep until a signal is caught. Even though our parent does not catch any signals, this puts the parent to sleep until it receives the SIGTERM signal from the child. The default action of this signal is to terminate the process, which is fine for this example. The reason we make the parent wait for the child is to measure an accurate clock time for this version of str_cli. Normally the child finishes after the parent, but since we measure the clock time using the shell's time command, the measurement ends when the parent terminates.

Notice the simplicity of this version, compared to the nonblocking I/O version shown earlier in this section. Our nonblocking version managed four different I/O streams at the same time, and since all four were nonblocking, we had to concern ourself with partial reads and writes for all four streams. But in the fork version, each process handles only two I/O streams, copying from one to the other. There is no need for nonblocking I/O because if there is no data to read from the input stream, there is nothing to write to the corresponding output stream.

Timing of `str_cli`

We have now shown four different versions of the `str_cli` function. We summarize the clock time required for these versions, along with a version using threads (Figure 23.2), when copying 2000 lines from a Solaris 2.5 client to a server with an RTT of 175 ms:

- 354.0 sec, stop-and-wait (Figure 5.5),
- 12.3 sec, `select` and blocking I/O (Figure 6.13),
- 6.9 sec, nonblocking I/O (Figure 15.3),
- 8.7 sec, `fork` (Figure 15.10), and
- 8.5 sec, threaded version (Figure 23.2).

Our nonblocking I/O version is almost twice as fast as our version using blocking I/O with `select`. Our simple version using `fork` is slower than our nonblocking I/O version. Nevertheless, given the complexity of the nonblocking I/O code, versus the `fork` code, we recommend the simple approach.

15.3 Nonblocking `connect`

When a TCP socket is set nonblocking and then `connect` is called, `connect` returns immediately with an error of EINPROGRESS but the TCP three-way handshake continues. We then check for either a successful or unsuccessful completion of the connection establishment using `select`. There are three uses for a nonblocking `connect`.

1. We can overlap other processing with the three-way handshake. A `connect` takes one round-trip time to complete (Section 2.5) and this can be anywhere from a few milliseconds on a LAN to hundreds of milliseconds or a few seconds on a WAN. There might be other processing we wish to perform during this time.

2. We can establish multiple connections at the same time using this technique. This has become popular with Web browsers, and we show an example of this in Section 15.5.

3. Since we wait for the connection establishment to complete using `select`, we can specify a time limit for `select`, allowing us to shorten the timeout for the `connect`. Many implementations have a timeout for `connect` that is between 75 seconds and several minutes. There are times when an application wants a shorter timeout, and using a nonblocking `connect` is one way to accomplish this. Section 13.2 talks about other ways to place timeouts on socket operations.

As simple as the nonblocking `connect` sounds, there are details that we must handle.

- Even though the socket is nonblocking, if the server to which we are connecting is on the same host, the connection establishment normally takes place immediately when we call `connect`. We must handle this scenario.

- Berkeley-derived implementations (and Posix.1g) have the following two rules regarding `select` and nonblocking `connect`s: (1) when the connection completes successfully, the descriptor becomes writable (p. 531 of TCPv2), and (2) when the connection establishment encounters an error, the descriptor becomes both readable and writable (p. 530 of TCPv2).

  > These two rules regarding `select` fall out from our rules in Section 6.3 about the conditions that make a descriptor ready. A TCP socket is writable if there is available space in the send buffer (which will always be the case for a connecting socket, since we have not yet written anything to the socket) *and* the socket is connected (which occurs only when the three-way handshake completes). A pending error causes a socket to be both readable and writable.

There are many portability problems with nonblocking `connect`s that we mention in the examples that follow.

15.4 Nonblocking `connect`: Daytime Client

Figure 15.11 shows our function `connect_nonb`, which performs a nonblocking `connect`. We replace the call to `connect` in Figure 1.5 with

```
if (connect_nonb(sockfd, (SA) &servaddr, sizeof(servaddr), 0) < 0)
    err_sys("connect error");
```

The first three arguments are the normal arguments to `connect` and the fourth argument is the number of seconds to wait for the connection to complete. A value of 0 implies no timeout on the `select`; hence the kernel will use its normal TCP connection establishment timeout.

Set socket nonblocking

9–10   We call `fcntl` to set the socket nonblocking.

11–14   We initiate the nonblocking `connect`. The error we expect is `EINPROGRESS`, indicating that the connection has started but is not yet complete (p. 466 of TCPv2). Any other error is returned to the caller

Overlap processing with connection establishment

15   At this point we can do whatever we want while we wait for the connection to complete.

Check for immediate completion

16–17   If the nonblocking `connect` returned 0, the connection is complete. As we have said, this can occur when the server is on the same host as the client.

lib/connect_nonb.c

```
 1 #include    "unp.h"

 2 int
 3 connect_nonb(int sockfd, const SA *saptr, socklen_t salen, int nsec)
 4 {
 5     int     flags, n, error;
 6     socklen_t len;
 7     fd_set  rset, wset;
 8     struct timeval tval;

 9     flags = Fcntl(sockfd, F_GETFL, 0);
10     Fcntl(sockfd, F_SETFL, flags | O_NONBLOCK);

11     error = 0;
12     if ( (n = connect(sockfd, (struct sockaddr *) saptr, salen)) < 0)
13         if (errno != EINPROGRESS)
14             return (-1);

15     /* Do whatever we want while the connect is taking place. */

16     if (n == 0)
17         goto done;              /* connect completed immediately */

18     FD_ZERO(&rset);
19     FD_SET(sockfd, &rset);
20     wset = rset;
21     tval.tv_sec = nsec;
22     tval.tv_usec = 0;

23     if ( (n = Select(sockfd + 1, &rset, &wset, NULL,
24                  nsec ? &tval : NULL)) == 0) {
25         close(sockfd);          /* timeout */
26         errno = ETIMEDOUT;
27         return (-1);
28     }
29     if (FD_ISSET(sockfd, &rset) || FD_ISSET(sockfd, &wset)) {
30         len = sizeof(error);
31         if (getsockopt(sockfd, SOL_SOCKET, SO_ERROR, &error, &len) < 0)
32             return (-1);        /* Solaris pending error */
33     } else
34         err_quit("select error: sockfd not set");

35   done:
36     Fcntl(sockfd, F_SETFL, flags);  /* restore file status flags */

37     if (error) {
38         close(sockfd);          /* just in case */
39         errno = error;
40         return (-1);
41     }
42     return (0);
43 }
```

lib/connect_nonb.c

Figure 15.11 Issue a nonblocking connect.

Call `select`

18-24   We call `select` and wait for the socket to be ready for either reading or writing. We zero out `rset`, turn on the bit corresponding to `sockfd` in this descriptor set, and then copy `rset` into `wset`. This assignment is probably a structure assignment, since descriptor sets are normally represented as structures. We also initialize the `timeval` structure and then call `select`. If the caller specifies a fourth argument of 0 (use the default timeout) we must specify a null pointer as the final argument to `select` and not a `timeval` structure with a value of 0 (which means do not wait at all).

Handle timeouts

25-28   If `select` returns 0, the timer expired, and we return `ETIMEDOUT` to the caller. We also close the socket, to prevent the three-way handshake from proceeding any farther.

Check for readability or writability

29-34   If the descriptor is readable or writable, we call `getsockopt` to fetch the socket's pending error (`SO_ERROR`). If the connection completed successfully, this value will be 0. If the connection encountered an error, this value is the `errno` value corresponding to the connection error (e.g., `ECONNREFUSED`, `ETIMEDOUT`, etc.). We also encounter our first portability problem. If an error occurred, Berkeley-derived implementations of `getsockopt` return 0 with the pending error returned in our variable `error`. But Solaris causes `getsockopt` itself to return –1 with `errno` set to the pending error. Our code handles both scenarios.

Turn off nonblocking and return

36-42   We restore the file status flags and return. If our `error` variable is nonzero from `getsockopt`, that value is stored in `errno` and the function returns –1.

As we said earlier, there are portability problems with various socket implementations and nonblocking connects. First, it is possible for the connection to complete and for data to arrive from the peer before `select` is called. In this case the socket will be both readable and writable on success, the same as if the connection had failed. Our code in Figure 15.11 handles this scenario by calling `getsockopt` and checking the pending error for the socket.

Next is how to determine whether the connection completed successfully or not, if we cannot assume that writability is the only way success is returned. Various solutions have been posted to Usenet. These would replace our call to `getsockopt` in Figure 15.11.

1. Call `getpeername` instead of `getsockopt`. If this fails with `ENOTCONN`, the connection failed and we must then call `getsockopt` with `SO_ERROR` to fetch the pending error for the socket.

2. Call `read` with a length of 0. If the `read` fails, the `connect` failed and the `errno` from `read` indicates the reason for the connection failure. If the connection succeeded, `read` should return 0.

3. Call `connect` again. It should fail and if the error is `EISCONN`, the socket is already connected and the first connection succeeded.

Unfortunately nonblocking `connect`s are one of the most nonportable areas of network programming. Be prepared for portability problems, especially with older implementations. A simpler technique is to create a thread (Chapter 23) to handle the connection.

Interrupted `connect`

What happens if our call to `connect` on a normal blocking socket is interrupted, say, by a caught signal, before TCP's three-way handshake completes? Assuming the `connect` is not automatically restarted, it returns `EINTR`. But we cannot call `connect` again to wait for the connection to complete. Doing so will return `EADDRINUSE`.

What we must do in this scenario is call `select`, just as we have done in this section for a nonblocking `connect`. Then `select` returns when the connection completes successfully (making the socket writable) or when the connection fails (making the socket readable and writable).

> Posix.1g explicitly specifies what a call to the XTI function `t_connect` does when interrupted by a caught signal but says nothing about how to handle this with `connect`. What we just described corresponds to the handling of this scenario by Berkeley-derived kernels.

15.5 Nonblocking `connect`: Web Client

A real-world example of nonblocking `connect`s started with the Netscape Web client (Section 13.4 of TCPv3). The client establishes an HTTP connection with a Web server and fetches a home page. On that page are often numerous references to other Web pages. Instead of fetching these other pages serially, one at a time, the client can fetch more than one at the same time, using nonblocking `connect`s. Figure 15.12 shows an example of establishing multiple connections in parallel. The leftmost scenario shows all three connections performed serially. We assume that the first connection takes 10 units of time, the second 15, and the third 4, for a total of 29 units of time.

In the middle scenario we perform two connections in parallel. At time 0 the first two connections are started, and when the first of these finishes, we start the third. The total time is almost halved, from 29 to 15, but realize that this is the ideal case. If the parallel connections are sharing a common link (say the client is behind a dialup modem link to the Internet) each can compete against each other for the limited resources, and all the individual connection times might get longer. For example, the time of 10 might be 15, the time of 15 might be 20, and the time of 4 might be 6. Nevertheless, the total time would be 21, still shorter than the serial scenario.

In the third scenario we perform three connections in parallel, and we again assume that there is no interference between the three connections (the ideal case). But the total time is the same (15 units) as the second scenario given the example times that we choose.

When dealing with Web clients, the first connection is done by itself, followed by multiple connections for the references found in the data from that first connection. We show this in Figure 15.13.

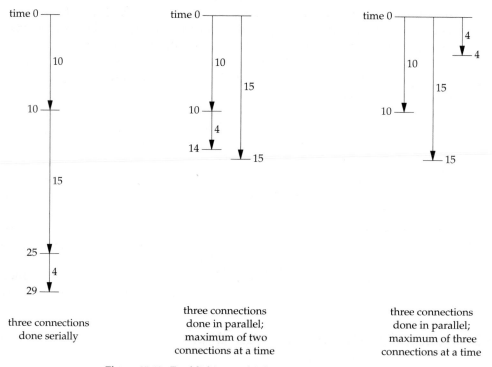

Figure 15.12   Establishing multiple connections in parallel.

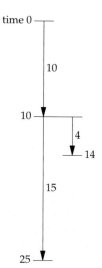

Figure 15.13   Complete first connection, then multiple connections in parallel.

As even further optimization, the client can start parsing the data that is returned for the first connection, before the first connection completes, and initiate additional connections as soon as it knows that additional connections are needed.

Since we are doing multiple nonblocking `connect`s at the same time, we cannot use our `connect_nonb` function from Figure 15.11, because it does not return until the connection is established. Instead we must keep track of multiple connections ourself.

Our program will read up to 20 files from a Web server. We specify as command-line arguments the maximum number of parallel connections, the server's hostname, and then each of the filenames to fetch from the server. A typical execution of our program is:

```
solaris % web 3 www.foobar.com / image1.gif image2.gif \
image3.gif image4.gif image5.gif \
image6.gif image7.gif
```

The command-line arguments specify three simultaneous connections, the server's hostname, the filename for the home page (/ the server's root page), and seven files to then read (which in this example are all GIF images). These seven files would normally be referenced on the home page, and a Web client would read the home page and parse the HTML to obtain these filenames. We do not want to complicate this example with HTML parsing, so we just specify the filenames on the command line.

This is a larger example so we will show it in pieces. Figure 15.14 is our `web.h` header that each file includes.

——————————————————————————— nonblock/web.h
```
 1 #include    "unp.h"

 2 #define MAXFILES    20
 3 #define SERV        "80"            /* port number or service name */

 4 struct file {
 5     char    *f_name;               /* filename */
 6     char    *f_host;               /* hostname or IPv4/IPv6 address */
 7     int     f_fd;                  /* descriptor */
 8     int     f_flags;               /* F_xxx below */
 9 } file[MAXFILES];

10 #define F_CONNECTING    1          /* connect() in progress */
11 #define F_READING       2          /* connect() complete; now reading */
12 #define F_DONE          4          /* all done */

13 #define GET_CMD     "GET %s HTTP/1.0\r\n\r\n"

14              /* globals */
15 int    nconn, nfiles, nlefttoconn, nlefttoread, maxfd;
16 fd_set rset, wset;

17              /* function prototypes */
18 void    home_page(const char *, const char *);
19 void    start_connect(struct file *);
20 void    write_get_cmd(struct file *);
```
——————————————————————————— nonblock/web.h

Figure 15.14 web.h header.

Define `file` structure

2-13   The program reads up to MAXFILES files from the Web server. We maintain a file structure with information about each file: its name (copied from the command-line argument), the hostname or IP address of the server the file from, the socket descriptor being used for the file, and a set of flags to specify what we are doing with this file (connecting, reading, or done).

Define globals and function prototypes

14-20   We define the global variables and function prototypes for our functions that we describe shortly.

       Figure 15.15 shows the first part of the main program.

—— *nonblock/web.c*
```
 1 #include    "web.h"

 2 int
 3 main(int argc, char **argv)
 4 {
 5     int     i, fd, n, maxnconn, flags, error;
 6     char    buf[MAXLINE];
 7     fd_set  rs, ws;

 8     if (argc < 5)
 9         err_quit("usage: web <#conns> <hostname> <homepage> <file1> ...");
10     maxnconn = atoi(argv[1]);

11     nfiles = min(argc - 4, MAXFILES);
12     for (i = 0; i < nfiles; i++) {
13         file[i].f_name = argv[i + 4];
14         file[i].f_host = argv[2];
15         file[i].f_flags = 0;
16     }
17     printf("nfiles = %d\n", nfiles);

18     home_page(argv[2], argv[3]);

19     FD_ZERO(&rset);
20     FD_ZERO(&wset);
21     maxfd = -1;
22     nlefttoread = nlefttoconn = nfiles;
23     nconn = 0;
```
—— *nonblock/web.c*

Figure 15.15 First part of simultaneous connect: globals and start of main.

Process command-line arguments

11-17   The file structure is filled in with the relevant information from the command-line arguments.

Read home page

18   The function home_page, which we show next, creates a TCP connection, sends a command to the server, and then reads the home page. This is the first connection, which is done by itself, before we start establishing multiple connections in parallel.

Initialize globals

19-23   Two descriptor sets, one for reading and one for writing, are initialized. `maxfd` is the maximum descriptor for `select` (which we initialize to −1, since descriptors are nonnegative), `nlefttoread` is the number of files remaining to be read (when this reaches 0 we are finished), `nlefttoconn` is the number of files that still need a TCP connection, and `nconn` is the number of connections currently open (which can never exceed the first command-line argument).

Figure 15.16 shows the `home_page` function that is called once when the `main` function begins.

```
                                                            ───── nonblock/home_page.c
 1 #include    "web.h"

 2 void
 3 home_page(const char *host, const char *fname)
 4 {
 5     int     fd, n;
 6     char    line[MAXLINE];

 7     fd = Tcp_connect(host, SERV);    /* blocking connect() */

 8     n = snprintf(line, sizeof(line), GET_CMD, fname);
 9     Writen(fd, line, n);

10     for ( ; ; ) {
11         if ( (n = Read(fd, line, MAXLINE)) == 0)
12             break;                  /* server closed connection */

13         printf("read %d bytes of home page\n", n);
14         /* do whatever with data */
15     }
16     printf("end-of-file on home page\n");
17     Close(fd);
18 }
                                                            ───── nonblock/home_page.c
```

Figure 15.16 home_page function.

Establish connection with server

7   Our `tcp_connect` establishes a connection with the server.

Send HTTP command to server; read reply

8-17   An HTTP GET command is issued for the home page (often named /). The reply is read (we do not do anything with the reply) and the connection is closed.

The next function, `start_connect` shown in Figure 15.17, initiates a nonblocking connect.

Create socket, set nonblocking

7-13   We call our `host_serv` function (Figure 11.5) to look up and convert the hostname and service name, returning a pointer to an array of `addrinfo` structures. We use only the first structure. A TCP socket is created and the socket is set nonblocking.

nonblock/start_connect.c

```
 1 #include     "web.h"

 2 void
 3 start_connect(struct file *fptr)
 4 {
 5     int      fd, flags, n;
 6     struct addrinfo *ai;

 7     ai = Host_serv(fptr->f_host, SERV, 0, SOCK_STREAM);

 8     fd = Socket(ai->ai_family, ai->ai_socktype, ai->ai_protocol);
 9     fptr->f_fd = fd;
10     printf("start_connect for %s, fd %d\n", fptr->f_name, fd);

11         /* Set socket nonblocking */
12     flags = Fcntl(fd, F_GETFL, 0);
13     Fcntl(fd, F_SETFL, flags | O_NONBLOCK);

14         /* Initiate nonblocking connect to the server. */
15     if ( (n = connect(fd, ai->ai_addr, ai->ai_addrlen)) < 0) {
16         if (errno != EINPROGRESS)
17             err_sys("nonblocking connect error");
18         fptr->f_flags = F_CONNECTING;
19         FD_SET(fd, &rset);        /* select for reading and writing */
20         FD_SET(fd, &wset);
21         if (fd > maxfd)
22             maxfd = fd;

23     } else if (n >= 0)           /* connect is already done */
24         write_get_cmd(fptr);     /* write() the GET command */
25 }
```

nonblock/start_connect.c

Figure 15.17 Initiate nonblocking connect.

Initiate nonblocking connect

14–22   The nonblocking connect is initiated and the file's flag is set to F_CONNECTING. The socket descriptor is turned on in both the read set and the write set, since select will wait for either condition as an indication that the connection has finished. We also update maxfd, if necessary.

Handle connection complete

23–24   If connect returns success, the connection is already complete and the function write_get_cmd (shown next) sends a command to the server.

We set the socket nonblocking for the connect but never reset it to its default blocking mode. This is OK because we write only a small amount of data to the socket (the GET command in the next function) and we assume that this command is much smaller than the socket send buffer. Even if write returns a short count because of the nonblocking flag, our writen function handles this. Leaving the socket nonblocking has no effect on the subsequent reads that are performed because we always call select to wait for the socket to become readable.

Figure 15.18 shows the function `write_get_cmd`, which sends an HTTP GET command to the server.

```
                                                    ——— nonblock/write_get_cmd.c
 1 #include    "web.h"

 2 void
 3 write_get_cmd(struct file *fptr)
 4 {
 5     int     n;
 6     char    line[MAXLINE];

 7     n = snprintf(line, sizeof(line), GET_CMD, fptr->f_name);
 8     Writen(fptr->f_fd, line, n);
 9     printf("wrote %d bytes for %s\n", n, fptr->f_name);

10     fptr->f_flags = F_READING;   /* clears F_CONNECTING */

11     FD_SET(fptr->f_fd, &rset);   /* will read server's reply */
12     if (fptr->f_fd > maxfd)
13         maxfd = fptr->f_fd;
14 }
                                                    ——— nonblock/write_get_cmd.c
```

Figure 15.18 Send an HTTP GET command to the server.

Build command and send it

7–9   The command is built and written to the socket.

Set flags

10–13   The file's F_READING flag is set, which also clears the F_CONNECTING flag (if set). This indicates to the main loop that this descriptor is ready for input. The descriptor is also turned on in the read set and `maxfd` updated, if necessary.

We now return to the `main` function in Figure 15.19, picking up from where we left off in Figure 15.15. This is the main loop of the program: as long as there are more files to process (`nlefttoread` is greater than 0), start another connection if possible, and then `select` on all active descriptors, handling both nonblocking connection completions and the arrival of data.

Can we initiate another connection?

24–35   If we are not at the specified limit of simultaneous connections, and there are additional connections to establish, find a file that we have not yet processed (indicated by a f_flags of 0), and call `start_connect` to initiate the connection. The number of active connections is incremented (`nconn`) and the number of connections remaining to be established is decremented (`nlefttoconn`).

`select`: wait for something to happen

36–37   `select` waits for either readability or writability. Descriptors that have a nonblocking `connect` in progress will be enabled in both sets, while descriptors with a completed connection that are waiting for data from the server will be enabled in just the read set.

nonblock/web.c

```
24    while (nlefttoread > 0) {
25        while (nconn < maxnconn && nlefttoconn > 0) {
26                /* find a file to read */
27            for (i = 0; i < nfiles; i++)
28                if (file[i].f_flags == 0)
29                    break;
30            if (i == nfiles)
31                err_quit("nlefttoconn = %d but nothing found", nlefttoconn);
32            start_connect(&file[i]);
33            nconn++;
34            nlefttoconn--;
35        }
36
37        rs = rset;
38        ws = wset;
39        n = Select(maxfd + 1, &rs, &ws, NULL, NULL);
40
41        for (i = 0; i < nfiles; i++) {
42            flags = file[i].f_flags;
43            if (flags == 0 || flags & F_DONE)
44                continue;
45            fd = file[i].f_fd;
46            if (flags & F_CONNECTING &&
47                (FD_ISSET(fd, &rs) || FD_ISSET(fd, &ws))) {
48                n = sizeof(error);
49                if (getsockopt(fd, SOL_SOCKET, SO_ERROR, &error, &n) < 0 ||
50                    error != 0) {
51                    err_ret("nonblocking connect failed for %s",
52                            file[i].f_name);
53                }
54                    /* connection established */
55                printf("connection established for %s\n", file[i].f_name);
56                FD_CLR(fd, &wset);  /* no more writeability test */
57                write_get_cmd(&file[i]);    /* write() the GET command */
58
59            } else if (flags & F_READING && FD_ISSET(fd, &rs)) {
60                if ( (n = Read(fd, buf, sizeof(buf))) == 0) {
61                    printf("end-of-file on %s\n", file[i].f_name);
62                    Close(fd);
63                    file[i].f_flags = F_DONE;   /* clears F_READING */
64                    FD_CLR(fd, &rset);
65                    nconn--;
66                    nlefttoread--;
67                } else {
68                    printf("read %d bytes from %s\n", n, file[i].f_name);
69                }
70            }
71        }
72    }
73    exit(0);
74 }
```

nonblock/web.c

Figure 15.19 Main loop of main function.

Handle all ready descriptors

39–55   We now process each element in the array of `file` structures to determine which descriptors need processing. If the `F_CONNECTING` flag is set and the descriptor is on in either the read set or the write set, the nonblocking `connect` is finished. As we described with Figure 15.11, we call `getsockopt` to fetch the pending error for the socket. If this value is 0, the connection completed successfully. In that case we turn off the descriptor in the write set and call `write_get_cmd` to send the HTTP request to the server.

See if descriptor has data

56–67   If the `F_READING` flag is set and the descriptor is ready for reading, we call `read`. If the connection was closed by the other end, we close the socket, set the `F_DONE` flag, turn off the descriptor in the read set, and decrement the number of active connections and the total number of connections to be processed.

There are two optimizations that we do not perform in this example (to avoid complicating it even more). First, we could terminate the `for` loop in Figure 15.19 when we have processed the number of descriptors that `select` said were ready. Next, we could decrease the value of `maxfd` when possible, to save `select` from examining descriptor bits that are no longer set. Since the number of descriptors that this code deals with at any one time is probably less than 10, and not in the thousands, it is doubtful that either of these optimizations is worth the additional complications.

Performance of Simultaneous Connections

What is the performance gain in establishing multiple connections at the same time? Figure 15.20 shows the clock time required to fetch a Web server's home page, followed by nine image files from that server. The RTT to the server is about 150 ms. The home page size was 4017 bytes and the average size of the nine image files was 1621 bytes. TCP's segment size was 512 bytes. We also include in this figure, for comparison, values for a version of this program that we develop in Section 23.9 using threads.

# Simultaneous connections	Clock time (seconds), nonblocking	Clock time (seconds), threads
1	6.0	6.3
2	4.1	4.2
3	3.0	3.1
4	2.8	3.0
5	2.5	2.7
6	2.4	2.5
7	2.3	2.3
8	2.2	2.3
9	2.0	2.2

Figure 15.20 Clock time for various numbers of simultaneous connections.

Most of the improvement is obtained with three simultaneous connections (the clock time is halved) and the performance increase is much less with four or more simultaneous connections.

> We provide this example using simultaneous connects because it is a nice example using nonblocking I/O and one whose performance impact can be measured. It is also a feature used by a popular Web application, the Netscape browser. There are pitfalls in this technique if there is any congestion in the network. Chapter 21 of TCPv1 describes TCP's slow start and congestion avoidance algorithms in detail. When multiple connections are established from a client to a server, there is no communication between the connections at the TCP layer. That is, if one connection encounters a packet loss, the other connections to the same server are not notified, and it is highly probable that the other connections will soon encounter packet loss unless they slow down. These additional connections are sending more packets into an already congested network. This technique also increases the load at any given time on the server.

15.6 Nonblocking `accept`

We stated in Chapter 6 that a listening socket is returned as readable by `select` when a completed connection is ready to be `accepted`. Therefore, if we are using `select` to wait for incoming connections, we should not need to set the listening socket nonblocking, because if `select` tells us that the connection is ready, `accept` should not block.

Unfortunately there is a timing problem that can trip us up here [Gierth 1996]. To see this problem we modify our TCP echo client (Figure 5.4) to establish the connection and then send an RST to the server. Figure 15.21 shows this new version.

Set `SO_LINGER` socket option

16–19   Once the connection is established we set the `SO_LINGER` socket option, setting the `l_onoff` flag to 1 and the `l_linger` time to 0. As stated in Section 7.5, this causes an RST to be sent on a TCP socket when the connection is closed. We then `close` the socket.

Next, we modify our TCP server from Figures 6.21 and 6.22 to pause after `select` returns that the listening socket is readable, but before calling `accept`. In the following code from the beginning of Figure 6.22 the two lines preceded by a plus sign are new.

```
        if (FD_ISSET(listenfd, &rset)) {      /* new client connection */
+            printf("listening socket readable\n");
+            sleep(5);
             clilen = sizeof(cliaddr);
             connfd = Accept(listenfd, (SA *) &cliaddr, &clilen);
```

What we are simulating here is a busy server that cannot call `accept` as soon as `select` returns that the listening socket is readable. Normally this slowness on the part of the server is not a problem (indeed this is why a queue of completed connections is maintained), but when combined with the RST from the client, after the connection is established, we can have a problem.

In Section 5.11 we noted that when the client aborts the connection before the server calls `accept`, Berkeley-derived implementations do not return the aborted connection

—————————————————————————— nonblock/tcpcli03.c
```
 1 #include     "unp.h"

 2 int
 3 main(int argc, char **argv)
 4 {
 5     int     sockfd;
 6     struct linger ling;
 7     struct sockaddr_in servaddr;

 8     if (argc != 2)
 9         err_quit("usage: tcpcli <IPaddress>");

10     sockfd = Socket(AF_INET, SOCK_STREAM, 0);

11     bzero(&servaddr, sizeof(servaddr));
12     servaddr.sin_family = AF_INET;
13     servaddr.sin_port = htons(SERV_PORT);
14     Inet_pton(AF_INET, argv[1], &servaddr.sin_addr);

15     Connect(sockfd, (SA *) &servaddr, sizeof(servaddr));

16     ling.l_onoff = 1;             /* cause RST to be sent on close() */
17     ling.l_linger = 0;
18     Setsockopt(sockfd, SOL_SOCKET, SO_LINGER, &ling, sizeof(ling));
19     Close(sockfd);

20     exit(0);
21 }
```
—————————————————————————— nonblock/tcpcli03.c

Figure 15.21 TCP echo client that creates connection and sends an RST.

to the server, while other implementations should return ECONNABORTED but often return EPROTO instead. Consider a Berkeley-derived implementation.

- The client establishes the connection and then aborts it as in Figure 15.21.

- select returns readable to the server process, but it takes the server a short time to call accept.

- Between the server's return from select and its calling accept, the RST is received from the client.

- The completed connection is removed from the queue and we assume that no other completed connections exist.

- The server calls accept, but since there are no completed connections, it blocks.

The server will remain blocked in the call to accept until some other client establishes a connection. But in the meantime, assuming a server like Figure 6.22, the server is blocked in the call to accept and will not handle any other ready descriptors.

> This problem is somewhat similar to the denial of service attack described in Section 6.8, but with this new bug the server breaks out of the blocked accept as soon as another client establishes a connection.

The fix for this problem is to

1. always set a listening socket nonblocking if we use `select` to tell us when a connection is ready to be `accepted`, and

2. ignore the following errors on the subsequent call to `accept`: EWOULDBLOCK (for Berkeley-derived implementations, when the client aborts the connection), ECONNABORTED (for Posix.1g implementations, when the client aborts the connection), EPROTO (for SVR4 implementations, when the client aborts the connection), and EINTR (if signals are being caught).

15.7 Summary

Our example of nonblocking reads and writes in Section 15.2 took our `str_cli` echo client and modified it to use nonblocking I/O on the TCP connection to the server. `select` is normally used with nonblocking I/O, to determine when a descriptor is readable or writable. This version of our client is the fastest version that we show, although the code modifications are nontrivial. We then showed that it is simpler to divide the client into two pieces using `fork`, and we employ the same technique using threads in Figure 23.2.

Nonblocking `connects` let us do other processing while TCP's three-way handshake takes place, instead of being blocked in the call to `connect`. Unfortunately these are also nonportable, with different implementations having different ways of indicating that the connection completed OK or encountered an error. We used nonblocking connects to develop a new client, which is similar to a Web client, that opens multiple TCP connections at the same time to reduce the clock time required to fetch numerous files from a server. Initiating multiple connections like this can reduce the clock time but is also "network unfriendly," with regard to TCP's congestion avoidance.

Exercises

15.1   In our discussion of Figure 15.10 we mentioned that the parent must call `shutdown`, not `close`. Why?

15.2   What happens in Figure 15.10 if the server process terminates prematurely, the child receives the end-of-file and terminates, but the child does not notify the parent?

15.3   What happens in Figure 15.10 if the parent dies unexpectedly before the child, and the child then reads an end-of-file on the socket?

15.4   What happens in Figure 15.11 if we remove the two lines

```
        if (n == 0)
            goto done;        /* connect completed immediately */
```

15.5   In Section 15.3 we said that it is possible for data to arrive for a socket before `connect` returns. How can this happen?

16

`ioctl` *Operations*

16.1 Introduction

The `ioctl` function has traditionally been the system interface used for everything that didn't fit into some other nicely defined category. Posix is getting rid of `ioctl`, by creating specific wrapper functions to replace `ioctl`s whose functionality is being standardized by Posix. For example, the Unix terminal interface was traditionally accessed using `ioctl` but Posix.1 created 12 new functions for terminals: `tcgetattr` to get the terminal attributes, `tcflush` to flush pending input or output, and so on. In a similar vein, Posix.1g is replacing one `ioctl`: the new `sockatmark` function (Section 21.3) replaces the `SIOCATMARK` `ioctl`. Nevertheless numerous `ioctl`s remain for implementation-dependent features related to network programming: obtaining the interface information, and accessing the routing table and the ARP cache, for example.

This chapter provides an overview of the `ioctl` requests related to network programming, but many of these are implementation dependent. Additionally, newer Berkeley-derived implementations use sockets in the `AF_ROUTE` domain (routing sockets) to accomplish many of these operations. We cover routing sockets in Chapter 17.

A common use of `ioctl` by network programs (typically servers) is to obtain information on all the host's interfaces when the program starts: the interface addresses, whether the interface supports broadcasting, whether the interface supports multicasting, and so on. We develop our own function to return this information and provide an implementation using `ioctl` in this chapter, and another implementation using routing sockets in Chapter 17.

425

16.2   `ioctl` Function

This function affects an open file, referenced by the *fd* argument.

```
#include <unistd.h>

int ioctl(int fd, int request, ... /* void *arg */ );
```

Returns: 0 if OK, –1 on error

The third argument is always a pointer, but the type of pointer depends on the *request*.

> 4.4BSD defines the second argument to be an `unsigned long` instead of an `int`, but that is not a problem, since header files define the constants that are used for this argument.
>
> Some implementations specify the third argument as a `void *` pointer, instead of the ANSI C ellipsis notation.
>
> There is no standard for the header to include to define the function prototype for `ioctl`, since it is not standardized by Posix. Many systems define it in `<unistd.h>`, as we show, but traditional BSD systems define it in `<sys/ioctl.h>`.

We can divide the *request*s related to networking into six categories.

- socket operations
- file operations
- interface operations
- ARP cache operations
- routing table operations
- streams system (Chapter 33)

Recall from Figure 7.15 that not only do some of the `ioctl` operations overlap some of the `fcntl` operations (e.g., setting a socket nonblocking), but there are also some operations that can be specified more than one way using `ioctl` (e.g., setting the process group ownership of a socket).

Figure 16.1 lists the *request*s, along with the datatype of what the *arg* address must point to. The following sections describe these requests in more detail.

16.3   Socket Operations

There are three `ioctl` requests explicitly for sockets (pp. 551–553 of TCPv2). All three require that the third argument to `ioctl` be a pointer to an integer.

SIOCATMARK   Return through the integer pointed to by the third argument a nonzero value if the socket's read pointer is currently at the out-of-band mark, or a zero value if the read pointer is not at the out-of-band mark. We describe out-of-band data in more detail in Chapter 21. Posix.1g replaces this request with the `sockatmark` function and we show an implementation of this new function using `ioctl` in Section 21.3.

Category	request	Description	Datatype
socket	SIOCATMARK	at out-of-band mark ?	int
	SIOCSPGRP	set process ID or process group ID of socket	int
	SIOCGPGRP	get process ID or process group ID of socket	int
file	FIONBIO	set/clear nonblocking flag	int
	FIOASYNC	set/clear asynchronous i/o flag	int
	FIONREAD	get # bytes in receive buffer	int
	FIOSETOWN	set process ID or process group ID of socket	int
	FIOGETOWN	get process ID or process group ID of socket	int
interface	SIOCGIFCONF	get list of all interfaces	struct ifconf
	SIOCSIFADDR	set interface address	struct ifreq
	SIOCGIFADDR	get interface address	struct ifreq
	SIOCSIFFLAGS	set interface flags	struct ifreq
	SIOCGIFFLAGS	get interface flags	struct ifreq
	SIOCSIFDSTADDR	set point-to-point address	struct ifreq
	SIOCGIFDSTADDR	get point-to-point address	struct ifreq
	SIOCGIFBRDADDR	get broadcast address	struct ifreq
	SIOCSIFBRDADDR	set broadcast address	struct ifreq
	SIOCGIFNETMASK	get subnet mask	struct ifreq
	SIOCSIFNETMASK	set subnet mask	struct ifreq
	SIOCGIFMETRIC	get interface metric	struct ifreq
	SIOCSIFMETRIC	set interface metric	struct ifreq
	SIOC*xxx*	(many more; implementation dependent)	
ARP	SIOCSARP	create/modify ARP entry	struct arpreq
	SIOCGARP	get ARP entry	struct arpreq
	SIOCDARP	delete ARP entry	struct arpreq
routing	SIOCADDRT	add route	struct rtentry
	SIOCDELRT	delete route	struct rtentry
streams	I_*xxx*	(see Section 33.5)	

Figure 16.1 Summary of networking ioctl requests.

SIOCGPGRP   Return through the integer pointed to by the third argument either the process ID or the process group ID that is set to receive the SIGIO or SIGURG signal for this socket. This request is identical to an fcntl of F_GETOWN and we note in Figure 7.15 that Posix.1g standardizes the fcntl.

SIOCSPGRP   Set either the process ID or the process group ID to receive the SIGIO or SIGURG signal for this socket from the integer pointed to by the third argument. This request is identical to an fcntl of F_SETOWN and we note in Figure 7.15 that Posix.1g standardizes the fcntl.

16.4 File Operations

The next group of requests begin with FIO and may apply to certain types of files, in addition to sockets. We cover only the requests that apply to sockets (p. 553 of TCPv2).

The following five requests all require that the third argument to ioctl point to an integer.

FIONBIO   The nonblocking flag for the socket is cleared or turned on, depending
               whether the third argument to ioctl points to a zero or nonzero value,
               respectively. This request accomplishes the same effect as the
               O_NONBLOCK file status flag that can be set and cleared with the
               F_SETFL command to the fcntl function.

FIOASYNC   The flag that governs the receipt of asynchronous I/O signals (SIGIO)
               for the socket is cleared or turned on, depending whether the third
               argument to ioctl points to a zero or nonzero value, respectively.
               This flag accomplishes the same effect as the O_ASYNC file status flag
               that can be set and cleared with the F_SETFL command to the fcntl
               function.

FIONREAD   Return in the integer pointed to by the third argument to ioctl the
               number of bytes currently in the socket receive buffer. This feature also
               works for files, pipes, and terminals. We said more about this request
               in Section 13.7.

FIOSETOWN   Equivalent to SIOCSPGRP for a socket.

FIOGETOWN   Equivalent to SIOCGPGRP for a socket.

16.5 Interface Configuration

One of the first steps employed by many programs that deal with the network interfaces on a system is to obtain from the kernel all the interfaces configured on the system. This is done with the SIOCGIFCONF request, which uses the ifconf structure, which in turn uses the ifreq structure, both of which are shown in Figure 16.2.

Before calling ioctl we allocate a buffer and an ifconf structure and then initialize the latter. We show a picture of this in Figure 16.3 (p. 430), assuming our buffer size is 1024 bytes. The third argument to ioctl is a pointer to our ifconf structure.

If we assume that the kernel returns two ifreq structures, we could have the arrangement shown in Figure 16.4 (p. 430) when the ioctl returns. The shaded regions have been modified by ioctl. The buffer has been filled in with the two structures and the ifc_len member of the ifconf structure has been updated to reflect the amount of information stored in the buffer. We assume in this figure that each ifreq structure occupies 32 bytes.

A pointer to an ifreq structure is also used as an argument to the remaining interface ioctls shown in Figure 16.1, which we describe in Section 16.7. Notice that each ifreq structure contains a union and there are numerous #defines to hide the fact that these fields are members of a union. All the references to the individual members are made using the defined names. Be aware that some systems have added many implementation-dependent members to the ifr_ifru union.

```
───────────────────────────────────────────────────────────── <net/if.h>
struct ifconf {
    int   ifc_len;                   /* size of buffer, value-result */
    union {
        caddr_t ifcu_buf;            /* input from user -> kernel */
        struct  ifreq *ifcu_req;     /* return from kernel -> user */
    } ifc_ifcu;
};
#define  ifc_buf  ifc_ifcu.ifcu_buf /* buffer address */
#define  ifc_req  ifc_ifcu.ifcu_req /* array of structures returned */

#define  IFNAMSIZ    16

struct ifreq {
    char    ifr_name[IFNAMSIZ];      /* interface name, e.g., "le0" */
    union {
        struct  sockaddr ifru_addr;
        struct  sockaddr ifru_dstaddr;
        struct  sockaddr ifru_broadaddr;
        short   ifru_flags;
        int     ifru_metric;
        caddr_t ifru_data;
    } ifr_ifru;
};
#define  ifr_addr       ifr_ifru.ifru_addr      /* address */
#define  ifr_dstaddr    ifr_ifru.ifru_dstaddr   /* other end of p-to-p link */
#define  ifr_broadaddr  ifr_ifru.ifru_broadaddr /* broadcast address */
#define  ifr_flags      ifr_ifru.ifru_flags     /* flags */
#define  ifr_metric     ifr_ifru.ifru_metric    /* metric */
#define  ifr_data       ifr_ifru.ifru_data      /* for use by interface */
───────────────────────────────────────────────────────────── <net/if.h>
```

Figure 16.2 ifconf and ifreq structures used with various interface ioctl requests.

16.6 get_ifi_info Function

Since many programs need to know all the interfaces on a system, we will develop a function of our own named get_ifi_info that returns a linked list of structures, one for each interface that is currently "up." In this section we will implement this function using the SIOCGIFCONF ioctl and in Chapter 17 we will develop a version using routing sockets.

> BSD/OS provides a function named getifaddrs with similar functionality.

> Searching the entire BSD/OS 2.1 source tree shows that 12 programs issue the SIOCGIFCONF ioctl to determine the interfaces that are present.

We first define the ifi_info structure in a new header named unpifi.h, shown in Figure 16.5.

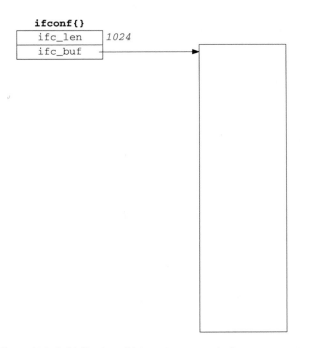

Figure 16.3 Initialization of ifconf structure before SIOCGIFCONF.

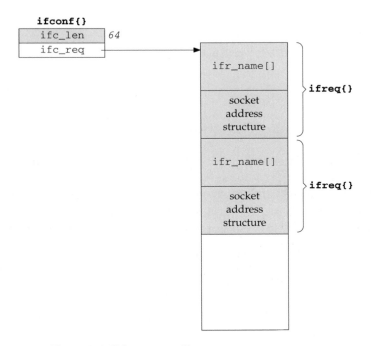

Figure 16.4 Values returned by SIOCGIFCONF.

―― *ioctl/unpifi.h*
```
 1 /* Our own header for the programs that need interface configuration info.
 2    Include this file, instead of "unp.h". */

 3 #ifndef __unp_ifi_h
 4 #define __unp_ifi_h

 5 #include    "unp.h"
 6 #include    <net/if.h>

 7 #define IFI_NAME    16          /* same as IFNAMSIZ in <net/if.h> */
 8 #define IFI_HADDR    8          /* allow for 64-bit EUI-64 in future */

 9 struct ifi_info {
10     char    ifi_name[IFI_NAME]; /* interface name, null terminated */
11     u_char  ifi_haddr[IFI_HADDR];   /* hardware address */
12     u_short ifi_hlen;           /* #bytes in hardware address: 0, 6, 8 */
13     short   ifi_flags;          /* IFF_xxx constants from <net/if.h> */
14     short   ifi_myflags;        /* our own IFI_xxx flags */
15     struct sockaddr *ifi_addr;  /* primary address */
16     struct sockaddr *ifi_brdaddr;   /* broadcast address */
17     struct sockaddr *ifi_dstaddr;   /* destination address */
18     struct ifi_info *ifi_next;  /* next of these structures */
19 };

20 #define IFI_ALIAS    1          /* ifi_addr is an alias */

21                     /* function prototypes */
22 struct ifi_info *get_ifi_info(int, int);
23 struct ifi_info *Get_ifi_info(int, int);
24 void    free_ifi_info(struct ifi_info *);

25 #endif  /* __unp_ifi_h */
```
―― *ioctl/unpifi.h*

Figure 16.5 `unpifi.h` header.

9–19   A linked list of these structures is returned by our function, each structure's
`ifi_next` member pointing to the next one. We return in this structure just the information that a typical application is probably interested in: the interface name, the hardware address (e.g., an Ethernet address), the interface flags (to let the application
determine if the interface supports broadcasting or multicasting, or is a point-to-point
interface), and the interface address, the broadcast address, and the destination address
for a point-to-point link. All of the memory used to hold the `ifi_info` structures,
along with the socket address structures contained within, are obtained dynamically.
Therefore we also provide a `free_ifi_info` function to free all this memory.

> Most hardware addresses today are 48-bit MAC addresses (e.g., Ethernet, token ring, etc.). But
> there is a trend toward 64-bit identifiers, called *EUI-64* [IEEE 1997b]. IPv6 addresses contain
> an EUI-64 value in the low-order 64 bits (Section A.5), and there is a simple way to encapsulate
> a 48-bit MAC address within a 64-bit EUI. We therefore allocate enough room in our
> `ifi_info` structure for a 64-bit identifier and also store the length of the hardware address.

Before showing the implementation of our `get_ifi_info` function, we show a
simple program that calls this function and then outputs all the information. This

program is a miniature version of the `ifconfig` program and is shown in Figure 16.6.

—————————————————————————————————————— ioctl/prifinfo.c

```
 1 #include    "unpifi.h"

 2 int
 3 main(int argc, char **argv)
 4 {
 5     struct ifi_info *ifi, *ifihead;
 6     struct sockaddr *sa;
 7     u_char *ptr;
 8     int    i, family, doaliases;

 9     if (argc != 3)
10         err_quit("usage: prifinfo <inet4|inet6> <doaliases>");
11     if (strcmp(argv[1], "inet4") == 0)
12         family = AF_INET;
13 #ifdef  IPV6
14     else if (strcmp(argv[1], "inet6") == 0)
15         family = AF_INET6;
16 #endif
17     else
18         err_quit("invalid <address-family>");
19     doaliases = atoi(argv[2]);
20     for (ifihead = ifi = Get_ifi_info(family, doaliases);
21          ifi != NULL; ifi = ifi->ifi_next) {
22         printf("%s: <", ifi->ifi_name);
23         if (ifi->ifi_flags & IFF_UP)           printf("UP ");
24         if (ifi->ifi_flags & IFF_BROADCAST)    printf("BCAST ");
25         if (ifi->ifi_flags & IFF_MULTICAST)    printf("MCAST ");
26         if (ifi->ifi_flags & IFF_LOOPBACK)     printf("LOOP ");
27         if (ifi->ifi_flags & IFF_POINTOPOINT)  printf("P2P ");
28         printf(">\n");

29         if ( (i = ifi->ifi_hlen) > 0) {
30             ptr = ifi->ifi_haddr;
31             do {
32                 printf("%s%x", (i == ifi->ifi_hlen) ? "  " : ":", *ptr++);
33             } while (--i > 0);
34             printf("\n");
35         }
36         if ( (sa = ifi->ifi_addr) != NULL)
37             printf("  IP addr: %s\n",
38                     Sock_ntop_host(sa, sizeof(*sa)));
39         if ( (sa = ifi->ifi_brdaddr) != NULL)
40             printf("  broadcast addr: %s\n",
41                     Sock_ntop_host(sa, sizeof(*sa)));
42         if ( (sa = ifi->ifi_dstaddr) != NULL)
43             printf("  destination addr: %s\n",
44                     Sock_ntop_host(sa, sizeof(*sa)));
45     }
46     free_ifi_info(ifihead);
47     exit(0);
48 }
```

—————————————————————————————————————— ioctl/prifinfo.c

Figure 16.6 `prifinfo` program that calls our `get_ifi_info` function.

20-45   The program is a `for` loop that calls `get_ifi_info` once and then steps through all the `ifi_info` structures that are returned.

22-35   The interface name and flags are all printed. If the length of the hardware address is greater than 0, it is printed as hexadecimal numbers. (Our `get_ifi_info` function returns an `ifi_hlen` of 0 if it is not available.)

36-44   The three IP addresses are printed, if returned.

If we run this program on our host `solaris` (Figure 1.16) we have the following output:

```
solaris % prifinfo inet4 0
lo0: <UP MCAST LOOP >
  IP addr: 127.0.0.1
le0: <UP BCAST MCAST >
  IP addr: 206.62.226.33
  broadcast addr: 206.62.226.63
```

The first command-line argument of `inet4` specifies IPv4 addresses, and the second argument of 0 specifies that no address aliases are to be returned (we described IP address aliases in Section A.4). Note that under Solaris the hardware address of the Ethernet interface is not available.

If we add three alias addresses to the Ethernet interface (`le0`), with host IDs of 44, 45, and 46, and if we change the second command-line argument to 1, we have

```
solaris % prifinfo inet4 1
lo0: <UP MCAST LOOP >
  IP addr: 127.0.0.1
le0: <UP BCAST MCAST >
  IP addr: 206.62.226.33              primary IP address
  broadcast addr: 206.62.226.63
le0:1: <UP BCAST MCAST >
  IP addr: 206.62.226.44              first alias
  broadcast addr: 206.62.226.63
le0:2: <UP BCAST MCAST >
  IP addr: 206.62.226.45              second alias
  broadcast addr: 206.62.226.63
le0:3: <UP BCAST MCAST >
  IP addr: 206.62.226.46              third alias
  broadcast addr: 206.62.226.63
```

If we run the same program under BSD/OS, using the implementation of `get_ifi_info` from Figure 17.16 (which can easily obtain the hardware address), we have:

```
bsdi % prifinfo inet4 1
we0: <UP BCAST MCAST >
  0:0:c0:6f:2d:40
  IP addr: 206.62.226.66
  broadcast addr: 206.62.226.95
ef0: <UP BCAST MCAST >
  0:20:af:9c:ee:95
  IP addr: 206.62.226.35              primary IP address
  broadcast addr: 206.62.226.63
```

```
ef0: <UP BCAST MCAST >
  0:20:af:9c:ee:95
  IP addr: 206.62.226.50                      alias
  broadcast addr: 206.62.226.63
lo0: <UP MCAST LOOP >
  IP addr: 127.0.0.1
```

For this example we directed the program to print the aliases and we see that one alias is defined for the second Ethernet interface (ef0) with a host ID of 50.

> This output depends on how the interface alias addresses are established. In this example the alias address is assigned to the Ethernet interface ef0, and this was the common technique with BSD/OS 2.1. But with BSD/OS 3.0 the recommended technique is to assign the alias addresses to the loopback interface lo0.

We now show our implementation of get_ifi_info that uses the SIOCGIFCONF ioctl. Figure 16.7 shows the first part of the function, which obtains the interface configuration from the kernel.

lib/get_ifi_info.c

```
 1 #include     "unpifi.h"

 2 struct ifi_info *
 3 get_ifi_info(int family, int doaliases)
 4 {
 5     struct ifi_info *ifi, *ifihead, **ifipnext;
 6     int     sockfd, len, lastlen, flags, myflags;
 7     char    *ptr, *buf, lastname[IFNAMSIZ], *cptr;
 8     struct ifconf ifc;
 9     struct ifreq *ifr, ifrcopy;
10     struct sockaddr_in *sinptr;

11     sockfd = Socket(AF_INET, SOCK_DGRAM, 0);

12     lastlen = 0;
13     len = 100 * sizeof(struct ifreq);   /* initial buffer size guess */
14     for ( ; ; ) {
15         buf = Malloc(len);
16         ifc.ifc_len = len;
17         ifc.ifc_buf = buf;
18         if (ioctl(sockfd, SIOCGIFCONF, &ifc) < 0) {
19             if (errno != EINVAL || lastlen != 0)
20                 err_sys("ioctl error");
21         } else {
22             if (ifc.ifc_len == lastlen)
23                 break;                  /* success, len has not changed */
24             lastlen = ifc.ifc_len;
25         }
26         len += 10 * sizeof(struct ifreq);   /* increment */
27         free(buf);
28     }
29     ifihead = NULL;
30     ifipnext = &ifihead;
31     lastname[0] = 0;
```

lib/get_ifi_info.c

Figure 16.7 Issue SIOCGIFCONF request to obtain interface configuration.

Create an Internet socket

11   We create a UDP socket that will be used with the `ioctl`s. Either a TCP or a UDP socket can be used (p. 163 of TCPv2).

Issue SIOCGIFCONF request in a loop

12–28   A fundamental problem with the `SIOCGIFCONF` request is that some implementations do not return an error if the buffer is not large enough to hold the result. Instead, the result is truncated and success is returned (a return value of 0 from `ioctl`). This means the only way we know that our buffer is large enough is to issue the request, save the return length, issue the request again with a larger buffer, and compare the length with the saved value. Only if the two lengths are the same is our buffer large enough.

> Berkeley-derived implementations do not return an error if the buffer is too small (pp. 118–119 of TCPv2); the result is just truncated to fit the available buffer. Solaris 2.5, on the other hand, returns `EINVAL` if the returned length would be greater than or equal to the buffer length. But we cannot assume success if the returned length is less than the buffer size, because Berkeley-derived implementations can return less than the buffer size if another structure does not fit.

> Some implementations provide a `SIOCGIFNUM` request that returns the number of interfaces. This allows the application to then allocate a buffer of sufficient size before issuing the `SIOCGIFCONF` request, but this new request is not widespread.

> Allocating a fixed-sized buffer for the result from the `SIOCGIFCONF` request has become a problem with the growth of the Web, because large Web servers are allocating many alias addresses to a single interface. Solaris 2.5, for example, had a limit of 256 aliases per interface, but this limit increases to 8192 with 2.6. Sites with large numbers of aliases discovered that programs with fixed-size buffers for the interface information started failing. Even though Solaris returns an error if the buffer is too small, these programs allocate their fixed-size buffer, issue the `ioctl`, but then die if an error was returned.

12–15   We dynamically allocate a buffer, starting with room for 100 `ifreq` structures. We also keep track of the length returned by the last `SIOCGIFCONF` request in `lastlen` and initialize this to 0.

19–20   If an error of `EINVAL` is returned by `ioctl`, and we have not yet had a successful return (i.e., `lastlen` is still 0), we have not yet allocated a buffer large enough and continue through the loop.

22–23   If `ioctl` returns OK, then if the returned length equals `lastlen`, the length has not changed (our buffer is large enough) and we `break` out of the loop since we have all the information.

26–27   Each time around the loop we increase the buffer size to hold 10 more `ifreq` structures.

Initialize linked list pointers

29–31   Since we will be returning a pointer to the head of a linked list of `ifi_info` structures, we use the two variables `ifihead` and `ifipnext` to hold pointers to the list as we build it. This is the same technique that we described with Figure 11.34.

The next part of our `get_ifi_info` function, the beginning of the main loop, is shown in Figure 16.8.

```
                                                              ─── lib/get_ifi_info.c
32      for (ptr = buf; ptr < buf + ifc.ifc_len;) {
33          ifr = (struct ifreq *) ptr;

34 #ifdef  HAVE_SOCKADDR_SA_LEN
35          len = max(sizeof(struct sockaddr), ifr->ifr_addr.sa_len);
36 #else
37          switch (ifr->ifr_addr.sa_family) {
38 #ifdef  IPV6
39          case AF_INET6:
40              len = sizeof(struct sockaddr_in6);
41              break;
42 #endif
43          case AF_INET:
44          default:
45              len = sizeof(struct sockaddr);
46              break;
47          }
48 #endif  /* HAVE_SOCKADDR_SA_LEN */
49          ptr += sizeof(ifr->ifr_name) + len;     /* for next one in buffer */

50          if (ifr->ifr_addr.sa_family != family)
51              continue;            /* ignore if not desired address family */

52          myflags = 0;
53          if ( (cptr = strchr(ifr->ifr_name, ':')) != NULL)
54              *cptr = 0;           /* replace colon will null */
55          if (strncmp(lastname, ifr->ifr_name, IFNAMSIZ) == 0) {
56              if (doaliases == 0)
57                  continue;        /* already processed this interface */
58              myflags = IFI_ALIAS;
59          }
60          memcpy(lastname, ifr->ifr_name, IFNAMSIZ);

61          ifrcopy = *ifr;
62          Ioctl(sockfd, SIOCGIFFLAGS, &ifrcopy);
63          flags = ifrcopy.ifr_flags;
64          if ((flags & IFF_UP) == 0)
65              continue;            /* ignore if interface not up */

66          ifi = Calloc(1, sizeof(struct ifi_info));
67          *ifipnext = ifi;         /* prev points to this new one */
68          ifipnext = &ifi->ifi_next;  /* pointer to next one goes here */

69          ifi->ifi_flags = flags; /* IFF_xxx values */
70          ifi->ifi_myflags = myflags;     /* IFI_xxx values */
71          memcpy(ifi->ifi_name, ifr->ifr_name, IFI_NAME);
72          ifi->ifi_name[IFI_NAME - 1] = '\0';
                                                              ─── lib/get_ifi_info.c
```

Figure 16.8 Process interface configuration.

Step to next socket address structure

32-49   As we loop through all the `ifreq` structures, `ifr` points to each structure and we then increment `ptr` to point to the next one. But we must deal with newer systems that provide a length field for socket address structures, and older systems that do not provide this length. Even though the declaration in Figure 16.3 declares the socket address structure contained within the `ifreq` structure as a generic socket address structure, on newer systems this can be any type of socket address structure. Indeed, on 4.4BSD a datalink socket address structure is also returned for each interface (p. 118 of TCPv2). Therefore if the length member is supported, we must use its value to update our pointer to the next socket address structure. Otherwise we use a length based on the address family, using the size of the generic socket address structure (16 bytes) as the default.

> On systems that support IPv6, there is no standard as to whether or not the `SIOCGIFCONF` request returns IPv6 addresses. We put in a `case` for IPv6, for newer systems, just in case. The problem is that the `union` in the `ifreq` structure defines the returned addresses as generic 16-byte `sockaddr` structures, which are adequate for 16-byte IPv4 `sockaddr_in` structures, but too small for 24-byte IPv6 `sockaddr_in6` structures. If IPv6 addresses were returned, it would probably break existing code that assumes a fixed-size `sockaddr` structure in each `ifreq` structure.

50-51   We ignore any addresses from families other than those desired by the caller.

Handle aliases

52-60   We must detect any aliases that may exist for the interface, that is, additional addresses that have been assigned to the interface. Note from our examples following Figure 16.6 that under Solaris the interface name for an alias contains a colon, while under 4.4BSD the interface name does not change for an alias. To handle both cases we save the last interface name in `lastname` and only compare up to a colon, if present. If a colon is not present, we still ignore this interface if the name is equivalent to the last interface that we processed.

Fetch interface flags

61-65   We issue an `ioctl` of `SIOCGIFFLAGS` (Section 16.5) to fetch the interface flags. The third argument to `ioctl` is a pointer to an `ifreq` structure that must contain the name of the interface for which we want the flags. We make a copy of the `ifreq` structure before issuing the `ioctl`, because if we didn't, this request would overwrite the IP address of the interface, since both are members of the same `union` in Figure 16.2. If the interface is not up, we ignore it.

Allocate and initialize `ifi_info` structure

66-72   At this point we know that we will return this interface to the caller. We allocate memory for our `ifi_info` structure and add it to the end of the linked list that we are building. We copy the interface flags and name into the structure. We make certain that the interface name is null terminated, and since `calloc` initializes the allocated region to all zero bits, we know that `ifi_hlen` is initialized to 0.

Figure 16.9 contains the last part of our function.

―――――――――――――――――――――――――――――――――――― *ioctl/get_ifi_info.c*
```
73              switch (ifr->ifr_addr.sa_family) {
74              case AF_INET:
75                  sinptr = (struct sockaddr_in *) &ifr->ifr_addr;
76                  if (ifi->ifi_addr == NULL) {
77                      ifi->ifi_addr = Calloc(1, sizeof(struct sockaddr_in));
78                      memcpy(ifi->ifi_addr, sinptr, sizeof(struct sockaddr_in));
79 #ifdef  SIOCGIFBRDADDR
80                      if (flags & IFF_BROADCAST) {
81                          Ioctl(sockfd, SIOCGIFBRDADDR, &ifrcopy);
82                          sinptr = (struct sockaddr_in *) &ifrcopy.ifr_broadaddr;
83                          ifi->ifi_brdaddr = Calloc(1, sizeof(struct sockaddr_in));
84                          memcpy(ifi->ifi_brdaddr, sinptr, sizeof(struct sockaddr_in));
85                      }
86 #endif
87 #ifdef  SIOCGIFDSTADDR
88                      if (flags & IFF_POINTOPOINT) {
89                          Ioctl(sockfd, SIOCGIFDSTADDR, &ifrcopy);
90                          sinptr = (struct sockaddr_in *) &ifrcopy.ifr_dstaddr;
91                          ifi->ifi_dstaddr = Calloc(1, sizeof(struct sockaddr_in));
92                          memcpy(ifi->ifi_dstaddr, sinptr, sizeof(struct sockaddr_in));
93                      }
94 #endif
95                  }
96                  break;

97              default:
98                  break;
99              }
100         }
101     free(buf);
102     return (ifihead);              /* pointer to first structure in linked list */
103 }
```
―――――――――――――――――――――――――――――――――――― *ioctl/get_ifi_info.c*

Figure 16.9 Fetch and return interface addresses.

73-78   We copy the IP address that was returned from our original SIOCGIFCONF request in the structure we are building.

79-96   If the interface supports broadcasting, we fetch the broadcast address with an ioctl of SIOCGIFBRDADDR. We allocate memory for the socket address structure containing this address and add it to the ifi_info structure that we are building. Similarly, if the interface is a point-to-point interface, the SIOCGIFDSTADDR returns the IP address of the other end of the link.

> There is not a case for AF_INET6 because as we mentioned earlier, it is not known whether IPv6 implementations will return IPv6 addresses with the SIOCGIFCONF request or not.

Figure 16.10 shows the free_ifi_info function, which takes a pointer that was returned by get_ifi_info and frees all the dynamic memory.

——————————————————————————————— ioctl/get_ifi_info.c

```
104 void
105 free_ifi_info(struct ifi_info *ifihead)
106 {
107     struct ifi_info *ifi, *ifinext;

108     for (ifi = ifihead; ifi != NULL; ifi = ifinext) {
109         if (ifi->ifi_addr != NULL)
110             free(ifi->ifi_addr);
111         if (ifi->ifi_brdaddr != NULL)
112             free(ifi->ifi_brdaddr);
113         if (ifi->ifi_dstaddr != NULL)
114             free(ifi->ifi_dstaddr);
115         ifinext = ifi->ifi_next;    /* can't fetch ifi_next after free() */
116         free(ifi);                  /* the ifi_info{} itself */
117     }
118 }
```

——————————————————————————————— ioctl/get_ifi_info.c

Figure 16.10 `free_ifi_info` function: free dynamic memory allocated by `get_ifi_info`.

16.7 Interface Operations

As we showed in the previous section, the `SIOCGIFCONF` request returns the name and a socket address structure for each interface that is configured. There are a multitude of other requests that we can then issue to set or get all the other characteristics of the interface. The *get* version of these requests (`SIOCG`*xxx*) is often issued by the `netstat` program, and the *set* version (`SIOCS`*xxx*) is often issued by the `ifconfig` program. Any user can get the interface information, while it takes superuser privileges to set the information.

These requests take or return an `ifreq` structure whose address is specified as the third argument to `ioctl`. The interface is always identified by its name: `le0`, `lo0`, `ppp0`, or whatever in the `ifr_name` member.

Many of these requests use a socket address structure to specify or return an IP address or address mask with the application. For IPv4, the address or mask is contained in the `sin_addr` member of an Internet socket address structure.

`SIOCGIFADDR`   Return the unicast address in the `ifr_addr` member.

`SIOCSIFADDR`   Sets the interface address from the `ifr_addr` member. The initialization function for the interface is also called.

`SIOCGIFFLAGS`   Return the interface flags in the `ifr_flags` member. The names of the various flags are IFF_*xxx* and are defined by including the `<net/if.h>` header. The flags indicate, for example, if the interface is up (`IFF_UP`), if the interface is a point-to-point interface (`IFF_POINTOPOINT`), if the interface supports broadcasting (`IFF_BROADCAST`), and so on.

`SIOCSIFFLAGS`   Set the interface flags from the `ifr_flags` member.

SIOCGIFDSTADDR Return the point-to-point address in the `ifr_dstaddr` member.

SIOCSIFDSTADDR Set the point-to-point address from the `ifr_dstaddr` member.

SIOCGIFBRDADDR Return the broadcast address in the `ifr_broadaddr` member. The application must first fetch the interface flags and then issue the correct request: `SIOCGIFBRDADDR` for a broadcast interface or `SIOCGIFDSTADDR` for a point-to-point interface.

SIOCSIFBRDADDR Set the broadcast address from the `ifr_broadaddr` member.

SIOCGIFNETMASK Return the subnet mask in the `ifr_addr` member.

SIOCSIFNETMASK Set the subnet mask from the `ifr_addr` member.

SIOCGIFMETRIC   Return the interface metric in the `ifr_metric` member. The interface metric is maintained by the kernel for each interface but is used by the routing daemon `routed`. The interface metric is added to the hop count (to make an interface less favorable).

SIOCSIFMETRIC   Set the interface routing metric from the `ifr_metric` member.

In this section we have described the generic interface requests. Many implementations have added additional requests.

16.8 ARP Cache Operations

The ARP cache is also manipulated with the `ioctl` function. These requests use an `arpreq` structure, shown in Figure 16.11 and defined by including the `<net/if_arp.h>` header.

```
                                                            ── <net/if_arp.h>
struct arpreq {
    struct  sockaddr  arp_pa;      /* protocol address */
    struct  sockaddr  arp_ha;      /* hardware address */
    int               arp_flags;   /* flags */
};

#define  ATF_INUSE       0x01  /* entry in use */
#define  ATF_COM         0x02  /* completed entry (hardware addr valid) */
#define  ATF_PERM        0x04  /* permanent entry */
#define  ATF_PUBL        0x08  /* published entry (respond for other host) */
                                                            ── <net/if_arp.h>
```

Figure 16.11 `arpreq` structure used with `ioctl` requests for ARP cache.

The third argument to `ioctl` must point to one of these structures. The following three *request*s are supported:

SIOCSARP   Add a new entry to the ARP cache or modify an existing entry. `arp_pa` is an Internet socket address structure containing the IP address and arp_ha is a generic socket address structure with sa_family set to AF_UNSPEC and sa_data containing the hardware address (e.g., the 6-byte Ethernet address). The two flags ATF_PERM and ATF_PUBL can be specified by the application. The other two flags, ATF_INUSE and ATF_COM, are set by the kernel.

SIOCDARP   Delete an entry from the ARP cache. The caller specifies the Internet address for the entry to be deleted.

SIOCGARP   Get an entry from the ARP cache. The caller specifies the Internet address and the corresponding Ethernet address is returned along with the flags.

Only the superuser can add or delete an entry. These three requests are normally issued by the arp program.

> These ARP-related ioctl requests are not supported on some newer systems, which use routing sockets for these ARP operations.

Notice that there is no way with ioctl to list all the entries in the ARP cache. Most versions of the arp command, when invoked with the -a flag (list all entries in the ARP cache), read the kernel's memory (/dev/kmem) to obtain the current contents of the ARP cache. We will see an easier (and better) way to do this using sysctl in Section 17.4.

Example: Print Hardware Addresses of Host

We now use our my_addrs function from Figure 9.7 to return all of a host's IP addresses, followed by an ioctl of SIOCGARP for each IP address, to obtain and print the hardware addresses. We show our program in Figure 16.12.

Get list of addresses and loop through each one

12–13   We call my_addrs to obtain the host's IP addresses and then loop through each address.

Print IP address

14–17   We print the IP address using inet_ntop and then switch based on the address family returned by gethostbyname. We handle only IPv4 addresses, as vendors will probably not support IPv6 addresses with the SIOCGARP request.

Issue ioctl and print hardware address

18–26   We fill in the arp_pa structure as an IPv4 socket address structure containing the IPv4 address. ioctl is called and the resulting hardware address is printed.

Running this program on our solaris host gives:

```
solaris % prmac
206.62.226.33: 8:0:20:78:e3:e3
```

———————————————————————————————————— ioctl/prmac.c

```
 1 #include    "unp.h"
 2 #include    <net/if_arp.h>

 3 int
 4 main(int argc, char **argv)
 5 {
 6     int     family, sockfd;
 7     char    str[INET6_ADDRSTRLEN];
 8     char    **pptr;
 9     unsigned char *ptr;
10     struct arpreq arpreq;
11     struct sockaddr_in *sin;

12     pptr = my_addrs(&family);
13     for ( ; *pptr != NULL; pptr++) {
14         printf("%s: ", Inet_ntop(family, *pptr, str, sizeof(str)));
15         switch (family) {
16         case AF_INET:
17             sockfd = Socket(AF_INET, SOCK_DGRAM, 0);

18             sin = (struct sockaddr_in *) &arpreq.arp_pa;
19             bzero(sin, sizeof(struct sockaddr_in));
20             sin->sin_family = AF_INET;
21             memcpy(&sin->sin_addr, *pptr, sizeof(struct in_addr));

22             Ioctl(sockfd, SIOCGARP, &arpreq);

23             ptr = &arpreq.arp_ha.sa_data[0];
24             printf("%x:%x:%x:%x:%x:%x\n", *ptr, *(ptr + 1),
25                     *(ptr + 2), *(ptr + 3), *(ptr + 4), *(ptr + 5));
26             break;

27         default:
28             err_quit("unsupported address family: %d", family);
29         }
30     }
31     exit(0);
32 }
```

———————————————————————————————————— ioctl/prmac.c

Figure 16.12 Print a host's hardware addresses.

16.9 Routing Table Operations

Two ioctl requests are provided to operate on the routing table. These two requests
require that the third argument to ioctl be a pointer to an rtentry structure, which is
defined by including the <net/route.h> header. These requests are normally issued
by the route program. Only the superuser can issue these requests.

SIOCADDRT   Add an entry to the routing table.

SIOCDELRT   Delete an entry from the routing table.

There is no way with `ioctl` to list all the entries in the routing table. This operation is usually performed by the `netstat` program when invoked with the `-r` flag. This program obtains the routing table by reading the kernel's memory (`/dev/kmem`). As with listing the ARP cache, we will see an easier (and better) way to do this using `sysctl` in Section 17.4.

16.10 Summary

The `ioctl` commands that are used in network programs can be divided into six categories:

- socket operations (are we at the out-of-band mark?),
- file operations (set or clear the nonblocking flag),
- interface operations (return interface list, obtain broadcast address),
- ARP table operations (create, modify, get, delete),
- routing table operations (add or delete), and
- streams system (Chapter 33).

We will use the socket and file operations and obtaining the interface list is such a common operation that we developed our own function to do this. We will use this function numerous times in the remainder of the text. Only a few specialized programs use the `ioctl`s with the ARP cache and the routing table.

Exercises

16.1 In Section 16.7 we said that the broadcast address returned by the `SIOCGIFBRDADDR` request is returned in the `ifr_broadaddr` member. But on p. 173 of TCPv2 notice that it is returned in the `ifr_dstaddr` member. Does this matter?

16.2 Modify the `get_ifi_info` program to issue its first `SIOCGIFCONF` request for one `ifreq` structure and then increment the length each time around the loop by the size of one of these structures. Then put some statements in the loop to print the buffer size each time the request is issued, whether or not `ioctl` returns an error, and upon success print the returned buffer length. Run the `prifinfo` program and see how your system handles this request when the buffer size is too small. Also print the address family for any returned structures whose address family is not the desired value to see what other structures are returned by your system.

16.3 Modify the `get_ifi_info` function to return information about an alias address if the additional address is on a different subnet from the previous address for this interface. That is, our version in Section 16.5 ignored the aliases 206.62.226.44 through 206.62.226.46, which is OK since they are on the same subnet as the primary address for the interface, 206.62.226.33. But if, in this example, an alias is on a different subnet, say 192.3.4.5, return an `ifi_info` structure with the information about the additional address.

16.4 If your system supports the `SIOCGIFNUM` ioctl, then modify Figure 16.7 to issue this request and use the return value as the initial buffer size guess.

17

Routing Sockets

17.1 Introduction

Traditionally the Unix routing table within the kernel has been accessed using `ioctl` commands. In Section 16.9 we described the two commands that are provided: `SIOCADDRT` and `SIOCDELRT`, to add or delete a route. We also mentioned that no command exists to dump the entire routing table, and instead programs such as `netstat` read the kernel memory to obtain the contents of the routing table. One additional piece to this hodgepodge is that routing daemons such as `gated` need to monitor ICMP redirect messages that are received by the kernel, and they often do this by creating a raw ICMP socket (Chapter 25) and listening on this socket to all received ICMP messages.

4.3BSD Reno cleaned up the interface to the kernel's routing subsystem by creating the `AF_ROUTE` domain. The only type of socket supported in the route domain is a raw socket. Three types of operations are supported on a routing socket.

1. A process can send a message to the kernel by writing to a routing socket. For example, this is how routes are added and deleted.

2. A process can read a message from the kernel on a routing socket. This is how the kernel notifies a process that an ICMP redirect has been received and processed.

   Some operations involve both steps: for example, the process sends a message to the kernel on a routing socket asking for all the information on a given route, and the process reads back the response from the kernel on the routing socket.

3. A process can use the `sysctl` function (Section 17.4) to either dump the routing table or to list all the configured interfaces.

The first two operations require superuser privileges, while the last operation can be performed by any process.

> Technically, the third operation is not performed using a routing socket but invokes the generic sysctl function. But we will see that one of the input parameters is the address family, which is AF_ROUTE for the operations we describe in this chapter, and the information returned is in the same format as the information returned by the kernel on a routing socket. Indeed, the sysctl processing for the AF_ROUTE family is part of the routing socket code in a 4.4BSD kernel (pp. 632–643 of TCPv2).

> The sysctl utility appeared in 4.4BSD. Unfortunately not all implementations that support routing sockets provide sysctl. For example, AIX 4.2, Digital Unix 4.0, and Solaris 2.6 all support routing sockets, but none supports sysctl.

17.2 Datalink Socket Address Structure

We will encounter the datalink socket address structures as return values contained in some of the messages returned on a routing socket. Figure 17.1 shows the definition of the structure, defined by including <net/if_dl.h>.

```
struct sockaddr_dl {
    uint8_t      sdl_len;
    sa_family_t  sdl_family;   /* AF_LINK */
    uint16_t     sdl_index;    /* system assigned index, if > 0 */
    uint8_t      sdl_type;     /* IFT_ETHER, etc. from <net/if_types.h> */
    uint8_t      sdl_nlen;     /* name length, starting in sdl_data[0] */
    uint8_t      sdl_alen;     /* link-layer address length */
    uint8_t      sdl_slen;     /* link-layer selector length */
    char         sdl_data[12]; /* minimum work area, can be larger;
                                  contains i/f name and link-layer address */
};
```

Figure 17.1 Datalink socket address structure.

Each interface has a unique positive index, and we will see this returned by the if_nametoindex and if_nameindex functions later in this chapter, along with the IPv6 multicasting socket options in Chapter 19.

The sdl_data member contains both the name and link-layer address (e.g., the 48-bit MAC address for an Ethernet interface). The name begins at sdl_data[0] and is not null terminated. The link-layer address begins sdl_nlen bytes after the name. This header defines the following macro to return the pointer to the link-layer address:

```
#define LLADDR(s)  ((caddr_t)((s)->sdl_data + (s)->sdl_nlen))
```

These socket address structures are variable length (p. 89 of TCPv2). If the link-layer address and name exceed 12 bytes, the structure will be larger than 20 bytes. The size is normally rounded up to the next multiple of 4 bytes, on 32-bit systems. We will also see in Figure 20.3 that when one of these structures is returned by the IP_RECVIF socket option, all three lengths are 0 and there is no sdl_data member at all.

17.3 Reading and Writing

After a process creates a routing socket, it can send commands to the kernel by writing to the socket and read information from the kernel by reading from the socket. There are 12 different routing commands, 5 of which can be issued by the process. These are defined by including the `<net/route.h>` header and are shown in Figure 17.2.

Message type	To kernel?	From kernel?	Description	Structure type
RTM_ADD	•	•	add route	rt_msghdr
RTM_CHANGE	•	•	change gateway, metrics, or flags	rt_msghdr
RTM_DELADDR		•	address being removed from interface	ifa_msghdr
RTM_DELETE	•	•	delete route	rt_msghdr
RTM_GET	•	•	report metrics and other route information	rt_msghdr
RTM_IFINFO		•	interface going up, down, etc.	if_msghdr
RTM_LOCK	•	•	lock specified metrics	rt_msghdr
RTM_LOSING		•	kernel suspects route is failing	rt_msghdr
RTM_MISS		•	lookup failed on this address	rt_msghdr
RTM_NEWADDR		•	address being added to interface	ifa_msghdr
RTM_REDIRECT		•	kernel told to use different route	rt_msghdr
RTM_RESOLVE		•	request to resolve destination to link-layer address	rt_msghdr

Figure 17.2 Types of messages exchanged across a routing socket.

Three different structures are exchanged across a routing socket, as shown in the final column of this figure: `rt_msghdr`, `if_msghdr`, and `ifa_msghdr`, which we show in Figure 17.3.

```
struct rt_msghdr {      /* from <net/route.h> */
  u_short  rtm_msglen;    /* to skip over non-understood messages */
  u_char   rtm_version;   /* future binary compatibility */
  u_char   rtm_type;      /* message type */

  u_short  rtm_index;     /* index for associated ifp */
  int      rtm_flags;     /* flags, incl. kern & message, e.g., DONE */
  int      rtm_addrs;     /* bitmask identifying sockaddrs in msg */
  pid_t    rtm_pid;       /* identify sender */
  int      rtm_seq;       /* for sender to identify action */
  int      rtm_errno;     /* why failed */
  int      rtm_use;       /* from rtentry */
  u_long   rtm_inits;     /* which metrics we are initializing */
  struct rt_metrics  rtm_rmx; /* metrics themselves */
};
struct if_msghdr {      /* from <net/if.h> */
  u_short  ifm_msglen;    /* to skip over non-understood messages */
  u_char   ifm_version;   /* future binary compatibility */
  u_char   ifm_type;      /* message type */

  int      ifm_addrs;     /* like rtm_addrs */
  int      ifm_flags;     /* value of if_flags */
  u_short  ifm_index;     /* index for associated ifp */
  struct if_data  ifm_data;/* statistics and other data about if */
};
```

```
struct ifa_msghdr {    /* from <net/if.h> */
  u_short  ifam_msglen;  /* to skip over non-understood messages */
  u_char   ifam_version; /* future binary compatibility */
  u_char   ifam_type;    /* message type */

  int      ifam_addrs;   /* like rtm_addrs */
  int      ifam_flags;   /* value of ifa_flags */
  u_short  ifam_index;   /* index for associated ifp */
  int      ifam_metric;  /* value of ifa_metric */
};
```

Figure 17.3 The three structures returned with routing messages.

The first three members of each structure are the same: length, version, and type of message. The type is one of the constants from the first column in Figure 17.2. The length member allows an application to skip over message types that it does not understand.

The members `rtm_addrs`, `ifm_addrs`, and `ifam_addrs` are bitmasks specifying which of eight possible socket address structures follow the message. Figure 17.4 shows the constants and values for this bitmask, which are defined by including the `<net/route.h>` header.

Bitmask		Array index		
Constant	Value	Constant	Value	Socket address structure containing
RTA_DST	0x01	RTAX_DST	0	destination address
RTA_GATEWAY	0x02	RTAX_GATEWAY	1	gateway address
RTA_NETMASK	0x04	RTAX_NETMASK	2	network mask
RTA_GENMASK	0x08	RTAX_GENMASK	3	cloning mask
RTA_IFP	0x10	RTAX_IFP	4	interface name
RTA_IFA	0x20	RTAX_IFA	5	interface address
RTA_AUTHOR	0x40	RTAX_AUTHOR	6	author of redirect
RTA_BRD	0x80	RTAX_BRD	7	broadcast or point-to-point destination address
		RTAX_MAX	8	max #elements

Figure 17.4 Constants used to refer to socket address structures in routing messages.

When multiple socket address structures are present, they are always in the order shown in the table.

Example: Fetch and Print a Routing Table Entry

We now show an example using routing sockets. Our program takes a command-line argument consisting of an IPv4 dotted-decimal address and sends an `RTM_GET` message to the kernel for this address. The kernel looks up the address in its IPv4 routing table and returns an `RTM_GET` message with information about the routing table entry. For example, if we execute

```
bsdi # getrt 4.5.6.7
dest: 0.0.0.0
gateway: 206.62.226.62
netmask: 0.0.0.0
```

on our host `bsdi`, we see that this destination address uses the default route (which is stored in the routing table with a destination IP address of 0.0.0.0 and a mask of 0.0.0.0). The next-hop router is our router `gw` (recall Figure 1.16). If we execute

```
bsdi # getrt 206.62.226.32
dest: 206.62.226.32
gateway: AF_LINK, index=2
netmask: 255.255.255.224
```

specifying the main Ethernet as the destination, the destination is the network itself. The gateway is now the outgoing interface, returned as a `sockaddr_dl` structure with an interface index of 2.

Before showing the source code we show what we write to the routing socket in Figure 17.5 along with what is returned by the kernel.

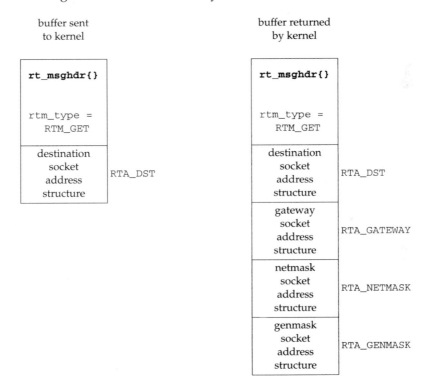

Figure 17.5 Data exchanged with kernel across routing socket for RTM_GET command.

We build a buffer containing an `rt_msghdr` structure followed by a socket address structure containing the destination address for the kernel to look up. The `rtm_type` is RTM_GET and the `rmt_addrs` is RTA_DST (recall Figure 17.4), indicating that the only socket address structure following the `rt_msghdr` structure is one containing the destination address. This command can be used with any protocol family (that provides a routing table) because the family of the address to look up is contained in the socket address structure.

After sending the message to the kernel we `read` back the reply, and it has the format shown in the right of Figure 17.5: an `rt_msghdr` structure followed by up to four socket address structures. Which of the four socket address structures get returned depends on the routing table entry and we are told which if the four by the value in the `rtm_addrs` member of the returned `rt_msghdr` structure. The family of each socket address structure is contained in the `sa_family` member, and as we saw in our examples earlier, one time the returned gateway was an IPv4 socket address structure and the next time it was a datalink socket address structure.

Figure 17.6 shows the first part of our program.

route/getrt.c
```
 1 #include      "unproute.h"

 2 #define BUFLEN  (sizeof(struct rt_msghdr) + 512)
 3                                /*  * sizeof(struct sockaddr_in6) = 192 */
 4 #define SEQ     9999

 5 int
 6 main(int argc, char **argv)
 7 {
 8     int     sockfd;
 9     char    *buf;
10     pid_t   pid;
11     ssize_t n;
12     struct rt_msghdr *rtm;
13     struct sockaddr *sa, *rti_info[RTAX_MAX];
14     struct sockaddr_in *sin;

15     if (argc != 2)
16         err_quit("usage: getrt <IPaddress>");

17     sockfd = Socket(AF_ROUTE, SOCK_RAW, 0);      /* need superuser privileges */

18     buf = Calloc(1, BUFLEN);    /* and initialized to 0 */

19     rtm = (struct rt_msghdr *) buf;
20     rtm->rtm_msglen = sizeof(struct rt_msghdr) + sizeof(struct sockaddr_in);
21     rtm->rtm_version = RTM_VERSION;
22     rtm->rtm_type = RTM_GET;
23     rtm->rtm_addrs = RTA_DST;
24     rtm->rtm_pid = pid = getpid();
25     rtm->rtm_seq = SEQ;
26     sin = (struct sockaddr_in *) (rtm + 1);
27     sin->sin_family = AF_INET;
28     Inet_pton(AF_INET, argv[1], &sin->sin_addr);

29     Write(sockfd, rtm, rtm->rtm_msglen);

30     do {
31         n = Read(sockfd, rtm, BUFLEN);
32     } while (rtm->rtm_type != RTM_GET || rtm->rtm_seq != SEQ ||
33              rtm->rtm_pid != pid);
```
route/getrt.c

Figure 17.6 First half of program to issue `RTM_GET` command on routing socket.

1-3   Our `unproute.h` header includes some files that are needed and then includes our `unp.h` file. The constant `BUFLEN` is the size of the buffer that we allocate to hold our message to the kernel, along with the kernel's reply. We need room for one `rt_msghdr` structure and possibly eight socket address structures (the maximum number that are ever returned on a routing socket). Since an IPv6 socket address structure is 24 bytes in size, the value of 512 is more than adequate.

Create routing socket

17   We create a raw socket in the `AF_ROUTE` domain, and as we said earlier, this requires superuser privileges. A buffer is allocated and initialized to 0.

Fill in `rt_msghdr` structure

18-25   We fill in the structure with our request. We store our process ID and a sequence number of our choosing in the structure. We will compare these values in the responses that we read, looking for the correct reply.

Fill in Internet socket address structure with destination

26-28   Following the `rt_msghdr` structure, we build a `sockaddr_in` structure containing the destination IPv4 address for the kernel to look up in its routing table. All we set are the address family and the address.

`write` message to kernel and `read` reply

29-33   We `write` the message to the kernel and `read` back the reply. Since other processes may have routing sockets open, and since the kernel passes a copy of all routing messages to all routing sockets, we must check the message type, sequence number, and process ID to verify that the message received is the one we are waiting for.

The last half of this program is shown in Figure 17.7. This half processes the reply.

―――――――――――――――――― route/getrt.c

```
34      rtm = (struct rt_msghdr *) buf;
35      sa = (struct sockaddr *) (rtm + 1);
36      get_rtaddrs(rtm->rtm_addrs, sa, rti_info);
37      if ( (sa = rti_info[RTAX_DST]) != NULL)
38          printf("dest: %s\n", Sock_ntop_host(sa, sa->sa_len));

39      if ( (sa = rti_info[RTAX_GATEWAY]) != NULL)
40          printf("gateway: %s\n", Sock_ntop_host(sa, sa->sa_len));

41      if ( (sa = rti_info[RTAX_NETMASK]) != NULL)
42          printf("netmask: %s\n", Sock_masktop(sa, sa->sa_len));

43      if ( (sa = rti_info[RTAX_GENMASK]) != NULL)
44          printf("genmask: %s\n", Sock_masktop(sa, sa->sa_len));

45      exit(0);
46  }
```

―――――――――――――――――― route/getrt.c

Figure 17.7 Last half of program to issue `RTM_GET` command on routing socket.

34-35   `rtm` points to the `rt_msghdr` structure and `sa` points to the first socket address structure that follows.

36   `rtm_addrs` is a bitmask of which of the eight possible socket address structure follow the `rt_msghdr` structure. Our `get_rtaddrs` function (which we show next)
takes this mask, and the pointer to the first socket address structure (`sa`), and fills in the
array `rti_info` with pointers to the corresponding socket address structures. Assuming that all four socket address structure shown in Figure 17.5 are returned by the kernel, the resulting `rti_info` array will be as shown in Figure 17.8.

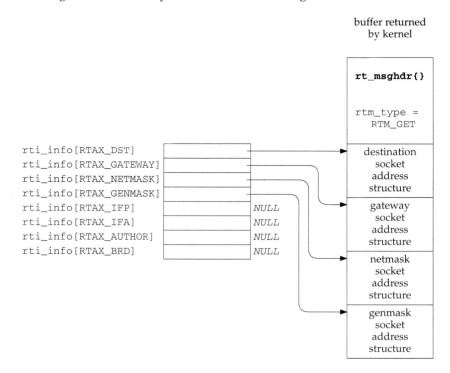

Figure 17.8 `rti_info` structure filled in by our `get_rtaddrs` function.

Our program then goes through the `rti_info` array, doing what it wants with all the
nonnull pointers in the array.

37–44   Each of the four possible addresses are printed, if present. We call our
`sock_ntop_host` function to print the destination address and the gateway address,
but call our `sock_masktop` to print the two masks. We show this new function shortly.

Figure 17.9 shows our `get_rtaddrs` function that we called from Figure 17.7.

Loop through eight possible pointers

17–23   RTAX_MAX is 8 in Figure 17.4, the maximum number of socket address structures
that are returned in a routing message from the kernel. The loop in this function looks
at each of the eight RTA_*xxx* bitmask constants from Figure 17.4 that can be set in the
`rtm_addrs`, `ifm_addrs`, or `ifam_addrs` members of the structures in Figure 17.3. If
the bit is set, the corresponding element in the `rti_info` array is set to the pointer to
the socket address structure; otherwise the array element is set to a null pointer.

libroute/get_rtaddrs.c

```
 1 #include     "unproute.h"

 2 /*
 3  * Round up 'a' to next multiple of 'size'
 4  */
 5 #define ROUNDUP(a, size) (((a) & ((size)-1)) ? (1 + ((a) | ((size)-1))) : (a))

 6 /*
 7  * Step to next socket address structure;
 8  * if sa_len is 0, assume it is sizeof(u_long).
 9  */
10 #define NEXT_SA(ap) ap = (struct sockaddr *) \
11     ((caddr_t) ap + (ap->sa_len ? ROUNDUP(ap->sa_len, sizeof (u_long)) : \
12                                   sizeof(u_long)))

13 void
14 get_rtaddrs(int addrs, struct sockaddr *sa, struct sockaddr **rti_info)
15 {
16     int     i;

17     for (i = 0; i < RTAX_MAX; i++) {
18         if (addrs & (1 << i)) {
19             rti_info[i] = sa;
20             NEXT_SA(sa);
21         } else
22             rti_info[i] = NULL;
23     }
24 }
```

libroute/get_rtaddrs.c

Figure 17.9 Build array of pointers to socket address structures in routing message.

Step to next socket address structure

2-12   The socket address structures are variable length, but this code assumes that each has an sa_len field specifying its length. There are two complications that must be handled. First, the two masks, the network mask and the cloning mask, can be returned in a socket address structure with an sa_len of 0, but this really occupies the size of an unsigned long. (Chapter 19 of TCPv2 discusses the cloning feature of the 4.4BSD routing table.) This value represents a mask of all zero bits, which we printed as 0.0.0.0 for the network mask of the default route in our earlier example. Second, each socket address structure can be padded at the end so that the next one begins on a specific boundary, which in this case is the size of an unsigned long (e.g., a 4-byte boundary for a 32-bit architecture). Although sockaddr_in structures occupy 16 bytes, which requires no padding, the masks often have padding at the end.

The last function that we must show for our example program is sock_masktop in Figure 17.10, which returns the presentation string for one of the two mask values that can be returned. Masks are stored in socket address structures. The sa_family member is undefined but they do contain an sa_len of 0, 5, 6, 7, or 8 for 32-bit IPv4 masks. When the length is greater than 0, the actual mask starts at the same offset from the beginning as does the IPv4 address in a sockaddr_in structure: 4 bytes from the

beginning of the structure (as shown in Figure 18.21, p. 577 of TCPv2), which is the
`sa_data[2]` member of the generic socket address structure.

```
                                                                  ─ libroute/sock_masktop.c
 1 #include    "unproute.h"

 2 char *
 3 sock_masktop(struct sockaddr *sa, socklen_t salen)
 4 {
 5     static char str[INET6_ADDRSTRLEN];
 6     unsigned char *ptr = &sa->sa_data[2];

 7     if (sa->sa_len == 0)
 8         return ("0.0.0.0");
 9     else if (sa->sa_len == 5)
10         snprintf(str, sizeof(str), "%d.0.0.0", *ptr);
11     else if (sa->sa_len == 6)
12         snprintf(str, sizeof(str), "%d.%d.0.0", *ptr, *(ptr + 1));
13     else if (sa->sa_len == 7)
14         snprintf(str, sizeof(str), "%d.%d.%d.0", *ptr, *(ptr + 1), *(ptr + 2));
15     else if (sa->sa_len == 8)
16         snprintf(str, sizeof(str), "%d.%d.%d.%d",
17                      *ptr, *(ptr + 1), *(ptr + 2), *(ptr + 3));
18     else
19         snprintf(str, sizeof(str), "(unknown mask, len = %d, family = %d)",
20                      sa->sa_len, sa->sa_family);
21     return (str);
22 }
                                                                  ─ libroute/sock_masktop.c
```

Figure 17.10 Convert a mask value to its presentation format.

7-21   If the length is 0, the implied mask is 0.0.0.0. If the length is 5, only the first byte of
the 32-bit mask is stored, with an implied value of 0 for the remaining 3 bytes. When
the length is 8, all 4 bytes of the mask are stored.

In this example we want to read the kernel's reply, because the reply contains the
information we are looking for. But in general the return value from our `write` to the
routing socket tells us if the command succeeded or not. If that is all the information we
need, we can call `shutdown` with a second argument of `SHUT_RD` to prevent a reply
from being sent. For example, if we are deleting a route, a return of 0 from `write`
means success, while an error return of `ESRCH` means the route could not be found
(p. 608 of TCPv2). Similarly, an error return of `EEXIST` from `write` when adding a
route means the entry already exists. In our example in Figure 17.6, if the routing table
entry does not exist (say our host does not have a default route), then `write` returns an
error of `ESRCH`.

17.4 `sysctl` Operations

Our main interest in routing sockets is the use of the `sysctl` function to examine both
the routing table and the interface list. Whereas the creation of a routing socket (a raw

socket in the AF_ROUTE domain) requires superuser privileges, any process can examine the routing table and the interface list using sysctl.

```
#include <sys/param.h>
#include <sys/sysctl.h>

int sysctl(int *name, u_int namelen, void *oldp, size_t *oldlenp,
           void *newp, size_t newlen);
```

Returns: 0 if OK, −1 on error

This function uses names that look like SNMP (Simple Network Management Protocol) MIB names (Management Information Base). Chapter 25 of TCPv1 talks about SNMP and its MIB in detail. These names are hierarchical.

The *name* argument is an array of integers specifying the name, and *namelen* specifies the number of elements in the array. The first element in the array specifies which subsystem of the kernel the request is directed to. The second element specifies some part of that subsystem, and so on. Figure 17.11 shows the hierarchical arrangement with some of the constants used at the first three levels.

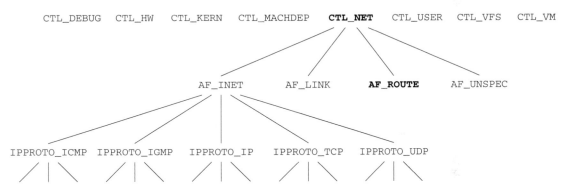

Figure 17.11 Hierarchical arrangement of sysctl names.

To fetch a value, *oldp* points to a buffer into which the kernel stores the value. *oldlenp* is a value–result argument: when the function is called the value pointed to by *oldlenp* specifies the size of this buffer, and on return the value contains the amount of data stored in the buffer by the kernel. If the buffer is not large enough, ENOMEM is returned. As a special case, *oldp* can be a null pointer and *oldlenp* a nonnull pointer, and the kernel determines how much data the call would have returned and returns this size through *oldlenp*.

To set a new value, *newp* points to a buffer of size *newlen*. If a new value is not being specified, *newp* should be a null pointer and *newlen* should be 0.

The sysctl manual page details all the various system information that can be obtained with this function: information on the filesystems, virtual memory, kernel limits, hardware, and so on. Our interest is in the networking subsystem, designated by the first element of the *name* array being set to CTL_NET. (The CTL_*xxx* constants are defined by including the <sys/sysctl.h> header.) The second element can then be

- AF_INET: get or set variables affecting the Internet protocols. The next level specifies the protocol using one of the IPPROTO_*xxx* constants. BSD/OS 3.0 provides about 30 variables at this level, controlling such features as whether the kernel should generate an ICMP redirect, whether TCP should use the RFC 1323 options, whether UDP checksums should be sent, and so on. We show an example of this use of sysctl at the end of this section.

- AF_LINK: get or set link-layer information, such as the number of PPP interfaces.

- AF_ROUTE: return information on either the routing table or the interface list. We describe this information shortly.

- AF_UNSPEC: get or set some socket layer variables, such as the maximum size of a socket send or receive buffer.

When the second element of the *name* array is AF_ROUTE, the third element (a protocol number) is always 0 (since there are not protocols within the AF_ROUTE family, as there are within the AF_INET family, for example), the fourth element is an address family, and the fifth and sixth levels specify what to do. We summarize this in Figure 17.12.

name[ ]	Return IPv4 routing table	Return IPv4 ARP cache	Return interface list
0	CTL_NET	CTL_NET	CTL_NET
1	AF_ROUTE	AF_ROUTE	AF_ROUTE
2	0	0	0
3	AF_INET	AF_INET	AF_INET
4	NET_RT_DUMP	NET_RT_FLAGS	NET_RT_IFLIST
5	0	RTF_LLINFO	0

Figure 17.12 sysctl information returned for route domain.

Three operations are supported, specified by *name*[4]. (The NET_RT_*xxx* constants are defined by including the <sys/socket.h> header.) The information returned by these three operations is returned through the *oldp* pointer in the call to sysctl. This buffer contains a variable number of RTM_*xxx* messages (Figure 17.2).

1. NET_RT_DUMP returns the routing table for the address family specified by *name*[3]. If this address family is 0, the routing tables for all address families are returned.

   The routing table is returned as a variable number of RTM_GET messages with each message followed by up to four socket address structures: the destination, gateway, network mask, and cloning mask of the routing table entry. We showed one of these messages on the right side of Figure 17.5 and our code in Figure 17.7 parsed one of these messages. All that changes with this sysctl operation is that one or more of these messages are returned by the kernel.

2. NET_RT_FLAGS returns the routing table for the address family specified by *name*[3] but only the routing table entries with an RTF_*xxx* flag value that

contains the flag specified by *name*[5]. All ARP cache entries in the routing table have the RTF_LLINFO flag bit set.

The information is returned in the same format as the previous item.

3. NET_RT_IFLIST returns information on all configured interfaces. If *name*[5] is nonzero, it is an interface index number, and only information on that interface is returned. (We say more about interface indexes in Section 17.6.) All the addresses assigned to each interface are also returned and if *name*[3] is nonzero, only addresses for that address family are returned.

For each interface one RTM_IFINFO message is returned, followed by one RTM_NEWADDR message for each address assigned to the interface. The RTM_IFINFO message is followed by one datalink socket address structure and each RTM_NEWADDR message is followed by up to three socket address structures: the interface address, the network mask, and the broadcast address. We show a picture of these two messages in Figure 17.13.

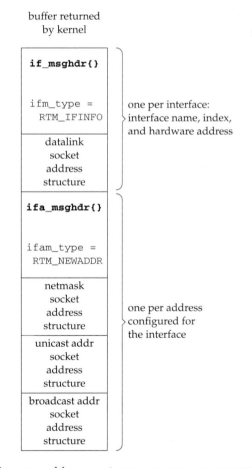

Figure 17.13 Information returned for sysctl, CTL_NET, NET_RT_IFLIST command.

As IPv6 support is added to 4.4BSD-derived kernels, support should be added for the *name*[1] member to be AF_INET6 (to set and fetch IPv6-specific variables), and for *name*[3] in Figure 17.12 to be AF_INET6 (to dump the IPv6 routing table, IPv6 neighbor cache, or to return IPv6 interface addresses).

Example: Determine If UDP Checksums Are Enabled

We now provide a simple example of sysctl with the Internet protocols to check whether UDP checksums are enabled. Some UDP applications (e.g., BIND) check whether UDP checksums are enabled when they start, and if not, try to enable them. Naturally it takes superuser privileges to enable a feature such as this, but all we do now is check whether the feature is enabled or not. Figure 17.14 is our program.

route/checkudpsum.c
```
 1 #include    "unproute.h"
 2 #include    <netinet/udp.h>
 3 #include    <netinet/ip_var.h>
 4 #include    <netinet/udp_var.h> /* for UDPCTL_xxx constants */

 5 int
 6 main(int argc, char **argv)
 7 {
 8     int    mib[5], val;
 9     size_t len;

10     mib[0] = CTL_NET;
11     mib[1] = AF_INET;
12     mib[2] = IPPROTO_UDP;
13     mib[3] = UDPCTL_CHECKSUM;

14     len = sizeof(val);
15     Sysctl(mib, 4, &val, &len, NULL, 0);
16     printf("udp checksum flag: %d\n", val);

17     exit(0);
18 }
```
route/checkudpsum.c

Figure 17.14   Check whether UDP checksums are enabled.

Include system headers

2–4   We must include the <netinet/udp_var.h> header to obtain the definition of the UDP sysctl constants. The two other headers are required for this header.

Call sysctl

10–16   We allocate an integer array with four elements and store the constants that correspond to the hierarchy shown in Figure 17.11. Since we are only fetching a variable, and not storing into a variable, we specify a null pointer for the *newp* argument to sysctl and a value of 0 for the *newlen* argument. *oldp* points to an integer variable of ours into which the result is stored and *oldlenp* points to a value–result variable for the size of this integer. The flag that we print will be either 0 (disabled) or 1 (enabled).

17.5 `get_ifi_info` Function

We now return to the example from Section 16.6: returning all the interfaces that are up as a linked list of `ifi_info` structures (Figure 16.5). The `prifinfo` program remains the same (Figure 16.6) but we now show a version of the `get_ifi_info` function that uses `sysctl` instead of the `SIOCGIFCONF` ioctl that was used in Figure 16.7.

We first show the function `net_rt_iflist` in Figure 17.15. This function calls `sysctl` with the `NET_RT_IFLIST` command to return the interface list for a specified address family.

```
                                                        ─── libroute/net_rt_iflist.c
 1 #include    "unproute.h"

 2 char *
 3 net_rt_iflist(int family, int flags, size_t *lenp)
 4 {
 5     int     mib[6];
 6     char    *buf;

 7     mib[0] = CTL_NET;
 8     mib[1] = AF_ROUTE;
 9     mib[2] = 0;
10     mib[3] = family;            /* only addresses of this family */
11     mib[4] = NET_RT_IFLIST;
12     mib[5] = flags;             /* interface index, or 0 */
13     if (sysctl(mib, 6, NULL, lenp, NULL, 0) < 0)
14         return (NULL);

15     if ( (buf = malloc(*lenp)) == NULL)
16         return (NULL);
17     if (sysctl(mib, 6, buf, lenp, NULL, 0) < 0)
18         return (NULL);

19     return (buf);
20 }
                                                        ─── libroute/net_rt_iflist.c
```

Figure 17.15 Call `sysctl` to return interface list.

7–14   The array `mib` is initialized as shown in Figure 17.12 to return the interface list and all configured addresses of the specified family. `sysctl` is then called twice. In the first call the third argument is null, which returns in the variable pointed to by `lenp` the buffer size required to hold all the interface information.

15–19   Space is then allocated for the buffer and `sysctl` is called again, this time with a nonnull third argument. This time the variable pointed to by `lenp` will contain upon return the amount of information stored in the buffer, and this variable is allocated by the caller. A pointer to the buffer is also returned to the caller.

> Since the size of the routing table or the number of interfaces can change between the two calls to `sysctl`, the value returned by the first call contains a 10% fudge factor (pp. 639–640 of TCPv2).

Figure 17.16 shows the first half of the `get_ifi_info` function.

―――――――――――――――――――――――――――――― *route/get_ifi_info.c*

```
 3  struct ifi_info *
 4  get_ifi_info(int family, int doaliases)
 5  {
 6      int     flags;
 7      char    *buf, *next, *lim;
 8      size_t  len;
 9      struct if_msghdr *ifm;
10      struct ifa_msghdr *ifam;
11      struct sockaddr *sa, *rti_info[RTAX_MAX];
12      struct sockaddr_dl *sdl;
13      struct ifi_info *ifi, *ifisave, *ifihead, **ifipnext;

14      buf = Net_rt_iflist(family, 0, &len);

15      ifihead = NULL;
16      ifipnext = &ifihead;

17      lim = buf + len;
18      for (next = buf; next < lim; next += ifm->ifm_msglen) {
19          ifm = (struct if_msghdr *) next;
20          if (ifm->ifm_type == RTM_IFINFO) {
21              if (((flags = ifm->ifm_flags) & IFF_UP) == 0)
22                  continue;        /* ignore if interface not up */

23              sa = (struct sockaddr *) (ifm + 1);
24              get_rtaddrs(ifm->ifm_addrs, sa, rti_info);
25              if ( (sa = rti_info[RTAX_IFP]) != NULL) {
26                  ifi = Calloc(1, sizeof(struct ifi_info));
27                  *ifipnext = ifi;    /* prev points to this new one */
28                  ifipnext = &ifi->ifi_next;  /* ptr to next one goes here */

29                  ifi->ifi_flags = flags;
30                  if (sa->sa_family == AF_LINK) {
31                      sdl = (struct sockaddr_dl *) sa;
32                      if (sdl->sdl_nlen > 0)
33                          snprintf(ifi->ifi_name, IFI_NAME, "%*s",
34                                  sdl->sdl_nlen, &sdl->sdl_data[0]);
35                      else
36                          snprintf(ifi->ifi_name, IFI_NAME, "index %d",
37                                  sdl->sdl_index);

38                      if ( (ifi->ifi_hlen = sdl->sdl_alen) > 0)
39                          memcpy(ifi->ifi_haddr, LLADDR(sdl),
40                                  min(IFI_HADDR, sdl->sdl_alen));
41                  }
42              }
```

――――――――――――――――――――――――――― *route/get_ifi_info.c*

Figure 17.16 `get_ifi_info` function, first half.

6-14   We declare the local variables and then call our `net_rt_iflist` function.

17-19   The `for` loop steps through each routing message in the buffer filled in by `sysctl`. We assume that the message is an `if_msghdr` structure and look at the `ifm_type` field. (Recall that the first three members of all three structures are identical so it doesn't matter which of the three structures we use to look at the type member.)

Check if interface is up

20-22   An `RTM_IFINFO` structure is returned for each interface. If the interface is not up, it is ignored.

Determine which socket address structures are present

23-24   `sa` points to the first socket address structure following the `if_msghdr` structure. Our `get_rtaddrs` function initializes the `rti_info` array, depending on which socket address structures are present.

Handle interface name

25-42   If the socket address structure with the interface name is present, an `ifi_info` structure is allocated and the interface flags are stored. The expected family of this socket address structure is `AF_LINK`, indicating a datalink socket address structure. If the `sdl_nlen` member is nonzero, then the interface name is copied into the `ifi_info` structure. Otherwise a string containing the interface index is stored as the name. If the `sdl_alen` member is nonzero, then the hardware address (e.g., the Ethernet address) is copied into the `ifi_info` structure and its length is also returned as `ifi_hlen`.

Figure 17.17 shows the second half of our `get_ifi_info` function, which returns the IP addresses for the interface.

Return IP addresses

43-63   An `RTM_NEWADDR` message is returned by `sysctl` for each address associated with the interface: the primary address and all aliases. If we have already filled in the IP address for this interface, then we are dealing with an alias. In that case, if the caller wants the alias address, we must allocate memory for another `ifi_info` structure, copy the fields that have been filled in, and then fill in the addresses that have been returned.

Return broadcast and destination addresses

64-73   If the interface supports broadcasting, the broadcast address is returned and if the interface is a point-to-point interface, the destination address is returned.

route/get_ifi_info.c

```
43              } else if (ifm->ifm_type == RTM_NEWADDR) {
44                  if (ifi->ifi_addr) {    /* already have an IP addr for i/f */
45                      if (doaliases == 0)
46                          continue;

47                          /* we have a new IP addr for existing interface */
48                      ifisave = ifi;
49                      ifi = Calloc(1, sizeof(struct ifi_info));
50                      *ifipnext = ifi;    /* prev points to this new one */
51                      ifipnext = &ifi->ifi_next;  /* ptr to next one goes here */
52                      ifi->ifi_flags = ifisave->ifi_flags;
53                      ifi->ifi_hlen = ifisave->ifi_hlen;
54                      memcpy(ifi->ifi_name, ifisave->ifi_name, IFI_NAME);
55                      memcpy(ifi->ifi_haddr, ifisave->ifi_haddr, IFI_HADDR);
56                  }
57                  ifam = (struct ifa_msghdr *) next;
58                  sa = (struct sockaddr *) (ifam + 1);
59                  get_rtaddrs(ifam->ifam_addrs, sa, rti_info);

60                  if ( (sa = rti_info[RTAX_IFA]) != NULL) {
61                      ifi->ifi_addr = Calloc(1, sa->sa_len);
62                      memcpy(ifi->ifi_addr, sa, sa->sa_len);
63                  }
64                  if ((flags & IFF_BROADCAST) &&
65                      (sa = rti_info[RTAX_BRD]) != NULL) {
66                      ifi->ifi_brdaddr = Calloc(1, sa->sa_len);
67                      memcpy(ifi->ifi_brdaddr, sa, sa->sa_len);
68                  }
69                  if ((flags & IFF_POINTOPOINT) &&
70                      (sa = rti_info[RTAX_BRD]) != NULL) {
71                      ifi->ifi_dstaddr = Calloc(1, sa->sa_len);
72                      memcpy(ifi->ifi_dstaddr, sa, sa->sa_len);
73                  }
74          } else
75              err_quit("unexpected message type %d", ifm->ifm_type);
76      }
77      /* "ifihead" points to the first structure in the linked list */
78      return (ifihead);               /* ptr to first structure in linked list */
79  }
```

route/get_ifi_info.c

Figure 17.17 get_ifi_info function, second half.

17.6   Interface Name and Index Functions

RFC 2133 [Gilligan et al. 1997] defines four functions that deal with interface names and indexes. These four functions are used with IPv6 multicasting, as we describe in Chapter 19. The basic concept is that each interface has a unique name and a unique positive index (0 is never used as an index).

```
#include <net/if.h>

unsigned int if_nametoindex(const char *ifname);
```
                                    Returns: positive interface index if OK, 0 on error
```
char *if_indextoname(unsigned int ifindex, char *ifname);
```
                                    Returns: pointer to interface name if OK, NULL on error
```
struct if_nameindex *if_nameindex(void);
```
                                    Returns: nonnull pointer if OK, NULL on error
```
void if_freenameindex(struct if_nameindex *ptr);
```

`if_nametoindex` returns the index of the interface whose name is *ifname*. `if_indextoname` returns a pointer to the interface name, given its *ifindex*. The *ifname* argument points to a buffer of size `IFNAMSIZ` (defined by including the `<net/if.h>` header; also shown in Figure 16.2) that the caller must allocate to hold the result, and this pointer is also the return value upon success.

`if_nameindex` returns a pointer to an array of `if_nameindex` structures:

```
struct if_nameindex {
  unsigned int   if_index;   /* 1, 2, ... */
  char          *if_name;   /* null terminated name: "le0", ... */
};
```

The final entry in this array contains a structure with an `if_index` of 0 and an `if_name` that is a null pointer. The memory for this array along with the names pointed to by the array members is dynamically obtained and is returned by calling `if_freenameindex`.

We now provide an implementation of these four functions using routing sockets.

`if_nametoindex` Function

Figure 17.18 shows the `if_nametoindex` function.

————————————————————————————— libroute/if_nametoindex.c

```
 1 #include    "unpifi.h"
 2 #include    "unproute.h"

 3 unsigned int
 4 if_nametoindex(const char *name)
 5 {
 6     unsigned int index;
 7     char    *buf, *next, *lim;
 8     size_t  len;
 9     struct if_msghdr *ifm;
10     struct sockaddr *sa, *rti_info[RTAX_MAX];
11     struct sockaddr_dl *sdl;

12     if ( (buf = net_rt_iflist(0, 0, &len)) == NULL)
13         return (0);

14     lim = buf + len;
15     for (next = buf; next < lim; next += ifm->ifm_msglen) {
16         ifm = (struct if_msghdr *) next;
17         if (ifm->ifm_type == RTM_IFINFO) {
18             sa = (struct sockaddr *) (ifm + 1);
19             get_rtaddrs(ifm->ifm_addrs, sa, rti_info);
20             if ( (sa = rti_info[RTAX_IFP]) != NULL) {
21                 if (sa->sa_family == AF_LINK) {
22                     sdl = (struct sockaddr_dl *) sa;
23                     if (strncmp(&sdl->sdl_data[0], name, sdl->sdl_nlen) == 0) {
24                         index = sdl->sdl_index;    /* save before free() */
25                         free(buf);
26                         return (index);
27                     }
28                 }
29             }
30         }
31     }
32     free(buf);
33     return (0);                    /* no match for name */
34 }
```

————————————————————————————— libroute/if_nametoindex.c

Figure 17.18 Return an interface index given its name.

Get interface list

12-13   Our `net_rt_iflist` function returns the interface list.

Process only `RTM_IFINFO` messages

17-30   We process the messages in the buffer (Figure 17.13), looking only for the `RTM_IFINFO` messages. When we find one, we call our `get_rtaddrs` function to set up the pointers to the socket address structures and if an interface name structure is present (the `RTAX_IFP` element of the `rti_info` array), the interface name is compared to the argument.

`if_indextoname` Function

The next function, `if_indextoname`, is shown in Figure 17.19.

—————————————————————————— libroute/if_indextoname.c
```
 1 #include    "unpifi.h"
 2 #include    "unproute.h"

 3 char *
 4 if_indextoname(unsigned int index, char *name)
 5 {
 6     char    *buf, *next, *lim;
 7     size_t  len;
 8     struct if_msghdr *ifm;
 9     struct sockaddr *sa, *rti_info[RTAX_MAX];
10     struct sockaddr_dl *sdl;

11     if ( (buf = net_rt_iflist(0, index, &len)) == NULL)
12         return (NULL);

13     lim = buf + len;
14     for (next = buf; next < lim; next += ifm->ifm_msglen) {
15         ifm = (struct if_msghdr *) next;
16         if (ifm->ifm_type == RTM_IFINFO) {
17             sa = (struct sockaddr *) (ifm + 1);
18             get_rtaddrs(ifm->ifm_addrs, sa, rti_info);
19             if ( (sa = rti_info[RTAX_IFP]) != NULL) {
20                 if (sa->sa_family == AF_LINK) {
21                     sdl = (struct sockaddr_dl *) sa;
22                     if (sdl->sdl_index == index) {
23                         strncpy(name, sdl->sdl_data, sdl->sdl_nlen);
24                         name[sdl->sdl_nlen] = 0;    /* null terminate */
25                         free(buf);
26                         return (name);
27                     }
28                 }
29             }
30         }
31     }
32     free(buf);
33     return (NULL);                    /* no match for index */
34 }
```
—————————————————————————— libroute/if_indextoname.c

Figure 17.19 Return an interface name given its index.

This function is nearly identical to the previous function, but instead of looking for an interface name, we compare the interface index against the caller's argument. Also, the second argument to our `net_rt_iflist` function is the desired index, so the result should contain the information for only the desired interface. When a match is found, the interface name is returned and it is also null terminated.

`if_nameindex` Function

The next function, `if_nameindex`, returns an array of `if_nameindex` structures, containing all the interface names and addresses. It is shown in Figure 17.20.

libroute/if_nameindex.c

```
 1 #include    "unpifi.h"
 2 #include    "unproute.h"

 3 struct if_nameindex *
 4 if_nameindex(void)
 5 {
 6     char    *buf, *next, *lim;
 7     size_t  len;
 8     struct if_msghdr *ifm;
 9     struct sockaddr *sa, *rti_info[RTAX_MAX];
10     struct sockaddr_dl *sdl;
11     struct if_nameindex *result, *ifptr;
12     char    *namptr;

13     if ( (buf = net_rt_iflist(0, 0, &len)) == NULL)
14         return (NULL);

15     if ( (result = malloc(len)) == NULL)     /* overestimate */
16         return (NULL);
17     ifptr = result;
18     namptr = (char *) result + len;      /* names start at end of buffer */

19     lim = buf + len;
20     for (next = buf; next < lim; next += ifm->ifm_msglen) {
21         ifm = (struct if_msghdr *) next;
22         if (ifm->ifm_type == RTM_IFINFO) {
23             sa = (struct sockaddr *) (ifm + 1);
24             get_rtaddrs(ifm->ifm_addrs, sa, rti_info);
25             if ( (sa = rti_info[RTAX_IFP]) != NULL) {
26                 if (sa->sa_family == AF_LINK) {
27                     sdl = (struct sockaddr_dl *) sa;
28                     namptr -= sdl->sdl_nlen + 1;
29                     strncpy(namptr, &sdl->sdl_data[0], sdl->sdl_nlen);
30                     namptr[sdl->sdl_nlen] = 0;   /* null terminate */
31                     ifptr->if_name = namptr;
32                     ifptr->if_index = sdl->sdl_index;
33                     ifptr++;
34                 }
35             }
36         }
37     }
38     ifptr->if_name = NULL;       /* mark end of array of structs */
39     ifptr->if_index = 0;
40     free(buf);
41     return (result);             /* call can free() this when done */
42 }
```

libroute/if_nameindex.c

Figure 17.20 Return all the interface names and indexes.

Get interface list; allocate room for result

13-18   We call our `net_rt_iflist` function to return the interface list. We also use the returned size as the size of the buffer that we allocate to contain the array of `if_nameindex` structures that we return. This is an overestimate but is simpler than making two passes through the interface list: one to count the number of interfaces and the total sizes of the names, and another to fill in the information. We create the `if_nameindex` array at the beginning of this buffer and store the interface names starting at the end of the buffer.

Process only `RTM_IFINFO` messages

22-36   We process all the messages looking for the `RTM_IFINFO` messages, and the datalink socket address structures that follow. The interface name and index are stored in the array that we are building.

Terminate array

38-39   The final entry in the array has a null `if_name` and an index of 0.

`if_freenameindex` Function

The final function, shown in Figure 17.21, frees the memory that was allocated for the array of `if_nameindex` structures and the names contained therein.

libroute/if_nameindex.c
```
43 void
44 if_freenameindex(struct if_nameindex *ptr)
45 {
46     free(ptr);
47 }
```
libroute/if_nameindex.c

Figure 17.21   Free the memory allocated by `if_nameindex`.

This function is trivial because we stored both the array of structures and the names in the same buffer. If we had called `malloc` for each name, then to free the memory we would have to go through the entire array, `free` the memory for each name, and then free the array.

17.7   Summary

The last of the socket address structures that we encounter in this text are `sockaddr_dl` structures, the variable-length datalink socket address structures. Berkeley-derived kernels associate these with interfaces, returning the interface index, name, and hardware address in one of these structures.

Five types of messages can be written to a routing socket by a process and 12 different messages can be returned by the kernel asynchronously on a routing socket. We showed an example where the process asks the kernel for information on a routing table entry, and the kernel responds with all the details. These kernel responses contain up to eight socket address structures and we have to parse this message to obtain each piece of information.

The `sysctl` function is a general way to fetch and store operating system parameters. The information that we are interested in with `sysctl` is

- dumping the interface list,
- dumping the routing table, and
- dumping the ARP cache.

The changes required by IPv6 to the sockets API include four functions to map between interface names and their indexes. Each interface is assigned a unique positive index. Berkeley-derived implementations already associate an index with each interface, so we are easily able to implement these functions using `sysctl`.

Exercises

17.1 What would you expect the `sdl_len` field of a datalink socket address structure to contain for a device named `eth10` whose link-layer address is a 64-bit IEEE EUI-64 address?

17.2 In Figure 17.6 disable the `SO_USELOOPBACK` socket option before calling `write`. What happens?

18

Broadcasting

18.1 Introduction

In this chapter we describe *broadcasting* and the next chapter describes *multicasting*. All the examples in the text so far have dealt with *unicasting*: a process talking to exactly one other process. Indeed, TCP works with only unicast addresses, although UDP supports other paradigms. Figure 18.1 shows a comparison of the different types of addressing.

Type	IPv4 ?	IPv6 ?	TCP ?	UDP ?	# interfaces identified	# interfaces delivered to
unicast	•	•	•	•	one	one
anycast		•	not yet	•	a set	one in set
multicast	opt.	•		•	a set	all in set
broadcast	•			•	all	all

Figure 18.1   Different forms of addressing.

We have added *anycasting* to this figure because IPv6 plans to support it in the future. But today it is an idea that has not yet been implemented. It is described in RFC 1546 [Partridge, Mendez, and Milliken 1993].

The important points in this figure are:

- Multicasting support is optional in IPv4 but mandatory in IPv6.

- Broadcasting support is not provided in IPv6: any IPv4 application that uses broadcasting must be recoded for IPv6 to use multicasting instead.

- Broadcasting and multicasting require UDP; they do not work with TCP.

One use for broadcasting is to locate a server on the local subnet when the server is assumed to be on the local subnet but its unicast IP address is not known. This is sometimes called *resource discovery*. Another use is to minimize the network traffic on a LAN when there are multiple clients communicating with a single server. There are numerous examples of Internet applications that use broadcasting for this purpose.

- ARP (Address Resolution Protocol). Although this is a fundamental part of IPv4, and not a user application, ARP broadcasts a request on the local subnet that says "will the system with an IP address of a.b.c.d please identify yourself and tell me your hardware address."

- BOOTP (Bootstrap Protocol). The client assumes a server is on the local subnet and sends its request to the broadcast address (often 255.255.255.255, since the client doesn't yet know its IP address, its subnet mask, or the limited broadcast address of the subnet).

- NTP (Network Time Protocol). In one common scenario, an NTP client is configured with the IP address of one or more servers to use, and the client polls the servers at some frequency (every 64 seconds or longer). The client updates its clock using sophisticated algorithms based on the time-of-day returned by the servers and the round-trip time to the servers. But on a broadcast LAN, instead of making each of the clients poll a single server, the server can broadcast the current time every 64 seconds for all the clients on the local subnet, reducing the amount of network traffic.

- Routing daemons. The most commonly used routing daemon, `routed`, broadcasts its routing table on a LAN. This allows all other routers attached to the LAN to receive these routing announcements, without each router having to be configured with the IP addresses of its neighbor routers. This feature is also used (many would say "misused") by hosts on the LAN listening to these routing announcements and updating their routing tables accordingly.

We must note that multicasting can replace both uses of broadcasting (resource discovery and reducing network traffic) and we describe the problems with broadcasting later in this chapter and the next chapter.

> Broadcasting to reduce network traffic on a LAN can have an undesirable interaction with diskless systems. Assume an NTP server broadcasts the current time every 64 seconds. If the NTP daemon on all the diskless clients gets paged out of main memory during this time, then every 64 seconds each of these diskless clients receives an NTP datagram and immediately reads the NTP daemon into main memory from its disk server, also on the LAN. Every 64 seconds there is a surge of LAN activity as each diskless client pages in the NTP daemon. Periodicity of this form can be seen with broadcast applications. Fortunately the decreasing price of disk drives is making diskless systems extinct.

18.2   Broadcast Addresses

If we denote an IPv4 address as {*netid, subnetid, hostid*}, then we have four types of broadcast addresses. We denote a field containing all one bits as −1.

1. Subnet-directed broadcast address: {*netid, subnetid, −1*}. This addresses all the interfaces on the specified subnet. For example, if we use an 8-bit subnet ID with the class B address 128.7, then 128.7.6.255 would be the subnet-directed broadcast address for all interfaces on the 128.7.6 subnet.

    Normally routers do not forward these broadcasts (pp. 226−227 of TCPv2). In Figure 18.2 we show a router connected to the two subnets 128.7.1 and 128.7.6.

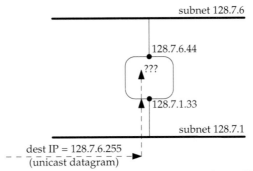

Figure 18.2 Does a router forward a subnet-directed broadcast?

The router receives a unicast IP datagram on the 128.7.1 subnet with a destination address of 128.7.6.255 (the subnet-directed broadcast address of another interface). The router normally does not forward the datagram onto the 128.7.6 subnet. Some systems have a configuration option that allows subnet-directed broadcasts to be forwarded (Appendix E of TCPv1).

2. All-subnets-directed broadcast address: {*netid, −1, −1*}. This addresses all subnets on the specified network. This type of address is rarely, if ever, used.

3. Network-directed broadcast address: {*netid, −1*}. This type of address is used on a network that does not use subnetting, which is almost nonexistent today.

4. Limited broadcast address: {−1, −1, −1} or 255.255.255.255. Datagrams destined to this address must never be forwarded by a router.

Of the four types of broadcast addresses, the subnet-directed broadcast address is the most common today. But some older systems still send datagrams destined to 255.255.255.255. Also, some older systems do not understand a subnet-directed broadcast address and only interpret datagrams sent to 255.255.255.255 as a broadcast.

> The intent of 255.255.255.255 is to be used as the destination address during the bootstrap process by applications such as TFTP and BOOTP that do not yet know the node's IP address.
>
> The question is: what does a host do when an application sends a UDP datagram to 255.255.255.255? Most hosts allow this (assuming the process has set the SO_BROADCAST socket option) and convert the destination address to the subnet-directed broadcast address of the outgoing interface. BSD/OS 3.0 has a new socket option, IP_ONESBCAST, and when set, the destination IP address for broadcasts is set to 255.255.255.255 by the kernel, regardless of which broadcast address (subnet-directed or limited) is specified as the destination of the sendto.

Another question is: what does a multihomed host do when the application sends a UDP datagram to 255.255.255.255? Some systems send a single broadcast on the primary interface (the first interface that was configured) with the destination IP address set to the subnet-directed broadcast address of that interface (p. 736 of TCPv2). Other systems send one copy of the datagram out from each broadcast-capable interface. Section 3.3.6 of RFC 1122 [Braden 1989] "takes no stand" on this issue. For portability, however, if an application needs to send a broadcast out from all broadcast-capable interfaces, it should obtain the interface configuration (Section 16.6) and do one `sendto` for each broadcast-capable interface with the destination set to that interface's broadcast address.

18.3 Unicast versus Broadcast

Before looking at broadcasting let's make certain we understand the steps that take place when a UDP datagram is sent to a unicast address. Figure 18.3 shows three hosts on an Ethernet.

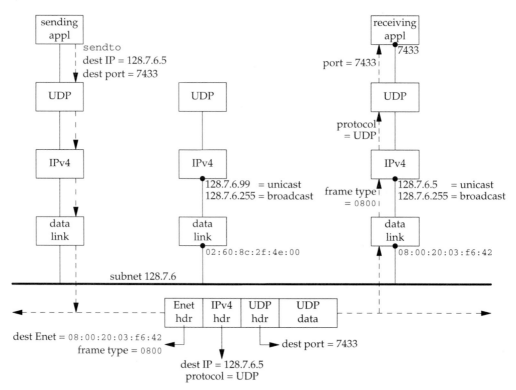

Figure 18.3 Unicast example of a UDP datagram.

The subnet address of the Ethernet is 128.7.6 with 8 bits being used as the subnet ID and 8 bits for the host ID. The application on the left host calls `sendto` on a UDP socket, sending a datagram to 128.7.6.5, port 7433. The UDP layer prepends a UDP header and passes the UDP datagram to the IP layer. IP prepends an IPv4 header, determines the outgoing interface, and in the case of an Ethernet, ARP is invoked to determine the

Ethernet address corresponding to the destination IP address: 08:00:20:03:f6:42. The packet is then sent as an Ethernet frame with that 48-bit address as the destination Ethernet address. The frame type field of the Ethernet frame will be 0800, specifying an IPv4 packet. The frame type for an IPv6 packet is 86dd.

The Ethernet interface on the host in the middle sees the frame pass by and compares the destination Ethernet address with its own Ethernet address (02:60: 9c:2f:4e:00). Since they are not equal, the interface ignores the frame. With a unicast frame there is no overhead whatsoever to this host. The interface ignores the frame.

The Ethernet interface on the host on the right also sees the frame pass by and when it compares the destination Ethernet address with its own Ethernet address, they are equal. This interface reads in the entire frame, probably generates a hardware interrupt when the frame is complete, and the device driver reads the frame from the interface memory. Since the frame type is 0800, the packet is placed onto the IP input queue.

When the IP layer processes the packet, it first compares the destination IP address (128.7.6.5) with all of its own IP addresses. (Recall that a host can be multihomed. Also recall our discussion of the strong end system model and the weak end system model in Section 8.8.) Since the destination address is one of the host's own IP addresses, the packet is accepted.

The IP layer then looks at the protocol field in the IPv4 header, and its value will be 17 for UDP. The IP datagram is passed to UDP.

The UDP layer looks at the destination port (and possibly the source port too, if the UDP socket is connected) and in our example places the datagram onto the appropriate socket receive queue. The process is awakened, if necessary, to read the newly received datagram.

The key point in this example is that a unicast IP datagram is received by only the one host specified by the destination IP address. No other hosts on the subnet are affected.

We now consider a similar example, on the same subnet, but with the sending application writing a UDP datagram to the subnet-directed broadcast address: 128.7.6.255. Figure 18.4 shows the arrangement.

When the host on the left sends the datagram, it notices that the destination IP address is the subnet-directed broadcast address and maps this into the Ethernet address of 48 one bits: ff:ff:ff:ff:ff:ff. This causes *every* Ethernet interface on the subnet to receive the frame. The two hosts on the right of this figure that are running IPv4 will both receive the frame. Since the Ethernet frame type is 0800, both hosts pass the packet to the IP layer. Since the destination IP address matches the broadcast address for each of the two hosts, and since the protocol field is 17 (UDP), both hosts pass the packet up to UDP.

The host on the right passes the UDP datagram to the application that has bound UDP port 520. Nothing special need be done by an application to receive a broadcast UDP datagram: it just creates a UDP socket and binds the application's port number to the socket.

But on the host in the middle, no application has bound UDP port 520. The host's UDP code then discards the received datagram. This host must *not* send an ICMP port unreachable, as doing so could generate a *broadcast storm*: a condition where lots of

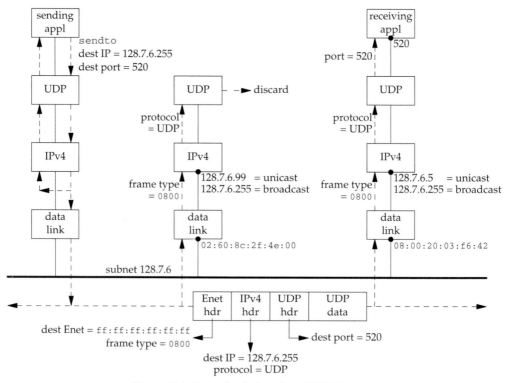

Figure 18.4 Example of a broadcast UDP datagram.

hosts on the subnet generate a response at about the same time, leading to the network being unusable for a few seconds.

In this example we also show the datagram that is output by the host on the left being delivered to itself. This is a property of broadcasts: by definition a broadcast goes to every host on the subnet, which includes the sender (pp. 109–110 of TCPv2). We also assume that the sending application has bound the port that it is sending to (520), so it will receive a copy of each broadcast datagram that it sends. (In general, however, there is no requirement that a process bind a UDP port to which it sends datagrams.)

> In this example we show a logical loopback, performed by either the IP layer or the datalink layer making a copy (pp. 109–110 of TCPv2) and sending the copy up the protocol stack. A network could use a physical loopback, but this can lead to problems in the case of network faults (such as an unterminated Ethernet).

This example shows the fundamental problem with broadcasting: every IPv4 host on the subnet that is not participating in the application must completely process the broadcast UDP datagram all the way up the protocol stack, through and including the UDP layer, before discarding the datagram. (Recall our discussion following Figure 8.21.) Also, every non-IP host on the subnet (say a host running Novell's IPX) must also receive the entire frame at the datalink layer before discarding the frame (assuming the host does not support the frame type, which would be 0800 for an IPv4 datagram). For applications that generate IP datagrams at a high rate (audio or video, for example) this unnecessary processing can severely affect these other hosts on the subnet. We will see in the next chapter how multicasting gets around this problem.

> Our choice of UDP port 520 in Figure 18.4 is intentional. This is the port used by the routed daemon to exchange RIP (Routing Information Protocol) packets. All routers on a subnet that are using RIP will send a broadcast UDP datagram every 30 seconds. If there are 200 hosts on the subnet, which includes two routers using RIP, 198 hosts will have to process (and discard) these broadcast datagrams every 30 seconds, assuming none of the 198 hosts is running routed.

18.4 dg_cli Function Using Broadcasting

We modify our dg_cli function one more time, this time allowing it to broadcast to the standard UDP daytime server (Figure 2.13), and printing all the replies. The only change we make to the main function (Figure 8.7) is to change the destination port number to 13:

```
servaddr.sin_port = htons(13);
```

We first compile this modified main function with the unmodified dg_cli function from Figure 8.8 and run it on the host bsdi.

```
bsdi % udpcli01 206.62.226.63
hi
sendto error: Permission denied
```

The command-line argument is the subnet-directed broadcast address for the attached Ethernet. We type a line of input, the program calls sendto, and the error EACCES is returned. The reason we receive the error is that we are not allowed to send a datagram to a broadcast destination address unless we explicitly tell the kernel that we will be broadcasting. We do this by setting the SO_BROADCAST socket option (Section 7.5).

> Berkeley-derived implementations implement this sanity check. Solaris 2.5, on the other hand, accepts the datagram destined for the broadcast address even if we do not specify the socket option. Posix.1g says that the kernel "may" return the error.
>
> Broadcasting was a privileged operation with 4.2BSD and the SO_BROADCAST socket option did not exist. This option was added to 4.3BSD and any process was allowed to set the option.

We now modify our dg_cli function as shown in Figure 18.5. This version sets the SO_BROADCAST socket option and prints all the replies received within 5 seconds.

Allocate room for server's address, set socket option

11-13   malloc allocates room for the server's address to be returned by recvfrom. The SO_BROADCAST socket option is set and a signal handler is installed for SIGCHLD.

Read line, send to socket, read all replies

14-24   The next two steps, fgets and sendto, are similar to previous versions of this function. But since we are sending a broadcast datagram we can receive multiple

―― bcast/dgclibcast1.c

```
 1 #include    "unp.h"

 2 static void recvfrom_alarm(int);

 3 void
 4 dg_cli(FILE *fp, int sockfd, const SA *pservaddr, socklen_t servlen)
 5 {
 6     int     n;
 7     const int on = 1;
 8     char    sendline[MAXLINE], recvline[MAXLINE + 1];
 9     socklen_t len;
10     struct sockaddr *preply_addr;

11     preply_addr = Malloc(servlen);

12     Setsockopt(sockfd, SOL_SOCKET, SO_BROADCAST, &on, sizeof(on));

13     Signal(SIGALRM, recvfrom_alarm);

14     while (Fgets(sendline, MAXLINE, fp) != NULL) {

15         Sendto(sockfd, sendline, strlen(sendline), 0, pservaddr, servlen);

16         alarm(5);
17         for ( ; ; ) {
18             len = servlen;
19             n = recvfrom(sockfd, recvline, MAXLINE, 0, preply_addr, &len);
20             if (n < 0) {
21                 if (errno == EINTR)
22                     break;      /* waited long enough for replies */
23                 else
24                     err_sys("recvfrom error");
25             } else {
26                 recvline[n] = 0;    /* null terminate */
27                 printf("from %s: %s",
28                         Sock_ntop_host(preply_addr, servlen), recvline);
29             }
30         }
31     }
32 }

33 static void
34 recvfrom_alarm(int signo)
35 {
36     return;                      /* just interrupt the recvfrom() */
37 }
```

―― bcast/dgclibcast1.c

Figure 18.5 dg_cli function that broadcasts.

replies. We call recvfrom in a loop and print all the replies received within 5 seconds. After 5 seconds, SIGALRM is generated, our signal handler is called, and recvfrom returns the error EINTR.

Print each received reply

25–29   For each reply received we call sock_ntop_host which in the case of IPv4 returns strings containing the dotted-decimal IP address and port number of the server. These are printed along with the server's reply.

If we run the program, specifying the subnet-directed broadcast address of 206.62.226.63, we see the following:

```
bsdi % udpcli01 206.62.226.63
hi
from 206.62.226.35: Sat Jun 14 12:19:36 1997
from 206.62.226.40: Sat Jun 14 12:19:36 1997
from 206.62.226.34: Sat Jun 14 12:19:36 1997
from 206.62.226.43: Sat Jun 14 12:19:36 1997
from 206.62.226.37: Sat Jun 14 12:19:36 1997
from 206.62.226.42: Sat Jun 14 12:19:36 1997
hello
from 206.62.226.35: Sat Jun 14 12:19:43 1997
from 206.62.226.40: Sat Jun 14 12:19:43 1997
from 206.62.226.34: Sat Jun 14 12:19:43 1997
from 206.62.226.43: Sat Jun 14 12:19:43 1997
from 206.62.226.42: Sat Jun 14 12:19:43 1997
from 206.62.226.37: Sat Jun 14 12:19:43 1997
```

Each time we must type a line of input to generate the output UDP datagram. Each time we receive six replies and this includes the sending host. As we said earlier, the definition of a broadcast datagram is *all* the hosts on the attached network, including the sender. Each reply is unicast, because the source address of the request, which is used by each server as the destination address of the reply, is a unicast address.

All the systems report the same time because all run NTP. We see that only six of the nine nodes on this subnet (Figure 1.16) respond. The remaining two hosts and the one router do not respond to the requests, since the requests are sent to a broadcast address.

IP Fragmentation and Broadcasts

Berkeley-derived kernels do not allow a broadcast datagram to be fragmented. If the size of an IP datagram that is being sent to a broadcast address exceeds the outgoing interface MTU, EMSGSIZE is returned (pp. 233–234 of TCPv2). This is a policy decision that has existed since 4.2BSD. There is nothing that prevents a kernel from fragmenting a broadcast datagram, but the feeling is that broadcasting puts enough load on the network as it is, so there is no need to multiply this load by the number of fragments.

We can see this scenario with our program in Figure 18.5. We redirect standard input to a file containing a 2000-byte line, which will require fragmentation on an Ethernet.

```
bsdi % udpcli01 206.62.226.63 < 2000line
sendto error: Message too long
```

> AIX, BSD/OS, Digital Unix, and UnixWare all implement this limitation, although UnixWare does not send the datagram but does not return an error either. Both Linux and Solaris fragment datagrams sent to a broadcast address. For portability, however, an application that

needs to broadcast should limit its datagrams to 1472 bytes, since the Ethernet MTU is normally the smallest for a LAN.

18.5 Race Conditions

A *race condition* is usually when multiple processes are accessing data that is shared among them but the correct outcome depends on the execution order of the processes. Since the execution order of processes on typical Unix systems is nondeterministic, sometimes the outcome is correct but sometimes the outcome is wrong. The hardest type of race conditions to debug are those in which the outcome is normally correct and only occasionally is the outcome wrong. We talk more about these types of race conditions in Chapter 23, when we discuss mutual exclusion variables and condition variables. Race conditions are always a concern with threads programming since so much data is shared among all the threads (e.g., all the global variables).

Race conditions of a different type often exist when dealing with signals. The problem occurs because a signal can normally be delivered at anytime while our program is executing. Posix.1 allows us to *block* a signal from being delivered, but this is often of little use while we are performing I/O operations.

An example is an easy way to see this problem. A race condition exists in Figure 18.5; take a few minutes and see if you can find it. (*Hint*: Where can we be executing when the signal is delivered?) You can also force the condition to occur as follows: change the argument to `alarm` from 5 to 1, and add `sleep(1)` immediately before the `printf`.

When we make these changes to the function and then type the first line of input, the line is sent as a broadcast and we set the `alarm` for 1 second in the future. We block in the call to `recvfrom` and the first reply then arrives for our socket, probably within a few milliseconds. The reply is returned by `recvfrom` but we then go to sleep for 1 second. Additional replies are received, and they are placed into our socket's receive buffer. But while we are asleep, the `alarm` timer expires and the SIGALRM signal is generated: our signal handler is called, and it just returns and interrupts the `sleep` in which we are blocked. We then loop around and read the queued replies, with a 1 second pause each time we print a reply. But when we have read all the replies we block again in the call to `recvfrom` but the timer is not running. We will block forever in `recvfrom`. The fundamental problem is that our intent is for our signal handler to interrupt a blocked `recvfrom`, but the signal can be delivered at any time, and we can be executing anywhere in the infinite `for` loop when the signal is delivered.

We now examine four different solutions to this problem: one incorrect solution and three different correct solutions.

Blocking and Unblocking the Signal

Our first (incorrect) solution reduces the window of error by blocking the signal from being delivered while we are executing the remainder of the `for` loop. Figure 18.6 shows the new version.

bcast/dgclibcast3.c

```
 1 #include     "unp.h"

 2 static void recvfrom_alarm(int);

 3 void
 4 dg_cli(FILE *fp, int sockfd, const SA *pservaddr, socklen_t servlen)
 5 {
 6     int      n;
 7     const int on = 1;
 8     char     sendline[MAXLINE], recvline[MAXLINE + 1];
 9     sigset_t sigset_alrm;
10     socklen_t len;
11     struct sockaddr *preply_addr;

12     preply_addr = Malloc(servlen);

13     Setsockopt(sockfd, SOL_SOCKET, SO_BROADCAST, &on, sizeof(on));

14     Sigemptyset(&sigset_alrm);
15     Sigaddset(&sigset_alrm, SIGALRM);

16     Signal(SIGALRM, recvfrom_alarm);

17     while (Fgets(sendline, MAXLINE, fp) != NULL) {

18         Sendto(sockfd, sendline, strlen(sendline), 0, pservaddr, servlen);

19         alarm(5);
20         for ( ; ; ) {
21             len = servlen;
22             Sigprocmask(SIG_UNBLOCK, &sigset_alrm, NULL);
23             n = recvfrom(sockfd, recvline, MAXLINE, 0, preply_addr, &len);
24             Sigprocmask(SIG_BLOCK, &sigset_alrm, NULL);
25             if (n < 0) {
26                 if (errno == EINTR)
27                     break;      /* waited long enough for replies */
28                 else
29                     err_sys("recvfrom error");
30             } else {
31                 recvline[n] = 0;    /* null terminate */
32                 printf("from %s: %s",
33                         Sock_ntop_host(preply_addr, servlen), recvline);
34             }
35         }
36     }
37 }

38 static void
39 recvfrom_alarm(int signo)
40 {
41     return;                          /* just interrupt the recvfrom() */
42 }
```

bcast/dgclibcast3.c

Figure 18.6 Block signals while executing within the `for` loop.

Declare signal set and initialize

14–15   We declare a signal set, initialize it to the empty set (`sigemptyset`), and then turn on the bit corresponding to SIGALRM (`sigaddset`).

Unblock and block signal

21–24   Before calling `recvfrom` we unblock the signal (so that it can be delivered while we are blocked) and then block the signal as soon as `recvfrom` returns. If the signal is generated (i.e., the timer expires) while the signal is blocked, the kernel remembers this fact but cannot deliver the signal (i.e., call our signal handler) until the signal is unblocked. This is the fundamental difference between the *generation* of a signal and its *delivery*. Chapter 10 of APUE provides additional details on all these facets of Posix.1 signal handling.

If we compile and run this program, it appears to work fine, but then most programs with a race condition work most of the time! There is still a problem: the unblocking of the signal, the call to `recvfrom`, and the blocking of the signal are all independent system calls. Assume `recvfrom` returns with the final datagram reply and the signal is delivered between the `recvfrom` and the blocking of the signal. The next call to `recvfrom` will block forever. We have reduced the window, but the problem still exists.

A variation of this solution is to have the signal handler set a global flag when the signal is delivered.

```
static void
recvfrom_alarm(int signo)
{
    had_alarm = 1;
    return;
}
```

The flag is initialized to 0 each time `alarm` is called. Our `dg_cli` function checks this flag before calling `recvfrom` and does not call it if the flag is nonzero.

```
for ( ; ; ) {
    len = servlen;
    Sigprocmask(SIG_UNBLOCK, &sigset_alrm, NULL);
    if (had_alarm == 1)
        break;
    n = recvfrom(sockfd, recvline, MAXLINE, 0, preply_addr, &len);
```

If the signal was generated during the time it was blocked (after the previous return from `recvfrom`) and when the signal is unblocked in this piece of code, it will be delivered before `sigprocmask` returns, setting our flag. But there is still a small window of time between the testing of the flag and the call to `recvfrom` when the signal can be generated and delivered, and if this happens, the call to `recvfrom` will block forever (assuming, of course, no additional replies are received).

Blocking and Unblocking the Signal with `pselect`

One correct solution is to use `pselect` (Section 6.9) as shown in Figure 18.7.

——————————————————————— bcast/dgclibcast4.c

```
 1 #include    "unp.h"

 2 static void recvfrom_alarm(int);

 3 void
 4 dg_cli(FILE *fp, int sockfd, const SA *pservaddr, socklen_t servlen)
 5 {
 6     int    n;
 7     const int on = 1;
 8     char    sendline[MAXLINE], recvline[MAXLINE + 1];
 9     fd_set rset;
10     sigset_t sigset_alrm, sigset_empty;
11     socklen_t len;
12     struct sockaddr *preply_addr;

13     preply_addr = Malloc(servlen);

14     Setsockopt(sockfd, SOL_SOCKET, SO_BROADCAST, &on, sizeof(on));

15     FD_ZERO(&rset);

16     Sigemptyset(&sigset_empty);
17     Sigemptyset(&sigset_alrm);
18     Sigaddset(&sigset_alrm, SIGALRM);

19     Signal(SIGALRM, recvfrom_alarm);

20     while (Fgets(sendline, MAXLINE, fp) != NULL) {
21         Sendto(sockfd, sendline, strlen(sendline), 0, pservaddr, servlen);

22         Sigprocmask(SIG_BLOCK, &sigset_alrm, NULL);
23         alarm(5);
24         for ( ; ; ) {
25             FD_SET(sockfd, &rset);
26             n = pselect(sockfd + 1, &rset, NULL, NULL, NULL, &sigset_empty);
27             if (n < 0) {
28                 if (errno == EINTR)
29                     break;
30                 else
31                     err_sys("pselect error");
32             } else if (n != 1)
33                 err_sys("pselect error: returned %d", n);

34             len = servlen;
35             n = Recvfrom(sockfd, recvline, MAXLINE, 0, preply_addr, &len);
36             recvline[n] = 0;    /* null terminate */
37             printf("from %s: %s",
38                     Sock_ntop_host(preply_addr, servlen), recvline);
39         }
40     }
41 }

42 static void
43 recvfrom_alarm(int signo)
44 {
45     return;                      /* just interrupt the recvfrom() */
46 }
```
——————————————————————— bcast/dgclibcast4.c

Figure 18.7 Blocking and unblocking signals with pselect.

22–33   We block `SIGALRM` and call `pselect`. The final argument to `pselect` is a pointer to our `sigset_empty` variable, which is a signal set with no signals blocked, that is, all signals unblocked. `pselect` will save the current signal mask (which has `SIGALRM` blocked), test the specified descriptors, block if necessary with the signal mask set to the empty set, but before returning the signal mask of the process is reset to its value when `pselect` was called. The key to `pselect` is that the setting of the signal mask, the testing of the descriptors, and the resetting of the signal mask are atomic operations with regard to the calling process.

34–38   If our socket is readable, we call `recvfrom` knowing it will not block.

As we mentioned in Section 6.9, `pselect` is new with Posix.1g and none of the systems in Figure 1.16 support the function. Nevertheless, Figure 18.8 shows a simple, albeit incorrect, implementation. Our reason for showing this incorrect implementation is to show the three steps involved: setting of the signal mask to the value specified by the caller along with saving the current mask, testing the descriptors, and resetting the signal mask.

―― *lib/pselect.c*

```
 9 #include    "unp.h"

10 int
11 pselect(int nfds, fd_set *rset, fd_set *wset, fd_set *xset,
12         const struct timespec *ts, const sigset_t *sigmask)
13 {
14     int      n;
15     struct timeval tv;
16     sigset_t savemask;

17     if (ts != NULL) {
18         tv.tv_sec = ts->tv_sec;
19         tv.tv_usec = ts->tv_nsec / 1000;   /* nanosec -> microsec */
20     }
21     sigprocmask(SIG_SETMASK, sigmask, &savemask);   /* caller's mask */
22     n = select(nfds, rset, wset, xset, (ts == NULL) ? NULL : &tv);
23     sigprocmask(SIG_SETMASK, &savemask, NULL);  /* restore mask */

24     return (n);
25 }
```

―― *lib/pselect.c*

Figure 18.8   Simple, incorrect implementation of `pselect`.

Using `sigsetjmp` and `siglongjmp`

Another correct way to solve our problem is not to use the ability of a signal handler to interrupt a blocked system call, but to call `siglongjmp` from the signal handler instead. This is called a *nonlocal goto* because we can use it to jump from one function back to another. Figure 18.9 demonstrates this technique.

Allocate jump buffer

4   We allocate a jump buffer that will be used by our function and its signal handler.

——————————————————————————————— bcast/dgclibcast5.c

```
 1 #include    "unp.h"
 2 #include    <setjmp.h>

 3 static void recvfrom_alarm(int);
 4 static sigjmp_buf jmpbuf;

 5 void
 6 dg_cli(FILE *fp, int sockfd, const SA *pservaddr, socklen_t servlen)
 7 {
 8     int     n;
 9     const int on = 1;
10     char    sendline[MAXLINE], recvline[MAXLINE + 1];
11     socklen_t len;
12     struct sockaddr *preply_addr;

13     preply_addr = Malloc(servlen);

14     Setsockopt(sockfd, SOL_SOCKET, SO_BROADCAST, &on, sizeof(on));

15     Signal(SIGALRM, recvfrom_alarm);

16     while (Fgets(sendline, MAXLINE, fp) != NULL) {

17         Sendto(sockfd, sendline, strlen(sendline), 0, pservaddr, servlen);

18         alarm(5);
19         for ( ; ; ) {
20             if (sigsetjmp(jmpbuf, 1) != 0)
21                 break;
22             len = servlen;
23             n = Recvfrom(sockfd, recvline, MAXLINE, 0, preply_addr, &len);
24             recvline[n] = 0;    /* null terminate */
25             printf("from %s: %s",
26                     Sock_ntop_host(preply_addr, servlen), recvline);
27         }
28     }
29 }

30 static void
31 recvfrom_alarm(int signo)
32 {
33     siglongjmp(jmpbuf, 1);
34 }
```

——————————————————————————————— bcast/dgclibcast5.c

Figure 18.9 Use of `sigsetjmp` and `siglongjmp` from signal handler.

Call `sigsetjmp`

20–23   When we call `sigsetjmp` directly from our `dg_cli` function, it establishes the jump buffer and returns 0. We proceed on and call `recvfrom`.

Handle `SIGALRM` and call `siglongjmp`

30–34   When the signal is delivered, we call `siglongjmp`. This causes the `sigsetjmp` in the `dg_cli` function to return with a return value equal to the second argument (1), which must be a nonzero value. This will cause the `for` loop in `dg_cli` to terminate.

Using `sigsetjmp` and `siglongjmp` in this fashion guarantees that we will not block forever in `recvfrom` because of a signal delivered at an inopportune time. The only potential for a problem occurs if the signal is delivered while `printf` is in the middle of its output. To prevent this we should combine the signal blocking and unblocking from Figure 18.6 with the nonlocal goto.

Using IPC from Signal Handler to Function

There is yet another correct way to solve our problem. Instead of having the signal handler just return and hopefully interrupt a blocked `recvfrom`, we have the signal handler use IPC (interprocess communication) to notify our `dg_cli` function that the timer has expired. This is somewhat similar to the proposal we made earlier for the signal handler to set the global `had_alarm` when the timer expired, because that global variable was being used as a form of IPC (shared memory between our function and the signal handler). The problem with that solution, however, was our function had to test this variable, and this led to timing problems if the signal was delivered at about the same time.

What we use in Figure 18.10 is a pipe within our process, with the signal handler writing 1 byte to the pipe when the timer expires, and our `dg_cli` function reading that byte to know when to terminate its `for` loop. What makes this such a nice solution is that the testing for the pipe being readable is done using `select`. We test for either the socket being readable or the pipe being readable.

Create pipe

15   We create a normal Unix pipe and two descriptors are returned. `pipefd[0]` is the read end and `pipefd[1]` is the write end.

> We could also use `socketpair` and get a full-duplex pipe. On some systems, notably SVR4, a normal Unix pipe is always full-duplex and we can read from either end and write to either end.

`select` on both socket and read end of pipe

23–30   We `select` on both the socket and the read end of the pipe.

45–50   When `SIGALRM` is delivered, our signal handler writes 1 byte to the pipe, making the read end readable. Our signal handler also returns, possible interrupting `select`. Therefore if `select` returns `EINTR`, we ignore the error, knowing that the read end of the pipe will also be readable, and that will terminate the `for` loop.

`read` from pipe

38–41   When the read end of the pipe is readable, we `read` the null byte that the signal handler wrote and ignore it. But this tells us that the timer expired, so we `break` out of the infinite `for` loop.

---

bcast/dgclibcast6.c

```
1 #include    "unp.h"

2 static void recvfrom_alarm(int);
3 static int pipefd[2];
```

```
 4 void
 5 dg_cli(FILE *fp, int sockfd, const SA *pservaddr, socklen_t servlen)
 6 {
 7     int     n, maxfdp1;
 8     const int on = 1;
 9     char    sendline[MAXLINE], recvline[MAXLINE + 1];
10     fd_set  rset;
11     socklen_t len;
12     struct sockaddr *preply_addr;

13     preply_addr = Malloc(servlen);

14     Setsockopt(sockfd, SOL_SOCKET, SO_BROADCAST, &on, sizeof(on));

15     Pipe(pipefd);
16     maxfdp1 = max(sockfd, pipefd[0]) + 1;

17     FD_ZERO(&rset);

18     Signal(SIGALRM, recvfrom_alarm);

19     while (Fgets(sendline, MAXLINE, fp) != NULL) {
20         Sendto(sockfd, sendline, strlen(sendline), 0, pservaddr, servlen);

21         alarm(5);
22         for ( ; ; ) {
23             FD_SET(sockfd, &rset);
24             FD_SET(pipefd[0], &rset);
25             if ( (n = select(maxfdp1, &rset, NULL, NULL, NULL)) < 0) {
26                 if (errno == EINTR)
27                     continue;
28                 else
29                     err_sys("pselect error");
30             }
31             if (FD_ISSET(sockfd, &rset)) {
32                 len = servlen;
33                 n = Recvfrom(sockfd, recvline, MAXLINE, 0, preply_addr, &len);
34                 recvline[n] = 0;    /* null terminate */
35                 printf("from %s: %s",
36                         Sock_ntop_host(preply_addr, servlen), recvline);
37             }
38             if (FD_ISSET(pipefd[0], &rset)) {
39                 Read(pipefd[0], &n, 1);    /* timer expired */
40                 break;
41             }
42         }
43     }
44 }

45 static void
46 recvfrom_alarm(int signo)
47 {
48     Write(pipefd[1], "", 1);    /* write 1 null byte to pipe */
49     return;
50 }
```
                                                                             —— bcast/dgclibcast6.c

Figure 18.10 Using a pipe as IPC from signal handler to our function.

18.6 Summary

Broadcasting sends a datagram that all hosts on the attached subnet receive. The disadvantage in broadcasting is that every host on the subnet must process the datagram, up through the UDP layer in the case of a UDP datagram, even if the host is not participating in the application. For high data rate applications, such as audio or video, this can place an excessive processing load on these hosts. We will see in the next chapter that multicasting solves this problem because only the hosts that are interested in the application receive the datagram.

Using a version of our UDP echo client that sends a broadcast to the daytime server and then prints all the replies that are received within 5 seconds, lets us look at race conditions with the SIGALRM signal. Since the use of the alarm function and the SIGALRM signal is a common way to place a timeout on a read operation, this subtle error is common in networking applications. We showed one incorrect way to solve the problem, and three correct ways:

- using pselect,
- using sigsetjmp and siglongjmp, and
- using IPC (typically a pipe) from the signal handler to the main loop.

Exercises

18.1 Run the UDP client using the dg_cli function that broadcasts: Figure 18.5. How many replies do you receive? Are the replies always in the same order? Do the hosts on your network have synchronized clocks?

18.2 When talking about the fragmentation of broadcast datagrams at the end of Section 18.4, we said that for portability an application should limit its broadcast datagrams to 1472 bytes. Where does this magic number come from?

18.3 Put some printfs in Figure 18.10 after select returns to see whether it returns an error or readability for one of the two descriptors. When the alarm expires, does your system return EINTR or readability on the pipe?

18.4 Run a tool such as tcpdump, if available, and look for broadcast packets on your LAN; tcpdump ether broadcast is the tcpdump command. To which protocol suites do the broadcasts belong?

19

Multicasting

19.1 Introduction

As shown in Figure 18.1, a unicast address identifies a *single* interface, a broadcast address identifies *all* interfaces on the subnet, and a multicast address identifies a *set* of interfaces. Unicasting and broadcasting are the endpoints of the addressing spectrum (one or all) and the intent of multicasting is to provide the capability of addressing something in between these endpoints. A multicast datagram should be received only by the interfaces that are interested in the datagram, that is, by the interfaces on the hosts that are running applications that wish to participate in the multicast session. Also, broadcasting is normally limited to a LAN whereas multicasting can be used on a LAN or across a WAN. Indeed, applications on the MBone (Section B.2) multicast across the entire Internet on a daily basis.

The additions to the sockets API to support multicasting are simple: five socket options: three that affect the sending of UDP datagrams to a multicast address, and two that affect the host's reception of multicast datagrams.

19.2 Multicast Addresses

When describing multicast addresses we must distinguish between IPv4 and IPv6.

IPv4 Class D Addresses

Class D addresses, in the range 224.0.0.0 through 239.255.255.255, are the multicast addresses in IPv4 (Figures A.3 and A.4). The low-order 28 bits of the class D address form the multicast *group ID* and the 32-bit address is called the *group address*.

Figure 19.1 shows how multicast addresses are mapped into Ethernet addresses. This mapping for IPv4 multicast addresses is described in RFC 1112 [Deering 1989] for Ethernets, in RFC 1390 [Katz 1993] for FDDI networks, and in RFC 1469 [Pusateri 1993] for token-ring networks. We also show the mapping for IPv6 multicast addresses to allow easy comparison of the resulting Ethernet addresses.

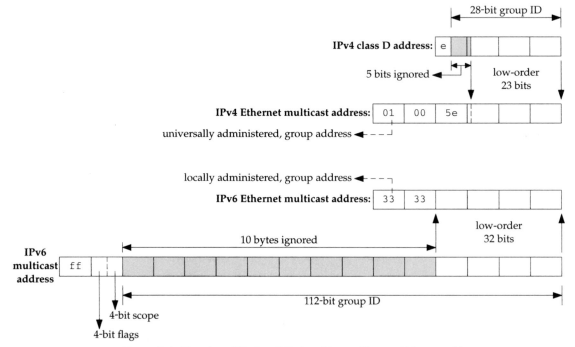

Figure 19.1 Mapping of IPv4 and IPv6 multicast address to Ethernet addresses.

Considering just the IPv4 mapping, the high-order 24 bits of the Ethernet address are always `01:00:5e`. The next bit is always 0 and the low-order 23 bits are copied from the low-order 23 bits of the multicast group address. The high-order 5 bits of the group address are ignored in the mapping. This means that 32 multicast addresses map to a single Ethernet address: the mapping is not one-to-one.

The low-order 2 bits of the first byte of the Ethernet address identify the address as a universally administered group address. Universally administered means the high-order 24 bits have been assigned by the IEEE and group addresses are recognized and handled specially by receiving interfaces.

There are a few special IPv4 multicast addresses.

- 224.0.0.1 is the *all-hosts* group. All multicast-capable hosts on a subnet must join this group on all multicast-capable interfaces. (We talk about what it means to join a multicast group shortly.)

- 224.0.0.2 is the *all-routers* group. All multicast routers on a subnet must join this group on all multicast-capable interfaces.

The range 224.0.0.0 through 224.0.0.255 (which we can also write as 224.0.0.0/24) is called *link local*. These addresses are reserved for low-level topology discovery or maintenance protocols, and datagrams destined to any of these addresses are never forwarded by a multicast router. We say more about the scope of various IPv4 multicast addresses after looking at the IPv6 multicast addresses.

IPv6 Multicast Addresses

The high-order byte of an IPv6 multicast address has the value `ff`. Figure 19.1 shows the mapping from a 16-byte IPv6 multicast address into a 6-byte Ethernet address. The low-order 32 bits of the group address are copied into the low-order 32 bits of the Ethernet address. The high-order 2 bytes of the Ethernet address are `33:33`. This mapping for Ethernets is specified in RFC 1972 [Crawford 1996a], the same mapping for FDDI is in RFC 2019 [Crawford 1996b], and the token ring mapping is in [Thomas 1997].

The low-order 2 bits of the first byte of the Ethernet address specify the address as a locally administered group address. Locally administered means there is no guarantee that the address is unique to IPv6. There could be other protocol suites besides IPv6 sharing the network and using the same high-order 2 bytes of the Ethernet address. As we mentioned earlier, group addresses are recognized and handled specially by receiving interfaces.

The 4-bit IPv6 multicast flags differentiate between a *well-known* multicast group (a value of 0) and a *transient* multicast group (a value of 1). The upper 3 bits of this field are reserved. IPv6 multicast addresses also have a 4-bit *scope* field that we discuss shortly.

There are a few special IPv6 multicast addresses.

- `ff02::1` is the *all-nodes* group. All multicast-capable hosts on a subnet must join this group on all multicast-capable interfaces. This is similar to the IPv4 224.0.0.1 multicast address.

- `ff02::2` is the *all-routers* group. All multicast routers on a subnet must join this group on all multicast-capable interfaces. This is similar to the IPv4 224.0.0.2 multicast address.

Since only the low-order 32 bits of the IPv6 multicast address are used when mapping to the hardware address, [Hinden and Deering 1997] recommend that the 10 bytes to the left of these 32 bits in Figure 19.1 be 0 when assigning new multicast addresses, at least until these 10 bytes are needed in the future.

Scope of Multicast Addresses

IPv6 multicast addresses have an explicit 4-bit *scope* field that specifies how "far" the multicast packet will travel. IPv6 packets also have a hop limit field that limits the number of times the packet is forwarded by a router. The following values have been assigned to the scope field:

     1: node-local
     2: link-local
     5: site-local
     8: organization-local
   14: global

The remaining values are unassigned or reserved. A node-local datagram must not be output by an interface and a link-local datagram must never be forwarded by a router. What defines a site or an organization is up to the administrators of the multicast routers at that site or organization. IPv6 multicast addresses that differ only in scope represent different groups.

IPv4 does not have a separate scope field for multicast packets. Historically the IPv4 TTL field in the IP header has doubled as a multicast scope field: a TTL of 0 means node-local, 1 means link-local, up through 32 means site-local, up through 64 means region-local, up through 128 means continent-local (whatever that is), and up through 255 are unrestricted in scope (global). This double usage of the TTL field has led to difficulties, as detailed in [Meyer 1997].

Although use of the IPv4 TTL field for scoping is accepted and recommended practice, administrative scoping is preferred, when possible. This defines the range 239.0.0.0 through 239.255.255.255 as the *administratively scoped IPv4 multicast space* ([Meyer 1997]). This is the high end of the multicast address space. Addresses in this range are assigned locally by an organization but are not guaranteed to be unique across organizational boundaries. An organization must configure its boundary routers (multicast routers at the boundary of the organization) not to forward multicast packets destined to any of these addresses.

The administratively scoped IPv4 multicast addresses are then divided into local scope and organization-local scope, the former being similar (but not semantically equivalent) to the IPv6 site-local scope. We summarize the different scoping rules in Figure 19.2.

Scope	IPv6	IPv4	
	scope	TTL scope	administrative scope
node-local	1	0	
link-local	2	1	224.0.0.0 to 224.0.0.255
site-local	5	<32	239.255.0.0 to 239.255.255.255
organization-local	8		239.192.0.0 to 239.195.255.255
global	14	<255	224.0.1.0 to 238.255.255.255

Figure 19.2 Scope of IPv4 and IPv6 multicast addresses.

19.3 Multicasting versus Broadcasting on A LAN

We now return to the examples in Figures 18.3 and 18.4 to show what happens in the case of multicasting. We use IPv4 for the example shown in Figure 19.3, but the steps are similar for IPv6.

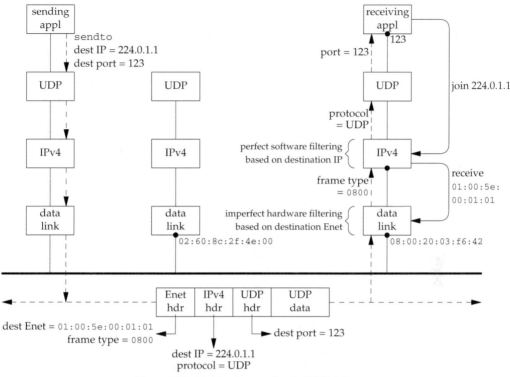

Figure 19.3 Multicast example of a UDP datagram.

The receiving application on the rightmost host starts and creates a UDP socket, binds port 123 to the socket, and then joins the multicast group 224.0.1.1. We will see shortly that this "join" operation is done by calling setsockopt. When this happens, the IPv4 layer saves the information internally and then tells the appropriate datalink to receive Ethernet frames destined to 01:00:5e:00:01:01 (Section 12.11 of TCPv2). This is the Ethernet address corresponding to the multicast address that the application has just joined using the mapping that we showed in Figure 19.1.

The next step is for the sending application on the leftmost host to create a UDP socket and send a datagram to 224.0.1.1, port 123. Nothing special is required to send a multicast datagram: the application does not have to join the multicast group. The sending host converts the IP address into the corresponding Ethernet destination address and the frame is sent. Notice that the frame contains both the destination Ethernet address (which is examined by the interfaces) and the destination IP address (which is examined by the IP layers).

We assume that the host in the middle is not IPv4 multicast capable (since support for IPv4 multicasting is optional). This host ignores the frame completely because (1) the destination Ethernet address does not match the address of the interface, (2) the destination Ethernet address is not the Ethernet broadcast address, and (3) the interface has not been told to receive any group addresses (those with the low-order bit of the high-order byte set to 1, as in Figure 19.1).

The frame is received by the datalink on the right, based on what we call *imperfect filtering* done by the interface using the Ethernet destination address. We say this is imperfect because it is normally the case that when the interface is told to receive frames destined to one specific Ethernet group address, it can receive frames destined to other Ethernet group addresses too.

> When told to receive frames destined to a specific Ethernet group address, many current Ethernet interface cards apply a hash function to the address, calculating a value between 0 and 63. One of 64 bits in an array is then turned on. When a frame passes by on the cable that is destined for a group address, the same hash function is applied by the interface to the destination address (which is the first field in the frame), calculating a value between 0 and 63. If the corresponding bit in the array is on, the frame is received; otherwise it is ignored. Newer interface cards increase the size of the bit array from 64 to 512, reducing the probability that an interface will receive frames in which it is not interested. Over time, as more and more applications use multicasting, this size will probably increase even more. Some interface cards today already have perfect filtering. Other interface cards have no multicast filtering at all, and when told to receive a specific group address must receive all multicast frames (sometimes called *multicast promiscuous* mode). One popular interface card does perfect filtering for 16 group addresses as well as having a 512-bit hash table. Even if the interface performs perfect filtering, perfect software filtering at the IP layer is still required because the mapping from the IP multicast address to the hardware address is not one-to-one.

Assuming that the datalink on the right receives the frame, since the Ethernet frame type is IPv4, the packet is passed to the IP layer. Since the received packet was destined to a multicast IP address, the IP layer compares this address against all the multicast addresses that applications on this host have joined. We call this *perfect filtering* since it is based on the entire 32-bit class D address in the IPv4 header. In this example the packet is accepted by the IP layer and passed to the UDP layer, which in turn passes the datagram to the socket that is bound to port 123.

There are three more scenarios that we do not show in Figure 19.3.

1. A host running an application that has joined the multicast address 225.0.1.1. Since the upper 5 bits of the group address are ignored in the mapping to the Ethernet address, this host's interface will also be receiving frames with an Ethernet destination address of 01:00:5e:00:01:01. In this case the packet will be discarded by the perfect filtering in the IP layer.

2. A host running an application that has joined some multicast group whose corresponding Ethernet address just happens to be one that the interface receives when it is programmed to receive 01:00:5e:00:01:01 (i.e., the interface card performs imperfect filtering). This frame will be discarded either by the datalink layer or by the IP layer.

3. A packet destined to the same group, 224.0.1.1, but a different port, say 4000. The rightmost host in Figure 19.3 still receives the packet, and it is accepted by the IP layer, but assuming a socket does not exist that has bound port 4000, the packet will be discarded by the UDP layer.

> This demonstrates that for a process to receive a multicast datagram the process must join the group and bind the port.

19.4 Multicasting on a WAN

Multicasting on a single LAN, as we discussed in the previous section, is simple. One host sends a multicast packet and any interested host receives the packet. The benefit in multicasting over broadcasting is reducing the load on all the hosts not interested in the multicast packets.

Multicasting is also beneficial on WANs. Consider the WAN shown in Figure 19.4.

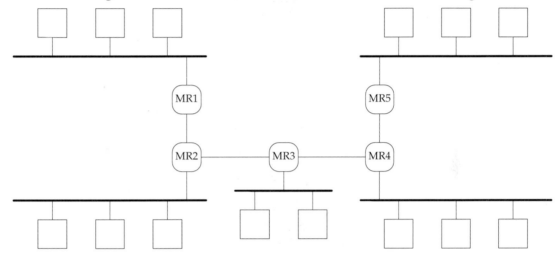

Figure 19.4 Five LANs connected with five multicast routers.

We show five LANs connected with five multicast routers.

Next assume that some program is started on five of the hosts (say a program that listens to a multicast audio session) and those five programs join a given multicast group. Each of the five hosts then joins that multicast group. We also assume that the multicast routers are all communicating with their neighbor multicast router using a *multicast routing protocol*, which we designate as just *MRP*. We show this in Figure 19.5.

When a process on a host joins a multicast group, that host sends an IGMP message to any attached multicast routers telling them that the host has just joined that group. The multicast routers then exchange this information using the multicast routing protocol so that each multicast router knows what to do if it receives a packet destined to the multicast address.

> Multicast routing is still a research topic and could easily consume a book on its own. [Maufer and Semeria 1997] provide an introduction and overview.

We now assume that a process on the host on the top left starts sending packets destined to the multicast address. Say this process is sending the audio packets that the multicast receivers are waiting to receive. We show these packets in Figure 19.6.

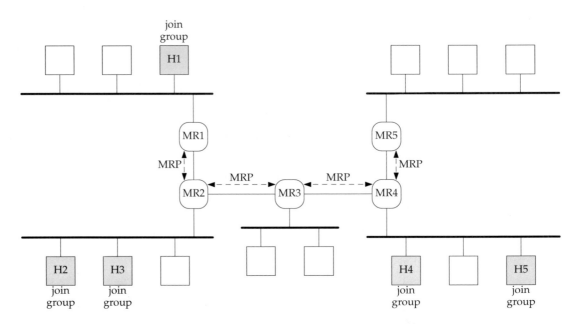

Figure 19.5   Five hosts join a multicast group on a WAN.

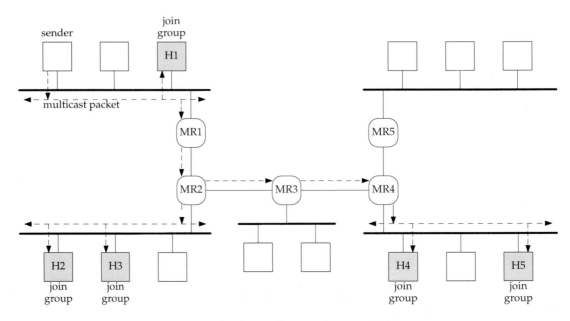

Figure 19.6   Sending multicast packets on a WAN.

We can follow the steps takes as the multicast packets go from the sender to all the receivers.

- The packets are multicast on the top left LAN by the sender. The receiver H1 receives these (since it has joined the group) as does MR1 (since a multicast router must receive all multicast packets).

- MR1 forwards the multicast packet to MR2, because the multicast routing protocol has informed MR1 that MR2 needs to receive packets destined to this group.

- MR2 multicasts the packet onto its attached LAN, since hosts H2 and H3 belong to the group. It also makes a copy of the packet and sends it to MR3.

  Making a copy of the packet, as MR2 does here, is something unique to multicast forwarding. A unicast packet is never duplicated as it is forwarded by routers.

- MR3 sends the multicast packet to MR4 but MR3 does not multicast a copy on its attached LAN, because we assume none of the hosts on the LAN has joined the group.

- MR4 multicasts the packet onto its attached LAN, since hosts H4 and H5 belong to the group. It does not make a copy and send it to MR5, because none of the hosts on MR5's attached LAN belong to the group and MR4 knows this based on the multicast routing information it has exchanged with MR5.

Two less desirable alternatives to multicasting on a WAN are *broadcast flooding* and sending individual copies to each receiver. In the first case the packets would be broadcast by the sender, and each router would broadcast the packet out each of its interfaces, except the arriving interface. It should be obvious that this increases the number of uninterested hosts and routers that must deal with the packet.

In the second case the sender must know the IP address of all the receivers and send each one a copy. With the five receivers that we show in Figure 19.6 this would require five packets on the sender's LAN, four packets going from MR1 to MR2, and two packets going from MR2 to MR3 to MR4.

19.5 Multicast Socket Options

The API support for multicasting requires only five new socket options. Figure 19.7 shows these five socket options, and the datatype of the argument expected in the call to getsockopt or setsockopt for IPv4 and IPv6. A pointer to a variable of the datatype shown is the fourth argument to getsockopt and setsockopt. All 10 of these options are valid with setsockopt, but the four that join and leave a multicast group are not allowed with getsockopt.

Command	Datatype	Description
IP_ADD_MEMBERSHIP	struct ip_mreq	join a multicast group
IP_DROP_MEMBERSHIP	struct ip_mreq	leave a multicast group
IP_MULTICAST_IF	struct in_addr	specify default interface for outgoing multicasts
IP_MULTICAST_TTL	u_char	specify TTL for outgoing multicasts
IP_MULTICAST_LOOP	u_char	enable or disable loopback of outgoing multicasts
IPV6_ADD_MEMBERSHIP	struct ipv6_mreq	join a multicast group
IPV6_DROP_MEMBERSHIP	struct ipv6_mreq	leave a multicast group
IPV6_MULTICAST_IF	u_int	specify default interface for outgoing multicasts
IPV6_MULTICAST_HOPS	int	specify hop limit for outgoing multicasts
IPV6_MULTICAST_LOOP	u_int	enable or disable loopback of outgoing multicasts

Figure 19.7 Multicast socket options.

> The IPv4 TTL and loopback options take a u_char argument, while the IPv6 hop limit and
> loopback options take an int and a u_int argument, respectively. A common programming
> error with the IPv4 multicast options is to call setsockopt with an int argument to specify
> the TTL or loopback (which is not allowed; pp. 354–355 of TCPv2), since most of the other
> socket options in Figure 7.1 have integer arguments. The change with IPv6 should be less
> error prone.

We now describe each of these five socket options in more detail. Notice that the
five options are conceptually identical between IPv4 and IPv6; only the name and argument type differs.

IP_ADD_MEMBERSHIP, IPV6_ADD_MEMBERSHIP

Join a multicast group on a specified local interface. We specify the local interface with one of its unicast addresses for IPv4 or with the interface index for
IPv6. The following two structures are used when joining or leaving a group:

```
struct ip_mreq {
  struct in_addr    imr_multiaddr;    /* IPv4 class D multicast addr */
  struct in_addr    imr_interface;    /* IPv4 addr of local interface */
};

struct ipv6_mreq {
  struct in6_addr   ipv6mr_multiaddr; /* IPv6 multicast addr */
  unsigned int      ipv6mr_interface; /* interface index, or 0 */
};
```

If the local interface is specified as the wildcard address (INADDR_ANY for IPv4)
or an index of 0 for IPv6, then the local interface is chosen by the kernel.

We say that a host belongs to a given multicast group on a given interface if one
or more processes currently belongs to that group on that interface.

More than one join is allowed on a given socket but each join must be for a different multicast address, or for the same multicast address but on a different
interface from previous joins for that address on this socket. This can be used
on a multihomed host where, for example, one socket is created and then for
each interface a join is performed for a given multicast address.

Recall from Figure 19.2 that IPv6 multicast addresses have an explicit scope field as part of the address. As we noted, IPv6 multicast addresses that differ only in scope represent different groups. Therefore, if an implementation of the Network Time Protocol wanted to receive all NTP packets, regardless of scope, it would have to join `ff01::101` (node-local), `ff02::101` (link-local), `ff05::101` (site-local), `ff08::101` (organization-local), and `ff0e::101` (global). All the joins could be performed on a single socket, and the `IPV6_PKTINFO` socket option could be set (Section 20.8) to have `recvmsg` return the destination address of each datagram.

> Most implementations have a limit on the number of joins that are allowed per socket This limit is 20 for Berkeley-derived implementations.
>
> When the interface on which to join is not specified, Berkeley-derived kernels look up the multicast address in the normal IP routing table and use the resulting interface (p. 357 of TCPv2). Some systems install a route for all multicast addresses (that is, a route with a destination of 224.0.0.0/8 for IPv4) upon initialization to handle this scenario.
>
> The change was made with IPv6 to use an interface index to specify the interface, instead of the local unicast address that is used with IPv4, to allow joins on unnumbered interfaces and tunnel endpoints. This is why the interface name and index functions that we described in Section 17.6 were introduced with RFC 2133 [Gilligan et al. 1997].

`IP_DROP_MEMBERSHIP`, `IPV6_DROP_MEMBERSHIP`

Leave a multicast group on a specified local interface. The same structures that we just showed for joining a group are used with this socket option. If the local interface is not specified (that is, the value is `INADDR_ANY` for IPv4 or an interface index of 0 for IPv6), the first matching multicasting group membership is dropped.

If a process joins a group but never explicitly leaves the group, when the socket is closed (either explicitly or on process termination), the membership is dropped automatically. It is possible for multiple processes on a host to each join the same group, in which case the host remains a member of that group until the last process leaves the group.

`IP_MULTICAST_IF`, `IPV6_MULTICAST_IF`

Specify the interface for outgoing multicast datagrams sent on this socket. This interface is specified as either an `in_addr` structure for IPv4 or an interface index for IPv6. If the value specified is `INADDR_ANY` for IPv4 or an interface index of 0 for IPv6, this removes any interface previously assigned by this socket option, and the system will choose the interface each time a datagram is sent.

Be careful to distinguish between the local interface specified (or chosen) when a process joins a group (the interface on which arriving multicast datagrams will be received), and the local interface specified (or chosen) when a multicast datagram is output.

Berkeley-derived kernels choose the default interface for an outgoing multicast datagram by searching the normal IP routing table for a route to the destination multicast address, and the corresponding interface is used. This is the same technique used to choose the receiving interface if the process does not specify one when joining a group. The assumption is that if a route exists for a given multicast address (perhaps the default route in the routing table), then the resulting interface should be use for input and output.

`IP_MULTICAST_TTL`, `IPV6_MULTICAST_HOPS`

Set the IPv4 TTL or the IPv6 hop limit for outgoing multicast datagrams. If this is not specified, both default to 1, which restricts the datagram to the local subnet.

`IP_MULTICAST_LOOP`, `IPV6_MULTICAST_LOOP`

Enable or disable local loopback of multicast datagrams. By default loopback is enabled: a copy of each multicast datagram sent by a process on the host will also be looped back and processed as a received datagram by that host, if the host belongs to that multicast group on the outgoing interface.

This is similar to broadcasting, where we saw that broadcasts sent on a host are also processed as a received datagram on that host (Figure 18.4). (But with broadcasting there is no way to disable this loopback.) This means that if a process belongs to the multicast group to which it is sending datagrams, it will receive its own transmissions.

> The loopback that is being described here is an internal loopback performed at the IP layer or higher. Should the interface hear its own transmissions, RFC 1112 [Deering 1989] requires that the driver discard these copies. This RFC also states that the loopback option defaults on as "a performance optimization for upper-layer protocols that restrict the membership of a group to one process per host (such as a routing protocol)."

The first two pairs of socket options (`ADD_MEMBERSHIP` and `DROP_MEMBERSHIP`) affect the *receiving* of multicast datagrams, while the last three pairs affect the *sending* of multicast datagrams (outgoing interface, TTL or hop limit, and loopback). We mentioned earlier that nothing special is required to send a multicast datagram. If none of the multicast socket options is specified before sending a multicast datagram, the interface for the outgoing datagram will be chosen by the kernel, the TTL or hop limit will be 1, and a copy will be looped back.

To receive a multicast datagram a process must join the multicast group and it must also `bind` a UDP socket to the port number that will be used as the destination port number for datagrams sent to the group. The two operations are distinct and both are required. Joining the group tells the host's IP layer and datalink layer to receive multicast datagrams sent to that group. Binding the port is how the application specifies to UDP that it wants to receive datagrams sent to that port. Some applications also `bind` the multicast address to the socket, in addition to the port. This prevents any other datagrams that might be received for that port from being delivered to the socket.

> Historically, Berkeley-derived implementations only require that *some* socket on the host join the multicast group, not necessarily the socket that binds the port and then receives the

multicast datagrams. There is the potential, however, with these implementations for multi-cast datagrams to be delivered to applications that are not multicast aware. Newer multicast kernels now require that the process bind the port and set any multicast socket option for the socket, the latter being an indication that the application is multicast aware. The most common multicast socket option to set is a join of the group. Solaris 2.5 differs slightly and only delivers received multicast datagrams to a socket that has both joined the group and bound the port. For portability, all multicast applications should join the group and bind the port.

Some older multicast-capable hosts do not allow the bind of a multicast address to a socket. For portability an application may wish to ignore a bind error for a multicast address.

19.6 `mcast_join` and Related Functions

Although the five multicast socket options for IPv4 are similar to the five multicast socket options for IPv6, there are enough differences that protocol-independent code using multicasting becomes complicated with lots of `#ifdefs`. A better solution is to hide the differences within the following eight functions.

```
#include "unp.h"

int mcast_join(int sockfd, const struct sockaddr *addr, socklen_t salen,
               const char *ifname, u_int ifindex);

int mcast_leave(int sockfd, const struct sockaddr *addr, socklen_t salen);

int mcast_set_if(int sockfd, const char *ifname, u_int ifindex);

int mcast_set_loop(int sockfd, int flag);

int mcast_set_ttl(int sockfd, int ttl);

                                        All above return: 0 if OK, –1 on error

int mcast_get_if(int sockfd);

                            Returns: nonnegative interface index if OK, –1 on error

int mcast_get_loop(int sockfd);

                                Returns: current loopback flag if OK, –1 on error

int mcast_get_ttl(int sockfd);

                            Returns: current TTL or hop limit if OK, –1 on error
```

`mcast_join` joins the multicast group whose IP address is contained within the socket address structure pointed to by *sa*, and whose length is specified by *salen*. We can specify the interface on which to join the group by either the interface name (a nonnull *ifname*) or a nonzero interface index (*ifindex*). If neither is specified, the kernel chooses the interface on which the group is joined. Recall that with IPv6 the interface is specified to the socket option by its index. If a name is specified for an IPv6 socket, we call `if_nametoindex` to obtain the index. With the IPv4 socket option the interface is specified by its unicast IP address. If a name is specified for an IPv4 socket, we call `ioctl` with a request of `SIOCGIFADDR` to obtain the unicast IP address for the interface. If an index is specified for an IPv4 socket, we first call `if_indextoname` to obtain the name and then process the name as just described.

> An interface name, such as `le0` or `ether0`, is normally the way users specify interfaces, and not with either the IP address or the index. `tcpdump`, for example, is one of the few programs that lets the user specify an interface, and its `-i` option takes an interface name as the argument.

`mcast_leave` leaves the multicast group whose IP address is contained within the socket address structure pointed to by *sa*.

`mcast_set_if` sets the default interface index for outgoing multicast datagrams. If *ifname* is nonnull, then it specifies the interface name; otherwise if *ifindex* is greater than 0, then it specifies the interface index. For IPv6 the name is mapped to an index using `if_nametoindex`. For IPv4 the mapping from either a name or an index into the interface's unicast IP address is done as described for `mcast_join`.

`mcast_set_loop` sets the loopback option to either 0 or 1, and `mcast_set_ttl` sets either the IPv4 TTL or the IPv6 hop limit. The three `mcast_get_XXX` functions return the corresponding value.

Example: `mcast_join` Function

Figure 19.8 shows the first half of our `mcast_join` function. This half handles an IPv4 socket

Handle index

11–19   The IPv4 multicast address in the socket address structure is copied into an `ip_mreq` structure. If an index was specified, `if_indextoname` is called, storing the name into our `ifreq` structure. If this succeeds, we branch ahead to issue the `ioctl`.

Handle name

20–27   The caller's name is copied into an `ifreq` structure and an `ioctl` of `SIOCGIFADDR` returns the unicast address associated with this name. Upon success the IPv4 address is copied into the `imr_interface` member of the `ip_mreq` structure.

Specify default

28–29   If an index was not specified, and a name was not specified, the interface is set to the wildcard address, telling the kernel to choose the interface.

30–31   `setsockopt` performs the join.

—— *lib/mcast_join.c*

```
 1 #include    "unp.h"
 2 #include    <net/if.h>

 3 int
 4 mcast_join(int sockfd, const SA *sa, socklen_t salen,
 5             const char *ifname, u_int ifindex)
 6 {
 7     switch (sa->sa_family) {
 8     case AF_INET:{
 9             struct ip_mreq mreq;
10             struct ifreq ifreq;

11             memcpy(&mreq.imr_multiaddr,
12                    &((struct sockaddr_in *) sa)->sin_addr,
13                    sizeof(struct in_addr));

14             if (ifindex > 0) {
15                 if (if_indextoname(ifindex, ifreq.ifr_name) == NULL) {
16                     errno = ENXIO;  /* i/f index not found */
17                     return (-1);
18                 }
19                 goto doioctl;
20             } else if (ifname != NULL) {
21                 strncpy(ifreq.ifr_name, ifname, IFNAMSIZ);
22               doioctl:
23                 if (ioctl(sockfd, SIOCGIFADDR, &ifreq) < 0)
24                     return (-1);
25                 memcpy(&mreq.imr_interface,
26                        &((struct sockaddr_in *) &ifreq.ifr_addr)->sin_addr,
27                        sizeof(struct in_addr));
28             } else
29                 mreq.imr_interface.s_addr = htonl(INADDR_ANY);

30             return (setsockopt(sockfd, IPPROTO_IP, IP_ADD_MEMBERSHIP,
31                                &mreq, sizeof(mreq)));
32         }
```

—— *lib/mcast_join.c*

Figure 19.8 Join a multicast group: IPv4 socket.

The second half of the function, which handles IPv6 sockets, is shown in Figure 19.9.

Handle index, name, or default

36–48   First the IPv6 multicast address is copied from the socket address structure into the ipv6_mreq structure. If an index was specified, it is stored in the ipv6mr_interface member. Else, if a name was specified, the index is obtained by calling if_nametoindex. Otherwise the interface index is set to 0 for setsockopt, telling the kernel to choose the interface. The group is joined.

```
                                                                      ─────────── lib/mcast_join.c
33 #ifdef  IPV6
34     case AF_INET6:{
35            struct ipv6_mreq mreq6;

36            memcpy(&mreq6.ipv6mr_multiaddr,
37                    &((struct sockaddr_in6 *) sa)->sin6_addr,
38                    sizeof(struct in6_addr));

39            if (ifindex > 0)
40                mreq6.ipv6mr_interface = ifindex;
41            else if (ifname != NULL)
42                if ( (mreq6.ipv6mr_interface = if_nametoindex(ifname)) == 0) {
43                    errno = ENXIO;   /* i/f name not found */
44                    return (-1);
45                } else
46                    mreq6.ipv6mr_interface = 0;

47            return (setsockopt(sockfd, IPPROTO_IPV6, IPV6_ADD_MEMBERSHIP,
48                                &mreq6, sizeof(mreq6)));
49        }
50 #endif

51     default:
52         errno = EPROTONOSUPPORT;
53         return (-1);
54     }
55 }
```
─── lib/mcast_join.c

Figure 19.9   Join a multicast group: IPv6 socket.

Example: `mcast_set_loop` Function

Figure 19.10 shows our `mcast_set_loop` function.

Since the argument is a socket descriptor, and not a socket address structure, we call our `sockfd_to_family` function to obtain the address family of the socket. The appropriate socket option is set.

We do not show the source code for all remaining `mcast_XXX` functions, but it is freely available (see the Preface).

19.7 `dg_cli` Function Using Multicasting

We modify our `dg_cli` function from Figure 18.5 by just removing the call to `setsockopt`. As we said earlier, none of the multicast socket options needs to be set to send a multicast datagram, if the default settings for the outgoing interface, TTL, and loopback option are OK. We run our program specifying the all-hosts group as the destination address:

—— *lib/mcast_set_loop.c*

```
 1 #include    "unp.h"

 2 int
 3 mcast_set_loop(int sockfd, int onoff)
 4 {
 5     switch (sockfd_to_family(sockfd)) {
 6     case AF_INET:{
 7             u_char   flag;

 8             flag = onoff;
 9             return (setsockopt(sockfd, IPPROTO_IP, IP_MULTICAST_LOOP,
10                               &flag, sizeof(flag)));
11         }

12 #ifdef  IPV6
13     case AF_INET6:{
14             u_int    flag;

15             flag = onoff;
16             return (setsockopt(sockfd, IPPROTO_IPV6, IPV6_MULTICAST_LOOP,
17                               &flag, sizeof(flag)));
18         }
19 #endif

20     default:
21         errno = EPROTONOSUPPORT;
22         return (-1);
23     }
24 }
```

—— *lib/mcast_set_loop.c*

Figure 19.10 Set the multicast loopback option.

```
solaris % udpcli01 224.0.0.1
hi there
from 206.62.226.40: Fri Jul 18 13:02:41 1997    Linux
from 206.62.226.35: Fri Jul 18 13:02:41 1997    BSD/OS
from 206.62.226.43: Fri Jul 18 13:02:41 1997    AIX
from 206.62.226.34: Fri Jul 18 13:02:41 1997    BSD/OS
from 206.62.226.42: Fri Jul 18 13:02:41 1997    Digital Unix
```

The five hosts respond because each host is multicast capable and has therefore joined
the all-hosts group, and because a process has bound the destination UDP port (13, the
daytime server). Therefore the arriving multicast datagram is delivered to the socket.
This server is normally part of inetd. Each reply is unicast, because the source address
of the request, which is used by each server as the destination address of the reply, is a
unicast address.

> The host sunos5 is the only multicast-capable host on the subnet that does not respond. We
> mentioned earlier that Solaris requires that the socket join the group, which is not the case for
> this example using the standard daytime server.

IP Fragmentation and Multicasts

We mentioned at the end of Section 18.4 that most systems do not allow the fragmentation of a broadcast datagram as a policy decision. Fragmentation is OK with multicasting, as we can easily verify using the same file with a 2000-byte line.

```
bsdi % udpcli01 224.0.0.1 < 2000line
from 206.62.226.35: Fri Jul 18 14:31:50 1997
from 206.62.226.34: Fri Jul 18 14:31:50 1997
from 206.62.226.40: Fri Jul 18 14:31:50 1997
from 206.62.226.43: Fri Jul 18 14:31:50 1997
from 206.62.226.42: Fri Jul 18 14:31:50 1997
```

Many implementations derived from 4.4BSD have a bug in the fragmentation of multicast datagrams: none of the fragments after the first are sent as link-layer multicasts.

19.8   Receiving MBone Session Announcements

To receive a multimedia conference on the MBone (Section B.2) a site needs to know only the multicast address of the conference and the UDP ports for the conference's data streams (audio and video, for example). *SAP*, the Session Announcement Protocol [Handley 1996], describes the way this is done (the packet headers and the frequency with which these announcements are multicast to the MBone) and *SDP*, the Session Description Protocol [Handley and Jacobson 1997], describes the contents of these announcements (how the multicast addresses and UDP port numbers are specified). A site wishing to announce a session on the MBone periodically sends a multicast packet containing a description of the session to a well-known multicast group and UDP port. Sites on the MBone run a program named sdr to receive these announcements. This program does a lot: not only does it receive session announcements but it also provides an interactive user interface that displays the information and lets the user send announcements.

In this section we develop a simple program that only receives these session announcements to show an example of a simple multicast receiving program. Our goal is to show the simplicity of a multicast receiver, and not to delve into the details of this one application.

Figure 19.11 shows our main program that receives the periodic SAP/SDP announcements.

Well-known name and well-known port

2–3   The multicast address assigned for SAP announcements is 224.2.127.254 and its name is sap.mcast.net. All of the well-known multicast addresses (see ftp://ftp.isi.edu/in-notes/iana/assignments/multicast-addresses) appear in the DNS under the mcast.net hierarchy. The well-known UDP port is 9875.

Create UDP socket

12–17   We call our udp_client function to look up the name and port, and it fills in the appropriate socket address structure. We use the defaults if no command-line

—————————————————————————— mysdr/main.c

```
 1 #include    "unp.h"

 2 #define SAP_NAME     "sap.mcast.net"     /* default group name and port */
 3 #define SAP_PORT     "9875"

 4 void    loop(int, socklen_t);

 5 int
 6 main(int argc, char **argv)
 7 {
 8     int      sockfd;
 9     const int on = 1;
10     socklen_t salen;
11     struct sockaddr *sa;

12     if (argc == 1)
13         sockfd = Udp_client(SAP_NAME, SAP_PORT, (void **) &sa, &salen);
14     else if (argc == 4)
15         sockfd = Udp_client(argv[1], argv[2], (void **) &sa, &salen);
16     else
17         err_quit("usage: mysdr <mcast-addr> <port#> <interface-name>");

18     Setsockopt(sockfd, SOL_SOCKET, SO_REUSEADDR, &on, sizeof(on));
19     Bind(sockfd, sa, salen);

20     Mcast_join(sockfd, sa, salen, (argc == 4) ? argv[3] : NULL, 0);

21     loop(sockfd, salen);         /* receive and print */

22     exit(0);
23 }
```

—————————————————————————— mysdr/main.c

Figure 19.11 main program to receive SAP/SDP announcements.

arguments are specified; otherwise we take the multicast address, port, and interface name from the command-line arguments.

bind port

18–19 We set the SO_REUSEADDR socket option to allow multiple instances of this program to run on a host, and bind the port to the socket. By binding the multicast address to the socket we prevent the socket from receiving any other UDP datagrams that may be received for the port. Binding this multicast address is not required, but it provides filtering by the kernel of packets in which we are not interested.

Join multicast group

20 We call our mcast_join function to join the group. If the interface name was specified as a command-line argument, it is passed to our function; otherwise we let the kernel choose the interface on which the group is joined.

21 We call our loop function, shown in Figure 19.12, to read and print all the announcements.

```
                                                                    —— mysdr/loop.c
 1 #include    "unp.h"

 2 void
 3 loop(int sockfd, socklen_t salen)
 4 {
 5     char    buf[MAXLINE + 1];
 6     socklen_t len;
 7     ssize_t n;
 8     struct sockaddr *sa;
 9     struct sap_packet {
10         uint32_t sap_header;
11         uint32_t sap_src;
12         char    sap_data[1];
13     } *sapptr;

14     sa = Malloc(salen);

15     for ( ; ; ) {
16         len = salen;
17         n = Recvfrom(sockfd, buf, MAXLINE, 0, sa, &len);
18         buf[n] = 0;                /* null terminate */

19         sapptr = (struct sap_packet *) buf;
20         if ((n -= 2 * sizeof(uint32_t)) <= 0)
21             err_quit("n = %d", n);
22         printf("From %s\n%s\n", Sock_ntop(sa, len), sapptr->sap_data);
23     }
24 }
                                                                    —— mysdr/loop.c
```

Figure 19.12 Loop that receives and prints SAP/SDP announcements.

Packet format

9–13   `sap_packet` describes the SDP packet: a 32-bit SAP header, followed by a 32-bit source address, followed by the actual announcement. The announcement is simply lines of ISO 8859–1 text and cannot exceed 1024 bytes. Only one session announcement is allowed in each UDP datagram.

Read UDP datagram, print sender and contents

15–23   `recvfrom` waits for the next UDP datagram destined to our socket. When one arrives we place a null byte at the end of the buffer and skip over the two header fields, and print the result. We also print the IP address and port number of the sender of the multicast announcement.

Figure 19.13 shows some typical output from our program.

```
solaris % mysdr
From 128.102.84.134/2840
v=0
o=shuttle 3050400397 3051818822 IN IP4 128.102.84.134
s=NASA - Shuttle STS-79 Mission Coverage
i=Pre-launch and mission coverage of Shuttle Mission STS-79.  Launch expected 9/
16/96 with a mission duration anticipated of 9-10 days.  STS-79 is the 4th in a
```

```
series of joint docking missions between the Shuttle and the MIR Space Station.
This session is being offered by NASA - Ames Research Center as a public service
 to the MBone community.
u=http://www-pao.ksc.nasa.gov/kscpao/kscpao.htm
p=NASA ARC Digital Video Lab (415) 604-6145
e=NASA ARC Digital Video Lab <mallard@mail.arc.nasa.gov>
c=IN IP4 224.2.86.28/127
t=3051608400 3052472400
m=audio 19432 RTP/AVP 0
m=video 61192 RTP/AVP 31
```

Figure 19.13   Typical SAP/SDP announcement.

This announcement describes the NASA coverage on the MBone of a space shuttle mission. The SDP session description consists of numerous lines of the form

> *type=value*

where the *type* is always one character and is case significant. The *value* is a structured text string that depends on the *type*. Spaces are not allowed around the equals sign. v=0 is the version.

o= is the origin. `shuttle` is the username, `3050400397` is the session ID, `3051818822` is the version number for this announcement, `IN` is the network type, `IP4` is the address type, and `128.102.84.134` is the address. The five-tuple consisting of the username, session ID, network type, address type, and address form a globally unique identifier for the session.

s= defines the session name, and i= is information about the session. We have wrapped the latter every 80 characters. u= provides a URI (Uniform Resource Identifier) for more information about the session, and p= and e= provide a phone number and email address of someone responsible for the conference.

c= provides the connection information, which in this example specifies that it is IP based, using IPv4, with a multicast address of 224.2.86.28 and a TTL of 127. t= provides the starting time and stopping time, both in NTP units, which are seconds since January 1, 1900, UTC. The m= lines are the media announcements. The first of these two lines specifies that the audio is on port 19432 and its format is RTP, the Real-time Transport Protocol, using AVP, the Audio/Video Profile, with payload type 0 (which is a PCM coded signal channel audio, encoded at 8 Khz). The next m= line specifies that the video is on port 61192 and the RTP/AVP payload type of 31 is ITU H.261 video format. Notice that the audio and video are both multicast to the same address (224.2.86.28) but to different ports. This means that if a host wants only one of the two, both will be received by the IP layer once the host joins the group and the unwanted data will be discarded by UDP.

19.9   Sending and Receiving

The MBone session announcement program in the previous section received only multicast datagrams. We now develop a simple program that sends and receives multicast

datagrams. Our program consists of two parts. The first part sends a multicast datagram to a specific group every 5 seconds and the datagram contains the sender's hostname and process ID. The second part is an infinite loop that joins the multicast group
to which the first part is sending and prints every received datagram (containing the
hostname and process ID of the sender). This allows us to start the program on multiple hosts on a LAN and easily see which host is receiving datagrams from which
senders.

Figure 19.14 shows the `main` function for our program.

```
                                                                   ─── mcast/main.c
 1 #include    "unp.h"

 2 void    recv_all(int, socklen_t);
 3 void    send_all(int, SA *, socklen_t);

 4 int
 5 main(int argc, char **argv)
 6 {
 7     int       sendfd, recvfd;
 8     const int on = 1;
 9     socklen_t salen;
10     struct sockaddr *sasend, *sarecv;

11     if (argc != 3)
12         err_quit("usage: sendrecv <IP-multicast-address> <port#>");

13     sendfd = Udp_client(argv[1], argv[2], (void **) &sasend, &salen);

14     recvfd = Socket(sasend->sa_family, SOCK_DGRAM, 0);

15     Setsockopt(recvfd, SOL_SOCKET, SO_REUSEADDR, &on, sizeof(on));

16     sarecv = Malloc(salen);
17     memcpy(sarecv, sasend, salen);
18     Bind(recvfd, sarecv, salen);

19     Mcast_join(recvfd, sasend, salen, NULL, 0);
20     Mcast_set_loop(sendfd, 0);

21     if (Fork() == 0)
22         recv_all(recvfd, salen);     /* child -> receives */

23     send_all(sendfd, sasend, salen);     /* parent -> sends */
24 }
                                                                   ─── mcast/main.c
```

Figure 19.14   Create sockets, `fork`, and start sender and receiver.

We create two sockets, one for sending and one for receiving. We want the receiving socket to `bind` the multicast group and port, say 239.255.1.2 port 8888. (Recall that
we could just `bind` the wildcard IP address and port 8888, but binding the multicast
address prevents the socket from receiving any other datagrams that might arrive destined for port 8888.) We then want the receiving socket to join the multicast group. The
sending socket will send datagrams to this same multicast address and port, say
239.255.1.2 port 8888. But if we try to use a single socket for sending and receiving, the
source protocol address is 239.255.1.2.8888 from the `bind` (using `netstat` notation)

and the destination protocol address for the `sendto` is also 239.255.1.2.8888. But the source protocol address that is bound to the socket becomes the source IP address of the UDP datagram, and RFC 1122 [Braden 1989] forbids an IP datagram from having a source IP address that is a multicast address or a broadcast address. (See Exercise 19.2 also.) Therefore we create two sockets: one for sending and one for receiving.

Create sending socket

13   Our `udp_client` function creates the sending socket, processing the two command-line arguments that specify the multicast address and port number. This function also returns a socket address structure that is ready for calls to `sendto` along with the length of this socket address structure.

Create receiving socket and `bind` multicast address and port

14–18   We create the receiving socket, using the same address family that was used for the sending socket. We set the `SO_REUSEADDR` socket option to allow multiple instances of this program to run at the same time on a host. We then allocate room for a socket address structure for this socket, copy its contents from the sending socket address structure (whose address and port were taken from the command-line arguments), and `bind` the multicast address and port to the receiving socket.

Join multicast group and turn off loopback

19–20   We call our `mcast_join` function to join the multicast group on the receiving socket, and our `mcast_set_loop` function to disable the loopback feature on the sending socket. For the join we specify the interface name as a null pointer and the interface index as 0, telling the kernel to choose the interface.

`fork` and call appropriate functions

21–23   We `fork` and then the child is the receive loop and the parent is the send loop.

Our `send_all` function, which sends one multicast datagram every 5 seconds, is shown in Figure 19.15. The `main` function passes as arguments the socket descriptor, a pointer to a socket address structure containing the multicast destination and the port, and the structure's length.

Obtain hostname and form datagram contents

9–11   We obtain the hostname from the `uname` function and build the output line containing it and the process ID.

Send datagram, then go to sleep

12–15   We send a datagram and then `sleep` for 5 seconds.

The `recv_all` function, which is the infinite receive loop, is shown in Figure 19.16.

Allocate socket address structure

9   A socket address structure is allocated to receive the sender's protocol address for each call to `recvfrom`.

Read and print datagrams

10–15   Each datagram is read by `recvfrom`, null terminated, and printed.

```
                                                                    mcast/send.c
1 #include      "unp.h"
2 #include      <sys/utsname.h>

3 #define SENDRATE    5              /* send one datagram every 5 seconds */

4 void
5 send_all(int sendfd, SA *sadest, socklen_t salen)
6 {
7     static char line[MAXLINE];   /* hostname and process ID */
8     struct utsname myname;

9     if (uname(&myname) < 0)
10        err_sys("uname error");;
11    snprintf(line, sizeof(line), "%s, %d\n", myname.nodename, getpid());

12    for ( ; ; ) {
13        Sendto(sendfd, line, strlen(line), 0, sadest, salen);

14        sleep(SENDRATE);
15    }
16 }
                                                                    mcast/send.c
```

Figure 19.15 Send a multicast datagram every 5 seconds.

```
                                                                    mcast/recv.c
1 #include      "unp.h"

2 void
3 recv_all(int recvfd, socklen_t salen)
4 {
5     int      n;
6     char     line[MAXLINE + 1];
7     socklen_t len;
8     struct sockaddr *safrom;

9     safrom = Malloc(salen);

10    for ( ; ; ) {
11        len = salen;
12        n = Recvfrom(recvfd, line, MAXLINE, 0, safrom, &len);

13        line[n] = 0;                 /* null terminate */
14        printf("from %s: %s", Sock_ntop(safrom, len), line);
15    }
16 }
                                                                    mcast/recv.c
```

Figure 19.16 Receive all multicast datagrams for a group that we have joined.

19.10 SNTP: Simple Network Time Protocol

NTP, the Network Time Protocol, is a sophisticated protocol for synchronizing clocks across a WAN or a LAN, and can often achieve millisecond accuracy. RFC 1305 [Mills

1992] describes the protocol in detail and RFC 2030 [Mills 1996] describes SNTP, a simplified version intended for hosts that do not need the complexity of a complete NTP implementation. It is common for a few hosts on a LAN to synchronize their clocks across the Internet to other NTP hosts, and then redistribute this time on the LAN using either broadcasting or multicasting.

In this section we develop an SNTP client that listens for NTP broadcasts or multicasts on all attached networks and then prints the time difference between the NTP packet and the host's current time-of-day. We do not try to adjust the time-of-day, as that takes superuser privileges, although that would be a trivial addition to the code.

The file `ntp.h`, shown in Figure 19.17, contains some basic definitions of the NTP packet format.

ssntp/ntp.h
```
 1 #define JAN_1970    2208988800UL    /* 1970 - 1900 in seconds */

 2 struct l_fixedpt {                  /* 64-bit fixed-point */
 3     uint32_t int_part;
 4     uint32_t fraction;
 5 };

 6 struct s_fixedpt {                  /* 32-bit fixed-point */
 7     u_short int_part;
 8     u_short fraction;
 9 };

10 struct ntpdata {                    /* NTP header */
11     u_char   status;
12     u_char   stratum;
13     u_char   ppoll;
14     int      precision:8;
15     struct s_fixedpt distance;
16     struct s_fixedpt dispersion;
17     uint32_t refid;
18     struct l_fixedpt reftime;
19     struct l_fixedpt org;
20     struct l_fixedpt rec;
21     struct l_fixedpt xmt;
22 };

23 #define VERSION_MASK    0x38
24 #define MODE_MASK       0x07

25 #define MODE_CLIENT     3
26 #define MODE_SERVER     4
27 #define MODE_BROADCAST  5
```
ssntp/ntp.h

Figure 19.17 `ntp.h` header: NTP packet format and definitions.

2–22   `l_fixedpt` defines the 64-bit fixed point values used by NTP for timestamps and `s_fixedpt` defines the 32-bit fixed point values that are also used by NTP. The `ntpdata` structure is the 48-byte NTP packet format.

Figure 19.18 shows the `main` function.

```
                                                                  ——— ssntp/main.c
 1 #include    "sntp.h"

 2 int
 3 main(int argc, char **argv)
 4 {
 5     int     sockfd;
 6     char    buf[MAXLINE];
 7     ssize_t n;
 8     socklen_t salen, len;
 9     struct ifi_info *ifi;
10     struct sockaddr *mcastsa, *wild, *from;
11     struct timeval now;

12     if (argc != 2)
13         err_quit("usage: ssntp <IPaddress>");

14     sockfd = Udp_client(argv[1], "ntp", (void **) &mcastsa, &salen);

15     wild = Malloc(salen);
16     memcpy(wild, mcastsa, salen);   /* copy family and port */
17     sock_set_wild(wild, salen);
18     Bind(sockfd, wild, salen);   /* bind wildcard */

19 #ifdef  MCAST
20         /* obtain interface list and process each one */
21     for (ifi = Get_ifi_info(mcastsa->sa_family, 1); ifi != NULL;
22          ifi = ifi->ifi_next) {
23         if (ifi->ifi_flags & IFF_MULTICAST)
24             Mcast_join(sockfd, mcastsa, salen, ifi->ifi_name, 0);
25         printf("joined %s on %s\n",
26                 Sock_ntop(mcastsa, salen), ifi->ifi_name);
27     }
28 #endif

29     from = Malloc(salen);
30     for ( ; ; ) {
31         len = salen;
32         n = Recvfrom(sockfd, buf, sizeof(buf), 0, from, &len);
33         Gettimeofday(&now, NULL);
34         sntp_proc(buf, n, &now);
35     }
36 }
                                                                  ——— ssntp/main.c
```

Figure 19.18 main function.

Get multicast IP address

12-14   When the program is executed, the user must specify the multicast address to join as the command-line argument. With IPv4 this would be 224.0.1.1 or the name ntp.mcast.net. With IPv6 this would be ff05::101 for the site-local scope NTP. Our udp_client function allocates space for a socket address structure of the correct type (either IPv4 or IPv6) and stores the multicast address and port in that structure. If this program is run on a host that does not support multicasting, any IP address can be specified, as only the address family and port are used from this structure. Note that our `udp_client` function does not `bind` the address to the socket; it just creates the socket and fills in the socket address structure.

Bind wildcard address to socket

15-18   We allocate space for another socket address structure and fill it in by copying the structure that was filled in by `udp_client`. This sets the address family and port. We call our `sock_set_wild` function to set the IP address to the wildcard and then call `bind`.

Get interface list

20-22   Our `get_ifi_info` function returns information on all the interfaces and addresses. The address family that we ask for is taken from the socket address structure that was filled in by `udp_client` based on the command-line argument.

Join the multicast group

23-24   We call our `mcast_join` function to join the multicast group specified by the command-line argument for each multicast-capable interface. All these joins are done on the one socket that this program uses. As we said earlier, there is normally a limit of 20 joins per socket, but few multihomed hosts have that many interfaces.

Read and process all NTP packets

29-35   Another socket address structure is allocated to hold the address returned by `recvfrom` and the program enters an infinite loop, reading all the NTP packets that the host receives and calling our `sntp_proc` function (described next) to process the packet. Since the socket was bound to the wildcard address, and since the multicast group was joined on all multicast-capable interfaces, the socket should receive any unicast, broadcast, or multicast NTP packet that the host receives. Before calling `sntp_proc` we call `gettimeofday` to fetch the current time, because `sntp_proc` calculates the difference between the time in the packet and the current time.

Our `sntp_proc` function, shown in Figure 19.19, processes the actual NTP packet.

Validate packet

10-21   We first check the size of the packet and then print the version, mode, and server stratum. If the mode is `MODE_CLIENT`, then the packet is a client request, not a server reply, and we ignore it.

Obtain transmit time from NTP packet

22-34   The field in the NTP packet that we are interested in is `xmt`, the transmit timestamp, which is the 64-bit fixed-point time at which the packet was sent by the server. Since NTP timestamps count seconds beginning in 1900 and Unix timestamps count seconds beginning in 1970, we first subtract `JAN_1970` (the number of seconds in these 70 years) from the integer part.

The fractional part is a 32-bit unsigned integer between 0 and 4,294,967,295, inclusive. This is copied from a 32-bit integer (`useci`) to a double precision floating-point variable (`usecf`) and then divided by 4,294,967,296 (2^{32}). The result is greater than or equal to 0.0 and less than 1.0. We multiply this by 1,000,000, the number of microseconds in a second, storing the result as a 32-bit unsigned integer in the variable `useci`.

ssntp/sntp_proc.c

```
 1 #include    "sntp.h"

 2 void
 3 sntp_proc(char *buf, ssize_t n, struct timeval *nowptr)
 4 {
 5     int      version, mode;
 6     uint32_t nsec, useci;
 7     double   usecf;
 8     struct timeval curr, diff;
 9     struct ntpdata *ntp;

10     if (n < sizeof(struct ntpdata)) {
11         printf("\npacket too small: %d bytes\n", n);
12         return;
13     }
14     ntp = (struct ntpdata *) buf;
15     version = (ntp->status & VERSION_MASK) >> 3;
16     mode = ntp->status & MODE_MASK;
17     printf("\nv%d, mode %d, strat %d, ", version, mode, ntp->stratum);
18     if (mode == MODE_CLIENT) {
19         printf("client\n");
20         return;
21     }
22     nsec = ntohl(ntp->xmt.int_part) - JAN_1970;
23     useci = htonl(ntp->xmt.fraction);    /* 32-bit integer fraction */
24     usecf = useci;              /* integer fraction -> double */
25     usecf /= 4294967296.0;       /* divide by 2**32 -> [0, 1.0) */
26     useci = usecf * 1000000.0;   /* fraction -> parts per million */

27     curr = *nowptr;              /* make a copy as we might modify it below */
28     if ( (diff.tv_usec = curr.tv_usec - useci) < 0) {
29         diff.tv_usec += 1000000;
30         curr.tv_sec--;
31     }
32     diff.tv_sec = curr.tv_sec - nsec;
33     useci = (diff.tv_sec * 1000000) + diff.tv_usec;    /* diff in microsec */
34     printf("clock difference = %d usec\n", useci);
35 }
```

ssntp/sntp_proc.c

Figure 19.19 sntp_proc function: process the SNTP packet.

This is the number of microseconds and will be between 0 and 999,999 (see Exercise 19.8). We convert to microseconds because the Unix timestamp returned by gettimeofday is returned as two integers: the number of seconds since January 1, 1970, UTC, along with the number of microseconds. We then calculate and print the difference between the host's time-of-day and the NTP server's time-of-day, in microseconds.

One thing that our program does not take into account is the network delay between the server and the client. But we assume that the NTP packets are normally received as a broadcast or multicast on a LAN, in which case the network delay should be only a few milliseconds.

If we run this program on our host `solaris` with an NTP server on our host `bsdi` that is multicasting NTP packets to the Ethernet every 64 seconds, we have the following output:

```
solaris # ssntp 224.0.1.1
joined 224.0.1.1.123 on lo0
joined 224.0.1.1.123 on le0

v3, mode 5, strat 3, clock difference = 621 usec

v3, mode 5, strat 3, clock difference = 1205 usec

v3, mode 5, strat 3, clock difference = 1664 usec

v3, mode 5, strat 3, clock difference = 2291 usec

v3, mode 5, strat 3, clock difference = 2942 usec

v3, mode 5, strat 3, clock difference = 3558 usec
```

To run our program we first terminated the normal NTP server running on this host, so when our program starts the time is very close to the server's time. We see this host is losing about 600 microseconds every 64 seconds, or about 810 ms in 24 hours.

19.11 SNTP (Continued)

We now expand our SNTP example with additional features. First, when the program starts it creates one socket per unicast address, one socket per broadcast address, and one socket per interface on which the multicast group is joined, instead of the single socket used in Section 19.10. The purpose of this is to determine the destination address of the packets that we receive. Second, when the program starts it broadcasts and multicasts an SNTP client request out from all attached interfaces, to get an initial estimate of the difference.

Warning: This code should not be taken as the recommended way to code an SNTP client. Our goal is to understand more about broadcasting and multicasting, especially on a multihomed host or router, along with the loopback property of broadcasts and multicasts. We pick SNTP to show these properties, because it is a useful, real-world application. Our client sends an SNTP client request out from all broadcast-capable and multicast-capable interfaces when it starts to show how some programs perform resource discovery when they start. This is not recommended for an SNTP client. A better technique is just to listen for server broadcasts or server multicasts as in Section 19.10.

Figure 19.20 is an overview of the functions that comprise our program. We first call our `get_ifi_info` program from Section 16.6 to obtain the interface list. For each interface we create a UDP socket and `bind` the unicast address, create another UDP socket and `bind` the broadcast address, and create another UDP socket and `bind` the NTP multicast group (224.0.1.1) and join the multicast group on that interface. Our `sntp_send` function sends a broadcast request out from each broadcast-capable socket to any NTP server on the attached subnet for the current time, and sends a multicast

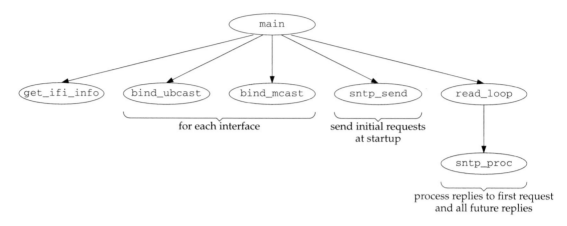

Figure 19.20 Overview of functions in our SNTP client.

request out from all multicast-capable sockets. The purpose of this first batch of sends is to find all the NTP servers on the attached subnets and to get an initial estimate of the current time.

The program then enters an infinite loop, read_loop, reading any replies that arrive. We first expect replies from some of the datagrams sent by sntp_send, and after that we should just receive the periodic transmissions from all NTP servers on any attached subnet. Most NTP servers that are broadcasting or multicasting send one datagram every 64 seconds. sntp_proc is the same function shown in Figure 19.19 that processes a received NTP packet.

We start our code presentation with Figure 19.21, our own sntp.h header that is included by all our programs. The ntp.h header that it includes is the same one shown in Figure 19.17.

Define Addrs structure

3–12   We define a structure of type Addrs that contains the information that we need for each address returned for a given interface. Since each ifi_info structure returned by our get_ifi_info function can have two addresses (a unicast address and a broadcast address, for example), we need to maintain two of our own Addrs structures, one for each address. The addr_sa member points to the socket address structure that is returned by get_ifi_info and addr_salen is its length. We save a pointer to the interface name in addr_ifname, and this will be used for multicasting. We will create one socket for each address, and the descriptor is saved in addr_fd. We also need to know if this socket has been bound to a broadcast address or a multicast address, and this is saved in the addr_flags member.

sntp/sntp.h

```
 1 #include   "unpifi.h"
 2 #include   "ntp.h"

 3 #define MAXNADDRS   128         /* max # of addresses to bind() */
 4 typedef struct {
 5     struct sockaddr *addr_sa;   /* ptr to bound address */
 6     socklen_t addr_salen;       /* socket address length */
 7     const char *addr_ifname;    /* interface name, for multicasting */
 8     int     addr_fd;            /* socket descriptor */
 9     int     addr_flags;         /* ADDR_xxx flags (see below) */
10 } Addrs;

11 Addrs    addrs[MAXNADDRS];      /* the actual array of structs */
12 int      naddrs;                /* index into the array */

13 #define ADDR_BCAST  1
14 #define ADDR_MCAST  2

15 const int on;                   /* for setsockopt() */

16              /* function prototypes */
17 void    bind_mcast(const char *, SA *, socklen_t, int);
18 void    bind_ubcast(SA *, socklen_t, int, int, int);
19 void    read_loop(void);
20 void    sntp_proc(char *, ssize_t nread, struct timeval *);
21 void    sntp_send(void);
```

sntp/sntp.h

Figure 19.21 sntp.h header.

Figure 19.22 shows the main function.

Get well-known multicast address and well-known port

10–14   The command-line argument is normally the name ntp.mcast.net, which maps into the multicast address 224.0.1.1. The service name is ntp. Our udp_client function allocates space for a socket address structure of the correct type (either IPv4 or IPv6) and stores the multicast address and port in that structure. If this program is run on a host that does not support multicasting, any IP address can be specified, as only the port will be used from this structure. We then close this socket, as the purpose of calling udp_client was just to fill in the socket address structure.

Get interface list

15–17   Our get_ifi_info function returns information on all the interfaces and addresses. The address family that we ask for is taken from the socket address structure that was filled in by udp_client based on the command-line argument.

Process each unicast and broadcast address

18–22   We call our bind_ubcast function one or two times for each address. The first time the final argument is 0, meaning the first argument points to the unicast address, and the next time it is 1, meaning the first argument points to the broadcast address. A value of 1 as the second argument to get_ifi_info tells it to return information about

```
                                                                    —— sntp/main.c
 1 #include     "sntp.h"

 2 const int on = 1;                   /* for setsockopt() flags */

 3 int
 4 main(int argc, char **argv)
 5 {
 6     int      sockfd, port;
 7     socklen_t salen;
 8     struct ifi_info *ifi;
 9     struct sockaddr *mcastsa, *wild;

10     if (argc != 2)
11         err_quit("usage: sntp <IPaddress>");

12     sockfd = Udp_client(argv[1], "ntp", (void **) &mcastsa, &salen);
13     port = sock_get_port(mcastsa, salen);
14     Close(sockfd);

15         /* obtain interface list and process each one */
16     for (ifi = Get_ifi_info(mcastsa->sa_family, 1); ifi != NULL;
17         ifi = ifi->ifi_next) {
18         bind_ubcast(ifi->ifi_addr, salen, port,
19                   ifi->ifi_myflags & IFI_ALIAS, 0);   /* unicast */

20         if (ifi->ifi_flags & IFF_BROADCAST)
21             bind_ubcast(ifi->ifi_brdaddr, salen, port,
22                       ifi->ifi_myflags & IFI_ALIAS, 1);   /* bcast */

23 #ifdef  MCAST
24         if (ifi->ifi_flags & IFF_MULTICAST)
25             bind_mcast(ifi->ifi_name, mcastsa, salen,
26                       ifi->ifi_myflags & IFI_ALIAS);   /* mcast */
27 #endif
28     }

29     wild = Malloc(salen);       /* socket address struct for wildcard */
30     memcpy(wild, mcastsa, salen);
31     sock_set_wild(wild, salen);
32     bind_ubcast(wild, salen, port, 0, 0);

33     sntp_send();                /* send first queries */

34     read_loop();                /* never returns */
35 }
                                                                    —— sntp/main.c
```

Figure 19.22 main function.

alias addresses. We then pass the IFI_ALIAS flag to our bind_XXX functions, letting each function decide how to handle alias addresses, as we will see shortly.

Join multicast group

23–27   If the interface is multicast capable, we call our bind_mcast function for each unicast address also, as we want to join the multicast group on each interface.

Bind wildcard address

29-32   After processing all the interface information, we allocate another socket address structure and copy its contents from the one filled in by `udp_client`. We then call our `sock_set_wild` function to store the appropriate wildcard address in the structure. `bind_ubcast` creates a socket and binds the wildcard address to it. This handles datagrams that arrive destined for some other address, such as 255.255.255.255, which we are unable to bind.

Send initial requests and read all subsequent replies

33-34   `sntp_send` broadcasts an SNTP request out from all broadcast-capable interfaces and multicasts an SNTP request out from all multicast-capable interfaces. `read_loop` then reads any replies to these requests, along with any future NTP broadcast or multicast packets that are received.

Figure 19.23 shows the sockets that will be created for our host `bsdi`. Recall from Figure 1.16 that this host is really a router with two Ethernet interfaces. We showed the interfaces and their unicast and broadcast IP addresses in the examples following Figure 16.6, although now we assume that there are no alias addresses. We will create nine sockets and `bind` the same port nine times.

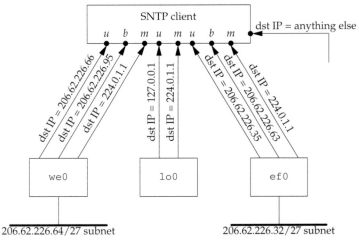

Figure 19.23   Nine sockets created by our SNTP client on host `bsdi`.

We have labeled the bottom eight sockets with *u*, *b*, or *m*, if the socket has bound a unicast address, broadcast address, or multicast address. We show the destination IP address of the packets that will be received on each socket and note that the socket bound to 0.0.0.0 on the right can receive packets destined to any other IP address (often 255.255.255.255) arriving on any interface.

Our `bind_ubcast` function is shown in Figure 19.24. This function is called for all unicast addresses, all broadcast addresses, and the wildcard address. The final argument in the three calls from Figure 19.22 is 1 only for a broadcast address.

```
                                                                          ─ sntp/bind_ubcast.c
 1 #include    "sntp.h"

 2 void
 3 bind_ubcast(struct sockaddr *sabind, socklen_t salen, int port,
 4             int alias, int bcast)
 5 {
 6     int     i, fd;

 7         /* first see if we've already bound this address */
 8     for (i = 0; i < naddrs; i++) {
 9         if (sock_cmp_addr(addrs[i].addr_sa, sabind, salen) == 0)
10             return;
11     }

12     fd = Socket(sabind->sa_family, SOCK_DGRAM, 0);

13     sock_set_port(sabind, salen, port);

14     Setsockopt(fd, SOL_SOCKET, SO_REUSEADDR, &on, sizeof(on));

15     printf("binding %s\n", Sock_ntop(sabind, salen));
16     if (bind(fd, sabind, salen) < 0) {
17         if (errno == EADDRINUSE) {
18             printf("  (address already in use)\n");
19             close(fd);
20             return;
21         } else
22             err_sys("bind error");
23     }
24     addrs[naddrs].addr_sa = sabind;        /* save ptr to sockaddr{} */
25     addrs[naddrs].addr_salen = salen;
26     addrs[naddrs].addr_fd = fd;
27     if (bcast)
28         addrs[naddrs].addr_flags = ADDR_BCAST;
29     naddrs++;
30 }
                                                                          ─ sntp/bind_ubcast.c
```

Figure 19.24 bind_ubcast function: create socket for unicast or broadcast address.

See if address has already been bound

7–11   We first check if this address has already been bound. While this will not happen for a unicast address, in the case of aliases that share the same broadcast address, we want to bind the broadcast address only one time.

Create socket and bind address

12–23   We create a UDP socket, set the port, and then set the SO_REUSEADDR socket option (since we are binding the same port for each address). We bind the address to the socket. The socket address structure in which we store the port for the bind is the one filled in and returned by get_ifi_info. We allow the bind to fail, which should happen only if the NTP daemon is itself running on this host.

Save information about this socket

24–29   The information is saved in our `Addrs` structure, including a flag if this address is a broadcast address.

For multicast-capable interfaces we need to create a socket, bind the well-known port, and then join the multicast group on the interface. This is done by our `bind_mcast` function, shown in Figure 19.25.

```
                                                               ——— sntp/bind_mcast.c
 1 #include    "sntp.h"

 2 void
 3 bind_mcast(const char *ifname, SA *mcastsa, socklen_t salen, int alias)
 4 {
 5 #ifdef  MCAST
 6     int     fd;
 7     struct sockaddr *msa;

 8     if (alias)
 9         return;                     /* only one mcast join per interface */

10     printf("joining %s on %s\n", Sock_ntop_host(mcastsa, salen), ifname);

11     fd = Socket(mcastsa->sa_family, SOCK_DGRAM, 0);

12     Setsockopt(fd, SOL_SOCKET, SO_REUSEADDR, &on, sizeof(on));
13     Bind(fd, mcastsa, salen);

14     Mcast_join(fd, mcastsa, salen, ifname, 0);

15     addrs[naddrs].addr_sa = mcastsa;
16     addrs[naddrs].addr_salen = salen;
17     addrs[naddrs].addr_ifname = ifname;      /* save pointer, not string copy */
18     addrs[naddrs].addr_fd = fd;
19     addrs[naddrs].addr_flags = ADDR_MCAST;
20     naddrs++;
21 #endif
22 }
                                                               ——— sntp/bind_mcast.c
```

Figure 19.25 `bind_mcast` function: join multicast group on interface.

Create socket and bind

8–13   If this address is an alias, we return immediately, as we need only join the multicast group once per interface, regardless of how many unicast addresses are aliased to the interface. The socket is created and the multicast group and well-known port are bound to the socket.

Join multicast group and save information

14–20   The multicast group is joined on the interface. We save the information in our `Addrs` structure. The `mcastsa` pointer that is saved in the `addr_sa` member points to the one socket address structure that was allocated by the call to our `udp_client` function in the `main` function. The `addr_sa` member for each multicast-capable interface points to this same structure, but that is OK, as the structure is never modified. The addr_ifname pointer points to the interface name string in the ifi_info structure, which is OK because our free_ifi_info function is never called to free this memory.

The next function is sntp_send, shown in Figure 19.26, which is called by main after all the interface information has been processed, and all the sockets have been created.

―――――――――――――――――――――――――――――― *sntp/sntp_send.c*

```
 1 #include    "sntp.h"

 2 void
 3 sntp_send(void)
 4 {
 5     int     fd;
 6     Addrs   *aptr;
 7     struct ntpdata msg;

 8         /* use the socket bound to 0.0.0.0/123 for sending */
 9     fd = addrs[naddrs - 1].addr_fd;
10     Setsockopt(fd, SOL_SOCKET, SO_BROADCAST, &on, sizeof(on));

11     bzero(&msg, sizeof(msg));
12     msg.status = (0 << 6) | (3 << 3) | MODE_CLIENT;      /* see RFC 2030 */

13     for (aptr = &addrs[0]; aptr < &addrs[naddrs]; aptr++) {
14         if (aptr->addr_flags & ADDR_BCAST) {
15             printf("sending broadcast to %s\n",
16                     Sock_ntop(aptr->addr_sa, aptr->addr_salen));
17             Sendto(fd, &msg, sizeof(msg), 0,
18                     aptr->addr_sa, aptr->addr_salen);
19         }
20 #ifdef  MCAST
21         if (aptr->addr_flags & ADDR_MCAST) {
22                 /* must first set outgoing i/f appropriately */
23             Mcast_set_if(fd, aptr->addr_ifname, 0);
24             Mcast_set_loop(fd, 0);  /* disable loopback */

25             printf("sending multicast to %s on %s\n",
26                     Sock_ntop(aptr->addr_sa, aptr->addr_salen),
27                     aptr->addr_ifname);
28             Sendto(fd, &msg, sizeof(msg), 0,
29                     aptr->addr_sa, aptr->addr_salen);
30         }
31 #endif
32     }
33 }
```

―――――――――――――――――――――――――――――― *sntp/sntp_send.c*

Figure 19.26 sntp_send function: broadcast and multicast SNTP requests.

Set SO_BROADCAST socket option and form request

8-12   Instead of creating a socket just for sending, we use the socket bound to the wildcard address for the calls to sendto. Since the IP address is the wildcard, the kernel uses the primary unicast address of the outgoing interface as the source IP address of the UDP datagram. We first set the SO_BROADCAST socket option. We then form the

SNTP request: we set LI (the leap indicator) to 0, the version to 3, and the mode to
CLIENT_MODE. These are the only fields that need be set in a client request.

Send broadcast request

14–19   If the address is a broadcast address, the request is broadcast.

Send multicast request

21–30   If the address is a multicast address we first specify the outgoing interface for multicasts on the socket (our mcast_set_if function) and then disable multicast loopback
on this socket (our mcast_set_loop function). If we did not disable the loopback feature, we could receive many copies of this packet on all the receiving sockets (see Exercise 19.11). The datagram is sent to the multicast address.

> This code shows a typical paradigm for multicast applications, which we can summarize as
>
> ```
> for (each interface) {
>     mcast_set_if( ... );
>     sendto( ... );
> }
> ```
>
> A datagram is sent out from each interface, so the outgoing interface must be set using the
> socket option before each sendto. This involves an additional system call for each datagram
> that is output. An alternative is to create one sending socket for each interface and set the out-
> going interface for each socket one time after it is created. We will see in Section 20.8 that IPv6
> allows the outgoing interface to be specified as ancillary data with a call to sendmsg, reducing
> the number of system calls in this scenario.
>
> There is also a class of multicast applications that does not care about the outgoing interface,
> sending only one datagram at a time, and letting the kernel choose the outgoing interface.

Using Figure 19.23 as our example, five datagrams would be sent by sntp_send:
one on each broadcast and multicast socket. Nothing is sent on the unicast sockets.

The next function is read_loop, and we show the first half in Figure 19.27. This
function is called at the end of the main function, and it just reads from all the sockets
that were created: any broadcast, multicast, or unicast NTP packets that appear on any
of the host's interfaces. We expect most NTP packets to be received as broadcasts or
multicasts, but responses to the queries sent by sntp_send will be unicast.

Allocate multiple buffers and socket address structures

4–19   We allocate two buffers in which we receive datagrams, two socket address structures in which the corresponding source address is stored, and two variables that hold
the size of the corresponding datagram. The index corresponding to the current datagram is in currb, and the index corresponding to the last datagram is in lastb. One
index will have the value 0 and the other will have the value 1. The reason we need
storage for two datagrams is that we will receive multiple copies of all multicast datagrams and we want to detect the copies and just ignore them. Even on a host with only
a single interface, a multicast NTP packet can be received at the socket bound to that
interface *and* the socket bound to the wildcard address (see Exercise 19.10).

These multiple copies occur in this example with multicasting because we have
bound the same port multiple times: once per interface and again for the wildcard.

sntp/read_loop.c

```
 1 #include    "sntp.h"
 2 static int        check_loop(struct sockaddr *, socklen_t);
 3 static int        check_dup(socklen_t);

 4 static char       buf1[MAXLINE], buf2[MAXLINE];
 5 static char       *buf[2] = { buf1, buf2 };
 6 struct sockaddr *from[2];
 7 static size_t     nread[2] = { -1, -1 };
 8 static int        currb = 0, lastb = 1;

 9 void
10 read_loop(void)
11 {
12     int     nsel, maxfd;
13     Addrs   *aptr;
14     fd_set  rset, allrset;
15     socklen_t len;
16     struct timeval now;

17         /* allocate two socket address structures */
18     from[0] = Malloc(addrs[0].addr_salen);
19     from[1] = Malloc(addrs[0].addr_salen);

20     maxfd = -1;
21     for (aptr = &addrs[0]; aptr < &addrs[naddrs]; aptr++) {
22         FD_SET(aptr->addr_fd, &allrset);
23         if (aptr->addr_fd > maxfd)
24             maxfd = aptr->addr_fd;
25     }
```

sntp/read_loop.c

Figure 19.27   `read_loop` function: first half.

Recall from our discussion of the SO_REUSEADDR socket option in Chapter 7 that one copy of a multicast or broadcast datagram is delivered to each matching socket, while a unicast datagram is delivered to just one socket. Our socket bound to the wildcard address matches every received multicast packet.

If we didn't care to know which address a given multicast packet was destined to, we could just create one socket and bind the multicast address (224.0.1.1) and the well-known port (123) to it, and always receive just a single copy. This is what we did in our example in Figure 19.11. What complicates this SNTP example is that we want to know the destination address of each datagram.

Prepare descriptor set for `select`

20–25   We prepare a descriptor set for `select` and calculate the maximum of all the descriptors that we can read from.

The second half of our `read_loop` function is shown in Figure 19.28. It calls `select` to wait for one or more of the descriptors to be readable, then reads the datagram, and processes the SNTP packet.

sntp/read_loop.c
```
26      for ( ; ; ) {
27          rset = allrset;
28          nsel = Select(maxfd + 1, &rset, NULL, NULL, NULL);

29          Gettimeofday(&now, NULL);   /* get time when select returns */

30          for (aptr = &addrs[0]; aptr < &addrs[naddrs]; aptr++) {
31              if (FD_ISSET(aptr->addr_fd, &rset)) {
32                  len = aptr->addr_salen;
33                  nread[currb] = recvfrom(aptr->addr_fd,
34                                          buf[currb], MAXLINE, 0,
35                                          from[currb], &len);
36                  if (aptr->addr_flags & ADDR_MCAST) {
37                      printf("%d bytes from %s", nread[currb],
38                              Sock_ntop(from[currb], aptr->addr_salen));
39                      printf(" multicast to %s", aptr->addr_ifname);

40                  } else if (aptr->addr_flags & ADDR_BCAST) {
41                      printf("%d bytes from %s", nread[currb],
42                              Sock_ntop(from[currb], aptr->addr_salen));
43                      printf(" broadcast to %s",
44                              Sock_ntop(aptr->addr_sa, aptr->addr_salen));

45                  } else {
46                      printf("%d bytes from %s", nread[currb],
47                              Sock_ntop(from[currb], aptr->addr_salen));
48                      printf(" to %s",
49                              Sock_ntop(aptr->addr_sa, aptr->addr_salen));
50                  }

51                  if (check_loop(from[currb], aptr->addr_salen)) {
52                      printf(" (ignored)\n");
53                      continue;   /* it's one of ours, looped back */
54                  }
55                  if (check_dup(aptr->addr_salen)) {
56                      printf(" (dup)\n");
57                      continue;   /* it's a duplicate */
58                  }
59                  sntp_proc(buf[lastb], nread[lastb], &now);

60                  if (--nsel <= 0)
61                      break;      /* all done with selectable descriptors */
62              }
63          }
64      }
65  }
```
sntp/read_loop.c

Figure 19.28 read_loop function: second half.

select and then get current time-of-day

27–29   As soon as select returns, we call gettimeofday to fetch the current time, which
will be used to calculate the difference from the time in the SNTP packet.

Determine which descriptor is readable

30–50   We check each descriptor to see which one is readable, call `recvfrom`, print how the datagram was received (broadcast, multicast, or unicast), and on which interface it was received.

Check for loopback

51–54   Our `check_loop` function returns 1 if the packet is one of our own that was looped back. We disabled multicast loopback in Figure 19.26, but there is no way to disable the automatic loopback of broadcast packets that we send.

Check for duplicate

55–58   Since we can receive multiple copies of any received multicast packet and any received broadcast packet, our `check_dup` function checks whether the current packet is an exact duplicate of the previous packet, and if so, returns 1.

Process SNTP packet

59   At this point the packet is not a loopback copy and is not a duplicate so we call our `sntp_proc` function (Figure 19.19) to process the NTP packet.

Our `check_loop` function, shown in Figure 19.29, checks whether the packet is a loopback copy of a packet that we sent.

```
                                                                  sntp/read_loop.c
66 int
67 check_loop(struct sockaddr *sa, socklen_t salen)
68 {
69     Addrs   *aptr;

70     for (aptr = &addrs[0]; aptr < &addrs[naddrs]; aptr++) {
71         if (sock_cmp_addr(sa, aptr->addr_sa, salen) == 0)
72             return (1);           /* it is one of our addresses */
73     }
74     return (0);
75 }
                                                                  sntp/read_loop.c
```

Figure 19.29 `check_loop` function: return 1 if datagram is one that we sent.

Check sender's address

70–74   To check for a loopback copy we go through all the addresses in our `Addrs` array and compare them against the source IP address of the received datagram.

Our `check_dup` function is shown in Figure 19.30 and it checks whether the received datagram is a complete copy of the previous datagram.

Check length, sender's address, and contents

80–88   We consider the datagram a copy if the lengths of the two datagrams are the same, if the two sender protocol addresses are the same, and if the actual contents of the two datagrams are the same. If the datagram is not a duplicate, the indexes `currb` and `lastb` are swapped. Notice that the call to `sntp_proc` at the end of Figure 19.28

```
                                                                ── sntp/read_loop.c
76 int
77 check_dup(socklen_t salen)
78 {
79     int     temp;

80     if (nread[currb] == nread[lastb] &&
81         memcmp(from[currb], from[lastb], salen) == 0 &&
82         memcmp(buf[currb], buf[lastb], nread[currb]) == 0) {
83         return (1);                    /* it is a duplicate */
84     }
85     temp = currb;                      /* swap currb and lastb */
86     currb = lastb;
87     lastb = temp;
88     return (0);
89 }
                                                                ── sntp/read_loop.c
```

Figure 19.30 check_dup function: return 1 if datagram is a duplicate.

passes the datagram indexed by lastb because the call to check_dup swaps the indexes for the next call to recvfrom.

Recall the nine sockets shown in Figure 19.23. Figure 19.31 shows the output when we run the program on our host bsdi with an NTP server running on the host solaris. The first nine lines show the sockets that are created, the IP addresses that are bound to the sockets, and the interfaces on which the multicast group is joined.

The next five lines show the packets that are sent by sntp_send: one packet to each broadcast address and one packet to each multicast address.

The next six lines show the first five datagrams that are received on the various sockets. These datagrams are all received in response to the queries sent by sntp_send. The first datagram is ignored because it is a loopback copy of one of the broadcasts that we sent (look at the source address). The second datagram is from the NTP server (the mode of 4 is MODE_SERVER from Figure 19.17) on the host solaris (206.62.26.33), which is an NTP version 3 server running at stratum 3. The time difference between the two hosts is about 116 ms. The next three datagrams are ignored: the first is a loopback copy of our broadcast to the other Ethernet, and the next two are loopback copies of our two broadcasts received on the wildcard socket. What has happened here with the two broadcasts that were sent is that one copy of each was looped back, and then one copy of each loopback packet was delivered to the socket that was bound to the corresponding broadcast address, and another copy of each loopback packet was delivered to the wildcard socket. Two broadcasts generated four loopback copies. With multicasting we can turn off these loopback copies, but we are unable to do this with broadcasting.

The final five lines correspond to four received datagrams and these four datagrams correspond to one received NTP packet from the host solaris. The first datagram is received as a multicast and is processed to yield a time difference of about 117 ms. The next three datagrams are duplicates of this multicast packet received on the two other

```
bsdi % sntp
binding 206.62.226.66.123          we0:  Ethernet unicast
binding 206.62.226.95.123          we0:  Ethernet broadcast
joining 224.0.1.1 on we0           we0:  multicast
binding 206.62.226.35.123          ef0:  Ethernet unicast
binding 206.62.226.63.123          ef0:  Ethernet broadcast
joining 224.0.1.1 on ef0           ef0:  multicast
binding 127.0.0.1.123              lo0:  loopback
joining 224.0.1.1 on lo0           lo0:  multicast
binding 0.0.0.0.123                wildcard

sending broadcast to 206.62.226.95.123
sending multicast to 224.0.1.1.123 on we0
sending broadcast to 206.62.226.63.123
sending multicast to 224.0.1.1.123 on ef0
sending multicast to 224.0.1.1.123 on lo0

48 bytes from 206.62.226.66.123 broadcast to 206.62.226.95.123 (ignored)
48 bytes from 206.62.226.33.123 to 206.62.226.35.123
v3, mode 4, strat 3, clock difference = -116013 usec
48 bytes from 206.62.226.35.123 broadcast to 206.62.226.63.123 (ignored)
48 bytes from 206.62.226.66.123 to 0.0.0.0.123 (ignored)
48 bytes from 206.62.226.35.123 to 0.0.0.0.123 (ignored)

48 bytes from 206.62.226.33.123 multicast to we0
v3, mode 5, strat 3, clock difference = -117043 usec
48 bytes from 206.62.226.33.123 multicast to ef0 (dup)
48 bytes from 206.62.226.33.123 multicast to lo0 (dup)
48 bytes from 206.62.226.33.123 to 0.0.0.0.123 (dup)
```

Figure 19.31 Output from our sntp program.

sockets that are bound to the same IP address and port (224.0.1.1.123), and on the socket bound to just the same port (0.0.0.0.123).

If we continue running the program in this environment, we see that every 64 seconds the NTP server on solaris multicasts an NTP packet, and our program receives four copies. The first of the four copies is processed, and the remaining three are duplicates that are ignored.

19.12 Summary

A multicast application starts by joining the multicast group assigned to the application. This tells the IP layer to join the group, which in turns tells the datalink layer to receive multicast frames that are sent to the corresponding hardware layer multicast address. Multicasting takes advantage of the hardware filtering present on most interface cards, and the better the filtering, the fewer the number of undesired packets that are received. Using this hardware filtering reduces the load on all the other hosts that are not participating in the application.

Multicasting on a WAN requires multicast-capable routers and a multicast routing protocol. Until all the routers on the Internet are multicast capable, a virtual network, the MBone (Section B.2) is being used.

Five socket options provide the API for multicasting:

- join a multicast group on an interface,
- leave a multicast group,
- set the default interface for outgoing multicasts,
- set the TTL or hop limit for outgoing multicasts, and
- enable or disable loopback of multicasts.

The first two are for receiving, and the last three are for sending. There is enough difference between the five IPv4 socket options and the five IPv6 socket options that protocol-independent multicasting code becomes littered with #ifdefs very quickly. We developed eight functions of our own, all beginning with mcast_, that can help in writing multicast applications that work with either IPv4 or IPv6.

Exercises

19.1   Build the program shown in Figure 18.9 and run it specifying an IP address on the command line of 224.0.0.1. What happens?

19.2   Modify the program in the previous example to bind 224.0.0.1 and port 0 to its socket. Run it. Are you allowed to bind a multicast address to the socket? If you have a tool such as tcpdump, watch the packets on the network. What is the source IP address of the datagram you send?

19.3   One way to tell which hosts on your subnet are multicast capable is to ping the all-hosts group: 224.0.0.1. Try this.

19.4   If we type ping 224.0.0.1 on our host unixware, which is not multicast capable, we get the following output:

```
unixware % ping 224.0.0.1
PING 224.0.0.1: 56 data bytes
64 bytes from gw.kohala.com (206.62.226.62): icmp_seq=0. time=0. ms
64 bytes from gw.kohala.com (206.62.226.62): icmp_seq=1. time=0. ms
64 bytes from gw.kohala.com (206.62.226.62): icmp_seq=2. time=0. ms
```

What is happening?

19.5   One way to locate any multicast routers on your subnet is to ping the all routers group: 224.0.0.2. Try this.

19.6   One way to tell if your host is connected to the MBone is to run our program from Section 19.8, wait a few minutes, and see if any session announcements appear. Try this and see if you receive any announcements.

19.7   The session ID and version in the o= line in Figure 19.13 are often NTP timestamps. Do the values shown make sense?

19.8 Go through the calculations in Figure 19.19 when the fractional part of the NTP timestamp is 1,073,741,824 (one-quarter of 2^{32}).

Redo these calculations for the largest possible integer fraction ($2^{32} - 1$).

19.9 In Figures 19.24 and 19.25 we set the SO_REUSEADDR socket option to allow the same port to be bound multiple times. But in Figure 19.25 we are performing completely duplicate bindings for each multicast address (224.0.1.1) and port 123, and we see three of these in Figure 19.31. How can we do this on a Berkeley-derived kernel without setting the SO_REUSEPORT socket option instead of SO_REUSEADDR?

19.10 The final line in Figure 19.31 shows a multicast datagram being received by the socket that was bound to the wildcard address. But if we run our SNTP client under Solaris 2.5, this socket does not receive the multicast datagrams. Why?

19.11 In the example shown in Figure 19.31, if we had not disabled multicast loopback in Figure 19.26, how many additional copies would be received?

19.12 Modify the implementation of mcast_set_if for IPv4 to remember each interface name for which it obtains the IP address to prevent calling ioctl again for that interface.

20

Advanced UDP Sockets

20.1 Introduction

This chapter is a collection of various topics that affect applications using UDP sockets. First is determining the destination address of a UDP datagram, and the interface on which the datagram was received, because a socket bound to a UDP port and the wildcard address can receive unicast, broadcast, and multicast datagrams, on any interface.

TCP is a byte-stream protocol and it uses a sliding window, so there is no such thing as a record boundary or allowing the sender to overrun the receiver with data. With UDP, however, each input operation corresponds to a UDP datagram (a record) so the problem arises of what happens when the received datagram is larger than the application's input buffer.

UDP is unreliable but there are applications where it makes sense to use UDP instead of TCP. We discuss the factors affecting when UDP can be used instead of TCP. In these UDP applications we must include some features to make up for UDP's unreliability: a timeout and retransmission, to handle lost datagrams, and sequence numbers to match the replies to the requests. We develop a set of functions that we can call from our UDP applications to handle these details.

If the implementation does not support the IP_RECVDSTADDR socket option, then one way to determine the destination IP address of a UDP datagram is to bind all the interface addresses and use select. We showed one example of this in Section 19.11 and work with this technique some more in this chapter.

Most UDP servers are iterative but there are applications that exchange multiple UDP datagrams between the client and server, requiring some form of concurrency. TFTP is the common example and we discuss how this is done, both with and without inetd.

The final topic is the per-packet information that can be specified as ancillary data for an IPv6 datagram: specifying the source IP address, the sending interface, the outgoing hop limit, and the next-hop address. Similar information—the destination IP address, received interface, and received hop limit—can be returned with an IPv6 datagram.

20.2 Receiving Flags, Destination IP Address, and Interface Index

Historically `sendmsg` and `recvmsg` have been used only to pass descriptors across Unix domain sockets (Section 14.7), and even this was rare. But the use of these two functions is increasing for two reasons.

1. The `msg_flags` member, which was added to the `msghdr` structure with 4.3BSD Reno, returns flags to the application. We summarized these flags in Figure 13.7.

2. Ancillary data is being used to pass more and more information between the application and the kernel. We will see in Chapter 24 that IPv6 continues this trend.

As an example of `recvmsg` we will write a function named `recvfrom_flags` that is similar to `recvfrom` but also returns

1. the returned `msg_flags` value,

2. the destination address of the received datagram (from the `IP_RECVDSTADDR` socket option), and

3. the index of the interface on which the datagram was received (the `IP_RECVIF` socket option).

To return the last two items we define the following structure in our `unp.h` header:

```
struct in_pktinfo {
  struct in_addr  ipi_addr;    /* destination IPv4 address */
  int             ipi_ifindex; /* received interface index */
};
```

We have purposely chosen the structure name and member names to be similar to the IPv6 `in6_pktinfo` structure that returns the same two items for an IPv6 socket (Section 20.8). Our `recvfrom_flags` function will take a pointer to an `in_pktinfo` structure as an argument, and if this pointer is nonnull, return the structure through the pointer.

A design problem with this structure is what to return if the `IP_RECVDSTADDR` information is not available (i.e., the implementation does not support the socket option). The interface index is easy to handle because a value of 0 can indicate that the index is not known. But all 32-bit values for an IP address are valid. What we have chosen is to return a value of all zeros (0.0.0.0) as the destination address when the actual value is not available. While this is a valid IP address, it is never allowed as the destination IP address (RFC 1122 [Braden 1989]); it is valid only as the source IP address when a host is bootstrapping and does not yet know its IP address.

> Unfortunately Berkeley-derived kernels do accept IP datagrams destined to 0.0.0.0 (pp. 218–219 of TCPv2). These are obsolete broadcasts generated by 4.2BSD-derived kernels.

We now show the first half of our `recvfrom_flags` function in Figure 20.1. This function is intended to be used with a UDP socket.

advio/recvfromflags.c

```
 1 #include    "unp.h"
 2 #include    <sys/param.h>        /* ALIGN macro for CMSG_NXTHDR() macro */

 3 #ifdef  HAVE_SOCKADDR_DL_STRUCT
 4 #include    <net/if_dl.h>
 5 #endif

 6 ssize_t
 7 recvfrom_flags(int fd, void *ptr, size_t nbytes, int *flagsp,
 8               SA *sa, socklen_t *salenptr, struct in_pktinfo *pktp)
 9 {
10     struct msghdr msg;
11     struct iovec iov[1];
12     ssize_t n;

13 #ifdef  HAVE_MSGHDR_MSG_CONTROL
14     struct cmsghdr *cmptr;
15     union {
16         struct cmsghdr cm;
17         char    control[CMSG_SPACE(sizeof(struct in_addr)) +
18                     CMSG_SPACE(sizeof(struct in_pktinfo))];
19     } control_un;

20     msg.msg_control = control_un.control;
21     msg.msg_controllen = sizeof(control_un.control);
22     msg.msg_flags = 0;
23 #else
24     bzero(&msg, sizeof(msg));    /* make certain msg_accrightslen = 0 */
25 #endif

26     msg.msg_name = sa;
27     msg.msg_namelen = *salenptr;
28     iov[0].iov_base = ptr;
29     iov[0].iov_len = nbytes;
30     msg.msg_iov = iov;
31     msg.msg_iovlen = 1;

32     if ( (n = recvmsg(fd, &msg, *flagsp)) < 0)
33         return (n);

34     *salenptr = msg.msg_namelen;    /* pass back results */
35     if (pktp)
36         bzero(pktp, sizeof(struct in_pktinfo));    /* 0.0.0.0, i/f = 0 */
```

advio/recvfromflags.c

Figure 20.1 `recvfrom_flags` function: call `recvmsg`.

Include files

2-5   To use the CMSG_NXTHDR macro requires including the <sys/param.h> header. We also need to include the <net/if_dl.h> header, which defines the sockaddr_dl structure, in which the received interface index is returned.

Function arguments

6-8   The function arguments are similar to recvfrom, except the fourth argument is now a pointer to an integer flag (so that we can return the flags returned by recvmsg) and the seventh argument is new: it is a pointer to an in_pktinfo structure that will contain the destination IPv4 address of the received datagram and the interface index on which the datagram was received.

Implementation differences

13-25   When dealing with the msghdr structure, and the various MSG_*xxx* constants, we encounter lots of differences between various implementations. Our way of handling these differences is to use C's conditional inclusion feature (#ifdef). If the implementation supports the msg_control member, space is allocated to hold the values returned by both the IP_RECVDSTADDR and IP_RECVIF socket options, and the appropriate members are initialized.

Fill in `msghdr` structure and call `recvmsg`

26-36   A msghdr structure is filled in and recvmsg is called. The values of the msg_namelen and msg_flags members must be passed back to the caller; they are value-result arguments. We also initialize the caller's in_pktinfo structure, setting the IP address to 0.0.0.0 and the interface index to 0.

          Figure 20.2 shows the second half of our function.
37-40   If the implementation does not support the msg_control member, we just set the returned flags to 0 and return. The remainder of the function handles the msg_control information.

Return if no control information

41-44   We return the msg_flags value and then return to the caller if (a) there is no control information, (b) the control information was truncated, or (c) the caller does not want an in_pktinfo structure returned.

Process ancillary data

45-46   We process any number of ancillary data objects using the CMSG_FIRSTHDR and CMSG_NXTHDR macros.

Process `IP_RECVDSTADDR`

47-54   If the destination IP address was returned as control information (Figure 13.9), it is returned to the caller.

Process `IP_RECVIF`

55-63   If the index of the received interface was returned as control information, it is returned to the caller. Figure 20.3 shows the contents of the ancillary data object that is returned.

advio/recvfromflags.c

```
37 #ifndef HAVE_MSGHDR_MSG_CONTROL
38     *flagsp = 0;                  /* pass back results */
39     return (n);
40 #else

41     *flagsp = msg.msg_flags;      /* pass back results */
42     if (msg.msg_controllen < sizeof(struct cmsghdr) ||
43              (msg.msg_flags & MSG_CTRUNC) || pktp == NULL)
44              return (n);

45     for (cmptr = CMSG_FIRSTHDR(&msg); cmptr != NULL;
46          cmptr = CMSG_NXTHDR(&msg, cmptr)) {

47 #ifdef  IP_RECVDSTADDR
48         if (cmptr->cmsg_level == IPPROTO_IP &&
49             cmptr->cmsg_type == IP_RECVDSTADDR) {

50             memcpy(&pktp->ipi_addr, CMSG_DATA(cmptr),
51                   sizeof(struct in_addr));
52             continue;
53         }
54 #endif

55 #ifdef  IP_RECVIF
56         if (cmptr->cmsg_level == IPPROTO_IP &&
57             cmptr->cmsg_type == IP_RECVIF) {
58             struct sockaddr_dl *sdl;

59             sdl = (struct sockaddr_dl *) CMSG_DATA(cmptr);
60             pktp->ipi_ifindex = sdl->sdl_index;
61             continue;
62         }
63 #endif
64         err_quit("unknown ancillary data, len = %d, level = %d, type = %d",
65                 cmptr->cmsg_len, cmptr->cmsg_level, cmptr->cmsg_type);
66     }
67     return (n);
68 #endif  /* HAVE_MSGHDR_MSG_CONTROL */
69 }
```

advio/recvfromflags.c

Figure 20.2 recvfrom_flags function: return flags and destination address.

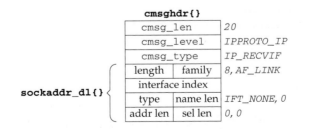

Figure 20.3 Ancillary data object returned for IP_RECVIF.

Recall the datalink socket address structure in Figure 17.1. The data returned in the ancillary data object is one of these structures, but the three lengths are 0 (name length, address length, and selector length). Therefore there is no need for any of the data that follows these lengths, so the size of the structure should be 8 bytes, and not the 20 that we show in Figure 17.1. The information that we return is the interface index.

Example: Print Destination IP Address and Datagram-Truncated Flag

To test our function we modify our `dg_echo` function (Figure 8.4) to call `recvfrom_flags` instead of `recvfrom`. We show this new version of `dg_echo` in Figure 20.4.

advio/dgechoaddr.c

```
 1 #include    "unpifi.h"

 2 #undef  MAXLINE
 3 #define MAXLINE 20                  /* to see datagram truncation */

 4 void
 5 dg_echo(int sockfd, SA *pcliaddr, socklen_t clilen)
 6 {
 7     int     flags;
 8     const int on = 1;
 9     socklen_t len;
10     ssize_t n;
11     char    mesg[MAXLINE], str[INET6_ADDRSTRLEN], ifname[IFNAMSIZ];
12     struct in_addr in_zero;
13     struct in_pktinfo pktinfo;

14 #ifdef  IP_RECVDSTADDR
15     if (setsockopt(sockfd, IPPROTO_IP, IP_RECVDSTADDR, &on, sizeof(on)) < 0)
16         err_ret("setsockopt of IP_RECVDSTADDR");
17 #endif
18 #ifdef  IP_RECVIF
19     if (setsockopt(sockfd, IPPROTO_IP, IP_RECVIF, &on, sizeof(on)) < 0)
20         err_ret("setsockopt of IP_RECVIF");
21 #endif
22     bzero(&in_zero, sizeof(struct in_addr));    /* all 0 IPv4 address */

23     for ( ; ; ) {
24         len = clilen;
25         flags = 0;
26         n = Recvfrom_flags(sockfd, mesg, MAXLINE, &flags,
27                         pcliaddr, &len, &pktinfo);
28         printf("%d-byte datagram from %s", n, Sock_ntop(pcliaddr, len));
29         if (memcmp(&pktinfo.ipi_addr, &in_zero, sizeof(in_zero)) != 0)
30             printf(", to %s", Inet_ntop(AF_INET, &pktinfo.ipi_addr,
31                                     str, sizeof(str)));
32         if (pktinfo.ipi_ifindex > 0)
33             printf(", recv i/f = %s",
34                     If_indextoname(pktinfo.ipi_ifindex, ifname));
35 #ifdef  MSG_TRUNC
36         if (flags & MSG_TRUNC)
37             printf(" (datagram truncated)");
38 #endif
```

```
39 #ifdef  MSG_CTRUNC
40          if (flags & MSG_CTRUNC)
41              printf(" (control info truncated)");
42 #endif
43 #ifdef  MSG_BCAST
44          if (flags & MSG_BCAST)
45              printf(" (broadcast)");
46 #endif
47 #ifdef  MSG_MCAST
48          if (flags & MSG_MCAST)
49              printf(" (multicast)");
50 #endif
51          printf("\n");

52          Sendto(sockfd, mesg, n, 0, pcliaddr, len);
53      }
54 }
```
————————————————————————————————————— advio/dgechoaddr.c

Figure 20.4 `dg_echo` function that calls our `recvfrom_flags` function.

Change `MAXLINE`

2–3   We remove the existing definition of `MAXLINE` that occurs in our `unp.h` header and redefine it to be 20. We do this to see what happens when we receive a UDP datagram that is larger than the buffer that we pass to the input function (`recvmsg` in this case).

Set `IP_RECVDSTADDR` and `IP_RECVIF` socket options

14–21   If the `IP_RECVDSTADDR` socket option is defined, it is turned on. Similarly the `IP_RECVIF` socket option is turned on.

> Unfortunately tests of this form are not adequate because some systems (e.g., Solaris 2.5) define `IP_RECVDSTADDR` even though it is not supported. Therefore we let the call to `setsockopt` fail, and if this happens we just print a message and continue. We cannot even check for a specific error, as different implementations return different errors when a socket option is not implemented. For example, in 4.4BSD `getsockopt` returns `ENOPROTOOPT` for an unknown error, but `setsockopt` returns `EINVAL`. But the multicast socket options in 4.4BSD return `EOPNOTSUPP` for an unknown option.

Read datagram, print source IP address and port

24–28   The datagram is read by calling `recvfrom_flags`. The source IP address and port of the server's reply are converted to presentation format by `sock_ntop`.

Print destination IP address

29–31   If the returned IP address is not 0, it is converted to presentation format by `inet_ntop` and printed.

Print name of received interface

32–34   If the returned interface index is not 0, its name is obtained by calling `if_indextoname` and printed.

Test various flags

35–51   We then test four additional flags and print a message if any are on.

If we run our server under BSD/OS 3.0 on the host bsdi (which is multihomed), we can see the various destination IP addresses and the various flags:

```
bsdi % udpserv01
9-byte datagram from 206.62.226.33.41164, to 206.62.226.35, recv i/f = ef0
13-byte datagram from 206.62.226.65.1057, to 206.62.226.95, recv i/f = we0
   (broadcast)
4-byte datagram from 206.62.226.33.41176, to 224.0.0.1, recv i/f = ef0
   (multicast)
20-byte datagram from 127.0.0.1.4632, to 127.0.0.1, recv i/f = lo0
   (datagram truncated)
9-byte datagram from 206.62.226.33.41178, to 206.62.226.66, recv i/f = ef0
```

We have wrapped the lines that print a flag in parentheses, for readability. To generate these five lines of output we ran our sock program (Section C.3) on various hosts.

1. The first line is from the host solaris, destined to 206.62.226.35, one of the unicast addresses of the server host.

2. The second line is from the host laptop, destined to 206.62.226.95, the broadcast address of the Ethernet shared by the client and server (Figure 1.16). The interface changes from the first line, as we expect. Our server receives the broadcast and the MSG_BCAST flag is set, indicating that the datagram was received as a link-layer broadcast.

3. The third line is from the host solaris, destined to 224.0.0.1, the all-hosts multicast group address. All multicast-capable hosts on the subnet must belong to this group. Our server receives the multicast because the BSD/OS operating system is multicast capable and the destination port matches our server's port. The MSG_MCAST flag is set, indicating that the datagram was received as a link-layer multicast.

4. The fourth line is from the host itself, destined to 127.0.0.1, the loopback address. The interface is lo0, as we expect. Also, this time we typed in a 41-byte line at the client (which we do not show). The server only receives the first 20 bytes of the datagram and the MSG_TRUNC flag is set, indicating that the datagram was truncated.

5. The final line is from the host solaris but destined to 206.62.226.66, the unicast address of this server host on its other Ethernet (Figure 1.16). The server still receives the datagram (because the host implements the weak end system model, as described in Section 8.8) but the destination IP address (206.62.226.66) does not match the address of the interface on which the datagram was received.

> Earlier Berkeley-derived implementations ignored the IP_RECVDSTADDR socket option when the received datagram was a broadcast or a multicast (p. 776 of TCPv2). Newer releases fix this bug.

> If the destination address is 255.255.255.255, BSD/OS converts this to the broadcast address of the received interface.

20.3 Datagram Truncation

The example in the previous section shows that under BSD/OS when a UDP datagram arrives that is larger than the application's buffer, recvmsg sets the MSG_TRUNC flag in the msg_flags member of the msghdr structure (Figure 13.7). All Berkeley-derived implementations that support the msghdr structure with the msg_flags member provide this notification.

> This is an example of a flag that must be returned from the kernel to the process. We mentioned in Section 13.3 that one design problem with the recv and recvfrom functions is that their *flags* argument is an integer, which allows flags to be passed from the process to the kernel but not vice versa.

Unfortunately not all implementations handle a larger-than-expected UDP datagram in this fashion. There are three possible scenarios.

1. Discard the excess bytes and return the MSG_TRUNC flag to the application. This requires that the application call recvmsg to receive the flag.

2. Discard the excess bytes but do not tell the application.

3. Keep the excess bytes and return them in subsequent read operations on the socket.

We have already seen the first type of behavior under BSD/OS. The second type of behavior is seen under Solaris 2.5: the excess bytes are discarded but since its msghdr structure does not support the msg_flags member, there is no way to return the error to the application.

> Posix.1g specifies the first type of behavior: discarding the excess bytes and setting the MSG_TRUNC flag. Early releases of SVR4 exhibited the third type of behavior.

Since there are such variations in how implementations handle datagrams that are larger than the application's receive buffer, one way to detect the problem is to always allocate an application buffer 1 byte greater than the largest datagram the application should ever receive. If a datagram is ever received whose length equals this buffer, consider it an error.

20.4 When to Use UDP Instead Of TCP

In Sections 2.3 and 2.4 we described the major differences between UDP and TCP. Given that TCP is reliable while UDP is not, the question arises: when should we use UDP instead of TCP, and why? We first list the advantages of UDP.

- As we show in Figure 18.1, UDP supports broadcasting and multicasting. Indeed, UDP *must* be used if the application uses broadcasting or multicasting. We discussed these two addressing modes in Chapters 18 and 19.

- UDP has no connection setup or teardown. With regard to Figure 2.5, UDP requires only two packets to exchange a request and a reply (assuming the size of each is less than the minimum MTU between the two end systems). TCP requires about 10 packets, assuming that a new TCP connection is established for each request–reply exchange.

  Also important in this number-of-packet analysis is the number of packet round trips required to obtain the reply. This becomes important if the latency exceeds the bandwidth, as described in Appendix A of TCPv3. That text shows that the minimum *transaction time* for a UDP request–reply is RTT + SPT where *RTT* is the round-trip time between the client and server, and *SPT* is the server processing time for the request. With TCP, however, if a new TCP connection is used for the request–reply, the minimum transaction time is $2 \times RTT + SPT$, one RTT greater than the UDP time. TCPv3 and Section 13.9 of this text also describe a modification to TCP, called T/TCP or "TCP for Transactions" that normally obviates the need for the TCP three-way handshake, allowing T/TCP to equal UDP's RTT + SPT transaction time.

It should be obvious with regard to the second point that if a TCP connection is used for multiple request–reply exchanges, then the cost of the connection establishment and teardown is amortized across all the requests and replies, and this is normally a better design than using a new connection for each request–reply. Nevertheless, there are applications that use a new TCP connection for each request–reply (e.g., HTTP) and there are applications in which the client and server exchange one request–reply (e.g., the DNS) and then might not talk to each other for hours or days.

We now list the features of TCP that are not provided by UDP, which means that an application must provide these features itself, if they are necessary to the application. We use the qualifier "necessary" because not all the features are needed by all applications. For example, dropped segments might not need to be retransmitted for a real-time audio application, if the receiver can interpolate the missing data. Also, for simple request–reply transactions, windowed flow control might not be needed if the two ends agree ahead of time on the size of the largest request and reply.

- Positive acknowledgments, retransmission of lost packets, duplicate detection, and sequencing of packets reordered by the network. TCP acknowledges all data, allowing lost packets to be detected. The implementation of these two features requires that every TCP data segment contain a sequence number that can then be acknowledged. It also requires that TCP estimate a retransmission time-out value for the connection and that this value be updated continually as network traffic between the two end systems changes.

- Windowed flow control. A receiving TCP tells the sender how much buffer space it has allocated for receiving data, and the sender cannot exceed this. That is, the amount of unacknowledged data at the sender can never exceed the receiver's advertised window.

- Slow start and congestion avoidance. This is a form of flow control imposed by the sender to determine the current network capacity and to handle periods of congestion. All current TCPs must support these two features and we know from experience (before these algorithms were implemented in the late 1980s) that protocols that do not "back off" in the face of congestion just make the congestion worse (e.g., [Jacobson 1988]).

In summary we can state the following recommendations:

- UDP *must* be used for broadcast or multicast applications. Any form of desired error control must be added to the clients and servers, but applications often use broadcasting or multicasting when some (assumed small) amount of error is OK (such as lost packets for audio or video). Multicast applications requiring reliable delivery have been built (e.g., multicast file transfer) but we must decide whether the performance gain in using multicasting (sending one packet to N destinations, versus sending N copies of the packet across N TCP connections) outweighs the added complexity required within the application to provide reliable communications.

- UDP *can* be used for simple request–reply applications but error detection must then be built into the application. Minimally this involves acknowledgments, timeouts, and retransmission. Flow control is often not an issue for reasonably sized requests and responses. We provide an example of these features in a UDP application in Section 20.5. The factors to consider here are how often the client and server communicate (could a TCP connection be left up between the two?) and how much data is exchanged (if multiple packets are normally required, then the cost of the TCP connection establishment and teardown becomes less of a factor).

- UDP *should not* be used for bulk data transfer (e.g., file transfer). The reason is that windowed flow control, congestion avoidance, and slow start must all be built into the application, along with the features from the previous bullet, which means we are reinventing TCP within the application. We should let the vendors focus on better TCP performance and concentrate our efforts on the application itself.

There are exceptions to these rules, especially in existing applications. TFTP, for example, uses UDP for bulk data transfer. UDP was chosen for TFTP because it is simpler to implement than TCP in bootstrap code (800 lines of C code for UDP versus 4500 lines for TCP in TCPv2, for example), and because TFTP is used only to bootstrap systems on a LAN, and not for bulk data transfer across WANs. But this requires that TFTP include its own sequence number field for acknowledgments, along with a timeout and retransmission capability.

NFS is another exception to the rule: it also uses UDP for bulk data transfer (although some might claim it is really a request–reply application, albeit using large requests and replies). This is partly historical, because in the mid-1980s when it was designed, UDP implementations were faster than TCP, and NFS was used only on LANs, where packet loss is often orders of magnitude less than on WANs. But as NFS started being used across WANs in the early 1990s, and as TCP implementations passed UDP in terms of bulk data transfer performance, NFS version 3 was designed to support TCP, and most vendors are now providing NFS over both UDP or TCP. Similar reasoning (UDP being faster than TCP in the mid-1980s along with a predominance of LANs over WANs) led the precursor of the DCE remote procedure call (RPC) package (the Apollo NCS package) to also choose UDP over TCP, although current implementations support both UDP and TCP.

We might be tempted to say that UDP usage is decreasing compared to TCP, with good TCP implementations being as fast as the network today, and with fewer application designers wanting to reinvent TCP within their UDP application. But the predicted increase in multimedia applications over the next decade will see an increase in UDP usage, since multimedia usually implies multicasting, which requires UDP.

20.5   Adding Reliability to a UDP Application

If we are going to use UDP for a request–reply application, as mentioned in the previous section, then we *must* add two features to our client:

1.   timeout and retransmission to handle datagrams that are discarded, and

2.   sequence numbers so the client can verify that a reply is for the the appropriate request.

These two features are part of most existing UDP applications that use the simple request–reply paradigm: DNS resolvers, SNMP agents, TFTP, and RPC, for example. We are not trying to use UDP for bulk data transfer—our intent is for an application that sends a request and waits for a reply.

> By definition a datagram is unreliable; therefore we purposely do not call this a "reliable datagram service." Indeed, the term "reliable datagram" is an oxymoron. What we are showing is an application that adds reliability on top of an unreliable datagram service (UDP).

Adding sequence numbers is simple. The client prepends a sequence number to each request and the server must echo this number back to the client in the reply. This lets the client verify that a given reply is for the request that was issued.

The old-fashioned method for handling timeout and retransmission was to send a request and wait for N seconds. If no response was received, retransmit and wait another N seconds. After this has happened some number of times, give up. This is a linear retransmit timer. (Figure 6.8 of TCPv1 shows an example of a TFTP client that uses this technique. Many TFTP clients still use this method.)

The problem with this technique is that the amount of time required for a datagram to make a round trip on an internet can vary from fractions of a second on a LAN to many seconds on a WAN. Factors affecting the round-trip time (RTT) are distance, network speed, and congestion. Additionally, the RTT between a client and server can change rapidly with time, as network conditions change. We must use a timeout and retransmission algorithm that takes into account the actual RTTs that we measure along with the changes in the RTT over time. Much work has been focused on this area, mostly relating to TCP, but the same ideas apply to any network application.

We want to calculate the retransmission timeout (*RTO*) to use for every packet that we send. To calculate this we measure the RTT: the actual round-trip time for a packet. Every time we measure an RTT we update two statistical estimators: *srtt* is the smoothed RTT estimator and *rttvar* is the smoothed mean deviation estimator. The latter is a good approximation of the standard deviation, but easier to compute since it does not involve a square root. Given these two estimators, the *RTO* to use is *srtt* plus four times *rttvar*. [Jacobson 1988] provides all the details on these calculations, which we can summarize in the following four equations:

$$delta = measuredRTT - srtt$$

$$srtt \leftarrow srtt + g \times delta$$

$$rttvar \leftarrow rttvar + h(\,|\,delta\,| - rttvar)$$

$$RTO = srtt + 4 \times rttvar$$

delta is the difference between the measured RTT and the current smoothed RTT estimator (*srtt*). *g* is the gain applied to the RTT estimator and equals ⅛. *h* is the gain applied to the mean deviation estimator and equals ¼.

> The two gains and the multiplier 4 in the *RTO* calculation are purposely powers of 2, so they can be calculated using shift operations instead of multiplying or dividing. Indeed the TCP kernel implementation (Section 25.7 of TCPv2) is normally performed using fixed-point arithmetic for speed, but for simplicity we use floating-point calculations in our code that follows.

Another point made in [Jacobson 1988] is that when the retransmission timer expires, an *exponential backoff* must be used for the next *RTO*. For example, if our first *RTO* is 2 seconds, and the reply is not received in this time, then the next *RTO* is 4 seconds. If there is still no reply, the next *RTT* is 8 seconds, and then 16, and so on.

Jacobson's algorithms tell us how to calculate the *RTO* each time we measure an RTT and how to increase the *RTO* when we retransmit. But a problem arises when we have to retransmit a packet and then receive a reply. This is called the *retransmission ambiguity problem*. Figure 20.5 shows three possible scenarios when our retransmission timer expires.

- The request is lost, or
- the reply is lost, or
- the *RTO* is too small.

When the client receives a reply to a request that was retransmitted, it cannot tell to which request the reply corresponds. In the example on the right the reply corresponds to the original request, while in the two other examples the reply corresponds to the retransmitted request.

Karn's algorithm [Karn and Partridge 1987] handles this scenario with the following rules that apply whenever a reply is received for a request that was retransmitted.

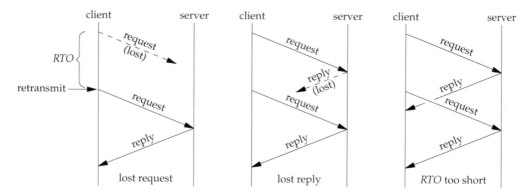

Figure 20.5 Three scenarios when retransmission timer expires.

- If an RTT was measured, do not use it to update the estimators since we do not know to which request the reply corresponds.

- Since this reply arrived before our retransmission timer expired, reuse this *RTO* for the next packet. Only when we receive a reply to a request that is not retransmitted will we update the RTT estimators and recalculate the *RTO*.

It is not hard to take Karn's algorithm into account when coding our RTT functions, but it turns out that an even better and more elegant solution exists. This solution is from the TCP extensions for "long fat pipes" (networks with either a high bandwidth, a long RTT, or both), which are documented in RFC 1323 [Jacobson, Braden, and Borman 1992]. In addition to prepending a sequence number to each request, which the server must echo back, we also prepend a *timestamp* that the server must also echo. Each time we send a request we store the current time in the timestamp. When a reply is received, we calculate the RTT of that packet as the current time minus the timestamp that was echoed by the server in its reply. Since every request carries a timestamp that is echoed by the server, we can calculate the RTT of *every* reply that we receive. There is no longer any ambiguity at all. Furthermore, since all the server does is echo the client's timestamp, the client can use any units desired for the timestamps and there is no requirement at all that the client and server have synchronized clocks.

Example

We now put all of this together in an example. We start with our UDP client `main` function from Figure 8.7 and just change the port number from `SERV_PORT` to 7 (the standard echo server, Figure 2.13).

Figure 20.6 is the `dg_cli` function. The only change from Figure 8.8 is to replace the calls to `sendto` and `recvfrom` with a call to our new function `dg_send_recv`.

Before showing our `dg_send_recv` function and our RTT functions that it calls, Figure 20.7 shows an outline of how we add reliability to a UDP client. All the functions beginning with `rtt_` are shown shortly.

——————————————————————— rtt/dg_cli.c

```
 1 #include    "unp.h"

 2 ssize_t Dg_send_recv(int, const void *, size_t, void *, size_t,
 3                      const SA *, socklen_t);

 4 void
 5 dg_cli(FILE *fp, int sockfd, const SA *pservaddr, socklen_t servlen)
 6 {
 7     ssize_t n;
 8     char    sendline[MAXLINE], recvline[MAXLINE + 1];

 9     while (Fgets(sendline, MAXLINE, fp) != NULL) {

10         n = Dg_send_recv(sockfd, sendline, strlen(sendline),
11                          recvline, MAXLINE, pservaddr, servlen);

12         recvline[n] = 0;          /* null terminate */
13         Fputs(recvline, stdout);
14     }
15 }
```
——————————————————————— rtt/dg_cli.c

Figure 20.6 dg_cli function that calls our dg_send_recv function.

```
static sigjmp_buf   jmpbuf;

{
    . . .
    form request

    signal(SIGALRM, sig_alrm); /* establish signal handler */
    rtt_newpack();             /* initialize rexmt counter to 0 */
sendagain:
    sendto();

    alarm(rtt_start());        /* set alarm for RTO seconds */
    if (sigsetjmp(jmpbuf, 1) != 0) {
        if (rtt_timeout())     /* double RTO, retransmitted enough? */
            give up
        goto sendagain;        /* retransmit */
    }
    do {
        recvfrom();
    } while (wrong sequence#);

    alarm(0);                  /* turn off alarm */
    rtt_stop();                /* calculate RTT and update estimators */

    process reply
    . . .
}
void
sig_alrm(int signo)
{
    siglongjmp(jmpbuf, 1);
}
```

Figure 20.7 Outline of RTT functions and when they are called.

When a reply is received but the sequence number is not the one expected, we call `recvfrom` again, but we do not retransmit the request and we do not restart the retransmission timer that is running. Notice in the rightmost example in Figure 20.5 that the final reply from the retransmitted request will be in the socket receive buffer the next time the client sends a new request. That is OK as the client will read this reply, notice that the sequence number is not the one expected, discard the reply, and call `recvfrom` again.

We call `sigsetjmp` and `siglongjmp` to avoid the race condition with the `SIGALRM` signal that we described in Section 18.5.

Figure 20.8 shows the first half of our `dg_send_recv` function.

1-5   We include a new header `unprtt.h`, shown in Figure 20.10, that defines the `rtt_into` structure that maintains the RTT information for a client. We define one of these structures, and numerous other variables.

Define `msghdr` structures and `hdr` structure

6-10   We want to hide the fact from the caller that we prepend a sequence number and a timestamp to each packet. The easiest way to do this is to use `writev`, writing our header (the `hdr` structure) followed by the caller's data, as a single UDP datagram. Recall that the output for `writev` on a datagram socket is a single datagram. This is easier than forcing the caller to allocate room at the front of its buffer for our use and is also faster than copying our header and the caller's data into one buffer (that we would have to allocate) for a single `sendto`. But since we are using UDP and have to specify a destination address, we must use the `iovec` capability of `sendmsg` and `recvmsg`, instead of `sendto` and `recvfrom`. Recall from Section 13.5 that some systems have a newer `msghdr` structure with ancillary data, while older systems still have the access rights members at the end of the structure. To avoid complicating the code with `#ifdefs` to handle these differences, we declare two `msghdr` structures as `static`, forcing their initialization to all zero bits by C and then just ignore the unused members at the end of the structures.

Initialize first time we are called

20-24   The first time we are called we call the `rtt_init` function.

Fill in `msghdr` structures

25-41   We fill in the two `msghdr` structures that are used for output and input. We increment the sending sequence number for this packet but do not set the sending timestamp until we send the packet (since it might be retransmitted, and each retransmission needs the current timestamp).

The second half of the function, along with the `sig_alrm` signal handler, is shown in Figure 20.9 (p. 548).

rtt/dg_send_recv.c

```
 1 #include    "unprtt.h"
 2 #include    <setjmp.h>

 3 #define RTT_DEBUG

 4 static struct rtt_info rttinfo;
 5 static int rttinit = 0;
 6 static struct msghdr msgsend, msgrecv;  /* assumed init to 0 */
 7 static struct hdr {
 8    uint32_t seq;                /* sequence # */
 9    uint32_t ts;                 /* timestamp when sent */
10 } sendhdr, recvhdr;

11 static void sig_alrm(int signo);
12 static sigjmp_buf jmpbuf;

13 ssize_t
14 dg_send_recv(int fd, const void *outbuff, size_t outbytes,
15             void *inbuff, size_t inbytes,
16             const SA *destaddr, socklen_t destlen)
17 {
18    ssize_t n;
19    struct iovec iovsend[2], iovrecv[2];

20    if (rttinit == 0) {
21        rtt_init(&rttinfo);      /* first time we're called */
22        rttinit = 1;
23        rtt_d_flag = 1;
24    }
25    sendhdr.seq++;
26    msgsend.msg_name = destaddr;
27    msgsend.msg_namelen = destlen;
28    msgsend.msg_iov = iovsend;
29    msgsend.msg_iovlen = 2;
30    iovsend[0].iov_base = &sendhdr;
31    iovsend[0].iov_len = sizeof(struct hdr);
32    iovsend[1].iov_base = outbuff;
33    iovsend[1].iov_len = outbytes;

34    msgrecv.msg_name = NULL;
35    msgrecv.msg_namelen = 0;
36    msgrecv.msg_iov = iovrecv;
37    msgrecv.msg_iovlen = 2;
38    iovrecv[0].iov_base = &recvhdr;
39    iovrecv[0].iov_len = sizeof(struct hdr);
40    iovrecv[1].iov_base = inbuff;
41    iovrecv[1].iov_len = inbytes;
```

rtt/dg_send_recv.c

Figure 20.8 dg_send_recv function: first half.

```
                                                               ───────── rtt/dg_send_recv.c
42      Signal(SIGALRM, sig_alrm);
43      rtt_newpack(&rttinfo);        /* initialize for this packet */

44    sendagain:
45      sendhdr.ts = rtt_ts(&rttinfo);
46      Sendmsg(fd, &msgsend, 0);

47      alarm(rtt_start(&rttinfo)); /* calc timeout value & start timer */

48      if (sigsetjmp(jmpbuf, 1) != 0) {
49          if (rtt_timeout(&rttinfo) < 0) {
50              err_msg("dg_send_recv: no response from server, giving up");
51              rttinit = 0;         /* reinit in case we're called again */
52              errno = ETIMEDOUT;
53              return (-1);
54          }
55          goto sendagain;
56      }
57      do {
58          n = Recvmsg(fd, &msgrecv, 0);
59      } while (n < sizeof(struct hdr) || recvhdr.seq != sendhdr.seq);

60      alarm(0);                        /* stop SIGALRM timer */
61          /* calculate & store new RTT estimator values */
62      rtt_stop(&rttinfo, rtt_ts(&rttinfo) - recvhdr.ts);

63      return (n - sizeof(struct hdr));    /* return size of received datagram */
64 }

65 static void
66 sig_alrm(int signo)
67 {
68      siglongjmp(jmpbuf, 1);
69 }
                                                               ───────── rtt/dg_send_recv.c
```

Figure 20.9   dg_send_recv function: second half.

Establish signal handler

42-43   A signal handler is established for SIGALRM and rtt_newpack sets the retransmission counter to 0.

Send datagram

45-47   The current timestamp is obtained by rtt_ts and stored in the hdr structure that is prepended to the user's data. A single UDP datagram is sent by sendmsg. The variable alrm_flag is set to 0, and this flag is then set to 1 by the signal handler. rtt_start returns the number of seconds for this timeout and the SIGALRM is scheduled by calling alarm.

Establish jump buffer

48   We establish a jump buffer for our signal handler with sigsetjmp. We wait for the next datagram to arrive by calling recvmsg. (We discussed the use of sigsetjmp and siglongjmp along with SIGALRM with Figure 18.9.) If the alarm timer expires, sigsetjmp returns 1.

Handle timeout

49-55   When a timeout occurs, `rtt_timeout` calculates the next *RTO* (the exponential backoff) and returns −1 if we should give up, or 0 if we should retransmit. If we give up we set `errno` to `ETIMEDOUT` and return to the caller.

Call `recvmsg`, compare sequence numbers

57-59   We wait for a datagram to arrive by calling `recvmsg`. When it returns, the datagram's length must be at least the size of our `hdr` structure and its sequence number must equal the sequence number that was sent. If either comparison is false, `recvmsg` is called again.

Turn off alarm and update RTT estimators

60-62   When the expected reply is received, the pending `alarm` is turned off and `rtt_stop` updates the RTT estimators. `rtt_ts` returns the current timestamp, and the timestamp from the received datagram is subtracted from this, giving the RTT.

`SIGALRM` handler

65-69   `siglongjmp` is called, causing the `sigsetjmp` in `dg_send_recv` to return 1.

We now look at the various RTT functions that were called by `dg_send_recv`. Figure 20.10 shows the `unprtt.h` header.

```
                                                                    —————— lib/unprtt.h
 1 #ifndef __unp_rtt_h
 2 #define __unp_rtt_h

 3 #include     "unp.h"

 4 struct rtt_info {
 5     float    rtt_rtt;           /* most recent measured RTT, seconds */
 6     float    rtt_srtt;          /* smoothed RTT estimator, seconds */
 7     float    rtt_rttvar;        /* smoothed mean deviation, seconds */
 8     float    rtt_rto;           /* current RTO to use, seconds */
 9     int      rtt_nrexmt;        /* #times retransmitted: 0, 1, 2, ... */
10     uint32_t rtt_base;          /* #sec since 1/1/1970 at start */
11 };

12 #define RTT_RXTMIN      2       /* min retransmit timeout value, seconds */
13 #define RTT_RXTMAX     60       /* max retransmit timeout value, seconds */
14 #define RTT_MAXNREXMT   3       /* max #times to retransmit */

15                     /* function prototypes */
16 void     rtt_debug(struct rtt_info *);
17 void     rtt_init(struct rtt_info *);
18 void     rtt_newpack(struct rtt_info *);
19 int      rtt_start(struct rtt_info *);
20 void     rtt_stop(struct rtt_info *, uint32_t);
21 int      rtt_timeout(struct rtt_info *);
22 uint32_t rtt_ts(struct rtt_info *);

23 extern int rtt_d_flag;          /* can be set nonzero for addl info */

24 #endif  /* __unp_rtt_h */
                                                                    —————— lib/unprtt.h
```

Figure 20.10 `unprtt.h` header.

rtt_info structure

4-11   This structure contains the variables necessary to time the packets between a client and server. The first four variables are from the equations given near the beginning of this section.

12-14   These constants define the minimum and maximum retransmission timeouts and the maximum number of times we retransmit.

Figure 20.11 shows a macro and the first two of our RTT functions.

```
                                                                    ─── lib/rtt.c
 1 #include     "unprtt.h"

 2 int     rtt_d_flag = 0;              /* debug flag; can be set nonzero by caller */

 3 /*
 4  * Calculate the RTO value based on current estimators:
 5  *      smoothed RTT plus four times the deviation.
 6  */
 7 #define RTT_RTOCALC(ptr) ((ptr)->rtt_srtt + (4.0 * (ptr)->rtt_rttvar))

 8 static float
 9 rtt_minmax(float rto)
10 {
11      if (rto < RTT_RXTMIN)
12          rto = RTT_RXTMIN;
13      else if (rto > RTT_RXTMAX)
14          rto = RTT_RXTMAX;
15      return (rto);
16 }

17 void
18 rtt_init(struct rtt_info *ptr)
19 {
20      struct timeval tv;

21      Gettimeofday(&tv, NULL);
22      ptr->rtt_base = tv.tv_sec;   /* #sec since 1/1/1970 at start */

23      ptr->rtt_rtt = 0;
24      ptr->rtt_srtt = 0;
25      ptr->rtt_rttvar = 0.75;
26      ptr->rtt_rto = rtt_minmax(RTT_RTOCALC(ptr));
27      /* first RTO at (srtt + (4 * rttvar)) = 3 seconds */
28 }
                                                                    ─── lib/rtt.c
```

Figure 20.11 RTT_RTOCALC macro, rtt_minmax and rtt_init functions.

3-8   The RTT_RTOCALC macro calculates the *RTO* as the RTT estimator plus four times the mean deviation estimator.

8-16   rtt_minmax makes certain that the *RTO* is between the upper and lower limits in the unprtt.h header.

17-28   rtt_init is called by dg_send_recv the first time any packet is sent. gettimeofday returns the current time and date, in the same timeval structure that we saw with select (Section 6.3). We save only the current number of seconds since the Unix Epoch, which is 00:00:00 January 1, 1970, Coordinated Universal Time (UTC). The measured RTT is set to 0 and the RTT and mean deviation estimators are set to 0 and 0.75, respectively, giving an initial *RTO* of 3 seconds.

> The gettimeofday function is not yet part of Posix.1 and might not be supported by some older implementations. It is required by Unix 98. We use it because it is quite common and it provides microsecond resolution on many hosts. An alternate function is the Posix.1 times function, but its resolution depends on the "clock tick" used by the kernel, normally 100 ticks per second, for a resolution of 10 ms.

Figure 20.12 shows the next three RTT functions.

```
                                                                  lib/rtt.c
34 uint32_t
35 rtt_ts(struct rtt_info *ptr)
36 {
37     uint32_t ts;
38     struct timeval tv;

39     Gettimeofday(&tv, NULL);
40     ts = ((tv.tv_sec - ptr->rtt_base) * 1000) + (tv.tv_usec / 1000);
41     return (ts);
42 }

43 void
44 rtt_newpack(struct rtt_info *ptr)
45 {
46     ptr->rtt_nrexmt = 0;
47 }

48 int
49 rtt_start(struct rtt_info *ptr)
50 {
51     return ((int) (ptr->rtt_rto + 0.5));     /* round float to int */
52         /* return value can be used as: alarm(rtt_start(&foo)) */
53 }
                                                                  lib/rtt.c
```

Figure 20.12 rtt_ts, rtt_newpack, and rtt_start functions.

34–42 rtt_ts returns the current timestamp for the caller to store as an unsigned 32-bit integer in the datagram being sent. We obtain the current time and date from gettimeofday and then subtract the number of seconds when rtt_init was called (the value saved in rtt_base). We convert this to milliseconds and also convert the microsecond value returned by gettimeofday into milliseconds. The timestamp is then the sum of these two value in milliseconds.

The difference between two calls to rtt_ts is the number of milliseconds between the two calls. But we store the millisecond timestamps in an unsigned 32-bit integer, instead of a timeval structure.

43–47 rtt_newpack just sets the retransmission counter to 0. This function should be called whenever a new packet is sent for the first time.

48–53 rtt_start returns the current *RTO* in seconds. The return value can then be used as the argument to alarm.

rtt_stop, shown in Figure 20.13, is called after a reply is received to update the RTT estimators and calculate the new *RTO*.

─── *lib/rtt.c*
```
62 void
63 rtt_stop(struct rtt_info *ptr, uint32_t ms)
64 {
65     double  delta;

66     ptr->rtt_rtt = ms / 1000.0; /* measured RTT in seconds */

67     /*
68      * Update our estimators of RTT and mean deviation of RTT.
69      * See Jacobson's SIGCOMM '88 paper, Appendix A, for the details.
70      * We use floating point here for simplicity.
71      */

72     delta = ptr->rtt_rtt - ptr->rtt_srtt;
73     ptr->rtt_srtt += delta / 8; /* g = 1/8 */

74     if (delta < 0.0)
75         delta = -delta;            /* |delta| */

76     ptr->rtt_rttvar += (delta - ptr->rtt_rttvar) / 4;    /* h = 1/4 */

77     ptr->rtt_rto = rtt_minmax(RTT_RTOCALC(ptr));
78 }
```
─── *lib/rtt.c*

Figure 20.13 rtt_stop function: update RTT estimators and calculate new *RTO*.

62–78   The argument is the measured RTT, obtained by the caller by subtracting the received timestamp in the reply from the current timestamp (rtt_ts). The equations at the beginning of this section are then applied, storing new values for rtt_srtt, rtt_rttvar, and rtt_rto.

The final function, rtt_timeout, is shown in Figure 20.14. This function is called when the retransmission timer expires.

─── *lib/rtt.c*
```
83 int
84 rtt_timeout(struct rtt_info *ptr)
85 {
86     ptr->rtt_rto *= 2;            /* next RTO */

87     if (++ptr->rtt_nrexmt > RTT_MAXNREXMT)
88         return (-1);                /* time to give up for this packet */
89     return (0);
90 }
```
─── *lib/rtt.c*

Figure 20.14 rtt_timeout function: apply exponential backoff.

86   The current *RTO* is doubled: this is the exponential backoff.
87–89   If we have reached the maximum number of retransmissions, −1 is returned to tell the caller to give up; otherwise 0 is returned.

As an example, our client was run twice to two different echo servers across the Internet in the morning on a weekday. Five hundred lines were sent to each server. Eight packets were lost to the first server and 16 packets were lost to the second server. Of the 16 lost to the second server, one packet was lost twice in a row: that is, the packet had to be retransmitted two times before a reply was received. All other lost packets were handled with a single retransmission. We could verify that these packets were really lost by printing the sequence number of each received packet. If a packet is just delayed, and not lost, after the retransmission two replies will be received by the client: one corresponding to the original transmission that was delayed, and one corresponding to the retransmission. Notice we are unable to tell when we retransmit whether it was the client's request or the server's reply that was discarded.

> For the first edition of this book the author wrote a UDP server that randomly discarded packets to test this client. That is no longer needed; all we have to do is run the client to a server across the Internet, and we are almost guaranteed of some packet loss!

20.6 Binding Interface Addresses

One common use for our `get_ifi_info` function is with UDP applications that need to monitor all interfaces on a host to know when a datagram arrives, on which interface it arrives. This allows the receiving program to know the destination address of the UDP datagram, since that address is what determines the socket to which a datagram is delivered, even if the host does not support the `IP_RECVDSTADDR` socket option.

> Recall our discussion at the end of Section 20.2. If the host employs the common weak end system model, the destination IP address may differ from the IP address of the receiving interface. In this case all we can determine is the destination address of the datagram, which need not be an address assigned to the received interface. To determine the receiving interface requires either the `IP_RECVIF` or `IPV6_PKTINFO` socket option.

> Earlier we showed an example of binding all the interface addresses in Section 19.11 with our SNTP example.

Figure 20.15 is the first part of a simple example of this technique with a UDP server that binds all the unicast addresses, all the broadcast addresses, and finally the wildcard address.

Call `get_ifi_info` to obtain interface information

11-12   `get_ifi_info` obtains all the IPv4 addresses, including aliases, for all interfaces. The program then loops through each returned `ifi_info` structure.

Create UDP socket and `bind` unicast address

13-20   A UDP socket is created and the unicast address is bound to it. We also set the `SO_REUSEADDR` socket option, as we are binding the same port (`SERV_PORT`) for all the IP addresses.

> Not all implementations require that this socket option be set. Berkeley-derived implementations, for example, do not require the option and allow a new `bind` of an already bound port if

advio/udpserv03.c

```
 1 #include     "unpifi.h"

 2 void    mydg_echo(int, SA *, socklen_t, SA *);

 3 int
 4 main(int argc, char **argv)
 5 {
 6     int      sockfd;
 7     const int on = 1;
 8     pid_t   pid;
 9     struct ifi_info *ifi, *ifihead;
10     struct sockaddr_in *sa, cliaddr, wildaddr;

11     for (ifihead = ifi = Get_ifi_info(AF_INET, 1);
12          ifi != NULL; ifi = ifi->ifi_next) {

13             /* bind unicast address */
14         sockfd = Socket(AF_INET, SOCK_DGRAM, 0);

15         Setsockopt(sockfd, SOL_SOCKET, SO_REUSEADDR, &on, sizeof(on));

16         sa = (struct sockaddr_in *) ifi->ifi_addr;
17         sa->sin_family = AF_INET;
18         sa->sin_port = htons(SERV_PORT);
19         Bind(sockfd, (SA *) sa, sizeof(*sa));
20         printf("bound %s\n", Sock_ntop((SA *) sa, sizeof(*sa)));

21         if ( (pid = Fork()) == 0) {  /* child */
22             mydg_echo(sockfd, (SA *) &cliaddr, sizeof(cliaddr), (SA *) sa);
23             exit(0);              /* never executed */
24         }
```

advio/udpserv03.c

Figure 20.15 First part of UDP server that binds all addresses.

the new IP address being bound (a) is not the wildcard, and (b) differs from all the IP addresses that are already bound to the port. Solaris 2.5, however, requires this option for the second bind of a unicast address to the same port to succeed.

fork child for this address

21-24   A child is forked and the function mydg_echo is called for the child. This function waits for any datagram to arrive on this socket and echoes it back to the sender.

Figure 20.16 shows the next part of the main function, which handles broadcast addresses.

Bind broadcast address

25-41   If the interface supports broadcasting, a UDP socket is created and the broadcast address is bound to it. This time we allow the bind to fail with an error of EADDRINUSE because if an interface has multiple addresses (aliases) on the same subnet, then each of the different unicast addresses will have the same broadcast address. We showed an example of this following Figure 16.6. In this scenario we expect only the first bind to succeed.

advio/udpserv03.c

```
25            if (ifi->ifi_flags & IFF_BROADCAST) {
26                    /* try to bind broadcast address */
27                sockfd = Socket(AF_INET, SOCK_DGRAM, 0);
28                Setsockopt(sockfd, SOL_SOCKET, SO_REUSEADDR, &on, sizeof(on));

29                sa = (struct sockaddr_in *) ifi->ifi_brdaddr;
30                sa->sin_family = AF_INET;
31                sa->sin_port = htons(SERV_PORT);
32                if (bind(sockfd, (SA *) sa, sizeof(*sa)) < 0) {
33                    if (errno == EADDRINUSE) {
34                        printf("EADDRINUSE: %s\n",
35                                Sock_ntop((SA *) sa, sizeof(*sa)));
36                        continue;
37                    } else
38                        err_sys("bind error for %s",
39                                Sock_ntop((SA *) sa, sizeof(*sa)));
40                }
41                printf("bound %s\n", Sock_ntop((SA *) sa, sizeof(*sa)));

42                if ( (pid = Fork()) == 0) {  /* child */
43                    mydg_echo(sockfd, (SA *) &cliaddr, sizeof(cliaddr),
44                            (SA *) sa);
45                    exit(0);         /* never executed */
46                }
47            }
48      }
```

advio/udpserv03.c

Figure 20.16 Second part of UDP server that binds all addresses.

fork **child**

42–46   A child is spawned and it calls the function `mydg_echo`.

The final part of the `main` function is shown in Figure 20.17. This code binds the wildcard address to handle any destination addresses other than the unicast and broadcast addresses that we have already bound. The only datagrams that should arrive on this socket should be those destined to the limited broadcast address (255.255.255.255).

Create socket and bind wildcard address

49–61   A UDP socket is created, the `SO_REUSEADDR` socket option is set, and the wildcard IP address is bound. A child is spawned, which calls the `mydg_echo` function.

main **function terminates**

62   The `main` function terminates, and the server continues executing as all the children that were spawned.

The function `mydg_echo`, which is executed by all the children, is shown in Figure 20.18.

advio/udpserv03.c
```
49          /* bind wildcard address */
50      sockfd = Socket(AF_INET, SOCK_DGRAM, 0);
51      Setsockopt(sockfd, SOL_SOCKET, SO_REUSEADDR, &on, sizeof(on));

52      bzero(&wildaddr, sizeof(wildaddr));
53      wildaddr.sin_family = AF_INET;
54      wildaddr.sin_addr.s_addr = htonl(INADDR_ANY);
55      wildaddr.sin_port = htons(SERV_PORT);
56      Bind(sockfd, (SA *) &wildaddr, sizeof(wildaddr));
57      printf("bound %s\n", Sock_ntop((SA *) &wildaddr, sizeof(wildaddr)));

58      if ( (pid = Fork()) == 0 ) {   /* child */
59          mydg_echo(sockfd, (SA *) &cliaddr, sizeof(cliaddr), (SA *) sa);
60          exit(0);                    /* never executed */
61      }
62      exit(0);
63  }
```
advio/udpserv03.c

Figure 20.17   Final part of UDP server that binds all addresses.

advio/udpserv03.c
```
64  void
65  mydg_echo(int sockfd, SA *pcliaddr, socklen_t clilen, SA *myaddr)
66  {
67      int     n;
68      char    mesg[MAXLINE];
69      socklen_t len;

70      for ( ; ; ) {
71          len = clilen;
72          n = Recvfrom(sockfd, mesg, MAXLINE, 0, pcliaddr, &len);
73          printf("child %d, datagram from %s", getpid(),
74                  Sock_ntop(pcliaddr, len));
75          printf(", to %s\n", Sock_ntop(myaddr, clilen));

76          Sendto(sockfd, mesg, n, 0, pcliaddr, clilen);
77      }
78  }
```
advio/udpserv03.c

Figure 20.18   mydg_echo function.

New argument

64-65   The fourth argument to this function is the IP address that was bound to the socket. This socket should receive only datagrams destined to that IP address. If the IP address is the wildcard, then the socket should receive only datagrams that are not matched by some other socket bound to the same port.

Read datagram and echo reply

70-77   The datagram is read with recvfrom and sent back to the client with sendto. This function also prints the client's IP address and the IP address that was bound to the socket.

We now run this program on our host `bsdi` after establishing three alias address for the `ef0` Ethernet interface. The three aliases have host IDs of 50, 51, and 52, but all have the same broadcast address of 206.62.226.63.

```
bsdi % udpserv03
bound 206.62.226.66.9877             unicast address of we0 interface
bound 206.62.226.95.9877             broadcast address of we0 interface
bound 206.62.226.35.9877             primary unicast address of ef0 interface
bound 206.62.226.63.9877             broadcast address of ef0 interface
bound 206.62.226.50.9877             first unicast alias
EADDRINUSE: 206.62.226.63.9877
bound 206.62.226.51.9877             second unicast alias
EADDRINUSE: 206.62.226.63.9877
bound 206.62.226.52.9877             third unicast alias
EADDRINUSE: 206.62.226.63.9877
bound 127.0.0.1.9877                 loopback interface
bound 0.0.0.0.9877                   wildcard
```

Note that the three `bind`s of the broadcast addresses for the aliases fail, as we expect. We can check that all these sockets are bound to the indicated IP address and port using `netstat`:

```
bsdi % netstat -na | grep 9877
udp        0        0   *.9877                    *.*
udp        0        0   127.0.0.1.9877            *.*
udp        0        0   206.62.226.52.9877        *.*
udp        0        0   206.62.226.51.9877        *.*
udp        0        0   206.62.226.50.9877        *.*
udp        0        0   206.62.226.63.9877        *.*
udp        0        0   206.62.226.35.9877        *.*
udp        0        0   206.62.226.95.9877        *.*
udp        0        0   206.62.226.66.9877        *.*
```

We should note that our design of one child process per socket is for simplicity, and other designs are possible. For example, to reduce the number of processes the program could manage all the descriptors itself using `select`, never calling `fork`. The problem with this design is the added code complexity. While it is easy to use `select` for all the descriptors, we would have to maintain some type of mapping of each descriptor to its bound IP address (probably an array of structures), so we could print the destination IP address when a datagram was read from a socket. (We used this solution in Section 19.11.) It is often simpler to use a single process or a single thread for one operation or descriptor, instead of having a single process multiplex many different operations or descriptors.

20.7 Concurrent UDP Servers

Most UDP servers are iterative: the server waits for a client request, reads the request, processes the request, sends back the reply, and then waits for the next client request. But when the processing of the client request takes a long time, some form of concurrency is desired.

The definition of a "long time" is whatever is considered too much time for another client to wait while the current client is serviced. For example, if two client requests arrive within 10 ms of each other, and it takes an average of 5 seconds of clock time to service a client, then the second client will have to wait about 10 seconds for its reply, instead of about 5 seconds if the request were handled as soon as it arrived.

With TCP it is simple to just `fork` a new child (or create a new thread as we will see in Chapter 23) and let the child handle the new client. What simplifies this server concurrency when TCP is being used is that every client connection is unique: the TCP socket pair is unique for every connection. But with UDP we must deal with two different types of servers.

1. First is a simple UDP server that reads a client request, sends a reply, and is then finished with the client. In this scenario the server that reads the client request can `fork` a child and let it handle the request. The "request," that is, the contents of the datagram and the socket address structure containing the client's protocol address, are passed to the child in its memory image from `fork`. The child then sends its reply directly to the client.

2. Second is a UDP server that exchanges multiple datagrams with the client. The problem is that the only port number that the client knows for the server is its well-known port. The client sends the first datagram of its request to that port, but how does the server distinguish between subsequent datagrams from that client, and new requests? The typical solution to this problem is for the server to create a new socket for each client, `bind` an ephemeral port to that socket, and use that socket for all its replies. This requires that the client look at the port number of the server's first reply and send subsequent datagrams for this request to that port.

An example of the second type of UDP server is TFTP, the Trivial File Transfer Protocol. To transfer a file using TFTP normally requires many datagrams (hundreds or thousands, depending on the file size), because the protocol sends only 512 bytes per datagram. The client sends a datagram to the server's well-known port (69) specifying the file to send or receive. The server reads the request but sends its reply from another socket that it creates and binds to an ephemeral port. All subsequent datagrams between the client and server for this file use the new socket. This allows the main TFTP server to continue to handle other client requests, which arrive at port 69, while this file transfer takes place (perhaps seconds or even minutes).

If we assume a stand-alone TFTP server (i.e., not invoked by `inetd`), we have the scenario shown in Figure 20.19. We assume that the ephemeral port bound by the child to its new socket is 2134.

If `inetd` is used, the scenario involves one more step. Recall from Figure 12.6 that most UDP servers specify the *wait-flag* as `wait`. In our description following Figure 12.10 we said that this causes `inetd` to stop selecting on the socket until its child terminates, allowing its child to read the datagram that has arrived on the socket. Figure 20.20 shows the steps involved.

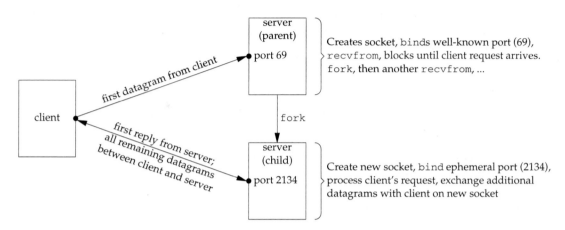

Figure 20.19 Processes involved in stand-alone concurrent UDP server.

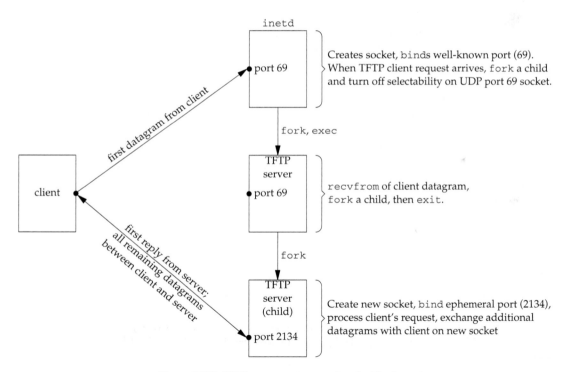

Figure 20.20 UDP concurrent server invoked by inetd.

The TFTP server that is the child of inetd calls recvfrom and reads the client request. It then forks a child of its own, and that child will process the client request. The TFTP server then calls exit, sending SIGCHLD to inetd, which we said tells inetd to again select on the socket bound to UDP port 69.

20.8 IPv6 Packet Information

IPv6 allows an application to specify up to four pieces of information for an outgoing datagram:

1. the source IPv6 address,
2. the outgoing interface index,
3. the outgoing hop limit, and
4. the next-hop address.

This information is sent as ancillary data with `sendmsg`. Three similar pieces of information can be returned for a received packet, and they are returned as ancillary data with `recvmsg`:

1. the destination IPv6 address,
2. the arriving interface index, and
3. the arriving hop limit.

Figure 20.21 summarizes the contents of the ancillary data, which we discuss shortly.

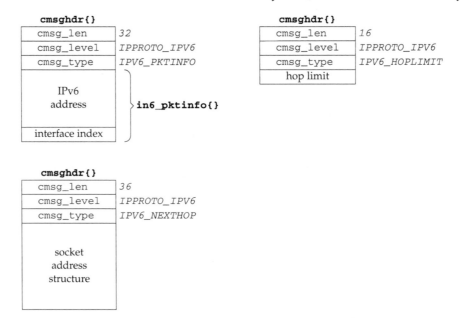

Figure 20.21 Ancillary data for IPv6 packet information.

An `in6_pktinfo` structure contains either the source IPv6 address and the outgoing interface index for an outgoing datagram, or the destination IPv6 address and the arriving interface index for a received datagram:

```
struct in6_pktinfo {
  struct in6_addr ipi6_addr;    /* src/dst IPv6 address */
  int             ipi6_ifindex; /* send/recv interface index */
};
```

This structure is defined by including the `<netinet/in.h>` header. In the `cmsghdr` structure containing this ancillary data, the `cmsg_level` member will be `IPPROTO_IPV6`, the `cmsg_type` member will be `IPV6_PKTINFO`, and the first byte of data will be the first byte of the `in6_pktinfo` structure. In the example in Figure 20.21 we assume no padding between the `cmsghdr` structure and the data, and 4 bytes for an integer.

Nothing special need be done to send this information: just specify the control information as ancillary data for `sendmsg`. But this information is returned as ancillary data by `recvmsg` only if the application has enabled the `IPV6_PKTINFO` socket option.

Outgoing and Arriving Interface

Interfaces on an IPv6 node are identified by small positive integers, as we discussed in Section 17.6. Recall that no interface is ever assigned an index of 0. When specifying the outgoing interface, if the `ipi6_ifindex` value is 0, the kernel will choose the outgoing interface. If the application specifies an outgoing interface for a multicast packet, the interface specified by the ancillary data overrides any interface specified by the `IPV6_MULTICAST_IF` socket option, for this datagram only.

Source and Destination IPv6 Address

The source IPv6 address is normally specified by calling `bind`. But supplying the source address together with the data may require less overhead. This option also allows a server to guarantee that the source address of its reply equals the destination address of the client's request, a feature that some clients require and which is hard to accomplish with IPv4 (Exercise 20.4).

When specifying the source IPv6 address as ancillary data, if the `ipi6_addr` member of the `in6_pktinfo` structure is `IN6ADDR_ANY_INIT`, then (a) if an address is currently bound to the socket, it is used as the source address, or (b) if no address is currently bound to the socket, the kernel will choose the source address. If the `ipi6_addr` member is not the unspecified address, but the socket has already bound a source address, then the `ipi6_addr` value overrides the already-bound source address for this output operation only. The kernel will verify that the requested source address is indeed a unicast address assigned to the node.

When the `in6_pktinfo` structure is returned as ancillary data by `recvmsg`, the `ipi6_addr` member contains the destination IPv6 address from the received packet. This is similar in concept to the `IP_RECVDSTADDR` socket option for IPv4.

Specifying and Receiving the Hop Limit

The outgoing hop limit is normally specified with either the `IPV6_UNICAST_HOPS` socket option for unicast datagrams (Section 7.8) or the `IPV6_MULTICAST_HOPS` socket option for multicast datagrams (Section 19.5). Specifying the hop limit as ancillary data lets us override either the kernel's default or a previously specified value, for either a unicast destination or a multicast destination, for a single output operation. Returning the received hop limit is useful for programs such as `traceroute` and for a class of IPv6 applications that need to verify that the received hop limit is 255 (e.g., that the packet has not been forwarded).

The received hop limit is returned as ancillary data by `recvmsg` only if the application has enabled the `IPV6_HOPLIMIT` socket option. In the `cmsghdr` structure containing this ancillary data, the `cmsg_level` member will be `IPPROTO_IPV6`, the `cmsg_type` member will be `IPV6_HOPLIMIT`, and the first byte of data will be the first byte of the integer hop limit. We showed this in Figure 20.21. Realize that the value returned as ancillary data is the actual value from the received datagram, while the value returned by a `getsockopt` of the `IPV6_UNICAST_HOPS` option is the default value that the kernel will use for outgoing datagrams on the socket.

Nothing special need be done to specify the outgoing hop limit: just specify the control information as ancillary data for `sendmsg`. The normal values for the hop limit are between 0 and 255, inclusive, but if the integer value is –1, this tells the kernel to use its default.

> The hop limit is not contained in the `in6_pktinfo` structure for the following reason. Some UDP servers want to respond to client requests by sending their reply out the same interface on which the request was received and with the source IPv6 address of the reply equal to the destination IPv6 address of the request. To do this the application can enable just the `IPV6_PKTINFO` socket option and then use the received control information from `recvmsg` as the outgoing control information for `sendmsg`. The application need not examine or modify the `in6_pktinfo` structure at all. But if the hop limit were contained in this structure, the application would have to parse the received control information and change the hop limit member, since the received hop limit is not the desired value for an outgoing packet.

Specifying the Next Hop Address

The `IPV6_NEXTHOP` ancillary data object specifies the next hop for the datagram as a socket address structure. In the `cmsghdr` structure containing this ancillary data, the `cmsg_level` member is `IPPROTO_IPV6`, the `cmsg_type` member is `IPV6_NEXTHOP`, and the first byte of data is the first byte of the socket address structure.

In Figure 20.21 we show an example of this ancillary data object, assuming that the socket address structure is a 24-byte `sockaddr_in6` structure. In this case the node identified by that address must be a neighbor of the sending host. If that address equals the destination IPv6 address of the datagram, then this is equivalent to the existing `SO_DONTROUTE` socket option. Setting this option requires superuser privileges.

20.9 Summary

There are applications that want to know the destination IP address and the received interface for a UDP datagram. The `IP_RECVDSTADDR` and `IP_RECVIF` socket options can be enabled to return this information as ancillary data with each datagram. Similar information, along with the received hop limit, can be returned for IPv6 sockets by enabling the `IPV6_PKTINFO` socket option.

Despite all the features provided by TCP that are not provided by UDP, there are times to use UDP. UDP must be used for broadcasting or multicasting. UDP can be used for simple request–reply scenarios, but some form of reliability must then be added to the application. UDP should not be used for bulk data transfer.

We added reliability to our UDP client in Section 20.5 by detecting lost packets using a timeout and retransmission. We modified our retransmission timeout dynamically by adding a timestamp to each packet and keeping track of two estimators: the RTT and its mean deviation. We also added a sequence number to verify that a given reply is the one expected. Our client still employed a simple stop-and-wait protocol, but that is the type of application for which UDP can be used.

Exercises

20.1 In Figure 20.18 why are there two calls to `printf`.

20.2 Can `dg_send_recv` (Figures 20.8 and 20.9) ever return 0?

20.3 Recode `dg_send_recv` to use `select` and its timer, instead of using `alarm`, `SIGALRM`, `sigsetjmp`, and `siglongjmp`.

20.4 How can an IPv4 server guarantee that the source address of its reply equals the destination address of the client's request (e.g., similar to the functionality provided by the `IPV6_PKTINFO` socket option)?

20.5 The `main` function in Section 20.6 is protocol dependent on IPv4. Recode it to be protocol independent. Require the user to specify one or two command-line arguments, the first being an optional IP address (e.g., 0.0.0.0 or 0::0), and the second being a required port number. Then call `udp_client` just to obtain the address family, port number, and length of the socket address structure.

What happens if you call `udp_client`, as suggested, without specifying a *hostname* argument, because `udp_client` does not specify the `AI_PASSIVE` hint to `getaddrinfo`?

20.6 Run the client in Figure 20.6 to an echo server across the Internet after modifying the RTT functions to print each RTT. Also modify the `dg_send_recv` function to print each received sequence number. Plot the resulting RTTs along with the estimators for the RTT and its mean deviation.

21

Out-of-Band Data

21.1 Introduction

Many transport layers have the concept of *out-of-band* data, which is sometimes called *expedited data*. The idea is that something important occurs at one end of the connection and that end wants to tell its peer quickly. By "quickly" we mean that this notification should be sent before any "normal" (sometimes called "in-band") data that is already queued to be sent. That is, out-of-band data is considered higher priority than the normal data. But instead of using two connections between the client and server, out-of-band data is mapped onto the existing connection.

Unfortunately once we get beyond the general concepts, and down to the real world, almost every transport layer has a different implementation of out-of-band data. In this chapter we focus on TCP's model of out-of-band data, provide numerous small examples of how it is handled by the sockets API, and then use it to write some simple client–server heartbeat functions that can detect when the peer process either crashes or is unreachable.

21.2 TCP Out-of-Band Data

TCP does not have true *out-of-band data*. Instead, TCP provides an *urgent mode* that we now describe. Assume a process has written N bytes of data to a TCP socket and that data is queued by TCP in the socket send buffer, waiting to be sent to the peer. We show this in Figure 21.1 and have labeled the data bytes 1 through N.

socket send buffer

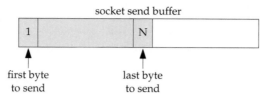

Figure 21.1 Socket send buffer containing data to send.

The process now writes a single byte of out-of-band data, containing the ASCII
character a, using the send function and the MSG_OOB flag:

```
send(fd, "a", 1, MSG_OOB);
```

TCP places the data in the next available position in the socket send buffer and sets its
urgent pointer for this connection to be the next available location. We show this in Figure 21.2 and have labeled the out-of-band byte "OOB."

socket send buffer

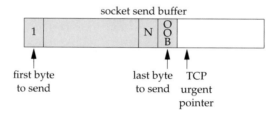

Figure 21.2   Socket send buffer after 1 byte of out-of-band data is written by application.

> TCP's urgent pointer has a sequence number one greater than the byte of data that is written
> with the MSG_OOB flag. As discussed on pp. 292–296 of TCPv1, this is a historical artifact that
> is now emulated by all implementations. As long as the sending TCP and the receiving TCP
> agree on the interpretation of TCP's urgent pointer, all is OK.

> In Section 7.9 we mentioned the new TCP_STDURG socket option that can change this interpre-
> tation of which byte the urgent pointer points to. This option should never need to be set.

Given the state of the TCP socket send buffer shown in Figure 21.2, the next segment sent by TCP will have its URG flag set in the TCP header and the urgent offset
field in the TCP header will point to the byte following the out-of-band byte. But this
segment may or may not contain the byte that we have labeled as OOB. Whether the
OOB byte is sent depends on the number of bytes ahead of it in the socket receive buffer, the segment size that TCP is sending to the peer, and the current window advertised
by the peer.

> We have used the terms *urgent pointer* and *urgent offset*. At the TCP level the two are different.
> The 16-bit value in the TCP header is called the urgent offset and it must be added to the
> sequence number field in the header to obtain the 32-bit urgent pointer. TCP looks at the
> urgent offset only if another bit in the header is set, and this bit is called the *URG flag*. From a
> programming perspective we need not worry about this detail and just refer to TCP's urgent
> pointer.

This is an important characteristic of TCP's urgent mode: the TCP header indicates that the sender has entered urgent mode (i.e., the URG flag is set along with the urgent offset), but the actual byte of data referred to by the urgent pointer need not be sent. Indeed, if the sending TCP is flow control stopped (the receiver's socket receive buffer is full, so its TCP has advertised a window of 0 to the sending TCP), the urgent notification is sent without any data (pp. 1016–1017 of TCPv2) as we show in Figures 21.10 and 21.11. This is one reason why applications use TCP's urgent mode (i.e., out-of-band data): the urgent notification is *always* sent to the peer TCP even if the flow of data is stopped by TCP's flow control.

What happens if we send multiple bytes of out-of-band data, as in

```
send(fd, "abc", 3, MSG_OOB);
```

In this example TCP's urgent pointer points one beyond the final byte; that is, the final byte (the c) is considered the out-of-band byte.

Now that we have covered the sending of out-of-band data let's look at it from the receiver's side.

1. When TCP receives a segment with the URG flag set, the urgent pointer is examined to see whether this pointer refers to *new* out-of-band data. That is, whether this is the first time TCP's urgent mode has referenced this particular byte in the stream of data from the sender to the receiver. It is common for the sending TCP to send multiple segments (typically over a short period of time) containing the URG flag but with the urgent pointer pointing to the same byte of data. Only the first of these segments causes the receiving process to be notified that new out-of-band data has arrived.

2. The receiving process is notified when a new urgent pointer arrives. First the SIGURG signal is sent to the owner of the socket, assuming either fcntl or ioctl has been called to establish an owner for the socket (Figure 7.15), and assuming the process has established a signal handler for this signal. Second, if the process is blocked in a call to select waiting for this socket descriptor to have an exception condition, select returns.

    These two potential notifications to the receiving process take place when a new urgent pointer arrives, regardless whether the actual byte of data pointed to by the urgent pointer has arrived at the receiving TCP.

3. When the actual byte of data pointed to by the urgent pointer arrives at the receiving TCP, the data byte can be pulled out-of-band or left inline. By default the SO_OOBINLINE socket option is *not* set for a socket so the single byte of data is not placed into the socket receive buffer. Instead, the data byte is placed into a separate 1-byte out-of-band buffer for this connection (pp. 986–988 of TCPv2). The only way for the process to read from this special 1-byte buffer is to call recv, recvfrom, or recvmsg and specify the MSG_OOB flag.

    If, however, the process sets the SO_OOBINLINE socket option, then the single byte of data referred to by TCP's urgent pointer is left in the normal socket receive buffer. The process cannot specify the MSG_OOB flag to read the data byte in this case. The process will know when it reaches this byte of data by checking the *out-of-band mark* for this connection, as we describe in Section 21.3.

Some errors are possible.

1. If the process asks for out-of-band data (e.g., specifying the MSG_OOB flag) but the peer has not sent any, EINVAL is returned.

2. If the process has been notified that the peer has sent an out-of-band byte (e.g., by SIGURG or select), and the process tries to read it, but that byte has not yet arrived, EWOULDBLOCK is returned. All the process can do at this point is read from the socket receive buffer (possibly discarding the data if it has no room to store the data), to make space in the buffer so that the peer TCP can send the out-of-band byte.

3. If the process tries to read the same out-of-band byte multiple times, EINVAL is returned.

4. If the process has set the SO_OOBINLINE socket option and then tries to read the out-of-band data by specifying MSG_OOB, EINVAL is returned.

Simple Example Using SIGURG

We now show a trivial example of sending and receiving out-of-band data. Figure 21.3 shows the sending program.

———————————————————————————————————— *oob/tcpsend01.c*
```
 1 #include      "unp.h"

 2 int
 3 main(int argc, char **argv)
 4 {
 5      int     sockfd;

 6      if (argc != 3)
 7          err_quit("usage: tcpsend01 <host> <port#>");

 8      sockfd = Tcp_connect(argv[1], argv[2]);

 9      Write(sockfd, "123", 3);
10      printf("wrote 3 bytes of normal data\n");
11      sleep(1);

12      Send(sockfd, "4", 1, MSG_OOB);
13      printf("wrote 1 byte of OOB data\n");
14      sleep(1);

15      Write(sockfd, "56", 2);
16      printf("wrote 2 bytes of normal data\n");
17      sleep(1);
```

```
18      Send(sockfd, "7", 1, MSG_OOB);
19      printf("wrote 1 byte of OOB data\n");
20      sleep(1);

21      Write(sockfd, "89", 2);
22      printf("wrote 2 bytes of normal data\n");
23      sleep(1);

24      exit(0);
25  }
```
───────────────────────────────────── oob/tcpsend01.c

Figure 21.3 Simple out-of-band sending program.

Nine bytes are sent, with a 1-second `sleep` between each output operation. The purpose of the pause is to let each `write` or `send` be transmitted as a single TCP segment and received as such by the other end. We talk later about some of the timing considerations with out-of-band data. When we run this program we see the expected output:

```
solaris % tcpsend01 bsdi 9999
wrote 3 bytes of normal data
wrote 1 byte of OOB data
wrote 2 bytes of normal data
wrote 1 byte of OOB data
wrote 2 bytes of normal data
```

Figure 21.4 is the receiving program.

Establish signal handler and socket owner

16–17   The signal handler for `SIGURG` is established and `fcntl` sets the owner of the connected socket.

> Notice that we do not establish the signal handler until `accept` returns. There is a small probability that out-of-band data can arrive after our TCP completes the three-way handshake but before `accept` returns, which we would miss. But if we established the signal handler before calling `accept` and also set the owner of the listening socket (which carries over to the connected socket), then if out-of-band data arrives before `accept` returns, our signal handler won't yet have a value for `connfd`. If this scenario is important for the application, it should have initialized `connfd` to –1, check for this value in the signal handler, and if true just set a flag for the main loop to check after `accept` returns.

18–25   The process reads from the socket, printing each string that is returned by `read`. When the sender terminates the connection, the receiver then terminates.

`SIGURG` handler

27–36   Our signal handler calls `printf`, reads the out-of-band byte by specifying the `MSG_OOB` flag, and then prints the returned data. Notice that we ask for up to 100 bytes in the call to `recv`, but as we will see shortly, only 1 byte is ever returned as out-of-band data.

> As stated earlier, calling the unsafe `printf` function from a signal handler is not recommended. We do it just to see what's happening with our programs.

———————————————————— oob/tcprecv01.c

```
 1 #include    "unp.h"

 2 int     listenfd, connfd;

 3 void    sig_urg(int);

 4 int
 5 main(int argc, char **argv)
 6 {
 7     int     n;
 8     char    buff[100];

 9     if (argc == 2)
10         listenfd = Tcp_listen(NULL, argv[1], NULL);
11     else if (argc == 3)
12         listenfd = Tcp_listen(argv[1], argv[2], NULL);
13     else
14         err_quit("usage: tcprecv01 [ <host> ] <port#>");

15     connfd = Accept(listenfd, NULL, NULL);

16     Signal(SIGURG, sig_urg);
17     Fcntl(connfd, F_SETOWN, getpid());

18     for ( ; ; ) {
19         if ( (n = Read(connfd, buff, sizeof(buff) - 1)) == 0) {
20             printf("received EOF\n");
21             exit(0);
22         }
23         buff[n] = 0;                /* null terminate */
24         printf("read %d bytes: %s\n", n, buff);
25     }
26 }

27 void
28 sig_urg(int signo)
29 {
30     int     n;
31     char    buff[100];

32     printf("SIGURG received\n");
33     n = Recv(connfd, buff, sizeof(buff) - 1, MSG_OOB);
34     buff[n] = 0;                /* null terminate */
35     printf("read %d OOB byte: %s\n", n, buff);
36 }
```

———————————————————— oob/tcprecv01.c

Figure 21.4 Simple out-of-band receiving program.

Here is the output when we run the receiving program, and then run the sending program from Figure 21.3.

```
bsdi % tcprecv01 9999
read 3 bytes: 123
SIGURG received
read 1 OOB byte: 4
read 2 bytes: 56
```

```
SIGURG received
read 1 OOB byte: 7
read 2 bytes: 89
received EOF
```

The results are as we expect. Each sending of out-of-band data by the sender generates SIGURG for the receiver, which then reads the single out-of-band byte.

Simple Example Using `select`

We now redo our out-of-band receiver to use `select` instead of the SIGURG signal. Figure 21.5 is the receiving program.

——— *oob/tcprecv02.c*
```
 1 #include    "unp.h"

 2 int
 3 main(int argc, char **argv)
 4 {
 5     int     listenfd, connfd, n;
 6     char    buff[100];
 7     fd_set  rset, xset;

 8     if (argc == 2)
 9         listenfd = Tcp_listen(NULL, argv[1], NULL);
10     else if (argc == 3)
11         listenfd = Tcp_listen(argv[1], argv[2], NULL);
12     else
13         err_quit("usage: tcprecv02 [ <host> ] <port#>");

14     connfd = Accept(listenfd, NULL, NULL);

15     FD_ZERO(&rset);
16     FD_ZERO(&xset);
17     for ( ; ; ) {
18         FD_SET(connfd, &rset);
19         FD_SET(connfd, &xset);

20         Select(connfd + 1, &rset, NULL, &xset, NULL);

21         if (FD_ISSET(connfd, &xset)) {
22             n = Recv(connfd, buff, sizeof(buff) - 1, MSG_OOB);
23             buff[n] = 0;        /* null terminate */
24             printf("read %d OOB byte: %s\n", n, buff);
25         }
26         if (FD_ISSET(connfd, &rset)) {
27             if ( (n = Read(connfd, buff, sizeof(buff) - 1)) == 0) {
28                 printf("received EOF\n");
29                 exit(0);
30             }
31             buff[n] = 0;        /* null terminate */
32             printf("read %d bytes: %s\n", n, buff);
33         }
34     }
35 }
```
——— *oob/tcprecv02.c*

Figure 21.5 Receiving program that uses `select` to be notified of out-of-band data.

15-20   The process calls `select` waiting for either normal data (the read set, `rset`) or out-of-band data (the exception set, `xset`). In each case the received data is printed.

When we run this program and then run the same sending program as earlier (Figure 21.3), we encounter the following error:

```
bsdi % tcprecv02 8888
read 3 bytes: 123
read 1 OOB byte: 4
recv error: Invalid argument
```

The problem is that `select` indicates an exception condition until the process reads *beyond* the out-of-band data (pp. 530–531 of TCPv2). We cannot read the out-of-band data more than once because after we read it the first time, the kernel clears the 1-byte out-of-band buffer. When we call `recv` specifying the `MSG_OOB` flag the second time, BSD/OS returns `EINVAL` while Solaris 2.5 returns `EAGAIN`. (Posix.1g specifies `EINVAL` as the error for this condition.)

The solution is to `select` for an exception condition only after reading normal data. Figure 21.6 is a modification of Figure 21.5 that handles this scenario correctly.

5   We declare a new variable named `justreadoob` that indicates whether we just read out-of-band data or not. This flag determines whether or not to `select` for an exception condition.

26-27   When we set the `justreadoob` flag we must also clear the bit for this descriptor in the exception set.

The program now works as expected.

21.3 `sockatmark` Function

Whenever out-of-band data is received, there is an associated *out-of-band mark*. This is the position in the normal stream of data *at the sender* when the sending process sent the out-of-band byte. The receiving process determines whether or not it is at the out-of-band mark by calling the `sockatmark` function while it reads from the socket.

```
#include <sys/socket.h>

int sockatmark(int sockfd);
```
Returns: 1 if at out-of-band mark, 0 if not at mark, −1 on error

This function is an invention of Posix.1g. Posix is replacing all `ioctl`s with functions.

Figure 21.7 (p. 574) shows an implementation of this function using the commonly found `SIOCATMARK` `ioctl`.

oob/tcprecv03.c

```
 1 #include    "unp.h"

 2 int
 3 main(int argc, char **argv)
 4 {
 5     int     listenfd, connfd, n, justreadoob = 0;
 6     char    buff[100];
 7     fd_set  rset, xset;

 8     if (argc == 2)
 9         listenfd = Tcp_listen(NULL, argv[1], NULL);
10     else if (argc == 3)
11         listenfd = Tcp_listen(argv[1], argv[2], NULL);
12     else
13         err_quit("usage: tcprecv03 [ <host> ] <port#>");

14     connfd = Accept(listenfd, NULL, NULL);

15     FD_ZERO(&rset);
16     FD_ZERO(&xset);
17     for ( ; ; ) {
18         FD_SET(connfd, &rset);
19         if (justreadoob == 0)
20             FD_SET(connfd, &xset);

21         Select(connfd + 1, &rset, NULL, &xset, NULL);

22         if (FD_ISSET(connfd, &xset)) {
23             n = Recv(connfd, buff, sizeof(buff) - 1, MSG_OOB);
24             buff[n] = 0;          /* null terminate */
25             printf("read %d OOB byte: %s\n", n, buff);
26             justreadoob = 1;
27             FD_CLR(connfd, &xset);
28         }
29         if (FD_ISSET(connfd, &rset)) {
30             if ( (n = Read(connfd, buff, sizeof(buff) - 1)) == 0) {
31                 printf("received EOF\n");
32                 exit(0);
33             }
34             buff[n] = 0;          /* null terminate */
35             printf("read %d bytes: %s\n", n, buff);
36             justreadoob = 0;
37         }
38     }
39 }
```

oob/tcprecv03.c

Figure 21.6 Modification of Figure 21.5 to select for an exception condition correctly.

lib/sockatmark.c

```
1 #include    "unp.h"

2 int
3 sockatmark(int fd)
4 {
5     int     flag;

6     if (ioctl(fd, SIOCATMARK, &flag) < 0)
7         return (-1);
8     return (flag != 0 ? 1 : 0);
9 }
```

lib/sockatmark.c

Figure 21.7 sockatmark function implemented using ioctl.

The out-of-band mark applies regardless whether the receiving process is receiving the out-of-band data inline (the SO_OOBINLINE socket option) or out-of-band (the MSG_OOB flag). One common use of the out-of-band mark is for the receiver to treat all of the data specially until the mark is passed.

Example

We now show a simple example to illustrate the following two features of the out-of-band mark.

1. The out-of-band mark always points one beyond the final byte of normal data. This means that, if the out-of-band data is received inline, sockatmark returns true if the next byte to be read is the byte that was sent with the MSG_OOB flag. Alternately, if the SO_OOBINLINE socket option is not enabled, then sockatmark returns true if the next byte of data is the first byte that was sent following the out-of-band data.

2. A read operation always stops at the out-of-band mark (pp. 519–520 of TCPv2). That is, if there are 100 bytes in the socket receive buffer but only 5 bytes until the out-of-band mark, and the process performs a read asking for 100 bytes, only the 5 bytes up until the mark are returned. This forced stop at the mark is to allow the process to call sockatmark to determine if the buffer pointer is at the mark.

Figure 21.8 is our sending program. It sends 3 bytes of normal data, 1 byte of out-of-band data, followed by another byte of normal data. There are no pauses between each output operation.

Figure 21.9 is the receiving program. This program does not use the SIGURG signal or select. Instead, it calls sockatmark to determine when the out-of-band byte is encountered.

————————————————————— oob/tcpsend04.c

```
 1 #include    "unp.h"

 2 int
 3 main(int argc, char **argv)
 4 {
 5      int     sockfd;

 6      if (argc != 3)
 7          err_quit("usage: tcpsend04 <host> <port#>");

 8      sockfd = Tcp_connect(argv[1], argv[2]);

 9      Write(sockfd, "123", 3);
10      printf("wrote 3 bytes of normal data\n");

11      Send(sockfd, "4", 1, MSG_OOB);
12      printf("wrote 1 byte of OOB data\n");

13      Write(sockfd, "5", 1);
14      printf("wrote 1 byte of normal data\n");

15      exit(0);
16 }
```

————————————————————— oob/tcpsend04.c

Figure 21.8 Sending program.

————————————————————— oob/tcprecv04.c

```
 1 #include    "unp.h"

 2 int
 3 main(int argc, char **argv)
 4 {
 5      int     listenfd, connfd, n, on = 1;
 6      char    buff[100];

 7      if (argc == 2)
 8          listenfd = Tcp_listen(NULL, argv[1], NULL);
 9      else if (argc == 3)
10          listenfd = Tcp_listen(argv[1], argv[2], NULL);
11      else
12          err_quit("usage: tcprecv04 [ <host> ] <port#>");

13      Setsockopt(listenfd, SOL_SOCKET, SO_OOBINLINE, &on, sizeof(on));

14      connfd = Accept(listenfd, NULL, NULL);
15      sleep(5);

16      for ( ; ; ) {
17          if (Sockatmark(connfd))
18              printf("at OOB mark\n");

19          if ( (n = Read(connfd, buff, sizeof(buff) - 1)) == 0) {
20              printf("received EOF\n");
21              exit(0);
22          }
23          buff[n] = 0;              /* null terminate */
24          printf("read %d bytes: %s\n", n, buff);
25      }
26 }
```

————————————————————— oob/tcprecv04.c

Figure 21.9 Receiving program that calls sockatmark.

Set SO_OOBINLINE socket option

13   We want to receive the out-of-band data inline, so we must set the SO_OOBINLINE socket option. But if we wait until accept returns and set the option on the connected socket, the three-way handshake is complete and out-of-band data may have already arrived. Therefore we must set this option for the listening socket, knowing that all socket options carry over from the listening socket to the connected socket (Section 7.4).

sleep after connection accepted

14-15   The receiver sleeps after the connection is accepted to let all the data from the sender be received. This allows us to demonstrate that a read stops at the out-of-band mark, even though additional data is in the socket receive buffer.

Read all the data from the sender

16-25   The program calls read in a loop, printing the received data. But before calling read, sockatmark checks if the buffer pointer is at the out-of-band mark.
            When we run this program we have the following output:

```
bsdi % tcprecv04 6666
read 3 bytes: 123
at OOB mark
read 2 bytes: 45
received EOF
```

Even though all the data has been received by the receiving TCP when read is called the first time (because the receiving process calls sleep), only 3 bytes are returned because the mark is encountered. The next byte read is the out-of-band byte (with a value of 4) because we told the kernel to place the out-of-band data inline.

Example

We now show another simple example to illustrate two additional features of out-of-band data, both of which we mentioned earlier.

1. TCP sends notification of out-of-band data (its urgent pointer) even though it is flow-control stopped from sending data.

2. A receiving process can be notified that the sender has sent out-of-band data (with the SIGURG signal or by select) *before* the out-of-band data arrives. If the process then calls recv specifying MSG_OOB and the out-of-band data has not arrived, an error of EWOULDBLOCK is returned.

Figure 21.10 is the sending program.

9-19   This process sets the size of its socket send buffer to 32768, writes 16384 bytes of normal data, and then sleeps for 5 seconds. We will see shortly that the receiver sets the size of its socket receive buffer to 4096, so these operations by the sender guarantee that the sending TCP fills the receiver's socket receive buffer. The sender then sends 1 byte of out-of-band data, followed by 1024 bytes of normal data, and terminates.

―― oob/tcpsend05.c

```
 1 #include    "unp.h"

 2 int
 3 main(int argc, char **argv)
 4 {
 5     int     sockfd, size;
 6     char    buff[16384];

 7     if (argc != 3)
 8         err_quit("usage: tcpsend04 <host> <port#>");

 9     sockfd = Tcp_connect(argv[1], argv[2]);

10     size = 32768;
11     Setsockopt(sockfd, SOL_SOCKET, SO_SNDBUF, &size, sizeof(size));

12     Write(sockfd, buff, 16384);
13     printf("wrote 16384 bytes of normal data\n");
14     sleep(5);

15     Send(sockfd, "a", 1, MSG_OOB);
16     printf("wrote 1 byte of OOB data\n");

17     Write(sockfd, buff, 1024);
18     printf("wrote 1024 bytes of normal data\n");

19     exit(0);
20 }
```

―― oob/tcpsend05.c

Figure 21.10 Sending program.

Figure 21.11 shows the receiving program.

14-20   The receiving process sets the size of the listening socket's receive buffer to 4096. This size will carry over to the connected socket after the connection is established. The process then accepts the connection, establishes a signal handler for SIGURG, and establishes the owner of the socket. The main loop calls pause in an infinite loop.

22-31   The signal handler calls recv to read the out-of-band data.

When we start the receiver and then the sender, here is the output from the sender.

```
solaris % tcpsend05 bsdi 5555
wrote 16384 bytes of normal data
wrote 1 byte of OOB data
wrote 1024 bytes of normal data
```

As expected, all the data fits into the sender's socket send buffer, and it terminates. Here is the output from the receiver.

```
bsdi % tcprecv05 5555
SIGURG received
recv error: Resource temporarily unavailable
```

The error string printed by our err_sys function corresponds to EAGAIN, which is the same as EWOULDBLOCK in BSD/OS. TCP sends the out-of-band notification to the receiving TCP, which then generates the SIGURG signal for the receiving process. But when recv is called specifying the MSG_OOB flag, the out-of-band byte cannot be read.

———————————————————————————— oob/tcprecv05.c

```
 1 #include     "unp.h"

 2 int     listenfd, connfd;

 3 void    sig_urg(int);

 4 int
 5 main(int argc, char **argv)
 6 {
 7     int     size;

 8     if (argc == 2)
 9         listenfd = Tcp_listen(NULL, argv[1], NULL);
10     else if (argc == 3)
11         listenfd = Tcp_listen(argv[1], argv[2], NULL);
12     else
13         err_quit("usage: tcprecv05 [ <host> ] <port#>");

14     size = 4096;
15     Setsockopt(listenfd, SOL_SOCKET, SO_RCVBUF, &size, sizeof(size));

16     connfd = Accept(listenfd, NULL, NULL);

17     Signal(SIGURG, sig_urg);
18     Fcntl(connfd, F_SETOWN, getpid());

19     for ( ; ; )
20         pause();
21 }

22 void
23 sig_urg(int signo)
24 {
25     int     n;
26     char    buff[2048];

27     printf("SIGURG received\n");
28     n = Recv(connfd, buff, sizeof(buff) - 1, MSG_OOB);
29     buff[n] = 0;                    /* null terminate */
30     printf("read %d OOB byte\n", n);
31 }
```

———————————————————————————— oob/tcprecv05.c

Figure 21.11 Receiving program.

The solution is for the receiver to make room in its socket receive buffer by reading the normal data that is available. This will cause its TCP to advertise a nonzero window to the sender, which will eventually let the sender transmit the out-of-band byte.

> We note two related issues in Berkeley-derived implementations (pp. 1016–1017 of TCPv2). First, even if the socket send buffer is full, an out-of-band byte is always accepted by the kernel from the process for sending to the peer. Second, when the process sends an out-of-band byte, a TCP segment is immediately sent that contains the urgent notification. All the normal TCP output checks (Nagle algorithm, silly-window avoidance, etc.) are bypassed.

Example

Our next example demonstrates that there is only a single out-of-band mark for a given TCP connection, and if new out-of-band data arrives before the receiving process reads some existing out-of-band data, the previous mark is lost.

Figure 21.12 is the sending program, which is similar to Figure 21.8 with the addition of another send of out-of-band data, followed by one more write of normal data.

—— oob/tcpsend06.c

```
 1 #include     "unp.h"

 2 int
 3 main(int argc, char **argv)
 4 {
 5     int     sockfd;

 6     if (argc != 3)
 7         err_quit("usage: tcpsend04 <host> <port#>");

 8     sockfd = Tcp_connect(argv[1], argv[2]);

 9     Write(sockfd, "123", 3);
10     printf("wrote 3 bytes of normal data\n");

11     Send(sockfd, "4", 1, MSG_OOB);
12     printf("wrote 1 byte of OOB data\n");

13     Write(sockfd, "5", 1);
14     printf("wrote 1 byte of normal data\n");

15     Send(sockfd, "6", 1, MSG_OOB);
16     printf("wrote 1 byte of OOB data\n");

17     Write(sockfd, "7", 1);
18     printf("wrote 1 byte of normal data\n");

19     exit(0);
20 }
```

—— oob/tcpsend06.c

Figure 21.12 Sending two out-of-band bytes in rapid succession.

There are no pauses in the sending, allowing all the data to be sent to the receiving TCP quickly.

The receiving program is identical to Figure 21.9, which sleeps for 5 seconds after accepting the connection to allow the data to arrive at its TCP. Here is the receiving program's output:

```
bsdi % tcprecv06 5555
read 5 bytes: 12345
at OOB mark
read 2 bytes: 67
received EOF
```

The arrival of the second out-of-band byte (the 6) overwrites the mark that was stored when the first out-of-band byte arrived (the 4). As we said, there is only one out-of-band mark per TCP connection.

21.4 TCP Out-of-Band Data Summary

All our examples using out-of-band data so far have been trivial. Unfortunately out-of-band data gets messy when we consider the timing problems that may arise. The first point to consider is that the concept of out-of-band data really conveys three different pieces of information to the receiver.

1. The fact that the sender went into urgent mode. The receiving process can be notified of this with either the SIGURG signal or with select. This *notification* is transmitted immediately after the sender sends the out-of-band byte, because we saw in Figure 21.11 that TCP sends the notification even if it is flow-control stopped from sending any data to the receiver. This notification might cause the receiver to go into some special mode of processing for any subsequent data that it receives.

2. The *position* of the out-of-band byte; that is, where it was sent with regard to the rest of data from the sender: the out-of-band mark.

3. The actual *value* of the out-of-band byte. Since TCP is a byte-stream protocol that does not interpret the data sent by the application, this can be any 8-bit value.

With TCP's urgent mode we can think of the URG flag as being the notification, the urgent pointer as being the mark, and the byte of data as itself.

The problems with this concept of out-of-band data are that (a) there is only one TCP urgent pointer per connection, (b) there is only one out-of-band mark per connection, and (c) there is only a single 1-byte out-of-band buffer per connection (which is an issue only if the data is not being read inline). We saw with Figure 21.12 that an arriving mark overwrites any previous mark that the process has not yet encountered. If the data is being read inline, previous out-of-band bytes are not lost when new out-of-band data arrives, but the mark is lost.

One common use of out-of-band data is with Rlogin, when the client interrupts the program that it is running on the server (pp. 393–394 of TCPv1). The server needs to tell the client to discard all queued output because up to one window's worth of output may be queued to send from the server to the client. The server sends a special byte to the client, telling it to flush all output, and this byte is sent as out-of-band data. When the client receives the SIGURG signal, it just reads from the socket until it encounters the mark, discarding everything up through the mark. (Pp. 398–401 of TCPv1 contain an example of this use of out-of-band data, along with the corresponding tcpdump output.) In this scenario, if the server were to send multiple out-of-band bytes in quick succession, it doesn't affect the client, as the client just reads up through the final mark, discarding all the data.

In summary, the usefulness of out-of-band data depends on why it is being used by the application. If the purpose is to tell the peer to discard the normal data, up through the mark, then losing an intermediate out-of-band byte and its corresponding mark is of no consequence. But if it is important that no out-of-band bytes be lost, then the data must be received inline. Furthermore, the data bytes that are sent as out-of-band data should be differentiated from normal data since intermediate marks can be overwritten when a new mark is received, effectively mixing the out-of-band bytes with the normal data. Telnet, for example, sends its own commands in the normal stream of data between the client and server, prefixing its commands with a byte of 255. (To send this value as data then requires two successive bytes of 255.) This lets it differentiate its commands from the normal user data but requires that the client and server process each byte of data looking for commands.

21.5 Client–Server Heartbeat Functions

We now develop some simple heartbeat functions for our echo client and server. These functions can detect the early failure of either the peer host or the communications path to the peer.

Before showing these functions we must provide some caveats. First, some people want to use the TCP keepalive feature (the SO_KEEPALIVE socket option) to provide this functionality, but TCP doesn't send a keepalive probe until the connection has been idle for 2 hours. When people discover this, their next question is how to modify the keepalive parameters down to a much lower value (often on the order of seconds) to detect a failure faster. While it is possible on many systems to shorten TCP's keepalive timer parameters (see Appendix E of TCPv1), these parameters are normally maintained on a per-kernel basis, not a per-socket basis, so changing them affects all sockets that enable this option. Also, the keepalive option was never intended for this purpose (high-frequency polling).

Second, a temporary loss in connectivity between two end systems is not always a bad thing. TCP was designed to cope with this, and Berkeley-derived TCP implementations will retransmit for 8–10 minutes before giving up on a connection. Newer IP routing protocols (e.g., OSPF) can detect the failure of a link and possibly come up with an alternate path in a short time (e.g., on the order of seconds). Therefore one must examine their application to determine whether terminating a connection after not hearing from the peer after 5 or 10 seconds is a good thing or not. Some applications require this type of functionality, but most do not.

We will use TCP's urgent mode to poll the peer on a regular basis; we assume once a second in the description below, along with a 5-second limit, but these can be changed by the application. Figure 21.13 shows the arrangement of the client and server.

In this example the client sends an out-of-band byte to the server once a second, and the receipt of this by the server causes it to send an out-of-band byte back to the client. Each needs to know if the other disappears or is unreachable. The client and server increment their cnt variable once a second and the receipt of an out-of-band byte resets this variable to 0. Should the counter reach 5 (that is, the process has not received an out-of-band byte from its peer in 5 seconds), a failure is assumed. Both client and server use the SIGURG signal to be notified when the out-of-band byte arrives. We note in the middle of this figure that the data, echoed data, and the out-of-band bytes are all exchanged across a single TCP connection.

Our client main function is unchanged from Figure 5.4. Our str_cli function (which we do not show) has only three simple changes from the version in Figure 6.13.

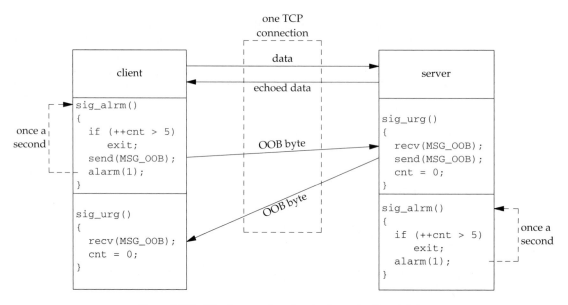

Figure 21.13 Client–server heartbeat using out-of-band data.

1. We call our `heartbeat_cli` function before entering the `for` loop, to set up the client heartbeat feature:

   ```
   heartbeat_cli(sockfd, 1, 5);
   ```

   The second argument is the polling frequency in seconds, and the third argument is the number of seconds with no response before giving up on the connection.

2. If `select` returns an error of `EINTR`, we `continue` to go around the loop and call `select` again. Note in Figure 21.13 that the client now catches two signals, `SIGALRM` and `SIGURG`, so we must be prepared to handle an interrupted system call.

3. Instead of calling `fputs` to write the echoed line to standard output we call `writen`. We do this because we are catching two signals, which we just said can interrupt slow system calls, and some versions of the standard I/O library do not handle interrupted system calls correctly [Korn and Vo 1991].

Figure 21.14 shows the three functions that provide the client heartbeat functionality.

Global variables

2–5   The first three variables are copies of the arguments to `heartbeat_cli`: the socket descriptor (which the signal handlers need to send and receive the out-of-band data), the frequency of the `SIGALRM`s, and the total number of `SIGALRM`s with no response from the server before the client considers the server or the connection dead. The variable `nprobes` counts the number of `SIGALRM`s since the last reply from the server.

————————————————————————————— oob/heartbeatcli.c

```
 1 #include    "unp.h"

 2 static int servfd;
 3 static int nsec;                    /* #seconds betweeen each alarm */
 4 static int maxnprobes;              /* #probes w/no response before quit */
 5 static int nprobes;                 /* #probes since last server response */
 6 static void sig_urg(int), sig_alrm(int);

 7 void
 8 heartbeat_cli(int servfd_arg, int nsec_arg, int maxnprobes_arg)
 9 {
10     servfd = servfd_arg;            /* set globals for signal handlers */
11     if ( (nsec = nsec_arg) < 1)
12         nsec = 1;
13     if ( (maxnprobes = maxnprobes_arg) < nsec)
14         maxnprobes = nsec;
15     nprobes = 0;

16     Signal(SIGURG, sig_urg);
17     Fcntl(servfd, F_SETOWN, getpid());

18     Signal(SIGALRM, sig_alrm);
19     alarm(nsec);
20 }

21 static void
22 sig_urg(int signo)
23 {
24     int     n;
25     char    c;

26     if ( (n = recv(servfd, &c, 1, MSG_OOB)) < 0) {
27         if (errno != EWOULDBLOCK)
28             err_sys("recv error");
29     }
30     nprobes = 0;                     /* reset counter */
31     return;                          /* may interrupt client code */
32 }

33 static void
34 sig_alrm(int signo)
35 {
36     if (++nprobes > maxnprobes) {
37         fprintf(stderr, "server is unreachable\n");
38         exit(0);
39     }
40     Send(servfd, "1", 1, MSG_OOB);
41     alarm(nsec);
42     return;                          /* may interrupt client code */
43 }
```

————————————————————————————— oob/heartbeatcli.c

Figure 21.14 Client heartbeat functions.

`heartbeat_cli` function

7-20   The `heartbeat_cli` function validates and saves the arguments. Signal handlers are established for `SIGURG` and `SIGALRM` and the owner of the socket is set to the process ID. `alarm` schedules the first `SIGALRM`.

`SIGURG` handler

21-32   This signal is generated when an out-of-band notification arrives. We try to read the out-of-band byte, but if it has not arrived (`EWOULDBLOCK`) that is OK. Notice that we are not receiving the out-of-band data inline, which would interfere with the client's reading of its normal data.

Since the server is still alive, `nprobes` is reset to 0.

`SIGALRM` handler

33-43   This signal is generated at a regular interval. The counter `nprobes` is incremented, and if it has reached `maxnprobes`, we assume the server host has either crashed or is unreachable. In this example we terminate the client process, although other designs could be used: a signal could be sent to the main loop, or another argument to `heartbeat_cli` could be a client function that is called when it appears that the server is dead.

A byte containing the character 1 is sent as out-of-band data (there is no meaning implied by this value) and `alarm` schedules the next `SIGALRM`.

Our server `main` function is identical to the one in Figure 5.12. The only modification to our `str_echo` function from Figure 5.3 is to add the line

```
heartbeat_serv(sockfd, 1, 5);
```

before the `for` loop. This call initializes the heartbeat function for the server.

Figure 21.15 shows the server heartbeat functions.

`heartbeat_serv` function

7-19   The variable declarations and the function `heartbeat_serv` are nearly identical to those for the client.

`SIGURG` handler

20-32   When an out-of-band notification is received by the server, it tries to read the byte. As with the client, if the out-of-band byte has not arrived, that is OK. The out-of-band byte is echoed back to the client as out-of-band data. Notice that if `recv` returns `EWOULDBLOCK`, then whatever happens to be in the automatic variable `c` is echoed back to the client. We do not use the value of the out-of-band byte for any purpose, so this is OK. All that is important is to send 1 byte of out-of-band data, whatever that byte happens to be. `nprobes` is reset to 0 since we just received notification that the client is alive.

`SIGALRM` handler

33-42   `nprobes` is incremented and if it has reached the caller-specified value of `maxnprobes`, the server process is terminated. Otherwise the next `SIGALRM` is scheduled.

oob/heartbeatserv.c
```
 1 #include    "unp.h"

 2 static int servfd;
 3 static int nsec;                 /* #seconds between each alarm */
 4 static int maxnalarms;           /* #alarms w/no client probe before quit */
 5 static int nprobes;              /* #alarms since last client probe */
 6 static void sig_urg(int), sig_alrm(int);

 7 void
 8 heartbeat_serv(int servfd_arg, int nsec_arg, int maxnalarms_arg)
 9 {
10     servfd = servfd_arg;         /* set globals for signal handlers */
11     if ( (nsec = nsec_arg) < 1)
12         nsec = 1;
13     if ( (maxnalarms = maxnalarms_arg) < nsec)
14         maxnalarms = nsec;

15     Signal(SIGURG, sig_urg);
16     Fcntl(servfd, F_SETOWN, getpid());

17     Signal(SIGALRM, sig_alrm);
18     alarm(nsec);
19 }

20 static void
21 sig_urg(int signo)
22 {
23     int     n;
24     char    c;

25     if ( (n = recv(servfd, &c, 1, MSG_OOB)) < 0) {
26         if (errno != EWOULDBLOCK)
27             err_sys("recv error");
28     }
29     Send(servfd, &c, 1, MSG_OOB);    /* echo back out-of-band byte */

30     nprobes = 0;                 /* reset counter */
31     return;                      /* may interrupt server code */
32 }

33 static void
34 sig_alrm(int signo)
35 {
36     if (++nprobes > maxnalarms) {
37         printf("no probes from client\n");
38         exit(0);
39     }
40     alarm(nsec);
41     return;                      /* may interrupt server code */
42 }
```
oob/heartbeatserv.c

Figure 21.15 Server heartbeat functions.

21.6   Summary

TCP does not have true out-of-band data. It provides an urgent pointer that is sent in the TCP header to the peer as soon as the sender goes into urgent mode. The receipt of this pointer by the other end of the connection tells that process that the sender has gone into urgent mode, and the pointer points to the final byte of urgent data. But all the data is still sent subject to TCP's normal flow control.

The sockets API maps TCP's urgent mode into what it calls out-of-band data. The sender goes into urgent mode by specifying the MSG_OOB flag in a call to send. The final byte of data in this call is considered the out-of-band byte. The receiver is notified when its TCP receives a new urgent pointer by either the SIGURG signal, or by select indicating that the socket has an exception condition pending. By default TCP takes the out-of-band byte out of the normal stream of data and places it into its own 1-byte out-of-band buffer that the process reads by calling recv with the MSG_OOB flag. Alternately the receiver can set the SO_OOBINLINE socket option, in which case the out-of-band byte is left in the normal stream of data. Regardless of which method is used by the receiver, the socket layer maintains an out-of-band mark in the data stream and will not read through the mark with a single input operation. The receiver determines if it has reached the mark by calling the sockatmark function.

Out-of-band data is not heavily used. Telnet and Rlogin use it, as does FTP, but FTP's use is only because early implementations did not provide an I/O multiplexing feature. Out-of-band data was designed at a time when resources were scarce (i.e., processor memory and CPU time). When designing new applications that need a second, high-priority, non-flow-controlled channel between the peers, we should consider a second TCP connection instead of using out-of-band data.

Exercises

21.1   Is there a difference between the single function call

```
send(fd, "ab", 2, MSG_OOB);
```

and the two function calls

```
send(fd, "a", 1, MSG_OOB);
send(fd, "b", 1, MSG_OOB);
```

21.2   Redo Figure 21.6 to use poll instead of select.

21.3   Modify the sig_alrm function in Figures 21.14 and 21.15 to write a message to STDERR_FILENO each time it is called and the nprobes counter is already greater than 0 (e.g., the previous probe was lost). Run the client and server on two hosts on the same LAN and see how often the message is printed. Redirect the client's standard input to a large text file and redirect its standard output to a temporary file. Run the client again, and compare the output file with the input file to make certain no data was lost. Is the message printed more often when lots of data is exchanged? Now run the client and server on two hosts across a WAN and compare the results with the LAN.

21.4   Rewrite the client–server heartbeat functions to use a second TCP connection, instead of using urgent data. Run the same tests from the previous exercise and compare the results.

22

Signal-Driven I/O

22.1 Introduction

Signal-driven I/O is when we tell the kernel to notify us with a signal when something happens on a descriptor. Historically this has been called *asynchronous I/O*, but the signal-driven I/O that we describe is not true asynchronous I/O. The latter is normally defined as the process performing the I/O operation (say a read or write), with the kernel returning immediately after the kernel initiates the I/O operation. The process continues executing while the I/O takes place. Some form of notification is then provided to the process when the operation is complete or encounters an error. We compared the various types of I/O that are normally available in Section 6.2 and showed the difference between signal-driven I/O and asynchronous I/O.

Notice that the nonblocking I/O that we described in Chapter 15 is not asynchronous I/O either. With nonblocking I/O the kernel does not return after initiating the I/O operation; the kernel returns immediately only if the operation cannot be completed without putting the process to sleep.

> Posix.1 provides true asynchronous I/O with its aio_*XXX* functions. These functions let the process specify whether or not a signal is generated when the I/O completes, and which signal to generate.

Berkeley-derived implementations support signal-driven I/O for sockets and terminal devices using the SIGIO signal. SVR4 supports signal-driven I/O for streams devices using the SIGPOLL signal, which is then equated to SIGIO.

22.2 Signal-Driven I/O for Sockets

To use signal-driven I/O with a socket (SIGIO) requires the process to perform the following three steps:

1. A signal handler must be established for the SIGIO signal.
2. The socket owner must be set, normally with the F_SETOWN command of fcntl (Figure 7.15).
3. Signal-driven I/O must be enabled for the socket, normally with the F_SETFL command of fcntl to turn on the O_ASYNC flag (Figure 7.15).

> The O_ASYNC flag is new with Posix.1g. None of the systems in Figure 1.16 support the flag. In Figure 22.4 we enable signal-driven I/O with the FIOASYNC ioctl instead. Notice the bad choice of names by Posix.1g: the name O_SIGIO would have been a better choice for the new flag.
>
> We should establish the signal handler *before* setting the owner of the socket. Under Berkeley-derived implementations the order of the two function calls does not matter, because the default action of SIGIO is to be ignored. Therefore if we were to reverse the order of the two function calls, there is a small chance that a signal could be generated after the call to fcntl but before the call to signal, but if that happens the signal is just discarded. Under SVR4, however, SIGIO is defined to be SIGPOLL in the <sys/signal.h> header and the default action of SIGPOLL is to terminate the process. Therefore under SVR4 we want to be certain the signal handler is installed before setting the owner of the socket.

Although setting a socket for signal-driven I/O is easy, the hard part is determining what conditions cause SIGIO to be generated for the socket owner. This depends on the underlying protocol.

SIGIO with UDP Sockets

Using signal-driven I/O with UDP is simple. The signal is generated whenever

- a datagram arrives for the socket, or
- an asynchronous error occurs on the socket.

Hence, when we catch SIGIO for a UDP socket, we call recvfrom to either read the datagram that arrived or to obtain the asynchronous error. We talked about asynchronous errors with regard to UDP sockets in Section 8.9. Recall that these are generated only if the UDP socket is connected.

> SIGIO is generated for these two conditions by the calls to sorwakeup on pp. 775, 779, and 784 of TCPv2.

SIGIO with TCP Sockets

Unfortunately signal-driven I/O is next to useless with a TCP socket. The problem is that the signal is generated too often, and the occurrence of the signal does not tell us what happened. As noted on p. 439 of TCPv2, the following conditions all cause `SIGIO` to be generated for a TCP socket (assuming signal-driven I/O is enabled):

- a connection request has completed on a listening socket,
- a disconnect request has been initiated,
- a disconnect request has completed,
- half of a connection has been shut down,
- data has arrived on a socket,
- data has been sent from a socket (i.e., the output buffer has free space), or
- an asynchronous error occurred.

For example, if one is both reading from and writing to a TCP socket, `SIGIO` is generated when new data arrives and when data previously written is acknowledged, and there is no way to distinguish between the two in the signal handler. If `SIGIO` is used in this scenario, the TCP socket should be set nonblocking to prevent a `read` or `write` from blocking. We should consider using `SIGIO` only with a listening TCP socket, because the only condition that generates `SIGIO` for a listening socket is the completion of a new connection.

The only real-world use of signal-driven I/O with sockets that the author was able to find is the NTP (Network Time Protocol) server, which uses UDP. The main loop of the server receives a datagram from a client and sends a response. But there is a non-negligible amount of processing to do for each client's request (more than our trivial echo server). It is important for the server to record accurate timestamps for each received datagram, since that value is returned to the client and then used by the client to calculate the round-trip time to the server. Figure 22.1 shows two ways to build such a UDP server.

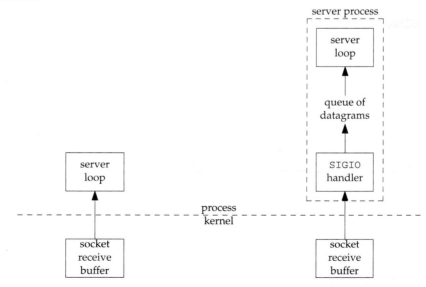

Figure 22.1　Two different ways to build a UDP server.

Most UDP servers (including our echo server from Chapter 8) are designed as shown in the left of this figure. But the NTP server uses the technique shown on the right side: when a new datagram arrives, it is read by the SIGIO handler, which also records the time at which the datagram arrived. The datagram is then placed on another queue within the process from which it will be removed by and processed by the main server loop. Although this complicates the server code, it provides accurate timestamps of arriving datagrams.

> Recall from Figure 20.4 that the process can set the IP_RECVDSTADDR socket option to receive the destination address of a received UDP datagram. One could argue that two additional pieces of information that should also be returned for a received UDP datagram are an indication of the received interface (which can differ from the destination address, if the host employs the common weak end system model), and the time at which the datagram arrived.

> For IPv6 the IPV6_PKTINFO socket option (Section 20.8) returns the received interface. For IPv4, we discussed the IP_RECVIF socket option in Section 20.2.

> FreeBSD also provides the SO_TIMESTAMP socket option, which returns the time at which the datagram was received as ancillary data in a timeval structure. Linux provides an SIOCGSTAMP ioctl that returns a timeval structure containing the time at which the datagram was received.

22.3 UDP Echo Server Using SIGIO

We now provide an example similar to the right side of Figure 22.1: a UDP server that uses the SIGIO signal to receive arriving datagrams. This example also illustrates the use of Posix reliable signals.

We do not change the client at all from Figures 8.7 and 8.8 and the server main function does not change from Figure 8.3. The only changes that we make are to the dg_echo function, which we show in the next four figures. Figure 22.2 shows the global declarations.

Queue of received datagrams

3–12   The SIGIO signal handler places arriving datagrams onto a queue. This queue is an array of DG structures that we treat as a circular buffer. Each structure contains a pointer to the received datagram, its length, a pointer to a socket address structure containing the protocol address of the client, and the size of the protocol address. QSIZE of these structures are allocated and we will see in Figure 22.4 that the dg_echo function calls malloc to allocate memory for all the datagrams and socket address structures. We also allocate a diagnostic counter, cntread, that we examine shortly. Figure 22.3 shows the array of structures, assuming that the first entry points to a 150-byte datagram and that the length of its associated socket address structure is 16.

Array indexes

13–15   iget is the index of the next array entry for the main loop to process and iput is the index of the next array entry for the signal handler to store into. nqueue is the total number of datagrams on the queue for the main loop to process.

——————————————————————————————————— sigio/dgecho01.c

```
 1 #include    "unp.h"

 2 static int sockfd;

 3 #define QSIZE      8          /* size of input queue */
 4 #define MAXDG   4096          /* maximum datagram size */

 5 typedef struct {
 6     void    *dg_data;         /* ptr to actual datagram */
 7     size_t  dg_len;           /* length of datagram */
 8     struct sockaddr *dg_sa;   /* ptr to sockaddr{} w/client's address */
 9     socklen_t dg_salen;       /* length of sockaddr{} */
10 } DG;
11 static DG dg[QSIZE];          /* the queue of datagrams to process */
12 static long cntread[QSIZE + 1]; /* diagnostic counter */

13 static int iget;              /* next one for main loop to process */
14 static int iput;              /* next one for signal handler to read into */
15 static int nqueue;            /* #on queue for main loop to process */
16 static socklen_t clilen;      /* max length of sockaddr{} */

17 static void sig_io(int);
18 static void sig_hup(int);
```
——————————————————————————————————— sigio/dgecho01.c

Figure 22.2 Global declarations.

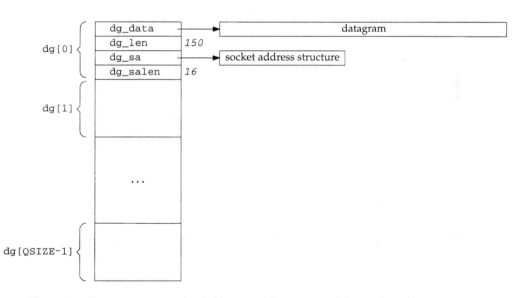

Figure 22.3 Data structures used to hold received datagrams and their socket address structures.

Figure 22.4 shows the main server loop, the dg_echo function.

sigio/dgecho01.c

```
19 void
20 dg_echo(int sockfd_arg, SA *pcliaddr, socklen_t clilen_arg)
21 {
22     int     i;
23     const int on = 1;
24     sigset_t zeromask, newmask, oldmask;

25     sockfd = sockfd_arg;
26     clilen = clilen_arg;

27     for (i = 0; i < QSIZE; i++) {     /* init queue of buffers */
28         dg[i].dg_data = Malloc(MAXDG);
29         dg[i].dg_sa = Malloc(clilen);
30         dg[i].dg_salen = clilen;
31     }
32     iget = iput = nqueue = 0;

33     Signal(SIGHUP, sig_hup);
34     Signal(SIGIO, sig_io);
35     Fcntl(sockfd, F_SETOWN, getpid());
36     Ioctl(sockfd, FIOASYNC, &on);
37     Ioctl(sockfd, FIONBIO, &on);

38     Sigemptyset(&zeromask);      /* init three signal sets */
39     Sigemptyset(&oldmask);
40     Sigemptyset(&newmask);
41     Sigaddset(&newmask, SIGIO); /* the signal we want to block */

42     Sigprocmask(SIG_BLOCK, &newmask, &oldmask);
43     for ( ; ; ) {
44         while (nqueue == 0)
45             sigsuspend(&zeromask);   /* wait for a datagram to process */

46             /* unblock SIGGIO */
47         Sigprocmask(SIG_SETMASK, &oldmask, NULL);

48         Sendto(sockfd, dg[iget].dg_data, dg[iget].dg_len, 0,
49                 dg[iget].dg_sa, dg[iget].dg_salen);

50         if (++iget >= QSIZE)
51             iget = 0;

52             /* block SIGIO */
53         Sigprocmask(SIG_BLOCK, &newmask, &oldmask);
54         nqueue--;
55     }
56 }
```

sigio/dgecho01.c

Figure 22.4 dg_echo function: server main processing loop.

Initialize queue of received datagrams

27–32   The socket descriptor is saved in a global since the signal handler needs it. The queue of received datagrams is initialized.

Establish signal handlers and set socket flags

33–37   Signal handlers are established for SIGHUP (which we use for diagnostic purposes) and SIGIO. The socket owner is set using fcntl and the signal-driven and non-blocking I/O flags are set using ioctl.

> We mentioned earlier that the O_ASYNC flag with fcntl is the Posix.1g way to specify asynchronous I/O, but since most systems do not yet support it, we use ioctl instead. While most systems do support the O_NONBLOCK flag to set nonblocking, we show the ioctl method here.

Initialize signal sets

38–41   Three signal sets are initialized: zeromask (which never changes), oldmask (which contains the old signal mask when we block SIGIO), and newmask. sigaddset turns on the bit corresponding to SIGIO in newmask.

Block SIGIO and wait for something to do

42–45   sigprocmask stores the current signal mask of the process in oldmask and then logically ORs newmask into the current signal mask. This blocks SIGIO and returns the current signal mask. We then enter the for loop and test the nqueue counter. As long as this counter is 0, there is nothing to do and we call sigsuspend. This Posix function saves the current signal mask internally and then sets the current signal mask to the argument (zeromask). Since zeromask is an empty signal set, this enables all signals. sigsuspend returns after a signal has been caught and the signal handler returns. (It is an unusual function because it *always* returns an error, EINTR.) But before returning, sigsuspend always sets the signal mask to its value when the function was called, which in this case is the value of newmask, so we are guaranteed that when sigsuspend returns, SIGIO is blocked. That is why we can test the flag nqueue, knowing that while we are testing it, a SIGIO signal cannot be delivered.

> Consider what would happen if SIGIO were not blocked while we tested the variable nqueue, which is shared between the main loop and the signal handler. We could test nqueue and find it 0, but immediately after this test, the signal is delivered and nqueue gets set to 1. We then call sigsuspend and go to sleep, effectively missing the signal. We are never awakened from the call to sigsuspend unless another signal occurs. This is similar to the race condition we described in Section 18.5.

Unblock SIGIO and send reply

46–51   We unblock SIGIO by calling sigprocmask to set the signal mask of the process to the value that was saved earlier (oldmask). The reply is then sent by sendto. The iget index is incremented and if its value is the number of elements in the array, its value is set back to 0. We treat the array as a circular buffer. Notice that we do not need SIGIO blocked while modifying iget, because this index is used only by the main loop; it is never modified by the signal handler.

Block SIGIO

52–54   SIGIO is blocked and the value of nqueue is decremented. We must block the signal while modifying this variable, since it is shared between the main loop and the signal handler. Also, we need SIGIO blocked when we test nqueue at the top of the loop.

An alternate technique is to remove both calls to `sigprocmask` that are within the `for` loop, which avoids unblocking the signal and then blocking it later. The problem, however, is that this executes the entire loop with the signal blocked, which decreases the responsiveness of the signal handler. Datagrams should not get lost because of this change (assuming the socket receive buffer is large enough), but the delivery of the signal to the process will be delayed the entire time that the signal is blocked. One goal when coding applications that perform signal handling should be to block the signal for the minimum amount of time.

Figure 22.5 shows the `SIGIO` signal handler.

——— *sigio/dgecho01.c*
```
57 static void
58 sig_io(int signo)
59 {
60      ssize_t len;
61      int     nread;
62      DG      *ptr;

63      for (nread = 0;;) {
64          if (nqueue >= QSIZE)
65              err_quit("receive overflow");

66          ptr = &dg[iput];
67          ptr->dg_salen = clilen;
68          len = recvfrom(sockfd, ptr->dg_data, MAXDG, 0,
69                 ·              ptr->dg_sa, &ptr->dg_salen);
70          if (len < 0) {
71              if (errno == EWOULDBLOCK)
72                  break;              /* all done; no more queued to read */
73              else
74                  err_sys("recvfrom error");
75          }
76          ptr->dg_len = len;

77          nread++;
78          nqueue++;
79          if (++iput >= QSIZE)
80              iput = 0;

81      }
82      cntread[nread]++;               /* histogram of #datagrams read per signal */
83 }
```
——— *sigio/dgecho01.c*

Figure 22.5 `SIGIO` handler.

The problem that we encounter when coding this signal handler is that Posix signals are normally *not* queued. This means that, if we are in the signal handler, which guarantees that the signal is blocked, and the signal occurs two more times, the signal is delivered only one more time.

> Posix.1 provides some realtime signals that *are* queued, but other signals such as `SIGIO` are normally not queued.

Consider the following scenario. A datagram arrives and the signal is delivered. The signal handler reads the datagram and places it onto the queue for the main loop. But while the signal handler is executing, two more datagrams arrive, causing the signal to be generated two more times. But since the signal is blocked, when the signal handler returns, it is called only one more time. The second time the signal handler executes, it reads the second datagram, but the third datagram is left on the socket receive queue. This third datagram will be read only if and when a fourth datagram arrives. When the fourth datagram arrives, it is the third datagram that is read and placed on the queue for the main loop, not the fourth one.

Because signals are not queued, the descriptor that is set for signal-driven I/O is normally set nonblocking also. We then code our SIGIO handler to read in a loop, terminating only when the read returns EWOULDBLOCK.

Check for queue overflow

64–65   If the queue is full, we terminate. There are other ways to handle this (e.g., additional buffers could be allocated) but for our simple example we just terminate.

Read datagram

66–76   recvfrom is called on the nonblocking socket. The array entry indexed by iput is where the datagram is stored. If there are no datagrams to read, break jumps out of the for loop.

Increment counters and index

77–80   nread is a diagnostic counter of the number of datagrams read per signal. nqueue is the number of datagrams for the main loop to process.

82   Before the signal handler returns, it increments the counter corresponding to the number of datagrams read per signal. We print this array in Figure 22.6 when the SIGHUP signal is delivered, as diagnostic information.

The final function (Figure 22.6) is the SIGHUP signal handler, which prints the cntread array. This counts the number of datagrams read per signal.

———————————————————————————————— sigio/dgecho01.c
```
84 static void
85 sig_hup(int signo)
86 {
87     int     i;

88     for (i = 0; i <= QSIZE; i++)
89         printf("cntread[%d] = %ld\n", i, cntread[i]);
90 }
```
———————————————————————————————— sigio/dgecho01.c

Figure 22.6 SIGHUP handler.

To illustrate that signals are not queued and that we must set the socket nonblocking in addition to setting the signal-driven I/O flag, we will run this server with six clients simultaneously. Each client sends 3645 lines for the server to echo and each client is started from a shell script in the background, so that all clients are started at about the same time. When all the clients have terminated, we send the SIGHUP signal to the server, causing it to print its cntread array:

```
bsdi % udpserv01
cntread[0] = 2
cntread[1] = 21838
cntread[2] = 12
cntread[3] = 1
cntread[4] = 0
cntread[5] = 1
cntread[6] = 0
cntread[7] = 0
cntread[8] = 0
```

Most of the time the signal handler reads only one datagram, but there are times when more than one is ready. The nonzero counter for cntread[0] is when the signal is generated while the signal handler is executing, but before the signal handler returns, it reads all pending datagrams. When the signal handler is called again, there are no datagrams left to read. Finally, we can verify that the weighted sum of the array elements $(21838 \times 1 + 12 \times 2 + 1 \times 3 + 1 \times 5 = 21870)$ equals 6 (the number of clients) times 3645 lines per client.

22.4 Summary

Signal driven I/O has the kernel notify us with the SIGIO signal when "something" happens on a socket.

- With a connected TCP socket there are numerous conditions that can cause this notification, making this feature of little use.
- With a listening TCP socket this notification occurs when a new connection is ready to be accepted.
- With UDP this notification means either a datagram arrived or an asynchronous error arrived, and in both cases we call recvfrom.

We modified our UDP echo server to use signal-driven I/O, using a technique similar to that used by NTP: read the datagram as soon as possible after it arrives, to obtain an accurate timestamp for its arrival and then queue it for later processing.

Exercises

22.1   An alternate design for the loop in Figure 22.4 is the following:

```
for ( ; ; ) {
    Sigprocmask(SIG_BLOCK, &newmask, &oldmask);
    while (nqueue == 0)
        sigsuspend(&zeromask);   /* wait for a datagram to process */
    nqueue--;

        /* unblock SIGGIO */
    Sigprocmask(SIG_SETMASK, &oldmask, NULL);

    Sendto(sockfd, dg[iget].dg_data, dg[iget].dg_len, 0,
            dg[iget].dg_sa, dg[iget].dg_salen);

    if (++iget >= QSIZE)
        iget = 0;
}
```

Is this modification OK?

23

Threads

23.1 Introduction

In the traditional Unix model, when a process needs something performed by another entity, it `forks` a child process and lets the child perform the processing. Most network servers under Unix are written this way, as we have seen in our concurrent server examples: the parent `accepts` the connection, `forks` a child, and the child handles the client. While this paradigm has served well for many years, there are problems with `fork`:

- `fork` is expensive. Memory is copied from the parent to the child, all descriptors are duplicated in the child, and so on. Current implementations use a technique called *copy-on-write*, which avoids a copy of the parent's data space to the child until the child needs its own copy, but regardless of this optimization, `fork` is expensive.

- Interprocess communication (IPC) is required to pass information between the parent and child *after* the `fork`. Information from the parent to the child *before* the `fork` is easy, since the child starts with a copy of the parent's data space and with a copy of all the parent's descriptors. But returning information from the child to the parent takes more work.

Threads help with both problems. Threads are sometimes called *lightweight processes* since a thread is "lighter weight" than a process. That is, thread creation can be 10–100 times faster than process creation.

All threads within a process share the same global memory. This makes the sharing of information easy between the threads, but along with this simplicity comes the problem of *synchronization*. But more than just the global variables are shared. All threads within a process share:

- process instructions,
- most data,
- open files (e.g., descriptors),
- signal handlers and signal dispositions,
- current working directory, and
- user and group IDs.

But each thread has its own:

- thread ID,
- set of registers, including program counter and stack pointer,
- stack (for local variables and return addresses),
- `errno`,
- signal mask, and
- priority.

> One analogy is to think of signal handlers as a type of thread as we discussed in Section 11.14. That is, in the traditional Unix model we have the main flow of execution (one thread) and a signal handler (another thread). If the main flow is in the middle of updating a linked list when a signal occurs, and the signal handler also tries to update the linked list, havoc normally results. The main flow and the signal handler share the same global variables, but each has its own stack.

In this text we cover Posix threads, also called *Pthreads*. These were standardized in 1995 as part of the Posix.1c standard and most versions of Unix will support them in the future. We will see that all the Pthread functions begin with `pthread_`. This chapter is an introduction to threads, so that we can use threads in our network programs. For additional details see [Butenhof 1997].

23.2   Basic Thread Functions: Creation and Termination

In this section we cover five basic thread functions and then use these in the next two sections to recode our TCP client–server using threads instead of `fork`.

`pthread_create` Function

When a program is started by `exec`, a single thread is created, called the *initial thread* or *main thread*. Additional threads are created by `pthread_create`.

```
#include <pthread.h>

int pthread_create(pthread_t *tid, const pthread_attr_t *attr,
                   void *(*func)(void *), void *arg);
```

Returns: 0 if OK, positive E*xxx* value on error

Each thread within a process is identified by a *thread ID*, whose datatype is `pthread_t` (often an `unsigned int`). On successful creation of a new thread, its ID is returned through the pointer *tid*.

Each thread has numerous *attributes*: its priority, its initial stack size, whether it should be a daemon thread or not, and so on. When a thread is created, we can specify these attributes by initializing a `pthread_attr_t` variable that overrides the default. We normally take the default, in which case we specify the *attr* argument as a null pointer.

Finally, when we create a thread, we specify a function for it to execute. The thread starts by calling this function and then terminates either explicitly (by calling `pthread_exit`) or implicitly (by letting this function return). The address of the function is specified as the *func* argument, and this function is called with a single pointer argument, *arg*. If we need multiple arguments to the function, we must package them into a structure and then pass the address of this structure as the single argument to the start function.

Notice the declarations of *func* and *arg*. The function takes one argument, a generic pointer (`void *`), and returns a generic pointer (`void *`). This lets us pass one pointer (to anything we want) to the thread, and lets the thread return one pointer (again, to anything we want).

The return value from the Pthread functions is normally 0 if OK or nonzero on an error. But unlike the socket functions, and most system calls, which return −1 on an error and set `errno` to a positive value, the Pthread functions return the positive error indication as the function's return value. For example, if `pthread_create` cannot create a new thread because we have exceeded some system limit on the number of threads, the function return value is `EAGAIN`. The Pthread functions do not set `errno`. The convention of 0 for OK or nonzero for an error is fine, since all the E*xxx* values in <sys/errno.h> are positive. A value of 0 is never assigned to one of the E*xxx* names.

`pthread_join` Function

We can wait for a given thread to terminate by calling `pthread_join`. Comparing threads to Unix processes, `pthread_create` is similar to `fork`, and `pthread_join` is similar to `waitpid`.

```
#include <pthread.h>

int pthread_join(pthread_t tid, void **status);
```
                                        Returns: 0 if OK, positive E*xxx* value on error

We must specify the *tid* of the thread that we wish to wait for. Unfortunately, there is no way to wait for any of our threads (similar to `waitpid` with a process ID argument of −1). We return to this problem when we discuss Figure 23.13.

If the *status* pointer is nonnull, the return value from the thread (a pointer to some object) is stored in the location pointed to by *status*.

`pthread_self` Function

Each thread has an ID that identifies it within a given process. The thread ID is returned by `pthread_create` and we saw it was used by `pthread_join`. A thread fetches this value for itself using `pthread_self`.

```
#include <pthread.h>

pthread_t pthread_self(void);
```

                                                            Returns: thread ID of calling thread

Comparing threads to Unix processes, `pthread_self` is similar to `getpid`.

`pthread_detach` Function

A thread is either *joinable* (the default) or *detached*. When a joinable thread terminates, its thread ID and exit status are retained until another thread calls `pthread_join`. But a detached thread is like a daemon process: when it terminates all its resources are released and we cannot wait for it to terminate. If one thread needs to know when another thread terminates, it is best to leave the thread as joinable.

The `pthread_detach` function changes the specified thread so that it is detached.

```
#include <pthread.h>

int pthread_detach(pthread_t tid);
```

                                                      Returns: 0 if OK, positive Exxx value on error

This function is commonly called by the thread that wants to detach itself, as in

```
pthread_detach(pthread_self());
```

`pthread_exit` Function

One way for a thread to terminate is to call `pthread_exit`.

```
#include <pthread.h>

void pthread_exit(void *status);
```

                                                                       Does not return to caller

If the thread is not detached, its thread ID and exit status are retained for a later `pthread_join` by some other thread in the calling process.

The pointer *status* must not point to an object that is local to the calling thread, since that object disappears when the thread terminates.

There are two other ways for a thread to terminate.

- The function that started the thread (the third argument to pthread_create) can return. Since this function must be declared as returning a void pointer, that return value is the exit status of the thread.

- If the main function of the process returns or if any thread calls exit, the process terminates, including any threads.

23.3 str_cli Function Using Threads

Our first example using threads is to recode the str_cli function from Figure 15.10, which uses fork, to use threads. Recall that we have provided numerous other versions of this function: the original in Figure 5.5 used a stop-and-wait protocol, which we showed was far from optimal for batch input, Figure 6.13 used blocking I/O and the select function, and the version starting with Figure 15.3 used nonblocking I/O. Figure 23.1 shows the design of our threads version.

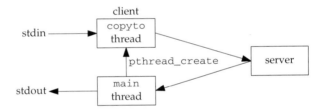

Figure 23.1 Recoding str_cli to use threads.

Figure 23.2 shows the str_cli function using threads.

unpthread.h header

1 This is the first time we have encountered the unpthread.h header. It includes our normal unp.h header, followed by the Posix.1 <pthread.h> header, and then defines the function prototypes for our wrapper versions of the pthread_XXX functions (Section 1.4), which all begin with Pthread_.

Save arguments in externals

10-11 The thread that we are about to create needs the values of the two arguments to str_cli: fp, the standard I/O FILE pointer for the input file, and sockfd, the TCP socket that is connected to the server. For simplicity we store these two values in external variables. An alternative technique is to put the two values into a structure and then pass a pointer to the structure as the argument to the thread that we are about to create.

Create new thread

12 The thread is created and the new thread ID is saved in tid. The function that is executed by the new thread is copyto. No arguments are passed to the thread.

```
                                                      ─── threads/strclithread.c
 1 #include    "unpthread.h"

 2 void   *copyto(void *);

 3 static int sockfd;              /* global for both threads to access */
 4 static FILE *fp;

 5 void
 6 str_cli(FILE *fp_arg, int sockfd_arg)
 7 {
 8     char    recvline[MAXLINE];
 9     pthread_t tid;

10     sockfd = sockfd_arg;        /* copy arguments to externals */
11     fp = fp_arg;

12     Pthread_create(&tid, NULL, copyto, NULL);

13     while (Readline(sockfd, recvline, MAXLINE) > 0)
14         Fputs(recvline, stdout);
15 }

16 void *
17 copyto(void *arg)
18 {
19     char    sendline[MAXLINE];

20     while (Fgets(sendline, MAXLINE, fp) != NULL)
21         Writen(sockfd, sendline, strlen(sendline));

22     Shutdown(sockfd, SHUT_WR);  /* EOF on stdin, send FIN */

23     return (NULL);
24         /* return (i.e., thread terminates) when end-of-file on stdin */
25 }
                                                      ─── threads/strclithread.c
```

Figure 23.2 str_cli function using threads.

Main thread loop: copy socket to standard output

13–14   The main thread calls readline and fputs, copying from the socket to the standard output.

Terminate

15   When the str_cli function returns, the main function terminates by calling exit (Section 5.4). When this happens, *all* threads in the process are terminated. In the normal scenario the other thread has already terminated when it read an end-of-file on standard input. But in case the server terminates prematurely (Section 5.12), calling exit terminates the other thread, which is what we want.

copyto thread

16–25   This thread just copies from standard input to the socket. When it reads an end-of-file on standard input, a FIN is sent across the socket by shutdown and the thread returns. The return from this function (which started the thread) terminates the thread.

At the end of Section 15.2 we provided measurements for the five different implementation techniques that we have used with our `str_cli` function. We note that the threads version that we just presented took 8.5 seconds, slightly faster than the version using `fork` (which we expect) but slower than the nonblocking I/O version. Nevertheless, comparing the complexity of the nonblocking I/O version (Section 15.2) versus the simplicity of the threads version, we still recommend using threads instead of nonblocking I/O.

23.4 TCP Echo Server Using Threads

We now redo our TCP echo server from Figure 5.2, using one thread per client, instead of one child process per client. We also make it protocol independent, using our `tcp_listen` function. Figure 23.3 shows the server.

—— threads/tcpserv01.c

```
 1 #include    "unpthread.h"

 2 static void *doit(void *);       /* each thread executes this function */

 3 int
 4 main(int argc, char **argv)
 5 {
 6     int     listenfd, connfd;
 7     socklen_t addrlen, len;
 8     struct sockaddr *cliaddr;

 9     if (argc == 2)
10         listenfd = Tcp_listen(NULL, argv[1], &addrlen);
11     else if (argc == 3)
12         listenfd = Tcp_listen(argv[1], argv[2], &addrlen);
13     else
14         err_quit("usage: tcpserv01 [ <host> ] <service or port>");

15     cliaddr = Malloc(addrlen);

16     for ( ; ; ) {
17         len = addrlen;
18         connfd = Accept(listenfd, cliaddr, &len);

19         Pthread_create(NULL, NULL, &doit, (void *) connfd);
20     }
21 }

22 static void *
23 doit(void *arg)
24 {
25     Pthread_detach(pthread_self());
26     str_echo((int) arg);          /* same function as before */
27     Close((int) arg);             /* we are done with connected socket */
28     return (NULL);
29 }
```

—— threads/tcpserv01.c

Figure 23.3 TCP echo server using threads.

Create a thread

16-20   When `accept` returns, we call `pthread_create` instead of `fork`. The first argument is a null pointer, since we do not care about the thread ID. The single argument that we pass to the `doit` function is the connected socket descriptor, `connfd`.

> We cast the integer descriptor `connfd` to be a `void` pointer. ANSI C does not guarantee that this works. It works only on systems on which the size of an integer is less than or equal to the size of a pointer. Fortunately most Unix implementations have this property (Figure 1.17). We talk more about this shortly.

Thread function

22-29   `doit` is the function executed by the thread. The thread detaches itself, since there is no reason for the main thread to wait for each thread that it creates. The function `str_echo` does not change from Figure 5.3. When this function returns, we must `close` the connected socket, since the thread shares all descriptors with the main thread. With `fork`, the child did not need to `close` the connected socket because the child then terminated and all open descriptors are closed on process termination. (See Exercise 23.2.)

Also notice that the main thread does not close the connected socket, which we always did with a concurrent server that calls `fork`. This is because all threads within a process share the descriptors, so if the main thread were to call `close`, it would terminate the connection. Creating a new thread does not affect the reference counts for open descriptors, which is different from `fork`.

There is a subtle error in this program, which we describe in detail in Section 23.5. Can you spot the error? (See Exercise 23.5.)

Passing Arguments to New Threads

We mentioned that in Figure 23.3 we cast the integer variable `connfd` to be a `void` pointer, but this is not guaranteed to work on all systems. To handle this correctly requires additional work.

First notice that we cannot just pass the address of `connfd` to the new thread. That is, the following does not work.

```
int
main(int argc, char **argv)
{
    int    listenfd, connfd;
    ...

    for ( ; ; ) {
        len = addrlen;
        connfd = Accept(listenfd, cliaddr, &len);

        Pthread_create(&tid, NULL, &doit, &connfd);
    }
}
```

```
static void *
doit(void *arg)
{
    int  connfd;

    connfd = *((int *) arg);
    Pthread_detach(pthread_self());
    str_echo((int) arg);        /* same function as before */
    Close((int) arg);           /* we are done with connected socket */
    return(NULL);
}
```

From an ANSI C perspective this is OK: we are guaranteed that we can cast the integer pointer to be a void * and then cast this pointer back to an integer pointer. The problem is what this pointer points to.

There is one integer variable connfd in the main thread and each call to accept overwrites this variable with a new value (the connected descriptor). The following scenario can occur:

- accept returns, connfd is stored into (say the new descriptor is 5), and the main thread calls pthread_create. The pointer to connfd (not its contents) is the final argument to pthread_create.

- A thread is created and the doit function is scheduled to start executing.

- Another connection is ready and the main thread runs again (before the newly created thread). accept returns, connfd is stored into (say the new descriptor is now 6), and the main thread calls pthread_create.

Even though two threads are created, both will operate on the final value stored into connfd, which we assume is 6. The problem is that multiple threads are accessing a shared variable (the integer value in connfd) with no synchronization. In Figure 23.3 we solved this problem by passing the *value* of connfd to pthread_create, instead of a pointer to the value. This is fine given the way that C passes integer values to a called function (a copy of the value is pushed onto the stack for the called function).

Figure 23.4 shows a better solution to this problem.

16–21   Each time we call accept we first call malloc and allocate space for an integer variable, the connected descriptor. This gives each thread its own copy of the connected descriptor.

27–28   The thread fetches the value of the connected descriptor and then calls free to release the memory.

Historically the malloc and free functions have been nonreentrant. That is, calling either function from a signal handler while the main thread is in the middle of one of these two functions has been a recipe for disaster, because of static data structures that are manipulated by these two functions. How can we call these two functions in Figure 23.4? Posix.1 requires that these two functions, along with many others, be *thread-safe*. This is normally done by some form of synchronization performed within the library functions that is transparent to us.

threads/tcpserv02.c

```
 1 #include      "unpthread.h"

 2 static void *doit(void *);        /* each thread executes this function */

 3 int
 4 main(int argc, char **argv)
 5 {
 6     int     listenfd, *iptr;
 7     socklen_t addrlen, len;
 8     struct sockaddr *cliaddr;

 9     if (argc == 2)
10         listenfd = Tcp_listen(NULL, argv[1], &addrlen);
11     else if (argc == 3)
12         listenfd = Tcp_listen(argv[1], argv[2], &addrlen);
13     else
14         err_quit("usage: tcpserv01 [ <host> ] <service or port>");

15     cliaddr = Malloc(addrlen);

16     for ( ; ; ) {
17         len = addrlen;
18         iptr = Malloc(sizeof(int));
19         *iptr = Accept(listenfd, cliaddr, &len);

20         Pthread_create(NULL, NULL, &doit, iptr);
21     }
22 }

23 static void *
24 doit(void *arg)
25 {
26     int     connfd;

27     connfd = *((int *) arg);
28     free(arg);

29     Pthread_detach(pthread_self());
30     str_echo(connfd);               /* same function as before */
31     Close(connfd);                  /* we are done with connected socket */
32     return (NULL);
33 }
```

threads/tcpserv02.c

Figure 23.4 TCP echo server using threads with more portable argument passing.

Thread-Safe Functions

Posix.1 requires that all the functions defined by Posix.1 and by the ANSI C standard be thread-safe, with the exceptions listed in Figure 23.5.

Unfortunately Posix.1g says nothing about thread safety with regard to the networking API functions. The last five lines in this table are from Unix 98. We talked about the nonreentrant property of gethostbyname and gethostbyaddr in Section 11.14. We mentioned that even though some vendors have defined thread-safe

Need not be thread-safe	Must be thread-safe	Comment
asctime	asctime_r	
	ctermid	thread-safe only if nonnull argument
ctime	ctime_r	
getc_unblocked		
getchar_unlocked		
getgrid	getgrid_r	
getgrnam	getgrnam_r	
getlogin	getlogin_r	
getpwnam	getpwnam_r	
getpwuid	getpwuid_r	
gmtime	gmtime_r	
localtime	localtime_r	
putc_unlocked		
putchar_unlocked		
rand	rand_r	
readdir	readdir_r	
strtok	strtok_r	
	tmpnam	thread-safe only if nonnull argument
ttyname	ttyname_r	
gethost*XXX*		
getnet*XXX*		
getproto*XXX*		
getserv*XXX*		
inet_ntoa		

Figure 23.5   Thread-safe functions.

versions whose names end in _r, there is no standard for these functions, and they should be avoided. All of the nonreentrant get*XXX* functions were summarized in Figure 9.9.

We see from this figure that the common technique for making a function thread-safe is to define a new function whose name ends in _r. Two of the functions are thread-safe only if the caller allocates space for the result and passes that pointer as the argument to the function.

23.5 Thread-Specific Data

When writing the code for Chapter 27 the author stumbled over a common programming error when converting a nonthreaded application to use threads. The error was only found when running the server in Figure 27.27, but the error is not in that figure, but in the readline function that is called to handle each client. The same function is called by Figure 23.3.

As with many other thread-related programming errors the failure was nondeterministic. In fact, the programs in Figures 23.4 and 27.27 both worked, but the error was found when running the timing tests for the threaded version in Figure 27.29. But the version in Figure 27.29 worked when the client and server were on the same host, yet failed at different points with the error "client request for 0 bytes" from our web_child function (Figure 27.8) when the client and server were on different hosts. After a few hours of futile debugging, it finally dawned on the author that in the process of speeding up the readline function (Figure 3.16) static variables were added (Figure 3.17). This speedup breaks the function when called from different threads within a single process.

This is a common problem when converting existing functions to run in a threads environment and there are various solutions.

1. Use thread-specific data. This is nontrivial and then converts the function into one that works only on systems with threads support. The advantage to this approach is that the calling sequence does not change and all the changes go into the library function and not the applications that call the function. We show a version of readline that is thread-safe by using thread-specific data later in this section.

2. Change the calling sequence so that the caller packages all the arguments into a structure, and also store in that structure the static variables from Figure 3.17. This was also done, and Figure 23.6 shows the new structure and the new function prototypes.

```
typedef struct {
    int       read_fd;        /* caller's descriptor to read from */
    char      *read_ptr;      /* caller's buffer to read into */
    size_t    read_maxlen;    /* caller's max #bytes to read */
                    /* next three are used internally by the function */
    int       rl_cnt;         /* initialize to 0 */
    char      *rl_bufptr;     /* initialize to rl_buf */
    char      rl_buf[MAXLINE];
} Rline;

void    readline_rinit(int, void *, size_t, Rline *);
ssize_t readline_r(Rline *);
ssize_t Readline_r(Rline *);
```

Figure 23.6 Data structure and function prototype for reentrant version of readline.

These new functions can be used on threaded and nonthreaded systems but all the applications that call readline must change.

3. Ignore the speedups introduced in Figure 3.17 and go back to the older version in Figure 3.16.

Thread-specific data is a common technique for making an existing function thread-safe. Before describing the Pthread functions that work with thread-specific data, we describe the concept and a *possible* implementation, because the functions appear more complicated than they really are.

Part of the complication in all the threads books that the author has seen is that their descriptions of thread-specific data read like the Pthreads standard, talking about key–value pairs and keys being opaque objects. We describe thread-specific data in terms of *indexes* and *pointers*, because common implementations use a small integer index for the key, and the value associated with the index is just a pointer to a region that the thread `malloc`s.

Each system supports a limited number of thread-specific data items. Posix.1 requires this limit be no less than 128 (per process), and we assume this limit in the following example. The system (probably the threads library) maintains one array of structures per process, which we call `Key` structures, as we show in Figure 23.7.

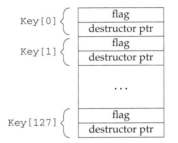

Figure 23.7 Possible implementation of thread-specific data.

The flag in the `Key` structure indicates whether this array element is currently in use, and all the flags are initialized to be "not in use." When a thread calls `pthread_key_create` to create a new thread-specific data item, the system searches through its array of `Key` structures and finds the first one not in use. Its index, 0 through 127, is called the *key* and this index is returned to the calling thread. We talk about the "destructor pointer," the other member of the `Key` structure, shortly.

In addition to the process-wide array of `Key` structures, the system maintains numerous pieces of information about each thread within a process. We call this a `Pthread` structure and part of this information is a 128-element array of pointers, which we call the `pkey` array. We show this in Figure 23.8.

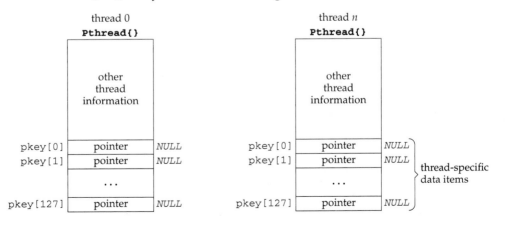

Figure 23.8 Information maintained by the system about each thread.

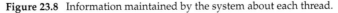

All entries in the `pkey` array are initialized to null pointers. These 128 pointers are the "values" associated with each of the possible 128 "keys" in the process.

When we create a key with `pthread_key_create`, the system tells us its key (index). Each thread can then store a value (pointer) for the key, and each thread normally obtains the pointer by calling `malloc`. Part of the confusion with thread-specific data is that the pointer is the value in the key–value pair, but the *real* thread-specific data is whatever this pointer points to.

We now go through an example of how thread-specific data is used, assuming that our `readline` function uses thread-specific data to maintain per-thread state across successive calls to the function. Shortly we will show the code for this, modifying our `readline` function to follow these steps.

1. A process is started and multiple threads are created.

2. One of the threads will be the first to call `readline` and it in turn calls `pthread_key_create`. The system finds the first unused `Key` structure in Figure 23.7 and returns its index (0–127) to the caller. We assume an index of 1 in this example.

   We will use the `pthread_once` function to guarantee that `pthread_key_create` is called only by the first thread to call `readline`.

3. `readline` calls `pthread_getspecific` to get the `pkey[1]` value (the "pointer" in Figure 23.8 for this key of 1) for this thread, and the returned value is a null pointer. Therefore `readline` calls `malloc` to allocate the memory that it needs to keep the per-thread information across successive calls to `readline` for this thread. `readline` initializes this memory as needed and calls `pthread_setspecific` to set the thread-specific data pointer (`pkey[1]`) for this key to point to the memory that it just allocated. We show this in Figure 23.9, assuming that the calling thread is thread 0 in the process.

   In this figure we note that the `Pthread` structure is maintained by the system (probably the thread library), but the actual thread-specific data that we `malloc` is maintained by our function (`readline` in this case). All that `pthread_setspecific` does is set the pointer for this key in the `Pthread` structure to point to our allocated memory. Similarly, all that `pthread_getspecific` does is return that pointer to us.

4. Another thread, say thread *n*, calls `readline`, perhaps while thread 0 is still executing within `readline`.

   `readline` calls `pthread_once` to initialize the key for this thread-specific data item, but since it has already been called, it is not called again.

5. `readline` calls `pthread_getspecific` to fetch the `pkey[1]` pointer for this thread, and a null pointer is returned. This thread then calls `malloc` followed by `pthread_setspecific`, just like thread 0, initializing its thread-specific data for this key (1). We show this in Figure 23.10.

6. Thread *n* continues executing in `readline`, using and modifying its own thread-specific data.

```
    if ( (ptr = pthread_getspecifi
        ptr = Malloc( ... );
        pthread_setspecific(rl_key
        /* initialize memory point
    }
    ...
    /* use the values pointed to b
}
```

Every time readline is called, it calls pointed to by its *onceptr* argument (the c tain that its *init* function is called o readline_once, creates the thread-spe which readline then uses in pthread_setspecific.

The pthread_getspecific and p fetch and store the value associated wi "pointer" in Figure 23.8. What this poin mally it points to dynamically allocated m

```
#include <pthread.h>

void *pthread_getspecific(pthread_

                           Returns: po

int pthread_setspecific(pthread_key
```

Notice that the argument to pthread_key function stores the value assigned to the k functions are the key itself (probably a sma

Example: readline Function Using Thread-Sp

We now show a complete example of thre version of our readline function from Fi the calling sequence.

Figure 23.11 shows the first part of the pthread_once_t variable, the readline_once function, and our Rlin we must maintain on a per-thread basis.

Destructor

4–8   Our destructor function just frees the m

One-time Function

9–13   We will see that our one-time function just creates the key that is used by readli

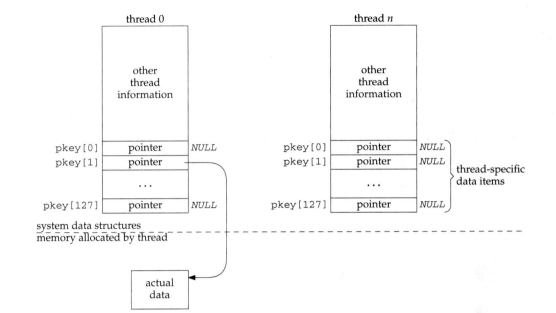

Figure 23.9 Associating malloced region with thread-specific data pointer.

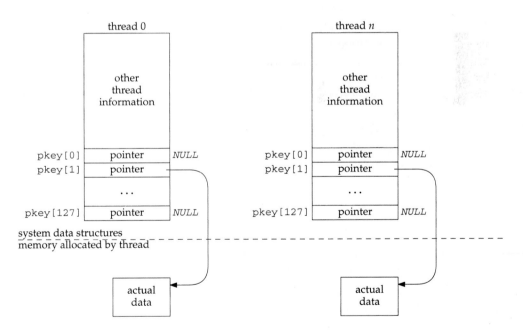

Figure 23.10 Data structures after thread *n* initializes its thread-specific data.

One item we have not addressed is
thread has called our `readline` func
that needs to be freed. This is where t
When the thread that creates the thread
one argument to this function is a poin
nates, the system goes through that
destructor function for each nonnull p
destructor" is the function pointer sto
the thread-specific data is free when a t

The first two functions that are no
data are `pthread_once` and `pthread`

```
#include <pthread.h>

int pthread_once(pthread_once_t

int pthread_key_create(pthread_k
```

`pthread_once` is normally called ev
specific data, but `pthread_once` uses
guarantee that the *init* function is called
`pthread_key_create` must be ca
cess. The key is returned through the
argument is a nonnull pointer, will be
thread has stored a value for this key.
Typical usage of these two functions

```
pthread_key_t    rl_key;
pthread_once_t   rl_once = PTHREA

void
readline_destructor(void *ptr)
{
    free(ptr);
}

void
readline_once(void)
{
    pthread_key_create(&rl_key, 
}

ssize_t
readline( ... )
{
    ...

pthread_once(&rl_once, readli
```

threads/readline.c

```
 1 #include    "unpthread.h"

 2 static pthread_key_t rl_key;
 3 static pthread_once_t rl_once = PTHREAD_ONCE_INIT;

 4 static void
 5 readline_destructor(void *ptr)
 6 {
 7     free(ptr);
 8 }

 9 static void
10 readline_once(void)
11 {
12     Pthread_key_create(&rl_key, readline_destructor);
13 }

14 typedef struct {
15     int     rl_cnt;           /* initialize to 0 */
16     char    *rl_bufptr;       /* initialize to rl_buf */
17     char    rl_buf[MAXLINE];
18 } Rline;
```

threads/readline.c

Figure 23.11   First part of thread-safe `readline` function.

Rline structure

14–18   Our `Rline` structure contains the three variables that caused the problem by being declared `static` in Figure 3.17. One of these structures will be dynamically allocated per thread, and then released by our destructor function.

Figure 23.12 shows the actual `readline` function and the function `my_read` that it calls. This figure is a modification of Figure 3.17.

`my_read` function

19–35   The first argument to the function is now a pointer to the `Rline` structure that was allocated for this thread (the actual thread-specific data).

Allocate thread-specific data

42   We first call `pthread_once` so that the first thread that calls `readline` in this process calls `readline_once` to create the thread-specific data key.

Fetch thread-specific data pointer

43–46   `pthread_getspecific` returns the pointer to the `Rline` structure for this thread. But if this is the first time this thread has called `readline`, the return value is a null pointer. In this case we allocate space for an `Rline` structure and the `rl_cnt` member is initialized to 0 by `calloc`. We then store this pointer for this thread by calling `pthread_setspecific`. The next time this thread calls `readline`, `pthread_getspecific` will return this pointer that was just stored.

threads/readline.c

```
19 static ssize_t
20 my_read(Rline *tsd, int fd, char *ptr)
21 {
22     if (tsd->rl_cnt <= 0) {
23       again:
24         if ( (tsd->rl_cnt = read(fd, tsd->rl_buf, MAXLINE)) < 0) {
25             if (errno == EINTR)
26                 goto again;
27             return (-1);
28         } else if (tsd->rl_cnt == 0)
29             return (0);
30         tsd->rl_bufptr = tsd->rl_buf;
31     }
32     tsd->rl_cnt--;
33     *ptr = *tsd->rl_bufptr++;
34     return (1);
35 }

36 ssize_t
37 readline(int fd, void *vptr, size_t maxlen)
38 {
39     int     n, rc;
40     char    c, *ptr;
41     Rline   *tsd;

42     Pthread_once(&rl_once, readline_once);
43     if ( (tsd = pthread_getspecific(rl_key)) == NULL) {
44         tsd = Calloc(1, sizeof(Rline));      /* init to 0 */
45         Pthread_setspecific(rl_key, tsd);
46     }
47     ptr = vptr;
48     for (n = 1; n < maxlen; n++) {
49         if ( (rc = my_read(tsd, fd, &c)) == 1) {
50             *ptr++ = c;
51             if (c == '\n')
52                 break;
53         } else if (rc == 0) {
54             if (n == 1)
55                 return (0);      /* EOF, no data read */
56             else
57                 break;           /* EOF, some data was read */
58         } else
59             return (-1);         /* error, errno set by read() */
60     }

61     *ptr = 0;
62     return (n);
63 }
```

threads/readline.c

Figure 23.12 Second part of thread-safe `readline` function.

23.6   Web Client and Simultaneous Connections (Continued)

We now revisit the Web client example from Section 15.5 and recode it using threads instead of nonblocking `connect`s. With threads we can leave the sockets in their default blocking mode and create one thread per connection. It is OK for each thread to block in its call to `connect`, as the kernel will just run some other thread that is ready.

Figure 23.13 shows the first part of the program, the globals and the start of the `main` function.

―― *threads/web01.c*
```
 1 #include     "unpthread.h"
 2 #include     <thread.h>              /* Solaris threads */

 3 #define MAXFILES     20
 4 #define SERV         "80"            /* port number or service name */

 5 struct file {
 6     char    *f_name;                /* filename */
 7     char    *f_host;                /* hostname or IP address */
 8     int     f_fd;                   /* descriptor */
 9     int     f_flags;                /* F_xxx below */
10     int     f_tid;                  /* thread ID */
11 } file[MAXFILES];
12 #define F_CONNECTING    1           /* connect() in progress */
13 #define F_READING       2           /* connect() complete; now reading */
14 #define F_DONE          4           /* all done */

15 #define GET_CMD     "GET %s HTTP/1.0\r\n\r\n"

16 int     nconn, nfiles, nlefttoconn, nlefttoread;

17 void    *do_get_read(void *);
18 void    home_page(const char *, const char *);
19 void    write_get_cmd(struct file *);

20 int
21 main(int argc, char **argv)
22 {
23     int     i, n, maxnconn;
24     pthread_t tid;
25     struct file *fptr;

26     if (argc < 5)
27         err_quit("usage: web <#conns> <IPaddr> <homepage> file1 ...");
28     maxnconn = atoi(argv[1]);

29     nfiles = min(argc - 4, MAXFILES);
30     for (i = 0; i < nfiles; i++) {
31         file[i].f_name = argv[i + 4];
32         file[i].f_host = argv[2];
33         file[i].f_flags = 0;
34     }
35     printf("nfiles = %d\n", nfiles);

36     home_page(argv[2], argv[3]);
```

```
37     nlefttoread = nlefttoconn = nfiles;
38     nconn = 0;
```
———————————————————————————————————— threads/web01.c

Figure 23.13 Globals and start of main function.

Globals

1-16   We #include <thread.h>, in addition to the normal <pthread.h> because we need to use Solaris threads in addition to Pthreads, as we describe shortly.

10   We have added one member to the file structure: f_tid, the thread ID. The remainder of this code is similar to Figure 15.15. With this threads version we do not use select and therefore do not need any descriptor sets or the variable maxfd.

36   The home_page function that is called is unchanged from Figure 15.16.

Figure 23.14 shows the main processing loop of the main thread.

———————————————————————————————————— threads/web01.c
```
39     while (nlefttoread > 0) {
40         while (nconn < maxnconn && nlefttoconn > 0) {
41                 /* find a file to read */
42             for (i = 0; i < nfiles; i++)
43                 if (file[i].f_flags == 0)
44                     break;
45             if (i == nfiles)
46                 err_quit("nlefttoconn = %d but nothing found", nlefttoconn);
47             Pthread_create(&tid, NULL, &do_get_read, &file[i]);
48             file[i].f_tid = tid;
49             file[i].f_flags = F_CONNECTING;
50             nconn++;
51             nlefttoconn--;
52         }
53         if ( (n = thr_join(0, &tid, (void **) &fptr)) != 0)
54             errno = n, err_sys("thr_join error");
55         nconn--;
56         nlefttoread--;
57         printf("thread id %d for %s done\n", tid, fptr->f_name);
58     }
59     exit(0);
60 }
```
———————————————————————————————————— threads/web01.c

Figure 23.14 Main processing loop of main function.

If possible, create another thread

40-52   If we are allowed to create another thread (nconn is less than maxnconn), we do so. The function that each new thread executes is do_get_read and the argument is the pointer to the file structure.

Wait for any thread to terminate

53-54   We call the Solaris thread function thr_join with a first argument of 0 to wait for any one of our threads to terminate. Unfortunately Pthreads does not provide a way to wait for *any* one of our threads to terminate; the `pthread_join` function makes us specify exactly which thread we wish to wait for. We will see in Section 23.9 that the Pthreads solution for this problem is more complicated, requiring us to use a condition variable for the terminating thread to notify the main thread when it is done.

> The solution that we show, using the Solaris thread `thr_join` function is not portable to all environments. Nevertheless, we want to show this version of our Web client example using threads without having to complicate the discussion with condition variables and mutexes. Fortunately one is able to mix Pthreads with Solaris threads under Solaris.
>
> When the author complained on Usenet about the inability of `pthread_join` to wait for *any* thread to terminate, a few people who had worked on the Pthreads standard justified this design decision, claiming that the `pthread_join` cannot be everything to everybody. The claim is also made that in the process model, there is a parent–child relationship so the ability of `wait` or `waitpid` to wait for any child makes sense. But in a threads environment there is no hierarchical relationship similar to parent–child, so waiting for any thread to terminate does not make sense. The thread whose status is returned by a wait-for-any function need not be one that the calling thread created. They added that if someone really needs to wait for any thread, it can be implemented (nontrivially) using condition variables, as we show shortly. Regardless of these arguments, the author considers the design of `pthread_join` flawed.

Figure 23.15 shows the `do_get_read` function, which is executed by each thread. This function establishes the TCP connection, sends an HTTP `GET` command to the server, and reads the server's reply.

Create TCP socket, establish connection

68–71   A TCP socket is created and a connection is established by our `tcp_connect` function. The socket is a normal blocking socket, so the thread will block in the call to `connect`, until the connection is established.

Write request to server

72   `write_get_cmd` builds the HTTP `GET` command and sends it to the server. We do not show this function again, as the only difference from Figure 15.18 is that the threads version does not call `FD_SET` and does not use `maxfd`.

Read server's reply

73–82   The server's reply is then read. When the connection is closed by the server, the `F_DONE` flag is set, and the function returns, terminating the thread.

We also do not show the `home_page` function, as it is identical to the version shown in Figure 15.16.

We return to this example, replacing the Solaris `thr_join` function with the more portable Pthreads solution, but we must first discuss mutexes and condition variables.

23.7   Mutexes: Mutual Exclusion

Notice in Figure 23.14 that when a thread terminates the main loop decrements both `nconn` and `nlefttoread`. We could have placed these two decrements in the function

————————————————————————————— threads/web01.c
```
61 void *
62 do_get_read(void *vptr)
63 {
64     int     fd, n;
65     char    line[MAXLINE];
66     struct file *fptr;

67     fptr = (struct file *) vptr;

68     fd = Tcp_connect(fptr->f_host, SERV);
69     fptr->f_fd = fd;
70     printf("do_get_read for %s, fd %d, thread %d\n",
71             fptr->f_name, fd, fptr->f_tid);

72     write_get_cmd(fptr);            /* write() the GET command */

73         /* Read server's reply */
74     for ( ; ; ) {
75         if ( (n = Read(fd, line, MAXLINE)) == 0)
76             break;                 /* server closed connection */

77         printf("read %d bytes from %s\n", n, fptr->f_name);
78     }
79     printf("end-of-file on %s\n", fptr->f_name);
80     Close(fd);
81     fptr->f_flags = F_DONE;        /* clears F_READING */

82     return (fptr);                 /* terminate thread */
83 }
```
————————————————————————————— threads/web01.c

Figure 23.15 do_get_read function.

do_get_read, letting each thread decrement these two counters immediately before the thread terminates. But this would be a subtle, yet significant, concurrent programming error.

The problem with placing the code in the function that each thread executes is that these two variables are global, not thread-specific. If one thread is in the middle of decrementing a variable, that thread is suspended, and another thread executes and decrements the same variable, an error can result. For example, assume that the C compiler turns the decrement operator into three instructions: load from memory into a register, decrement the register, and store from the register into memory. Consider the following possible scenario:

1. Thread A is running and it loads the value of nconn (3) into a register.

2. The system switches threads from A to B. A's registers are saved, and B's registers are restored.

3. Thread B executes the three instructions corresponding to the C expression nconn--, storing the new value of 2.

4. Sometime later the system switches threads from B to A. A's registers are restored and A continues where it left off, at the second machine instruction in the three-instructions sequence: the value of the register is decremented from 3 to 2 and the value of 2 is stored in nconn.

The end result is that nconn is 2 when it should be 1. This is wrong.

These types of concurrent programming errors are hard to find for numerous reasons. First, they occur rarely. Nevertheless, it is an error and it will fail (Murphy's Law). Secondly, the error is hard to duplicate, since it depends on the nondeterministic timing of many events. Lastly, on some systems the hardware instructions might be atomic; that is, there exists a hardware instruction to decrement an integer in memory (instead of the three-instruction sequence that we assumed above) and the hardware cannot be interrupted during this instruction. But this is not guaranteed by all systems, so the code works on one system but not on another.

We call threads programming *concurrent programming* or *parallel programming* since multiple threads can be running concurrently (in parallel), accessing the same variables. While the error scenario that we just discussed assumes a single CPU system, the potential for error also exists if threads A and B are running at the same time, on different CPUs on a multiprocessor system. With normal Unix programming we do not encounter these concurrent programming problems, because with fork nothing besides descriptors are shared between the parent and child. We will, however, encounter this same type of problem when we discuss shared memory between processes.

We can easily demonstrate this problem with threads. Figure 23.17 is a simple program that creates two threads and then has each thread increment a global variable 5000 times.

We exacerbate the potential for a problem by fetching the current value of counter, printing the new value, and then storing the new value. If we run this program we have the output shown in Figure 23.16.

```
4: 1
4: 2
4: 3
4: 4
                    this continues as thread 4 executes
4: 517
4: 518
5: 518              thread 5 now executes
5: 519
5: 520
                    this continues as thread 5 executes
5: 926
5: 927
4: 519              thread 4 now executes, stored value is wrong
4: 520
```

Figure 23.16 Output from the program in Figure 23.17.

```
                                                         ——— threads/example01.c
 1 #include    "unpthread.h"

 2 #define NLOOP 5000

 3 int     counter;              /* this is incremented by the threads */

 4 void    *doit(void *);

 5 int
 6 main(int argc, char **argv)
 7 {
 8     pthread_t tidA, tidB;

 9     Pthread_create(&tidA, NULL, &doit, NULL);
10     Pthread_create(&tidB, NULL, &doit, NULL);

11         /* wait for both threads to terminate */
12     Pthread_join(tidA, NULL);
13     Pthread_join(tidB, NULL);

14     exit(0);
15 }

16 void *
17 doit(void *vptr)
18 {
19     int     i, val;

20     /*
21      * Each thread fetches, prints, and increments the counter NLOOP times.
22      * The value of the counter should increase monotonically.
23      */

24     for (i = 0; i < NLOOP; i++) {
25         val = counter;
26         printf("%d: %d\n", pthread_self(), val + 1);
27         counter = val + 1;
28     }

29     return (NULL);
30 }
                                                         ——— threads/example01.c
```

Figure 23.17 Two threads that increment a global variable incorrectly.

Notice the error the first time the system switches from thread 4 to thread 5: the value 518 is stored by each thread. This happens numerous times through the 10,000 lines of output.

The nondeterministic nature of this type of problem is also evident if we run the program a few times: each time the end result is different from the previous run of the program. Also, if we redirect the output to a disk file, sometimes the error does not occur, since the program runs faster, providing fewer opportunities to switch between the threads. The greatest number of errors occurs when we run the program interactively, writing the output to the (slow) terminal, but saving the output in a file using the Unix `script` program (discussed in detail in Chapter 19 of APUE).

The problem that we just discussed, multiple threads updating a shared variable, is the simplest of these problems. The solution is to protect the shared variable with a *mutex* (which stands for "mutual exclusion") and access the variable only when we hold the mutex. In terms of Pthreads, a mutex is a variable of type `pthread_mutex_t`. We lock and unlock the mutex using the following two functions.

```
#include <pthread.h>

int pthread_mutex_lock(pthread_mutex_t *mptr);

int pthread_mutex_unlock(pthread_mutex_t *mptr);
```

Both return: 0 if OK, positive E*xxx* value on error

If we try to lock a mutex that is already locked by some other thread, we are blocked until the mutex is unlocked.

If a mutex variable is statically allocated, we must initialize it to the constant `PTHREAD_MUTEX_INITIALIZER`. We will see in Section 27.8 that if we allocate a mutex in shared memory we must initialize it at run time by calling the `pthread_mutex_init` function.

> Some systems (e.g., Solaris) define `PTHREAD_MUTEX_INITIALIZER` to be 0, so omitting this initialization is OK, since statically allocated variables are automatically initialized to 0. But there is no guarantee that this is OK and other systems (e.g., Digital Unix) define the initializer to be nonzero.

Figure 23.18 is a corrected version of Figure 23.17 that uses a single mutex to lock the counter between the two threads.

── *threads/example02.c*

```
 1 #include    "unpthread.h"

 2 #define NLOOP 5000

 3 int     counter;              /* this is incremented by the threads */
 4 pthread_mutex_t counter_mutex = PTHREAD_MUTEX_INITIALIZER;

 5 void    *doit(void *);

 6 int
 7 main(int argc, char **argv)
 8 {
 9     pthread_t tidA, tidB;

10     Pthread_create(&tidA, NULL, &doit, NULL);
11     Pthread_create(&tidB, NULL, &doit, NULL);

12         /* wait for both threads to terminate */
13     Pthread_join(tidA, NULL);
14     Pthread_join(tidB, NULL);

15     exit(0);
16 }
```

```
17 void *
18 doit(void *vptr)
19 {
20     int     i, val;

21     /*
22      * Each thread fetches, prints, and increments the counter NLOOP times.
23      * The value of the counter should increase monotonically.
24      */

25     for (i = 0; i < NLOOP; i++) {
26         Pthread_mutex_lock(&counter_mutex);

27         val = counter;
28         printf("%d: %d\n", pthread_self(), val + 1);
29         counter = val + 1;

30         Pthread_mutex_unlock(&counter_mutex);
31     }

32     return (NULL);
33 }
```
threads/example02.c

Figure 23.18   Corrected version of Figure 23.17 using a mutex to protect the shared variable.

We declare a mutex named `counter_mutex` and this mutex must be locked by the thread before the thread manipulates the `counter` variable. When we run this program, the output is always correct: the value is incremented monotonically and the final value printed is always 10,000.

How much overhead is involved with mutex locking? The programs in Figures 23.17 and 23.18 were changed to loop 50,000 times, and timed while the output was directed to /dev/null. The difference in CPU time from the incorrect version with no mutual exclusion to the correct version that used a mutex was 10%. This tells us that mutex locking is not a large overhead.

23.8   Condition Variables

A mutex is fine to prevent simultaneous access to a shared variable, but we need something else to let us go to sleep waiting for some condition to occur. Let's demonstrate this with an example. We return to our Web client in Section 23.6 and replace the Solaris `thr_join` with `pthread_join`. But we cannot call the Pthread function until we know that a thread has terminated. We first declare a global that counts the number of terminated threads and protect it with a mutex.

```
int             ndone;          /* number of terminated threads */
pthread_mutex_t ndone_mutex = PTHREAD_MUTEX_INITIALIZER;
```

We then require that each thread increment this counter when it terminates, being careful to use the associated mutex.

```
void *
do_get_read(void *vptr)
{
    ...

    Pthread_mutex_lock(&ndone_mutex);
    ndone++;
    Pthread_mutex_unlock(&ndone_mutex);

    return(fptr);          /* terminate thread */
}
```

This is fine, but how do we code the main loop? It needs to lock the mutex continually and check if any threads have terminated.

```
while (nlefttoread > 0) {
    while (nconn < maxnconn && nlefttoconn > 0) {
            /* find a file to read */
        ...
    }

        /* See if one of the threads is done */
    Pthread_mutex_lock(&ndone_mutex);
    if (ndone > 0) {
        for (i = 0; i < nfiles; i++) {
            if (file[i].f_flags & F_DONE) {
                Pthread_join(file[i].f_tid, (void **) &fptr);

                /* update file[i] for terminated thread */
                ...
            }
        }
    }
    Pthread_mutex_unlock(&ndone_mutex);
}
```

While this is OK, it means the main loop *never* goes to sleep; it just loops, checking ndone every time around the loop. This is called *polling* and is considered a waste of CPU time.

We want a method for the main loop to go to sleep until one of its threads notifies it that something is ready. A *condition variable*, in conjunction with a mutex, provides this facility. The mutex provides mutual exclusion and the condition variable provides a signaling mechanism.

In terms of Pthreads, a condition variable is a variable of type pthread_cond_t. They are used with the following two functions.

```
#include <pthread.h>

int pthread_cond_wait(pthread_cond_t *cptr, pthread_mutex_t *mptr);

int pthread_cond_signal(pthread_cond_t *cptr);
```

                                    Both return: 0 if OK, positive E*xxx* value on error

---

The term "signal" in the second function's name does not refer to a Unix SIG*xxx* signal.

An example is the easiest way to explain these functions. Returning to our Web client example, the counter `ndone` is now associated with both a condition variable and a mutex:

```
int             ndone;
pthread_mutex_t ndone_mutex = PTHREAD_MUTEX_INITIALIZER;
pthread_cond_t  ndone_cond  = PTHREAD_COND_INITIALIZER;
```

A thread notifies the main loop that it is terminating by incrementing the counter while its mutex lock is held and by signaling the condition variable:

```
Pthread_mutex_lock(&ndone_mutex);
ndone++;
Pthread_cond_signal(&ndone_cond);
Pthread_mutex_unlock(&ndone_mutex);
```

The main loop then blocks in a call to `pthread_cond_wait`, waiting to be signaled by a terminating thread:

```
while (nlefttoread > 0) {
    while (nconn < maxnconn && nlefttoconn > 0) {
            /* find a file to read */
        ...
    }

        /* Wait for one of the threads to terminate */
    Pthread_mutex_lock(&ndone_mutex);
    while (ndone == 0)
        Pthread_cond_wait(&ndone_cond, &ndone_mutex);

    for (i = 0; i < nfiles; i++) {
        if (file[i].f_flags & F_DONE) {
            Pthread_join(file[i].f_tid, (void **) &fptr);

            /* update file[i] for terminated thread */
            ...
        }
    }
    Pthread_mutex_unlock(&ndone_mutex);
}
```

Notice that the variable `ndone` is still checked only while the mutex is held. Then, if there is nothing to do, `pthread_cond_wait` is called. This puts the calling thread to sleep *and* releases the mutex lock that it holds. Furthermore, when the thread returns from `pthread_cond_wait` (after some other thread has signaled it), the thread again holds the mutex.

Why is a mutex always associated with a condition variable? The "condition" is normally the value of some variable that is shared between the threads. The mutex is required to allow this variable to be set and tested by the different threads. For example, if we did not have the mutex in the example code just shown, the main loop would test it as follows:

```
                    /* Wait for one of the threads to terminate */
            while (ndone == 0)
                Pthread_cond_wait(&ndone_cond, &ndone_mutex);
```

But there is a possibility that the last of the threads increments `ndone` after the test of `ndone == 0`, but before the call to `pthread_cond_wait`. If this happens, this last "signal" is lost, and the main loop would block forever, waiting for something that will never occur again.

This is the same reason that `pthread_cond_wait` must be called with the associated mutex locked, and why this function unlocks the mutex and puts the calling thread to sleep as a single, atomic operation. If this function did not unlock the mutex, and then lock it again when it returns, the thread would have to do unlock and lock the mutex, and the code would look like:

```
                    /* Wait for one of the threads to terminate */
            Pthread_mutex_lock(&ndone_mutex);
            while (ndone == 0) {
                Pthread_mutex_unlock(&ndone_mutex);
                Pthread_cond_wait(&ndone_cond, &ndone_mutex);
                Pthread_mutex_lock(&ndone_mutex);
            }
```

But again, there is a possibility that the final thread could terminate and increment the value of `ndone` between the call to `pthread_mutex_unlock` and `pthread_cond_wait`.

Normally `pthread_cond_signal` awakens one thread that is waiting on the condition variable. There are instances when a thread knows that multiple threads should be awakened, in which case `pthread_cond_broadcast` will wake up *all* threads that are blocked on the condition variable.

```
    #include <pthread.h>

    int pthread_cond_broadcast(pthread_cond_t *cptr);

    int pthread_cond_timedwait(pthread_cond_t *cptr, pthread_mutex_t *mptr,
                               const struct timespec *abstime);
```
                                        Both return: 0 if OK, positive E*xxx* value on error

`pthread_cond_timedwait` lets a thread place a limit on how long it will block. *abstime* is a `timespec` structure (as we defined with the `pselect` function, Section 6.9) that specifies the system time when the function must return, even if the condition variable has not been signaled yet. If this timeout occurs, ETIME is returned.

This time value is an *absolute time*; it is not a *time delta*. That is, *abstime* is the system time—the number of seconds and nanoseconds past January 1, 1970, UTC—when the function should return. This differs from both `select` and `pselect`, which specify the number of seconds and microseconds (nanoseconds for `pselect`) until some time in the future when the function should return. The normal procedure is to call `gettimeofday` to obtain the current time (as a `timeval` structure!), copy this into a `timespec` structure, adding in the desired time limit. For example,

```
struct timeval  tv;
struct timespec ts;

if (gettimeofday(&tv, NULL) < 0)
    err_sys("gettimeofday error");
ts.tv_sec  = tv.tv_sec + 5;      /* 5 seconds in future */
ts.tv_nsec = tv.tv_usec * 1000;  /* microsec to nanosec */

pthread_cond_timedwait( ... , &ts);
```

The advantage in using an absolute time, instead of a delta time, is if the function prematurely returns (perhaps because of a caught signal). The function can be called again, without having to change the contents of the `timespec` structure. The disadvantage, however, is having to call `gettimeofday` before the function can be called the first time.

> Posix.1 defines a new `clock_gettime` function that returns the current time as a `timespec` structure.

23.9 Web Client and Simultaneous Connections (Continued)

We now recode our Web client from Section 23.6, removing the call to the Solaris `thr_join` function and replacing it with a call to `pthread_join`. As discussed in that section, we now must specify exactly which thread we are waiting for. To do this we will use a condition variable, as described in Section 23.8.

The only change to the globals (Figure 23.13) is to add one new flag and the condition variable:

```
#define   F_JOINED        8   /* main has pthread_join'ed */

int             ndone;        /* number of terminated threads */
pthread_mutex_t ndone_mutex = PTHREAD_MUTEX_INITIALIZER;
pthread_cond_t  ndone_cond  = PTHREAD_COND_INITIALIZER;
```

The only change to the `do_get_read` function (Figure 23.15) is to increment `ndone` and signal the main loop before the thread terminates:

```
        printf("end-of-file on %s\n", fptr->f_name);
        Close(fd);
        fptr->f_flags = F_DONE;    /* clears F_READING */

        Pthread_mutex_lock(&ndone_mutex);
        ndone++;
        Pthread_cond_signal(&ndone_cond);
        Pthread_mutex_unlock(&ndone_mutex);

        return(fptr);       /* terminate thread */
    }
```

Most changes are in the main loop, Figure 23.14, the new version of which we show in Figure 23.19.

```
                                                                      threads/web03.c
43      while (nlefttoread > 0) {
44          while (nconn < maxnconn && nlefttoconn > 0) {
45                  /* find a file to read */
46              for (i = 0; i < nfiles; i++)
47                  if (file[i].f_flags == 0)
48                      break;
49              if (i == nfiles)
50                  err_quit("nlefttoconn = %d but nothing found", nlefttoconn);

51              Pthread_create(&tid, NULL, &do_get_read, &file[i]);
52              file[i].f_tid = tid;
53              file[i].f_flags = F_CONNECTING;
54              nconn++;
55              nlefttoconn--;
56          }

57              /* Wait for one of the threads to terminate */
58          Pthread_mutex_lock(&ndone_mutex);
59          while (ndone == 0)
60              Pthread_cond_wait(&ndone_cond, &ndone_mutex);

61          for (i = 0; i < nfiles; i++) {
62              if (file[i].f_flags & F_DONE) {
63                  Pthread_join(file[i].f_tid, (void **) &fptr);

64                  if (&file[i] != fptr)
65                      err_quit("file[i] != fptr");
66                  fptr->f_flags = F_JOINED;    /* clears F_DONE */
67                  ndone--;
68                  nconn--;
69                  nlefttoread--;
70                  printf("thread %d for %s done\n", fptr->f_tid, fptr->f_name);
71              }
72          }
73          Pthread_mutex_unlock(&ndone_mutex);
74      }

75      exit(0);
76  }
```
                                                                      threads/web03.c

Figure 23.19 Main processing loop of `main` function.

If possible, create another thread

44–56   This code has not changed.

Wait for a thread to terminate

57–60   To wait for one of the threads to terminate we wait for `ndone` to be nonzero. As discussed in Section 23.8, the test must be done while the mutex is locked, and the sleep is performed by `pthread_cond_wait`.

Handle terminated thread

61–73   When a thread has terminated, we go through all the `file` structures to find the appropriate thread, call `pthread_join`, and then set the new `F_JOINED` flag.

Figure 15.20 shows the timing for this version, along with the timing of the version using nonblocking `connects`.

23.10 Summary

The creation of a new thread is normally faster than the creation of a new process with `fork`. This alone can be an advantage in heavily used network servers. Threads programming, however, is a new paradigm that requires more discipline.

All threads in a process share the global variables and descriptors, allowing this information to be shared between different threads. But this sharing introduces synchronization problems and the Pthread synchronization primitives that we must use are mutexes and condition variables. Synchronization of shared data is a required part of almost every threaded application.

When writing functions that can be called by threaded applications, these functions must be thread-safe. Thread-specific data is one technique that helps with this, and we showed an example with our `readline` function.

We return to the threads model in Chapter 27 with another server design in which the server creates a pool of threads when it starts. An available thread from this pool handles the next client request.

Exercises

23.1 Compare the descriptor usage in a server using `fork` versus a server using a thread, assuming 100 clients are being serviced at the same time.

23.2 What happens in Figure 23.3 if the thread does not `close` the connected socket when `str_echo` returns?

23.3 In Figures 5.5 and 6.13 we print "server terminated prematurely" when we expect an echoed line from the server but receive an end-of-file instead (recall Section 5.12). Modify Figure 23.2 to print this message too, when appropriate.

23.4 Modify Figures 23.11 and 23.12 so that they can compile on a system that does not support threads.

23.5 To see the error with the `readline` function that is used in Figure 23.4, build that program and start the server. Then build the TCP echo client from Figure 6.13 that works in a batch mode correctly. Find a large text file on your system and start the client three times in a batch mode, reading from the large text file and writing its output to a temporary file. If possible, run the clients on a different host from the server. If the three clients terminate correctly (often they hang), look at their temporary output files and compare them to the input file.

Now build a version of the server using the correct `readline` function from Section 23.5. Rerun the test with three clients, and all three clients should now work. You should also put a `printf` in the `readline_destructor` function, the `readline_once` function, and in the call to `malloc` in `readline`. This shows that the key is created only one time, but the memory is allocated for every thread, and that the destructor function is called for every thread.

24

IP Options

24.1 Introduction

IPv4 allows up to 40 bytes of options to follow the fixed 20-byte header. Although 10 different options are defined, the most commonly used is the source route option. Access to these options is through the IP_OPTIONS socket option and we demonstrate this with an example that uses source routing.

IPv6 allows extension headers to occur between the fixed 40-byte IPv6 header and the transport layer header (e.g., ICMPv6, TCP, or UDP). Six different extension headers are currently defined. Unlike the IPv4 approach, access to the IPv6 extension headers is through a functional interface instead of forcing the user to understand the actual details of how the headers appear in the IPv6 packet.

24.2 IPv4 Options

In Figure A.1 we show options following the 20-byte IPv4 header. As noted there, the 4-bit header length field limits the total size of the IPv4 header to 15 32-bit words (60 bytes), so the size of the IP options is limited to 40 bytes. Ten different options are defined for IPv4.

1. NOP: no-operation. A 1-byte option typically used for padding to make a later option fall on a 4-byte boundary.

2. EOL: end-of-list. A 1-byte option that terminates option processing. Since the total size of the IP options must be a multiple of 4 bytes, EOL bytes follow the final option.

3. LSRR: loose source and record route (Section 8.5 of TCPv1). We show an example of this shortly.

4. SSRR: strict source and record route (Section 8.5 of TCPv1). We show an example of this shortly.

5. Timestamp (Section 7.4 of TCPv1).

6. Record route (Section 7.3 of TCPv1).

7. Basic security.

8. Extended security.

9. Stream identifier (obsolete).

10. Router alert. This is a new option described in RFC 2113 [Katz 1997]. This option is included in IP datagrams that should be examined by all routers that forward the datagram.

Chapter 9 of TCPv2 provides further details on the kernel processing of the first six options and the indicated sections in TCPv1 provide examples of their use. RFC 1108 [Kent 1991] has additional details on the two security options, which are not widely used.

The `getsockopt` and `setsockopt` functions (with a *level* of `IPPROTO_IP` and an *optname* of `IP_OPTIONS`) fetch and set the IP options. The fourth argument to `getsockopt` and `setsockopt` is a pointer to a buffer (whose size is 44 bytes or less), and the fifth argument is the size of this buffer. The reason that the size of this buffer can be 4 bytes larger than the maximum size of the options is because of the way the source route option is handled, as we describe shortly. Other than the two source route options, the format of what goes into the buffer is the format of the options when placed into the IP datagram.

When the IP options are set using `setsockopt`, the specified options will then be sent on all IP datagrams on that socket. This works for TCP, UDP, and raw IP sockets. To clear these options call `setsockopt` and specify either a null pointer as the fourth argument or a value of 0 as the fifth argument (the length).

> Setting the IP options for a raw IP socket does not work on all implementations if the `IP_HDRINCL` socket option (which we describe in the next chapter) is also set. Many Berkeley-derived implementations do not send the options set with `IP_OPTIONS` when `IP_HDRINCL` is enabled, because the application can set its own IP options in the IP header that it builds (pp. 1056–1057 of TCPv2). Other systems (e.g., FreeBSD) allow the user to specify IP options using either the `IP_OPTIONS` socket options, or setting `IP_HDRINCL` and including them in the IP header that it builds, but not both.

When `getsockopt` is called to fetch the IP options for a connected TCP socket that was created by `accept`, all that is returned is the reversal of the source route option received with the client's SYN for the listening socket (p. 931 of TCPv2). The source route is automatically reversed by TCP because the source route specified by the client was from the client to the server, but the server needs to use the reverse of this route in datagrams it sends to the client. If no source route accompanied the SYN, then the value–result length returned by `getsockopt` through its fifth argument will be 0. For all other TCP sockets and for all UDP sockets and raw IP sockets, calling `getsockopt` to fetch the IP options just returns a copy of whatever IP options have been set by `setsockopt` for the socket. Note that for a raw IP socket the received IP header, including any IP options, is always returned by the input functions, so the received IP options are always available.

> Berkeley-derived kernels have never returned a received source route, or any other IP options, for a UDP socket. The code shown on p. 775 of TCPv2 to return the IP options has existed since 4.3BSD Reno, but has always been commented out since it does not work. This makes it impossible for a UDP application to use the reverse of a received route for datagrams back to the sender.

> Many Berkeley-derived kernels panic (i.e., the system halts) if `getsockopt` or `setsockopt` is called for a raw IP socket. But it takes superuser privileges to create a raw IP socket and there are many more malevolent deeds that someone with superuser privileges can do to a system.

24.3 IPv4 Source Route Options

A *source route* is a list of IP addresses specified by the sender of the IP datagram. If the source route is *strict*, then the datagram must pass through each listed node and only the listed nodes. That is, all the nodes listed in the source route must be neighbors. But if the source route is *loose*, the datagram must pass through each listed node but can also pass through other nodes that do not appear in the source route.

> IPv4 source routing is controversial. [Cheswick and Bellovin 1994, p. 26] advocate disabling the feature on all your routers, and many organizations and service providers do this. One legitimate use for source routing is to detect asymmetric routes using the Traceroute program, as demonstrated on pp. 108–109 of TCPv1, although as more and more routers on the Internet disable source routing, even this use disappears. Nevertheless, specifying and receiving source routes is part of the sockets API and needs to be described.

IPv4 source routes are called *source and record routes*, LSRR for the loose option and SSRR for the strict option, because as the datagram passes through all the listed nodes each one replaces its listed address with the address of the outgoing interface. This allows the receiver to take this new list and reverse it to follow the reverse path back to the sender. Examples of these two source routes, along with the corresponding `tcpdump` output, is in Section 8.5 of TCPv1.

We specify a source route as an array of IPv4 addresses, prefixed by three 1-byte fields, as shown in Figure 24.1. This is the format of the buffer that we will pass to `setsockopt`.

NOP	code	len	ptr	IP addr #1	IP addr #2	IP addr #3	. . .	IP addr #9	dest IP addr
1	1	1	1	4 bytes	4 bytes	4 bytes		4 bytes	4 bytes

(← 44 bytes →)

Figure 24.1 Passing a source route to the kernel.

We place a NOP before the source route option, which causes all the IP addresses to be aligned on a 4-byte boundary. This is not required but takes no additional space (the IP options are always padded to be a multiple of 4 bytes) and aligns the addresses.

In this figure we show up to 10 IP addresses in the route, but the first listed address is removed from the source route option and becomes the destination address of the IP datagram. Although there is room for only nine IP addresses in the 40-byte IP option space (do not forget the 3-byte option header that we are about to describe), there are actually 10 IP addresses in an IPv4 header, when the destination address is included.

The *code* is either 0x83 for an LSRR option or 0x89 for an SSRR option. The *len* that we specify is the size of the option in bytes, including the 3-byte header, and including the extra destination address at the end. It will be 11 for a route consisting of one IP address, 15 for a route consisting of two IP addresses, and so on, up to a maximum of 43. The NOP is not part of the option and is not included in the *len* field but is included in the size of the buffer that we specify to setsockopt. When the first address in the list is removed from the source route option and placed into the destination address field of the IP header, this *len* value is decremented by 4 (Figures 9.32 and 9.33 of TCPv2). *ptr* is a pointer or offset of the next IP address to be processed in the route, and we initialize it to 4, which points to the first IP address. The value of this field increases by 4 as the datagram is processed by each listed node.

We now develop three functions to initialize, create, and process a source route option. Our functions handle only a source route option. While it is possible to combine a source route with other IP options (such as a timestamp), the options other than the two source route options are rarely used. Figure 24.2 is the first function inet_srcrt_init along with some static variables that are used as an option is being built.

```
                                                                    ── ipopts/sourceroute.c
 1 #include    "unp.h"
 2 #include    <netinet/in_systm.h>
 3 #include    <netinet/ip.h>

 4 static u_char *optr;          /* pointer into options being formed */
 5 static u_char *lenptr;        /* pointer to length byte in SRR option */
 6 static int ocnt;              /* count of # addresses */

 7 u_char *
 8 inet_srcrt_init(void)
 9 {
10     optr = Malloc(44);        /* NOP, code, len, ptr, up to 10 addresses */
11     bzero(optr, 44);          /* guarantees EOLs at end */
12     ocnt = 0;
13     return (optr);            /* pointer for setsockopt() */
14 }
                                                                    ── ipopts/sourceroute.c
```

Figure 24.2 inet_srcrt_init function: initialize before storing a source route.

Initialize

10–13   We allocate a maximum sized buffer of 44 bytes and set it to 0. The value of the EOL option is 0, so this initializes the entire option to EOL bytes. The pointer to the option is returned to the caller and will be passed as the fourth argument to `setsockopt`.

The next function, `inet_srcrt_add`, adds one IPv4 address to the source route being constructed.

```
                                                                ── ipopts/sourceroute.c
15 int
16 inet_srcrt_add(char *hostptr, int type)
17 {
18     int     len;
19     struct addrinfo *ai;
20     struct sockaddr_in *sin;

21     if (ocnt > 9)
22         err_quit("too many source routes with: %s", hostptr);

23     if (ocnt == 0) {
24         *optr++ = IPOPT_NOP;     /* NOP for alignment */
25         *optr++ = type ? IPOPT_SSRR : IPOPT_LSRR;
26         lenptr = optr++;         /* we fill in the length later */
27         *optr++ = 4;             /* offset to first address */
28     }
29     ai = Host_serv(hostptr, "", AF_INET, 0);
30     sin = (struct sockaddr_in *) ai->ai_addr;
31     memcpy(optr, &sin->sin_addr, sizeof(struct in_addr));
32     freeaddrinfo(ai);

33     optr += sizeof(struct in_addr);
34     ocnt++;
35     len = 3 + (ocnt * sizeof(struct in_addr));
36     *lenptr = len;
37     return (len + 1);            /* size for setsockopt() */
38 }
                                                                ── ipopts/sourceroute.c
```

Figure 24.3 `inet_srcrt_add` function: add one IPv4 address to a source route.

Arguments

15–16   The first argument points to either a hostname or a dotted-decimal IP address, and the second argument is 0 for a loose source route or nonzero for a strict source route. We will see that the type of the first address added to the route determines whether the route is loose or strict.

Check for overflow and then initialize

21–28   We check that too many addresses are not specified and then initialize if this is the first address. As we mentioned, we always place a NOP before the source route option. We save a pointer to the *len* field and will store this value as each address is added to the list.

Obtain binary IP address and store in route

29–37   Our `host_serv` function handles either a hostname or a dotted-decimal string and we store the resulting binary address in the list. We update the *len* field and return the total size of the buffer (including the NOP) that the caller must pass to `setsockopt`.

When a received source route is returned to the application by `getsockopt`, the format is different from Figure 24.1. We show the received format in Figure 24.4.

IP addr #1	NOP	code	len	ptr	IP addr #2	IP addr #3	IP addr #4	...	dest IP addr
4 bytes	1	1	1	1	4 bytes	4 bytes	4 bytes		4 bytes

(spanning label: 44 bytes)

Figure 24.4 Format of source route option returned by `getsockopt`.

First, the order of the addresses has been reversed by the kernel from the ordering in the received source route. What we mean by "reversed" is that if the received source route contains the four addresses A, B, C, and D, in that order, the reverse of this route is D, C, B, and then A. The first 4 bytes contain the first IP address in the list, followed by a 1-byte NOP (for alignment), followed by the 3-byte source route option header, followed by the remaining IP addresses. Up to nine IP addresses can follow the 3-byte header, and the *len* field in the returned header will have a maximum value of 39. Since the NOP is always present, the length returned by `getsockopt` will always be a multiple of 4 bytes.

The format shown in Figure 24.4 is defined in `<netinet/ip_var.h>` as the following structure:

```
#define MAX_IPOPTLEN    40

struct ipoption {
  struct in_addr ipopt_dst;  /* first-hop dst if source routed */
  char           ipopt_list[MAX_IPOPTLEN];  /* options proper */
};
```

In Figure 24.5 we find it just as easy to parse the data ourselves, instead of using this structure.

This returned format differs from the format that we pass to `setsockopt`. If we wanted to convert the format in Figure 24.4 to the format in Figure 24.1 we would have to right-shift the addresses that follow the 3-byte header by 4 bytes and move the first IP address that precedes the header immediately after the header. Fortunately we do not have to do this, as Berkeley-derived implementations automatically use the reverse of a received source route for a TCP socket. That is, the information shown in Figure 24.4 is returned by `getsockopt` for our information only. We do not have to call `setsockopt` to tell the kernel to use this route for IP datagrams sent on the TCP connection—the kernel does that automatically. We will see an example of this shortly with our TCP server.

The next of our source route functions takes a received source route, in the format shown in Figure 24.4, and prints the information. We show our `inet_srcrt_print` function in Figure 24.5.

Save first IP address, skip any NOPs

45–47   The first IP address in the buffer is saved and any NOPs that follow are skipped over.

ipopts/sourceroute.c

```
39 void
40 inet_srcrt_print(u_char *ptr, int len)
41 {
42     u_char  c;
43     char    str[INET_ADDRSTRLEN];
44     struct in_addr *hop1;

45     memcpy(&hop1, ptr, sizeof(struct in_addr));
46     ptr += sizeof(struct in_addr);

47     while ( (c = *ptr++) == IPOPT_NOP) ;      /* skip any leading NOPs */

48     if (c == IPOPT_LSRR)
49         printf("received LSRR: ");
50     else if (c == IPOPT_SSRR)
51         printf("received SSRR: ");
52     else {
53         printf("received option type %d\n", c);
54         return;
55     }
56     printf("%s ", Inet_ntop(AF_INET, &hop1, str, sizeof(str)));

57     len = *ptr++ - sizeof(struct in_addr);  /* subtract "hop1" */
58     ptr++;                        /* skip over pointer */
59     while (len > 0) {
60         printf("%s ", Inet_ntop(AF_INET, ptr, str, sizeof(str)));
61         ptr += sizeof(struct in_addr);
62         len -= sizeof(struct in_addr);
63     }
64     printf("\n");
65 }
```

ipopts/sourceroute.c

Figure 24.5 inet_srcrt_print function: print a received source route.

Check for source route option

48–64   We only print the information for a source route, and from the 3-byte header we check the *code*, fetch the *len*, and skip over the *ptr*. We then print all the IP addresses that follow the 3-byte header.

Example

We now modify our TCP echo client to specify a source route and our TCP echo server to print a received source route. Figure 24.6 is our client.

Process command-line arguments

8–23   We call our inet_srcrt_init function to initialize the source route. Each hop is specified by either a -g option (loose) or a -G option (strict). The type of the first IP address (loose or strict) specifies the type of the source route. (We do this for simplicity. Clearly we could add code to check that all are of the same type.) Our inet_srcrt_add function adds each address to the route.

—————————————————————————————————————— ipopts/tcpcli01.c

```
 1 #include    "unp.h"

 2 int
 3 main(int argc, char **argv)
 4 {
 5     int     c, sockfd, len = 0;
 6     u_char *ptr;
 7     struct addrinfo *ai;

 8     if (argc < 2)
 9         err_quit("usage: tcpcli01 [ -[gG] <hostname> ... ] <hostname>");

10     ptr = inet_srcrt_init();

11     opterr = 0;                    /* don't want getopt() writing to stderr */
12     while ( (c = getopt(argc, argv, "g:G:")) != -1) {
13         switch (c) {
14         case 'g':                  /* loose source route */
15             len = inet_srcrt_add(optarg, 0);
16             break;

17         case 'G':                  /* strict source route */
18             len = inet_srcrt_add(optarg, 1);
19             break;

20         case '?':
21             err_quit("unrecognized option: %c", c);
22         }
23     }

24     if (optind != argc - 1)
25         err_quit("missing <hostname>");

26     ai = Host_serv(argv[optind], SERV_PORT_STR, AF_INET, SOCK_STREAM);

27     sockfd = Socket(ai->ai_family, ai->ai_socktype, ai->ai_protocol);

28     if (len > 0) {
29         len = inet_srcrt_add(argv[optind], 0);   /* dest at end */
30         Setsockopt(sockfd, IPPROTO_IP, IP_OPTIONS, ptr, len);
31         free(ptr);
32     }
33     Connect(sockfd, ai->ai_addr, ai->ai_addrlen);

34     str_cli(stdin, sockfd);    /* do it all */

35     exit(0);
36 }
```

—————————————————————————————————————— ipopts/tcpcli01.c

Figure 24.6 TCP echo client that specifies a source route.

This is our first encounter with the Posix.2 getopt function. The third argument is a character string specifying the characters that we allow as command-line arguments, g and G in this example. Each is followed by a colon, indicating that the option takes an argument. This function works with four global variables that are defined by including <unistd.h>:

```
extern char    *optarg;
extern int     optind, opterr, optopt;
```

Before calling getopt we set opterr to 0 to prevent the function from writing error messages to standard error in the case of an error, because we handle these ourself. Posix.2 states that if the first character of the third argument is a colon, this also prevents the function from writing to standard error, but not all implementations support this.

Handle destination address and create socket

24–27   The final command-line argument is the hostname or dotted-decimal address of the server and our host_serv function processes it. We are not able to call our tcp_connect function, because we must specify the source route between the calls to socket and connect. The latter initiates the three-way handshake and we want the initial SYN and all subsequent packets to use this source route.

28–34   If a source route is specified, we must add the server's IP address to the end of the list of IP addresses (Figure 24.1). setsockopt installs the source route for this socket. We then call connect, followed by our str_cli function (Figure 5.5).

Our TCP server is almost identical to the code shown in Figure 5.12, with the following changes. First, we allocate space for the options:

```
int       len;
u_char    *opts;

opts = Malloc(44);
```

We then fetch the IP options after the call to accept, but before the call to fork:

```
len = 44;
Getsockopt(connfd, IPPROTO_IP, IP_OPTIONS, opts, &len);
if (len > 0) {
    printf("received IP options, len = %d\n", len);
    inet_srcrt_print(opts, len);
}
```

If the received SYN from the client does not contain any IP options, the len variable will contain 0 on return from getsockopt (it is a value–result argument). As mentioned earlier, we do not have to do anything to cause TCP to use the reverse of the received source route: that is done automatically by TCP (p. 931 of TCPv2). All we are doing by calling getsockopt is obtaining a copy of the reversed source route. If we do not want TCP to use this route, we call setsockopt after accept returns, specifying a fifth argument (the length) of 0, and this removes any IP options currently in use. The source route has already been used by TCP for the second segment of the three-way handshake (Figure 2.5) but if we remove the options, IP will use whatever route it calculates for future packets to this client.

We now show an example of our client–server when we specify a source route. We run our client on the host solaris as follows:

```
solaris % tcpcli01 -g gw -g sunos5 bsdi
```

This sends the IP datagrams from solaris to the router gw (Figure 1.16), to the host sunos5, and then to the host bsdi, which is running the server. The two intermediate systems, gw and sunos5, must forward source routed datagrams for this example to work.

When the connection is established at the server, it outputs the following:

```
bsdi % tcpserv01
received IP options, len = 16
received LSRR: 206.62.226.36 206.62.226.62 206.62.226.33
```

The first IP address printed is the first hop of the reverse path (sunos5, as shown in Figure 24.4), and the next two addresses are in the order that is used by the server to send datagrams back to the client. If we watch the client–server exchange using tcpdump, we can see the source route option on every datagram in both directions.

> Unfortunately the operation of the IP_OPTIONS socket option has never been documented, so you may encounter variations on systems that are not derived from the Berkeley source code. For example, under Solaris 2.5 the first address returned in the buffer by getsockopt (Figure 24.4) is not the first-hop address for the return route, but the address of the peer. Nevertheless, the reversed route used by TCP is correct. Also, Solaris 2.5 precedes all source route options with four NOPs, limiting the option to eight IP addresses, instead of the real limit of nine.

Deleting A Received Source Route

Unfortunately source routes present a security hole. Starting with the Net/1 release (1989), the rlogind and rshd servers had code similar to the following:

```
u_char  buf[44];
char    lbuf[BUFSIZ];
int     optsize;

optsize = sizeof(buf);
if (getsockopt(0, IPPROTO_IP, IP_OPTIONS,
               buf, &optsize) == 0 && optsize != 0) {
    /* format the options as hex numbers to print in lbuf[] */
    syslog(LOG_NOTICE,
           "Connection received using IP options (ignored):%s", lbuf);
    setsockopt(0, ipproto, IP_OPTIONS, NULL, 0);
}
```

If a connection arrives with any IP options (the value of optsize returned by getsockopt is nonzero), then a message is logged using syslog and setsockopt is called to clear the options. This prevents any future TCP segments sent on this connection from using the reverse of the received source route. This technique is now known to be inadequate, because by the time the application receives the connection, the TCP three-way handshake is complete, and the second segment (the server's SYN-ACK in Figure 2.5) has already followed the reverse of the source route back to the client (or at least to one of the intermediate hops listed in the source route, which is where the hacker is located). Since the hacker has seen TCP's sequence numbers in both directions, even if no more packets are sent with the source route, the hacker can still send packets to the server, with the correct sequence number.

The only solution for this potential problem is to forbid all TCP connections that arrive with a source route, when you are using the source IP address for some form of validation (as do `rlogind` and `rshd`). Replace the call to `setsockopt` in the code fragment just shown with a closing of the just-accepted connection and a termination of the newly spawned server. The second segment of the three-way handshake has already been sent, but the connection should not be left open.

24.4   IPv6 Extension Headers

We do not show any options with the IPv6 header in Figure A.2 (it is always 40 bytes in length) but an IPv6 header can be followed by optional *extension headers*.

1. Hop-by-hop options must immediately follow the 40-byte IPv6 header. There are no hop-by-hop options currently defined that are usable by an application.

2. Destination options. None are currently defined that are usable by an application.

3. Routing header. This is a source routing option, similar in concept to what we described for IPv4 in Section 24.3.

4. Fragmentation header. This header is automatically generated by a host that fragments an IPv6 datagram and then processed by the final destination when it reassembles the fragments.

5. Authentication header (AH). The use of this header is documented in RFC 1826 [Atkinson 1995a] and [Kent and Atkinson 1997a].

6. Encapsulating security payload (ESP) header. The use of this header is documented in RFC 1827 [Atkinson 1995b] and [Kent and Atkinson 1997b].

We said the fragmentation header is handled entirely by the kernel, and a proposal for socket options to handle the AH and ESP headers is in [McDonald 1997]. This leaves the first three options, which we discuss in the next two sections.

24.5   IPv6 Hop-by-Hop Options and Destination Options

The hop-by-hop and destination options have a similar format, shown in Figure 24.7. The 8-bit *next header* field identifies the next header that follows this extension header. The 8-bit *header extension length* is the length of this extension header, in units of 8 bytes, but not including the first 8 bytes. For example, if this extension header occupies 8 bytes, then its header extension length is 0. If this extension header occupies 16 bytes, then its header extension length is 1, and so on. These two headers are padded to be a multiple of 8 bytes with either the `pad1` option, or with the `padN` option, described shortly.

The hop-by-hop options header and the destination options header each hold any number of individual options, which have the format shown in Figure 24.8.

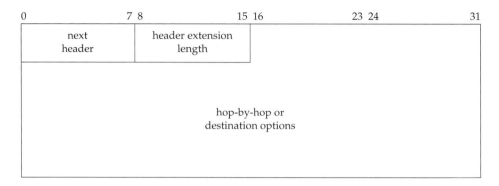

Figure 24.7 Format of hop-by-hop and destinations options.

Figure 24.8 Format of individual hop-by-hop and destination options.

This is called *TLV coding* because each option appears with its type, length, and value. The 8-bit *type* field identifies the option type. Additionally the two high-order bits specifies what an IPv6 node does with this option if it does not understand the option:

00   Skip over this option and continue processing the header.

01   Discard the packet.

10   Discard the packet and send an ICMP parameter problem type 2 error (Figure A.16) to the sender, regardless of whether or not the packet's destination is a multicast address.

11   Discard the packet and send an ICMP parameter problem type 2 error (Figure A.16) to the sender. But the error is sent only of the packet's destination is not a multicast address.

The next high-order bit specifies whether or not the option data changes en route:

0   The option data does not change en route.

1   The option data may change en route.

The low-order 5 bits then specify the option.

The 8-bit *length* field specifies the length of the option data in bytes. The type field and this length field are not included in this length.

The two pad options are defined in RFC 1883 [Hinden and Deering 1995] and can be used in either the hop-by-hop options header or in the destination options header. The *jumbo payload length*, a hop-by-hop option, is also defined in RFC 1883, and it is generated when needed, and processed when received entirely by the kernel. A new hop-by-hop option is proposed for IPv6 in [Katz et al. 1997], similar to the IPv4 router alert. We show these in Figure 24.9.

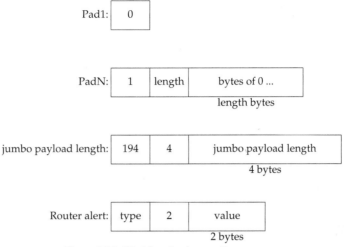

Figure 24.9 IPv6 hop-by-hop options.

The pad1 byte is the only option without a length and value. It provides 1 byte of padding. The padN option is used when 2 or more bytes of padding are required. For 2 bytes of padding, the length of this option would be 0 and the option would consist of just the type field and the length field. For 3 bytes of padding, the length would be 1, and 1 byte of 0 would follow this length. The jumbo payload length option provides a datagram length of 32 bits and is used when the 16-bit payload length field in Figure A.2 is inadequate.

   We show these options because each hop-by-hop and destination option also has an associated *alignment requirement*, written as $xn + y$. This means that the option must appear at an integer multiple of x bytes from the start of the header, plus y bytes. For example, the alignment requirement of the jumbo payload option is $4n + 2$, and this is to force the 4-byte option value (the jumbo payload length) to be on a 4-byte boundary. The reason that the y value is 2 for this option is because of the 2 bytes that appear at the beginning of each hop-by-hop and destination options header (Figure 24.7).

   The hop-by-hop options and the destination options are normally specified as ancillary data with sendmsg and returned as ancillary data by recvmsg. Nothing special need be done by the application to send either or both of these options; just specify them in a call to sendmsg. But to receive these options, the corresponding socket option must be enabled: IPV6_HOPOPTS for the hop-by-hop options, and IPV6_DSTOPTS for the destination options. For example, to enable both options to be returned:

```
const int  on = 1;

setsockopt(sockfd, IPPROTO_IPV6, IPV6_HOPOPTS, &on, sizeof(on));
setsockopt(sockfd, IPPROTO_IPV6, IPV6_DSTOPTS, &on, sizeof(on));
```

Figure 24.10 shows the format of the ancillary data objects used to send and receive hop-by-hop and destination options.

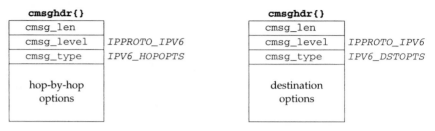

Figure 24.10   Ancillary data objects for hop-by-hop and destination options.

Unlike the other IPv6 ancillary data objects that we have described (Figure 20.21) it is up to each implementation as to what is passed between the user and the kernel as the cmsg_data portion of these objects. Instead of defining these contents, six functions are defined to create and process these ancillary data objects. The following four functions build an option to send.

```
#include <netinet/in.h>

int inet6_option_space(int nbytes);

                                    Returns: number of bytes required to hold option

int inet6_option_init(void *buf, struct cmsghdr **cmsgp, int type);

                                                    Returns: 0 if OK, −1 on error

int inet6_option_append(struct cmsghdr *cmsg, const uint8_t *typep,
                        int multx, int plusy);

                                                    Returns: 0 if OK, −1 on error

uint8_t *inet6_option_alloc(struct cmsghdr *cmsg, int datalen,
                           int multx, int plusy);

                          Returns: pointer to option type field if OK, NULL on error
```

inet6_option_space returns the number of bytes required to hold an option, including the cmsghdr structure at the beginning and any pad bytes at the end. The *nbytes* argument is the size of the structure defining the option, which must include any pad bytes at the beginning (the value y in the alignment term $xn + y$), the option type, length, and data.

inet6_option_init is called once per ancillary data object that will contain either a hop-by-hop option or a destination option. *buf* points to the buffer that will contain the ancillary data object. *cmsgp* is the address of a pointer to a cmsghdr structure, and this function initializes this structure in the buffer pointed to by buf and returns a pointer to this structure in *cmsgp*. *type* is either IPV6_HOPOPTS or

IPV6_DSTOPTS and is stored in the cmsg_type member of the cmsghdr structure that
is built.

inet6_option_append appends either a hop-by-hop option or a destination
option into an ancillary data object that was initialized by inet6_option_init. *cmsg*
is a pointer to the cmsghdr structure that was initialized by inet6_option_init.
typep is a pointer to the 8-bit option type, which must be followed by the 8-bit option
length, and the option data (TLV). The caller sets these values before calling this function. *multx* and *plusy* are the two terms *x* and *y* in the alignment requirement for this
option.

The previously described function requires the caller to build the option's TLV and
then pass a pointer as the *typep* argument and the option is then copied into the ancillary data object. Alternately, the inet6_option_alloc function returns a pointer to
the ancillary data object, and the caller must then store the options TLV into the ancillary data object. *cmsg* is a pointer to the cmsghdr structure that was initialized by
inet6_option_init. *datalen* is the value of the length byte for this option, and this is
required to calculate if any padding must be appended to the option. *multx* and *plusy*
are the two terms *x* and *y* in the alignment requirement for this option.

The remaining two functions process a received option.

```
#include <netinet/in.h>

int inet6_option_next(const struct cmsghdr *cmsg, uint8_t **tptrp);

                     Returns: 0 if another option to process, –1 on end of options or error

int inet6_option_find(const struct cmsghdr *cmsg, uint8_t *tptrp, int type);

                                                Returns: 0 if OK, –1 on error
```

inet6_option_next processes the next option in a buffer. *cmsghdr* points to a
cmsghdr structure of which the cmsg_level must be IPPROTO_IPV6 and the
cmsg_type must be either IPV6_HOPOPTS or IPV6_DSTOPTS. The first time this
function is called for a given ancillary data object, *tptrp* must be a null pointer and then
each time this function returns, *tptrp* points to the 8-bit option type field of the next
option to process. The value of *tptrp* is used by the function to remember its place in
the ancillary data object from one call to the next. When the last option has been processed, the return value is –1 and *tptrp* is a null pointer. If an error occurs, the return
value if –1 and *tptrp* is a nonnull pointer.

inet6_option_find is similar to the previous function, but it lets the caller specify the option type to search for (the *type* argument) instead of always returning the next
option.

24.6 IPv6 Routing Header

The IPv6 routing header is used for source routing in IPv6. The first 2 bytes of the routing header are the same as we showed in Figure 24.7: a *next header* field followed by a

header extension length. The next 2 bytes specify the *routing type* and the number of *segments left* (i.e., how many listed nodes are still to be visited). Only one type of routing header is specified, type 0, and we show its format in Figure 24.11.

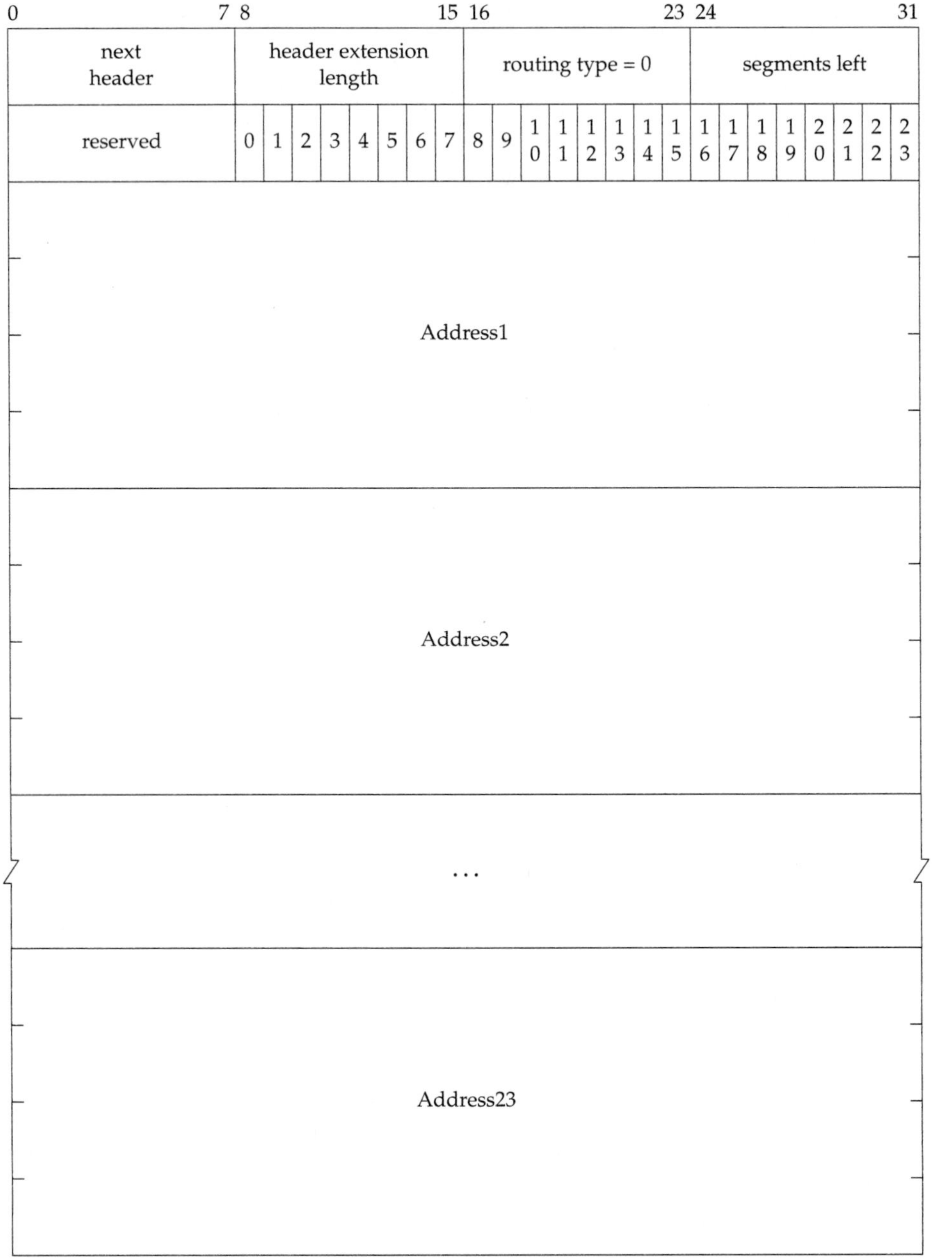

0	7	8	15	16	23	24	31

next header	header extension length	routing type = 0	segments left

reserved	0 1 2 3 4 5 6 7 8 9 10 11 12 13 14 15 16 17 18 19 20 21 22 23

Address1

Address2

. . .

Address23

Figure 24.11 IPv6 routing header.

Up to 23 addresses can appear in the routing header and *segments left* is between 1 and 23. The 24 bits that we label from 0 to 23 form the *strict/loose bit map*: a value of 1 means the corresponding address is a *strict* hop (that node must be a neighbor of the previously listed node) and a value of 0 means the corresponding address is a *loose* hop (that node need not be a neighbor). The bit labeled 1 corresponds to Address1, the bit labeled 2 correspond to Address 2, and so on. The bit labeled 0 is for the first hop. RFC 1883 [Hinden and Deering 1995] specifies the details of how the header is processed as the packet travels to the final destination, along with a detailed example.

The routing header is normally specified as ancillary data with `sendmsg` and returned as ancillary data by `recvmsg`. Nothing special need be done by the application to send the header: just specify it in a call to `sendmsg`. But to receive the routing header, the `IPV6_RTHDR` socket option must be enabled, as in

```
const int  on = 1;

setsockopt(sockfd, IPPROTO_IPV6, IPV6_RTHDR, &on, sizeof(on));
```

Figure 24.12 shows the format of the ancillary data object used to send and receive the routing header. Similar to the ancillary data objects for the hop-by-hop and destination options (Figure 24.10), it is up to each implementation as to what is passed between the user and the kernel as the `cmsg_data` portion of this object. Eight functions are defined to create and process the routing header. The following four functions build an option to send.

```
#include <netinet/in.h>

size_t inet6_rthdr_space(int type, int segments);
```
Returns: positive number of bytes if OK, 0 on error

```
struct cmsghdr *inet6_rthdr_init(void *buf, int type);
```
Returns: nonnull pointer if OK, NULL on error

```
int inet6_rthdr_add(struct cmsghdr *cmsg, const struct in6_addr *addr,
                    unsigned int flags);
```
Returns: 0 if OK, –1 on error

```
int inet6_rthdr_lasthop(struct cmsghdr *cmsg, unsigned int flags);
```
Returns: 0 if OK, –1 on error

`inet6_rthdr_space` returns the number of bytes required to hold an ancillary data object containing a routing header of the specified *type* (normally specified as `IPV6_RTHDR_TYPE_0`) with the specified number of *segments*. This size includes the `cmsghdr` structure.

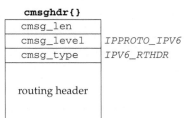

Figure 24.12 Ancillary data object for IPv6 routing header.

`inet6_rthdr_space` and `inet6_option_space` both return the number of bytes required for one type of ancillary data object but neither allocates the memory. This is in case the caller wants to allocate a larger buffer to hold other ancillary data objects too.

`inet6_rthdr_init` initializes the buffer pointed to by *buf* to contain an ancillary data object with a routing header of the specified *type*. The return value is the pointer to the `cmsghdr` structure that is built in the buffer, and this pointer is then used as an argument to the next two functions. The `cmsg_level` and `cmsg_type` members are initialized.

`inet6_rthdr_add` adds the IPv6 address pointed to by `addr` to the end of the routing header being constructed. The *flags* argument is either `IPV6_RTHDR_LOOSE` or `IPV6_RTHDR_STRICT`. Upon success the `cmsg_len` member is updated to account for the new address.

`inet6_rthdr_lasthop` specifies the *flags* (`IPV6_RTHDR_LOOSE` or `IPV6_RTHDR_STRICT`) for the final hop. Realize that a routing header with *N* addresses has *N* + *1* hops. This requires *N* calls to `inet6_rthdr_add` and one call to `inet6_rthdr_lasthop`.

The following four functions deal with a received routing header.

```
#include <netinet/in.h>

int inet6_rthdr_reverse(const struct cmsghdr *in, struct cmsghdr *out);
```
                                                                   Returns: 0 if OK, −1 on error

```
int inet6_rthdr_segments(const struct cmsghdr *cmsg);
```
                                          Returns: number of segments in routing header if OK, −1 on error

```
struct in6_addr *inet6_rthdr_getaddr(struct cmsghdr *cmsg, int index);
```
                                                         Returns: nonnull pointer if OK, NULL on error

```
int inet6_rthdr_getflags(const struct cmsghdr *cmsg, int index);
```
                                                       Returns: loose/strict flag if OK, −1 on error

`inet6_rthdr_reverse` takes a routing header that was received as ancillary data (pointed to by *in*) and creates a new routing header (in the buffer pointed to by *out*) that sends datagrams along the reverse of that path. The reversal can occur in place; that is, the *in* and *out* pointers can point to the same buffer.

`inet6_rthdr_segments` returns the number of segments in the routing header described by *cmsg*. Upon success, the return value is between 1 and 23, inclusive.

`inet6_rthdr_getaddr` returns a pointer to the IPv6 address specified by *index* in the routing header described by *cmsg*. *index* must have a value between 1 and the value returned by `inet6_rthdr_segments`, inclusive.

`inet6_rthdr_getflags` returns `IPV6_RTHDR_LOOSE` or `IPV6_RTHDR_STRICT` corresponding to *index* (which must have a value between 0 and the value returned by `inet6_rthdr_segments`, inclusive) in the routing header described by *cmsg* for the routing header

> Addresses are indexed starting at 1, and the loose/strict flags are indexed starting at 0, as we show in Figure 24.11. This is consistent with the notation in RFC 1883 [Hinden and Deering 1995].

24.7 IPv6 Sticky Options

We have described the use of ancillary data with `sendmsg` and `recvmsg` to send and receive six different ancillary data objects:

1. IPv6 packet information: the `in6_pktinfo` structure containing either the destination address and outgoing interface index, or the source address and the arriving interface index (Figure 20.21).

2. The outgoing hop limit or the received hop limit (Figure 20.21).

3. The next-hop address (Figure 20.21).

4. Hop-by-hop options (Figure 24.10).

5. Destination options (Figure 24.10).

6. Routing header (Figure 24.12).

We summarized the `cmsg_level` and `cmsg_type` values for these objects, along with the values for the other ancillary data object in Figure 13.11.

Instead of sending these options in every call to `sendmsg`, we can set the `IPV6_PKTOPTIONS` socket option instead. When setting this option the fourth argument points to a buffer containing all the ancillary data objects that should be sent with all packets on this socket. The format of this buffer is exactly as if the buffer were specified as ancillary data to `sendmsg`. These options are called "sticky" because once they are set, they remain set until cleared (setting the socket option with a length of 0). But these sticky options can be overridden on a per-packet basis for a UDP socket or for a raw IPv6 socket by specifying ancillary data in a call to `sendmsg`. If any ancillary data is specified in a call to `sendmsg`, none of the sticky options is sent with that datagram.

The concept of sticky options can also be used with TCP, because ancillary data is never sent or received by `sendmsg` or `recvmsg` on a TCP socket. Instead, a TCP application can set the `IPV6_PKTOPTIONS` socket option and specify any of the six ancillary data objects mentioned at the beginning of this section. These objects then affect all packets sent on this socket.

A TCP application can also call `getsockopt` for the `IPV6_PKTOPTIONS` socket option to retrieve these ancillary data objects. In this case the kernel maintains only the options from the most recently received segment and for those options that the application has explicitly said that it wants (by enabling the corresponding socket option).

24.8 Summary

The most commonly used of the 10 defined IPv4 options is the source route, but its use is dwindling these days because of security concerns. Access to the IPv4 header options is through the `IP_OPTIONS` socket option.

IPv6 defines six extension headers, although as of this writing support for these options is minimal. Access to the IPv6 extension headers is through a functional interface, obviating the need to understand their actual format in the packet. These extension headers are written as ancillary data with `sendmsg` and returned as ancillary data with `recvmsg`.

Exercises

24.1   In our IPv4 source route example at the end of Section 24.3 what changes at the server if instead of specifying the hostname `gw` to the client, we specify the other IP address of this router: 206.85.40.74 from Figure 1.16?

24.2   In our IPv4 source route example at the end of Section 24.3 what changes if we specify each intermediate node to the client with the `-G` option, instead of the `-g` option?

24.3   The length of the buffer specified to `setsockopt` for the `IP_OPTIONS` socket option must be a multiple of 4 bytes. What would be do if we did not place a NOP at the beginning of the buffer, as shown in Figure 24.1?

24.4   How does `ping` receive a source route when the IP Record Route option is used (described in Section 7.3 of TCPv1)?

24.5   In the example code from the `rlogind` server at the end of Section 24.3 that clears a received source route, why is the socket descriptor argument for `getsockopt` and `setsockopt` 0?

24.6   For many years the code that we showed at the end of Section 24.3 that clears a received source route looked like:

```
optsize = 0;
setsockopt(0, ipproto, IP_OPTIONS, NULL, &optsize);
```

What is wrong with this code? Does it matter?

25

Raw Sockets

25.1 Introduction

Raw sockets provide three features not provided by normal TCP and UDP sockets.

1. Raw sockets let us read and write ICMPv4, IGMPv4, and ICMPv6 packets. The Ping program, for example, sends ICMP echo requests and receives ICMP echo replies. (We develop our own version of the Ping program in Section 25.5.) The multicast routing daemon, `mrouted`, sends and receives IGMPv4 packets.

   This capability also allows applications that are built using ICMP or IGMP to be handled entirely as user processes, instead of putting more code into the kernel. The router discovery daemon (`in.rdisc` under Solaris 2.x; Appendix F of TCPv1 describes how to obtain the source code for a publicly available version), for example, is built this way. It processes two ICMP messages (router advertisement and router solicitation) that the kernel knows nothing about.

2. With a raw socket a process can read and write IPv4 datagrams with an IPv4 protocol field that is not processed by the kernel. Recall the 8-bit IPv4 protocol field in Figure A.1. Most kernels only process datagrams containing values of 1 (ICMP), 2 (IGMP), 6 (TCP), and 17 (UDP). But many other values are defined for the protocol field: RFC 1700 [Reynolds and Postel 1994] lists all the values. For example, the OSPF routing protocol does not use TCP or UDP but uses IP directly, setting the protocol field of the IP datagram to 89. The `gated` program that implements OSPF must use a raw socket to read and write these IP datagrams since they contain a protocol field that the kernel knows nothing about. This capability will carry over to IPv6 also.

3. With a raw socket a process can build its own IPv4 header, using the
   IP_HDRINCL socket option. This can be used, for example, to build our own
   UDP or TCP packets, and we show an example of this in Section 26.6.

This chapter describes raw socket creation, input, and output. We then develop versions of the Ping and Traceroute programs that work with both IPv4 and IPv6.

25.2 Raw Socket Creation

The steps involved in creating a raw socket are as follows:

1. The socket function creates a raw socket when the second argument is
   SOCK_RAW. The third argument (the protocol) is normally nonzero. For example, to create an IPv4 raw socket we would write

   ```
   int     sockfd;

   sockfd = socket(AF_INET, SOCK_RAW, protocol);
   ```

   where *protocol* is one of the constants IPPROTO_*xxx* defined by including the
   <netinet/in.h> header, such as IPPROTO_ICMP. Be aware that just because
   a protocol has its name defined in this header, such as IPPROTO_EGP, does not
   mean that the kernel supports it.

   Only the superuser can create a raw socket. This prevents normal users from
   writing their own IP datagrams to the network.

2. The IP_HDRINCL socket option can be set:

   ```
   const int  on = 1;

   if (setsockopt(sockfd, IPPROTO_IP, IP_HDRINCL, &on, sizeof(on)) < 0)
       error
   ```

   We describe the effect of this socket option in the next section.

3. bind can be called on the raw socket, but this is rare. This function sets only the
   local address: there is no concept of a port number with a raw socket. With
   regard to output, calling bind sets the source IP address that will be used for
   datagrams sent on the raw socket (but only if the IP_HDRINCL socket option is
   not set). If bind is not called, the kernel sets the source IP address to the primary IP address of the outgoing interface.

4. connect can be called on the raw socket, but this is rare. This function sets
   only the foreign address: again, there is no concept of a port number with a raw
   socket. With regard to output, calling connect lets us call write or send
   instead of sendto, since the destination IP address is already specified.

25.3 Raw Socket Output

Output on a raw socket is governed by the following rules:

1. Normal output is performed by calling `sendto` or `sendmsg` and specifying the destination IP address. `write`, `writev`, or `send` can also be called if the socket has been connected.

2. If the `IP_HDRINCL` option is not set, the starting address of the data for the kernel to write specifies the first byte following the IP header, because the kernel will build the IP header and prepend it to the data from the process. The kernel sets the protocol field of the IPv4 header that it builds to the third argument from the call to `socket`.

3. If the `IP_HDRINCL` option is set, the starting address of the data for the kernel to write specifies the first byte of the IP header. The amount of data to write must include the size of the caller's IP header. The process builds the entire IP header, except (a) the IPv4 identification field can be set to 0, which tells the kernel to set this value, and (b) the kernel always calculates and stores the IPv4 header checksum.

4. The kernel fragments raw packets that exceed the outgoing interface MTU.

> Unfortunately the `IP_HDRINCL` socket option has never been documented, specifically with regard to the byte ordering of the fields in the IP header. On Berkeley-derived kernels all fields are in network byte order except `ip_len` and `ip_off`, which are in host byte order (pp. 233 and 1057 of TCPv2). On Linux, however, all the fields must be in network byte order.

> The `IP_HDRINCL` socket option was introduced with 4.3BSD Reno. Before this the only way for an application to specify its own IP header in packets sent on a raw IP socket was to apply a kernel patch that was introduced in 1988 by Van Jacobson to support Traceroute. This patch required the application to create a raw IP socket specifying a *protocol* of `IPPROTO_RAW`, which has a value of 255 (and is a reserved value and must never appear as the protocol field in an IP header).

> The functions that perform input and output on raw sockets are some of the simplest in the kernel. For example, in TCPv2 each function requires about 40 lines of C code (pp. 1054–1057), compared to TCP input at about 2000 lines and TCP output at about 700 lines.

Our description of the `IP_HDRINCL` socket option is for 4.4BSD. Earlier versions, such as Net/2, filled in more fields in the IP header when this option was set.

With IPv4 it is the responsibility of the user process to calculate and set any header checksums contained in whatever follows the IPv4 header. For example, in our Ping program (Figure 25.13) we must calculate the ICMPv4 checksum and store it in the ICMPv4 header before calling `sendto`.

IPv6 Differences

There are a few differences with raw IPv6 sockets [Stevens and Thomas 1997].

- All fields in the protocol headers sent or received on a raw IPv6 socket are in network byte order.

- There is nothing similar to the IPv4 `IP_HDRINCL` socket option with IPv6. Complete IPv6 packets cannot be read or written on an IPv6 raw socket. Almost all fields in an IPv6 header and all extension headers are available to the application through socket options or ancillary data (see Exercise 25.1). Should an application need to read or write complete IPv6 datagrams, datalink access (described in Chapter 26) must be used.

- Checksums on raw IPv6 sockets are handled differently, as described shortly.

`IPV6_CHECKSUM` Socket Option

For an ICMPv6 raw socket the kernel always calculates and stores the checksum in the ICMPv6 header. This differs from an ICMPv4 raw socket, where the application must do this itself (compare Figures 25.13 and 25.15). While ICMPv4 and ICMPv6 both require the sender to calculate the checksum, ICMPv6 includes a pseudoheader in its checksum (we discuss the concept of a pseudoheader when we calculate the UDP checksum in Figure 26.13). One of the fields in this pseudoheader is the source IPv6 address, and normally the application lets the kernel choose this value. To prevent the application from having to try to choose this address just to calculate the checksum, it is easier to let the kernel calculate the checksum.

For other raw IPv6 sockets (i.e., those created with a third argument to `socket` other than `IPPROTO_ICMPV6`) a socket option tells the kernel whether to calculate and store a checksum in outgoing packets and verify the checksum in received packets. By default this option is disabled, and it is enabled by setting the option value to a nonnegative value, as in

```
int  offset = 2;

if (setsockopt(sockfd, IPPROTO_IPV6, IPV6_CHECKSUM,
               &offset, sizeof(offset)) < 0)
    error
```

This not only enables checksums on this socket, it also tells the kernel the byte offset of the 16-bit checksum: 2 bytes from the start of the application data in this example. To disable the option it must be set to −1. When enabled the kernel will calculate and store the checksum for outgoing packets sent on the socket and also verify the checksums for packets received on the socket.

25.4 Raw Socket Input

The first question that we must answer regarding raw socket input is: which received IP datagrams does the kernel pass to raw sockets? The following rules apply:

1. Received UDP packets and received TCP packets are *never* passed to a raw socket. If a process wants to read IP datagrams containing UDP or TCP packets, the packets must be read at the datalink layer, as described in Chapter 26.

2. *Most* ICMP packets are passed to a raw socket, after the kernel has finished processing the ICMP message. Berkeley-derived implementations pass all received ICMP packets to a raw socket other than echo request, timestamp request, and address mask request (pp. 302–303 of TCPv2). These three ICMP messages are processed entirely by the kernel.

3. *All* IGMP packets are passed to a raw socket, after the kernel has finished processing the IGMP message.

4. *All* IP datagrams with a protocol field that the kernel does not understand are passed to a raw socket. The only kernel processing done on these packets is the minimal verification of some IP header fields: the IP version, IPv4 header checksum, the header length, and the destination IP address (pp. 213–220 of TCPv2).

5. If the datagram arrives in fragments, nothing is passed to a raw socket until all fragments have arrived and have been reassembled.

When the kernel has an IP datagram to pass to the raw sockets, all raw sockets for all processes are examined, looking for all matching sockets. A copy of the IP datagram is delivered to *each* matching socket. The following tests are performed for each raw socket and only if all three tests are true is the datagram delivered to the socket.

1. If a nonzero *protocol* is specified when the raw socket is created (the third argument to `socket`), then the received datagram's protocol field must match this value, or the datagram is not delivered to this socket.

2. If a local IP address is bound to the raw socket by `bind`, then the destination IP address of the received datagram must match this bound address, or the datagram is not delivered to this socket.

3. If a foreign IP address was specified for the raw socket by `connect`, then the source IP address of the received datagram must match this connected address, or the datagram is not delivered to this socket.

Notice that if a raw socket is created with a *protocol* of 0, and neither `bind` nor `connect` is called, then that socket receives a copy of *every* raw datagram that the kernel passes to raw sockets.

Whenever a received datagram is passed to a raw IPv4 socket, the entire datagram, including the IP header, is passed to the process. We mentioned in the previous section that the IPv6 header and any extension headers are never passed to a raw IPv6 socket.

In the IPv4 header passed to the application, `ip_len`, `ip_off`, and `ip_id` are host byte ordered, but the remaining fields are network byte ordered. Under Linux, all fields are left as network byte ordered.

We mentioned in the previous section that all fields in a datagram passed to a raw IPv6 socket are left in their network byte order.

ICMPv6 Type Filtering

A raw ICMPv4 socket receives most ICMPv4 messages received by the kernel. But ICMPv6 is a superset of ICMPv4, including the functionality of ARP and IGMP (Section 2.2). Therefore a raw ICMPv6 socket can potentially receive many more packets compared to a raw ICMPv4 socket. But most applications using a raw socket are interested in only a small subset of all ICMP messages.

To reduce the number of packets passed from the kernel to the application across a raw ICMPv6 socket, an application-specified filter is provided. A filter is declared with a datatype of `struct icmp6_filter`, which is defined by including `<netinet/icmp6.h>`. The current filter for a raw ICMPv6 socket is set and fetched using `setsockopt` and `getsockopt` with a *level* of `IPPROTO_ICMPV6` and an *optname* of `ICMP6_FILTER`.

Six macros operate on the `icmp6_filter` structure.

```
#include <netinet/icmp6.h>

void ICMP6_FILTER_SETPASSALL(struct icmp6_filter *filt);
void ICMP6_FILTER_SETBLOCKALL(struct icmp6_filter *filt);

void ICMP6_FILTER_SETPASS(int msgtype, struct icmp6_filter *filt);
void ICMP6_FILTER_SETBLOCK(int msgtype, struct icmp6_filter *filt);

int  ICMP6_FILTER_WILLPASS(int msgtype, const struct icmp6_filter *filt);
int  ICMP6_FILTER_WILLBLOCK(int msgtype, const struct icmp6_filter *filt);
```
                                    Both return: 1 if filter will pass (block) message type, 0 otherwise

The *filt* argument to all the macros is a pointer to an `icmp6_filter` variable that is modified by the first four macros and examined by the final two macros. The *msgtype* argument is a value between 0 and 255 specifying the ICMP message type.

The `SETPASSALL` macro specifies that all message types are to be passed to the application, while the `SETBLOCKALL` macros specifies that no message types are to be passed. By default, when an ICMPv6 raw socket is created, all ICMPv6 message types are passed to the application.

The `SETPASS` macro enables one specific message type to be passed to the application while the `SETBLOCK` macro blocks one specific message type. The `WILLPASS` macro returns 1 if the specified message type is passed by the filter, or 0 otherwise, while the `WILLBLOCK` macro returns 1 if the specified message type is blocked by the filter, or 0 otherwise.

As an example, consider an application that wants to receive only ICMPv6 router advertisements:

```
struct icmp6_filter  myfilt;

fd = Socket(AF_INET6, SOCK_RAW, IPPROTO_ICMPV6);

ICMP6_FILTER_SETBLOCKALL(&myfilt);
ICMP6_FILTER_SETPASS(ND_ROUTER_ADVERT, &myfilt);
Setsockopt(fd, IPPROTO_ICMPV6, ICMP6_FILTER, &myfilt, sizeof(myfilt));
```

We first block all message types (since the default is to pass all message types) and then pass only router advertisements.

25.5 Ping Program

In this section we develop and present a version of the Ping program that works with both IPv4 and IPv6. We develop our own program, instead of presenting the publicly available source code for two reasons. First, the publicly available Ping program suffers from a common programming disease known as *creeping featurism*: it supports a dozen different options. Our goal in examining a Ping program is to understand the network programming concepts and techniques, without being distracted with all these options. Our version of Ping supports only one option and is about five times smaller than the public version. Second, the public version works with only IPv4 and we want to show a version that also supports IPv6.

The operation of Ping is extremely simple: an ICMP echo request is sent to some IP address and that node responds with an ICMP echo reply. These two ICMP messages are supported under both IPv4 and IPv6. Figure 25.1 shows the format of the ICMP messages.

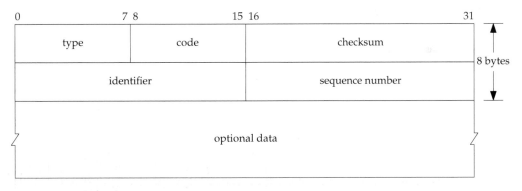

Figure 25.1 Format of ICMPv4 and ICMPv6 echo request and echo reply messages.

Figures A.15 and A.16 shows the *type* values for these messages and also shows that the *code* is 0. We will see that we set the *identifier* to the process ID of the Ping process and we increment the *sequence number* by one for each packet that we send. We store the 8-byte timestamp of when the packet is sent as the optional data. The rules of ICMP require that the *identifier*, *sequence number*, and any optional data be returned in the echo reply. Storing the timestamp in the packet lets us calculate the RTT when the reply is received.

Figure 25.2 shows some examples of our program. The first uses IPv4 and the second uses IPv6. Note the pound-sign prompt, signifying the superuser, as it takes superuser privileges to create a raw socket.

```
solaris # ping gemini.tuc.noao.edu
PING gemini.tuc.noao.edu (140.252.4.54): 56 data bytes
64 bytes from 140.252.4.54: seq=0, ttl=248, rtt=37.542 ms
64 bytes from 140.252.4.54: seq=1, ttl=248, rtt=34.596 ms
64 bytes from 140.252.4.54: seq=2, ttl=248, rtt=29.204 ms
64 bytes from 140.252.4.54: seq=3, ttl=248, rtt=52.630 ms

solaris # ping 6bone-router.cisco.com
PING 6bone-router.cisco.com (5f00:6d00:c01f:700:1:60:3e11:6770): 56 data bytes
64 bytes from 5f00:6d00:c01f:700:1:60:3e11:6770: seq=0, hlim=255, rtt=116.802 ms
64 bytes from 5f00:6d00:c01f:700:1:60:3e11:6770: seq=1, hlim=255, rtt=129.321 ms
64 bytes from 5f00:6d00:c01f:700:1:60:3e11:6770: seq=2, hlim=255, rtt=109.297 ms
64 bytes from 5f00:6d00:c01f:700:1:60:3e11:6770: seq=3, hlim=255, rtt=78.216 ms
```

Figure 25.2 Sample output from our Ping program.

Figure 25.3 is an overview of the functions that comprise our Ping program.

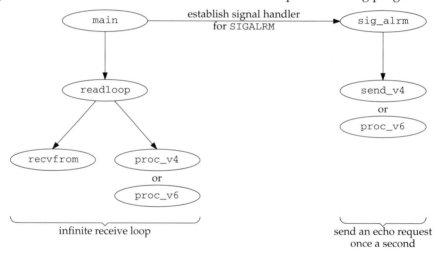

Figure 25.3 Overview of the functions in our Ping program.

The program operates in two parts: one half reads everything received on a raw socket, printing the ICMP echo replies, and the other half sends an ICMP echo request once a second. The second half is driven by a SIGALRM signal once a second.

Figure 25.4 shows our ping.h header that is included by all our program files.

ping/ping.h

```
1 #include    "unp.h"
2 #include    <netinet/in_systm.h>
3 #include    <netinet/ip.h>
4 #include    <netinet/ip_icmp.h>
```

```
 5 #define BUFSIZE      1500

 6               /* globals */
 7 char    recvbuf[BUFSIZE];
 8 char    sendbuf[BUFSIZE];

 9 int     datalen;              /* #bytes of data, following ICMP header */
10 char    *host;
11 int     nsent;               /* add 1 for each sendto() */
12 pid_t   pid;                 /* our PID */
13 int     sockfd;
14 int     verbose;

15               /* function prototypes */
16 void    proc_v4(char *, ssize_t, struct timeval *);
17 void    proc_v6(char *, ssize_t, struct timeval *);
18 void    send_v4(void);
19 void    send_v6(void);
20 void    readloop(void);
21 void    sig_alrm(int);
22 void    tv_sub(struct timeval *, struct timeval *);

23 struct proto {
24     void    (*fproc) (char *, ssize_t, struct timeval *);
25     void    (*fsend) (void);
26     struct sockaddr *sasend;   /* sockaddr{} for send, from getaddrinfo */
27     struct sockaddr *sarecv;   /* sockaddr{} for receiving */
28     socklen_t salen;           /* length of sockaddr{}s */
29     int     icmpproto;         /* IPPROTO_xxx value for ICMP */
30 } *pr;

31 #ifdef  IPV6

32 #include    "ip6.h"           /* should be <netinet/ip6.h> */
33 #include    "icmp6.h"         /* should be <netinet/icmp6.h> */

34 #endif
```
── *ping/ping.h*

Figure 25.4 `ping.h` header.

Include IPv4 and ICMPv4 headers

1–22   We include the basic IPv4 and ICMPv4 headers, define some global variables, and our function prototypes.

Define `proto` structure

23–30   We use the `proto` structure to handle the differences between IPv4 and IPv6. This structure contains two function pointers, two pointers to socket address structures, the size of the socket address structures, and the protocol value for ICMP. The global pointer `pr` will point to one of these structures that we will initialize for either IPv4 or IPv6.

Include IPv6 and ICMPv6 headers

31–34   We include two headers that define the IPv6 and ICMPv6 structures and constants ([Stevens and Thomas 1997]).

The `main` function is shown in Figure 25.5.

```
 1 #include    "ping.h"

 2 struct proto proto_v4 =
 3 {proc_v4, send_v4, NULL, NULL, 0, IPPROTO_ICMP};

 4 #ifdef  IPV6
 5 struct proto proto_v6 =
 6 {proc_v6, send_v6, NULL, NULL, 0, IPPROTO_ICMPV6};
 7 #endif

 8 int     datalen = 56;            /* data that goes with ICMP echo request */

 9 int
10 main(int argc, char **argv)
11 {
12     int     c;
13     struct addrinfo *ai;

14     opterr = 0;                  /* don't want getopt() writing to stderr */
15     while ( (c = getopt(argc, argv, "v")) != -1) {
16         switch (c) {
17         case 'v':
18             verbose++;
19             break;

20         case '?':
21             err_quit("unrecognized option: %c", c);
22         }
23     }

24     if (optind != argc - 1)
25         err_quit("usage: ping [ -v ] <hostname>");
26     host = argv[optind];

27     pid = getpid();
28     Signal(SIGALRM, sig_alrm);

29     ai = Host_serv(host, NULL, 0, 0);

30     printf("PING %s (%s): %d data bytes\n", ai->ai_canonname,
31             Sock_ntop_host(ai->ai_addr, ai->ai_addrlen), datalen);

32         /* initialize according to protocol */
33     if (ai->ai_family == AF_INET) {
34         pr = &proto_v4;
35 #ifdef IPV6
36     } else if (ai->ai_family == AF_INET6) {
37         pr = &proto_v6;
38         if (IN6_IS_ADDR_V4MAPPED(&(((struct sockaddr_in6 *)
39                                 ai->ai_addr)->sin6_addr)))
40             err_quit("cannot ping IPv4-mapped IPv6 address");
41 #endif
42     } else
43         err_quit("unknown address family %d", ai->ai_family);
```

```
44         pr->sasend = ai->ai_addr;
45         pr->sarecv = Calloc(1, ai->ai_addrlen);
46         pr->salen = ai->ai_addrlen;

47         readloop();

48         exit(0);
49 }
```

── *ping/main.c*

Figure 25.5 main function.

Define `proto` structures for IPv4 and IPv6

2-7   We define a `proto` structure for IPv4 and for IPv6. The socket address structure pointers are initialized to null pointers, as we do not yet know whether we will use IPv4 or IPv6.

Length of optional data

8   We set the amount of optional data that gets sent with the ICMP echo request to 56 bytes. This will yield an 84-byte IPv4 datagram (20-byte IPv4 header and 8-byte ICMP header) or a 104-byte IPv6 datagram. Any data that accompanies an echo request must be sent back in the echo reply. We will store the time at which we send an echo request in the first 8 bytes of this data area and then use this to calculate and print the RTT when the echo reply is received.

Handle command-line options

14-28   The only command-line option that we support is –v, which will cause us to print most received ICMP messages. (We do not print echo replies belonging to another copy of Ping that is running.) A signal handler is established for SIGALRM and we will see that this signal is generated once a second and causes an ICMP echo request to be sent.

Process hostname argument

29-46   A hostname or IP address string is a required argument and it is processed by our `host_serv` function. The returned `addrinfo` structure contains the protocol family, either AF_INET or AF_INET6. We initialize the `pr` global to the correct `proto` structure. We also make certain that an IPv6 address is not really an IPv4-mapped IPv6 address by calling IN6_IS_ADDR_V4MAPPED, because even though the returned address is an IPv6 address, IPv4 packets will be sent to the host. (We could switch and use IPv4 when this happens.) The socket address structure that has already been allocated by the `getaddrinfo` function is used as the one for sending, and another socket address structure of the same size is allocated for receiving.

47   The function `readloop` is where the processing takes place, and we show this in Figure 25.6.

Create socket

10-11   A raw socket of the appropriate protocol is created. The call to setuid sets our effective user ID to our real user ID. The program must have superuser privileges to create the raw socket, but now that the socket is created, we can give up the extra privileges. It is always best to give up this extra privilege when it is no longer needed, just in case the program has a latent bug that someone could exploit.

ping/readloop.c

```
 1 #include    "ping.h"

 2 void
 3 readloop(void)
 4 {
 5     int     size;
 6     char    recvbuf[BUFSIZE];
 7     socklen_t len;
 8     ssize_t n;
 9     struct timeval tval;

10     sockfd = Socket(pr->sasend->sa_family, SOCK_RAW, pr->icmpproto);
11     setuid(getuid());           /* don't need special permissions any more */

12     size = 60 * 1024;           /* OK if setsockopt fails */
13     setsockopt(sockfd, SOL_SOCKET, SO_RCVBUF, &size, sizeof(size));

14     sig_alrm(SIGALRM);          /* send first packet */

15     for ( ; ; ) {
16         len = pr->salen;
17         n = recvfrom(sockfd, recvbuf, sizeof(recvbuf), 0, pr->sarecv, &len);
18         if (n < 0) {
19             if (errno == EINTR)
20                 continue;
21             else
22                 err_sys("recvfrom error");
23         }
24         Gettimeofday(&tval, NULL);
25         (*pr->fproc) (recvbuf, n, &tval);
26     }
27 }
```

ping/readloop.c

Figure 25.6 readloop function.

Set socket receive buffer size

12–13   We try to set the socket receive buffer size to 61,440 bytes (60×1024), which should be larger than the default. We do this in case the user pings either the IPv4 broadcast address or a multicast address, either of which can generate lots of replies. By making the buffer larger, there is a smaller chance that the socket receive buffer will overflow.

Send first packet

14   We call our signal handler, which we will see sends a packet and schedules a SIGALRM for 1 second in the future. It is not common to see a signal handler called directly, as we do here, but it is OK. A signal handler is just a C function, even though it is normally called asynchronously by the kernel.

Infinite loop reading all ICMP messages

15–26   The main loop of the program is an infinite loop that reads all packets returned on the raw ICMP socket. We call gettimeofday to record the time that the packet was received and then call the appropriate protocol function (proc_v4 or proc_v6) to process the ICMP message.

Figure 25.8 shows the `proc_v4` function, which processes all received ICMPv4 messages. You may want to refer to Figure A.1, which shows the format of the IPv4 header. Also realize that when the ICMPv4 message is received by the process on the raw socket, the kernel has already verified that the basic fields in the IPv4 header and in the ICMPv4 header are valid (pp. 214 and 311 of TCPv2).

Get pointer to ICMP header

10-14   The IPv4 header length field is multiplied by 4, giving the size of the IPv4 header in bytes. (Remember that an IPv4 header can contain options.) This lets us set `icmp` to point to the beginning of the ICMP header. Figure 25.9 shows the various headers, pointers, and lengths used by the code.

Check for ICMP echo reply

15-19   If the message is an ICMP echo reply, then we must check the identifier field to see if this reply is in response to a request that our process sent. If the Ping program is running multiple times on this host, each process gets a copy of all received ICMP messages.

20-25   We calculate the RTT by subtracting the time the message was sent (contained in the optional data portion of the ICMP reply) from the current time (pointed to by the `tvrecv` function argument). The RTT is converted from microseconds to milliseconds and printed, along with the sequence number field and the received TTL. The sequence number field lets the user see if packets are dropped, reordered, or duplicated, and the TTL gives an indication of the number of hops between the two hosts.

Print all received ICMP messages if verbose option specified

26-30   If the user specified the `-v` command-line option, we print the type and code fields from all other received ICMP messages.

Figure 25.7 shows the `tv_sub` function, which subtracts two `timeval` structures, storing the result in the first structure.

————————————————————————————————— lib/tv_sub.c

```
 1 #include    "unp.h"

 2 void
 3 tv_sub(struct timeval *out, struct timeval *in)
 4 {
 5     if ((out->tv_usec -= in->tv_usec) < 0) {    /* out -= in */
 6         --out->tv_sec;
 7         out->tv_usec += 1000000;
 8     }
 9     out->tv_sec -= in->tv_sec;
10 }
```

————————————————————————————————— lib/tv_sub.c

Figure 25.7 `tv_sub` function: subtract two `timeval` structures.

The processing of ICMPv6 messages is handled by the `proc_v6` function, shown in Figure 25.10 (p. 669). It is similar to the `proc_v4` function.

—————————————————————————————— ping/proc_v4.c

```
 1 #include    "ping.h"

 2 void
 3 proc_v4(char *ptr, ssize_t len, struct timeval *tvrecv)
 4 {
 5     int      hlen1, icmplen;
 6     double   rtt;
 7     struct ip *ip;
 8     struct icmp *icmp;
 9     struct timeval *tvsend;

10     ip = (struct ip *) ptr;       /* start of IP header */
11     hlen1 = ip->ip_hl << 2;       /* length of IP header */

12     icmp = (struct icmp *) (ptr + hlen1);   /* start of ICMP header */
13     if ( (icmplen = len - hlen1) < 8)
14         err_quit("icmplen (%d) < 8", icmplen);

15     if (icmp->icmp_type == ICMP_ECHOREPLY) {
16         if (icmp->icmp_id != pid)
17             return;               /* not a response to our ECHO_REQUEST */
18         if (icmplen < 16)
19             err_quit("icmplen (%d) < 16", icmplen);

20         tvsend = (struct timeval *) icmp->icmp_data;
21         tv_sub(tvrecv, tvsend);
22         rtt = tvrecv->tv_sec * 1000.0 + tvrecv->tv_usec / 1000.0;

23         printf("%d bytes from %s: seq=%u, ttl=%d, rtt=%.3f ms\n",
24                 icmplen, Sock_ntop_host(pr->sarecv, pr->salen),
25                 icmp->icmp_seq, ip->ip_ttl, rtt);

26     } else if (verbose) {
27         printf("  %d bytes from %s: type = %d, code = %d\n",
28                 icmplen, Sock_ntop_host(pr->sarecv, pr->salen),
29                 icmp->icmp_type, icmp->icmp_code);
30     }
31 }
```

—————————————————————————————— ping/proc_v4.c

Figure 25.8 proc_v4 function: process ICMPv4 message.

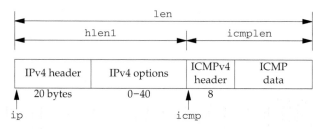

Figure 25.9 Headers, pointers, and lengths in processing ICMPv4 reply.

—————————————————————————— ping/proc_v6.c

```
 1 #include     "ping.h"

 2 void
 3 proc_v6(char *ptr, ssize_t len, struct timeval *tvrecv)
 4 {
 5 #ifdef  IPV6
 6     int     hlen1, icmp6len;
 7     double  rtt;
 8     struct ip6_hdr *ip6;
 9     struct icmp6_hdr *icmp6;
10     struct timeval *tvsend;

11     ip6 = (struct ip6_hdr *) ptr;    /* start of IPv6 header */
12     hlen1 = sizeof(struct ip6_hdr);
13     if (ip6->ip6_nxt != IPPROTO_ICMPV6)
14         err_quit("next header not IPPROTO_ICMPV6");

15     icmp6 = (struct icmp6_hdr *) (ptr + hlen1);
16     if ( (icmp6len = len - hlen1) < 8)
17         err_quit("icmp6len (%d) < 8", icmp6len);

18     if (icmp6->icmp6_type == ICMP6_ECHO_REPLY) {
19         if (icmp6->icmp6_id != pid)
20             return;                  /* not a response to our ECHO_REQUEST */
21         if (icmp6len < 16)
22             err_quit("icmp6len (%d) < 16", icmp6len);

23         tvsend = (struct timeval *) (icmp6 + 1);
24         tv_sub(tvrecv, tvsend);
25         rtt = tvrecv->tv_sec * 1000.0 + tvrecv->tv_usec / 1000.0;

26         printf("%d bytes from %s: seq=%u, hlim=%d, rtt=%.3f ms\n",
27                 icmp6len, Sock_ntop_host(pr->sarecv, pr->salen),
28                 icmp6->icmp6_seq, ip6->ip6_hlim, rtt);

29     } else if (verbose) {
30         printf("  %d bytes from %s: type = %d, code = %d\n",
31                 icmp6len, Sock_ntop_host(pr->sarecv, pr->salen),
32                 icmp6->icmp6_type, icmp6->icmp6_code);
33     }
34 #endif  /* IPV6 */
35 }
```

—————————————————————————— ping/proc_v6.c

Figure 25.10 proc_v6 function: process received ICMPv6 message.

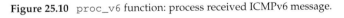
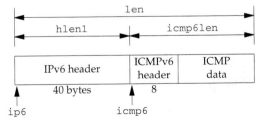

Figure 25.11 Headers, pointers, and lengths in processing ICMPv6 reply.

Get pointer to ICMPv6 header

11-17   The size of the IPv6 header is fixed (40 bytes) and we ensure that the next header is ICMPv6. (Recall that the extension headers, if any, are never returned as normal data, but as ancillary data.) Figure 25.11 shows the various headers, pointers, and lengths used by the code.

Check for ICMP echo reply

18-28   If the ICMP message type is an echo reply, we check the identifier field to see if the reply is for us. If so, we calculate the RTT and then print it along with the sequence number and the IPv6 hop limit.

Print all received ICMP messages if verbose option specified

29-33   If the user specified the -v command-line option, we print the type and code fields from all other received ICMP messages.

> If the -v option is not specified, we could establish an ICMPv6 filter (the ICMP6_FILTER socket option described in Section 25.4) so that only echo replies are returned on our socket by the kernel.

Our signal handler for the SIGALRM signal is the sig_alrm function, shown in Figure 25.12. We saw in Figure 25.6 that our readloop function calls this signal handler once at the beginning to send the first packet. This function just calls the protocol-dependent function to send an ICMP echo request (send_v4 or send_v6) and then schedules another SIGALRM for 1 second in the future.

—— ping/sig_alrm.c

```
1 #include    "ping.h"

2 void
3 sig_alrm(int signo)
4 {
5       (*pr->fsend) ();

6       alarm(1);
7       return;                        /* probably interrupts recvfrom() */
8 }
```

—— ping/sig_alrm.c

Figure 25.12 sig_alrm function: SIGALRM signal handler.

The function send_v4, shown in Figure 25.13, builds an ICMPv4 echo request message and writes it to the raw socket.

Build ICMPv4 message

7-12   The ICMPv4 message is built. The identifier field is set to our process ID and the sequence number field is set to the global nsent, which is then incremented for the next packet. The current time-of-day is stored in the data portion of the ICMP message.

Calculate ICMP checksum

13-15   To calculate the ICMP checksum we set the checksum field to 0 and call the function in_cksum, storing the result in the checksum field. The ICMPv4 checksum is calculated from the ICMPv4 header and any data that follows.

—————————————————————————————————— *ping/send_v4.c*

```
 1 #include    "ping.h"

 2 void
 3 send_v4(void)
 4 {
 5     int     len;
 6     struct icmp *icmp;

 7     icmp = (struct icmp *) sendbuf;
 8     icmp->icmp_type = ICMP_ECHO;
 9     icmp->icmp_code = 0;
10     icmp->icmp_id = pid;
11     icmp->icmp_seq = nsent++;
12     Gettimeofday((struct timeval *) icmp->icmp_data, NULL);

13     len = 8 + datalen;          /* checksum ICMP header and data */
14     icmp->icmp_cksum = 0;
15     icmp->icmp_cksum = in_cksum((u_short *) icmp, len);

16     Sendto(sockfd, sendbuf, len, 0, pr->sasend, pr->salen);
17 }
```
—————————————————————————————————— *ping/send_v4.c*

Figure 25.13 send_v4 function: build an ICMPv4 echo request message and send it.

Send datagram

16   The ICMP message is sent on the raw socket. Since we have not set the IP_HDRINCL socket option, the kernel builds the IPv4 header and prepends it to our buffer.

The Internet checksum is the ones-complement sum of the 16-bit values to be check-summed. If the data length is an odd number, then 1 byte of 0 is logically appended to the end of the data, just for the checksum computation. This algorithm is used for the IPv4, ICMPv4, IGMPv4, ICMPv6, UDP, and TCP checksums. RFC 1071 [Braden, Borman, and Partridge 1988] contains additional information and some numerical examples. Section 8.7 of TCPv2 talks about this algorithm in more detail and shows a more efficient implementation. Our in_cksum function, shown in Figure 25.14, calculates the checksum.

Internet checksum algorithm

1–27   The first while loop calculates the sum of all the 16-bit values. If the length is odd, then the final byte is added in to the sum. The algorithm that we show in Figure 25.14 is the simple algorithm, fine for a Ping program, but inadequate for the high volume of checksum computations performed by the kernel.

This function is taken from the public domain version of Ping.

The final function for our Ping program is send_v6, shown in Figure 25.15 (p. 673), which builds and sends an ICMPv6 echo request.

—————————————————————————————— libfree/in_cksum.c

```
 1 unsigned short
 2 in_cksum(unsigned short *addr, int len)
 3 {
 4     int    nleft = len;
 5     int    sum = 0;
 6     unsigned short *w = addr;
 7     unsigned short answer = 0;

 8     /*
 9      * Our algorithm is simple, using a 32 bit accumulator (sum), we add
10      * sequential 16 bit words to it, and at the end, fold back all the
11      * carry bits from the top 16 bits into the lower 16 bits.
12      */
13     while (nleft > 1) {
14         sum += *w++;
15         nleft -= 2;
16     }

17         /* mop up an odd byte, if necessary */
18     if (nleft == 1) {
19         *(unsigned char *) (&answer) = *(unsigned char *) w;
20         sum += answer;
21     }
22         /* add back carry outs from top 16 bits to low 16 bits */
23     sum = (sum >> 16) + (sum & 0xffff);    /* add hi 16 to low 16 */
24     sum += (sum >> 16);         /* add carry */
25     answer = ~sum;              /* truncate to 16 bits */
26     return (answer);
27 }
```

—————————————————————————————— libfree/in_cksum.c

Figure 25.14 in_cksum function: calculate the Internet checksum.

The send_v6 function is similar to send_v4, but notice that it does not compute the ICMPv6 checksum. As we mentioned earlier in the chapter, since the ICMPv6 checksum uses the source address from the IPv6 header in its computation, this checksum is calculated by the kernel for us, after the kernel chooses the source address.

25.6 Traceroute Program

In this section we develop our own version of the Traceroute program. Like the Ping program that we developed in the previous section, we develop and present our own version, instead of presenting the publicly available version. We do this because we need a version that supports both IPv4 and IPv6, and we do not want to be distracted with lots of options that are not germane to our discussion of network programming.

Traceroute lets us determine the path that IP datagrams follow from our host to some other destination. Its operation is simple and Chapter 8 of TCPv1 covers it in

ping/send_v6.c

```
 1 #include    "ping.h"

 2 void
 3 send_v6()
 4 {
 5 #ifdef  IPV6
 6     int    len;
 7     struct icmp6_hdr *icmp6;

 8     icmp6 = (struct icmp6_hdr *) sendbuf;
 9     icmp6->icmp6_type = ICMP6_ECHO_REQUEST;
10     icmp6->icmp6_code = 0;
11     icmp6->icmp6_id = pid;
12     icmp6->icmp6_seq = nsent++;
13     Gettimeofday((struct timeval *) (icmp6 + 1), NULL);

14     len = 8 + datalen;            /* 8-byte ICMPv6 header */

15     Sendto(sockfd, sendbuf, len, 0, pr->sasend, pr->salen);
16         /* kernel calculates and stores checksum for us */
17 #endif  /* IPV6 */
18 }
```

ping/send_v6.c

Figure 25.15 send_v6 function: build and send an ICMPv6 echo request message.

detail with numerous examples of its usage. Traceroute uses the IPv4 TTL field or the IPv6 hop limit field and two ICMP messages. It starts by sending a UDP datagram to the destination with a TTL (or hop limit) of 1. This datagram causes the first hop router to return an ICMP "time exceeded in transit" error. The TTL is then increased by one and another UDP datagram sent, which locates the next router in the path. When the UDP datagram reaches the final destination, the goal is to have that host return an ICMP "port unreachable" error. This is done by sending the UDP datagram to a random port that is (hopefully) not in use on that host.

Early versions of Traceroute were able to set the TTL field in the IPv4 header only by setting the IP_HDRINCL socket option and then building its own IPv4 header. Current systems, however, provide the IP_TTL socket option that lets us specify the TTL to use for outgoing datagrams. (This socket option was introduced with the 4.3BSD Reno release.) It is easier to set this socket option than to build a complete IPv4 header (although we show how to build our own IPv4 and UDP headers in Section 26.6). The IPv6 IPV6_UNICAST_HOPS socket option lets us control the hop limit field for IPv6 datagrams.

Figure 25.16 shows our trace.h header, which all of our program files include.

1–11   We include the standard IPv4 headers that define the IPv4, ICMPv4, and UDP structures and constants. The rec structure defines the data portion of the UDP datagram that we send, but we will see that we never need to examine this data. It is sent mainly for debugging purposes.

traceroute/trace.h

```
 1 #include    "unp.h"
 2 #include    <netinet/in_systm.h>
 3 #include    <netinet/ip.h>
 4 #include    <netinet/ip_icmp.h>
 5 #include    <netinet/udp.h>

 6 #define BUFSIZE     1500

 7 struct rec {                    /* of outgoing UDP data */
 8     u_short rec_seq;            /* sequence number */
 9     u_short rec_ttl;            /* TTL packet left with */
10     struct timeval rec_tv;      /* time packet left */
11 };

12            /* globals */
13 char    recvbuf[BUFSIZE];
14 char    sendbuf[BUFSIZE];

15 int     datalen;                /* #bytes of data, following ICMP header */
16 char    *host;
17 u_short sport, dport;
18 int     nsent;                  /* add 1 for each sendto() */
19 pid_t   pid;                    /* our PID */
20 int     probe, nprobes;
21 int     sendfd, recvfd;         /* send on UDP sock, read on raw ICMP sock */
22 int     ttl, max_ttl;
23 int     verbose;

24            /* function prototypes */
25 char    *icmpcode_v4(int);
26 char    *icmpcode_v6(int);
27 int     recv_v4(int, struct timeval *);
28 int     recv_v6(int, struct timeval *);
29 void    sig_alrm(int);
30 void    traceloop(void);
31 void    tv_sub(struct timeval *, struct timeval *);

32 struct proto {
33     char    *(*icmpcode) (int);
34     int     (*recv) (int, struct timeval *);
35     struct sockaddr *sasend;    /* sockaddr{} for send, from getaddrinfo */
36     struct sockaddr *sarecv;    /* sockaddr{} for receiving */
37     struct sockaddr *salast;    /* last sockaddr{} for receiving */
38     struct sockaddr *sabind;    /* sockaddr{} for binding source port */
39     socklen_t salen;            /* length of sockaddr{}s */
40     int     icmpproto;          /* IPPROTO_xxx value for ICMP */
41     int     ttllevel;           /* setsockopt() level to set TTL */
42     int     ttloptname;         /* setsockopt() name to set TTL */
43 } *pr;

44 #ifdef  IPV6

45 #include    "ip6.h"             /* should be <netinet/ip6.h> */
46 #include    "icmp6.h"           /* should be <netinet/icmp6.h> */

47 #endif
```

traceroute/trace.h

Figure 25.16 trace.h header.

Define `proto` structure

32–43   As with our Ping program in the previous section, we handle the protocol differences between IPv4 and IPv6 by defining a `proto` structure that contains function pointers, pointers to socket address structures, and other constants that differ between the two IP versions. The global `pr` will be set to point to one of these structures that is initialized for either IPv4 or IPv6, after the destination address is processed by the `main` function (since the destination address is what specifies whether we use IPv4 or IPv6).

Include IPv6 headers

44–47   We include the headers that define the IPv6 and ICMPv6 structures and constants.

The `main` function is shown in Figure 25.17. It processes the command-line arguments, initializes the `pr` pointer for either IPv4 or IPv6, and calls our `traceloop` function.

traceroute/main.c

```
 1 #include     "trace.h"

 2 struct proto proto_v4 =
 3 {icmpcode_v4, recv_v4, NULL, NULL, NULL, NULL, 0,
 4  IPPROTO_ICMP, IPPROTO_IP, IP_TTL};

 5 #ifdef  IPV6
 6 struct proto proto_v6 =
 7 {icmpcode_v6, recv_v6, NULL, NULL, NULL, NULL, 0,
 8  IPPROTO_ICMPV6, IPPROTO_IPV6, IPV6_UNICAST_HOPS};
 9 #endif

10 int     datalen = sizeof(struct rec);   /* defaults */
11 int     max_ttl = 30;
12 int     nprobes = 3;
13 u_short dport = 32768 + 666;

14 int
15 main(int argc, char **argv)
16 {
17      int     c;
18      struct addrinfo *ai;

19      opterr = 0;                    /* don't want getopt() writing to stderr */
20      while ( (c = getopt(argc, argv, "m:v")) != -1) {
21          switch (c) {
22          case 'm':
23              if ( (max_ttl = atoi(optarg)) <= 1)
24                  err_quit("invalid -m value");
25              break;

26          case 'v':
27              verbose++;
28              break;

29          case '?':
30              err_quit("unrecognized option: %c", c);
31          }
32      }
```

```
33      if (optind != argc - 1)
34          err_quit("usage: traceroute [ -m <maxttl> -v ] <hostname>");
35      host = argv[optind];

36      pid = getpid();
37      Signal(SIGALRM, sig_alrm);

38      ai = Host_serv(host, NULL, 0, 0);

39      printf("traceroute to %s (%s): %d hops max, %d data bytes\n",
40              ai->ai_canonname,
41              Sock_ntop_host(ai->ai_addr, ai->ai_addrlen),
42              max_ttl, datalen);

43      /* initialize according to protocol */
44      if (ai->ai_family == AF_INET) {
45          pr = &proto_v4;
46 #ifdef  IPV6
47      } else if (ai->ai_family == AF_INET6) {
48          pr = &proto_v6;
49          if (IN6_IS_ADDR_V4MAPPED(&(((struct sockaddr_in6 *) ai->ai_addr)->sin6_add
50              err_quit("cannot ping IPv4-mapped IPv6 address");
51 #endif
52      } else
53          err_quit("unknown address family %d", ai->ai_family);

54      pr->sasend = ai->ai_addr;    /* contains destination address */
55      pr->sarecv = Calloc(1, ai->ai_addrlen);
56      pr->salast = Calloc(1, ai->ai_addrlen);
57      pr->sabind = Calloc(1, ai->ai_addrlen);
58      pr->salen = ai->ai_addrlen;

59      traceloop();

60      exit(0);
61 }
```
                                                              — *traceroute/main.c*

Figure 25.17 main function for Traceroute program.

Define `proto` structures

2–9   We define the two `proto` structures, one for IPv4 and one for IPv6, although the pointers to the socket address structures are not allocated until the end of this function.

Set defaults

10–13   The maximum TTL or hop limit that the program uses defaults to 30, although we provide the −m command-line option to let the user change this. For each TTL we send three probe packets, but this could be changed with another command-line option. The initial destination port is 32768 + 666 and this will be incremented by one each time we send a UDP datagram. We hope that these ports are not in use on the destination host when the datagrams finally reach the destination, but there is no guarantee.

Process command-line arguments

19–37   The −v command-line option causes most received ICMP messages to be printed.

Process hostname or IP address argument and finish initialization

38-58   The destination hostname or IP address is processed by our host_serv function, returning a pointer to an addrinfo structure. Depending on the type of returned address, IPv4 or IPv6, we finish initializing the proto structure, store the pointer in the pr global, and allocate additional socket address structures of the correct size.

59   The function traceloop, shown in Figure 25.18, sends the datagrams and reads the returned ICMP messages. This is the main loop of the program.

Create two sockets

9-11   We need two sockets: a raw socket on which we read all returned ICMP messages and a UDP socket on which we send the probe packets with the increasing TTLs. After creating the raw socket, we reset our effective user ID to our real user ID, since we no longer require superuser privileges.

Bind source port of UDP socket

12-15   We bind a source port to the UDP socket that is used for sending, using the low-order 15 bits of our process ID with the high-order bit set to 1. Since it is possible for multiple copies of the Traceroute program to be running at any given time, we need a way to determine if a received ICMP message was generated in response to one of our datagrams, or in response to a datagram sent by another copy of the program. We use the source port in the UDP header to identify the sending process because the returned ICMP message always returns the UDP header from the datagram that caused the ICMP error.

Establish signal handler for SIGALRM

16   We establish our function sig_alrm as the signal handler for SIGALRM because each time we send a UDP datagram we wait 3 seconds for an ICMP message before sending the next probe.

———————————————————————————————————— *traceroute/traceloop.c*

```
 1 #include    "trace.h"

 2 void
 3 traceloop(void)
 4 {
 5     int     seq, code, done;
 6     double  rtt;
 7     struct rec *rec;
 8     struct timeval tvrecv;

 9     recvfd = Socket(pr->sasend->sa_family, SOCK_RAW, pr->icmpproto);
10     setuid(getuid());             /* don't need special permissions any more */

11     sendfd = Socket(pr->sasend->sa_family, SOCK_DGRAM, 0);

12     pr->sabind->sa_family = pr->sasend->sa_family;
13     sport = (getpid() & 0xffff) | 0x8000;   /* our source UDP port# */
14     sock_set_port(pr->sabind, pr->salen, htons(sport));
15     Bind(sendfd, pr->sabind, pr->salen);

16     sig_alrm(SIGALRM);
```

```
17        seq = 0;
18        done = 0;
19        for (ttl = 1; ttl <= max_ttl && done == 0; ttl++) {
20            Setsockopt(sendfd, pr->ttllevel, pr->ttloptname, &ttl, sizeof(int));
21            bzero(pr->salast, pr->salen);

22            printf("%2d  ", ttl);
23            fflush(stdout);

24            for (probe = 0; probe < nprobes; probe++) {
25                rec = (struct rec *) sendbuf;
26                rec->rec_seq = ++seq;
27                rec->rec_ttl = ttl;
28                Gettimeofday(&rec->rec_tv, NULL);

29                sock_set_port(pr->sasend, pr->salen, htons(dport + seq));
30                Sendto(sendfd, sendbuf, datalen, 0, pr->sasend, pr->salen);

31                if ( (code = (*pr->recv) (seq, &tvrecv)) == -3)
32                    printf(" *");    /* timeout, no reply */
33                else {
34                    char    str[NI_MAXHOST];

35                    if (sock_cmp_addr(pr->sarecv, pr->salast, pr->salen) != 0) {
36                        if (getnameinfo(pr->sarecv, pr->salen, str, sizeof(str),
37                                        NULL, 0, 0) == 0)
38                            printf(" %s (%s)", str,
39                                    Sock_ntop_host(pr->sarecv, pr->salen));
40                        else
41                            printf(" %s",
42                                    Sock_ntop_host(pr->sarecv, pr->salen));
43                        memcpy(pr->salast, pr->sarecv, pr->salen);
44                    }
45                    tv_sub(&tvrecv, &rec->rec_tv);
46                    rtt = tvrecv.tv_sec * 1000.0 + tvrecv.tv_usec / 1000.0;
47                    printf("  %.3f ms", rtt);

48                    if (code == -1) /* port unreachable; at destination */
49                        done++;
50                    else if (code >= 0)
51                        printf(" (ICMP %s)", (*pr->icmpcode) (code));
52                }
53                fflush(stdout);
54            }
55            printf("\n");
56        }
57 }
```
—— traceroute/traceloop.c

Figure 25.18 `traceloop` function: main processing loop.

Main loop; set TTL or hop limit and send three probes

17–28   The main loop of the function is a double nested `for` loop. The outer loop starts the
TTL or hop limit at 1, and increases it by 1, while the inner loop sends three probes
(UDP datagrams) to the destination. Each time the TTL changes, we call `setsockopt`
to set the new value using either the `IP_TTL` or `IPV6_UNICAST_HOPS` socket option.

Each time around the outer loop we initialize the socket address structure pointed to by `salast` to 0. This structure will be compared to the socket address structure returned by `recvfrom` when the ICMP message is read, and if the two structures are different, the IP address from the new structure is printed. Using this technique the IP address corresponding to the first probe for each TTL is printed, and should the IP address change for a given value of the TTL (say a route changes while we are running the program) the new IP address is then printed.

Set destination port and send UDP datagram

29-30   Each time a probe packet is sent, the destination port in the `sasend` socket address structure is changed by calling our `sock_set_port` function. The reason for changing the port for each probe is that when we reach the final destination, all three probes are sent to a different port, and hopefully at least one of the ports is not in use. `sendto` sends the UDP datagram.

Read ICMP message

31-53   One of our functions `recv_v4` or `recv_v6` calls `recvfrom` to read and process the ICMP messages that are returned. These two functions return −3 if a timeout occurs (telling us to send another probe if we haven't sent three for this TTL), −2 if an ICMP "time exceeded in transit" error is received, −1 if an ICMP "port unreachable" error is received (which means we have reached the final destination), or the nonnegative ICMP code if some other ICMP destination unreachable error is received.

Print reply

33-53   As we mentioned earlier, if this is the first reply for a given TTL, or if the IP address of the node sending the ICMP message has changed for this TTL, we print the hostname and IP address, or just the IP address (if the call to `getnameinfo` doesn't return the hostname). The RTT is calculated as the time difference from when we sent the probe to the time the ICMP message is returned and printed.

Our `recv_v4` function is shown in Figure 25.19.

―――――――――――――――――――――――――――――――――――― *traceroute/recv_v4.c*

```
 1 #include     "trace.h"

 2 /*
 3  * Return: -3 on timeout
 4  *            -2 on ICMP time exceeded in transit (caller keeps going)
 5  *            -1 on ICMP port unreachable (caller is done)
 6  *         >= 0 return value is some other ICMP unreachable code
 7  */

 8 int
 9 recv_v4(int seq, struct timeval *tv)
10 {
11     int      hlen1, hlen2, icmplen;
12     socklen_t len;
13     ssize_t n;
14     struct ip *ip, *hip;
15     struct icmp *icmp;
16     struct udphdr *udp;
```

```
17      alarm(3);
18      for ( ; ; ) {
19          len = pr->salen;
20          n = recvfrom(recvfd, recvbuf, sizeof(recvbuf), 0, pr->sarecv, &len);
21          if (n < 0) {
22              if (errno == EINTR)
23                  return (-3);     /* alarm expired */
24              else
25                  err_sys("recvfrom error");
26          }
27          Gettimeofday(tv, NULL); /* get time of packet arrival */

28          ip = (struct ip *) recvbuf;      /* start of IP header */
29          hlen1 = ip->ip_hl << 2; /* length of IP header */

30          icmp = (struct icmp *) (recvbuf + hlen1);   /* start of ICMP header */
31          if ( (icmplen = n - hlen1) < 8)
32              err_quit("icmplen (%d) < 8", icmplen);

33          if (icmp->icmp_type == ICMP_TIMXCEED &&
34              icmp->icmp_code == ICMP_TIMXCEED_INTRANS) {
35              if (icmplen < 8 + 20 + 8)
36                  err_quit("icmplen (%d) < 8 + 20 + 8", icmplen);

37              hip = (struct ip *) (recvbuf + hlen1 + 8);
38              hlen2 = hip->ip_hl << 2;
39              udp = (struct udphdr *) (recvbuf + hlen1 + 8 + hlen2);
40              if (hip->ip_p == IPPROTO_UDP &&
41                  udp->uh_sport == htons(sport) &&
42                  udp->uh_dport == htons(dport + seq))
43                  return (-2);     /* we hit an intermediate router */

44          } else if (icmp->icmp_type == ICMP_UNREACH) {
45              if (icmplen < 8 + 20 + 8)
46                  err_quit("icmplen (%d) < 8 + 20 + 8", icmplen);

47              hip = (struct ip *) (recvbuf + hlen1 + 8);
48              hlen2 = hip->ip_hl << 2;
49              udp = (struct udphdr *) (recvbuf + hlen1 + 8 + hlen2);
50              if (hip->ip_p == IPPROTO_UDP &&
51                  udp->uh_sport == htons(sport) &&
52                  udp->uh_dport == htons(dport + seq)) {
53                  if (icmp->icmp_code == ICMP_UNREACH_PORT)
54                      return (-1);     /* have reached destination */
55                  else
56                      return (icmp->icmp_code);   /* 0, 1, 2, ... */
57              }
58          } else if (verbose) {
59              printf(" (from %s: type = %d, code = %d)\n",
60                      Sock_ntop_host(pr->sarecv, pr->salen),
61                      icmp->icmp_type, icmp->icmp_code);
62          }
63          /* Some other ICMP error, recvfrom() again */
64      }
65  }
```

traceroute/recv_v4.c

Figure 25.19 `recv_v4` function: read and process ICMPv4 messages.

Set alarm and read each ICMP message

17–27   An alarm is set for 3 seconds in the future and the function enters a loop that calls `recvfrom`, reading each ICMPv4 message returned on the raw socket.

> This function contains the same race condition that we described in Section 18.5 with regard to a `SIGALRM` interrupting a read operation.

Get pointer to ICMP header

28–32   `ip` points to the beginning of the IPv4 header (recall that a read on a raw socket always returns the IP header), and `icmp` points to the beginning of the ICMP header. Figure 25.20 shows the various headers, pointers, and lengths used by the code.

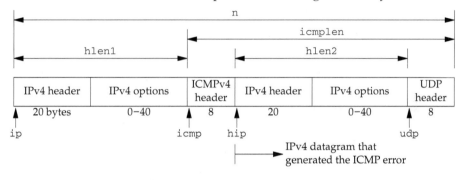

Figure 25.20 Headers, pointers, and lengths in processing ICMPv4 error.

Process ICMP time exceeded in transit message

33–43   If the ICMP message is a "time exceeded in transit" message, it is possibly a reply to one of our probes. `hip` points to the IPv4 header that is returned in the ICMP message, following the 8-byte ICMP header. `udp` points to the UDP header that follows. If the ICMP message was generated by a UDP datagram and if the source and destination ports of that datagram are the values that we sent, then this is a reply to our probe from an intermediate router.

Process ICMP port unreachable message

44–57   If the ICMP message is a "destination unreachable," then we look at the UDP header returned in the ICMP message to see if the message is a response to our probe. If so, and if the ICMP code is "port unreachable" we return −1 as we have reached the final destination. If the ICMP message is from one of our probes, but it is not a "port unreachable," then that ICMP code value is returned. A common example of this is a firewall returning some other unreachable code for the destination host that we are probing.

Handle other ICMP messages

58–62   All other ICMP messages are printed if the `-v` flag was specified.

The next function, `recv_v6`, is shown in Figure 25.22 and is the IPv6 equivalent to the previously described function. This function is nearly identical to `recv_v4`, except for the different constant names and the different structure member names. Also, the size of the IPv6 header is a fixed 40 bytes, while with IPv4 we had to fetch the header length field and multiply it by 4 to account for any IP options. Figure 25.21 shows the various headers, pointers, and lengths used by the code.

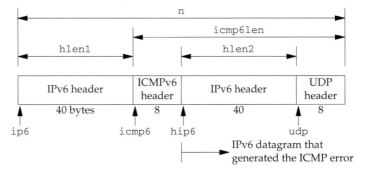

Figure 25.21 Headers, pointers, and lengths in processing ICMPv6 error.

We define two functions, `icmpcode_v4` and `icmpcode_v6`, that can be called from the bottom of the `traceloop` function to print a description string corresponding to an ICMP destination unreachable error. Figure 25.23 (p. 684) shows just the IPv6 function. The IPv4 function is similar, albeit longer, as there are more ICMPv4 destination unreachable codes (Figure A.15).

The final function in our Traceroute program is our SIGALRM handler, the `sig_alrm` function shown in Figure 25.24 (p. 684). All this function does is return, causing an error return of EINTR from the `recvfrom` in either `recv_v4` or `recv_v6`.

traceroute/recv_v6.c
```
 1 #include    "trace.h"

 2 /*
 3  * Return: -3 on timeout
 4  *          -2 on ICMP time exceeded in transit (caller keeps going)
 5  *          -1 on ICMP port unreachable (caller is done)
 6  *       >= 0 return value is some other ICMP unreachable code
 7  */

 8 int
 9 recv_v6(int seq, struct timeval *tv)
10 {
11 #ifdef  IPV6
12     int     hlen1, hlen2, icmp6len;
13     ssize_t n;
14     socklen_t len;
15     struct ip6_hdr *ip6, *hip6;
16     struct icmp6_hdr *icmp6;
17     struct udphdr *udp;

18     alarm(3);
```

```
19      for ( ; ; ) {
20          len = pr->salen;
21          n = recvfrom(recvfd, recvbuf, sizeof(recvbuf), 0, pr->sarecv, &len);
22          if (n < 0) {
23              if (errno == EINTR)
24                  return (-3);    /* alarm expired */
25              else
26                  err_sys("recvfrom error");
27          }
28          Gettimeofday(tv, NULL); /* get time of packet arrival */

29          ip6 = (struct ip6_hdr *) recvbuf;   /* start of IPv6 header */
30          hlen1 = sizeof(struct ip6_hdr);

31          icmp6 = (struct icmp6_hdr *) (recvbuf + hlen1);     /* ICMP hdr */
32          if ( (icmp6len = n - hlen1) < 8)
33              err_quit("icmp6len (%d) < 8", icmp6len);

34          if (icmp6->icmp6_type == ICMP6_TIME_EXCEEDED &&
35              icmp6->icmp6_code == ICMP6_TIME_EXCEED_TRANSIT) {
36              if (icmp6len < 8 + 40 + 8)
37                  err_quit("icmp6len (%d) < 8 + 40 + 8", icmp6len);

38              hip6 = (struct ip6_hdr *) (recvbuf + hlen1 + 8);
39              hlen2 = sizeof(struct ip6_hdr);
40              udp = (struct udphdr *) (recvbuf + hlen1 + 8 + hlen2);
41              if (hip6->ip6_nxt == IPPROTO_UDP &&
42                  udp->uh_sport == htons(sport) &&
43                  udp->uh_dport == htons(dport + seq))
44                  return (-2);    /* we hit an intermediate router */

45          } else if (icmp6->icmp6_type == ICMP6_DST_UNREACH) {
46              if (icmp6len < 8 + 40 + 8)
47                  err_quit("icmp6len (%d) < 8 + 40 + 8", icmp6len);

48              hip6 = (struct ip6_hdr *) (recvbuf + hlen1 + 8);
49              hlen2 = 40;
50              udp = (struct udphdr *) (recvbuf + hlen1 + 8 + hlen2);
51              if (hip6->ip6_nxt == IPPROTO_UDP &&
52                  udp->uh_sport == htons(sport) &&
53                  udp->uh_dport == htons(dport + seq)) {
54                  if (icmp6->icmp6_code == ICMP6_DST_UNREACH_NOPORT)
55                      return (-1);    /* have reached destination */
56                  else
57                      return (icmp6->icmp6_code);     /* 0, 1, 2, ... */
58              }
59          } else if (verbose) {
60              printf(" (from %s: type = %d, code = %d)\n",
61                      Sock_ntop_host(pr->sarecv, pr->salen),
62                      icmp6->icmp6_type, icmp6->icmp6_code);
63          }
64          /* Some other ICMP error, recvfrom() again */
65      }
66 #endif
67 }
```
——— *traceroute/recv_v6.c*

Figure 25.22 `recv_v6` function: read and process ICMPv6 messages.

—————————————————————————————— traceroute/icmpcode_v6.c

```
 1 #include     "trace.h"

 2 char *
 3 icmpcode_v6(int code)
 4 {
 5     switch (code) {
 6     case ICMP6_DST_UNREACH_NOROUTE:
 7         return ("no route to host");
 8     case ICMP6_DST_UNREACH_ADMIN:
 9         return ("administratively prohibited");
10     case ICMP6_DST_UNREACH_NOTNEIGHBOR:
11         return ("not a neighbor");
12     case ICMP6_DST_UNREACH_ADDR:
13         return ("address unreachable");
14     case ICMP6_DST_UNREACH_NOPORT:
15         return ("port unreachable");
16     default:
17         return ("[unknown code]");
18     }
19 }
```
—————————————————————————————— traceroute/icmpcode_v6.c

Figure 25.23   Return the string corresponding to an ICMPv6 unreachable code.

—————————————————————————————— traceroute/sig_alrm.c

```
 1 #include     "trace.h"

 2 void
 3 sig_alrm(int signo)
 4 {
 5     return;                    /* just interrupt the recvfrom() */
 6 }
```
—————————————————————————————— traceroute/sig_alrm.c

Figure 25.24   `sig_alrm` function.

Example

We first show an example using IPv4:

```
solaris # traceroute gemini.tuc.noao.edu
traceroute to gemini.tuc.noao.edu (140.252.3.54): 30 hops max, 12 data bytes
 1 gw.kohala.com (206.62.226.62)  3.839 ms  3.595 ms  3.722 ms
 2 tuc-1-s1-9.rtd.net (206.85.40.73)  42.014 ms  21.078 ms  18.826 ms
 3 frame-gw.ttn.ep.net (198.32.152.9)  39.283 ms  24.598 ms  50.037 ms
 4 tucson-nap-1.arizona.edu (198.32.152.248)  44.350 ms  78.109 ms  47.003 ms
 5 Butch-ENET-BONE.Telcom.Arizona.EDU (128.196.11.5)  29.849 ms  46.664 ms  83.571 ms
 6 gateway.tuc.noao.edu (140.252.104.1)  37.376 ms  36.430 ms  30.555 ms
 7 gemini.tuc.noao.edu (140.252.3.54)  70.476 ms  43.555 ms  88.716 ms
```

Here is an example using IPv6. We have wrapped the long lines for a more readable output.

```
solaris # traceroute ipng9.ipng.nist.gov
traceroute to ipng9.ipng.nist.gov (5f00:3100:8106:3300:0:c0:3302:5a):
30 hops max, 12 data bytes
 1    6bone-router.cisco.inner.net (5f00:6d00:c01f:700:1:60:3e11:6770)
               185.869 ms *  127.082 ms
 2    buzzcut.ipv6.nrl.navy.mil (5f00:3000:84fa:5a00::5)
               187.736 ms  199.455 ms  172.839 ms
 3    ipng9.ipng.nist.gov (5f00:3100:8106:3300:0:c0:3302:5a)
               206.762 ms *  441.081 ms
```

In this example the second probe with a hop limit of 1 timed out, as did the second probe with a hop limit of 3.

25.7 An ICMP Message Daemon

Receiving asynchronous ICMP errors on a UDP socket has been, and continues to be, a problem. The ICMP errors are received by the kernel but are rarely delivered to the application that needs to know. In the sockets API we have seen that it requires connecting the UDP socket to one IP address to receive these errors (Section 8.11). The reason for this limitation is that the only error return from `recvfrom` is an integer `errno` code, and if the application sends datagrams to multiple destinations and then calls `recvfrom`, this function cannot tell the application which datagram encountered an error.

We will see in Section 31.4 that XTI improves on this (slightly) by returning an error from its equivalent of `recvfrom` and then the application must call another function (`t_rcvuderr`) to obtain the actual error and the destination address and port number from the datagram that caused the error. The problem with this solution, however, is that the kernel probably keeps information on only one of these asynchronous errors at a time. If the application sends (say) three datagrams, and two elicit ICMP errors, only one is returned to the application.

In this section we provide a different solution that does not require any kernel changes. We provide an ICMP message daemon, `icmpd`, that creates a raw ICMPv4 socket and a raw ICMPv6 socket and receives all ICMP messages that the kernel passes these two raw sockets. It also creates a Unix domain stream socket, `binds` it to the pathname `/tmp/icmpd`, and listens for incoming client `connects` to this pathname. We show this in Figure 25.25.

A UDP application (which is a client to the daemon) first creates its UDP socket, the socket for which it wants to receive asynchronous errors. The application must `bind` an ephemeral port to this socket, for reasons we discuss later. It then creates a Unix domain socket and `connects` to this daemon's well-known pathname. We show this in Figure 25.26.

The application then "passes" its UDP socket to the daemon across the Unix domain connection using *descriptor passing*, as we described in Section 14.7. This gives the daemon a copy of the socket so that it can call `getsockname` and obtain the port number bound to the socket. We show this passing of the socket in Figure 25.27.

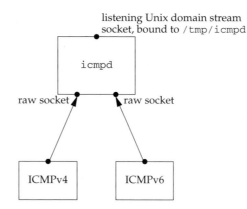

Figure 25.25   icmpd daemon: initial sockets created.

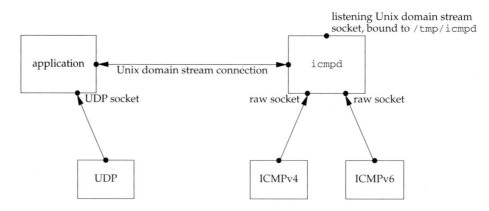

Figure 25.26   Application creates its UDP socket and a Unix domain connection to the daemon.

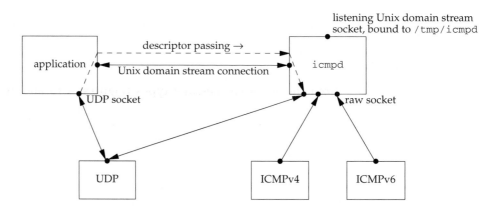

Figure 25.27   Passing UDP socket to daemon across Unix domain connection.

After the daemon obtains the port number bound to the UDP socket, it closes its copy of the socket, taking us back to the arrangement shown in Figure 25.26.

> If the host supports credential passing (Section 14.8), the application could also send its credentials to the daemon. The daemon could then check whether this user should be allowed access to this facility.

From this point on any ICMP errors that the daemon receives that are in response to UDP datagrams sent from the port bound to the application's UDP socket cause the daemon to send a message (which we describe shortly) across the Unix domain socket to the application. The application must therefore use `select` or `poll` awaiting data on either the UDP socket or the Unix domain socket.

We now look at the source code for an application using this daemon, and then the daemon itself. We start with Figure 25.28, our header that is included by both the application and the daemon.

—————————————————————————————————————— icmpd/unpicmpd.h

```
 1 #ifndef __unpicmp_h
 2 #define __unpicmp_h

 3 #include    "unp.h"

 4 #define ICMPD_PATH        "/tmp/icmpd"     /* server's well-known pathname */

 5 struct icmpd_err {
 6     int     icmpd_errno;          /* EHOSTUNREACH, EMSGSIZE, ECONNREFUSED */
 7     char    icmpd_type;           /* actual ICMPv[46] type */
 8     char    icmpd_code;           /* actual ICMPv[46] code */
 9     socklen_t icmpd_len;          /* length of sockaddr{} that follows */
10     struct sockaddr icmpd_dest;   /* may be bigger */
11     char    icmpd_fill[MAXSOCKADDR - sizeof(struct sockaddr)];
12 };

13 #endif   /* __unpicmp_h */
```

—————————————————————————————————————— icmpd/unpicmpd.h

Figure 25.28 `unpicmpd.h` header.

4–12   We define the server's well-known pathname and the `icmpd_err` structure that is passed from the server to the application whenever an ICMP message is received that should be passed to this application.

6–8   A problem is that the ICMPv4 message types differ numerically (and sometimes conceptually) from the ICMPv6 message types (Figures A.15 and A.16). The actual ICMP *type* and *code* values are returned, but we also map these into an `errno` value (`icmpd_errno`), similar to the final column in Figures A.15 and A.16. The application can deal with this value, instead of the protocol-dependent ICMPv4 or ICMPv6 values. Figure 25.29 shows the ICMP messages that are handled, and their mapping into an `errno` value. The daemon returns five types of ICMP errors.

   1. Port unreachable, indicating that no socket is bound to the destination port at the destination IP address.

icmpd_errno	ICMPv4 error	ICMPv6 error
ECONNREFUSED	port unreachable	port unreachable
EMSGSIZE	fragmentation needed but DF set	packet too big
EHOSTUNREACH	time exceeded	time exceeded
EHOSTUNREACH	source quench	
EHOSTUNREACH	all other destination unreachables	all other destination unreachables

Figure 25.29 `icmpd_errno` mapping from ICMPv4 and ICMPv6 errors.

2. Packet too big, which is used with path MTU discovery. Currently there is no API defined to allow a UDP application to perform path MTU discovery. What often happens on kernels that support path MTU discovery for UDP is the receipt of this ICMP error causes the kernel to record the new path MTU value in the kernel's routing table, but the UDP application that sent the datagram that got discarded is not notified. Instead, the application must time out and retransmit the datagram, in which case the kernel will find the new (and smaller) MTU in its routing table, and the kernel will then fragment the datagram. Passing this error back to the application lets the application retransmit sooner, and perhaps the application can reduce the size of the datagrams it sends.

3. The time exceeded error is normally seen with a code of 0, indicating that either the IPv4 TTL or IPv6 hop limit reached 0. This often indicates a routing loop, which might be a transient error.

4. ICMPv4 source quenches, while deprecated by RFC 1812 [Baker 1995], may be sent by routers (or by misconfigured hosts acting as routers). They indicate that the packet has been discarded, and we therefore treat them like a destination unreachable. Note that IPv6 does not have a source quench error.

5. All other destination unreachables indicate that the packet has been discarded.

10   The `icmpd_dest` member is a socket address structure containing the destination IP address and port of the datagram that generated the ICMP error. This member will be either a `sockaddr_in` structure for IPv4 or a `sockaddr_in6` structure for IPv6. If the application is sending datagrams to multiple destinations, it probably has one socket address structure per destination. By returning this information in a socket address structure, the application can compare it against its own structures to find the one that caused the error.

11   The `icmpd_fill` member pads out the `icmpd_err` structure to accommodate the largest possible socket address structure.

UDP Echo Client That Uses Our `icmpd` Daemon

We now modify our UDP echo client, the `dg_cli` function to use our `icmpd` daemon. Figure 25.30 shows the first half of the function.

——————————————————————————— icmpd/dgcli01.c

```
 1 #include    "unpicmpd.h"

 2 void
 3 dg_cli(FILE *fp, int sockfd, const SA *pservaddr, socklen_t servlen)
 4 {
 5     int     icmpfd, maxfdp1;
 6     char    sendline[MAXLINE], recvline[MAXLINE + 1];
 7     fd_set  rset;
 8     ssize_t n;
 9     struct timeval tv;
10     struct icmpd_err icmpd_err;

11     Sock_bind_wild(sockfd, pservaddr->sa_family);

12     icmpfd = Tcp_connect("/unix", ICMPD_PATH);
13     Write_fd(icmpfd, "1", 1, sockfd);
14     n = Read(icmpfd, recvline, 1);
15     if (n != 1 || recvline[0] != '1')
16         err_quit("error creating icmp socket, n = %d, char = %c",
17                     n, recvline[0]);

18     FD_ZERO(&rset);
19     maxfdp1 = max(sockfd, icmpfd) + 1;
```

——————————————————————————— icmpd/dgcli01.c

Figure 25.30   First half of `dg_cli` application.

2–3   The function arguments are the same as all previous versions of this function.

`bind` wildcard address and ephemeral port

11   We call our `sock_bind_wild` function to `bind` the wildcard IP address and an ephemeral port to the UDP socket. We do this so that the copy of this socket that we pass to the daemon has bound a port, as the daemon needs to know this port.

> The daemon could also do this `bind`, if a local port has not already been bound to the socket that it receives, but this does not work in all environments. Under SVR4 implementations, such as Solaris 2.5, in which sockets are not part of the kernel, when one process `binds` a port to a shared socket, the other process with a copy of that socket gets strange errors when it tries to use the socket. The easiest solution is to require the application to `bind` the local port before passing the socket to the daemon.

Establish Unix domain connection to daemon

12   We call our `tcp_connect` function to create a Unix domain stream socket and `connect` to the daemon's well-known pathname. (Recall from Section 11.5 that our implementation of `getaddrinfo` supports Unix domain sockets.)

Send UDP socket to daemon, await daemon's reply

13–17   We call our `write_fd` function from Figure 14.13 to send a copy of our UDP socket to the daemon. We also send a single byte of data, the character "1," because some implementations do not like passing a descriptor without any data. The daemon sends back a single byte of data, consisting of the character "1" to indicate success. Any other reply indicates an error.

18–19   We initialize a descriptor set and calculate the first argument for `select` (the maximum of the two descriptors, plus one).

The last half of our client is shown in Figure 25.31. This is the loop that reads a line from standard input, sends the line to the server, reads back the server's reply, and writes the reply to standard output.

```
                                                                ── icmpd/dgcli01.c
20      while (Fgets(sendline, MAXLINE, fp) != NULL) {
21          Sendto(sockfd, sendline, strlen(sendline), 0, pservaddr, servlen);

22          tv.tv_sec = 5;
23          tv.tv_usec = 0;
24          FD_SET(sockfd, &rset);
25          FD_SET(icmpfd, &rset);
26          if ( (n = Select(maxfdp1, &rset, NULL, NULL, &tv)) == 0) {
27              fprintf(stderr, "socket timeout\n");
28              continue;
29          }
30          if (FD_ISSET(sockfd, &rset)) {
31              n = Recvfrom(sockfd, recvline, MAXLINE, 0, NULL, NULL);
32              recvline[n] = 0;       /* null terminate */
33              Fputs(recvline, stdout);
34          }
35          if (FD_ISSET(icmpfd, &rset)) {
36              if ( (n = Read(icmpfd, &icmpd_err, sizeof(icmpd_err))) == 0)
37                  err_quit("ICMP daemon terminated");
38              else if (n != sizeof(icmpd_err))
39                  err_quit("n = %d, expected %d", n, sizeof(icmpd_err));
40              printf("ICMP error: dest = %s, %s, type = %d, code = %d\n",
41                      Sock_ntop(&icmpd_err.icmpd_dest, icmpd_err.icmpd_len),
42                      strerror(icmpd_err.icmpd_errno),
43                      icmpd_err.icmpd_type, icmpd_err.icmpd_code);
44          }
45      }
46  }
                                                                ── icmpd/dgcli01.c
```

Figure 25.31 Last half of dg_cli application.

Call select

22–29   Since we are calling select we can easily place a timeout on our wait for the echo server's reply. We set this to 5 seconds, enable both descriptors for readability, and call select. If a timeout occurs, we print a message and go back to the top of the loop.

Print server's reply

30–34   If a datagram is returned by the server, we print it to standard output.

Handle ICMP error

35–44   If our Unix domain connection to the icmpd daemon is readable, we try to read an icmpd_err structure. If this succeeds, we print the relevant information that the daemon returns.

> strerror is an example of a simple, almost trivial, function that should be more portable than it is. First, ANSI C and Posix.1 say nothing about an error return from the function. The Solaris 2.5 manual page says that the function returns a null pointer if the argument is out of range. But this means code like

```
printf("%s", strerror(arg));
```

is incorrect, because `strerror` can return a null pointer. But the UnixWare 2.1 implementation, along with all the source code implementations that the author could find, handle an invalid argument by returning a pointer to a string such as "Unknown error." This makes sense and means the code above is fine. But Unix 98 changes this and says that because no return value is reserved to indicate an error, if the argument is out of range, the function sets `errno` to `EINVAL`. (They do not say anything about the returned pointer in the case of an error.) This means that completely conforming code must set `errno` to 0, call `strerror`, test whether `errno` equals `EAGAIN`, and print some other message in case of an error.

UDP Echo Client Examples

We now show some examples of this client, before looking at the daemon source code. We first send datagrams to an IP address that is not connected to the Internet.

```
solaris % udpcli01 192.3.4.5 echo
hi there
socket timeout
and hello
socket timeout
```

We expect ICMP host unreachables to be returned by some router, but none are received. Instead, our application times out. We show this to reiterate that a timeout is still required, and the generation of ICMP messages such as "host unreachable" may not occur. We then ran this example about 30 seconds later and did receive the expected ICMP error:

```
solaris % udpcli01 192.3.4.5 echo
hello
ICMP error: dest = 192.3.4.5.7, No route to host, type = 3, code = 1
```

Our next example sends a datagram to the standard echo server on a host that is not running the server. We receive an ICMPv4 port unreachable, as expected.

```
solaris % udpcli01 gemini.tuc.noao.edu echo
hello, world
ICMP error: dest = 140.252.4.54.7, Connection refused, type = 3, code = 3
```

`icmpd` Daemon

We start the description of our `icmpd` daemon with the `icmpd.h` header, shown in Figure 25.32.

`client` array

2–17   Since the daemon can handle any number of clients, we use an array of `client` structures to keep the information about each client. This is similar to the data structures we used in Section 6.8. In addition to the descriptor for the Unix domain connection to the client, we also store the address family of the client's UDP socket `AF_INET` or `AF_INET6`) and the port number bound to this socket. We also declare the function prototypes and the globals shared by these functions.

Figure 25.33 shows the first half of the `main` function.

icmpd/icmpd.h

```
 1 #include     "unpicmpd.h"

 2 struct client {
 3     int       connfd;          /* Unix domain stream socket to client */
 4     int       family;          /* AF_INET or AF_INET6 */
 5     int       lport;           /* local port bound to client's UDP socket */
 6     /* network byte ordered */
 7 } client[FD_SETSIZE];

 8                     /* globals */
 9 int    fd4, fd6, listenfd, maxi, maxfd, nready;
10 fd_set  rset, allset;
11 socklen_t addrlen;
12 struct sockaddr *cliaddr;

13              /* function prototypes */
14 int    readable_conn(int);
15 int    readable_listen(void);
16 int    readable_v4(void);
17 int    readable_v6(void);
```

icmpd/icmpd.h

Figure 25.32 icmpd.h header for icmpd daemon.

icmpd/icmpd.c

```
 1 #include     "icmpd.h"

 2 int
 3 main(int argc, char **argv)
 4 {
 5     int    i, sockfd;

 6     if (argc != 1)
 7         err_quit("usage: icmpd");

 8     maxi = -1;                 /* index into client[] array */
 9     for (i = 0; i < FD_SETSIZE; i++)
10         client[i].connfd = -1;  /* -1 indicates available entry */
11     FD_ZERO(&allset);

12     fd4 = Socket(AF_INET, SOCK_RAW, IPPROTO_ICMP);
13     FD_SET(fd4, &allset);
14     maxfd = fd4;

15 #ifdef  IPV6
16     fd6 = Socket(AF_INET6, SOCK_RAW, IPPROTO_ICMPV6);
17     FD_SET(fd6, &allset);
18     maxfd = max(maxfd, fd6);
19 #endif

20     listenfd = Tcp_listen("/unix", ICMPD_PATH, &addrlen);
21     FD_SET(listenfd, &allset);
22     maxfd = max(maxfd, listenfd);
23     cliaddr = Malloc(addrlen);
```

icmpd/icmpd.c

Figure 25.33 First half of main function: create sockets.

Initialize `client` array

9–10   The `client` array is initialized by setting the connected socket member to –1.

Create sockets

12–23   Three sockets are created: a raw ICMPv4 socket, a raw ICMPv6 socket, and a Unix domain stream socket. We call our `tcp_listen` function to create the latter, which also binds its well-known pathname to the socket and calls `listen`. This is the socket to which clients `connect`. The maximum descriptor is also calculated for `select` and a socket address structure is allocated for calls to `accept`.

Figure 25.34 shows the second half of the `main` function, which is an infinite loop that calls `select`, waiting for any of the daemon's descriptors to be readable.

—————————————————————————————— icmpd/icmpd.c
```
24      for ( ; ; ) {
25          rset = allset;
26          nready = Select(maxfd + 1, &rset, NULL, NULL, NULL);

27          if (FD_ISSET(listenfd, &rset))
28              if (readable_listen() <= 0)
29                  continue;

30          if (FD_ISSET(fd4, &rset))
31              if (readable_v4() <= 0)
32                  continue;

33 #ifdef  IPV6
34          if (FD_ISSET(fd6, &rset))
35              if (readable_v6() <= 0)
36                  continue;
37 #endif

38          for (i = 0; i <= maxi; i++) {    /* check all clients for data */
39              if ( (sockfd = client[i].connfd) < 0)
40                  continue;
41              if (FD_ISSET(sockfd, &rset))
42                  if (readable_conn(i) <= 0)
43                      break;      /* no more readable descriptors */
44          }
45      }
46      exit(0);
47 }
```
—————————————————————————————— icmpd/icmpd.c

Figure 25.34   Second half of `main` function: handle readable descriptor.

Check listening Unix domain socket

27–29   The listening Unix domain socket is tested first and if ready, `readable_listen` is called. The variable `nready`, the number of descriptors that `select` returns as readable, is a global. Each of our `readable_XXX` function decrements this variable and returns its new value as the return value of the function. When this value reaches 0, all the readable descriptors have been processed and `select` is called again.

Check raw ICMP sockets

30-37 The raw ICMPv4 socket is tested, and then the raw ICMPv6 socket.

Check connected Unix domain sockets

38-44 We then check whether any of the connected Unix domain sockets are readable. Readability on any of these sockets means that the client has sent a descriptor, or that the client has terminated.

Figure 25.35 shows the `readable_listen` function, called when the daemon's listening socket is readable. This indicates a new client connection.

```
                                                              —— icmpd/readable_listen.c
 1 #include    "icmpd.h"

 2 int
 3 readable_listen(void)
 4 {
 5     int     i, connfd;
 6     socklen_t clilen;

 7     clilen = addrlen;
 8     connfd = Accept(listenfd, cliaddr, &clilen);

 9         /* find first available client[] structure */
10     for (i = 0; i < FD_SETSIZE; i++)
11         if (client[i].connfd < 0) {
12             client[i].connfd = connfd;  /* save descriptor */
13             break;
14         }
15     if (i == FD_SETSIZE)
16         err_quit("too many clients");
17     printf("new connection, i = %d, connfd = %d\n", i, connfd);

18     FD_SET(connfd, &allset);    /* add new descriptor to set */
19     if (connfd > maxfd)
20         maxfd = connfd;         /* for select() */
21     if (i > maxi)
22         maxi = i;               /* max index in client[] array */

23     return (--nready);
24 }
                                                              —— icmpd/readable_listen.c
```

Figure 25.35 Handle new client connections.

7-23 The connection is accepted and the first available entry in the `client` array is used. The code in this function was copied from the beginning of Figure 6.22.

When a connected socket is readable, our `readable_conn` function is called (Figure 25.36), and its argument is the index of this client in the `client` array.

Read client data and possibly a descriptor

13-18 We call our `read_fd` function from Figure 14.11 to read the data and possibly a descriptor. If the return value is 0, the client has closed its end of the connection, possibly by terminating.

——— *icmpd/readable_conn.c*

```
 1 #include    "icmpd.h"

 2 int
 3 readable_conn(int i)
 4 {
 5     int     unixfd, recvfd;
 6     char    c;
 7     ssize_t n;
 8     socklen_t len;
 9     union {
10         char    buf[MAXSOCKADDR];
11         struct sockaddr sock;
12     } un;

13     unixfd = client[i].connfd;
14     recvfd = -1;
15     if ( (n = Read_fd(unixfd, &c, 1, &recvfd)) == 0) {
16         err_msg("client %d terminated, recvfd = %d", i, recvfd);
17         goto clientdone;        /* client probably terminated */
18     }
19         /* data from client; should be descriptor */
20     if (recvfd < 0) {
21         err_msg("read_fd did not return descriptor");
22         goto clienterr;
23     }
```

——— *icmpd/readable_conn.c*

Figure 25.36 Read data and possible descriptor from client.

One design decision was whether to use a Unix domain stream socket between the application and the daemon, or a Unix domain datagram socket. The application's UDP socket can be passed over either type of Unix domain socket. The reason we use a stream socket is to detect when a client terminates. All its descriptors are automatically closed when it terminates, including its Unix domain connection to the daemon, which tells the daemon to remove this client from the `client` array. Had we used a datagram socket, we would not know when the client terminates.

19–23   If the client has not closed the connection, then we expect a descriptor.

The second half of our `readable_conn` function is shown in Figure 25.37.

Get port number bound to UDP socket

24–28   `getsockname` is called so the daemon can obtain the port number bound to the socket. Since we do not know what size buffer to allocate for the socket address structure, we declare a `union` of a character array and a generic socket address structure. This guarantees that the character array is suitably aligned for a socket address structure, something that we are not guaranteed if we just declared a character array by itself. We discussed this problem with Figure 11.7, and in that program we called `malloc` to guarantee the alignment.

29–36   The address family of the socket is stored in the `client` structure, along with the port number. If the port number is 0, we call our `sock_bind_wild` function to `bind` the wildcard address and an ephemeral port to the socket, but as we mentioned earlier, this does not work on SVR4 implementations.

icmpd/readable_conn.c

```
24      len = sizeof(un.buf);
25      if (getsockname(recvfd, (SA *) un.buf, &len) < 0) {
26          err_ret("getsockname error");
27          goto clienterr;
28      }
29      client[i].family = un.sock.sa_family;
30      if ((client[i].lport = sock_get_port(&un.sock, len)) == 0) {
31          client[i].lport = sock_bind_wild(recvfd, client[i].family);
32          if (client[i].lport <= 0) {
33              err_ret("error binding ephemeral port");
34              goto clienterr;
35          }
36      }
37      Write(unixfd, "1", 1);      /* tell client all OK */
38      FD_SET(unixfd, &allset);
39      if (unixfd > maxfd)
40          maxfd = unixfd;
41      if (i > maxi)
42          maxi = i;
43      Close(recvfd);              /* all done with client's UDP socket */
44      return (--nready);

45  clienterr:
46      Write(unixfd, "0", 1);      /* tell client error occurred */
47  clientdone:
48      Close(unixfd);
49      if (recvfd >= 0)
50          Close(recvfd);
51      FD_CLR(unixfd, &allset);
52      client[i].connfd = -1;
53      return (--nready);
54  }
```

icmpd/readable_conn.c

Figure 25.37   Get port number that client has bound to its UDP socket.

Tell client OK

37–42   One byte consisting of the character "1" is sent back to the client. The new descriptor is added to the set of descriptors for `select` and `maxfd` and `maxi` are updated if necessary.

`close` client's UDP socket

43   We are finished with the client's UDP socket and `close` it. This descriptor was passed to us by the client and is therefore a copy; hence the UDP socket is still open in the client.

Handle errors and termination of client

45–53   If an error occurs, a byte of "0" is written back to the client. When the client terminates, our end of the Unix domain connection is closed, and that descriptor is removed from the set of descriptors for `select`. The `connfd` member of the `client` structure is set to –1, indicating it is available.

Our `readable_v4` function is called when the raw ICMPv4 socket is readable. We show the first half in Figure 25.38. This code is similar to the ICMPv4 code shown earlier in Figures 25.8 and 25.19.

icmpd/readable_v4.c

```
 1 #include     "icmpd.h"
 2 #include     <netinet/in_systm.h>
 3 #include     <netinet/ip.h>
 4 #include     <netinet/ip_icmp.h>
 5 #include     <netinet/udp.h>

 6 int
 7 readable_v4(void)
 8 {
 9     int     i, hlen1, hlen2, icmplen, sport;
10     char    buf[MAXLINE];
11     char    srcstr[INET_ADDRSTRLEN], dststr[INET_ADDRSTRLEN];
12     ssize_t n;
13     socklen_t len;
14     struct ip *ip, *hip;
15     struct icmp *icmp;
16     struct udphdr *udp;
17     struct sockaddr_in from, dest;
18     struct icmpd_err icmpd_err;

19     len = sizeof(from);
20     n = Recvfrom(fd4, buf, MAXLINE, 0, (SA *) &from, &len);

21     printf("%d bytes ICMPv4 from %s:",
22             n, Sock_ntop_host((SA *) &from, len));

23     ip = (struct ip *) buf;        /* start of IP header */
24     hlen1 = ip->ip_hl << 2;        /* length of IP header */

25     icmp = (struct icmp *) (buf + hlen1);   /* start of ICMP header */
26     if ( (icmplen = n - hlen1) < 8)
27         err_quit("icmplen (%d) < 8", icmplen);

28     printf(" type = %d, code = %d\n", icmp->icmp_type, icmp->icmp_code);
```

icmpd/readable_v4.c

Figure 25.38 Process received ICMPv4 datagram, first half.

This function prints some information about every received ICMPv4 message. This was done for debugging when developing this daemon and could be output based on a command-line argument.

Figure 25.39 shows the last half of our `readable_v4` function.

icmpd/readable_v4.c

```
29     if (icmp->icmp_type == ICMP_UNREACH ||
30         icmp->icmp_type == ICMP_TIMXCEED ||
31         icmp->icmp_type == ICMP_SOURCEQUENCH) {
32         if (icmplen < 8 + 20 + 8)
33             err_quit("icmplen (%d) < 8 + 20 + 8", icmplen);

34         hip = (struct ip *) (buf + hlen1 + 8);
35         hlen2 = hip->ip_hl << 2;
36         printf("\tsrcip = %s, dstip = %s, proto = %d\n",
37                 Inet_ntop(AF_INET, &hip->ip_src, srcstr, sizeof(srcstr)),
38                 Inet_ntop(AF_INET, &hip->ip_dst, dststr, sizeof(dststr)),
39                 hip->ip_p);
40         if (hip->ip_p == IPPROTO_UDP) {
41             udp = (struct udphdr *) (buf + hlen1 + 8 + hlen2);
42             sport = udp->uh_sport;

43                 /* find client's Unix domain socket, send headers */
44             for (i = 0; i <= maxi; i++) {
45                 if (client[i].connfd >= 0 &&
46                     client[i].family == AF_INET &&
47                     client[i].lport == sport) {

48                     bzero(&dest, sizeof(dest));
49                     dest.sin_family = AF_INET;
50 #ifdef  HAVE_SOCKADDR_SA_LEN
51                     dest.sin_len = sizeof(dest);
52 #endif
53                     memcpy(&dest.sin_addr, &hip->ip_dst,
54                             sizeof(struct in_addr));
55                     dest.sin_port = udp->uh_dport;

56                     icmpd_err.icmpd_type = icmp->icmp_type;
57                     icmpd_err.icmpd_code = icmp->icmp_code;
58                     icmpd_err.icmpd_len = sizeof(struct sockaddr_in);
59                     memcpy(&icmpd_err.icmpd_dest, &dest, sizeof(dest));

60                         /* convert type & code to reasonable errno value */
61                     icmpd_err.icmpd_errno = EHOSTUNREACH;   /* default */
62                     if (icmp->icmp_type == ICMP_UNREACH) {
63                         if (icmp->icmp_code == ICMP_UNREACH_PORT)
64                             icmpd_err.icmpd_errno = ECONNREFUSED;
65                         else if (icmp->icmp_code == ICMP_UNREACH_NEEDFRAG)
66                             icmpd_err.icmpd_errno = EMSGSIZE;
67                     }
68                     Write(client[i].connfd, &icmpd_err, sizeof(icmpd_err));
69                 }
70             }
71         }
72     }
73     return (--nready);
74 }
```

icmpd/readable_v4.c

Figure 25.39 Process received ICMPv4 datagram, second half.

Check message type, notify application

29–31   The only ICMPv4 messages that we pass to the application are destination unreachable, time exceeded, and source quench (Figure 25.29).

Check for UDP error, find client

34–42   hip points to the IP header that is returned following the ICMP header. This is the IP header of the datagram that elicited the ICMP error. We verify that this IP datagram is a UDP datagram and then fetch the source UDP port number from the UDP header following the IP header.

43–55   A search is made of all the client structures for a matching address family and port. If a match is found, an IPv4 socket address structure is built containing the destination IP address and port from the UDP datagram that caused the error.

Build icmpd_err structure

56–70   An icmpd_err structure is built that is sent to the client across the Unix domain connection to this client. The ICMPv4 message type and code are first mapped into an errno value, as described with Figure 25.29.

ICMPv6 errors are handled by our readable_v6 function, the first half of which is shown in Figure 25.40. The ICMPv6 handling is similar to the code in Figures 25.10 and 25.22.

The second half of our readable_v6 function is shown in Figure 25.41 (p. 701). This code is similar to Figure 25.39: it checks the type of ICMP error, checks that the datagram that caused the error was a UDP datagram, and then builds the icmpd_err structure that is sent to the client.

———————————————————————————————————— icmpd/readable_v6.c

```
 1 #include      "icmpd.h"
 2 #include      <netinet/in_systm.h>
 3 #include      <netinet/ip.h>
 4 #include      <netinet/ip_icmp.h>
 5 #include      <netinet/udp.h>

 6 #ifdef  IPV6
 7 #include      "ip6.h"                /* should be <netinet/ip6.h> */
 8 #include      "icmp6.h"              /* should be <netinet/icmp6.h> */
 9 #endif

10 int
11 readable_v6(void)
12 {
13 #ifdef  IPV6
14     int     i, hlen1, hlen2, icmp6len, sport;
15     char    buf[MAXLINE];
16     char    srcstr[INET6_ADDRSTRLEN], dststr[INET6_ADDRSTRLEN];
17     ssize_t n;
18     socklen_t len;
19     struct ip6_hdr *ip6, *hip6;
20     struct icmp6_hdr *icmp6;
21     struct udphdr *udp;
22     struct sockaddr_in6 from, dest;
23     struct icmpd_err icmpd_err;

24     len = sizeof(from);
25     n = Recvfrom(fd6, buf, MAXLINE, 0, (SA *) &from, &len);

26     printf("%d bytes ICMPv6 from %s:",
27             n, Sock_ntop_host((SA *) &from, len));

28     ip6 = (struct ip6_hdr *) buf;   /* start of IPv6 header */
29     hlen1 = sizeof(struct ip6_hdr);
30     if (ip6->ip6_nxt != IPPROTO_ICMPV6)
31         err_quit("next header not IPPROTO_ICMPV6");

32     icmp6 = (struct icmp6_hdr *) (buf + hlen1);
33     if ( (icmp6len = n - hlen1) < 8)
34         err_quit("icmp6len (%d) < 8", icmp6len);

35     printf(" type = %d, code = %d\n", icmp6->icmp6_type, icmp6->icmp6_code);
```

———————————————————————————————————— icmpd/readable_v6.c

Figure 25.40 Process received ICMPv6 datagram, first half.

icmpd/readable_v6.c

```
36      if (icmp6->icmp6_type == ICMP6_DST_UNREACH ||
37          icmp6->icmp6_type == ICMP6_PACKET_TOO_BIG ||
38          icmp6->icmp6_type == ICMP6_TIME_EXCEEDED) {
39          if (icmp6len < 8 + 40 + 8)
40              err_quit("icmp6len (%d) < 8 + 40 + 8", icmp6len);

41          hip6 = (struct ip6_hdr *) (buf + hlen1 + 8);
42          hlen2 = sizeof(struct ip6_hdr);
43          printf("\tsrcip = %s, dstip = %s, next hdr = %d\n",
44                  Inet_ntop(AF_INET6, &hip6->ip6_src, srcstr, sizeof(srcstr)),
45                  Inet_ntop(AF_INET6, &hip6->ip6_dst, dststr, sizeof(dststr)),
46                  hip6->ip6_nxt);
47          if (hip6->ip6_nxt == IPPROTO_UDP) {
48              udp = (struct udphdr *) (buf + hlen1 + 8 + hlen2);
49              sport = udp->uh_sport;

50                  /* find client's Unix domain socket, send headers */
51              for (i = 0; i <= maxi; i++) {
52                  if (client[i].connfd >= 0 &&
53                      client[i].family == AF_INET6 &&
54                      client[i].lport == sport) {

55                      bzero(&dest, sizeof(dest));
56                      dest.sin6_family = AF_INET6;
57 #ifdef  HAVE_SOCKADDR_SA_LEN
58                      dest.sin6_len = sizeof(dest);
59 #endif
60                      memcpy(&dest.sin6_addr, &hip6->ip6_dst,
61                          sizeof(struct in6_addr));
62                      dest.sin6_port = udp->uh_dport;

63                      icmpd_err.icmpd_type = icmp6->icmp6_type;
64                      icmpd_err.icmpd_code = icmp6->icmp6_code;
65                      icmpd_err.icmpd_len = sizeof(struct sockaddr_in6);
66                      memcpy(&icmpd_err.icmpd_dest, &dest, sizeof(dest));

67                          /* convert type & code to reasonable errno value */
68                      icmpd_err.icmpd_errno = EHOSTUNREACH;   /* default */
69                      if (icmp6->icmp6_type == ICMP6_DST_UNREACH) {
70                          if (icmp6->icmp6_code == ICMP_UNREACH_PORT)
71                              icmpd_err.icmpd_errno = ECONNREFUSED;
72                          else if (icmp6->icmp6_code == ICMP_UNREACH_NEEDFRAG)
73                              icmpd_err.icmpd_errno = EMSGSIZE;
74                      }
75                      Write(client[i].connfd, &icmpd_err, sizeof(icmpd_err));
76                  }
77              }
78          }
79      }
80      return (--nready);
81 #endif
82 }
```

icmpd/readable_v6.c

Figure 25.41 Process received ICMPv6 datagram, second half.

25.8 Summary

Raw sockets provide three capabilities:

1. We can read and write ICMPv4, IGMPv4, and ICMPv6 packets.
2. We can read and write IP datagrams with a protocol field that the kernel does not handle.
3. We can build our own IPv4 header, normally used for diagnostic purposes (or by hackers, unfortunately).

Two commonly used diagnostic tools, Ping and Traceroute, use raw sockets, and we have developed our own versions of both that support IPv4 and IPv6. We also developed our own `icmpd` daemon that provides access to ICMP errors for a UDP socket. This example also provides an example of descriptor passing across a Unix domain socket between a client and server that are unrelated.

Exercises

25.1   We said that almost all fields in an IPv6 header and all extension headers are available to the application through socket options or ancillary data. What information in an IPv6 datagram is *not* available to an application?

25.2   What happens in Figure 25.39 if for some reason the client stops reading from its Unix domain connection to the `icmpd` daemon, and lots of ICMP errors arrive for the client? What is the easiest solution?

25.3   If we specify the subnet-directed broadcast address to our Ping program, it works. That is, a broadcast ICMP echo request is sent as a link-layer broadcast, even though we do not set the `SO_BROADCAST` socket option. Why?

25.4   What happens with our Ping program if we ping the all-hosts multicast group, 224.0.0.1 on a multihomed host?

26

Datalink Access

26.1 Introduction

Providing access to the datalink layer for an application is a powerful feature that is available with most current operating systems. This provides the following capabilities:

- The ability to watch the packets received by the datalink layer, allowing programs such as tcpdump to be run on normal computer systems (as opposed to dedicated hardware devices to watch packets). When combined with the capability of the network interface to go into a *promiscuous mode*, this allows an application to watch all the packets on the local cable, not just the packets destined for the host on which the program is running.

- The ability to run certain programs as normal applications instead of as part of the kernel. For example, most Unix versions of an RARP server are normal applications that read RARP requests from the datalink (RARP requests are not IP datagrams) and then write the reply back to the datalink.

The three common methods to access the datalink layer under Unix are the BSD Packet Filter (BPF), the SVR4 Data Link Provider Interface (DLPI), and the Linux SOCK_PACKET interface. We present an overview of these three but then describe libpcap, the publicly available packet capture library. This library works with all three and using this library makes our programs independent of the actual datalink access provided by the operating system. We describe this library by developing a program that sends DNS queries to a name server (we build our own UDP datagrams and write them to a raw socket) and reading the reply using libpcap to determine if the name server enables UDP checksums.

26.2 BPF: BSD Packet Filter

4.4BSD and many other Berkeley-derived implementations support BPF, the BSD packet filter. The implementation of BPF is described in Chapter 31 of TCPv2. The history of BPF, a description of the BPF pseudomachine, and a comparison with the SunOS 4.1.x NIT packet filter is provided in [McCanne and Jacobson 1993].

Each datalink driver calls BPF right before a packet is transmitted and right after a packet is received, as shown in Figure 26.1.

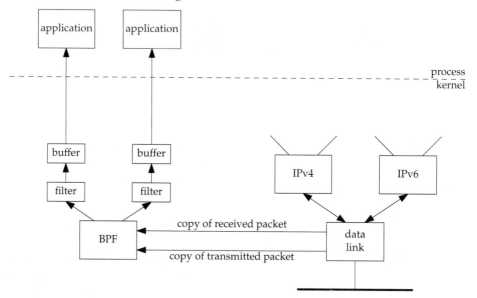

Figure 26.1 Packet capture using BPF.

Examples of these calls are in Figures 4.11 and 4.19 of TCPv2 for an Ethernet interface. The reason for calling BPF as soon as possible after reception and as late as possible before transmission is to provide accurate timestamps.

While it is not hard to provide a tap into the datalink to catch all packets, the power of BPF is in its filtering capability. Each application that opens a BPF device can load its own filter that is then applied by BPF to each packet. While some filters are simple (`udp` or `tcp` receives only UDP or TCP packets), others can examine fields in the packet headers for certain values. For example,

```
tcp and port 80 and tcp[13:1] & 0x7 != 0
```

was used in Chapter 14 of TCPv3 to collect only TCP segments to or from port 80 that had either the SYN, FIN, or RST flags on. The expression `tcp[13:1]` refers to the 1-byte value starting at byte offset 13 from the start of the TCP header.

BPF implements a register-based filter machine that applies the application-specific filters to each received packet. While one can write their own filter programs in the machine language of this pseudomachine (which is described on the BPF manual page), the simplest interface is to compile ASCII strings (such as the one beginning with `tcp` that we just showed) into this machine language using the `pcap_compile` function that we describe in Section 26.6.

Three techniques are used by BPF to reduce its overhead.

1. The BPF filtering is within the kernel, which minimizes the amount of data copied from BPF to the application. This copy, from kernel space to user space, is expensive. If every packet were copied, BPF could have trouble keeping up with fast datalinks.

2. Only a portion of each packet is passed by BPF to the application. This is called the *capture length*. Most applications need only the packet headers, not the packet data. This also reduces the amount of data that is copied by BPF to the application. `tcpdump`, for example, defaults this value to 68, which allows room for a 14-byte Ethernet header, a 20-byte IP header, a 20-byte TCP header, and 14 bytes of data. But to print additional information for other protocols (e.g., DNS and NFS) requires the user to increase this value when `tcpdump` is run.

3. BPF buffers the data destined for an application and this buffer is copied to the application only when the buffer is full, or when the *read timeout* expires. This timeout value can be specified by the application. `tcpdump`, for example, sets the timeout to 1000 ms, while the RARP daemon sets it to 0 (since there are few RARP packets, and the RARP server needs to send a response as soon as it receives the request). The purpose of the buffering is to reduce the number of system calls. The same number of packets are still copied between BPF and the application, but each system call has an overhead, and reducing the number of system calls always reduces the overhead. (Figure 3.1 of APUE compares the overhead of the `read` system call, for example, when reading a given file in different chunk sizes varying between 1 byte and 131,072 bytes.)

    Although we show only a single buffer in Figure 26.1, BPF maintains two buffers for each application and fills one while the other is being copied to the application. This is the standard *double buffering* technique.

In Figure 26.1 we show only the BPF reception of packets: packets received by the datalink from below (the network) and packets received by the datalink from above (IP). The application can also write to BPF, causing packets to be sent out the datalink, but most applications read only from BPF. There is no reason to write to BPF to send IP datagrams, because the `IP_HDRINCL` socket option allows us to write any type of IP datagram desired, including the IP header. (We show an example of this in Section 26.6.) The only reason to write to BPF is to send our own network packets that are not IP datagrams. The RARP daemon does this, for example, to send its RARP replies, which are not IP datagrams.

To access BPF one must open a BPF device that is not currently open. For example, one would try `/dev/bpf0` and if the error return is `EBUSY`, then try `/dev/bpf1`, and so on. Once the device is opened, about a dozen `ioctl` commands set the characteristics of the device: load the filter, set the read timeout, set the buffer size, attach a datalink to the BPF device, enable promiscuous mode, and so on. I/O is then performed using `read` and `write`.

26.3 DLPI: Data Link Provider Interface

SVR4 provides datalink access through DLPI, the Data Link Provider Interface. DLPI is a protocol-independent interface designed by AT&T that interfaces to the service provided by the datalink layer [Unix International 1991]. Access to DLPI is by sending and receiving streams messages.

To tap into the datalink layer the application simply `opens` the device (e.g., `le0`) and attaches it using the DLPI `DL_ATTACH_REQ` request. But for efficient operation two additional streams modules are normally pushed onto the stream: `pfmod`, which performs packet filtering within the kernel, and `bufmod`, which buffers the data destined for the application. We show this in Figure 26.2.

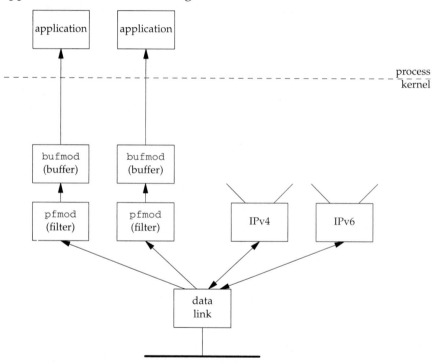

Figure 26.2 Packet capture using DLPI, `pfmod`, and `bufmod`.

Conceptually this is similar to what we described in the previous section for BPF: `pfmod` supports filtering within the kernel using a pseudomachine and `bufmod` reduces the amount of data and the number of system calls by supporting a capture length and a read timeout.

One interesting difference, however, is the type of pseudomachine supported by the BPF and `pfmod` filters. The BPF filter is a directed acyclic control flow graph (CFG) while pfmod uses a boolean expression tree. The former maps naturally into code for a register machine while the latter maps naturally into code for a stack machine [McCanne and Jacobson 1993]. This paper shows that the CFG implementation used by BPF is normally 3 to 20 times faster than the boolean expression tree, depending on the complexity of the filter.

26.4 Linux: `SOCK_PACKET`

To receive packets from the datalink layer under Linux we create a socket of type SOCK_PACKET. To do this we must have superuser privileges (similar to creating a raw socket), and the third argument to socket must be a nonzero value specifying the Ethernet frame type. For example, to receive all frames from the datalink, we write

```
fd = socket(AF_INET, SOCK_PACKET, htons(ETH_P_ALL));
```

This would return frames for all protocols that the datalink receives. If we wanted only IPv4 frames, the call would be

```
fd = socket(AF_INET, SOCK_PACKET, htons(ETH_P_IP));
```

Other constants for the final argument are ETH_P_ARP and ETH_P_IPV6, for example.

Specifying a protocol of ETH_P_ALL tells the datalink which frame types to pass to the socket for the frames that the datalink receives. If the datalink supports a promiscuous mode (e.g., an Ethernet) then the device must also be put into a promiscuous mode, if desired. This is done by an ioctl of SIOCGIFFLAGS to fetch the flags, setting the IFF_PROMISC flag, and then storing the flags with SIOCSIFFLAGS.

Comparing this Linux feature to BPF and DLPI there are some differences.

1. The Linux feature provides no kernel buffering and no kernel filtering. There is a normal socket receive buffer, but multiple frames cannot be buffered together and passed to the application with a single read. This increases the overhead involved in copying the potentially voluminous amounts of data from the kernel to the application.

2. The Linux feature provides no filtering by device. If ETH_P_IP is specified in the call to socket, then all IPv4 packets from all devices (Ethernets, PPP links, SLIP links, and the loopback device, for example) are passed to the socket. A generic socket address structure is returned by recvfrom and the sa_data member contains the device name (e.g., eth0). The application must then discard data from any device in which it is not interested. The problem again is too much data can be returned to the application, which can be a problem when monitoring a high-speed network.

26.5 `libpcap`: Packet Capture Library

The packet capture library, libpcap, provides implementation-independent access to the underlying packet capture facility provided by the operating system. Currently it supports only the reading of packets (although adding a few lines of code to the library lets one write datalink packets too).

Support currently exists for BPF under Berkeley-derived kernels, DLPI under Solaris 2.x, NIT under SunOS 4.1.x, the Linux SOCK_PACKET socket, and a few other operating systems. This library is used by tcpdump. About 25 functions comprise the library but rather than just describe the functions, we will show the actual use of the common functions in a complete example in the following section. All the library functions begin with the pcap_ prefix. The pcap manual page describes these functions in more detail.

The library is publicly available from ftp://ftp.ee.lbl.gov/libpcap.tar.Z.

26.6 Examining the UDP Checksum Field

We now develop an example that sends a UDP datagram containing a DNS query to a name server and reads the reply using the packet capture library. The goal of the example is to determine whether the name server computes a UDP checksum or not. With IPv4 the computation of a UDP checksum is optional. Most current systems enable these checksums by default but unfortunately older systems, notably SunOS 4.1.x, disable these checksums by default. All systems today, and especially a system running a name server, should *always* run with UDP checksums enabled, as corrupted datagrams can corrupt the server's database.

Enabling or disabling UDP checksums is normally done on a systemwide basis, as described in Appendix E of TCPv1.

We build our own UDP datagram (the DNS query) and write it to a raw socket. We could use a normal UDP socket to send the query, but we want to show how to use the IP_HDRINCL socket option to build a complete IP datagram. But we can never obtain the UDP checksum when reading from a normal UDP socket and we can never read UDP or TCP packets using a raw socket (Section 25.4). Therefore we must use the packet capture facility to obtain the entire UDP datagram containing the name server's reply. We then examine the UDP checksum field in the UDP header and if it is 0, the server does not have UDP checksums enabled.

Figure 26.3 summarizes the operation of our program. We write our own UDP datagrams to the raw socket and read back the replies using libpcap. Notice that UDP also receives the name server reply, and it will respond with an ICMP port unreachable, because it knows nothing about the source port number that our application chooses. The name server will ignore this ICMP error. We also note that it is harder to write a test program of this form that uses TCP, even though we are easily able to write our own TCP segments, because any reply to the TCP segments that we generate will normally cause our TCP to respond with an RST to whomever we sent the segment.

One way around this is to send the TCP segments with a source IP address that belongs to the attached subnet but is not currently assigned to some other node. Add an ARP entry to the

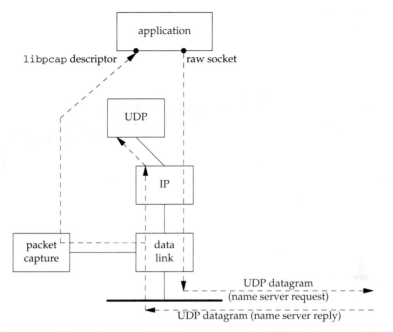

Figure 26.3 Our application to check if a name server has UDP checksums enabled.

sending host for this new IP address so that the sending host will answer ARP requests for this new address. But do not configure the new IP address as an alias. This will cause the IP stack on the sending host to discard packets received for this new IP address, assuming that the sending host is not acting as a router.

Figure 26.4 is a summary of the functions that comprise our program.

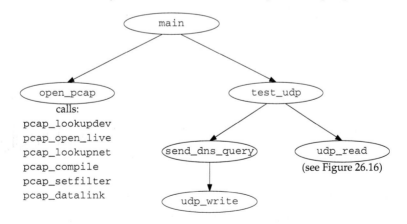

Figure 26.4 Summary of functions for our udpcksum program.

Figure 26.5 shows the header udpcksum.h, which includes our basic unp.h header along with various system headers that are needed to access the structure definitions for the IP and UDP packet headers.

———————————————————————————————— udpcksum/udpcksum.h

```
 1 #include    "unp.h"
 2 #include    <pcap.h>

 3 #include    <netinet/in_systm.h>     /* required for ip.h */
 4 #include    <netinet/in.h>
 5 #include    <netinet/ip.h>
 6 #include    <netinet/ip_var.h>
 7 #include    <netinet/udp.h>
 8 #include    <netinet/udp_var.h>
 9 #include    <net/if.h>
10 #include    <netinet/if_ether.h>

11 #define LOCALPORT    "39123"     /* source port (default) */
12 #define TTL_OUT      64          /* outgoing TTL */

13                     /* declare global variables */
14 extern struct sockaddr *dest, *local;
15 extern socklen_t destlen, locallen;
16 extern int datalink;
17 extern char *device;
18 extern pcap_t *pd;
19 extern int rawfd;
20 extern int snaplen;
21 extern int verbose;
22 extern int zerosum;

23                       /* function prototypes */
24 void    cleanup(int);
25 char    *next_pcap(int *);
26 void    open_pcap(void);
27 void    test_udp(void);
28 void    udp_write(char *, int);
29 struct udpiphdr *udp_read(void);
```

———————————————————————————————— udpcksum/udpcksum.h

Figure 26.5 udpcksum.h header.

3–10   Additional Internet headers are required to deal with the IP and UDP header fields.
11–29   We define some global variables and prototypes for our own functions that we show shortly.

The first part of the main function is shown in Figure 26.6.

Check number of command-line arguments

20–21   The program requires at least two arguments: the hostname or IP address that is running the DNS server and the service name (domain) or port number (53) of the server. We do not show the usage function; it just prints a summary of the command format and terminates.

udpcksum/main.c

```
 1 #include     "udpcksum.h"

 2                /* define global variables */
 3 struct sockaddr *dest, *local;
 4 socklen_t destlen, locallen;

 5 int     datalink;               /* from pcap_datalink(), in <net/bpf.h> */
 6 char    *device;                /* pcap device */
 7 int     fddipad;                /* HACK; for libpcap if FDDI defined */
 8 pcap_t *pd;                     /* packet capture struct pointer */
 9 int     rawfd;                  /* raw socket to write on */
10 int     snaplen = 200;          /* amount of data to capture */
11 int     verbose;
12 int     zerosum;                /* send UDP query with no checksum */

13 static void usage(const char *);

14 int
15 main(int argc, char *argv[])
16 {
17     int      c, on = 1;
18     char     *ptr, localname[1024], *localport;
19     struct addrinfo *aip;

20     if (argc < 2)
21         usage("");

22     /*
23      * Need local IP address for source IP address for UDP datagrams.
24      * Can't specify 0 and let IP choose, as we need to know it for
25      * the pseudo-header to calculate the UDP checksum.
26      * Both localname and localport can be overridden by -l option.
27      */

28     if (gethostname(localname, sizeof(localname)) < 0)
29         err_sys("gethostname error");
30     localport = LOCALPORT;
```

udpcksum/main.c

Figure 26.6 main function: definitions.

Obtain local hostname

28–30   Since we will be building our own IP and UDP headers, we must know the source
IP address when we write the UDP datagram. We cannot leave it as 0 and let IP choose
the address, because the address is part of the UDP pseudoheader (which we describe
shortly) that we must use for the UDP checksum computation. Therefore we call
gethostname to obtain the host's name. We also default the source port to the value in
udpcksum.h.

The next part of the main function, shown in Figure 26.7, processes the
command-line arguments.

———————————————————————————————— *udpcksum/main.c*

```
31      opterr = 0;                    /* don't want getopt() writing to stderr */
32      while ( (c = getopt(argc, argv, "0i:l:v")) != -1) {
33          switch (c) {

34          case '0':
35              zerosum = 1;
36              break;

37          case 'i':
38              device = optarg;      /* pcap device */
39              break;

40          case 'l':                  /* local IP address and port#: a.b.c.d.p */
41              if ( (ptr = strrchr(optarg, '.')) == NULL)
42                  usage("invalid -l option");

43              *ptr++ = 0;            /* null replaces final period */
44              localport = ptr;       /* service name or port number */
45              strncpy(localname, optarg, sizeof(localname));
46              break;

47          case 'v':
48              verbose = 1;
49              break;

50          case '?':
51              usage("unrecognized option");
52          }
53      }
```

———————————————————————————————— *udpcksum/main.c*

Figure 26.7 `main` function: process command-line arguments.

Process command-line options

31–36   We call `getopt` to process the command-line arguments. The `-0` option lets us send our UDP query without a UDP checksum to see if the server handles this differently from a datagram with a checksum.

37–39   The `-i` option lets us specify the interface on which to receive the server's reply. If this is not specified, the packet capture library chooses one, which might not be correct on a multihomed host. This is one way reading from a packet capture device differs from reading from a normal socket: with a socket we can wildcard the local address, allowing us to receive packets arriving on any interface. But with a packet capture device we receive arriving packets on only one interface.

> We note that the Linux SOCK_PACKET feature does not limit its datalink capture to a single device. Nevertheless, `libpcap` provides this filtering based on either its default or on our `-i` option.

40–46   The `-l` option lets us specify the source IP address and port number. The port (or a service name) is taken as the string following the final period, and the source IP address is taken as everything before the final period.

The last part of the `main` function is shown in Figure 26.8.

```
—————————————————————————————————————— udpcksum/main.c
54    if (optind != argc - 2)
55        usage("missing <host> and/or <serv>");

56        /* convert destination name and service */
57    aip = host_serv(argv[optind], argv[optind + 1], AF_INET, SOCK_DGRAM);
58    dest = aip->ai_addr;          /* don't freeaddrinfo() */
59    destlen = aip->ai_addrlen;

60        /* convert local name and service */
61    aip = host_serv(localname, localport, AF_INET, SOCK_DGRAM);
62    local = aip->ai_addr;         /* don't freeaddrinfo() */
63    locallen = aip->ai_addrlen;

64    /*
65     * Need a raw socket to write our own IP datagrams to.
66     * Process must have superuser privileges to create this socket.
67     * Also must set IP_HDRINCL so we can write our own IP headers.
68     */

69    rawfd = Socket(dest->sa_family, SOCK_RAW, 0);

70    Setsockopt(rawfd, IPPROTO_IP, IP_HDRINCL, &on, sizeof(on));

71    open_pcap();                   /* open packet capture device */

72    setuid(getuid());              /* don't need superuser privileges any more */

73    Signal(SIGTERM, cleanup);
74    Signal(SIGINT, cleanup);
75    Signal(SIGHUP, cleanup);

76    test_udp();

77    cleanup(0);
78 }
—————————————————————————————————————— udpcksum/main.c
```

Figure 26.8 `main` function: convert hostnames and service names, create socket.

Process destination name and port, then local name and port

54–63 We verify that exactly two command-line arguments remain: the destination host-name and service name. We call `host_serv` to convert these into a socket address structure, the pointer to which we save in `dest`. We then do the same conversion of the local hostname and port, saving the pointer to the socket address structure in `local`.

Create raw socket and open packet capture device

64–71 We create a raw socket and enable the `IP_HDRINCL` socket option. This option lets us write complete IP datagrams, including the IP header. The function `open_pcap` opens the packet capture device, and we show this function next.

Change permissions and establish signal handlers

72–75 We need superuser privileges to create a raw socket. We normally need superuser privileges to open the packet capture device, but this depends on the implementation. For example, with BPF the administrator can set the permissions of the `/dev/bpf` devices to whatever is desired for that system. We now give up these additional permissions, assuming the program file is set-user-ID. If the process has superuser privileges, calling `setuid` sets our real user ID, effective user ID, and saved set-user-ID to our real user ID (`getuid`). We establish signal handlers in case the user terminates the program before it is done.

Perform test and cleanup

76–77   The function `test_udp` (Figure 26.10) performs the test and then returns. `cleanup` (Figure 26.18) prints summary statistics from the packet capture library and terminates the process.

Figure 26.9 shows the `open_pcap` function, which we called from the `main` function to open the packet capture device.

Choose packet capture device

10–14   If the packet capture device was not specified (the `-i` command-line option), then `pcap_lookupdev` chooses a device. It issues the `SIOCGIFCONF` ioctl and chooses the lowest numbered device that is up, but not the loopback. Many of the `pcap` library functions fill in an error string if an error occurs. The sole argument to this function is an array that is filled in with an error string.

Open device

15–17   `pcap_open_live` opens the device. The term "live" refers to an actual device being opened, instead of a save file containing previously saved packets. The first argument is the device name, the second is the number of bytes to save per packet (`snaplen`, which we initialized to 200 in Figure 26.6), the third is a promiscuous flag, the fourth is a timeout value in milliseconds, and the fifth is a pointer to an error message array.

If the promiscuous flag is set, the interface is placed into promiscuous mode, causing it to receive all packets passing by on the wire. This is the normal mode for `tcpdump`. For our example, however, the DNS server replies will be sent to our host.

The timeout argument is a read timeout. Instead of having the device return a packet to the process every time a packet is received (which could be inefficient, invoking lots of copies of individual packets from the kernel to the process), a packet is returned only when either the device's read buffer is full, or when the read timeout expires. If the read timeout is set to 0, every packet is returned as soon as it is received.

Obtain network address and subnet mask

18–23   `pcap_lookupnet` returns the network address and subnet mask for the packet capture device. We must specify the subnet mask in the call to `pcap_compile` that follows, because the packet filter needs this to determine if an IP address is a subnet-directed broadcast address.

Compile packet filter

24–30   `pcap_compile` takes a filter string (which we build in the `cmd` array) and compiles it into a filter program (stored in `fcode`). This will select the packets that we wish to receive.

udpcksum/pcap.c

```
1 #include     "udpcksum.h"

2 #define CMD       "udp and src host %s and src port %d"

3 void
4 open_pcap(void)
5 {
6     uint32_t localnet, netmask;
7     char    cmd[MAXLINE], errbuf[PCAP_ERRBUF_SIZE], str1[INET_ADDRSTRLEN],
8             str2[INET_ADDRSTRLEN];
9     struct bpf_program fcode;

10    if (device == NULL) {
11        if ( (device = pcap_lookupdev(errbuf)) == NULL)
12            err_quit("pcap_lookup: %s", errbuf);
13    }
14    printf("device = %s\n", device);

15        /* hardcode: promisc=0, to_ms=500 */
16    if ( (pd = pcap_open_live(device, snaplen, 0, 500, errbuf)) == NULL)
17        err_quit("pcap_open_live: %s", errbuf);

18    if (pcap_lookupnet(device, &localnet, &netmask, errbuf) < 0)
19        err_quit("pcap_lookupnet: %s", errbuf);
20    if (verbose)
21        printf("localnet = %s, netmask = %s\n",
22                Inet_ntop(AF_INET, &localnet, str1, sizeof(str1)),
23                Inet_ntop(AF_INET, &netmask, str2, sizeof(str2)));

24    snprintf(cmd, sizeof(cmd), CMD,
25            Sock_ntop_host(dest, destlen),
26            ntohs(sock_get_port(dest, destlen)));
27    if (verbose)
28        printf("cmd = %s\n", cmd);
29    if (pcap_compile(pd, &fcode, cmd, 0, netmask) < 0)
30        err_quit("pcap_compile: %s", pcap_geterr(pd));

31    if (pcap_setfilter(pd, &fcode) < 0)
32        err_quit("pcap_setfilter: %s", pcap_geterr(pd));

33    if ( (datalink = pcap_datalink(pd)) < 0)
34        err_quit("pcap_datalink: %s", pcap_geterr(pd));
35    if (verbose)
36        printf("datalink = %d\n", datalink);
37 }
```

udpcksum/pcap.c

Figure 26.9 open_pcap function: open and initialize packet capture device.

Load filter program

31-32   pcap_setfilter takes the filter program that we just compiled and loads it into the packet capture device. This initiates the capturing of the packets that we selected with the filter.

Determine datalink type

33–36   `pcap_datalink` returns the type of datalink for the packet capture device. We need this when receiving packets to determine the size of the datalink header that will be at the beginning of each packet that we read (Figure 26.14).

After calling `open_pcap`, the `main` function calls `test_udp`, which we show in Figure 26.10. This function sends a DNS query and reads the server's reply.

―― *udpcksum/udpcksum.c*
```
47 void
48 test_udp(void)
49 {
50     volatile int nsent = 0, timeout = 3;
51     struct udpiphdr *ui;

52     Signal(SIGALRM, sig_alrm);

53     if (sigsetjmp(jmpbuf, 1)) {
54         if (nsent >= 3)
55             err_quit("no response");
56         printf("timeout\n");
57         timeout *= 2;           /* exponential backoff: 3, 6, 12 */
58     }
59     canjump = 1;                /* siglongjmp is now OK */

60     send_dns_query();
61     nsent++;

62     alarm(timeout);
63     ui = udp_read();
64     canjump = 0;
65     alarm(0);

66     if (ui->ui_sum == 0)
67         printf("UDP checksums off\n");
68     else
69         printf("UDP checksums on\n");
70     if (verbose)
71         printf("recevied UDP checksum = %x\n", ui->ui_sum);
72 }
```
―― *udpcksum/udpcksum.c*

Figure 26.10 `test_udp` function: send queries and read responses.

`volatile` variables

50   We want the two automatic variables `nsent` and `timeout` to retain their value after a `siglongjmp` from the signal handler back to this function. An implementation is allowed to restore automatic variables back to their value when `sigsetjmp` was called (p. 178 of APUE), but adding the `volatile` qualifier prevents this from happening.

Establish signal handler and jump buffer

52–53   A signal handler is established for `SIGALRM` and `sigsetjmp` establishes a jump buffer for `siglongjmp`. (These two functions are described in detail in Section 10.15 of

APUE.) The second argument of 1 to `sigsetjmp` tells it to save the current signal mask, since we will call `siglongjmp` from our signal handler.

Handle `siglongjmp`

54-58   This code is executed only when `siglongjmp` is called from our signal handler. This indicates that a timeout occurred: we sent a request and never received a reply. If we have sent three requests, we terminate. Otherwise we print a message and multiply the timeout value by 2. This is an *exponential backoff*, which we also described in Section 20.5. The first timeout will be for 3 seconds, then 6, and then 12.

The reason we use `sigsetjmp` and `siglongjmp` in this example, rather than just catching `EINTR` (as in Figure 13.1), is because the packet capture library reading functions (which are called by our `udp_read` function) restart a read operation when `EINTR` is returned. Since we do not want to modify the library functions to return this error, our only solution is to catch the `SIGALRM` signal and perform a nonlocal goto, returning control to our code instead of the library code.

Send DNS query and read reply

60-65   `send_dns_query` (Figure 26.12) sends a DNS query to a name server. `udp_read` (Figure 26.14) reads the reply. We call `alarm` to prevent the read from blocking forever. If the specified timeout period (in seconds) expires, `SIGALRM` is generated and our signal handler calls `siglongjmp`.

Examine received UDP checksum

66-71   If the received UDP checksum is 0, the server did not calculate and send a checksum.

Figure 26.11 shows our signal handler, `sig_alrm`, which handles the `SIGALRM` signal.

```
                                                          udpcksum/udpcksum.c
 1 #include     "udpcksum.h"
 2 #include     <setjmp.h>

 3 static sigjmp_buf jmpbuf;
 4 static int canjump;

 5 void
 6 sig_alrm(int signo)
 7 {
 8     if (canjump == 0)
 9         return;
10     siglongjmp(jmpbuf, 1);
11 }
                                                          udpcksum/udpcksum.c
```

Figure 26.11 `sig_alrm` function: handle `SIGALRM` signal.

8-10   The flag `canjump` was set in Figure 26.10 after the jump buffer was initialized by `sigsetjmp`. If the flag has been set, `siglongjmp` causes the flow of control to act as if the `sigsetjmp` in Figure 26.10 had returned with the return value of 1.

Figure 26.12 shows the `send_dns_query` function that sends a UDP query to a DNS server. This function builds the application data, a DNS query.

———————————————————————————————— *udpcksum/udpcksum.c*
```
16 void
17 send_dns_query(void)
18 {
19     size_t  nbytes;
20     char    buf[sizeof(struct udpiphdr) + 100], *ptr;
21     short   one;

22     ptr = buf + sizeof(struct udpiphdr);    /* leave room for IP/UDP headers */

23     *((u_short *) ptr) = htons(1234);    /* identification */
24     ptr += 2;
25     *((u_short *) ptr) = htons(0x0);     /* flags */
26     ptr += 2;
27     *((u_short *) ptr) = htons(1);   /* #questions */
28     ptr += 2;
29     *((u_short *) ptr) = 0;      /* #answer RRs */
30     ptr += 2;
31     *((u_short *) ptr) = 0;      /* #authority RRs */
32     ptr += 2;
33     *((u_short *) ptr) = 0;      /* #additional RRs */
34     ptr += 2;

35     memcpy(ptr, "\001a\014root-servers\003net\000", 20);
36     ptr += 20;
37     one = htons(1);
38     memcpy(ptr, &one, 2);        /* query type = A */
39     ptr += 2;
40     memcpy(ptr, &one, 2);        /* query class = 1 (IP addr) */
41     ptr += 2;

42     nbytes = 36;
43     udp_write(buf, nbytes);
44     if (verbose)
45         printf("sent: %d bytes of data\n", nbytes);
46 }
```
———————————————————————————————— *udpcksum/udpcksum.c*

Figure 26.12 `send_dns_query` function: send a query to a DNS server.

Initialize buffer pointer

20-22   `buf` has room for a 20-byte IP header, an 8-byte UDP header, and 100 bytes of user data. `ptr` is set to point to the first byte of user data.

Build DNS query

23-34   To understand the details of the UDP datagram built by this function requires an understanding of the DNS message format. This is found in Section 14.3 of TCPv1. We set the identification field to 1234, the flags to 0, the number of questions to 1, and then the number of answer resource records (RRs), the number of authority RRs, and the number of additional RRs to 0.

> The `<arpa/nameser.h>` header defines a `HEADER` datatype for the first 12 bytes of a query
> header. We find it just as easy to store these 12 bytes ourselves for the simple query we are
> building.

35–41   We then form the single question that follows in the message: an A query for the IP
addresses of the host `a.root-servers.net`. This domain name is stored in 20 bytes
and consists of 4 labels: the 1-byte label `a`, the 12-byte label `root-servers` (remember
that `\014` is an octal character constant), the 3-byte label `net`, and the root label whose
length is 0. The query type is 1 (called an A query) and the query class is also 1.

Write UDP datagram

42–45   This message consists of 36 bytes of user data (eight 2-byte fields and the 20-byte
domain name). We call our function `udp_write` to build the UDP and IP headers, and
then to write the IP datagram to our raw socket.

Figure 26.13 shows our function `udp_write`, which builds the IP and UDP headers
and then writes the datagram to the raw socket.

Initialize packet header pointers

11–13   `ip` points to the beginning of the IP header (an `ip` structure) and `ui` points to the
same location, but the structure `udpiphdr` is the combined IP and UDP headers.

Update lengths

14–17   `ui_len` is the UDP length: the number of bytes of user data plus the size of the
UDP header (8 bytes). `userlen` (the number of bytes of user data that follows the UDP
header) is incremented by 28 (20 bytes for the IP header and 8 bytes for the UDP
header) to reflect the total size of the IP datagram.

Fill in UDP header and calculate UDP checksum

18–35   When the UDP checksum is calculated, it includes not only the UDP header and the
UDP data, but also fields from the IP header. These additional fields from the IP header
form what is called the *pseudoheader*. The inclusion of the pseudoheader provides additional verification that if the checksum is correct then the datagram was delivered to the
correct host and to the correct protocol code. These statements initialize the fields in the
IP header that form the pseudoheader. The code is somewhat obtuse but is explained in
Section 23.6 of TCPv2. The end result is storing the UDP checksum in the `ui_sum`
member if the `zerosum` flag (the `-0` command-line argument) is not set.

If the calculated checksum is 0, the value `0xffff` is stored instead. In ones-
complement arithmetic the two values are the same, but UDP sets the checksum to 0 to
indicate that the sender did not store a UDP checksum. Notice that we did not check
for a calculated checksum of 0 in Figure 25.13 because the ICMPv4 checksum is
required: the value of 0 does not indicate the absence of a checksum.

> We note that Solaris 2.x, for x < 6, has a bug with regard to checksums for TCP segments or
> UDP datagrams sent on a raw socket with the `IP_HDRINCL` socket option set. The kernel cal-
> culates the checksum and we must set the `ui_sum` field to the UDP length.

Fill in IP header

36–49   Since we have set the `IP_HDRINCL` socket option, we must fill in most fields in the

IP header. (Section 25.3 discusses these writes to a raw socket when this socket option is set.) We set the identification field to 0 (ip_id), which tells IP to set this field. IP also calculates the IP header checksum. sendto writes the IP datagram.

—————————————————————————————— udpcksum/udpwrite.c

```
 6 void
 7 udp_write(char *buf, int userlen)
 8 {
 9      struct udpiphdr *ui;
10      struct ip *ip;

11          /* Fill in and checksum UDP header */
12      ip = (struct ip *) buf;
13      ui = (struct udpiphdr *) buf;
14              /* add 8 to userlen for pseudo-header length */
15      ui->ui_len = htons((u_short) (sizeof(struct udphdr) + userlen));
16              /* then add 28 for IP datagram length */
17      userlen += sizeof(struct udpiphdr);

18      ui->ui_next = 0;
19      ui->ui_prev = 0;
20      ui->ui_x1 = 0;
21      ui->ui_pr = IPPROTO_UDP;
22      ui->ui_src.s_addr = ((struct sockaddr_in *) local)->sin_addr.s_addr;
23      ui->ui_dst.s_addr = ((struct sockaddr_in *) dest)->sin_addr.s_addr;
24      ui->ui_sport = ((struct sockaddr_in *) local)->sin_port;
25      ui->ui_dport = ((struct sockaddr_in *) dest)->sin_port;
26      ui->ui_ulen = ui->ui_len;
27      ui->ui_sum = 0;
28      if (zerosum == 0) {
29 #ifdef notdef                    /* change to ifndef for Solaris 2.x, x < 6 */
30          if ( (ui->ui_sum = in_cksum((u_short *) ui, userlen)) == 0)
31              ui->ui_sum = 0xffff;
32 #else
33          ui->ui_sum = ui->ui_len;
34 #endif
35      }
36          /* Fill in rest of IP header; */
37          /* ip_output() calcuates & stores IP header checksum */
38      ip->ip_v = IPVERSION;
39      ip->ip_hl = sizeof(struct ip) >> 2;
40      ip->ip_tos = 0;
41 #ifdef  linux
42      ip->ip_len = htons(userlen);    /* network byte order */
43 #else
44      ip->ip_len = userlen;        /* host byte order */
45 #endif
46      ip->ip_id = 0;               /* let IP set this */
47      ip->ip_off = 0;              /* frag offset, MF and DF flags */
48      ip->ip_ttl = TTL_OUT;

49      Sendto(rawfd, buf, userlen, 0, dest, destlen);
50 }
```

—————————————————————————————— udpcksum/udpwrite.c

Figure 26.13 udp_write function: build UDP and IP headers and write IP datagram to raw socket.

The next function is `udp_read`, shown in Figure 26.14, which was called from Figure 26.10.

——————————————————————————————————— udpcksum/udpread.c

```
 7 struct udpiphdr *
 8 udp_read(void)
 9 {
10     int     len;
11     char    *ptr;
12     struct ether_header *eptr;

13     for ( ; ; ) {
14         ptr = next_pcap(&len);

15         switch (datalink) {
16         case DLT_NULL:          /* loopback header = 4 bytes */
17             return (udp_check(ptr + 4, len - 4));

18         case DLT_EN10MB:
19             eptr = (struct ether_header *) ptr;
20             if (ntohs(eptr->ether_type) != ETHERTYPE_IP)
21                 err_quit("Ethernet type %x not IP", ntohs(eptr->ether_type));
22             return (udp_check(ptr + 14, len - 14));

23         case DLT_SLIP:          /* SLIP header = 24 bytes */
24             return (udp_check(ptr + 24, len - 24));

25         case DLT_PPP:           /* PPP header = 24 bytes */
26             return (udp_check(ptr + 24, len - 24));

27         default:
28             err_quit("unsupported datalink (%d)", datalink);
29         }
30     }
31 }
```

——————————————————————————————————— udpcksum/udpread.c

Figure 26.14 `udp_read` function: read next packet from packet capture device.

14-29   Our function `next_pcap` (Figure 26.15) returns the next packet from the packet capture device. Since the datalink headers differ depending on the actual device type, we branch based on the value returned by the `pcap_datalink` function.

> These magic offsets of 4, 14, and 24 are shown in Figure 31.9 of TCPv2. The 24-byte offsets shown for SLIP and PPP are for BSD/OS 2.1.
>
> Despite having the qualifier "10MB" in the name `DLT_EN10MB`, this datalink type is also used for 100 Mbit/sec Ethernet.

Our function `udp_check` (Figure 26.17) examines the packet and verifies fields in the IP and UDP headers.

Figure 26.15 shows the `next_pcap` function, which returns the next packet from the packet capture device.

—————————————————————————————————— udpcksum/pcap.c

```
38 char *
39 next_pcap(int *len)
40 {
41     char    *ptr;
42     struct pcap_pkthdr hdr;

43         /* keep looping until packet ready */
44     while ( (ptr = (char *) pcap_next(pd, &hdr)) == NULL) ;

45     *len = hdr.caplen;            /* captured length */
46     return (ptr);
47 }
```

—————————————————————————————————— udpcksum/pcap.c

Figure 26.15 next_pcap function: return next packet.

43–44   We call the library function `pcap_next`, which returns the next packet. A pointer to the packet is returned as the return value of the function and the second argument points to a `pcap_pkthdr` structure, which is also filled in on return:

```
struct pcap_pkthdr {
  struct timeval  ts;     /* timestamp */
  bpf_u_int32     caplen; /* length of portion captured */
  bpf_u_int32     len;    /* length this packet (off wire) */
};
```

The timestamp is when the packet capture device read the packet, as opposed to the actual delivery of the packet to the process, which could be some time later. `caplen` is the amount of data that was captured (recall that we set our variable `snaplen` to 200 in Figure 26.6, and then this was the second argument to `pcap_open_live` in Figure 26.9). The purpose of the packet capture facility is to capture the packet headers, and not all the data in each packet. `len` is the full length of the packet on the wire. `caplen` will always be less than or equal to `len`.

45–46   The captured length is returned through the pointer argument and the return value of the function is the pointer to the packet. Keep in mind that the "pointer to the packet" points to the datalink header, which is the 14-byte Ethernet header in the case of an Ethernet frame, or a 4-byte pseudo-link header in the case of the loopback interface.

If we look at the implementation of `pcap_next` in the library, it shows the division of labor between the different functions. We show this in Figure 26.16. Our application calls the `pcap_` functions and some of these functions are device independent, while others are dependent on the type of packet capture device. For example, we show that the BPF implementation calls `read`, while the DLPI implementation calls `getmsg` and the Linux implementation calls `recvfrom`.

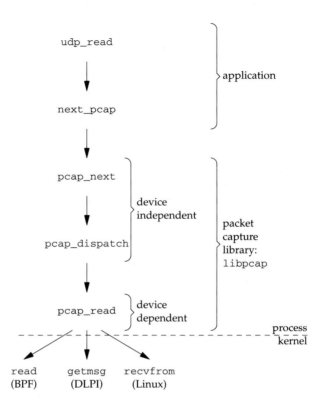

Figure 26.16 Arrangement of function calls to read from packet capture library.

Our function `udp_check` verifies numerous fields in the IP and UDP headers. It is shown in Figure 26.17. We must do these verifications because when the packet is passed to us by the packet capture device, the IP layer has not yet seen the packet. This differs from a raw socket.

44–61   The packet length must include at least the IP and UDP headers. The IP version is verified along with the IP header length and the IP header checksum. If the protocol field indicates a UDP datagram, the function returns the pointer to the combined IP/UDP header. Otherwise the program terminates, since the packet capture filter that we specified in our call to `pcap_setfilter` in Figure 26.9 should not return any other type of packet.

——— udpcksum/udpread.c
```
38 struct udpiphdr *
39 udp_check(char *ptr, int len)
40 {
41     int     hlen;
42     struct ip *ip;
43     struct udpiphdr *ui;

44     if (len < sizeof(struct ip) + sizeof(struct udphdr))
45         err_quit("len = %d", len);

46         /* minimal verification of IP header */
47     ip = (struct ip *) ptr;
48     if (ip->ip_v != IPVERSION)
49         err_quit("ip_v = %d", ip->ip_v);
50     hlen = ip->ip_hl << 2;
51     if (hlen < sizeof(struct ip))
52         err_quit("ip_hl = %d", ip->ip_hl);
53     if (len < hlen + sizeof(struct udphdr))
54         err_quit("len = %d, hlen = %d", len, hlen);

55     if ( (ip->ip_sum = in_cksum((u_short *) ip, hlen)) != 0)
56         err_quit("ip checksum error");

57     if (ip->ip_p == IPPROTO_UDP) {
58         ui = (struct udpiphdr *) ip;
59         return (ui);
60     } else
61         err_quit("not a UDP packet");
62 }
```
——— udpcksum/udpread.c

Figure 26.17 udp_check function: verify fields in IP and UDP headers.

——— udpcksum/cleanup.c
```
 2 void
 3 cleanup(int signo)
 4 {
 5     struct pcap_stat stat;

 6     fflush(stdout);
 7     putc('\n', stdout);

 8     if (verbose) {
 9         if (pcap_stats(pd, &stat) < 0)
10             err_quit("pcap_stats: %s\n", pcap_geterr(pd));
11         printf("%d packets received by filter\n", stat.ps_recv);
12         printf("%d packets dropped by kernel\n", stat.ps_drop);
13     }
14     exit(0);
15 }
```
——— udpcksum/cleanup.c

Figure 26.18 cleanup function.

The `cleanup` function shown in Figure 26.18 is called by the `main` function immediately before the program terminates, and also as the signal handler if the user aborts the program (Figure 26.7).

Fetch and print packet capture statistics

8–13 `pcap_stats` fetches the packet capture statistics: the total number of packets received by the filter and the number of packets dropped by the kernel.

Example

We first run our program with the `-0` command-line option to verify that the name server responds to datagrams that arrive with no checksum. We also specify the `-v` flag.

```
solaris # udpcksum -0 -v connix.com domain
device = le0
localnet = 206.62.226.32, netmask = 255.255.255.224
cmd = udp and src host 198.69.10.4 and src port 53
datalink = 1
sent: 36 bytes of data
UDP checksums on
recevied UDP checksum = ad39

2 packets received by filter
0 packets dropped by kernel
```

Next we run our program to a name server that does not have UDP checksums enabled.

```
solaris # udpcksum -v gw.pacbell.com domain
device = le0
localnet = 206.62.226.32, netmask = 255.255.255.224
cmd = udp and src host 192.150.170.2 and src port 53
datalink = 1
sent: 36 bytes of data
UDP checksums off
recevied UDP checksum = 0

1 packets received by filter
0 packets dropped by kernel
```

26.7 Summary

With raw sockets we have the capability to read and write IP datagrams that the kernel does not understand, and with access to the datalink layer we can extend that capability to read and write *any* type of datalink frame, not just IP datagrams. `tcpdump` is probably the most commonly used program that accesses the datalink layer directly.

Different operating systems have different ways of accessing the datalink layer. We looked at the Berkeley-derived BPF, SVR4's DLPI, and the Linux `SOCK_PACKET`. But we can ignore all their differences and still write portable code using the freely available packet capture library, `libpcap`.

Exercises

26.1   What is the purpose of the `canjump` flag in Figure 26.11?

26.2   In our `udpcksum` program, common error replies are an ICMP port unreachable (the destination is not running a name server) or an ICMP host unreachable. In either case we need not wait for a timeout of our `udp_read` in Figure 26.10 because the ICMP error is essentially a reply to our DNS query. Modify the program to catch these ICMP errors.

27

Client–Server Design Alternatives

27.1 Introduction

We have several choices for the type of process control to use when writing a Unix server.

- Our first server, Figure 1.9, was an *iterative server*, but there are a limited number of scenarios where this is recommended, because the server cannot process a pending client until it has completely serviced the current client.

- Figure 5.2 was our first *concurrent server* and it called `fork` to spawn a child process for every client. Traditionally most Unix servers fall into this category.

- In Section 6.8 we developed a different version of our TCP server consisting of a single process using `select` to handle any number of clients.

- In Figure 23.3 we modified our concurrent server to create one thread per client, instead of one process per client.

There are two other modifications to the concurrent server design that we look at in this chapter.

- *Preforking* has the server call `fork` when it starts, creating a pool of child processes. One process from the currently available pool handles each client request.

- *Prethreading* has the server create a pool of available threads when it starts, and one thread from the pool handles each client.

There are numerous details with preforking and prethreading that we examine in this chapter: what if there are not enough processes or threads in the pool? what if there are too many processes or threads in the pool? how can the parent and its children or threads synchronize with each other?

Clients are typically easier to write than servers because there is less process control in a client. Nevertheless, we have already examined various ways to write our simple echo client, and we summarize these in Section 27.2.

In this chapter we look at nine different server designs and we run each server against the same client. Our client–server scenario is typical of the Web: the client sends a small request to the server and the server responds with data back to the client. Some of the servers we have already discussed in detail (e.g., the concurrent server with one `fork` per client) while the preforked and prethreaded servers are new and therefore discussed in detail in this chapter.

We run multiple instances of a client against each server, measuring the CPU time required to service a fixed number of client requests. Instead of scattering all our CPU timings throughout the chapter, we summarize them in Figure 27.1 and refer to this figure throughout the chapter. We note that the times in this figure measure the CPU time required *only for process control* and the iterative server is our baseline that we subtract from the actual CPU time, because an iterative server has no process control overhead. We include the baseline times of 0.0 in this figure to reiterate this point. We use the term *process control CPU time* in this chapter to denote this difference from the baseline for a given system.

Row	Server description	Process control CPU time, seconds (difference from baseline)		
		Solaris	DUnix	BSD/OS
0	Iterative server (baseline measurement; no process control)	0.0	0.0	0.0
1	Concurrent server, one `fork` per client request	504.2	168.9	29.6
2	Prefork with each child calling `accept`		6.2	1.8
3	Prefork with file locking to protect `accept`	25.2	10.0	2.7
4	Prefork with thread mutex locking to protect `accept`	21.5		
5	Prefork with parent passing socket descriptor to child	36.7	10.9	6.1
6	Concurrent server, create one thread per client request	18.7	4.7	
7	Prethreaded with mutex locking to protect `accept`	8.6	3.5	
8	Prethreaded with main thread calling `accept`	14.5	5.0	

Figure 27.1 Timing comparisons of the various servers discussed in this chapter.

We ran the various servers on three hosts: `sunos5` (Solaris 2.5.1), `alpha` (Digital Unix 4.0b), and `bsdi` (BSD/OS 3.0). Notice that not all of the servers can be run on all three hosts. For example, row 2 cannot be run on most SVR4 hosts (as we discuss in Section 27.7) and none of the threaded servers can be run under BSD/OS (since the kernel does not support threads). The three server hosts are of different architectures, so we are not able to compare the timing between the three server hosts. The intent of these timings is to see how the different server designs compare on a given host, and not to compare different hardware architectures and operating systems. For example, row 7, the prethreaded server with mutex locking to protect the accept is the fastest server under both Solaris and Digital Unix, while row 2 is the fastest under BSD/OS.

All of these server timings were obtained by running the client shown in Figure 27.4 on two different hosts on the same subnet as the server. For all tests both clients spawned five children to create five simultaneous connections to the server, for a maximum of 10 simultaneous connections at the server at any time. Each client requested 4000 bytes from the server across the connection. For those tests involving a preforked or a prethreaded server, the server created 15 children or 15 threads when it started.

# children or # threads	Process control CPU time, seconds (difference from baseline)					
	prefork, no locking around accept (row 2)		prefork, file locking around accept (row 3)			prethreaded, mutex locking around accept (row 7)
	DUnix	BSD/OS	Solaris	DUnix	BSD/OS	Solaris
15	6.2	1.8	25.2	10.0	2.7	8.6
30	7.8	3.5	27.3	11.2	5.6	10.0
45	8.9	5.5	29.7	13.1	8.7	19.6
60	10.1	6.9	34.2	14.3	11.2	28.6
75	11.4	8.7	39.8	16.0	13.7	29.3
90	12.6	10.9	130.1	17.6	15.5	28.6
105	13.2	12.0		19.7	17.6	30.4
120	15.7	13.5		22.0	19.2	29.4

Figure 27.2 Effect of extraneous children or threads on server CPU time.

child # or thread #	#clients serviced										
	prefork, no locking around accept (row 2)		prefork, file locking around accept (row 3)			prefork, descriptor passing (row 5)			prethreaded, thread locking around accept (row 7)	
	DUnix	BSD/OS	Solaris	DUnix	BSD/OS	Solaris	DUnix	BSD/OS	Solaris	DUnix
0	318	333	347	335	335	1006	718	530	333	335
1	343	340	328	334	335	950	647	529	323	337
2	326	335	332	334	332	720	589	509	333	338
3	317	335	335	333	333	582	554	502	328	311
4	309	332	338	333	331	485	526	501	329	345
5	344	331	340	335	335	457	501	495	322	332
6	340	333	335	330	332	385	447	488	324	355
7	337	333	343	334	333	250	389	484	360	322
8	340	332	324	333	334	105	314	460	341	336
9	309	331	315	333	336	32	208	443	348	337
10	356	334	326	333	331	14	62	59	358	334
11	354	333	340	334	338	9	18	0	331	340
12	356	334	330	333	333	4	14	0	321	317
13	302	332	331	333	331	1	12	0	329	326
14	349	332	336	333	331	0	1	0	320	335
	5000	5000	5000	5000	5000	5000	5000	5000	5000	5000

Figure 27.3 Number of clients or threads serviced by each of the 15 children or threads.

Some server designs involve creating a pool of child processes or a pool of threads. Another item that we look at is the effect of too many children or too many threads. Figure 27.2 summarizes these results and we discuss these numbers in the appropriate sections.

Another topic that we consider when we have a collection of child processes or threads to service the clients is the distribution of the client requests to the available pool. Figure 27.3 summarizes these distributions and we discuss each column in the appropriate section.

27.2   TCP Client Alternatives

We have already examined various client designs, but it is worth summarizing their strengths and weaknesses.

1. Figure 5.5 was the basic TCP client. There were two problems with this program. First, while it is blocked awaiting user input, it does not see network events, such as the peer closing the connection. Additionally it operates in a stop-and-wait mode, making it inefficient for batch processing.

2. Figure 6.9 was the next iteration and by using `select` the client was notified of network events while waiting for user input. The problem, however, is that this program did not handle batch mode correctly. Figure 6.13 corrected this problem by using the `shutdown` function.

3. Figure 15.3 began the presentation of our client using nonblocking I/O.

4. The first of our clients that went beyond the single-process, single-thread design was Figure 15.9, which used `fork` with one process handling the client-to-server data, and the other process handling the server-to-client data.

5. Figure 23.2 used two threads, instead of two processes.

At the end of Section 15.2 we summarized the timing differences between these various versions. As we noted there, although the nonblocking I/O version was the fastest, the code was more complex, and using either two processes or two threads simplifies the code.

27.3   TCP Test Client

Figure 27.4 shows the client that we will use to test all the variations of our server.

10–12   Each time we run the client we specify the hostname or IP address of the server, the server's port, the number of children for the client to `fork` (allowing us to initiate multiple connections to the same server concurrently), the number of requests each child should send to the server, and the number of bytes to request the server to return each time.

——— server/client.c

```
 1 #include    "unp.h"

 2 #define MAXN    16384           /* max #bytes to request from server */

 3 int
 4 main(int argc, char **argv)
 5 {
 6     int    i, j, fd, nchildren, nloops, nbytes;
 7     pid_t  pid;
 8     ssize_t n;
 9     char   request[MAXLINE], reply[MAXN];

10     if (argc != 6)
11         err_quit("usage: client <hostname or IPaddr> <port> <#children> "
12                  "<#loops/child> <#bytes/request>");
13     nchildren = atoi(argv[3]);
14     nloops = atoi(argv[4]);
15     nbytes = atoi(argv[5]);
16     snprintf(request, sizeof(request), "%d\n", nbytes);      /* newline at end */

17     for (i = 0; i < nchildren; i++) {
18         if ( (pid = Fork()) == 0) {   /* child */
19             for (j = 0; j < nloops; j++) {
20                 fd = Tcp_connect(argv[1], argv[2]);

21                 Write(fd, request, strlen(request));

22                 if ( (n = Readn(fd, reply, nbytes)) != nbytes)
23                     err_quit("server returned %d bytes", n);

24                 Close(fd);      /* TIME_WAIT on client, not server */
25             }
26             printf("child %d done\n", i);
27             exit(0);
28         }
29         /* parent loops around to fork() again */
30     }

31     while (wait(NULL) > 0)      /* now parent waits for all children */
32         ;
33     if (errno != ECHILD)
34         err_sys("wait error");

35     exit(0);
36 }
```
——— server/client.c

Figure 27.4 TCP client program for testing our various servers.

17–30   The parent calls `fork` for each child, and each child establishes the specified number of connections with the server. On each connection the child sends a line specifying the number of bytes for the server to return, and then the child reads that amount of data from the server. The parent just `waits` for all the children to terminate. Notice that the client closes each TCP connection, so TCP's TIME_WAIT state occurs on the client, not on the server. This is a difference between our client–server and normal HTTP connections.

When we measure the various servers in this chapter we execute the client as

```
% client 206.62.226.36 8888 5 500 4000
```

This creates 2500 TCP connections to the server: 500 connections from each of five children. On each connection 5 bytes are sent from the client to the server ("4000\n") and 4000 bytes are transferred from the server back to the client. We run the client from two different hosts to the same server, providing a total of 5000 TCP connections, with a maximum of 10 simultaneous connections at the server at any given time.

> Sophisticated benchmarks exist for testing various Web servers. One is called WebStone and is available from `http://www.sgi.com/Products/WebFORCE/WebStone`. We do not need anything this sophisticated to make some general comparisons of the various server design alternatives that we examine in this chapter.

We now present the nine different server designs.

27.4 TCP Iterative Server

An iterative TCP server processes each client's request completely before moving on to the next client. Iterative TCP servers are rare but we showed one in Figure 1.9: a simple daytime server.

We do, however, have a use for an iterative server in comparing the various servers in this chapter. If we run the client as

```
% client 206.62.226.36 8888 1 5000 4000
```

to an iterative server, we get the same number of TCP connections (5000) and the same amount of data transferred across each connection. But since the server is iterative, there is *no process control whatsoever* performed by the server. This gives us a baseline measurement of the CPU time required to handle this number of clients that we can then subtract from all the other server measurements. From a process control perspective the iterative server is the fastest possible, because it performs no process control. We then compare the *differences* from this baseline in Figure 27.1.

We do not show our iterative server, as it is a trivial modification to the concurrent server that we present in the next section.

27.5 TCP Concurrent Server, One Child per Client

Traditionally a concurrent TCP server calls `fork` to spawn a child to handle each client. This allows the server to handle numerous clients at the same time, one client per process. The only limit on the number of clients is the operating system limit on the number of child processes for the user ID under which the server is running. Figure 5.12 is an example of a concurrent server and most TCP servers are written in this fashion.

The problem with these concurrent servers is the amount of CPU time that it takes to `fork` a child for each client. Years ago (the late 1980s), when a busy server handled hundreds or perhaps even a few thousand clients per day, this was OK. But the explosion of the World Wide Web (WWW) has changed this attitude. Busy Web servers measure the number of TCP connections per day in the millions. This is for an individual host, and the busiest sites run multiple hosts, distributing the load among the hosts. (Section 14.2 of TCPv3 talks about a common way to distribute this load using what is called "DNS round robin.") Later sections describe various techniques that avoid the per-client `fork` incurred by a concurrent server but concurrent servers are still common.

Figure 27.5 shows the `main` function for our concurrent TCP server.

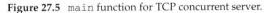

```
                                                                    server/serv01.c
 1 #include    "unp.h"

 2 int
 3 main(int argc, char **argv)
 4 {
 5     int     listenfd, connfd;
 6     pid_t   childpid;
 7     void    sig_chld(int), sig_int(int), web_child(int);
 8     socklen_t clilen, addrlen;
 9     struct sockaddr *cliaddr;

10     if (argc == 2)
11         listenfd = Tcp_listen(NULL, argv[1], &addrlen);
12     else if (argc == 3)
13         listenfd = Tcp_listen(argv[1], argv[2], &addrlen);
14     else
15         err_quit("usage: serv01 [ <host> ] <port#>");
16     cliaddr = Malloc(addrlen);

17     Signal(SIGCHLD, sig_chld);
18     Signal(SIGINT, sig_int);

19     for ( ; ; ) {
20         clilen = addrlen;
21         if ( (connfd = accept(listenfd, cliaddr, &clilen)) < 0) {
22             if (errno == EINTR)
23                 continue;        /* back to for() */
24             else
25                 err_sys("accept error");
26         }
27         if ( (childpid = Fork()) == 0) {     /* child process */
28             Close(listenfd);     /* close listening socket */
29             web_child(connfd);   /* process the request */
30             exit(0);
31         }
32         Close(connfd);              /* parent closes connected socket */
33     }
34 }
                                                                    server/serv01.c
```

Figure 27.5 `main` function for TCP concurrent server.

This function is similar to Figure 5.12: it calls `fork` for each client connection and handles the `SIGCHLD` signals from the terminating children. This function, however, we have made protocol independent by calling our `tcp_listen` function. We do not show the `sig_chld` signal handler: it is the same as Figure 5.11, with the `printf` removed.

We also catch the `SIGINT` signal, generated when we type our terminal interrupt key. We do this after the client completes to print the CPU time required for the program. Figure 27.6 shows the signal handler. This is an example of a signal handler that does not return.

—————————————————————————————— *server/serv01.c*
```
35 void
36 sig_int(int signo)
37 {
38     void    pr_cpu_time(void);
39     pr_cpu_time();
40     exit(0);
41 }
```
—————————————————————————————— *server/serv01.c*

Figure 27.6 Signal handler for `SIGINT`.

Figure 27.7 shows the `pr_cpu_time` function that is called by the signal handler.

—————————————————————————————— *server/pr_cpu_time.c*
```
 1 #include     "unp.h"
 2 #include     <sys/resource.h>

 3 #ifndef HAVE_GETRUSAGE_PROTO
 4 int      getrusage(int, struct rusage *);
 5 #endif

 6 void
 7 pr_cpu_time(void)
 8 {
 9     double  user, sys;
10     struct rusage myusage, childusage;

11     if (getrusage(RUSAGE_SELF, &myusage) < 0)
12         err_sys("getrusage error");
13     if (getrusage(RUSAGE_CHILDREN, &childusage) < 0)
14         err_sys("getrusage error");

15     user = (double) myusage.ru_utime.tv_sec +
16         myusage.ru_utime.tv_usec / 1000000.0;
17     user += (double) childusage.ru_utime.tv_sec +
18         childusage.ru_utime.tv_usec / 1000000.0;
19     sys = (double) myusage.ru_stime.tv_sec +
20         myusage.ru_stime.tv_usec / 1000000.0;
21     sys += (double) childusage.ru_stime.tv_sec +
22         childusage.ru_stime.tv_usec / 1000000.0;

23     printf("\nuser time = %g, sys time = %g\n", user, sys);
24 }
```
—————————————————————————————— *server/pr_cpu_time.c*

Figure 27.7 `pr_cpu_time` function: print total CPU time.

The getrusage function is called twice to return the resource utilization of both the calling process (RUSAGE_SELF) and of all the terminated children of the calling process (RUSAGE_CHILDREN). The values printed are the total user time (CPU time spent in the user process) and the total system time (CPU time spent within the kernel executing on behalf of the calling process).

Returning to Figure 27.5, it calls the function web_child to handle each client request. Figure 27.8 shows this function.

———————————————————————————————————— *server/web_child.c*

```
 1 #include     "unp.h"

 2 #define MAXN     16384              /* max #bytes that a client can request */

 3 void
 4 web_child(int sockfd)
 5 {
 6     int      ntowrite;
 7     ssize_t nread;
 8     char     line[MAXLINE], result[MAXN];

 9     for ( ; ; ) {
10         if ( (nread = Readline(sockfd, line, MAXLINE)) == 0)
11             return;              /* connection closed by other end */

12         /* line from client specifies #bytes to write back */
13         ntowrite = atol(line);
14         if ((ntowrite <= 0) || (ntowrite > MAXN))
15             err_quit("client request for %d bytes", ntowrite);

16         Writen(sockfd, result, ntowrite);
17     }
18 }
```

———————————————————————————————————— *server/web_child.c*

Figure 27.8 web_child function to handle each client's request.

After the client establishes the connection with the server, the client writes a single line specifying the number of bytes the server must return to the client. This is somewhat similar to HTTP: the client sends a small request and the server responds with the desired information (often an HTML file or a GIF image, for example). In the case of HTTP the server normally closes the connection after sending back the requested data, although newer versions are using *persistent connections*, holding the TCP connection open for additional client requests. In our web_child function the server allows additional requests from the client, but we saw in Figure 27.4 that our client sends only one request per connection and the client then closes the connection.

Row 1 of Figure 27.1 shows the timing result for this concurrent server. When compared to the subsequent lines in this figure, we see that the concurrent server requires the most amount of CPU time, which is what we expect with one fork per client.

> One server design that we do not measure in this chapter is one invoked by inetd, which we
> covered in Section 12.5. From a process control perspective a server invoked by inetd

involves a `fork` and an `exec`, so the CPU time will be even greater than the times shown in row 1 of Figure 27.1.

27.6 TCP Preforked Server, No Locking around `accept`

Our first of the "enhanced" TCP servers uses a technique called *preforking*. Instead of doing one `fork` per client, the server preforks some number of children when it starts, and then the children are ready to service the clients as each client connection arrives. Figure 27.9 shows a scenario where the parent has preforked N children and two clients are currently connected.

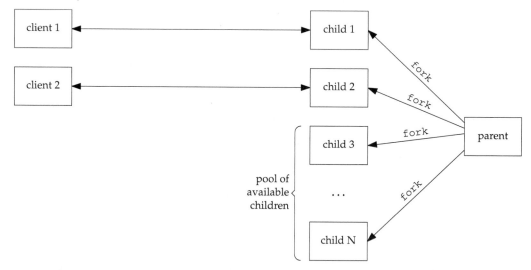

Figure 27.9 Preforking of children by server.

The advantage of this technique is that new clients can be handled without the cost of a `fork` by the parent. The disadvantage is that the parent must guess when it starts how many children to prefork. If the number of clients at any time ever equals the number of children, additional clients are ignored until a child is available. But recall from Section 4.5 that the clients are not completely ignored. The kernel will complete the three-way handshake for any additional clients, up to the `listen` backlog for this socket, and then pass the completed connections to the server when it calls `accept`. But the client application can notice a degradation in response time because even though its `connect` might return immediately, its first request might not be handled by the server for some time.

With some extra coding the server can always handle the client load. What the parent must do is continually monitor the number of available children, and if this value drops below some threshold, the parent must `fork` additional children. Also, if the number of available children exceeds another threshold, the parent can terminate some of the excess children, because when we discuss Figure 27.2 we will see that having too many available children can degrade performance too.

But before worrying about these enhancements, let's examine the basic structure of this type of server. Figure 27.10 shows the main function for the first version of our pre-forked server.

```
                                                              server/serv02.c
 1 #include    "unp.h"

 2 static int nchildren;
 3 static pid_t *pids;

 4 int
 5 main(int argc, char **argv)
 6 {
 7     int     listenfd, i;
 8     socklen_t addrlen;
 9     void    sig_int(int);
10     pid_t   child_make(int, int, int);

11     if (argc == 3)
12         listenfd = Tcp_listen(NULL, argv[1], &addrlen);
13     else if (argc == 4)
14         listenfd = Tcp_listen(argv[1], argv[2], &addrlen);
15     else
16         err_quit("usage: serv02 [ <host> ] <port#> <#children>");
17     nchildren = atoi(argv[argc - 1]);
18     pids = Calloc(nchildren, sizeof(pid_t));

19     for (i = 0; i < nchildren; i++)
20         pids[i] = child_make(i, listenfd, addrlen);      /* parent returns */

21     Signal(SIGINT, sig_int);

22     for ( ; ; )
23         pause();                      /* everything done by children */
24 }
                                                              server/serv02.c
```

Figure 27.10 main function for preforked server.

11–18   An additional command-line argument is the number of children to prefork. An array is allocated to hold the process IDs of the children, which we need when the program terminates, to allow the main function to terminate all the children.

19–20   Each child is created by child_make, which we examine in Figure 27.12.

Our signal handler for SIGINT, which we shown in Figure 27.11, differs from Figure 27.6.

30–34   getrusage reports on the resource utilization of *terminated* children, so we must terminate all the children before calling pr_cpu_time. We do this by sending SIGTERM to each child, and then we wait for all the children.

Figure 27.12 shows the child_make function, which is called by main to create each child.

7–9   fork creates each child and only the parent returns. The child calls the function child_main, which we show in Figure 27.13 and which is an infinite loop.

———————————————————————————————— server/serv02.c
```
25 void
26 sig_int(int signo)
27 {
28     int     i;
29     void    pr_cpu_time(void);

30         /* terminate all children */
31     for (i = 0; i < nchildren; i++)
32         kill(pids[i], SIGTERM);
33     while (wait(NULL) > 0)        /* wait for all children */
34         ;
35     if (errno != ECHILD)
36         err_sys("wait error");

37     pr_cpu_time();
38     exit(0);
39 }
```
———————————————————————————————— server/serv02.c

Figure 27.11 Signal handler for `SIGINT`.

———————————————————————————————— server/child02.c
```
1 #include    "unp.h"

2 pid_t
3 child_make(int i, int listenfd, int addrlen)
4 {
5     pid_t   pid;
6     void    child_main(int, int, int);

7     if ( (pid = Fork()) > 0)
8         return (pid);              /* parent */

9     child_main(i, listenfd, addrlen);   /* never returns */
10 }
```
———————————————————————————————— server/child02.c

Figure 27.12 `child_make` function: create each child.

———————————————————————————————— server/child02.c
```
11 void
12 child_main(int i, int listenfd, int addrlen)
13 {
14     int     connfd;
15     void    web_child(int);
16     socklen_t clilen;
17     struct sockaddr *cliaddr;

18     cliaddr = Malloc(addrlen);

19     printf("child %ld starting\n", (long) getpid());
20     for ( ; ; ) {
21         clilen = addrlen;
22         connfd = Accept(listenfd, cliaddr, &clilen);

23         web_child(connfd);        /* process the request */
24         Close(connfd);
25     }
26 }
```
———————————————————————————————— server/child02.c

Figure 27.13 `child_main` function: infinite loop executed by each child.

20-25   Each child calls `accept` and when this returns, the function `web_child` (Figure 27.8) handles the client request. The child continues in this loop until terminated by the parent.

4.4BSD Implementation

If you have never seen this type of arrangement (multiple processes calling `accept` on the same listening descriptor), you probably wonder how it can even work. It's worth a short digression on how this is implemented in Berkeley-derived kernels (e.g., as presented in TCPv2).

The parent creates the listening socket before spawning any children and recall that all descriptors are duplicated in each child each time `fork` is called. Figure 27.14 shows the arrangement of the `proc` structures (one per process), the one `file` structure for the listening descriptor and the one `socket` structure.

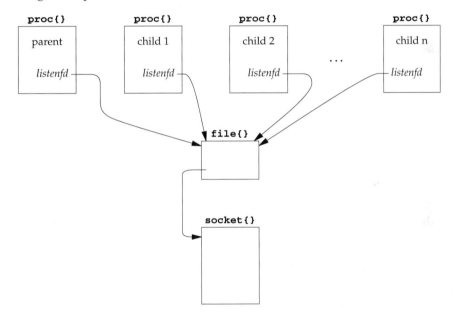

Figure 27.14 Arrangement of `proc`, `file`, and `socket` structures.

Descriptors are just an index in an array in the `proc` structure that reference a `file` structure. One of the properties of the duplication of descriptors in the child that occurs with `fork` is that a given descriptor in the child references the same `file` structure as that same descriptor in the parent. Each `file` structure has a reference count which starts at one when the file or socket is opened and is incremented by one each time `fork` is called or each time the descriptor is duped. In our example with N children, the reference count in the `file` structure would be N + 1 (don't forget the parent that still has the listening descriptor open, even though the parent never calls `accept`).

When the program starts, N children are created, and all N call `accept` and all are put to sleep by the kernel (line 140, p. 458 of TCPv2). When the first client connection arrives, all N children are awakened. This is because all N have gone to sleep on the same "wait channel," the `so_timeo` member of the `socket` structure, because all N share the same listening descriptor, which points to the same `socket` structure. Even though all N are awakened, the first of the N to run will obtain the connection and the remaining N − 1 will all go back to sleep, because when each of the remaining N − 1 execute the statement on line 135 of p. 458 of TCPv2, the queue length will be 0 since the first child to run already took the connection.

This is sometimes called the *thundering herd* problem because all N are awakened even though only one will obtain the connection. Nevertheless, the code works, with the performance side effect of waking up too many processes each time a connection is ready to be `accepted`. We now measure this performance effect.

Effect of Too Many children

The CPU time of 1.8 for the BSD/OS server in row 2 of Figure 27.1 is for 15 children and a maximum of 10 simultaneous clients. We can measure the effect of the thundering herd problem by just increasing the number of children for the same maximum number of clients (10). We show these CPU times in Figure 27.2, for this example, and for two other examples that we discuss in future sections. Here we discuss only the `accept` blocking and save discussion of the remaining three columns for later sections.

We see an increase in the CPU time every time we add another 15 (unneeded) children. To avoid the thundering herd problem we do not want too many extra children hanging around.

> Some Unix kernels have a function, often named `wakeup_one`, that wakes up only one process that is waiting for some event, instead of waking up all processes waiting for the event [Schimmel 1994]. The BSD/OS kernel does not have such a function.

Distribution of Connections to the Children

The next thing to examine is the distribution of the client connections to the pool of available children that are blocked in the call to `accept`. To collect this information we modify the `main` function to allocate an array of long integer counters in shared memory, one counter per child. This is done with

```
long    *cptr, *meter(int);    /* for counting #clients/child */

cptr = meter(nchildren);       /* before spawning children */
```

Figure 27.15 shows the `meter` function.

We use anonymous memory mapping, if supported (e.g., 4.4BSD), or the mapping of `/dev/zero` (e.g., SVR4). Since the array is created by `mmap` before the children are spawned, the array is then shared between this process (the parent) and all of its children that are created later by `fork`.

We then modify our `child_main` function (Figure 27.13) so that each child increments its counter when `accept` returns and our `SIGINT` handler prints this array after all the children are terminated.

——————————————————————————— server/meter.c
```
 1 #include    "unp.h"
 2 #include    <sys/mman.h>

 3 /*
 4  * Allocate an array of "nchildren" longs in shared memory that can
 5  * be used as a counter by each child of how many clients it services.
 6  * See pp. 467-470 of "Advanced Programming in the Unix Environment".
 7  */

 8 long *
 9 meter(int nchildren)
10 {
11     int     fd;
12     long    *ptr;

13 #ifdef  MAP_ANON
14     ptr = Mmap(0, nchildren * sizeof(long), PROT_READ | PROT_WRITE,
15                 MAP_ANON | MAP_SHARED, -1, 0);
16 #else
17     fd = Open("/dev/zero", O_RDWR, 0);

18     ptr = Mmap(0, nchildren * sizeof(long), PROT_READ | PROT_WRITE,
19                 MAP_SHARED, fd, 0);
20     Close(fd);
21 #endif

22     return (ptr);
23 }
```
——————————————————————————— server/meter.c

Figure 27.15 `meter` function to allocate an array in shared memory.

Figure 27.3 shows the distribution. When the available children are blocked in the call to `accept`, the kernel's scheduling algorithm distributes the connections uniformly to all the children.

`select` Collisions

While looking at this example under 4.4BSD we can also examine another poorly understood, but rare phenomenon. Section 16.13 of TCPv2 talks about *collisions* with the `select` function and how the kernel handles this possibility. A collision occurs when multiple processes call `select` on the same descriptor, because room is allocated in the `socket` structure for only one process ID to be awakened when the descriptor is ready. If multiple processes are waiting for the same descriptor, the kernel must wake up *all* processes that are blocked in a call to `select`, since it doesn't know which processes are affected by the descriptor that just became ready.

We can force `select` collisions with our example by preceding the call to `accept` in Figure 27.13 with a call to `select`, waiting for readability on the listening socket. The children will spend their time blocked in this call to `select` instead of in the call to `accept`. Figure 27.16 shows the portion of the `child_main` function that changes, using plus signs to note the lines that have changed from Figure 27.13.

```
        printf("child %ld starting\n", (long) getpid());
+       FD_ZERO(&rset);
        for ( ; ; ) {
+           FD_SET(listenfd, &rset);
+           Select(listenfd+1, &rset, NULL, NULL, NULL);
+           if (FD_ISSET(listenfd, &rset) == 0)
+               err_quit("listenfd readable");
+
            clilen = addrlen;
            connfd = Accept(listenfd, cliaddr, &clilen);

            web_child(connfd);        /* process the request */
            Close(connfd);
        }
```

Figure 27.16 Modification to Figure 27.13 to block in `select` instead of `accept`.

If we make this change and then examine the BSD/OS kernel's `nselcoll` counter before and after, we see 1814 collisions one time we run the sever, and 2045 collisions the next time. Since the two clients create a total of 5000 connections for each run of the server, this corresponds to about 35–40% of the calls to `select` invoking a collision.

If we compare the BSD/OS server's CPU time for this example, the value of 1.8 in Figure 27.1 increases to 2.9 when we add the call to `select`. Part of this increase is probably because of the additional system call (since we are calling `select` and `accept`, instead of just `accept`) and another part is probably because of the kernel overhead in handling the collisions.

The lesson to be learned from this discussion is when multiple processes are blocking on the same descriptor, it is better to block in a function such as `accept`, instead of blocking in `select`.

27.7 TCP Preforked Server, File Locking around `accept`

The implementation that we just described for 4.4BSD that allows multiple processes to call `accept` on the same listening descriptor works only with Berkeley-derived kernels that implement `accept` within the kernel. System V kernels, which implement `accept` as a library function, do not allow this. Indeed, if we run the server from the previous section on Solaris 2.5 (an SVR4-based kernel) with multiple children, soon after the clients start connecting to the server a call to `accept` in one of the children returns EPROTO, which means a protocol error.

> The reasons for this problem with the SVR4 library version of `accept` arise from the streams implementation (Chapter 33) and the fact that the library `accept` is not an atomic operation. Solaris 2.6 fixes this problem but the problem still exists in most other SVR4 implementations.

The solution is for the application to place a *lock* of some form around the call to `accept`, so that only one process at a time is blocked in the call to `accept`. The remaining children will be blocked trying to obtain the lock.

There are various ways to provide this locking around the call to `accept`, as we describe in the second volume of this series. In this section we use Posix file locking with the `fcntl` function.

The only change to the `main` function (Figure 27.10) is adding a call to our `my_lock_init` function before the loop that creates the children:

```
+    my_lock_init("/tmp/lock.XXXXXX");   /* one lock file for all children */
     for (i = 0; i < nchildren; i++)
          pids[i] = child_make(i, listenfd, addrlen); /* parent returns */
```

The `child_make` function remains the same as Figure 27.12. The only change to our `child_main` function (Figure 27.13) is to obtain a lock before calling `accept` and release the lock after `accept` returns:

```
     for ( ; ; ) {
          clilen = addrlen;
+         my_lock_wait();
          connfd = Accept(listenfd, cliaddr, &clilen);
+         my_lock_release();

          web_child(connfd);          /* process the request */
          Close(connfd);
     }
```

Figure 27.17 shows our `my_lock_init` function that uses Posix file locking.

—— *server/lock_fcntl.c*
```
 1 #include     "unp.h"

 2 static struct flock lock_it, unlock_it;
 3 static int lock_fd = -1;
 4                     /* fcntl() will fail if my_lock_init() not called */

 5 void
 6 my_lock_init(char *pathname)
 7 {
 8     char    lock_file[1024];

 9         /* must copy caller's string, in case it's a constant */
10     strncpy(lock_file, pathname, sizeof(lock_file));
11     Mktemp(lock_file);

12     lock_fd = Open(lock_file, O_CREAT | O_WRONLY, FILE_MODE);
13     Unlink(lock_file);             /* but lock_fd remains open */

14     lock_it.l_type = F_WRLCK;
15     lock_it.l_whence = SEEK_SET;
16     lock_it.l_start = 0;
17     lock_it.l_len = 0;

18     unlock_it.l_type = F_UNLCK;
19     unlock_it.l_whence = SEEK_SET;
20     unlock_it.l_start = 0;
21     unlock_it.l_len = 0;
22 }
```
—— *server/lock_fcntl.c*

Figure 27.17 `my_lock_init` function using Posix.1 file locking.

9-13   The caller specifies a pathname template as the argument to `my_lock_init` and the `mktemp` function creates a unique pathname based on this template. A file is then created with this pathname and immediately `unlinked`. By removing the pathname from the directory, if the program crashes, the file completely disappears. But as long as one or more processes have the file open (i.e., the file's reference count is greater than 0), the file itself is not removed. (This is the fundamental difference between removing a pathname from a directory and closing an open file.)

14-21   Two `flock` structures are initialized: one to lock the file and one to unlock the file. The range of the file that is locked starts at byte offset 0 (a `l_whence` of `SEEK_SET` with `l_start` set to 0). Since `l_len` is set to 0, this specifies that the entire file is locked. We never write anything to the file (its length is always 0) but that is OK: the advisory lock is still handled correctly by the kernel.

> The author first initialized these structures when they were declared, using
>
> ```
> static struct flock   lock_it = { F_WRLCK, 0, 0, 0, 0 };
> static struct flock   unlock_it = { F_UNLCK, 0, 0, 0, 0 };
> ```
>
> but there are two problems. First, there is no guarantee that the constant SEEK_SET is 0. But more importantly, there is no guarantee by Posix as to the order of the members in the structure. On Solaris and Digital Unix the `l_type` member is the first one in the structure, but on BSD/OS it is not. All Posix guarantees is that the members that Posix requires are present in the structure. Posix does not guarantee the order of the members, and Posix also allows additional, non-Posix members, to be in the structure. Therefore, initializing a structure to anything other than all zeros should always be done by actual C code, and not by an initializer when the structure is allocated.
>
> An exception to this rule is when the structure initializer is provided by the implementation. For example, when initializing a Pthread mutex lock in Chapter 23 we wrote
>
> ```
> pthread_mutex_t  mlock = PTHREAD_MUTEX_INITIALIZER;
> ```
>
> The `pthread_mutex_t` datatype is often a structure, but the initializer is provided by the implementation and can differ from one implementation to the next.

Figure 27.18 shows the two functions that lock and unlock the file. These are just calls to `fcntl`, using the structures that were initialized in Figure 27.17.

This new version of our preforked server now works on SVR4 systems by assuring that only one child process at a time is blocked in the call to `accept`. Comparing rows 2 and 3 in Figure 27.1 for the Digital Unix and BSD/OS servers shows that this type of locking adds to the server's process control CPU time.

> Release 1.1 of the Apache Web server, `http://www.apache.org`, preforks its children and then uses either the technique in the previous section (all children blocked in the call to `accept`), if the implementation allows this, or uses file locking around the `accept`.

Effect of Too Many children

We can check this version to see if the same thundering herd problem exists, which we described in the previous section. Figure 27.2 shows the results when we increase the number of unneeded children. With the Solaris column that uses file locking around the

```
                                                               ——— server/lock_fcntl.c
23 void
24 my_lock_wait()
25 {
26     int     rc;

27     while ( (rc = fcntl(lock_fd, F_SETLKW, &lock_it)) < 0) {
28         if (errno == EINTR)
29             continue;
30         else
31             err_sys("fcntl error for my_lock_wait");
32     }
33 }

34 void
35 my_lock_release()
36 {
37     if (fcntl(lock_fd, F_SETLKW, &unlock_it) < 0)
38         err_sys("fcntl error for my_lock_release");
39 }
                                                               ——— server/lock_fcntl.c
```

Figure 27.18 my_lock_wait and my_lock_release functions using fcntl.

accept we are only able to measure up through 75 children, as the next step (90) does something that causes the CPU time to increase a lot. One possible reason is that the system ran out of memory with all the processes and started swapping.

Distribution of Connections to the Children

We can examine the distribution of the clients to the pool of available children by using the function that we described with Figure 27.15. Figure 27.3 shows the result. All three operating systems distribute the file locks uniformly to the waiting processes.

27.8 TCP Preforked Server, Thread Locking around accept

As we mentioned there are various ways to implement locking between processes. The Posix file locking in the previous section is portable to all Posix-compliant systems, but it involves filesystem operations, which can take time. In this section we use thread locking, taking advantage of the fact that this can be used not only for locking between the threads within a given process, but also for locking between different processes.

Our main function remains the same as in the previous section, as do our child_make and child_main functions. The only thing that changes is our three locking functions. To use thread locking between different processes requires that (1) the mutex variable be stored in memory that is shared between all the processes, and (2) the thread library must be told that the mutex is shared among different processes.

> This also requires that the thread library support the PTHREAD_PROCESS_SHARED attribute. Digital Unix 4.0b does not, so we cannot run this server under this operating system.

There are various ways to share memory between different processes, as we describe in the second volume of this series. In our example we will use the `mmap` function with the `/dev/zero` device, which works under Solaris and other SVR4 kernels. Figure 27.19 shows our `my_lock_init` function.

server/lock_pthread.c

```
 1 #include    "unpthread.h"
 2 #include    <sys/mman.h>

 3 static pthread_mutex_t *mptr;    /* actual mutex will be in shared memory */

 4 void
 5 my_lock_init(char *pathname)
 6 {
 7     int     fd;
 8     pthread_mutexattr_t mattr;

 9     fd = Open("/dev/zero", O_RDWR, 0);

10     mptr = Mmap(0, sizeof(pthread_mutex_t), PROT_READ | PROT_WRITE,
11               MAP_SHARED, fd, 0);
12     Close(fd);

13     Pthread_mutexattr_init(&mattr);
14     Pthread_mutexattr_setpshared(&mattr, PTHREAD_PROCESS_SHARED);
15     Pthread_mutex_init(mptr, &mattr);
16 }
```

server/lock_pthread.c

Figure 27.19 `my_lock_init` function using Pthread locking between processes.

9–12   We open `/dev/zero` and then call `mmap`. The number of bytes that are mapped is the size of a `pthread_mutex_t` variable. The descriptor is then closed, which is OK, because the descriptor has been memory mapped.

13–15   In our previous Pthread mutex examples we initialized the global or static mutex variable using the constant `PTHREAD_MUTEX_INITIALIZER` (e.g., Figure 23.18). But with a mutex in shared memory we must call some Pthread library functions to tell the library that the mutex is in shared memory and that it will be used for locking between different processes. We first initialize a `pthread_mutexattr_t` structure with the default attributes for a mutex and then set the `PTHREAD_PROCESS_SHARED` attribute. (The default for this attribute is `PTHREAD_PROCESS_PRIVATE`, allowing use only within a single process.) `pthread_mutex_init` then initializes the mutex with these attributes.

Figure 27.20 shows our `my_lock_wait` and `my_lock_release` functions. Each is now just a call to a Pthread function to lock or unlock the mutex.

Comparing rows 3 and 4 in Figure 27.1 for the Solaris server shows that thread mutex locking is faster than file locking.

27.9 TCP Preforked Server, Descriptor Passing

The final modification to our preforked server is to have only the parent call `accept` and then "pass" the connected socket to one child. This gets around the possible need

```
                                                      ———— server/lock_pthread.c
17 void
18 my_lock_wait()
19 {
20     Pthread_mutex_lock(mptr);
21 }

22 void
23 my_lock_release()
24 {
25     Pthread_mutex_unlock(mptr);
26 }
                                                      ———— server/lock_pthread.c
```

Figure 27.20 `my_lock_wait` and `my_lock_release` functions using Pthread locking.

for locking around the call to accept in all the children but requires some form of descriptor passing from the parent to the children. This technique also complicates the code somewhat because the parent must keep track of which children are busy and which are free to pass a new socket to a free child.

In the previous preforked examples the process never cared which child received a client connection. The operating system handled this detail, giving one of the children the first call to accept or giving one of the children the file lock or the mutex lock. The first five columns of Figure 27.3 also show that the three operating systems that we are measuring do this in a fair, round-robin fashion.

With this example we need to maintain a structure of information about each child. We show our child.h header in Figure 27.21 that defines our Child structure.

```
                                                      ———— server/child.h
1 typedef struct {
2     pid_t    child_pid;          /* process ID */
3     int      child_pipefd;       /* parent's stream pipe to/from child */
4     int      child_status;       /* 0 = ready */
5     long     child_count;        /* #connections handled */
6 } Child;

7 Child  *cptr;                    /* array of Child structures; calloc'ed */
                                                      ———— server/child.h
```

Figure 27.21 `Child` structure.

We store the child's process ID, the parent's stream pipe descriptor that is connected to the child, the child's status, and a count of the number of clients that the child has handled. We will print this counter in our SIGINT handler to see the distribution of the client requests among the children.

Let us first look at the child_make function, which we show in Figure 27.22. We create a stream pipe, a Unix domain stream socket (Chapter 14), before calling fork. After the child is created, the parent closes one descriptor (sockfd[1]) and the child closes the other descriptor (sockfd[0]). Furthermore, the child duplicates its end of the stream pipe (sockfd[1]) onto standard error, so that each child just reads and writes to standard error to communicate with the parent. This gives us the arrangement shown in Figure 27.23.

server/child05.c

```
 1 #include    "unp.h"
 2 #include    "child.h"

 3 pid_t
 4 child_make(int i, int listenfd, int addrlen)
 5 {
 6     int     sockfd[2];
 7     pid_t   pid;
 8     void    child_main(int, int, int);

 9     Socketpair(AF_LOCAL, SOCK_STREAM, 0, sockfd);

10     if ( (pid = Fork()) > 0) {
11         Close(sockfd[1]);
12         cptr[i].child_pid = pid;
13         cptr[i].child_pipefd = sockfd[0];
14         cptr[i].child_status = 0;
15         return (pid);            /* parent */
16     }
17     Dup2(sockfd[1], STDERR_FILENO);     /* child's stream pipe to parent */
18     Close(sockfd[0]);
19     Close(sockfd[1]);
20     Close(listenfd);                    /* child does not need this open */
21     child_main(i, listenfd, addrlen);   /* never returns */
22 }
```

server/child05.c

Figure 27.22 `child_make` function descriptor passing preforked server.

Figure 27.23 Stream pipe after parent and child both close one end.

After all the children are created, we have the arrangement shown in Figure 27.24. We close the listening socket in each child, as only the parent calls `accept`. We show that the parent must handle the listening socket along with all the stream sockets. As you might guess, the parent uses `select` to multiplex all these descriptors.

Figure 27.25 shows the `main` function. The changes from previous versions of this function are that descriptor sets are allocated and the bits corresponding to the listening socket along with the stream pipe to each child are turned on in the set. The maximum descriptor value is also calculated. We allocate memory for the array of `Child` structures. The main loop is driven by a call to `select`.

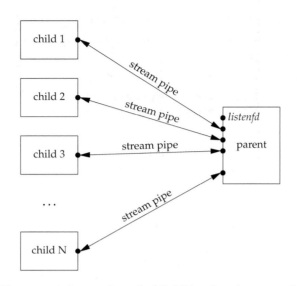

Figure 27.24 Stream pipes after all children have been created.

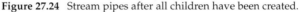

server/serv05.c

```
 1 #include     "unp.h"
 2 #include     "child.h"

 3 static int nchildren;

 4 int
 5 main(int argc, char **argv)
 6 {
 7     int     listenfd, i, navail, maxfd, nsel, connfd, rc;
 8     void    sig_int(int);
 9     pid_t   child_make(int, int, int);
10     ssize_t n;
11     fd_set  rset, masterset;
12     socklen_t addrlen, clilen;
13     struct sockaddr *cliaddr;

14     if (argc == 3)
15         listenfd = Tcp_listen(NULL, argv[1], &addrlen);
16     else if (argc == 4)
17         listenfd = Tcp_listen(argv[1], argv[2], &addrlen);
18     else
19         err_quit("usage: serv05 [ <host> ] <port#> <#children>");

20     FD_ZERO(&masterset);
21     FD_SET(listenfd, &masterset);
22     maxfd = listenfd;
23     cliaddr = Malloc(addrlen);

24     nchildren = atoi(argv[argc - 1]);
25     navail = nchildren;
26     cptr = Calloc(nchildren, sizeof(Child));
```

```
27              /* prefork all the children */
28      for (i = 0; i < nchildren; i++) {
29          child_make(i, listenfd, addrlen);    /* parent returns */
30          FD_SET(cptr[i].child_pipefd, &masterset);
31          maxfd = max(maxfd, cptr[i].child_pipefd);
32      }

33      Signal(SIGINT, sig_int);

34      for ( ; ; ) {
35          rset = masterset;
36          if (navail <= 0)
37              FD_CLR(listenfd, &rset);    /* turn off if no available children */
38          nsel = Select(maxfd, &rset, NULL, NULL, NULL);

39              /* check for new connections */
40          if (FD_ISSET(listenfd, &rset)) {
41              clilen = addrlen;
42              connfd = Accept(listenfd, cliaddr, &clilen);

43              for (i = 0; i < nchildren; i++)
44                  if (cptr[i].child_status == 0)
45                      break;        /* available */

46              if (i == nchildren)
47                  err_quit("no available children");
48              cptr[i].child_status = 1;    /* mark child as busy */
49              cptr[i].child_count++;
50              navail--;

51              n = Write_fd(cptr[i].child_pipefd, "", 1, connfd);
52              Close(connfd);
53              if (--nsel == 0)
54                  continue;        /* all done with select() results */
55          }
56              /* find any newly-available children */
57          for (i = 0; i < nchildren; i++) {
58              if (FD_ISSET(cptr[i].child_pipefd, &rset)) {
59                  if ( (n = Read(cptr[i].child_pipefd, &rc, 1)) == 0)
60                      err_quit("child %d terminated unexpectedly", i);
61                  cptr[i].child_status = 0;
62                  navail++;
63                  if (--nsel == 0)
64                      break;        /* all done with select() results */
65              }
66          }
67      }
68  }
```

server/serv05.c

Figure 27.25 `main` function that uses descriptor passing.

Turn off listening socket if no available children

36–37   The counter `navail` keeps track of the number of available children. If this counter is 0, the listening socket is turned off in the descriptor set for `select`. This prevents us from `accepting` a new connection for which there is no available child. The kernel still queues these incoming connections, up to the `listen` backlog, but we do not want to `accept` them until we have a child ready to process the client.

accept new connection

39-55   If the listening socket is readable, a new connection is ready to `accept`. We find the first available child and pass the connected socket to the child using our `write_fd` function from Figure 14.13. We write 1 byte along with the descriptor, but the recipient does not look at the contents of this byte. The parent closes the connected socket.

We always start looking for an available child with the first entry in the array of `Child` structures. This means the first children in the array always receive new connections to process before later elements in the array. We will verify this when we discuss Figure 27.3 and look at the `child_count` counters after the server terminates. If we didn't want this bias toward earlier children, we could remember which child received the most previous connection and start our search one element past that one each time, circling back to the first element when we reach the end. There is no advantage in doing this (it really doesn't matter which child handles a client request if multiple children are available), unless the operating system scheduling algorithm penalizes processes with longer total CPU times. Spreading the load more evenly among all the children would tend to average out their total CPU times.

Handle any newly available children

56-66   We will see that our `child_main` function writes a single byte back to the parent across the stream pipe when the child has finished with a client. That makes the parent's end of the stream pipe readable. We `read` the single byte (ignoring its value) and then mark the child as available. Should the child terminate unexpectedly, its end of the stream pipe will be close, and the `read` returns 0. We catch this and terminate, but a better approach is to log the error and spawn a new child to replace the one that terminated.

Our `child_main` function is shown in Figure 27.26.

Wait for descriptor from parent

32-33   This function differs from the ones in the previous two sections, because our child no longer calls `accept`. Instead the child blocks in a call to `read_fd` waiting for the parent to pass it a connected socket descriptor to process.

Tell parent we are ready

38   When we have finished with the client we `write` 1 byte across the stream pipe to tell the parent we are available.

In Figure 27.1 comparing rows 4 and 5 for our Solaris server we see that this server is slower than the version in the previous section that used thread locking between the children. Comparing rows 3 and 5 for our Digital Unix and BSD/OS servers leads to a similar conclusion: passing a descriptor across the stream pipe to each child, and writing a byte back across the stream pipe from the child takes more time than locking and unlocking either a mutex in shared memory or a file lock.

```
                                                                        ── server/child05.c
23 void
24 child_main(int i, int listenfd, int addrlen)
25 {
26     char    c;
27     int     connfd;
28     ssize_t n;
29     void    web_child(int);

30     printf("child %ld starting\n", (long) getpid());
31     for ( ; ; ) {
32         if ( (n = Read_fd(STDERR_FILENO, &c, 1, &connfd)) == 0)
33             err_quit("read_fd returned 0");
34         if (connfd < 0)
35             err_quit("no descriptor from read_fd");

36         web_child(connfd);        /* process the request */
37         Close(connfd);

38         Write(STDERR_FILENO, "", 1);    /* tell parent we're ready again */
39     }
40 }
                                                                        ── server/child05.c
```

Figure 27.26 child_main function: descriptor passing, preforked server.

Figure 27.3 shows the distribution of the child_count counters in the Child structure, which we print in the SIGINT handler when the server is terminated. The earlier children do handle more clients, as we discussed with Figure 27.25.

27.10 TCP Concurrent Server, One Thread per Client

The last five sections have focused on one process per client, both one fork per client and preforking some number of children. If the server supports threads, we can use threads instead of child processes.

Our first threaded version is shown in Figure 27.27. It is a modification of Figure 27.5 that creates one thread per client, instead of one process per client. This version is very similar to Figure 23.3.

Main thread loop

19-23   The main thread blocks in a call to accept and each time a client connection is returned a new thread is created by pthread_create. The function executed by the new thread is doit and its argument is the connected socket.

Per-thread function

25-33   The doit function detaches itself so the main thread does not have to wait for it and calls our web_client function (Figure 27.4). When that function returns the connected socket is closed.

server/serv06.c
```
 1 #include     "unpthread.h"

 2 int
 3 main(int argc, char **argv)
 4 {
 5     int     listenfd, connfd;
 6     void    sig_int(int);
 7     void    *doit(void *);
 8     pthread_t tid;
 9     socklen_t clilen, addrlen;
10     struct sockaddr *cliaddr;

11     if (argc == 2)
12         listenfd = Tcp_listen(NULL, argv[1], &addrlen);
13     else if (argc == 3)
14         listenfd = Tcp_listen(argv[1], argv[2], &addrlen);
15     else
16         err_quit("usage: serv06 [ <host> ] <port#>");
17     cliaddr = Malloc(addrlen);

18     Signal(SIGINT, sig_int);

19     for ( ; ; ) {
20         clilen = addrlen;
21         connfd = Accept(listenfd, cliaddr, &clilen);

22         Pthread_create(&tid, NULL, &doit, (void *) connfd);
23     }
24 }

25 void *
26 doit(void *arg)
27 {
28     void    web_child(int);

29     Pthread_detach(pthread_self());
30     web_child((int) arg);
31     Close((int) arg);
32     return (NULL);
33 }
```
server/serv06.c

Figure 27.27 `main` function for TCP threaded server.

We note from Figure 27.1 that this simple threaded version is faster on both Solaris and Digital Unix than even the fastest of the preforked versions. This one-thread-per-client version is also many times faster than the one-child-per-client version (row 1).

In Section 23.5 we noted three alternatives for converting a function that is not thread-safe into one that is thread-safe. Our web_child function calls our readline function, and the version shown in Figure 3.17 is not thread-safe. Alternatives 2 and 3 from Section 23.5 were timed with the example in Figure 27.27. The speedup from alternative 3 to alternative 2 was less than one percent, probably because readline is used only to read the 5-character count from the client. Therefore, for simplicity we use the less efficient version from Figure 3.16 for the threaded server examples in this chapter.

27.11 TCP Prethreaded Server, per-Thread `accept`

We found earlier in this chapter that it is faster to prefork a pool of children than to create one child for every client. On a system that supports threads it is reasonable to expect a similar speedup by creating a pool of threads when the server starts, instead of creating a new thread for every client. The basic design of this server is to create a pool of threads and then let each thread call `accept`. Instead of having each thread block in the call to `accept`, we will use a mutex lock (similar to Section 27.8) that allows only one thread at a time to call `accept`. There is no reason to use file locking to protect the call to `accept` from all the threads, because with multiple threads in a single process we know that a mutex lock can be used.

Figure 27.28 shows the `pthread07.h` header that defines a `Thread` structure that maintains some information about each thread.

———————————————————————————————— server/pthread07.h

```
1 typedef struct {
2     pthread_t thread_tid;        /* thread ID */
3     long    thread_count;        /* #connections handled */
4 } Thread;
5 Thread *tptr;                    /* array of Thread structures; calloc'ed */

6 int     listenfd, nthreads;
7 socklen_t addrlen;
8 pthread_mutex_t mlock;
```

———————————————————————————————— server/pthread07.h

Figure 27.28 `pthread07.h` header.

We also declare a few globals, such as the listening socket descriptor and a mutex variable that all the threads need to share.

Figure 27.29 shows the `main` function.

———————————————————————————————— server/serv07.c

```
1 #include    "unpthread.h"
2 #include    "pthread07.h"

3 pthread_mutex_t mlock = PTHREAD_MUTEX_INITIALIZER;

4 int
5 main(int argc, char **argv)
6 {
7     int     i;
8     void    sig_int(int), thread_make(int);

9     if (argc == 3)
10        listenfd = Tcp_listen(NULL, argv[1], &addrlen);
11    else if (argc == 4)
12        listenfd = Tcp_listen(argv[1], argv[2], &addrlen);
13    else
14        err_quit("usage: serv07 [ <host> ] <port#> <#threads>");
15    nthreads = atoi(argv[argc - 1]);
16    tptr = Calloc(nthreads, sizeof(Thread));
```

```
17     for (i = 0; i < nthreads; i++)
18         thread_make(i);              /* only main thread returns */

19     Signal(SIGINT, sig_int);

20     for ( ; ; )
21         pause();                     /* everything done by threads */
22 }
```
—— *server/serv07.c*

Figure 27.29 `main` function for prethreaded TCP server.

The `thread_make` and `thread_main` functions are shown in Figure 27.30.

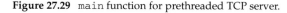
——— *server/pthread07.c*
```
 1 #include     "unpthread.h"
 2 #include     "pthread07.h"

 3 void
 4 thread_make(int i)
 5 {
 6     void    *thread_main(void *);

 7     Pthread_create(&tptr[i].thread_tid, NULL, &thread_main, (void *) i);
 8     return;                       /* main thread returns */
 9 }

10 void *
11 thread_main(void *arg)
12 {
13     int      connfd;
14     void     web_child(int);
15     socklen_t clilen;
16     struct sockaddr *cliaddr;

17     cliaddr = Malloc(addrlen);

18     printf("thread %d starting\n", (int) arg);
19     for ( ; ; ) {
20         clilen = addrlen;
21         Pthread_mutex_lock(&mlock);
22         connfd = Accept(listenfd, cliaddr, &clilen);
23         Pthread_mutex_unlock(&mlock);
24         tptr[(int) arg].thread_count++;

25         web_child(connfd);       /* process the request */
26         Close(connfd);
27     }
28 }
```
——— *server/pthread07.c*

Figure 27.30 `thread_make` and `thread_main` functions.

Create thread

7   Each thread is created and executes the `thread_main` function. The only argument is the index number of the thread.

21–23   The `thread_main` function calls the functions `pthread_mutex_lock` and `pthread_mutex_unlock` around the call to `accept`.

In Figure 27.1, comparing rows 6 and 7, we see that this latest version of our server is faster than the create-one-thread-per-client version under both Solaris and Digital Unix. We expect this, since we create the pool of threads only once, when the server starts, instead of creating one thread per client. Indeed, this version of our server is the fastest on these two hosts.

Figure 27.3 shows the distribution of the `thread_count` counters in the `Thread` structure, which we print in the `SIGINT` handler when the server is terminated. The uniformity of this distribution is caused by the thread scheduling algorithm that appears to cycle through all the threads in order, when choosing which thread receives the mutex lock.

> On a Berkeley-derived kernel such as Digital Unix we do not need any locking around the call to `accept` and can make a version of Figure 27.30 without any mutex locking and unlocking. Doing so, however, increases the process control CPU time from 3.5 seconds for row 7 in Figure 27.1 to 3.9 seconds. If we look at the two components of the CPU time, the user time and the system time, without any locking the user time decreases (because the locking is done in the threads library which executes in user space) but the system time increases (the kernel's thundering herd as all threads blocked in `accept` are awakened when a connection arrives). Since some form of mutual exclusion is required, to return each connection to a single thread, it is faster for the threads to do this themselves than for the kernel.

27.12 TCP Prethreaded Server, Main Thread `accept`

Our final server design using threads has the main thread create a pool of threads when it starts, and then only the main thread calls `accept` and passes each client connection to one of the available threads in the pool. This is similar to the descriptor passing version in Section 27.9.

The design problem is how does the main thread "pass" the connected socket to one of the available threads in the pool. There are various ways to implement this. We could use descriptor passing, as we did earlier, but there's no need to pass a descriptor from one thread to another, since all the threads and all the descriptors are in the same process. All the receiving thread needs to know is the descriptor number. Figure 27.31 shows the `pthread08.h` header that defines a `Thread` structure, identical to Figure 27.28.

server/pthread08.h
```
1 typedef struct {
2     pthread_t thread_tid;        /* thread ID */
3     long     thread_count;       /* #connections handled */
4 } Thread;
5 Thread *tptr;                    /* array of Thread structures; calloc'ed */

6 #define MAXNCLI 32
7 int      clifd[MAXNCLI], iget, iput;
8 pthread_mutex_t clifd_mutex;
9 pthread_cond_t clifd_cond;
```
server/pthread08.h

Figure 27.31 `pthread08.h` header.

Define shared array to hold connected sockets

6–9   We also define a `clifd` array in which the main thread will store the connected socket descriptors. The available threads in the pool take one of these connected sockets and service the corresponding client. `iput` is the index into this array of the next entry to be stored into by the main thread and `iget` is the index of the next entry to be fetched by one of the threads in the pool. Naturally this data structure that is shared between all the threads must be protected and we use a mutex along with a condition variable.

Figure 27.32 is the `main` function.

Create the pool of threads

23–25   `thread_make` creates each of the threads.

Wait for each client connection

27–38   The main thread blocks in the call to `accept`, waiting for each client connection to arrive. When one arrives, the connected socket is stored in the next entry in the `clifd` array, after obtaining the mutex lock on the array. We also check that the `iput` index has not caught up with the `iget` index, which indicates that our array is not big enough. The condition variable is signaled and the mutex is released, allowing one of the threads in the pool to service this client.

The `thread_make` and `thread_main` functions are shown in Figure 27.33. The former is identical to the version in Figure 27.30.

Wait for client descriptor to service

17–26   Each thread in the pool tries to obtain a lock on the mutex that protects the `clifd` array. When the lock is obtained, there is nothing to do if the `iget` and `iput` indexes are equal. In that case the thread goes to sleep by calling `pthread_cond_wait`. It will be awakened by the call to `pthread_cond_signal` in the main thread after a connection is accepted. When the thread obtains a connection, it calls `web_child`.

The times in Figure 27.1 show that this server is slower than the one in the previous section, in which each thread called `accept` after obtaining a mutex lock. The reason is that this section's example requires both a mutex and a condition variable, compared to just a mutex in Figure 27.30.

If we examine the histogram of the number of clients serviced by each thread in the pool, it is similar to the final column in Figure 27.3. This means the threads library cycles through all the available threads when doing the wakeup based on the condition variable when the main thread calls `pthread_cond_signal`.

server/serv08.c

```
 1 #include     "unpthread.h"
 2 #include     "pthread08.h"

 3 static int nthreads;
 4 pthread_mutex_t clifd_mutex = PTHREAD_MUTEX_INITIALIZER;
 5 pthread_cond_t clifd_cond = PTHREAD_COND_INITIALIZER;

 6 int
 7 main(int argc, char **argv)
 8 {
 9     int    i, listenfd, connfd;
10     void   sig_int(int), thread_make(int);
11     socklen_t addrlen, clilen;
12     struct sockaddr *cliaddr;

13     if (argc == 3)
14         listenfd = Tcp_listen(NULL, argv[1], &addrlen);
15     else if (argc == 4)
16         listenfd = Tcp_listen(argv[1], argv[2], &addrlen);
17     else
18         err_quit("usage: serv08 [ <host> ] <port#> <#threads>");
19     cliaddr = Malloc(addrlen);

20     nthreads = atoi(argv[argc - 1]);
21     tptr = Calloc(nthreads, sizeof(Thread));
22     iget = iput = 0;

23         /* create all the threads */
24     for (i = 0; i < nthreads; i++)
25         thread_make(i);            /* only main thread returns */

26     Signal(SIGINT, sig_int);

27     for ( ; ; ) {
28         clilen = addrlen;
29         connfd = Accept(listenfd, cliaddr, &clilen);

30         Pthread_mutex_lock(&clifd_mutex);
31         clifd[iput] = connfd;
32         if (++iput == MAXNCLI)
33             iput = 0;
34         if (iput == iget)
35             err_quit("iput = iget = %d", iput);
36         Pthread_cond_signal(&clifd_cond);
37         Pthread_mutex_unlock(&clifd_mutex);
38     }
39 }
```

server/serv08.c

Figure 27.32 main function for prethreaded server.

server/pthread08.c

```
 1 #include    "unpthread.h"
 2 #include    "pthread08.h"

 3 void
 4 thread_make(int i)
 5 {
 6     void    *thread_main(void *);

 7     Pthread_create(&tptr[i].thread_tid, NULL, &thread_main, (void *) i);
 8     return;                     /* main thread returns */
 9 }

10 void *
11 thread_main(void *arg)
12 {
13     int     connfd;
14     void    web_child(int);

15     printf("thread %d starting\n", (int) arg);
16     for ( ; ; ) {
17         Pthread_mutex_lock(&clifd_mutex);
18         while (iget == iput)
19             Pthread_cond_wait(&clifd_cond, &clifd_mutex);
20         connfd = clifd[iget];   /* connected socket to service */
21         if (++iget == MAXNCLI)
22             iget = 0;
23         Pthread_mutex_unlock(&clifd_mutex);
24         tptr[(int) arg].thread_count++;

25         web_child(connfd);      /* process the request */
26         Close(connfd);
27     }
28 }
```

server/pthread08.c

Figure 27.33 `thread_make` and `thread_main` functions.

27.13 Summary

In this chapter we have looked at nine different server designs and run them all against the same Web-style client, comparing the amount of CPU time spent performing process control:

0. iterative server (baseline measurement; no process control),
1. concurrent server, one `fork` per client,
2. prefork with each child calling `accept`,
3. prefork with file locking to protect `accept`,
4. prefork with thread mutex locking to protect `accept`,
5. prefork with parent passing socket descriptor to child,
6. concurrent server, create one thread per client request,
7. prethreaded with mutex locking to protect `accept`, and
8. prethreaded with main thread calling `accept`.

We can make a few summary comments.

- First, if the server is not heavily used, the traditional concurrent server model, with one `fork` per client is fine. This can even be combined with `inetd`, letting it handle the accepting of each connection. The remainder of our comments are meant for heavily used servers, such as Web servers.

- Creating a pool of children or a pool of threads reduces the process control CPU time compared to the traditional one-`fork`-per-client design, by a factor of 10 or more. The coding is not complicated but what is required, above and beyond the examples that we have shown, is a monitoring the number of free children and increasing or decreasing this number as the number of clients being served changes dynamically.

- Some implementations allow multiple children or threads to block in a call to `accept` while on other implementations we must place some type of lock around the call to `accept`. Either file locking or Pthread mutex locking can be used.

- Having all the children or threads call `accept` is normally simpler and faster than having the main thread call `accept` and then pass the descriptor to the child or thread.

- Having all the children or threads block in a call to `accept` is preferable over blocking in a call to `select`, because of the potential for `select` collisions.

- Using threads is normally faster than using processes. But the choice of one-child-per-client or one-thread-per-client depends on what the operating system provides and can also depend on what other programs, if any, are invoked to service each client. For example, if the server that `accepts` the client's connection calls `fork` and `exec`, it can be faster to `fork` a single threaded process than to `fork` a multithreaded process.

Exercises

27.1   In Figure 27.14 why does the parent keep the listening socket open, instead of closing it after all the children are created?

27.2   Can you recode the server in Section 27.9 to use a Unix domain datagram socket instead of a Unix domain stream socket? What changes?

27.3   Run the client and as many of the servers as your environment supports, and compare your results with those reported in this chapter.

Part 4

XTI: X/Open Transport Interface

28

XTI: TCP Clients

28.1 Introduction

Figure 1.15 showed that the sockets API was introduced in 1983 with 4.2BSD and initially worked with the TCP/IP protocol suite and the Unix domain protocols. During the mid-1980s, before Posix.1 was complete, there was still a rift within the Unix community between "Berkeley Unix" and "AT&T Unix." In the networking world, the claim was that TCP/IP would be replaced "shortly" with the OSI protocols.

In 1986 AT&T introduced a different networking API called TLI (Transport Layer Interface) with Release 3.0 of System V (SVR3). Although there are numerous similarities between TLI and sockets, TLI was modeled after the OSI Transport Service Definition. SVR3 also provided the first commercial release of the streams subsystem, which we say more about in Chapter 33. Unfortunately SVR3 did not include any networking protocols such as TCP/IP: it included only the streams and TLI building blocks. This led to a few companies providing third-party networking protocols for System V, usually TCP/IP and some preliminary implementations of the OSI protocols. System V Release 4 (SVR4) in 1990 finally provided the TCP/IP protocols as part of the basic operating system.

We mentioned X/Open in Section 1.10. In 1988 they released a modification of TLI called XTI: the *X/Open Transport Interface*. XTI is basically a superset of TLI and has gone through several versions. We describe XTI instead of TLI in this text because the Posix.1g standard started with XTI, not TLI. What we describe in the following chapters is XTI as specified for Unix 98 [Open Group 1997], which is nearly identical to the Posix.1g XTI.

XTI uses the term *communications provider* to describe the protocol implementation. The commonly available communications providers are for the Internet protocols, that is, TCP and UDP. The term *communications endpoint* refers to an object that is created and maintained by a communications provider and then used by an application. These endpoints are referred to by file descriptors. We will often shorten these two terms to just *provider* and *endpoint*.

> TLI referred to these as the *transport provider* and the *transport endpoint*.

All the XTI functions begin with `t_`. The header that the application includes to obtain all the XTI definitions is `<xti.h>`. Some Internet-specific definitions are obtained by including `<xti_inet.h>`.

We discuss XTI in the following order:

- TCP clients,
- name and address functions,
- TCP servers,
- UDP clients and servers,
- options,
- streams, and
- additional functions.

Our discussion of XTI is shorter than our discussion of sockets because the network programming *techniques* are the same. What changes are the function names, function arguments, and some of the nitty-gritty details (e.g., accepting TCP connections), but there is no need to duplicate every one of the sockets examples using XTI.

28.2 `t_open` Function

The first step in establishing a communications endpoint is to open the Unix device that identifies the particular communications provider. This function returns a descriptor (a small integer) that is used by the other XTI functions.

```
#include <xti.h>
#include <fcntl.h>

int t_open(const char *pathname, int oflag, struct t_info *info);
```

> Returns: 0 if OK, −1 on error

The actual *pathname* to use depends on the implementation, but typical values for TCP/IP endpoints are `/dev/tcp`, `/dev/udp`, or `/dev/icmp`. Typical values for loopback endpoints are `/dev/ticots`, `/dev/ticotsord`, and `/dev/ticlts`.

The *oflag* argument specifies the open flags. Its value is `O_RDWR`. For a nonblocking endpoint the flag `O_NONBLOCK` is logically ORed with `O_RDWR`.

> This XTI function is similar to the `socket` function. Both return a file descriptor that is associated with a user-specified protocol.

The `t_info` structure is a collection of integer values that describe the protocol-dependent features of the provider. This structure is returned through the *info* pointer, if this argument is not a null pointer. This is our first encounter with one of the XTI structures that begins with t_. There are seven of these structures, which we say more about in Section 28.4.

```
struct t_info {
  t_scalar_t  addr;      /* max #bytes of communications protocol address */
  t_scalar_t  options;   /* max #bytes of protocol-specific options */
  t_scalar_t  tsdu;      /* max #bytes of transport service data unit (TSDU) */
  t_scalar_t  etsdu;     /* max #bytes of expedited TSDU (ETSDU) */
  t_scalar_t  connect;   /* max #bytes of data on conn. establishment */
  t_scalar_t  discon;    /* max #bytes of data on t_XXXdis() & t_XXXreldata() */
  t_scalar_t  servtype;  /* service type supported */
  t_scalar_t  flags;     /* other information (new with XTI) */
};
```

> This is our first encounter with the t_scalar_t datatype, which is new with Unix 98. Older implementations use a long integer for all these members, but this presents a problem on 64-bit architectures as we discussed in Section 1.11. t_scalar_t and t_uscalar_t are therefore defined to be int32_t and uint32_t, respectively.

Before describing each of the members of the t_info structure, we show some typical values for TCP and UDP, in Figures 28.1 and 28.2, which we explain shortly.

	AIX 4.2	DUnix 4.0B	HP-UX 10.30	Solaris 2.6	UnixWare 2.1.2
addr	16	16	16	16	16
options	512	4096	1024	504	360
tsdu	0	0	0	0	0
etsdu	−1	−1	−1	−1	−1
connect	−2	−2	−2	−2	−2
discon	−2	−2	−2	−2	−2
servtype	T_COTS_ORD	T_COTS_ORD	T_COTS_ORD	T_COTS_ORD	T_COTS_ORD

Figure 28.1 t_info values for TCP.

	AIX 4.2	DUnix 4.0B	HP-UX 10.30	Solaris 2.6	UnixWare 2.1.2
addr	16	16	16	16	16
options	512	768	256	468	328
tsdu	8192	9216	65508	65508	65508
etsdu	−2	−2	−2	−2	−2
connect	−2	−2	−2	−2	−2
discon	−2	−2	−2	−2	−2
servtype	T_CLTS	T_CLTS	T_CLTS	T_CLTS	T_CLTS

Figure 28.2 t_info values for UDP.

We are interested in three cases for each of the first six variables in the t_info structure: ≥0, −1 (also called T_INFINITE), and −2 (also called T_INVALID).

addr   This specifies the maximum size in bytes of a protocol-specific address. A value of −1 indicates there is no limit to the size. A value of −2 indicates there is no user access to the protocol addresses.

The value of 16 shown for TCP and UDP is the size of a `sockaddr_in` structure. For an IPv6 endpoint this value will probably be the size of a `sockaddr_in6` structure.

options   This specifies the size in bytes of the protocol-specific options. A value of −1 indicates there is no limit to the size. A value of −2 indicates there is no user access to the options. We talk more about XTI options in Chapter 32.

As we can see in the examples, there is little commonality amongst the various implementations, with the size ranging from 256 to 1024 bytes.

tsdu   TSDU stands for "transport service data unit." This variable specifies the maximum size in bytes of a record whose boundaries are preserved from one endpoint to the other. A value of zero indicates that the communications provider does not support the concept of a TSDU, although it supports a byte stream of data (i.e., no record boundaries). A value of −1 indicates there is no limit to the size. A value of −2 indicates that the transport of normal data is not supported (a rare condition).

For TCP the value is always 0, since TCP provides a byte-stream service without any record boundaries. The predominant value for UDP is 65508, which is wrong. The maximum size of an IP datagram is 65535 bytes (the 16-bit total length field in Figure A.1), so the maximum size of a UDP datagram is 65535 minus 20 (for the IP header) minus 8 (for the UDP header), or 65507.

etsdu   ETSDU stands for "expedited transport service data unit" and this variable specifies the maximum size in bytes of an ETSDU. This is what we called out-of-band data in Chapter 21. A value of zero indicates that the communications provider does not support the concept of ETSDU, although it supports a byte stream of out-of-band data (i.e., record boundaries are not preserved in the out-of-band data). A value of −1 indicates there is no limit to the size. A value of −2 indicates that the transport of expedited data is not supported.

As we expect, UDP does not support any form of out-of-band data. TCP supports the concept, but there is no limit to the amount of out-of-band data that the application can send. (Recall our discussion of TCP's urgent mode in Section 21.2.)

connect   Some connection-oriented protocols support the transfer of user data along with a connection request. This variable specifies the maximum amount of this data. A value of −1 indicates there is no limit to the size. A value of −2 indicates that the communications provider does not support this feature.

TCP does not support this feature, so its value is always −2, and since UDP is not a connection-oriented protocol, its value is also −2. The connection-oriented OSI transport layer supports this feature.

Note that TCP allows sending data with a SYN, as described on pp. 14–16 of TCPv3. Sockets and XTI, however, provide no way to cause TCP to send data with a SYN.

Nevertheless, what this member of the t_info structure is referring to is something different (e.g., the capability provided by the OSI transport layer).

discon   Some connection-oriented protocols support the transfer of user data along with a disconnection request. We will see the possibility of this when we discuss the t_snddis and t_rcvdis functions later in this chapter. This variable specifies the maximum amount of this data. A value of –1 indicates there is no limit to the size. A value of –2 indicates that the communications provider does not support this feature. This variable also specifies the amount of user data that can be sent with an orderly release, using the t_sndreldata and t_rcvreldata functions, which we describe in Section 34.10.

TCP does not support this feature, but it is supported by the OSI transport layer.

servtype   This specifies the type of service provided by the communications provider. There are three possibilities which we show in Figure 28.3.

servtype	Description
T_COTS	connection-oriented service, without orderly release
T_COTS_ORD	connection-oriented service, with orderly release
T_CLTS	connectionless service

Figure 28.3 Types of service provided by communications providers.

TCP is connection oriented with orderly release and UDP is connectionless.

flags   This member, which is new with XTI, specifies additional flags for the communications provider. The two constants shown in Figure 28.4 are defined by including the <xti.h> header that can be returned in this member.

flag	Description
T_SENDZERO	provider supports 0-length writes
T_ORDRELDATA	provider supports orderly release data (t_sndreldata and t_rcvreldata)

Figure 28.4 Values for flags member of t_info structure.

TCP does not support 0-length writes, but UDP does (resulting in a 28-byte IP datagram, with just an IP header and a UDP header, but no data). TCP does not support the T_ORDRELDATA flag either.

28.3 t_error and t_strerror Functions

Recall that most of the socket functions (e.g., socket, bind, connect, and so on) return –1 when they encounter an error and set the variable errno to provide additional information about the error. The XTI functions normally return −1 on an error and set the variable t_errno to provide additional information about the error. (Recall our discussion of errno in Section 23.1 and how it is a per-thread variable. In a threads environment t_errno must also be a per-thread variable.) t_errno is similar to errno in that it is set only when an error occurs and it is not cleared on successful calls.

All the XTI error codes are defined as a result of including <xti.h> and begin with T, as in TBADADDR (incorrect address format), TBADF (illegal transport descriptor), and so on.

One special error value is TSYSERR and when it is returned in t_errno, it tells the application to look at the value in errno for the system error indication.

The two functions t_error and t_strerror are provided to help format error messages resulting from XTI functions.

```
#include <xti.h>

int t_error(const char *msg);
```
Returns: 0

```
const char *t_strerror(int errnum);
```
Returns: pointer to message

t_error produces a message on the standard error output. This message consists of the string pointed to by *msg* (assuming this pointer is nonnull) followed by a colon and a space, followed by a message string corresponding to the current value of t_errno. If t_errno equals TSYSERR, then a message string is also output corresponding to the current value of errno. Finally a newline is output.

t_strerror returns a string describing the value of *errnum*, which is assumed to be one of the possible t_errno values. Unlike t_error, t_strerror does nothing special if this value is TSYSERR.

The program in Figure 28.5 shows the use of these two XTI error functions, along with our err_xti function. (We describe the latter in Section D.4.)

xtiintro/strerror.c

```
 1 #include     "unpxti.h"

 2 int
 3 main(int argc, char **argv)
 4 {
 5     printf("%s\n", t_strerror(TPROTO));

 6     errno = ETIMEDOUT;
 7     printf("%s\n", t_strerror(TSYSERR));

 8     t_errno = TSYSERR;
 9     errno = ETIMEDOUT;
10     t_error("t_error says");
```

```
11      t_errno = TSYSERR;
12      errno = ETIMEDOUT;
13      err_xti("err_xti says");

14      exit(0);
15  }
```
—— *xtiintro/strerror.c*

Figure 28.5 Example of `t_error` and `t_strerror` functions.

The output from this program is

```
aix % strerror
XTI protocol error
system error
t_error says: system error, Connection timed out
err_xti says: system error: Connection timed out
```

28.4 `netbuf` Structures and XTI Structures

XTI defines seven structures that are used to pass information between the application and the XTI functions. One of these, the `t_info` structure that we described in Section 28.2, is just a collection of integer values that describe protocol-dependent features of the provider. The remaining six structures each contain between one and three `netbuf` structures. The `netbuf` structure defines a buffer that is used to pass data from the application to the XTI function or vice versa.

```
struct netbuf {
  unsigned int  maxlen;   /* maximum size of buf */
  unsigned int  len;      /* actual amount of data in buf */
  void          *buf;     /* data (char* before Posix.1g) */
};
```

Figure 28.6 shows the six XTI structures that contain one or more `netbuf` structures, and the various other members of the XTI structure.

Datatype	XTI structure					
	t_bind	t_call	t_discon	t_optmgmt	t_uderr	t_unitdata
struct netbuf	addr	addr			addr	addr
struct netbuf		opt		opt	opt	opt
struct netbuf		udata	udata			udata
t_scalar_t					error	
t_scalar_t				flags		
unsigned int	qlen					
int			reason			
int		sequence	sequence			

Figure 28.6 Six XTI structures and their members.

These six XTI structures that contain the `netbuf` structures are always passed by reference between the application and the XTI function. That is, we pass the address of the XTI structure as an argument to an XTI function. Therefore the XTI function can always read and update any of the three members of the `netbuf` structure (although none of the functions change the `maxlen` member).

The use of the three members of the `netbuf` structure depends on which direction the structure is being passed: from the application to the XTI function, or vice versa, as shown in Figure 28.7. We also note whether the XTI function reads the value of the member or writes the value of the member.

Member	Data from application to XTI	Data from XTI to application
`maxlen`	Ignored.	Read-only. Size of buffer pointed to by `buf`. XTI function will not store more than this amount of data in `buf`. If 0, then nothing is returned and `len` and `buf` are ignored.
`len`	Read-only. Application sets this to amount of data pointed to by `buf`.	Write-only. XTI function sets this member to the actual amount of data stored in `buf`, and this value will always be less than or equal to the value of `maxlen`.
`buf`	Pointer to data stored by application and then processed by XTI function.	Pointer to data stored by XTI function and then processed by application.

Figure 28.7   Processing of three members of `netbuf` structure.

If XTI has more data to return than `maxlen` allows, the XTI call fails with `t_errno` set to `TBUFOVFLW`.

Since the address of the `netbuf` structure is always passed to an XTI function, and since the structure contains both the size of the buffer (`maxlen`) and the amount of data actually stored in the buffer (`len`), there is no need in XTI for all the value–result arguments used with sockets.

28.5   `t_bind` Function

This function assigns the local address to an endpoint and activates the endpoint. In the case of TCP or UDP the local address is an IP address and a port.

```
#include <xti.h>

int t_bind(int fd, const struct t_bind *request, struct t_bind *return);
```
                                                          Returns: 0 if OK, −1 on error

The second and third arguments point to `t_bind` structures:

```
struct t_bind {
    struct netbuf  addr;    /* protocol-specific address */
    unsigned int   qlen;    /* max# of outstanding connections (if server) */
};
```

The endpoint is specified by *fd*. There are three cases to consider for the *request* argument.

request == NULL
> The caller does not care what local address gets assigned to the endpoint. The provider selects an address. The value of the qlen element is assumed to be zero (see below).

request != NULL, but *request->addr.len* == 0
> The caller does not care what local address gets assigned to the endpoint, and again the provider selects an address. Unlike the previous case, however, the caller can now specify a nonzero value for the qlen member of the *request* structure.

request != NULL, and *request->addr.len* > 0
> The caller specifies a local address for the communications provider to assign to the communications endpoint.

Whether the application specifies the address or whether the provider selects an address, the provider returns the address that it assigns to the endpoint in the *return* structure. If the *return* argument is a null pointer, the provider does not return the actual address.

The value of qlen has meaning only for a connection-oriented server: it specifies the maximum number of connections to queue for this endpoint. It is possible for this value to be changed by the provider, in which case the qlen element of the *return* structure indicates the actual value supported by the provider. We say more about this value and measure the actual number of connections queued for various values of qlen with Figure 30.14.

Notice that the addr member of the t_bind structure is an actual netbuf structure, and not a pointer to one of these structures. We will see that this is common to these XTI structures: most contain one or more netbuf structures within the t_*XXX* structure.

> If XTI cannot bind the requested address, the error TADDRBUSY is returned. If TLI encountered this problem, it could bind another local address to the endpoint, requiring the caller to then compare the assigned address to the requested address.

> The XTI method for the caller telling the provider to select an appropriate address is more generic than the method used by bind. For example, with TCP and UDP over IPv4 we must specify an Internet address of INADDR_ANY and a port of zero for the provider to select the local address. This is IPv4-specific and not generic to bind.

> The qlen value corresponds to the backlog argument specified to listen. For a connection-oriented server, the t_bind function does the same work as the bind and listen functions.

> A connection-oriented XTI client must call t_bind before calling t_connect (which we describe next). This differs from connect, which calls bind internally, if the socket has not been bound.

28.6   `t_connect` Function

A connection-oriented client initiates a connection with a server by calling `t_connect`. The client specifies the server's protocol address (e.g., IP address and port for a TCP server).

```
#include <xti.h>

int t_connect(int fd, const struct t_call *sendcall, struct t_call *recvcall);
```
Returns: 0 if OK, −1 on error

The second and third arguments point to a `t_call` structure:

```
struct t_call {
  struct netbuf  addr;      /* protocol-specific address */
  struct netbuf  opt;       /* protocol-specific options */
  struct netbuf  udata;     /* user data to accompany connection request */
  int            sequence;  /* for t_listen() & t_accept() functions */
};
```

The `t_call` structure pointed to by the *sendcall* argument specifies the information needed by the transport provider to establish the connection: the `addr` structure specifies the server's address, `opt` specifies any protocol-specific options desired by the caller, and `udata` contains any user data to be transferred to the server during connection establishment. (Recall from Figure 28.1 that TCP does not support any user data being sent with the connection request.) The `sequence` member has no significance for this function but is used when this structure is used with the `t_accept` function.

On return from this function, the `t_call` structure pointed to by the *recvcall* argument contains information associated with the connection that is returned by the communications provider to the caller: the `addr` structure contains the address of the peer process, `opt` contains any protocol-dependent optional data associated with the connection, and `udata` contains any user data returned by the peer's transport provider during connection establishment. Again, the `sequence` member has no meaning.

The contents of the `opt` structure are protocol dependent. The caller can set the `len` field of this structure to 0, telling the communications provider to use default values for any connection options. We talk more about XTI options in Chapter 32.

The caller can specify a null pointer for the *recvcall* argument, if the return information about the connection is not desired.

By default, this function does not return until the connection is completed, or an error occurs. We discuss how to perform a nonblocking connect in Section 34.3.

We saw in Section 4.3 that common errors when establishing a TCP connection are receiving an RST, receiving an ICMP destination unreachable, and timing out. Unfortunately, when one of these common errors occurs, `t_connect` returns −1, but `t_errno` is set to `TLOOK`, requiring more code to determine the exact reason. We discuss this problem in Sections 28.9 and 28.10 and show an example in Figure 28.13.

The `t_connect` function is similar to the `connect` function.

28.7 `t_rcv` and `t_snd` Functions

By default, XTI applications cannot call the normal `read` and `write` functions (unless the `tirdwr` module is pushed onto the stream, as we describe in Section 28.12). Instead XTI applications must call `t_rcv` and `t_snd`.

```
#include <xti.h>

int t_rcv(int fd, void *buff, unsigned int nbytes, int *flagsp);

int t_snd(int fd, const void *buff, unsigned int nbytes, int flags);
```
                    Both return: number of bytes read or written if OK, −1 on error

The first three arguments are similar to the first three arguments to `read` and `write`: descriptor, buffer pointer, and number of bytes to read or write.

> The input and output functions in the sockets API all use `size_t` for the buffer size, and `ssize_t` for the return value. The XTI functions use `unsigned int` and `int`.

The *flags* argument to `t_snd` is either zero, or some combination of the constants shown in Figure 28.8.

flag	Description
`T_EXPEDITED`	send or receive expedited (out-of-band) data
`T_MORE`	there is more data to send or receive

Figure 28.8 *flags* for `t_rcv` and `t_snd`.

`T_EXPEDITED` is used with `t_snd` to send out-of-band data (Section 34.12). This flag is set on return from `t_rcv` when out-of-band data is received.

`T_MORE` is provided so that multiple `t_rcv` or `t_snd` function calls can read or write what the protocol considers a logical record. This feature applies only to those protocols that support the concept of records. We show an example of this flag with the `t_rcvudata` function and the record-oriented UDP protocol in Figure 31.7. This flag is also used with TCP when reading out-of-band data, as we describe in Section 34.12, but is never used with normal TCP data.

> XTI defines a `T_PUSH` flag that tells the provider to send all the data that is has accumulated but not yet sent. This flag is used with XTI over SNA (IBM's Systems Network Architecture) but should not be used with TCP, and more specifically does *not* cause TCP's PUSH flag to be set.

Note that the *flags* argument to `t_snd` is an integer value, while the corresponding argument for `t_rcv` is a pointer to an integer. But the value pointed to by *flagsp* for `t_tcv` is not a true value–result argument, because its value is not examined by the function; it is set only on return.

Both of these functions return the actual number of bytes read or written. The return value from `t_snd` can be less than *nbytes* if the endpoint is nonblocking or if a signal is caught by the process.

These two functions correspond to the send and recv functions. The XTI T_EXPEDITED flag corresponds to MSG_OOB, although with XTI we cannot specify this flag to t_rcv.

Recall with a TCP socket that the receipt of a FIN causes read to return 0 and the receipt of an RST causes read to return −1, with errno set to ECONNRESET. t_rcv behaves differently when either of these conditions occur on an XTI endpoint:

- When a TCP FIN is received for an XTI endpoint, t_rcv returns −1 with t_errno set to TLOOK. The XTI function t_look must then be called, and it returns T_ORDREL. This is called an *orderly release indication*.

- When a TCP RST is received for an XTI endpoint, t_rcv returns −1 with t_errno set to TLOOK. The XTI function t_look must then be called, and it returns T_DISCONNECT. This is called a *disconnect* or an *abortive release*.

We first discuss the t_look function, followed by the orderly release and abortive release functions.

28.8 t_look Function

Various *events* can occur for an XTI endpoint and these events can occur *asynchronously*. By that we mean that the application can be performing some task when an unrelated event occurs on the endpoint. Some events indicate an error condition (T_UDERR, an error in a previously sent datagram) while other events are not an error (T_EXDATA, the arrival of expedited data).

For example, assume the application calls t_snd to send data to the peer, but right before this something happens at the peer and the peer process sends an RST and terminates. This unexpected event (having received an RST when the application calls t_snd) is passed to the application by having t_snd return −1 with t_errno set to TLOOK. The application then calls t_look to determine what happened (e.g., which event occurred) on the endpoint. The event in this case will be T_DISCONNECT, the receipt of a disconnect (an RST).

```
#include <xti.h>

int t_look(int fd);
```
Returns: event (Figure 28.9) if OK, −1 on error

The integer value returned by this function corresponds to one of the nine events shown in Figure 28.9.

When an event occurs on an XTI endpoint, it is considered *outstanding* until it is *consumed*. Figure 28.10 shows which XTI functions consume the XTI events and also shows that two events are consumed by calling t_look.

Event	Description
T_CONNECT	connection confirmation received
T_DATA	normal data received
T_DISCONNECT	disconnect received
T_EXDATA	expedited data received
T_GODATA	flow control restrictions on normal data lifted
T_GOEXDATA	flow control restrictions on expedited data lifted
T_LISTEN	connect indication received
T_ORDREL	orderly release indication received
T_UDERR	error in previously sent datagram

Figure 28.9 Events for an XTI endpoint.

Event	Cleared by t_look?	Consuming function
T_CONNECT		t_connect, t_rcvconnect
T_DATA		t_rcv, t_rcvv, t_rcvudata, t_rcvvudata
T_DISCONNECT		t_rcvdis
T_EXDATA		t_rcv, t_rcvv
T_GODATA	yes	t_snd, t_sndv, t_sndudata, t_sndvudata
T_GOEXDATA	yes	t_snd, t_sndv
T_LISTEN		t_listen
T_ORDREL		t_rcvrel
T_UDERR		t_rcvuderr

Figure 28.10 XTI events and which functions consume the event.

For the t_connect function on a blocking endpoint (the default), the T_CONNECT event is handled by the function itself and not seen by the application. In the example we were considering (the receipt of a FIN when we call t_snd) this figure shows that we must call t_rcvrel to clear the event.

> At the beginning of this section we described how the receipt of an RST generates a T_DISCONNECT event for the endpoint. Until Unix 98 the receipt of a FIN would generate a T_ORDREL event for the endpoint. Unix 98 makes this optional.

28.9 t_sndrel and t_rcvrel Functions

XTI supports two ways of releasing a connection: an *orderly release* and an *abortive release*. The differences are that an abortive release does not guarantee the delivery of any outstanding data, while the orderly release guarantees this. All communications providers must support an abortive release, while the support of an orderly release is optional. Recall, however, from Figure 28.1 that TCP provides an orderly release.

We can send and receive an orderly release with the following functions.

```
#include <xti.h>

int t_sndrel(int fd);

int t_rcvrel(int fd);
```
Both return: 0 if OK, −1 on error

To understand the semantics of an orderly release, we must remember that a connection-oriented protocol is usually a full-duplex connection between the two processes. The data transfer in one direction is independent of the data being transferred in the other direction. Figure 28.11 shows one use of these functions with TCP, to take advantage of TCP's half-close.

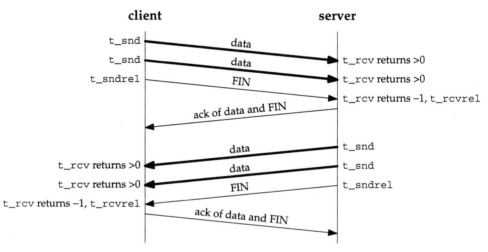

Figure 28.11   TCP's half-close using XTI.

A process issues an orderly release by calling t_sndrel. This tells the provider that the application has no more data to send on this endpoint. For a TCP endpoint, TCP sends a FIN to the peer (after any data that is already queued to be sent to the peer). The process that calls t_sndrel can continue to receive data, it can still read from the descriptor, but it can no longer write to the descriptor.

> This function performs the same action as shutdown with a second argument of SHUT_WR (1) on a TCP socket.

A process acknowledges the receipt of a connection release by calling the t_rcvrel function. This process can still write to the descriptor but it can no longer read from the descriptor.

> There is nothing in the sockets API comparable to t_rcvrel. The receipt of a FIN is delivered to the process as an end-of-file (e.g., read returns 0).

> This feature of XTI forces the application to deal with the full-duplex orderly release, even if the application is not interested in using this feature, as we will see in Figure 28.13.

28.10 t_snddis and t_rcvdis Functions

The following two functions handle an abortive release (a disconnect).

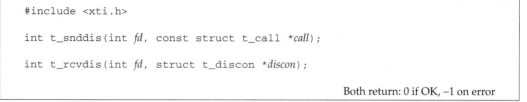

```
#include <xti.h>

int t_snddis(int fd, const struct t_call *call);

int t_rcvdis(int fd, struct t_discon *discon);
```
Both return: 0 if OK, −1 on error

The t_snddis function is used for two different purposes:

- to perform an abortive release of an existing connection, which in terms of TCP causes an RST to be sent, and
- to reject a connection request.

For an abortive release of an existing connection, the *call* argument can be a null pointer, in which case no information is sent to the peer process. Otherwise, the interpretation of the fields in the t_call structure is shown in Figure 28.12.

Member	Disconnection of existing connection	Rejection of new connection
addr	ignored	ignored
opt	ignored	ignored
udata	optional	optional
sequence	ignored	required

Figure 28.12 t_call structure used with t_snddis.

The optional udata member specifies user data to accompany the disconnection, but we saw in Figure 28.1 (the discon member of the t_info structure) that this is not supported by TCP.

> An abortive release is generated by a sockets application by setting the SO_LINGER socket option, setting l_onoff to a nonzero value and l_linger to 0, and then closing the socket (Chapter 7).

When a T_DISCONNECT event occurs on an XTI endpoint (e.g., an RST is received by TCP), the application must receive the abortive release by calling t_rcvdis. If the *discon* argument is a nonnull pointer, a t_discon structure is filled in with the reason for the abortive release.

```
struct t_discon {
  struct netbuf  udata;     /* user data */
  int            reason;    /* protocol-specific reason code */
  int            sequence;
};
```

The udata member contains the optional user data that accompanied the disconnect, reason is a protocol-dependent reason for the disconnect, and sequence is applicable only for servers that are receiving connections.

> There is nothing in the sockets API comparable to t_rcvdis. The receipt of an RST is delivered to the process as an input error (e.g., read returns −1) with errno set to ECONNRESET. Writing to a socket that has received an RST generates SIGPIPE.

28.11 XTI TCP Daytime Client

We now recode our TCP daytime client from Figure 1.5 using XTI. Figure 28.13 shows the function.

——————————————————————————— xtiintro/daytimecli01.c

```
 1 #include    "unpxti.h"

 2 int
 3 main(int argc, char **argv)
 4 {
 5     int    tfd, n, flags;
 6     char   recvline[MAXLINE + 1];
 7     struct sockaddr_in servaddr;
 8     struct t_call tcall;
 9     struct t_discon tdiscon;

10     if (argc != 2)
11         err_quit("usage: daytimecli01 <IPaddress>");

12     tfd = T_open(XTI_TCP, O_RDWR, NULL);

13     T_bind(tfd, NULL, NULL);

14     bzero(&servaddr, sizeof(servaddr));
15     servaddr.sin_family = AF_INET;
16     servaddr.sin_port = htons(13);  /* daytime server */
17     Inet_pton(AF_INET, argv[1], &servaddr.sin_addr);

18     tcall.addr.maxlen = sizeof(servaddr);
19     tcall.addr.len = sizeof(servaddr);
20     tcall.addr.buf = &servaddr;

21     tcall.opt.len = 0;            /* no options with connect */
22     tcall.udata.len = 0;          /* no user data with connect */

23     if (t_connect(tfd, &tcall, NULL) < 0) {
24         if (t_errno == TLOOK) {
25             if ( (n = T_look(tfd)) == T_DISCONNECT) {
26                 tdiscon.udata.maxlen = 0;
27                 T_rcvdis(tfd, &tdiscon);
28                 errno = tdiscon.reason;
29                 err_sys("t_connect error");
30             } else
31                 err_quit("unexpected event after t_connect: %d", n);
32         } else
33             err_xti("t_connect error");
34     }
```

```
35      for ( ; ; ) {
36          if ( (n = t_rcv(tfd, recvline, MAXLINE, &flags)) < 0) {
37              if (t_errno == TLOOK) {
38                  if ( (n = T_look(tfd)) == T_ORDREL) {
39                      T_rcvrel(tfd);
40                      break;
41                  } else if (n == T_DISCONNECT) {
42                      tdiscon.udata.maxlen = 0;
43                      T_rcvdis(tfd, &tdiscon);
44                      errno = tdiscon.reason;     /* probably ECONNRESET */
45                      err_sys("server terminated prematurely");
46                  } else
47                      err_quit("unexpected event after t_rcv: %d", n);
48              } else
49                  err_xti("t_rcv error");
50          }
51          recvline[n] = 0;           /* null terminate */
52          fputs(recvline, stdout);
53      }
54      exit(0);
55  }
```
—— *xtiintro/daytimecli01.c*

Figure 28.13 Daytime client using XTI.

unpxti.h header

1   We define our own unpxti.h header that we #include in all our XTI programs. We show this header in Section D.3.

Create endpoint, bind any local address

12–13   t_open creates the XTI endpoint and we let the system choose its local protocol address by calling t_bind with a null second argument.

Specify server's address and port

14–22   We fill in an Internet socket address structure with the server's IP address and port, identical to Figure 1.5. We then fill in a t_call structure to point to this socket address structure and we also set the len members of the opt and udata structure to 0, indicating no options and no user data.

> There is nothing in XTI that requires the t_call structure to point to a sockaddr_in structure for IPv4. Nevertheless, almost all Unix implementations implement XTI with the Internet protocols using the sockaddr_in structure to pass the protocol address between the application and the provider. In protocol-independent code the use of this structure should be hidden from the application. We show how to do this in the next chapter.

Establish connection

23–34   t_connect establishes the connection, which in this case performs TCP's three-way handshake. As we mentioned earlier, if the connection establishment fails with one of the common errors, t_connect returns TLOOK and we then call t_look to find the event, calling t_rcvdis if the event is T_DISCONNECT. In this case we also store the reason for the disconnect in errno and call our err_sys function to print the appropriate error message.

Read from server, copy to standard output

35-53   We read the data from the server with t_rcv, printing the data on the standard output, until we hit the end of the connection.

Handle orderly release and disconnect

37-47   When t_rcv returns an error, if t_errno is TLOOK we call t_look to obtain the current event for the endpoint. If that event is T_ORDREL, we call t_rcvrel; otherwise if it is T_DISCONNECT, we call t_rcvdis.

If we run this program to the same set of hosts as in Section 4.3, we see the following output. First we connect to a host that is running the daytime server.

```
unixware % daytimecli01 206.62.226.35
Tue Feb  4 15:00:26 1997
```

Next we specify a nonexistent host on the local subnet.

```
unixware % daytimecli01 206.62.226.55
t_connect error: Connection timed out
```

Next we specify a router that is not running a daytime server, receiving an RST in response to our SYN.

```
unixware % daytimecli01 140.252.1.4
t_connect error: Connection refused
```

Finally we specify an IP address that is not connected to the Internet, receiving an ICMP host unreachable in response to our SYNs.

```
unixware % daytimecli01 192.3.4.5
t_connect error: No route to host
```

XTI and Sockets Interoperability

We note in the first example shown with our XTI daytime client, connecting to the server on the host bsdi (206.62.226.35), the server is written using sockets but our client is written using XTI. Nevertheless, the client communicates fine with the server. Similarly we could write a daytime server using XTI and it would communicate fine with our client from Figure 1.5 that uses sockets.

This interoperability is provided by the Internet protocol suite and has nothing to do with sockets or XTI. A client written using TCP or UDP interoperates with a server using the same transport protocol if the client and server speak the same *application protocol*, regardless of what API is used to write either the client or the server. It is the application protocol (e.g., HTTP, FTP, Telnet, and so on) and the transport layer (TCP or UDP) that determine the interoperability. The API we use to write either the client or server makes no difference.

29

XTI: Name and Address Functions

29.1 Introduction

XTI itself says nothing about name and address translation. The only functions required by Unix 98 in this area are the ones we covered in Chapter 9: `gethostbyname`, `gethostbyaddr`, `getservbyname`, and the like. Nevertheless, since many implementations of XTI are on SVR4-derived systems, most of these provide the name and address functions derived from SVR4: what we call the `netconfig` and `netdir` functions. These functions are called the "Network selection and name-to-address mapping facility" in SVR4.

In our client in Section 28.11 we filled in an Internet socket address structure with an IP address and a port number. This is protocol dependent and our goal in this chapter is to avoid knowing the contents of the `netbuf` structure, handling it instead as an opaque structure. We should start with a hostname and a service name, call some functions, and the end result should be a `netbuf` structure, ready for a call to `t_connect`, for example, in a TCP client. This is similar to our use of the `getaddrinfo` function in Section 11.2.

> One problem with the omission of the functions that we will describe from any standard is the lack of a definitive description as to how they operate. For example, most implementations of `netdir_getbyname` accept either a name or a decimal port number for a TCP or UDP service name, but other implementations accept only a name and not a port number.

783

29.2 `/etc/netconfig` File and `netconfig` Functions

The starting point for XTI name and address mapping is the `/etc/netconfig` file. This is a text file with one line for each supported protocol. Some typical values for the fields for each protocol are shown in Figure 29.1.

Network ID	Semantics	Flags	Protocol family	Protocol name	Device
tcp	tpi_cots_ord	v	inet	tcp	/dev/tcp
udp	tpi_clts	v	inet	udp	/dev/udp
icmp	tpi_raw	–	inet	icmp	/dev/icmp
rawip	tpi_raw	–	inet	–	/dev/rawip
ticlts	tpi_clts	v	loopback	–	/dev/ticlts
ticots	tpi_cots	v	loopback	–	/dev/ticots
ticotsord	tpi_cots_ord	v	loopback	–	/dev/ticotsord
spx	tpi_cots_ord	v	netware	spx	/dev/nspx2
ipx	tpi_clts	v	netware	ipx	/dev/ipx

Figure 29.1 Typical entries in the `/etc/netconfig` file.

There are actually seven fields for each line of the file but we do not show the final field, which specifies one or more libraries for directory lookups for that network. Typical values for this final field for the Internet protocols are `/usr/lib/tcpip.so` or `/usr/lib/resolv.so`. These are normally dynamically loadable libraries that provide the network-specific portion of the name-to-address translations.

The network IDs for the four Internet protocols are as we expect. The next three rows are loopback entries (`ti` stands for "transport independent"), and the final two rows are for the Novell Netware protocols (which we do not discuss in this text).

The values shown for the network semantics for the Internet protocols correspond to the service types shown in Figure 28.1, with the exception of `tpi_raw`, which is used for ICMP and raw IP. Note that TCP provides a connection-oriented service with an orderly release, as we saw in Figure 28.1.

The only flag currently defined is `v`, which means the entry is visible to the NETPATH library routines (described shortly).

The device name is used as the argument to `t_open`.

The network services library provides numerous functions to read the `netconfig` file. The function `setnetconfig` opens the file and the function `getnetconfig` then reads the next entry in the file. `endnetconfig` closes the file and releases any memory that was allocated.

> The term *network services library* is from System V and usually refers to the library that is specified to the linker as `-lnsl`. This library, say `/usr/lib/libnsl.so`, contains all the XTI library functions as well as the functions we are about to describe.

```
    #include <netconfig.h>

    void *setnetconfig(void);
```

Returns: nonnull pointer if OK, NULL on error

```
    struct netconfig *getnetconfig(void *handle);
```

Returns: nonnull pointer if OK, NULL on end-of-file

```
    int endnetconfig(void *handle);
```

Returns: 0 if OK, −1 on error

The pointer returned by setnetconfig (called a *handle*) is then used as the argument to the remaining two functions. Each entry in the file is returned as a netconfig structure:

```
struct netconfig {
   char            *nc_netid;     /* "tcp", "udp", etc. */
   unsigned long   nc_semantics;  /* NC_TPI_CLTS, etc. */
   unsigned long   nc_flag;       /* NC_VISIBLE, etc. */
   char            *nc_protofmly; /* "inet", "loopback", etc. */
   char            *nc_proto;     /* "tcp", "udp", etc. */
   char            *nc_device;    /* device name for network id */
   unsigned long   nc_nlookups;   /* # of entries in nc_lookups */
   char            **nc_lookups;  /* list of lookup libraries */
   unsigned long   nc_unused[8];
};
```

The first six members in this structure correspond to the six columns in Figure 29.1. If we wrote a program that looked like the following outline

```
void   *handle;
struct netconfig   *nc;

handle = setnetconfig();
while ( (nc = getnetconfig(handle)) != NULL) {
    /* print netconfig structure */
}
endnetconfig(handle);
```

and assuming the netconfig file were as shown in Figure 29.1, nine netconfig structures would be printed, one per line of the figure, and in that order.

29.3 NETPATH Variable and netpath Functions

The getnetconfig function returns the next entry in the file, letting us go through the entire file, line by line. But for interactive programs (typically clients) we want the searching of the file limited only to the protocols that the user is interested in. This is done by allowing the user to set an environment variable named NETPATH and then using the following functions instead of the netconfig functions described in the previous section.

```
#include <netconfig.h>

void *setnetpath(void);
```
Returns: nonnull pointer if OK, NULL on error

```
struct netconfig *getnetpath(void *handle);
```
Returns: nonnull pointer if OK, NULL on end-of-file

```
int endnetpath(void *handle);
```
Returns: 0 if OK, −1 on error

For example, we could set the environment variable with the KornShell as

```
export NETPATH=udp:tcp
```

Using this setting, if we coded a program as shown in the following outline

```
void   *handle;
struct netconfig  *nc;

handle = setnetpath();
while ( (nc = getnetpath(handle)) != NULL) {
    /* print netconfig structure */
}
endnetpath(handle);
```

only two entries would be printed, one for UDP followed by one for TCP. The order of the two structures returned now corresponds to the order of the protocols in the environment variable, and not to the order in the netconfig file.

If the NETPATH environment variable is not set, all visible entries are returned, in their order in the netconfig file.

29.4 `netdir` Functions

The netconfig and netpath functions let us find a desired protocol. We also need to look up a hostname and a service name, based on the protocol that we choose with the netconfig or netpath functions. This is provided by the netdir_getbyname function.

```
#include <netdir.h>

int netdir_getbyname(const struct netconfig *ncp,
                     const struct nd_hostserv *hsp,
                     struct nd_addrlist **alpp);
```
Returns: 0 if OK, nonzero on error

```
void netdir_free(void *ptr, int type);
```

The first function converts a hostname and service name into an address. *ncp* points to a netconfig structure that was returned by getnetconfig or getnetpath. We must also fill in an nd_hostserv structure with the hostname and service name and pass a pointer to this structure as the second argument.

```
struct nd_hostserv {
    char  *h_host;              /* hostname */
    char  *h_serv;              /* service name */
};
```

The third argument points to a pointer to an nd_addrlist structure, and on success *alpp* contains a pointer to one of these structures:

```
struct nd_addrlist {
    int             n_cnt;    /* number of netbufs */
    struct netbuf   *n_addrs; /* array of netbufs containing the addrs */
};
```

Notice that this nd_addrlist structure points to an array of one or more netbuf structures, each of which contains one of the host's addresses. (Recall that a host can be multihomed.)

For example, using an example similar to Figure 11.1, where the hostname is bsdi (which has two IP addresses) and the service name is domain (TCP and UDP ports 53), then Figure 29.2 shows the information returned by netdir_getbyname, assuming that the netconfig structure used as the first argument to this function was for TCP.

> We again assume that the format used by the provider to represent an Internet address is the sockaddr_in structure. While this is common, it is not required.

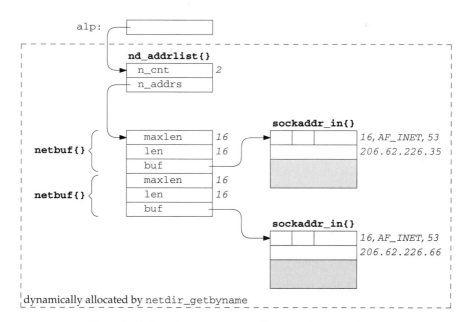

Figure 29.2 Data structures returned by netdir_getbyname.

The final argument to `netdir_getbyname` for this example would be a pointer to our `alp` variable.

When we have finished with these dynamically allocated structures, we call `netdir_free` with *ptr* pointing to the `nd_addrlist` structure, and *type* set to `ND_ADDRLIST`.

The reverse conversion—given a `netbuf` structure containing an address, return the hostname and service name—is provided by `netdir_getbyaddr`.

```
#include <netdir.h>

int netdir_getbyaddr(const struct netconfig *ncp,
                      struct nd_hostservlist **hslpp,
                      const struct netbuf *addr);
```
                                                      Returns: 0 if OK, nonzero on error

The first and third arguments provide the input: a pointer to a `netconfig` structure and a pointer to a `netbuf` structure. The result is a pointer to an `nd_hostservlist` structure, and this pointer is stored in *`*hslpp`*.

```
struct nd_hostservlist {
  int                 h_cnt;      /* number of nd_hostservs */
  struct nd_hostserv  *h_hostservs; /* the hostname/service-name pairs */
};
```

This structure in turn points to an array of one or more `nd_hostserv` structures. The memory for the `nd_hostservlist` structure, the array of `nd_hostserv` structures that it points to, and the hostname and service name strings that this last structure points to are all dynamically allocated. This space is freed by calling `netdir_free` with a *type* of `ND_HOSTSERVLIST`.

29.5   `t_alloc` and `t_free` Functions

One of the requirements for protocol independence with an API is knowing the size of the protocol's addresses without having to know the exact format of the address. With sockets, this size is provided by the `ai_addrlen` member of the `addrinfo` structure that is returned by the `getaddrinfo` function (Section 11.2). With XTI, this size is provided by the `addr` member of the `t_info` structure that is returned by the `t_open` function.

Given this size, the next step is to dynamically allocate the required structures. With sockets we only had to worry about socket address structures and we just called `malloc` when necessary (e.g., Figure 27.5). But with XTI there are six structures (Figure 28.6), each of which contains one or more `netbuf` structures. These `netbuf` structures point to a buffer whose size depends on the size of the protocol address (such as the `addr` member of the `t_call` structure in Section 28.6). To simplify the dynamic allocation of these XTI structures and the `netbuf` structures that they contain, the `t_alloc` and `t_free` functions are provided.

```
#include <xti.h>

void *t_alloc(int fd, int structtype, int fields);

                                    Returns: nonnull pointer if OK, NULL on error

int t_free(void *ptr, int structtype);

                                              Returns: 0 if OK, −1 on error
```

The *structtype* argument specifies which of the seven XTI structures is to be allocated or freed and must be one of the constants shown in Figure 29.3.

The *fields* argument lets us specify that space for one or more `netbuf` structures should also be allocated and initialized appropriately. *fields* is the bitwise-OR of the constants shown in Figure 29.4. Recall from Figure 28.6 that the `netbuf` structure is always named `addr`, `opt`, or `udata`.

structtype	Type of structure
`T_BIND`	`struct t_bind`
`T_CALL`	`struct t_call`
`T_DIS`	`struct t_discon`
`T_INFO`	`struct t_info`
`T_OPTMGMT`	`struct t_optmgmt`
`T_UDERROR`	`struct t_uderr`
`T_UNITDATA`	`struct t_unitdata`

Figure 29.3 *structtype* argument for `t_alloc` and `t_free`.

fields	Allocate and initialize
`T_ALL`	all relevant fields of the given structure

`T_ADDR`
`T_OPT`
`T_UDATA`
	`addr` field of `t_bind`, `t_call`, `t_uderr`, or `t_unitdata`
	`opt` field of `t_optmgmt`, `t_call`, `t_uderr`, or `t_unitdata`
	`udata` field of `t_call`, `t_discon`, or `t_unitdata`

Figure 29.4 *fields* argument for `t_alloc`.

The reason for these different values of the *fields* argument is that some of the XTI structures contain more than one `netbuf` structure, and we might not want to allocate space for all the buffers. For example, the `t_call` structure that we showed in Section 28.6, contains three `netbuf` structures.

```
struct t_call {
  struct netbuf   addr;      /* protocol-specific address */
  struct netbuf   opt;       /* protocol-specific options */
  struct netbuf   udata;     /* user data */
  int             sequence;  /* applies only to t_listen() func */
};
```

Specifying some combination of `T_ADDR`, `T_OPT`, and `T_UDATA` gives us complete control of the allocation. We will normally use `T_ALL` for our examples, because this is the simplest. (See also Exercise 29.2.)

Given the values in Figure 28.1 for AIX 4.2, if we call t_alloc with an *fd* that refers to a TCP endpoint, *structtype* of T_CALL, and *fields* of T_ALL, we get the picture shown in Figure 29.5 on return.

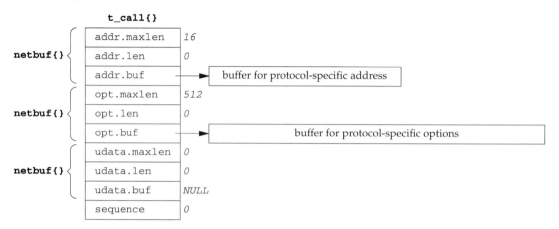

Figure 29.5 Allocation of structures and buffers by t_alloc.

This call to t_alloc allocates space for the t_call structure, which contains three netbuf structures. One buffer is allocated for the protocol-specific address (the addr member) and another for the protocol-specific options (the opt member). The two buf pointers are initialized along with the two maxlen members, and the two len members are set to 0. The third netbuf structure is not used for TCP (the user data to accompany the connection request), so the two lengths in the udata member are set to 0 and the buffer pointer is set to a null pointer.

The t_free function frees a structure that was previously allocated by t_alloc. The *structtype* argument specifies the type of the structure, and the constants shown in Figure 29.3 are used for this. t_free not only frees the memory that was allocated for the structure specified by *structtype*, but it also first checks any netbuf structures contained therein and releases the memory used by those buffers. In our example in Figure 29.5, t_free would first release the two buffers, and then the t_call structure.

29.6 t_getprotaddr Functions

The t_getprotaddr function returns both the local and foreign protocol addresses associated with an endpoint.

```
#include <xti.h>

int t_getprotaddr(int fd, struct t_bind *localaddr, struct t_bind *peeraddr);
```

                                                           Returns: 0 if OK, −1 on error

The addr member (a netbuf structure) of the two t_bind structures is used by this function. When the function is called, the maxlen and buf members of the netbuf structures specify where the result is to be stored. A maxlen of 0 indicates that the corresponding address should not be returned. On return the len members of the netbuf structures contain the size of the address that was stored in buf. This value will be 0 for the local address, if it has not yet been bound, and will be 0 for the peer address, if the endpoint has not yet been connected.

> TLI had an undocumented function named t_getname that could return both the local protocol address and the foreign protocol address.

> The t_getprotaddr function is a combination of both getsockname and getpeername.

> If we are interested in only one of the two addresses, we must still allocate a t_bind structure for the unwanted address and set its maxlen to 0. A simpler design would allow us to specify a null pointer for either of the two arguments when we do not want that address returned.

29.7 xti_ntop Function

We want a simple way to print an XTI protocol address (simpler than netdir_getbyaddr) so we write our own function xti_ntop to do this, similar to our sock_ntop function in Section 3.8. Most XTI implementations provide two functions named taddr2uaddr and uaddr2taddr. The term taddr refers to a *transport address*, contained in a netbuf structure, and the term uaddr refers to a *universal address*, a human-readable text string, stored as a null-terminated C string. These implementations print IPv4 universal addresses as six decimal numbers separated by five decimal points, with the first four numbers being the dotted-decimal IPv4 address and the final two numbers being the 2 bytes of the TCP or UDP port number.

The problem with these two functions, however, is that they require an argument to a netconfig structure, which gives information about the protocol whose address is being converted. But XTI addresses for IPv4 and IPv6 are self-defining. For example, when an IPv4 addresses is stored within a netbuf structure, the address is really a socket address structure and the first member is the address family, AF_INET. The length of this netbuf structure is 16 bytes (e.g., the addr row in Figures 28.1 and 28.2). We expect IPv6 addresses to be stored as sockaddr_in6 structures, with an address family of AF_INET6 and a length of 24 bytes. We are not guaranteed that all XTI addresses stored in netbuf structures are self-defining like this, but IPv4 and IPv6 addresses will be.

> Self-defining may be too strong a term. It is possible for some other protocol suite to use a 16-byte address whose first 2 bytes just happen to equal the constant AF_INET. But practically speaking, this should not be a problem.

We must then choose how to pass the protocol address to our function. Our first choice would be one of the XTI t_*XXX* structures. But for clients the protocol address of the server is in the addr member of a t_call structure (Section 28.6), for servers the protocol address of the client is in the addr member of a t_bind structure (Section 30.2), and for any endpoint the local and foreign addresses returned by t_getprotaddr are in a t_bind structure. Since there is no consistency here (if we passed a pointer to one of these structures, we would also have to pass a flag indicating the type of structure), we will skip the XTI structures and pass a pointer to a netbuf structure to our function instead.

```
#include "unpxti.h"

char *xti_ntop(const struct netbuf *np);
                                          Returns: nonnull pointer if OK, NULL on error
```

The argument is a pointer to a netbuf structure containing the address. The result is stored in static storage within the function. On success the return value is a pointer to the string containing the presentation format of the address.

We will use another function named xti_ntop_host, with the same calling sequence, that formats only the IP address, ignoring the port number.

> These two functions are similar to the code shown in Figure 3.13. We do not show the source code, but it is freely available (see the Preface).

29.8 tcp_connect Function

We can now combine the getnetpath function, which returns information about one or more protocols with the netdir_getbyname function, which looks up a hostname and service and redo our tcp_connect function from Section 11.8 to use XTI instead of sockets and getaddrinfo. We show this function in Figure 29.6.

Initialize

13-15   setnetpath opens the netconfig file. The nd_hostserv structure is initialized with pointers to the hostname and service name.

Get next entry from netconfig file

16-18   getnetpath searches the netconfig file for the next protocol in the NETPATH variable. If the protocol is not TCP, we ignore the entry. Since we are looking for only the entry for TCP, we could call

```
ncp = getnetconfigent("tcp");
```

to locate just this entry. The call

```
freenetconfigent(ncp);
```

would then free the memory allocated by getnetconfigent. But since we would also like this code to work with IPv6, we go through the loop looking at each netconfig structure. Currently it is not known what the entry in the netconfig file will look like for TCP over IPv6, and how the XTI name functions will handle IPv6.

libxti/tcp_connect.c

```
 1 #include     "unpxti.h"

 2 int
 3 tcp_connect(const char *host, const char *serv)
 4 {
 5     int     tfd, i;
 6     void    *handle;
 7     struct t_call tcall;
 8     struct t_discon tdiscon;
 9     struct netconfig *ncp;
10     struct nd_hostserv hs;
11     struct nd_addrlist *alp;
12     struct netbuf *np;

13     handle = Setnetpath();

14     hs.h_host = (char *) host;
15     hs.h_serv = (char *) serv;

16     while ( (ncp = getnetpath(handle)) != NULL) {
17         if (strcmp(ncp->nc_proto, "tcp") != 0)
18             continue;

19         if (netdir_getbyname(ncp, &hs, &alp) != 0)
20             continue;

21             /* try each server address */
22         for (i = 0, np = alp->n_addrs; i < alp->n_cnt; i++, np++) {
23             tfd = T_open(ncp->nc_device, O_RDWR, NULL);

24             T_bind(tfd, NULL, NULL);

25             tcall.addr.len = np->len;
26             tcall.addr.buf = np->buf;    /* pointer copy */
27             tcall.opt.len = 0;   /* no options */
28             tcall.udata.len = 0;     /* no user data with connect */

29             if (t_connect(tfd, &tcall, NULL) == 0) {
30                 endnetpath(handle);      /* success, connected to server */
31                 netdir_free(alp, ND_ADDRLIST);
32                 return (tfd);
33             }
34             if (t_errno == TLOOK && t_look(tfd) == T_DISCONNECT) {
35                 t_rcvdis(tfd, &tdiscon);
36                 errno = tdiscon.reason;
37             }
38             t_close(tfd);
39         }
40         netdir_free(alp, ND_ADDRLIST);
41     }
42     endnetpath(handle);
43     return (-1);
44 }
```

libxti/tcp_connect.c

Figure 29.6 tcp_connect function for XTI.

Search for hostname and service name

19–20   `netdir_getbyname` looks up the hostname and service name, using the `netconfig` structure returned by `getnetpath`.

Go through all server addresses

21–28   This loop tries each returned address for the server, calling `t_open`, `t_bind`, and `t_connect` for each address, until a connection is established, or until all the addresses have been tried. The `t_call` structure is initialized from the `netbuf` structure returned by `netdir_getbyname`.

Connection succeeds

29–33   If the connection succeeds, we clean up and return the connected descriptor. `endnetpath` frees the memory allocated for the `netconfig` structure and closes the `netconfig` file, and `netdir_free` frees all the memory starting with the `nd_addrlist` structure (Figure 29.2).

Handle `t_connect` errors

34–38   If `t_connect` fails, we check for `TLOOK` and call `t_rcvdis` if the connection was refused. We set `errno` to the protocol-dependent error code for the caller to examine. The endpoint is closed.

Finished with all addresses

40–41   After all the addresses have been tried, the `nd_addrlist` structure and the array of `netbuf` structures pointed to by it are freed by `netdir_free`. The `while` loop will keep going through the `netconfig` file, possibly returning additional protocols to try.

> `getaddrinfo` combines the call to `getnetpath` with the testing for the correct protocol or semantics, with the call to `netdir_getbyname`.
>
> An XTI endpoint that fails connection establishment can still be used in another call to `t_connect`. That is, we could move the calls to `t_open` and `t_bind` outside the `for` loop, calling these two functions once for each time through the `while` loop. Naturally, we would also move the call to `t_close` outside the `for` loop. With sockets, however, when a call to `connect` fails, the socket is no longer usable and must be closed (see Figure 11.6, for example).
>
> But there is a subtle problem with this approach with XTI. The problem appears when the host to which we are trying to connect has multiple addresses, and the connection establishment fails. In this scenario the local port never changes and each call to `t_connect` for the next address is delayed by an exponential backoff from the previous call to `t_connect`, because all these connection establishments are from the same local endpoint. That is, if the first call to `t_connect` fails, the next call to `t_connect` might be delayed by 1 second, and if this fails the next call to `t_connect` might be delayed by 2 seconds, and so on. To avoid this problem we `t_close` the endpoint when `t_connect` fails and then create a new endpoint for the next call to `t_connect`.

Example

We now use our `tcp_connect` function and redo our protocol independent daytime client from Figure 11.7 using XTI instead of sockets. Our XTI version is in Figure 29.7.

xtiintro/daytimecli02.c

```
 1 #include    "unpxti.h"

 2 int
 3 main(int argc, char **argv)
 4 {
 5     int     tfd, n, flags;
 6     char    recvline[MAXLINE + 1];
 7     struct t_bind *bound, *peer;
 8     struct t_discon tdiscon;

 9     if (argc != 3)
10         err_quit("usage: daytimecli02 <hostname/IPaddress> <service/port#>");

11     tfd = Tcp_connect(argv[1], argv[2]);

12     bound = T_alloc(tfd, T_BIND, T_ALL);
13     peer = T_alloc(tfd, T_BIND, T_ALL);
14     T_getprotaddr(tfd, bound, peer);
15     printf("connected to %s\n", Xti_ntop(&peer->addr));

16     for ( ; ; ) {
17         if ( (n = t_rcv(tfd, recvline, MAXLINE, &flags)) < 0) {
18             if (t_errno == TLOOK) {
19                 if ( (n = T_look(tfd)) == T_ORDREL) {
20                     T_rcvrel(tfd);
21                     break;
22                 } else if (n == T_DISCONNECT) {
23                     T_rcvdis(tfd, &tdiscon);
24                     errno = tdiscon.reason;     /* probably ECONNRESET */
25                     err_sys("server terminated prematurely");
26                 } else
27                     err_quit("unexpected event after t_rcv: %d", n);
28             } else
29                 err_xti("t_rcv error");
30         }
31         recvline[n] = 0;          /* null terminate */
32         fputs(recvline, stdout);
33     }
34     exit(0);
35 }
```

xtiintro/daytimecli02.c

Figure 29.7 Protocol independent daytime client.

Establish connection

11   We call our tcp_connect function from Figure 29.6 to look up the hostname and service name and establish the connection.

Print peer's protocol address

12–15   We allocate two t_bind structures and call t_getprotaddr to obtain the local protocol address and the peer's protocol address. We print the peer's address by calling our xti_ntop function.

Read data from server until EOF

16–33   The reading of the data from the server is identical to the code in Section 28.11.

We can run the program as follows:

```
unixware % daytimecli02 aix daytime
connected to 206.62.226.43.13
Fri Feb  7 13:28:24 1997
```

29.9 Summary

In SVR4 implementations of XTI network selection is normally done using the
`/etc/netconfig` file and the function `netdir_getbyname` then looks up the hostname and service name, returning an array of `netbuf` structures, one per address and
service. This is similar to the `getaddrinfo` function in Chapter 11. The reverse mapping, from the protocol address to the presentation form, is done by
`netdir_getbyaddr`, which is similar to `getnameinfo`.

Since so many structures are used by XTI, the seven *t_XXX* structures, and the
`netbuf` structures contained therein, two functions are provided to dynamically allocate and free these structures: `t_alloc` and `t_free`.

Exercises

29.1   `getnetconfig` returns a pointer to a structure that it fills in, similar to `gethostbyname`.
But we said the latter function was not thread-safe. Is `getnetconfig` thread-safe, and if
so, how does it do this?

29.2   Write a program that calls `t_alloc` twice for a `t_call` structure for a TCP endpoint. The
first time specify the third argument as `T_ALL` and the second time specify the third argu-
ment as `T_ADDR|T_OPT|T_UDATA`. What happens?

29.3   Why does `t_free` require a *structtype* argument?

29.4   In Figure 29.6 why don't we initialize the `nd_hostserv` structure as

```
struct nd_hostserv hs = { host, serv };
```

30

XTI: TCP Servers

30.1 Introduction

Undoubtedly the most confusing aspect of XTI is the handling of incoming connections by a connection-oriented server. With sockets we just call `accept` and all the details are handled by the kernel or by the sockets library. In the case of TCP, arriving SYNs from clients are placed onto an incomplete connection queue for that endpoint (Figure 4.6). When the three-way handshake completes, `accept` returns (Figure 2.5). If multiple connections are on the completed connection queue, they are returned in a FIFO order by `accept`. In the real world (Figure 4.9) the number of completed connections is normally 0 while the number of incomplete connections is often nonzero.

The *intent* of the XTI model (which is based on the design of the OSI transport service) is to allow the transport layer to tell the server process when a SYN arrives from a client (called a *connect indication*), passing the client's protocol address (IP address and port) to the server. The server process is then allowed to either accept or reject the connection request. The server's TCP, in this model, would not send its SYN/ACK or its RST until the server process tells it what to do. This model is shown in Figure 30.1.

Notice the server's function calls: the first call to `t_bind` (with a nonzero `qlen`) indicates that the endpoint will be accepting incoming connections, `t_listen` returns when the connection is "available" (we say more about this shortly), and the server must then call `t_open`, `t_bind`, and `t_accept` to accept the connection. LISTEN indicates the endpoint's TCP state (Figure 2.4).

When the server process receives notification of the connection request it can also choose not to accept the connection, calling `t_snddis` to reject the request. We show this in Figure 30.2. The *intent* here is that the server is notified when the SYN arrives (the connect indication) and chooses not to accept the connection (perhaps based on the client's IP address or port number, or on the user data sent with the connection request,

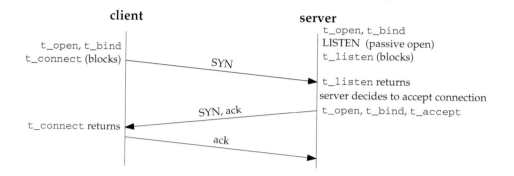

Figure 30.1 Intended model when XTI server accepts connection request.

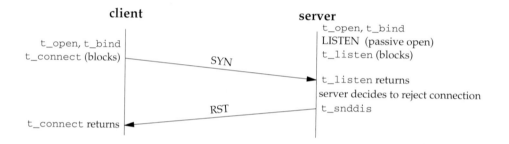

Figure 30.2 Intended model when XTI server rejects connection request.

if supported by the protocol). The application then calls `t_snddis`, causing an RST to be sent instead of completing the three-way handshake. This would make the client's call to `t_connect` return an error.

> Recall from our sockets discussion and the time line in Figure 2.5 that a sockets server can never cause a client's `connect` to fail, because `accept` returns when the three-way handshake completes, one-half of an RTT after `connect` returns. If a sockets server doesn't like a client (perhaps based on the client's IP address or port returned by `accept`), all the server can do is terminate the connection, either with a normal `close` (sending a FIN) or by first setting the `SO_LINGER` socket option and then calling `close` (sending an RST).

We have italicized the word *intent* when describing the XTI scenario because this is not what really happens. This scenario was the intent of the OSI protocols, but most existing TCP implementations automatically accept incoming connection requests (as long as the complete and incomplete connection queues are not full) and do not notify the server process until the three-way handshake is complete.

> The technique of notifying the application when the SYN arrives and then not completing the three-way handshake until the application indicates whether it wants to accept or reject the connection request is sometimes called a *lazy accept*. At least two historical implementations of TLI, from The Wollongong Group and Sequent Computer Systems, performed lazy accepts.

Both have changed to the de facto "standard" method of returning from t_listen when the three-way handshake completes. One reason for the change is that the lazy accept breaks most implementations of FTP.

Posix.1g also requires that when t_listen returns successfully for a TCP endpoint, this indicates a completed connection, and not a connect indication.

[Jacobson 1994] notes that 4.4BSD was supposed to provide a per-socket option to allow a lazy accept with the sockets API for TCP, but this was never implemented. 4.4BSD supports the lazy accept for the OSI protocols.

30.2 t_listen Function

The normal scenario for a connection-oriented XTI server is to call the following functions.

```
listenfd = t_open( ... );        /* create listening endpoint */
t_bind(listenfd, ... );          /* t_bind.qlen > 0 */

for ( ; ; ) {
    t_listen(listenfd, ... );    /* blocks awaiting connection */
    connfd = t_open( ... );      /* create new fd for connected endpoint */
    t_bind(connfd, NULL, NULL);  /* any local addr */
    t_accept(listenfd, connfd, ... );  /* accept on new fd */

    ...             /* process connected endpoint */

    t_close(connfd);
}
```

t_listen is the function that normally blocks, waiting for a connection from a client.

```
#include <xti.h>

int t_listen(int fd, struct t_call *call);
```
Returns: 0 if OK, –1 on error

We described the t_call structure when we described the t_connect function but show it again here:

```
struct t_call {
  struct netbuf   addr;      /* protocol-specific address */
  struct netbuf   opt;       /* protocol-specific options */
  struct netbuf   udata;     /* user data to accompany connection request */
  int             sequence;  /* for t_listen() & t_accept() functions */
};
```

The structure returned through the *call* pointer contains relevant parameters of the connection: addr contains the protocol address of the client, opt contains any protocol-specific options, and udata contains any user data that was sent along with the connection request (which is not supported by TCP). The sequence variable contains a unique value that identifies this connection request. This value will be used when we call t_accept (or t_snddis) to identify which connection to accept (or reject).

Although this function appears similar to the accept function, it is different, as t_listen waits only for a connection to arrive; it does not accept the connection. To do that, the XTI user has to call the t_accept function.

Although *sequence* is an integer, some implementations store an address in this member. Do not assume it is a small integer like a descriptor.

30.3 `tcp_listen` Function

We now write our own function that creates a listening endpoint on which incoming connections can be accepted. The calling sequence is identical to the function of the same name shown in Figure 11.8.

Initialize

16–18   setnetconfig opens the /etc/netconfig file. If the host argument is a null pointer, we pass the special string HOST_SELF to netdir_getbyname. This causes the listening socket to be bound to the wildcard address (0.0.0.0 for IPv4).

Find matching protocol

19–22   We process each line of the /etc/netconfig file looking for the TCP protocol. Notice that we use getnetconfig for a server, while in Figure 29.6 we called getnetpath for a client. This is because a server should not assume that the NETPATH environment variable is set to anything meaningful, since the server might be started by an initialization script or from the command line. Clients, on the other hand, are normally started from an interactive shell on behalf of a user and can assume the variable might be set by the user.

Look up hostname and service name

23–27   netdir_getbyname looks up the hostname and service name, using the pointer to the netconfig structure for the desired protocol.

Open device

28–29   t_open opens the appropriate device (such as /dev/tcp) and we save a copy of this device name in the external xti_serv_dev. We do this because the caller of tcp_listen will need to call t_open again, once per connection, and needs this device name to maintain protocol independence. With the sockets version of tcp_listen we didn't need to save anything like this, because accept (not the process) automatically creates the new socket for each connection.

> This technique is not thread-safe. This is an unfortunate side effect of requiring the application to maintain state information (the name of the device) between the call to t_open for the listening descriptor, and the later calls to t_open for each connected descriptor. One way to make this operation thread-safe is to call strdup to copy the device name into dynamically allocated storage and then return the pointer through another argument to tcp_listen, for the caller to free.

libxti/tcp_listen.c

```
 1 #include    "unpxti.h"
 2 #include    <limits.h>          /* PATH_MAX */

 3 char    xti_serv_dev[PATH_MAX + 1];

 4 int
 5 tcp_listen(const char *host, const char *serv, socklen_t *addrlenp)
 6 {
 7      int     listenfd;
 8      void    *handle;
 9      char    *ptr;
10      struct t_bind tbind;
11      struct t_info tinfo;
12      struct netconfig *ncp;
13      struct nd_hostserv hs;
14      struct nd_addrlist *alp;
15      struct netbuf *np;

16      handle = Setnetconfig();

17      hs.h_host = (host == NULL) ? HOST_SELF : (char *) host;
18      hs.h_serv = (char *) serv;

19      while ( (ncp = getnetconfig(handle)) != NULL &&
20              strcmp(ncp->nc_proto, "tcp") != 0) ;

21      if (ncp == NULL)
22          return (-1);

23      if (netdir_getbyname(ncp, &hs, &alp) != 0) {
24          endnetconfig(handle);
25          return (-2);
26      }
27      np = alp->n_addrs;            /* use first address */

28      listenfd = T_open(ncp->nc_device, O_RDWR, &tinfo);
29      strncpy(xti_serv_dev, ncp->nc_device, sizeof(xti_serv_dev));

30      tbind.addr = *np;             /* copy entire netbuf{} */
31          /* can override LISTENQ constant with environment variable */
32      if ( (ptr = getenv("LISTENQ")) != NULL)
33          tbind.qlen = atoi(ptr);
34      else
35          tbind.qlen = LISTENQ;
36      T_bind(listenfd, &tbind, NULL);

37      netdir_free(alp, ND_ADDRLIST);
38      endnetconfig(handle);

39      if (addrlenp)
40          *addrlenp = tinfo.addr; /* size of protocol addresses */
41      return (listenfd);
42 }
```

libxti/tcp_listen.c

Figure 30.3 XTI tcp_listen function: create listening endpoint.

Enter TCP's LISTEN state

30-36   We call `t_bind`, binding the address returned by `netdir_getbyname` to the endpoint. By setting the `qlen` member of the `t_bind` structure nonzero, this indicates a listening endpoint, and in the case of TCP the endpoint enters the LISTEN state. (We are talking about TCP's LISTEN state here. The XTI state is called `T_IDLE`.) Incoming connections will now be accepted by the transport provider. We let the environment variable `LISTENQ` override the default value of this constant from our `unp.h` header. We have similar code in our `Listen` wrapper function for the sockets `listen` function (Figure 4.8).

Free memory, return values

37-41   We call `netdir_free` and `endnetconfig` to free the allocated memory. We return the size of the protocol addresses (if requested) and the return value of the function is the listening endpoint.

   Notice that we do not call `t_listen` as that is where the server blocks awaiting the incoming connection.

30.4   `t_accept` Function

Once the `t_listen` function indicates that a connection has arrived, we choose whether to accept the request or not. To accept the request the `t_accept` function is called.

```
#include <xti.h>

int t_accept(int listenfd, int connfd, struct t_call *call);
```
Returns: 0 if OK, −1 on error

listenfd specifies the endpoint where the connection arrived; that is, this is the endpoint that was the argument to `t_listen`. The *connfd* argument specifies the endpoint where the connection is to be established. Normally the server creates a new endpoint, *connfd*, to receive the connection.

   The *call* argument identifies which connection is being accepted (in case multiple connections are pending, which we talk about shortly), and its value is whatever was returned by `t_listen`.

   Notice that it is the server's responsibility to create the new endpoint for a server. This is usually done by calling `t_open` between the calls to `t_listen` and `t_accept`.

> We also have the option of specifying the same descriptor for *listenfd* and *connfd*; that is, we accept the new connection on the listening endpoint. But if we do this, no further connections are accepted by the provider until we have finished with this connection (e.g., this is an iterative server). It only makes sense in this scenario to set the `qlen` to one. Given the limitations of this scenario, and the need of most real-world servers to handle multiple connections at the same time, we won't show any examples of this.

30.5 `xti_accept` **Function**

We now write a simple function named `xti_accept` to perform the steps required to accept a connection using XTI. In the common case we should write something like the following for our XTI server applications:

```
listenfd = Tcp_listen( ... );  /* create listening endpoint */

for ( ; ; ) {
    connfd = Xti_accept(listenfd, ... );  /* block, then accept */

    ...     /* process connfd */

    t_close(connfd);
}
```

This is similar to the sockets code, just replacing `accept` with `xti_accept`.

```
#include "unpxti.h"

int xti_accept(int listenfd, struct netbuf *cliaddr, int rdwr);
                                        Returns: nonnegative descriptor if OK, –1 on error
```

On success, the return value is the new connected descriptor, the client's address is returned in the `netbuf` structure pointed to by *cliaddr*, and if the *rdwr* argument is nonzero, our `xti_rdwr` function is called for the connected endpoint.

We show a simple version of our `xti_accept` function in Figure 30.4. We say "simple" because we will see shortly that it can fail when multiple connections are ready at the same time. We will fix this in Section 30.8.

Wait for connection

8–9   A `t_call` structure is allocated to hold the information about the client's connection. `t_listen` blocks, waiting for a connection.

Create new endpoint and bind any local address

10–12   A new endpoint is created by `t_open`, using the pathname that was saved in the external variable `xti_serv_dev` by `tcp_listen`. Any local address is bound to the endpoint. This call to `t_bind` is optional. If we do not bind something to the endpoint, it will be unbound when `t_accept` is called, and the communications provider will bind it automatically to some address that is appropriate.

Accept the connection

13   `t_accept` accepts the connection. `t_accept` knows which connection to accept by looking at the `sequence` member of the `t_call` structure, which was filled in by `t_listen` to identify this particular connection.

Allow **read** and **write**, if desired

14–15   If the caller specifies a nonzero *rdwr* argument, our `xti_rdwr` function pushes the `tirdwr` module onto the stream, allowing `read` and `write` to be used instead of `t_rcv` and `t_snd`.

```
                                                            ————— libxti/xti_accept_simple.c
 1 #include    "unpxti.h"

 2 int
 3 xti_accept(int listenfd, struct netbuf *cliaddr, int rdwr)
 4 {
 5     int     connfd;
 6     u_int   n;
 7     struct t_call *tcallp;

 8     tcallp = T_alloc(listenfd, T_CALL, T_ALL);

 9     T_listen(listenfd, tcallp); /* blocks */

10         /* following assumes caller called tcp_listen() */
11     connfd = T_open(xti_serv_dev, O_RDWR, NULL);
12     T_bind(connfd, NULL, NULL);
13     T_accept(listenfd, connfd, tcallp);

14     if (rdwr)
15         Xti_rdwr(connfd);

16     if (cliaddr) {                  /* return client's protocol address */
17         n = min(cliaddr->maxlen, tcallp->addr.len);
18         memcpy(cliaddr->buf, tcallp->addr.buf, n);
19         cliaddr->len = n;
20     }
21     T_free(tcallp, T_CALL);
22     return (connfd);
23 }
                                                            ————— libxti/xti_accept_simple.c
```

Figure 30.4 Simple version of `xti_accept` function.

Return client's protocol address

16–20   The caller can specify a nonnull *cliaddr* argument that points to a `netbuf` structure. That structure must be initialized by the caller to point to a buffer in which the client's protocol address is returned. We ensure we do not overflow the caller's buffer and then set the `len` member to the size of the address that we return.

Clean up and return

21–22   The `t_call` structure is freed and the connected descriptor is returned.

30.6 Simple Daytime Server

We now rewrite our simple daytime server from Figure 11.10 using XTI, calling our `tcp_listen` and `xti_accept` functions.

Create endpoint

10–17   `tcp_listen` creates the listening endpoint. We allocate memory for the client's protocol address and initialize our `netbuf` structure for this purpose.

——————————————————————————————— xtiintro/daytimesrv01.c

```
 1 #include    "unpxti.h"

 2 int
 3 main(int argc, char **argv)
 4 {
 5     int    listenfd, connfd;
 6     char    buff[MAXLINE];
 7     time_t   ticks;
 8     socklen_t addrlen;
 9     struct netbuf cliaddr;

10     if (argc == 2)
11         listenfd = Tcp_listen(NULL, argv[1], &addrlen);
12     else if (argc == 3)
13         listenfd = Tcp_listen(argv[1], argv[2], &addrlen);
14     else
15         err_quit("usage: daytimetcpsrv01 [ <host> ] <service or port>");
16     cliaddr.buf = Malloc(addrlen);
17     cliaddr.maxlen = addrlen;

18     for ( ; ; ) {
19         connfd = Xti_accept(listenfd, &cliaddr, 0);
20         printf("connection from %s\n", Xti_ntop(&cliaddr));

21         ticks = time(NULL);
22         snprintf(buff, sizeof(buff), "%.24s\r\n", ctime(&ticks));
23         T_snd(connfd, buff, strlen(buff), 0);

24         T_close(connfd);
25     }
26 }
```

——————————————————————————————— xtiintro/daytimesrv01.c

Figure 30.5 Daytime server using XTI.

Wait for connection and accept it

19-20   Our xti_accept function waits for the connection, creates a new endpoint, returns the connected descriptor, and returns the client's IP address and port number. We print the client's protocol address using our xti_ntop function.

Generate daytime output

21-24   Calling time and then ctime generates the current time and date in a human-readable format, and t_snd sends this back to the client across the connection. The endpoint is closed with t_close.

Notice that we simply call t_close when have finished sending data. Since TCP provides an orderly release, this sends a FIN and goes through the normal four-packet connection termination sequence (Figure 2.5), but t_close returns immediately.

This is identical to calling close on a TCP socket.

If we want to wait until the peer TCP receives our data and sends its FIN, we must call `t_sndrel` to send our FIN and then wait for the FIN from the peer with `t_rcvrel`. We would replace the call to `T_close` at the end of Figure 30.5 with the following:

```
T_sndrel(connfd);
while ( (n = t_rcv(connfd, buff, MAXLINE, &flags)) >= 0)
    ;
if (t_errno == TLOOK) {
    if ( (n = T_look(connfd)) == T_ORDREL) {
        T_rcvrel(connfd);
    } else if (n == T_DISCONNECT) {
        T_rcvdis(connfd, NULL);
    } else
        err_quit("unexpected event after t_rcv: %d", n);
} else
    err_xti("t_rcv error");
T_close(connfd);
```

`t_sndrel` sends the FIN and we must then wait for an orderly release indication at which time we call `t_rcvrel`. To do this we call `t_rcv`, ignoring any data that may arrive.

> This scenario is similar to calling `shutdown` for a socket and then waiting until `read` returns an end-of-file (Figure 7.8).

> With XTI we can also cause a `t_close` or `close` to linger, if there is still data queued to send to the peer, instead of returning immediately. This is done by setting the `XTI_LINGER` option, which we describe in Section 32.3. This is similar to the `SO_LINGER` socket option.

30.7 Multiple Pending Connections

We have alluded to the complexity involved when multiple connections arrive at nearly the same time for a listening endpoint. To demonstrate this problem we return to our TCP server in Figure 27.5. We used this server to measure the process control time required for various types of servers. We can run the client that we wrote for this server (Figure 27.4) and specify the number of children to `fork`, establishing multiple connections with the server.

Figure 30.6 shows the server, which is just Figure 27.5 coded to use XTI instead of sockets.

10–22   We call our `tcp_listen` and `xti_accept` functions that we developed earlier in this chapter.

SIGINT handler

31–37   Our signal handler calls our internal `xti_accept_dump` function, and we use this to collect the counters shown in Figure 30.13. This function prints the `count` member of each `cli` structure (Figure 30.7).

———————————————————————————— xtiserver/serv01.c

```
 1 #include     "unpxti.h"

 2 int
 3 main(int argc, char **argv)
 4 {
 5     int     listenfd, connfd;
 6     pid_t   childpid;
 7     void    sig_chld(int), sig_int(int), web_child(int);
 8     socklen_t addrlen;
 9     struct netbuf cliaddr;

10     if (argc == 2)
11         listenfd = Tcp_listen(NULL, argv[1], &addrlen);
12     else if (argc == 3)
13         listenfd = Tcp_listen(argv[1], argv[2], &addrlen);
14     else
15         err_quit("usage: serv01 [ <host> ] <port#>");
16     cliaddr.buf = Malloc(addrlen);
17     cliaddr.maxlen = addrlen;

18     Signal(SIGCHLD, sig_chld);
19     Signal(SIGINT, sig_int);

20     for ( ; ; ) {
21         connfd = Xti_accept(listenfd, &cliaddr, 1);
22         printf("connection from %s\n", Xti_ntop(&cliaddr));

23         if ( (childpid = Fork()) == 0) {      /* child process */
24             Close(listenfd);    /* close listening socket */
25             web_child(connfd);  /* process the request */
26             exit(0);
27         }
28         Close(connfd);              /* parent closes connected socket */
29     }
30 }

31 void
32 sig_int(int signo)
33 {
34     void    xti_accept_dump(void);

35     xti_accept_dump();
36     exit(0);
37 }
```

———————————————————————————— xtiserver/serv01.c

Figure 30.6 TCP concurrent server to demonstrate multiple connection problem.

If we start this server to listen on TCP port 9999

```
unixware % serv01 9999
```

and run the client from another host as

```
solaris % client unixware 9999 1 600 4000
```

everything works fine. (1 is the number of children to `fork`, 600 is the number of connections per child, and 4000 is the number of bytes per connection.) Our server works because we tell the client to spawn only one child, so the connections arrive serially at the server from this one client.

If we change the third command-line argument from 1 to 2, however, we get the following error almost immediately from our server:

```
t_accept error: event requires attention
```

The problem is that two connections arrive at the server at about the same time—one connection from each of the two children. TCP's three-way handshake takes place for both connections because the server's TCP establishes the connections.

While the server TCP is establishing the connections, our server process is blocked in a call to `t_listen` from our server's call to `xti_accept`. When the first connection completes the three-way handshake, `t_listen` returns, and then `t_open` and `t_accept` are called. But when `t_accept` is called for this first connection, the second connection has completed the three-way handshake and is also ready to be accepted. The rules of XTI now dictate that instead of `t_accept` completing the first connection, it returns an error with `t_errno` set to `TLOOK` ("event requires attention"). The event pending is `T_LISTEN` (a connect indication is pending) because there is another connection pending (the second connection).

What is happening here is that `t_accept` always returns an error if there is another connection ready. What we have to do is call `t_listen` to receive all the connect indications, saving the `t_call` structure for each connection, and then call `t_accept` for each connection.

> Why does XTI accept connections in this bizarre manner? If `t_listen` really returned when the client's SYN arrived (Figure 30.1), then forcing the server to call `t_listen` on all SYNs that have arrived, before calling `t_accept` for any single connection, gives the server process the opportunity to choose the order in which it accepts the pending connections. The server might prioritize them, for example, based on the IP address or port number returned by `t_listen` or based on the user data that might accompany the connection request (which is not supported by TCP). But given that `t_listen` does not return for TCP until the three-way handshake completes, all this feature does is add (needless) complexity to the server.

> What we just described corresponds to XTI in Unix 95. Posix.1g and Unix 98 change the description of `t_accept` to say that it *may* fail with `t_errno` set to `TLOOK`. Nevertheless we must be prepared for `t_accept` to fail in this fashion.

30.8 `xti_accept` Function (Revisited)

We now redo our simple `xti_accept` function from Figure 30.4 into one that is more robust. There are two scenarios that we must handle.

- `t_accept` failing because there is another connection pending (`t_look` will return `T_LISTEN`), and

- `t_accept` failing because a pending connection has received an RST (`t_look` will return `T_DISCONNECT`).

To handle these semantics we must maintain a queue of pending connections. The potential size of this queue is the value of `qlim` when we called `t_bind` for the listening endpoint. There are lots of possible data structures that we can use to keep track of the pending connections. For simplicity we will use a simple stack (array) of `cli` structures. Each structure contains the connected descriptor, a diagnostic counter of how often the structure is used, and a pointer to a `t_call` structure.

Let's assume that three clients establish connections with our server at about the same time. The server TCP will complete all three of the three-way handshakes and when the first one is returned by `t_listen` we use the `cli[0]` structure in our array, as shown in Figure 30.7.

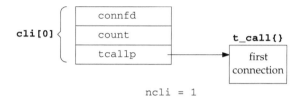

ncli = 1

Figure 30.7   Data structures after first client connection returned by `t_listen`.

`connfd` is the new descriptor that we create by calling `t_open`, on which the connection will be accepted. `count` is a diagnostic counter that we examine shortly with our test program. `tcallp` is a pointer to a `t_call` structure that is filled in by `t_listen` and then passed to `t_accept`. It contains the client's protocol address (the `addr` member) and the connection identifier (the `sequence` member). We also keep a counter (`ncli`) of the number of entries in our array of `cli` structures, and its value would be 1.

Assume that we call `t_accept` to accept this first connection, but `t_accept` returns an error of `TLOOK` and `t_look` returns `T_LISTEN`. We must then call `t_listen` again to fetch the next connection. We just add another entry to our `cli` array and increment `ncli`. We show this in Figure 30.8.

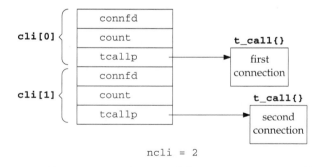

ncli = 2

Figure 30.8   Data structures after second client connection returned by `t_listen`.

We always call `t_accept` for the "last" entry in the array, the one whose array index is `ncli-1`. This causes us to process the connections on a last-in, first-out basis (LIFO), instead of the first-in, first-out (FIFO) that one might expect. It is not hard to change this, if desired, but adds complexity.

Figure 4.9 shows that even on a moderately busy Web server, it is rare for more than one completed connection to be ready for the application to accept at any given time. Therefore the simplicity of our design is practical.

At this point we call t_accept for cli[1] but assume it also returns an error of TLOOK and t_look then returns T_LISTEN. We must add another entry to our array, cli[2], as shown in Figure 30.9.

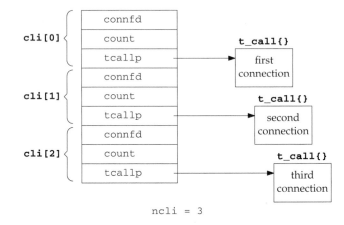

ncli = 3

Figure 30.9   Data structures after third client connection returned by t_listen.

At this point we have three connections pending and we now call t_accept for cli[2]. But now assume that the first client (cli[0]) has just aborted its connection by sending an RST. Once again the call to t_accept fails with an error of TLOOK, but this time t_look returns T_DISCONNECT. We must now call t_rcvdis to receive the disconnect. Recall that one entry in the t_discon structure that this function fills in is the sequence identifier of the connection that was aborted (Section 28.10). We must use this to search our array of cli structures, looking for the entry whose t_call structure has a matching sequence. We then move the entries "up" by one, overwriting cli[0] with cli[1], and then overwriting cli[1] with cli[2]. We also decrement ncli and have the data structures shown in Figure 30.10.

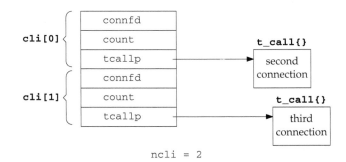

ncli = 2

Figure 30.10   Data structures after first connection is aborted.

We call t_accept (again) for cli[1] but assume this time it succeeds. We then remove the cli[1] entry from the array, decrement ncli to become 1, and pass the third connection back to the caller of xti_accept. Remember that everything described so far in this example, starting with the first call to t_listen, has taken place in our xti_accept function. This is now the first time this function has returned a connected descriptor to the caller.

The next time xti_accept is called, ncli will be 1, and t_accept is called for cli[0]. Assuming it succeeds, the second connection is returned to the caller.

We now show the source code for our xti_accept function, the first half of which is in Figure 30.11.

```
                                                                    ─── libxti/xti_accept.c
 1 #include    "unpxti.h"

 2 static int ncli = -1, ndisconn;
 3 static struct cli {
 4     int      connfd;                  /* connected fd or -1 if disconnected */
 5     int      count;
 6     struct t_call *tcallp;           /* ptr to t_alloc'ed structure */
 7 } *cli;                              /* cli[0], cli[1], ..., cli[ncli-1] are in use */

 8 int
 9 xti_accept(int listenfd, struct netbuf *cliaddr, int rdwr)
10 {
11     int      i, event;
12     u_int    n;
13     char     *ptr;
14     struct t_discon tdiscon;

15     if (ncli == -1) {                /* initialize first time through */
16         if (cli != NULL)
17             err_quit("already initialized");
18         if ( (ptr = getenv("LISTENQ")) != NULL)
19             n = atoi(ptr);
20         else
21             n = LISTENQ;
22         cli = Calloc(n, sizeof(struct cli));
23         for (i = 0; i < n; i++)
24             cli[i].tcallp = T_alloc(listenfd, T_CALL, T_ALL);
25         ncli = 0;
26     }
                                                                    ─── libxti/xti_accept.c
```

Figure 30.11 xti_accept function: first part.

Declare static variables

2-7   The counter ncli, another diagnostic counter of aborted connections ndisconn, and a pointer to our array of cli structures are declared as static.

Initialize the first time we are called

15-26   The first time we are called we allocate an array of cli structures, the number of entries in the array being the constant LISTENQ or the value of the environment variable of the same name. This will be the same value as tcp_listen used in the call to `t_bind`. For every element in the array we then call `t_alloc` to allocate a `t_call` structure and store the returned pointer in our `cli` structure.

> In a threads environment this one copy of the `cli` array and its `ncli` counter must be protected to allow multiple threads to call `xti_accept` at the same time.

The second half of the function is shown in Figure 30.12.

Wait for a connection

28–35   If our array is empty, we must call `t_listen` and wait for a connection. This call to `t_listen` is where the listening server spends most of its time. When `t_listen` returns, the client's protocol address and the connection identifier have been saved in the `t_call` structure by `t_listen`. We call `t_open` to create a new endpoint on which the connection will be accepted and bind this endpoint to any local address.

Call `t_accept`; return on success

36–46   We call `t_accept` to accept the connection specified by `cli[ncli-1]`, and if it succeeds we return this connected descriptor to the caller. We also call our `xti_rdwr` function, if the caller want to use `read` and `write`, and optionally return the client's protocol address.

Handle additional pending connections

47–53   If `t_accept` returns `TLOOK` and `t_look` returns `T_LISTEN`, another connection is pending and we must call `t_listen` to receive the information about this new connection. We note that this call will not block, since the endpoint has a `T_LISTEN` event pending. We also call `t_open` and `t_bind` and save the information in the array entry `cli[ncli]`.

Handle disconnection of pending connection

54–66   If `t_accept` returns `TLOOK` and `t_look` returns `T_DISCONNECT`, one of the connections that has already been returned by `t_listen` has been aborted by the client. We call `t_rcvdis` to obtain the information about the aborted connection (i.e., its `sequence`) and then search our array for the matching entry. When we find the matching entry we calculate the number of entries beyond the one being aborted (n) and call `memmove` to move the remaining entries. We call `memmove`, instead of `memcpy`, because the former correctly handles overlapping fields, which we will have in this scenario (see Exercise 30.3).

We can test our server from Figure 30.6 using this new version of `xti_accept` and it works as expected with multiple clients. We also want to see how often `t_accept` returns an error because of an additional pending connection. To see this we write a simple function that prints the `count` member of the `cli` structure, and the `ndisconn` counter (which we describe shortly), and then call this function from the server parent's `SIGINT` signal handler (Figure 30.6). Figure 30.13 (p. 814) shows the results with the server on UnixWare 2.1.2 and the client on Solaris 2.5.1. We vary the number of client children from 1 to 4, always issuing a total of 600 connections from all the children.

libxti/xti_accept.c

```
27      for ( ; ; ) {
28          if (ncli == 0) {            /* need to wait for a connection */
29              T_listen(listenfd, cli[ncli].tcallp);   /* block here */

30                  /* following assumes caller called tcp_listen() */
31              cli[ncli].connfd = T_open(xti_serv_dev, O_RDWR, NULL);
32              T_bind(cli[ncli].connfd, NULL, NULL);
33              cli[ncli].count++;
34              ncli++;
35          }
36          if (t_accept(listenfd, cli[ncli - 1].connfd,
37                      cli[ncli - 1].tcallp) == 0) {
38              ncli--;                /* success */
39              if (rdwr)
40                  Xti_rdwr(cli[ncli].connfd);

41              if (cliaddr) {        /* return client's protocol address */
42                  n = min(cliaddr->maxlen, cli[ncli].tcallp->addr.len);
43                  memcpy(cliaddr->buf, cli[ncli].tcallp->addr.buf, n);
44                  cliaddr->len = n;
45              }
46              return (cli[ncli].connfd);

47          } else if (t_errno == TLOOK) {
48              if ( (event = T_look(listenfd)) == T_LISTEN) {
49                  T_listen(listenfd, cli[ncli].tcallp);   /* won't block */
50                  cli[ncli].connfd = T_open(xti_serv_dev, O_RDWR, NULL);
51                  T_bind(cli[ncli].connfd, NULL, NULL);
52                  cli[ncli].count++;
53                  ncli++;

54              } else if (event == T_DISCONNECT) {
55                  T_rcvdis(listenfd, &tdiscon);
56                  for (i = 0; i < ncli; i++) {
57                      if (cli[i].tcallp->sequence == tdiscon.sequence) {
58                          T_close(cli[i].connfd);
59                          ndisconn++;
60                          ncli--;
61                          if ( (n = ncli - i) > 0)
62                              memmove(&cli[i], &cli[i + 1],
63                                      n * sizeof(struct cli));
64                          break;
65                      }
66                  }
67              } else
68                  err_quit("unexpected t_look event %d", event);
69          } else
70              err_xti("unexpected t_accept error");
71      }
72  }
```

libxti/xti_accept.c

Figure 30.12 xti_accept function: second half.

Server counter	#client children			
	1	2	3	4
`cli[0].count`	600	309	95	102
`cli[1].count`		291	286	121
`cli[2].count`			219	235
`cli[3].count`				142
Total	600	600	600	600

Figure 30.13 Counter of how often t_accept returns T_LISTEN.

Even with only two clients, each establishing 300 connections, one after the other, at about the same time, t_accept returns TLOOK with T_LISTEN about half the time.

> Why do we see multiple completed connections ready for the server to accept so often in this scenario, when we showed earlier (Figure 4.9) that on a busy Web server this is a rare occurrence? One reason is that we are forcing this scenario in Figure 30.13 with all the connections coming from a client on the same LAN. Second, the rate of the connections, 600 in about 12 seconds, corresponds to more than 4 million connections per day. Lastly, we purposely ran this example on a slow server (a 75-Mhz Pentium CPU) to test the handling of multiple pending connections with our xti_accept function. We can summarize this scenario as being infrequent enough in the real world so that handling them in a LIFO order by our xti_accept function is fine, but since the scenario can and does occur, the server must handle it.

To test this server with a client that aborts just-established connections we modify our client from Figure 27.4 by changing the innermost loop to the following:

```
    for (j = 0; j < nloops; j++) {
        fd = Tcp_connect(argv[1], argv[2]);

+       if (i == 2 && (j % 3) == 0) {
+           struct linger   ling;
+
+           ling.l_onoff = 1;
+           ling.l_linger = 0;
+           Setsockopt(fd, SOL_SOCKET, SO_LINGER, &ling, sizeof(ling));
+           Close(fd);
+
+           /* and just continue on for this client connection ... */
+           fd = Tcp_connect(argv[1], argv[2]);
+       }

        Write(fd, request, strlen(request));

        if ( (n = Readn(fd, reply, nbytes)) != nbytes)
            err_quit("server returned %d bytes", n);

        Close(fd);          /* TIME_WAIT on client, not server */
    }
```

The lines preceded by a plus sign are new. This modification causes the third child (i equals 2) to abort every third just-completed connection. To send the RST we set the SO_LINGER socket option accordingly and close the socket. We then create another connection and continue with the loop. The effect on the server depends on the timing: some RSTs may arrive between the server's call to t_listen and its call to t_accept (and we count these with our ndisconn counter to verify that the code is exercised). Others may arrive before t_listen notifies the server of the connection, and others may arrive after the connection is accepted.

XTI Queue Length versus Listen Backlog

The XTI queue length and the listen backlog are similar but not identical. First, there has never been an exact specification of what the listen backlog means. We saw in Figure 4.10 that current systems differ in their interpretation.

Posix.1g states that the XTI queue length value specifies the number of "outstanding connect indications" that the provider should support for the endpoint. An outstanding connect indication is one that has been passed to the application by the provider but not yet accepted or rejected. The provider *may* queue more connect indications than specified but must ensure that there are never more than qlen delivered to the application that are still outstanding at any given time.

If the implementation passed connect indications to the application when they arrived (i.e., when the client SYN arrives at the server), then this form of application queueing might make sense. But given that a TCP connection is completely established before the application is notified, there is no real need for the application to queue these connections.

As usual, the way to make any sense out of standards is to see what the implementations really provide when we specify different values for the qlen. We modified Figure E.15 to work with XTI instead of sockets and ran the program on our five systems that support XTI. The results are shown in Figure 30.14.

request qlen	AIX 4.2		DUnix 4.0B		HP-UX 10.30		Solaris 2.6		UWare 2.1.2	
	return qlen	actual #conns	return qlen	actual #conns	return qlen	actual #conns	return qlen	actual #conns	return qlen	actual #conns
0	0	0	0	0	0	0	0	0		0
1	1	3	1	2	1	1	1	1		1
2	2	6	2	4	2	2	2	2		2
3	3	8	3	6	3	3	3	3		3
4	4	11	4	8	4	4	4	4		4
5	5	13	5	10	5	5	5	5		5
6	5	13	6	12	6	6	6	6		6
7	5	13	7	14	7	7	7	7		7
8	5	13	8	16	8	8	8	8		8
9	5	13	9	18	9	9	9	9		9
10	5	13	10	20	10	10	10	10		10
11	5	13	11	22	11	11	11	11		11
12	5	13	12	24	12	12	12	12		12
13	5	13	13	26	13	13	13	13		13
14	5	13	14	28	14	13	14	14		14

Figure 30.14 Actual number of queued connections for values of XTI qlen.

Recall from Section 28.5 that the third argument to t_bind is a pointer to a t_bind structure that is filled in upon return by the provider. By looking at the qlen member of this structure we can see what the provider sets this to. (XTI calls this a "negotiated" value.) We note that most systems return the value that was specified, unless a smaller value is supported (AIX). One system (UnixWare) does not return the value.

None of the systems allow any connections when the qlen is 0 (which differs from a listen backlog of 0 in Figure 4.10), and two of the systems returned an error from t_connect (HP-UX and Solaris). Some of the implementations queue more connections than specified by qlen (AIX and Digital Unix), but the remaining three do not.

> Here we are measuring the number of connections queued by the provider, not by the application, but it is this queueing by the provider in which we are most interested.

Setting the Server's Listening Queue Length to 1

One way to avoid the complication involved in accepting XTI connections is to set the qlen member of the t_bind structure to 1. But the problem with this solution is that many implementations will then queue only one client connection (Figure 30.14) and then ignore all other arriving SYNs until this connection is accepted.

We can test this feature with our server from this section. We again run the server on UnixWare 2.1.2, which queues only one connection when the specified qlen is 1. Like the numbers in Figure 30.13, we vary the number of client children that are issuing connections between 1 and 4, but this time we measure the clock time (in seconds) required for the fixed number of connections (600).

Queue	#client children			
length	1	2	3	4
1	10.6	12.2	15.6	13.2
1024	10.6	10.2	10.3	10.4

Figure 30.15   Clock time for 600 total connections, varying number of children and listen queue.

For a queue length of 1, the clock time increases as the number of children increases. This is caused by many of the client SYNs being ignored by the server, because one connection has filled the queue, and the client must retransmit the SYN. But when the queue length is greater than the number of simultaneous connections, the clock time decreases for the few number of children that we are testing here.

These numbers verify our previous statement: a queue length of 1 is unrealistic for a real-world server.

30.9 Summary

Accepting client connections with XTI is much harder than the same operation with sockets. As we described, the reason for the added complexity is to allow protocols to provide a lazy accept, where the application is notified when the connect request arrives, and not when the connection establishment is complete. TCP implementations do not provide a lazy accept, and Unix 98 no longer requires t_accept to return an event of T_LISTEN when another connection is pending, but for backward compatibility XTI servers must handle this scenario.

Exercises

30.1 We mentioned in Section 30.2 that some implementations store a pointer in the sequence member of the t_call structure that is filled in by t_listen. What happens on a 64-bit architecture?

30.2 Why do we add one to PATH_MAX in the declaration of xti_serv_dev in Figure 30.3?

30.3 In Figure 30.12 we call memmove and mention that this is needed since the source and destination overlap. Assume a 4-byte array, with elements x[0] through x[3] (drawn from left to right) and assume that we want to delete x[1], moving the next two elements "left" by 1 byte, leaving three elements. Draw a picture of the source field and destination field. Then describe what happens if the copy operation starts from the beginning of the source field to the beginning of the destination (copying from right to left). Then describe what happens if the copy operation starts from the end of the source field to the end of the destination (copying from left to right). Does memcpy guarantee in which direction the copy takes place?

30.4 Recode Figure E.15 to use XTI instead of sockets.

30.5 Recode Figures 30.11 and 30.12 to use a linked list of cli structures instead of the fixed-size array that we used for simplicity. Allocate the structures dynamically.

31

XTI: UDP Clients and Servers

31.1 Introduction

XTI provides three functions for connectionless clients and servers: `t_sndudata` to send a datagram, `t_rcvudata` to receive a datagram, and `t_rcvuderr` to obtain information about an asynchronous error. With sockets we had the option of calling `connect` for a UDP application, but XTI does not provide that choice.

31.2 `t_rcvudata` and `t_sndudata` Functions

These two functions are used with connectionless protocols (such as UDP) to receive and send datagrams.

```
#include <xti.h>

int t_rcvudata(int fd, struct t_unitdata *unitdata, int *flagsp);

int t_sndudata(int fd, struct t_unitdata *unitdata);
```
                                                    Both return: 0 if OK, −1 on error

For the `t_sndudata` function the `t_unitdata` structure specifies the destination address, any options, and the actual data to send.

```
struct t_unitdata {
  struct netbuf  addr;    /* protocol-specific address */
  struct netbuf  opt;     /* protocol-specific options */
  struct netbuf  udata;   /* user data */
};
```

For the `t_rcvudata` function this structure specifies where to store the sender's proto-col address, any received options, and the actual data.

Both of these functions return 0 if everything is OK, or −1 on an error. This differs from most read and write functions that usually return the number of bytes transferred. With `t_rcvudata` the size of the received datagram is returned as the `udata.len` member of the `t_unitdata` structure. `t_sndudata` does not return the number of bytes written; it just returns 0 on success (i.e., the entire datagram has been copied into the kernel's buffers).

The integer pointed to by *flagsp* is similar to the final argument to `t_rcv`: it is not a value–result argument because its value is not examined by the function; it is set only on return. The `T_MORE` flag is returned if another call to `t_rcvudata` is required to read more of the datagram (i.e., what remains of the datagram exceeds the length of the receive buffer). We show an example of this in Section 31.6.

> These two XTI functions correspond to the `sendto` and `recvfrom` functions.

31.3 `udp_client` Function

Before showing a UDP example using XTI we will write a function named `udp_client`, with the same calling sequence as shown in Section 11.10, that creates an XTI endpoint for a UDP client. This function, shown in Figure 31.1, handles the host-name and service name conversions described in Chapter 29.

Look up hostname and service name

12–19   The calls to `getnetpath` and `netdir_getbyname` are similar to the calls described in Figure 29.6.

Open device, bind any local address

20–21   `t_open` opens the appropriate device and `t_bind` binds any local address to the endpoint.

Allocate `t_unitdata` structure

22   `t_alloc` allocates a `t_unitdata` structure but only the `addr` structure within, not the `opt` or `udata` structures. We do not allocate the `opt` structure because per-datagram options are rare with UDP (Chapter 32). We do not allocate the `udata` struc-ture because the range of UDP datagram sizes is large, up to 65507 bytes as shown in Figure 28.2, but few applications deal with these maximum-sized datagrams. Since most applications deal with smaller datagrams (a few thousand bytes at the most), it makes more sense for the application to allocate the data buffer itself, based on its needs.

Use first returned address for server

23–25   The `addr` structure is filled in with the first address returned for the server. Fig-ure 31.2 (p. 822) shows the data structures involved, assuming that two `netbuf` struc-tures are returned for the specified hostname and service name, and assuming that the implementation uses the `sockaddr_in` structure to represent IPv4 addresses.

libxti/udp_client.c

```
 1 #include     "unpxti.h"

 2 int
 3 udp_client(const char *host, const char *serv, void **vptr, socklen_t *lenp)
 4 {
 5     int     tfd;
 6     void    *handle;
 7     struct netconfig *ncp;
 8     struct nd_hostserv hs;
 9     struct nd_addrlist *alp;
10     struct netbuf *np;
11     struct t_unitdata *tudptr;

12     handle = Setnetpath();

13     hs.h_host = (char *) host;
14     hs.h_serv = (char *) serv;

15     while ( (ncp = getnetpath(handle)) != NULL) {
16         if (strcmp(ncp->nc_proto, "udp") != 0)
17             continue;

18         if (netdir_getbyname(ncp, &hs, &alp) != 0)
19             continue;

20         tfd = T_open(ncp->nc_device, O_RDWR, NULL);

21         T_bind(tfd, NULL, NULL);

22         tudptr = T_alloc(tfd, T_UNITDATA, T_ADDR);

23         np = alp->n_addrs;       /* use first server address */
24         tudptr->addr.len = min(tudptr->addr.maxlen, np->len);
25         memcpy(tudptr->addr.buf, np->buf, tudptr->addr.len);

26         endnetpath(handle);
27         netdir_free(alp, ND_ADDRLIST);

28         *vptr = tudptr;          /* return pointer to t_unitdata{} */
29         *lenp = tudptr->addr.maxlen;   /* and size of addresses */
30         return (tfd);
31     }
32     endnetpath(handle);
33     return (-1);
34 }
```

libxti/udp_client.c

Figure 31.1 udp_client function for XTI.

The addr.maxlen value should be the same as the maxlen values in the structure returned by netdir_getbyname (16 for IPv4), but we use the min macro to be certain we do not overflow the destination of the memcpy. We show four lengths of 0 and two null pointers for the opt and udata structures, since t_alloc initializes these members to these values because we told it to allocate and initialize only the addr structure with the T_ADDR argument.

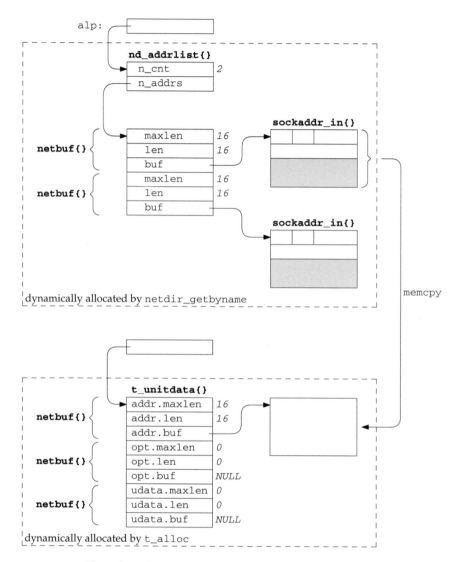

Figure 31.2 Data structures during call to udp_client.

Free memory and return

26–33   endnetpath frees the memory allocated for the netconfig structure and netdir_free releases the memory that it allocated (Figure 31.2). The pointer to the t_unitdata structure is returned to the caller, along with the size of the protocol addresses and the descriptor for the endpoint. We return the size of the protocol addresses as addr.maxlen instead of addr.len, because this value is returned for the caller to use in a call to malloc. Should the addresses be variable-length, we should return the maximum size, and not just the size of this address.

Example: Daytime Client

We now use our udp_client function to recode our protocol-independent daytime client from Figure 11.12 to use XTI, which we show in Figure 31.3.

————————————————————————————— xtiudp/daytimeudpcli1.c
```
 1 #include     "unpxti.h"

 2 int
 3 main(int argc, char **argv)
 4 {
 5     int     tfd, flags;
 6     char    recvline[MAXLINE + 1];
 7     socklen_t addrlen;
 8     struct t_unitdata *sndptr, *rcvptr;

 9     if (argc != 3)
10         err_quit("usage: daytimeudpcli <hostname> <service>");

11     tfd = Udp_client(argv[1], argv[2], (void **) &sndptr, &addrlen);

12     rcvptr = T_alloc(tfd, T_UNITDATA, T_ADDR);

13     printf("sending to %s\n", Xti_ntop_host(&sndptr->addr));

14     sndptr->udata.maxlen = MAXLINE;
15     sndptr->udata.len = 1;
16     sndptr->udata.buf = recvline;
17     recvline[0] = 0;                /* 1-byte datagram containing null byte */
18     T_sndudata(tfd, sndptr);

19     rcvptr->udata.maxlen = MAXLINE;
20     rcvptr->udata.buf = recvline;
21     T_rcvudata(tfd, rcvptr, &flags);
22     recvline[rcvptr->udata.len] = 0;    /* null terminate */
23     printf("from %s: %s", Xti_ntop_host(&rcvptr->addr), recvline);

24     exit(0);
25 }
```
————————————————————————————— xtiudp/daytimeudpcli1.c

Figure 31.3 UDP daytime client using XTI and our udp_client function.

Create endpoint

11-13   We call our udp_client function to create the XTI endpoint and to allocate a t_unitdata structure that we will use for sending datagrams. We allocate another t_unitdata structure that we will use for receiving replies. We call our xti_ntop_host function to print the server's IP address.

Send datagram

14-18   We initialize the udata structure within the t_unitdata structure to point to our recvline buffer and to contain one byte of 0. t_sndudata sends the datagram to the server.

> We should be able to send a 0-byte UDP datagram, given our discussion with Figure 28.4, but many implementations of XTI do not allow this.

Read reply

19–23   We initialize the `udata` structure for the receiving `t_unitdata` structure and call `t_rcvudata` to read the server's reply. The reply is null terminated and printed to standard output, along with the server's address.

This example shares all the unreliable UDP properties of our sockets client in Figure 11.12: the client will block forever in the call to `t_rcvudata` if there is no response. If we run the client to a host that is running the server, the output is as we expect.

```
unixware % daytimeudpcli1 bsdi daytime
sending to 206.62.226.35
from 206.62.226.35: Fri Feb 28 17:23:40 1997
```

What if we send a datagram to this same host, but to a UDP port that no process has bound? We expect an ICMP port unreachable error to be returned. Recall with our sockets client, if the client does not call `connect`, this error is not returned to the client. There is nothing similar to `connect` for a UDP endpoint with XTI, but we see that the error is returned to our client and our `T_rcvudata` wrapper function prints an error:

```
unixware % daytimeudpcli1 bsdi 9999
sending to 206.62.226.35
t_rcvudata error: event requires attention
```

When an asynchronous error is received for a UDP endpoint, `t_rcvudata` returns an error of `TLOOK` and we must call `t_rcvuderr` to determine the actual error. We discuss this in the next section.

31.4 `t_rcvuderr` Function: Asynchronous Errors

For a connectionless protocol, errors can be returned asynchronously. That is, a datagram can be correctly transmitted by the protocol stack, only to have an error in it detected somewhere else in the network. Common errors with UDP datagrams are to elicit an ICMP port unreachable from the destination host or an ICMP host unreachable from some intermediate router. When this ICMP error is received at some later time by the provider, it requires some form of notification from the provider to the process and some means for the process to determine the actual error. As shown at the end of the previous section, XTI provides this notification by setting `t_errno` to `TLOOK` when we call `t_rcvudata` to indicate that an error occurred on a previously sent datagram. We can then call the `t_rcvuderr` function to determine what happened and to clear the error status.

```
#include <xti.h>

int t_rcvuderr(int fd, struct t_uderr *uderr);
```
                                                       Returns: 0 if OK, –1 on error

If the *uderr* pointer is nonnull, a `t_uderr` structure is filled in with information about the error.

```
struct t_uderr {
  struct netbuf  addr;   /* protocol-specific address */
  struct netbuf  opt;    /* protocol-specific options */
  t_scalar_t     error;  /* protocol-specific error */
};
```

The `addr` structure contains the destination address of the datagram that caused the error, the `opt` structure contains any protocol-specific options from the datagram that caused the error, and `error` contains a protocol-specific error code. For UDP, `error` is normally one of the `errno` values from `<sys/errno.h>`.

If *uderr* is a null pointer, this clears the error status without returning any information.

Example: ICMP Port Unreachable

We now recode our client from Figure 31.3 to handle asynchronous errors. This is shown in Figure 31.4.

Handle asynchronous errors

23–33   What has changed from Figure 11.12 is the call to our wrapper function `T_rcvudata` is replaced with a call to `t_rcvudata`, and we handle an asynchronous error by calling `t_rcvuderr`, printing the returned error code.

If we run this program and send a datagram to a host that does not support the daytime protocol, we receive the ICMP port unreachable error from `t_rcvuderr`:

```
unixware % daytimeudpcli2 gateway.tuc.noao.edu daytime
sending to 140.252.104.1
error 146 for datagram sent to 140.252.104.1

unixware % grep 146 /usr/include/sys/errno.h
#define ECONNREFUSED    146       /* Connection refused */
```

We see that the `error` value returned in the `t_uderr` structure is the `errno` value corresponding to the ICMP error (Figure A.15).

> Unfortunately, as nice as this design feature appears (returning ICMP errors for XTI UDP endpoints), there are still problems. First, there is no requirement that the provider notify the application when these errors occur. With UnixWare 2.1.2, for example, ICMP port unreachables are returned to the application, but ICMP host unreachables are not. Also, if we modify our client to send three datagrams to three different servers and then read all the replies, but two of the datagrams elicit an ICMP port unreachable error, only the first of these two errors is returned to the application by `t_rcvuderr`. This is because the provider maintains only one error per endpoint. All of these problems are what led us to develop an independent way of notifying a datagram application of asynchronous errors: our `icmpd` daemon in Section 25.7.

> Notice that all we receive is the error code and the destination address of the datagram that caused the error. Another piece of information that is not returned is the source address of who returned the error (e.g., the source address of the ICMP error).

——————————————————————————————— xtiudp/daytimeudpcli2.c

```
 1 #include    "unpxti.h"

 2 int
 3 main(int argc, char **argv)
 4 {
 5     int     tfd, flags;
 6     char    recvline[MAXLINE + 1];
 7     socklen_t addrlen;
 8     struct t_unitdata *sndptr, *rcvptr;
 9     struct t_uderr *uderr;

10     if (argc != 3)
11         err_quit("usage: a.out <hostname or IPaddress> <service or port#>");

12     tfd = Udp_client(argv[1], argv[2], (void **) &sndptr, &addrlen);

13     rcvptr = T_alloc(tfd, T_UNITDATA, T_ADDR);
14     uderr = T_alloc(tfd, T_UDERROR, T_ADDR);

15     printf("sending to %s\n", Xti_ntop_host(&sndptr->addr));

16     sndptr->udata.maxlen = MAXLINE;
17     sndptr->udata.len = 1;
18     sndptr->udata.buf = recvline;
19     recvline[0] = 0;               /* 1-byte datagram containing null byte */
20     T_sndudata(tfd, sndptr);

21     rcvptr->udata.maxlen = MAXLINE;
22     rcvptr->udata.buf = recvline;
23     if (t_rcvudata(tfd, rcvptr, &flags) == 0) {
24         recvline[rcvptr->udata.len] = 0;     /* null terminate */
25         printf("from %s: %s", Xti_ntop_host(&rcvptr->addr), recvline);
26     } else {
27         if (t_errno == TLOOK) {
28             T_rcvuderr(tfd, uderr);
29             printf("error %ld for datagram sent to %s\n",
30                     uderr->error, Xti_ntop_host(&uderr->addr));
31         } else
32             err_xti("t_rcvudata error");
33     }
34     exit(0);
35 }
```

——————————————————————————————— xtiudp/daytimeudpcli2.c

Figure 31.4 UDP client using XTI that handles asynchronous errors.

31.5 udp_server Function

We can also recode our udp_server function from Figure 11.14 to use XTI, and we
show this in Figure 31.5.

libxti/udp_server.c

```
 1 #include    "unpxti.h"

 2 int
 3 udp_server(const char *host, const char *serv, socklen_t *addrlenp)
 4 {
 5     int    tfd;
 6     void   *handle;
 7     struct t_bind tbind;
 8     struct t_info tinfo;
 9     struct netconfig *ncp;
10     struct nd_hostserv hs;
11     struct nd_addrlist *alp;
12     struct netbuf *np;

13     handle = Setnetconfig();

14     hs.h_host = (host == NULL) ? HOST_SELF : (char *) host;
15     hs.h_serv = (char *) serv;

16     while ( (ncp = getnetconfig(handle)) != NULL &&
17             strcmp(ncp->nc_proto, "udp") != 0) ;

18     if (ncp == NULL)
19         return (-1);

20     if (netdir_getbyname(ncp, &hs, &alp) != 0)
21         return (-2);
22     np = alp->n_addrs;              /* use first address */

23     tfd = T_open(ncp->nc_device, O_RDWR, &tinfo);

24     tbind.addr = *np;              /* copy entire netbuf{} */
25     tbind.qlen = 0;                /* not used for connectionless server */
26     T_bind(tfd, &tbind, NULL);

27     endnetconfig(handle);
28     netdir_free(alp, ND_ADDRLIST);

29     if (addrlenp)
30         *addrlenp = tinfo.addr; /* size of protocol addresses */
31     return (tfd);
32 }
```

libxti/udp_server.c

Figure 31.5 udp_server function using XTI.

Lookup protocol, host, and service

13–22   The beginning of the function is similar to our tcp_listen function (Figure 30.3), finding the protocol by calling getnetconfig and then calling netdir_getbyname to look up the hostname and service name.

Open device, bind server's IP address and port

23–28   t_open opens the correct device and t_bind binds the server's IP address (the wildcard address if the host argument is a null pointer) and port. The memory allocated by netdir_getbyname is returned by netdir_free.

Return address length and descriptor

29–31   The size of the protocol's addresses is returned if the final argument is a nonnull pointer, and the descriptor for the endpoint is the return value of the function.

Example: Daytime Server

We can now recode our simple daytime server from Figure 11.15 using XTI. We show this in Figure 31.6.

————————————————————— xtiudp/daytimeudpsrv2.c

```
 1 #include     "unpxti.h"
 2 #include     <time.h>

 3 int
 4 main(int argc, char **argv)
 5 {
 6     int      tfd, flags;
 7     char     buff[MAXLINE];
 8     time_t   ticks;
 9     struct t_unitdata *tud;

10     if (argc == 2)
11         tfd = Udp_server(NULL, argv[1], NULL);
12     else if (argc == 3)
13         tfd = Udp_server(argv[1], argv[2], NULL);
14     else
15         err_quit("usage: daytimeudpsrv [ <host> ] <service or port>");

16     tud = T_alloc(tfd, T_UNITDATA, T_ADDR);

17     for ( ; ; ) {
18         tud->udata.maxlen = MAXLINE;
19         tud->udata.buf = buff;
20         if (t_rcvudata(tfd, tud, &flags) == 0) {
21             printf("datagram from %s\n", Xti_ntop(&tud->addr));
22             ticks = time(NULL);
23             snprintf(buff, sizeof(buff), "%.24s\r\n", ctime(&ticks));
24             tud->udata.len = strlen(buff);
25             T_sndudata(tfd, tud);

26         } else if (t_errno == TLOOK)
27             T_rcvuderr(tfd, NULL);  /* just clear error */
28         else
29             err_xti("t_rcvudata error");
30     }
31 }
```

————————————————————— xtiudp/daytimeudpsrv2.c

Figure 31.6 UDP daytime server using XTI.

Create XTI endpoint

10–16   Our udp_server function creates the endpoint and binds the local IP address and port. We allocate a t_unitdata structure by calling t_alloc, specifying the T_ADDR argument, so that it allocates a buffer for only the protocol address.

Read request, send reply

17–30   The program then loops, reading a client request with `t_rcvudata` and sending a reply with `t_sndudata`. If one of our replies generates an asynchronous error, `t_rcvudata` will return an error with `t_errno` set to `TLOOK` and we handle the error by calling `t_rcvuderr`. Notice that the final argument to `t_rcvuderr` is a null pointer to clear the error without returning any information (since there is nothing for us to do when these errors occur). If we did not handle these errors as shown, but aborted if `t_rcvudata` returned an error, then any client could crash our server by sending a datagram to the server and then immediately terminating. When the reply was received by the client's host, it would respond with an ICMP port unreachable, causing the server's `t_rcvudata` to return an error. Therefore the handling of these asynchronous errors is mandatory for a UDP server written using XTI.

31.6   Reading a Datagram in Pieces

Recall our discussion of datagram truncation in Section 20.3 and the different scenarios when a datagram is read on a UDP socket, but the datagram length exceeds the number of bytes requested by the application. XTI handles this scenario differently.

Recall the final *flagsp* argument for `t_rcvudata`. If the application's buffer is not large enough to hold the next datagram on the queue, the number of bytes returned will be `udata.maxlen` and the `T_MORE` bit in the integer pointed to by the *flagsp* argument will be turned on. This flag tells the application to call `t_rcvudata` again to read the remainder of this datagram. The sender's address and options are returned by only the first call to `t_rcvudata` for a given datagram. For all subsequent calls to this function that read the remainder of the datagram, `addr.len` and `opt.len` members will be 0 on return.

We can show the use of this feature by modifying our client from Figure 31.4, as shown in Figure 31.7.

Redefine MAXLINE

2–3   We redefine the constant `MAXLINE` from our `unp.h` header to be 2 bytes, and this is the size of our `recvline` buffer.

Create endpoint, send datagram to server

12–22   This code has not changed from Figure 31.4.

Read reply, 2 bytes at a time

23–41   We now call `t_rvcudata` in a loop, until our `flags` variable does not have the `T_MORE` bit set. We print the server's IP address for only the first piece of the datagram, when the `addr.len` member is nonzero.

xtiudp/daytimeudpcli4.c

```
 1 #include    "unpxti.h"

 2 #undef  MAXLINE
 3 #define MAXLINE 2

 4 int
 5 main(int argc, char **argv)
 6 {
 7     int     tfd, flags;
 8     char    recvline[MAXLINE + 1];
 9     socklen_t addrlen;
10     struct t_unitdata *sndptr, *rcvptr;
11     struct t_uderr *uderr;

12     if (argc != 3)
13         err_quit("usage: a.out <hostname or IPaddress> <service or port#>");

14     tfd = Udp_client(argv[1], argv[2], (void **) &sndptr, &addrlen);

15     rcvptr = T_alloc(tfd, T_UNITDATA, T_ADDR);
16     uderr = T_alloc(tfd, T_UDERROR, T_ADDR);

17     printf("sending to %s\n", Xti_ntop_host(&sndptr->addr));

18     sndptr->udata.maxlen = MAXLINE;
19     sndptr->udata.len = 1;
20     sndptr->udata.buf = recvline;
21     recvline[0] = 0;              /* 1-byte datagram containing null byte */
22     T_sndudata(tfd, sndptr);

23     do {
24         rcvptr->udata.maxlen = MAXLINE;
25         rcvptr->udata.buf = recvline;
26         flags = 0;
27         if (t_rcvudata(tfd, rcvptr, &flags) == 0) {
28             recvline[rcvptr->udata.len] = 0;    /* null terminate */
29             if (rcvptr->addr.len > 0)
30                 printf("from %s: ", Xti_ntop_host(&rcvptr->addr));
31             printf("%s\n", recvline);
32         } else {
33             if (t_errno == TLOOK) {
34                 T_rcvuderr(tfd, uderr);
35                 printf("error %ld from %s\n",
36                         uderr->error, Xti_ntop_host(&uderr->addr));
37             } else
38                 err_xti("t_rcvudata error");
39             flags = 0;
40         }
41     } while (flags & T_MORE);
42     exit(0);
43 }
```

xtiudp/daytimeudpcli4.c

Figure 31.7 UDP client using XTI that reads returned datagram in pieces.

We now run this client to a daytime server.

```
unixware % daytimeudpcli4 bsdi daytime
sending to 206.62.226.35
from 206.62.226.35: Su
n
Ma
r
 2
 1
1:
53
:5
0
19
97
```

If we remove the newline from the `printf` format string for `recvline` (line 31, which we used only to show how much data was returned by `t_rcvudata`), we get the more familiar output:

```
unixware % daytimeudpcli4 bsdi daytime
sending to 206.62.226.35
from 206.62.226.35: Sun Mar  2 12:04:48 1997
```

31.7 Summary

The two XTI functions `t_rcvudata` and `t_sndudata` are similar to `recvfrom` and `sendto`. One new feature with XTI, which is not provided with sockets, is reading a datagram in pieces, having the `T_MORE` flag returned when there is more to read.

Asynchronous errors are returned with XTI by having `t_rcvudata` and `t_sndudata` return an error of `TLOOK`. We then call `t_rcvuderr` to obtain more protocol-dependent information about the error. This is better than the sockets approach (returning an asynchronous error only if the socket is connected), but even with the XTI approach asynchronous errors can be lost, and our application is still depending on the protocol stack to decide which ICMP errors to return. A better solution is to use a daemon like `icmpd` (Section 25.7) and return all the errors on a separate channel.

32

XTI Options

32.1 Introduction

Another of the mystery areas of XTI has been option processing. The standards and most manuals spend page after page describing the intricacies of option processing and option negotiation, providing no examples, and ending with a statement of the form "the details are protocol dependent."

The term *negotiation* is used heavily with XTI options. An option is not "set"; it is negotiated, meaning the provider may not set the option to exactly what we ask for. When an XTI option is negotiated, the actual value used by the provider is returned, so we can see what that value is.

Figure 32.1 shows all of the standard XTI options, both the generic options (those beginning with XTI_) and those for IPv4.

> Unix 98 prepended T_ to all the INET_, IP_, TCP_, and UDP_ names, but Posix.1g does not do this. For example, the UDP option is called UDP_CHECKSUM by Posix.1g. Unix 98 accepts these Posix.1g names as legacy names, but we will use the newer names in this text.

XTI classifies options as either *end-to-end* or *local*. End-to-end options normally cause some type of information to be sent to the peer across the network. An example is the IPv4 type-of-service field. It can be set by one endpoint (for either TCP or UDP), is carried in the IPv4 header, and is available to the other endpoint. The IPv4 header options and the UDP checksum are the two other end-to-end options in Figure 32.1. An example of a local option is T_IP_REUSEADDR, as this option affects the ability of the calling process to bind a port number that is already in use to its endpoint but has no effect on the data that is sent to the other endpoint.

Level	Name	Datatype	End-to-end	Absolute	Description
XTI_GENERIC	XTI_DEBUG	t_uscalar_t[]		•	enable debug tracing
	XTI_LINGER	t_linger{}		•	linger on close if data to send
	XTI_RCVBUF	t_uscalar_t			receive buffer size
	XTI_RCVLOWAT	t_uscalar_t			receive buffer low-water mark
	XTI_SNDBUF	t_uscalar_t			send buffer size
	XTI_SNDLOWAT	t_uscalar_t			send buffer low-water mark
T_INET_IP	T_IP_BROADCAST	u_int		•	permit sending of broadcast mesg
	T_IP_DONTROUTE	u_int		•	bypass routing table lookup
	T_IP_OPTIONS	u_char[]	•	•	IP header options
	T_IP_REUSEADDR	u_int		•	allow local address reuse
	T_IP_TOS	u_char	•	•	type-of-service and precedence
	T_IP_TTL	u_char		•	time-to-live
T_INET_TCP	T_TCP_KEEPALIVE	t_kpalive{}		•	periodically test if connection alive
	T_TCP_MAXSEG	t_uscalar_t			TCP MSS (read-only)
	T_TCP_NODELAY	t_uscalar_t		•	disable Nagle algorithm
T_INET_UDP	T_UDP_CHECKSUM	t_uscalar_t	•	•	enable UDP checksum

Figure 32.1   XTI options.

Some XTI options are classified as an *absolute requirement*, which we also show in Figure 32.1. When setting the value of an option with this property, if the requested value cannot be assigned to the option, failure is returned. If an option does not have this property, and we try to set the option to some value that is not within the range of supported values, the provider will change the requested value to be within the acceptable range. An example of the latter is the receive buffer size, XTI_RCVBUF, as most systems enforce a lower limit and an upper limit on this value. If we request a value less than the lower limit or greater than the upper limit, the value will be changed to the appropriate limit and the return is then "partial success."

XTI options are specified and received in the following ways:

1. Calling the t_optmgmt function lets us specify any options (end-to-end and local) that we desire. We can also call this function to obtain the current value or the default value of an option.

2. For a UDP endpoint we can specify our desired options (end-to-end and local) with each call to t_sndudata, using the opt member of the t_unitdata structure.

3. For a UDP endpoint any end-to-end options that arrive with the datagram are returned by t_rcvudata through the opt member of the t_unitdata structure.

4. For a TCP client we can specify our desired options (end-to-end and local) when calling t_connect, as the opt member of the t_call structure.

5. For a TCP server any end-to-end options that arrive with the connection are returned by t_listen through the opt member of the t_call structure.

The t_optmgmt function is a combination of the getsockopt and setsockopt functions. In the sockets API, however, there is no way to specify options when sending or receiving UDP datagrams, or when initiating or accepting TCP connections. The sendmsg and recvmsg functions provide the capability to specify and receive ancillary data, and this is used for IPv6 options.

Figure 32.2 summarizes the sending and receiving of options by the XTI functions.

Endpoint	Function	Return end-to-end only	Return end-to-end and local	Specify end-to-end and local
any endpoint	t_optmgmt		•	•
TCP endpoint	t_accept			•
	t_connect		•	•
	t_listen	•		
	t_rcvconnect		•	
UDP endpoint	t_rcvudata	•		
	t_rcvvudata	•		
	t_rcvuderr		•	
	t_sndudata			•
	t_sndvudata			•

Figure 32.2 XTI functions that can specify and return options.

Figure 32.2 indicates that we can specify options with t_accept. With TCP this is not possible, because the connection is already established when t_listen returns. Hence, any desired end-to-end options that we want to effect the three-way handshake must be specified for the listening endpoint.

32.2 t_opthdr Structure

XTI options are always specified and returned through a netbuf structure named opt that is a member of the t_call, t_optmgmt, t_uderr, and t_unitdata structures (Figure 28.6). The contents of the options buffer is one or more t_opthdr structures, each followed by an optional value.

```
struct t_opthdr {
  t_uscalar_t  len;     /* total length of option:
                           sizeof(struct t_opthdr) + length of value */
  t_uscalar_t  level;   /* protocol affected */
  t_uscalar_t  name;    /* option name */
  t_uscalar_t  status;  /* status value */
        /* followed by the option value, and then possible padding */
};
```

One difference from TLI to XTI is that TLI said nothing about the format of the options buffer other than it was implementation dependent. Many implementations of TLI used a structure named opthdr, which had only three elements: level, name, and len.

We show two of these XTI structures, pointed to by a netbuf structure that is part of a t_unitdata structure, in Figure 32.3.

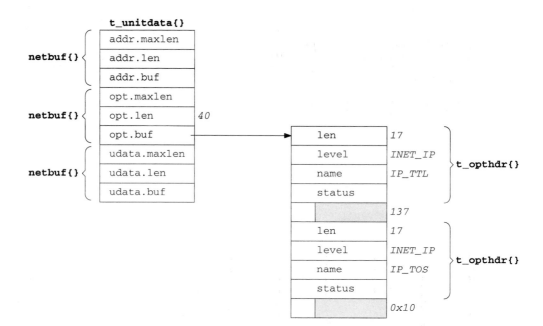

Figure 32.3 Example of two options pointed to by a netbuf structure.

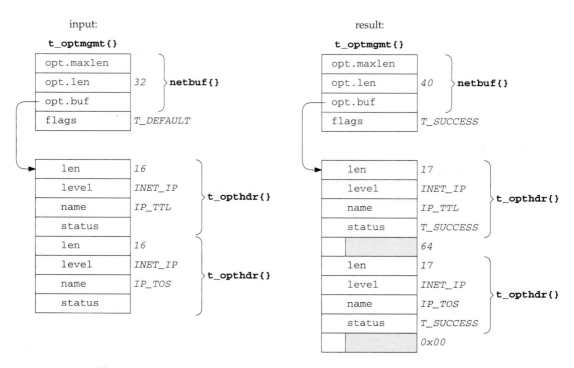

Figure 32.4 Requesting the default value of two options from t_optmgmt.

In Figure 32.3 we are specifying the IP TTL as 137 and the IP type-of-service as 0x10 (routine precedence and low delay). Each option value is a 1-byte u_char (Figure 32.1) and we show 3 bytes of padding after each value. We also assume here that a t_uscalar_t occupies 4 bytes; hence the total size of the option buffer is 40 bytes.

We show another example in Figure 32.4, this time a call to the t_optmgmt function, which we describe in Section 32.4. This function takes pointers to two t_optmgmt structures: one is the input and the other is the result.

In this example we are asking for the default values of the IP TTL and TOS options (the flags of T_DEFAULT) so we specify only a t_opthdr structure for each option without any value. The result is a copy of the input, with the default values returned after each of the t_opthdr structures. In the result structures the status member is also filled in.

> Unix 98, but not Posix.1g, defines three macros that can be used when processing a t_opthdr structure and the data that follows: T_OPT_FIRSTHDR, T_OPT_NEXTHDR, and T_OPT_DATA. These are similar to the three macros CMSG_FIRSTHDR, CMSG_NXTHDR, and CMSG_DATA used to process ancillary data with sockets, which we described in Section 13.6.

32.3 XTI Options

Most XTI options can be mapped directly to one of the socket options that we described in Chapter 7. Therefore our description of them here is brief. We also note that the header <xti_inet.h> must be included to define the constants for all the IP, TCP, and UDP options.

> Note that XTI does not define any way to multicast.

XTI_DEBUG Option

This option is similar to the SO_DEBUG socket option and normally supported by only TCP. This option is disabled by specifying an option header with no value. By this we mean that the len member of the t_opthdr structure is just the size of this structure (16 bytes, for example, in Figure 32.4).

XTI_LINGER Option

This option is similar to the SO_LINGER socket option and is supported by TCP. It specifies what to do when an endpoint is closed. The t_linger structure is

```
struct t_linger {
  t_scalar_t  l_onoff;    /* T_NO, T_YES */
  t_scalar_t  l_linger;   /* T_UNSPEC (use default), T_INFINITE,
                             or linger time in seconds */
};
```

We specified in Figure 32.1 that this option is an absolute value, but only the value of l_onoff is an absolute requirement; the value of l_linger is not an absolute requirement. That is, the implementation can place lower and upper limits on the linger time itself.

Unlike the SO_LINGER socket option, XTI_LINGER is not used to send an RST. t_snddis sends an RST.

XTI_RCVBUF and XTI_RCVLOWAT Options

These two options are similar to the SO_RCVBUF and SO_RCVLOWAT socket options. The first option specifies the size of the endpoint's receive buffer and the second the receive buffer low-water mark used with poll or select.

Figure 32.1 does not consider the XTI_RCVBUF option end-to-end, but with TCP's long fat pipe support (RFC 1323 [Jacobson, Braden, and Borman 1992]), this option does indeed have end-to-end significance since it affects TCP's window scale option that is negotiated with the three-way handshake.

XTI_SNDBUF and XTI_SNDLOWAT Options

These two options are similar to the SO_SNDBUF and SO_SNDLOWAT socket options. The first option specifies the size of the endpoint's send buffer and the second the send buffer low-water mark that is used with poll or select.

T_IP_BROADCAST Option

This option is similar to the SO_BROADCAST socket option. The value of this option is either T_YES or T_NO.

T_IP_DONTROUTE Option

This option is similar to the SO_DONTROUTE socket option. The value of this option is either T_YES or T_NO.

T_IP_OPTIONS Option

This option is similar to the IP_OPTIONS socket option. The value of this option is used as the IPv4 header options. An example of these options is provided in Chapter 24. The option is disabled if specified with no value (i.e., only a t_opthdr structure).

Calling t_optmgmt with a request of T_CURRENT returns the current value of the IP options that will be used in outgoing datagrams.

T_IP_REUSEADDR Option

This option is similar to the SO_REUSEADDR socket option. The value of this option is either T_YES or T_NO.

`T_IP_TOS` Option

This option is similar to the `IP_TOS` socket option. The option value is a combination of the IPv4 precedence field, from the values shown in Figure 32.5, with the IPv4 type-of-service field, from the values shown in Figure 32.6.

Constant	Value
T_ROUTINE	0
T_PRIORITY	1
T_IMMEDIATE	2
T_FLASH	3
T_OVERRIDEFLASH	4
T_CRITIC_ECP	5
T_INETCONTROL	6
T_NETCONTROL	7

Figure 32.5 IPv4 precedence values used with `T_IP_TOS` option.

Constant	Description
T_NOTOS	normal
T_LDELAY	minimize delay
T_HITHRPT	maximize throughput
T_HIREL	maximize reliability
T_LOCOST	minimize cost

Figure 32.6 IPv4 type-of-service values used with `T_IP_TOS` option.

The macro `SET_TOS` (defined by including the `<xti.h>` header) combines its first argument, a precedence value from Figure 32.5, with its second argument, a type-of-service value from Figure 32.6, and the result should be used with this XTI option.

Calling `t_optmgmt` with a request of `T_CURRENT` returns the current value of the option that will be used in outgoing datagrams.

`T_IP_TTL` Option

This option is similar to the `IP_TTL` socket option. The value of the option is the IPv4 time-to-live field. This option may be set to specify the value used in outgoing datagrams. There is no way, however, to obtain the TTL from a received datagram.

`T_TCP_KEEPALIVE` Option

This option is similar to the `SO_KEEPALIVE` socket option and controls the sending of keepalive packets on a TCP connection. This XTI option uses the following structure:

```
struct t_kpalive {
  t_scalar_t  kp_onoff;   /* T_NO (disable), T_YES (enable), or
                             T_YES|T_GARBAGE (enable & send garbage byte) */
  t_scalar_t  kp_timeout; /* timeout in minutes; T_UNSPEC means default */
};
```

This option is similar to the XTI_LINGER option in that the value of kp_onoff is an absolute requirement but the value of kp_timeout is not an absolute requirement.

> Sending a garbage byte should not be required and in fact T_GARBAGE was removed from Unix 98. The use of the garbage byte is discussed on p. 335 of TCPv1.

T_TCP_MAXSEG Option

This option is similar to the TCP_MAXSEG socket option. This option is read-only and returns the maximum segment size (MSS) for a TCP endpoint. Since this option is read-only, its value cannot be an absolute requirement.

T_TCP_NODELAY Option

This option is similar to the TCP_NODELAY socket option. The value of this option is either T_YES (disable the Nagle algorithm) or T_NO (the default, the Nagle algorithm is enabled). We say more about the Nagle algorithm in Section 7.9.

T_UDP_CHECKSUM Option

This XTI option is one of the end-to-end options; therefore it is always returned by t_rcvudata if received options are requested (i.e., if opt.maxlen is nonzero). The value of this option is either T_YES or T_NO.

> This option should *never* be enabled and providing the ability for an application to disable the sending of UDP checksums for an endpoint is a mistake. Examples exist of data corruption when UDP checksums are disabled and there is no reason to ever disable UDP checksums. The only use of this option should be to detect whether a peer has UDP checksums enabled.

32.4   t_optmgmt Function

The t_optmgmt function lets us perform the following operations with regard to XTI options:

- check whether one or more options are supported,
- obtain the default value of one or more options,
- obtain the current value of one or more options, and
- negotiate values for one or more options.

```
#include <xti.h>

int t_optmgmt(int fd, const struct t_optmgmt *request, struct t_optmgmt *result);
```

Returns: 0 if OK, −1 on error

We specify our request as a `t_optmgmt` structure, and one of these structures is returned as the result. If we are not interested in the result, we set the `maxlen` member of the structure pointed to by *result* to 0. We showed an example of these two structures in Figure 32.4.

```
struct t_optmgmt {
  struct netbuf  opt;     /* one or more t_opthdr structures */
  t_scalar_t     flags;   /* action on input, result on output */
};
```

The `flags` member of the *request* structure specifies the action desired by the caller:

T_CHECK	check whether the options are supported,
T_DEFAULT	return the default values of the options,
T_CURRENT	return the current values of the options, and
T_NEGOTIATE	negotiate values for the options.

We will examine each of these four operations in the following sections.

We are able to specify multiple options in a single call to `t_optmgmt` as shown in Figure 32.4. But if we do this all options must specify the same `level`. This is OK in Figure 32.4 because the `level` of both options is `T_INET_IP`. There is another complication when negotiating new values for multiple options in a single call to this function: the returned `flags` contains the worst single result, even though each option contains its own `status` return. To avoid these complications, it is simplest to manipulate just one option at a time in each call to `t_optmgmt`.

> This XTI function corresponds to the `getsockopt` and `setsockopt` functions.

32.5 Checking If an Option Is Supported and Obtaining the Default

Our first example of XTI options is to check which of the options listed in Figure 32.1 are supported on our system, and for each supported option, to print its default value. Figure 32.7 shows our program.

── *xtiopt/checkopts.c*

```
 1 #include     "unpxti.h"

 2 struct xti_opts {
 3   char          *opt_str;
 4   t_uscalar_t    opt_level;
 5   t_uscalar_t    opt_name;
 6   char         * (*opt_val_str)(struct t_opthdr *);
 7 } xti_opts[] = {
 8   "XTI_DEBUG",       XTI_GENERIC,    XTI_DEBUG,       xti_str_uscalard,
 9   "XTI_LINGER",      XTI_GENERIC,    XTI_LINGER,      xti_str_linger,
10   "XTI_RCVBUF",      XTI_GENERIC,    XTI_RCVBUF,      xti_str_uscalard,
11   "XTI_RCVLOWAT",    XTI_GENERIC,    XTI_RCVLOWAT,    xti_str_uscalard,
12   "XTI_SNDBUF",      XTI_GENERIC,    XTI_SNDBUF,      xti_str_uscalard,
13   "XTI_SNDLOWAT",    XTI_GENERIC,    XTI_SNDLOWAT,    xti_str_uscalard,
14   "T_IP_BROADCAST",  T_INET_IP,      T_IP_BROADCAST, xti_str_uiyn,
15   "T_IP_DONTROUTE",  T_INET_IP,      T_IP_DONTROUTE, xti_str_uiyn,
16   "T_IP_OPTIONS",    T_INET_IP,      T_IP_OPTIONS,   xti_str_uchard,
```

```
17    "T_IP_REUSEADDR",   T_INET_IP,    T_IP_REUSEADDR, xti_str_uiyn,
18    "T_IP_TOS",         T_INET_IP,    T_IP_TOS,       xti_str_ucharx,
19    "T_IP_TTL",         T_INET_IP,    T_IP_TTL,       xti_str_uchard,
20    "T_TCP_KEEPALIVE",  T_INET_TCP,   T_TCP_KEEPALIVE,xti_str_kpalive,
21    "T_TCP_MAXSEG",     T_INET_TCP,   T_TCP_MAXSEG,   xti_str_uscalard,
22    "T_TCP_NODELAY",    T_INET_TCP,   T_TCP_NODELAY,  xti_str_usyn,
23    "T_UDP_CHECKSUM",   T_INET_UDP,   T_UDP_CHECKSUM, xti_str_usyn,
24    NULL,               0,            0,              NULL
25 };

26 int
27 main(int argc, char **argv)
28 {
29     int     fd;
30     struct t_opthdr *topt;
31     struct t_optmgmt *req, *ret;
32     struct xti_opts *ptr;

33     if (argc != 2)
34         err_quit("usage: checkopts <device>");

35     fd = T_open(argv[1], O_RDWR, NULL);
36     T_bind(fd, NULL, NULL);

37     req = T_alloc(fd, T_OPTMGMT, T_ALL);
38     ret = T_alloc(fd, T_OPTMGMT, T_ALL);

39     for (ptr = xti_opts; ptr->opt_str != NULL; ptr++) {
40         topt = (struct t_opthdr *) req->opt.buf;
41         topt->level = ptr->opt_level;
42         topt->name = ptr->opt_name;
43         topt->len = sizeof(struct t_opthdr);
44         req->opt.len = topt->len;

45         req->flags = T_CHECK;
46         printf("%s: ", ptr->opt_str);
47         if (t_optmgmt(fd, req, ret) < 0) {
48             err_xti_ret("t_optmgmt error");
49         } else {
50             topt = (struct t_opthdr *) ret->opt.buf;
51             printf("%s", xti_str_flags(topt->status));

52             if (topt->status == T_SUCCESS || topt->status == T_READONLY) {
53                 req->flags = T_DEFAULT;
54                 if (t_optmgmt(fd, req, ret) < 0) {
55                     err_xti_ret("t_optmgmt error for T_DEFAULT");
56                 } else {
57                     topt = (struct t_opthdr *) ret->opt.buf;
58                     printf(", default = %s", (*ptr->opt_val_str) (topt));
59                 }
60             }
61             printf("\n");
62         }
63     }
64     exit(0);
65 }
```

xtiopt/checkopts.c

Figure 32.7 Check which XTI options are supported.

2–25   We define and initialize a structure defining all the XTI options from Figure 32.1. The final member of each array element is a pointer to a function that prints the value of the option. We need one function for each of the different option types. We do not show the source code for all these functions here.

Open device

35–38   We take the device name as a command-line argument and open the device. This lets us run the program twice, once for /dev/tcp and once for /dev/udp, as we expect different options to be supported by each provider. We bind any local address to the endpoint, because most calls to t_optmgmt require that the endpoint be bound. We also allocate two t_optmgmt structures, one for our request and one for the function's reply.

Call t_optmgmt for request of T_CHECK

39–48   We call t_optmgmt for each option in our xti_opts array, with a request flag of T_CHECK. We fill in our req structure, building a single t_opthdr structure in the opt buffer (Section 32.2). This structure contains just a t_opthdr structure, without any data (e.g., similar to the left side of Figure 32.4).

Call t_optmgmt for request of T_DEFAULT

49–62   If the first call to t_optmgmt succeeds, we print the status of the option. If the status is T_SUCCESS or T_READONLY, we call t_optmgmt again, this time with a request of T_DEFAULT. If this second call succeeds, we call the function pointed to by the opt_val_str member of our structure in Figure 32.7 to print the default value. When we call t_optmgmt the second time, we change only the flags member of our request structure. Since the pointer to this structure in the function prototype for t_optmgmt has the const qualifier, we know the structure was not changed by the first call.

We now run the program two times under AIX 4.2: first for TCP and then for UDP. Notice that AIX uses the device names /dev/xti/tcp and /dev/xti/udp.

```
aix % checkopts /dev/xti/tcp
XTI_DEBUG: T_SUCCESS, default = 0
XTI_LINGER: T_SUCCESS, default = T_NO, 0 sec
XTI_RCVBUF: T_SUCCESS, default = 16384
XTI_RCVLOWAT: T_SUCCESS, default = 1
XTI_SNDBUF: T_SUCCESS, default = 16384
XTI_SNDLOWAT: T_SUCCESS, default = 4096
T_IP_BROADCAST: T_SUCCESS, default = T_NO
T_IP_DONTROUTE: T_SUCCESS, default = T_NO
T_IP_OPTIONS: T_SUCCESS, default = 0 (length of value)
T_IP_REUSEADDR: T_SUCCESS, default = T_NO
T_IP_TOS: T_SUCCESS, default = 0x00
T_IP_TTL: T_SUCCESS, default = 0
T_TCP_KEEPALIVE: T_SUCCESS, default = T_NO, T_UNSPEC
T_TCP_MAXSEG: T_READONLY, default = 512
T_TCP_NODELAY: T_SUCCESS, default = T_NO
T_UDP_CHECKSUM: t_optmgmt error: incorrect option format
```

```
aix % checkopts /dev/xti/udp
XTI_DEBUG: T_SUCCESS, default = 0
XTI_LINGER: T_SUCCESS, default = T_NO, 0 sec
XTI_RCVBUF: T_SUCCESS, default = 41600
XTI_RCVLOWAT: T_SUCCESS, default = 1
XTI_SNDBUF: T_SUCCESS, default = 9216
XTI_SNDLOWAT: T_SUCCESS, default = 4096
T_IP_BROADCAST: T_SUCCESS, default = T_NO
T_IP_DONTROUTE: T_SUCCESS, default = T_NO
T_IP_OPTIONS: T_SUCCESS, default = 0 (length of value)
T_IP_REUSEADDR: T_SUCCESS, default = T_NO
T_IP_TOS: T_SUCCESS, default = 0x00
T_IP_TTL: T_SUCCESS, default = 0
T_TCP_KEEPALIVE: t_optmgmt error: incorrect option format
T_TCP_MAXSEG: t_optmgmt error: incorrect option format
T_TCP_NODELAY: t_optmgmt error: incorrect option format
T_UDP_CHECKSUM: T_NOTSUPPORT
```

The supported values are as we expect, other than the T_IP_TTL value. The T_UDP_CHECKSUM option that is not supported by TCP, and the three TCP options that are not supported by UDP cause t_optmgmt to return an error of TBADOPT. The UDP provider understands the T_UDP_CHECKSUM option but returns T_NOTSUPPORT since it is not supported. The string "(length of value)" that is printed for T_IP_OPTIONS indicates that the len member that was returned was 0, so there is no value to output.

32.6   Getting and Setting XTI Options

We now show examples of getting and setting XTI options. We define two functions of our own, xti_getopt and xti_setopt, that have identical calling sequences to getsockopt and setsockopt (Section 7.2).

```
#include "unpxti.h"

int xti_getopt(int fd, int level, int name, void *optval, socklen_t *optlen);

int xti_setopt(int fd, int level, int name, const void *optval, socklen_t optlen);
```
                                                    Both return: 0 if OK, −1 on error

These functions can simplify our XTI programs, since each comprises about 20−30 lines of C code.

xti_getopt Function

To fetch the current value of an XTI option we call t_optmgmt with the flags member of the request structure set to T_CURRENT. Figure 32.8 shows our xti_getopt function.

```
                                                                  ── libxti/xti_getopt.c
 1 #include      "unpxti.h"

 2 int
 3 xti_getopt(int fd, int level, int name, void *optval, socklen_t *optlenp)
 4 {
 5     int     rc, len;
 6     struct t_optmgmt *req, *ret;
 7     struct t_opthdr *topt;

 8     req = T_alloc(fd, T_OPTMGMT, T_ALL);
 9     ret = T_alloc(fd, T_OPTMGMT, T_ALL);
10     if (req->opt.maxlen == 0)
11         err_quit("xti_getopt: opt.maxlen == 0");

12     topt = (struct t_opthdr *) req->opt.buf;
13     topt->level = level;
14     topt->name = name;
15     topt->len = sizeof(struct t_opthdr);      /* just a t_opthdr{} */
16     req->opt.len = topt->len;

17     req->flags = T_CURRENT;
18     if (t_optmgmt(fd, req, ret) < 0) {
19         T_free(req, T_OPTMGMT);
20         T_free(ret, T_OPTMGMT);
21         return (-1);
22     }
23     rc = ret->flags;

24     if (rc == T_SUCCESS || rc == T_READONLY) {
25             /* copy back value and length */
26         topt = (struct t_opthdr *) ret->opt.buf;
27         len = topt->len - sizeof(struct t_opthdr);
28         len = min(len, *optlenp);
29         memcpy(optval, topt + 1, len);
30         *optlenp = len;
31     }
32     T_free(req, T_OPTMGMT);
33     T_free(ret, T_OPTMGMT);

34     if (rc == T_SUCCESS || rc == T_READONLY)
35         return (0);
36     return (-1);                        /* T_NOTSUPPORT */
37 }
                                                                  ── libxti/xti_getopt.c
```

Figure 32.8 xti_getopt function: get the current value of an XTI option.

Allocate request and reply structures

8-11   We call t_alloc to allocate room for a request structure and a reply structure. We
also verify that the size of the options buffer is nonzero.

> Older implementations of TLI often used a value of 0 for the size of the TCP options, meaning
> the application had to allocate its own buffer.

Fill in `t_opthdr` structure

12-16   We fill in a `t_opthdr` structure with the option's *level* and *name*. We do not specify any value in the request structure because this is not required when fetching the current value of an option.

Call `t_optmgmt` and return option value

17-31   We call `t_optmgmt` and then save the `flags` member in the returned structure. If the return value was `T_SUCCESS` or `T_READONLY`, we copy back the value of the option and its size. (The pointer expression `topt+1` points to the returned option value, which immediately follows the `t_opthdr` structure.) The final argument to our function is a value–result argument and we are careful not to overflow the caller's buffer (in case it is too small).

Free memory and return

32-36   We free the memory allocated by `t_alloc` and return 0 on success or −1 on an error.

`xti_setopt` Function

To set the value of an XTI option we call `t_optmgmt` with the `flags` member of the request structure set to `T_NEGOTIATE`. Figure 32.9 shows our `xti_setopt` function. This function is similar to the `xti_getopt` function in Figure 32.8 with a few exceptions.

Copy caller's value

12-19   We copy the caller's option value into the buffer that we build, placing it immediately following the `t_opthdr` structure.

Call `t_opmgmt`

20-26   The request `flags` is now `T_NEGOTIATE` for `t_optmgmt`.

Free memory and return

27-31   If the option value is not an absolute requirement the return value is `T_PARTSUCCESS`, which is OK.

XTI lets us set an option and fetch its value in a single call to `t_optmgmt`. This might be useful for an option whose value is not an absolute requirement (e.g., the send and receive buffer sizes). Using our functions requires a call to `xti_setopt` followed by a call to `xti_getopt`. We could have defined a function that does both, but the extra call to `xti_getopt` would rarely be the bottleneck of an application.

```
                                                                    libxti/xti_setopt.c
 1 #include    "unpxti.h"

 2 int
 3 xti_setopt(int fd, int level, int name, void *optval, socklen_t optlen)
 4 {
 5     int     rc;
 6     struct t_optmgmt *req, *ret;
 7     struct t_opthdr *topt;

 8     req = T_alloc(fd, T_OPTMGMT, T_ALL);
 9     ret = T_alloc(fd, T_OPTMGMT, T_ALL);
10     if (req->opt.maxlen == 0)
11         err_quit("xti_setopt: req.opt.maxlen == 0");

12     topt = (struct t_opthdr *) req->opt.buf;
13     topt->level = level;
14     topt->name = name;
15     topt->len = sizeof(struct t_opthdr) + optlen;
16     if (topt->len > req->opt.maxlen)
17         err_quit("optlen too big");
18     req->opt.len = topt->len;
19     memcpy(topt + 1, optval, optlen);   /* copy option value */

20     req->flags = T_NEGOTIATE;
21     if (t_optmgmt(fd, req, ret) < 0) {
22         T_free(req, T_OPTMGMT);
23         T_free(ret, T_OPTMGMT);
24         return (-1);
25     }
26     rc = ret->flags;

27     T_free(req, T_OPTMGMT);
28     T_free(ret, T_OPTMGMT);

29     if (rc == T_SUCCESS || rc == T_PARTSUCCESS)
30         return (0);
31     return (-1);                        /* T_FAILURE, T_NOTSUPPORT, T_READONLY */
32 }
                                                                    libxti/xti_setopt.c
```

Figure 32.9 xti_setopt function: set the value of an XTI option.

Example

We now use the two functions that were just shown. The program in Figure 32.10 fetches the current value of TCP's maximum segment size, sets the size of the send buffer to 65536, and then fetches and prints the size of the send buffer. If we compile and execute this program, its output is

```
aix % getsetopt
TCP mss = 512
send buffer size = 65536
```

xtiopt/getsetopt.c

```
 1 #include     "unpxti.h"

 2 int
 3 main(int argc, char **argv)
 4 {
 5     int     fd;
 6     socklen_t optlen;
 7     t_uscalar_t mss, sendbuff;

 8     fd = T_open(XTI_TCP, O_RDWR, NULL);
 9     T_bind(fd, NULL, NULL);

10     optlen = sizeof(mss);
11     Xti_getopt(fd, T_INET_TCP, T_TCP_MAXSEG, &mss, &optlen);
12     printf("TCP mss = %d\n", mss);

13     sendbuff = 65536;
14     Xti_setopt(fd, XTI_GENERIC, XTI_SNDBUF, &sendbuff, sizeof(sendbuff));

15     optlen = sizeof(sendbuff);
16     Xti_getopt(fd, XTI_GENERIC, XTI_SNDBUF, &sendbuff, &optlen);
17     printf("send buffer size = %d\n", sendbuff);

18     exit(0);
19 }
```

xtiopt/getsetopt.c

Figure 32.10 Example of our `xti_getopt` and `xti_setopt` functions.

32.7 Summary

XTI options are negotiated with the possibility that the provider returns a different value than we asked for. Although XTI option processing is very general, the simplest approach is to define two basic functions that look like `getsockopt` and `setsockopt` and call them from our application.

33

Streams

33.1 Introduction

Before describing some of the additional features of XTI, such as signal-driven I/O and out-of-band data, we need to understand some implementation details. XTI and the networking protocols are normally implemented using the streams system, as is the terminal I/O system on most SVR4-derived kernels.

In this chapter we provide an overview of the streams system and the functions used by an application to access a stream. Our goal is to understand the implementation of networking protocols within the streams framework. We also develop a simple TCP client using TPI, the interface into the transport layer that both XTI and sockets normally use on a system based on streams. Additional information on streams, including information on writing kernel routines that utilize streams, can be found in [Rago 1993].

> Streams were designed by Dennis Ritchie [Ritchie 1984] and first made widely available with SVR3 in 1986. They have never been standardized by Posix. The basic streams functions are required by Unix 98: `getmsg`, `getpmsg`, `putmsg`, `putpmsg`, `fattach`, and all of the streams `ioctl` commands. XTI is often implemented using streams. Any system derived from System V should provide streams, but the various 4.xBSD releases do not provide streams.

> The streams system is often written as STREAMS, but it is not even an acronym, so we write it as just *streams*.

> Be careful to distinguish between the stream I/O system that we are describing in this chapter, versus "standard I/O streams." The latter term is used when talking about the standard I/O library (e.g., functions such as `fopen`, `fgets`, `printf`, and the like).

849

33.2   Overview

Streams provide a full-duplex connection between a process and a *driver*, as shown in Figure 33.1. Although we describe the bottom box as a driver, this need not be associated with a hardware device; it can also be a pseudo-device driver (e.g., a software driver).

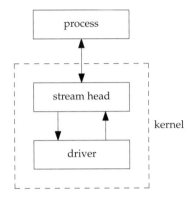

Figure 33.1   A stream shown between a process and a driver.

The *stream head* consists of the kernel routines that are invoked when the application makes a system call for a streams descriptor (e.g., `read`, `putmsg`, `ioctl`, and the like).

A process can dynamically add and remove intermediate processing *modules* between the stream head and the driver. A module performs some type of filtering on the messages going up and down a stream. We show this in Figure 33.2.

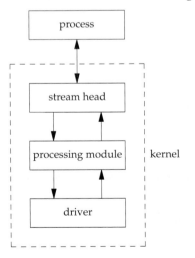

Figure 33.2   A stream with a processing module.

Any number of modules can be pushed onto a stream. When we say *push*, we mean that each new module gets inserted just below the stream head.

A special type of pseudo-device driver is a *multiplexor*, which accepts data from multiple sources. A streams-based implementation of the TCP/IP protocol suite, as found on SVR4 for example, could be as shown in Figure 33.3.

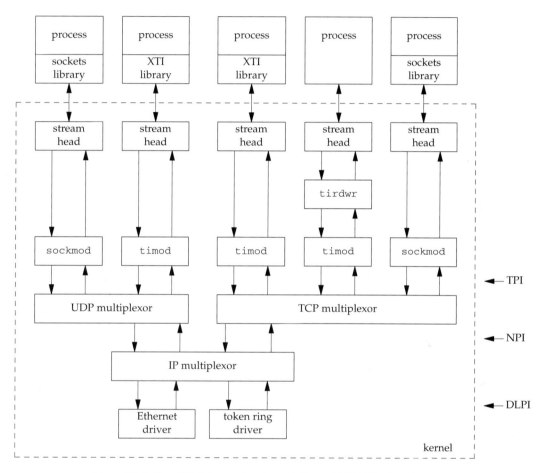

Figure 33.3 Simplified streams implementations of TCP/IP using streams.

- When a socket is created, the module `sockmod` is pushed onto the stream by the sockets library. It is the combination of the sockets library and the `sockmod` streams module that provides the sockets API to the process.

- When an XTI endpoint is created, the module `timod` is pushed onto the stream by the XTI library. It is the combination of the XTI library and the `timod` streams module that provides the XTI API to the process.

- We mentioned in Section 28.12 that the streams module `tirdwr` must normally be pushed onto a stream to use `read` and `write` with an XTI endpoint. The middle process using TCP in Figure 33.3 has done this. This process has probably abandoned the use of XTI by doing this, so we have removed the XTI library.

- Three service interfaces define the format of the networking messages exchanged up and down a stream. TPI, the *Transport Provider Interface* [Unix International 1992b], defines the interface provided by a transport-layer provider (e.g., TCP and UDP) to the modules above it. NPI, the *Network Provider Interface* [Unix International 1992a], defines the interface provided by a network-layer provider (e.g., IP). DLPI is the *Data Link Provider Interface* [Unix International 1991]. An alternate reference for TPI and DLPI, which contains sample C code, is [Rago 1993].

> The claim is regularly made to Usenet that "in a streams environment sockets are implemented on top of TLI (XTI)." This is false. As we can see in Figure 33.3, both sockets and XTI are implemented on top of TPI. This claim is often followed with "therefore TLI (XTI) is faster than sockets." This is also false. The TCP, UDP, and IP layers are the same, regardless of whether XTI or sockets are used. What changes is the user library and whether `timod` or `sockmod` is on the stream. But the author is not aware of any numbers comparing these libraries and modules, For the bottleneck of most applications (data transfer), the code path is probably similar for XTI and sockets, unless special optimizations have been applied to one and not the other.

Each component in a stream—the stream head, all processing modules, and the driver—contain at least one pair of *queues*: a write queue and a read queue. We show this in Figure 33.4.

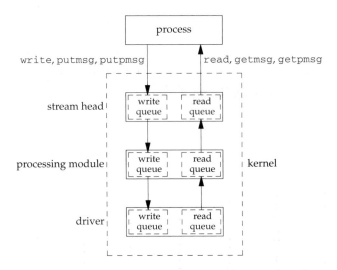

Figure 33.4   Each component in a stream has at least one pair of queues.

Message Types

Streams messages can be categorized as *high priority*, *priority band*, or *normal*. There are 256 different priority bands, between 0 and 255, with normal messages in band 0. The priority of a streams message is used for both queueing and flow control. By convention, high-priority messages are unaffected by flow control.

Figure 33.5 shows the ordering of the messages on a given queue.

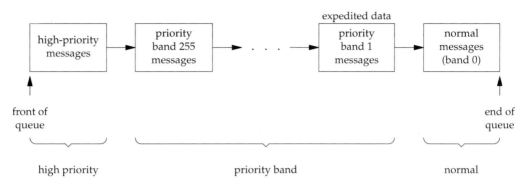

Figure 33.5 Ordering of streams messages on a queue, based on priority.

Although the streams system supports 256 different priority bands, networking protocols often use band 1 for expedited data and band 0 for normal data.

> TCP's out-of-band data is not considered true expedited data by TPI. Indeed, TCP uses band 0
> for both normal data and its out-of-band data (as we will verify in Figure C.4). The use of
> band 1 for expedited data is for protocols in which the expedited data (not just the urgent
> pointer, as in TCP) is sent ahead of normal data.

> Beware of the term *normal*. In releases before SVR4 there were no priority bands; there were
> just normal messages and priority messages. SVR4 implemented priority bands, requiring the
> getpmsg and putpmsg functions, which we describe shortly. The older priority messages
> were renamed high priority. The question is what to call the new messages, with priority
> bands between 1 and 255. Common terminology [Rago 1993] is to refer to everything other
> than high-priority messages as normal-priority messages and then subdivide these normal-
> priority messages into priority bands. The term *normal message* should always refer to a mes-
> sage with a band of 0.

Although we talk about normal-priority messages and high-priority messages,
there are about a dozen normal-priority message types and around 18 high-priority
message types. From an application's perspective, and the getmsg and putmsg functions that we are about to describe, we are interested in only three different types of
messages: M_DATA, M_PROTO, and M_PCPROTO (PC stands for "priority control" and
implies a high-priority message). Figure 33.6 shows how these three different message
types are generated by the write and putmsg functions.

Function	Control?	Data?	Flags	Message type generated
write		yes		M_DATA
putmsg	no	yes	0	M_DATA
putmsg	yes	don't care	0	M_PROTO
putmsg	yes	don't care	MSG_HIPRI	M_PCPROTO

Figure 33.6 Streams message types generated by write and putmsg.

We will see what we mean by control, data, and flags in our description of the `putmsg` function in the next section.

33.3 `getmsg` and `putmsg` Functions

The data transferred up and down a stream consists of messages and each message contains *control*, *data*, or both. If we use `read` and `write` on a stream, these transfer only data. To allow a process to read and write both data and control information, two new functions were added.

```
#include <stropts.h>

int getmsg(int fd, struct strbuf *ctlptr, struct strbuf *dataptr, int *flagsp);

int putmsg(int fd, const struct strbuf *ctlptr,
           const struct strbuf *dataptr, int flags);
```
                              Both return: nonnegative value if OK (see text), −1 on error

Both the control and data portions of the message are described by a `strbuf` structure:

```
struct strbuf {
    int    maxlen;      /* maximum size of buf */
    int    len;         /* actual amount of data in buf */
    char   *buf;        /* data */
};
```

> Note the similarity between the `strbuf` structure and the `netbuf` structure. The names of the three elements in each structure are identical.

> But the two lengths in the `netbuf` structure are unsigned integers, while the two lengths in the `strbuf` structure are signed integers. The reason is that some of the streams functions use a `len` or `maxlen` value of −1 to indicate something special.

We can send only control information, only data, or both using `putmsg`. To indicate the absence of control information we can either specify *ctlptr* as a null pointer, or set *ctlptr->len* to −1. The same technique is used to indicate no data.

If there is no control information, an `M_DATA` message is generated by `putmsg` (Figure 33.6); otherwise either an `M_PROTO` or an `M_PCPROTO` message is generated, depending on the *flags*. The *flags* argument to `putmsg` is 0 for a normal message or `RS_HIPRI` for a high-priority message.

The final argument to `getmsg` is a value–result argument. If the integer pointed to by *flagsp* is 0 when the function is called, the first message on the stream is returned (which can be normal or high priority). If the integer value is `RS_HIPRI` when the function is called, the function waits for a high-priority message to arrive at the stream head. In both cases the value stored in the integer pointed to by *flagsp* will be 0 or `RS_HIPRI`, depending on the type of message returned.

Assuming we pass nonnull *ctlptr* and *dataptr* values to `getmsg`, if there is no control information to return (i.e., an `M_DATA` message is being returned), this is indicated by setting *ctlptr->len* to −1 on return. Similarly, *dataptr->len* is set to −1 if there is no data to return.

The return value from putmsg is 0 if all is OK, or −1 on an error. But getmsg returns 0 only if the entire message was returned to the caller. If the control buffer is too small for all the control information, the return value is MORECTL (which is guaranteed to be nonnegative). Similarly if the data buffer is too small, MOREDATA can be returned. If both are too small, the logical OR of these two flags is returned.

33.4 `getpmsg` and `putpmsg` Functions

When support for different priority bands was added to streams with SVR4, the following two variants of getmsg and putmsg were added.

```
#include <stropts.h>

int getpmsg(int fd, struct strbuf *ctlptr,
            struct strbuf *dataptr, int *bandp, int *flagsp);

int putpmsg(int fd, const struct strbuf *ctlptr,
            const struct strbuf *dataptr, int band, int flags);
```
                                                           Both return: nonnegative value if OK, −1 on error

The *band* argument to putpmsg must be between 0 and 255, inclusive. If the *flags* argument is MSG_BAND, then a message is generated in the specified priority band. Setting *flags* to MSG_BAND and specifying a band of 0 is equivalent to calling putmsg. If *flags* is MSG_HIPRI, *band* must be 0, and a high-priority message is generated. (Note that this flag is named differently from the RS_HIPRI flag for putmsg.)

The two integers pointed to by bandp and flagsp are value–result arguments for getpmsg. The integer pointed to by *flagsp* for getpmsg can be MSG_HIPRI (to read a high-priority message), MSG_BAND (to read a message whose priority band is at least equal to the integer pointed to by *bandp*), or MSG_ANY (to read any message). On return the integer pointed to by *bandp* contains the band of the message that was read, and the integer pointed to by flagsp contains MSG_HIPRI (if a high-priority message was read) or MSG_BAND (if some other message was read).

33.5 `ioctl` Function

With streams we again encounter the ioctl function that we described in Chapter 16.

```
#include <stropts.h>

int ioctl(int fd, int request, ... /* void *arg */ );
```
                                                                       Returns: 0 if OK, −1 on error

The only change from the function prototype shown in Section 16.2 is the headers that must be included when dealing with streams.

There are about 30 requests that affect a stream head. Each request begins with `I_` and they are normally documented on the `streamio` manual page. We showed the `I_PUSH` request in Figure 28.14 when we pushed the `tirdwr` module onto a stream.

When we discuss signal-driven I/O with XTI in Section 34.11 we discuss the `I_SETSIG` request.

33.6 TPI: Transport Provider Interface

In Figure 33.3 we showed that TPI is the service interface into the transport layer from above. Both sockets and XTI use this interface in a streams environment. In Figure 33.3 it is a combination of the sockets library and `sockmod`, along with a combination of the XTI library and `timod` that exchange TPI messages with TCP and UDP.

TPI is a *message-based* interface. It defines the messages that are exchanged up and down a stream between the application (e.g., the XTI or sockets library) and the transport layer: the format of these messages and what operation each message performs. In many instances the application sends a request to the provider (such as "bind this local address") and the provider sends back a response ("OK" or "error"). Some events occur asynchronously at the provider (the arrival of a connection request for a server), causing a message or a signal to be sent up the stream.

We are able to bypass both XTI and sockets and use TPI directly. In this section we rewrite our simple daytime client using TPI, instead of sockets (Figure 1.5) or XTI (Figure 28.13). Using programming languages as an analogy, using sockets or XTI is like programming in a high-level language such as C or Pascal, while using TPI directly is like programming in assembler. We are not advocating the use of TPI directly in real applications. But examining how TPI works and developing this example gives us a better understanding of how the sockets library and the XTI library work in a streams environment.

Figure 33.7 is our `tpi_daytime.h` header.

```
                                                                  ── streams/tpi_daytime.h
 1 #include     "unpxti.h"
 2 #include     <sys/stream.h>
 3 #include     <sys/tihdr.h>

 4 void    tpi_bind(int, const void *, size_t);
 5 void    tpi_connect(int, const void *, size_t);
 6 ssize_t tpi_read(int, void *, size_t);
 7 void    tpi_close(int);
                                                                  ── streams/tpi_daytime.h
```

Figure 33.7 Our `tpi_daytime.h` header.

We need to include one additional streams header along with `<sys/tihdr.h>`, which contains the definitions of the structures for all the TPI messages.

Figure 33.8 is the `main` function for our daytime client.

—— streams/tpi_daytime.c

```
 1 #include    "tpi_daytime.h"

 2 int
 3 main(int argc, char **argv)
 4 {
 5     int     fd, n;
 6     char    recvline[MAXLINE + 1];
 7     struct sockaddr_in myaddr, servaddr;

 8     if (argc != 2)
 9         err_quit("usage: tpi_daytime <IPaddress>");

10     fd = Open(XTI_TCP, O_RDWR, 0);

11         /* bind any local address */
12     bzero(&myaddr, sizeof(myaddr));
13     myaddr.sin_family = AF_INET;
14     myaddr.sin_addr.s_addr = htonl(INADDR_ANY);
15     myaddr.sin_port = htons(0);

16     tpi_bind(fd, &myaddr, sizeof(struct sockaddr_in));

17         /* fill in server's address */
18     bzero(&servaddr, sizeof(servaddr));
19     servaddr.sin_family = AF_INET;
20     servaddr.sin_port = htons(13);  /* daytime server */
21     Inet_pton(AF_INET, argv[1], &servaddr.sin_addr);

22     tpi_connect(fd, &servaddr, sizeof(struct sockaddr_in));

23     for ( ; ; ) {
24         if ( (n = tpi_read(fd, recvline, MAXLINE)) <= 0) {
25             if (n == 0)
26                 break;
27             else
28                 err_sys("tpi_read error");
29         }
30         recvline[n] = 0;        /* null terminate */
31         fputs(recvline, stdout);
32     }
33     tpi_close(fd);
34     exit(0);
35 }
```

—— streams/tpi_daytime.c

Figure 33.8 `main` function for our daytime client written to TPI.

Open transport provider, bind local address

10-16   We open the device corresponding to the transport provider (normally `/dev/tcp`). We fill in an Internet socket address structure with `INADDR_ANY` and a port of 0, telling TCP to bind any local address to our endpoint. We call our own function `tpi_bind` (shown shortly) to do the bind.

Fill in server's address, establish connection

17–22   We fill in another Internet socket address structure with the server's IP address (taken from the command line) and port (13). We call our `tpi_connect` function to establish the connection.

Read data from server, copy to standard output

23–33   As in our other daytime clients, we just copy data from the connection to standard output, stopping when we receive the end-of-file from the server (e.g., the FIN). We have written this loop to look like our sockets client (Figure 1.5) instead of our XTI client (Figure 28.13), because our `tpi_read` function will convert an orderly release from the server into a return of 0. We then call our `tpi_close` function to close our endpoint.

Our `tpi_bind` function is shown in Figure 33.9.

Fill in `T_bind_req` structure

16–20   The `<sys/tihdr.h>` header defines the `T_bind_req` structure:

```
struct T_bind_req {
    long          PRIM_type;      /* T_BIND_REQ */
    long          ADDR_length;    /* address length */
    long          ADDR_offset;    /* address offset */
    unsigned long CONIND_number;  /* connect indications requested */
        /* followed by the protocol address for bind */
};
```

All TPI requests are defined as a structure that begins with a long integer type field. We define our own `bind_req` structure that begins with the `T_bind_req` structure, followed by a buffer containing the local address to be bound. TPI says nothing about the contents of this buffer; it is defined by the provider. TCP providers expect this buffer to contain a `sockaddr_in` structure.

We fill in the `T_bind_req` structure, setting the `ADDR_length` member to the size of the address (16 bytes for an Internet socket address structure) and `ADDR_offset` to the byte offset of the address (it immediately follows the `T_bind_req` structure). We are not guaranteed that this location is suitably aligned for the `sockaddr_in` structure that is stored there, so we call `memcpy` to copy the caller's structure into our `bind_req` structure. We set `CONIND_number` to 0, because we are a client, not a server.

Call `putmsg`

21–23   TPI requires that the structure that we just built be passed to the provider as one `M_PROTO` message. We therefore call `putmsg` specifying our `bind_req` structure as the control information, with no data and with a flag of 0.

Call `getmsg` to read high-priority message

24–30   The response to our `T_BIND_REQ` request will be either a `T_BIND_ACK` message or a `T_ERROR_ACK` message. These acknowledgment messages are sent as high-priority messages (`M_PCPROTO`) so we read them using `getmsg` with a flag of `RS_HIPRI`. Since the reply is a high-priority message, it will bypass any normal-priority messages on the stream.

streams/tpi_bind.c

```
 1 #include     "tpi_daytime.h"

 2 void
 3 tpi_bind(int fd, const void *addr, size_t addrlen)
 4 {
 5     struct {
 6         struct T_bind_req msg_hdr;
 7         char    addr[128];
 8     } bind_req;
 9     struct {
10         struct T_bind_ack msg_hdr;
11         char    addr[128];
12     } bind_ack;
13     struct strbuf ctlbuf;
14     struct T_error_ack *error_ack;
15     int     flags;

16     bind_req.msg_hdr.PRIM_type = T_BIND_REQ;
17     bind_req.msg_hdr.ADDR_length = addrlen;
18     bind_req.msg_hdr.ADDR_offset = sizeof(struct T_bind_req);
19     bind_req.msg_hdr.CONIND_number = 0;
20     memcpy(bind_req.addr, addr, addrlen);   /* sockaddr_in{} */

21     ctlbuf.len = sizeof(struct T_bind_req) + addrlen;
22     ctlbuf.buf = (char *) &bind_req;
23     Putmsg(fd, &ctlbuf, NULL, 0);

24     ctlbuf.maxlen = sizeof(bind_ack);
25     ctlbuf.len = 0;
26     ctlbuf.buf = (char *) &bind_ack;
27     flags = RS_HIPRI;
28     Getmsg(fd, &ctlbuf, NULL, &flags);
29     if (ctlbuf.len < (int) sizeof(long))
30         err_quit("bad length from getmsg");

31     switch (bind_ack.msg_hdr.PRIM_type) {
32     case T_BIND_ACK:
33         return;

34     case T_ERROR_ACK:
35         if (ctlbuf.len < (int) sizeof(struct T_error_ack))
36             err_quit("bad length for T_ERROR_ACK");
37         error_ack = (struct T_error_ack *) &bind_ack.msg_hdr;
38         err_quit("T_ERROR_ACK from bind (%d, %d)",
39                     error_ack->TLI_error, error_ack->UNIX_error);

40     default:
41         err_quit("unexpected message type: %d", bind_ack.msg_hdr.PRIM_type);
42     }
43 }
```

streams/tpi_bind.c

Figure 33.9 tpi_bind function: bind a local address to an endpoint.

These two messages are

```
struct T_bind_ack {
    long            PRIM_type;      /* T_BIND_ACK */
    long            ADDR_length;    /* address length */
    long            ADDR_offset;    /* address offset */
    unsigned long   CONIND_number;  /* connect ind to be queued */
        /* followed by the bound address */
};

struct T_error_ack {
    long            PRIM_type;      /* T_ERROR_ACK */
    long            ERROR_prim      /* primitive in error */
    long            TLI_error;      /* TLI error code */
    long            UNIX_error;     /* UNIX error code */
};
```

All these messages begin with the type, so we can read the reply assuming it is a T_BIND_ACK message, look at the type, and process the message accordingly. We do not expect any data from the provider, so we specify a null pointer as the third argument to getmsg.

> When we verify that the amount of control information returned is at least the size of a long integer, we must be careful to cast the sizeof value to an integer. The sizeof operator returns an unsigned integer value but it is possible for the returned len field to be −1. But since the less-than comparison is comparing a signed value on the left to an unsigned value on the right, the compiler casts the signed value to an unsigned value. On a twos-complement architecture, −1 considered as an unsigned value is very large, causing −1 to be greater than 4 (if we assume a long integer occupies 4 bytes).

Process reply

31–33   If the reply is T_BIND_ACK, the bind was successful, and we return. The actual address that was bound to the endpoint is returned in the addr member of our bind_ack structure, which we ignore.

34–39   If the reply is T_ERROR_ACK, we verify that the entire message was received and then print the three return values in the structure. In this simple program we terminate when an error occurs; we do not return to the caller.

We can see these errors from the bind request by changing our main function to bind some port other than 0. For example, if we try to bind port 1 (which requires superuser privileges, since it is a port less than 1024) we get

```
aix % tpi_daytime 206.62.226.33
T_ERROR_ACK from bind (3, 0)
```

The error EACCES has the value of 3 on this system. If we change the port to a value greater than 1023, but one that is currently in use by another TCP endpoint, we get

```
aix % tpi_daytime 206.62.226.33
T_ERROR_ACK from bind (23, 0)
```

The error EADDRBUSY has a value of 23 on this system.

This error is new with the TPI to support XTI. Older versions of TPI that support TLI would bind another unused port if the requested one was busy. This meant that a server binding a well-known port would have to compare the returned address (from the `T_bind_ack` message, which is returned by `t_bind` if the third argument is a nonnull pointer) to the requested address, and abort if they were not equal.

The next function, shown in Figure 33.10, is `tpi_connect`, which establishes the connection with the server.

Fill in request structure and send to provider

18-26   TPI defines a `T_conn_req` structure that contains the protocol address and options for the connection:

```
struct T_conn_req {
  long    PRIM_type;    /* T_CONN_REQ */
  long    DEST_length; /* destination address length */
  long    DEST_offset; /* destination address offset */
  long    OPT_length;  /* options length */
  long    OPT_offset;  /* options offset */
      /* followed by the protocol address and options for connection */
};
```

As in our `tpi_bind` function, we define our own structure named `conn_req` that includes a `T_conn_req` structure along with room for the protocol address. We fill in our `conn_req` structure, setting the two members dealing with options to 0. We call `putmsg` with only control information and a flag of 0 to send an `M_PROTO` message down the stream.

—————————————————————— streams/tpi_connect.c

```
 1 #include   "tpi_daytime.h"

 2 void
 3 tpi_connect(int fd, const void *addr, size_t addrlen)
 4 {
 5     struct {
 6         struct T_conn_req msg_hdr;
 7         char    addr[128];
 8     } conn_req;
 9     struct {
10         struct T_conn_con msg_hdr;
11         char    addr[128];
12     } conn_con;
13     struct strbuf ctlbuf;
14     union T_primitives rcvbuf;
15     struct T_error_ack *error_ack;
16     struct T_discon_ind *discon_ind;
17     int     flags;

18     conn_req.msg_hdr.PRIM_type = T_CONN_REQ;
19     conn_req.msg_hdr.DEST_length = addrlen;
20     conn_req.msg_hdr.DEST_offset = sizeof(struct T_conn_req);
21     conn_req.msg_hdr.OPT_length = 0;
22     conn_req.msg_hdr.OPT_offset = 0;
23     memcpy(conn_req.addr, addr, addrlen);   /* sockaddr_in{} */
```

```
24      ctlbuf.len = sizeof(struct T_conn_req) + addrlen;
25      ctlbuf.buf = (char *) &conn_req;
26      Putmsg(fd, &ctlbuf, NULL, 0);

27      ctlbuf.maxlen = sizeof(union T_primitives);
28      ctlbuf.len = 0;
29      ctlbuf.buf = (char *) &rcvbuf;
30      flags = RS_HIPRI;
31      Getmsg(fd, &ctlbuf, NULL, &flags);
32      if (ctlbuf.len < (int) sizeof(long))
33          err_quit("tpi_connect: bad length from getmsg");

34      switch (rcvbuf.type) {
35      case T_OK_ACK:
36          break;

37      case T_ERROR_ACK:
38          if (ctlbuf.len < (int) sizeof(struct T_error_ack))
39              err_quit("tpi_connect: bad length for T_ERROR_ACK");
40          error_ack = (struct T_error_ack *) &rcvbuf;
41          err_quit("tpi_connect: T_ERROR_ACK from conn (%d, %d)",
42                  error_ack->TLI_error, error_ack->UNIX_error);

43      default:
44          err_quit("tpi_connect: unexpected message type: %d", rcvbuf.type);
45      }

46      ctlbuf.maxlen = sizeof(conn_con);
47      ctlbuf.len = 0;
48      ctlbuf.buf = (char *) &conn_con;
49      flags = 0;
50      Getmsg(fd, &ctlbuf, NULL, &flags);
51      if (ctlbuf.len < (int) sizeof(long))
52          err_quit("tpi_connect2: bad length from getmsg");

53      switch (conn_con.msg_hdr.PRIM_type) {
54      case T_CONN_CON:
55          break;

56      case T_DISCON_IND:
57          if (ctlbuf.len < (int) sizeof(struct T_discon_ind))
58              err_quit("tpi_connect2: bad length for T_DISCON_IND");
59          discon_ind = (struct T_discon_ind *) &conn_con.msg_hdr;
60          err_quit("tpi_connect2: T_DISCON_IND from conn (%d)",
61                  discon_ind->DISCON_reason);

62      default:
63          err_quit("tpi_connect2: unexpected message type: %d",
64                  conn_con.msg_hdr.PRIM_type);
65      }
66  }
```

streams/tpi_connect.c

Figure 33.10 `tpi_connect` function: establish connection with server.

Read response

27–45   We call `getmsg` expecting to receive either a `T_OK_ACK` message

```
struct T_ok_ack {
  long    PRIM_type;        /* T_OK_ACK   */
  long    CORRECT_prim;     /* correct primitive */
};
```

if the connection establishment was started, or a T_ERROR_ACK message (which we showed earlier). In the case of an error, we terminate. Since we do not know what type of message we will receive, a union named T_primitives is defined as the union of all the possible requests and replies, and we allocate one of these that we use as the input buffer for the control information when we call getmsg.

Wait for connection establishment to complete

46-65   The successful T_OK_ACK message that was just received only tells us that the connection establishment was started. We must now wait for a T_CONN_CON message to tell us that the other end has confirmed the connection request.

```
struct T_conn_con {
  long    PRIM_type;        /* T_CONN_CON */
  long    RES_length;       /* responding address length */
  long    RES_offset;       /* responding address offset */
  long    OPT_length;       /* option length */
  long    OPT_offset;       /* option offset */
        /* followed by peer's protocol address and options */
};
```

We call getmsg again, but the expected message is sent as an M_PROTO message, not an M_PCPROTO message, so we set the flags to 0. If we receive the T_CONN_CON message, the connection is established, and we return, but if the connection was not established (either the peer process was not running, a timeout, or whatever), a T_DISCON_IND message is sent up the stream instead:

```
struct T_discon_ind {
  long    PRIM_type;        /* T_DISCON_IND */
  long    DISCON_reason;    /* disconnect reason */
  long    SEQ_number;       /* sequence number */
};
```

We can see the different errors that are returned by the provider. We first specify the IP address of a host that is not running the daytime server:

```
solaris26 % tpi_daytime 140.252.1.4
tpi_connect2: T_DISCON_IND from conn (146)
```

The error of 146 corresponds to ECONNREFUSED. Next we specify an IP address that is not connected to the Internet:

```
solaris26 % tpi_daytime 192.3.4.5
tpi_connect2: T_DISCON_IND from conn (145)
```

The error this time is ETIMEDOUT. But if we run our program again, specifying the same IP address, we get a different error:

```
solaris26 % tpi_daytime 192.3.4.5
tpi_connect2: T_DISCON_IND from conn (148)
```

The error this time is EHOSTUNREACH. The difference in the last two results is that the first time no ICMP host unreachable errors were returned, while the next time this error was returned.

The next function is tpi_read, shown in Figure 33.11. It reads data from a stream.

```
                                                                        ──── streams/tpi_read.c
 1 #include    "tpi_daytime.h"

 2 ssize_t
 3 tpi_read(int fd, void *buf, size_t len)
 4 {
 5     struct strbuf ctlbuf;
 6     struct strbuf datbuf;
 7     union T_primitives rcvbuf;
 8     int     flags;

 9     ctlbuf.maxlen = sizeof(union T_primitives);
10     ctlbuf.buf = (char *) &rcvbuf;

11     datbuf.maxlen = len;
12     datbuf.buf = buf;
13     datbuf.len = 0;

14     flags = 0;
15     Getmsg(fd, &ctlbuf, &datbuf, &flags);

16     if (ctlbuf.len >= (int) sizeof(long)) {
17         if (rcvbuf.type == T_DATA_IND)
18             return (datbuf.len);
19         else if (rcvbuf.type == T_ORDREL_IND)
20             return (0);
21         else
22             err_quit("tpi_read: unexpected type %d", rcvbuf.type);
23     } else if (ctlbuf.len == -1)
24         return (datbuf.len);
25     else
26         err_quit("tpi_read: bad length from getmsg");
27 }
                                                                        ──── streams/tpi_read.c
```

Figure 33.11 tpi_read function: read data from a stream.

Read control and data; process reply

9–26   This time we call getmsg to read both control information and data. The strbuf structure for the data points to the caller's buffer. Four different scenarios can occur on the stream.

- The data can arrive as an M_DATA message, and this is indicated by the returned control length set to –1. The data was copied into the caller's buffer by getmsg, and we just return the length of this data as the return value of the function.

- The data can arrive as a T_DATA_IND message, in which case the control information will be a T_data_ind structure:

```
struct T_data_ind {
  long    PRIM_type;  /* T_DATA_IND */
  long    MORE_flag;  /* more data */
};
```

If this message is returned, we ignore the MORE_flag member (it will never be set for a stream protocol such as TCP) and just return the length of the data that was copied into the caller's buffer by getmsg.

- A T_ORDREL_IND message is returned if all the data has been consumed and the next item is a FIN:

```
struct T_ordrel_ind {
  long    PRIM_type;      /* T_ORDREL_IND */
};
```

This is the orderly release that we described in Section 28.9. We just return 0, indicating to the caller that the end-of-file has been encountered on the connection.

- A T_DISCON_IND message is returned if a disconnect has been received. We discussed this in Section 28.10 and said this occurs in the case of TCP if an RST is received on an existing connection. We do not handle this scenario in this simple example, but we did handle it in Figure 28.13.

We can now explain the two different scenarios that we saw in Section 28.12 when we called read but had not pushed the tirdwr module onto the stream. In the first example, which generated the error "read error: Not a data message," the provider had sent a T_DATA_IND message up the stream as an M_PROTO message (since it had control and data). But read handles only M_DATA messages, hence the error.

In the second example the error was "read error: Bad message" but this appeared after the server's expected reply was received and printed. On this implementation the provider sent the data up the stream as an M_DATA message, so it was handled by read correctly. But the next message up the stream was a T_ORDREL_IND message, which read cannot handle.

Our final function is tpi_close, shown in Figure 33.12.

Send orderly release to peer

7–10   We build a T_ordrel_req structure

```
struct T_ordrel_req {
  long PRIM_type;   /* T_ORDREL_REQ */
};
```

and send it as an M_PROTO message using putmsg. This corresponds to the XTI t_sndrel function.

This example has given us a flavor for TPI. The application sends messages down a stream to the provider (requests) and the provider sends messages up the stream (replies). Some exchanges are a simple request–reply scenario (binding a local address) while others may take a while (establishing a connection), allowing us to do something

```
                                                              ── streams/tpi_close.c
 1 #include     "tpi_daytime.h"

 2 void
 3 tpi_close(int fd)
 4 {
 5     struct T_ordrel_req ordrel_req;
 6     struct strbuf ctlbuf;

 7     ordrel_req.PRIM_type = T_ORDREL_REQ;

 8     ctlbuf.len = sizeof(struct T_ordrel_req);
 9     ctlbuf.buf = (char *) &ordrel_req;
10     Putmsg(fd, &ctlbuf, NULL, 0);

11     Close(fd);
12 }
                                                              ── streams/tpi_close.c
```
Figure 33.12   tpi_close function: send an orderly release to peer.

while we wait for the reply. Our choice of writing a TCP client using TPI was done for
simplicity; writing a TCP server and handling connections as we described in Section 30.7 becomes much harder.

It should be obvious that the mapping from the XTI functions to TPI is very close.
On the other hand, the mapping from sockets to TPI is not as close. Nevertheless, both
the XTI and socket libraries handle lots of the details required by TPI, simplifying our
applications.

> We can compare the number of system calls required for the network operations that we have
> seen in this chapter, when using TPI versus a kernel that implements sockets within the kernel.
> Binding a local address takes two system calls with TPI, but only one with kernel sockets
> (TCPv2, p. 454). To establish a connection on a blocking descriptor takes three system calls
> with TPI, but only one with kernel sockets (TCPv2, p. 466).

33.7 Summary

XTI is often implemented using streams. Four new functions are provided to access the
streams subsystem, getmsg, getpmsg, putmsg, and putpmsg, and the existing ioctl
function is heavily used by the streams subsystem also.

TPI is the SVR4 streams interface from the upper layers into the transport layer. It is
used by both XTI and sockets, as shown in Figure 33.3. We developed a version of our
daytime client using TPI directly, as an example to show the message-based interface
that TPI uses.

Exercises

33.1   In Figure 33.12 we call putmsg to send the orderly release request down the stream and
then immediately close the stream. What happens if our orderly release request is lost by
the streams subsystem when the stream is closed?

34

XTI: Additional Functions

34.1 Introduction

In the previous chapters we have covered the XTI functions for

- TCP clients,
- hostname and service name lookups,
- TCP servers,
- UDP clients and servers,
- options, and
- the common streams implementation.

This chapter covers the remaining XTI functions.

34.2 Nonblocking I/O

An endpoint can be put into a nonblocking mode. This is done by specifying the O_NONBLOCK flag in the call to t_open when the endpoint is created, or at a later time with the fcntl function (as shown in Section 7.10).

The operation of some of the XTI functions changes when the endpoint is nonblocking.

- t_connect returns immediately with a return of −1 and t_errno set to TNODATA. With TCP this call initiates the three-way handshake, and we must call t_rcvconnect (Section 34.3) to wait for the connection establishment to complete.

- `t_rcvconnect` returns −1 with `t_errno` set to TNODATA if a connection is in progress but has not yet completed.

- `t_listen` returns immediately with a return of −1 and `t_errno` set to TNODATA when there are no connections ready for the application to call `t_accept`.

- The four receive functions, `t_rcv`, `t_rcvudata`, `t_rcvv`, and `t_rcvvudata`, return −1 with `t_errno` set to TNODATA if there is no data available. If some data is available, that data is returned, even though it may be less than asked for by the application. (The last two functions mentioned are new; we describe them in Section 34.8.)

- The four send functions, `t_snd`, `t_sndudata`, `t_sndv`, and `t_sndvudata`, return −1 with `t_errno` set to TFLOW if the provider is not able to accept any data. If some data can be accepted, then the return value might be less than the amount requested for `t_snd` and `t_sndv`. The two datagram functions write a complete datagram, or they return an error. (The last two of the four functions listed are new; we describe them in Section 34.9.)

34.3 `t_rcvconnect` Function

In the previous section we mentioned initiating a connection in the nonblocking mode and then waiting for the connection to complete by calling `t_rcvconnect`.

```
#include <xti.h>

int t_rcvconnect(int fd, struct t_call *recvcall);
```

Returns: 0 if OK, −1 on error

The sequence of steps typically used with this function are as follows:

1. An endpoint is created using `t_open` and set nonblocking.

2. `t_connect` initiates the connection establishment. Since the endpoint is in the nonblocking mode, this function returns immediately with a value of −1 and `t_errno` set to TNODATA.

3. At some later time the process calls `t_rcvconnect` to determine if the connection has completed. If the endpoint is no longer in a nonblocking mode (the process has turned off the nonblocking flag since calling `t_connect` in step 2), then `t_rcvconnect` blocks until the connection is established. If the endpoint is still in a nonblocking mode, then this call to `t_rcvconnect` either (a) returns immediately with a return value of 0 if the connection is established, or (b) returns a value of −1 with `t_errno` set to TNODATA if the connection is not yet established.

Note in the case of a blocking t_connect (the default), the provider returns the information in the t_call structure that is pointed to by the third argument to t_connect. But with a nonblocking t_connect, this information is returned in the t_call structure that is pointed to by the second argument to t_rcvconnect.

Unless the application converts the endpoint from nonblocking to blocking between the calls to t_connect and t_rcvconnect (steps 2 and 3 above), calling t_rcvconnect to determine when a nonblocking connection establishment completes is a waste of time, because the application must call t_rcvconnect in a loop of some form, waiting for the connection to complete (or an error to be returned). This is called *polling*. Better techniques for waiting for a nonblocking connection establishment to complete are to call either select or poll (Chapter 6), or to use signal-driven I/O (Section 34.11).

Recall our discussion of an interrupted connection establishment at the end of Section 15.4. With XTI, if a call to t_connect on a blocking endpoint is interrupted, we just call t_rcvconnect to wait for the connection establishment to complete.

34.4 t_getinfo Function

Recall the t_info structure that is returned by the t_open function (Section 28.2). The following function returns the same information to the caller.

```
#include <xti.h>

int t_getinfo(int fd, struct t_info *info);
```
                                                        Returns: 0 if OK, −1 on error

This function is called, for example, by t_alloc, to obtain the information about an endpoint that is already open for t_alloc to obtain the required buffer sizes.

34.5 t_getstate Function

Every transport endpoint has a *current state* associated with it. The following function returns the current state (an integer value) to the caller.

```
#include <xti.h>

int t_getstate(int fd);
```
                                                        Returns: current state if OK, −1 on error

The current state is specified by one of the constants shown in Figure 34.1. The final three columns indicate which states are valid for the different service types (Figure 28.3).

State	Description	T_COTS	T_COTS_ORD	T_CLTS
T_DATAXFER	data transfer	•	•	
T_IDLE	bound, but idle	•	•	•
T_INCON	incoming connection pending for passive endpoint	•	•	
T_INREL	incoming orderly release		•	
T_OUTCON	outgoing connection pending for active endpoint	•	•	
T_OUTREL	outgoing orderly release		•	
T_UNBND	unbound	•	•	•
T_UNINIT	uninitialized: starting and final state	•	•	•

Figure 34.1 Possible states of an XTI endpoint.

A state transition diagram can be developed to show exactly how the state of a transport endpoint changes as different XTI functions are called and as different events occur at the endpoint. This diagram would also show which XTI functions are allowed in the different states. For example, the only function call allowed in the T_UNINIT state is t_open and the new state becomes T_UNBND. Four events can occur in the T_UNBND state:

1. A successful return from t_close changes the state to T_UNINIT.

2. Calling t_optmgmt is allowed but does not change the state. (What this state transition diagram cannot show, however, is that the option processing might change depending on the state. For example, the T_UDP_CHECKSUM option behaves differently in the T_UNBND state, versus other states.)

3. A successful return from t_bind changes the state to T_IDLE.

4. Passing a connection to the endpoint (by t_accept) is allowed, and changes the state to T_DATAXFER.

Once we get past these first two states, however, the diagram becomes unwieldy, so we will not attempt to show it.

34.6   t_sync Function

Historically TLI was implemented as a library of functions in SVR3. Consider a program using TLI that calls exec as shown in Figure 34.2. Perhaps the program on the left is a listening server that waits for a connection to arrive and be accepted and then execs the program on the right to handle the client. (Remember that the process ID does not change across an exec, but the caller's memory is replaced with the new program that then begins execution at its main function.)

The problem encountered with this scenario in SVR3 was that state information is maintained in both the TLI library within the process and in the provider within the kernel. After an exec all of the state information in the library is discarded, and the library in the new program starts off fresh. The purpose of the t_sync function was to allow the new program (on the right in Figure 34.2) to synchronize the state of its library with the provider in the kernel.

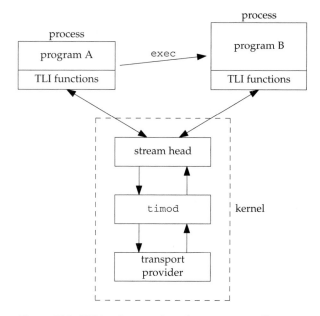

Figure 34.2 TLI implementation when a process calls exec.

With SVR4, however, the need to call t_sync for the scenario that we show in Figure 34.2 disappeared. The TLI library functions could detect the need for performing a synchronization themselves. For example, if the library has a variable declared as

```
static int  synced;     /* initialized to 0 when program starts */
```

then each function can begin with the sequence similar to the following:

```
int
t_connect(fd, ... )
{
    if (synced == 0)
        t_sync(fd);  /* also sets synced = 1 */

    ...
}
```

While this handles the case of a process calling exec, there is still one scenario, albeit rare, where t_sync is required: when multiple processes are sharing an XTI endpoint. In this scenario it is assumed that the processes are cooperating with each other and that each calls t_sync when it deems necessary (which depends, of course, on the specifics of the application). One example where t_sync might be necessary is in a parent–child relationship, if the parent calls t_listen and then the child calls t_accept. The parent would need to call t_sync to update its library copy of the endpoint state, which might change after the child calls t_accept.

```
#include <xti.h>

int t_sync(int fd);
```

Returns: current state if OK, –1 on error

The successful return from this function is one of the states shown in Figure 34.1.

> There is no operation similar to this function in the sockets API.

34.7 `t_unbind` Function

The effect of the `t_bind` function is undone by `t_unbind`.

```
#include <xti.h>

int t_unbind(int fd);
```

Returns: 0 if OK, –1 on error

This function disables the transport endpoint specified by *fd*. No further data will be accepted for this endpoint. `t_bind` may be called, however, to bind another local address to the endpoint.

> With sockets this operation can be performed only on a connected UDP socket by calling `bind` with an invalid address.

34.8 `t_rcvv` and `t_rcvvudata` Functions

These two functions extend the `t_rcv` and `t_rcvudata` functions to operate on a *vector* of buffers, instead of just a single buffer. They provide a *scatter read* capability.

> These two functions and the two described in the next section were introduced with Posix.1g.

> The concept of operating on a vector of buffers comes from the `readv` and `writev` functions, along with the `recvmsg` and `sendmsg` functions.

```
#include <xti.h>

int t_rcvv(int fd, struct t_iovec *iov, unsigned int iovcnt, int *flags);

int t_rcvvudata(int fd, struct t_unitdata *unitdata,
                struct t_iovec *iov, unsigned int iovcnt, int *flags);
```

Both return: number of bytes read or written if OK, –1 on error

The second argument to both functions is a pointer to an array of `t_iovec` structures:

```
struct t_iovec {
  void   *iov_base;   /* starting address of buffer */
  size_t  iov_len;    /* length of buffer in bytes */
}
```

The number of entries in the array is specified by the *iovcnt* argument. The limit on the number of entries in the array is given by the constant T_IOV_MAX, defined by including the <xti.h> header, whose value must be at least 16.

Comparing these new functions to their earlier counterparts we see the following:

- The buffer pointer and its length are the middle two arguments to t_rcv.

- The buffer pointers and their lengths are in an array of t_iovec structures for t_rcvv, and the middle two arguments for this function point to this array of structures and specify the number of entries in the array.

- The buffer pointer and its length are in the udata member of the t_unitdata structure for t_rcvudata. Also, this function returns 0 upon success, with the actual length of the received datagram in the udata.len member of the t_unitdata structure.

- The buffer pointers and their lengths are in an array of t_iovec structures for t_rcvvudata. The third argument to this function is a pointer to this array of structures and the fourth argument is the number of entries in the array. A pointer to a t_unitdata structure is the second argument to this function and the addr and opt member are still used (for the sender's protocol address and any received options), but the udata member is ignored. This function returns the number of bytes in the datagram as its return value, not 0.

34.9 t_sndv and t_sndvudata Functions

These two functions extend the t_snd and t_sndudata functions to operate on a *vector* of buffers, instead of just a single buffer. They are the send counterparts of the two functions described in the previous section and provide a *gather write* capability.

```
#include <xti.h>

int t_sndv(int fd, struct t_iovec *iov, unsigned int iovcnt, int flags);
```

                                   Returns: number of bytes read or written if OK, −1 on error

```
int t_sndvudata(int fd, struct t_unitdata *unitdata,
                struct t_iovec *iov, unsigned int iovcnt);
```

                                                      Returns: 0 if OK, −1 on error

The *iov* argument to both functions is a pointer to an array of t_iovec structures, which we showed in the previous section. The number of entries in the array is specified by the *iovcnt* argument.

The output buffers are specified by the two middle arguments to t_sndv, replacing the two middle arguments to t_snd. For the datagram functions, the output buffer is specified by the udata member of the t_unitdata structure with t_sndudata but by the *iov* vector with t_sndvudata. The udata member of the t_unitdata structure is ignored by t_sndvudata.

34.10 t_rcvreldata and t_sndreldata Functions

If we send an orderly release with t_sndrel (Section 28.9) we cannot send data with the orderly release notification (the only argument to the function is a descriptor), but if we send a disconnect with t_snddis (Section 28.10), we can send data (the udata member of the t_call structure). We find the same limitation for t_rcvrel, compared to t_rcvdis. To get around this limitation XTI invented two new functions that send and receive data with an orderly release.

```
#include <xti.h>

int t_sndreldata(int fd, const struct t_discon *discon);

int t_rcvreldata(int fd, struct t_discon *discon);
```

Both return: 0 if OK, −1 on error

The difference between these two functions and t_sndrel and t_rcvrel is the addition of the second argument (a pointer to a t_discon structure).

These functions are useful only when the provider supports the sending of data with an orderly release, as indicated by the T_ORDRELDATA flag in the flag member of the t_info structure (Figure 28.4). If supported, the amount of orderly release data is limited to the value of the discon member of the t_info structure.

> TCP does not support this optional feature.

34.11 Signal-Driven I/O

Signal-driven I/O is provided by the streams system, not XTI. The signal name is SIGPOLL and the signal is not delivered just because the process installs a signal handling function for the signal. The process must also tell the kernel that it wants to receive the signal by issuing the I_SETSIG streams ioctl request, specifying which conditions should generate the signal. This is similar to what we must do to receive the SIGIO and SIGURG signals that we described for the sockets API.

The third argument to ioctl is an integer value that specifies the conditions for which a SIGPOLL signal should be generated. If this value is 0, the process will no longer receive the SIGPOLL signal for the stream. This value can also be formed as the logical OR of the following constants:

S_BANDURG   If this flag is specified in conjunction with S_RDBAND, the SIGURG signal will be generated instead of SIGPOLL when a message in a priority band greater than 0 can be read.

S_ERROR   The stream is in error.

S_HANGUP   A hangup message has reached the stream head.

S_HIPRI   A high-priority message can be read.

S_INPUT   This is equivalent to S_RDNORM | S_RDBAND and means that a message with any band (including 0) can be read.

S_OUTPUT   The write queue just below the stream head is no longer flow controlled for normal messages (band 0).

S_MSG   A streams signal message is at the front of the stream's read queue.

S_RDNORM   A normal message (band 0) can be read.

S_RDBAND   A message in a priority band greater than 0 can be read.

S_WRNORM   Equivalent to S_OUTPUT.

S_WRBAND   The write queue is no longer flow controlled for messages in a priority band greater than 0.

> The S_BANDURG flag is used by the sockets API when it is implemented using streams.
>
> There is no output equivalent for S_HIPRI. This is because putmsg and putpmsg do not block when sending a high-priority message: these messages are not flow controlled.
>
> The streams signal SIGPOLL is used for both signal-driven I/O and for the notification of the arrival of out-of-band data. This corresponds to the two signals SIGIO and SIGURG that we described with the sockets API.

The default action for SIGPOLL is to terminate the process, so when using this signal we must establish the signal handler and then call ioctl to enable the signal.

> There is a conflict between the default action of SIGPOLL, which we just said terminates the process, and SIGIO. Posix.1g specifies that the default action of SIGIO is to be ignored. Since SVR4 systems define these two signals to be the same, these systems will have to change the default action for SIGPOLL to be ignored, to be Posix.1g compliant.

Even though the SIGPOLL signal can be generated for numerous conditions, typical applications that do not deal with out-of-band data are interested in only S_RDNORM and S_WRNORM.

34.12 Out-of-Band Data

Out-of-band data is called *expedited data* by XTI. Support for this feature is provided by the transport provider and the streams system. We mentioned in Chapter 33 that out-of-band data is often implemented as normal-priority data in priority band 1. Normal data (i.e., not out-of-band data) is in priority band 0.

> We also mentioned in Chapter 33 that since TCP's out-of-band data is not true expedited data (in the XTI sense), it is actually implemented in band 0, not band 1.

Everything that we said in Chapter 21 about the support for out-of-band data with TCP, and the mapping of TCP's urgent mode into out-of-band data, applies to XTI just like sockets.

Out-of-band data is sent with the XTI t_snd function by specifying a *flags* argument of T_EXPEDITED. This flag value is also returned to the caller by the t_rcv function.

We cannot use the read and write functions when writing an application that deals with out-of-band data (recall our xti_rdwr function in Section 28.12). We must use t_snd and t_rcv.

Since TCP's out-of-band data corresponds to normal-priority messages in band 0, to receive SIGPOLL when out-of-band data arrives requires that we specify S_RDNORM when we call ioctl with a request of I_SETSIG (Section 34.11). Since this also generates the signal when normal data arrives, if we want to differentiate between normal data and out-of-band data, we must call t_look from our signal handler and check for either T_DATA or T_EXDATA (Figure 28.9). XTI sets the event T_EXDATA as soon as a TCP segment with an urgent pointer is received, and this event remains set until all data up through the urgent pointer has been received.

> SIGPOLL corresponds to the SIGURG signal for sockets.

If using poll to await the arrival of out-of-band data (Section 6.10), the events member of the pollfd structure must be set to POLLRDNORM since it appears as normal data in band 0. We will verify that TCP's out-of-band data appears as normal data to poll in Figures 34.4 and C.5. Also note that this treatment of out-of-band data with XTI differs from sockets, which considers out-of-band data as belonging to a priority band.

> Using poll corresponds to calling select and waiting for an exception condition, but poll does not tell us what type of data arrived: we must call t_look and t_rcv.

> Recall that by default the sockets API removes a received out-of-band byte from the normal stream of data, placing it into its own special 1-byte buffer that the application reads using recv with the MSG_OOB flag. There is nothing similar to this mode with XTI: TCP's out-of-band data is always received inline, something we have to enable with sockets using the SO_OOBINLINE socket option.

We now look at a few examples to see how signal-driven I/O and poll work with XTI's out-of-band data.

Example Using SIGPOLL

Figure 34.3 is a program that uses SIGPOLL to be notified when data is available on an XTI endpoint.

——————————————————————————————————— xtioob/tcprecv01.c
```
 1 #include     "unpxti.h"

 2 #define NREAD    100

 3 int     listenfd, connfd;

 4 void    sig_poll(int);

 5 int
 6 main(int argc, char **argv)
 7 {
 8     int     n, flags;
 9     char    buff[NREAD + 1];     /* +1 for null at end */

10     if (argc == 2)
11         listenfd = Tcp_listen(NULL, argv[1], NULL);
12     else if (argc == 3)
13         listenfd = Tcp_listen(argv[1], argv[2], NULL);
14     else
15         err_quit("usage: tcprecv01 [ <host> ] <port#>");

16     connfd = Xti_accept(listenfd, NULL, NULL);

17     Signal(SIGPOLL, sig_poll);
18     Ioctl(connfd, I_SETSIG, S_RDNORM);

19     for ( ; ; ) {
20         flags = 0;
21         if ( (n = t_rcv(connfd, buff, NREAD, &flags)) < 0) {
22             if (t_errno == TLOOK) {
23                 if ( (n = T_look(connfd)) == T_ORDREL) {
24                     printf("received T_ORDREL\n");
25                     exit(0);
26                 } else
27                     err_quit("unexpected event after t_rcv: %d", n);
28             }
29             err_xti("t_rcv error");
30         }
31         buff[n] = 0;              /* null terminate */
32         printf("read %d bytes: %s, flags = %s\n",
33             n, buff, Xti_flags_str(flags));
34     }
35 }

36 void
37 sig_poll(int signo)
38 {
39     printf("SIGPOLL received, event = %s\n", Xti_tlook_str(connfd));
40 }
```
——————————————————————————————————— xtioob/tcprecv01.c

Figure 34.3 Receive normal and out-of-band data using `SIGPOLL` on an XTI endpoint.

Create listening endpoint and wait for connection

10-16   We call our `tcp_listen` function to create a listening endpoint and then our `xti_accept` function waits for a connection to arrive and accepts it.

Establish signal handler

17-18   We call `signal` to establish a signal handler for `SIGPOLL` and then call `ioctl` to enable the signal to be generated when normal data arrives for the endpoint.

Loop, reading data

19-34   We call `t_rcv` to receive the data, handling an orderly release when the peer closes the connection. We print the data bytes that are received, along with the `flags` returned by `t_rcv`. Our function `xti_flags_str` returns a pointer to a message describing the flags that are passed as an argument.

Signal handler

36-40   Our signal handler just prints a message that includes the current event for the endpoint. Our function `xti_tlook_str` calls `t_look` and returns a pointer to a message describing the current event for the endpoint.

We start this program and then run the program from Figure 21.3 as the client. Here is the output from our server:

```
unixware % tcprecv01 9999
read 3 bytes: 123, flags = 0
SIGPOLL received, event = T_EXDATA
read 1 bytes: 4, flags = T_EXPEDITED
SIGPOLL received, event = T_DATA
read 2 bytes: 56, flags = 0
SIGPOLL received, event = T_EXDATA
read 1 bytes: 7, flags = T_EXPEDITED
SIGPOLL received, event = T_DATA
read 2 bytes: 89, flags = 0
SIGPOLL received, event = T_ORDREL
received T_ORDREL
```

The first 3 bytes are received as normal data but `SIGPOLL` is not generated. This is a timing issue. Recall from Figure 2.5 that the client's `connect` (or `t_connect` if XTI is being used) returns one-half an RTT before the server's `accept` (or `t_accept`), given how the TCP three-way handshake operates. This gives the client a head start in sending its first segment of data, and we see in this example that the first 3 bytes arrive before we establish our signal handler.

We then receive `SIGPOLL` and the event is `T_EXDATA`. `t_rcv` returns a flag of `T_EXPEDITED`. We can see from the remaining lines of output that each time a TCP segment arrives, `SIGPOLL` is generated, and we must call `t_look` to see what event has occurred.

When we have read all the data and are notified that the client closed its end of the connection, the signal is generated and the event is `T_ORDREL`, as expected.

Example Using `poll`

Our next example, shown in Figure 34.4, uses the `poll` function.

—————————————————————————————————— xtioob/tcprecv03.c

```
 1 #include     "unpxti.h"

 2 #define NREAD    100

 3 int      listenfd, connfd;

 4 int
 5 main(int argc, char **argv)
 6 {
 7     int      n, flags;
 8     char     buff[NREAD + 1];     /* +1 for null at end */
 9     struct pollfd pollfd[1];

10     if (argc == 2)
11         listenfd = Tcp_listen(NULL, argv[1], NULL);
12     else if (argc == 3)
13         listenfd = Tcp_listen(argv[1], argv[2], NULL);
14     else
15         err_quit("usage: tcprecv03 [ <host> ] <port#>");

16     connfd = Xti_accept(listenfd, NULL, NULL);

17     pollfd[0].fd = connfd;
18     pollfd[0].events = POLLIN;

19     for ( ; ; ) {
20         Poll(pollfd, 1, INFTIM);

21         printf("revents = %x\n", pollfd[0].revents);
22         if (pollfd[0].revents & POLLIN) {
23             flags = 0;
24             if ( (n = t_rcv(connfd, buff, NREAD, &flags)) < 0) {
25                 if (t_errno == TLOOK) {
26                     if ( (n = T_look(connfd)) == T_ORDREL) {
27                         printf("received T_ORDREL\n");
28                         exit(0);
29                     } else
30                         err_quit("unexpected event after t_rcv: %d", n);
31                 }
32                 err_xti("t_rcv error");
33             }
34             buff[n] = 0;         /* null terminate */
35             printf("read %d bytes: %s, flags = %s\n",
36                     n, buff, Xti_flags_str(flags));
37         }
38     }
39 }
```

—————————————————————————————————— xtioob/tcprecv03.c

Figure 34.4   Receive normal and out-of-band data using `poll` on an XTI endpoint.

Wait for client connection

10–16   The creation of the listening endpoint and accepting the client's connection have not changed from Figure 34.3.

Prepare for `poll`

17–18   We allocate a 1-element `pollfd` array and initialize it to tell us when normal or priority data arrives for our connected endpoint.

Call `poll`

19–38   We call `poll` with an infinite time limit. When it returns, we print the `revents` member of our `pollfd` structure to see what type of data has arrived. If the event is `POLLIN`, we call `t_rcv` to read the data and print the data and the returned flags.

We run this program with Figure 21.3 as the client (the same client as in the previous example).

```
unixware % tcprecv03 7777
revents = 1
read 3 bytes: 123, flags = 0
revents = 1
read 1 bytes: 4, flags = T_EXPEDITED
revents = 1
read 2 bytes: 56, flags = 0
revents = 1
read 1 bytes: 7, flags = T_EXPEDITED
revents = 1
read 2 bytes: 89, flags = 0
revents = 1
received T_ORDREL
```

Each time `poll` returns, the event is 1, which is `POLLIN` on this system. `t_rcv` tells us the type of data being returned through the returned flags.

34.13 Loopback Transport Providers

Many implementations of XTI provide a loopback transport provider. The names in the `netconfig` file are normally `ticlts`, `ticots`, and `ticotsord` for the three types of XTI providers (Figure 28.3). The `ti` prefix stands for "transport independent." These three names are also the filenames in the `/dev` directory for `t_open`.

Unix domain sockets are often implemented on streams-based systems using two of these three providers: `ticlts` is used for `SOCK_DGRAM` sockets, and either `ticots` or `ticotsord` is used for `SOCK_STREAM` sockets, depending which of the two appears first in the `netconfig` file.

One point to be aware of, when using these providers directly with XTI, is that the addresses used are called *flex addresses*, which are just arbitrary strings of one or more bytes. These addresses are not null terminated; their length is specified by the `len` member of the `netbuf` structure containing the address. But the `addr` member of the `t_info` structure can be returned as –1 (`T_INFINITE`), causing `t_alloc` not to allocate a buffer for the address.

> One of the differences between TLI and XTI is the handling of `T_INFINITE` by `t_alloc`. TLI would allocate a 1024-byte buffer by default, while XTI does not allocate a buffer.

34.14 **Summary**

Nonblocking I/O is enabled for an XTI endpoint by specifying the O_NONBLOCK in the call to t_open, or anytime later with fcntl. The changes are similar to the changes with sockets when an endpoint is made nonblocking, with the exception of a nonblocking t_connect. We can wait for this to complete with the t_rcvconnect function.

Four new I/O functions are defined by XTI to operate on vectors of buffers: t_rcvv, t_rcvvudata, t_sndv, and t_sndvudata.

Signal-driven I/O is enabled for an XTI endpoint using ioctl, and we also must specify all the conditions under which the signal is to be generated: one of the S_*xxx* functions. Out-of-band data is sent by t_snd when the T_EXPEDITED flag is set. Nothing special need be done to receive out-of-band data: t_rcv returns a flag of T_EXPEDITED. A signal can also be generated when out-of-band data arrives.

Appendix A

IPv4, IPv6, ICMPv4, and ICMPv6

A.1   Introduction

This appendix is an overview of IPv4, IPv6, ICMPv4, and ICMPv6. This material provides additional background that may be helpful in understanding the discussion of TCP and UDP in Chapter 2. Some features of IP and ICMP are also used in some of the advanced chapters: IP options (Chapter 24), along with the Ping and Traceroute programs (Chapter 25), for example.

A.2   IPv4 Header

The IP layer provides a connectionless and unreliable datagram delivery service (RFC 791 [Postel 1981a]). IP makes its best effort to deliver an IP datagram to the specified destination, but there is no guarantee that the datagram arrives. Any desired reliability must be added by the upper layers. In the case of a TCP application, this is performed by TCP itself. In the case of a UDP application, this must be done by the application itself, since UDP is unreliable, and we show an example of this in Section 20.5.

One of the most important functions of the IP layer is *routing*. Every IP datagram contains the source address and the destination address. Figure A.1 shows the format of an IPv4 header.

- The 4-bit *version* is 4. This has been the version of IP in use since the early 1980s.

- The *header length* is the length of the entire IP header, including any options, in 32-bit words. The maximum value for this 4-bit field is 15, giving a maximum IP

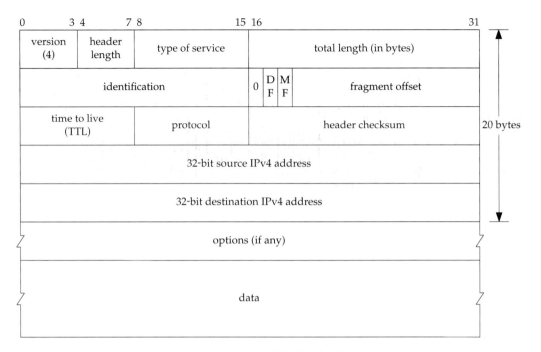

Figure A.1 Format of the IPv4 header.

header length of 60 bytes. Therefore, with the fixed portion of the header occupying 20 bytes, this allows for up to 40 bytes of options.

- The 8-bit *type-of-service* field (TOS) is composed of a 3-bit precedence field (which is ignored), 4 bits specifying the type-of-service, and an unused bit that must be 0. We can set this field with the IP_TOS socket option (Figure 7.12).

- The 16-bit *total length* is the total length in bytes of the IP datagram including the IPv4 header. The amount of data in the datagram is this field minus four times the header length. This field is required because some datalinks pad the frame to some minimum length (e.g., Ethernet) and it is possible for the size of a valid IP datagram to be less than the datalink minimum.

- The 16-bit *identification* field is set to a different value for each IP datagram and is used with fragmentation and reassembly (Section 2.9).

- The *DF* bit (don't fragment), the *MF* bit (more fragments), and the 13-bit *fragment offset* field are also used with fragmentation and reassembly.

- The 8-bit *time-to-live* field (TTL) is set by the sender and then decremented by one by each router that forwards the datagram. The datagram is discarded by any router that decrements the value to 0. This limits the lifetime of any IP datagram to 255 hops. A common default for this field is 64 but we can query and change this default with the IP_TTL and IP_MULTICAST_TTL socket options (Section 7.6).

- The 8-bit *protocol* field specifies the type of data contained in the IP datagram. Typical values are 1 (ICMPv4), 2 (IGMPv4), 6 (TCP), and 17 (UDP). These values are specified in RFC 1700 [Reynolds and Postel 1994].

- The 16-bit *header checksum* is calculated over just the IP header (including any options). The algorithm is the standard Internet checksum algorithm, a simple 16-bit ones-complement addition, which we show in Figure 25.14.

- The *source IPv4 address* and the *destination IPv4 address* are both 32-bit fields.

- We describe the *options* field in Section 24.2 and show an example of the IPv4 source route option in Section 24.3.

A.3 IPv6 Header

Figure A.2 shows the format of an IPv6 header (RFC 1883 [Deering and Hinden 1995]).

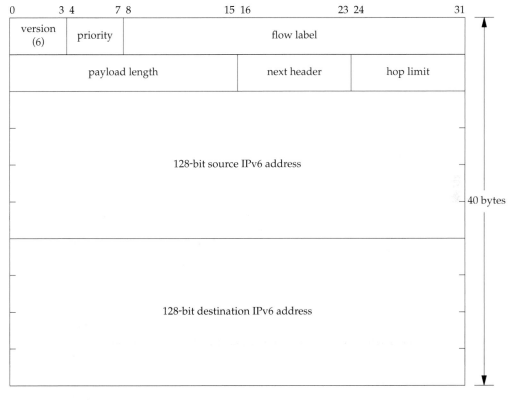

Figure A.2 Format of the IPv6 header.

- The 4-bit *version* is 6. Since this field occupies the first four bits of the first byte of the header (similar to the IPv4 version, Figure A.1), it allows a receiving IP stack that supports both versions to differentiate between the two versions.

During the development of IPv6 in the early 1990s, before the version number of 6 was assigned, the protocol was called *IPng*, for "IP next generation." You may still encounter references to IPng.

- The 4-bit priority field is set by the sender.

> The usefulness of this field is still a research topic. RFC 1883 [Hinden and Deering 1995] defines two sets of values for this field: values 0 through 7 identify traffic that backs off in response to congestion (e.g., TCP data) and values 8 through 15 identify traffic that does not back off in response to congestion (e.g., real-time packets sent at a constant rate). As of mid-1997 the proposal is that these 4 bits have no significance to receivers but the sender can set the low-order bit to indicate that the traffic is "interactive" (i.e., delay is more important than throughput). These 4 bits can also be rewritten by routers for private purposes.

- The 24-bit *flow label* can be chosen randomly by the application for a given socket. (The use of this field is still experimental.) A *flow* is a sequence of packets from a particular source to a particular destination for which the source desires special handling by intervening routers. For a given flow, once the flow label is chosen by the source, it does not change. A flow label of 0 (the default) identifies packets that do not belong to a flow.

  The combination of the priority and flow label fields is called the *flow information*. Both fields are contained in the `sin6_flowinfo` member of the `sockaddr_in6` socket address structure (Figure 3.4).

- The 16-bit *payload length* is the length in bytes of everything following the 40-byte IPv6 header. A value of 0 means the length requires more than 16 bits and is contained in a jumbo payload option (Figure 24.9). This is called a *jumbogram*.

- The 8-bit *next header* field is similar to the IPv4 protocol field. Indeed, when the upper layer is basically unchanged, the same values are used, such as 6 for TCP and 17 for UDP. There were so many changes from ICMPv4 to ICMPv6 that the latter was assigned a new value of 58.

- The 8-bit *hop limit* is similar to the IPv4 TTL field. The hop limit is decremented by one by each router that forwards the packet and the packet is discarded by any router that decrements the value to 0. The default value for this field can be set and fetched with the `IPV6_UNICAST_HOPS` and `IPV6_MULTICAST_HOPS` socket options (Section 7.8). The `IPV6_HOPLIMIT` socket option also lets us set this field and obtain its value from a received datagram.

- The *source IPv6 address* and the *destination IPv6 address* are both 128-bit fields.

> An IPv6 datagram can have numerous headers following the 40-byte IPv6 header. That is why the field is called the "next header" and not the "protocol." An IPv4 datagram has only a single protocol header following the IPv4 header.
>
> Early specifications of IPv4 had routers decrement the TTL by either one or the number of seconds that the router held the packet, whichever was greater. Hence the name "time-to-live."

In reality, however, the field was always decremented by one. IPv6 calls for its hop limit field to always be decremented by one, hence the name change from IPv4.

The most significant change from IPv4 to IPv6 is, of course, the larger IPv6 address fields. Another change is simplifying the IPv6 header because the simpler the header, the faster the header can be processed by a router. We can note other changes between the headers.

- There is no IPv6 header length field since there are no options in the header. There are optional headers that follow the fixed 40-byte IPv6 header, but each of these has its own length field.

- The two IPv6 addresses are aligned on a 64-bit boundary if the header itself is 64-bit aligned. This can speed up processing on 64-bit architectures.

- There are no fragmentation fields in the IPv6 header because there is a separate fragmentation header for this purpose. This design decision was made because fragmentation is the exception, and exceptions should not slow down normal processing.

- The IPv6 header does not include its own checksum. This is because all the upper layers—TCP, UDP, and ICMPv6—have their own checksum that includes the upper-layer header, the upper-layer data, and the following fields from the IPv6 header: IPv6 source address, IPv6 destination address, payload length, and next header. By omitting the checksum from the header, routers that forward the packet need not recalculate a header checksum after they modify the hop limit. Again, speed of forwarding by routers is the key point.

In case this is your first encounter with IPv6, we also note the following major differences from IPv4 to IPv6:

- There is no broadcasting with IPv6 (Chapter 18). Multicasting (Chapter 19), which is optional with IPv4, is mandatory with IPv6.

- IPv6 routers do not fragment packets that they forward. Fragmentation with IPv6 is performed only by the originating host.

- IPv6 requires support for authentication and security options.

- IPv6 requires support for path MTU discovery (Section 2.9). Technically this support is optional and could be omitted from minimal implementations such as bootstrap loaders, but if a node does not implement this feature, it cannot send datagrams larger than the IPv6 minimum link MTU (576 bytes; Section 2.9).

A.4   IPv4 Addresses

A 32-bit IPv4 address has one of the five formats shown in Figure A.3. Historically, an organization was assigned either a class A, B, or C network ID and it could do whatever it wanted with the host ID portion of the address. But that changed in the mid-1990s with the advent of *classless* addresses, which we talk about shortly.

IPv4 addresses are usually written as four decimal numbers, separated by decimal points. This is called *dotted-decimal notation* and each decimal number represents one of the 4 bytes of the 32-bit address. The first of the four decimal numbers identifies the address class, as shown in Figure A.4.

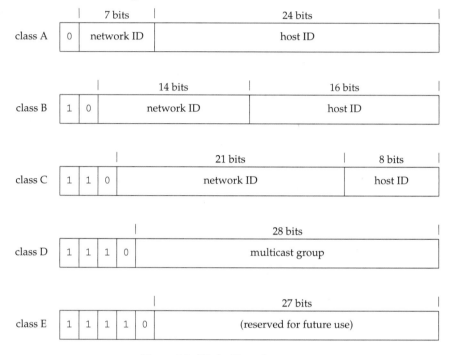

Figure A.3   IPv4 address formats.

Class	Range
A	0.0.0.0 to 127.255.255.255
B	128.0.0.0 to 191.255.255.255
C	192.0.0.0 to 223.255.255.255
D	224.0.0.0 to 239.255.255.255
E	240.0.0.0 to 247.255.255.255

Figure A.4   Ranges for the five different classes of IPv4 addresses.

Classless Addresses and CIDR

IPv4 addresses are now considered classless. That is, we can ignore the distinction between class A, B, and C addresses and the implied boundaries between the network ID and the host ID shown in Figure A.3 for class A, B, and C addresses. Instead, whenever an IPv4 network address is assigned to an organization, what is assigned is a 32-bit network address and a corresponding 32-bit mask. Bits of 1 in the mask cover the network address and bits of 0 in the mask cover the host. Since the bits of 1 in the mask are always contiguous from the leftmost bit, and the bits of 0 in the mask are always contiguous from the rightmost bit, this address mask can also be specified as a *prefix length* that denotes the number of contiguous bits of 1 starting from the left. For example, class A addresses have an implied mask of 255.0.0.0 or a prefix length of 8, class B addresses have an implied mask of 255.255.0.0 or a prefix length of 16, and class C addresses have an implied mask of 255.255.255.0 or a prefix length of 24.

But the advantage of classless addresses is that we are no longer restricted to just these three fixed prefix lengths of 8, 16, and 24 for class A, B, and C addresses. Instead, addresses can be assigned with different prefix lengths. For example, using classless addresses an Internet Service Provider (ISP) can take one class C address and assign it to four different customers, each with a mask of 255.255.255.192, which is a prefix length of 26. Each of the four customers then has 6 bits (instead of 8) to play with, in terms of choosing a subnet boundary (if any) and then assigning subnet IDs and host IDs. (We talk about subnetting shortly.)

All IPv4 addresses assigned today for the Internet are classless. The same concept is used with IPv6 addresses. IPv4 network addresses are normally written as a dotted-decimal number, followed by a slash, followed by the prefix length. Figure 1.16 showed examples of this.

Using classless addresses requires classless routing, and this is normally called CIDR (RFC 1519 [Fuller et al. 1993]). The goals of CIDR usage are to decrease the size of the Internet backbone routing tables and to reduce the rate of IPv4 address depletion. Section 10.8 of TCPv1 talks more about CIDR.

Subnet Addresses

IPv4 addresses are normally *subnetted* (RFC 950 [Mogul and Postel 1985]). This adds another level to the address hierarchy:

- network ID (assigned to site),
- subnet ID (chosen by site), and
- host ID (chosen by site).

The boundary between the network ID and the subnet ID is fixed by the prefix length of the assigned network address. This prefix length is normally assigned by the organization's ISP. But the boundary between the subnet ID and the host ID is chosen by the site. All the hosts on a given subnet share a common *subnet mask* and this mask specifies the boundary between the subnet ID and the host ID. Bits of 1 in the subnet mask cover the network ID and subnet ID, and bits of 0 cover the host ID.

For example, consider the author's subnets in Figure 1.16. The assigned network address from the ISP is 206.62.226.0/24, which is an entire class C network. The author then divides the remaining 8 bits into a 3-bit subnet ID and a 5-bit host ID. Figure A.5 shows this. The subnet mask for these addresses is 0xffffffe0 or 255.255.255.224.

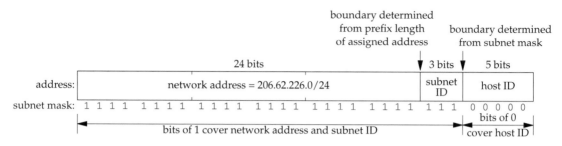

Figure A.5 24-bit network address with 3-bit subnet ID and 5-bit host ID.

The top subnet in Figure 1.16 has the three subnet bits set to `001` and we designate this subnet as 206.62.226.32/27. The "/27" notation indicates that the subnet mask comprises the leftmost 27 bits. We are using this prefix notation for both the overall network address, 206.62.226.0/24, and for the subnet addresses, such as 206.62.226.32/27. The hosts on this subnet will have addresses between 206.62.226.33 and 206.62.226.62, and the address with a host ID of all one bits, 206.62.226.63, is the subnet broadcast address (Section 18.2). The other subnet in Figure 1.16 has the three subnet bits set to `010` and we designate this as 206.62.226.64/27.

> When the subnetting of IP addresses started in the mid-1980s a noncontiguous subnet mask was allowed but not recommended (RFC 950 [Mogul and Postel, 1985]). But with the current use of classless addresses, noncontiguous subnet masks are no longer allowed. IPv6 also requires that all address masks be contiguous starting at the leftmost bit.

> RFC 950 recommends not using the two subnets with a subnet ID of all zero bits or all one bits. Some software today supports these two forms of subnet IDs.

As another example of subnetting from Figure 1.16, consider the bottom subnet. The assigned network address for `noao.edu` is 140.252.0.0/16, which is an entire class B network. NOAO then divides the remaining 16 bits into an 8-bit subnet ID and an 8-bit host ID, which is typical for organizations with class B addresses. We show this in Figure A.6.

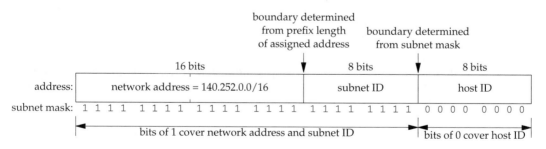

Figure A.6 16-bit network address with 8-bit subnet ID and 8-bit host ID.

The subnet mask is `0xffffff00` or 255.255.255.0. The subnet that we show has a subnet ID of 1 and we designate this subnet as 140.252.1.0/24.

Loopback Addresses

By convention the address 127.0.0.1 is assigned to the loopback interface. Anything sent to this IP address loops around and becomes IP input. We often use this address when testing a client and server on the same host. This address is normally known by the name `INADDR_LOOPBACK`.

> Any address on the network 127/8 can be assigned to the loopback interface, but 127.0.0.1 is common.

Unspecified Address

The address consisting of 32 zero bits is the IPv4 unspecified address. In an IPv4 packet it can appear only as the source address in packets sent by a node that is bootstrapping before the node learns its IP address. In the sockets API this address is called the wildcard address and is normally known by the name `INADDR_ANY`.

Multihoming and Address Aliases

Traditionally the definition of a *multihomed* host has been a host with multiple interfaces: two Ethernets, for example, or an Ethernet and a point-to-point link. Each interface must have a unique IPv4 address. When counting interfaces to determine if a host is multihomed, the loopback interface does not count.

A router, by definition, is multihomed since it forwards packets that arrive on one interface out another interface. But a multihomed host is not a router unless it forwards packets. Indeed, a multihomed host must not assume it is a router just because the host has multiple interfaces; it must not act as a router unless it has been configured to do so (typically by the administrator enabling a configuration option).

The term multihoming, however, is more general and covers two different scenarios (Section 3.3.4 of RFC 1122 [Braden 1989]).

1. A host with multiple interfaces is multihomed and each interface must have its own IP address. This is the traditional definition.

2. Newer hosts have the capability of assigning multiple IP addresses to a given physical interface. Each additional IP address, after the first (primary), is called an *alias* or a *logical interface*. Often the aliased IP addresses share the same subnet address as the primary address but have different host IDs. But it is also possible for the aliases to have a completely different network address or subnet addresses from the primary. We show an example of aliased addresses in Section 16.6.

Hence the definition of a multihomed host is one with multiple interfaces, regardless of whether those interfaces are physical or logical.

> Multihoming is also used in another context. A network that has multiple connections to the Internet is also called multihomed. For example, some sites have two connections to the Internet, instead of one, providing a backup capability.

A.5   IPv6 Addresses

IPv6 addresses comprise 128 bits and are usually written as eight 16-bit hexadecimal numbers. There are no address classes, per se, as we have with IPv4; instead the high-order bits of the 128-bit address imply the type of address ([Hinden and Deering 1997]). Figure A.7 shows the different values of the high-order bits and what type of address these bits imply.

Allocation	Format prefix
reserved	0000 0000
unassigned	0000 0001
reserved for NSAP	0000 001
reserved for IPX	0000 010
unassigned	0000 011
unassigned	0000 1
unassigned	0001
aggregatable global unicast addresses	001
unassigned	010
unassigned	011
unassigned	100
unassigned	101
unassigned	110
unassigned	1110
unassigned	1111 0
unassigned	1111 10
unassigned	1111 110
unassigned	1111 1110 0
link-local unicast address	1111 1110 10
site-local unicast address	1111 1110 11
multicast addresses	1111 1111

Figure A.7   Meaning of high-order bits of IPv6 addresses.

These high-order bits are called the *format prefix*. For example, if the high-order 3 bits are 001, the address is called a *aggregatable global unicast address*. If the high-order 8 bits are 11111111 (0xff), it is a multicast address. If the high-order 8 bits are 00000000, the address is reserved, and we will see some examples of these addresses.

Aggregatable Global Unicast Addresses

Probably the most common form of IPv6 address will be the aggregatable global unicast address, which in Figure A.7 begins with a 3-bit prefix of 001. These addresses will replace the IPv4 class A, B, and C addresses.

> The original IPv6 address specification, RFC 1884 [Hinden and Deering 1995], called for *provider-based unicast addresses* with the 3-bit prefix of 010. These are described in RFC 2073 [Rekhter et al. 1997]. At the IETF (Internet Engineering Task Force) meeting in March 1997, however, the decision was made to proceed with a different form of unicast address.

The format of aggregation-based unicast addresses are defined in [Hinden, O'Dell, and Deering 1997] and contain the following fields, starting at the leftmost bit and going right:

- format prefix (001),
- TLA ID (top-level aggregation identifier),
- NLA ID (next-level aggregation identifier),
- SLA ID (site-level aggregation identifier; e.g., subnet ID), and
- interface identifier.

Figure A.8 shows an example of a aggregatable global unicast address.

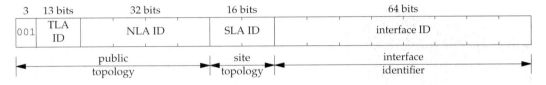

Figure A.8 IPv6 aggregatable global unicast addresses.

The interface ID must be constructed in IEEE *EUI-64* format [IEEE 1997b]. This is a superset of the 48-bit IEEE 802 MAC addresses that are assigned to most LAN interface cards. This identifier should be automatically assigned for an interface, based on its hardware MAC address when possible. Details for constructing EUI-64 based interface identifiers are in Appendix A of [Hinden and Deering 1997].

6bone Test Addresses

The 6bone is a virtual network used for early testing of the IPv6 protocols (Section B.3). As of this writing the aggregatable global unicast addresses are not yet being assigned, although there are plans to use a special format of these addresses on the 6bone ([Hinden, Fink, and Postel 1997]). Instead, the address format shown in Figure A.9, which is documented in RFC 1897 [Hinden and Postel 1996], is being used for all nodes on the 6bone.

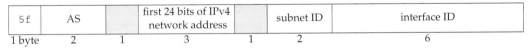

Figure A.9 IPv6 test addresses for 6bone.

These addresses are considered temporary, and nodes using these addresses will have to renumber when aggregatable global unicast addresses are assigned.

The high-order byte is 0x5f. The 16-bit *AS* field is the *autonomous system number* assigned to the organization or to its ISP. These are used with IPv4 to identify routing domains. The next field is the high-order 24 bits of the node's current IPv4 address. The *subnet ID* is whatever the organization chooses and the *interface ID* is normally the 48-bit IEEE 802 MAC address.

In Section 9.2 we showed the IPv6 address for the host `solaris` in Figure 1.16 as `5f1b:df00:ce3e:e200:0020:0800:2078:e3e3`. The AS is 7135 (`0x1bdf`) and 206.62.226 is `0xce3ee2`. The subnet ID is `0x0020` and the low-order 48 bits are the MAC address of the host's Ethernet card.

IPv4-Mapped IPv6 Addresses

IPv4-mapped IPv6 addresses allow IPv6 applications on hosts supporting both IPv4 and IPv6 to communicate with IPv4-only hosts during the transition of the Internet to IPv6. These addresses are automatically created by DNS resolvers (Figure 9.5) when a query is made by an IPv6 application for the IPv6 addresses of a host, but that host has only IPv4 addresses.

We saw in Figure 10.4 that using this type of address with an IPv6 socket causes an IPv4 datagram to be sent to the IPv4 host. These addresses are not stored in any DNS data files—they are created when needed by a resolver.

Figure A.10 shows the format of these addresses The low-order 32 bits contain an IPv4 address.

0000 0000	FFFF	IPv4 address
80 bits	16	32

Figure A.10   IPv4-mapped IPv6 address.

When writing an IPv6 address, a consecutive string of zeros can be abbreviated with two colons. Also, the embedded IPv4 address is written using dotted-decimal notation. For example, we can abbreviate the IPv4-mapped IPv6 address `0:0:0:0:0:FFFF:206.62.226.33` as `::FFFF:206.62.226.33`.

IPv4-Compatible IPv6 Addresses

IPv4-compatible IPv6 addresses are also used during the transition from IPv4 to IPv6. The administrator for a host supporting both IPv4 and IPv6 that does not have a neighbor IPv6 router should create a DNS AAAA record containing an IPv4-compatible IPv6 address. Any other IPv6 host with an IPv6 datagram to send to an IPv4-compatible IPv6 address will then *encapsulate* the IPv6 datagram with an IPv4 header and this is called an *automatic tunnel*. We talk more about tunneling in Section B.3 and show an example of this type of IPv6 datagram encapsulated within an IPv4 header in Figure B.2. Each tunnel on the 6bone, however, is *configured* (e.g., set up by an administrator in a startup file), whereas with IPv4-compatible IPv6 addresses only the address is configured by hand (e.g., placed into a DNS data file as a AAAA record) and the tunneling is then automatic.

Figure A.11 shows the format of an IPv4-compatible IPv6 address.

0000 0000	0000	IPv4 address
80 bits	16	32

Figure A.11   IPv4-compatible IPv6 address.

type	code	Description	Handled by or `errno`
0	0	echo reply	user process (Ping)
3		destination unreachable:	
	0	network unreachable	EHOSTUNREACH
	1	host unreachable	EHOSTUNREACH
	2	protocol unreachable	ECONNREFUSED
	3	port unreachable	ECONNREFUSED
	4	fragmentation needed but DF bit set	EMSGSIZE
	5	source route failed	EHOSTUNREACH
	6	destination network unknown	EHOSTUNREACH
	7	destination host unknown	EHOSTUNREACH
	8	source host isolated (obsolete)	EHOSTUNREACH
	9	destination network administratively prohibited	EHOSTUNREACH
	10	destination host administratively prohibited	EHOSTUNREACH
	11	network unreachable for TOS	EHOSTUNREACH
	12	host unreachable for TOS	EHOSTUNREACH
	13	communication administratively prohibited	(ignored)
	14	host precedence violation	(ignored)
	15	precedence cutoff in effect	(ignored)
4	0	source quench	kernel for TCP, ignored by UDP
5		redirect:	
	0	redirect for network	kernel updates routing table
	1	redirect for host	kernel updates routing table
	2	redirect for type-of-service and network	kernel updates routing table
	3	redirect for type-of-service and host	kernel updates routing table
8	0	echo request	kernel generates reply
9	0	router advertisement	user process
10	0	router solicitation	user process
11		time exceeded:	
	0	TTL equals 0 during transit	user process
	1	TTL equals 0 during reassembly	user process
12		parameter problem:	
	0	IP header bad (catchall error)	ENOPROTOOPT
	1	required option missing	ENOPROTOOPT
13	0	timestamp request	kernel generates reply
14	0	timestamp reply	user process
15	0	information request (obsolete)	(ignored)
16	0	information reply (obsolete)	user process
17	0	address mask request	kernel generates reply
18	0	address mask reply	user process

Figure A.15 Handling of the ICMP message types by 4.4BSD.

type	code	Description	Handled by or `errno`
1		destination unreachable:	
	0	no route to destination	EHOSTUNREACH
	1	administratively prohibited (firewall filter)	EHOSTUNREACH
	2	not a neighbor (incorrect strict source route)	EHOSTUNREACH
	3	address unreachable (any other reason)	EHOSTDOWN
	4	port unreachable (UDP)	ECONNREFUSED
2	0	packet too big	kernel does PMTU discovery
3		time exceeded:	
	0	hop limit exceeded in transit	user process
	1	fragment reassembly time exceeded	user process
4		parameter problem:	
	0	erroneous header field	ENOPROTOOPT
	1	unrecognized next header	ENOPROTOOPT
	2	unrecognized option	ENOPROTOOPT
128	0	echo request (Ping)	kernel generates reply
129	0	echo reply (Ping)	user process (Ping)
130	0	group membership query	user process
131	0	group membership report	user process
132	0	group membership reduction	user process
133	0	router solicitation	user process
134	0	router advertisement	user process
135	0	neighbor solicitation	user process
136	0	neighbor advertisement	user process
137	0	redirect	kernel updates routing table

Figure A.16 ICMPv6 messages.

The notation "user process" means that the kernel does not process the message and it is up to a user process with a raw socket to handle the message. We must also note that different implementations may handle certain messages differently. For example, although Unix systems normally handle router solicitations and router advertisements in a user process, other implementations might handle these messages in the kernel.

ICMPv6 clears the high-order bit of the *type* field for the error messages (*types* 1–4) and sets this bit for the informational messages (*types* 128–137).

Appendix B

Virtual Networks

B.1 Introduction

When a new feature is added to TCP, such as the long fat pipe support defined in RFC 1323, support is required only in the hosts using TCP; no changes are required in the routers. These RFC 1323 changes, for example, are slowly appearing in host implementations of TCP and when a new TCP connection is established each end can determine if the other end supports the new feature. If both hosts support the feature, it can be used.

This differs from changes being made to the IP layer, such as multicasting at the end of the 1980s and IPv6 in the mid-1990s, because these new features require changes in all the hosts *and* all the routers. But people want to start using the new features without having to wait for all the systems to be upgraded. To do this a *virtual network* is established on top of the existing IPv4 Internet using *tunnels*.

B.2 The MBone

Our first example of a virtual network that is built using tunnels is the MBone, which started around 1992 [Eriksson 1994]. If two or more hosts on a LAN support multicasting, multicast applications can be run on all these hosts and communicate with each other. To connect this LAN to some other LAN that also has multicast-capable hosts a tunnel is configured between one host on each of the LANs, as shown in Figure B.1. We show the following numbered steps in this figure.

1. An application on the source host, MH1, sends a multicast datagram to a class D address.

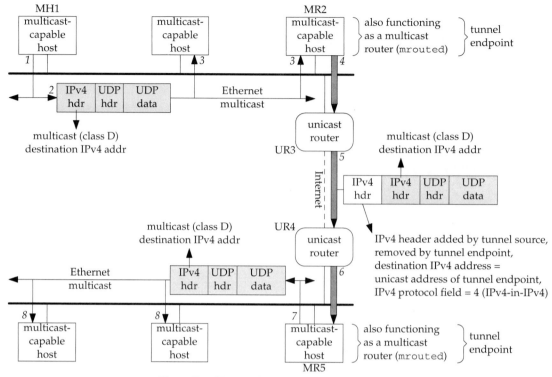

Figure B.1 IPv4-in-IPv4 encapsulation used on MBone.

2. We show this as a UDP datagram, since most multicast applications use UDP. We talk more about multicasting and how to send and receive multicast datagrams in Chapter 19.

3. The datagram is received by all the multicast-capable hosts on the LAN, including MR2. We note that MR2 is also functioning as a multicast router, running the `mrouted` program, which performs multicast routing.

4. MR2 prepends another IPv4 header at the front of the datagram with the destination IPv4 address of this new header set to the unicast address of the tunnel endpoint, MR5. This unicast address is configured by the administrator of HR2 and is read by the `mrouted` program when it starts up. Similarly the unicast address of HR2 is configured for MR5, the other end of the tunnel. The protocol field in the new IPv4 header is set to 4, which is the value for IPv4-in-IPv4 encapsulation. The datagram is sent to the next-hop router, UR3, which we explicitly denote as a unicast router. That is, UR3 does not understand multicasting, which is the whole reason we are using a tunnel. The shaded portion of the IPv4 datagram has not changed from what was sent in step 1, other than the decrementing of the TTL field in the shaded IPv4 header.

5. UR3 looks at the destination IPv4 address in the outermost IPv4 header and forwards the datagram to the next-hop router, UR4, another unicast router.

6. UR4 delivers the datagram to its destination, MR5, the tunnel endpoint.

7. MR5 receives the datagram and since the protocol field indicates IPv4-in-IPv4 encapsulation, it removes the first IPv4 header and then outputs the remainder of the datagram (a copy of what was multicast on the top LAN) as a multicast datagram on its LAN.

8. All the multicast-capable hosts on the lower LAN receive the multicast datagram.

The end result is that the multicast datagram sent on the top LAN also gets transmitted as a multicast datagram on the lower LAN. This occurs even though the two routers that we show attached to these two LANs, and all the Internet routers between these two routers, are not multicast capable.

In this example we show the multicast routing function being performed by the `mrouted` program running on one host on each LAN. This is how the MBone started. But around 1996 multicast routing functionality started appearing in the routers from most major router vendors. If the two unicast routers UR3 and UR4 in Figure B.1 were multicast capable, then we would not need to run `mrouted` at all, and UR3 and UR4 would function as the multicast routers. But if there still exist other routers between UR3 and UR4 that are not multicast capable, then a tunnel is still required. But the tunnel endpoints would then be MR3 (a multicast-capable replacement for UR3) and MR4 (a multicast-capable replacement for UR4), not MR2 and MR5.

> In the scenario that we show in Figure B.1 every multicast packet appears twice on the top LAN and twice on the bottom LAN: once as a multicast packet, and again as a unicast packet within the tunnel as the packet goes between the host running `mrouted` and the next-hop unicast router (e.g., between MR2 and UR3, and between UR4 and MR5). This extra copy is the cost of tunneling. The advantage in replacing the two unicast routers UR3 and UR4 in Figure B.1 with multicast-capable routers (what we called MR3 and MR4) is to avoid this extra copy of every multicast packet from appearing on the LANs. Even if MR3 and MR4 must then establish a tunnel between themselves, because some intermediate routers between them (that we do not show) are not multicast capable, this is still advantageous since it avoids the duplicate copies on each LAN.

B.3   The 6bone

The 6bone is a virtual network that was created in 1996 for reasons similar to the MBone: users with islands of IPv6-capable hosts wanted to connect them together using a virtual network without waiting for all the intermediate routers to become IPv6-capable. Figure B.2 shows an example of two IPv6-capable LANs connected with a tunnel across IPv4-only routers. We show the following numbered steps in this figure.

1. Host H1 on the top LAN sends an IPv6 datagram containing a TCP segment to host H4 on the bottom LAN. We designate these two hosts as "IPv6 hosts" but both probably run IPv4 also. The IPv6 routing table on H1 specifies that host HR2 is the next-hop router and an IPv6 datagram is sent to this host

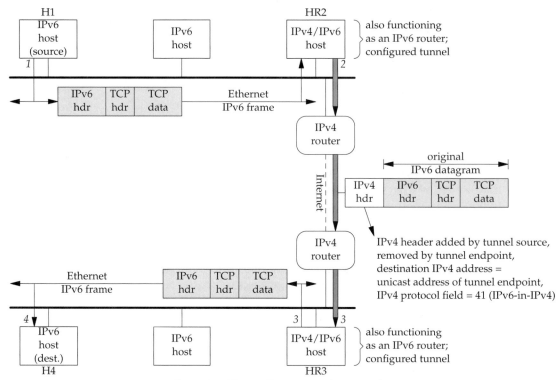

Figure B.2 IPv6-in-IPv4 encapsulation on 6bone.

2. Host HR2 has a configured tunnel to host HR3. This configured tunnel allows IPv6 datagrams to be sent between the two tunnel endpoints across an IPv4 internet by encapsulating the IPv6 datagram in an IPv4 datagram (called "IPv6-in-IPv4 encapsulation"). The IPv4 protocol field has a value of 41. We note that the two IPv4/IPv6 hosts at the ends of the tunnel, HR2 and HR3, are both acting as IPv6 routers since they are forwarding IPv6 datagrams that they receive on one interface out another interface. The configured tunnel counts as an interface, even though it is a virtual interface, and not a physical interface.

3. The tunnel endpoint, HR3, receives the encapsulated datagram, strips off the IPv4 header, and sends the IPv6 datagram onto its LAN.

4. The destination, H4, receives the IPv6 datagram.

The goal for these virtual networks is that over time, as the intermediate routers gain the required functionality (multicast routing in terms of the MBone and IPv6 routing in terms of the 6bone), the virtual networks disappear. We describe both of these virtual networks since some of the examples in the text use the MBone and the 6bone.

Appendix C

Debugging Techniques

This appendix contains some hints and techniques for debugging network applications. No one technique is the answer for everyone; instead there are various tools that we should be familiar with, and then use whatever works in our environment.

C.1 System Call Tracing

Many versions of Unix provide a system call tracing facility. This can often provide a valuable debugging technique.

Working at this level we need to differentiate between a *system call* and a *function*. The former is an entry point into the kernel and that is what we are able to trace with the tools we will look at in this section. Posix, and most other standards, use the term function to describe what appear to the users to be functions, even though on some implementations they may be system calls. For example, on a Berkeley-derived kernel `socket` is a system call even though it appears to be a normal C function to the application programmer. But under SVR4 we will see shortly that it is a library function in the sockets library that issues calls to `putmsg` and `getmsg`, these latter two being the actual system calls.

In this section we examine the system calls involved in running our daytime client. We showed the sockets version in Figure 1.5 and the XTI version in Figure 28.13.

SVR4 Streams-Based Sockets Library

We start with a streams-based implementation of sockets, as found under SVR4. The `truss` program is provided by SVR4 to run a program and trace the system calls that are executed. We run this program as

```
unixware % truss  -o truss.out  -v getmsg,putmsg,ioctl \
daytimetcpcli  140.252.1.54
```

(We have wrapped this long command onto two lines.) The -o option directs the output to a file (there is often lots of output from this technique), and the -v option turns on verbose tracing for the three specified system calls. This will show us additional information about the arguments for these system calls.

The beginning of the output (about 40 lines) deals with linking the program with dynamic libraries using memory-mapped I/O. This is done using open and mmap. (The latter system call is described in Section 12.9 of APUE and is not relevant to our discussion of networking APIs.) We omit these lines of output.

Next is the opening of the /etc/netconfig file, followed by a read of the entire file (806 bytes).

```
open("/etc/netconfig", O_RDONLY, 0666)              = 3
 . . .
read(3, " t c p\t t p i _ c o t s".., 8192)         = 806
read(3, 0x0804A6B8, 8192)                           = 0
 . . .
close(3)                                            = 0
```

We have omitted some calls to ioctl and lseek that are not relevant to our discussion. Whenever we do this we show a line with three dots. The value of 3 at the right side of the equals sign for the call to open is the returned descriptor. The call to read asks for 8192 bytes but the return value is 806 (the size of the file). The next call to read returns 0 (end-of-file). truss also shows the first 12 bytes returned by read (beginning with tcp) and this is the start of the first line of the file. The file is then closed. We would guess that this reading of the netconfig file is finished when the sockets library starts, with our first call to socket.

The next system call is an open of /dev/tcp and the returned descriptor is again 3.

```
open("/dev/tcp", O_RDWR, 027776333624)              = 3
ioctl(3, I_FIND, "sockmod")                         = 0
ioctl(3, I_PUSH, "sockmod")                         = 0
 . . .
ioctl(3, I_STR, 0x080467E4)                         = 0
        cmd=TI_BIND timout=-1 len=32 dp=0x0804ABA8
 . . .
```

The ioctl that follows the open checks whether the module sockmod is already on the stream. The return value is 0 indicating that it is not on the stream, so an ioctl of I_PUSH pushes it onto the stream. This is followed by numerous ioctls for the stream and lots of signal handling (which we omit). The ioctl of I_STR sends an internal streams ioctl message and the command is TI_BIND. The length of 32 probably indicates a T_BIND_REQ, which consists of four 4-byte fields in the T_bind_req structure (which we discussed with Figure 33.9), followed by a 16-byte sockaddr_in structure. This is probably a bind of any local address being performed by the sockets library when we call connect on an unbound socket.

We would expect to see a putmsg followed by a getmsg here, as in our tpi_bind function.

We then see the first call to `putmsg` and it is for control information only, with a flag of 0.

```
putmsg(3, 0x08046958, 0x00000000, 0)              = 0
        ctl:  maxlen=428   len=36    buf=0x0804ABA8
getmsg(3, 0x08046924, 0x08046918, 0x08046934)   = 0
        ctl:  maxlen=428   len=8     buf=0x0804ABA8
        dat:  maxlen=128   len=-1    buf=0x08046898
getmsg(3, 0x08046964, 0x08046958, 0x0804697C)   = 0
        ctl:  maxlen=428   len=56    buf=0x0804ABA8
        dat:  maxlen=128   len=-1    buf=0x080468D8
```

The length of 36 is probably a `T_CONN_REQ` request (Figure 33.10): five 4-byte values followed by a 16-byte `sockaddr_in` structure. The next `getmsg` returns 8 bytes of control information without any data, and this is probably a `T_OK_ACK` message (Figure 33.10). The next `getmsg` returns 56 bytes of control information without any data, and this is probably a `T_CONN_CON` message (Figure 33.10): five 4-byte fields, a 16-byte `sockaddr_in` structure, and 20 bytes of options. We can only guess that the final 20 bytes are options, based on the size of a `t_opthdr` structure (four 4-byte fields, Section 32.2), followed by the 1-byte `IP_TOS` option (the only end-to-end option from Figure 32.1 that we would expect to have returned at this point), followed by 3 bytes of padding (see also Figure 32.3).

The next system call is `getmsg`, and it returns 8 bytes of control information and 26 bytes of data. This is probably a `T_DATA_IND` message.

```
getmsg(3, 0x08046AEC, 0x08046AE0, 0x08046B14)   = 0
        ctl:  maxlen=428   len=8     buf=0x0804ABA8
        dat:  maxlen=4096  len=26    buf=0x08046BB0
write(1, " F  r  i     A  p  r     4     0".., 26)   = 26
getmsg(3, 0x08046AEC, 0x08046AE0, 0x08046B14)   = 0
        ctl:  maxlen=428   len=-1    buf=0x0804ABA8
        dat:  maxlen=4096  len=0     buf=0x08046BB0
_exit(0)
```

Our client then calls `write` to standard output (descriptor 1) for the 26 bytes of data. The next call to `getmsg` returns no control information and 0 bytes of data, probably an indication from the provider that the end-of-file has been encountered.

> We would expect to receive a `T_ORDREL_IND` message at this point.

SVR4 Streams-Based XTI Library

Our next example is a streams-based XTI library, Solaris 2.6. We expect the system calls to be similar to our calls in Section 33.6.

After the library mapping with `mmap`, we find the call to `open` for the TCP transport provider, followed by a check for `timod` and then a push of this module onto the stream.

```
    . . .
open("/dev/tcp", O_RDWR)                         = 3
ioctl(3, I_FIND, "timod")                        = 0
ioctl(3, I_PUSH, "timod")                        = 0
```

We then find numerous calls to `ioctl` along with signal handling (which we omit). One of these calls to `ioctl` appears to be in response to our call to `t_bind`, and it appears that the XTI library does the bind by issuing this `ioctl` to `timod`. (This is similar to what we saw with the sockets-over-streams example earlier with UnixWare.)

The first call to `putmsg` sends 36 bytes of control information and no data. This is probably a `T_CONN_REQ` request from our call to `t_connect`.

```
...
putmsg(3, 0xEFFFE7F4, 0x00000000, 0)              = 0
        ctl: maxlen=912  len=36   buf=0x0002BAB8: "\0\0\0\0\0\0\010"..
getmsg(3, 0xEFFFE710, 0xEFFFE700, 0xEFFFE71C)     = 0
        ctl: maxlen=912  len=8    buf=0x0002C1E8: "\0\0\013\0\0\0\0\0"
        dat: maxlen=0    len=-1   buf=0x00000000
        flags:  0x0001
getmsg(3, 0xEFFFE7F4, 0xEFFFE770, 0xEFFFE77C)     = 0
        ctl: maxlen=912  len=36   buf=0x0002BAB8: "\0\0\0\f\0\0\010"..
        dat: maxlen=0    len=-1   buf=0x00000000
        flags:  0x0000
```

We also see that Solaris prints the first 8 bytes of the buffer in hexadecimal with C escapes. For the call to `putmsg` we have 7 bytes of 0 followed by a byte of `0x10` (16). But this is really two 4-byte fields: the first 4 bytes are the `T_CONN_REQ` request (which has a value of 0), followed by the length of the destination address (16).

The first call to `getmsg` in the previous output returns a `T_OK_ACK` message, and the next returns a `T_CONN_CON` message. We can tell the type of the first returned message because the value of `T_OK_ACK` is 19 (`0x13`) and the next 4 bytes indicate the primitive that is being acknowledged (the `T_CONN_REQ`, which we said has a value of 0). We can tell the type of the second returned message because the value of `T_CONN_CON` is 12 (which is printed as the C escape for the formfeed character, `\f`), followed by the length of the peer's address (16, printed as `0x10`).

Solaris prints the flags variable that is pointed to by the final argument to `getmsg` and we see the first call returns a value of 1 (which is `MSG_HIPRI`, as we expect since the `T_OK_ACK` message is an `M_PCPROTO` message) and the second call returns a value of 0 (a normal message, as expected). We also notice that the Solaris `T_CONN_CON` does not appear to return any options (the length of 36), whereas our UnixWare example earlier appeared to return 20 bytes of options.

The next system call of interest is another call to `getmsg`, probably in response to our call to `t_rcv`. This call returns 26 bytes of data and no control information, probably an `M_DATA` message with the server's response.

```
getmsg(3, 0xEFFFE7EC, 0xEFFFE7DC, 0xEFFFE81C)     = 0
        ctl: maxlen=912  len=-1   buf=0x0002BAB8
        dat: maxlen=4096 len=26   buf=0xEFFFE8D0: " F r i   A p r  "..
        flags:  0x0000
write(1, " F r i   A p r   4   1".., 26)          = 26
getmsg(3, 0xEFFFE7EC, 0xEFFFE7DC, 0xEFFFE81C)     = 0
        ctl: maxlen=912  len=4    buf=0x0002BAB8: "\0\0\017"
        dat: maxlen=4096 len=-1   buf=0xEFFFE8D0
        flags:  0x0000
...
_exit(0)
```

Our client calls `write` and the next call to `getmsg` returns a `T_ORDREL_IND` message (4 bytes of control with no data). The value of `T_ORDREL_IND` is 23, which is printed as `0x17`.

BSD Kernel Sockets

Our next example is BSD/OS, a Berkeley-derived kernel in which all the socket functions are system calls. The system call tracing program is `ktrace`. This writes the trace information to a file (whose default name is `ktrace.out`), which we print with `kdump`. We execute our sockets client as

```
bsdi % ktrace daytimetcpcli 206.62.226.43
Fri Apr  4 17:24:30 1997
```

We then execute `kdump` to output the trace information to standard output.

```
13187 daytimetcpcli CALL   socket(0x2,0x1,0)
13187 daytimetcpcli RET    socket 3

13187 daytimetcpcli CALL   connect(0x3,0xefbfc9a0,0x10)
13187 daytimetcpcli RET    connect 0

13187 daytimetcpcli CALL   read(0x3,0xefbfc9b0,0x1000)
13187 daytimetcpcli GIO    fd 3 read 26 bytes
      "Fri Apr  4 17:24:30 1997\r\n"
13187 daytimetcpcli RET    read 26/0x1a

...

13187 daytimetcpcli CALL   write(0x1,0x9000,0x1a)
13187 daytimetcpcli GIO    fd 1 wrote 26 bytes
      "Fri Apr  4 17:24:30 1997\r\n"
13187 daytimetcpcli RET    write 26/0x1a

13187 daytimetcpcli CALL   read(0x3,0xefbfc9b0,0x1000)
13187 daytimetcpcli GIO    fd 3 read 0 bytes
      ""
13187 daytimetcpcli RET    read 0

13187 daytimetcpcli CALL   exit(0)
```

13187 is the process ID. `CALL` identifies a system call, `RET` is the return, and `GIO` stands for generic process I/O. We see the calls to `socket` and `connect`, followed by the call to `read` that returns 26 bytes. Our client writes these bytes to standard output and then the next call to `read` returns 0 (end-of-file).

Solaris 2.6 Kernel Sockets

Solaris 2.x is based on SVR4 and all the releases before 2.6 have implemented sockets as shown in Figure 33.3. One problem, however, with all SVR4 implementations that implement sockets in this fashion, is that they rarely provide 100% compatibility with Berkeley-derived kernel sockets. To provide additional compatibility, Solaris 2.6 changes the implementation technique and implements sockets using a `sockfs` filesystem. This provides kernel sockets, as we can verify using `truss` on our sockets client.

```
solaris26 % truss -v connect daytimetcpcli 198.69.10.4
Sat Apr  5 11:32:07 1997
```

After the normal library linking, the first system call we see is to so_socket, a system call invoked by our call to socket.

```
so_socket(2, 2, 0, "", 1)                         = 3
connect(3, 0xEFFFE8C8, 16)                        = 0
        name = 198.69.10.4/13
read(3, " S a t   A p r   5   1".., 4096)         = 26
 ...
Sat Apr  5 11:32:07 1997
write(1, " S a t   A p r   5   1".., 26)          = 26
read(3, 0xEFFFE8D8, 4096)                         = 0
 ...
_exit(0)
```

The first three arguments to so_socket are our three arguments to socket.

We then see that connect is a system call, and truss, when invoked with the -v connect flag, prints the contents of the socket address structure pointed to by the second argument (the IP address and port number). The only system calls that we have replaced with ellipses are a few dealing with standard input and standard output.

> One side effect of this new implementation is the addition of 18 system calls to the kernel.

C.2   Standard Internet Services

Be familiar with the standard Internet services described in Figure 2.13. We have used the daytime service many times for testing our clients. The discard service is convenient port to which we can send data. The echo service is similar to the echo server that we have used throughout the text.

> Many sites now prevent access to these services through their firewalls, because of some denial-of-service attacks using these services in 1996 (Exercise 12.3). Nevertheless, you can hopefully use these services within your own network.

C.3   sock Program

The author's sock program first appeared in TCPv1, where it was frequently used to generate special case conditions, most of which were then examined in the text using tcpdump. The handy thing about the program is that it generates so many different scenarios, saving us from having to write special test programs.

We do not show the source code for the program in this text (it is over 2000 lines of C), but the source code is freely available (see the Preface).

The program operates in one of four modes, and each mode can use either TCP or UDP.

1. Standard input, standard output client (Figure C.1).

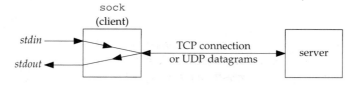

Figure C.1 sock client, standard input, standard output.

In the client mode everything read from standard input is written to the network, and everything received from the network is written to standard output. The server's IP address and port must be specified and in the case of TCP an active open is performed.

2. Standard input, standard output server. This mode is similar to the previous mode, except the program binds a well-known port to its socket and in the case of TCP performs a passive open.

3. Source client (Figure C.2).

Figure C.2 sock program as source client.

The program performs a fixed number of writes to the network of some specified size.

4. Sink server (Figure C.3).

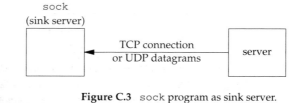

Figure C.3 sock program as sink server.

The program performs a fixed number of reads from the network.

These four operating modes correspond to the following four commands:

```
sock [ options ] hostname service
sock [ options ] -s [ hostname ] service
sock [ options ] -i hostname service
sock [ options ] -is [ hostname ] service
```

where *hostname* is a hostname or IP address and *service* is a service name or port number. In the two server modes the wildcard address is bound, unless the optional *hostname* is specified.

About 40 command-line options can also be specified, and these drive the optional features of the program. We will not detail these options here, but almost every socket option described in Chapter 7 can be set. Executing the program without any arguments prints a summary of the options:

```
-b n   bind n as client's local port number
-c     convert newline to CR/LF & vice versa
-f a.b.c.d.p  foreign IP address = a.b.c.d, foreign port# = p
-g a.b.c.d  loose source route
-h     issue TCP half-close on standard input EOF
-i     "source" data to socket, "sink" data from socket (w/-s)
-j a.b.c.d  join multicast group
-k     write or writev in chunks
-l a.b.c.d.p  client's local IP address = a.b.c.d, local port# = p
-n n   #buffers to write for "source" client (default 1024)
-o     do NOT connect UDP client
-p n   #ms to pause before each read or write (source/sink)
-q n   size of listen queue for TCP server (default 5)
-r n   #bytes per read() for "sink" server (default 1024)
-s     operate as server instead of client
-u     use UDP instead of TCP
-v     verbose
-w n   #bytes per write() for "source" client (default 1024)
-x n   #ms for SO_RCVTIMEO (receive timeout)
-y n   #ms for SO_SNDTIMEO (send timeout)
-A     SO_REUSEADDR option
-B     SO_BROADCAST option
-D     SO_DEBUG option
-E     IP_RECVDSTADDR option
-F     fork after connection accepted (TCP concurrent server)
-G a.b.c.d  strict source route
-H n   IP_TOS option (16=min del, 8=max thru, 4=max rel, 2=min cost)
-I     SIGIO signal
-J n   IP_TTL option
-K     SO_KEEPALIVE option
-L n   SO_LINGER option, n = linger time
-N     TCP_NODELAY option
-O n   #ms to pause after listen, but before first accept
-P n   #ms to pause before first read or write (source/sink)
-Q n   #ms to pause after receiving FIN, but before close
-R n   SO_RCVBUF option
-S n   SO_SNDBUF option
-T     SO_REUSEPORT option
-U n   enter urgent mode before write number n (source only)
-V     use writev() instead of write(); enables -k too
-W     ignore write errors for sink client
-X n   TCP_MAXSEG option (set MSS)
-Y     SO_DONTROUTE option
-Z     MSG_PEEK
-2     IP_ONESBCAST option (255.255.255.255) for broadcast
```

C.4   Small Test Programs

Another useful debugging technique, one that the author uses all the time when writing books, is writing small test programs to see how one specific feature works in a carefully constructed test case. It helps when writing test small test programs to have a set of library wrapper functions and some simple error functions, such as the ones we have used throughout this text. This reduces the amount of code that we have to write but still provides the required testing for errors.

Example: XTI Out-of-Band Data, Which Band?

As an example of this technique, combined with system call tracing, we will answer the question: "how does XTI send out-of-band data in TCP?" We establish a TCP connection with a server, followed by a call to t_snd, sending 1 byte with the T_EXPEDITED flag set. Figure C.4 shows our simple test program.

```
                                                                    debug/test01.c
 1 #include     "unpxti.h"

 2 int
 3 main(int argc, char **argv)
 4 {
 5     int     tfd;

 6     if (argc != 3)
 7         err_quit("usage: test01 <hostname/IPaddress> <service/port#>");

 8     tfd = Tcp_connect(argv[1], argv[2]);

 9     t_snd(tfd, "", 1, T_EXPEDITED);

10     exit(0);
11 }
                                                                    debug/test01.c
```

Figure C.4 Simple test program to see how XTI sends TCP out-of-band data.

We then run this program under Solaris 2.6 using truss to trace the system calls.

```
solaris26 % truss -v putmsg,putpmsg test01 198.69.10.4 discard
```

The final lines of output are

```
putpmsg(3, 0xEFFFF7D4, 0xEFFFF7C0, 0, 0x0004)   = 0
       ctl:   maxlen=8    len=8    buf=0xEFFFF7CC: "\0\0\004\0\0\0\0"
       dat:   maxlen=1    len=1    buf=0x00015318: "\0"
```

which answers our question. The third argument to putpmsg is 0, the band number. The value of 4 in the first 4 bytes of the control buffer is T_EXDATA_REQ (expedited data request), indicating that the XTI library sends this message to the provider as a normal message in band 0.

Example: XTI Out-of-Band Data, Which poll Event?

Our next question regarding TCP out-of-band data and XTI is which of the possible input events from Figure 6.23 should we poll for when awaiting out-of-band data:

POLLIN, POLLRDNORM, POLLRDBAND, or POLLPRI? This time we start with our simple XTI server Figure 30.5, producing the program shown in Figure C.5.

—— *debug/test03.c*

```
 1 #include     "unpxti.h"

 2 int
 3 main(int argc, char **argv)
 4 {
 5     int     listenfd, connfd, n, flags;
 6     char    buff[MAXLINE];
 7     struct pollfd fds[1];

 8     if (argc == 2)
 9         listenfd = Tcp_listen(NULL, argv[1], NULL);
10     else if (argc == 3)
11         listenfd = Tcp_listen(argv[1], argv[2], NULL);
12     else
13         err_quit("usage: daytimetcpsrv01 [ <host> ] <service or port>");

14     connfd = Xti_accept(listenfd, NULL, 0);

15     fds[0].fd = connfd;
16     fds[0].events = POLLIN | POLLRDNORM | POLLRDBAND | POLLPRI;
17     for ( ; ; ) {
18         n = poll(fds, 1, INFTIM);
19         printf("poll returned %d, revents = 0x%x\n", n, fds[0].revents);

20         n = T_rcv(connfd, buff, sizeof(buff), &flags);
21         printf("received %d bytes, flags = %d\n", n, flags);
22     }
23 }
```

—— *debug/test03.c*

Figure C.5 Simple test program to check how to poll for TCP out-of-band data.

We set all four conditions in our input events, and print the returned events. We then call t_rcv and print the number of bytes returned along with the returned flags.

We want to send this program normal data and out-of-band data, and to do this we run our sock program on another host as the client:

```
solaris % sock  -v  -i  -w 1  -n 3  -U 2  -p 4000  192.9.5.9  8888
connected on 206.62.226.33.34560 to 192.9.5.9.8888
TCP_MAXSEG = 1460
wrote 1 bytes
wrote 1 byte of urgent data
wrote 1 bytes
wrote 1 bytes
```

The -v flag turns on the verbose flag, -i causes the program to write data to the network (the source client mode), -w 1 says to write 1 byte at a time, -n 3 says to perform three writes, -U 2 says to write 1 byte of urgent data immediately before the second write, and -p 4000 causes a pause of 4000 ms (4 sec) after every write. We start our test program and then start our sock program, and here is the output from our test program:

```
solaris26 % test03 8888
poll returned 1, revents = 0x41
received 1 bytes, flags = 0
poll returned 1, revents = 0x41
received 1 bytes, flags = 2
poll returned 1, revents = 0x41
received 1 bytes, flags = 0
poll returned 1, revents = 0x41
received 1 bytes, flags = 0
poll returned 1, revents = 0x41
t_rcv error: An event requires attention
```

Each time the returned events are POLLIN and POLLRDNORM, telling us that the arrival of TCP's out-of-band data is not handled specially by poll. (We look up the values for the 2 bits in the returned event of 0x41 in the <sys/poll.h> header. When writing small test programs like this, it is normally easier and faster to print these values numerically and then look up the values in the appropriate headers.) But t_rcv returns a flag of 2 (T_EXPEDITED) when it returns the out-of-band byte.

C.5   tcpdump Program

An invaluable tool when dealing with network programming is a tool such as tcpdump. This program reads the packets from the network and prints lots of information about the packets. It also has the capability of printing only those packets that match some criteria that we specify. For example,

```
% tcpdump '(udp and port daytime) or icmp'
```

prints only the UDP datagrams with a source or destination port of 13 (the daytime server), or ICMP packets. The command

```
% tcpdump 'tcp and port 80 and tcp[13:1] & 2 != 0'
```

prints only the TCP segments with a source or destination port of 80 (the HTTP server) that have the SYN flag set. The SYN flag has a value of 2 in the byte with an offset of 13 from the start of the TCP header. The command

```
% tcpdump 'tcp and tcp[0:2] > 7000 and tcp[0:2] <= 7005'
```

prints only TCP segments with a source port between 7001 and 7005. The source port starts at byte offset 0 in the TCP header and occupies 2 bytes.

Appendix A of TCPv1 details the operation of this program in more detail.

> This program is available from ftp.ee.lbl.gov and works under many different flavors of Unix. It was written by Van Jacobson, Craig Leres, and Steven McCanne.

> Some vendors supply a program of their own with similar functionality. For example, Solaris 2.x provides the snoop program. The advantage in tcpdump is that it works under so many versions of Unix, and using a single tool in a heterogeneous environment, instead of a different tool for each environment, is a big advantage.

C.6   `netstat` Program

We have used the `netstat` program many times throughout the text. This program serves multiple purposes.

- It shows the status of networking endpoints. We showed this in Section 5.6, when we followed the status of our endpoint as we started our client and server.

- It shows the multicast groups that a host belongs to on each interface. The `-ia` flags are the normal way to show this, or the `-g` flags under Solaris 2.x.

- It shows the per-protocol statistics with the `-s` option. We showed this in Section 8.13, when looking at the lack of flow control with UDP.

- It displays the routing table with the `-r` option and the interface information with the `-i` option. We showed this in Section 1.9, where we used `netstat` to discover the topology of our network.

There are other uses of `netstat` and most vendors have added their own features. Check the manual page on your system.

C.7   `lsof` Program

The name `lsof` stands for "list open files." Like `tcpdump`, it is a publicly available tool that is handy for debugging and has been ported to many versions of Unix.

One common use for `lsof` with networking is to find which process has a socket open on a specified IP address or port. `netstat` tells us which IP addresses and ports are in use, and the state of the TCP connections but it does not identify the process. For example, to find which process provides the daytime server, we execute

```
solaris % lsof -i TCP:daytime
COMMAND  PID  USER  FD   TYPE      DEVICE  SIZE/OFF   INODE NAME
inetd    222  root  15u  inet  0xf5a801f8      0t0     TCP *:daytime
```

This tells us the command (this service is provided by the `inetd` server), its process ID, the owner, descriptor (15 and the `u` means it is open for read–write), the type of socket, the address of its protocol control block, the size or offset of the file (not meaningful for a socket), the protocol type, and the name.

One common use for this program is when we start a server that binds its well-known port, and get the error that the address is already in use. We then use `lsof` to find the process that is using the port.

Since `lsof` reports on open files, it cannot report on network endpoints that are not associated with an open file: TCP endpoints in the TIME_WAIT state.

> `ftp://vic.cc.purdue.edu/pub/tools/unix/lsof` is the location for this program. It was written by Vic Abell.

> Some vendors supply their own utility that does similar things. For example, BSD/OS supplies the `fstat` program. The advantage in `lsof` is that it works under so many versions of Unix, and using a single tool in a heterogeneous environment, instead of a different tool for each environment, is a big advantage.

Appendix D

Miscellaneous Source Code

D.1 `unp.h` Header

Almost every program in the text includes our `unp.h` header, shown in Figure D.1. This header includes all the standard system headers that most network programs need, along with some general system headers. It also defines constants such as MAXLINE and ANSI C function prototypes for the functions that we define in the text (e.g., `readline`) and all the wrapper functions that we use. We do not show these prototypes.

lib/unp.h

```
 1 /* Our own header.  Tabs are set for 4 spaces, not 8 */

 2 #ifndef __unp_h
 3 #define __unp_h

 4 #include    "../config.h"       /* configuration options for current OS */
 5                                 /* "../config.h" is generated by configure */

 6 /* If anything changes in the following list of #includes, must change
 7    acsite.m4 also, for configure's tests. */

 8 #include    <sys/types.h>       /* basic system data types */
 9 #include    <sys/socket.h>      /* basic socket definitions */
10 #include    <sys/time.h>        /* timeval{} for select() */
11 #include    <time.h>            /* timespec{} for pselect() */
12 #include    <netinet/in.h>      /* sockaddr_in{} and other Internet defns */
13 #include    <arpa/inet.h>       /* inet(3) functions */
14 #include    <errno.h>
15 #include    <fcntl.h>           /* for nonblocking */
16 #include    <netdb.h>
17 #include    <signal.h>
```

```
18 #include    <stdio.h>
19 #include    <stdlib.h>
20 #include    <string.h>
21 #include    <sys/stat.h>         /* for S_xxx file mode constants */
22 #include    <sys/uio.h>          /* for iovec{} and readv/writev */
23 #include    <unistd.h>
24 #include    <sys/wait.h>
25 #include    <sys/un.h>           /* for Unix domain sockets */

26 #ifdef   HAVE_SYS_SELECT_H
27 #include    <sys/select.h>       /* for convenience */
28 #endif

29 #ifdef   HAVE_POLL_H
30 #include    <poll.h>             /* for convenience */
31 #endif

32 #ifdef   HAVE_STRINGS_H
33 #include    <strings.h>          /* for convenience */
34 #endif

35 /* Three headers are normally needed for socket/file ioctl's:
36  * <sys/ioctl.h>, <sys/filio.h>, and <sys/sockio.h>.
37  */
38 #ifdef   HAVE_SYS_IOCTL_H
39 #include    <sys/ioctl.h>
40 #endif
41 #ifdef   HAVE_SYS_FILIO_H
42 #include    <sys/filio.h>
43 #endif
44 #ifdef   HAVE_SYS_SOCKIO_H
45 #include    <sys/sockio.h>
46 #endif

47 #ifdef   HAVE_PTHREAD_H
48 #include    <pthread.h>
49 #endif

50 /* OSF/1 actually disables recv() and send() in <sys/socket.h> */
51 #ifdef   __osf__
52 #undef   recv
53 #undef   send
54 #define recv(a,b,c,d)    recvfrom(a,b,c,d,0,0)
55 #define send(a,b,c,d)    sendto(a,b,c,d,0,0)
56 #endif

57 #ifndef INADDR_NONE
58 #define INADDR_NONE 0xffffffff  /* should have been in <netinet/in.h> */
59 #endif

60 #ifndef SHUT_RD                 /* these three Posix.1g names are quite new */
61 #define SHUT_RD     0           /* shutdown for reading */
62 #define SHUT_WR     1           /* shutdown for writing */
63 #define SHUT_RDWR   2           /* shutdown for reading and writing */
64 #endif
65 #ifndef INET_ADDRSTRLEN
66 #define INET_ADDRSTRLEN     16  /* "ddd.ddd.ddd.ddd\0"
```

```
 67                                    1234567890123456 */
 68 #endif

 69 /* Define following even if IPv6 not supported, so we can always allocate
 70    an adequately-sized buffer, without #ifdefs in the code. */
 71 #ifndef INET6_ADDRSTRLEN
 72 #define INET6_ADDRSTRLEN    46  /* max size of IPv6 address string:
 73                         "xxxx:xxxx:xxxx:xxxx:xxxx:xxxx:xxxx:xxxx" or
 74                         "xxxx:xxxx:xxxx:xxxx:xxxx:xxxx:ddd.ddd.ddd.ddd\0"
 75                          1234567890123456789012345678901234567890123456 */
 76 #endif

 77 /* Define bzero() as a macro if it's not in standard C library. */
 78 #ifndef HAVE_BZERO
 79 #define bzero(ptr,n)         memset(ptr, 0, n)
 80 #endif

 81 /* Older resolvers do not have gethostbyname2() */
 82 #ifndef HAVE_GETHOSTBYNAME2
 83 #define gethostbyname2(host,family)     gethostbyname((host))
 84 #endif

 85 /* The structure returned by recvfrom_flags() */
 86 struct in_pktinfo {
 87     struct in_addr ipi_addr;    /* dst IPv4 address */
 88     int     ipi_ifindex;        /* received interface index */
 89 };

 90 /* We need the newer CMSG_LEN() and CMSG_SPACE() macros, but few
 91    implementations support them today.  These two macros really need
 92    an ALIGN() macro, but each implementation does this differently. */
 93 #ifndef CMSG_LEN
 94 #define CMSG_LEN(size)       (sizeof(struct cmsghdr) + (size))
 95 #endif
 96 #ifndef CMSG_SPACE
 97 #define CMSG_SPACE(size)     (sizeof(struct cmsghdr) + (size))
 98 #endif

 99 /* Posix.1g requires the SUN_LEN() macro but not all implementations define
100    it (yet).  Note that this 4.4BSD macro works regardless whether there is
101    a length field or not. */
102 #ifndef SUN_LEN
103 #define SUN_LEN(su) \
104    (sizeof(*(su)) - sizeof((su)->sun_path) + strlen((su)->sun_path))
105 #endif

106 /* Posix.1g renames "Unix domain" as "local IPC".
107    But not all systems define AF_LOCAL and AF_LOCAL (yet). */
108 #ifndef AF_LOCAL
109 #define AF_LOCAL    AF_UNIX
110 #endif
111 #ifndef PF_LOCAL
112 #define PF_LOCAL    PF_UNIX
113 #endif

114 /* Posix.1g requires that an #include of <poll.h> define INFTIM, but many
115    systems still define it in <sys/stropts.h>.  We don't want to include
```

```
116    all the streams stuff if it's not needed, so we just define INFTIM here.
117     This is the standard value, but there's no guarantee it is -1. */
118 #ifndef INFTIM
119 #define INFTIM          (-1)     /* infinite poll timeout */
120 #ifdef  HAVE_POLL_H
121 #define INFTIM_UNPH              /* tell unpxti.h we defined it */
122 #endif
123 #endif

124 /* Following could be derived from SOMAXCONN in <sys/socket.h>, but many
125    kernels still #define it as 5, while actually supporting many more */
126 #define LISTENQ    1024        /* 2nd argument to listen() */

127 /* Miscellaneous constants */
128 #define MAXLINE     4096        /* max text line length */
129 #define MAXSOCKADDR  128        /* max socket address structure size */
130 #define BUFFSIZE    8192        /* buffer size for reads and writes */

131 /* Define some port number that can be used for client-servers */
132 #define SERV_PORT       9877    /* TCP and UDP client-servers */
133 #define SERV_PORT_STR  "9877"   /* TCP and UDP client-servers */
134 #define UNIXSTR_PATH    "/tmp/unix.str"    /* Unix domain stream cli-serv */
135 #define UNIXDG_PATH     "/tmp/unix.dg"  /* Unix domain datagram cli-serv */

136 /* Following shortens all the type casts of pointer arguments */
137 #define SA  struct sockaddr

138 #define FILE_MODE   (S_IRUSR | S_IWUSR | S_IRGRP | S_IROTH)
139                     /* default file access permissions for new files */
140 #define DIR_MODE    (FILE_MODE | S_IXUSR | S_IXGRP | S_IXOTH)
141                     /* default permissions for new directories */

142 typedef void Sigfunc (int);     /* for signal handlers */

143 #define min(a,b)    ((a) < (b) ? (a) : (b))
144 #define max(a,b)    ((a) > (b) ? (a) : (b))

145 #ifndef HAVE_ADDRINFO_STRUCT
146 #include    "../lib/addrinfo.h"
147 #endif

148 #ifndef HAVE_IF_NAMEINDEX_STRUCT
149 struct if_nameindex {
150     unsigned int if_index;      /* 1, 2, ... */
151     char  *if_name;             /* null terminated name: "le0", ... */
152 };
153 #endif

154 #ifndef HAVE_TIMESPEC_STRUCT
155 struct timespec {
156     time_t  tv_sec;             /* seconds */
157     long    tv_nsec;            /* and nanoseconds */
158 };
159 #endif
```

—— *lib/unp.h*

Figure D.1 Our header unp.h.

D.2   `config.h` Header

The GNU `autoconf` tool was used to aid in the portability of all the source code in this text. It is available from `ftp://prep.ai.mit.edu/pub/gnu/`. This tool generates a shell script named `configure` that you must run after downloading the software onto your system. This script determines the features provided by your Unix system: do socket address structures have a length field? is multicasting supported? are datalink socket address structures supported? and so on, generating a header named `config.h`. This header is the first header included by our `unp.h` header in the previous section. Figure D.2 shows the `config.h` header for BSD/OS 3.0.

The lines beginning with `#define` in column 1 are for features that the system provides. The lines that are commented out and contain `#undef` are features that the system does not provide.

———————————————————————————— i386-pc-bsdi3.0/config.h

```
 1 /* config.h.  Generated automatically by configure.  */
 2 /* Define the following if you have the corresponding header */
 3 #define CPU_VENDOR_OS "i386-pc-bsdi3.0"
 4 /* #undef   HAVE_NETCONFIG_H */      /* <netconfig.h> */
 5 /* #undef   HAVE_NETDIR_H */         /* <netdir.h> */
 6 #define HAVE_PTHREAD_H 1             /* <pthread.h> */
 7 #define HAVE_STRINGS_H 1             /* <strings.h> */
 8 /* #undef   HAVE_XTI_INET_H */       /* <xti_inet.h> */
 9 #define HAVE_SYS_FILIO_H 1           /* <sys/filio.h> */
10 #define HAVE_SYS_IOCTL_H 1           /* <sys/ioctl.h> */
11 #define HAVE_SYS_SELECT_H 1          /* <sys/select.h> */
12 #define HAVE_SYS_SOCKIO_H 1          /* <sys/sockio.h> */
13 #define HAVE_SYS_SYSCTL_H 1          /* <sys/sysctl.h> */
14 #define HAVE_SYS_TIME_H 1            /* <sys/time.h> */

15 /* Define if we can include <time.h> with <sys/time.h> */
16 #define TIME_WITH_SYS_TIME 1

17 /* Define the following if the function is provided */
18 #define HAVE_BZERO 1
19 #define HAVE_GETHOSTBYNAME2 1
20 /* #undef   HAVE_PSELECT */
21 #define HAVE_VSNPRINTF 1

22 /* Define the following if the function prototype is in a header */
23 /* #undef   HAVE_GETADDRINFO_PROTO */      /* <netdb.h> */
24 /* #undef   HAVE_GETNAMEINFO_PROTO */      /* <netdb.h> */
25 #define HAVE_GETHOSTNAME_PROTO 1           /* <unistd.h> */
26 #define HAVE_GETRUSAGE_PROTO 1             /* <sys/resource.h> */
27 #define HAVE_HSTRERROR_PROTO 1             /* <netdb.h> */
28 /* #undef   HAVE_IF_NAMETOINDEX_PROTO */   /* <net/if.h> */
29 #define HAVE_INET_ATON_PROTO 1             /* <arpa/inet.h> */
30 #define HAVE_INET_PTON_PROTO 1             /* <arpa/inet.h> */
31 /* #undef   HAVE_ISFDTYPE_PROTO */         /* <sys/stat.h> */
32 /* #undef   HAVE_PSELECT_PROTO */          /* <sys/select.h> */
33 #define HAVE_SNPRINTF_PROTO 1              /* <stdio.h> */
34 /* #undef   HAVE_SOCKATMARK_PROTO */       /* <sys/socket.h> */

35 /* Define the following if the structure is defined. */
```

```
36 /* #undef    HAVE_ADDRINFO_STRUCT */          /* <netdb.h> */
37 /* #undef    HAVE_IF_NAMEINDEX_STRUCT */       /* <net/if.h> */
38 #define HAVE_SOCKADDR_DL_STRUCT 1              /* <net/if_dl.h> */
39 #define HAVE_TIMESPEC_STRUCT 1                 /* <time.h> */

40 /* Define the following if feature is provided. */
41 #define HAVE_SOCKADDR_SA_LEN 1        /* sockaddr{} has sa_len member */
42 #define HAVE_MSGHDR_MSG_CONTROL 1     /* msghdr{} has msg_control member */

43 /* Names of XTI devices for TCP and UDP */
44 /* #undef    HAVE_DEV_TCP */                   /* most XTI have devices here */
45 /* #undef    HAVE_DEV_XTI_TCP */               /* AIX has them here */
46 /* #undef    HAVE_DEV_STREAMS_XTISO_TCP */     /* OSF 3.2 has them here */

47 /* Define the following to the appropriate datatype, if necessary */
48 /* #undef    int8_t */                 /* <sys/types.h> */
49 /* #undef    int16_t */                /* <sys/types.h> */
50 /* #undef    int32_t */                /* <sys/types.h> */
51 #define uint8_t unsigned char          /* <sys/types.h> */
52 #define uint16_t unsigned short        /* <sys/types.h> */
53 #define uint32_t unsigned int          /* <sys/types.h> */
54 /* #undef    size_t */                 /* <sys/types.h> */
55 /* #undef    ssize_t */                /* <sys/types.h> */
56 /* socklen_t should be typedef'd as uint32_t, but configure defines it
57    to be an unsigned int, as it is needed early in the compile process,
58    sometimes before some implementations define uint32_t. */
59 #define socklen_t unsigned int         /* <sys/socket.h> */
60 #define sa_family_t SA_FAMILY_T        /* <sys/socket.h> */
61 #define SA_FAMILY_T uint8_t

62 #define t_scalar_t int32_t             /* <xti.h> */
63 #define t_uscalar_t uint32_t           /* <xti.h> */

64 /* Define the following, if system suports the feature */
65 #define IPV4 1                /* IPv4, uppercase V name */
66 #define IPv4 1                /* IPv4, lowercase v name, just in case */
67 /* #undef    IPV6 */          /* IPv6, uppercase V name */
68 /* #undef    IPv6 */          /* IPv6, lowercase v name, just in case */
69 #define UNIXDOMAIN 1          /* Unix domain sockets */
70 #define UNIXdomain 1          /* Unix domain sockets */
71 #define MCAST 1               /* multicasting support */
```
——— *i386-pc-bsdi3.0/config.h*

Figure D.2 Our `config.h` header for BSD/OS 3.0.

D.3   `unpxti.h` Header

All our XTI programs include a header named `unpxti.h`, which is shown in Figure D.3. As with the listing of our `unp.h` header in Section D.1, we omit all the function prototypes. We also omit the definitions of the `T_` names between `T_INET_TCP` and `T_IP_BROADCAST`, as they are nearly identical.

─── *libxti/unpxti.h*

```
 1 #ifndef __unp_xti_h
 2 #define __unp_xti_h

 3 #include    "unp.h"

 4 #include    <xti.h>
 5 #ifdef  HAVE_XTI_INET_H
 6 #include    <xti_inet.h>
 7 #endif
 8 #ifdef  HAVE_NETCONFIG_H
 9 #include    <netconfig.h>
10 #endif
11 #ifdef  HAVE_NETDIR_H
12 #include    <netdir.h>
13 #endif

14 #ifdef  INFTIM_UNPH
15 #undef  INFTIM                    /* was not in <poll.h>, undef for <stropts.h> */
16 #endif

17 #include    <stropts.h>

18 /* Provide compatibility with the new names prepended with T_
19    in XNS Issue 5, which are not in Posix.1g. */

20 #ifndef T_INET_TCP
21 #define T_INET_TCP      INET_TCP
22 #endif
   ...
56 #ifndef T_IP_BROADCAST
57 #define T_IP_BROADCAST  IP_BROADCAST
58 #endif

59 /* Define the appropriate devices for t_open(). */
60 #ifdef  HAVE_DEV_TCP
61 #define XTI_TCP     "/dev/tcp"
62 #define XTI_UDP     "/dev/udp"
63 #endif
64 #ifdef  HAVE_DEV_XTI_TCP
65 #define XTI_TCP     "/dev/xti/tcp"
66 #define XTI_UDP     "/dev/xti/udp"
67 #endif
68 #ifdef  HAVE_DEV_STREAMS_XTISO_TCP
69 #define XTI_TCP     "/dev/streams/xtiso/tcp+"   /* + for XPG4 */
70 #define XTI_UDP     "/dev/streams/xtiso/udp+"   /* + for XPG4 */
71 #endif

72          /* device to t_open() for t_accept(); set by tcp_listen() */
73 extern char xti_serv_dev[];
```
─── *libxti/unpxti.h*

Figure D.3 Our header unpxti.h for XTI programs.

D.4   Standard Error Functions

We define our own set of error functions that are used throughout the text to handle error conditions. The reason for our own error functions is to let us write our error handling with a single line of C code, as in

```
if (error condition)
    err_sys (printf format with any number of arguments);
```

instead of

```
if (error condition) {
    char buff[200];
    snprintf(buff, sizeof(buff), printf format with any number of arguments);
    perror(buff);
    exit(1);
}
```

Our error functions use the variable-length argument list facility from ANSI C. See Section 7.3 of [Kernighan and Ritchie 1988] for additional details.

Figure D.4 lists the differences between the various error functions. If the global integer `daemon_proc` is nonzero, the message is passed to `syslog` with the indicated level; otherwise the error is output to standard error.

Function	strerror (errno) ?	Terminate ?	syslog level
err_dump	yes	abort();	LOG_ERR
err_msg	no	return;	LOG_INFO
err_quit	no	exit(1);	LOG_ERR
err_ret	yes	return;	LOG_INFO
err_sys	yes	exit(1);	LOG_ERR
err_xti	yes	exit(1);	LOG_ERR
err_xti_ret	yes	return;	LOG_INFO

Figure D.4 Summary of our standard error functions.

Figure D.5 shows the first five functions from Figure D.4.

—— *lib/error.c*

```
 1 #include    "unp.h"

 2 #include    <stdarg.h>          /* ANSI C header file */
 3 #include    <syslog.h>          /* for syslog() */

 4 int     daemon_proc;            /* set nonzero by daemon_init() */

 5 static void err_doit(int, int, const char *, va_list);

 6 /* Nonfatal error related to a system call.
 7  * Print a message and return. */

 8 void
 9 err_ret(const char *fmt,...)
10 {
```

```
11      va_list ap;

12      va_start(ap, fmt);
13      err_doit(1, LOG_INFO, fmt, ap);
14      va_end(ap);
15      return;
16 }

17 /* Fatal error related to a system call.
18  * Print a message and terminate. */

19 void
20 err_sys(const char *fmt,...)
21 {
22      va_list ap;

23      va_start(ap, fmt);
24      err_doit(1, LOG_ERR, fmt, ap);
25      va_end(ap);
26      exit(1);
27 }

28 /* Fatal error related to a system call.
29  * Print a message, dump core, and terminate. */

30 void
31 err_dump(const char *fmt,...)
32 {
33      va_list ap;

34      va_start(ap, fmt);
35      err_doit(1, LOG_ERR, fmt, ap);
36      va_end(ap);
37      abort();                        /* dump core and terminate */
38      exit(1);                        /* shouldn't get here */
39 }

40 /* Nonfatal error unrelated to a system call.
41  * Print a message and return. */

42 void
43 err_msg(const char *fmt,...)
44 {
45      va_list ap;

46      va_start(ap, fmt);
47      err_doit(0, LOG_INFO, fmt, ap);
48      va_end(ap);
49      return;
50 }

51 /* Fatal error unrelated to a system call.
52  * Print a message and terminate. */

53 void
54 err_quit(const char *fmt,...)
55 {
56      va_list ap;
```

```
57        va_start(ap, fmt);
58        err_doit(0, LOG_ERR, fmt, ap);
59        va_end(ap);
60        exit(1);
61 }

62 /* Print a message and return to caller.
63  * Caller specifies "errnoflag" and "level". */

64 static void
65 err_doit(int errnoflag, int level, const char *fmt, va_list ap)
66 {
67        int      errno_save, n;
68        char     buf[MAXLINE];

69        errno_save = errno;           /* value caller might want printed */
70 #ifdef   HAVE_VSNPRINTF
71        vsnprintf(buf, sizeof(buf), fmt, ap);    /* this is safe */
72 #else
73        vsprintf(buf, fmt, ap);       /* this is not safe */
74 #endif
75        n = strlen(buf);
76        if (errnoflag)
77            snprintf(buf + n, sizeof(buf) - n, ": %s", strerror(errno_save));
78        strcat(buf, "\n");

79        if (daemon_proc) {
80            syslog(level, buf);
81        } else {
82            fflush(stdout);              /* in case stdout and stderr are the same */
83            fputs(buf, stderr);
84            fflush(stderr);
85        }
86        return;
87 }
```
—— *lib/error.c*

Figure D.5 Our standard error functions.

Appendix E

Solutions to Selected Exercises

Chapter 1

1.3 Under AIX we get

```
aix % daytimetcpcli 206.62.226.33
socket error: Addr family not supported by protocol
```

To find more information on this error we first use `grep` to search for the string `Addr` in the `<sys/errno.h>` header.

```
aix % grep Addr /usr/include/sys/errno.h
#define EAFNOSUPPORT 66 /* Address family not supported by protocol family */
#define EADDRINUSE   67 /* Address already in use */
```

The first is the `errno` returned by `socket`. We then look at the manual page:

```
aix % man socket
```

Most manual pages give additional, albeit terse, information toward the end under a heading of the form "Errors."

1.4 We change the first declaration to be

```
int    sockfd, n, counter = 0;
```

We add the statement

```
counter++;
```

as the first statement of the `while` loop. Finally we execute

```
printf("counter = %d\n", counter);
```

before terminating. The value printed is always 1.

1.5   We declare an int named i and change the call to write to be

```
for (i = 0; i < strlen(buff); i++)
    Write(connfd, &buff[i], 1);
```

The results vary, depending on the client host and the server host. If the client and server are on the same host, the counter is normally 1, which means even though the server does 26 writes, the data is returned by a single read. But if the client runs under Solaris 2.5.1 and the server runs under BSD/OS 3.0, the counter is normally 2. If we watch the packets on the Ethernet, we see the first character is sent in a packet by itself, but the next packet contains the remaining 25 characters. (Our discussion of the Nagle algorithm in Section 7.9 explains the reason for this behavior.) If the client runs under BSD/OS 3.0 and the server runs under Solaris 2.5.1, the counter is now 26. If we watch the packets we see each character sent in its own packet.

The purpose of this example is to reiterate that different TCPs do different things with the data and our application must be prepared to read the data as a stream of bytes, until the end of the data stream is encountered.

Chapter 2

2.1   All RFCs are available at no charge through electronic mail, anonymous FTP, or the World Wide Web. A starting point is http://www.internic.net. The directory ftp://ds.internic.net/rfc is one location for RFCs. The starting point is to fetch the current RFC index, normally the file rfc-index. Look at the entry for RFC 1340, with a title of "Assigned Numbers," and note that it has been made obsolete by RFC 1700. Although RFC 1700 is current at the time of writing, it will probably be obsolete by the time you read this. Go backward from these obsolete RFCs and find the current (i.e., highest numbered) of the "Assigned Numbers" RFC.

The section of this RFC titled "Version Numbers" identifies the various IP version numbers. Version 0 is reserved, version 1–3 are unassigned, and version 5 is the Internet Stream protocol.

2.2   If we search the RFC index (see the solution to the previous exercise) with an editor of some form, looking for the term "Stream," we find that RFC 1819 defines Version 2 of the Internet Stream Protocol. Whenever looking for information that might be covered by an RFC, the RFC index should be searched.

2.3   With IPv4 this generates a 576-byte IP datagram (20 bytes for the IPv4 header and 20 bytes for the TCP header), the minimum reassembly buffer size with IPv4.

2.4   In this example the server performs the active close, not the client.

2.5   The host on the token ring cannot send packets with more than 1460 bytes of data, because the MSS it received was 1460. The host on the Ethernet can send packets with up to 4096 bytes of data, but it will not exceed the MTU of the outgoing interface (the Ethernet) to avoid fragmentation. TCP cannot exceed the MSS announced by the other end, but it can always send less than this amount.

2.6   The "Protocol Numbers" section of the Assigned Numbers RFC shows a value of 89 for OSPF.

Chapter 3

3.1   In C a function cannot change the value of an argument that is passed by value. For a called function to modify a value passed by the caller requires that the caller pass a pointer to the value to be modified.

3.2   The pointer must be incremented by the number of bytes read or written, but C does not allow a `void` pointer to be incremented (since the compiler does not know the datatype pointed to).

Chapter 4

4.1   Look at the definitions for the constants beginning with `INADDR_` other than `INADDR_ANY` (which is all zero bits) and `INADDR_NONE` (which is all one bits). For example, the class D multicast address `INADDR_MAX_LOCAL_GROUP` is defined as `0xe00000ff` with the comment "224.0.0.255," which is clearly in host byte order.

4.2   Here are the new lines added after the call to `connect`:

```
len = sizeof(cliaddr);
Getsockname(sockfd, (SA *) &cliaddr, &len);
printf("local addr: %s\n",
        Sock_ntop((SA *) &cliaddr, sizeof(cliaddr), NULL));
```

This requires a declaration of `len` as a `socklen_t` and a declaration of `cliaddr` as a `struct sockaddr_in`. Notice that the value–result argument for `getsockname` (`len`) must be initialized before the call to the size of the variable pointed to by the second argument. The most common programming error with value–result arguments is to forget this initialization.

4.3   When the child calls `close`, the reference count is decremented from 2 to 1, so a FIN is not sent to the client. Later, when the parent calls `close`, the reference count is decremented to 0 and the FIN is sent.

4.4   `accept` returns EINVAL, since the first argument is not a listening socket.

4.5   Without a call to `bind` the call to `listen` assigns an ephemeral port to the listening socket.

Chapter 5

5.1   The duration of the TIME_WAIT state should be between 1 and 4 minutes, giving an MSL between 30 seconds and 2 minutes.

5.2   Our client–server programs do not work with a binary file. Assume the first 3 bytes in the file are binary 1, binary 0, and a newline. The call to `fgets` in

Figure 5.5 reads up to MAXLINE-1 characters, or until a newline is encountered, or up through the end-of-file. In this example it will read the first three characters and then terminate the string with a null byte. But our call to strlen in Figure 5.5 returns 1, since it stops at the first null byte. One byte is sent to the server, but the server blocks in its call to readline, waiting for a newline character. The client blocks waiting for the server's reply. This is called a *deadlock*: both processes are blocked waiting for something that will never arrive from the other one. The problem here is that fgets signifies the end of the data that it returns with a null byte, so the data that it reads cannot contain any null bytes.

5.3   Telnet converts the input lines into NVT ASCII (Section 26.4 of TCPv1), which means terminating every line with the 2-character sequence of a CR (carriage return) followed by an LF (linefeed). Our client adds only a newline, which is actually a linefeed character. Nevertheless, we can use the Telnet client to communicate with our server as our server echoes back every character, including the CR that precedes each newline.

5.4   No, the final two segments of the connection termination sequence are not sent. When the client sends the data to the server, after we kill the server child (the "another line"), the server TCP responds with an RST. The RST aborts the connection and also prevents the server end of the connection (the end that did the active close) from passing through the TIME_WAIT state.

5.5   Nothing changes because the server process that is started on the server host creates a listening socket and is waiting for new connection requests to arrive. What we send in step 3 is a data segment destined for an ESTABLISHED TCP connection. Our server with the listening socket never sees this data segment, and the server TCP still responds to it with an RST.

5.6   Figure E.1 shows the program. Running this program under AIX generates

```
aix % tsigpipe 206.62.226.34
SIGPIPE received
write error: Broken pipe
```

The initial sleep of 2 seconds is to let the daytime server send its reply and close its end of the connection. Our first write sends a data segment to the server, which responds with an RST (since the daytime server has completely closed its socket). Note that our TCP allows us to write to a socket that has received a FIN. The second sleep lets the server's RST be received, and our second write generates SIGPIPE. Since our signal handler returns, write returns an error of EPIPE.

5.7   Assuming the server host supports the *weak end system model* (which we describe in Section 8.8) everything works. That is, the server host will accept an incoming IP datagram (which contains a TCP segment in this case) arriving on the leftmost datalink even though the destination IP address is the address of the rightmost datalink. We can test this by running our server on our host bsdi (Figure 1.16) and then starting the client on our host solaris but specifying the other IP address of the server (206.62.226.66) to the client. After the connection is

tcpcliserv/tsigpipe.c

```
 1 #include    "unp.h"

 2 void
 3 sig_pipe(int signo)
 4 {
 5     printf("SIGPIPE received\n");
 6     return;
 7 }

 8 int
 9 main(int argc, char **argv)
10 {
11     int     sockfd;
12     struct sockaddr_in servaddr;

13     if (argc != 2)
14         err_quit("usage: tcpcli <IPaddress>");

15     sockfd = Socket(AF_INET, SOCK_STREAM, 0);

16     bzero(&servaddr, sizeof(servaddr));
17     servaddr.sin_family = AF_INET;
18     servaddr.sin_port = htons(13);  /* daytime server */
19     Inet_pton(AF_INET, argv[1], &servaddr.sin_addr);

20     Signal(SIGPIPE, sig_pipe);

21     Connect(sockfd, (SA *) &servaddr, sizeof(servaddr));

22     sleep(2);
23     Write(sockfd, "hello", 5);
24     sleep(2);
25     Write(sockfd, "world", 5);

26     exit(0);
27 }
```

tcpcliserv/tsigpipe.c

Figure E.1 Generate `SIGPIPE`.

established, if we run `netstat` on the server we see that the local IP address is the destination IP address from the client's SYN, not the IP address of the datalink on which the SYN arrived (as we mentioned in Section 4.4).

5.8   Our client was on a little-endian Intel system, where the 32-bit integer with a value of 1 is stored as shown in Figure E.2.

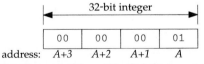

Figure E.2 Representation of the 32-bit integer 1 in little-endian format.

The 4 bytes are sent across the socket in the order *A*, *A+1*, *A+2*, and *A+3* where they are stored in the big-endian format, as shown in Figure E.3.

01	00	00	00
A	A+1	A+2	A+3

Figure E.3 Representation of the 32-bit integer from Figure E.2 in big-endian format.

This value of `0x01000000` is interpreted as 16,777,216. Similarly the integer 2 sent by the client will be interpreted at the server as `0x02000000`, or 33,554,432. The sum of these two integers is 50,331,648, or `0x03000000`. When this big-endian value on the server is sent to the client, it is interpreted on the client as the integer value 3.

But the 32-bit integer value of −22 is represented on the little-endian system as shown in Figure E.4, assuming a two's complement representation of negative numbers.

ff	ff	ff	ea
A+3	A+2	A+1	A

Figure E.4 Representation of the 32-bit integer −22 in little-endian format.

This is interpreted on the big-endian server as `0xeaffffff`, or −352,321,537. Similarly the little-endian representation of −77 is `0xffffffb3` but this is represented on the big-endian server as `0xb3ffffff`, or −1,275,068,417. The addition on the server yields a binary result of `0x9efffffe`, or −1,627,389,954. This big-endian value is sent across the socket to the client where it is interpreted as the little-endian value `0xfeffff9e`, or −16,777,314, which is the value printed in our example.

5.9   The technique is correct (converting the binary values to network byte order) but the two functions `htonl` and `ntohl` cannot be used. Even though the `l` in these functions once meant "long," these functions operate on 32-bit integers (Section 3.4). On a 64-bit system a `long` will probably occupy 64 bits, and these two functions will not work correctly. One might define two new functions, `hton64` and `ntoh64`, to solve this problem, but this will not work on systems that represent `long`s using 32 bits.

5.10 In the first scenario the server blocks forever in the call to `readn` in Figure 5.20 because the client sends two 32-bit values but the server is waiting for two 64-bit values. Swapping the client and server between the two hosts causes the client to send two 64-bit values, but the server reads only the first 64 bits, interpreting it as two 32-bit values. The second 64-bit value remains in the server's socket receive buffer. The server writes back two 32-bit values and the client will block forever in its call to `readn` in Figure 5.19, waiting to read two 64-bit values.

5.11 IP's routing function looks at the destination IP address (the server's IP address) and searches the routing table to determine the outgoing interface and the next hop (Chapter 9 of TCPv1). The primary IP address of the outgoing interface is used as the source IP address, assuming the socket has not already bound a local IP address.

Chapter 6

6.1   The array of integers is contained within a structure and C allows structures to be assigned across an equals sign.

6.2   If `select` tells us that the socket is writable, the socket send buffer has room for 8192 bytes, but we call `write` for this blocking socket with a buffer length of 8193 bytes, `write` can block, waiting for room for the final byte. Read operations on a blocking socket will always return a short count if some data is available but write operations on a blocking socket will block until all the data can be accepted by the kernel. Therefore when using `select` to test for writability, we must set the socket nonblocking to avoid blocking.

6.3   If both descriptors are readable, only the first test is performed, the test of the socket. But this does not break the client; it just makes it less efficient. That is, if `select` returns with both descriptors readable, the first `if` is true, causing a `readline` from the socket followed by an `fputs` to standard output. The next `if` is skipped (because of the `else` that we prepended) but `select` is then called again and immediately finds standard input readable and returns immediately. The key concept here is that what clears the condition of "standard input being readable" is not `select` returning, but reading from the descriptor.

6.4   Use the `getrlimit` function to fetch the values for the `RLIMIT_NOFILE` resource and then call `setrlimit` to set the current soft limit (`rlim_cur`) to the hard limit (`rlim_max`). For example, under Solaris 2.5 the soft limit is 64 but any process can increase this to the default hard limit of 1024.

`getrlimit` and `setrlimit` are not part of Posix.1 but are required by Unix 98.

6.5   The server application continually sends data to the client, which the client TCP acknowledges and throws away.

6.6   `shutdown` always sends a FIN while `close` sends a FIN only if the descriptor reference count is 1 when `close` is called.

6.7   `readline` returns an error, and our `Readline` wrapper function terminates the server. Server's must be more robust than this. Notice that we handle this condition in Figure 6.26, although even that code is inadequate. Consider what happens if connectivity is lost between the client and server and one of the server's responses eventually times out. The error returned could be `ETIMEDOUT`.

In general, a server should not abort for errors such as these. It should log the error, close the socket, and continue servicing other clients. Realize that handling an error of this type by aborting is unacceptable in a server such as this one, where one process is handling all clients. But if the server were a child handling just one client, then having that one child abort would not affect the parent (which we assume handles all new connections and spawns the children) or any of the other children that are servicing other clients.

Chapter 7

7.2   Figure E.5 shows one solution to this exercise. We have removed the printing of the data string returned by the server as that value is not needed.

——————————————————————————— sockopt/rcvbuf.c

```
 1 #include      "unp.h"
 2 #include      <netinet/tcp.h>      /* for TCP_MAXSEG */

 3 int
 4 main(int argc, char **argv)
 5 {
 6     int       sockfd, rcvbuf, mss;
 7     socklen_t len;
 8     struct sockaddr_in servaddr;

 9     if (argc != 2)
10         err_quit("usage: rcvbuf <IPaddress>");

11     sockfd = Socket(AF_INET, SOCK_STREAM, 0);

12     len = sizeof(rcvbuf);
13     Getsockopt(sockfd, SOL_SOCKET, SO_RCVBUF, &rcvbuf, &len);
14     len = sizeof(mss);
15     Getsockopt(sockfd, IPPROTO_TCP, TCP_MAXSEG, &mss, &len);
16     printf("defaults: SO_RCVBUF = %d, MSS = %d\n", rcvbuf, mss);

17     bzero(&servaddr, sizeof(servaddr));
18     servaddr.sin_family = AF_INET;
19     servaddr.sin_port = htons(13);   /* daytime server */
20     Inet_pton(AF_INET, argv[1], &servaddr.sin_addr);

21     Connect(sockfd, (SA *) &servaddr, sizeof(servaddr));

22     len = sizeof(rcvbuf);
23     Getsockopt(sockfd, SOL_SOCKET, SO_RCVBUF, &rcvbuf, &len);
24     len = sizeof(mss);
25     Getsockopt(sockfd, IPPROTO_TCP, TCP_MAXSEG, &mss, &len);
26     printf("after connect: SO_RCVBUF = %d, MSS = %d\n", rcvbuf, mss);

27     exit(0);
28 }
```

——————————————————————————— sockopt/rcvbuf.c

Figure E.5   Print socket receive buffer size and MSS before and after connection establishment.

First, there is no "correct" output from this program. The results vary from system to system. Some systems (notably Solaris 2.5.1 and earlier) always return 0 for the socket buffer sizes, preventing us from seeing what happens with this value across the connection.

With regard to the MSS, the value printed before connect is the implementation default (often 536 or 512) while the value printed after connect depends on a possible MSS option from the peer. On a local Ethernet, for example, the value after connect could be 1460. After a connect to a server on a remote network, however, the MSS may be similar to the default, unless your system supports path

MTU discovery. If possible, run a tool like `tcpdump` (Section C.5) while the program is running to see the actual MSS option on the SYN segment from the peer.

With regard to the socket receive buffer size, many implementations round this value up after the connection is established to a multiple of the MSS. Another way to see the socket receive buffer size after the connection establishment is to watch the packets using a tool like `tcpdump` and look at TCP's advertised window.

7.3 Allocate a `linger` structure named `ling` and initialize it as

```
str_cli(stdin, sockfd);

ling.l_onoff = 1;
ling.l_linger = 0;
Setsockopt(sockfd, SOL_SOCKET, SO_LINGER, &ling, sizeof(ling));

exit(0);
```

This should cause the client TCP to terminate the connection with an RST instead of the normal four segment exchange. The server child's call to `readline` returns an error of ECONNRESET and the message printed is

```
readline error: Connection reset by peer
```

The client socket should not go through the TIME_WAIT state, even though the client did the active close.

7.4 The first client calls `setsockopt`, `bind`, and `connect`. But between the first client's calls to `bind` and `connect` if the second client calls `bind`, EADDRINUSE is returned. But as soon as the first client connects to the peer, the second client's `bind` will work, since the first client's socket is then connected. The only way to handle this is for the second client to try calling `bind` multiple times if EADDRINUSE is returned and not give up the first time the error is returned. (This race condition was pointed out in the Posix.1g standard.)

7.5 We run the program on a host without multicast support (UnixWare 2.1.2).

```
unixware % sock -s 9999 &                        start first server with wildcard
[1]     29697
unixware % sock -s 206.62.226.37 9999            try second server but without -A
can't bind local address: Address already in use
unixware % sock -s -A 206.62.226.37 9999 &   try again with -A; works
[2]     29699
unixware % sock -s -A 127.0.0.1 9999 &       third server, with -A; works
[3]     29700
unixware % netstat -na | grep 9999
tcp     0       0   127.0.0.1.9999          *.*               LISTEN
tcp     0       0   206.62.226.37.9999      *.*               LISTEN
tcp     0       0   *.9999                  *.*               LISTEN
```

7.6 We first try on a host without multicast support (UnixWare 2.1.2).

```
unixware % sock -s -u -A 206.62.226.37 8888 &      first one starts
[4]     29707
```

```
unixware % sock -s -u -A 206.62.226.37 8888
can't bind local address: Address already in use    cannot start another
```

We specify the SO_REUSEADDR option for both instances, but it does not work.

We now try this on a host that supports multicasting but does not support the SO_REUSEPORT option (Solaris 2.6).

```
solaris26 % sock -s -u 8888 &                       first one starts
[1]    1135
solaris26 % sock -s -u 8888
can't bind local address: Address already in use
solaris26 % sock -s -u -A 8888 &                    try second again with -A; works
solaris26 % netstat -na | grep 8888                 and we can see the duplicate bindings
      *.8888                          Idle
      *.8888                          Idle
```

On this system we do not need to specify SO_REUSEADDR for the first bind, only for the second.

Finally we run this scenario under BSD/OS 3.0, which supports multicasting and the SO_REUSEPORT option. We first try SO_REUSEADDR for both servers, but this does not work.

```
bsdi % sock -u -s -A 7777 &
[1]    17610
bsdi % sock -u -s -A 7777
can't bind local address: Address already in use
```

Next we try SO_REUSEPORT but only for the second server, not for the first. This does not work since a completely duplicate binding requires the option for all sockets that share the binding.

```
bsdi % sock -u -s 8888 &
[1]    17612
bsdi % sock -u -s -T 8888
can't bind local address: Address already in use
```

Finally we specify SO_REUSEPORT for both servers, and this works.

```
bsdi % sock -u -s -T 9999 &
[1]    17614
bsdi % sock -u -s -T 9999 &
[2]    17615
bsdi % netstat -na | grep 9999
udp        0        0  *.9999                      *.*
udp        0        0  *.9999                      *.*
```

7.7 This does nothing because Ping uses an ICMP socket and the SO_DEBUG socket option affects only TCP sockets. The description for the SO_DEBUG socket option has always been something generic such as "this option enables debugging in the respective protocol layer" but the only protocol layer to implement the option has been TCP.

7.8   Figure E.6 shows the time line.

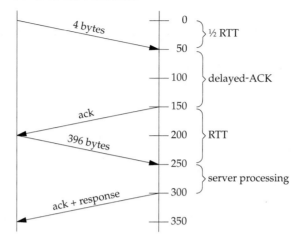

Figure E.6 Interaction of Nagle algorithm with delayed-ACK.

7.9   Setting the `TCP_NODELAY` socket option causes the data from the second `write` to be sent immediately, even though the connection has a small packet outstanding. We show this in Figure E.7. The total time in this example is just over 150 ms.

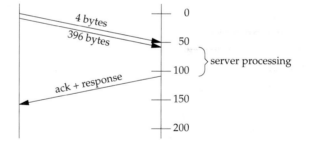

Figure E.7 Avoidance of Nagle algorithm by setting `TCP_NODELAY` socket option.

7.10   The advantage to this solution is reducing the number of packets, as we show in Figure E.8.

7.11   Section 4.2.3.2 states "the delay MUST be less than 0.5 seconds, and in a stream of full-sized segments there SHOULD be an ACK for at least every second segment." Berkeley-derived implementations delay an ACK by at most 200 ms (p. 821 of TCPv2).

7.12   The server parent in Figure 5.2 spends most of its time blocked in the call to `accept` and the child in Figure 5.3 spends most of its time blocked in the call to `read`, which is called by `readline`. The keepalive option has no effect on a listening socket so the parent is not affected should the client host crash. The child's

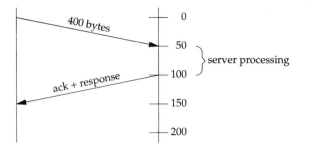

Figure E.8 Using `writev` instead of setting the `TCP_NODELAY` socket option.

read will return an error of ETIMEDOUT, sometime around 2 hours after the last data exchange across the connection.

7.13   The client in Figure 5.5 spends most of its time blocked in the call to `fgets`, which in turn is blocked in some type of read operation on standard input within the standard I/O library. When the keepalive timer expires around 2 hours after the last data exchange across the connection, and all the keepalive probes fail to elicit a response from the server, the socket's pending error is set to ETIMEDOUT. But the client is blocked in the call to `fgets` on standard input and will not see this error until it performs a read or write on the socket. This is one reason why we modified Figure 5.5 to use `select` in Chapter 6.

7.14   This client spends most of its time blocked in the call to `select`, which will return the socket as readable as soon as the pending error is set to ETIMEDOUT (as we described in the previous solution).

7.15   Only two segments, not four. There is a very low probability that the two systems will have timers that are exactly synchronized; hence one end's keepalive timer will expire shortly before the other's. The first one to expire sends the keepalive probe, causing the other end to ACK this probe. But the receipt of the keepalive probe causes the keepalive timer on the host with the (slightly) slower clock to be reset for 2 hours in the future.

7.16   The original sockets API did not have a `listen` function. Instead, the fourth argument to `socket` contained socket options, and SO_ACCEPTCON was used to specify a listening socket. When `listen` was added, the flag stayed around, but is now set only by the kernel (p. 456 of TCPv2).

Chapter 8

8.1   Yes. The `read` returns 4096 bytes of data but the `recvfrom` returns 2048 (the first of the two datagrams). A `recvfrom` on a datagram socket never returns more than one datagram, regardless of how much the application asks for.

8.2   If the protocol uses variable-length socket address structures, `clilen` could be too large. We will see in Chapter 14 that this is OK with Unix domain socket address structures, but the correct way to code the function is to use the actual length returned by `recvfrom` as the length for `sendto`.

8.4 Running `ping` like this is an easy way to see ICMP messages that are received by the host on which `ping` is being run. We reduce the number of packets sent from the normal one per second just to reduce the output. If we run our UDP client on our host `solaris`, specifying the server's IP address as 206.62.226.42, and also run the `ping` program, we get the following output:

```
solaris % ping -v -I 60 127.0.0.1
PING 127.0.0.1: 56 data bytes
64 bytes from localhost (127.0.0.1): icmp_seq=0. time=2. ms
ICMP Port Unreachable from gateway alpha.kohala.com (206.62.226.42)
 for udp from solaris.kohala.com (206.62.226.33)
            to alpha.kohala.com (206.62.226.42) port 9877
```

8.5 It probably has a socket receive buffer size, but data is never accepted for a listening TCP socket. Most implementations do not preallocate memory for socket send buffers or socket receive buffers. The socket buffer sizes specified with the SO_SNDBUF and SO_RCVBUF socket options are just upper limits for that socket.

8.6 We run the `sock` program on the multihomed host `bsdi` specifying the `-u` option (use UDP) and the `-l` option (specifying the local IP address and port).

```
bsdi % sock -u -l 206.62.226.66.4444 206.62.226.42 8888
hello
recv error: Connection refused
```

The local IP address is the lower Ethernet in Figure 1.16, but the datagram must go out the upper Ethernet to get to the destination. The "Connection refused" error that is returned is because the `sock` program calls `connect` and the server host returns an ICMP port unreachable. Watching the network with `tcpdump` shows that the source IP address is the one that was bound by the client, not the outgoing interface address.

```
14:39:46.211130 206.62.226.66.4444 > 206.62.226.42.8888: udp 6
14:39:46.211656 206.62.226.42 > 206.62.226.66: icmp: 206.62.226.42
                                        udp port 8888 unreachable
```

8.7 Putting a `printf` in the client should introduce a delay between each datagram, allowing the server to receive more datagrams. Putting a `printf` in the server should cause the server to lose more datagrams.

8.8 The largest IPv4 datagram is 65535 bytes, limited by the 16-bit total length field in Figure A.1. The IP header requires 20 bytes and the UDP header requires 8 bytes, leaving a maximum of 65507 bytes for user data. With IPv6, without jumbogram support, the size of the IPv6 header is 40 bytes, leaving a maximum of 65487 bytes for user data.

Figure E.9 shows the new version of `dg_cli`. If you forget to set the send buffer size, Berkeley-derived kernels return an error of EMSGSIZE from `sendto`, since the size of the socket send buffer is normally less than required for a maximum sized UDP datagram (be sure to do Exercise 7.1). But if we set the client's socket

udpcliserv/dgclibig.c

```
 1 #include    "unp.h"

 2 #undef   MAXLINE
 3 #define MAXLINE 65507

 4 void
 5 dg_cli(FILE *fp, int sockfd, const SA *pservaddr, socklen_t servlen)
 6 {
 7     int     size;
 8     char    sendline[MAXLINE], recvline[MAXLINE + 1];
 9     ssize_t n;

10     size = 70000;
11     Setsockopt(sockfd, SOL_SOCKET, SO_SNDBUF, &size, sizeof(size));
12     Setsockopt(sockfd, SOL_SOCKET, SO_RCVBUF, &size, sizeof(size));

13     Sendto(sockfd, sendline, MAXLINE, 0, pservaddr, servlen);

14     n = Recvfrom(sockfd, recvline, MAXLINE, 0, NULL, NULL);

15     printf("received %d bytes\n", n);
16 }
```

udpcliserv/dgclibig.c

Figure E.9 Writing the maximum size UDP/IPv4 datagram.

buffer sizes as shown in Figure E.9 and run the client program, nothing is returned by the server. We can verify that the client's datagram is sent to the server by running tcpdump, but if we put a printf in the server, it's call to recvfrom does not return the datagram. The problem is that the server's UDP socket receive buffer is smaller than the datagram that we are sending, so the datagram is discarded and not delivered to the socket. On a BSD/OS system we can verify this by running netstat -s and looking at the "dropped due to full socket buffers" counter, before and after our big datagram is received. The final solution is to modify the server, setting its socket send and receive buffer sizes.

On most networks a 65535-byte IP datagram is fragmented. Recall from Section 2.9 that an IP layer must support a reassembly buffer size of only 576 bytes. Therefore you may encounter hosts that will not receive the maximum sized datagrams sent in this exercise. Also, many Berkeley-derived implementations, including 4.4BSD-Lite2, have a sign bug that prevents UDP from accepting a datagram larger than 32767 bytes (line 95 of p. 770 of TCPv2).

Chapter 9

9.1   Figure E.10 shows our program that calls gethostbyaddr.

names/hostent2.c

```
 1 #include    "unp.h"

 2 int
 3 main(int argc, char **argv)
 4 {
 5     char    *ptr, **pptr;
```

```
 6        char      str[INET6_ADDRSTRLEN];
 7        struct hostent *hptr;

 8        while (--argc > 0) {
 9            ptr = *++argv;
10            if ( (hptr = gethostbyname(ptr)) == NULL) {
11                err_msg("gethostbyname error for host: %s: %s",
12                        ptr, hstrerror(h_errno));
13                continue;
14            }
15            printf("official hostname: %s\n", hptr->h_name);

16            for (pptr = hptr->h_aliases; *pptr != NULL; pptr++)
17                printf("    alias: %s\n", *pptr);

18            switch (hptr->h_addrtype) {
19            case AF_INET:
20 #ifdef  AF_INET6
21            case AF_INET6:
22 #endif
23                pptr = hptr->h_addr_list;
24                for ( ; *pptr != NULL; pptr++) {
25                    printf("\taddress: %s\n",
26                            Inet_ntop(hptr->h_addrtype, *pptr, str, sizeof(str)));

27                    if ( (hptr = gethostbyaddr(*pptr, hptr->h_length,
28                                        hptr->h_addrtype)) == NULL)
29                        printf("\t(gethostbyaddr failed)\n");
30                    else if (hptr->h_name != NULL)
31                        printf("\tname = %s\n", hptr->h_name);
32                    else
33                        printf("\t(no hostname returned by gethostbyaddr)\n");
34                }
35                break;

36            default:
37                err_ret("unknown address type");
38                break;
39            }
40        }
41        exit(0);
42 }
```

—————————————————————————————————— names/hostent2.c

Figure E.10 Modification to Figure 9.4 to call `gethostbyaddr`.

This program works fine for a host with a single IP address. If we run the program in Figure 9.4 for a host with four IP addresses we get

```
solaris % hostent gemini.tuc.noao.edu
official hostname: gemini.tuc.noao.edu
        address: 140.252.8.54
        address: 140.252.4.54
        address: 140.252.3.54
        address: 140.252.1.11
```

But if we run the program in Figure E.10 for the same host only the first IP address is output:

```
solaris % hostent2 gemini.tuc.noao.edu
official hostname: gemini.tuc.noao.edu
        address: 140.252.8.54
        name = gemini.tuc.noao.edu
```

The problem is that the two functions gethostbyname and gethostbyaddr share the same hostent structure, as we show at the beginning of Section 11.14. When our new program calls gethostbyaddr, it reuses this structure along with the storage that the structure points to (i.e., the h_addr_list array of pointers), wiping out the remaining three IP addresses returned by gethostbyname.

9.2   If your system does not supply the reentrant version of gethostbyaddr (which we describe in Section 11.15), then you must make a copy of the array of pointers returned by gethostbyname, along with the data pointed to by this array, before calling gethostbyaddr.

9.3   The my_addrs function is shown in Figure E.11 and the main function in Figure E.12.

names/myaddrs1.c
```
 1 #include     "unp.h"
 2 #include     <sys/param.h>

 3 char **
 4 my_addrs(int *addrtype)
 5 {
 6     struct hostent *hptr;
 7     char    myname[MAXHOSTNAMELEN];

 8     if (gethostname(myname, sizeof(myname)) < 0)
 9         return (NULL);

10     if ( (hptr = gethostbyname(myname)) == NULL)
11         return (NULL);

12     *addrtype = hptr->h_addrtype;
13     return (hptr->h_addr_list);
14 }
```
names/myaddrs1.c

Figure E.11 Version of Figure 9.7 that calls gethostname.

9.4   If gethostbyname returns a hostent structure specifying one or more IPv6 addresses, h_length will be 16. This will overflow the sockaddr_in structure, writing over whatever happens to follow it in memory. This resolver option should be set *only* if the program is prepared to deal with IPv6 addresses, which our program is not. This example also shows why the length argument to memcpy should be the size of the destination, sizeof(struct in_addr) in this example, and not the size of the source, hp->h_length, even if the two should be the same.

9.5   The chargen server sends data to the client until the client closes the connection (i.e., until you abort the client).

names/prmyaddrs1.c

```
 1 #include     "unp.h"

 2 char  **my_addrs(int *);

 3 int
 4 main(int argc, char **argv)
 5 {
 6     int     addrtype;
 7     char  **pptr, buf[INET6_ADDRSTRLEN];

 8     if ( (pptr = my_addrs(&addrtype)) == NULL)
 9         err_quit("my_addrs error");

10     for ( ; *pptr != NULL; pptr++)
11         printf("\taddress: %s\n",
12                 Inet_ntop(addrtype, *pptr, buf, sizeof(buf)));

13     exit(0);
14 }
```

names/prmyaddrs1.c

Figure E.12   Test program for Figures 9.7 and E.11.

9.6   As mentioned with Figure 9.3, this is a feature of newer releases of BIND. Figure E.13 shows the modified version. The order of the tests on the hostname string is important. We call inet_pton first, as it is a fast, in-memory test for whether or not the string is a valid dotted-decimal IP address. Only if this fails do we call gethostbyname, which typically involves some network resources and some time.

If the string is a valid dotted-decimal IP address, we make our own array of pointers (addrs) to the single IP address, allowing the loop using pptr to remain the same.

Since the address has already been converted to binary in the socket address structure, we change the call to memcpy in Figure 9.8 to call memmove instead, because when a dotted-decimal IP address is entered, the source and destination fields are the same in this call. Exercise 30.3 talks about overlapping fields with memcpy and memmove.

names/daytimetcpcli2.c

```
 1 #include     "unp.h"

 2 int
 3 main(int argc, char **argv)
 4 {
 5     int     sockfd, n;
 6     char    recvline[MAXLINE + 1];
 7     struct sockaddr_in servaddr;
 8     struct in_addr **pptr, *addrs[2];
 9     struct hostent *hp;
10     struct servent *sp;

11     if (argc != 3)
12         err_quit("usage: daytimetcpcli2 <hostname> <service>");
```

```
13          bzero(&servaddr, sizeof(servaddr));
14          servaddr.sin_family = AF_INET;

15          if (inet_pton(AF_INET, argv[1], &servaddr.sin_addr) == 1) {
16              addrs[0] = &servaddr.sin_addr;
17              addrs[1] = NULL;
18              pptr = &addrs[0];
19          } else if ((hp = gethostbyname(argv[1])) != NULL) {
20              pptr = (struct in_addr **) hp->h_addr_list;
21          } else
22              err_quit("hostname error for %s: %s", argv[1], hstrerror(h_errno));

23          if ( (n = atoi(argv[2])) > 0)
24              servaddr.sin_port = htons(n);
25          else if ((sp = getservbyname(argv[2], "tcp")) != NULL)
26              servaddr.sin_port = sp->s_port;
27          else
28              err_quit("getservbyname error for %s", argv[2]);

29          for ( ; *pptr != NULL; pptr++) {
30              sockfd = Socket(AF_INET, SOCK_STREAM, 0);

31              memmove(&servaddr.sin_addr, *pptr, sizeof(struct in_addr));
32              printf("trying %s\n",
33                      Sock_ntop((SA *) &servaddr, sizeof(servaddr)));

34              if (connect(sockfd, (SA *) &servaddr, sizeof(servaddr)) == 0)
35                  break;                  /* success */
36              err_ret("connect error");
37              close(sockfd);
38          }
39          if (*pptr == NULL)
40              err_quit("unable to connect");

41          while ( (n = Read(sockfd, recvline, MAXLINE)) > 0) {
42              recvline[n] = 0;            /* null terminate */
43              Fputs(recvline, stdout);
44          }
45          exit(0);
46      }
```
——— *names/daytimetcpcli2.c*

Figure E.13   Allow dotted-decimal IP address or hostname, port number or service name.

9.7   Figure E.14 shows the program.

——— *names/daytimetcpcli3.c*
```
1 #include     "unp.h"

2 int
3 main(int argc, char **argv)
4 {
5      int     sockfd, n;
6      char    recvline[MAXLINE + 1];
7      struct sockaddr_in servaddr;
8      struct sockaddr_in6 servaddr6;
9      struct sockaddr *sa;
10     socklen_t salen;
11     struct in_addr **pptr;
```

```
12      struct hostent *hp;
13      struct servent *sp;

14      if (argc != 3)
15          err_quit("usage: daytimetcpcli3 <hostname> <service>");

16      if ( (hp = gethostbyname(argv[1])) == NULL)
17          err_quit("hostname error for %s: %s", argv[1], hstrerror(h_errno));

18      if ( (sp = getservbyname(argv[2], "tcp")) == NULL)
19          err_quit("getservbyname error for %s", argv[2]);

20      pptr = (struct in_addr **) hp->h_addr_list;
21      for ( ; *pptr != NULL; pptr++) {
22          sockfd = Socket(hp->h_addrtype, SOCK_STREAM, 0);

23          if (hp->h_addrtype == AF_INET) {
24              sa = (SA *) &servaddr;
25              salen = sizeof(servaddr);
26          } else if (hp->h_addrtype == AF_INET6) {
27              sa = (SA *) &servaddr6;
28              salen = sizeof(servaddr6);
29          } else
30              err_quit("unknown addrtype %d", hp->h_addrtype);

31          bzero(sa, salen);
32          sa->sa_family = hp->h_addrtype;
33          sock_set_port(sa, salen, sp->s_port);
34          sock_set_addr(sa, salen, *pptr);

35          printf("trying %s\n", Sock_ntop(sa, salen));

36          if (connect(sockfd, sa, salen) == 0)
37              break;                  /* success */
38          err_ret("connect error");
39          close(sockfd);
40      }
41      if (*pptr == NULL)
42          err_quit("unable to connect");

43      while ( (n = Read(sockfd, recvline, MAXLINE)) > 0) {
44          recvline[n] = 0;            /* null terminate */
45          Fputs(recvline, stdout);
46      }
47      exit(0);
48  }
```

———————————————————————————— names/daytimetcpcli3.c

Figure E.14   Modification of Figure 9.8 to work with IPv4 and IPv6.

We use the h_addrtype value returned by gethostbyname to determine the type of address. We also use our sock_set_port and sock_set_addr functions (Section 3.8) to set these two fields in the appropriate socket address structure.

Although this program works, it has two limitations. First, we must handle all the differences, looking at h_addrtype and then setting sa and salen appropriately. A better solution is to have a library function that not only looks up the hostname and the service name but also fills in the entire socket address structure (e.g., `getaddrinfo` in Section 11.2). Second, this program compiles only on hosts that support IPv6. To make this compile on an IPv4-only host would add numerous `#ifdefs` to the code, complicating it.

We return to the concept of protocol independence in Chapter 11 and see better ways to accomplish it.

Chapter 10

10.1 Here are the relevant excepts (e.g., with the login and directory listings omitted).

```
solaris % ftp bsdi
Connected to bsdi.kohala.com.
220 bsdi.kohala.com FTP server ...
...
230 Guest login ok, access restrictions apply.
ftp> debug
Debugging on (debug=1).
ftp> dir
---> PORT 206,62,226,33,129,145
200 PORT command successful.
---> LIST
150 Opening ASCII mode data connection for /bin/ls.

...

solaris % ftp sunos5
Connected to sunos5.kohala.com.
220 sunos5.kohala.com FTP server ...
...
230 Guest login ok, access restrictions apply.
ftp> debug
Debugging on (debug=1).
ftp> dir
---> LPRT 6,16,95,27,223,0,206,62,226,0,0,32,8,0,32,120,227,227,2,129,148
200 LPRT command successful.
---> LIST
150 ASCII data connection for /bin/ls (5f1b:df00:ce3e:e200:20:800:2078:e3e3,
3172) (0 bytes).
```

Chapter 11

11.1 Allocate a big buffer (larger than any socket address structure) and call `getsockname`. The third argument is a value–result argument that returns the actual size of the protocol's addresses. Unfortunately, this works only for protocols with fixed-length socket address structures (e.g., IPv4 and IPv6) but is not guaranteed to work with protocols that can return variable-length socket address structures (e.g., Unix domain sockets, Chapter 14).

11.2 We first allocate arrays to hold the hostname and service name:

```
char    host[NI_MAXHOST], serv[NI_MAXSERV];
```

After `accept` returns, we call `getnameinfo` instead of `sock_ntop`:

```
if (getnameinfo(cliaddr, len, host, NI_MAXHOST, serv, NI_MAXSERV,
                NI_NUMERICHOST | NI_NUMERICSERV) == 0)
    printf("connection from %s.%s\n", host, serv);
```

Since this is a server, we specify the NI_NUMERICHOST and NI_NUMERICSERV flags, to avoid a DNS look and a lookup of `/etc/services`.

11.3   The first problem is that the second server cannot `bind` the same port as the first server because the `SO_REUSEADDR` socket option is not set. The easiest way to handle this is to make a copy of the `udp_server` function, rename it `udp_server_reuseaddr`, have it set the socket option, and call this new function from the server.

11.4   If the variable were global, `getaddrinfo` would not be thread-safe.

11.5   Yes. `ftp://ftp.isi.edu/in-notes/iana/assignments/port-numbers` shows that the service names `c1/1` and `914c/g` both contain slashes.

11.6   When the client outputs "Trying 206.62.226.35..." `gethostbyname` has returned the IP address. Any client pause before this is the time taken by the resolver to look up the hostname. The output "Connected to bsdi.kohala.com." means `connect` has returned. Any pause between these two lines of output is the time taken by `connect` to establish the connection.

Chapter 12

12.1   The `close` of the descriptors in `daemon_init` closes the listening TCP socket that was created by `tcp_listen`. Since programs that we write as a daemon might be executed from one of the system startup scripts, we should not assume that any error message can be written to a terminal. All error messages, even a startup error such as an invalid command-line argument, should be logged using `syslog`.

12.2   The TCP versions of the `echo`, `discard`, and `chargen` servers all run as a child process after being `fork`ed by `inetd`, because these three run until the client terminates the connection. The other two TCP servers, `time` and `daytime`, do not require a `fork` because their service is trivial to implement (get the current time and date, format it, write it, and close the connection), so these two are handled directly by `inetd`. All five UDP services are handled without a `fork` because each service generates a single datagram in response to the client datagram that triggers the service. These five are therefore handled directly by `inetd`.

12.3   This is a well-known denial of service attack ([CERT 1996a]). The first datagram from port 7 causes the `chargen` server to send a datagram back to port 7. This is echoed and sends another datagram to the `chargen` server. This loop continues. One solution, implemented in BSD/OS, is to refuse datagrams to any of the internal servers if the source port of the incoming datagram belongs to any of the internal servers. Another common solution is to disable these internal services, either through `inetd` on each host, or at a organizations's router to the Internet.

12.4 The client's IP address and port are obtained from the socket address structure filled in by `accept`.

The reason `inetd` does not do this for a UDP socket is because the `recvfrom` to read the datagram is performed by the actual server that is `exec`ed, and not by `inetd` itself.

`inetd` could read the datagram specifying the `MSG_PEEK` flag (Section 13.7), just to obtain the client's IP address and port, but leaving the datagram in place for the actual server to read.

Chapter 13

13.1 If no handler had been set, the return from the first call to `signal` will be `SIG_DFL` and the call to `signal` to reset the handler just sets it back to its default.

13.3 Here is just the `for` loop:

```
for ( ; ; ) {
    if ( (n = Recv(sockfd, recvline, MAXLINE, MSG_PEEK)) == 0)
        break;         /* server closed connection */

    Ioctl(sockfd, FIONREAD, &npend);
    printf("%d bytes from PEEK, %d bytes pending\n", n, npend);

    n = Read(sockfd, recvline, MAXLINE);
    recvline[n] = 0;    /* null terminate */
    Fputs(recvline, stdout);
}
```

13.4 The data is still output because the falling off the end of the `main` function is the same as returning from this function, and the `main` function is called by the C startup routine as

```
exit(main(argc, argv));
```

Hence `exit` is called, and the standard I/O cleanup routine is called.

Chapter 14

14.1 The `unlink` removes the pathname from the filesystem and when the client calls `connect` at a later time, the `connect` will fail. The server's listening socket is not affected, but no clients will be able to `connect` after the `unlink`.

14.2 The client cannot `connect` to the server even if the pathname still exists, because for the `connect` to succeed a Unix domain socket must be currently open and bound to that pathname (Section 14.4).

14.3 When the server prints the client's protocol address by calling `sock_ntop`, the output is "datagram from (no pathname bound)" because no pathname is bound to the client's socket by default.

One solution is to specifically check for a Unix domain socket in `udp_client` and `udp_connect` and `bind` a temporary pathname to the socket. This puts the protocol dependency in the library function, where it belongs, and not in our application.

14.4   Even though we force 1-byte `writes` by the server for its 26-byte reply, putting the `sleep` in the client guarantees that all 26 segments are received before `read` is called, causing `read` to return the entire reply. This is just to confirm (again) that TCP is a byte stream with no inherent record markers.

To use the Unix domain protocols we start the client and server with the two command-line arguments `/local` (or `/unix`) and `/tmp/daytime` (or any other temporary pathname that you wish to use). Nothing changes: 26 bytes are returned by `read` each time the client runs.

Since the server specifies the `MSG_EOR` flag for each `send`, each byte is considered a logical record, and `read` returns 1 byte each time it is called. What is happening here is that Berkeley-derived implementations support the `MSG_EOR` flag, by default. This is undocumented, however, and should not be used in production code. We use it here as an example of the difference between a byte stream and a record-oriented protocol. From an implementation perspective, each output operation goes into an mbuf (memory buffer) and the `MSG_EOR` flag is retained by the kernel with the mbuf as the mbuf goes from the sending socket to the receiving socket's receive buffer. When `read` is called, the `MSG_EOR` flag is still attached to each mbuf, so the generic kernel `read` routine (which supports the `MSG_EOR` flag since some protocols use the flag) returns each byte by itself. Had we used `recvmsg` instead of `read`, the `MSG_EOR` flag would be returned in the `msg_flags` member each time `recvmsg` returned 1 byte. This does not work with TCP because the sending TCP never looks at the `MSG_EOR` flag in the mbuf that it is sending, and even if it did, there is no way to pass this flag to the receiving TCP in the TCP header. (Thanks to Matt Thomas for pointing out this undocumented "feature.")

14.5   Figure E.15 shows an implementation of this program. We show an XTI version in Figure E.21.

―――――――――――――――――――――――――――――――――――――― *debug/backlog.c*
```
 1 #include    "unp.h"

 2 #define PORT        9999
 3 #define ADDR        "127.0.0.1"
 4 #define MAXBACKLOG  100

 5               /* globals */
 6 struct sockaddr_in serv;
 7 pid_t   pid;                    /* of child */

 8 int     pipefd[2];
 9 #define pfd pipefd[1]           /* parent's end */
10 #define cfd pipefd[0]           /* child's end */

11              /* function prototypes */
12 void    do_parent(void);
```

```
13 void    do_child(void);

14 int
15 main(int argc, char **argv)
16 {
17     if (argc != 1)
18         err_quit("usage: backlog");

19     Socketpair(AF_UNIX, SOCK_STREAM, 0, pipefd);

20     bzero(&serv, sizeof(serv));
21     serv.sin_family = AF_INET;
22     serv.sin_port = htons(PORT);
23     Inet_pton(AF_INET, ADDR, &serv.sin_addr);

24     if ( (pid = Fork()) == 0)
25         do_child();
26     else
27         do_parent();

28     exit(0);
29 }

30 void
31 parent_alrm(int signo)
32 {
33     return;                          /* just interrupt blocked connect() */
34 }

35 void
36 do_parent(void)
37 {
38     int     backlog, j, k, junk, fd[MAXBACKLOG + 1];

39     Close(cfd);
40     Signal(SIGALRM, parent_alrm);

41     for (backlog = 0; backlog <= 14; backlog++) {
42         printf("backlog = %d: ", backlog);
43         Write(pfd, &backlog, sizeof(int));  /* tell child value */
44         Read(pfd, &junk, sizeof(int));  /* wait for child */

45         for (j = 1; j <= MAXBACKLOG; j++) {
46             fd[j] = Socket(AF_INET, SOCK_STREAM, 0);
47             alarm(2);
48             if (connect(fd[j], (SA *) &serv, sizeof(serv)) < 0) {
49                 if (errno != EINTR)
50                     err_sys("connect error, j = %d", j);
51                 printf("timeout, %d connections completed\n", j - 1);
52                 for (k = 1; k < j; k++)
53                     Close(fd[k]);
54                 break;              /* next value of backlog */
55             }
56             alarm(0);
57         }
58         if (j > MAXBACKLOG)
59             printf("%d connections?\n", MAXBACKLOG);
60     }
```

```
61      backlog = -1;                    /* tell child we're all done */
62      Write(pfd, &backlog, sizeof(int));
63 }

64 void
65 do_child(void)
66 {
67      int      listenfd, backlog, junk;
68      const int on = 1;

69      Close(pipefd[1]);

70      Read(cfd, &backlog, sizeof(int));    /* wait for parent */
71      while (backlog >= 0) {
72          listenfd = Socket(AF_INET, SOCK_STREAM, 0);
73          Setsockopt(listenfd, SOL_SOCKET, SO_REUSEADDR, &on, sizeof(on));
74          Bind(listenfd, (SA *) &serv, sizeof(serv));
75          Listen(listenfd, backlog);   /* start the listen */

76          Write(cfd, &junk, sizeof(int));      /* tell parent */

77          Read(cfd, &backlog, sizeof(int));    /* just wait for parent */
78          Close(listenfd);             /* closes all queued connections too */
79      }
80 }
```
——————————————————————————— debug/backlog.c

Figure E.15 Determine actual number of queued connections for different *backlog* values.

Chapter 15

15.1 The descriptor is shared between the parent and child, so it has a reference count of 2. If the parent calls `close`, this just decrements the reference count from 2 to 1 and since it is still greater than 0, a FIN is not sent. This is another reason for the `shutdown` function: to force a FIN to be sent even if the descriptor's reference count is greater than 0.

15.2 The parent will keep writing to the socket that has received a FIN, and the first segment sent to the server will elicit an RST in response. The next `write` after this will send `SIGPIPE` to the parent as we discussed in Section 5.12.

15.3 When the child calls `getppid` to send `SIGTERM` to the parent, the returned process ID will be 1, the `init` process, which inherits all children whose parents terminate while their children are still running. The child will try to send the signal to the `init` process, but will not have adequate permission. But if there is a chance that this client could run with superuser privileges, allowing it to send this signal to `init`, then the return value of `getppid` should be tested before sending the signal.

15.4 If these two lines are removed, `select` is called. But `select` will return immediately because with the connection established the socket is writable. This test and `goto` are to avoid the unnecessary call to `select`.

15.5 This can happen if the server immediately sends data when its `accept` returns, and if the client host is busy when the second packet of the three-way handshake arrives to complete the connection at the client end (Figure 2.5). SMTP servers, for example, immediately write to a new connection, before reading from it, to send a greeting message to the client.

Chapter 16

16.1   No, it does not matter because the first three members of the union in Figure 16.2 are socket address structures.

Chapter 17

17.1   The sdl_nlen member will be 5 and the sdl_alen member will be 8. This requires 21 bytes, so the size is rounded up to 24 bytes (p. 89 of TCPv2), assuming a 32-bit architecture.

17.2   The kernel's response is never sent to this socket. This socket option determines whether the kernel sends its reply to the sending process, as discussed on pp. 649–650 of TCPv2. It defaults to on, since most processes want the replies. But disabling the option prevents the replies from being sent to the sender.

Chapter 18

18.1   If you get more than a few replies, they should not be in the same order each time. The sending host, however, is normally the first reply, since the datagrams to and from it do not appear on the actual network.

18.2   1472 is the Ethernet MTU (1500) minus 20 bytes for the IPv4 header and minus 8 bytes for the UDP header.

18.3   Under BSD/OS when the signal handler writes the byte to the pipe and then returns, select returns EINTR. It is called again and returns readability on the pipe.

Chapter 19

19.1   When we run the program the output is:

```
solaris % udpcli05 224.0.0.1
hi
from 206.62.226.34: Thu Jun 19 17:28:32 1997
from 206.62.226.43: Thu Jun 19 17:28:32 1997
from 206.62.226.42: Thu Jun 19 17:28:32 1997
from 206.62.226.40: Thu Jun 19 17:28:32 1997
from 206.62.226.35: Thu Jun 19 17:28:32 1997
```

The five responding hosts are running AIX, BSD/OS, Digital Unix, and Linux. The only multicast-capable nodes not responding are those running Solaris 2.5 and the Cisco router.

What is happening here is that the destination address of the UDP datagram is 224.0.0.1, the all-hosts group that all multicast-capable nodes must join. The UDP datagram is sent as a multicast Ethernet frame and all the multicast-capable nodes receive the datagram, since they all belong to the group. The responding hosts all pass the received datagram to the UDP daytime server (normally part of `inetd`) even though that socket has not joined the group. The Solaris implementation, however, requires that the destination socket must join the group to receive the datagram.

This example demonstrates that a UDP program that was never designed to respond to multicast datagrams can receive these datagrams. We saw the same thing happen with this daytime example in Chapter 18: a UDP program that was never designed to respond to broadcast datagrams can receive these datagrams.

19.2   Figure E.16 shows a simple modification to the `main` function to `bind` the multicast address and port 0.

mcast/udpcli06.c

```
 1 #include     "unp.h"

 2 int
 3 main(int argc, char **argv)
 4 {
 5      int      sockfd;
 6      socklen_t salen;
 7      struct sockaddr *cli, *serv;

 8      if (argc != 2)
 9          err_quit("usage: udpcli06 <IPaddress>");

10      sockfd = Udp_client(argv[1], "daytime", (void **) &serv, &salen);

11      cli = Malloc(salen);
12      memcpy(cli, serv, salen);   /* copy socket address struct */
13      sock_set_port(cli, salen, 0);   /* and set port to 0 */
14      Bind(sockfd, cli, salen);

15      dg_cli(stdin, sockfd, serv, salen);

16      exit(0);
17 }
```

mcast/udpcli06.c

Figure E.16 UDP client `main` function that `bind`s a multicast address.

Unfortunately on the three systems that this was tried on, BSD/OS, Digital Unix, and Solaris 2.5, all allow the `bind` and then send the UDP datagrams with a multicast source IP address. The five responding systems (the same ones as in the previous exercise) all swap the source and destination IP addresses in the reply, so all five replies are multicast! Nothing happens on the multicast-capable client hosts with the replies that they receive, because the destination port of the replies is the ephemeral port that the client kernel chose when the multicast address was bound, and there were no sockets bound to that port. ICMP port unreachables are not generated in response to a UDP datagram that is multicast.

19.3   If we do this from our host `solaris`, which is multicast capable, we get:

```
solaris % ping 224.0.0.1
PING 224.0.0.1: 56 data bytes
64 bytes from solaris.kohala.com (206.62.226.33): icmp_seq=0. time=4. ms
64 bytes from linux.kohala.com (206.62.226.40): icmp_seq=0. time=9. ms
64 bytes from aix.kohala.com (206.62.226.43): icmp_seq=0. time=11. ms
64 bytes from bsdi.kohala.com (206.62.226.35): icmp_seq=0. time=13. ms
64 bytes from alpha.kohala.com (206.62.226.42): icmp_seq=0. time=15. ms
64 bytes from sunos5.kohala.com (206.62.226.36): icmp_seq=0. time=17. ms
64 bytes from bsdi2.kohala.com (206.62.226.34): icmp_seq=0. time=54. ms
64 bytes from gw.kohala.com (206.62.226.62): icmp_seq=0. time=75. ms
^?
----224.0.0.1 PING Statistics----
1 packets transmitted, 8 packets received, 8.00 times amplification
round-trip (ms)  min/avg/max = 4/24/75
```

Every host from the top Ethernet in Figure 1.16 responds (including the sender, of course) except `unixware`, which is not multicast capable.

19.4   Since the kernel is not multicast capable it treats the destination as a normal IP address. It looks up 224.0.0.1 in the normal IP routing table and matches the default route, which points to the router `gw` (recall Figure 1.16). A unicast ICMP echo request is sent to this router with the destination IP address of 224.0.0.1 and the hardware address of that router's Ethernet interface (that is, the hardware address is not a multicast address). The router accepts the received packet because it is addressed to its interface and the destination IP address is a multicast group that the router belongs to.

19.5   If we do this from our host `solaris` we get:

```
solaris % ping 224.0.0.2
PING 224.0.0.2: 56 data bytes
64 bytes from bsdi.kohala.com (206.62.226.35): icmp_seq=0. time=3. ms
64 bytes from gw.kohala.com (206.62.226.62): icmp_seq=0. time=24. ms
^?
----224.0.0.2 PING Statistics----
1 packets transmitted, 2 packets received, 2.00 times amplification
round-trip (ms)  min/avg/max = 3/13/24
```

We expect `bsdi` to respond, as it is the multicast router on the subnet with a tunnel to the MBone (Section B.2) and is running `mrouted`. The router `gw` also responds, but it is not acting as a multicast router.

19.7   In Figure 19.17 we see that NTP timestamps are the number of seconds since January 1, 1900. There are 31,536,000 seconds in a year ($365 \times 24 \times 60 \times 60$) so the two values are about 96.7 years (ignoring leap years), which makes sense. Also, the version number of this announcement is greater than the session ID (which we expect was assigned when the session was first announced), which also makes sense.

19.8   The value 1,073,741,824 is converted to a floating-point number and divided by 4,294,967,296, yielding 0.250. This is multiplied by 1,000,000, yielding 250,000, which in microseconds is one-quarter of a second.

The largest fraction is 4,294,967,295, which divided by 4,294,967,296 yields 0.99999999976716935634. Multiplying this by 1,000,000 and truncating to an integer yields 999,999, the largest value for the number of microseconds.

19.9 In our discussion of these two socket options in Section 7.5 we noted that SO_REUSEADDR is considered equivalent to SO_REUSEPORT if the IP address being bound is a multicast address. This simplifies the portability of our code, because if this were not the case we would have to write:

```
#ifdef SO_REUSEPORT
    Setsockopt(fd, SOL_SOCKET, SO_REUSEPORT, &on, sizeof(on));
#else
    Setsockopt(fd, SOL_SOCKET, SO_REUSEADDR, &on, sizeof(on));
#endif
```

19.10 Some systems will not deliver a multicast datagram to a socket unless that socket has joined the multicast group. Just binding the port is inadequate on these systems. Solaris 2.5 operates in this fashion. Berkeley-derived implementations, on the other hand, deliver the datagram to all matching sockets, regardless of whether that particular socket has joined the group. Recall that our bind_ubcast function is called from Figure 19.22 to bind the socket to the wildcard address, so the multicast group is not joined on this socket.

19.11 Twelve additional datagrams would be received: three multicasts are sent in Figure 19.31 and each one is then delivered to four matching sockets (three multicast sockets plus the wildcard socket).

Chapter 20

20.1 Recall that sock_ntop uses its own static buffer to hold the result. If we call it twice as arguments in a call to printf, the second call overwrites the result of the first call.

20.2 Yes, if the reply contains 0 bytes of user data (i.e., just an hdr structure).

20.3 Since select does not modify the timeval structure that specifies its time limit, you need to note the time when the first packet is sent (this is already returned in units of milliseconds by rtt_ts). If select returns with the socket being readable, note the current time, and if recvmsg is called again, calculate the new timeout for select.

20.4 The common technique is to create one socket per interface address, as we did in Sections 19.11 and 20.6, and send the reply from the same socket on which the request arrived.

20.5 Calling getaddrinfo without a hostname argument and without the AI_PASSIVE flag set causes it to assume the localhost: 0::1 (IPv6) and 127.0.0.1 (IPv4). Recall that an IPv6 socket address structure is returned before an IPv4 socket address structure by getaddrinfo, assuming IPv6 is supported. If both protocols are supported on the host, the call to socket in udp_client will succeed with the family equal to AF_INET6.

Figure E.17 is the protocol-independent version of this program.

————————————————— advio/udpserv04.c

```c
 1 #include      "unpifi.h"

 2 void     mydg_echo(int, SA *, socklen_t);

 3 int
 4 main(int argc, char **argv)
 5 {
 6     int      sockfd, family, port;
 7     const int on = 1;
 8     pid_t  pid;
 9     socklen_t salen;
10     struct sockaddr *sa, *wild;
11     struct ifi_info *ifi, *ifihead;

12     if (argc == 2)
13         sockfd = Udp_client(NULL, argv[1], (void **) &sa, &salen);
14     else if (argc == 3)
15         sockfd = Udp_client(argv[1], argv[2], (void **) &sa, &salen);
16     else
17         err_quit("usage: udpserv04 [ <host> ] <service or port>");
18     family = sa->sa_family;
19     port = sock_get_port(sa, salen);
20     Close(sockfd);                 /* we just want family, port, salen */

21     for (ifihead = ifi = Get_ifi_info(family, 1);
22          ifi != NULL; ifi = ifi->ifi_next) {

23             /* bind unicast address */
24         sockfd = Socket(family, SOCK_DGRAM, 0);
25         Setsockopt(sockfd, SOL_SOCKET, SO_REUSEADDR, &on, sizeof(on));

26         sock_set_port(ifi->ifi_addr, salen, port);
27         Bind(sockfd, ifi->ifi_addr, salen);
28         printf("bound %s\n", Sock_ntop(ifi->ifi_addr, salen));

29         if ( (pid = Fork()) == 0) {   /* child */
30             mydg_echo(sockfd, ifi->ifi_addr, salen);
31             exit(0);                /* never executed */
32         }
33         if (ifi->ifi_flags & IFF_BROADCAST) {
34                 /* try to bind broadcast address */
35             sockfd = Socket(family, SOCK_DGRAM, 0);
36             Setsockopt(sockfd, SOL_SOCKET, SO_REUSEADDR, &on, sizeof(on));

37             sock_set_port(ifi->ifi_brdaddr, salen, port);
38             if (bind(sockfd, ifi->ifi_brdaddr, salen) < 0) {
39                 if (errno == EADDRINUSE) {
40                     printf("EADDRINUSE: %s\n",
41                             Sock_ntop(ifi->ifi_brdaddr, salen));
42                     continue;
43                 } else
44                     err_sys("bind error for %s",
45                             Sock_ntop(ifi->ifi_brdaddr, salen));
46             }
47             printf("bound %s\n", Sock_ntop(ifi->ifi_brdaddr, salen));
```

```
48                    if ( (pid = Fork()) == 0) {   /* child */
49                        mydg_echo(sockfd, ifi->ifi_brdaddr, salen);
50                        exit(0);            /* never executed */
51                    }
52              }
53        }
54        /* bind wildcard address */
55        sockfd = Socket(family, SOCK_DGRAM, 0);
56        Setsockopt(sockfd, SOL_SOCKET, SO_REUSEADDR, &on, sizeof(on));
57        wild = Malloc(salen);
58        memcpy(wild, sa, salen);     /* copy family and port */
59        sock_set_wild(wild, salen);
60        Bind(sockfd, wild, salen);
61        printf("bound %s\n", Sock_ntop(wild, salen));
62        if ( (pid = Fork()) == 0) {   /* child */
63            mydg_echo(sockfd, wild, salen);
64            exit(0);                  /* never executed */
65        }
66        exit(0);
67 }
68 void
69 mydg_echo(int sockfd, SA *myaddr, socklen_t salen)
70 {
71        int      n;
72        char     mesg[MAXLINE];
73        socklen_t len;
74        struct sockaddr *cli;
75        cli = Malloc(salen);
76        for ( ; ; ) {
77            len = salen;
78            n = Recvfrom(sockfd, mesg, MAXLINE, 0, cli, &len);
79            printf("child %d, datagram from %s",
80                    getpid(), Sock_ntop(cli, len));
81            printf(", to %s\n", Sock_ntop(myaddr, salen));
82            Sendto(sockfd, mesg, n, 0, cli, salen);
83        }
84 }
```
—— *advio/udpserv04.c*

Figure E.17 Protocol-independent version of program from Section 20.6.

Chapter 21

21.1 Yes. In the first example 2 bytes are sent with a single urgent pointer that points
to the byte following the b. But in the second example (the two function calls),
first the a is sent with an urgent pointer that points just beyond it, and this is followed by another TCP segment containing the b with a different urgent pointer
that points just beyond it.

21.2   Figure E.18 shows the version using `poll`.

oob/tcprecv03p.c

```
 1 #include     "unp.h"

 2 int
 3 main(int argc, char **argv)
 4 {
 5     int     listenfd, connfd, n, justreadoob = 0;
 6     char    buff[100];
 7     struct pollfd pollfd[1];

 8     if (argc == 2)
 9         listenfd = Tcp_listen(NULL, argv[1], NULL);
10     else if (argc == 3)
11         listenfd = Tcp_listen(argv[1], argv[2], NULL);
12     else
13         err_quit("usage: tcprecv03p [ <host> ] <port#>");

14     connfd = Accept(listenfd, NULL, NULL);

15     pollfd[0].fd = connfd;
16     pollfd[0].events = POLLRDNORM;
17     for ( ; ; ) {
18         if (justreadoob == 0)
19             pollfd[0].events |= POLLRDBAND;

20         Poll(pollfd, 1, INFTIM);

21         if (pollfd[0].revents & POLLRDBAND) {
22             n = Recv(connfd, buff, sizeof(buff) - 1, MSG_OOB);
23             buff[n] = 0;            /* null terminate */
24             printf("read %d OOB byte: %s\n", n, buff);
25             justreadoob = 1;
26             pollfd[0].events &= ~POLLRDBAND;     /* turn bit off */
27         }
28         if (pollfd[0].revents & POLLRDNORM) {
29             if ( (n = Read(connfd, buff, sizeof(buff) - 1)) == 0) {
30                 printf("received EOF\n");
31                 exit(0);
32             }
33             buff[n] = 0;            /* null terminate */
34             printf("read %d bytes: %s\n", n, buff);
35             justreadoob = 0;
36         }
37     }
38 }
```

oob/tcprecv03p.c

Figure E.18   Version of Figure 21.6 using `poll` instead of `select`.

Chapter 22

22.1   No, the modification introduces an error. The problem is that `nqueue` is decremented before the array entry `dg[iget]` is processed, allowing the signal handler to read a new datagram into this array element.

Chapter 23

23.1   In the `fork` example there will be 101 descriptors in use, one listening socket and 100 connected sockets. But each of the 101 processes (one parent, 100 children) has just one descriptor open (ignoring any others, such as standard input, if the server is not daemonized). In the threaded server, however, there are 101 descriptors in the single process. Each thread (including the main thread) is handling one descriptor.

23.2   The final two segments of the TCP connection termination—the server's FIN and the client's ACK of this FIN—will not be exchanged. This leaves the client's end of the connection in the FIN_WAIT_2 state (Figure 2.4). Berkeley-derived implementations will time out the client's end when it remains in the state for just over 11 minutes (pp. 825–827 of TCPv2).

23.3   This message should be printed by the main thread when it reads an end-of-file from the socket *and* the other thread is still running. A simple way to do this is to declare another external named `done` that is initialized to 0. Before the thread `copyto` returns, it sets this variable to 1. The main thread checks this variable, and if 0, prints the error message. Since only one thread sets the variable, there is no need for any synchronization.

Chapter 24

24.1   Nothing changes at the server. First, that router employs the common weak end system model, so it accepts the incoming datagrams from the Ethernet even though the destination address is that of its other interface. Next, with an IPv4 source route the forwarding host replaces its address in the list with the address of the outgoing interface. That outgoing interface is the Ethernet interface (206.62.226.62), regardless of which address the packet is sent to.

24.2   Nothing changes. All the systems are neighbors, so a strict source route is identical to a loose source route.

24.3   We would place an EOL (a byte of 0) at the end of the buffer.

24.4   Since `ping` creates a raw socket (Chapter 25), it receives the complete IP header, including any IP options, on every datagram that it reads with `recvfrom`.

24.5   Because `rlogind` is invoked by `inetd` (Section 12.5).

24.6   The problem is that the fifth argument to `setsockopt` is the pointer to the length, instead of the length. This bug was probably fixed when ANSI C prototypes were first used.

As it turns out the bug is harmless, because as we mentioned, to clear the IP_OPTIONS socket option we can specify either a null pointer as the fourth argument or a fifth argument (the length) of 0 (p. 269 of TCPv2).

Chapter 25

25.1   The version number field and the next header field in the IPv6 header are not available. The payload length field is available as either an argument to one of the output functions or as the return value from one of the input functions, but if a jumbo payload option is required, that actual option itself is not available to an application. The fragment header is also not available to an application.

25.2   Eventually the client's socket receive buffer will fill, causing the daemon's `write` to block. We do not want this to happen, as that stops the daemon from handling any more data on any of its sockets. The easiest solution is for the daemon to set its end of the Unix domain connection to the client nonblocking. The daemon must then call `write` instead of the wrapper function `Write` and just ignore an error of EWOULDBLOCK.

25.3   Berkeley-derived kernels, by default, allow broadcasting on a raw socket (p. 1057 of TCPv2). The SO_BROADCAST socket option needs to be specified only for UDP sockets.

25.4   Our program does not check for a multicast address and does not set the IP_MULTICAST_IF socket option. Therefore the kernel chooses the outgoing interface, probably by searching the routing table for 224.0.0.1. We also do not set the IP_MULTICAST_TTL field, so it defaults to 1, which is OK.

Chapter 26

26.1   This flag indicates that the jump buffer has been set by `sigsetjmp` (Figure 26.10). While the flag may seem superfluous, there is a chance that the signal can be delivered after the signal handler is established, but before the call to `sigsetjmp`. Even if the program doesn't cause the signal to be generated, signals can also be generated in other ways (such as with the `kill` command).

Chapter 27

27.1   The parent keeps the listening socket open in case it needs to `fork` additional children at some later time (which would be an enhancement to our code).

27.2   Yes, a datagram socket can be used to pass a descriptor instead of using a stream socket. With a datagram socket the parent does not receive an end-of-file on its end of the stream pipe when a child terminates prematurely, but the parent could use SIGCHLD for this purpose. Realize that one difference in this scenario, where SIGCHLD can be used versus our `icmpd` daemon in Section 25.7, is that in the latter there was not a parent–child relationship between the client and server, so the end-of-file on the stream pipe was the only way for the server to detect the disappearance of a client.

Chapter 28

28.1   Not usually, because the only type of application that sets the `qlen` member nonzero is a connection-oriented server (e.g., TCP). But servers normally bind their well-known port, instead of letting the system choose an ephemeral port. One exception is an RPC (remote procedure call) server, which binds an ephemeral port and then registers the port with the RPC port mapper.

28.2   The receipt of an ICMP destination unreachable in response to a SYN is not a fatal error. TCP should retransmit the SYN some number of times, or until its retransmission timer expires.

28.3   A `write` to a socket that has received an RST generates `SIGPIPE`. If the process does nothing with this signal, its default action terminates the process. If the process ignores the signal, `write` returns an error of `EPIPE`.

Chapter 29

29.1   Yes, the function is thread-safe. `setnetconfig` dynamically allocates the memory used to hold the `netconfig` structure, and the arrays that it points to. This memory is released by `endnetconfig`. Be careful not to reference the `netconfig` structure returned by `getnetconfig` after calling `endnetconfig`, as that memory has been freed.

29.2   Figure E.19 shows the program.

—————————————————————————————————— debug/test06.c
```
 1 #include     "unpxti.h"

 2 int
 3 main(int argc, char **argv)
 4 {
 5     int     fd;
 6     struct t_call *tcall;

 7     fd = T_open(XTI_TCP, O_RDWR, NULL);

 8     tcall = T_alloc(fd, T_CALL, T_ALL);
 9     printf("first t_alloc OK\n");

10     tcall = T_alloc(fd, T_CALL, T_ADDR | T_OPT | T_UDATA);
11     printf("second t_alloc OK\n");

12     exit(0);
13 }
```
—————————————————————————————————— debug/test06.c

Figure E.19   Compare `T_ALL` versus specifying each `netbuf` structure.

When we execute this program the output is

```
alpha % test06
first t_alloc OK
t_alloc error: system error: Invalid argument
```

A TCP endpoint does not support user data with a connection request (the value of –2 for the `connect` row in Figure 28.1). When `T_ALL` is specified, these unsupported structures are skipped by `t_alloc` and we saw in Figure 29.5 that `udata.len` is set to 0 and the `udata.buf` is set to a null pointer. But if we specify each of the three `netbuf` structures as the third argument to `t_alloc`, instead of `T_ALL`, an error is returned if any of the specified fields are unsupported. This is another reason to always use `T_ALL`.

29.3 The function cannot tell the type of structure given just its pointer. If `t_free` released only the structure, this argument would not be required. But since it goes through the structure and releases any buffers pointed to by `netbuf` structures within the structure, it must know the type of structure.

29.4 We are not guaranteed of the order of the elements with the structure.

Chapter 30

30.1 This technique does not work because an integer is normally stored in 32 bits, while pointers require 64 bits (Figure 1.17).

30.2 The Posix.1 `PATH_MAX` constant does not include the terminating null byte.

30.3 In Figure E.20 we first draw the 4-byte array and the two 2-byte fields, which shows the overlap of the source and destination.

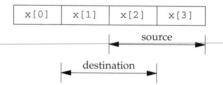

Figure E.20 Source and destination of copy operation overlap.

If the copy is done from the beginning of the source to the beginning of the destination, as in the C fragment

```
while (nbytes--)
    *dst++ = *src++;
```

then two assignment statements are executed:

```
x[1] = x[2];
x[2] = x[3];
```

which is correct. But if the copy is done in the other direction, as in the C fragment

```
src += nbytes;
dst += nbytes;
while (nbytes--)
    *--dst = *--src;
```

then the two assignment statements are

```
x[2] = x[3];
x[1] = x[2];
```

which is wrong (why?). There is no guarantee in which direction memcpy copies; hence when the fields overlap, memmove must be called. memmove handles the overlap by copying in the "correct" direction, depending on the relationship between the source and destination.

30.4 Figure E.21 shows the two functions do_parent and do_child. **The only change prior to this from Figure E.15 is to #include unpxti.h instead of unp.h.**

——————————————————————————————————— debug/qlen.c

```
35 void
36 do_parent(void)
37 {
38     int     qlen, j, k, junk, fd[MAXBACKLOG + 1];
39     struct t_call tcall;

40     Close(cfd);
41     Signal(SIGALRM, parent_alrm);

42     for (qlen = 0; qlen <= 14; qlen++) {
43         printf("qlen = %d: ", qlen);
44         Write(pfd, &qlen, sizeof(int));      /* tell child value */
45         Read(pfd, &junk, sizeof(int));   /* wait for child */

46         for (j = 0; j <= MAXBACKLOG; j++) {
47             fd[j] = T_open(XTI_TCP, O_RDWR, NULL);
48             T_bind(fd[j], NULL, NULL);

49             tcall.addr.maxlen = sizeof(serv);
50             tcall.addr.len = sizeof(serv);
51             tcall.addr.buf = &serv;
52             tcall.opt.len = 0;
53             tcall.udata.len = 0;

54             alarm(2);
55             if (t_connect(fd[j], &tcall, NULL) < 0) {
56                 if (errno != EINTR)
57                     err_xti("t_connect error, j = %d", j);
58                 printf("timeout, %d connections completed\n", j - 1);
59                 for (k = 1; k < j; k++)
60                     T_close(fd[k]);
61                 break;          /* next value of qlen */
62             }
63             alarm(0);
64         }
65         if (j > MAXBACKLOG)
66             printf("%d connections?\n", MAXBACKLOG);
67     }
68     qlen = -1;                       /* tell child we're all done */
69     Write(pfd, &qlen, sizeof(int));
70 }
```

```
71 void
72 do_child(void)
73 {
74     int      listenfd, qlen, junk;
75     struct t_bind tbind, tbindret;

76     Close(pipefd[1]);

77     Read(cfd, &qlen, sizeof(int));   /* wait for parent */
78     while (qlen >= 0) {
79         listenfd = T_open(XTI_TCP, O_RDWR, NULL);

80         tbind.addr.maxlen = sizeof(serv);
81         tbind.addr.len = sizeof(serv);
82         tbind.addr.buf = &serv;
83         tbind.qlen = qlen;

84         tbindret.addr.maxlen = 0;
85         tbindret.addr.len = 0;

86         T_bind(listenfd, &tbind, &tbindret);
87         printf("returned qlen = %d, ", tbindret.qlen);
88         fflush(stdout);

89         Write(cfd, &junk, sizeof(int));      /* tell parent */

90         Read(cfd, &qlen, sizeof(int));   /* just wait for parent */
91         T_close(listenfd);       /* closes all queued connections too */
92     }
93 }
```
—— *debug/qlen.c*

Figure E.21   Determine actual number of queued connections for different `qlen` values.

Chapter 33

33.1   We are assuming here that the default for the protocol is an orderly release when the stream is closed, which is true for TCP.

Bibliography

All RFCs are available at no charge through electronic mail, anonymous FTP, or the World Wide Web. A starting point is `http://www.internic.net`. The directory `ftp://ds.internic.net/rfc` is one location for RFCs. URLs are not specified for the RFCs.

Items marked "Internet Draft" are works in progress of the IETF (Internet Engineering Task Force). These drafts expire six months after publication. The appropriate version of the draft may change after this book is published, or the draft may be published as an RFC. They are available at no charge across the Internet, similar to the RFCs. `ftp://ds.internic.net/internet-drafts` is a major repository for Internet Drafts. The filename portion of the URL for each Internet Draft is included, since the filename contains the version number.

Whenever an electronic copy was found of a paper or report referenced in this bibliography, its URL is included. Be aware that these URLs can change over time, and readers are encouraged to check the Errata for this text on the author's home page for any changes: `http://www.kohala.com/~rstevens`.

Albitz, P., and Liu, C. 1997. *DNS and BIND, Second Edition.* O'Reilly & Associates, Sebastopol, Calif.

Almquist, P. 1992. "Type of Service in the Internet Protocol Suite," RFC 1349, 28 pages (July).
> How to use the type-of-service field in the IPv4 header.

Atkinson, R. J. 1995a. "IP Authentication Header," RFC 1826, 13 pages (Aug.).

Atkinson, R. J. 1995b. "IP Encapsulating Security Payload (ESP)," RFC 1827, 12 pages (Aug.).

Baker, F., ed. 1995. "Requirements for IP Version 4 Routers," RFC 1812, 175 pages (June).

Borman, D. A. 1997a. "Re: Frequency of RST Terminated Connections," January 30, 1997, end2end-interest mailing list.

    `http://www.kohala.com/~rstevens/borman.97jan30.txt`

Borman, D. A. 1997b. "TCP and UDP over IPv6 Jumbograms," RFC 2147, 3 pages (May).

Borman, D. A. 1997c. "Re: SYN/RST cookies," June 6, 1997, tcp-impl mailing list.

    `http://www.kohala.com/~rstevens/borman.97jun06.txt`

Braden, R. T., ed. 1989. "Requirements for Internet Hosts—Communication Layers," RFC 1122, 116 pages (Oct.).

    The first half of the Host Requirements RFC. This half covers the link layer, IPv4, ICMPv4, IGMPv4, ARP, TCP, and UDP.

Braden, R. T. 1992a. "TIME-WAIT Assassination Hazards in TCP," RFC 1337, 11 pages (May).

Braden, R. T. 1992b. "Extending TCP for Transactions—Concepts," RFC 1379, 38 pages (Nov.).

Braden, R. T. 1993. "TCP Extensions for High Performance: An Update," Internet Draft, 10 pages (June).

    `http://www.kohala.com/~rstevens/tcplw-extensions.txt`
    This is an update to RFC 1323 [Jacobson, Braden, and Borman 1992] that never got published as an RFC, but an update to RFC 1323 should appear someday.

Braden, R. T. 1994. "T/TCP—TCP Extensions for Transactions, Functional Specification," RFC 1644, 38 pages (July).

Braden, R. T., Borman, D. A., and Partridge, C. 1988. "Computing the Internet Checksum," RFC 1071, 24 pages (Sept.).

Bradner, S. 1996. "The Internet Standards Process—Revision 3," RFC 2026, 36 pages (Oct.).

Butenhof, D. R. 1997. *Programming with POSIX Threads.* Addison-Wesley, Reading, Mass.

CERT. 1996a. "UDP Port Denial-of-Service Attack," Advisory CA-96.01, Computer Emergency Response Team, Pittsburgh, Pa. (Feb.).

    `ftp://info.cert.org/pub/cert_advisories/CA-96.01.UDP_service_denial`

CERT. 1996b. "TCP SYN Flooding and IP Spoofing Attacks," Advisory CA-96.21, Computer Emergency Response Team, Pittsburgh, Pa. (Sept.).

    `ftp://info.cert.org/pub/cert_advisories/CA-96.21.tcp_syn_flooding`

Cheswick, W. R., and Bellovin, S. M. 1994. *Firewalls and Internet Security: Repelling the Wily Hacker.* Addison-Wesley, Reading, Mass.

Comer, D. E., and Lin, J. C. 1994. "TCP Buffering and Performance Over an ATM Network," Purdue Technical Report CSD-TR 94-026, Purdue University, West Lafayette, Ind. (Mar.).

    `ftp://gwen.cs.purdue.edu/pub/lin/TCP.atm.ps.Z`

Conta, A., and Deering, S. E. 1995. "Internet Control Message Protocol (ICMPv6) for the Internet Protocol Version 6 (IPv6) Specification," RFC 1885, 20 pages (Dec.).

Crawford, M. 1996a. "A Method for the Transmission of IPv6 Packets over Ethernet Networks," RFC 1972, 4 pages (Aug.).

Crawford, M. 1996b. "A Method for the Transmission of IPv6 Packets over FDDI Networks," RFC 2019, 6 pages (Oct.).

Deering, S. E. 1989. "Host Extensions for IP Multicasting," RFC 1112, 17 pages (Aug.).

Deering, S. E., and Hinden, R. 1995. "Internet Protocol, Version 6 (IPv6) Specification," RFC 1883, 37 pages (Dec.).

Dewar, R. B. K., and Smosna, M. 1990. *Microprocessors: A Programmer's View.* McGraw-Hill, New York.

Eriksson, H. 1994. "MBONE: The Multicast Backbone," *Communications of the ACM*, vol. 37, no. 8, pp. 54–60 (Aug.).

Fenner, W. C. 1997. Private Communication.

Fuller, V., Li, T., Yu, J. Y., and Varadhan, K. 1993. "Classless Inter-Domain Routing (CIDR): An Address Assignment and Aggregation Strategy," RFC 1519, 24 pages (Sept.).

Garfinkel, S. L., and Spafford, E. H. 1996. *Practical UNIX and Internet Security, Second Edition.* O'Reilly & Associates, Sebastopol, Calif.

Gierth, A. 1996. Private Communication.

Gilligan, R. E., Thomson, S., Bound, J., and Stevens, W. R. 1997. "Basic Socket Interface Extensions for IPv6," RFC 2133, 32 pages (Apr.).

Handley, M. 1996. "SAP: Session Announcement Protocol," Internet Draft, 14 pages (Nov.).
```
draft-ietf-mmusic-sap-00.txt
```

Handley, M., and Jacobson, V. 1997. "SDP: Session Description Protocol," Internet Draft (Mar.).
```
draft-ietf-mmusic-sdp-03.txt
```

Hinden, R., and Deering, S. E. 1995. "IP Version 6 Addressing Architecture," RFC 1884, 18 pages (Dec.).

Hinden, R., and Deering, S. E. 1997. "IP Version 6 Addressing Architecture," Internet Draft, 25 pages (July).
```
draft-ietf-ipngwg-addr-arch-v2-02.txt
```
This document should replace RFC 1884 [Hinden and Deering 1995] when it becomes an RFC.

Hinden, R., Fink, R., and Postel, J. B. 1997. "IPv6 Testing Address Allocation," Internet Draft, 4 pages (July).
```
draft-ietf-ipngwg-testv2-addralloc-01.txt
```
This document should replace RFC 1897 [Hinden and Postel 1996] when it becomes an RFC.

Hinden, R., O'Dell, M., and Deering, S. E. 1997. "An IPv6 Aggregatable Global Unicast Address Format," Internet Draft, 9 pages (July).
```
draft-ietf-ipngwg-unicast-aggr-02.txt
```
This document should replace RFC 2073 [Rekhter et al. 1997] when it becomes an RFC.

Hinden, R., and Postel, J. B. 1996. "IPv6 Testing Address Allocation," RFC 1897, 4 pages (Jan.).

IEEE. 1996. "Information Technology—Portable Operating System Interface (POSIX)—Part 1: System Application Program Interface (API) [C Language]," IEEE Std 1003.1, 1996 Edition, Institute of Electrical and Electronics Engineers, Piscataway, N. J. (July).

> This version of Posix.1 contains the 1990 base API, the 1003.1b realtime extensions (1993), the 1003.1c pthreads (1995), and the 1003-1i technical corrections (1995). This is also International Standard ISO/IEC 9945-1: 1996 (E). Ordering information on IEEE standards and draft standards is available at `http://www.ieee.org`.

IEEE. 1997a. "Information Technology—Portable Operating System Interface (POSIX)—Part xx: Protocol Independent Interfaces (PII)," P1003.1g/D6.6, Institute of Electrical and Electronics Engineers, Piscataway, N. J. (Mar.).

> This should be the final draft of Posix.1g. Unfortunately, the IEEE does not make these drafts available online.

IEEE. 1997b. *Guidelines for 64-bit Global Identifier (EUI-64) Registration Authority.* Institute of Electrical and Electronics Engineers, Piscataway, N. J.

> `http://standards.ieee.org/db/oui/tutorials/EUI64.html`

Jacobson, V. 1988. "Congestion Avoidance and Control," *Computer Communication Review*, vol. 18, no. 4, pp. 314–329 (Aug.).

> `ftp://ftp.ee.lbl.gov/papers/congavoid.ps.Z`
> A classic paper describing the slow start and congestion avoidance algorithms for TCP.

Jacobson, V. 1994. "Re: half baked anycastoff idea...," June 27, 1994, end2end-interest mailing list.

> `http://www.kohala.com/~rstevens/vanj.94jun27.txt`

Jacobson, V., Braden, R. T., and Borman, D. A. 1992. "TCP Extensions for High Performance," RFC 1323, 37 pages (May).

> Describes the window scale option, the timestamp option, and the PAWS algorithm, along with the reasons these modifications are needed. [Braden 1993] updates this RFC.

Jacobson, V., Braden, R. T., and Zhang, L. 1990. "TCP Extensions for High-Speed Paths," RFC 1185, 21 pages (Oct.).

Josey, A., ed. 1997. *Go Solo 2: The Authorized Guide to Version 2 of the Single UNIX Specification.* Prentice Hall, Upper Saddle River, N.J.

Joy, W. N. 1994. Private Communication.

Karn, P., and Partridge, C. 1987. "Improving Round-Trip Time Estimates in Reliable Transport Protocols," *Computer Communication Review*, vol. 17, no. 5, pp. 2–7 (Aug.).

> `ftp://sics.se/users/craig/karn-partridge.ps`

Katz, D. 1993. "Transmission of IP and ARP over FDDI Network," RFC 1390, 11 pages (Jan.).

Katz, D. 1997. "IP Router Alert Option," RFC 2113, 4 pages (Feb.).

Katz, D., Atkinson, R. J., Partridge, C., and Jackson, A. 1997. "IPv6 Router Alert Option," Internet Draft, 5 pages (June).

> `draft-ietf-ipngwg-ipv6-router-alert-02.txt`

Kent, S. T. 1991. "U.S. Department of Defense Security Options for the Internet Protocol," RFC 1108, 17 pages (Nov.).

Kent, S. T., and Atkinson, R. J. 1997a. "IP Authentication Header," Internet Draft, 22 pages (July).

    draft-ietf-ipsec-auth-header-01.txt

Kent, S. T., and Atkinson, R. J. 1997b. "IP Encapsulating Security Payload (ESP)," Internet Draft, 19 pages (July).

    draft-ietf-ipsec-esp-v2-00.txt

Kernighan, B. W., and Pike, R. 1984. *The UNIX Programming Environment.* Prentice Hall, Englewood Cliffs, N.J.

Kernighan, B. W., and Ritchie, D. M. 1988. *The C Programming Language, Second Edition.* Prentice Hall, Englewood Cliffs, N.J.

Korn, D. G., and Vo, K. P. 1991. "SFIO: Safe/Fast String/File IO," *Proceedings of the 1991 Summer USENIX Conference*, pp. 235–255, Nashville, Tenn.

    A description of an alternative to the standard I/O library. The source code is available from
    http://www.research.att.com/sw/tools/reuse.

Lanciani, D. 1996. "Re: sockets: AF_INET vs. PF_INET," Message-ID: <3561@news.IPSWITCH.COM>, Usenet, comp.protocols.tcp-ip Newsgroup (Apr.).

    http://www.kohala.com/~rstevens/lanciani.96apr10.txt

Maslen, T. M. 1997. "Re: gethostbyXXXX() and Threads," Message-ID <maslen.862463530 @shellx>, Usenet, comp.programming.threads Newsgroup (May).

    http://www.kohala.com/~rstevens/maslen.97may01.txt

Maufer, T., and Semeria, C. 1997. "Introduction to IP Multicast Routing," Internet Draft (Mar.).

    draft-ietf-mboned-intro-multicast-02.txt

McCann, J., Deering, S. E., and Mogul, J. C. 1996. "Path MTU Discovery for IP version 6," RFC 1981, 15 pages (Aug.).

McCanne, S., and Jacobson, V. 1993. "The BSD Packet Filter: A New Architecture for User-Level Packet Capture," *Proceedings of the 1993 Winter USENIX Conference*, pp. 259–269, San Diego, Calif.

    ftp://ftp.ee.lbl.gov/papers/bpf-usenix93.ps.Z

McDonald, D. L. 1997. "A Simple IP Security API Extension to BSD Sockets," Internet Draft, 12 pages (Mar.).

    draft-mcdonald-simple-ipsec-api-01.txt

McDonald, D. L., Phan, B. G., and Atkinson, R. J. 1996. "A Socket-Based Key Management API (and surrounding infrastructure)," *Proceedings of the INET'96 Conference*, pp. 53–63 (June), Montreal, Quebec.

    http://www.cs.hut.fi/ssh/crypto/pf-key.ps

McDonald, D. L., Metz, C. W., and Phan, B. G. 1997. "PF_KEY Key Management API, Version 2," Internet Draft, 67 pages (July).

    draft-mcdonald-pf-key-v2-03.txt

McKusick, M. K., Bostic, K., Karels, M. J., and Quarterman, J. S. 1996. *The Design and Implementation of the 4.4BSD Operating System.* Addison-Wesley, Reading, Mass.

Meyer, D. 1997. "Administratively Scoped IP Multicast," Internet Draft, 7 pages (June).
    `draft-ietf-mboned-admin-ip-space-03.txt`

Mills, D. L. 1992. "Network Time Protocol (Version 3): Specification, Implementation, and Analysis," RFC 1305, 113 pages (Mar.).

Mills, D. L. 1996. "Simple Network Time Protocol (SNTP) Version 4 for IPv4, IPv6 and OSI," RFC 2030, 18 pages (Oct.).

Mogul, J. C., and Deering, S. E. 1990. "Path MTU Discovery," RFC 1191, 19 pages (Apr.).

Mogul, J. C., and Postel, J. B. 1985. "Internet Standard Subnetting Procedure," RFC 950, 18 pages (Aug.).

Nemeth, E. 1997. Private Communication.

Open Group, The. 1997. *CAE Specification, Networking Services (XNS), Issue 5.* The Open Group, Reading, Berkshire, U.K.

> This is the specification for sockets and XTI in Unix 98. This manual also has appendices describing the use of XTI with NetBIOS, the OSI protocols, SNA, and the Netware IPX and SPX protocols. Three appendices cover the use of both sockets and XTI with ATM.

Partridge, C., Mendez, T., and Milliken, W. 1993. "Host Anycasting Service," RFC 1546, 9 pages (Nov.).

Partridge, C., and Pink, S. 1993. "A Faster UDP," *IEEE/ACM Transactions on Networking,* vol. 1, no. 4, pp. 429–440 (Aug.).

Paxson, V. 1996. "End-to-End Routing Behavior in the Internet," *Computer Communication Review,* vol. 26, no. 4, pp. 25–38 (Oct.).
    `ftp://ftp.ee.lbl.gov/papers/routing.SIGCOMM.ps.Z`

Piscitello, D. M. 1994. "FTP Operation Over Big Address Records (FOOBAR)," RFC 1639, 5 pages (June).

Plauger, P. J. 1992. *The Standard C Library.* Prentice Hall, Englewood Cliffs, N.J.

Postel, J. B. 1980. "User Datagram Protocol," RFC 768, 3 pages (Aug.).

Postel, J. B., ed. 1981a. "Internet Protocol," RFC 791, 45 pages (Sept.).

Postel, J. B. 1981b. "Internet Control Message Protocol," RFC 792, 21 pages (Sept.).

Postel, J. B., ed. 1981c. "Transmission Control Protocol," RFC 793, 85 pages (Sept.).

Pusateri, T. 1993. "IP Multicast Over Token-Ring Local Area Networks," RFC 1469, 4 pages (June).

Rago, S. A. 1993. *UNIX System V Network Programming.* Addison-Wesley, Reading, Mass.

Rekhter, Y., Lothberg, P., Hinden, R., Deering, S. E., and Postel, J. B. 1997. "An IPv6 Provider-Based Unicast Address Format," RFC 2073, 7 pages (Jan.).

Reynolds, J. K., and Postel, J. B. 1994. "Assigned Numbers," RFC 1700, 230 pages (Oct.).

> Changes to some of the information contained in this RFC can occur before the RFC is updated. All the tables of information in the RFC are taken from files in the directory `ftp://ftp.isi.edu/in-notes/iana/assignments`, and these files are updated as changes occur. The RFC contains the URLs for the files in this directory, and these files should be consulted for the latest information.

Ritchie, D. M. 1984. "A Stream Input-Output System," *AT&T Bell Laboratories Technical Journal*, vol. 63, no. 8, pp. 1897–1910 (Oct.).

Salus, P. H. 1994. *A Quarter Century of Unix.* Addison-Wesley, Reading, Mass.

Salus, P. H. 1995. *Casting the Net: From ARPANET to Internet and Beyond.* Addison-Wesley, Reading, Mass.

Schimmel, C. 1994. *UNIX Systems for Modern Architectures: Symmetric Multiprocessing and Caching for Kernel Programmers.* Addison-Wesley, Reading, Mass.

Srinivasan, R. 1995. "XDR: External Data Representation Standard," RFC 1832, 24 pages (Aug.).

Stevens, W. R. 1992. *Advanced Programming in the UNIX Environment.* Addison-Wesley, Reading, Mass.

> All the details of Unix programming. Referred to through this text as APUE.

Stevens, W. R. 1994. *TCP/IP Illustrated, Volume 1: The Protocols.* Addison-Wesley, Reading, Mass.

> A complete introduction to the Internet protocols. Referred to through this text as TCPv1.

Stevens, W. R. 1996. *TCP/IP Illustrated, Volume 3: TCP for Transactions, HTTP, NNTP, and the UNIX Domain Protocols.* Addison-Wesley, Reading, Mass.

> Referred to through this text as TCPv3.

Stevens, W. R., and Thomas, M. 1997. "Advanced Sockets API for IPv6," Internet Draft (July).

> `draft-stevens-advanced-api-04.txt`

Tanenbaum, A. S. 1987. *Operating Systems Design and Implementation.* Prentice Hall, Englewood Cliffs, N.J.

Thomas, S. 1997. "Transmission of IPv6 Packets over Token Ring Networks," Internet Draft, 10 pages (June).

> `draft-ietf-ipngwg-trans-tokenring-00.txt`

Thomson, S., and Huitema, C. 1995. "DNS Extensions to Support IP version 6," RFC 1886, 5 pages (Dec.).

Torek, C. 1994. "Re: Delay in re-using TCP/IP port," Message-ID <199501010028.QAA16863 @elf.bsdi.com>, Usenet, comp.unix.wizards Newsgroup (Dec.).

> `http://www.kohala.com/~rstevens/torek.94dec31.txt`

Unix International. 1991. "Data Link Provider Interface Specification," Revision 2.0.0, Unix International, Parsippany, N. J. (Aug.).

> `http://www.kohala.com/~rstevens/dlpi.2.0.0.ps`
> A newer version of this specification is available online from The Open Group at `http://www.rdg.opengroup.org/pubs/catalog/web.htm`.

Unix International. 1992a. "Network Provider Interface Specification," Revision 2.0.0, Unix International, Parsippany, N. J. (Aug.).

> `http://www.kohala.com/~rstevens/npi.2.0.0.ps`

Unix International. 1992b. "Transport Provider Interface Specification," Revision 1.5, Unix International, Parsippany, N. J. (Dec.).

> `http://www.kohala.com/~rstevens/tpi.1.5.ps`
> A newer version of this specification is available online from The Open Group at `http://www.rdg.opengroup.org/pubs/catalog/web.htm`.

Vixie, P. A. 1996. Private Communication.

Wright, G. R., and Stevens, W. R. 1995. *TCP/IP Illustrated, Volume 2: The Implementation.* Addison-Wesley, Reading, Mass.

> The implementation of the Internet protocols in the 4.4BSD-Lite operating system. Referred to through this text as TCPv2.

Index

Networking is a field that is pockmarked with acronyms. Rather than provide a separate glossary (with most of the entries being acronyms), this index also serves as a glossary for all the acronyms used in the book. The primary entry for the acronym appears under the acronym name. For example, all references to the Internet Control Message Protocol appear under ICMP. The entry under the compound term "Internet Control Message Protocol" refers back to the main entry under ICMP.

The notation "definition of" appearing with a C function refers to the boxed function prototype for that function, its primary description. The "definition of" notation for a structure refers to its primary definition. Some functions also contain the notation "source code" if the source code implementation for that function appears in the text.

Structure Definitions